*Feasting on the Gospels
Mark*

Editorial Board

GENERAL EDITORS

Cynthia A. Jarvis (Presbyterian Church (U.S.A.)), Minister, The Presbyterian Church of Chestnut Hill, Philadelphia, Pennsylvania

E. Elizabeth Johnson (Presbyterian Church (U.S.A.)), J. Davison Philips Professor of New Testament, Columbia Theological Seminary, Decatur, Georgia

VOLUME EDITORS

Christine Chakoian (Presbyterian Church (U.S.A.)), Pastor, First Presbyterian Church of Lake Forest, Lake Forest, Illinois

Gary W. Charles (Presbyterian Church (U.S.A.)), Pastor, Central Presbyterian Church, Atlanta, Georgia

Jaime Clark-Soles (American Baptist Churches USA), Associate Professor of New Testament, Perkins School of Theology, Dallas, Texas

Stephanie Buckhanon Crowder (National Baptist Convention, Christian Church [Disciples of Christ]), Adjunct Faculty, New Testament Studies, McCormick Theological Seminary, Chicago, Illinois

R. Alan Culpepper (Baptist [Cooperative Baptist Fellowship]), Dean and Professor of New Testament, McAfee School of Theology, Mercer University, Atlanta, Georgia

Mark Douglas (Presbyterian Church (U.S.A.)), Professor of Christian Ethics and Director, Master of Arts in Theological Studies Program, Columbia Theological Seminary, Decatur, Georgia

Mary F. Foskett (Baptist [Cooperative Baptist Fellowship]), Professor of Religion and Director of WFU Humanities Institute, Wake Forest University, Winston-Salem, North Carolina

Martha Moore-Keish (Presbyterian Church (U.S.A.)), Associate Professor of Theology, Columbia Theological Seminary, Decatur, Georgia

D. Cameron Murchison (Presbyterian Church (U.S.A.)), Professor Emeritus of Ministry, Columbia Theological Seminary, Decatur, Georgia

Carmen Nanko-Fernández (Roman Catholic Church), Associate Professor of Hispanic Theology and Ministry, Catholic Theological Union, Chicago, Illinois

Stanley P. Saunders (Christian Church [Disciples of Christ]), Associate Professor of New Testament, Columbia Theological Seminary, Decatur, Georgia

Richard F. Ward (United Church of Christ), Fred B. Craddock Professor of Homiletics and Worship, Phillips Theological Seminary, Tulsa, Oklahoma

CONSULTING EDITORS

David L. Bartlett (American Baptist Churches USA), Professor Emeritus of New Testament, Columbia Theological Seminary, Decatur, Georgia

Barbara Brown Taylor (The Episcopal Church), Butman Professor of Religion, Piedmont College, Demorest, Georgia

PROJECT MANAGER

Joan Murchison, Columbia Theological Seminary, Decatur, Georgia

PROJECT COMPILER

Mary Lynn Darden, Columbia Theological Seminary, Decatur, Georgia

A Feasting on the Word® Commentary

Feasting on the Gospels

Mark

CYNTHIA A. JARVIS and E. ELIZABETH JOHNSON

General Editors

WESTMINSTER
JOHN KNOX PRESS
LOUISVILLE · KENTUCKY

© 2014 Westminster John Knox Press

2014 paperback edition
Originally published in hardback in the United States
by Westminster John Knox Press in 2014
Louisville, Kentucky

14 15 16 17 18 19 20 21 22 23—10 9 8 7 6 5 4 3 2 1

All rights reserved. No part of this book may be reproduced or transmitted in any form or by any means, electronic or mechanical, including photocopying, recording, or by any information storage or retrieval system, without permission in writing from the publisher. For information, address Westminster John Knox Press, 100 Witherspoon Street, Louisville, Kentucky 40202-1396. Or contact us online at www.wjkbooks.com.

Scripture quotations from the New Revised Standard Version of the Bible are copyright © 1989 by the Division of Christian Education of the National Council of the Churches of Christ in the U.S.A. and are used by permission. Scripture quotations marked NASB are taken from the *New American Standard Bible,* © 1960, 1962, 1963, 1968, 1971, 1972, 1973, 1975, 1977 by The Lockman Foundation. Used by permission. Scripture quotations marked NIV are from *The Holy Bible, New International Version.* Copyright © 1973, 1978, 1984 International Bible Society. Used by permission of Zondervan Bible Publishers. Scripture quotations marked RSV are from the Revised Standard Version of the Bible, copyright © 1946, 1952, 1971, and 1973 by the Division of Christian Education of the National Council of the Churches of Christ in the U.S.A., and are used by permission.

Excerpt from Huub Oosterhuis, "He Did Not Want to Be Far," *TheWorshipbook* (Philadelphia: The Westminster Press, 1975) is reprinted by permission of the WCC Publications.

Excerpt from "If Christ Is Charged with Madness," by Thomas Troeger © Oxford University Press Inc. 1986. Assigned to Oxford University Press 2010. Reproduced by permission. All rights reserved.

Excerpt from "Silence! Frenzied, Unclean Spirit," by Thomas Troeger © Oxford University Press Inc. 1986. Assigned to Oxford University Press 2010. Reproduced by permission. All rights reserved.

Book design by Drew Stevens
Cover design by Lisa Buckley and Dilu Nicholas

Library of Congress Cataloging-in-Publication Data

Feasting on the Gospels : a feasting on the WordTM commentary / Cynthia A. Jarvis and E. Elizabeth Johnson, general editors. — First edition.
    volumes cm
  Includes index.
  ISBN 978-0-664-23162-0 (v. 3: hardback)
  ISBN 978-0-664-23394-5 (v. 2: hardback)
  ISBN 978-0-664-23540-6 (v. 1: hardback)
 1. Bible. Matthew—Commentaries. I. Jarvis, Cynthia A., editor of compilation.
  BS2575.52.F37 2013
  226'.2077—dc23

2013004484

ISBN 978-0-664-25991-4 (v. 3 paperback)
ISBN 978-0-664-23974-9 (v. 2 paperback)
ISBN 978-0-664-23973-2 (v. 1 paperback)

♾ The paper used in this publication meets the minimum requirements of the American National Standard for Information Sciences—Permanence of Paper for Printed Library Materials, ANSI Z39.48-1992.

Contents

vii	Publisher's Note	242	Mark 8:31–33
		248	Mark 8:34–9:1
ix	Series Introduction	254	Mark 9:2–8
		260	Mark 9:9–13
		266	Mark 9:14–29
2	Mark 1:1–8	272	Mark 9:30–32
8	Mark 1:9–11	278	Mark 9:33–37
14	Mark 1:12–13	284	Mark 9:38–41
20	Mark 1:14–15	290	Mark 9:42–50
26	Mark 1:16–20	296	Mark 10:1–12
32	Mark 1:21–28	302	Mark 10:13–16
38	Mark 1:29–34	308	Mark 10:17–22
44	Mark 1:35–39	314	Mark 10:23–31
50	Mark 1:40–45	320	Mark 10:32–34
56	Mark 2:1–12	326	Mark 10:35–45
62	Mark 2:13–17	332	Mark 10:46–52
68	Mark 2:18–22	338	Mark 11:1–10
74	Mark 2:23–28	344	Mark 11:11–26
80	Mark 3:1–6	350	Mark 11:27–33
86	Mark 3:7–12	356	Mark 12:1–12
92	Mark 3:13–19a	362	Mark 12:13–17
98	Mark 3:19b–30	368	Mark 12:18–27
104	Mark 3:31–35	374	Mark 12:28–34
110	Mark 4:1–9	380	Mark 12:35–37
116	Mark 4:10–20	386	Mark 12:38–40
122	Mark 4:21–25	392	Mark 12:41–44
128	Mark 4:26–29	398	Mark 13:1–8
134	Mark 4:30–34	404	Mark 13:9–13
140	Mark 4:35–41	410	Mark 13:14–23
146	Mark 5:1–20	416	Mark 13:24–27
152	Mark 5:21–24a, 35–43	422	Mark 13:28–31
158	Mark 5:24b–34	428	Mark 13:32–37
164	Mark 6:1–6a	434	Mark 14:1–2, 10–11
170	Mark 6:6b–13	440	Mark 14:3–9
176	Mark 6:14–29	446	Mark 14:12–16
182	Mark 6:30–44	452	Mark 14:17–21
188	Mark 6:45–52	458	Mark 14:22–25
194	Mark 6:53–56	464	Mark 14:26–31
200	Mark 7:1–23	470	Mark 14:32–42
206	Mark 7:24–30	476	Mark 14:43–52
212	Mark 7:31–37	482	Mark 14:53–65
218	Mark 8:1–10	488	Mark 14:66–72
224	Mark 8:11–21	494	Mark 15:1–5
230	Mark 8:22–26	500	Mark 15:6–15
236	Mark 8:27–30	506	Mark 15:16–20

512	Mark 15:21–32
518	Mark 15:33–41
524	Mark 15:42–47
530	Mark 16:1–8
536	Mark 16:9–20
543	*Contributors*
549	*Author Index*

Publisher's Note

Feasting on the Gospels is a seven-volume series that follows in the proud tradition of *Feasting on the Word: Preaching the Revised Common Lectionary*. Whereas *Feasting on the Word* provided commentary on only the texts in the lectionary, *Feasting on the Gospels* will cover every passage of the four Gospels. *Feasting on the Gospels* retains the popular approach of *Feasting on the Word* by providing four perspectives on each passage—theological, pastoral, exegetical, and homiletical—to stimulate and inspire preaching, teaching, and discipleship.

Westminster John Knox Press is grateful to the members of the large *Feasting* family who have given so much of themselves to bring this new series to life. General editors Cynthia A. Jarvis and E. Elizabeth Johnson stepped from their service on the editorial board of *Feasting on the Word* to the editorship of *Feasting on the Gospels* without missing a beat. Their commitment, energy, and unflagging enthusiasm made this work possible. The project manager, Joan Murchison, and project compiler, Mary Lynn Darden, continued their remarkable work, bringing thousands of pieces and hundreds of authors together seamlessly.

The editorial board did enormous work under grueling deadlines and did it with excellence and good humor. The hundreds of writers who participated—scholars, preachers, and teachers—gave much of themselves to help create this bountiful feast. David Bartlett and Barbara Brown Taylor took the time and care to help conceive this new project even as they were finishing their excellent work as general editors of *Feasting on the Word*.

Finally, we are again indebted to Columbia Theological Seminary for their partnership. As they did with *Feasting on the Word*, they provided many resources and personnel to help make this series possible. We are grateful in particular to seminary President Stephen Hayner and Dean of Faculty and Executive Vice President Deborah Mullen.

It is with joy that we welcome you to this feast, in hopes that it will nourish you as you proclaim the Word to all of God's people.

Westminster John Knox Press

Series Introduction

At their best, people who write about Scripture are conversation partners. They enter the dialogue between the biblical text and the preacher or teacher or interested Christian and add perspectives gained from experience and disciplined attention. They contribute literary, historical, linguistic, and theological insights gathered over the millennia to the reader's first impressions of what is going on in a text. This conversation is essential if the reading of Scripture is to be fruitful in the church. It keeps reading the Bible from being an exercise in individual projection or uncritical assumption. That said, people who comment on the Bible should never become authorities. While a writer may indeed know more about the text than the reader does, he or she nevertheless writes from a particular perspective shaped by culture, ethnicity, gender, education, and theological tradition. In this regard, the writer of a commentary is no different from the writers and readers of Scripture.

The model for this series on the Gospels is the lectionary-based resource *Feasting on the Word* (Westminster John Knox Press, 2008–2011), now widely used by ministers as they prepare to preach. As central as the task of preaching is to the health of congregations, Scripture is the Word that calls the whole community of faith into being and sends out those addressed as witnesses to the Word in the world. Whether read devotionally by those gathered to pray or critically by others gathered to study, the Bible functions in a myriad of ways to undergird, support, and nurture the Christian life of individuals and communities. Those are the reasons that Westminster John Knox Press has taken the next step in the *Feasting* project to offer *Feasting on the Gospels*, a series in the style of *Feasting on the Word* with two major differences. First, all four Gospels are considered in their entirety, a *lectio continua* of sorts that leaves nothing out. Second, while *Feasting on the Word* is addressed specifically to preachers, *Feasting on the Gospels* is addressed to all who want to deepen their understanding of the Gospels—Bible study leaders and class members, seasoned preachers and seminarians, believers and skeptics.

The advantage of *Feasting on the Gospels* is that the reader encounters multiple perspectives on each text—not only the theological, exegetical, pastoral, and homiletical emphases that shape the essays, but also the ecumenical, social, ethnic, and cultural perspectives of the authors. Unlike a single-author commentary, which sustains a particular view of a given interpreter throughout, *Feasting on the Gospels* offers readers a broad conversation that engages the text from many angles. In a church as diverse as the twenty-first-century church is, such deliberate engagement with many voices is imperative and, we hope, provocative.

A few observations about the particular challenges posed by the Gospels are in order here. The Gospels were written in a time when fledgling Christian communities—probably in their second generation—were just beginning to negotiate their relationships with Judaism (within which they were conceived and born), a community that was itself in the process of redefinition after the destruction of the Second Temple in 70 CE. Some of that negotiation was marked by great tension and sometimes outright hostility. The temptation for Christian readers to read anti-Semitism into texts that portray intra-Jewish conflict has beset the church almost from its beginnings. Our editors have been particularly mindful of this when dealing with essays on texts where the temptation to speak contemptuously of Jews and Judaism might threaten faithful interpretation.

A second observation involves the New Testament manuscript tradition. In *Feasting on the Gospels* we identify and comment on significant manuscript variants such as Mark 16:9–20 and John 7:53–8:11, something we did not have to contend with in *Feasting on the Word*. We identify those variant readings the way the NRSV does, except that we talk about "other ancient manuscripts" rather than the "other ancient authorities" of the NRSV notes.

The twelve members of our editorial board come from a broad swath of American Christianity: they are members or ministers of Presbyterian, Baptist, United Church of Christ, Roman Catholic, and Disciples of Christ churches. Some of them are academics who serve on the faculties of theological schools; others are clergy serving congregations. All of them are extraordinarily hardworking, thoughtful, and perceptive readers of Scripture, of the church, and of the world. The writers whose work comprises these volumes represent an even wider cross section of the church, most of them from North America, but a significant number from around the world, particularly the global South.

We could not have undertaken this work without the imagination, advice, and support of David Dobson, Editorial Director at Westminster John Knox Press, and his colleagues Don McKim, Marianne Blickenstaff, Michele Blum, and Julie Tonini. We are deeply grateful to David L. Bartlett and Barbara Brown Taylor, our mentors in the *Feasting on the Word* project, who continued to offer hands-on assistance with *Feasting on the Gospels*. We thank President Stephen A. Hayner and Dean Deborah F. Mullen of Columbia Theological Seminary and the congregation of The Presbyterian Church of Chestnut Hill in Philadelphia, Pennsylvania, who made possible our participation in the project. Joan Murchison, who as Project Manager kept all of us and our thousands of essays in order and enforced deadlines with great good humor, is once again the beloved Hammer. Mary Lynn Darden, our compiler, who corralled not only the essays but also information about their authors and editors, brought all the bits and pieces together into the books you see now.

To the preachers, teachers, Bible study leaders, and church members who will read the Gospels with us, we wish you happy feasting.

Cynthia A. Jarvis
E. Elizabeth Johnson

Feasting on the Gospels
Mark

Mark 1:1–8

¹ The beginning of the good news of Jesus Christ, the Son of God. ²As it is written in the prophet Isaiah,
"See, I am sending my messenger ahead of you,
   who will prepare your way;
³ the voice of one crying in the wilderness:
   'Prepare the way of the Lord,
   make his paths straight,'"
⁴John the baptizer appeared in the wilderness, proclaiming a baptism of repentance for the forgiveness of sins. ⁵And people from the whole Judean country-

Theological Perspective

Most stories in the Bible begin with a human being—Abram and Sarai, Naomi and Ruth, James and John. Yes, there are exceptions—the creation story most especially. Two of the four Gospels begin from the human side—with a genealogy in Matthew, and Zechariah and Elizabeth in Luke. Even John, which begins with the creation through the Word, includes "all people" in the opening verses of its Prologue (John 1:4). Mark simply begins with "the beginning of the good news of Jesus Christ, the Son of God" (v. 1). Yes, Jesus is human as well as divine, but the human side of Jesus' advent (his birth, his childhood, his call) gets no space in Mark.

Mark is the story of an invasion, an invasion of this world by God and God's reign. Most human invasions involve some preparation—planning out the route, softening up the resistance, spreading some propaganda regarding the invaders. In some very basic way, John the Baptist serves this purpose. However, in Mark, even John's work seems perfunctory, and rushed, and orchestrated somewhere offstage ("John the baptizer appeared in the wilderness," v. 4). This is an invasion that is going forward without any invitation. This is an invasion that neither expects nor requires any real receptivity on the part of those for whom the invasion is planned (as the whole Gospel will make clear; nobody "gets" it,

Pastoral Perspective

The Gospel according to Mark begins with one of the finest opening lines in biblical literature. This grand sentence introduces the story of Jesus as good news.

Today there is a heart hunger for good news. One unofficial means of documenting this hunger is through church prayer chains. Nearly every congregation has one, and it is almost always fully occupied with the concerns of parishioners, their family members, and friends. Meanwhile, every congregation is full of concerns that never make it to the prayer chain because people keep their thoughts stored in their hearts until they utter them to God. Someone has cancer. Another is looking for work. Here a heart is heavy with grief, and a dreadful worry weighs upon another soul. There is no end to the list of concerns. Tennyson's line still obtains: "Never morning wore / To evening, but some heart did break."[1] The pastoral task is to speak to these broken hearts, offering the strength and help to be found in God's good news in Jesus Christ.

Today there is a particular hunger for good news from religion. Religion has become associated with bad news, harsh attitudes, and caustic spirits. The treatment of women, of children, of gays and

---

1. *In Memoriam A.H.H.*, 6, lines 7–8, in *Tennyson's Poetry*, ed. Robert W. Hill, 2nd ed. (New York: W. W. Norton, 1999), 209.

side and all the people of Jerusalem were going out to him, and were baptized by him in the river Jordan, confessing their sins. ⁶Now John was clothed with camel's hair, with a leather belt around his waist, and he ate locusts and wild honey. ⁷He proclaimed, "The one who is more powerful than I is coming after me; I am not worthy to stoop down and untie the thong of his sandals. ⁸I have baptized you with water; but he will baptize you with the Holy Spirit."

Exegetical Perspective

Mark's introduction to his narrative anchors the church's gospel in continuity with Jesus, Scripture, and John the Baptist.

The Church's Gospel Is in Continuity with Jesus (v. 1). The discussion here presented understands 1:1 to be Mark's title for his narrative as a whole (as in the NRSV). The word "gospel" (*euangelion*), "good news," refers to the church's message of God's saving act in Jesus, the message proclaimed by the church of Mark's day and ours. It does not here refer to a book representing the life and teaching of Jesus, a meaning the word did not attain until the middle of the second century. Thus Mark 1:1 does not mean "the Gospel begins here" (a gratuitous comment in any case).

Mark's first word, *archē*, can mean "beginning, source, and/or norm." English has no single word with all three connotations; here it has overtones of all three English words. There were many versions of the Christian message in Mark's day, as in ours. Not all were equally valid, and some were dangerously perverse. The author wants to provide direction for how the gospel can be authentically proclaimed. He does this not by stating a creed or list of principles to which the Christian message should conform, but by claiming that the narrative to follow is the beginning, source, and norm for the church's proclamation of the gospel.

Homiletical Perspective

With its collection of powerful, world-changing stories, Mark's Gospel provides rich fodder for the preacher. Even the very first line offers fertile material: "The beginning of the good news of Jesus Christ, Son of God." Most scholars understand this brief sentence to be a title summarizing Mark's purpose for writing the book, to tell the story of God's "good news" made present in the advent of Jesus Christ. Unlike the later Gospel writers, Mark does not say he intends to give a full and final account of things. In fact, most scholars believe that Mark does not offer a conventional conclusion to his narrative, where things are wrapped up neatly, as we find in the other Gospels. Instead, his Gospel actually ends in 16:8 with an empty tomb.

The unfinished nature of his testimony, juxtaposed to this strong, affirmative opening statement, suggests that for Mark, the life, ministry, death, and even the resurrection of Jesus Christ are not the end of the story. They are, instead, the events that set the gospel in motion. The "good news" story of Jesus Christ, Son of God, is an ongoing one, continuing into the story of the church's birth and expansion, and into the lives of those who meet the living Christ today.

Most of the time, however, modern Christians experience the story of Jesus as ancient history, far

Mark 1:1–8

Theological Perspective

with the exception of the demons and the centurion, 15:39). This is an invasion that only *begins* in the life, death, and resurrection of Jesus Christ (the last of which gets almost no coverage in Mark), because it is an invasion that is still going on.

To say that the Gospel of Mark emphasizes *God's* initiative in salvation is a gross understatement. This is not a story of a people crying out and God coming down (as in Exodus). This is not a story of God infiltrating the world through the righteousness of Joseph (Matthew) or the obedience of Mary (Luke). No, this is the story of a God who will bring in his reign, come hell or high water. Ready or not, here God comes!

One way to think about this is to focus on *Mark's hearers*, a mostly Gentile community of believers under persecution in the 70s CE. They would prefer a Messiah who would appreciate their willingness to work with him toward the overthrow of the empire that has them in its grip. He could nurture a group of dedicated disciples, train them in the disciplines required for his service, then lead them on to victory. "The beginning of the good news of Jesus Christ, the Son of God, and his faithful minions." However, this Gospel ends with the death of a suffering Messiah, and the women running away in fear. Take that, you revolutionary zealots!

Another, and perhaps more productive, way to think about this is in relationship to *us*. It is not just that we would prefer a victorious Messiah to a suffering Messiah. That is relatively easy to swallow. What is a tad more difficult to accept and give thanks for is a God who is coming regardless. No asking or preparing or cooperation on our part at all. You call that "good news"?

Yes, by all means, yes. Is that not what this beginning, theologically, is all about?

This then would be a good occasion to review some basic theology, like "prevenient grace." We thank God not only for coming to us, but for preparing our receptivity to God's approach, no thanks to us. "This effectual call is of God's free and special grace alone, not from anything at all foreseen in man, who is altogether passive therein, until, being quickened by the Holy Spirit, he is thereby enabled to answer this call, and to embrace the grace offered and conveyed in it."[1] Yes, this is an invasion.

This would be a good occasion to think a little, theologically, about how we share this news with

Pastoral Perspective

lesbians, of different races, and even of visitors to our church pews has led to the idea that religion, not only Christianity, is something that comes down hard on people. The more negatively religion is perceived, the less appealing the life of faith appears. We have before us a golden opportunity and responsibility to do what Mark did for the world, when he opened his book the way he did. We can present the Christian message as good news.

Today there is a heart hunger for good news rooted in something historic. Many of us moderns suffer from a kind of tyranny of the latest. Under this tyranny we tend to think the times in which we live are unprecedented in terms of their difficulty and complexity. David McCullough had this tyranny in mind when he wrote *1776*. His book about that crucial year in American history was his response to the terrorist attacks of September 11, 2001. Without denying the severity of those attacks or their impact upon the nation, he reacted against those who stated that our country had never before faced an ordeal that severe. McCullough wrote *1776* to say we had faced such a time before and had survived.[2]

Some such word can be helpful today. Think only of issues facing the church. There is no question that life in twenty-first-century North America poses strong challenges to the church. A people faced with these difficulties can think them unprecedented, and so strong that congregations have impossible odds against them.

Pastoral help can come from digging down into history, particularly in Scripture, to discover the resources to be found there. Mark anchors the story he is about to tell in the Scriptures, particularly in the prophets. The material from Isaiah was more than six hundred years old when Mark put it to use. He realized he was writing for the present, but he drew upon the past. Like Mark we can find yesterday full of profound help for today. Stability can come when we see that the faith we profess has seen people through all manner of circumstances, and there is no reason to believe it will be undone by those that we face.

Moving to something more specific than the general need for good news, think about the present-day need for a word about guilt. John the Baptist's message and work turned people toward the forgiveness of sin. People flocked into the wilderness to hear him. Even taking the hyperbole of Mark 1:5 ("all the

---

1. The Westminster Confession of Faith (6.065), in *The Constitution of the Presbyterian Church (U.S.A.)*, Part 1, *Book of Confessions* (Louisville, KY: Office of the General Assembly, 2002), 134.

2. Justin Ravitz, "Author Interview: David McCullough," www.bomc.com. May 21, 2005.

Exegetical Perspective

The church does not merely continue the message of Jesus, but proclaims its faith that, in Jesus, God has acted definitively to reveal and make real God's own character and saving action. The church does not replicate Jesus' own message. In the light of Easter, the church proclaims God's saving act in the Christ event, but can do this legitimately only if the church's message is inseparably bound to the story of the crucified and risen Jesus.

The Church's Gospel Is in Continuity with the Scripture (vv. 2–3). In Mark, Jesus appears on the stage of history for the first time in 1:9, when he comes to be baptized by John. Prior to any action on the narrative stage, the audience hears an off-stage, transcendent voice speaking in the words of Scripture (actually a mélange of three different texts [Exod. 23:20; Mal. 3:1; Isa. 40:3]). Mark claims, as does the New Testament in general, that the plan of God revealed in the Jewish Scriptures finds its goal and fulfillment in the event of Jesus Christ. Mark is distinctive in presenting these Scripture texts as a transcendent scene in which the "I" that speaks represents the voice of God, speaking to "you," a second transcendent figure, "the Lord" (the text of Malachi has been adjusted to get this effect). It is not until Mark 12:36, in a similar use of Scripture, that Jesus the Messiah is explicitly identified with the transcendent Lord. The Lord has a "way," and God is sending a messenger before the Lord to prepare his way.

Thus, before the narrative curtain opens, the audience has a transcendent framework within which to interpret the figures in the story. God is the actor, who sends both John and Jesus. There is no explicit doctrine of preexistence here, as in the letters of Paul and the Gospel of John. However, when Jesus appears in 1:9, the audience already knows his transcendent identity as the church's Lord, sent by God. The figures in the narrative will not know this until after the cross and resurrection. The messianic secret is already adumbrated in the opening words of the Gospel; the later adoptionist heresy is already implicitly rejected. The meaning of Mark's story, like the Scripture texts with which he begins, becomes clear only in retrospect, in the light of the resurrection.

The Church's Gospel Is in Continuity with John the Baptist (vv. 4–8). The historical John was a Jewish eschatological prophet calling Israel to repentance in view of the impending advent of God's judgment. John baptized those who responded as the nucleus of a renewed and purified Israel. He was

Homiletical Perspective

removed from our own. They may acknowledge it to be their most essential identity-shaping story, offering powerful insights into who God is and who we are in relation to God. That said, do they or we fully comprehend the implications of a story whose central figure, Jesus, is not simply a historical role model, but is instead the risen and living Lord?

What could it mean for congregations to believe that we, here today, are part of this ongoing story of good news, that the end of the story has not yet been written? Can we imagine ourselves as players in God's drama of redemption? What role might we discover God calling us to assume in God's unfinished story of grace and reconciliation and love? Where might we discover we have failed to take up that responsibility? Most importantly, where do we see Jesus, the "good news" made flesh, inviting us to join him in the ongoing work of reconciliation in the life of our world today?

In this first sentence, Mark uses language that echoes that of the creation stories. "In the beginning," says Genesis, God created all that is, on earth and in the heavens. Here Mark declares another "beginning," a *new* creation—the beginning of the "good news." In Mark's day, followers of the still-new Christian faith were experiencing significant persecution at the hands of the Roman Empire. The Greek word Mark uses for this new thing that is happening because of the coming of Jesus is *euangelion*, "gospel." This term was often used in his time to refer to the peace, prosperity, and good life that came from a grand military victory by the empire.

It is a bold move for Mark to dare to suggest that it is the Son of God, Jesus Christ, rather than Caesar, who makes this hope- and peace-filled kind of new life possible. In our present day, where military ventures across the world have produced hollow victories at best, it is a good reminder for us as well that our true security and redemption come from the hands of God and not from human might. Moreover, in a time when there is a plethora of bad news, we hear from Mark the life-giving good news that all is not finished, that God is still in the process of making all things new.

Mark's story of good news begins with a look back to the prophets. "As it is written in the prophet Isaiah, 'See, I am sending my messenger ahead of you, who will prepare your way'" (v. 2). In this new beginning, God's long-standing promises are being fulfilled. These very first words connect the new story of Jesus, which was foretold by the prophets of old, with the ongoing story of God. The messenger

Mark 1:1–8

Theological Perspective

others. Do we wait until we see signs of approachability and receptivity and cooperation on the part of others? No, we start living out the reality of the kingdom now, come hell or high water. "The mission of God in Christ gives shape and substance to the life and work of the Church. In Christ, the Church participates in God's mission for the transformation of creation and humanity by proclaiming to all people the good news of God's love, offering to all people the grace of God at font and table, and calling all people to discipleship in Christ."[2] Again, this is an invasion.

This might be a good occasion to think a little about how we go about worship. Do we make it more accessible, more user friendly, more intelligible and adaptable to the norms of our communities and cultures? Not if it gets in the way of an invasion, the invasion of God's presence and reign made manifest in Jesus Christ. In that great paraphrase of Psalm 98, we might join in singing Isaac Watts's words: "Joy to the world! The Lord is come. Let earth receive her King. Let every heart prepare him room, and heaven and nature sing; and heaven and nature sing, and heaven, and heaven and nature sing."[3] Every Lord's Day is an invasion.

Yes, it is true that much of Mark's Gospel will deal with how this invasion upends our expectations, revealing a Messiah who rules from a cross, not a throne. It thus will demand a deep and sacrificial response on our part. Now, at the beginning, let us note how this good news *begins*. With an invasion. At God's initiative. The bus has left the station. Get *out of* the way, or get *on* the way. Yes, get ready. Good news is coming—*like fire*.

RICHARD N. BOYCE

Pastoral Perspective

people") into account, and so lowering our estimates of the crowd, it must have been at least large enough to attract attention. John must have gained this hearing because his message about forgiveness spoke to a real need that was troubling souls.

Look out upon any congregation. The presence of guilt, though carefully hidden, is not difficult to see. A middle-aged daughter is torn between the time she would like to spend with her husband, children, and grandchildren, and the attention she feels she has to give to her elderly and increasingly frail mother. A father in his seventies is estranged from his son, and he feels much of it is his fault for failing to be a better father. Sitting nearby is a couple whose marriage survived the infidelity of one of them, but that one still lives with the guilt of having been untrue. Not far away is a youth who has the fresh memory of one of those fights adolescents have with parents; hurtful words were spoken, and they cannot be taken back. All this is present on a single Sunday, considering only one side of the sanctuary. The whole church hungers for some good news concerning the guilt they feel. Speak about this helpfully, and people will come out to hear, even as they came to John.

The idea of the wilderness presents another pastoral theme. Mark must want us to notice the wilderness, for he mentions it twice. The pastoral task is not necessarily one of helping people see that their lives can be likened to a wilderness; important as diagnosis is, diagnosis is not yet treatment; much less is it cure. The larger pastoral task is helping people hear the word of God in their wildernesses.

Mark provides clues as to what the resources in the wilderness are today. He points to Isaiah, and to John's ministry of proclamation and baptism. He heralds the coming Christ. Effective pastoral care and preaching and teaching today, speaking to persons who experience some expression of wilderness in their lives, picks up on these clues and points people to the strengthening help of God found in Scripture, assembly, preaching, sacrament, and, above all, in Christ himself.

MARK E. YURS

---

2. *The Constitution of the Presbyterian Church (U.S.A.)*, Part 2, *Book of Order* (Louisville, KY: Office of the General Assembly, 2011), 1.
3. *The Presbyterian Hymnal* (Louisville, KY: Westminster/John Knox Press, 1990), 40.

Exegetical Perspective

an independent figure with his own message, his own disciples, and a considerable following who continued alongside those of Jesus as a parallel community, and sometimes as a competing group (see Matt. 3:7–12; Luke 3:1–9, 16–17; 11:1; John 3:25; 4:1; Acts 19:1–7). The historical reality—that some members of the early Christian community had earlier belonged to the Baptist movement, that John never became a disciple of Jesus, and that Jesus himself had been baptized by John—was problematic for some early Christian teachers.

Each of the Gospel writers deals with this in his own way, each showing that Jesus, not John, was the true savior sent from God. In Mark, John has no independent message; all he has to say has been concentrated on one figure, the Mighty One to come. For Mark, this is Messiah Jesus, so that John is no longer a rival preacher of a competing movement, but has been incorporated into the saving Christian message as the forerunner of the Messiah. The point of Mark's brief paragraph about John, however, is not merely to neutralize the competition, but to frame the significance of Jesus in the story he is about to tell.

Although Mark's narrative Gospel begins without birth and childhood stories, when Jesus appears for baptism at 1:9, he is not a transcendent visitor from the heavenly world without antecedents in the nitty-gritty of historical reality. He emerges from the history in which God has been active through the ages, the history of hope and promise documented in the Scripture, the same history in which John the Baptist plays his own appointed role in God's plan. John had promised the "Mighty One" to come. Mark understands Jesus to be this Mighty One. The first thing said of Jesus is that he has a "way" (v. 3). By Mark's time, the Gospel's readers know that this way leads to the cross (though the characters in the story have a devil of a time accepting this). How can the one "crucified in weakness" (2 Cor. 13:4) be the Mighty One of divine power? This tensive question drives the plot of Mark's Gospel.

M. EUGENE BORING

Homiletical Perspective

John prepares the way for Jesus through his proclamation of baptism, repentance, confession, and forgiveness. In a twist peculiar to him, Mark does not begin with a call to repentance. Instead, he says that John called people to come and be baptized for the forgiveness of sins. Repentance and confession are necessary pieces of the forgiveness God bestows, but the first act is God's gracious, cleansing gift of the waters of baptism.

Mark does not begin his narrative in the "churches" of Jesus' day or even among the religious people of the time. Instead, it is John, a man living on the fringes of society, far from the halls of power, who first points to God's coming grace. From the wilderness, he calls out to the people, offering forgiveness for their sins. They come, says Mark, "people from the whole Judean countryside and all the people of Jerusalem" (v. 5).

Something about the message from this outsider draws them. This man who lived on locusts and wore the clothes of a beggar, who took no credit for himself but pointed always beyond himself to the "more powerful" one who is to come, attracted a crowd. Unlike the religious institutions of Jesus' day, whose laws and requirements for sacrifices placed heavy burdens on those who desired to make their lives right with their God, John, the outsider, offered something new. Baptism and forgiveness were God's gift to those who confessed and repented of their sins. No longer were the poor and marginalized excluded by their lack of resources or access to the traditional means of restitution.

Could it be that then—and perhaps now as well—God's message of good news can be heard most clearly outside the trappings of institutions? Do our churches unintentionally exclude the very people who most need to hear God's good news? From what "wilderness" places may God be speaking a fresh new word to us today, if we only have ears to hear?

LEAH MCKELL HORTON

Mark 1:9–11

⁹In those days Jesus came from Nazareth of Galilee and was baptized by John in the Jordan. ¹⁰And just as he was coming up out of the water, he saw the heavens torn apart and the Spirit descending like a dove on him. ¹¹And a voice came from heaven, "You are my Son, the Beloved; with you I am well pleased."

Theological Perspective

Just as Mark's Gospel leads off with an invasion of this world by God and God's reign, so in Jesus' baptism, this invasion continues. The verbs following Jesus as subject are essentially *passive* or those of a spectator: he came, was baptized, just as he was coming up out of the water, he saw. In contrast, the verbs following God as subject (either stated or implied) are *active*: the heavens are torn apart, the Spirit is descending, and a voice comes out of heaven. While other passages describe this intervention in more cosmic terms (e.g., "O that you would tear open the heavens and come down," Isa. 64:1), here God's invasion becomes personal; this is not just an encounter, but a possession.

Many readers have written on the Gospel of Mark as a series of exorcisms (Ched Myers's *Binding the Strong Man* comes first to mind). Jesus commands demons and spirits and illnesses to "come out" of those they have possessed, but Jesus' baptism reads like the reverse of an exorcism. At the beginning of his ministry, while he is watching and listening and coming up out of the water, he is possessed by the Spirit and a divine "occupation" begins.

Early theologians worried over the implications of such an "adult onset" invasion, leading to discussions of "adoptionism," the notion that Jesus was born only human, and was later adopted as the Son of God.

Pastoral Perspective

"In those days Jesus came from Nazareth of Galilee." Most of our people do not hesitate to say Jesus came in those days, but they know *those* days are not *these* days. They know *those* days are not *their* days. They think of Bible days as long ago and far away, and they wonder if what took place then and there has bearing on their lives here and now. Pastoral preaching and teaching cross the bridge from "those days" when "Jesus came from Nazareth" into these days that surround parishioners now.

Mark does not linger long at the baptism of Jesus, but he stays just long enough to point to the spiritual power at work in Jesus' arrival on the public scene. It is as if Mark says Jesus' appearance out of Nazareth is an answer to an old prayer. The prophet had long ago prayed, "O that you would tear open the heavens and come down" (Isa. 64:1). This is precisely what takes place near the Jordan after Jesus is baptized.

Mark goes on to suggest the appearance of Jesus is like a new creation. Back in the first chapter of Genesis, God pronounced as good all that God had made. Here, at the baptism of Jesus, a voice speaks from heaven announcing God's delight in Jesus. The arrival of Jesus to take up his public life is the dawn of a new day, the fresh morning light of a new creation.

That was then. This is now. Whether from the pulpit, in the classroom, or on a hospital visit,

Exegetical Perspective

It is virtually certain that Jesus was baptized by John the Baptist, an event that was interpreted in a variety of ways in early Christianity prior to Mark. The events behind the text have already been interpreted in the biblical texts, often in multidimensional ways. The preacher, teacher, or interpreter of Scripture is to bring out this (frequently multifaceted) meaning of the text, and allow it to enter into dialogue with the contemporary world and life. What does the story of Jesus' baptism mean in the Markan narrative?

Baptism as Public Identification. The first time the audience sees Jesus in the Markan narrative, he is coming from Nazareth to be baptized by John. This is the author's choice; he could have introduced Jesus some other way. Neither Luke nor John narrates Jesus' baptism; they refer to it only obliquely. Both Matthew and Luke introduce Jesus in their birth and childhood stories. Only Mark makes baptism front and center in the Jesus story. So also, near the conclusion of Jesus' ministry, in a key discussion of the meaning of discipleship, Jesus points to the disciples being united with him in baptism as central (10:35–40). In Mark's situation, as in our own time, believers were tempted to keep their faith a personal, private thing. In baptism, one publicly identifies with Jesus.

Homiletical Perspective

The powerful one is coming, and the preacher would do well simply to pay attention to Mark's unique beginning. Mark has proclaimed him the "Son of God." John has unequivocally asserted that he is unworthy even to untie the sandals of this individual, who will baptize not simply with water but also with the Holy Spirit. Given these remarkable introductions, it is surprising how quietly Jesus appears on the scene in this Gospel. There is none of the expected fanfare. There are no angel heralds or guiding stars announcing his arrival, as in the other Gospels. Instead, Jesus shows up for the first time in Mark in the midst of the crowds of sinners who have come from near and far to be doused by John in the muddy waters of the Jordan. No special attention is drawn to him. He simply goes down into the water with all the rest.

When high priests and kings of Mark's day were preparing to take office, inaugural ceremonies of anointing were performed. The pouring of oil symbolized to onlookers that the individual had been chosen by God for this important role. It was believed that through the ritual of anointing, God's spirit came to rest upon the anointed one. Jesus commences his work with an anointing, but not a kingly one. There are no precious oils. Instead, his anointing begins with his descent into the waters of baptism.

Mark 1:9–11

Theological Perspective

Even John Calvin worried over why the Spirit who had "formerly dwelt in Christ" should then descend on him "at that time."[1] If the reader notes the fact that the Spirit is cited in the passage that precedes this passage (1:8) and in the passage that follows (1:12), then the real issue is not whether Jesus was possessed before or after this particular occasion, but what such a dramatic possession, here at the beginning of his public ministry, implies—for him and for us.

Several things, theologically, might be said.

This Is God's Story. Following from the preceding section in Mark, it is clear that this is a story about God's initiative. God and God's reign are coming, ready or not. While human beings, and the Son of God, may and will participate in this invasion, this is an operation planned and unleashed by God. The actor in this baptismal scene is clearly God. Jesus comes, submits, and receives. Yes, this is a coronation and an installation as such, but the Messiah here, as in Psalm 2, is an agent and an instrument of the God who reigns. "Now therefore, O kings, be wise; be warned, O rulers of the earth" (Ps. 2:10). God's reign has come to earth, in the person of this Jesus, who is now possessed with "the kingdom, the power, and the glory" of his heavenly Sovereign. This is a story about God.

There Is a Battle for Possession Going On. While Jesus will demonstrate his power over demons and storms and the principalities and powers of this world throughout the ensuing Gospel, and while the crowds and the authorities will repeatedly worry over the "authority" with which this Jesus heals and exorcises and teaches, the source of Jesus' power and authority is here, at the beginning, made clear. In order for Jesus to dispossess others, he must first be possessed. In order for Jesus to invade and occupy the territory of others, he must first be invaded and occupied himself. "No one can enter a strong man's house and plunder his property without first tying up the strong man; then indeed the house can be plundered," Jesus later says to those who accuse him of being possessed by Beelzebul (3:27). Jesus has no power to plunder Beelzebul's property unless he has first been invaded and occupied. That is what is happening in Jesus' baptism, as told by Mark. That is what is happening in our own baptisms, as properly understood.

---

1. Calvin decides finally that this particular descent is less for Jesus' sake than for our own, "so that believers might learn to contemplate with reverence, his divine power, and that the weakness of his flesh might not make him despised" (*Calvin's Commentaries* [Grand Rapids: Baker Book House, 1989], 16:204).

Pastoral Perspective

ministers who say the heavens were torn open, but say no more, are boring at best. Pastoral encounters that help people hear tearing of the heavens now are full of interest. Where and how are the heavens now opening? Where and how is the Spirit descending? How is the God who makes all things new creating anew today? Preaching and teaching that venture to answer these questions, moving responsibly from those days to these days, will always have a hearing.

We cannot predict where the tearing will be. That is not for us to know with certainty, but we can do our best to name where the tearing was most recently. For example, the voice of a man dying of cancer broke as he told his pastor he had just received a card from someone else in the congregation, a woman who only weeks before was in a terrible automobile accident: "With all she has on her mind, she thought of me!" Did that simple card not tear heaven open for that man and bring God down to him?

In a Bible study class where the participants were sharing how they came to be more deeply involved in church life, one woman testified that when she was in high school, one Sunday during worship she had the sudden realization that there really is something to religion, that there really is Someone big out there, and she vowed she wanted to be part of it. Did heaven not tear open for her that Sunday morning? Surely her testimony was a tearing for those who heard it during the Bible class.

In like manner we can go on naming events that hit us "out of the blue" as experiences of the heavens tearing open. Doing so puts the present tense into our verbs and helps people think of God as near. That is pastoral.

Pastoral preaching and teaching try not only to bridge the gap between Bible days and the current day. It also seeks to connect Christian doctrine with the living questions of personal experience. The question of baptism, for example, may be particularly alive for a young couple new to parenthood and perhaps new to the church. Depending upon their religious backgrounds, they may have differing views on the subject. They may be trying to cope with the uninvited viewpoints imposed upon them by the members of their extended family or by persons within their circle of friends. Not every question around baptism can be answered by way of this text about Jesus' baptism, but some can. A visit at the time of baptism or a teaching sermon about the meaning of this sacrament can offer just the right pastoral touch of helpful guidance.

Exegetical Perspective

Solidarity with Sinful Humanity. Mark has presented John as preaching "baptism of repentance for the forgiveness of sins" (1:4) and described those who were baptized as "confessing their sins" (1:5). Without a word of explanation from the narrator or protest from John, Jesus comes and is baptized along with all the rest. Does this mean that Mark thought of Jesus as a sinner who repented and confessed his sins when he accepted John's baptism? Before we answer too quickly, we might ponder another scene near the end of Jesus' ministry. A seeker addresses Jesus as "good teacher" and is surprisingly corrected: "Why do you call me good? No one is good but God alone" (10:18). Such scenes are unique to Mark; both are corrected by the other Gospels to avoid the implication that Jesus is a sinner (e.g., Matt. 3:13–15 adds an explanation that explains Jesus' baptism as different from the others, and Matt. 19:17 removes the objectionable element from Mark). Mark himself has no such nervousness; it is in fact his narrative that raises such questions and evokes such explanations from the other Gospel writers.

This does not mean that he considers Jesus to be a sinner; this question in the abstract apparently had not occurred to him. He has no reflection on systemic evil and whether Jesus, like other human beings, participated in it. However, the baptismal scene in Mark makes it clear that if a firm line is drawn between the holy, sinless God and sinful humanity, Jesus takes his stand on the human side of that line in solidarity with sinful humanity. Jesus' "confession of sin" was his identification with his fellow human beings.

Declared to Be Son of God. There is more here than meets the eye. The heavens are split, and the heavenly voice declares that Jesus is God's Son. In Mark, this revelation comes only to Jesus—and the audience of this Gospel, who begin to be aware that they know things the human characters in the story do not and cannot yet know. "Son of God" is a key term for Mark in identifying Jesus' significance. Some manuscripts include this phrase in the title (1:1). Jesus is declared to be Son of God in this opening scene (1:11), in the transfiguration scene in the middle of the narrative (9:7), when he finally makes this claim himself at his trial (14:62), and when the centurion confesses him to be Son of God in the climactic crucifixion scene (15:39). There is no question that this title is deeply important to Mark. What does it mean?

The designation "Son of God" has several meanings in Mark's context: in biblical and Jewish texts

Homiletical Perspective

This one, who has come to save God's people, is not marked for his role in the ordinary way. Jesus, the Messiah, takes on an unexpected identity right from the start. Rather than being set apart from the rest of us sinners, he partakes of the same baptism, joining all the unclean there in the waters. Just as our ministry begins when we come up out of the waters, forgiven and freed to be God's people, ready to share the good news with the world, so also Jesus' public ministry begins with his baptism. There follows only the brief account of his sojourn and testing in the wilderness before Mark has Jesus speak his inaugural words: "The time is fulfilled, and the kingdom of God has come near; repent, and believe in the good news" (v. 15).

Jesus was baptized alongside sinners, but Jesus' baptism was not like anyone else's. Mark says that as Jesus came up out of the water, "he saw the heavens torn apart and the Spirit descending like a dove on him" (v. 10). Then God spoke to him, calling him "my Son, the Beloved" (v. 11). Something momentous is happening. This is no ordinary man. It is not clear that anyone else present at the river heard and saw the same things that Jesus did. Mark's readers are offered this inside view of Jesus' commissioning.

The language Mark attributes to God comes from Scriptures that would have been familiar to his readers and would have confirmed Jesus' significance. In Psalm 2:7 God speaks to his anointed Messiah, saying, "You are my son; today I have begotten you." Isaiah 42:1 speaks of a chosen one in whom God delights. Hinting of the events to come, Abraham is told in Genesis 22:2 to take his beloved son and offer him as a sacrifice. People who encounter Jesus in Mark's Gospel do not recognize him, but Mark's readers are given strong evidence that this man, Jesus, is God's own beloved Son, the promised one, who has been empowered by no less than the Holy Spirit.

Mark does not offer insight into the feelings or thoughts of Jesus, John, or anyone else present for this momentous event except God. As Jesus comes out of the water, says Mark, the heavens are "torn apart." This is not a gentle cranking open of a window, but a violent wrenching of a hole in the ceiling that bounds heaven and earth. "Tearing" does not happen neatly, or with a tool. Hands are usually involved. God's hands, in this case, rip open the sky, creating a gap through which God speaks to his beloved as he begins his work on earth.

Mark uses this same language at the moment of Jesus' death when the temple veil, also a symbolic barrier between God and the creation, is torn in two, perhaps by God's grief. The tearing of the heavens is

Mark 1:9–11

Theological Perspective

In baptism, we are possessed by the same power and for the same reason. We are now ready to listen to the liturgy more carefully. Yes, we can celebrate the Spirit descending like a dove on us and those we love. Yes, we can wonder at the voice of the liturgist saying to us and other brothers and sisters in Christ, "You are my sons and daughters, my Beloved; with you I am well pleased." Yet one must also sense the heavens being torn open and the Spirit descending, not just to comfort and commend, but to possess.

Listen to this baptismal liturgy:

Do you renounce all evil, and powers in the world which defy God's righteousness and love?

I renounce them.

Do you renounce the ways of sin that separate you from the love of God?

I renounce them.

Do you turn to Jesus Christ and accept him as your Lord and Savior?

I do.

Will you be Christ's faithful disciple, obeying his Word and showing his love, to your life's end?

I will, with God's help.[2]

This is an exorcism in reverse. We are possessed in order to possess others.

Yes, much of this language seems archaic and, worse, coercive and violent; and so it would be, and so would Mark's Gospel be—if this sovereign power were not most clearly shown by the Possessed One's suffering love on the cross. The truth is that we live in a world of principalities and powers ("And though this world, with devils filled, Should threaten to undo us"[3]). We are all possessed by Someone. Mark 1:9–11 makes this crystal clear. By whom is Jesus possessed, and with whom would he then possess others? Get ready. *God's* kingdom is coming.

RICHARD N. BOYCE

Pastoral Perspective

More difficult than the question of Christian baptism is the question of what is meant by the term "Trinity." All three persons of the Trinity are active in the passage about the baptism of Jesus, and questions about each person abound. Even the most seasoned saint sitting in the pews has questions about this historic and complicated piece of doctrine. Why does the church believe in the Trinity? Is this old doctrine still vital in the present day? If we must give the doctrine of Three-in-One serious consideration still, do we have to use the old language? What new language is there, and does it help or hurt to make use of it? These are living questions that call out for an answer.

Pastoral leaders can also be prophetic. Here let "prophetic" mean serving as a voice for persons who feel they have no voice or who are afraid to speak up for themselves. There may be strong reason to be prophetic around the subject of parenting. It is safe to suppose that the congregation includes sons and daughters whose hearts silently ache for some vocal or demonstrative expression of love from their father or mother. The proud affirmation spoken over Jesus by the voice from heaven provides the pastor with an opportunity to take up the side of these children and advocate for them. What more Godlike thing can there be than to use word and deed to express your love for and delight in your children? A sermon or lesson on this text, perhaps on Father's Day, can call for this Godlikeness and so help improve relationships and strengthen lives.

MARK E. YURS

---

2. *The Book of Common Worship* (Louisville, KY: Westminster/John Knox Press, 1993), 407–8.
3. Martin Luther, in *The Presbyterian Hymnal* (Louisville, KY: Westminster/John Knox Press, 1990), 260.

Exegetical Perspective

the phrase can refer to the people of Israel (Exod. 4:22); to true, eschatological Israelites, Israel-as-Israel-was-meant-to-be (*Pss. Sol.* 17:27); to the ideal Israelite, the truly righteous person (Wis. 2:1–20); to the Judean king, adopted by God at the coronation ritual (Ps. 2:7; cf. 2 Sam. 7:14); to divine beings, members of the heavenly court (Gen. 6:2, 4; Job 1:6); to the eschatological savior figure, identified as Son of God, Son of Man, and Messiah (*4 Ezra* 7:28; 12:25; 13:37, 52). Christians sometimes referred to themselves and other believers as sons or children of God, especially in their exalted eschatological status (Matt. 5:9; Luke 20:36; Rom. 8:14; Gal. 3:26). Hellenistic heroes and miracle workers were sometimes regarded as filled with divine power and were sometimes considered to be sons of the gods. Some Roman emperors claimed to be God's son.

The Markan audience knows that God has designated Jesus as God's own Son. They cannot know what this means from a priori definitions, but only from the Markan story. A beginning is made in this text. The voice of God speaks in words of Scripture. The Markan reader is already accustomed to this from 1:2–3. "You are my Son" is from Psalm 2:7, the coronation ritual for the Judean king. It is combined with "With you I am well pleased," from a Greek translation of Isaiah 42:1, introducing the Servant of YHWH. The king, like the Servant, is endowed with the powerful Spirit of God to accomplish God's purpose.

At Jesus' baptism, this divine power comes on Jesus (1:10). The kings of Israel, like all other kings, exercise power by violence and military might. The Servant exercises this ultimate power in service for others, ultimately suffering and dying for their sake (Isa. 52:13–53:12). How can God's royal power be combined with weakness and suffering? Mark offers no explanation, but invites the reader into the story world where this baptismal vision becomes reality.

M. EUGENE BORING

Homiletical Perspective

a dramatic and vivid image suggesting action, intention, and even emotion on God's part (see also Isa. 64). In choosing this language, which graphically depicts a new connection between heaven and earth, Mark helps us understand something of what God is doing in the advent of Jesus. For many, this is joyous good news: God, who was once far away, has drawn close. For others, God loose among us feels more akin to a dangerous, threatening, alien invasion.

In contrast to the violent image of the breaching of the sky, the Spirit is described as coming down upon, or "into," Jesus "like a dove." This gentle image of anointing is then followed by God's loving words of affirmation. The means by which God bestows power upon Jesus suggests that his power will not be the kind of worldly power given to kings, who wield swords and spears and chariots. Instead, his power is the power of one who has come to love and serve, to heal and feed and redeem. It is the inner power of spirit, not the earthly power of might.

Finally, God not only calls Jesus "my Son" but also proclaims him "my Beloved." This term of endearment is usually reserved for those who are especially dearly loved, as one's spouse or child is. In this simple phrase, then, God's heart is laid bare. Jesus is God's precious one. Anyone who loves so deeply is vulnerable to great pain and loss. As we know, God still offers this treasured one on our behalf. The cost of Jesus' advent and the events that are about to unfold is well known. The death of his "Beloved" will surely strike deep into the heart of God. Nonetheless, God proclaims that Jesus' life, which challenges anything that opposes God's love, even, finally, at the cost of his own life, is a life well pleasing to God.

LEAH MCKELL HORTON

Mark 1:12–13

¹²And the Spirit immediately drove him out into the wilderness. ¹³He was in the wilderness forty days, tempted by Satan; and he was with the wild beasts; and the angels waited on him.

Theological Perspective

If you have read or preached through the first two sections of Mark using this commentary, you *immediately* (to use a favorite Markan word) recognize Mark 1:12–14 as a "three-peat." Once again Jesus is less actor than acted upon. He is driven into the wilderness, he is tempted by Satan, he is with the wild beasts, and the angels wait on him. From the beginning until now, Someone else is controlling this story, Someone else is invading this world, Someone else is preparing Jesus as this One's emissary. While Jesus is about to break forth as an exorcist and teacher and preacher par excellence, here at the start he is less a leader than one who is led (note that while Jesus is "led up by the Spirit" in Matthew and Luke, he is "driven out" by the Spirit in Mark). As he was possessed, now he is tested and waited upon.

Now all of this is about to change.

Now, having been commissioned and tested, Jesus, for the first time in Mark, becomes the *active* subject of an *active* verb. In verse 14, Jesus comes to Galilee (as he came from Nazareth in v. 9). He then "proclaims" in verse 14 and "says" in verse 15. Without the context, the reader might miss the punch. This is still God's story, and this is still God's invasion, but now someone other than God or the Holy Spirit begins to act.

Pastoral Perspective

Whatever the circumstances of the congregation—urban or rural, large or small, liberal or conservative—someone in the church is battling temptation. Because Mark does not name the temptations Jesus faced, his spare account can help people see their own temptations in the light of Christ and master them with the strength that comes from God. When, as in Matthew and Luke, the action focuses on particular temptations faced by Jesus, it can be hard for people to identify with what is happening. His temptations are not theirs. Mark's account invites those in the congregation to consider their own temptations in the wilderness.

To be tempted is to be enticed to veer from the path one believes to be good and right, proper and true. When and how are people enticed to veer from the good and the true today? Where and how do they run into temptation? A profitable exercise that helps the pastor connect with the congregation involves sitting down with pen and pad and listing the known temptations before the congregation. The best way to start such a list is to begin with one's own temptations. The ones we name may be familiar wild beasts, or they may be surprises that come growling as if out of nowhere. If the exercise teaches nothing else, it drives home the point that no minister can address temptation without touching some nerve.

Exegetical Perspective

Biblical teaching and preaching must attend carefully to what is not in the text, as well as what is there.

What Is Not There. In the earlier and longer Q version of this story preserved in Matthew and Luke, there is a scribal-like debate on the meaning of Jesus' role as Son of God and the nature of his forthcoming mission, with Scripture cited by both Jesus and Satan. In Mark, there is *no conversation, no dialogue, no debate*. The Markan Jesus has not yet spoken. Jesus' first words are heard in 1:17: "Follow me."

There is *no fasting, prayer, or hunger*. The *angels* do not appear only at the end of the forty-day period, as in Matthew 4:11, but sustain Jesus throughout, as in the case of Elijah's forty-day struggle in the wilderness (1 Kgs. 19:1–8).

There is *no meditation, reflection, prayer, or psychologizing*. Mark does not speculate on what Jesus was thinking about, does not psychologize Jesus or romantically picture him pondering the meaning of his baptismal experience.

There is no *moralizing. Peirazō* can mean either "tempt" in the moral/ethical sense (e.g., Gal. 6:1) or "test" in the sense of determining whether something or someone is strong enough to endure. In this scene, Jesus is not being tempted, but tested. Jesus has just been declared Son of God and filled with the

Homiletical Perspective

Jesus has barely had time to dry off the baptismal waters when he is "driven" into the wilderness by the Spirit. The very same Spirit that descended upon Jesus in the form of a gentle bird now propels this grown man out into the deserted place, where wild beasts and demons are known to roam. The first surprise of this short passage is the unexpected role God's Spirit plays in sending Jesus to the place of testing and temptation. A more predictable storyline would have made Satan responsible for driving Jesus into the wilderness to face this difficult ordeal. However, the Gospel is clear. God sends Jesus there.

Many in Mark's audience would immediately have remembered the long history of God's people being put to the test in the wilderness, in order to prepare them to be faithful to God when they returned to their more settled lives. Therefore, even though it might seem that the same Spirit who had appeared as a sign of God's favor in baptism was now abandoning Jesus to the wild places, the long history of God testing people in the wilderness instead suggests that some kind of testing or preparation time is ahead.

The wilderness holds all kinds of associations for the people of Israel. The Israelites had spent a good deal of time there. In the wilderness they showed their allegiance to God, following Moses year after

Mark 1:12–13

Theological Perspective

The first act is *proclamation*. One could argue that, from beginning to ending, the Bible is an oracular event. God speaks, and a cosmos is created. Moses speaks, and Pharaoh relents. Prophets speak, and kings change their courses. While Genesis 1 leaves it to the reader to speculate just how human beings are made "in the image" of God, surely part of the correspondence is the fact that we communicate through speaking and hearing. While Jesus in Mark uses hands and feet and even saliva (7:33 and 8:23) to signal the kingdom, the main thing Jesus employs is his *voice*, which even the winds and waves obey (4:39).

It cannot be accidental, then, that the first action Jesus takes in Mark is proclamation. It surely is providential that through proclamation Jesus continues to speak and act today: "The preached Word or sermon is to be based upon the written Word. It is a proclamation of Scripture in the conviction that through the Holy Spirit Jesus Christ is present to the gathered people, offering grace and calling for obedience."[1] While God gathers, forgives, redeems, instructs, and sends God's people in worship, God's primary instrument is the human voice, in Mark and in sanctuaries today.

The content of the proclamation is the kingdom of God drawn near. While Jesus becomes present to gathered community through the proclamation of God's Word, the content of the proclamation is not solely the person of Jesus. Jesus does not come to Galilee saying simply, "Here I am!" No, this is not what Mark identifies as "the good news of God" (v. 14). Here is how Mark summarizes the content of Jesus' proclamation: "The time is fulfilled, and the kingdom of God has come near" (v. 15). While the life, death, and resurrection of Jesus are surely the first fruit of this kingdom; and while the way Jesus lives and the way Jesus dies in Mark embody the character of this kingdom; Jesus uses his hands and feet, his voice and saliva, his life and his death to signal the advent of a new age breaking into this world.

In the words of a recent statement of faith:

> We believe Christ gives us and demands of us lives in pilgrimage toward God's kingdom.... Our confidence and hope for ourselves and other people do not rest in the powers and achievements of this world, but in the coming and hidden presence of God's kingdom. Christ calls each of us to a life appropriate to that kingdom: to serve as he has served us; to take up our cross, risking the

---

1. *The Constitution of the Presbyterian Church (U.S.A.), Part II, Book of Order* (Louisville, KY: The Office of the General Assembly, 2011), 89.

Pastoral Perspective

When preaching or teaching about temptation, it is important to avoid moralizing. Moralistic ministers tell people what to do without guiding them toward the resources they need in order to do the right thing. Moralistic sermons, for instance, are often trite, unable to attract much interest among listeners and leaving the congregation powerless to change their lives in any way that matters. In the case of the text before us now, it would do little good to tell people to resist temptation. They already know they are supposed to do that. However, the majority of our people could use help in finding the resources they need to stand up to temptation when it comes— whether in the form of some ominous beast or, more likely, in the form of something more subtle and coy.

We suppose Jesus had strength to stand up to temptation because he was divine. However, Mark allows us to imagine Jesus did not battle on the basis of his resources alone. Mark says the angels ministered to him.

One task of pastoral care and preaching and teaching is to name angels who minister to us and help us resist trouble today. This pastoral exercise avoids the faults of moralistic preaching and helps the hearer lay hold of the strength that comes from God. In dealing with these angels, we do not need to think of beings with wings and halos and harps. We can think instead of any agent of divine mercy and strength that seems to bring heavenly help to situations full of beasts.

Who, then, are these angels? Naming the angels of present-day experience calls for another list that begins with what the minister has found to be filled with the help of God. What could be called the angel of laughter might be first on the list. We know laughter is good medicine. Perhaps laughter is an angel sent from God to help and to strengthen.

A woman told her pastor about how she and her two siblings were helped through the agony of admitting their mother, affected by an advancing dementia, into a nursing home. There were tears, of course, but also laughter over some of the odd things their mother would say, especially at times when a bit of comic relief was needed most. They were not laughing at their mother, by any means, but some angelic spirit of respite was coming to minister to them through from their mother's strange comments and peculiar observations. They looked upon the laughter as a godsend.

Examples of survival through struggle can be another kind of angel who ministers in the wilderness. One young woman was decimated by

Exegetical Perspective

power of God, the Holy Spirit. The world lies in the power of Satan, the Evil One who has previously prevailed against all comers. The promised eschatological savior appears, filled with the power of God. Will Jesus meet the test? The scene closes without rendering a verdict, but in the opening scene of Jesus' public ministry the demonic world cringes before him (1:23–26); he strides through Galilee casting out demons (1:34, 39) and declares that he has bound the prince of demons and is ransacking his kingdom (3:23–27). Jesus was tested, and prevailed.

What Is There. The Spirit *casts Jesus out* into the wilderness. The word is *ekballō*, the same term used for Jesus' exorcisms. He will later cast out unclean spirits; here, the Holy Spirit casts him out. This is reminiscent of the earlier reversal: John promised a Mighty One who would baptize with the Holy Spirit—but instead of baptizing and dispensing the Spirit, Jesus himself is baptized and receives the Spirit. This toying with language and theology is deadly serious: Jesus does not merely fulfill the hopes and promises of salvation already in place; he redefines, reforms, and reverses expectations, even as he fulfills them. The parade example is the fundamental Christian confession. If the Messiah is *Jesus*, then messiahship is not only fulfilled but redefined.

The *wilderness*—mentioned twice within six words, despite the fact that Jesus is already in the wilderness where John is baptizing—is not mere geography but theology. *Wilderness*, combined with *forty days,* conjures up the history of Israel, the forty years of in-between time after Egypt but before the promised land, the time of threat in the realm of deprivation and death, away from other people, when Israel was totally dependent on God (Deut. 8).

While the presence of *angels* is clearly a positive, victorious image, as elsewhere in Mark (8:38; 13:27), the reference to *wild animals/beasts* is not so clear. *Thērion* can refer simply to undomesticated wildlife, part of God's good creation (as in Gen. 1:24). The term also is used of the monstrous beasts of apocalyptic imagery, Satan's cohorts (Rev. 13:17–18; 20:10). Mark leaves the image for the imagination of the audience. He has a firm doctrine of God the Creator of all (10:6; 13:19), and one would be true to Mark by imagining Jesus as a second Adam, at home with the restored creation (Isa. 11:6–8; Mark is very dependent on Isaiah's imagery elsewhere, as we have already seen in 1:3). One would also be true to Mark by imagining Jesus, as he encounters Satan, confronting the anticreation beastly cosmic powers,

Homiletical Perspective

year, on the trek from Egypt to the promised land. In the wilderness they broke that trust when they fashioned others gods. In the wilderness they sought to provide for themselves, hoarding manna rather than relying on God's promises of food. In the wilderness God made and renewed covenants with the people. There they learned how to be faithful to an unseen God, depending on promises made with words instead of on human-made idols, as they had in the past. The wilderness was also the place where God delivered them.

For most of us today, wilderness is a symbolic state rather than an actual, physical place. When we recall times spent "in the wilderness," we usually think of times when the future felt frightening, when the path ahead was unknown, when all hope seemed to have vanished, when we felt completely alone, far from rescue, abandoned by all the things and people we trust. Even though few of us have spent time in an actual, physical wilderness, we have heard enough to imagine what it is like and to fear it.

Preaching this text offers an opportunity to reflect on the various places—in individual lives and in the world—where "wilderness" exists. It also encourages us to consider what we can learn from such experiences and how we are called by God to work to liberate people, just as Jesus did, from all such harsh, life-threatening places.

There is good news to be found in Mark's mention in this passage of the presence of angels who minister to Jesus. We have hope because the same Spirit that accompanied Jesus and provided for his care during this time of testing has now come to dwell with us. When we find ourselves in those places where we see nothing but empty, terrifying space around us, we too can trust that we are not there all alone. No desolation is so complete that God is not there with us. The Spirit accompanies us into the wild as well as the settled places in our lives. Like Jesus, we may find that we are strengthened by even the most trying times along the way.

Unlike the other Gospels, Mark does not describe Satan's temptations of Jesus. We are familiar with the detailed conversations Satan has with Jesus in Luke and Matthew, where Satan unsuccessfully tries to entice Jesus with food and power and glory. Mark simply says that Satan tempted Jesus. The dictionary defines temptation as the "incitement of desire." In a contemporary world where millions of dollars are spent by marketers and advertisers to "incite our desires," we preachers are sure to find rich material in this passage. For instance, what will it take for us

Mark 1:12–13

Theological Perspective

consequences of faithful discipleship; to walk by faith, not sight, to hope for what we have not seen.[2]

Note that the proper response to this proclamation is repentance and trust that this good news is true. It is time to get aboard. It is hard to miss the fact that Mark's Gospel would be a very different work if Jesus' proclamation had simply been heard and received. The same is true today. However, the rest of Mark's Gospel makes clear that this proclamation leads to a battle among the principalities and powers. In the person and proclamation of this Jesus, an invasion has begun that will stir up the demons, set the authorities plotting, and lead to scenes where the disciples deny him, the crowds shout for his crucifixion, and the soldiers mock him.

A similar struggle is set up in our hearts and in our world when this same "good news" is proclaimed. Only now we know the whole story; and now we have the same Spirit helping us to repent and trust the proclamation Jesus long ago brought to Galilee. Even so, Brian Blount warns all of Jesus' followers who would join in this proclamation of the kingdom's arrival: "Jesus' preaching is boundary-breaking, socially and politically challenging behavior. Contemporary believers who limit their preaching to pulpiteering follow rules of righteous rhetoric, but not Mark's way of the Lord."[3] Yes, it is time to get aboard—as preachers and hearers today.

RICHARD N. BOYCE

Pastoral Perspective

disappointment. Her dreams for her future were so damaged that she was more than tempted to despair. What kept her from being destroyed by despair were the noble examples of her mother and one of her grandmothers. These two older women each had been through terrible ordeals of their own, and both came out strong, happy, and full of faith and character. Neither the mother nor the grandmother had a set of wings, a halo, or a harp—at least none anyone could see—but each fine example was a ministering angel nonetheless.

Naming angels can be a happy exercise of pastoral care. Then what should we do about Satan? The figure of Satan occupies no small place in this text. Shall this figure occupy much of a place—if any—in our preaching?

Karl Barth taught that the devil and demons are subjects we should not linger over for long. The very thing they are waiting for, Barth said, is for us to "find them dreadfully interesting and give them our serious . . . attention."[1]

Theologian Donald G. Bloesch, my teacher and someone who draws deeply from Barth, refers to Augustine's comparison of the devil to a mean but chained dog. The dog's bark is vicious and alarming to passersby, but the tether or fence keeps it from getting loose to attack and do harm.[2] The devil, this image suggests, is similarly boisterous and frightening but, because of our union with Christ, harmless to the Christian.

Thus we can come to the latter part of the text and help people walk courageously and confidently past what is otherwise frightening and menacing. Once we sort through all the metaphors, the pastoral and encouraging word is this: even a wilderness can be faced if you look for the angels God sends to the tempted and the troubled. This is true even if the wilderness has Satan and wild beasts.

MARK E. YURS

---

2. A Declaration of Faith 9.5 Presbyterian Church in the United States (1976), http://www.pcusa.org/media/uploads/theologyandworship/pdfs/decoffaith.pdf.
3. Brian Blount, notes on Mark in *The Discipleship Study Bible* (Louisville, KY: Westminster John Knox Press, 2008), 1752.

1. Karl Barth, *Church Dogmatics*, III/3, trans. G. W. Bromiley and R. J. Ehrlich (Edinburgh: T. & T. Clark, 1960), 519.
2. Donald G. Bloesch, *Essentials of Evangelical Theology* (San Francisco: Harper & Row, 1979), 2:134.

Exegetical Perspective

and overcoming them in the hidden victory in the wilderness. This already evokes the apocalyptic imagery that is the framework for the Markan story as a whole.

The Markan Cosmic Apocalyptic Stage and Jesus' Role in the Grand Scheme of Things. Scholarship has long since outgrown the view of the older liberal theology of two generations ago, when Mark, the shortest (and "simplest") Gospel, was understood as simply presenting the historical Jesus, unfortunately spoiled by the later christological and apocalyptic views of the other New Testament writers. While Mark too had his "little apocalypse" (chap. 13), once this was excised, the Markan Jesus could be seen as a model of liberal idealism.

We now see that the Markan narrative throughout is cast in an apocalyptic, cosmic framework. Mark presupposes a grand narrative: God the Creator of all does not abandon the world when it rebels against its Creator. God called Israel as an instrument of the divine purpose for the whole world, sent the Son at the climax of Israel's and all human history, and will shortly bring the whole universe back to its proper life under the divine rule. The meaning of life and history is revealed in the advent of the Messiah, who calls believers to be witnesses to this good news. The whole drama is played out on a cosmic apocalyptic stage. Before beginning his life's work, the representative of God's definitive act of salvation is tested by the ultimate power of evil, and emerges victorious.

The victory is already won, but it is a hidden victory. The narrative that follows reveals that, to be sure, there are still demonic powers at work, but Jesus and his followers face a defeated enemy, and can live their lives confidently, between the times that look back to God's definitive victory and forward to its vindication. Human beings, even those who suppose that they have outgrown myth and are too postmodern for such grand narratives, may be deeply surprised and grateful to find in Mark's story of Jesus what they have been looking for without ever being able to articulate it. However, they must first be brought within hearing distance.

M. EUGENE BORING

Homiletical Perspective

to resist the daily temptations we face to turn away from God's will and ways in pursuit of other "gods"?

Mark understands Satan to be the leader of all the forces that are at work in the world resisting God's rule and reign. Throughout his Gospel, he tells stories of Jesus' encounters with demons, Satan's minions, who possess people, cripple them, and wreak havoc in their lives. Many of Jesus' healing miracles involve exorcising demons so that people can be freed from the destructive powers that bind them and keep them from enjoying fruitful relationships with others and with God. At the very beginning of Jesus' ministry, Mark describes Satan going to great lengths to lure Jesus off his given path.

Whether we imagine an actual physical being who offers Jesus every possible opportunity to abandon God's way, or simply the man Jesus wrestling internally with all the reasons and excuses any human might consider for turning away from the difficult task at hand, what we do know is that Satan did not succeed. Jesus emerges from the desert and announces that the kingdom of God is at hand. Satan's wilderness assault failed. Jesus' mission was not stopped before it began.

When we find ourselves in the wilderness, we too are tempted to preserve ourselves, to do whatever is necessary to stay alive, to relieve our own fears or pain or anxieties as quickly as possible, no matter the cost in pain and harm to those around us. In those moments, Mark's terse verses offer us a reminder that God's Spirit dwells in us, just as it did with Jesus, and remains with us in even the most difficult places. Therefore we are freed from the ever-present human temptation to preserve ourselves, because we can live in trust that we have already been rescued. In every circumstance, our lives rest in the hands of the one who came to save.

LEAH MCKELL HORTON

Mark 1:14–15

¹⁴Now after John was arrested, Jesus came to Galilee, proclaiming the good news of God, ¹⁵and saying, "The time is fulfilled, and the kingdom of God has come near; repent, and believe in the good news."

Theological Perspective

The beginning of Jesus' Galilean ministry in Mark's Gospel follows his baptism and temptation. Jesus came to Galilee, after the arrest of John, "proclaiming the good news of God" and then announced his message: "The time is fulfilled, and the kingdom of God has come near; repent, and believe in the good news" (vv. 14–15).

This passage is a summary statement that introduces themes present throughout Mark's Gospel. These form the core of what Jesus' disciples and, later, the early Christian church preached and taught. Mark 1:15 is not a fixed theological formula, as if Jesus had only "one sermon" and just delivered it in a variety of places. Instead, the themes here open into the ways Jesus explained and expounded them throughout his ministry, in different contexts. They open into what the church developed in its theological understandings, in light of the revelation in Scripture and God's work expressed through the biblical canon.

All four Gospels use the Greek verb *erchesthai* in their various accounts to indicate Jesus "came" to Galilee (Mark 1:14), to Capernaum (Matt. 4:13), and to Nazareth (Luke 4:16), and was seen by John the Baptist "coming" to him (John 1:29). As the Gospel narratives develop, this "coming" of Jesus means the kingdom of God comes as well.

Pastoral Perspective

When John the Baptist's ministry ended, the interim time and liminal space of Jesus' ministry in Galilee began. Immediately after John was put in prison, Jesus came to Galilee proclaiming the good news of God. "The time [*kairos*] has been fulfilled," Jesus said—not just chronological time but the season of God's redemptive work in history. Jesus of Nazareth, the Son of God, was culturally situated at a specific time and in a particular place. For us to understand his ministry we must return imaginatively to its setting in first-century Galilee.

It was not just a pure chance that Jesus chose Galilee for his ministry. Here among the oppressed and marginalized people of Jesus' time, God began the new work of the kingdom. Galilee was neither a religious center nor an intellectual center in Jesus' day. It appears to have been outside the mainstream of Israel's socioeconomic and political life. Galilee was the home of simple people: the hardworking, marginal, oppressed, left out, and the exploited. Jesus announced good news not in metropolitan centers but in small villages—not in Sepphoris or Tiberias but in Capernaum and Bethsaida—in fields, by the lake, and along "the way." Galilee was liminal geographically, economically, politically, and religiously.

If Jerusalem was the place of rejection for Jesus, then Galilee was the place of the kingdom. It was

Exegetical Perspective

Mark 1:14–15 is aptly described as the "seam" between the Markan Prologue (1:1–13) and the beginning of Jesus' Galilean ministry (1:16–8:27). It gathers the themes of expectation and fulfillment that are introduced in Mark's citation of Isaiah 40:3 (1:2) and recitation of the preaching of John the Baptist (1:7), while simultaneously giving those themes concrete expression in time ("after John was arrested") and place ("Jesus came to Galilee").

That Jesus comes "after John was arrested" does more than set the temporal significance, however. The Greek verb "was arrested" (*paradothēnai*) is used throughout Mark (eighteen times, ten in the account of Jesus' arrest and trial, chaps. 14–15) and conveys two closely related senses: to "betray" and to "hand over." The latter is the sense here, and it finds its closest parallel in the use of the verb in the arrest and trial of Jesus (15:1, 10, 15). There, the sense is that Jesus is being drawn into the events of the passion according to God's design, a design that Jesus accepts, however reluctantly (9:31; 10:33).

Is the same sense at work here? Does the "handing over" of John connote not only a political event but an eschatological one, the end of the anticipation of God's kingdom and the beginning of its arrival? Certainly the announcement of verse 15 that "the kingdom of God has come near" seems to support

Homiletical Perspective

It is rarely good homiletical form to quote Greek in the pulpit, suggesting the preacher knows Scripture in a way the congregation does not. This text from Mark might suggest a powerful exception.

Read the first chapter of Mark's Gospel in the Greek and the word *metanoeite* leaps off the page. First, John the Baptist shouts to the long line of sinners flooding to the Jordan: *Metanoeite!* Still dripping wet from his own baptism, Jesus shouts *Metanoeite!* to anyone who will listen. *Metanoeite!* is a Greek verb that is plural in number, present in tense, active in voice, and imperative in mood. *Metanoeite!* is not a quiet whisper from Jesus to a close friend; it is a booming call to anyone within earshot. The present tense and imperative mood of this Greek verb gives *Metanoeite!* a recurring urgency, something that is always the *kairos*—the right time, the pregnant moment—to do or to do *again*.

In English, *Metanoeite!* is typically rendered as: "repent." Unfortunately, "repent" limps around most churches today, handicapped by misuse and overuse. In the church's past, the cry of "Repent!" evoked scary images of wild-eyed preachers thumping their Bibles and haranguing any sinner in sight. Today, mainline congregations are happy to donate "repent" to denominations and sects that love its harsh and severe sound, using it as a theological dagger, an

Mark 1:14–15

Theological Perspective

What Jesus preached was "the good news [gospel] of God." This can be interpreted as meaning God is the subject of the phrase; and thus it describes God's own good news—the message that the time is fulfilled and God has come near (in Greek this is a "subjective genitive"). It can also be seen as describing God as the object of the phrase, referring to the good news "about" God that Jesus brings: waiting and preparation are fulfilled, and God's kingdom is ready to appear ("objective genitive"). Theologically, both constructions are true. Jesus preaches about God; and the news Jesus proclaims is God's own good news, originating in God.

Three elements form the content of Jesus' message.

The Time Is Fulfilled. Jesus' proclamation is that with his coming and the opening of his ministry, "the fullness of time" has come (Gal. 4:4). It is not that historical circumstances were waiting to be "ripe," so Jesus could make an entrance into the world. Instead, with his coming, time has now received its "fullness" and, ultimately, its meaning. As Karl Barth put it: "The mission of the Son actually brings the fullness of time with it, and not *vice versa*. With the mission of the Son, with His entry into the time process, a new era of time has dawned, so far-reaching in its consequences that it may be justly called the fullness of all time."[1] We now live in the midst of this "fullness" brought by Jesus. So all our time and activities are to express this new era and reality.

The Kingdom of God Has Come Near. There is ambiguity with the Greek term *ēngiken*, which can mean "has arrived" or "has come near." The best understanding is that "even though the kingdom has not arrived in power, it is already present in a hidden way in Jesus' ministry. For in proclaiming the kingdom, in exorcising demons, and in doing mighty works, Jesus makes God's rule present."[2] This is the amazement displayed through Jesus' ministry. In his life and work, a sense of the present reality of God's kingdom emerges, through the elements and actions Jesus taught his followers to look for and observe. They see this in Jesus' "mighty deeds," healings, exorcisms, and "signs," but also in the numerous parables that begin, "The kingdom of God [or heaven] is like . . ." In Jesus, God's kingdom reign is realized. This

---

1. Karl Barth, *Church Dogmatics*, III/2, ed. G. W. Bromiley and T. F. Torrance, repr. (Edinburgh: T. & T. Clark, 1968), 459.
2. Frank J. Matera, *New Testament Theology: Exploring Diversity and Unity* (Louisville, KY: Westminster John Knox Press, 2007), 9.

Pastoral Perspective

the place where Jesus healed the sick, confronted the authorities, fed the hungry, and crossed social barriers. When people heard him and witnessed his works, they exclaimed, "What is this? A new teaching—with authority!" (1:27). Jesus spoke truth to power when he responded to the scribes by forgiving the paralyzed man's sins and healing him (2:6, 11). Jesus crossed social and religious barriers when he "sat at dinner in Levi's house" with the tax collectors and "sinners" gathered there (2:15). The "country of the Gerasenes" (5:1), where he encountered the man possessed of a legion of demons in a cemetery, was liminal space between Galilee and the Decapolis. Death is always a liminal time, and Mark recognizes its liminality by reporting that when Jairus summoned Jesus to heal his dying daughter, Jesus took only three of his disciples and the child's parents with him "and went in where the child was" (5:40). On the Galilean mountain where Jesus was transfigured, another time and place so liminal that it still defies interpretation, a cloud overshadowed Jesus and a voice came from the cloud affirming Jesus' divine sonship and instructing his disciples to "listen to him!" (9:7). It is significant, therefore, that Mark's Gospel ends with Jesus going ahead of the disciples to Galilee and the angel at the tomb sending the disciples back to Galilee (16:7).

For many immigrants and racial ethnic minorities in the United States, the beginning of Jesus' ministry in Galilee speaks a significant word of hope to the hardship of their lives lived in a liminal place. *Galilean Journey* by Virgilio Elizondo[1] introduces a Mexican American theological perspective and understanding of this hope and promise. Similarly, *From a Liminal Place* by Sang Hyun Lee[2] offers an Asian American theological perspective and understanding of the promise of Jesus' ministry from a liminal space.

Both Elizondo and Lee claim that God is in strategic alliance with the marginalized to usher in the new heaven and the new earth through the creative potentials of liminality. Lee develops Victor Turner's ritual theory, in which liminality is that creative space of being in the in-between where one becomes more open to new possibilities: open to the new, to the *communitas*, and to prophetic knowledge and action.

---

1. Virgilio Elizondo, *Galilean Journey: The Mexican-American Promise* (Maryknoll, NY: Orbis Books, 1983).
2. Sang Hyun Lee, *From a Liminal Place: An Asian American Theology* (Minneapolis: Fortress Press, 2010).

Exegetical Perspective

this line of thinking. At the very least, the use of the term here presages its use in the passion narrative and reminds us that even as John is arrested and slain, so will it be with Jesus.

Jesus comes "preaching the good news of God." Behind the English translation "good news" is the Greek word *euangelion,* often translated "gospel." Again, the choice of vocabulary is hardly accidental. Mark opens his narrative with what is often considered a title: "The beginning of the good news [gospel] of Jesus Christ, the Son of God" (v. 1); the same noun appears both there and here. What is the difference between "the good news of Jesus Christ" and "the good news of God"? It is often suggested that the "good news of Jesus Christ" in verse 1 is the story of the life, death, and resurrection of Jesus contained within Mark; and that *euangelion* is the name of a genre of literature of which Mark (the first of the four canonical Gospels) is the earliest example. If so, then "the good news of God" is perhaps a broader term, intended to describe the content of Jesus' proclamation of God's transforming grace.

It is also true that Roman imperial decrees were called *euangelia.* To the extent that Mark is trading on this fact, it may indicate a co-opting of the term for Christian use: the Gospel demands a response with no less urgency than do the decrees of the emperor. In any case, the term "good news" or "gospel" is not a neutral term. Whether used to describe the contents of Mark's story or of Jesus' preaching, the clear implication is that the "news" is transformative. Having heard it, one is expected—indeed, compelled—to respond.

Verse 15 unpacks the contents of this "good news of God." The "good news" is both informational and imperative in content. Verse 15a contains two statements: "the time [*kairos*] is fulfilled," and "the kingdom of God [*basileia tou theou*] has come near." Both of these statements are openly eschatological in nature; that is, they imply the arrival of God's anticipated future in a manner that evokes a response. *Kairos* is the Greek term implying a moment of particular significance, a moment of decision. The arrival of a "kairotic" moment forces an immediate response, simply because its arrival implies a change in life and circumstance.

The term itself is not specific about the nature of the kairotic change. Filling in the content is the role of the second statement: that the "kingdom of God has come near." The "kingdom of God" has a long history in Scripture, reaching back into the Old Testament. Ancient Israel expected the reign of God to

Homiletical Perspective

ominous threat to "change your ways!" before the heavenly storm, brewing overhead, showers its judgment upon you.

Unfortunately, that is not how Mark uses *metanoeite.* This enticing verb in Mark has an almost irresistible allure. After his baptism, and having survived the temptations in the desert, Jesus arrives in Galilee to announce that God's reign is within breathing distance: "*Metanoeite!* Believing the gospel!" (1:15). Without question, *Metanoeite!* carries with it the notion that we have some changing to do, some new directions to take; its primary orientation, though, is toward God's future rather than our past. In Mark, *Metanoeite!* is an invitation to trust in a future made possible by the grace of God.

The first word Jesus speaks in Mark's Gospel is "*Metanoeite!*" Why? Because in Jesus, God makes it possible for God's people to do more than rerun the past. That is the gospel, the good news, the glad tidings toward which Jesus invites us to stop, turn, or turn again, and hold on to for dear life. *Metanoeite!* says our Lord; *things do not have to stay the way they are now!* In fact, to follow Jesus means that things *cannot* stay the way they are.

Just ask Peter, James, Andrew, Levi, and John—the first five disciples—none of whom applied for the job. Just ask Peter's mother-in-law, whose fever cooled with Jesus' soothing touch, or the leper whose life was no longer defined by his disease after he met with Jesus. Just ask those friends who lowered the paralytic through the roof, or the man whose withered hand caught more of Jesus' attention than obeying 4,352 Sabbath regulations!

Not everyone hears *Metanoeite!* as good news. Some spend their lives insisting that things stay just the way they are; they expend every ounce of energy making sure that things remain the same. Sometimes those people are preachers, and sometimes those people sit in the pews. Who needs to repent when nothing needs changing? Throughout Mark's Gospel, the religious leaders are so dead set on maintaining the religious status quo that they lose sight of the One for whom life is meant to be lived.

Metanoeite! means that every old way of living is going to change, every wall of resistance to God's future is going to fall, including the most formidable wall of sin. That is why Jesus not only tells the paralytic to pick up his bed and walk, but says, "Your sins are forgiven." In these four words, Jesus announces what every human being, including the most strident religious leader, needs to know: sin is real. Sin too often gets the best of us, reduces us, demeans us, and

Mark 1:14–15

Theological Perspective

is why early church theologians such as Tertullian and Origen referred to the kingdom as *autobasileia*, a "self-kingdom"—a kingdom expressed in Jesus Christ himself.

At the same time, Jesus pointed toward the final kingdom, yet to come. Notably, this is a reality for which his disciples are to pray (Matt. 6:10) and that will be a future, eschatological event (Matt. 8:11; Mark 14:25; Luke 13:29).

This is the familiar tension of the "already, but not yet." The kingdom has come in Jesus Christ but awaits final fulfillment according to God's will.

Repent, and Believe in the Good News. Jesus' affirmative and indicative words are followed by the imperative. The announcement of the kingdom has consequences in the lives of those who receive this proclamation.

To repent is to have a complete reorientation of life, a "turning" from one direction to another. Biblically and theologically, repentance relates to confession of sin and the ongoing movement of one's life and love away from self-interest and self-centeredness, toward the life called for by the new realities of believing in the "good news"—the Christian gospel, the message of salvation in Jesus Christ. This is the direction of the New Testament teachings and in a sense the whole rhythm of the Christian life itself: repent and believe; believe and repent.

Repenting and believing are ongoing dimensions of Christian experience. Calvin said we must "strive toward repentance," "devote ourselves to it throughout life, and pursue it to the very end if we would abide in Christ."[3] Theologians stress that repentance is not a "work," an action we do to gain God's favor. Repentance and new directions in life emerge from the mercy and goodness God gives, from the "good news" of salvation and the kingdom present in Jesus Christ. The astounding good news of the kingdom brings sorrow for sin. It calls for lives of obedience and service to God in Christ as disciples. Our whole Christian lives are spent trying to understand and live out the implications of believing the "good news."

DONALD K. MCKIM

Pastoral Perspective

Anthropologist Victor Turner in *The Ritual Process: Structure and Anti-structure*[3] provides the foundation for both Lee's and Elizondo's marginal theory. The Galileans were marginalized people who were located in a liminal socioeconomic and political setting. The structurally inferior are often the morally and ritually superior; secular weakness is sacred power. John's incarceration in Herod's prison would not stop the work of proclaiming the good news. Jesus takes up the baton and continues the good work. On the other hand, John has prepared the way for Jesus to unfold the mystery of God, in the spirit of the Judean wilderness, where the divine power and human sinfulness are in confluence with one another.

Jesus, an exemplar of God's strategic alliance with the marginalized, provides a way for all ethnic Americans to reclaim the potential of liminality. In Jesus' preaching, we can experience the transforming power of God, *metanoia*, redirecting our lives to begin the new earth and new heaven. This is the power. With specific times and specific places, God's promise of good news is proclaimed, creating new *communitas* for the people of God.

The liminal space and time, which many churches may experience during their interim period in pastoral transitions, teach us something of the beginning of Jesus' work for humanity in Galilee. The good news is the invitation to the wilderness where the liminal, in-between time and place can help the congregation in transition to envision greater things.

Each of us can be the liminal space in which the kingdom can become reality for others. Our heart can be a little Galilee. What was known as a marginal, forgotten, and barren land in Jesus' time suddenly became a center of God's salvation history for all humanity. Jesus is asking us to turn around (*metanoia*) from our own preconceived belief system to accept Jesus' real presence in Galilee. This is the hope of God's kingdom and the good news Jesus came to announce. It is an invitation for all of us (not just racial ethnic minorities) to enter liminal spaces and times and let the kingdom begin its work in us.

PAUL JUNGGAP HUH

---

3. John Calvin, *Institutes of the Christian Religion*, trans. Ford Lewis Battles, 2 vols. (Philadelphia: Westminster Press, 1960), 3.3.20.

3. Victor Turner, *The Ritual Process* (Chicago: Aldine Publishing Co., 1969).

Exegetical Perspective

be a time of peace, justice, and deliverance from the various social, economic, and political ills suffered at the hands of its conquerors (e.g., Isa. 52:7). The coming reign of God was also a day on which God would sweep away all that was contrary to God's will—including Israel's own disobedience and waywardness (Amos 5:18–20). By the time of the writing of the apocalyptic section of Daniel (Dan. 7–12), the kingdom of God is associated with the anticipated consummation of human history as a whole, and its arrival is occasioned by the coming of "one like a human being" (Heb.: "son of man," *ben adam*; see Dan. 7:13–14), a term that Jesus uses to refer to himself throughout Mark.

Verbs in both phrases are indicative perfect, indicating action accomplished from the point of view of the speaker. Thus Jesus regards "the time" as having now been "fulfilled" and God's kingdom as having in his presence "come near." The implication is clear: in Jesus the *kairos* has reached its moment of fulfillment, and the expectations of the faith community for justice, peace, and deliverance are satisfied. What remains to be explored is the meaning of this fulfillment and satisfaction: how is it possible that these eschatological hopes and dreams may be fulfilled in one who commands no army and wears no crown? What sort of kingdom is it whose king is "handed over" to die an ignominious death at the hands of foreign powers? This is the overarching question to which Mark addresses his story.

Mark 1:14–15 thus stands at the intersection between question and answer, expectation and fulfillment. Having raised the hope of the Lord's coming with John's proclamation, Mark 1:14–15 offers the "good news" that this hope is realized in Jesus. That realization will be tested throughout Mark, by the religious authorities, demonic forces, the power of Rome, and ultimately even death itself. The question "what sort of kingdom is this?" awaits Mark's unfolding narrative, as does the assessment of how good this good news truly is.

PAUL K. HOOKER

Homiletical Perspective

makes us less than what God intends for our lives, both as individuals and as communities.

In Mark 1:14–15 Jesus speaks what the people will see when the anonymous paralytic man stands upright in Capernaum: years; walls of sin start to crumble. Then on the third day, when God's grace overcomes even the sinful tyranny of the cross and death, the wall of sin collapses. That explains the imperative urgency for God's people to respond to *Metanoeite!*

Since *Metanoeite!* is in the present tense, it carries with it the idea of continuous action. You do not just repent once and be done with it. Would it not be wonderful if all our fresh starts would result in totally changed people and churches and nations? We know better. No sooner are New Year's resolutions made than they are broken. No sooner do we promise to be a kinder and gentler nation than we act in ways that portray anything but kindness and gentleness. No sooner do we paint the church as a place of high moral virtue than another leader is arrested for an immoral act, even while the church closes its doors to the human need on its doorstep.

Do not forget that *Metanoeite!* is a plural verb. Over the years, in English, we have downsized this powerful Greek verb into a singular, private affair. Of course, a person's decision whether or not to follow Jesus *is* deeply personal, but *Metanoeite!* is a plural imperative that extends beyond one's personal decision. Mark refuses to reduce *Metanoeite!* to a privatized response, as though the invitation of Jesus involved "just me and Jesus." Mark will have none of that. "Believing the gospel" is a group effort. Christian life is lived in community, always in community, no matter how many blemishes or scars.

So, on the Sunday when the congregation considers Mark 1:14–15, what if the first word for the preacher is a Greek verb, *metanoeite!* an ancient word that speaks with contemporary urgency in a world and even a church that too often settles for far less than Jesus' vision of the imminent reign of God.

GARY W. CHARLES

Mark 1:16–20

¹⁶As Jesus passed along the Sea of Galilee, he saw Simon and his brother Andrew casting a net into the sea—for they were fishermen. ¹⁷And Jesus said to them, "Follow me and I will make you fish for people." ¹⁸And immediately they left their nets and followed him. ¹⁹As he went a little farther, he saw James son of Zebedee and his brother John, who were in their boat mending the nets. ²⁰Immediately he called them; and they left their father Zebedee in the boat with the hired men, and followed him.

Theological Perspective

The power and authority of Jesus' words are experienced in the call to his first disciples. Two sets of brothers—Simon (Peter) and Andrew, James and John—are called from their tasks of fishing. They respond immediately and decisively. Their tasks as fishers give way to a "higher calling" (Calvin), which is to "fish for people" (v. 17). Leaving jobs and families shows their willingness to obey. Their call begins an allegiance to Jesus that is paradigmatic for all Christian disciples. This is captured in Peter's later confession: "You are the Messiah" (8:29).

Call. Calls come throughout the Scripture, from Abraham and Sarah, to Moses, to Paul, to the church (Rom. 8:28, 30; 1 Cor. 1:2, etc.). These decisive actions are by God or Jesus Christ. God is always the subject, the one who does the calling. God issues the word; it is up to humans to respond.

The call of the first disciples is a model of God's calling, since the call comes from Jesus and is directed to ordinary people. It is a call to follow Jesus. In this sense, it is an act of God's election in Jesus Christ. It expresses the choice to bring these fisher folk into God's kingdom, as disciples of Jesus Christ. They are elected or called for a specific purpose, to fish for people. As Karl Barth noted, they have a "commission to seek and gather" people, as

Pastoral Perspective

Jesus' calling of the first disciples looks simple in its description. Unlike in previous passages, however, Mark is writing in great detail and with striking emphasis. The story is not only about the calling of the disciples, but also about how to follow Jesus Christ, who is proclaiming God's good news. The calling of the fishermen is a graphic lesson in discipleship.

Jesus' urgent call required the disciples to respond by following right away. We do not know whether they were beginning or ending a day of fishing, but this does not matter. Following Christ is an act of the present, no matter how important your current work is. Leave the nets behind!

In this strong call from Jesus, we see the disciples completely surrendering, although what is more striking than the disciples' surrender is the power of Jesus' leadership. In this fast-changing age, churches everywhere are seeking strong leadership. Jesus' decisive leadership in calling his disciples can serve as a model for church leaders today. We need to educate God's people as imaginative and resilient leaders for faith communities, but it is important to note that Jesus did not invite the fishermen simply to follow his teachings. He did not offer them a trial period, free of risk. He offered no promises of ease or success. Instead, his call was direct, personal, and unconditional: "You follow me."

Exegetical Perspective

The public ministry of Jesus (Mark 1:16–8:27) begins not with a spectacular miracle or a pyrotechnic speech, but with a recruitment story. Jesus' first act is to recruit four followers. The story is simple and without ornament: he merely commands them to "get behind him" (v. 17), and so they do.

The story of Jesus' call to Simon and Andrew, James and John, has its closest biblical parallel in the prophetic call narratives of the OT (e.g., Isa. 6:1–13; Jer. 1:4–19; Ezek. 1:1–3:15). Mark 1:16–20 is perhaps most like the call of Elisha by Elijah in 1 Kings 19:19–21. In that story, Elijah "passes by" Elisha (note the similarity to the verbs of Mark 1:16, 19) and throws his prophetic mantle on him, symbolizing a summons to follow. Elisha follows, but begs to be released to "kiss my father and my mother" (1 Kgs. 19:20); Elijah acquiesces, and Elisha goes back to the team of oxen with which he was plowing and slaughters them as a sacrifice before setting out to follow Elijah.

Note the differences. Unlike Elijah, Jesus offers the four fishermen no prophetic mantle, but only commands their attention. The four do not return either to their work (v. 16) or to their father (v. 20), but simply and "immediately" (Gk. *euthys*, v. 18) "leave" and follow. Mark's Jesus calls his followers with an authority greater even than Elijah, the

Homiletical Perspective

Preaching on Mark, especially Mark 1, can leave preachers and congregations breathless. To fuel the rapid-fire movement of this chapter, Mark stitches each scene together with his favorite adverb, *euthys*. Often translated "immediately," this adverb is Mark's kindling to set the fire of his Gospel aflame. There is something about Jesus, says Mark, that demands our attention—immediately.

Just before our text, Jesus has preached his first sermon with two powerful indicatives—"the time is fulfilled" and "the kingdom of God is at hand." The two indicatives fuel two key imperatives—"repent" and "believe." Repent, not hoping that someday God may come near. Repent, because in Jesus God *has* come near. Believe, not hoping that one day God will come among us. Believe, because in Jesus God *is* among us.

Mark then moves into this passage to show the two imperatives in action. Walking along the Sea of Galilee and without one word of explanation, Jesus calls out, "Follow me," first to Peter and Andrew, who are casting their nets into the sea, and then to James and John, who are mending their nets. He calls. They follow. The word common to both brief scenes is "immediately." Immediately Jesus calls and immediately they follow. Whatever you do with this passage, be sure that you do not go lightly on the urgency.

Mark 1:16–20

Theological Perspective

those who fish seek and gather fish in their nets. This calling is "their election through Jesus. It is their election to belong to Him. And it is their election for the purpose for which He Himself is elected, for the proclamation to many, for the creation of the Church with its task in relation to the world, that the candle placed on the candlestick should illumine all that are in the house."[1]

Throughout the New Testament, "to call" takes on a technical sense for the overall work of salvation and means, quite clearly, the divine calling issued by God in Jesus Christ, by which, as Barth said, a person is "transplanted" into a new state "as a Christian, is made a participant in the promise (Eph. 1:18, 4:4) bound up with this new state and assumes the duty (Eph. 4:1; 2 Pet. 1:10) corresponding to this state. This calling is holy (2 Tim. 1:9). It is heavenly (Heb. 3:1). It comes, therefore, from above (Phil. 3:14)."[2]

"Follow Me." The call to follow is specifically the call to follow Jesus Christ. Given the conviction that this is the most important call in life, no other person or force could enact a call that has more significance or can make such a radical change for our lives. Christ transforms all previous "callings" in light of the one, central calling, which is to follow him. It is Jesus who sets his new disciples into motion, in mission and ministry, establishing them in salvation, and providing new life for them as participants in the kingdom of God. The Christian's union with Christ, by faith (Gal. 2:20), means our lives are "hidden with Christ in God" and Christ is our life (Col. 3:3, 4). We follow Jesus.

Jesus' call was to these ordinary, working people. He spoke a human word that led them to be united with Jesus and the mission he gave them. John Calvin noted that "Christ takes complete fools, both uneducated and ignorant of doctrine, as subjects for His fine training, for renewal by the grace of His Spirit, that they may excel all the wise men of the world."[3]

Theologically this indicates there is nothing inherent in the disciples themselves that commended them to be Jesus' first disciples. So also there is nothing inherent in any of us that commends us to becoming Christian persons and Christ's contemporary disciples. God uses "the likes of us," such as we are—sinners as we are—to be witnesses to Jesus Christ

Pastoral Perspective

Dave Gibbons, an Asian American pastor of a fast-growing multicultural church in southern California, New Song Community, proposes a liquid leadership for the changing twenty-first century.[1] Sharing his personal experience as a third-culture-raised child who belonged in neither the Asian nor the American way, Gibbons presents liquid leadership as a creative and fresh way of doing ministry and church from the global perspective. Just as the water in which fish live surrounds them and flows in a stream, so our leadership must be encompassing and address the flow of the culture in which we live.

In every instance of leadership there is also followership.[2] The people who turn out to be the best leaders are those who have previously been the best followers. The nature of leadership can perhaps be understood by turning the coin over and studying followership. The call and response is all about building a mutual relationship of trust through interactive communication between the leader and his or her followers.

This mutuality between leader and follower is especially true for the church. The gospel is for all people. Proclamation cannot be the work of one person. It requires teamwork. Each member of the team must have the same goal as Jesus. Giving up one's own purpose, each person must embrace the purpose of Jesus Christ. We become members of the team as Jesus passes by our lives, observing as we cast our nets into the sea of life. He is searching with his gentle eyes and calling our names, urging us to leave our nets to follow him.

Calling them by their names in Mark's Gospel, we can assume Jesus knew who they were. "Fisher for people" is the catch promise for Simon and Andrew. James and John left their nets, left their father, left their boat, and left their fellow workers. Would they have second thoughts? Mark does not deal with this. He simply tells us that they left everything and followed immediately.

Cesáreo Gabaráin captures Jesus' call to discipleship in a Hispanic hymn that teaches how to follow when the call is made. It tells of Jesus who has come to the lakeshore and seeks not wise people or wealthy people. "You only wanted that I should follow,"[3] sings one who has very little property. There is

---

1. Karl Barth, *Church Dogmatics*, IV/3.2, ed. G. W. Bromiley and T. F. Torrance, repr. (Edinburgh: T. & T. Clark, 1967), 444; cf. 588–89.
2. Ibid., III/4:600.
3. John Calvin, commentary on Luke 5:10, from *A Harmony of the Gospels: Matthew, Mark and Luke*, ed. David W. Torrance and Thomas F. Torrance, trans. A. W. Morrison, in *Calvin's New Testament Commentaries*, 12 vols., reprint (Grand Rapids: Eerdmans, 1980), 1:157.

1. Dave Gibbons, *The Monkey and the Fish: Liquid Leadership for a Third-Culture Church* (Grand Rapids: Zondervan, 2009).
2. There are many books about followership, e.g., Ronald E. Riggio, Ira Chaleff, and Jean Lipman-Blumen, eds., *The Art of Followership: How Great Followers Create Great Leaders and Organizations* (San Francisco: Jossey-Bass, 2008).
3. Cesáreo Gabaráin in *The Presbyterian Hymnal* (Louisville, KY: Westminster/John Knox Press, 1990), 377.

Exegetical Perspective

prophet whose return was expected to herald the arrival of God's kingdom. He who comes bearing in himself the fulfillment of the kingdom (1:15) demands of those whom he encounters an "immediate" response that waits for no tidying of personal loose ends before acting (see also Mark 3:31–35).

The narrative of the call of the four fishermen is structured in two parallel episodes. In each, Jesus is moving ("passed along," v. 16; "went a little farther," v. 19); in each he speaks ("said to them," v. 17; "called them," v. 20); and in each they "leave" something (nets, v. 18; father, v. 20) and "follow."

At the center of this parallel activity, however, is Jesus' singular statement that focuses the entire pericope: "Follow me and I will make you fish for people" (v. 17). English translations may give the impression that this is a conditional promise: *If* you follow me, *then* I will make you fish for people. The Greek eliminates this meaning, however. The phrase translated "Follow me" is *deute opisō mou,* and it should be rendered with a sharply imperative tone: "Here! Behind me!" (see 12:7, the language of the tenants as they resolve to kill the vineyard owner's son). Jesus is not inviting company for a pleasant seaside walk; he is summoning followers to participate in the kairotic moment of the coming of God's kingdom.

The image of "fishing for people" (Gk. *halieis anthrōpōn*) plays deliberately on the fact that the four are already fishermen, but there is more here than mere wordplay. In Jeremiah 16:16–18 the prophet anticipates a day on which God will send out "fishermen" to capture wayward and iniquitous Israel. In Mark, the four are called to the task of capturing people to Jesus. The usual interpretation attached to "fishing for people" is evangelistic: those who follow Jesus seek to capture other followers. In light of the strongly eschatological character of Mark 1:14–15, it is more likely that this capturing of people echoes Jeremiah's capturing of Israel to God in anticipation of both the judgment and the redemption associated with the arrival of God's kingdom. Jesus' recruitment of the four fishermen is not an appeal for evangelists so much as it is the beginning of the gathering of the eschatological fellowship in the reign of God. Such a reading would accord well with the urgent nature of the call, the sense of immediacy and near-impatience of this text.

The reactions of the four are consistent with such a sense of Jesus' call. Simon and Andrew "immediately" leave their nets and follow. Commentators have made much of the fact that a few verses later

Homiletical Perspective

Preachers and congregations may ask a number of reasonable questions at this point: What about the businesses they left behind? Were none of these men married, with wives, with children, with responsibilities? What about the commandment to honor your father and mother, as James and John leave father Zebedee to mend their stinking fishing nets? What were these four men saying yes to? Why was it more compelling to follow Jesus than to stay nicely nestled in their familiar routines? Reasonable questions, all. Mark answers none of them, nor should the preacher. Instead, Mark tugs at our arms and says, "Move along, immediately!"

The one thing we learn from Mark is that Jesus has a new vocation in mind for these four fishers. Preachers would be wise to listen to Ted Smith, who argues that verse 17 should not be translated, "Follow me and I will make you fish for people." Smith contends,

> This makes it sound as if fishing for people were a *task*. The better translation receives fishing for people as a new *identity*. A literal translation might read, "Follow me, and I will make you to become fishers for people." There is a world of difference between "I will make you fish" and "I will make you to become fishers." "I will make you fish" gives us one more activity to work into our datebooks.... "fish for people. How about every fourth Monday? Can anyone else do fourth Mondays?" But "I will make you to become fishers"? That promises a whole new life.[1]

Christian congregations tend to be composed of well-ordered folks who live well-ordered lives. For those averse to change, the Jesus we meet in Mark 1:16–20 can cause serious indigestion. Without a word of warning, he inserts himself smack in the middle of four ordinary lives and says, "Follow me—immediately." Pick another passage, preachers, if you think you or your congregations can keep regular hours, follow regular routines, and lead regular lives and follow this Jesus.

I am often astonished by how many people see following Jesus as optional equipment in life, like buying an extended warranty on a car. "Yes, I would like to purchase the 'Christian' option, just in case there is something to this Jesus, then, we are well covered." This is not the Jesus we meet in the first Gospel. Mark introduces us to a Jesus who is not interested in our occasional curiosity or our arm's

---

1. Ted Smith, "Homiletical Perspective," in *Feasting on the Word, Year B, Volume 1* (Louisville, KY: Westminster John Knox Press, 2008), 289.

Mark 1:16–20

Theological Perspective

and participants in God's mission and reign in the world. This points us to the work of the Holy Spirit in salvation and to the recognition that the grace and faith we receive are gifts to us, by God's Spirit, and not generated by us. We follow Jesus as our Lord and Savior by the work of the Spirit within us.

Response. The discipleship into which Jesus' first followers entered comes with a cost. The disciples' response, as recorded by Mark, was immediate and decisive. Twice in this passage, Mark uses "immediately" to describe the response. Simon and Andrew left their nets and James and John their father Zebedee and followed Jesus.

We do not know the ins and outs of what was involved for those disciples. The point is that their attachment and loyalty to Jesus overtook and transcended their allegiances and connections with the structures of life that had been most significant for them, prior to Jesus' call. Jobs and family were left behind in light of the call to this new vocation.

Whatever the details, these decisions could not have been easy or without pain. They represented a radical transformation of life and a launch into an uncertain—and dangerous—future. The disciples' response led Dietrich Bonhoeffer famously to say that when Christ calls a person, he calls that person to come and die. This is the ultimate "cost of discipleship." While we are not all called directly to forsake our current contexts to follow Jesus, our responses to following Jesus can lead to costly consequences in many ways. The witness of Christians through the ages attests to this reality.

Jesus formed a community of disciples, to learn and serve. By God's grace, we too hear and respond to the call to follow.

DONALD K. MCKIM

Pastoral Perspective

no money to buy food and no weapons to fight with. The poorest of the poor people have no choice but to follow Christ. It is a desperate situation that calls for a radical decision. Like many immigrants who leave their family and social network behind, the singer follows the call of Jesus to a new land and a new vision for life.

For our technologically nomadic world, what would it mean to leave the media network behind when we are called to follow Jesus? "Leave [*aphentes*] the nets behind" presents many different challenges and applications for us living in the twenty-first century. The word *aphentes* is also used for "forgive" in Mark 11:25 and Luke 17:3. It presents complete surrender of our body, soul, and even emotions for the new direction we are following.

When Jesus began his ministry in Galilee, he proclaimed that God's kingdom was at hand. It was the good news for all people, especially for Galileans, who heard the gospel in their backyard. Now the challenge is for Galileans to leave the comfort of their homes and their families. The Galilean fishermen left their homes to live with Jesus in the wilderness, journeying together, not knowing where they would end up.

It was neither the palace nor the temple but a cross and an empty tomb to which Jesus was leading the disciples. Perhaps they did not know what it meant to follow Christ until death; however, it was the only way to fulfill Christ's promise of "fishing for people." The command to "take up their cross and follow me" (8:34) hovers over the call to discipleship. John's arrest (1:14) is ominous, and leads soon enough to his death. The authorities, religious and political, soon conspire to destroy Jesus (3:6), and the work of the kingdom requires that Jesus make his way to Jerusalem, where "the Son of Man must undergo great suffering" (8:31). Those who would follow Jesus will therefore ultimately have to decide what that call means to them when they see the silhouette of a cross on a hill.

PAUL JUNGGAP HUH

Exegetical Perspective

Mark makes clear that Simon has a house and a family (1:29), and that Simon's abrupt abandonment of his family would have had a catastrophic effect on their economic security. Similarly, the family of Zebedee has a boat (v. 19) and hired hands (v. 20), implying the existence of some sort of business; James and John would have been heirs to the family livelihood, and their decision to follow Jesus would thus have posed a familial crisis.

Such interpretations depend to a certain extent on assumptions not immediately evident in the text, and may therefore be questionable. However, this may miss the point. The reactions of the four are best understood in light of the eschatological nature of Jesus' call. Such a call is disruptive, transformative, reorienting, and radical. It forces those who hear it out of their quotidian preoccupations and into a focus solely on this one who is the bearer of the kingdom.

It is worthy of note that nowhere in this text are the four fishermen invited to become "disciples" (though Jesus will use this term later). In Hellenistic culture, the term "disciple" (Gk. *mathētēs*) evoked images of students who attached themselves to a teacher by their own choice or mutual arrangement (as did the students of Socrates or Plato). By contrast, there is no hint of volition or choice on the part of the four fishermen. Instead, Jesus issues the eschatological summons, and they follow. The initiative belongs to Jesus, not to them.

Finally, both this pericope and its immediate predecessor make clear that the geographical context is Galilee (1:14, 16). Commentators have noted that in Mark 16:7, the angels tell the women at the door of the empty tomb that Jesus "is going ahead of you to Galilee." The reference serves as a literary bracket for the Gospel, beginning and ending it in the same place. It also serves a theological point: the place where the eschatological moment is announced in 1:14–15 and where the eschatological fellowship is created in 1:16–20 is the place where the moment is revealed in all its meaning and the fellowship is joined across the barrier of death.

PAUL K. HOOKER

Homiletical Perspective

length respect; he is interested in claiming and transforming our lives—immediately!

It takes courage to preach the Jesus we meet in Mark. I grew up in a sea of childhood civic Christianity that always preferred the polite "Christian" option rather than being engaged by the often impolite, living Lord. The Jesus I met in church was always well mannered, had encouraging words to say, especially to the children. He loved his mother, obeyed his father, performed marvelous miracles, and did not do anything that might disrupt decent and orderly church life.

The Jesus whom preachers and congregations meet in Mark bears little resemblance to the civic Jesus of my childhood. He is not looking for allegiance or amazement; he is looking to turn us around, to shake us up, to make us become fishers for people adrift in the sea of casual faith or no faith at all. The Jesus we meet in Mark not only promises to change our lives; he promises to transform them. He is not looking for us to make a decision to follow him eventually, when the time is right, when we have more information, when the economy is better, when the children are older, or when we are nearing retirement.

The Jesus we meet in Mark is looking for us to make a decision immediately, and then immediately again tomorrow and the day after tomorrow. There is nothing provisional or conditional about Jesus' call. There are no promises or guarantees. It is an absolute, person-centered call: You follow me. Preach any of Mark, especially Mark 1:16–20, and be prepared to deal with and be dealt with by anyone but the well-behaved Lord of my childhood who never expected much of us. Expect to be encountered by the relentless and transforming Lord who expects everything of us and right now!

Preach that Jesus and your congregation will meet Mark's Jesus who never leaves us as he found us, who is not looking for and will not settle for casual curiosity or convenient compliance. Preach that Jesus who wants nothing less than our complete attention. Preach that Jesus who is ready to lead preachers and congregations into a whole new life—immediately!

GARY W. CHARLES

Mark 1:21–28

²¹They went to Capernaum; and when the sabbath came, he entered the synagogue and taught. ²²They were astounded at his teaching, for he taught them as one having authority, and not as the scribes. ²³Just then there was in their synagogue a man with an unclean spirit, ²⁴and he cried out, "What have you to do with us, Jesus of Nazareth? Have you come to destroy us? I know who you are, the Holy One of God." ²⁵But Jesus rebuked him, saying, "Be silent, and come out of him!" ²⁶And the unclean spirit, convulsing him and crying with a loud voice, came out of him. ²⁷They were all amazed, and they kept on asking one another, "What is this? A new teaching—with authority! He commands even the unclean spirits, and they obey him." ²⁸At once his fame began to spread throughout the surrounding region of Galilee.

Theological Perspective

Mark's description of Jesus' early acts of ministry embraces two emphases found throughout Jesus' life: teaching and healing. These take place in the context of the synagogue at Capernaum, showing Jesus' participation in his Jewish context.

Jesus teaches in the synagogue, with definite results. The people "were astounded at his teaching, for he taught them as one having authority, and not as the scribes." Throughout the Gospels, people are amazed at what Jesus says and does. He is recognized as a "teacher" and a "rabbi" and frequently portrayed as teaching, in various settings.

The amazement sets in with the contrast the people perceive in the content and manner of Jesus' teaching, compared to the scribes. Jesus teaches as one with "authority" (Gk. *exousia*; also "power"). Inherent in what Jesus teaches is evidently that which hits people hard with a sense of truth and significance they are not used to experiencing from their leaders. No mention is made of Jesus' use of gimmicks or manipulations. His "authority" strikes home because it opens new ways of thought and experience, leaving listeners "astounded." Just as Jesus' "word" of invitation enlists his first disciples in life-changing commitments, so his "word" now elicits deep response in his hearers. The power of Jesus' word occurs over and over in the Gospel narratives.

Pastoral Perspective

People were astounded by his teaching. There was a power in his proclamation. There was power in his healing. There was a power in his silencing of the unclean spirit. The main theme of this passage concerns the question of authority in Jesus' teaching.

The encounter between Jesus and the unclean spirit unfolds abruptly, with the rather violent intrusion of divine power. Our human existence is so constantly surrounded with violent acts of injustice that the only way for Jesus to reach humanity is by countering with a form of divine power. He casts out the unclean spirit. When the evil spirit shakes the man violently and comes out of him with a shriek, the people at the Capernaum synagogue on that Sabbath are surprised and amazed. Perhaps they are scared. The spiritual fight between the unclean spirit and the Holy One of God continues throughout Mark's Gospel.

Jesus' command in verse 25 against evil spirits is *epitimaō*, which means "to rebuke." In the authority and power of Jesus' stern command, the spirit is not able to hide in the body of its victim any longer. According to Mark, this is the very first act of Jesus' ministry, right after he pronounces the reign of God and calls the disciples to follow him. Now Jesus demonstrates his power in the presence of his followers. The very first miracle is performed in the middle of a

Exegetical Perspective

This pericope might appear to contain two stories, especially given the paragraph break between verses 22 and 23 in most English versions (but not the NRSV). In fact, the narrative is a single unit whose setting is the synagogue at Capernaum (v. 21). Mark signals the connection between the two episodes with the adverb "immediately" (Gk. *euthys*) in verse 23, temporally connecting the two episodes. The more important connection is the common vocabulary of the two sections. In verses 21–22 we are told that Jesus taught, and that his "teaching" (*didachē*) possessed "authority" (*exousia*). We are not given the content of that teaching, however. In verses 23–28, Jesus exorcises a demon, and the reaction of the crowd to the exorcism is that this is a "new teaching—with authority" (*didachē kainē kat' exousian*). The implication is clear: what Jesus teaches in the synagogue is not a body of propositional knowledge; it is the embodiment of authority over the forces of evil. The "teaching" is not so much what is said as who is saying it. However, that begs the question: how is an exorcism a "new teaching"? Mark's answer: When the teacher and exorcist is in himself the kingdom of God, "drawn near" (1:15).

The worshipers in the synagogue are "astounded" at this teaching (v. 22), recognizing it as distinct from that of the "scribes." The scribes (Gk.

Homiletical Perspective

The title that the editors of the NRSV use to describe these verses is "The Man with an Unclean Spirit." How unfortunate. So let me begin with a word of caution to my colleagues who preach and teach: beware of titles, yours or someone else's. Titles can entice and invite the reader/listener into a deeper engagement with a text; but in this case the title sends the reader/listener looking for answers to questions that Mark is not interested in addressing. This title misdirects Mark's focus onto a man possessed by an unclean spirit and onto the unclean spirit itself, while Mark does not choose to focus on either.

If Mark does not focus on the man with an unclean spirit, the unclean spirit itself, or even on the act of exorcism leading to the casting out of the unclean spirit, then where does he focus? Anyone preaching on Mark 1:21–28 will want to pay attention to some common words/themes that appear throughout the first Gospel. The most obvious word/theme in this text is "teach." While Mark's Gospel does not have an extended teaching segment from the mountain (Matthew) or the plain (Luke) and the writer does not pepper his testimony with parables, for Mark, Jesus is the consummate teacher, and Jesus distinguishes himself from other teachers in the synagogue because he teaches with "authority" (another prominent Markan theme). These early verses in the

Mark 1:21–28

Theological Perspective

Jesus' word in action is dramatically experienced again when Jesus is confronted by a "man with an unclean spirit" (v. 23). Here the unclean spirit speaks through the man who is possessed. The reality of such forces is taken for granted by the New Testament writers, and Jesus' miracles of exorcism and healing display his power over such powers. The New Testament does not show direct interest in these forces in themselves. Its interest is in the clash between Jesus and these powers, and the victory of Jesus when the confrontations take place. Jesus (and later his disciples) are able to liberate those who are oppressed by such "unclean spirits," since the power of God is stronger than all lordless powers that oppose God's reign. In his crucifixion, resurrection, and ascension, Jesus' victory over such powers is established (Col. 2:14–15; 1 Pet. 3:22).

The unclean spirit recognizes Jesus as "the Holy One of God," who has come "to destroy us" (either multiple spirits in the man or speaking on behalf of all unclean spirits in general; v. 24). Jesus' word of rebuke and command silences the spirits as they convulse the man and come "out of him" (v. 26). Again, the word of Jesus carries effect and establishes Jesus' power while also healing the man of his affliction. The crowds recognize Jesus' authoritative teaching and actions, even over "unclean spirits." As a result, Jesus' fame begins to spread through Galilee.

The Gospels are filled with Jesus' "miracles" and accounts of the acts of power that take place through him. This fact embarrassed some earlier generations of biblical interpreters who sought to provide rational "explanations" for the miraculous and to relegate these accounts to the "prescientific" status of the biblical writers. Today, the miracle stories of Jesus are sometimes said to be stumbling blocks to faith for those enmeshed in a scientific culture.

However, the miracle stories are significant as expressions of the authority and power of Jesus and as signs of the kingdom of God (Matt. 11:5; Luke 7:22). In the life and ministry of Jesus, his authority over all powers is exhibited in miracle accounts. These, in themselves, are a witness to the kingdom of God, which is underway and characterized by such acts, and to the future time when the reign of God is established in all its fullness.

In another theological sense, Karl Barth has said that what "always takes place" in the miracle stories is that "in and with them a completely new and astonishing light—and in all its different

Pastoral Perspective

simple teaching lesson. After the dramatic exorcism, notice that the people respond, "What is this? A new teaching?" (v. 27). Word and work are intertwined such that the power at work in the exorcism is still active whenever Jesus' word is proclaimed.

In this story, miracles are only a part of Jesus' teaching ministry. The focus of the narrative is not necessarily on the miracle itself. In fact, miracles sometimes confuse people and lead them to misunderstand Jesus' true identity (8:11–33). The story of Jesus' Galilean ministry begins with this dramatic act of God's power. It is not merely a miracle story about casting out an evil spirit. There is much more life to it. The only one who knows the identity of the teacher is the unclean spirit! How is it that Jesus' name is confessed not by the religious leaders or the congregation in the synagogue, but by the spirit that opposes Jesus? What sort of confession is this?

Midway through the Gospel, Peter confesses, "You are the Messiah" (8:29), but he still does not understand the nature of Jesus' messiahship, in particular that it will require him to suffer and die. The only true confession comes in the last scene of the passion narrative. Having heard Jesus' cry and then seeing him die, the centurion—a Gentile—confesses, "Truly this man was God's Son!" (15:39). Jesus' teaching reveals that the genuine confession of our faith needs to wait until the time of the cross and resurrection of Christ. Until then, Jesus, the Holy One of God, silences the unclean spirit so that it will not reveal his identity. Who he is must be kept secret until the right time. The identity of Jesus is always hidden in Mark's narrative. Ultimately, Jesus' identity is revealed, not by his mighty acts or his teachings, but by his death. According to Mark, Jesus' identity is an eternal mystery and cannot be revealed until it can be understood in the light of his crucifixion and resurrection.

If this story were set in our time, how would the unclean spirit present itself? Such spirits come to us and take possession of our lives in the form of obsession and fear. All kinds of addictions (to alcohol, drug, narcotics, sex, money, and power) might be identified as evil spirits whose presence in us is manifest in anger and violence.

However, the unclean spirits of addictions are only one manifestation of the world's opposition to Jesus' authority and power that called forth his rebuke. The religious leaders were called evil when they opposed Jesus (2:1–3:6). Nature's power to destroy life was silenced by Jesus (4:37–39). Peter, Jesus' most intimate friend and advocate, was also rebuked (8:33).

Exegetical Perspective

grammateis) were scholars of Torah, and their exegetical method was to clarify one passage by examining others using the same vocabulary, informed by the comments of previous scholarship (a method that continues to be useful in our own time). The temptation is strong to read verse 22 as a condemnation of scholarly study in favor of "spiritual insight" that relies on no authority but itself.

Not only does this miss the point of the text, focusing on scribal scholarship instead of on Jesus himself; it also misunderstands the role of all human interpreters of Scripture. As a careful reading of Mark makes clear, Jesus is unique among all "teachers" in that he is the kingdom of God drawn near, the eschatological future breaking into history. All authority rests ultimately on the authority of God, expressed in the one who is, as the demonic powers will shortly confess, the "Holy One of God." Only Jesus can teach as he teaches, because only he is Jesus. For anyone else to presume to take his place is arrogance and folly.

The nature of that authority is immediately revealed in the exorcism in verses 23–28. The story of the exorcism conforms to the well-understood conventions of miracle stories in almost all ancient literature. There is a problem that must be resolved (v. 23, a man with an "unclean spirit"), an action on the part of Jesus that resolves the problem (v. 25, Jesus commands the spirit to "come out of him"), some evidence that the action effects a resolution (v. 26, the spirit "convulses" the man and comes out), and a reaction on the part of the observers (v. 27, they are "amazed" and discuss with each other this "new teaching—with authority").

While this structure recounts the actions necessary to the story, the additional details convey key elements in determining its significance. In these details, the confrontation between Jesus and the unclean spirit is the centerpiece. The spirit's question, usually translated "What have you to do with us?" (Gk. *ti hēmin kai soi*, v. 24), is probably best understood, "What do we have in common with you?" The words are less a question than a challenge; the spirit perceives Jesus as invading its (their) domain. Indeed, the next statement confirms this: they "know who you are, the Holy One of God" (v. 24). To the spirit, Jesus belongs in the kingdom of God, not in the sphere of history. The kingdom has drawn near, though, eradicating old boundaries and claiming history and creation for the kingdom.

Modern readers often struggle with stories of demon possession and exorcism. We understand

Homiletical Perspective

first chapter establish what will be a conflict until the hour of his crucifixion: whose teaching has divine authority—that of the leaders of synagogues and the religious parties in Jerusalem or that of Jesus?

What would it mean for the church today to be engaged seriously and intensively with the teaching of Jesus as Mark presents it? For Mark, Jesus "teaches" by his actions as much as his words; he is not a visiting lecturer, someone whom you listen to and then decide later if you can endorse his teaching. Jesus is someone to follow (see 1:16–20); and in the following, you will listen and see "teaching" that will transform your life, teaching with authority/power (Gk. *exousia*). Throughout the Gospel, and especially in this passage, questions of authority/power are central, and they are raised not simply by those in the synagogue but also by a community of demons possessing an anonymous man.

Mark's Jesus is not for the casual Christian who is glad to give Jesus an affectionate nod and happy to have Jesus as an occasional colleague. From 1:1, the narrator tells us that with the reign of God set loose in the world, no sphere of authority/power will hold sway against the divine authority/power of Jesus. In Mark's Gospel Jesus is no one's colleague or buddy or chum. Jesus is "the Christ," "the Son of God" (1:1).

For Mark, Jesus teaches with authority/power. Therefore he is not one choice teacher among many good teachers out there; he is the one teacher whose life is stamped with the divine seal of God. Too often in postmodern America, if Jesus is discussed at all, he is considered as one teacher in a pantheon of other great teachers. Not for Mark. In Mark's Gospel, Jesus is the one teacher worth attending to by setting everything else aside. In Mark, as evidenced in this passage, even the most demonic forces of the day recognize the teaching, healing, life-giving authority/power of Jesus. What would it mean for the church to preach Mark's Jesus and watch people wake from their Sunday worship yawns?

Invite those inside and outside your congregations who find Christianity a curious, premodern, religious sect, fascinated with magic and obsessed with the scientifically absurd, to read this passage. In Mark 1:21–28, "There are no incantations, no magic words, no props, no ceremonies or rituals. It is also important to see that there is no struggle. From the very first, Jesus stands before a defeated enemy."[1] Magic produces amazement (almost never

---

1. M. Eugene Boring, *Mark, A Commentary*, The New Testament Library (Louisville, KY: Westminster John Knox Press, 2006), 65.

Mark 1:21–28

Theological Perspective

manifestations the same light—was cast on the human situation."[1] God in Jesus Christ relates to those in need.

Among the things Barth said about miracle stories, three concepts can be adapted.

God Is Directly Interested in People. Jesus showed interest, care, and love for the humans he came to "seek out and to save" (Luke 19:10). God's care is crystallized in the establishment of God's kingdom in Jesus Christ who, as the kingdom himself, enacts the mind and heart of God in the Gospel stories. Nowhere does the flame of love for humans burn brighter than in miracle stories. Here Jesus frees and liberates those who suffer, a paradigm of his wider work of salvation. All suggestions that the gospel is limited to "spiritual matters" or that the church should not be involved in ministries of healing and mental and physical relief are rejected on the basis of Jesus' healing miracles.

***God Is at Our Sides and All That Causes Suffering to Us Is "Painful and Alien and Antithetical" to God.*[2]** Liberation theologians speak of God as on the side of the poor. This is true and is wide enough to mean that God is with all who suffer, in whatever ways. God in Jesus enters into our sufferings. In Jesus' kingdom activities, he expressed "a defiance of the power of destruction which enslaves [humans], of *phthora* [destruction] in all its forms."[3] Jesus' exorcism of the unclean spirits is this action against the forces of ruin that rob life of the fullness God wants us to experience.

Jesus Conveys God's Free Grace. All the healing miracles are acts of Jesus' love and care, and the free grace he came to bring to the world. Jesus was "full of grace and truth" (John 1:14). This grace was offered freely as Jesus healed persons in body and soul. This free grace given in Jesus underlies all our efforts to heal and bring relief to those who suffer: "We love because he first loved us" (1 John 4:19).

Jesus' word of authority and actions in healing can continue today through the church's proclamation and enacting the kingdom of God that Jesus brought and is.

DONALD K. MCKIM

Pastoral Perspective

In addition, when we are fueled by our own pride, our unlimited claims for our limited knowledge can also serve as an evil spirit. When we engage in the interpretation of a text, therefore, we also need to allow Jesus' rebuke to create working space for us to accept silence and wait for the revealing of the mystery of Jesus' true identity. Our encounter with stories in Scripture such as this one requires us to silence our own prior understanding of who Christ is. Theologically trained pastors also need to put their scribe hats aside and put on the authority of Jesus when they preach.

Our own conviction and our own belief system as well as the unclean spirits within us can sometimes lead us to recognize the Holy One of God. Yet we must examine ourselves to clarify what purpose our confession is serving. Does our confession help others to recognize the Holy One of God as the unclean spirits within them are vanquished? The story leads us to see the importance of the teaching ministry as it guides people to recognize the ultimate authority in the words of Jesus.

Thomas Troeger has written a poignant hymn on this text:

> "Silence! Frenzied, unclean spirit," cried God's healing, Holy One.
> "Cease your ranting! Flesh can't bear it. Flee as night before the sun."[1]

To preach on this difficult periscope, we need to recognize ourselves as vulnerable and as the one who was possessed by an evil spirit. No one is exempt from the danger of a violent confrontation with the word of Jesus. We must trust and believe that Jesus has come not to destroy us but to restore, heal, and save, so that we may obey his loving authority. That indeed is a new teaching!

PAUL JUNGGAP HUH

---

1. Karl Barth, *Church Dogmatics*, IV/2, ed. Geoffrey W. Bromiley and Thomas F. Torrance, repr. (Edinburgh: T. & T. Clark, 1967), 220.
2. Ibid., 225.
3. Ibid., 232.

1. Thomas Troeger, "Silence! Frenzied, Unclean Spirit," in *Glory to God* (Louisville, KY: Westminster John Knox Press, 2013), 180.

Exegetical Perspective

persons afflicted with convulsions to be the victims of mental and physical illnesses, not hostages of evil. The temptation is always to psychologize these stories so that Jesus becomes more therapist than Messiah. Such interpretations miss the point. The confrontation described in this and other exorcism narratives in Mark (see also 5:1–20; 7:24–30; 9:14–29) is not the human interaction between Jesus and the afflicted man; it is the eschatological conflict of the kingdom of God and the forces of evil. In a significant sense, the synagogue and the afflicted man are little more than the stage on which is acted out this greater drama.

Jesus' only words in this episode are his commands to the unclean spirit: "Be silent, and come out of him!" (v. 25). Jesus silences the spirits because they make a claim that Jesus himself is not ready to reveal. Markan scholarship for more than a century has noted that Jesus either rebukes or corrects those who state openly that he is the Messiah or the Son of God (e.g., 8:30). The only point at which such confessions are not either rebuked or corrected is the Roman soldier's confession at the foot of the cross: "Truly this man was God's Son" (15:39). At the same time, the exorcisms and other healings testify to the inbreaking of the kingdom of God, a fact that all the rebukes and corrections cannot hide. The Gospel thus sets up a tension between the "hiding" of Jesus' identity as the bearer of God's kingdom and the simultaneous revelation of that identity in acts of exorcism and healing. In the last analysis, only Jesus' crucifixion and resurrection will resolve this tension, making clear that Jesus initiates God's promised kingdom through his self-sacrificial death on the cross.

The unclean spirit immediately obeys Jesus' command, in effect recognizing that its power over the human realm is ended. Jesus has indeed "come to destroy" the powers that threaten and demonize human life.

In the end, the "new teaching" demonstrated in the exorcism is that one "with authority" has come at the head of God's kingdom, to declare the eschatological moment and to reveal its power to alter the landscape of reality. Small wonder those who witnessed this teaching were "amazed."

PAUL K. HOOKER

Homiletical Perspective

a favorable term in Mark's Gospel), but amazement is not faith. In the great eschatological battle for the religious imagination that is Mark 1 (and arguably, the entire Gospel), Mark calls his audience not to amazement over the wonder-working deeds of Jesus, but to faith in the One who has already won the eschatological battle over Satan.

What would it mean for preachers to introduce congregations *not* to the "amazing Jesus" who performed miracles and cast out demons in Galilee and, if we believe hard enough, may yet do the same for us and others today? What would it mean for preachers to introduce congregations *not* to the "moralizing Jesus" who lived a truly good life and stands ready to be our best possible ethics coach? What would it mean for preachers to introduce congregations *not* to the "charming Jesus" who drew great crowds (a common theme in chapters 1–10) and who still holds the charisma to draw great crowds to fill our empty pews? What would it mean to preach the Jesus we meet in Mark's Gospel: the Jesus who will settle for nothing less than our wholehearted allegiance and unwavering trust and who silences even the most demonic voices of evil?

Preachers would do well to think long and hard about how to title this passage and how to title a sermon on this text. Dare to preach the Jesus who does not appear first in a manger in Mark's Gospel wrapped in swaddling clothes, but appears first knee-deep in the Jordan with the heavens ripped open, indicating that the reign of God is set loose on earth. Preach that Jesus, and it will not matter what you title the sermon. Just get out of the way, and stand not in amazement, but in faith, at what this Jesus can "teach" the church.

GARY W. CHARLES

Mark 1:29-34

²⁹As soon as they left the synagogue, they entered the house of Simon and Andrew, with James and John. ³⁰Now Simon's mother-in-law was in bed with a fever, and they told him about her at once. ³¹He came and took her by the hand and lifted her up. Then the fever left her, and she began to serve them.

³²That evening, at sundown, they brought to him all who were sick or possessed with demons. ³³And the whole city was gathered around the door. ³⁴And he cured many who were sick with various diseases, and cast out many demons; and he would not permit the demons to speak, because they knew him.

Theological Perspective

A remarkable feature in the healing of Simon's (Peter's) mother-in-law is the swift efficiency of Jesus' action. He says no words, offers no prayer, performs no command. In one brief sentence, the Gospel tells us that he takes her by the hand and lifts her up, the fever leaves her, and she is able to serve (v. 31). The simplicity, immediacy, and complete effectiveness of this healing is, in its own way, more impressive than the later, more complicated healing of the boy with convulsions (9:14–29), in which Jesus also takes someone by the hand and raises him up.

The drama in the story of Simon's mother-in-law is found in its lean decisiveness. The people in the house tell Jesus merely that she is ill. He goes, takes her hand, and raises her up, as simple as that. We could quibble that a more elaborate cure was necessary for the demon-possessed boy, but in so doing, we overlook the seriousness of the mother-in-law's incapacitating fever, which could be the precursor of an agonizing death. Rather, the stark immediacy evident in Jesus' healing follows closely upon the description of Jesus' teaching as that of "one with authority" (1:22, 27). He speaks as one with authority, and he heals in the same way.

As the Gospel progresses, and as his passion approaches, the crowds become more skeptical and hostile, and Jesus' apparently effortless, authoritative

Pastoral Perspective

The narrative moves quickly from the Gospel's beginning, from the way being prepared, to Jesus identified as God's Son, the Beloved, in the waters of baptism. He resists the temptations in the wilderness while John is arrested and Old Testament prophecy comes to a conclusion. The way is now prepared for the new covenant. Jesus gathers his first disciples, and they travel to Capernaum to begin his public ministry. On this first day on the job, he teaches in the synagogue and confronts the evil spirit. They travel to the home of Peter and Andrew, wherein their engagement raises several pastoral questions.

Why does Peter bring Jesus to their home? Since Jesus and the others are in Peter's hometown, maybe he and Andrew want to show them hospitality. Maybe they want to show these fairly new friends a little more about themselves, to introduce them to the family, to share another part of their lives. Maybe they want to bring Jesus into the presence of their relative. Since they tell Jesus of her sickness as soon as they arrive, they must have prior knowledge of her condition. Most likely, Peter hopes that Jesus, the one who can drive away spirits, can also heal this woman. If that is his plan, it works well.

Peter cannot heal her. That is not his role. Rather, his role is to bring the woman into contact with Jesus, and then to step back and pray for the miracle.

Exegetical Perspective

This brief episode is composed of two scenes. In the first, Jesus heals Simon's mother-in-law of a fever and she serves Jesus and his disciples dinner (1:29–31). In the second, as a result of that healing, people bring to Jesus "all" in the neighborhood who are afflicted with illness or demonic possession, so that "the whole city" comes to watch what Jesus will do (vv. 32–33).

Although the story is spare, it adds to the drama Mark has been portraying from the beginning of his book. The only four disciples named thus far in the story—two pairs of brothers, Simon and Andrew, and James and John (1:16–20)—accompany Jesus from Sabbath worship in the synagogue, where Jesus has exorcised a demon (1:21–28). They go to the home of Simon and Andrew, where Simon's mother-in-law lies sick. Mark says only that "as he approached he raised her up [*ēgeiren*] by grasping her hand [*kratēsas tēs cheiros*] and the fever left her" (v. 31, my trans.). Later Jesus will make the same move as he grasps the hand (*kratēsas tēs cheiros*) of Jairus's daughter, also to raise (*egeire*) her, this time from death rather than illness (5:41).

Although other miracle stories in Mark include more details—think, for instance, of the saliva Jesus puts on the tongue of the deaf man who cannot speak (7:33) and on the eyes of the blind man of

Homiletical Perspective

Preaching on texts about miraculous healing is never easy. The healing of Peter's mother-in-law and the others that show up at her door could be the focus for an uplifting sermon about the power of God in Jesus Christ to bring healing and restoration to sick and dying people. The flip side of healing stories is that they can also leave people with questions about God's loving mercy when a prayer for healing and recovery goes unanswered.

We must carefully consider how these moments of healing within Scripture are heard and understood by our hearers who face sickness and death. We must also examine our own answers to the questions of sickness and healing in order to speak thoughtfully about them in our sermons. How do we reconcile a loving God with tragedy and sickness in the world? What is the message of the gospel when overwhelming human brokenness still persists? Why are some healed while others suffer? Questions of theodicy are not new, but wrestling with them in sermon preparation will offer thoughtful theological substance to a sermon about the healing nature of God in the presence of tragedy, suffering, and disease.

This passage addresses the question of healing and sickness in a number of ways. First, it is important to remember that the healing and casting out of demons in the Gospel of Mark is more about Jesus

Mark 1:29–34

Theological Perspective

healings become more complicated. As hostility and doubt prevail, and people's expectations fail to match the reality of the gospel, so Jesus' ability to heal with a simple word or touch becomes compromised by their lack of faith.

With the story of Simon's mother-in-law, however, we are still at the beginning of Mark's Gospel. In this early, "honeymoon" period, Jesus is an object of fascination and the answer to desperate prayers. When the people learn that there is someone in town who can cure them of all manner of debilitating conditions, "the whole city was gathered around the door" (v. 33). The Gospel tells us that Jesus' fame is spreading throughout the region because of his healing and teaching (1:28), and from now on, the crowds come in droves, hang on every word, and beg for his healing touch.

This time cannot last. There is a sense of urgency in Mark's Gospel, first hinted in the prologue—make way! the kingdom is at hand!—as the narrative charges ahead from John's prophetic appearance to Jesus' being baptized and driven into the wilderness. All this happens in just a few short sentences (1:1–13). We feel that urgency in the swift healing of Simon's mother-in-law and in the pressing of the crowds. Jesus' time is limited, and yet the Gospel repeatedly tells us that not even the people closest to Jesus really know who Jesus is.

Jesus' current celebrity does not jive with weakness and suffering and the ignominy of crucifixion. The people perceive only that he can banish suffering and evil. That the one who heals and casts out demons must die helplessly on a cross does not make any sense, nor does the implication that his followers must also suffer. When the reality of his mission becomes clear, the crowds will turn on him (14:43b; 15:6–14), and his disciples will desert him and flee (14:50).

Still today we yearn to believe, wish for clear signs, and wait for Jesus to act decisively in our favor. Could it be that our doubt and our fear in response to Jesus and the demands of discipleship compromise Jesus' ability to heal and transform us? We continue to misunderstand who Jesus is, even though Mark's Gospel provides readers with an omniscient view of Jesus' ministry and mission. We, the readers, know the ending of the story. We know who Jesus is all along. As often as the author of this Gospel says that the people surrounding Jesus do not understand who he is, the Gospel reminds us that we do know. When the disciples abandon Jesus (14:50), when Peter denies him (14:68), and when the women run

Pastoral Perspective

That role is important—one often given to church folks. We feel so powerless to make a difference, to introduce someone to the faith, to transform a life, to heal a wound. We feel powerless because generally we are powerless. Rather, our role is to bring people into proximity with Jesus, to invite them into his presence, and to trust and pray that his transforming love and power will make the difference.

Why does Jesus heal her? Few folks would bother with this woman. The powers of society consider her a second- or third-class citizen. In her important work *Texts of Terror*, Phyllis Tribble writes honestly about biblical stories of brutality against women. While certainly biblical families knew the joy of love, women still were treated as property. So, as this story progresses, folks of power might ask, "Why bother with this simple woman?" A cynic might say that Jesus bothers with her because he is hungry. However, a closer reading of the Gospel attests that Jesus heals her because he is Jesus. That is what Jesus does. Mark's purpose in writing this Gospel was to tell the "beginning of the good news" (1:1). Jesus embodies good news (or "gospel") and brings that good news to the people. He brings that good news in the form that will best engage the people—some with feeding, some with accepting, some with protecting, some with saving, some with preaching, all with loving . . . and some with healing. At this moment in her life, the good news this woman needs is that of renewed health, and through that need Jesus shares the gospel. Why bother with this woman? That might be the same question church folks ask when we say, "Why bother with that homeless community that lives within twenty minutes of our church?" "Why bother with those kids who are falling behind in school because they do not understand the language?" "Why bother with folks who are being abused or bullied?" Why bother? For now, an initial response is "Because Jesus did."

What do we learn from the woman's response? Now that her healing is complete, she arises and begins serving. She demonstrates for those disciples present and for millennia of future disciples the proper response to an encounter with Jesus' gospel. We respond to the gospel by sharing it. We respond through ministry. The woman's ailment robbed her of an important ministry role—that of showing hospitality to friends and strangers. If her health were strong and she knew of Peter's plan to bring these friends, she certainly would have the house ready and a nice meal prepared. With her health restored through the good news, she responds in kind through humble service.

Exegetical Perspective

Bethsaida (8:22–26)—Jesus frequently heals with little more than a word. Sometimes he seems not even to be in control of his own ability to restore wholeness. He asks, "Who touched me?" when the woman with a hemorrhage evokes his healing power (5:30).

The last words of verse 31, "and she began to serve them," may hint at Simon's mother-in-law's gratitude for Jesus' healing her, although it is more likely a reminder that by this point in the narrative we have come to the end of a Sabbath day, and work is again permitted. This means that Jesus has twice done what the Pharisees will later label "not lawful" on the Sabbath (2:24), first by exorcising a demon in the synagogue and now by healing a woman in the home of Simon and Andrew.

Verses 32–34 are the first of several summary statements in Mark that record Jesus' growing reputation as a healer and exorcist.[1] So also Mark's detail that "he would not permit the demons to speak, because they knew him" (1:34) recalls the demoniac in the synagogue who shouts, "I know who you are, the Holy One of God" (1:24). Similarly, Mark says at 3:11, "Whenever the unclean spirits saw him, they fell down before him and shouted, 'You are the Son of God!'" Likewise the Gerasene cries out, "What have you to do with me, Jesus, Son of the Most High God?" (5:7). The Spirit of God casts Jesus out into the wilderness in the opening scene of Mark's book to size up his cosmic opponent Satan (1:13)[2] and he engages in hand-to-hand combat with the devil throughout the story. This is why the demons recognize Jesus when he confronts them; these opponents have faced each other on the battlefield before.

The first part of this episode features another theme that is prominent in Mark's Gospel: the disorientation and reorientation of family life provoked by the gospel. That Peter abandons the family business in 1:18, only to bring Jesus home two paragraphs later to heal his mother-in-law, shows that in the new age that is dawning conventional expectations about kinship are revised. In 3:13–19 Jesus calls the Twelve "to be with him" (3:14) and gives three of them symbolic names. In antiquity it is the father's

---

1. "Everyone is searching for you" (1:37); "So many gathered around that there was no longer room for them, not even in front of the door" (2:2); "He told his disciples to have a boat ready for him because of the crowd, so that they would not crush him; for he had cured many, so that all who had diseases pressed upon him to touch him" (3:9–10).
2. The word translated "tempted" there is better rendered "tested," because not a word is exchanged, as in Matthew or Luke, and what Satan and Jesus do is test each others' strength as enemies. Each is arrayed with his troops: Satan has the demons and Jesus has the beasts and the angels. He will add to that army human soldiers in the course of Mark's story.

Homiletical Perspective

than about the ones who are healed. The point of healing people of disease is to reveal that Jesus has the ultimate power to overthrow demons, cure the incurable, and give people life. People being healed is a sign of the kingdom of God and a glimpse of the future that God in Jesus Christ brings. Miraculous healing, therefore, tells us more about the personhood and mission of Jesus than about who should and should not be healed.

Second, these healing texts also offer an opportunity within the sermon to confront the false notion that health and safety are the only signs of God's presence. In our passage, Jesus is not afraid to enter into the places of sickness or stand in the midst of the darkest demons. Jesus goes to Peter's mother-in-law's bedside and touches her hand in order to raise her up (v. 31). Jesus allows the sick and possessed to come to him and welcomes them into his presence (v. 32). Jesus ultimately experiences suffering and death upon a cross with bandits around him (15:27). He is not absent in sickness and death but in the midst of it. Our congregations need to hear that God in Jesus Christ is with them in good times and bad times, in sickness and health, and will go with them even through the valley of the shadow of death.

A final consideration for a sermon dealing with God's role in healing and sickness is to point out that those who were healed and raised up to the fullness of life are still susceptible to sickness, demons, and death. Therefore, the ultimate meaning of Jesus' healing is more than the physical healing. The mother-in-law's sickness disconnects her from her community and her ability to offer hospitality to those in her home. The sick and possessed outside her home are also cut off from their community. Jesus' healing raises the mother-in-law to her family and restores those in the crowd to right relationship in their community.

The healing that undergirds the physical restoration is a spiritual restoration to relationship. In the act of physical healing, Jesus' power to destroy the power of suffering is made manifest. No longer can suffering cut us off from others, or demean us, or make us forget our place as a child of God within God's community. Our preaching can point to this kind of healing, even in the midst of physical pain and disease.

Feminist scholars rightly point out that Peter's mother-in-law is healed in order to fulfill her duty to serve the men in her household. Although we should address the subjugation of women within biblical texts and point out the patriarchal system of the

Mark 1:29–34

Theological Perspective

terrified from the empty tomb and say nothing to anyone (16:8), the Gospel challenges its readers to overcome fear and doubt, embrace the cross, and proclaim the gospel. Yet it is precisely when the cross must be embraced and the gospel proclaimed that we falter.

Even as it challenges us, this Gospel acknowledges human fallibilities. Of all the Gospels, Mark's shows us the most bumbling disciples and the most poignant portrait of Jesus, on the edge of despair in the garden. We still follow Jesus as bumbling disciples. Like the earliest followers of Jesus, our expectations are both immensely complicated and starkly simple.

Even though many of us are suspicious about miracles, we still desperately (if often secretly) plead for Jesus' help. Even though we know the scientific intricacies of healing, we still long for the calm, swift resolution of Jesus' taking us or our loved ones by the hand and lifting us up. As we watch the world around us consume itself, we wish (but often are not sure how to pray) that Jesus would step in like a superhero and make things right. In a skeptical age, we still hope that he has that authority. Like the first people who crowded around the door to the house in wonder and hope, we want to be amazed by Jesus' ability to create order out of chaos, and yet we do not quite understand why that authority also includes suffering and death. Like the women running from the tomb, we fear and doubt the meaning of the tomb's emptiness.

May we find new strength to serve in our belief in the One who reaches out his hand to lift us up. May we capture anew our faith that he himself was lifted up, and that he will lift us up, just so, in the end.

MARIANNE BLICKENSTAFF

Pastoral Perspective

Her story gives strength to folks whose ministries include humble service, from shoveling the snow to making parking lots safe for worshipers, to setting up tables for community meals, to changing diapers in the nursery, to removing a deer from the cemetery fence. She serves as an example when we worry that we have no gift to bring; she serves as a reminder when we engage in our ministries without due humility.

This woman's service demonstrates a faithful means of responding to Jesus' love. Lamar Williamson, retired professor from the Presbyterian School of Christian Education, compares her response to that of her son-in-law in the next story, where Peter tells Jesus of the people's needs without attempting to address them (though I would argue that Peter's response in our current story was appropriate). Williamson says, "This is the first of a series of incidents in which a woman represents a right response (the poor widow, 12:41–44; the woman with the ointment, 14:3–9; the women at the cross, 15:40–41; the women at the tomb, 16:1)."[1] These stories point to Mark's belief that all folks can make a contribution, and they challenge today's reader to listen to the silenced voices, the unassuming characters, and the overlooked ideas.

Finally, how do these final verses (vv. 32–34) speak to us? They again depict Jesus sharing the good news with the sick and the afflicted. Jesus does so despite the rise of his fame. He ministers despite the recognition of him by the evil spirits. He does so despite the reality that each life changed and each identity disclosed brings him closer to the cross. Still, Jesus shares the gospel because that is what Jesus does.

DAVID MICHAEL BENDER

---

1. Lamar Williamson, *Mark*, Interpretation (Louisville, KY: John Knox Press, 1983), 55.

Exegetical Perspective

responsibility to name children, and Jesus acts here to create a new family around himself.

That clearly does not sit well with his family of origin, for in the next paragraph they accuse him of being crazy (just as the scribes accuse him of being in cahoots with the devil), and Jesus replaces them with the "mother and brothers and sisters" who do God's will (3:20–35). His sneering neighbors in Nazareth accuse him of abandoning his sisters (6:1–6), and he warns that commitment to him and to the gospel will result in broken families: "Brother will betray brother to death, and a father his child, and children will rise against parents and have them put to death; and you will be hated by all because of my name" (13:12–13).[3]

Although Jesus calls his first disciples to leave their homes and families, and predicts disruption of family relationships because of the demands of faithfulness, the separation is not necessarily permanent, since in our passage Simon and Andrew take Jesus home with them. So also at 10:2–12 he uses Genesis 2:24 to interpret Deuteronomy 24:1–3 and forbid remarriage after divorce, and at 10:19 he reaffirms the commandment to honor parents (Exod. 20:12; Deut. 5:16). Mark makes no consistent replacement of the patriarchal family with the Christian family. Instead, he relativizes and redefines domestic relations within the Christian community. All relationships, even the most basic of parent and child or husband and wife, are secondary to the disciple's relationship to Jesus.

E. ELIZABETH JOHNSON

Homiletical Perspective

time, it is also important to preach on the broader implications of her healing for our congregations. The mother-in-law is feverish and therefore unable to offer hospitality to the company in her home. Through her healing, she is able to return to her normal and honorable place of tending to her guests. This should not validate the return of women to subordinate roles, but should be a call to place ourselves in the context of her healing and hospitality. Peter's mother-in-law does not have a name, and in good homiletical tradition this invites us to put ourselves (both male and female) in her place. By seeing ourselves as Peter's mother-in-law, we can preach on the theological undertones of what it means to be healed and to serve.

Our call to serve others is grounded in the fact that God in Jesus Christ has first served us and loved us. Jesus extends grace, compassion, healing, and hospitality to us and therefore we are called to extend grace, compassion, healing, and welcome to others. In the sermon we can explicitly name the places, events, and people through which we have been offered the grace and love of God. Within this celebration of God's love, we can empower our congregation to serve others in the world in similar ways. Preachers can explicitly name the ways in which the hearers can engage in service to others in the community.

An effective sermon always challenges the hearers to act out of the faith that arises from the grace and love of God in our lives. This does not have to be a cause-and-effect sermon, because often we are both the receiver of grace and the giver of grace at the same time. In serving others we receive grace. In serving others we receive love. In serving others we participate in the healing of the world.

ROBERT W. BREWER

---

3. E. Elizabeth Johnson, "'Who Is My Mother?' Family Values in the Gospel of Mark," in Beverly Roberts Gaventa and Cynthia L. Rigby, eds., *Blessed One: Protestant Perspectives on Mary* (Louisville, KY: Westminster John Knox Press, 2002), 32–46; E. Elizabeth Johnson, "Apocalyptic Family Values," *Interpretation* 56 (2002): 34–44.

Mark 1:35–39

> [35]In the morning, while it was still very dark, he got up and went out to a deserted place, and there he prayed. [36]And Simon and his companions hunted for him. [37]When they found him, they said to him, "Everyone is searching for you." [38]He answered, "Let us go on to the neighboring towns, so that I may proclaim the message there also; for that is what I came out to do." [39]And he went throughout Galilee, proclaiming the message in their synagogues and casting out demons.

Theological Perspective

The crowds have been pressing around him day after day, and Jesus takes time to find sacred space to be alone with God in prayer (v. 35). Though Jesus soon is interrupted by the breathless arrival of Simon and his companions, he manages to postpone the onrushing demands of his mission, however briefly, to refill the well of spiritual waters. His going out to a "deserted place" echoes his withdrawal into the wilderness before he started his ministry (1:12–13) and his transfiguration (9:2–13), which were both significant times of clarifying his identity and mission.

In a misunderstanding of Jesus' purposes typical of Mark's Gospel, Simon and his companions have different expectations and seem rather put out that Jesus has given them the slip. "Everyone is searching for you!" they say (v. 37). There is a modern-day press-corps aspect to the disciples in this passage. One can imagine them bursting with excitement and purpose as they lead Jesus back into the public eye. Everyone anticipates that Jesus will continue the popular program of teaching and healing there in Capernaum (vv. 33–34), where he has been a huge success.

Jesus has a different agenda: to go into the neighboring towns and proclaim his message there, "for that is what I came out to do" (v. 38; Luke 4:43). John Calvin anticipated an objection from Christians who

Pastoral Perspective

After Jesus heals Peter's relative, his fame quickly spreads throughout the land, perhaps too quickly for his own comfort. Soon his proclamation of the gospel will speak against other social, political, and religious forces, provoking many confrontations that will eventually lead him to the cross. For now, Jesus seems far from the cross and far from Jerusalem.

Jesus has enjoyed a successful, dynamic, exhausting first day of ministry full of preaching, healing, and breaking bread with others. The ministry fills the evening until the wee hours of the morning with more sickness and healing. Finally, Jesus needs a break, and he withdraws to an isolated place. This occasion is one of only three in this Gospel when Jesus finds himself alone, the others being his moments in prayer on the mountain and at Gethsemane (6:46–47; 14:35). Other attempts at isolation are unsuccessful. Once, he sneaks into a house looking to get away, only to encounter a Syrophoenician women in need of help (7:24). Even on the cross, he is not alone (15:27). Mark comically demonstrates Jesus' inability to find isolation by his definition of "alone": "When he was alone, those who were with him along with the twelve" (4:10). We can relate to Jesus' need for time alone to reconnect with God and with ourselves in the midst of the many demands of people who surround us.

Exegetical Perspective

The morning after Jesus heals Simon's mother-in-law and then, after dinner, cures a great horde of sick and demon-possessed people (1:29–34), he rises before the sun does and goes out to a deserted place to pray (v. 35). This is not the only time in Mark's story that Jesus withdraws from the crowd to pray. At 6:46, after he dismisses the great multitude that he has fed with no more than a little boy's lunch box, he goes up on a mountain to pray; and on the evening he is about to be arrested, he goes to a garden to pray (14:32–42). There, he invites his inner circle to join him: "pray that you may not come into the time of trial" (14:38).

All this confrontation of demonic forces and restoration of human wholeness is not for Mark a demonstration of Jesus' personal power or his unique identity so much as it is a disclosure of God's invasion of the creation. So Jesus prays to the God who is at work in him. God, who rips open the heavens at Jesus' baptism (1:10), whose Spirit hurls Jesus into the wilderness to confront Satan (1:12), and who rips the temple curtain from top to bottom as Jesus dies (15:38), is using this Jesus to reclaim the creation and its people.

Other important things happen very early in the morning (Gk. *prōi*, v. 35) in Mark too. The disciples see the fig tree Jesus has cursed the previous

Homiletical Perspective

The Gospel of Mark moves with unsettling speed from one event in Jesus' ministry to another without room to pause. It is day. It is night. It is the next day. Mark's overuse of the word "immediately" offers not only a sense of urgency but also a sense that this good news of Jesus Christ is an unstoppable force. In the first twenty-eight verses of the Gospel, Jesus is ushered in by John the Baptist, baptized, and tempted in the wilderness before he moves on to call the disciples, cast out demons, and amaze the crowd with his teaching. Jesus is on the move, and the good news is speeding toward the climactic confrontation with death that ends with an empty tomb and a proclamation that Jesus is in Galilee waiting to meet his disciples again (16:7). The speed of the Gospel offers the preacher an opportunity to match the fast-paced nature of this book with a sermon that displays the urgency and power of an unstoppable and uncontainable gospel. This gospel message is immediate, urgent, and necessary.

This section of Mark's narrative is known as the preaching tour, where Jesus journeys in just a few verses through the towns of Galilee proclaiming the message of the kingdom of God. Jesus' preaching tour is more than a series of speaking engagements; it is a succession of powerful proclamations coupled with the casting out of demons (v. 39). In the first place,

Mark 1:35–39

Theological Perspective

read this passage, that perhaps it would be better that ministers of the gospel stayed in one place, to "instruct perfectly the hearers whom they have once obtained." However, Calvin concludes, "it was necessary that Christ should travel, within a short period, throughout Judea, to awaken the minds of men, on all sides, as if by the sound of a trumpet, to hear the Gospel."[1]

Calvin describes the urgency of Jesus' mission; the narrative implies that he has no time to lose in reaching out to as many people as he can, and this means he does not stay in place for long. Those who accompany Jesus must also be continually on the move. Families and livelihoods necessarily are disrupted (e.g., 1:20). Indeed, the disciples say they have "left everything" to follow Jesus (10:28–30). Mark's Gospel likely was written during a tumultuous time for Jews and for the nascent church, after a great fire in Rome in 64 CE (for which Nero blamed the Christians and had many people tortured and executed) and during or after the first Jewish revolt (66–70 CE), when the Romans besieged Jerusalem, and sacked and burned the temple.

Mark's Gospel reflects a first-century Jewish eschatological expectation that God's messiah will soon come to set things right. But in Mark's view, Jesus was not the triumphant, conquering messiah people expected. Rather, he was a suffering messiah who embodied the suffering of the people. Abandoning homes, families, fields, and livelihoods to follow Jesus (10:28–30) reflects the reality of Mark's time, that to follow Jesus often meant the disruption of life as usual and sometimes even death at the hands of occupying forces. Mark's Gospel assured the people that their suffering would be vindicated and gave people something much bigger and long lasting for which they could hope: that God had the last word and that they would receive "a hundredfold" in the world to come (10:30).

The itinerancy, evangelism, and heightened apocalyptic expectation reflected in Mark's Gospel are not understood easily by most mainline Christians in North America today. We do not feel the same urgency that the first hearers felt. We live in relative peace and security. We are not occupied by a foreign power, and we are members of the dominant religion. We are suspicious of traveling missionaries, evangelists, and miraculous healings. How can we take to heart this passage in Mark?

---

1. John Calvin, *Commentary on Matthew, Mark, and Luke* (Grand Rapids: Christian Classics Ethereal Library, 1999), 169.

Pastoral Perspective

"While it is still dark" (v. 35) Jesus withdraws to a deserted place that provides solitude and rest, a much-needed Sabbath after an exhausting day. As our church folks live their lives in a twenty-four-hour cycle of work, family, fun, church, and other obligations, this story beckons all of us to spend some time in a deserted place of our own. Unfortunately Jesus' respite proves to be a brief one. When they notice Jesus is missing, Simon and his companions go searching for him. Even though they find him praying, this does not deter them from interrupting him. Peter approaches Jesus with the news that the people in town still need him. This simple statement raises a number of pastoral issues.

First, one might imagine that, having worked for many hours in this unimpressive town, Jesus assumes his ministry there is now complete, that the people have been served. We assume the same, sometimes, until we come to the bewildering understanding that, even in our tiny corner of the world, the call to ministry includes no definite or guaranteed ending. Likewise, folks in our pews understand the nearly universal reality of overscheduled lives with "to do" lists that grow longer by the hour. They understand how work begets more work, whether that work is outside the home or keeping a home and family in order, and how the intensity of work only increases if, like Jesus, they are successful in their work. Even those who are unemployed or underemployed know what it is to be overwhelmed by the anxiety and pressure of seeking employment. The need is limitless and resources are limited. Choices must be made.

With their statement to Jesus, "Everyone is searching for you," the disciples' unspoken message is clear. Their silence tells Jesus that the healing and services of the Savior continue to be in demand. They then try to convince Jesus to return to Capernaum. This statement represents the first, but not the last, attempt by the disciples to convince Jesus to follow their will, rather than his will. Later, they will tell Jesus to send the crowd away for food (6:36) when Jesus intends to feed them. Peter's rebuke of Jesus at his first death pronouncement presumes that Jesus' prediction of his death is inaccurate and his demise is avoidable (8:32). The disciples expect that Jesus will make one of them the greatest (9:34) and grant one to sit at his right hand (10:37). They never waver, though the Savior knows and preaches that the last shall be first. They urge him to silence one who is ministering in his name (9:38), though he refuses. They work to distance the children from him

Exegetical Perspective

day "withered away to its roots" (11:20). This prophetic sign action pronounces divine judgment on the temple cult and assures the disciples that the Christian community marked by faith, prayer, and forgiveness (11:23–25), the house "not made with hands" (14:58), will replace the temple as the locus of right worship.[1] At the conclusion of the parable of the Householder, Jesus warns that the master could return at any time: "in the evening, or at midnight, or at cockcrow, or at dawn" (13:35). These very moments will structure the passion narrative that is about to begin.[2] Finally, at 16:2, Mary, Mary, and Salome go to the tomb "very early" to anoint the body of a dead Jesus, only to encounter a live angel who tells them Jesus has been raised and is already on his way to Galilee to meet them.

All these events early in the morning are revelatory, moments when the disciples see Jesus for who he really is: the bearer of God's healing power, God's agent who defeats Satan, God's reformer who nurtures people's right worship, God's Messiah whose death and resurrection disclose God's love and justice.

In this first of Mark's early morning revelations, Simon and "his companions" (perhaps his brother Andrew and the Zebedee brothers, since they were present the day before) go hunting for Jesus. "Everyone is searching for you," they say (v. 37), which recalls Mark's earlier comment that "the whole city" gathered to see Jesus heal and exorcise at the home of Simon and Andrew (v. 33). This picture of the crowds who surround Jesus recurs through Mark's story. "So many gathered around that there was no longer room for them, not even in front of the door" (2:2); "He told his disciples to have a boat ready for him because of the crowd, so that they would not crush him; for he had cured many, so that all who had diseases pressed upon him to touch him" (3:9–10; cf. 4:1; 5:21; 9:15; 11:18).

Jesus replies, "Let us go on to the neighboring towns, so that I may proclaim the message there also" (v. 38). Jesus has actually said very little to this point in Mark's Gospel. At 1:15 he announces, "The time is fulfilled, and the kingdom of God has come near; repent, and believe in the good news." At 1:17 he says to Simon and Andrew, "Follow me and I will make you fish for people." At 1:25 he says to the demon in the synagogue, "Be silent, and come out of

---

1. Donald H. Juel, *Messiah and Temple: The Trial of Jesus in the Gospel of Mark*; SBLDS 31 (Missoula, MT: Scholars Press, 1977). Although Mark labels the temple charge "false testimony" (14:57), it points ironically to the truth.
2. Jesus shares his last meal with the disciples in the evening (14:1–17) and is arrested at night (14:46), the cock crows at the conclusion of his trial before the Sanhedrin (14:72), and at dawn he is handed over to Pilate (15:1–15).

Homiletical Perspective

it is intimately connected to people being healed and set free from the demons and diseases that bind them. In the second place, it is powerful, authoritative, and life giving. In the third place, Jesus' proclamation of the kingdom of God transforms lives.

Although preachers should not pretend to be Jesus, his preaching offers us a directive about what and how to preach today. Our preaching must be urgent and bold enough to set people free. Our preaching must be authoritative enough to confront the oppressive and binding forces of this world. It must proclaim the gospel that is demanding, transformative, and powerful enough to cast out demons.

If this passage in Mark tells us anything, it is a call to preach like Jesus. It is a call to preach as though the lives in our congregations depend on hearing the liberating words of the gospel—because they do! It is a call to believe that preaching can change our people and the world. This means confronting the darkest demons of our world with a gospel message that is immediate, life giving, and palpable.

Because of scientific and medical advances today, we do not label mental illness and tragic conditions as the work of a demonic force. We do not blame disease, illness, addiction, and tragedy on a personification of evil, but this does not make them any less of a powerful force in people's lives. Therefore, we must still confront and address these forces with the good news of God's kingdom. Powerful preaching that transforms lives and deepens faith engages the hard questions posed by painful conditions and frames them within the hope and promise of the gospel. Preaching like Jesus means that we ask questions such as: What does the gospel say in the face of a diagnosis of cancer? How does the gospel respond to unfathomable tragedy? How does the gospel address violence, abuse, addiction?

The answers to these questions are not easy, but we can offer some general ground rules based on our passage. First, we must make it clear to our congregation (as it is in this passage) that Jesus is in the ministry of casting out demons, not creating them. Second, we must proclaim that Jesus is present in the very places of tragedy, oppression, pain, disease, and diagnosis. The reality of evil does not negate the presence or power of God. Jesus shows up in the places of most need, even when the need is so strong and immediate that we miss his presence. We do not face the tragedy of life alone. Finally, we must preach with the power and authority of God in Jesus Christ that the demons of this world (whatever they may be) do not have the final say. Even though the demons in

Mark 1:35–39

Theological Perspective

Two clues provide a possible, if incomplete answer: Jesus proclaimed the message "in their synagogues," and he "cast out demons" (1:39). That he focused on proclaiming in the synagogues means that he went directly to the places where people came together (the same custom that Paul followed); he met with people in their congregations and proclaimed his message. This activity is what we continue to do in our churches today; we come together to pray, study, and have fellowship while we listen for Jesus' word to us. We hear the gospel proclaimed, and then we go out into the world to act on that word.

The second clue is in the detail of casting out demons, which in the context of the first-century world was not only miraculous, but also a very practical thing to do and, in Mark's Gospel, equated with healing. Jesus' preaching and healing were not a celebrity performance but the nitty-gritty ministry of taking care of people's immediate needs. Jesus' miracles were practical in nature: they brought God's wholeness to body and spirit. Later in the Gospel, Jesus performed miracles of feeding in addition to healing and preaching; he understood the physical as well as spiritual hungers of his people. Churches today continue to follow Jesus through missions of feeding, healing, visiting, and proclaiming good news in other tangible ways to those, both among us and far away, who despair and suffer.

Even though we may feel a disconnect between our own situation and the apocalyptic urgency of Mark's Gospel, and we may be uncomfortable with the model of abandoning homes and families to follow Jesus all over the countryside, we resonate with the urgency of turmoil and suffering in the world, and we try to meet those demands unselfishly. This is what we come out to do.

That said, given all the pressing demands of our lives, we also resonate with Jesus' need to withdraw from time to time for prayer and renewal, to consider our identity and mission.

MARIANNE BLICKENSTAFF

Pastoral Perspective

(10:13), while he welcomes these little ones in love. As Jesus' present-day disciples, we do the same. Who among us has not confused our own will with that of Jesus? Who among us has not said in word or in deed that we know better than God?

The second pastoral issue raised by this statement has to do with Jesus' response to the disciples' expectation of him. Would it not be tempting for Jesus to follow their guidance and to settle permanently in Capernaum? He would be their greatest local hero, the wise one with the mysterious powers who could solve all of their problems. This occasion presents one of several situations in the Gospel in which we imagine Jesus being tempted to utilize his authority for personal gain. The most obvious example occurs during his forty days in the wilderness (1:13). Another occurs when Peter tempts Jesus to retract his death prediction and to take his place on David's throne (8:31–33). Our church folks need to hear about how Jesus faces and rejects the temptation to live for himself, rather than for God. They face these same temptations for fame and glory and power, which can corrupt even the most faithful.

Finally, Jesus refuses the disciples' efforts to return him to Capernaum, for Jesus is called to "proclaim the message" in other towns (1:38). Thus far, Jesus' only proclamation has come at the arrest of John, when he "came to Galilee, proclaiming the good news of God, and saying, 'The time is fulfilled, and the kingdom of God has come near; repent, and believe in the good news'" (1:14–15). However, when we read about his next encounter in the next town, we find no proclamation of this or any other message. Not only does Jesus refrain from the public proclamation of the gospel, but he specifically instructs the one he heals to refrain from proclaiming this good news. Maybe Jesus demonstrates another type of proclamation—one where the power is in the deed, rather than the word. Maybe Jesus reminds folks that their greatest testimonies are often unspoken, the greatest sermons include few words, as we testify to the love of Jesus by demonstrating that love.

DAVID MICHAEL BENDER

Exegetical Perspective

him!" That is all. Mark says, though, that the people in the synagogue are amazed at Jesus' "new teaching," not only because it is "as one having authority, and not as the scribes" (1:22), but also because it seems to consist of both speech about the coming realm of God and also specific demonstrations of that realm in healings and exorcisms.

Jesus appears in this story as someone supremely confident of his vocation. This is "what I came out to do," he says (v. 38). "The game's afoot," as Sherlock Holmes used to say, quoting Shakespeare.[3] The hunt is on for God's enemies and everything that oppresses God's people: sickness and death, hunger and disability, despair and hopelessness. Jesus commences his ministry of preaching, healing, and exorcism at home and immediately (Mark's favorite adverb!) extends it beyond home. "And he went throughout Galilee, proclaiming the message in their synagogues and casting out demons" (v. 39). He does not stay in the Galilee to cast out demons, heal, and preach, but extends God's invasive redemption to non-Jews as well as to the historic people of God (7:31; 8:10).

Mark's pairing of "proclaiming the message" with "casting out demons" in 1:39 serves as an important reminder that preaching and teaching can never be limited to words spoken or concepts understood intellectually. A contemporary church that thinks it has remained faithful by keeping its theological skirts clean without getting its hands dirty in the mess of a broken and suffering world neither hears nor follows the Jesus of Mark's Gospel.

E. ELIZABETH JOHNSON

Homiletical Perspective

Mark continue to haunt people's lives, Jesus silences them on many occasions, and the resurrection finally silences their power and authority. If in our sermons we earnestly and humbly address the demons of our time with the good news of God's kingdom, as Jesus addressed them in his time, we will then preach with life-giving and life-sustaining hope.

The demand upon Jesus' time and energy in this fast-paced Gospel is intense. Although not a perfect analogy, the intensity of Jesus' mission can mirror the hectic schedules of modern-day folk. We must be careful not to directly compare our particular busyness with the mission of Jesus' ministry, but we can understand the pressure that comes from the constant demand of others, especially in times when "everyone is searching for you" (v. 37). Here, within the staccato pace of gospel proclamation and ministry, Jesus seeks out a moment of quiet rest (v. 35). This brief mention of Jesus' time of prayer can offer homiletical material for the importance of prayer in the middle of a frenetic and demanding life.

A sermon on prayer might identify the context of prayer with the urgency of Jesus' ministry in Mark's Gospel and with the demands that arise from such a mission. In this way, the challenge to action or the missional aspect of the sermon can be a call to engage in regular times of prayer as a necessary part of a busy life and demanding ministry. The preacher can allow the congregation to participate in prayer through a time of silence within the sermon or at the end of the sermon. This time of prayer can be framed as a moment for the congregation to focus on the power and presence of God, in order to ask for the strength and confidence to face any demon that may come their way.

ROBERT W. BREWER

---

3. William Shakespeare, *The Life of King Henry V*, Act 3, Scene I, in *The Complete Works of Shakespeare*, ed. Hardin Craig (Chicago: Scott, Foresman & Co., 1961), 749.

Mark 1:40–45

⁴⁰A leper came to him begging him, and kneeling he said to him, "If you choose, you can make me clean." ⁴¹Moved with pity, Jesus stretched out his hand and touched him, and said to him, "I do choose. Be made clean!" ⁴²Immediately the leprosy left him, and he was made clean. ⁴³After sternly warning him he sent him away at once, ⁴⁴saying to him, "See that you say nothing to anyone; but go, show yourself to the priest, and offer for your cleansing what Moses commanded, as a testimony to them." ⁴⁵But he went out and began to proclaim it freely, and to spread the word, so that Jesus could no longer go into a town openly, but stayed out in the country; and people came to him from every quarter.

Theological Perspective

Jesus exposes human constructions as being just that: human constructions. In doing so, he calls his hearers to discern what is God's creation, what is our creation, and, crucially, whether our creation contradicts God's.

The man who encounters Jesus is a leper. That is the identity that society has constructed for him through its rituals and norms. He has no need for a name; he is already described enough for Jesus' audience. He must scream "Unclean!" wherever he goes, so others can get out of his way and not risk impurity. Impurity, not contagion, is what others fear from him. Skin diseases are defined in Leviticus 13, purification from them in Leviticus 14. Leprosy can mean any number of skin diseases, not necessarily contagious, and the passage of illness from person to person is not entirely understood in Mark's era. So on top of his physical ailment (which I would imagine hurts), the leper faces a socially constructed inferior status that may not even be what we would today call medically necessary. In the midst of this constructed problem, the leper encounters Jesus.

I cannot help but hear his imploring as sarcastic: "Hey, Jesus, if you want, you can make me clean, huh?" My reasoning here is the total context of the passage: the scene makes better sense with Jesus being moved by anger (*orgistheis*) rather than

Pastoral Perspective

It was an ordinary Wednesday afternoon around Rock Spring Presbyterian Church in Atlanta, Georgia, years ago. Mrs. Bessie was in the kitchen making fried chicken and biscuits, and I was in the fellowship hall preparing for the meal and program less than an hour away. A man from the streets came knocking on the door. His clothes were tattered. He smelled of sweat and despair. His name was Joe-Rod Minus, and he needed help. I wondered if Minus was his real last name or if it served as a symbol of the value he felt he offered. If a minus indicates a loss or reduction, then minuses marked nearly every aspect of Joe-Rod's life. He had recently lost a good job, then lost his savings, and finally lost his marriage. The streets of Atlanta became his home, and he wandered into the church hurting, hopeless, and hungry.

To be honest, I felt inconvenienced by Joe-Rod's interruption, because I was busy preparing for an important church program, but it was a common practice of the servants at Rock Spring to welcome everyone around the tables for the Wednesday fellowship meal. Joe-Rod Minus would be no exception. Mrs. Bessie piled his plate high with chicken and biscuits, the sight of which brought a smile to Joe-Rod's face, shining the light of grace into the darkness of his day. Mrs. Bessie knew how to cook well, but more importantly she knew how to serve

Exegetical Perspective

Sharon Betcher's outstanding book *Spirit and the Politics of Disablement*[1] cautions us against reading the New Testament miracle stories merely as healings in which bodies are transformed into an idealized state, thereby making these stories "texts of terror" for those whose illnesses or disabilities place them in the realm of "otherness." The illnesses described in the miracle stories often refer to what the society demonizes or regards as God's punishment. Betcher's analysis is especially helpful with regard to "leprosy" in Mark 1:40–45: normal or "harmless" bodily functions are identified as unclean and used to legitimize social exclusion.

A leper comes to Jesus and asks to be made clean. Mark's decision not to mention the time or place of the meeting underlines the exemplary character of this healing. The action and speech of both actors parallel each other: the stretching out of the hand and the touch of Jesus correspond to the arrival and kneeling of the sick person. The request of the leper and the answer of Jesus also correspond. Mark describes the sick exclusively as a leper (v. 40)—the illness concerns the person as a whole. It is consistent that for Jesus' action compassion is mentioned.

---

1. Sharon Betcher, *Spirit and the Politics of Disablement* (Minneapolis: Fortress Press, 2007).

Homiletical Perspective

This third individual healing story in Mark's Gospel holds promise for the preacher on several fronts. First, this text introduces the theme of "untouchables" and how Jesus deals with them. People with leprosy were deemed to be untouchables in ancient Jewish society for at least three reasons. Physically, their skin diseases were thought to be contagious. Socially, they were forced to live in isolation outside the ordinary boundaries of neighborhood and community. Spiritually, they were considered "unclean" according to Levitical law (Lev. 13–14). In short, lepers were separated from the very individuals, communities, and rituals that might have brought healing and compassion into their lives.

The fact that Jesus not only heals this leper, but actually *touches* him is highly significant in this story. The Hebrew Scriptures record another instance of such a healing, the healing of Naaman the leper by the prophet Elisha (2 Kgs. 5:1–14), but in that story Elisha never touches the leper. In Mark's Gospel, Jesus' touch puts him at risk not only of contracting leprosy himself; it also makes him ritually "unclean."

The question of who the "untouchables" are in our society—physically, socially, and spiritually—is an interesting one to ponder. Certainly parallels have been drawn between lepers and people with HIV/AIDS. I helped write the history of the Riverside

Mark 1:40–45

Theological Perspective

compassion (*splanchnistheis*).[1] An angry Jesus is more likely to snort like a horse (*embrimēsamenos*) after cleansing the leper than is a compassionate Jesus. Oh, and touching a leper? That is a construct broken.

An angry Jesus, an angry Son of God, is another construct broken. How often is God's anger in the prophets regarded as hyperbole, anthropomorphism, or just the (obviously inferior) "God of the Old Testament"? Mark's Jesus, however, is thoroughly upset by this leper. He is perhaps even angry at the leprosy.[2] God angry at a disease! God is irrational?! Our organization of the world and its people and its God into nice categories is threatened by a touch and a snort from Jesus.

Jesus does not condemn all human constructs out of hand, though. Having cleansed the leper and restored him to human community (God's creation), Jesus orders him to go to the priest, as prescribed in Leviticus 14. Jesus in Mark does not usually have a high view of the temple or its officials, so the temple hierarchy is probably not being portrayed here as a divine creation. Rather, Jesus uses the human construct—priests—to reincorporate the leper into the divinely ordained community.

Mark uses this scene to call his listeners to discern which things are God's creation and which things are human creations. Mark offers some hints as to how his listeners can carry out this type of discernment today. We should not assume that just because we are the church we know what to do. When the unnamed woman anoints Jesus' feet, the disciples snort like horses and get an earful from Jesus! (14:3–9). Being in the inner circle guarantees nothing. Everyone has to discern.

Discernment takes the form of asking of Jesus what the leper sarcastically and unwittingly confessed: What does Jesus will (*thelō*, v. 41), and what is Jesus able (*dynata*, 14:36) to do? The answers lie elsewhere in Mark. Gordon Lathrop's *The Four Gospels on Sundays* is the latest book to argue that Mark is written as a "ring story," in which stories cycle in mutual interpretation, with rings building chiastically so that the middle of the story carries the meaning. Lathrop's interest is in the middle as is

---

1. In this I side with Francis J. Moloney, *The Gospel of Mark: A Commentary* (Peabody, MA: Hendrickson Publishers, 2002), 58. Also Joel Marcus, *Mark 1–8: A New Translation with Introduction and Commentary* (New York: Doubleday, 2000), 206. In favor of "compassion," see Donald H. Juel, *Mark* (Minneapolis: Augsburg, 1990), 44. Also John R. Donahue and Daniel J. Harrington, *The Gospel of Mark* (Collegeville, MN: Liturgical Press, 2002), 89.
2. Joel Marcus writes, "Jesus' rage is directed not at the man but at the demonic forces responsible for his affliction" (*Mark 1–8*, 209).

Pastoral Perspective

heaping helpings of compassion; and that day she did that far better than I.

Mark reminds us that Jesus had a way of either attracting or seeking out the minuses in life, and the leper in Mark's moving text would likely have seen himself as a minus. Certainly his society would have seen him that way. Jesus could very easily have rejected the leper, sending him away as so many likely had on numerous occasions, but he did not. Jesus turned a strange interruption into a sacred encounter. Jesus listened to the leper's plea, and he was moved by compassion. He reached out his hand and healed him. Before his encounter with Jesus, the text calls him "a leper," but after Jesus, he is called "the man." Jesus took away his minuses and left him whole. Jesus reinstated the man's dignity as a child of God.

Who among us does not get interrupted? Some interruptions might be more important than others, and some might be easier to handle, but at its heart each interruption is an indication of need. A child needs his shoes tied. A grieving spouse needs her hand held. A hungry person needs food. A person facing terminal illness needs strength. The finance committee needs your numbers for the budget. We all have moments when we feel as if we are less than we could be or should be, when we subtract value from the world, when we are minuses.

In that state, sometimes it takes a great deal of courage to ask for help and healing. Other times there is no choice, and that plea might be the only words we can utter; so we form them over and over until someone listens. Jesus shows us that, in response to another's plea, all we need to do is listen. If we listen and reach out our hand, minus beside minus, pointing to Jesus as the way, we can help each other to wholeness and a full recognition of what each person adds to God's creation.

If you listen, though, if you walk beside people and point them to Jesus for relief and affirmation of value, if you sow compassion, you must reap the consequences. If you genuinely help someone, she is going to tell other people. Those other people will remember and will seek you out when they need help. You know what that means? More interruptions. Jesus knew this. In fact, he might have even tried to avoid them. Maybe that was the reason Jesus asked the man not to tell anyone. He reminded the man how to incorporate himself back into society with offerings presented to the priest, but very clearly asked him not to say anything about how he was healed.

Exegetical Perspective

The noun *splanchna* is synonymous with our word for heart in the figurative sense, meaning the center of feeling. In antiquity the verb is often used when an attitude is invoked that leads to mercy. The text makes clear: Jesus causes the cleansing because his heart is touched. The passive "and he was made clean" (v. 42) indicates that it was God who healed the man.

The passage speaks of cleanness three times: the sick person asks for cleanness, Jesus promises it, and in verse 44 it appears in the ritual frame. One thing is striking: in the first part of the pericope, typical Jewish understandings of uncleanness play no significant role. The leper asks to be cleansed, and he is touched by Jesus, but this does not cause Jesus to become contaminated. Why might this be so? The explanation can be found in a closer examination of the differing ways leprosy was understood medically and socially in antiquity.

Lepra in the ancient medical texts and Jewish texts, such as Qumran or the Jewish medical book Kitab-al-Tabakh, is evaluated either as a therapeutic evacuation, as the result of an inadequate balance of bodily fluids, or as something caused by the influence of harmful environmental factors on the body, particularly the impact of hot climates. In one passage from the *Corpus Hippocraticum On Nutriment*, *lepra* appears at first sight as a harmless skin disease: "Ulceration, . . . *lepra*, . . . sometimes harms and sometimes helps, and sometimes neither harms nor helps."[2] A gloss in one manuscript suggests that "harm" means the illness makes its way into the depth as well as the surface of the body. "Neither harm nor help" indicates the infection remains merely on the surface. In some cases, therefore, *lepra* is a *therapeutic evacuation* (which nevertheless could be brought on by a fatally progressing illness) that rids the body of harmful materials.

Ancient people believed that the skin is one of the openings in the body through which harmful bodily substances can flow out, just as they would otherwise exit through another part of the body. Jewish and secular medical texts share a similar understanding of *lepra*. It is thus possible that *lepra* refers to a harmless skin secretion, or at least that it refers to conditions that might be regarded either positively or negatively from a medical standpoint. It is the social and ritual meanings attached to the condition more than the condition itself that Jesus must overcome.

The social implications come to the fore in some Old Testament texts that detail exclusion from the

---

2. *Corpus Hippocraticum On Nutriment*, http://daedalus.umkc.edu/hippocrates/HippocratesLoeb1/page.349.php?size=240x320; accessed May 15, 2013.

Homiletical Perspective

Church in New York City and was struck, while doing research there, to find that in the early 1980s many churches in New York would not even provide funerals for people who died of AIDS—so great was the fear of contagion. (Riverside Church was a notable exception.) I am reminded as well of health care professionals who, on a regular basis, carry on ministries of healing to people with all manners of conditions and diseases—sometimes at great risk to themselves.

Though it may be stretching to move beyond the physical parallels, we nevertheless would do well to ask, who are the social and spiritual "lepers" in our society today? Who are the people we in our churches and our social circles tend to shun or ostracize? People with addictions? People whose sins have been made public? People whose theologies or politics are radically different than our own? Jesus calls us to touch the untouchables, even at the risk of being seen to be like them, and thus to offer community to those who often need it the most.

A second theme for preaching is the faith and healing dynamic that takes place between the leper and Jesus. The leper starts his conversation with Jesus with a statement of faith: "If you choose, you can make me clean." Jesus responds (depending on which of the NRSV alternate readings you adopt) with either great "pity" for the man or great "anger" (v. 41a). The Greek verb, *splanchnizomai*, literally means "to have one's intestines turned."

Jesus clearly has great compassion for this man—and perhaps anger as well over his diseased state. This healing story—like every healing story—raises questions about why some people are cured by God and some are not. If, however, we focus only on that issue, we may miss the other dynamic that also plays itself out here: namely, the interplay between the faith of the believer and the faithfulness of God.

I have known people with cancer who have adopted, in faith, mantras that remind them of God's faithfulness and sovereignty, even when a cure does not come. "The sky is still blue" was the mantra of one person I know, "The sun still rises" the mantra of another. My own personal favorite is Julian of Norwich's "All shall be well, and all shall be well, and all manner of things shall be well." To adopt such mantras is not to deny illness or to adapt a naive approach to life. Rather, it is to say to God in faith, as the leper said, "If you will, you can make me whole." It is to profess faith that wholeness itself can come—even in the midst of grave disease.

Further, Jesus' reply of empathy and/or anger is often exactly what is needed by the one going

Mark 1:40–45

Theological Perspective

his writing. We are not reading the middle, here; we are reading an outer ring. In a chiasm, Lathrop tells us, the rings correspond. For example, a story built on the chiasm ABB'A' will be centered on B and B', and the transition between them, but the outer rings of A and A' will interpret each other also. The ring that interprets and is interpreted by 1:40–45 (and the stories that follow it) centers on chapters 14 and 15.[3]

In Mark 14, Jesus *wants* to eat the Passover, but dreads crucifixion and death, and he prays, "Father, you *are able* to . . . remove this cup from me; but, not what I *want*, but what you [*want*]" (14:36, my trans.). The cup of the Lord's Supper and the cup of the cross are to Mark the same cup. Perhaps we should ask ourselves if what we are doing or believing in our churches is consistent with the cup "given for all to drink." Perhaps we should ask if we who drink the cup in the worship of the church drink the cup of the cross along with those who suffer daily, or if the cup in our congregation really is given for all to drink. Whom have we "constructed out" of the life of our church? Who are the lepers? What might God do that we could consider "out of character"? Most of all, we should not forget what God *wants* in giving this cup to Jesus: triumph over sin, death, and the devil. Jesus might not be *able* to come down off of his cross, but God most certainly is *able* to save the world—and in Mark, God does.

TIMOTHY ANDREW LEITZKE

Pastoral Perspective

The man's joy, however, was too great to contain. He told everyone he saw. He could not believe that Jesus cared enough to make him a plus sign. He wanted everyone to know. The obvious result of the leper's healing was that Jesus became even more popular. He continued to preach, teach, and heal on the fringes of life with the people who dwelt on those fringes. People continued to come to Jesus, people who represented the minuses of life, looking for a word, a touch, some genuine expression of real love that the leper experienced so lavishly from him.

This stirring scene invites all who read it to consider the interruptions of ministry as opportunities, at the very least, to become better listeners. When a minus comes wandering by the church in search of help, it is tempting to view the interruption as an annoyance, but what if God means for the interruption to serve as an opportunity to share compassion? Rather than thinking of all the things we cannot do for those in need who come to us begging for help, what if we in the church were to find ways to say, "I will," to the suffering?[1] What if we just listen and point to Jesus? It is impossible to feel like a minus when we are focused on Jesus.

If we do that, though, word will get out. Our lives may well become one interruption after another, so much so that our to-do list for each and every day will have only one item on it: help people. Our days, like Jesus' days, will be filled with sacred interruptions, turning minus after minus into plus after plus, filling the earth with people whose joy in Jesus is too great to contain.

WAIN WESBERRY

---

3. Gordon W. Lathrop, *The Four Gospels on Sunday: The New Testament and the Reform of Christian Worship* (Minneapolis: Fortress Press, 2012), 82. Lathrop arranges Mark as follows: A: 1:2–20; B: 1:21–6:6a; C: 6:6b-8:21; D: 8:22–10:52; C': 11:1–13:37; B': 14:1–15:47; A': 16:1–8.

1. Lamar Williamson, *Mark*, Interpretation (Louisville, KY: Westminster John Knox Press, 1985), 58–62.

Exegetical Perspective

community, resulting in sociolocal isolation, and the precautions necessary to avoid the contamination of other people. The physician Caelius Aurelianus mentions a similar exclusion of sick people: "Others recommend further that in any city which has never before been plagued by this illness, one should kill a sick person if he is a stranger. A citizen, however, should be banished to a quite distant place or made to stay in cold regions in the interior of the country, away from all people, and be brought back when his health is shown to be better, so that other citizens may not be harmed through contact with this illness." Aurelianus also refers to the practice of various physicians who, as is also reported in the Jewish sources, argued in favor of the exclusion of the sick from the community.[3]

In the second part of the passage (vv. 43–45), the healed person is asked to be quiet, go to the priests, and to make the sacrifice demanded by Moses. The language Mark employs in this section is forceful, even explosive. Jesus "snorts" (*embrimasthai*) at the man, "casts him out" (*ekballein*), and goes away. Other characters now enter the story, including the priests and the people who come to Jesus. The mention of the "testimony" is also striking. This testimony probably contains the recognition of the remedial power of Jesus as well his loyalty to Torah. A new role falls to the sick person: he preaches. This is made clear by the verb *kēryssein*—to announce—and *diaphēmizein ton logon*–the word spread out. As a consequence, Jesus himself must stay "out in the country" ("lonesome places"), and people come to him "from everywhere."

Is this story a text of terror? I would argue against this view! The story speaks primarily to Jesus' heart being touched after seeing sickness and his reaction of extending a physical touch to the sufferer. The healing is concerned first with social reintegration. How does this text invite us to reach out and to touch those whose physical and social conditions cause them to be treated as "other" by the society? Are not all of us less than ideal? Does healing mean restoration to an ideal state, or inclusion as whole members of the human community despite our varied infirmities?

ANNETTE WEISSENRIEDER

Homiletical Perspective

through illness. To know that Jesus not only weeps with us in our times of serious illness, but also rages with us against the forces that still unleash diseases willy-nilly in our world is not only a great comfort to us; it is also a boost to our own faith.

Finally, this passage gives testimony to the power of preaching itself, and to the important role it plays in both Jesus' ministry and that of his followers. New Testament scholar Brian Blount argues that in Mark's Gospel, what we witness is a boundary-breaking, world-upending Jesus who inaugurates, through his very being, the apocalyptic reign of God in our midst. The vehicle through which God announces and effects that reign is preaching. "Preaching," he writes, "represents on a tactical, human level what God is doing on the mythological level, entering human reality with the purpose of transforming it."[1]

Thus Mark 1 begins with the highly effective preaching of John the Baptist (1:4–5), continues with the powerful preaching of Jesus (1:14–15), and concludes with this leper-turned-street-preacher who refuses to obey Jesus' instruction to him to "say nothing to anyone" (v. 44a) but instead "began to proclaim it freely, and to spread the word, so that Jesus could no longer go into town openly, but stayed out in the country; and people came to him from every quarter" (v. 45).

In many congregations, preaching is seen to be the purview of the clergy. Here, at the outset of Mark's Gospel, we are reminded that the preaching ministry of Jesus also belongs to all those who have encountered his boundary-breaking reign in our midst. We too are called to "go preach"; when we do, watch out! For the power of preaching is power that can literally upend and transform the world.

LEONORA TUBBS TISDALE

---

3. See Annette Weissenrieder, *Images of Illness in the Gospel of Luke. Insights of Ancient Medical Texts*, WUNT 164 (Tübingen: Mohr Siebeck, 2003).

1. Brian K. Blount, *Go Preach! Mark's Kingdom Message and the Black Church Today* (Maryknoll, NY: Orbis Books, 1998), 92.

Mark 2:1–12

¹When he returned to Capernaum after some days, it was reported that he was at home. ²So many gathered around that there was no longer room for them, not even in front of the door; and he was speaking the word to them. ³Then some people came, bringing to him a paralyzed man, carried by four of them. ⁴And when they could not bring him to Jesus because of the crowd, they removed the roof above him; and after having dug through it, they let down the mat on which the paralytic lay. ⁵When Jesus saw their faith, he said to the paralytic, "Son, your sins are forgiven." ⁶Now some of the scribes were sitting there, questioning in their hearts, ⁷"Why does this fellow speak in this way? It is blasphemy! Who can forgive sins but God alone?" ⁸At once Jesus perceived in his spirit that they were discussing these questions among themselves; and he said to them, "Why do you raise such questions in your hearts? ⁹Which is easier, to say to the paralytic, 'Your sins are forgiven,' or to say, 'Stand up and take your mat and walk'? ¹⁰But so that you may know that the Son of Man has authority on earth to forgive sins"—he said to the paralytic—¹¹"I say to you, stand up, take your mat and go to your home." ¹²And he stood up, and immediately took the mat and went out before all of them; so that they were all amazed and glorified God, saying, "We have never seen anything like this!"

Theological Perspective

Forgiveness is easy in theory, not necessarily in practice, for it entails great risks for everyone involved. Forgiveness is risky because it makes the forgiver vulnerable, in a "there's-a-hole-in-my-roof" sense.

This story of the forgiving and healing of the paralytic does not stand by itself. According to John Donahue and Daniel Harrington, Mark employs it as the first part of a five-part ring of stories, set in Capernaum, that ends with Jesus' healing of the man with the withered hand in a synagogue in 3:1–6. The ring's center, which is found in 2:18–22, focuses on fasting, the bridegroom, and newness.[1] Mark thus compares the "house meeting" in this scene (2:1–12) to an officially designated prayer meeting in 3:1–6; both are settings for conflict, with scribes here in the house, and later in the synagogue with Pharisees. The bridegroom's presence commences a time of newness, but also generates increasingly harsh responses from some.

The scene in 2:1–12 is also a ring in itself. Joel Marcus breaks it into five parts, centering on the controversy over forgiveness.[2] The point of the scene,

---

1. John R. Donahue and Daniel J. Harrington, *The Gospel of Mark* (Collegeville, MN: Liturgical Press, 2002), 97.
2. Marcus arranges the scene: A: Introduction 2:1–2; B: Spiritual Healing 2:3–5; C: Controversy 2:6–10a; B': Physical Healing 2:10b–12a; A': Conclusion 2:12b. See Joel Marcus, *Mark 1–8: A New Translation with Introduction and Commentary* (New York: Doubleday, 2000), 219.

Pastoral Perspective

Dilemmas often serve as defining moments in ministry—from responding to illnesses and deaths to solving problems related to church budgets, personnel, volunteer recruitment, and mission opportunities. A dilemma literally entails two options (A and B) between which one must choose. In Mark 2:1–12, there are dilemmas that Jesus faces and one that he presents. Like Jesus in this story, we often do not get to choose what dilemmas we will face on any given day, but we always have the ability to choose how we will deal with those dilemmas. As Jesus handles his dilemmas, he models for us masterful ways to deal with our own.

The scene in Mark opens with Jesus in someone's home, sharing insights about God's word. He is modeling good pastoral ministry, ministry shaped and defined by being with the people where they are. The people respond favorably to Jesus, and a large crowd fills the house. By this point in the narrative, we sense that something is about to happen, something significant. Some friends of a paralyzed man carry him toward the house where Jesus speaks, a house so chock full that not one more person could possibly squeeze in the door.

It would have been difficult to manage that crowd on two feet; imagine what it would have been like for four people to maneuver a stretcher through

Exegetical Perspective

Because illnesses are so filled with uncertainty, they often generate diverse interpretations. Medical experts can diagnose a problem, but may not be of help with regard to the interpretations we attach to the experience of illness. Various interpretive perspectives may be employed, including those that regard illness as sin. The common idea that illness is an experience to be interpreted conflicts with the medical ideal that an illness is a phenomenon devoid of intrinsic meaning. A patient might experience an illness as a calamity, while modern medicine views it as a coincidental clash of microorganisms. Are all interpretations of illness equal from both medical and theological perspectives? How can we make sense of a story like Mark 2:1–12, where illness and sin seem to be equated?

The healing of the paralytic is one of a series of healings in this portion of Mark. Several features suggest that the story may be a composite, combining a healing story (2:1–5b, 11–12) and a controversy (2:5c–10): (a) the phrase "Jesus says to the paralytic" (*legei tō paralytikō*) is repeated literally in verses 5b and 10b; (b) the scribes appear only from verse 6 on, but are missing in the final proclamation; (c) the four bearers are not mentioned again after verse 4; (d) the title "Son of Man" is introduced without explanation; and (e) the promise of forgiveness occurs abruptly

Homiletical Perspective

While there are many preaching possibilities from this text, two hold particular promise. The first is the relationship between sickness and sin, healing and forgiveness. The healing of the paralytic is the only miracle story in the Gospels in which the forgiveness of sins also occurs. Yet it has often been used in very harmful ways to assert a cause-and-effect connection between sickness and sin, particularly asserting that a person is sick or disabled because of his or her sin.

I remember some years ago being appalled to hear a well-known mainline preacher argue in a sermon that AIDS was the visitation of God's judgment against homosexuals. The troublesome assumptions were not only that homosexuality is a "sin," but also that God punishes sin by sending disease. In a similar way, persons with other diseases or disabilities have been made to feel guilty through the church's preaching that somehow they must be at fault if they are sick. More than a few have found themselves asking, "What did I do to bring this on? Why is God so displeased with me?"

While it is certainly the case that there are things people do that can result in physical harm to themselves (e.g., drunk driving or promiscuity), Kathy Black reminds us that physical symptoms of illness or disability are often caused by sins that have been committed *against* a person (e.g., by abuse), not *by*

Mark 2:1–12

Theological Perspective

if we accept Marcus's arrangement, is that Jesus has the authority to forgive. Combining Marcus's interpretation of this individual ring with the larger ring identified by Donahue and Harrington, one can see that this story is about the house meeting—that is, the early Christian liturgy—as a locus of forgiveness. That is to say, this episode calls upon the assembly to forgive. Forgiveness, we noted at the outset, is easily said, but the narrative suggests enacting it might not be so easy.

The crippled man's friends cut a hole in the roof in order to get him to Jesus. I have loved this scene ever since my father read it to me when I was a small child. In those days, the roof over my head was my father's concern; now, the roof over my head is my concern. I am not interested in having a hole torn in my roof, no matter who is visiting. The property damage and the threat to my other belongings and the integrity of my house is more than I want to consider. Mark's story implies that when Jesus is home, the house itself is vulnerable to the collateral damage of those who relentlessly seek him, his healing, and his forgiveness. The word is a word to the church.

A contemporary analogy to this is drawn in the work of Jewish theologian Emmanuel Levinas. Briefly, Levinas argues that in Western tradition philosophy has always noted the presence of an Other that is beyond the thinker, transcendent of the thinker's own being or person. René Descartes famously asserted this in his *Meditations on First Philosophy* when he argued that since he knew he was thinking and could conceive of something infinite, this infinite being must exist and must guarantee the truthfulness of Descartes's perceptions of reality around him. Levinas thinks that Descartes should have quit while he was ahead, with the fact that a thinker experiences an Other who transcends her. This Other is what interests Levinas, not for what the Other might do for philosophical foundations, but for what the Other might say to him. The other, by being different from Levinas's own person (or, the "same," as he puts it), calls the same into question. He writes, "A calling into question of the same . . . is brought about by the other. We name this calling into question of my spontaneity by the presence of the Other ethics."[3]

Perhaps this Other comes to expression in the tearing open of the roof. Perhaps the roof in Mark 2 is a way of keeping the Other at bay. The walls and

---

3. Emmanuel Levinas, *Totality and Infinity: An Essay on Exteriority*, trans. Alphonso Lingis (Pittsburgh: Duquesne University Press, 1969), 43.

Pastoral Perspective

this gathering. In short, the crowds make it difficult for the paralytic's friends to bear him to Jesus. One pastor cleverly suggests that the paralyzed man cannot be carried through the front door of the home "*because all of the church people are in the way, and they are refusing to move from their seats.*"[1] This is a dilemma indeed. Do they continue to try to work their way through the crowd, or do they go home in frustration to wait for a more opportune time to bring their friend to Jesus? Neither. They get creative and imaginative and decide to dig through the home's roof to lower their friend into the very presence of the one they seek. Their efforts serve as a striking example of perseverance in the face of challenge, creativity in the midst of adversity.

Although the floor is standing room only, Jesus certainly would have noticed someone digging through the roof. Indeed, everyone there would have noticed. Jesus pays close attention to their sweat and struggle, particularly as the paralytic parcel is dropped at his feet, and we come to our next dilemma. What will Jesus do? Will he make the man walk, or make his friends carry him away? Neither. Jesus forgives the sins of the paralytic. The text makes it clear that he has physical problems, but Jesus' words indicate that his primary problem is sin.

Though it is the primary problem of every human being, it is easy to be consumed with other, more visible issues. Markan scholar Lamar Williamson offers a word of insight and caution here. The story neither names a specific sin committed by the paralytic nor mentions anything at all about guilt; there is no specific connection between sin and sickness.[2] Jesus does not say that sin causes the paralysis. It may be helpful here to look beyond what Jesus says ("Son, your sins are forgiven," v. 5b) to what Jesus does. As Jesus is interrupted in an enormous and unusual way, he remains calm, pays close attention, and then responds. His response is a word of grace to the one in greatest apparent need, the paralytic, to ease his greatest yet least apparent discomfort, sin. More than that, Jesus is preparing those gathered for an even greater expression of grace that comes after the next dilemma in the story.

The suspicious scribes in the crowd are unsettled and offended by Jesus' pronouncement to the paralytic. They know that God alone has the power to forgive sins; therefore, for Jesus to pronounce

---

1. Otis Moss, "By Any Means Necessary," Mark 2:1–12, January 20, 2008; http://30goodminutes.org/csec/sermon/moss_5114.html; accessed March 23, 2012.
2. Lamar Williamson, *Mark*, Interpretation (Atlanta: John Knox Press, 1983), 64.

Exegetical Perspective

and the crowd's praise may refer only to the healing, not to the forgiveness (v. 12ac). Those who see the story as a composite usually argue that an original healing story was later extended by including the discussion of sin and forgiveness.

I believe, however, that the story is a coherent narrative structured around spatial contrasts between inside and outside, as well as above and below: Jesus is in the house, the crowd outside "in front of the door" (v. 2). The crowd hinders the four bearers carrying the paralytic from reaching the door to the house and from access to Jesus. The hindered horizontal approach gives way to a vertical approach. The sick person is lowered into the house through the roof. The continuing action takes place inside the house (vv. 5–11). Two parallel statements frame the interaction with the paralytic. In verse 5 Jesus forgives the man's sin, in verse 11 he asks him to move. Although the crowd first hinders the paralytic's access to Jesus, in verse 12 it clears the way for his departure.

The sick man is called a *paralytikos*, a term that comes from the stem "loose" or "detach," and can mean to detach from life. The paralysis is rooted in lack of strength and sensation. In the *Corpus Hippocraticum*, numerous passages associate the feebleness with a lack of *pneuma*-spirit in the body. Put simply, the body is supplied only with a small amount of *pneuma*. If a person lacks sufficient *pneuma*, he or she draws near to death.[1] In verses 1–11, the paralytic is passive: he is carried, he is let down into the house, he is commanded by Jesus. The paralyzed is completely dependent on help from others; the six active verbs in verses 3–4 show the readiness of his companions to help. The three actions attributed to the paralytic in verse 12 signal his transformation.

The correspondence of healing and forgiveness of sins in this story is found already in First Testament tradition, especially in Psalm 103:3 (102 LXX), where forgiveness of sin and healing stand side by side in a *parallelismus membrorum*. It is noteworthy that in Psalm 103:13 the compassion of God is compared to a father who turns to his children. Is it merely a coincidence that in verse 5c Jesus addresses the paralytic as a child? Psalm 103:20 refers twice to the word of God (*ton logon autou*) and in Mark 2:2b: "Jesus was speaking the word [*logon*] to them." This intertext thus confirms the interpretation of Mark 2:1–12 as a unified, coherent story.

---

1. See further Annette Weissenrieder and Gregor Etzelmüller, "Christentum und Medizin. Welche Kopplungen sind lebensförderlich?" in Etzelmüller and Weissenrieder, eds., *Religion und Krankheit* (Darmstadt: WBG, 2010).

Homiletical Perspective

the person. Consequently if we as preachers advocate a causal relationship between sin and sickness, we not only make troublesome assertions about the nature of God; we can also perpetuate the cycle of blaming the victim.[1]

Black joins a number of other scholars in pointing out that there is no cause-and-effect relationship between sin and sickness suggested in this biblical text. While Jesus does tell the paralytic that his sins are forgiven, he never once implies that he is sick because he sinned. Rather, as Donald Gowan reminds us, "Sin and sickness do come together in Jesus' work; not because one is necessarily the cause of the other, but because he came to save us from both. . . . Each involves a different kind of alienation."[2]

In this story Jesus breaks down the walls of alienation that divide this man from the larger community. By both forgiving his sins and curing his paralysis, Black asserts, "Jesus broke all the causes of alienation. The man was not only able to walk again, but he was also rid of the stigma that it was his fault."[3]

A second theme that emerges for preaching is the role the four friends (or neighbors or family members—we are never really told who they are) play in bringing the paralytic to Jesus. These four people have a tenacious, imaginative, and bold kind of compassion that results not only in their carrying this man for some distance on a cot, but also in finding a creative solution when they realize that direct access to Jesus is blocked by the crowds who are thronging around him. Undeterred, they lift this man high over their heads, carry him up on top of a roof, and literally dig their way through the sod and wood on the roof in order to lower him to Jesus!

The text tells us that "*when Jesus saw their faith*, he said to the paralytic, 'Son, your sins are forgiven'" (v. 5). It is important for preachers to note two things about this statement. First, the faith that is admired here is not merely the faith of the paralytic, but the faith of the community that surrounds and includes him. Second, while faith is not a prerequisite for healing here, Jesus appears to be moved by the faith of those who have enough compassion to (literally) make a way where there is no way and to bring this man to Jesus.

---

1. Kathy Black, *A Healing Homiletic: Preaching and Disability* (Nashville: Abingdon Press, 1996), 112–13. This book is one of the best resources I know for preaching on the healing stories of Jesus in a pastorally sensitive and theologically acute way.
2. Donald E. Gowan, "Salvation as Healing," *Ex Auditu* 5 (1989): 11, as quoted in Black, *A Healing Homiletic*.
3. Black, *A Healing Homiletic*, 121–22.

Mark 2:1–12

Theological Perspective

roof of a house are designed to keep out anything unwanted. Yet this house is special, because Jesus is visiting it. He has shown up at the meeting in the house, and therefore the purpose of this house meeting is forgiveness, and if those who need forgiveness cannot fit through the door, they might just have to tear a hole in the roof. Suddenly the barrier is gone, and those inside must acknowledge those outside. The Same must face the Other. The Other will critique the Same. "By what grounds do you *not* forgive us?" "What have *you* done that needs forgiving?" Of course, there is the unspoken question, "Will you be patching up the roof after this, or will you keep yourself open to having to forgive and be forgiven?"

Lest we be left with ethics only, with simply another rule we must follow, Jesus answers all of these questions with a miraculous healing. In so doing, he reminds us that ultimately the story is not about our response to the questions, but about Jesus' work on our behalf. The ultimate Other, God, is here in person, in the flesh, and has chosen to forgive. The very Other who critiques us also justifies us. Those who would tear a hole in the roof do so because they are seeking the Other who forgives us and will forgive them.

Mark's emphasis on the house meeting reassures us that God in Christ is present when the church meets. The Other will be with us at worship. God will call us to account, and God will forgive us. No matter how stodgy or stiff the worship, no matter how lively and vibrant the congregation, the Other will be there, forgiving, and making all things new.

TIMOTHY ANDREW LEITZKE

Pastoral Perspective

a person's sins forgiven is blasphemous in their eyes. Once more, Jesus is very perceptive, and he responds to the scribes' suspicion. He does what no other person can do: he forgives the paralytic's sins, and he tells the paralytic to stand up! The once paralyzed man stands up, takes his mat, and walks home. In this exchange, Jesus introduces the final dilemma: which is easier, to forgive sin or to make the paralytic walk? Neither. Both are equally easy and possible for Jesus. Both are equally impossible for anyone else.

The story ends with all the witnesses dazzled by the display of grace and goodness, of mercy and might, by the one who embodies all the character traits of the Son of Man, Jesus the Christ. It is a rare situation for all things to come together so well, but here we find Jesus combining the acts of forgiving sins and healing the sick. Jesus does what only the incarnate Christ can do, and he does so to provide inspiration to disciples of every age.

The church, along with all her leaders and servants, is invited and encouraged to cast many modern dilemmas in light of the grace found within the story. While Jesus' pronouncements bring grace to the dilemmas of the text, Jesus' presence is even more significant. Amid the crowd, the chaos, and the characters who doubt who he is and what he is capable of, Jesus maintains a presence of quiet confidence, a presence of approachability, a presence of trust in God, a presence that transforms despair into hope and anxiety into amazement. Jesus demonstrates that the answer to a dilemma might not be A or B. It might be a third, totally unexpected option, one visible only when we are calm, pay close attention, and respond with faith in his name.

WAIN WESBERRY

Exegetical Perspective

The narrative of Mark 2:1–12 transforms the connection between illness and sin: the illness is a visible expression of sin. The paralytic is apparently a sinner. The parallelism in verse 9 confirms this connection: "What is easier, *to say* to the paralytic, 'Your sins are forgiven,' or to say 'Get up, take your bed and go'?" (my trans.).

Jesus does not ask where the illness comes from or who has caused it. It is not about *guilt* or an explanation! What is crucial is that in the presence and actions of Jesus, sin and illness lose their power. Furthermore, forgiveness of sin and healing do not stand in a temporal or causal order: the sick person does not need to be forgiven prior to the cure. The physical restoration is no secondary addition, but integral with the forgiveness. Restoration is for the whole person.

This interpretation helps to clarify the scribes' reproach of blasphemy. The rhetorical question in verse 9 might suggest that the word of forgiveness is powerless. Precisely the opposite is true: though a sick person's healing was not an everyday experience in antiquity, such healing is possible, along with the forgiveness Jesus connects to it. The forgiveness of sins is a privilege of God (Exod. 34:7; Isa. 43:25; 44:22). When Jesus forgives sins, he claims divine authority for the Son of Man.

Jesus presumes the common ancient attribution of illness to sin; his actions overcome sin and illness alike. The German artist Matthias Grünewald's greatest work was an altarpiece painted for the infirmary of the Monastery of St. Anthony in Isenheim, Germany, whose monks were known for their care of those suffering from the plague and from skin diseases. Grünewald depicts the skin of the crucified Christ cruelly torn from plague sores. Through the painting the crucified Christ is saying to the sick of Isenheim, "I am in your skin!" Jesus Christ comes near to us, even in illness and death. Neither sin nor illness can separate us from God. God turns to the people even when we turn away.

ANNETTE WEISSENRIEDER

Homiletical Perspective

This text might lead local congregations to ask the following questions: What are we doing (either intentionally or unintentionally) as a faith community that is blocking access of others (especially those who are disabled or marginalized) to the worship and service of God? What tenacious, imaginative, and bold acts are we willing to undertake in order to make sure that those for whom we have compassion have full access to the life of our faith communities?

We often think of providing "access" as providing physical access to buildings through the addition of ramps and elevators and the like—which is certainly an important first step. However, there are other steps that can be taken. I think of a congregation that created a special class and regularly staffed it for the sake of a single child with special needs who was incapable of sitting through a worship service. Not only was the class a service to the child; it also allowed his parents to attend worship on a regular basis. Another congregation of my acquaintance lights a candle each Sunday during worship to signal its support for people who are struggling with addictions. A large New York City congregation entered into a lawsuit with the City of New York when the city demanded that the church remove the homeless people who sleep on its steps each night and the church refused. (The church ultimately won the suit.)

Who knows what creative and innovative possibilities we can come up with if we, like the four friends, care enough to "dig through" those obstacles that are blocking access to Jesus?

LEONORA TUBBS TISDALE

Mark 2:13–17

¹³Jesus went out again beside the sea; the whole crowd gathered around him, and he taught them. ¹⁴As he was walking along, he saw Levi son of Alphaeus sitting at the tax booth, and he said to him, "Follow me." And he got up and followed him.

¹⁵And as he sat at dinner in Levi's house, many tax collectors and sinners were also sitting with Jesus and his disciples—for there were many who followed him. ¹⁶When the scribes of the Pharisees saw that he was eating with sinners and tax collectors, they said to his disciples, "Why does he eat with tax collectors and sinners?" ¹⁷When Jesus heard this, he said to them, "Those who are well have no need of a physician, but those who are sick; I have come to call not the righteous but sinners."

Theological Perspective

"Those who are well have no need of a physician, but those who are sick." With these words, Jesus describes a great deal of his ministry in the Gospel of Mark. His first act in the Gospel takes place when he enters the synagogue in Capernaum and teaches. As he is speaking, a man with an unclean spirit jumps up and asks if Jesus has come to destroy them. Jesus commands the evil spirit to come out of him, and it does. The people are immediately amazed, and recognize that this teacher has authority and power, especially the power to heal those being afflicted and to liberate those being oppressed by evil spirits. After he leaves the synagogue, he heals Simon's mother-in-law of the fever afflicting her.

It is no wonder that very soon the people bring to him many who are sick, so that he might heal them, or those possessed with demons, so that he might cast them out. The power of Jesus to heal and cast out demons has a strongly magnetic effect on the people, and soon there are so many coming to him that he can no longer go into towns, but has to stay in the country to let people bring the sick and possessed to him.

Jesus came as a physician to heal the sick, and were this all he had come to do, it is likely he would have lived a long and happy life, celebrated by his generation as one of the most remarkable figures of

Pastoral Perspective

Thanks to social media, public discourse now takes place at lightning speed. The results are a mixed brew with large quantities of anonymous commentary stirred in, splashes of keen wit adding color, diced bits of video thrown in for extra spice.

The social media in Jesus' day consisted, apparently, of checking out who was eating with whom, and discussing the company kept. The buzz was this: Jesus and the disciples were not very particular about their dining partners. In fact, they had been spotted breaking bread with Levi and some of his crew. Unclean, despised, wrong side of the tracks—Jesus and his team are consorting with the enemy! Video to be posted any minute! Someone finally works up the nerve to say something directly to them. Do they not know proper church procedure: take it to the parking lot, and wait for word to leak back to those directly involved?

Had this played out in our time, the video would have indeed been posted, followed immediately by a barrage of outraged comments, shares, links to similar events, tweeted rumors. The whole episode would have gone viral in no time. Then the loyal defenders of Jesus and the disciples would take up the cause. Perhaps a separate Facebook page would be set up to defend Levi as a misunderstood victim in all this, a man simply trying to earn a living.

Exegetical Perspective

The Call of Levi. In the short span of just one chapter of the Gospel of Mark, and a few verses of the second, Jesus has begun his public ministry: spending time in the wilderness areas surrounding the river Jordan (1:9); calling Simon, Andrew, James, and John to follow him as they worked their fishing nets on the Sea of Galilee (1:16–20); teaching in Capernaum (1:21–27); healing the sick (1:29–31); and developing a large following of crowds, to the extent that people seeking Jesus' ministry had difficulty finding him or getting near to him (2:3–12).

The rapid narrative of Mark's Gospel continues as Jesus calls Levi, a tax collector, to join others in following him. As Mark tells us, Levi son of Alphaeus (referred to as Matthew in the parallel story in Matt. 9:9–13; also recounted in Luke 5:27–32), is sitting, and presumably working, at his tax booth beside the Sea of Galilee when Jesus calls him to follow. Like the fishermen a few verses before him, he gets up from his post and follows Jesus without question, doubt, or wonder.

As a tax collector, Levi was saddled with the reputation of being one who could (and would) demand more than was due from those individuals who crossed his path. He would keep the excess tax revenue for himself, thereby ensuring his own wealth

Homiletical Perspective

The narrative in Mark's Gospel is gathering steam. Driven by quick shifts from scene to scene, Mark's story is moving so fast that the reader or listener may have trouble catching her breath! Here is what the one preaching or teaching this text gets to do: press the pause button long enough to let the listener have a look around at what is happening in these two scenes. Help your own listeners imagine what is going on both within the frame of each episode and between the lines.

Jesus and his growing number of disciples have moved from the house in Capernaum back to the shore of the Sea of Galilee, one of Jesus' favorite spots for preaching and teaching. Mark does not tell us what is happening along the way. He only implies that the curious crowd was getting so large that Jesus had to seek out a larger venue for his work. Imagine the crowd. Who might be there that the modern reader or hearer could identify with? Someone who is impressed by Jesus' authority in an environment where respect for authority has declined? (1:22) Someone whose curiosity about Jesus has overcome indifference? (1:27) Someone wondering if Jesus' ministry is an agency of healing? (1:32–34) Someone who has heard about Jesus' willingness and power to forgive sins? (2:5)

Whenever Jesus acts or makes a move, whether in our world or in the world of Mark's Gospel, he

Mark 2:13–17

Theological Perspective

his day, with a steadily growing crowd of admirers. However, Jesus soon complicates this picture dramatically, and sets in motion the opposition that will bring him to his death, by revealing that his healing is only a sign of his larger mission. When the paralytic is lowered into the house in Capernaum, which is jammed full of people wanting to be helped by Jesus, Jesus responds by saying to the paralytic, "Son, your sins are forgiven."

This scene is astonishing on several grounds. First, the man was brought to him for healing, not for forgiveness. Second, the man does not confess his sin or acknowledge any guilt at all, nor is he said to repent. Third, Jesus forgives him by his own authority, and does not say that the Lord forgives him, as Nathan said to David. It is precisely here, when Jesus makes the surprising transition from healing and casting out demons to forgiving sin by his own authority, that the opposition to him begins. "Why does this fellow speak in this way? It is blasphemy! Who can forgive sins but God alone?" (v. 7). Jesus heals the paralytic to show that he has the authority to forgive sins. Thus the one who heals sickness and casts out demons does all this to show that in him is found the authority to forgive sin. This claim to an authority that belongs alone to God provokes the opposition that will bring him to his death.

Jesus continues to exercise his authority to forgive sins by calling Levi the tax collector to be his follower, and then by eating in Levi's home with other tax collectors and sinners. Jesus not only comes to forgive sin. He also goes so far as to identify himself with sinners and picks the most reprehensible of the lot, those who enriched themselves at the expense of their fellow Jews in the service of the Roman occupation.

The opposition to Jesus grows more pronounced as a consequence, leading the scribes and Pharisees to ask his disciples, "Why does he eat with tax collectors and sinners?" Jesus hears their question, and in response shows that his healing is in the service of his call to sinners. "Those who are well have no need of a physician, but those who are sick; I have come to call not the righteous but sinners" (v. 17). Jesus heals and casts out demons to show that he has come to call sinners to himself and to the kingdom. He has come to restore those who are outside the law, whose lives cannot be restored by the law. As a sign of this, he even heals on the Sabbath, to show that his work of restoration goes beyond the law, and even apparently against the law. He does this in order to heal those who are sick and to call those who are sinners.

Pastoral Perspective

Within a few short hours, the lines would all be blurred. Most would have an opinion and most would feel quite justified in the rightness of that opinion. Most would feel they had furthered the cause, however they defined it.

Is it possible that at least part of Jesus' intention was to blur the lines? If we had the benefit of a video that focused on his facial expressions, captured his body language, recorded his eye contact as he responded to his critics, what might we learn? Would we find Jesus tilting his head and looking directly into the eyes of those questioning him, with a slight smile forming on his lips as he says, "Those who are well have no need . . ."?

Was anyone in that group of critics actually "well"? Could anyone claim truthfully to be without sin? Had Jesus not, in fact, come for all, tax collector and scribe, self-aware sinner and self-presumed saint?

On any given Sunday we are worshiping with, preaching with, praying with those who are acutely aware that they need the Great Physician, as well as with those who are comfortable in their belief that they have no such need. On any given Sunday, who can honestly tell who is sick and who is healthy? Do we ever really know? Do we have the right to judge? Do we enter into worship aware of our own need?

Few extended families these days have not experienced the pain of addiction, divorce, and myriad other disruptions. Where such issues were once taboo, congregations now offer support and compassion. Even more of a challenge for many of the faithful is what to do with the scribes. It is one thing to accept imperfect people. It is quite another to begin to acknowledge our own need for the physician, to release the illusion of our self-sufficiency. Our society places an increasingly high value on being right, being sure, "having it all together." No one wants to be the last to know, to be left out of the loop.

While it is acceptable to admit needing our high-tech gadgets, our smart phones and laptops and tablets, it is as yet unacceptable—indeed a source of embarrassment—to admit we need help from actual humans. To admit we need help from the Holy One, a Higher Power, the God of tax collectors and scribes, prostitutes and Pharisees? Unthinkable. We may stay awake at night fearing the loss of our career or the lump felt under the skin. Our relationships may be in turmoil, and we may desperately hope no one can tell. As long as we look the part, as long as there are still Levis around to distract attention from us, we feel safe. Who is well? Who has no need?

Exegetical Perspective

at the expense of others. Because of this, those in his profession were distrusted and despised, held in contempt by both society and religious authorities as sinners. In spite of it being against cultural and religious norms of the day, Jesus goes to dinner at Levi's house and proceeds to eat with him and others gathered there. Three times in verses 15–16 Mark impresses upon his readers that Jesus and his disciples ate with "tax collectors and sinners," thereby placing Jesus squarely in the company of those less desirable.

What Does It Mean to Be a Disciple of Jesus Christ? These five verses offer an opportunity to consider this question. One key element that will be of interest to the reader/preacher is that this is the first time Mark uses the term "disciples" to name Jesus' followers. As Ched Myers, a commentator, educator, and activist, says, "It is of no small significance that Mark chooses this scene to introduce his term for 'disciples' (*tois mathētais*). It seems he wants to stress here that Jesus' disciples may freely mix with 'sinners,' because Jesus' repudiation of the debt code has made everyone equal again before God. There are now only sinners on the road to discipleship, as Jesus will argue in 2:17."[1]

These early moments of the Gospel of Mark make it clear that being a follower of Jesus, a disciple, requires that one engage a way of life that places one in the company of those on the margins of society. After all, according to Jesus in verse 17, "those who are well have no need of a physician, but those who are sick." He reminds all who have ears to hear that he has "come to call not the righteous but sinners."

Discipleship in Mark. There are many educators, pastors, and theologians who have written on the topic of Christian discipleship; those individuals will no doubt be consulted and considered as one seeks to interpret this text. However, it is important to return to the text itself to gain an understanding of what the Gospel of Mark understands discipleship to be. Mark portrays Jesus' disciples as a confused lot, continuously confounded by Jesus' teaching, yet eager to continue with him along his journey. Jesus' disciples are ones who go against the grain of tradition, who question Jesus' teaching because they do not comprehend it, and who want to understand yet fall short of Jesus' expectations time and again. They are the ones whom Jesus asks: "Who do people say

1. Ched Myers, *Binding the Strong Man: A Political Reading of Mark's Story of Jesus* (Maryknoll, NY: Orbis Books, 1988), 157.

Homiletical Perspective

generates profound questions about his destination, his identity in relationship to God, and what he is here to do. Questions like this: what type of person does Jesus call into discipleship? One example? Levi, son of Alphaeus. How long has it been since someone gave this tax collector his full name instead of calling him a name? One of the few details we get in the text is that Levi is at his day job in a tax booth. We do not know what kind of taxes he collects or how much money he makes by doing it. We do not even know why he decided at this moment in the story to respond to Jesus' call. What we can assume is that Levi is more likely to be called "Liar!" "Thief!" "Traitor!" than "Disciple." Until Jesus passes by, Levi sits in the pocket of an oppressive imperial system, an "outcast" among his people, considered to be outside the grace of God.

Your congregation may need only a reminder of what Levi's predicament was. What of those in our day whose means of employment (or lack thereof) leaves them feeling isolated or marginalized among "good" people? On the other hand, perhaps there are some in the congregation who regret that Jesus would have anything to do with someone like Levi, who is obviously making a living from his collaboration with a system of government that is brutal, repressive, and corrupt. Can such persons, lamenting the loss of a job or the controversial nature of the job they have, be counted as candidates for faithful discipleship? Jesus apparently hopes so.

What is missing in this call to Levi is Jesus' insistence that he "repent" or "get right with God" before he can qualify for effective discipleship. Later in this Gospel, Jesus will issue an invitation to a man of means to "go, sell what you own, and give the money to the poor" before becoming a disciple (10:17–23). That is not the case with Levi. Jesus does not stand in judgment of his occupation any more than he did with Simon and Andrew or James and John (1:17–20). Whether fishermen, whether those who collect taxes or unemployment, whether lawyers, homemakers, or pastors—it does not matter. Any and all, from whatever walk of life, are summoned to walk with Jesus in the direction of human need. The call to discipleship can certainly happen gradually over time, perhaps even a lifetime. However, the call to Levi suggests that a call to discipleship can happen in a moment. "Yes," says the new disciple, "I will start paying attention to this Jesus character and follow his lead!"

Levi's choice to follow Jesus takes him first to a dinner in a house (v. 15). Whose house was it? Did

Mark 2:13–17

Theological Perspective

It is precisely in light of this call that the Pharisees conspire with the Herodians regarding how to destroy him (3:6).

By calling sinners, Jesus provokes the sin of seeking to put him to death. The scribes and Pharisees were not considered sinners before Jesus came to call sinners, but were instead among the righteous that he did not come to call. By opposing Jesus and his call to tax collectors and sinners, the scribes and Pharisees make themselves the sinners into whose hands the Son of Man is betrayed. More than this, the desire of the opponents of Jesus to put him to death causes the disciples themselves to become sinners. Judas decides to betray Jesus when he tells his disciples he intends to die in Jerusalem. Once Jesus is arrested, the other disciples desert him, with one even fleeing away naked. And when Jesus is condemned by the high priest, Peter denies three times that he knows him. "But he began to curse, and swore an oath, 'I do not know this man you are talking about'" (14:71).

However, by making themselves into sinners as they oppose his call to sinners, the scribes and Pharisees make themselves into the very ones Jesus came to call. By betraying, deserting, and denying him, the disciples also make themselves into the sinners to whom Jesus was sent. Even Paul, who opposed Jesus because of his fellowship with sinners, became the very sinner that Jesus came to call. "The saying is sure and worthy of full acceptance, that Christ Jesus came into the world to save sinners—of whom I am the foremost" (1 Tim. 1:15).

RANDALL C. ZACHMAN

Pastoral Perspective

For Jesus, all the lines were blurred, if not erased. Let whoever is without sin cast the first stone. Father, forgive them. Today, I come and dine at your house. Follow me. Take, and eat, all of you. Woman, give me a drink. We come close to this line-blurring when we break bread together, the whole lot of us, scribes and Levis and disciples and would-be followers. Whether we approach the table, come and kneel, stand in a circle, or sit quietly in pews while the plates are passed, no one asks for a status update. Sinner or saint? Sick or well? Perhaps we should ask out loud what is implied. Are you hungry? Do you have need?

Aware or not, we break the bread and drink the cup. Jesus is dining at our house. The deacon who is convinced she is absolutely right about not veering from the way we have always done things, and the young man who struggles to stay on his medicines to quiet the voices in his head: they are hungry, and they are joining us today. The elderly gentleman who knows his days with us are very few and the single mother being dragged up the aisle by her energetic toddler are ready to receive what Jesus has to offer.

We take that crust of bread and taste the fruit of the vine too. Yes, it is meant for us. Especially, perhaps, for those of us who answer the call to look out for the ones in need. The physician's assistants, as it were. We need to be fed. We need the care of the Great Healer. There are no lines drawn, no right or wrong sides to take. No video to post. Jesus tilts his head, looks us in the eye, with perhaps a bit of a smile crossing his lips, saying, "Those who are well . . ."

JULIE PEEPLES

Exegetical Perspective

that I am? Who do you say that I am?" (8:27, 29). They are the ones to whom he proclaims shortly thereafter, "If any want to become my followers, let them deny themselves and take up their cross and follow me" (8:34).

Over the course of the Gospel, Mark recounts three passion predictions of Jesus, each saying essentially the same thing: Jesus "began to teach them that the Son of Man must undergo great suffering, and be rejected by the elders, the chief priests, and the scribes, and be killed, and after three days rise again" (8:31; 9:30–32; 10:32–34). Each time, the disciples respond in a different way—in shock and dismay (8:32), by arguing with one another (9:33), and by jostling with one another for power (10:35).

Each time, Jesus offers clues as to what the character of discipleship will be like for those who follow him. Jesus says, "If any want to become my followers, let them deny themselves and take up their cross and follow me. For those who want to save their life will lose it, and those who lose their life for my sake, and for the sake of the gospel, will save it" (8:34–35). "Whoever wants to be first must be last of all and servant of all" (9:35). "Whoever wishes to become great among you must be your servant, and whoever wishes to be first among you must be slave of all" (10:43–44). Jesus calls Levi from a position of vulnerability but potential wealth into a calling that makes him even more vulnerable, yet possessed of life. This is what discipleship means in the Gospel of Mark.

As one studies through the Gospel, the question of discipleship and what it means to follow Jesus will arise again and again. In each instance, the text offers opportunities to wrestle with what being a disciple means. That discussion will be rooted in the story of the call of Levi and in the early moments of the Gospel of Mark when Jesus makes it clear who his disciples are, what they must risk, and the company they are to keep if they follow him.

KATHRYN E. ANDERSON

Homiletical Perspective

Levi follow Jesus to Jesus' house? Did Jesus follow Levi to his?[1] The point for the preacher is what kind of group is there, who is watching, and what is the significance of the gathering. Have your congregation peek through the window or doorway of the house and see things from the point of view of the "scribes"(2:16). To go and sit down at that table and to enter into fellowship with this group would violate their idea of "holiness." For them, Bible and tradition drew clear boundaries around who and what was "pure" and "ritually clean." Holiness was performed out of love and respect for God, using proscribed sets of rituals that were carefully passed down through tradition. The "righteous" remembered the grace that God extended to them. In return, they performed the rituals and abided by the major divine laws for conduct and behavior. How are one's own ideas of purity and righteousness exposed here?

All of us have tried to corral God's grace in one way or another. Even faithful believers are sometimes confounded by God's inclusive ways and find themselves outside of what God is up to. Such is the case in this story where the insiders have become outsiders. The story says nothing, however, about a door or window being closed off to the joyful gathering inside. Jesus is in the company of those who have been scapegoats for social ills or wounded by exclusion. They have been maligned by those deep inside centers of power. Now, with this new inbreaking of God's realm, they find themselves in the presence of a "physician" who has the power to forgive, heal, and bring about a new relationship to God. Why not take a place at the table and join them?

RICHARD F. WARD

---

1. See the footnote in the NRSV.

Mark 2:18–22

¹⁸Now John's disciples and the Pharisees were fasting; and people came and said to him, "Why do John's disciples and the disciples of the Pharisees fast, but your disciples do not fast?" ¹⁹Jesus said to them, "The wedding guests cannot fast while the bridegroom is with them, can they? As long as they have the bridegroom with them, they cannot fast. ²⁰The days will come when the bridegroom is taken away from them, and then they will fast on that day.

²¹"No one sews a piece of unshrunk cloth on an old cloak; otherwise, the patch pulls away from it, the new from the old, and a worse tear is made. ²²And no one puts new wine into old wineskins; otherwise, the wine will burst the skins, and the wine is lost, and so are the skins; but one puts new wine into fresh wineskins."

Theological Perspective

"Why do John's disciples and the disciples of the Pharisees fast, but your disciples do not fast?" (v. 18). The people of Galilee notice a key difference between the followers of Jesus and the followers of John and the Pharisees. The latter practice fasting, but the former do not. It is not surprising that John's followers practice fasting, as John comes "proclaiming a baptism of repentance for the forgiveness of sins" (Mark 1:4). Starting with the Day of Atonement in Leviticus, fasting was associated with the confession of sin, in the hope of forgiveness by the Lord (Lev. 23:26–32). The people in Samuel's day fast and confess their sin in the same hope that God would deliver them from the Philistines. More importantly, the people fast and confess their sins in the aftermath of the destruction of Jerusalem and the exile to Babylon. Daniel fasts and confesses his sins while in Babylon contemplating the ruin of Jerusalem (Dan. 9:1–23).

The returned exiles collectively fast and confess their sin once the temple and the city of Jerusalem are restored after the exile (Neh. 9). When Joel proclaims that the Day of the Lord is coming with darkness and destruction, the Lord urges the people to turn to God with fasting, weeping, and mourning, in the hope that the Lord may yet relent and spare the people (Joel 2:1–19). By fasting, the disciples of John

Pastoral Perspective

The seemingly endless debate about "new" and "different" in church can get to be a challenge for pastors. Not that it is wrong or out of place, but church experts, clergy, and laity have debated and discussed contemporary versus traditional versus modern versus emergent versus emerging for so long now that what was thrown out in the opening rounds of the debate has cycled back as the new and different!

In the midst of these discussions, there are still the hospital calls, the weddings and funerals, the meetings and sermons to tend to. For many, ordinary life in ordinary congregations goes on. Is there perhaps something more for us in this passage, so often cited in the context of changing church life? Is there some piece of good news to grab on to here that goes beyond taking sides in a cultural/religious/musical/liturgical battle?

Here is one. The images speak of celebration: wedding, bridegroom, wine. In other words, this is not the time to fast. We can get so caught up in striving to do it right, to catch the newest and latest, to do church better, to outwit the megachurch down the road, and to play the numbers game, that we lose the ability simply to celebrate. We forget to enjoy the great company we are in. Jesus is with us. The party is on.

Here is another piece of good news. There is wine and there are wineskins. Fullness, provision,

Exegetical Perspective

Jesus begins his public ministry by going to Galilee, "proclaiming the good news of God, and saying, 'The time is fulfilled, and the kingdom of God has come near; repent, and believe in the good news'" (1:14–15). In the Gospel of Mark, the reign of God has come in Jesus, and is already here. Mark also holds that the reign of God is still coming into the world, and is not quite yet complete, though it will be in the fullness of time. From the very beginning, Jesus teaches, preaches, and indeed embodies this tension between the already and the not-yet of the reign of God. The "Question about Fasting," as Mark 2:18–22 is often named, plays with tensions between the already and not-yet of God's reign, but in ways that reverse our usual expectations. The story suggests that the time of celebration because of the bridegroom's presence is already here, during the ministry of Jesus, while the time of absence and waiting lies ahead.

In this passage (paralleled in Matt. 9:14–17 and Luke 5:33–39), Jesus responds to questions about why his disciples do not fast like the disciples of John and the disciples of the Pharisees (2:18). Jesus uses the analogy of a wedding banquet and a bridegroom (himself) to explain his disciples' actions.[1]

---
1. Those desiring further study of this passage would be well served to expand their inquiries to other Scriptures that also portray Jesus as the bridegroom, including Matt. 25:1–13; John 3:28–30; Eph. 5:21–33; and Rev. 19:9.

Homiletical Perspective

From time to time the practice of fasting will get a lot of press. Social activists know that fasting can be an effective means of calling attention to a justice issue. Prisoners go on a hunger strike to protest crowded conditions inside. A seminary student goes on a fast to raise awareness of the plight of underpaid workers in the food industry. A woman fasts for peace as a war heats up. Someone else might fast for health reasons. Every now and then an advertisement recommends a special cleansing fast for the improvement of one's physical condition. Another will fast during Lent or on a church retreat to become more attentive to how the Spirit of God is working in her or his life.

Fasting, for whatever reason, takes place in the hope that one's condition or political situation may change. Because we live in an age of conspicuous consumption and extreme poverty, the practice of fasting can startle. What startles us raises awareness about matters that need our attention.

The practice of fasting can also set questions of motive swirling around, like the questions raised in this text. Mark moves us from a query about who Jesus eats and drinks with to why he and his disciples do not fast. The "people" (v. 18) who are asking the question may represent the people in Mark's own community who were asking similar questions—or

Mark 2:18–22

Theological Perspective

and of the Pharisees remind themselves of the great destruction brought on Jerusalem and the people of Israel by their sin; by confessing their sin they seek to avert a similar fate coming upon them at the hands of the Lord.

By not having his disciples fast, Jesus reveals that he does not want his followers to dwell on the destruction that has overtaken Jerusalem in the past, but on the coming of the kingdom of God, which promises the ultimate restoration and vindication of Jerusalem and of Israel. He signifies this different expectation by speaking of himself as the bridegroom and of his followers as the wedding guests: "The wedding guests cannot fast while the bridegroom is with them, can they?" (v. 19). In this way, Jesus directly engages the image the prophets use to speak about the distress the Babylonians will bring upon Jerusalem. Jeremiah repeatedly warns Jerusalem that in the coming destruction the Lord "will bring to an end the sound of mirth and gladness, the voice of the bride and bridegroom" (Jer. 7:34). On the other hand, Jeremiah speaks of the restoration of Judah and Jerusalem in terms of the return of the voice of the bride and bridegroom, which is "the voice of mirth and the voice of gladness," "the voices of those who sing" (Jer. 33:11). Isaiah also speaks of the return of the Lord to Zion as the rejoicing of the bridegroom over his bride, to whom he will be bound forever. "For as a young man marries a young woman, so shall your builder marry you, and as the bridegroom rejoices over the bride, so shall your God rejoice over you" (Isa. 62:5). By speaking of himself as the bridegroom, Jesus clearly portrays himself as the beginning of the final restoration of Jerusalem, when the Lord will dwell with the people and they will never again fear being cast into exile away from their temple and land. The coming of the kingdom is the coming of the redemption of Israel, and so the disciples of Jesus cannot fast, because they must rejoice with the bridegroom who is in their midst.

If the presence of Jesus is the beginning of the ultimate restoration of Jerusalem, Judea, and Israel, then it makes sense that his disciples cannot observe fasting, since that looks to the past destruction of the people due to their sins, and seeks to avert future destruction and exile at the hands of the Lord. The new wine of rejoicing with the bridegroom, and of celebrating the return of the Lord to Zion once and for all, cannot be poured into the old wineskins of fasting and the confession of sin to avert future wrath. The future that Jesus proclaims is one of joy, not of sorrow; of feasting with the bridegroom, not

Pastoral Perspective

enough. We can so tie ourselves up into knots over changes and resisting them or introducing them that we forget to stop, look around. We never pause long enough to marvel at the astounding fact that we have been given enough. In Christ's presence there is fullness of life, abundance.

Is that awareness and the resulting gratitude not the best foundation for receiving the "new"? Indeed God is forever doing a new thing. However, if we approach the new and this news with fear and trepidation, or a sense that this is all about competing with the churches in our neighborhood, our denomination, our demographic; if we tiptoe up to the "new," dreading the ramifications and the angry responses and the sense of disorientation, the "new" will hardly be welcomed as gift. If we suspect there really is not enough to go around—enough love, enough grace, enough members, enough money—then anything new will be threatening.

How does this newness sound to the person in the pew who feels the world is moving way too fast and wishes it would all slow down a bit? How does this fall on the ears of the person who still cannot figure out how to use a cell phone, much less a smart phone? Where is the good news in "new" for the middle-aged woman just laid off from her job of twenty-two years, or the young family whose infant was just diagnosed with a serious disorder? In a culture that often worships the improved and the latest and whatever makes us feel good, how do we help people discern what needs to be cherished and what needs to be released? In a time when Jesus is often presented as a preserver of the status quo, the tried and true, the traditional, how can people move beyond the dissonance created by hearing Jesus promoting change?

The very images Jesus uses call us to something deeper than any simplistic "out with the old, in with the new" mantra. These can be especially helpful images for people struggling to emerge from difficult economic times and rapid social upheaval. If we take as our starting point that the bridegroom is yet with us and that we have, in fact, been given what we need, a different picture begins to emerge. Different questions begin to present themselves, offering possible ways forward.

Perhaps the new thing Jesus is doing involves calming our fears, releasing us from age-old anxieties. Jesus could be calling into question our increasingly fear-driven society. Maybe this ever-present bridegroom is reminding us that wedding parties are not solo affairs; we are not alone, even and especially

Exegetical Perspective

Lamar Williamson Jr. says it well: the image of Christ as bridegroom in this passage implies joy in the presence of Jesus, and celebration of the "already" dimension of the kingdom of God.[2] If the disciples would not fast at an actual wedding banquet, why would they fast when the bridegroom Jesus was with them? After all, the kingdom of God has come near; Jesus demands a new way of life from his disciples, one that goes against the grain of the societal and religious norms of the day.

Jesus then says, "the days will come when the bridegroom is taken away from them, and then they will fast on that day" (v. 20). This refers to the time when Jesus' earthly life and ministry will end. References to fasting during these moments indicate sorrow at the absence of Jesus and highlight the "not yet" dimension of the kingdom of God.[3] Jesus teaches that his presence ushers in a new way of being, a new way of living in response to the good news. The disciples do not fast because Jesus, the embodiment of the kingdom of God, is with them. There will be plenty of time to fast when Jesus has completed his earthly ministry, but already the kingdom of God has indeed come near. Those who follow Jesus as his disciples are to repent and trust in the good news that is present and in their midst. At the same time, they are to wait and watch for its arrival, feasting with great joy in the places where that kingdom will yet come to be in the fullness of time.

In the second part of this passage, Jesus continues his response to those who question him by making two references to the "old" and the "new." No one puts a new patch on an old garment, and young wine is meant for new, not old, wineskins. To fit the new into the old by force would be unthinkable. The old garment would simply tear with greater ease and be ruined. The new/good wine would potentially be lost if it were stored in older, less reliable vessels. Jesus has come to bring a new teaching. After all, Jesus' teaching is what led those who heard him at Capernaum to wonder and exclaim, "What is this? A new teaching—with authority! He commands even the unclean spirits, and they obey him" (1:27). All of Jesus' ministry and teaching points to the new age that has dawned with the coming of the kingdom of God. This teaching will put him in the crosshairs of the religious authorities who do not welcome—or are threatened by (in every age?)—Jesus' message of a new day dawning.

2. Lamar Williamson Jr., *Mark*, Interpretation series (Atlanta: John Knox Press, 1983), 68–69.
3. Ibid.

Homiletical Perspective

they may even represent the people in our communities today!

What is the point of fasting? Why do some faithful people fast and others do not? What does fasting have to do with discipleship? Is fasting something that some of us should consider? Mark's community was trying to establish its witness and how it understood itself in relation to Jesus. The question about fasting had deeper implications: Is Jesus with us? Has he "gone before us" into mission? Is Jesus absent just now and we await his return? If so, should we not be fasting like the disciples of John or the Pharisees?

Fasting was a regular practice among the Pharisees. At this point, take care. Do not jump to the conclusion that "Pharisees" are rigid, narrow-minded legalists who had nothing to contribute to the faithful service to God. Doing so would distort the historical record and, worse, contribute to poor relationships between temple, synagogue, and church. In Mark's narrative Pharisees are foils to Jesus, and their opposition does indeed harden into conspiracy as the plot develops. The preacher might reflect here on how religious zeal, from whatever group, can eventually harden into opposition to God's agents in our world.

In this story, though, the questions are about fasting. Fasting meant abstaining from sex, bathing, and eating certain foods. For the Pharisee, fasting was a sign of penitence and a means for preparing oneself for the coming reign of God.

The mention of "John's disciples" (v. 18) can serve as another teaching moment for the preacher. Some in the congregation may not be aware that a community associated with "the Baptist" competed for followers alongside Jesus' disciples. They too bore witness to the coming reign of God by fasting. For them, rejecting the comforts that others enjoyed was a way of purifying and preparing themselves for God's impending judgment. In time, the church would come to understand John's ministry as being the forerunner who announced Jesus' ministry as the harbinger of God's reign.

Mark does not spell out the ways that either the Pharisees or the disciples of John the Baptist imagined the coming reign of God. His emphasis rather is upon Jesus, who as the Son of God breaks in and breaks through human opposition to God and establishes a beachhead for God's reign. "The time is fulfilled," announces Jesus, "and the kingdom of God has come near" (1:15). According to Mark, the Pharisees and the disciples of John are waiting for something that is already unfolding before their eyes.

Mark 2:18–22

Theological Perspective

of fasting; of celebrating the mercy and love of God for Judah and Israel, not of confessing sin in light of the possibility of God's wrath.

However, Jesus qualifies this hope by saying that a time is coming when the bridegroom will be taken away, and then his followers will fast. The rejoicing of the present will be followed by fasting and mourning in the future. The bridegroom who is now with them will be crucified, and the people who crucify him will again see the destruction of the temple and the exile of the people from Jerusalem. "Do you see these great buildings? Not one stone will be left here upon another; all will be thrown down" (13:2).

Christians have for millennia seen the future fasting of which Jesus speaks in light of his crucifixion, and have cast a blind eye on the fasting of the Jewish community in light of the destruction of Jerusalem and the exile of the Jews from their land. It is possible to read the words of Jesus in a different way, and see the coming time of fasting for the disciples as one that joins the crucifixion of Jesus by the Romans to the destruction of Jerusalem by the Romans. Christians have rejoiced for far too long over the destruction of Jerusalem as revealing the divine vindication of Jesus over against his rejection by the Jews. It is hard to see how this could be a cause of rejoicing, since the restoration of Jerusalem of which Jesus so clearly spoke failed to materialize. Perhaps we could unite the fasting of the future of which Jesus speaks with the question of the disciples framed as a prayer: "Lord, is this the time when you will restore the kingdom to Israel?" (Acts 1:6).

RANDALL C. ZACHMAN

Pastoral Perspective

when we do not feel much like celebrating. Perhaps the new thing Jesus is doing is helping us rediscover the critical importance of real human relationships in an era of increasing social disconnection. The possibilities are endless. New things do not have to be shiny or expensive. They may not necessarily involve expansions and dislocations.

If Jesus is indeed with us, do we ever express any of this good news in our worship together, in our lives, in our learning and service? If Jesus is with us, do we share a sense of joy with others who visit with us? Is everyone welcome to this party?

Moreover, if God has provided the wine and the wineskins, if God has poured forth abundant grace and blessing, can we first remember to give thanks? Before all else, before wrestling with the questions over contemporary music or keeping the organ, remodeling the entryway or putting in a coffee bar, have we expressed deep gratitude for the life we have together?

If Jesus is with us and God still provides, we can look beyond the church walls with our fear in check, to see who has been left out of the party, or even locked out. We can be with the ones struggling to find a cup of clean water, their daily bread, a word of hope, some longed-for justice. If Jesus is with us, we may not be able to do so in the old-wineskins sort of ways, as in "here we are to rescue and save you." That way is not holding the wine very well anymore. The new-wineskins way has more to do with Jesus being present with all, and some of us discovering a party going on that we never knew about. Celebration and giving thanks to God can be acts of protest too. The powers of destruction and exclusion cannot stop the party. It is an open invitation. Come as you are. Talk about new and different! Thanks be to God.

JULIE PEEPLES

Exegetical Perspective

Everything that Jesus says and does in the Gospel from this point forward will be rooted in the struggle and tension between old and new. Jesus will go on to speak in parables about the kingdom of God, and each of these teachings will point in some way to the "new" that has come, and to the "old" that has gone away (also reflected later in 2 Cor. 5:17). Jesus will go on to teach and preach around the Sea of Galilee. All the while, those who hear him and follow him will struggle to grasp what it means to live in the tension between old and new, the kingdom at hand and the kingdom yet to come.

Even at the end of the Gospel, we will encounter the push and pull between old and new. In the face of death, the disciples (the women, in this instance) experience the ultimate encounter of the old with the new when the one who greets them at Jesus' empty tomb tells them, "Go, tell his disciples and Peter that he is going ahead of you to Galilee; there you will see him, just as he told you" (16:7). Even at the end, the "new" still prevails, for Mark sends the disciples (and us as readers) back to Galilee, back to the beginning where everything started—to begin again the journey of discipleship.

KATHRYN E. ANDERSON

Homiletical Perspective

Those who have been fasting and praying for God's representative to come and break the power of evil can now celebrate the fulfillment of God's promises.

We catch a glimpse of Mark's vision of God's reign by looking more closely at this text. Here is a wedding feast, and the bridegroom is present. The banquet table is being set. We have already seen in the preceding story who the guests are. They are those like Jesus who are religiously or socially suspect. Like so many today, their life circumstances make it nigh impossible to practice the kind of rigorous piety that distinguishes the disciples of John or the Pharisees. God is being wed to all God's people through the presence and ministry of Jesus. There is joy in this awareness, and a celebration is in order. Aspects of life in God's realm are already here, and all are welcome to participate.

There is, however, a time in the life of Jesus' disciples when fasting is appropriate. The realm of God is already here but has not yet come in its fullness, as those who struggle to survive may sense most acutely. One feels this most when one remembers the story of how Jesus' earthly ministry will end. It will seem for a time that the joy of Jesus' presence ends in the sorrow of the cross. Jesus in his crucifixion will present to God the brokenness of humanity and awaken in humankind the longing for the full manifestation of God's realm. Faithful disciples—whether of the Pharisees, or of John, or of Jesus—await this fulfillment.

When we celebrate the presence of Jesus among us or await the fulfillment of God's reign, we are nourished with new wine and clothed in fresh garments. New manifestations of the gospel do not quite fit in the old forms, patterns, and vessels provided. What disciples in every age come to discover about Jesus is that the way of life he teaches and embodies is fresh and new and does not easily conform to what they expect. Sip the new wine and look to the one beside you who is clothed anew in God's grace. You may be surprised!

RICHARD F. WARD

Mark 2:23–28

²³One sabbath he was going through the grainfields; and as they made their way his disciples began to pluck heads of grain. ²⁴The Pharisees said to him, "Look, why are they doing what is not lawful on the sabbath?" ²⁵And he said to them, "Have you never read what David did when he and his companions were hungry and in need of food? ²⁶He entered the house of God, when Abiathar was high priest, and ate the bread of the Presence, which it is not lawful for any but the priests to eat, and he gave some to his companions." ²⁷Then he said to them, "The sabbath was made for humankind, and not humankind for the sabbath; ²⁸so the Son of Man is lord even of the sabbath."

Theological Perspective

The letter of the law versus the spirit and intent of teaching is at the heart of this text—like its immediate predecessor, Mark 2:18–22. Even deeper than that, though, lies the question of what it means to live a life of faithfulness. Definitions of Sabbath seem to matter far less to Jesus than honoring the purposes of Sabbath and meeting real human need. His apparent intent in testing the legalistic religious authorities can be broadened in the early twenty-first century. Surely religious practices need to be challenged as we seek the true spirit of Sabbath. Yet can we also expand Jesus' reflections on human need by exploring the way we live our lives, whether in church or beyond, whether religious or not? Can the call to Sabbath provide much-needed healing for a frantic and anxious world?

Jesus' ongoing battle with the religious authorities reaches a new level here. Sabbath violation is serious business. Jesus reaches back into the tradition to make his initial argument. If David can do it, why not I?

Then he makes an important shift. The real purpose of Sabbath observance is not about *what* or *when*. It is *why*. Why do God's beloved creatures need a rest? God needed no rest at the conclusion of the original creative activity; God rested to model for humans, indeed for all creation, the need for rest.

Pastoral Perspective

The writer of Mark begins this Gospel with common features of the Gospel tradition: John the Baptist appears and baptizes Jesus, the devil tempts Jesus in the wilderness, and Jesus calls disciples. An exorcism performed in the synagogue is the first public act of Jesus recorded in this Gospel. This act reveals Jesus as an authoritative exorcist rebelling against the forces that hold God's people captive. Jesus' controversial behavior continues and expands in chapters 2 and 3. The rebellious Son of God forgives a man's sin and heals his paralysis, eats with sinners and tax collectors, breaks but does not reject laws of fasting, and then, in the story considered here, condones the plucking of grain on the Sabbath. Jesus, the lord of the Sabbath, concludes, "The sabbath was made for humankind, and not humankind for the sabbath." Sabbath is another expression of Jesus' revolt against the powers of this world that seek to bind and control us.

Although Jesus does not specifically mention corporate worship in this text, for him and his Jewish community, keeping the Sabbath probably included a sacred meal at home on Friday night, gathering in the synagogue or temple for worship on Saturday, and refraining from labor. Christians today generally consider Sunday as their Sabbath day. People who are unable to keep Sabbath on Sunday may choose

Exegetical Perspective

Most students of Mark's Gospel agree that Mark 2:1–3:6 is a unified text composed as a chiasm or concentric structure. Its form is outlined below.

```
A   2:1-12         healing and forgiveness
  B   2:13-17      table companionship with
                   sinners
    C   2:18-22    the old and the new in
                   conflict
  B'  2:23-28      Sabbath work and plucking
                   food
A'  3:1-6          healing on the Sabbath
```

The Pharisees' challenge to Jesus about his disciples' Sabbath practice belongs to this concentric structure in the B' position. What themes and similarities hold this concentric structure together, and what are the implications for this specific text from Mark (2:23-28)? The meaning of a chiasm depends on how one member (B' for our purposes) relates to its counterpart in the chiasm (B). In some way, B will enhance the meaning of B' and vice versa. Finally, B' will in some way relate to the central member (C). The central member of the structure (C) usually states the theme which its members will explore in various ways. For example, A and A' both deal with the meaning of healing, while B and B' deal with food and meals, the procuring of food by plucking

Homiletical Perspective

Nothing determines where you wind up quite as much as where you start. Most rich adults start as rich children; most PhD's and MDs have highly educated parents. Of course it matters what direction you head, what route you take, how long you journey; but your starting point, and that you ever even start, is just as decisive. One group following Jesus, the Pharisees, asked why another group of Jesus' followers, the disciples, did "what is not lawful on the sabbath" (v. 24). Jesus responded not by redefining Torah but by redefining Sabbath. Their starting places were so different it is a wonder Jesus and the Pharisees had any conversation at all.

Unless one imagines the Pharisees hiding in the grainfield waiting for passersby to violate the Sabbath, they must also have been following Jesus around Galilee. They do not follow long; their later appearances are variously described as one form or another of coming or being sent to test or argue with Jesus (7:1-2; 8:11; 10:2; 12:13). In the opening chapters, however, they seem to be questioning from the inside. More to the point, their questions, including the one in the present passage, may be understood as insider questions, seeking clarification and understanding. "Why does he eat with tax collectors and sinners?" (2:16). It is worth noting that, although Mark writes that the Pharisees "went out and

Mark 2:23–28

Theological Perspective

We need rest because we are not God. God knew our need from the outset. It was codified in the Ten Commandments. That codification inevitably led to misinterpretation. Here Jesus is not only a challenger of authority. He is an interpreter of the truth. As he interprets, he highlights the vast difference between being lawful and being faithful.

Perhaps the battle has been lost already. Blue laws are a thing of the past. Grocery stores never close, and we expect them to always be open. Benton Johnson makes the case that people of faith lost something when we abdicated the practice of Sabbath observance.[1] Surely we have lost something culturally, even as we live in a post-Christian culture. However the deeper impact is a spiritual one. Soccer practice and graduation ceremonies impinge on Sunday mornings. As more and more Americans check "none" in the religious affiliation surveys, and as cable television and the Internet are always "on," with smart phones always at our fingertips, the notion of "rest," let alone a time set apart for rest, seems quaint and foreign.

Jesus knows better, and we know better if we pay attention. We were made to rest, and not the other way around.

What does this say about those who exercise religious leadership? What does tending to such an impulse say to those who practice ministry today? Is it unwise, if not unfaithful, to work and work and produce and produce without caring for the primary vehicle of ministry, the soul? If we are religious leaders of any type, we too need to model such a practice, for our own living and for those with whom we offer leadership. We are not to turn a "day off" into an idol, and we may need to work at times when others are recreating. Pastoral availability will always be an issue. However, if we are to care for others and creation, we must care for self as well. This is much easier to preach than practice. Work will always be calling. Yet we are saved by grace, not by our work. In fact, our work is enhanced if the worker is rested.

All of us, servants and followers of all kinds, would do well to tune into rhythms of life. We would do well to recall that Jesus went away in order to reengage the world to which he had been called. The bottom line is that the Creator's creatures need rest in order to live the full lives we are intended to live. Such rest used to be woven into our cultural fabric.

---

1. Benton Johnson, "On Dropping the Subject: Presbyterians and Sabbath Observance in the Twentieth Century," in Milton J Coalter, John M. Mulder, and Louis B. Weeks, *The Presbyterian Predicament: Six Perspectives* (Louisville, KY: Westminster John Knox Press, 1990), 90-108.

Pastoral Perspective

another day of the week as a day of worship and rest. Others do not keep Sabbath at all—they do not worship or refrain from work on Sunday or any other day.

Sabbath in our society is often overlooked and neglected. Children's athletic events are held on Sunday mornings; people go to work, others go shopping or to the theater or participate in any number of activities that depend on Sunday laborers. Preachers work on Sunday! Even when we have a choice, we rarely refrain from work because it is Sunday—we wash the car or clean the house or mow the lawn. How can we support one another in the midst of pressures that make the shared practice of Sabbath so difficult?

Some congregations provide a worship opportunity on a day other than Sunday, especially for those who are unable to attend a regular Sunday worship event—Saturday late afternoon, or Wednesday evening, or even an early morning weekday. This provides for the worship part of keeping Sabbath. Finding a day or even part of a day to refrain from labor and focus on faith and family seems much more difficult in our society. Families can be encouraged to plan a night each week to dine together, read or discuss appropriate devotional material, and participate in a recreational activity such as a board game, art or music time, or a walk in the neighborhood. Naming and keeping a regular, weekly "Sabbath" evening is important for those who are unable to worship together, and even for those who also worship on Sunday morning.

For most of us, Sabbath means we need to stop our working, consuming, and spending in order to remember that God is the source of all love. If, as Jesus says, Sabbath was made for humankind, we need also be sensitive to the concerns of all those for whom keeping Sabbath may seem more a burden than a gift.

For the unemployed, a sermon stressing rest on the Sabbath may be difficult to hear. Parents unable to support their family because jobs are lost experience frustration, boredom, anxiety, and guilt. Their concern is not about taking time to rest; they suddenly have plenty of time for Sabbath. The part of the commandment with which they struggle is not about Sabbath. It is the other part of the commandment that they find difficult to hear and obey: "Six days you shall labor and do all your work" (Exod. 20:9). Sensitivity to those who are unable to keep the "work" part of the commandment is as important as proclaiming rest on the Sabbath.

Sabbath may pose a special challenge for retired people. What does "six days you shall labor and do

Exegetical Perspective

heads of grain for their hurried meal. The disciples enjoy an impromptu meal on the run with Jesus, and Jesus experiences table companionship with toll collectors and sinners.

It is also worth noting that the last half on the chiasm (B′ and A′) forms an inclusio on the issue of Sabbath observance (2:23; 2:27–28). Throughout the concentric structure, there is an escalation in the character of Jesus' adversaries. In 2:6 they are identified simply as "scribes," whereas in 2:16, they are identified as "scribes of the Pharisees." In 2:18 they are called "the disciples of the Pharisees," and "Pharisees" in 2:24, culminating in the ominous mention of "Pharisees" and "Herodians" (3:6). Since a major theme of the central member (C) is the conflict and collision of the old order and the new, the second half of the chiasm begins to spell out the who more than the what, although both issues will be important.

At first glance, it may seem strange that the Sabbath emerges as such an important and prominent matter. The reasons are substantial. Sabbath keeping is enshrined in the Decalogue and more fully elaborated than any other of the Ten Commandments. It is the only commandment rooted both in creation and in the exodus from Egypt. The Sabbath was the reminder of the liberation from slavery that made the Sabbath possible. The Sabbath was more than a day of rest for the individual Israelite. The commandment was a reminder that YHWH had chosen Israel to be a light to the nations. During the exile, Israel preserved its identity by keeping Sabbath and maintaining circumcision. The loss of sacred space was a given after the destruction of Israel and Judah, but they could keep sacred time in almost any space.

So it was no small matter that the disciples of Jesus violated the tradition of Torah obedience. Although there is some dispute over which commandments were being violated, it appears that the disciples have broken two: journeying beyond the village borders and "working" by plucking the grain for food. Either one would be considered provocative. It is possible to read the Pharisees as issuing an honor challenge: just as the disciples stand as a proxy for Jesus, the Pharisees see themselves as proxies protecting Torah. As a leader of his disciples who reflect his views, Jesus is responsible for what his disciples have done. The charge is a serious one.

At this point, hearers would expect Jesus to cite Torah or recite some oral Torah to justify his behavior. Instead, he cites 1 Samuel 21, in which David, a fugitive trying to escape Saul's murderous designs, manages to persuade Ahimelech to provision him

Homiletical Perspective

immediately conspired with the Herodians against him, how to destroy him" (3:6), they are completely absent from Mark's account of Jesus' betrayal, arrest, trial, and execution. Their last appearance in the Gospel is in the twelfth chapter (12:13).

Even more to the point, unless readers and interpreters of Scripture recognize that the first followers of Jesus had much more in common with the Pharisees than not, we will continue to misunderstand and misinterpret, and perpetuate ideas that lead to prejudice and bigotry.[1] There is no fight like a family fight—or as many families call it, Thanksgiving dinner.

Why are the disciples doing what it is not lawful to do on the Sabbath? Because they were hungry—or bored, or distracted, or not actually noticing what they were doing. It does not really matter. On one level the "dispute" is only a pretext for the saying with which the passage ends. Jesus' argument from Scripture (1 Sam. 21:1–6) about David's action as precedent is not especially apt; the incident Jesus cites has nothing to do with Sabbath, though it does involve eating. Of course Jesus had a long list of possibilities upon which to argue, "It is okay to violate Torah because David did" (we must forgo the historical question of whether David had any sense of a Torah that he might keep or violate).

The argument Jesus makes, even the form of the argument (if a=b, then c=b′; if David can eat *what* he should not, then the disciples can eat *when* they should not), is not original or compelling; but the starting point, What is Sabbath? is fascinating. "The sabbath was made for humankind, and not humankind for the sabbath" (v. 27). The starting point for understanding Sabbath is not the law, but humanity. Humanity is the measure of all things? Talk about a slippery slope. The next thing you know Jesus' followers will be eating the wrong things, with the wrong people, and enjoying it too much.

This conflict is not law versus gospel, but more like *Footloose* or *Dirty Dancing*. It is not that you and yours are doing something that I and mine do not, but that you are having a good time doing it, so it must be wrong. Make a list of all the things everyone used to know were wrong: dancing, shopping on Sunday, going to the movies, playing cards, tight jeans and short skirts, drinking alcohol, going all the way, divorce. Make another list of all the things everyone used to know were right: Jim Crow,

---

1. Amy-Jill Levine is responsible for two very helpful correctives: *The Misunderstood Jew* (New York: HarperOne, 2006) and the *Jewish Annotated New Testament* (New York: Oxford, 2011).

Mark 2:23–28

Theological Perspective

No longer. Now we must be more creative and intentional about seeking and claiming Sabbath. If we do not find rest somehow, then we will face much bigger implications about how we live our lives and how we live together.

A Sabbath prayer, from a contemporary Reform Jewish prayer book, captures the need eloquently: "Let me learn to pause, if only for this day. / Let me enter into a quiet world this day."[2]

The passage from Mark indicates that the religious authorities, charged with keeping the tradition, had missed the vision of Sabbath while preserving its appearance. They were so focused on the mandate that they missed the end of holiness. It is an easy mistake to make. This would not be the only matter over which they would battle with Jesus, but it is an important one. Healing, eating, meeting human need will trump a constricted and constricting interpretation of faith and its practice. The religious authorities will have their own issues with Jesus, and we know where this confrontation will lead. For now, we should remember that Sabbath observance is an important spiritual practice, a discipline worth pursuing in order that we might serve God as fully as we can. Perhaps we can reclaim Sabbath, not as a religious burden but as a gracious gift of faith.

As the text ends, Jesus exerts his lordship. The authorities will not be happy; this is one more example, to them, of Jesus' blasphemous ways. Yet even as he does that, it is to underscore the true meaning of Sabbath. God has built rest and recreation into the very fabric of creation itself. We need not be concerned about violating regulations if we seek faithful rest. We should be more concerned if we do not seek rest, rest that would honor the lord of the Sabbath, who needs us at our best if we are to serve with full gratitude and joy.

JOHN WILKINSON

Pastoral Perspective

all your work" mean for those who are retired? They worked hard for years, at home or away from home, and now many of their days are Sabbath-like. We can affirm the well-earned, more relaxed lifestyle of those enjoying retirement at the same time we encourage them to volunteer their time and energies in ways that may help others claim Sabbath time. Those who suffer from disabilities that prohibit work may have similar concerns. A word of encouragement and suggestions of ways to find meaning in their days, including Sunday, will be helpful. Retirees or those with disabilities might exchange Sabbath on Sunday for Sabbath on another day and appreciate a meaningful Sabbath from their regular routines spent in service to others.

Homebound congregational members may deeply miss worship with their community of faith. Sundays are long days for them. For years, they attended worship, took their children to Sunday school, sang in the choir, and visited with friends at church on Sundays. For them a true Sabbath requires meaningful reconnection with their community of faith. It is important for congregations to provide ways to include these members in worship. Technology now allows us to share worship in the home of an elderly person or a care center in real time. Active members can take turns making Sunday morning visits, bringing a bulletin, a hymnal, bread and wine to share during home worship. The pastor can welcome and name homebound members and their visitors in the announcements. Even one Sunday each month being able to keep Sabbath with their congregation will be a blessed event for these folks and for those who help them worship.

Jesus declared Sabbath a day of freedom from labor. When Sabbath is kept, whatever the day of the week, it is a gift to us from God. When we are able to let go of labor and find time to honor loving relationships with ourselves, others, and God, Sabbath becomes our gift to God.

DENA L. WILLIAMS

---

2. *Mishkan T'Filah: A Reform Siddur* (New York: Central Conference of American Rabbis, 2007), 7.

Exegetical Perspective

with the loaves of holy bread and Goliath's knife (not to cut the bread). David lies to procure the bread, pretending that others will join him on a mission sanctioned by Saul, who knows nothing of these maneuverings. To make matters murkier, Jesus perpetuates David's fabrication by noting that David confiscated the holy bread and gave some "to those who were with him" (2:26, my trans.), when there was no one with David.

What is the point of this appeal to David as a response to the Pharisees' honor challenge? Jesus identifies with David the fugitive, not David the king—with David on the run, seeking refuge from Saul. Jesus has shifted the ground from an argument about work to the issue of authority.

The Torah-obedient argument is moot. Jesus could have argued to determine whether he had journeyed or not, but he did not. He could have argued whether his disciples had worked or not, but he did not. The commandment regarding Sabbath keeping (resting on the seventh day as God rested after creation) was clear. No work! What constitutes work? What special provisions might be necessary to help someone in distress? The rabbis sought to be compassionate while keeping Torah.

Jesus identified with David the fugitive, the very note on which the concentric structure ends, "The Pharisees went out and immediately conspired with the Herodians against him, how to destroy him" (3:6), just like Saul and his minions. Jesus, the son of David, knows what it is like to be a fugitive, on the run.

The issue being acted out is the issue of authority. Who or what is an authority that can proclaim the coming reign of God, an authority greater even than the kingdom of David, greater even than the Sabbath keeping so central to Israel's life? This is what Jesus means when he speaks the aphorism about human beings, the Son of Man, and Sabbath keeping. Who has the authority to bring this to fruition? The Human One who is like a hidden David, a fugitive, and the once and future king. The answer depends on how the son of the fugitive reacts. Has he the authority to invent a new Sabbath order?

WILLIAM R. HERZOG II

Homiletical Perspective

male-only suffrage, prohibition of unions, McCarthyism, "our" dictators. What is your starting point?

Sabbath, like "shewbread" (NRSV "bread of the presence"), is a good thing. Inherently, with or without "For in six days the LORD made heaven and earth, the sea, and all that is in them, but rested the seventh day" (Exod. 20:11). The gift of Sabbath is as liable to corruption as anything else in creation, perhaps more. A friend is fond of saying that violating the Sabbath is the only sin we brag about: "I am so busy that I have no time to even think about rest." This is insane, but culturally sanctioned, aided and abetted by the church (have you looked at the "calendar of events" for Sunday on the back of your bulletin?).

Most churches and parishioners need to be encouraged to do more, give more, serve more, not because they are given to sloth and greed, but because the needs around them are so great. At the same time, they need to be encouraged to take the time and find the rhythm to be sufficiently rested and adequately formed for the call of God on their lives. God fashioned us to serve and love, and provided the gift of Sabbath to make both possible. One size of Sabbath, however, does not fit all. What renews one person would exhaust another; keeping score, getting it "right," may well be central to someone's spirituality. However, if it becomes a requirement for everyone's spirituality to be genuine, we are all in trouble. Does this mean anything goes? Please. That is not what Jesus said or suggested. Instead he offered a different starting point, a new legalism if you will. Does your way of keeping Sabbath give life, nourish, and renew? If the answer is yes, enjoy!

WILLIAM BROSEND

Mark 3:1–6

¹Again he entered the synagogue, and a man was there who had a withered hand. ²They watched him to see whether he would cure him on the sabbath, so that they might accuse him. ³And he said to the man who had the withered hand, "Come forward." ⁴Then he said to them, "Is it lawful to do good or to do harm on the sabbath, to save life or to kill?" But they were silent. ⁵He looked around at them with anger; he was grieved at their hardness of heart and said to the man, "Stretch out your hand." He stretched it out, and his hand was restored. ⁶The Pharisees went out and immediately conspired with the Herodians against him, how to destroy him.

Theological Perspective

Much goes on in these six brief verses. Mark offers a healing story, to be sure, but it is located in a larger arc, an extension and continuation of the debate about Sabbath. A contemporary engagement must address both aspects—Sabbath and healing—as well as the underlying confrontation with the religious authorities that will lead him, and us, to Holy Week.

Jesus' credibility is established as he again enters the synagogue. "They" (the religious authorities from 2:24) are watching closely. They all—Jesus included—notice a man with a withered hand. What will Jesus do? Jesus approaches the man; his healing will also serve as a lesson in Jesus' dispute with the Pharisees. If they did not get the point in the previous encounter (2:23–28), here it is more starkly transparent. This is not about the etiquette of meals or worship. This is about human well-being.

Doing good, caring for neighbor, trumps all regulations. What does that say to us today, whether we protest rules and regulations within the life of the church, or advocate for change in culture and politics? What trumps what? What priorities matter? Jesus' fierce testimony silences the critics. Either they have decided already and do not seek debate, or they have nothing to say—or both. Either way, their silence both angers and saddens Jesus. Again,

Pastoral Perspective

Mark's Jesus continues behavior considered by the Pharisees to be outrageous, rebellious, and unlawful. Knowing others will judge him for healing on the Sabbath, he preempts their challenge by asking, "Is it lawful to do good or to do harm on the sabbath?" (v. 4). The observers make no remarks. They leave in silence, then plot to kill Jesus. Why do these people want to destroy Jesus? What motivates the Pharisees and Herodians to use the healing of a man's withered hand as an excuse to try to entrap Jesus?

One motive involves the threat he poses to their version of the tradition, and thus to their authority and power with the people. Beginning in Mark 2, Jesus challenges traditions often used in distorted ways by those in power. Forgiveness of sin, for example, is tied to temple sacrifices and controlled by a corrupt priesthood; rules of purity restrict eating with those of lesser status in society; fasting is practiced in ways that bring honor to the person fasting rather than to God; the Sabbath is strictly maintained according to ancient rules, but neglects those in need.

Jesus, on the other hand, claims authority to forgive sin, eats with sinners and tax collectors, fails to fast according to the rules, and boldly honors the Sabbath as a perfectly acceptable day to restore and heal. Although questioned by the Pharisees and

Exegetical Perspective

The story of the Pharisees' challenge to Jesus about his disciples' Sabbath practice, Mark 3:1–6 (A'), closes the concentric structure that began with the healing of the paralytic (2:1–12). It depicts how the conflict and hostility between Jesus and his adversaries have escalated from scribes in a house setting (A, 2:1–12) to Herodians and Pharisees in a more dangerous power play aimed at destroying Jesus.

Throughout the episode, only Jesus speaks. Everyone else remains silent, and the silence witnesses to two strategies employed by Pharisees and Herodians. The first silence witnesses to what Paulo Freire calls "the culture of silence,"[1] which intimidates the oppressed and prevents them from finding their voice. It is one thing to rejoice in the healing of a paralytic in a house (2:1–12, A), but it is quite another matter to undermine the Sabbath by a public challenge in the synagogue (A'). A comparison between the two healings reveals how deep the hostility has become; nowhere is this more evident than in the closing line of each incident: the high praise of 2:12b (A) and the murderous intent of the Pharisees and Herodians (A'). The cacophony of voices praising God in the house (2:1) gives way to a fear-driven

---

1. See, for example, Paulo Freire, *The Politics of Education* (Granby, MA: Bergin & Garvey, 1985).

Homiletical Perspective

This is it, so we had better make the most of the opportunity. Most Christians think it happened at the temple, just before the tables got tossed, but that is not the way the Gospels tell the story. Only here, in the synagogue of Jesus' adopted hometown of Capernaum, is Jesus described as angry. Not just in Mark, but in the entire Bible; this is it. Actually it is his "look" that is described as angry: "He looked around at them with anger." His emotion is something even stronger: "He was grieved at their hardness of heart" (v. 5).

The unrighteous anger of those whose opposition to Jesus crystallizes in this passage has been building for weeks. The impression the passage creates is that what joins together a most unlikely alliance of Pharisees and Herodians is not healing on the Sabbath, but Jesus' "calling them out." The healing itself is unremarkable: a "withered hand," not exactly stage four brain cancer. The familiar pattern—demonstration of need, word/act of healing, proof of efficacy—is interrupted by the "dialogue" with those whose only interest in synagogue, Sabbath, and human need is gathering evidence. A sermon on this passage will depend on which loose thread the preacher pulls, a choice that may have more to do with the community with which one preaches than the passage itself. Most sermons do.

Mark 3:1–6

Theological Perspective

to what suffering and injustice is the church silent today?

Centuries ago, the framers of the Westminster Confession of Faith insisted that we keep Sabbath as we prepare our hearts, order our common affairs, observe "an holy rest," and take up "public and private" exercises of worship. Clearly this is what the authorities have in mind, but might the Westminster authors have had Mark 3 in mind? We are also to attend to "duties of necessity and mercy," they wrote.[1] How could Jesus—how could we—pass on such an opportunity to extend necessary mercy, particularly on the Sabbath?

The healing encounter plays only a small role here, and the healing itself is not described. Unlike some other healings, it takes no physical action of Jesus, but words alone, for the man to be restored. The details we seek, the physical description, are absent. Jesus' authoritative word is enough, embodying as it does God's healing mercy. Clearly, the word of the Lord of the Sabbath trumps all human words and theological interpretations.

Still, the matter of healing must be engaged. What do we do with the healing episodes as we read them in the twenty-first century? We want to believe, and yet our scientific, medically oriented world would point us in other directions. Not to believe would seem to dismiss a key component of the Gospel narrative: Jesus' healing power and the cumulative testimony of healing story after healing story. To look only at those receiving healing—often an outcast, one rejected and ignored by society and religion—as theologically and culturally important as that is, without considering the healing itself, seems to miss the full point. *Whom* Jesus healed mattered a great deal, but that he *did* heal mattered as well.

We who live in communities of faith have experienced inexplicable health recoveries. Terminal diagnoses have been transformed into years and years of fruitful living. We have also known extraordinary sufferings and sadnesses. Bad things do happen to people, good or bad or otherwise; so often a terminal cancer diagnosis will become just that. There seems to be no rhyme or reason. Rain *does* fall on the righteous and unrighteous alike.

This passage could launch a complex discussion about prayer and healing and the nature of faith. It could also launch a discussion of the vocation of health-care professionals, those who exercise their

---

1. Westminster Confession of Faith, in *The Constitution of the Presbyterian Church (U.S.A.)*, Part I, *Book of Confessions* (Louisville, KY: Office of the General Assembly, 2004), 6.119.

Pastoral Perspective

others, Jesus shows his compassion on behalf of the people and challenges tradition in order to minister to those in need. Pastors and leaders in communities of faith today are called by Jesus' example to challenge traditions that keep them from caring for those in need or are used to exclude and oppress others.

Conflict over tradition in the church today can seem petty to some and profound to others. Particular pews are known to "belong" to longtime members. Worship liturgies reflect a style of worship baby boomers learned in childhood. Inclusiveness at the Eucharist is inhibited by age and membership requirements. Like the Pharisees, congregations struggle with changes they view as threatening to long held practices, particularly when change is suggested by new members or new pastors. For instance, when a new pastor simplifies the order of worship in an effort to include visitors and new members, people are upset. A new member family expects their young children to be allowed to receive Holy Communion. Often the response is, "We have never allowed anyone to receive Communion until they are at least ten years old!" "This is the way we have always worshiped!" "Do we have a say any longer in how change happens here?"

Like the Pharisees, people feel threatened because they see changes in the way things happen as a challenge to their authority and power in the congregation. In the worst-case scenarios, the agents of change may, indeed, be "destroyed." Nevertheless, following Jesus' example, pastors and leaders in congregations are called by God's love for all people to challenge traditions in ways that lead to change whenever and wherever traditions are used in destructive ways.

A second motive for opposition to Jesus involves his mission. Jesus' mission to heal and restore fulfills the intent of the Sabbath as a day for doing good, even as it places him at odds with religious leaders. Likewise a pastor must call a congregation to carry out their mission to share God's love with the world, even when traditions are threatened and the pastor is placed at odds with those in power in a congregation. At other times, members are called to challenge pastors who may not understand a congregation's mission to serve others.

Whether one is on the side of tradition or change, the struggle is often over the mission of the church. Those who believe the church exists for the sake of the world may be frustrated by funds spent on buildings, dollars languishing in an endowment, the sacrifice of the mission in order to preserve

Exegetical Perspective

silence, no doubt the product of the presence of the powers that be or their proxies.

In a fear-controlled society, peasants want to remain as anonymous as possible. Certainly they do not want to be singled out, and they do not want to come to the attention of ruling elites or their proxies. To use the language of James C. Scott, oppressed peasants will maintain a "hidden transcript" of their view of events and conflicts, like the healing in the synagogue. The Herodians and the Pharisees will produce a "public transcript" of the same events.[2] In fact, the verb translated "accuse" means to bring a charge against (*katēgorēsōsin*, v. 1); this suggests that Jesus' adversaries are gathering documentation for their case, that is, the public transcript. Peasants will speak publicly only in platitudes, to mask their view of events and to avoid standing out, but then discuss matters among themselves with appropriate cautions against informers. Their hidden transcript will be largely oral and often sound superficially like the public transcript.

When Jesus heals the man with the withered hand, he is hurling an honor challenge at the Pharisees. The second silence reflects their response to the honor challenge. One who is challenged must decide how to respond. If he judges that the challenger is close enough in social standing to accept the challenge without loss of prestige and social standing, the riposte begins with no holds barred. If, however, the person or group deems the challenge beneath their dignity, they can reject the challenge with a put-down that shames the challenger(s). The ultimate put-down is to snub the challenger with silence and act as though the challenge never occurred. This is like erasing or "disappearing" the challenger as though he or she never existed.

Jesus enters the synagogue, the power base of the Pharisaic movement, surveys the scene, and notices a man with a withered hand standing in a conspicuous place, a "plant," a trap set by "them." "They watched him," not wanting to miss a moment of the implied challenge. Given what has been said of peasant villagers not wanting to stand out, Jesus may suspect that the man with the withered hand is not there of his own free will. He is the worm on the hook, the bait used to trap Jesus, possibly forced to assume this role or bear the consequences. Nobody says no to the Pharisees and Herodians when they come knocking, so he plays the role. The man's fellow villagers will

Homiletical Perspective

The homiletical question for every preaching opportunity is the same: What does the Holy Spirit want the people of God to hear from these texts on this occasion? Note first that this is not the same as asking, "What do I want to tell them about this passage?" The preacher may see ready analogies between the persons who are likely to be within the sound of her voice and the Pharisees and/or Herodians, folks who are in church for all the wrong reasons, who do not want to do good on the Sabbath or any other day, and so on. Topics will abound: religious legalism, access to health care, silent opposition to change, and let us not forget "righteous anger." All of these are topics that occur to the preacher but may never cross the mind of those with whom the sermon will be shared.

Just a guess—and each preacher is entitled to her own—but at least a few listeners may wonder how it is that folk could get so off track that they want to "destroy" another person for healing someone. There are many ways to approach this question. One that will be helpful in dealing with passage after passage—and so lay something of a hermeneutical foundation for sermons to come—is to talk about honor systems in ancient Mediterranean life.[1] One way or another, however, the fact that the ill or injured man is quite secondary to the story (classified form-critically as a controversy narrative, not a healing narrative) is important. If healing is a pretext in the text, it should not be central to the sermon.

So how is it that one becomes so threatened by another that even his or her goodness is seen as hostile and must be destroyed? Sin is a ready enough answer; we "hate the good and love the evil" (Mic. 3:2). Why, though, this particular sin, hating this particular good? The man's injury or illness would have kept him from working effectively, putting his life and the life of his family in jeopardy. How could anyone begrudge his healing, on any day?

There is a narrative explanation, but that is just a dodge: if the healing did not happen on the Sabbath, no controversy. Because this is a controversy narrative, no narrative. Which only pushes to the fore the question: why so much dispute about the Sabbath? The silence of Jesus' opponents demonstrates that they also know that the answer to his question—"Is

---

2. James C. Scott, *Domination and the Arts of Resistance: Hidden Transcripts* (New Haven, CT: Yale University Press, 1992).

1. Cultures recognize and organize status and position in ways overt (family name, profession, affiliations) and subtle (attire, accent, manners), which collectively form an honor system. Honor is "earned" by birth, community assent ("We have never seen anything like this!" Mark 2:12), office, and patronage (Luke 7:4–5). Honor may just as easily be called into question ("Where did this man get all this?" Mark 6:2). Jesus' action challenged the honor of those looking on by rejecting their "right" to regulate Sabbath activity.

Mark 3:1–6

Theological Perspective

gifts in the pursuit of healing and who embrace a sense of faithfulness as they engage their work. It could also launch a discussion of the role of the disabled, or differently abled, in the life of the faith community. What was this man's role?

We know nothing of the man at the synagogue. Might he have been a "plant" to provide an occasion for the rulers to accuse Jesus? Was he a temple regular, a deeply pious practitioner of the faith? Had others sought to care for him, and failed? These theological questions take on ethical and pastoral dimensions as we seek to connect with the dramatic dynamic of the encounter. We imagine the interaction as Jesus engages him and as he responds.

Even so, Mark is not focused on the healing, and the restored man is given just slightly more attention than that. He is healed, yet the healing serves primarily as a flesh-and-blood case against legalism. Eating grain was just the beginning; healing clearly raises the stakes and ratchets up the intensity of Jesus' conflict with his adversaries over Sabbath.

Rather than entertaining the possibility of healing, rather than embracing the miracle before them, the authorities miss the point altogether, as they play the legal card. In this healing moment, they add one more brick on the road to crucifixion, paved as it is by religious disrespect and perceived lack of piety. That is why the real offense is not the healing proper, but Jesus' revolutionary disregard for religious comfort zones and the turning inside out of all matters pious. Jesus knows the risk as well as the consequence.

So do we. At this point, we might surmise that the unnamed man with a withered hand would choose healing and life over law. What would we do? Would we, with Jesus, challenge religious convention, even if the risk is something less than death—for the good of those in need? What is our duty of necessity and mercy?

Mark tells us that Jesus is both angry and aggrieved. Both responses matter. As we make our offerings, as we offer our prayers, as we seek to travel the pathway of faith, how will we respond? From safety and comfort and convention? From radical discipleship? How will Jesus, the ultimate risk taker, respond?

JOHN WILKINSON

Pastoral Perspective

tradition. There may be disagreement as to whether funds should be spent on new altar ware or given to a local food bank. Some may see an endowment as a hedge against falling membership and giving. Others may see the fund as a means of hoarding resources needed to serve others. A focus on proclamation of the word and provision of the sacraments may come in tension with ministry with those in need.

Mark's Jesus clearly chooses mission over tradition whenever tradition interferes with compassion for all people. A congregational decision to choose mission over tradition needs to be made in a manner of inclusive love for those on both sides of the question. Sometimes a teacher or preacher from outside the congregation may be called to mediate conversations regarding such conflict, so that the focus is not on winning or losing, but on living in loving, faithful community. Jesus' leadership demonstrates courage in the face of opposition, yet he remains merciful and caring toward all people.

Finally, at various places in the Gospel stories Jesus confronts opposition even among his disciples. In the midst of acts of compassion, healing, and forgiveness of sin, Jesus is as stern with his disciples as he is here with the Pharisees. His godly mission calls him to both defend and admonish his followers. Congregations are called to treasure and nurture these traits in their pastors and other leaders. As they stand for justice in defending and admonishing even the faithful, trusted congregational leaders and pastors deserve honor and respect. They also need and deserve mercy and forgiveness. Leaders who know that they too are sinners saved by grace recognize their call to humble leadership.

A sermon based on this text might seem to come down heavily and ironically on the side of "law." A stern call from the pulpit to challenge traditions, even those blocking compassionate ministry, is probably not the most effective choice. A challenging sermon needs to be balanced with at least equal parts of love and compassion for all listeners, those invested in tradition as well as those seeking change. The love of the gospel need not be eclipsed by challenging demands to upset traditions. Preaching Jesus' compassion as law misses the point of God's love for all people.

DENA L. WILLIAMS

Exegetical Perspective

appreciate what he has done by helping to trap Jesus, and they can count on his saying nothing about it.

At this point, many a debater would slink away in total defeat. Jesus does just the opposite. He calls to the bait. The translation reads, "come [*egeire*] here," which means "rise up." The verb is used in conjunction with healing and other mighty acts. Resurrection power is everywhere, even in a booby-trapped synagogue.

Jesus brings the man with the withered hand front and center, the last place in the world he wants to be. There is more than a healing here; there is a Torah debate. Can Jesus offer enough cover for the healing? Jesus fills the silence with a scathing question: "Is it Torah obedient to do good or to harm on the Sabbath, to save or to kill?" (v. 4, my trans.). Do not miss the irony. While Jesus is healing the man, the Pharisees and Herodians are plotting to kill him; this hardly qualifies as saving life.

The conflict over Sabbath keeping is real for all the reasons mentioned in the preceding story. Keeping Sabbath is a fundamental identity marker for Israel, and Jesus threatens to take it away. Here is where the use of silence does not serve the Pharisees and Herodians well; they cannot win an honor challenge with an argument from silence. Moreover, Jesus has a card up his sleeve: he can heal the man—and he does.

The reaction following the healing reveals that there is a deeper problem in the synagogue than the Pharisees have accounted for, namely, a hardened heart. Their reaction to the healing reveals their hardness of heart. It is this, more than arguments over points of Torah, that draws out Jesus' anger (v. 5). Almost lost in the commotion is the restoration of the withered hand. In front of the community gathered in the synagogue, Jesus heals by his word alone; there are no aids of any kind. Is this a violation of Torah? Is this work in the absence of tools and jobs?

This story brings closure to the concentric structure in 2:1–3:6 and marks the end of the first segment of Mark's story (1:1–3:6). Mark has crafted a glimpse of the Gospel in miniature. The seeds of conflict sown in this section of Mark will come to fruition in the subsequent narrative.

WILLIAM R. HERZOG II

Homiletical Perspective

it lawful to do good or to do harm on the sabbath, to save life or to kill?" (v. 4)—is widely understood to be "Do good." One important aside: this is an argument within Judaism about how one keeps the Sabbath holy, not an argument between Jews, who are legalistic, and Jesus, who is not. Jesus was a Jew who kept the law. However—and this is equally important—with the exception of Saul of Tarsus, no one within Second Temple Judaism thought that keeping the law was an all-or-nothing proposition. Jews then and now sin and ask for and receive forgiveness, just like Christians. God did not suddenly start forgiving sinners on the first Easter.

Perhaps the greatest trap of this story is the already noted silence, almost absence, of the person who is healed. Because this is a controversy narrative, not only is the act of healing secondary; so is the person healed. The argument happens around him, even while it is fundamentally about what will happen to him. Most interpreters, and preachers, are comfortable with this, and preach accordingly. Is it lawful to do good? Who can set limits on when we decide to do good? How dare they!

Then here comes the sermon on opening wide the church doors to help others, setting aside old ways and habits that stand in the way. The sermons are always about whether or not we will "do unto others." We never imagine ourselves, or our listeners, as the poor guy with a "withered hand." Even when we are arguing about doing good, we always manage to be in control.

WILLIAM BROSEND

Mark 3:7–12

⁷Jesus departed with his disciples to the sea, and a great multitude from Galilee followed him; ⁸hearing all that he was doing, they came to him in great numbers from Judea, Jerusalem, Idumea, beyond the Jordan, and the region around Tyre and Sidon. ⁹He told his disciples to have a boat ready for him because of the crowd, so that they would not crush him; ¹⁰for he had cured many, so that all who had diseases pressed upon him to touch him. ¹¹Whenever the unclean spirits saw him, they fell down before him and shouted, "You are the Son of God!" ¹²But he sternly ordered them not to make him known.

Theological Perspective

Like Mark's Gospel itself, these six brief verses are packed with themes and plot points. The audience feels nearly breathless when considering all that is going on: the relocation of the locus of ministry, the growing crowds, a healing and casting out, and a stern rebuke about keeping secrets. Theological riches can be mined in many directions.

To follow the Markan flow, we begin first with Jesus' move to the sea. He is seeking to avoid the growing crowds, but they will have none of it. They follow him. Mark wants us to know that this ministry of invitation, preaching, healing and agitation is succeeding as it moves to a new setting. Faithful ministry is never solely about statistical success, but we need to know the elements of a compelling and engaging witness. Jesus' ministry is so successful, so persuasive, that he instructs his disciples to prepare a getaway vehicle in case the crowds become too threatening.

Why should the crowds *not* grow? He had cured so many. Perhaps he could cure them. One is not sure what to do with these healing stories. One thinks of the stereotypical faith healer with a big tent in a field. Worse yet, one thinks of a novel or movie or television show that parodies such activity: *Elmer Gantry*, or even an episode of *The Simpsons* in which Bart plays the role of a young faith healer. The plot

Pastoral Perspective

The writer of Mark focuses on interactions between Jesus and people who live on the fringe of society. Although many healthy people follow Jesus, those with disease are the ones who press toward him in order to touch him. So many make demands on him that he is in danger of being crushed. To escape the large crowds he takes to a boat on the lake. As at several other points in this Gospel, the unclean spirits see Jesus and identify him as the Son of God. Jesus responds by sternly ordering the spirits and those he heals not to tell anyone about him. So many people place demands on him, he is crushed, seeks escape, and seems to want no others to know of his healing abilities. This story illustrates the struggles involved in the call to follow Jesus. Those who seek to serve the needs of the world may find themselves exhausted and empty from the work. Does the call to serve inevitably bring exhaustion?

Mark's Gospel makes clear the needs of the people Jesus serves, including those with fevers, demons, unclean spirits, leprosy, paralysis, deafness, muteness, blindness; as well as tax collectors, "sinners," children, women, the hungry and thirsty, immigrants, beggars, widows, slaves, and those living in poverty. Jesus' response may be summed up in these words: "As he went ashore, he saw a great crowd; and

Exegetical Perspective

This passage summarizes the first section of Mark's Gospel (1:1–3:12). Both the beginning and the end of this opening section of the Gospel designate Jesus "the Son of God" (1:1; 3:12) and together form an *inclusio*, a framing of the first section of the Markan narrative. At first glance, this text may appear uninteresting and unimportant when compared with the more dramatic stories encountered in Mark 2, but looks can be deceiving. A walk through the story may surface some of these contrasts. It is useful to compare this summary (3:7–12) with the first summary (1:14–15). Everything that has occurred between these two summaries has interpreted the meaning of the "good news of God" and the "kingdom" that "is at hand," as well as the appropriate response, "repent and believe."

This story provides a preview of coming attractions and explores the implications of Jesus' ministry for Jesus himself and for those around him, both friend and foe. It begins with a verb, "withdraw" (*anechōrēsen*), which can refer to taking refuge or seeking seclusion. This may be Jesus' response to the plotting against his life mentioned in 3:6. This is more than a two-week vacation or a break for R and R. He is seeking safe space to continue his work.

The very activity of itinerating puts Jesus at risk in a world where the powers that be discourage

Homiletical Perspective

How do you preach a narrative transition, with a list of regions in Roman Palestine and claims of great crowds pressing on Jesus and a boat readied "so that they would not crush him"? How do you preach a healing and exorcism narrative that omits the healing and the exorcism but emphasizes the aftermath, "he sternly ordered them not to make him known"? How, in other words, do you preach Mark, not Jesus, the background, not the foreground, the silence before the proclamation in the next passage?

You do not; at least most preachers will not, which may be an opportunity missed, an opportunity for a particular kind of proclamation, and an opportunity for teaching that is as sorely needed as it is generally lacking. The numbers are stunning. Start with give or take 250,000,000, which, according to the famous "Ashtabula Liar's Study,"[1] is the number of residents of the United States who did not participate in formal worship last weekend. Of the roughly fifty million who did attend worship, what percentage participated in a formal Christian education opportunity? Exactly. The sermon is not only the primary place of proclamation; it is the primary occasion of Christian education. You had better be good.

---

1. Kirk Hadaway and Penny L. Marler, "Did you really go to church this week: behind the poll data," *Christian Century*, May 6, 1998, 472–75.

Mark 3:7–12

Theological Perspective

typically includes the faith healer being exposed for what he is; then through the attending humiliation he experiences a greater understanding of self—the true act of faith.

Jesus is no stereotypical faith healer. He combines his healing and curing with truth telling. His words that challenge conventional religious practice, coupled with his ability to change the lives of those who are suffering, guarantee that crowds will grow.

We do not know whether the religious authorities who had been testing him in earlier scenes have followed him to the sea, but we can presume, as they build their case against him, that they are aware of this growing threat. Even so, there are other witnesses to all that is unfolding. Each time he heals, each time he cures, he does more than banish a physical disease. He encounters unclean spirits. If no one else recognizes him, they do. They know he is the Son of God. In fact, Jesus seems to engage in an ongoing discourse with the spirits. They seem to recognize him for who he is earlier and more clearly than do the disciples and crowd—an ongoing theme in the Gospels and today. In spite of the growing crowds and increasing popularity, he insists that they keep quiet about who he truly is.

For readers two millennia later, the matter of Mark's "messianic secret" remains a challenging concept. Throughout Mark, Jesus withholds his full identity. Here he orders the spirits to remain silent. In other places he instructs those whom he has healed to tell no one. His parables often leave listeners searching for meaning, and even his closest followers—the disciples—do not fully comprehend who he is. Mark Allan Powell's *Introducing the New Testament*[1] outlines various scholarly theories as to why Jesus (via Mark) would seek to conceal his full identify. Whatever the reason, the readers are in on the secret, even if the original audience is not. What does Mark want *us* to know, and why?

We are to know that Jesus is a threat to the practices of institutional religion. That much is clear. His ministries of compassion happen in confrontational ways. They are a threat to the authorities, not only because he does things they cannot, but because, in doing so on the Sabbath, he challenges the very infrastructure of their livelihood, the bedrock of the status quo.

We are to know as well that Jesus is a threat not only to the practice of organized religion but also to

---
1. See Mark Allan Powell, *Introducing the New Testament* (Ada, MI: Baker Academic, 2009). section 6.7.

Pastoral Perspective

he had compassion for them, because they were like sheep without a shepherd" (6:34).

Jesus repeatedly meets the crush of crowds in order to heal and set people free from the power of sin. He decries ancient practices that have come to stand in the way of compassion. He renews tradition, challenges religious leaders and the self-righteous, and exposes the injustice of legal and political systems. It requires great courage and strength to claim such authority, and great compassion, in spite of dangers and weariness, to do so on behalf of vulnerable people. Jesus empowers his disciples to claim this divine authority for themselves and to instill among those they lead the necessary vision, compassion, and courage also to claim God's power on behalf of vulnerable, marginalized people.

However, for many, the ideal of compassion can either remain an abstraction or become an impossible responsibility. Although preachers often enough focus on Jesus as an example of a loving, forgiving, and compassionate person, they do not always name and support concrete ways for listeners to demonstrate compassion. Instilling concern or guilt is not sufficient. Encouragement to feed the hungry, for example, requires naming opportunities to provide direct aid, while at the same time attending to the systemic causes of hunger and seeking to empower marginalized people to act on their own behalf.

Jesus' compassion is not merely a feeling of pity; his compassion focuses on wholeness and justice on behalf of those in need. Real compassion entails actually getting to know people, understanding their needs and concerns, and sharing resources even at personal cost. Compassion may also mean shared suffering. In all these ways, compassion moves toward wholeness for both the recipient of care and the caregiver

When compassion is no longer an abstraction, its demands may quickly sap our strength. Many in our congregations, including pastors, feel crushed by the demands placed on them. We frequently experience "compassion fatigue." While health-care providers, clergy, social workers, and others in caregiving professions clearly face such demands, our society in general seems more and more beset by a bewildering array of demands that cause many to shut down. Reports of natural and social disasters and violence across the globe bring fear and feelings of inadequacy. Parents and others who care for children, especially given the alarming rise of autism spectrum disorder and depression in children, can be overwhelmed by the daily demands of their

Exegetical Perspective

peasants from traveling farther from the safety of their village than the nearest market town. Clearly Jesus is pushing the envelope, as the Herodians and Pharisees understand (3:6). He may be a possible threat if he is attracting crowds and stirring the deep discontent lying just beneath the surface of colonial occupation. Why else would crowds follow his teaching and hang on to every healing?

The list of places is not at all arbitrary. The list names Galilee as the center, and from there covers the three compass points of Judea, Jerusalem and Idumea (south), beyond the Jordan (east), and Tyre and Sidon (north). The Mediterranean was to the west. The Sea of Galilee was one primary place where Jesus healed the people and exorcised the demons. So the point of the geography lesson is to emphasize how widespread the Jesus movement had become. There is more. In the Roman Empire, the world was divided between the center and the periphery. Jerusalem with the temple was clearly at the center of Judean life, but it was peripheral to Roman interests and Roman temples for the region, which they administered through the client kingship of the house of Herod (read Herodians).

Jesus and the Jesus movement made a fundamental change in the center/periphery model of social and political control, first by rejecting the Roman/Herodian version of the model and then by creating a new model that undermined the work of the powers that be. By means of his itinerating, Jesus himself became the new center. So the center of the Jesus movement was wherever Jesus was, and it was much more difficult to keep track of a moving center. This is why, when Jesus withdrew, many "came to him" (v. 8). This innocent phrase translates the discipleship verb, *akoloutheō*, "follow." It is true that, in this context, the verb may carry the secondary meaning of "accompany." However, the two translations need not be mutually exclusive. The center is now on the move, even though the guardians of the moving periphery are lurking and seeking to destroy Jesus.

Who were the followers/disciples who came to Jesus? The first response would be to say that the crowd (*ochlos*) came to him, but Mark uses the phrase *poly plēthos*, meaning "many, many," a large group. Is the difference that great? The Romans and the client king who did their bidding held large groups in low regard. They called them *hoi polloi* and described them as *ochlos*. They were inconsequential scum who had to be controlled through violence and force. They were powerless and had to be kept

Homiletical Perspective

Mark 3:7–12 is an opportunity to explain what you think Mark was up to, why he approached the task the way he did, and what we might make of such claims about the size of the crowd and the silencing of demons and those healed (admittedly the latter not in this passage, but in Mark 1:44; 5:43; 7:36; 8:30).

Start with the crowd. The evangelistic goal is to demonstrate Jesus' growing popularity without saying, "Jesus was really popular," and to indicate how widespread his early healing ministry was without detailing fifty healing miracles, although it sometimes feels like Mark tells us about that many. How would you do it? Ideally like Mark, vividly and concisely, with a few details for verisimilitude. Did he get his geography right? More or less. Were the crowds really that big? Compared to what? Social-science critics have tempered some of our more wayward estimates of population in Roman Palestine, noting that ancient agriculture, aquifers, wells and cisterns, and aqueducts could not support the millions often described. A more realistic number for the whole of "Judea, Jerusalem, Idumea, beyond the Jordan, and the region around Tyre and Sidon" (v. 8) is 250,000; Jerusalem itself was not much larger than 50,000.[2] Mark, who goes with a number in "the feeding of the five thousand" (6:30–44), here emphasizes that people came from across the region, and seems to stress the fervor more than the masses. After all, ten people in a small space feels crowded. It was the press of the crowd, their urgency, more than their sheer number. How will you communicate fervor, the desperation of the crowd to touch the healer? That is the homiletical task.

The "silencing" theme has been explored again and again since Wrede, with varying levels of satisfaction.[3] Mark offers his own explanations, from crowd control (as early as 1:45) to resistance to demands and expectations for a "sign" (8:11–13). How does the preacher explain something as counterintuitive as "don't tell anyone that you were healed"? The question is important because the Gospels, beginning with Mark, are shot through with counterintuitive claims: the dead are alive, Rome is not in charge, the great buildings of Jerusalem will fall, God has taken on human flesh. That the sick are healed and the possessed liberated of their demons fits right in.

---

2. See especially Douglas E. Oakham, "How Large Is a 'Great Crowd'? (Mark 6:34)," in *Jesus and the Peasants* (Eugene, OR: Cascade Books, 2008), 46–52.
3. Wilhelm Wrede, *The Messianic Secret*, trans. J. C. G. Greig (Cambridge: J. Clarke, 1971).

Mark 3:7–12

Theological Perspective

any established authority, period. Even if people do not fully understand who he is, they flock to see him in increasing numbers. The threat, therefore, is not theoretical; it is real and it is growing.

To follow the trajectory in Mark's Gospel is to discover Jesus moving from place to place, calling people to follow, casting out, welcoming and including, healing, uttering provocative words and commands, sharing radical teachings. Every time he moves, the crowds following him grow larger. We who are invested in maintaining things as they are should pay heed. We who are seeking an authentic, transforming life experience should get on board. Either way, we know that change is coming.

At every turn in the road, we have a choice. Mark's fast-paced narrative draws us in and takes us along for a breathtaking ride. Opposition to Jesus is growing, but so are the crowds. Finally, some verses later, Jesus begins assembling his primary group of followers. Soon the Twelve will be chosen (see 6:7). They do not fully understand who he is. They do not fully understand the risk. Do we, generations later, understand any more clearly than they the risk or the opportunity?

At the outset of the twenty-first century, the church is evolving rapidly, some change driven by external realities and some by internal promptings. Either way, change is coming and change is difficult. It is easy to resonate with those maintaining the status quo, either to hold on to power or to give in to inertia. Change is difficult.

Can we really fully understand the demands of discipleship, the implications of following Jesus? Of course not. However, we can read the signs of the times and see evidence of his ministry all around us. So we follow, whether or not part of a growing crowd. Jesus will tell the truth. Jesus will make whole. His earlier followers were asked to keep a secret. We are not.

JOHN WILKINSON

Pastoral Perspective

responsibilities. Those who care for chronically ill relatives or aging parents also can be weighed down with a loved one's needs. Given all of these circumstances, there is a high likelihood that someone in a pew on any Sunday morning is weary of demands placed on her.

Anyone, apparently even the Son of God, can grow weary of caregiving. Naming and sharing concerns about this increasingly common phenomenon may offer encouragement to caregivers who experience guilt or shame when fatigue overtakes them. An offer of support from the pastor and congregation, a reminder to care for one's self under trying circumstances, and some recognition of those who give continual care can go a long way toward providing needed support. Pastors themselves need to be aware of their own vulnerability to discouragement as they seek to minister to others.

In every case, we are well served to remember it is not merely individuals who are called to compassion, but the church as a community, together sharing in and bearing witness to God's work of healing, justice, and making whole. The shared work of compassion is one of the factors for which ancient Christians first became known. When plagues, droughts, and disasters took place, many ancient people would flee. Christians stayed, offering basic care not only to their own, but to others, often at the cost of their own lives. These practices made them seem foolish to many.

American author Flannery O'Connor is credited with saying: "You shall know the truth and the truth shall make you odd." Living out the love of the gospel will generate a peculiar lifestyle in our time and place, not only among individuals but in the church as a whole. Love of God that leads to compassion and authoritative action can be isolating and dangerous, as Jesus himself found, especially in a world that so often overlooks those who are oppressed and vulnerable. Living as odd people, people who claim God's love, authority, and strength in order to practice compassion in daily life, does, indeed, set us free.

DENA L. WILLIAMS

Exegetical Perspective

submissive. Jesus was empowering a movement, no small threat to Herodians and Pharisees.

There are two other echoes emanating from Jesus' constant wandering. The first is Jesus leading a people (*poly plēthos*) in wandering through the wilderness. Many have noted the prevalence of sea crossings in Mark 4–8. The trips are an extension of his itinerary in the stops mentioned in 3:7–8. Taken together, they depict Jesus and his boat trips as an extension of his moving center.

The second echo is riskier and may seem less obvious, but does offer a region to explore for the venturesome. When a Roman commander won an auspicious victory, he was given "a Triumph." When Titus captured Jerusalem, he was given a Triumph that included parading of the spoils of war, prisoners, gladiatorial games, victims sold into slavery, culminating in bringing the conquered client king or military commanders to be sacrificed at the temple of Jupiter. The Roman general could receive a laurel wreath and testimonies to his skill. Did Jesus pick up on that custom and depict his wandering as a "triumph," albeit of a very different kind? Could he have lampooned the Roman ceremony?

More immediate and more urgent are the healings he performed. To emphasize their prominent place in Jesus' wanderings, Mark even shifts the word order—"many [*pollous*] had he healed" (v. 10, literal trans.)—to make his point. Healing carried great weight in a society that viewed illness as punishment from heaven. The healings set off a chain reaction as word spread among the villagers of Galilee. Remember that healing touched more than the individual; it restored the family and kinship relations.

No wonder the spirits cry out, "You are the Son of God" (v. 11), a confession that a Herodian or Pharisee could not make. Prudently speaking, sometimes silence is the best policy and the safest policy. Some things may be said "off stage," to use James C. Scott's language,[1] but not "on stage." The command to silence serves a useful purpose.

WILLIAM R. HERZOG II

Homiletical Perspective

Many of us, alas, do not do counterintuitive very well. We like our good news straight up, our power indisputable, our tombs forever empty, our healings and exorcisms celebrated universally. This is a homiletical and hermeneutical problem that must be addressed head-on, because the gospel does not work the way many people want it to.

Look again at Mark 3:11: "Whenever the unclean spirits saw him, they fell down before him and shouted, 'You are the Son of God!'" They got that right, so why not let them pass on the good news? Perhaps because the reader is not ready to understand what the claim means, and because demon-possessed evangelists are not the most reliable. Indeed, it is not until 15:39 that a character in Mark's Gospel, in this case the centurion, declares Jesus to be "Son of God" without some form of correction, rebuke, or silencing. In other words it is not possible to understand the proclamation that Jesus is the Son of God until he is dead. It does not get much more counterintuitive than that.

The evangelist is teaching us how to read the Gospel in this passage. The good news is "universal"—the people coming from everywhere, or as much of an everywhere as the setting in Roman Palestine makes possible. (Luke, of course, operates on a much larger horizon.) They come because they have heard "all that he was doing" (v. 8), and soon enough his family will come for the same reason, if not with the same attitude (3:21)—more Markan counterintuitive action. The reader is being taught not to "trust" in the healings and the exorcisms, and so being directed to the teaching and preaching of Jesus to come in chapter 4 and following. It is a different strategy than John's, who alternates sign with discourse, but it may well be where John learned the lesson. This may not seem like much of a passage, but the attentive preacher will find more than enough to fill the hour.

WILLIAM BROSEND

---

1. James C. Scott, *Domination and the Arts of Resistance: Hidden Transcripts* (New Haven, CT: Yale University Press, 1992).

Mark 3:13–19a

¹³He went up the mountain and called to him those whom he wanted, and they came to him. ¹⁴And he appointed twelve, whom he also named apostles, to be with him, and to be sent out to proclaim the message, ¹⁵and to have authority to cast out demons. ¹⁶So he appointed the twelve: Simon (to whom he gave the name Peter); ¹⁷James son of Zebedee and John the brother of James (to whom he gave the name Boanerges, that is, Sons of Thunder); ¹⁸and Andrew, and Philip, and Bartholomew, and Matthew, and Thomas, and James son of Alphaeus, and Thaddaeus, and Simon the Cananaean, ¹⁹and Judas Iscariot, who betrayed him.

Theological Perspective

Jesus had a plan. He would not declare "the message" alone. In the Galilean backwater he invested himself in a small group of individuals whom he called to participate in announcing the gospel, the good news of God's new day. On the mountain, Jesus assembled those apostles, the "sent ones" who would join him in carrying the word throughout Galilee and beyond. The apostolic arsenal was a small one; as one preacher says, "He called twelve not twelve hundred."[1] Why twelve? Well, there were twelve tribes of Israel, if you need symbols to start a movement. Perhaps it is better to pour yourself into an intense little band that will then teach others to retell the gospel story. Perhaps God's new day is so imminent that you have to act fast with as manageable and mobile a group as possible.

What are these apostles to do? With characteristic succinctness, the earliest Gospel describes the gathering of the Twelve, offering basic details and haunting imagery that is fascinating and troubling all at once. Essentially Jesus calls them "to be with him and to be sent out" (v. 14). They spend time with him on the mountain in apostolic spiritual formation and then go out on their own to make known what he has

---
1. Walter (Buddy) Shurden, "Small Things," sermon at the installation of Bob Setzer, Knollwood Baptist Church, Winston-Salem, NC, March 25, 2012.

Pastoral Perspective

The congregational nominating committee has finished its deliberations. Each member has a list of names and phone numbers. The task: phone the person on the top of the list, ask him or her to "prayerfully consider" serving as a deacon, elder, or other officeholder. If the committee is well organized, it might even have a set of expectations for each position. If the caller gets a no, the assignment is to move on to the next name.

"It is only a couple of meetings a month," the caller pleads. "I am sure you can fit it into your busy schedule."

These phone calls prompt a range of responses from "How did you get my name?" to "I am too busy." The most common response is, "I am not worthy."

Jesus followed no such protocol to appoint the Twelve. There is no evidence in the text that he weighed the strengths and weaknesses of each candidate or administered a Myers Briggs test to make sure he was getting a proper balance of personality types. As to worthiness, there is no attestation whatsoever.

Jesus simply calls "those he wanted," the disciples come to him, and he appoints them to be with him. Then out go the Twelve to proclaim the arrival of the kingdom, to carry on the work Jesus has begun, and to do it all with the authority of Jesus himself.

Exegetical Perspective

One of the dilemmas Jesus faces after healing the man with the withered hand is crowd control. The writer of the Gospel of Mark makes it clear that, as the healings of Jesus multiply, so does the number of people who follow him. As the miracles grow, so does the multitude. Thus, after enduring people "pressing upon him," Jesus physically comes apart from the crowd in order to select a chosen few.

Jesus goes to a mountain, sets aside space, in order to call twelve apostles and clarify their mission. Mark's inclusion of this mountainside appointment is not happenstance. Jewish readers in the author's community would readily recall Abraham's conversation with God on Mount Moriah (Gen. 22) and the revelation of God to Moses on Mount Sinai (Exod. 19). This is the first of four occasions in which Mark uses mountain settings for divine purposes (6:46; 9:2; 13:3). Thus Jesus' "calling" of the disciples, soon to be apostles, to himself on a mountain is not some ordinary feat, but is indeed the handiwork of God, or even God's divine crowd control.

The Twelve whom Jesus selects represent the twelve tribes of Jacob or Israel. These apostles are the recontextualization and ongoing embodiment of God's people in a new day and age. The *apostoloi*, those who are sent out, are the inauguration of a new family of God; they are new sons of Jacob. The

Homiletical Perspective

Great expectations and broken dreams: we fall in love and foresee the rest of our lives together. Then the relationship stumbles and collapses. We take a position that looks like our dream job, but soon find ourselves disillusioned by office politics. We move to a new church attracted by an initial sense of fellowship, only to discover a community fraught with petty jealousies and turf wars.

Great expectations and broken dreams: Mark the evangelist knows all about this pattern. He pictures Jesus calling and appointing the apostles "to be with him, and to be sent out to proclaim the message, and to have authority to cast out demons" (vv. 14–15). What great expectations come with their being chosen as apostles! It is hard to imagine a higher, holier calling than to exercise a ministry of presence to Christ, to give witness to the good news he embodied and taught, and to join him in driving out the fanatical powers that hold the world in thrall.

Now and then in the Gospel of Mark it looks as though the disciples will live up to these great expectations, especially in chapter 6, when Jesus sends them out two by two and Mark recounts: "So they went out and proclaimed that all should repent. They cast out many demons, and anointed with oil many who were sick and cured them" (6:12–13). When they returned they "gathered around Jesus, and told

Mark 3:13–19a

Theological Perspective

taught them. What do they announce? The earliest message seems to go like this: God's New Community is already here and its fullness lies just ahead. It brings new relationships with God and one another and is the good news of God's continuing action in the world. Those who understand should begin to act on the basis of that reality. "God's kingdom is within you," Jesus told them. "Now live like it is."

The text then adds an additional, intriguing element to the nature of the apostolic witness. Jesus gives them "authority to cast out demons" (v. 15). With no more detail than that and with so many human ills and evils to be confronted, what does that particular apostolic mandate mean? There are various possibilities.

1. Demons are real and require exorcism. The representatives of the New Community have the authority to deal with them. Even today, multiple Christian communions from Roman Catholics to Pentecostals maintain numerous theological and liturgical approaches aimed at ridding individuals of the debilitating spiritual beings that plague them. Throughout the Gospels, Jesus himself demonstrates such actions, casting out innumerable demons that wreak havoc in the lives of multiple persons. Many Christians believe that the authority to cast out demons remains a calling and a necessity in the Christian church.

2. When declaring the good news of God's New Community, the demonic must be confronted. A new day of the Spirit is dawning, and even the demons know it. Thus spiritual "warfare" is inevitable when the kingdom is at hand. The news may be good, but it is also dangerous. Evil cannot go unchallenged.

3. When the New Day dawns, the principalities and powers of this present age must be dealt with, explicitly or implicitly, wherever they appear. Literally or figuratively, some demons represent an assault on individuals, blatantly destroying human lives through excesses in alcohol, drugs, depression, despondence, injustice, cruelty, and abuse. (The list seems endless.)

4. Some sources of the demonic are more subtle, often occupying facets of an individual's life or the life of a community that are less immediately evident but no less imminently destructive. Jesus gives the apostles authority to confront them all, whatever their terrible manifestations.

The New Community will not come easily. It offers an inevitable challenge to and from the demonic in the world. What authority do

Pastoral Perspective

The striking thing about the Twelve is their utter lack of qualifications. Several are mere fishermen, one is a tax collector (read social pariah), and another, Simon the Cananaean, is a supernationalist. The rest are so undistinguished that the Synoptic writers and John cannot agree on their names. (Is it Levi or Matthew? Thaddeus or Lebaeus?) Do not forget Judas Iscariot, whom Mark labels as Jesus' betrayer, thus letting Simon Peter off the hook for his own betrayal of the Lord (14:66–72).

Forget for the moment that Mark portrays this dirty dozen as spectacularly dense regarding Jesus' messianic identity. The fact is, by the time Luke takes up the story of the early church, most of the Twelve have become bit players. Peter has a supporting role, but it is Paul and James, the brother of Jesus—not members of the original Twelve—who take center stage in Acts while the Twelve dissolve into the wings.

No doubt Mark has his own reasons for telling us how Jesus appointed the Twelve—not least of them being to link the first covenant with the second covenant begun in Jesus. What strikes this pastor is the close resemblance between the Twelve and the folks in ordinary congregations. The Twelve might not impress, but they sure do look like church.

First, there is Peter—too much sizzle and too little substance. He is rock solid at Caesarea Philippi (8:29) but cannot get his head around the concept of a suffering Messiah. He shines in the height of the storm, but sinks a few minutes later (Matt. 14:28–33). When push comes to shove in the courtyard of the high priest, Peter's oath of allegiance to Jesus (14:31) becomes an oath of disavowal (14:71).

Then the cock crows. Who knew a rock could weep?

Second, we have James and John, "Sons of Thunder." Nobody seems to know for sure where that peculiar nickname came from. One theory is that by the time the tradition reached Mark, the original moniker had become so corrupted that "Sons of Thunder" was the best Mark could make of it. Certainly there is nothing thunderous about their effort to claim dibs on the best seats in Glory Land (10:35–40). According to Matthew, it was the mother of the Sons of Thunder who suggested that Jesus promote them to the head of the class. So far as she is concerned, all her children are above average.

It is not a big leap from this crew to the followers of Jesus who make up the church today. Peter resembles the chair of the stewardship committee who tells the congregation she is doubling her pledge, but

Exegetical Perspective

sons born of Leah, Rachel, Bilhah, and Zilpah live anew through the work of these whom Jesus calls to himself in a lofty place. Mark as a writer does not employ *apostoloi* regularly. The term is used only one other time in the Gospel: when the apostles give an accounting of their mission efforts (6:30). This again reinforces the nuanced nature, mission, and purpose of this "new" Twelve.

From among the crowd Jesus chooses twelve whose tripartite purpose is to be with Jesus, to proclaim the message, and to cast out demons (vv. 14–15). Mark at this point does not clarify what it means to be with Jesus or what the message is. Until now Jesus' primary message has been that of healing the sick and curing persons who are demon-possessed. What is apparent is that the apostles must spend time with Jesus to learn what this message is. In addition they will continue his exorcising ministry.

The names of the Twelve vary in each of the Gospels (Matt. 10:1–4; Luke 6:12–16; John 1:42; Acts 1:13). In Matthew and Luke, Andrew is identified as Simon Peter's brother. This is not the case in Mark. Luke substitutes Matthew's Simon the Canaanite with Simon the Zealot while including two men named Judas. John does not give a complete list of twelve disciples, but gives Philip a primary role counter to his portrayal in the other Gospels. Acts focuses on efforts to replace Judas.

What is unique about Acts and the Synoptics is that all begin their lists with Peter, James, and John and end with Judas. In addition, all four of these characters receive literary qualifiers in their descriptions. Simon is Peter, "the rock" in Greek or Cephas in Aramaic. James and John are Sons of Thunder or Boanerges. Judas is the betrayer or traitor. Mark and the other Synoptic writers use such characterizations as a means of foreshadowing the role of these four in the ministry of Jesus. In this way, Mark continues to control and narrow the crowd by filtering the work of Jesus through the crowds, the Twelve, and now through four primary personalities.

Peter, James, and John appear on four other occasions in the Gospel of Mark (5:37; 9:2; 13:3; 14:33). They are on the Mount of Transfiguration (9:2) and the Mount of Olives (13:3). This trio not only has insight into what Jesus does on earth; they also are allowed to see more closely his relationship with the God of heaven and earth. They not only behold the majesty of Jesus during a transfiguration, but they witness Jesus struggling and in anguish as he prepares to die for them. By beginning the list of disciples with these three, Mark provides a literary

Homiletical Perspective

him all that they had done and taught" (6:30). That must have brought some genuine satisfaction to Jesus: the disciples were for the moment filling his great expectations.

However, their regaling Jesus with their stories of healing and teaching were to be the exception rather than the rule. From the moment Jesus appoints the apostles, Mark foreshadows the heartbreak that lies ahead. He ends the list of the disciples' names with an observation that draws a cloud over the whole gospel, "Judas Iscariot, who betrayed him" (v. 19). The great expectations will end in betrayal. Judas gets the rap, but the rest of the disciples are not much better than the traitor himself. For the most part they abandon the great expectations that Jesus named when "he went up the mountain and called to him those whom he wanted, and they came to him" (v. 13). Jesus wanted them "to be with him," but on the night of the Last Supper, when he asked them to keep awake while he prayed, they fell asleep on him three times (14:32–42). When Jesus was arrested, "all of them deserted him and fled" (14:50). So much for the great expectation that they would offer the ministry of personal presence to Christ!

Christ's call to them to "proclaim his message" fared no better than their ministry of presence in the garden at Christ's arrest. They could not proclaim what they did not understand, and their failure to understand Christ and his teaching is a recurring motif in Mark's Gospel. Jesus said to them, "Do you not understand this parable? Then how will you understand all the parables?" (4:13). "Then do you also fail to understand?" (7:18). "Do you still not perceive or understand? Are your hearts hardened? Do you have eyes, and fail to see? Do you have ears, and fail to hear?'" (8:17–18). Since they were baffled by his teaching, there was little likelihood of their proclaiming it to others. So much for the expectation of their preaching the gospel to the world!

As for the disciples' driving out demons, Mark describes a father who in exasperation recounts to Jesus, "'Teacher, I brought you my son; he has a spirit that makes him unable to speak; and whenever it seizes him, it dashes him down; and he foams and grinds his teeth and becomes rigid; and I asked your disciples to cast it out, but they could not do so.' He answered them, 'You faithless generation, how much longer must I be among you? How much longer must I put up with you?'" (9:17–19).

Great expectations and broken dreams: Mark knows the pattern, and in this last verse he portrays Jesus as frustrated and downhearted as any of us are

Mark 3:13–19a

Theological Perspective

contemporary apostles claim over current expressions of the demonic? Does the authority to cast them out remain?

Then there were the Twelve. Mark lists their names like a roll call at the first-ever Christian confirmation class. Jesus renames three of them: Simon becomes Peter the Rock (more on that later), while the brothers James and John received the dubious AKA "Sons of Thunder." Whatever did they do or had they done to warrant that less-than-flattering appellation? We learn more about some, though not all, of the Twelve as the story unfolds and the message deepens. Throughout the four Gospels, they are a terribly human lot, that inner group of persons whom Jesus "wanted," at once courageous and cowardly, committed and plodding, carrying the Good News into the world even as they seem to understand so little of it.

Last on the list is Judas Iscariot, "who betrayed him." Mark reminds us of that at the beginning of the story. Knowing how it all ends, Mark warns us from the start that there was one apostolic messenger who could not escape his own demons. In whatever way Christians may theologize about Judas, then and now—predestined pawn, kingdom-hastening agent, mistaken militant, would-be powerbroker—even the earliest apostolic community included the presence and the reality of the demonic, a timely reminder for those who would attribute some mythic purity to the first-century church.

As those who have read the end of the story are compelled to acknowledge, Judas was not the only apostle troubled by the demonic. A demon or two appear to have hunkered down in Simon, "to whom he gave the name Peter." Remember Peter's denials—three of them—in the post-Gethsemane darkness, some of them even punctuated "with curses" (14:66–72)? It took dawn and the crowing of the cock before Peter "broke down" and, brokenhearted, sent the demons flying.

What might Mark be trying to tell us in his introduction to this portion of the Jesus story? In the birth pangs of the New Community, even there, the demonic was inescapable. The news may be good, but it is never without danger, even in the most apostolic among us. Best to remember that from the start—"on the mountain"—before we all get to Golgotha.

BILL J. LEONARD

Pastoral Perspective

fails to follow through. The congregation thinks she is God's gift to fundraising, but the treasurer knows better. Simon the Zealot is the deacon who takes five minutes for a "minute for mission" during worship. Before he opens his mouth, the congregation has stopped listening. They have heard it all before.

In James one can see the sister who lords it over the choir from her seat in the alto section. In John one sees the brother who takes offense if his name is left off a thank-you list in the newsletter. Their mother? She is the helicopter parent who keeps texting her child during the youth group lock-in and torments the youth director with incessant e-mails.

Messy? Without a doubt. Imperfect? Of course. Less than God would have them be? Yes. Clearly the Twelve have a long way to go; but look what constitutes their apostolicity. Jesus calls them "*to be with him.*" It is through intimate, day-by-day association with Jesus that these twelve misfits become the twelve apostles. They do not cease to be who they are—"sinners in the sight of God justly deserving God's displeasure and without hope save in God's sovereign mercy"[1]—but after having been with Jesus, they are sent out with power and authority to accomplish amazing things (6:7–13).

Peter is still Rocky the Impetuous. James and John are still the Sons of Importunity. Simon's zealotry still makes him hard to live with. However, their life with Jesus makes them living proof that the reign of God has begun.

In many baptism liturgies, the sevenfold gifts of the Spirit are invoked. While laying hands upon the newly baptized, the minister asks God to send

> the spirit of counsel and might,
> the spirit of wisdom and understanding,
> the spirit of knowledge and the fear of the Lord,
> the spirit of joy in your presence.

The apostolic age has ended, but the apostolic faith continues. So long as the church is "with Jesus," so long as it is blessed with the joy of Christ's presence, it is leaning toward the kingdom.

BRANT S. COPELAND

---

1. *The Book of Church Order, Presbyterian Church in the United States, 1981–1982* (Atlanta: John Knox Press, 1981), 104.

Exegetical Perspective

window into the integral role Peter, James, and John will play later in the narrative. Additionally, the writer combines the use of a special setting, a mountain, with special people of Jesus' inner circle.

Although Mark names Judas Iscariot last, this does not mean he is the least of the apostles. He resurfaces later in Mark (14:43) as he undertakes what the writer foretells upon his appointment as an apostle. Mark labels Judas one who betrays (Gk. *paradidōmi*). Judas lives up to this description. He will indeed "give Jesus over to the hands of another." Mark's inclusion of and pairing the name Judas with the nomenclature "Iscariot" also prewarns the reader of this apostle's future actions. As "Iscariot" is possibly a derivative of "sicarii," little daggers used to assassinate, Judas will be a tool in the political assassination of Jesus. The name Judas appears at the end, but what he does in the Gospel overshadows this narrative positioning.

Jesus removes himself from the crowd by going to a high and lofty place where he chooses twelve to represent "the message." Whatever this message is, these twelve apostles must come to Jesus in order to be sent out by Jesus. The Gospel of Mark uses the geographical setting of a mountain as a means of focusing the reader's attention on the revelatory nature of this relationship and on those whom Jesus calls unto himself. The chosen must come apart from the crowd in order to get a better view of the one in whose presence they will receive power to cure those in the crowd who are hurting. As Mark specifically names the individuals who will proclaim and cast out demons, the author provides literary bookends to show which apostles will have more pronounced roles in the ministry of Jesus.

STEPHANIE BUCKHANON CROWDER

Homiletical Perspective

when the high expectations we have vested in our closest friends fail and fade. How are we to deal with this familiar pattern of human life? Does Mark want us to conclude that Jesus would have been wiser if his call to the disciples had not come with such high expectations?

No. I am convinced that is not Mark's purpose, because he later portrays Jesus teaching that "for God all things are possible" (10:27). This theological affirmation helps to explain why Mark so boldly portrays both the holy calling of the apostles and their failure to live up to it. Because all things are possible for God, Christ is free to have high expectations of those who follow him: there is no telling what God might accomplish, even through disciples as fallible and foolish as the apostles. Jesus certainly is not going to tone down his expectations of what human beings can accomplish through the empowering Spirit of the living God.

At the same time, Mark is a realist about human nature. He knows that just because Christ "called to him those whom he wanted" (v. 13), there is no guarantee they will fulfill their Lord's great expectations. Mark's portrayal of the apostles' calling and their subsequent failures constitutes a story sermon to all who count themselves disciples of Christ. If we were to write down an outline, it would go like this: Christ has great expectations of us and has no intention of lessening them. We disciples often fail to meet them, but that is no reason for despair, because all things are possible for God.

THOMAS H. TROEGER

Mark 3:19b–30

¹⁹ᵇThen he went home; ²⁰and the crowd came together again, so that they could not even eat. ²¹When his family heard it, they went out to restrain him, for people were saying, "He has gone out of his mind." ²²And the scribes who came down from Jerusalem said, "He has Beelzebul, and by the ruler of the demons he casts out demons." ²³And he called them to him, and spoke to them in parables, "How can Satan cast out Satan? ²⁴If a kingdom is divided against itself, that kingdom cannot stand. ²⁵And if a house is divided against itself, that house will not be able to stand. ²⁶And if Satan has risen up against himself and is divided, he cannot stand, but his end has come. ²⁷But no one can enter a strong man's house and plunder his property without first tying up the strong man; then indeed the house can be plundered.

²⁸"Truly I tell you, people will be forgiven for their sins and whatever blasphemies they utter; ²⁹but whoever blasphemes against the Holy Spirit can never have forgiveness, but is guilty of an eternal sin"— ³⁰for they had said, "He has an unclean spirit."

Theological Perspective

"Then he went home," the Markan text observes mundanely. For Jesus, home must have meant Nazareth, where what should have been a routine family visit became a heated controversy. Home can be like that for any of us, a confrontation with people who have known us the longest but often understand us the least. For Jesus of Nazareth, home could get hazardous. Remember his encounter in the synagogue there, as described in Luke 4? The hometown folks at first celebrated the return of "Joseph's son," inviting him to read and comment on the day's text (Isa. 61) and rejoicing that such grace should come from his mouth. Then, when his interpretation of the text included race-related commentary and illustrated God's care for certain questionable persons on the margins, the crowd became so "filled with rage" that they tried to "hurl him off the cliff" (Luke 4:28–29). In the synagogue at Nazareth, Jesus needed to keep his eyes on the nearest exit!

This time, as Mark tells it, popularity again prevailed before controversy. The text describes a time when the crowds were so substantial that Jesus and his entourage "could not even eat," gatherings that must have seemed half theological seminar, half local celebrity watch. Even then, however, another hullabaloo surfaced as Jesus' critics attacked both his ideas and his character. In a fascinating documentary film

Pastoral Perspective

"Mother, we're doing this for your own good."

The woman's son spoke these words from the witness stand during a competency hearing. He had been telling the judge about his mother's erratic behavior. She was up at all hours. She did not seem to know night from day. She left the water running and constantly neglected to turn off the burners on the kitchen stove. Her finances were a mess. She wrote checks to total strangers who appeared at her door. The time had come for the children to take charge, but she would have none of it. She fought her children all the way to the courthouse.

When the hearing was over and the judge had left the courtroom, she turned to her pastor. "My family hates me," she said.

Some commentators suggest that Jesus' family found him an embarrassment, a blot on the family name. They could not bear to hear people saying, "He has gone out of his mind" (v. 21). However, there is no reason to assume that Jesus' family is acting solely to preserve the family's honor. Just as likely, they want to "restrain him" for his own good.

Members of congregations who have struggled with mental illness or addictions in their own families are likely to hear this pericope differently from those who have not. Perhaps they will see themselves as the anxious relatives who are waiting outside the

Exegetical Perspective

There is an aphorism that states, "The road to hell is paved with good intentions."[1] While it is not certain whether the writer of the Gospel of Mark was familiar with the saying, it is clear in this pericope that many believe the good intentions of Jesus originated from some hellish force. Jesus' healing the man with the withered hand on the Sabbath is a watershed moment in Mark's narrative (3:1–6). This healing leads to other healings and, more particularly, to Jesus delivering persons from unclean spirits (3:11). All of this becomes the basis for Jesus' opponents to level charges of insanity and demonic activity against him.

The irony in this section of Mark's narrative is the reaction that Jesus receives when he goes home (v. 19b) to Capernaum in Galilee. This is supposed to be a place of comfort and support for Jesus but, from the beginning, Jesus experiences the total opposite. His own family misjudges him and seeks to restrain him, due to the accusations from the crowd. The antagonism against Jesus is so profound and comprehensive that adversaries from Jerusalem come to accuse him. They would have had to travel more than 100 miles to do this.

---

1. Many attribute an original variation of this quote to Bernard of Clairvaux (ca. 1150), who wrote, "Hell is full of good wishes and desires." http://www.englishclub.com/ref/esl/Sayings/Quizzes/Religion/The_road_to_hell_is_paved_with_good_intentions_917.htm; accessed July 21, 2011.

Homiletical Perspective

Nowadays it seems every cop-and-robber show that I watch involves someone shooting another person. But from the time I was growing up in the late 1950s I recall television scene after scene of someone breaking into a home and tying up the occupant, usually to a chair, with lots of rope and then gagging the victim's mouth. The bound person would usually make groaning sounds and try rocking the chair in order to get loose, but they were bound so tightly that the most they ever accomplished was to tip the chair over while the thief made off with their goods.

Although there was no television in Jesus' day, it is clear from this passage in Mark that the image of binding up a householder in order to plunder his or her goods was familiar to our ancient forebears. Jesus himself uses it to argue against the claim that it is "by the ruler of the demons he casts out demons" (v. 22). He precedes the image of binding a strong man with a highly logical argument: if he, Christ, were using demonic powers to cast out demons, then it would mean that there was a civil war going on in Satan's house. "'How can Satan cast out Satan? If a kingdom is divided against itself, that kingdom cannot stand. And if a house is divided against itself, that house will not be able to stand. And if Satan has risen up against himself and is divided, he cannot

Mark 3:19b–30

Theological Perspective

called *The People Who Take Up Serpents*, an Appalachian serpent handler reflects on the actions of her antagonists, noting, "They'll tell anything on you down in town."[1] So it seemed in Nazareth when the reproach began. The dispute concerned Jesus' very identity. Does he speak for God or Beelzebul, the biggest demon of them all? Then and now, Jesus' New Community can manifest "a sweet, sweet Spirit in this place," or provoke "the hosts of evil round us."[2]

That is when his family decided it was time to step in. From the first to the twenty-first century, citizens of Jesus' New Community can be a blessing or an embarrassment, at least insofar as their families are concerned. Families across the theological and social spectrum may celebrate or divide over loved ones who exemplify the Jesus Way and appear to carry it to its logical or illogical conclusions. The Markan text highlights one of the great theological questions confronting religious people in every era: who is a prophet and who is not, and how do you know the difference? Opinion was obviously split over Jesus himself. Should his family members "restrain" him because some in the community thought he had "gone out of his mind," or turn him loose to declare new insights, new revelations, as God's anointed messenger? The hometown friends and relatives seem unable to agree.

From the beginning, Jesus and his apostles had set themselves against the demonic, making confrontation with such disruptive forces a sign of the New Community. Others, however, were apparently convinced that Jesus harbored the Evil One himself. Thus they introduced a first-century theological conundrum, insisting that Jesus was casting out demons through demonic power, a devious bit of spiritual tomfoolery that proved he was a charlatan. The text flirts with dualism, that epic confrontation between the forces of good and evil, ideas influenced by Persian Zoroastrianism, no doubt, and dividing the Jews of Jesus' day. (For example, the Pharisees apparently believed in demons, while the Sadducees rejected that idea.) It was a volatile debate.

Jesus will not let the charges go unanswered. His response suggests that while Satan is surely wicked, he is certainly not stupid! The Evil One cannot contradict its own nature. Satan must by nature manifest and maintain the demonic, not facilitate deliverance from its grasp. As the King James Version translates

1. *The People Who Take Up Serpents*, Appalshop Film Productions, 1974.
2. See "There's a Sweet, Sweet Spirit in This Place" and "God of Grace and God of Glory," in *Celebrating Grace Hymnal* (Macon, GA: Celebrating Grace, Inc., 2010), #241 and #285.

Pastoral Perspective

crowded house, hoping for a moment alone with the one they love. They know what it is like to take part in a therapeutic intervention, to tell a loved one she is headed toward disaster if she does not enter treatment, to be told that they are "enablers" and should practice "tough love." They know how it is to feel guilty for acting and guilty for not acting.

Before we come down too hard on Jesus' family, we should spend some time standing where they stand. Why should they be outside looking in? Why should they have to bear the brunt of the choices Jesus makes? They did not sign up for this. Nobody asked them if they would like a member of their own family to be God's chosen Messiah.

It is harder to empathize with "the scribes who came down from Jerusalem." These are the religious authorities who have heard of Jesus' exploits in Galilee and have come north to assess the situation. For them, Jesus is a threat to the status quo and to their personal status as experts regarding the will of God. Unlike Jesus' family, who seem to want to whisk Jesus out of harm's way, the authorities want to condemn him on theological grounds. Jesus may appear to be doing God's work, they argue, but in fact he is the agent of Satan. "He has Beelzebul, and by the ruler of the demons he casts out demons" (v. 22).

It does not take long for modern theological disputes to turn similarly nasty. Reasoned discourse soon deteriorates into ad hominem attack. No better (or worse) example is the never-ending fight over human sexuality. It seems Christians cannot agree to disagree about the ordination of self-affirming homosexuals or the blessing of same-sex unions. We cannot allow our opponents to be merely mistaken. We insist that they have rejected the authority of the Bible, or they are fundamentalists hopelessly mired in homophobia. There is no middle ground. The "other" is "the agent of Satan."

Jesus refuses to join in the name-calling. Instead he offers a simple, commonsense reply to the religious authorities: "How can Satan cast out Satan?" (v. 23). It stands to reason that someone who goes round Galilee casting out demons is not doing Satan any favors. The religious authorities are so keen to condemn Jesus that they hurl an accusation devoid of internal logic. With a deftness that is almost humorous, Jesus points out the absurdity.

Then the conversation turns deadly serious. It is one thing to stick to one's tradition. It is another to deny the possibility that God might have something new to say, even if it comes through your presumed enemy. To witness the freedom Jesus brings—to see

Exegetical Perspective

What are the specific charges against Jesus? He is the embodiment of whatever is not good. He is a Beelzebub (v. 22). Jewish and Gentile readers in Mark's community would readily think of Baal, the Canaanite god of fertility. Baal in later religious history would also come to symbolize evil. Thus Jesus is akin to a sinister, foreign, strange deity. In addition he is under the control of the ruler of darkness (v. 22). The original idea of "satan" was a "ha-satan" figure or "accuser." This being incites David to number the people (1 Chr. 21:1), and is present as a member of the divine council in Job (chaps. 1–2). The concept of "satan" as an evil force or "Satan" as proper noun is a product of Diaspora character development prevalent circa the second century BCE.

Despite all of the good he has done, the crowd maintains that Jesus is bad. Jesus goes along with ominous assaults and uses a parable to respond to their accusations. Within the first-century-CE context of Mark's day, such parabolic literary devices were common. Like a proverb, an aphorism, or a fictitious narrative, a parable uses common language and everyday, ordinary cultural fixtures to teach a lesson or to invite the hearer into another ordering of reality. Here Jesus defends himself against those who believe him to be evil through the allegorical world of a parable by making reference to himself as Satan (v. 23). In the first place, he questions whether Satan as the strong man would act against the strong man. Why would the ruler of demons act against the ruler of demons?

In the second place, according to Jesus, Satan, as ruler of a kingdom, would not cause internal disorder within his own kingdom (vv. 24–25). Mark is using kingdom or *basileia* language to hint at the political nature of Jesus' parable (v. 24). The talk of destroying kingdoms and tearing down houses, along with Jesus' healing on the Sabbath, sets the stage for political drama in Mark's imperialistic setting. The destruction of the Jewish temple during the first Jewish-Roman War (66–70 CE) is the contextual center out of which Mark writes.

Later in Mark's three passion predictions (8:31; 9:31; 10:32), the language of Jesus will be more direct. For now, what Jesus does not say openly, he says in parables, letting symbolic utterance do the work for him. In this way, Mark also employs a widespread Greco-Roman rhetorical means to delineate what could have been common thoughts on evil and good.

As Jesus addresses the absurdity of political implosion and internal sabotage in this passage, he

Homiletical Perspective

stand, but his end has come'" (vv. 23b–26). Using three parallel "if" statements in a row, Jesus employs hard reasoning to reject the charge of his opponents. Then, as though reason were not enough to convince them, he turns to this startling image of violence and thievery: "'But no one can enter a strong man's house and plunder his property without first tying up the strong man; then indeed the house can be plundered'" (v. 27).

The clear implication is that Jesus is the thief who binds the strong man, Satan, in order to plunder his house. Jesus as thief! Jesus binding someone! Jesus plundering a house! I have never seen a stained-glass window featuring this as an image of Christ.

If you think about this image and place it in the context of the whole Gospel of Mark, it is profoundly revealing. Later in the Gospel the satanic powers, working through Judas, the religious establishment, the mob, and the Roman occupiers, will arrest and bind Jesus and rob him of his life. Mark uses the gutsy image of tying up a strong man and plundering his house in order to convey the intensity of Christ's struggle against the demonic powers. When the trial, flogging, and crucifixion take place later in the Gospel, it is as though the strong man whom Jesus had bound earlier has gotten loose and is now taking revenge on the Holy One who plundered his realm, casting out the powers of destruction that were his prized possessions.

The intensity of the struggle that engages Jesus is so great that his family poignantly misunderstands what he is doing. They come "to restrain him, for people were saying, 'He has gone out of his mind'" (v. 21b). Jesus appears to them to be crazy. When someone deliberately tangles with the demonic powers of this world, it can look like madness. I think of women and men who have bravely tried to eradicate prejudice and oppression. They are commonly greeted with the assumption of most people that the established powers will never be displaced, and those who try must be "out of their minds" to make what is surely a futile effort.

I once tried to condense these insights to a hymn text based on this very passage from the lectionary. In turning to poetry after having written more analytically about these matters, I hoped to capture something of the same pattern of thought that Christ uses in this passage: moving from a reasoned argument to the poetic idiom of parable. It is a model that I commend to preachers as they strive to convey the force of what Mark is portraying in this passage.

Mark 3:19b–30

Theological Perspective

it, Jesus' response becomes, "A house divided against itself cannot stand" (v. 25). Across the centuries, great theology turns into great literature. That superb English phrase found its way from Jesus to the mouth of Abraham Lincoln as he struggled to exorcise the demons of war from a divided, slavery-plagued republic. The lesson of the text continued.

The text then moves from debates over the demonic to the central issue: the New Community is "at hand," and it is dangerous business. If you are going to change the world, or attempt to bring about God's rule and reign in human life and human society, you have to confront the Evil One. In this great task, Jesus' strategy is clear. To get to the New Community, Jesus must tie up "the strong man" (v. 27), engaging in serious spiritual warfare. In spite of what his critics claim, Jesus' message and actions are not demonic. Rather, they challenge the very nature and presence of evil in the world.

Even then the critics were not silenced. "He has an unclean spirit," they insisted, in response to Jesus' (and the early church's) comments on what sins can and cannot be forgiven. Some biblical texts offer hope and hopelessness at the same time. The criticism continued, even if the critics were not sure what Jesus was talking about. Some of us still are not clear about what a "blasphemy against the Holy Spirit" might mean, but it does not sound promising.

Finally, what of us amid all this first-century talk of the demonic? We might consider this: to follow Jesus and his New Community is to risk familial misgivings, social ridicule, and theological confrontation, often from the people we thought would always understand. If the Jesus Way can create even fleeting moments when the "strong man" of demonic exploitation, injustice, and corruption is eventually "plundered" by "the old, old story of Jesus and his love," then is it not worth the struggle?[3] For a small taste of that good news, we might find courage to confront the whole world, even our own kinfolks.

These days, what specific demons do we need to "tie up"?

BILL J. LEONARD

Pastoral Perspective

the broken made whole, the shackled set free, the lowly raised up, and the banished restored—and to call *that* the work of Satan is to blaspheme the Holy Spirit. If there is an unforgivable sin, it is to put limits on the Triune God revealed in Jesus Christ through the Holy Spirit.

The leper-touching, demon-tossing, scribe-deflating Jesus challenges all our expectations about how God's Messiah is supposed to behave. In the process he can be an embarrassment, even to those of us who claim to love him. We can wrestle with him, argue with him, struggle to understand him, and even pretend not to know him. The one thing we cannot do is confuse him with Satan.

As an exercise in pastoral care, we might hold this story up as a mirror and encourage the congregation to take a good look. We might recognize ourselves in the confused and embarrassed faces of Jesus' family, but we might also notice a striking resemblance to those who would limit the Spirit's freedom to work in unexpected and unorthodox ways. After undergoing the scrutiny of this text, the congregation will be more than ready to sing:

> There's a wideness in God's mercy,
> Like the wideness of the sea;
> There's a kindness in God's justice
> that is more than liberty.
>
> There is no place where earth's sorrows
> Are more felt than up in heaven;
> There is no place where earth's failings
> Have such kindly judgment given.
>
> But we make His love too narrow
> By false limits of our own;
> And we magnify his strictness
> With a zeal He will not own.
>
> Was there ever kinder shepherd
> Half so gentle, half so sweet,
> As the Savior who would have us
> Come and gather at his feet?[1]

BRANT S. COPELAND

---

3. "I Love to Tell the Story," *Celebrating Grace Hymnal*, #581.

1. Frederick William Faber, 1854. For full text, see http://www.cyberhymnal.org/htm/t/h/e/therwide.htm; accessed November 26, 2012.

Exegetical Perspective

also expounds on the danger of questioning spiritual motives. People can sin and still receive forgiveness. People can blaspheme and still get a pardon. Nevertheless Jesus warns those who have traveled miles to accuse him, as well as individuals who are eating with him and members of his family, that there is a limit to God's remission of penalties. Blaming the Holy Spirit for evil is unforgivable (v. 29). It is the unpardonable sin. One may question the mission, but not the motive. One may question what is done, but must not cast doubt on the spiritual impetus for such actions. At this stage in Mark's story, Jesus warns religious leaders who may question what Jesus does to be careful with their skepticism of the source or rationale behind what happens.

Finally in this pericope, the "Spirit" is not just the "Spirit." In addressing the unforgivable act, Mark qualifies the "Spirit" as "Holy." This is only the third time Mark has made reference to the Spirit. The Spirit appears at the baptism of Jesus (1:10), and it leads him into the wilderness to be tempted (1:12). On two of the three occasions when Mark mentions the Spirit, the author also speaks of Satan. It is possible that within Mark's social location, a dualistic worldview was present in the minds of his readers. These same readers also lived within a polytheistic Greco-Roman world filled with innumerable gods. Mark's narrative employs these cultural linguistic codes. In addition, Mark's content reflects his own theological context. Jews in Mark's community were a people who worshiped the one God of Israel, and this God as good. However, when Mark tries to reach Gentiles with the message of the same God through Jesus, the author has to use socioreligious language that these readers can comprehend. The Gospel shows Mark code-switching for the sake of making the message of Jesus accessible to non-Jews.

Jesus goes home, not to find solace, but to wrestle with accusations of "Satanic" empowerment. In the end Mark does not focus on whether Jesus is evil. Mark concludes the section by bringing to the forefront the integral, good nature of the Holy Spirit as the motivating force in what Jesus does.

STEPHANIE BUCKHANON CROWDER

Homiletical Perspective

If Christ is charged with madness, it's madness that's divine,
a visionary gladness this world cannot confine,
the madness of conceiving what no one else can see,
then acting and believing so it will come to be.

Thus when Christ seized and plundered the demons' dark domain,
his friends and foes both wondered if he were not insane.
They charged his soul was riven, his heart and mind possessed
by forces he had driven from those who were distressed.

Christ spoke to all this ranting, a vivid, lucid word
a parable supplanting the charges he had heard.
"A house that is divided, a kingdom, soul or land
with raging wars inside it cannot survive and stand."

Despite his deft explaining, Christ still appeared distraught
to guardians maintaining accepted bounds of thought.
The force of faith in action seems madness to each age
and often the reaction is fear disguised as rage.

Yet earth needs heaven's madness to seize with grace and bind
the guilt, the hurt, the sadness, the fear and hate that blind.
Intrude, O Christ, impassioned with madness that's divine,
upon the world we've fashioned and give it your design.[1]

It may seem as though the world is mad enough as it is. Does it really need more madness? Yes, but madness of a different kind, what I call in the hymn "visionary gladness," a way of seeing the world that breaks through the rigidities and distortions of our established perspectives. We often hold the illusion that reason is the antidote to the world's madness, but this approach forgets that reason can be held in thrall to the world's madness. Mark gives witness to the deeper passion of the Spirit working through Jesus to bind the demonic forces of the world.

THOMAS H. TROEGER

---

1. Thomas H. Troeger, *Borrowed Light: Hymn Texts, Prayers, and Poems* (New York: Oxford University Press, 1994), 173–74.

Mark 3:31–35

³¹Then his mother and his brothers came; and standing outside, they sent to him and called him. ³²A crowd was sitting around him; and they said to him, "Your mother and your brothers and sisters are outside, asking for you." ³³And he replied, "Who are my mother and my brothers?" ³⁴And looking at those who sat around him, he said, "Here are my mother and my brothers! ³⁵Whoever does the will of God is my brother and sister and mother."

Theological Perspective

Jesus' family would not let it go. Mark deepens issues of familial tension with the simple line: "Then his mother and his brothers came" (v. 31). "Standing outside," they requested a meeting. Did they hope for a brief family visit? Was this a rescue or a kidnapping? Were they concerned for his safety or embarrassed by his behavior? Was this a friendly chat or a family intervention? Whatever their motive, his relatives showed up, "sent to him and called him" (v. 31).

For his part, Jesus apparently ignored them. His response in this text is less than welcoming to those who seem to have known him the longest, but perhaps understood him the least. He sent no messages, offered no welcome, and gave no special response to his "loved ones," even when informed that they were outside waiting. Instead of rushing to the family reunion, Jesus asked one of those rabbinical rhetorical questions addressed to listeners then and now: "Who are my mother and my brothers?" The messengers thought they were informing him about his biological family. He used the occasion to redefine the nature of family for those who joined him on the way to a New Community.

As the Gospels tell it, Jesus' family relations were sketchy at best. Even when selected encounters are detailed, Jesus seemed to be on a different wavelength, dealing with the meaning of family in modes

Pastoral Perspective

The cover story of the May 16, 2011, edition of the *Christian Century* is the kind of thing that keeps pastors up at night: "The Dis-membered Church: Attending Without Joining." The article discussed the increasing tendency of people to attend church without becoming formal members.[1] Apparently many in the millennial generation cannot see the point of having their names on the membership rolls. Is participation in the life of a worshiping community not enough?

Our text suggests that the nonjoiners are at least half right. Participation is more important than having one's name on the roll. Millennials are hypersensitive to the charge of hypocrisy. They want any association that they join to feel "authentic." They prefer "loose connections," the kind that do not keep them tied down or obligated to a particular creed or set of expectations. Gone are the days when church membership was an important indicator of social standing.

Far from an advantage, formal membership in a church can be a hindrance in today's America. Try telling your child's soccer coach that your family is committed to worship on Sunday mornings or the

---

1. Amy Frykholm, "Loose connections: What's happening to church membership?" *Christian Century*, May 16, 2011.

104 Feasting on the Gospels

Exegetical Perspective

The Gospel of Mark introduces the family of Jesus in 3:21. Until this time the only family connections mentioned refer to the disciples (1:16; 1:30). While Mark notes the appearance of relatives of Jesus in verse 21, the writer does not expound on who they are until verse 31. In addition, these relatives are not supportive of Jesus. Instead, they appear to be a dysfunctional family who is present to restrain Jesus (v. 21).

What is also unusual about the Gospel's presentation of Jesus' blood relatives is their physical placement in comparison to members of the multitude. Mark asserts that the mother, brothers, and sister(s) of Jesus are outsiders (v. 32). It is as if the author wants to distinguish between those inside and outside the circle of Jesus. Yes, the Twelve are called out from the multitude and appointed for special duties (3:14). Yes, Mark in listing the apostles tends to narrow the focus on Peter, James, John, and Judas (3:15–19). Now the writer wants to show that the ministry of Jesus calls for a reconstitution of family. There is insider and outsider language to this effect.

In verse 20 Mark records that while at home, Jesus eats. However, the crowd is so thick that he can hardly partake of his meal. Is Jesus eating inside of the house or outside? In verse 21 Mark writes that Jesus' family goes out to restrain him, implying that Jesus is outside eating in the midst of many people.

Homiletical Perspective

I have never forgotten the question a professor asked at the start of a course on ministry to families, even though it was more than forty years ago when I sat in his class: "What picture comes to mind when you hear the word 'family'? Is it the family pictured on the Sears Roebuck catalog?" The Sears Roebuck catalog was a thick mail-order catalog from which you could order just about anything, from clothing to tools and appliances. Each year it featured on its cover a family of four: a tall father, a slightly less tall mother, a middle-school-aged boy, and a grade-school girl. They were all robust, smiling, and dressed in clothes you could buy from the catalog.

The professor went on to describe other groupings of human beings that named their collective identity as family: two elderly, never-married women who had lived their whole adult lives together, a family of three generations who all dwelt in the same apartment, two gay men who were raising a child, the occupants of a residential home. The list went on and on, and then the professor observed how many ways the word "family" is used to describe much larger groups: churches, teams, organizations, buyers of particular brands. Again the list went on and on.

Once the professor had established the vast diversity of relationships that people called family,

Mark 3:31–35

Theological Perspective

that appeared to inform his own way of being in the world. One early account involves a confrontation between the adolescent Jesus and his frantic mother in the temple, where she discovered him after days of fruitless searching throughout Jerusalem. "Why have you treated us like this?" she demanded, only to receive her son's perplexed response: "Why are you searching for me? Did you not know that I must be in my Father's house?" (Luke 2:49). This exchange is the first of various instances when Jesus' interaction with his biological family offers insight into his broader mission and message in the world.

In chapter 3 of Mark's Gospel the meaning of the New Community moves beyond biology to a new way of conceiving the family and shaping human relationships. In this text a nameless messenger (disciple?) brought word that "your mother and your brothers and sisters are outside, asking for you" (v. 32). The family requested his presence but was left hanging. Instead, the situation became an occasion for Jesus to offer yet another illustration of the kind of gospel community he believed to be at hand, a community that he was mobilizing in Galilee. Right there on the spot he redefined the shape of family in the New Community. "Who are my brothers and mother?" he asked those gathered in his presence. Then, "looking at those who sat around him," Jesus answered his own question: "Here are my mother and my brothers!" (vv. 33–34). The people right in front of him represented that New Community. They had entered into the gospel journey with the strange Nazarene—a journey with multiple implications.

Then came a description of the "holy family" that is at once immediate and timeless: "Whoever does the will of God is my brother and sister and mother" (v. 35). By the time this specific passage ends, Jesus has transformed the implications of family from biology to spirituality. He has broadened it from his own genetic circle to a new assortment of brothers, sisters, mothers, and fathers who long to do God's will. In this New Community, traditional relationships, even hereditary ones, may be extended to other models of spiritual and familial communion.

Here as elsewhere in Mark's Gospel, Jesus seems to be coming of age, conceding to, challenging, and moving beyond family and other traditional connections, on the way to the New Community. Ideally, in that Community, relationships are as deep and abiding as that of one's family of origin. Doing "the will of God" becomes another sign of spiritual kinship, one not to be taken lightly. Thus, pursuing God's will offers the potential to strengthen and transform all

Pastoral Perspective

high school band director that your child will not be going on the band trip during Holy Week. You will not be nominated for the parent-of-the-year award.

For the Jesus of this passage, belonging is not a matter of formal—or even familial—association. The true members of his family are not his blood kin waiting outside, asking for him, but those crowding round him now, seeking the will of God. "Whoever does the will of God is my brother and sister and mother" (v. 35).

By redefining family, the Jesus of this text defines church. Imagine Mark's community sitting around this text in the same way those in the passage sat around Jesus. They look into each other's faces as they hear the Lord's words, "Here are my mother and my brothers" (v. 34). As Paul wrote to the Galatians, "There is no longer Jew or Greek, there is no longer slave or free, there is no longer male and female; for all of you are one in Christ Jesus" (Gal. 3:28).

Debates over the definition of "family" are also the stuff of modern headlines and magazine covers. Lesléa Newman's children's book *Heather Has Two Mommies*,[2] first published in 1989, was intended to convey a message about acceptance and tolerance, but was heartily criticized by those who felt it undermined the "traditional" family. In modern America, what does a traditional family look like? The congregation that hears this text might very well include families that could be described as blended, single-parent, multi-generational, or interracial. The theme of *Heather Has Two Mommies* was simple: the most important thing about any family is that all the people in it love each other. That message comes as good news to five-year-old Heather, but good news for some feels like bad news for others.

Without venturing too far from Mark's intent, it might be worth noting who is *not* among the members of Jesus' family standing outside that crowded house in Capernaum. The crowd tells Jesus, "Your mother and your brothers and sisters are outside, asking for you," but no mention is made of Jesus' father (v. 32). When Jesus preaches in his hometown synagogue, his indignant fellow Nazarenes murmur (perhaps with a sneer?), "Is not this the carpenter, the *son of Mary* and brother of James and Joses and Judas and Simon, and are not his sisters here with us?" (6:3).

The most likely explanation for the absence of Jesus' father as the head of the family in that

---

2. Lesléa Newman, *Heather Has Two Mommies* (Boston: Alyson Books, 1994).

Exegetical Perspective

In verse 31 Mark returns to the family. The writer now states more specifically that the mother and brothers of Jesus are outside. They are the ones who initially had come to restrain him. Now they "send to Jesus and call him" (v. 31). With this detail, Mark shows the crowd to be so large that Jesus' immediate family cannot readily get to him. Jesus is outside; his family is outside. However, the presence of many others is so overwhelming that those who are "really close" to Jesus, his family, cannot get to him.

Another possibility is that Jesus and the crowds are dining inside a house (v. 21). His brothers and mother stand outside and call for him to come out from where he is (v. 31). However, this would be inconsistent with Mark's previous statement that the family of Jesus was "coming out" to restrain him (v. 21). There would be no need for them to come out and subdue Jesus if they are already outside with the crowd.

The exact location of Jesus' dining points primarily to one fact: wherever Jesus is, his earthly family is not. If Jesus is dining inside, the writer clearly shows the family as being outside. If Jesus is having a meal outside, then members of his family have to come from the inside and move outside in order to help him. If Jesus and the family are both outside, the crowd separates them.

Through this insider-outsider language, Mark shows that the message of Jesus in this new day and age calls for a new family. Just as the twelve apostles represent twelve new tribes of Israel, those who hear the voice of Jesus constitute his new kin. Not only are the apostles called to leave their families; Jesus must distance himself from his own family.

Mark avers that the mother and brothers of Jesus seek him (v. 31). The inclusion of "sisters" in verse 32 is omitted in some ancient manuscripts. This omission is primarily due to Jesus' omission in that he mentions only his "mother and brothers" (v. 33). Most manuscripts agree with the presence of the singular form "sister" later in the pericope (v. 35). Although there is textual discrepancy over the insertion of "sisters," it is from the same Greek root, *adelphos*, as "brothers." In verse 35 Mark uses the feminine form *adelphē*. Whereas Mark's context is a patriarchal one, through the use of "sister" and "mother" the writer declares the presence of women in the ministry of Jesus.

While Jesus may not be excluding those in his immediate family, he does not give them a place of honor or appear to esteem them highly. This is an affront to first-century concepts of family. An

Homiletical Perspective

he shared case studies of how people felt about their families. The range of memories, associations, and feelings was as diverse as the range of relationships that they recognized as their family. For some the experience of family was positive, nurturing, and supportive; for others it was negative, abusive, and degrading; for most it was a complex blend of fulfillment and disappointment, companionship and conflict, gratitude and resentment, memories both treasured and terrifying.

I suppose the professor's lecture has stayed with me all these years because it has turned out to be true to my experience. Families do take extremely diverse forms, and families do awaken an astonishing range of memories and associations, and anyone who is going to preach on a passage about families would be wise to acknowledge this. The mere mention of the word is apt to touch off a plethora of different assumptions in a congregation, and there is probably no passage one could select from the Bible that would do this more powerfully than Mark 3:31–35. People bring freighted memories and feelings to the way Jesus interacts with his own immediate family. Listen to the passage from two different perspectives: first as a member of a loving family, and then as someone from an abusive family.

If we come from a close, supportive family, we may have difficulty hearing Jesus' response when he is informed, "Your mother and your brothers and sisters are outside, asking for you" (v. 32). Earlier in the same chapter we are told that what brings them is concern for his mental stability: his family "went out to restrain him, for people were saying, 'He has gone out of his mind'" (3:21). Since concern for Jesus' welfare has drawn his family to seek him out, imagine how cruel his response might sound to them when he looks at the crowd and says: "Here are my mother and my brothers! Whoever does the will of God is my brother and sister and mother" (vv. 34–35).

Listeners from loving families might understandably see Jesus as calloused to his own flesh and blood. Yet even the most loving families have their limitations. It is possible for such families to become ingrown, to share abundantly among themselves, but not to see beyond their own family circle to the immensity of human need that stretches all about them.

Now listen to the same passage as someone who was raised in an abusive family, in which one felt degraded by psychological and physical violence. Jesus' words might strike you as balm: you can

Mark 3:31–35

Theological Perspective

relationships dramatically. However, if the text is any indication, it may also create distance from those whose blood runs in a disciple's veins. The gospel nurtures familial relationships even as it can divide them.

Thus, to be "in Christ" is to belong to a new family, made brother or sister to a collection of individuals who have decided to follow the Jesus way as best they can. The people who seek to "do the will of God" for Jesus' sake are stuck with each other, becoming brothers and sisters, friends and mentors by God's grace. Just as none of us chooses our biological brothers and sisters, so we must beware of obsessive selectivity in relating to our sisters and brothers in Christ. Indeed, throughout the Gospels Jesus continually extends the boundaries of his spiritual family to a variety of public sinners, persons who are left behind physically, mentally, spiritually, and economically in one way or another.

The demands of that sort of spiritual family are no easier now than the day that Jesus' mother, sisters, and brothers showed up asking for him. His question to those first disciples, "Who are my mother and my brothers?" is with us yet.

In the end, Jesus' varied encounters with his kinfolks are intriguing incidents that reflect his ceaseless efforts to extend God's action in the world. His message is clear: the New Community is at hand. It will impact every aspect of life for those who are drawn to its promise. It will transform the way we understand who we are and what we are about as members of the body of Christ.

Mary makes a final Gospel appearance, of course. This time she is not "outside" but up close, "standing near the cross" of her son (John 19:25). In that poignant moment Jesus redefines family for "the disciple whom he loved" with these words to Mary: "Woman, here is your son," and to the disciple: "Here is your mother" (John 19:26–27). Family relationships, biological and spiritual, negotiated to the bitter end.

BILL J. LEONARD

Pastoral Perspective

patriarchal culture is that he is dead. A slur on Jesus' legitimacy (and Mary's honor) may also lie behind the text. Mark makes no mention of the birth order in Jesus' family, but if Jesus is the oldest son, familial obligations would fall most heavily upon him. We have already seen (chap. 1) how the call to follow him drew Jesus' disciples away from their own families. This text suggests that not only did Jesus leave his family behind to fulfill his messianic calling; he left a family that was particularly dependent on him. In some ways the text raises more pastoral issues than it solves.

The primary emphasis of the text, however, is on *doing* the will of God. In the context of Mark's Gospel, this means joining in the actions that herald God's reign (1:14–15). Whenever the church is participating in God's mission—housing the homeless, feeding the hungry, setting free the oppressed, working for peace—it is "being family."

Like textile workers at the turn of the last century, Florida tomato harvesters are still paid by the piece. The average piece rate at this writing is $0.50 for every thirty-two pounds of tomatoes they pick, a rate that has remained virtually unchanged since 1980. As a result of that stagnation, a worker today must pick more than 2.25 tons of tomatoes to earn minimum wage in a typical ten-hour workday—nearly twice the amount a worker had to pick to earn minimum wage thirty years ago, when the rate was $0.40 per bucket. Most farm workers, who today earn less than $12,000 a year, are routinely subjected to risk from pesticides and dangerous conditions in the fields.

A congregation in Florida's capital city finds itself specializing in showing hospitality to farm workers who travel from central and south Florida to lobby the state legislature for just labor practices. Each year during the legislative session, the church's modest fellowship hall is filled with people who sleep on pew cushions borrowed from the historic sanctuary, and the aroma of breakfast tortillas fills the morning air. In broken Spanish a representative of the congregation greets each arrival, *"Bienvenido, hermano. . . . Bienvenida, hermana"*: "Welcome, brother. . . . Welcome, sister."

Doing God's will is a family affair.

BRANT S. COPELAND

Exegetical Perspective

individual's worth and identity were tied to family status. A married woman was accorded a safe and well-protected social state of being. Although children had no rights and were expendable, they were secure in a family unit, unlike orphans and widows, who were at the mercy of the state or anyone who dared to care for them.

In declaring, "Here are my mother and my brothers" (v. 34), Jesus also does not mention "father." First-century-CE society was rooted in a patriarchal (male-rule), patrilineal (male-descendency), patrinomial (male-naming), and patrilocal (male-placement) society. What an assault this is to concepts of family embedded in Mark's society! Although the following quote is related to Luke's community, it is still apropos in addressing the social hierarchy in Mark's day just a decade earlier: "The status of a woman was tied to that of a male relative. Her identity and social belonging were situated outside of her self and her gender."[1] Mark's Jesus attempts to reconfigure this gender order.

For Mark's community listening to the words of Jesus, family was a group tied together through a spiritual bond. Jesus asseverates that those who dine and sit with him are members of his family. Whoever does God's will is his brother, mother, and sister. Thus family is a new group that does not limit the role of women. This group is not patriarchal. Mothers have a vital role to play. God is now the head of the household. This group is not male exclusively. It includes sisters who are on par with brothers in the work of Jesus.

STEPHANIE BUCKHANON CROWDER

Homiletical Perspective

finally belong to a family of love and grace, something for which you have ached all your life.

Even though our initial response to this story may have its origin in our origins, the story is told in Mark to lift us beyond the limitations of personal experience. To see the larger human community in all its diversity and need and wonder can be a graciously redemptive act for any of us, no matter what the experience of our immediate families has been.

Christ sets only one criterion for being a member of his larger family: that we do the will of God. Since Jesus thoroughly knows the Torah and the Scriptures, the will of God is not for him an amorphous abstraction or an empty pietism. The will of God is something he identifies later in Mark when a scribe asks him, "Which commandment is the first of all?" (12:28). Christ answers that the first commandment is to love God with all that we are and that the second is to love our neighbor as ourselves.

If we keep the first commandment, we will discover the unconditional acceptance and indestructible joy that not even the most loving human family can provide. If we have been abused by our families we will discover the overflowing grace that can heal our wounds. If we keep the second commandment, we will have developed a healthy self-love, the kind of inner affirmation that releases us from the feelings of self-loathing and negativity that abusive families inculcate. In other words, keeping the two great commandments is a way of doing the will of God, and in the doing of God's will we find ourselves healed and empowered. Far from weakening families, Christ's statement that "whoever does the will of God is my brother and sister and mother" (v. 35) nurtures those qualities that make us healthy members of our immediate family and faithful members of Christ's unbounded circle of grace and love.

THOMAS H. TROEGER

---

1. Stephanie Buckhanon Crowder, "The Gospel of Luke," in *True to Our Native Land: An African American Commentary* (Minneapolis: Fortress Press, 2007), 180.

Mark 4:1–9

¹Again he began to teach beside the sea. Such a very large crowd gathered around him that he got into a boat on the sea and sat there, while the whole crowd was beside the sea on the land. ²He began to teach them many things in parables, and in his teaching he said to them: ³"Listen! A sower went out to sow. ⁴And as he sowed, some seed fell on the path, and the birds came and ate it up. ⁵Other seed fell on rocky ground, where it did not have much soil, and it sprang up quickly, since it had no depth of soil. ⁶And when the sun rose, it was scorched; and since it had no root, it withered away. ⁷Other seed fell among thorns, and the thorns grew up and choked it, and it yielded no grain. ⁸Other seed fell into good soil and brought forth grain, growing up and increasing and yielding thirty and sixty and a hundredfold." ⁹And he said, "Let anyone with ears to hear listen!"

Theological Perspective

The set of parables in Mark 4 is the first explicit elaboration of the message of the kingdom of God in this Gospel. These parables interpret and elaborate on the statement at the beginning of Mark's Gospel (1:14–15) that concisely states the purpose of Jesus' ministry: "Jesus came to Galilee, proclaiming the good news of God, and saying, 'The time is fulfilled, and the kingdom of God has come near; repent, and believe in the good news.'" The parables of Mark 4 give an answer—or a range of answers—to the immediate questions about the nature, scope, and implications of the kingdom of God.

The story sketches the setting of this teaching very precisely. Jesus begins teaching on the shore of the Sea of Galilee. A large crowd quickly assembles, so large that Jesus gets into a boat, sits down in it, and continues his teaching from that vantage point. One can imagine that the large crowd quickly surges forward to the edge of the water, straining to hear the words of Jesus. Sounds travel well over water; perhaps this natural amplification of sound was part of Jesus' intent.

With a clear imperative, "Listen," Jesus begins to tell a story. Its images would have been familiar to his hearers, the story of a farmer with a pouch of grain. The crowd would have understood the process of sowing seed, cultivating the ground after the seed

Pastoral Perspective

"Listen! . . . Listen!" These imperatives bracket the whole parable. The opening call is an inviting plural: "You all: Listen!" The closing bracket is a focusing singular: to "the one who has ears to hear: Listen!" Something is up, and the hearer should pay attention. Listen!

Jesus begins and ends this encounter with a call to listen. In between, in a parable, he speaks about four different ways of hearing. Then he makes explicit to his closer friends that the parable's four different kinds of receptivity to seed are like four different kinds of hearing. So here we have a story about hearing, bracketed by commands to listen. If we are paying attention, if we are listening, perhaps we may *hear* Jesus' insistent emphasis on aural reception!

It seems common and popular these days in my denominational tradition to emphasize speaking and talking more than listening or hearing. A high value is placed on preaching and teaching, and rightly so. Speaking the Word is a primary instrument for God's revelation to humanity. So we speak, and we labor to speak faithfully. It is likely that you are reading this book in preparation to speak this Word. I am grateful that this series is not titled *Speaking the Gospels* but rather is rightly named *Feasting on the Gospels*—an activity whose ruminative nature has

Exegetical Perspective

The Setting (vv. 1-2). The colorful setting of Jesus by the Sea of Galilee in Mark 4:1-34 recalls Jesus' call of the first disciples by the sea (1:16-20), his earlier teaching of the crowd there (2:13), and his departure to the sea (3:7). His teaching from the boat is foreshadowed in 3:9, when he directs his disciples to have a boat ready for him because of the crowd.

The scene of Jesus seated in the boat with the crowd gathered on the shore in verses 1-2 communicates both his dignity as a teacher and his distance from or superiority to the crowd. Sitting was the usual posture affected by Jewish teachers (see Matt. 5:1). Thus far in Mark's Gospel we have learned that the kingdom of God was the central theme of Jesus' teaching and activity (1:15), and we have seen Jesus the exorcist, the healer, and the sage in action. We still do not know much about what he means by the kingdom of God, and what his role in it is. That is the purpose of his discourse in 4:1-34.

The most prominent literary vehicle that Jesus uses to teach about the kingdom of God is the parable. In a parable the speaker places one thing beside another. That is the basic meaning of the Greek verb *paraballō*. A parable is at its most basic level a comparison or an analogy.[1] The classic definition

---
1. John R. Donahue and Daniel J. Harrington, *The Gospel of Mark*, Sacra Pagina 2 (Collegeville, MN: Liturgical Press, 2002), 130.

Homiletical Perspective

This text has something of a surprise for the preacher who will be wrestling with it and for the congregation that will hear it. While the text contains the familiar parable about the sower and the seed, Mark's Gospel does not offer an explanation of the parable until a few verses later (4:13-20). Many of the people encountering this text will very likely think they know its meaning because they are aware of the allegorical interpretation that follows Jesus' explanation of why he speaks in parables (4:10-12). The first challenge for the preacher is to respect the text. This means he or she will need to stay with the text, working as carefully as possible to disentangle the parable from all the expected interpretations.

To this end, it is helpful for the preacher to focus on the action the text describes. Jesus is teaching outdoors. The normal setting for rabbinic teaching was in the synagogue. Jesus is out in the open and accessible to anyone who wants to come to him. A crowd has gathered. There is clearly something compelling about Jesus. On this occasion, Jesus tells a parable about a sower and his seed. He concludes the parable with a rather stark command for the people to listen.

The text calls for some review of what a parable is. Parables are a distinctive teaching and preaching device. Obviously the literature on parables is

Mark 4:1–9

Theological Perspective

had been scattered, and waiting for the harvest. Jesus gives no explanation, just another "Listen!" command at the end of the story.

Clearly the disciples, although certainly understanding the cultural context of the images, did not understand the meaning of the story. The uncertainty about the meaning of the parable continues even into the present. Although Jesus himself explains the parable in subsequent verses, a variety of interpretations have emerged, including at least these four: The first interpretation sees the fullness of the harvest in verse 20 as an eschatological promise after a time of struggle and resistance. The second interpretation understands the parable as a word of encouragement to the disciples. On this reading, Jesus is encouraging their faithfulness in the midst of challenge. The third interpretation emphasizes the imperatives at the beginning and end of the parable: "Listen!" This would seem to highlight the responsibility of the hearers. It is up to the attentive hearers to understand the word as it is sown by the sower. The fourth interpretation would see the parable as a summary of Jesus' own experience in his ministry. As he sows the word concerning the kingdom of God, the soil of the hearers receives him very differently.[1]

All of these interpretations, and more, are possible in encountering this parable. The prominent themes are discipleship, growth, readiness, and receptivity. The unavoidable connection between readiness and fruitfulness is a clear assumption of the parable. Martin Luther once said that the learned tongue, the ready ear, and the prepared heart are all related.[2] All are necessary for fruitful discipleship. Without any one of these, the "current" of discipleship is broken. Without a learned tongue, discipleship is misdirected. Without a ready ear, discipleship is paralyzed. Without a prepared heart, discipleship is resisted.

Theologically, the dynamics of readiness and response reach down deeply into the dynamics of divine and human agency. Theologically this parable, and the ones that follow it in this chapter, explore the mysterious connections between God's action and our action, between God's gracious initiative and our obedient response. These theological connections are not clearly stated in this parable; as a parable, it evokes, it suggests.

---

1. C. S. Mann, *Mark*, Anchor Bible 27 (Garden City, NY: Doubleday & Co., 1986), 261.
2. Martin Luther, *Luther's Works*, vol. 17, *Lectures on Isaiah*, ed. J. J. Pelikan (St. Louis: Concordia Publishing House, 1972), 194.

Pastoral Perspective

much to teach us about how we might obey Jesus' exhortation to listen.

In the next section, verses 10 through 20, Jesus makes it clear that there are four different ways of hearing, three of which yield no fruit. Some seeds get quickly eaten by birds, some seeds are scorched, and some seeds begin to sprout but get choked out. Jesus explains that some ground is too hard to be receptive; some receivers are too distracted to nurture the sprouts. However, there is one kind of receptivity, one kind of listening and hearing, which leads to fruit bearing.

Consider various feasting images. For some partiers, "feasting" conjures notions of hedonistic bacchanals, eating and drinking more than can be digested, ingesting more resources and calories than can possibly be metabolized or useful. Some of what is consumed is stored as fat; some is simply passed through and eliminated as waste. Such feasting is not a pretty sight. There is, though, another kind of feast marked by thankfulness more than gluttony, by mindfulness more than self-gratification. It is not about feeding my appetites and cravings; it is rather about savoring a gift with gratitude. I could talk about church potlucks that resemble the former more than the latter, but stories of church potlucks deserve their own essay.

In records from the desert fathers and mothers of the third and fourth centuries, we read of their slow, quiet, contemplative practice of listening to Scripture as a kind of rumination. Ruminative listening to Scripture was compared to the way the camel chews its cud, regurgitating a bit at a time, chewing it again and again until all of its nutrition has been received and embodied. *Ruminatio* was a prayerful way of attentively listening to the Word, different from a linear, cognitive, analytical treatment of the content. It was a deep hearing, inviting the Word to come and take residence deep in one's bowels, in the New Testament sense of bowels (Col. 3:12 KJV, "Put on therefore . . . bowels of mercies"; see also in KJV 2 Cor. 6:12; Phil. 1:8; Phil. 2:1; Phlm. 7; 1 John 3:17). These "bowels" (Gk. *splanchna*) are the seat of emotions and passions. From the ruminative perspective, the best response to hearing the Word may not be to chat about it, but rather to digest it slowly, internalize it deeply, and embody it thoroughly before beginning to talk about it.

A high school student was leading her first weekly Bible study series. She always felt pleased when the discussion was vigorous, but she felt like a bad leader when the discussion fell silent. Over the years she

Exegetical Perspective

of a parable comes from the British New Testament scholar C. H. Dodd (1884–1973), who described a parable as "a metaphor or simile drawn from nature or common life, arresting the hearer by its vividness or strangeness and leaving the mind in sufficient doubt about its precise application to tease it into active thought."[2]

The crowd that formed the audience for Jesus' discourse in Mark 4 presumably included Galilean farmers, and the three seed parables in 4:3–9; 4:26–29; and 4:30–32 would surely have piqued their interest and helped them to understand various aspects of the kingdom of God. The Hebrew equivalent of "parable" (*mashal*) has an even broader meaning, and includes proverbs and riddles. The somewhat obscure material in 4:10–12 and 4:21–25 and the allegorical interpretation of the parable of the Sower in 4:13–20 fit the broader Hebrew concept quite well.

The Parable of the Sower (vv. 3–9). The parable begins and ends with a call to pay attention: "Listen!" and "Let anyone with ears to hear listen!" In other words, this is important material. While the passage is traditionally called the parable of the Sower (see Matt. 13:18), the real focus is the four sowings; the first three are failures, and only the last one is a great success.

The narrative follows the rules for good storytelling (or even jokes). The use of repetition sets up a pattern of expectations. When the sower goes out to sow, there are three unsuccessful sowings—on a path, on rocky ground, and among thorns. The reasons for their lack of success are made clear: the birds ate the seeds on the way; the sun scorched the seeds on the rocky ground; and the thorns choked the seeds sown among them.

Why would a farmer be so careless and foolish as to sow seeds on a road, or in rocky ground, or among thorns? Some scholars have argued that the sower of the parable reflects ancient Palestinian farming practices by which sowing precedes plowing. Others have suggested that what we have here is "broadcasting," that is, sowing indiscriminately, in the hope that something will grow somewhere somehow. In the context of the parable, this could be a case of Markan irony where the sower casts seeds in places that no prudent sower would ever cast seeds.

In telling his story of the sowings, Jesus the good storyteller does not introduce unnecessary details.

2. Charles Harold Dodd, *The Parables of the Kingdom*, rev. ed. (New York: Scribner, 1961), 5.

Homiletical Perspective

extensive. The preacher needs to be clear about the nature and purposes of parables. As the sermon is being constructed, the preacher needs to determine how much instruction about parables is needed and how much attention is demanded by this particular parable. One good and straightforward explanation of parables is given by William Placher. Drawing on insights from C. H. Dodd, Paul Ricoeur, and John Dominic Crossan, Placher suggests that parables were used to lead listeners from a concrete and common experience into an uncertain and mysterious reflection that result in new insights.[1]

It is also possible for the preacher to invite people hearing this parable to recall other references to sowing and harvest in Jewish Scriptures, such as Hosea 2:23; 8:7, or to offer examples from Greek and Roman literature.[2]

A necessary question for the preacher to ask is, what was Jesus' purpose in telling this particular parable? The reference at the end of the parable to an extraordinary yield (v. 8) is clearly an encouraging message. The closing line in verse 9 is just as clearly an exhortation. The references to birds, rocky ground, and scorching sun all suggest opposition to what the sower is doing. There is no suggestion that the qualities of the seeds vary. It is the reception of the seeds that varies. Proclamation, sowing of the seeds, is not the problem, at least not in this parable. The parable describes both the generosity of the sower in sowing seeds and the difficulties encountered by the seeds. Hearing, the reception of the seeds, is where problems occur. No wonder Jesus ends the parable with the exhortation to hear, to listen, and to be receptive soil.

At some point in the sermon preparation, it will be helpful for the preacher to step back from the text and think about how the parable speaks to the preacher's specific congregation. Lamar Williamson offers two very helpful insights that are clearly supported by the text. He lifts up the motifs of exhortation and encouragement, and he identifies two audiences: the audience that first heard Jesus preach this parable and the early church that is listening to Mark's Gospel.[3]

A primary form of exhortation is preaching. The preacher needs to pay careful and disciplined attention to the call of Jesus that instructs people to listen

1. William Placher, *Mark*, Belief, A Theological Commentary on the Bible (Louisville, KY: Westminster John Knox Press, 2010), 70.
2. Adela Yarbro Collins, *Mark*, Hermeneia (Minneapolis: Fortress Press, 2007), 243.
3. Lamar Williamson Jr., *Mark*, Interpretation series (Louisville, KY: John Knox Press, 1983), 87.

Mark 4:1–9

Theological Perspective

A visual depiction of this parable has been created in the St. John's Bible, a beautiful contemporary illuminated manuscript of the Bible commissioned by the Benedictines of St. John's Abbey in Collegeville, Minnesota (http://www.saintjohnsbible.org/see/). The illustration of the parable of the Sower artistically reveals some of the theological dynamics of divine and human agency. A simple figure of the farmer, clearly identified as Jesus himself, is in the center of the illustration. The rows of soil—fertile, rocky, shallow, weedy—are at his feet. The illustration is enclosed by a rather ornate etched frame. The frame does not constrain the farmer. His sweeping arm as it scatters seeds breaks through the frame of the illustration. The seeds themselves are scattered beyond the frame into the text of the Gospel itself.

With these artistic decisions, the illustrator is making important theological claims about divine and human action. These claims include the affirmation that God is the sower who cannot be bound by the limits of human imagination. Even a fancy, ornate "frame" around God's action does not hinder God's action. Furthermore, the seeds of God's gracious action spread beyond where we would expect them to be, even beyond where we might wish them to be. We may want to limit the sowing of the seeds into just certain fields belonging to certain landowners, but the scattered seeds from God's arm spill out beyond the limits. Finally, the seeds of God's action are sown throughout Scripture; open any page of Scripture and some seeds will fall out.

This illustration is not, of course, a systematically theological articulation. It evokes. It points. It suggests that God flings seeds widely, beyond our boundaries and well beyond our expectations. It also suggests that human action and receptivity play a strong role in the fruitfulness of discipleship. In the kingdom of God, which this parable begins to sketch, God reigns in a lavish scattering of seeds. It is human response that either participates in God's kingdom by sprouting, flowering, and fruiting, or refuses to participate and dies from the scorching sun and hot wind.

LEANNE VAN DYK

Pastoral Perspective

came to realize that some of the most important hearing and learning happened in the silence. Even more, she learned that what really mattered was the quality of the fruit born from the word taking root in the learners' lives. That was far more valuable than the vigor of the discussion at the time of the study. As a matter of fact, she did not see much correlation between the vigor of the discussion and the impact of the Word on people's lives.

That high school student is a pastor now, and she has come to realize that some people use vigorous discussion as a way to avoid listening and hearing. In Bible study, the chattiness she once cherished sometimes seems more like the bloom that springs up in the rocky soil. It is exciting to see something green shooting forth from the hard earth; but without time to deepen the roots, the green shoots wither under the scorching sun.

That young pastor began to learn a way of engaging the Scriptures in a listening, contemplative, ruminating way. She learned that the analytical study in her head was indeed important, but the ruminative digestion in her bowels was just as important, if the word was to take root in her life.

I was raised in a Japanese American home that was significantly shaped by Japanese culture. Listening and attentiveness were valued far more than talkativeness. In that culture, if you have to use too many words to communicate, that may be a sign that you are not too sharp. Even the simple word for "noisy"—*yakamashii*—carries a pejorative sense. If a grownup said to a child: *yakamashii*, it was not just a description of the noise level; it was a judgment of character and an invitation to be quiet and listen. A loving parent could send that message very subtly, with no need to yell.

When Jesus begins and ends with "Listen!" I cannot help but hear a gentle *yakamashii*: prepare to listen and hear, in hope of a transformed life overflowing with an abundance of grain to share.

STEVEN TOSHIO YAMAGUCHI

Exegetical Perspective

Rather, having built up a pattern of failures in verses 4–7, he ends with a remarkable contrast between the failures and the one great success: the seeds sown in the good soil grow up, increase, and yield "thirty and sixty and a hundredfold" (v. 8). These numbers are not simply indicative of a good crop. Rather, they are "kingdom numbers," indicating growth beyond any sower's wildest imagining. The punch line is saved until the end of the story and comes as a surprise.

It is likely that the three seed parables in Mark 4:3–9, 26–29, and 30–32 once circulated as unit. The latter two begin with a notice that "the kingdom of God is like" seed growing by itself or like a mustard seed. No such introduction appears in the parable of the Sower. What then might it tell us about the kingdom of God?

In Mark's Gospel (and very likely in the early church and in Jesus' own ministry), the parable of the Sower helped explain the mixed reception that Jesus' proclamation of God's kingdom received. It concerned both the seed (the message about the kingdom of God) and the sower (Jesus the preacher of God's kingdom). It insists that there is nothing wrong with either the seed or the sower. The problem is with the soils in which the seed has been sown (as the allegorical interpretation in Mark 4:13–20 will make clear). The goodness of the seed is proved by the superabundant harvest that occurs in the fourth sowing. The goodness of the sower is proved by the final result of his preaching. What is needed is good soil. While the sower may be prodigal (in its positive sense of overly generous), he is not foolish.

The parable of the Sower was (and is) both an explanation why not everyone accepts Jesus' teaching and also a source of encouragement for his discouraged followers and maybe even for Jesus. Those who have ears to listen may now carry on Jesus' proclamation of God's kingdom in a spirit of confidence and with the certain hope that God will one day bring about a magnificent and superabundant harvest.

DANIEL J. HARRINGTON

Homiletical Perspective

to what he is saying. This may not be surprising, yet it is remarkably challenging. It is challenging, in part, because so often we seem to think we know what Jesus is saying or what he is going to say. In this text we are exhorted to listen anew for the biblical witness to Jesus in the Gospels, and to listen to all of that witness, not just our favorite sayings.

Likewise, the preacher can point with encouragement to the abundant harvest promised in the parable. It will be challenging to work with this promise of abundance, especially in a culture that readily equates abundance with numerical measurements. It is worth challenging a congregation to ask what abundance would look like in their individual lives as well as in the life of the congregation. Other passages could be helpful in presenting the challenge. At the end of another parable, in Luke's Gospel, the one about a man with great abundance, there is the exhortation that we are to be "rich toward God" (Luke 12:21). In John's Gospel Jesus says that he has come that people might have life in abundance (John 10:10). The parable in Mark's text is explicit about tremendous numerical yields. The book of Acts speaks of tremendous numerical growth in the early church. It is worth exploring the difference between seeking growth and seeking the faithfulness that allows God to make growth in many forms happen.

It may not be possible for the preacher to include a consideration of how both audiences heard Jesus, so it will be helpful for the preacher to determine which audience is most like his or her congregation. Some congregations—like the audience Jesus had—have a remarkable number of "new" Christians or people testing Christianity. Other congregations have many more experienced Christians who could well be exhorted to listen, as Mark's audience was exhorted to listen, that the harvest may be abundant.

LAIRD J. STUART

Mark 4:10–20

¹⁰When he was alone, those who were around him along with the twelve asked him about the parables. ¹¹And he said to them, "To you has been given the secret of the kingdom of God, but for those outside, everything comes in parables; ¹²in order that
 'they may indeed look, but not perceive,
  and may indeed listen, but not understand;
 so that they may not turn again and be forgiven.'"
¹³And he said to them, "Do you not understand this parable? Then how will you understand all the parables? ¹⁴The sower sows the word. ¹⁵These are the ones on the path where the word is sown: when they hear, Satan immediately

Theological Perspective

After the "sermon from the boat" at the beginning of Mark 4, the disciples draw Jesus aside and ask for a clarification. Jesus takes the time to explain the parable to his confused disciples. "The sower sows the word," says Jesus. This seems clear enough, but a critical ambiguity emerges. Is the sower Jesus? God the Father? The disciples? Jesus does not specify; each of these possibilities evokes a different meaning. The word that is sown is also not identified, although it is clear that this seed is bursting with potential and fruitfulness. For when it hits good soil, the harvest is astounding. Thirty-, sixty-, hundredfold harvests result, far exceeding what even a skillful farmer can expect. Such an abundant harvest suggests a comprehensive scope of "word" in this parable. The "word" is the words of Jesus; the words of the Law and the Prophets; the words of the eyewitnesses to Jesus' life, teachings, death, and resurrection; the words of Scripture; and the Word, Jesus himself. These are the seeds that are sown far and wide. The meaning of the soils is more precisely identified by Jesus. They are hearers that range from shallow and fickle to faithful and true. The quality of the soil makes all the difference in the longevity and sturdiness of the plant.

The explanation that Jesus gives his disciples touches on several theological themes, including divine sovereignty, conversion, and the shape of

Pastoral Perspective

Earlier Jesus had spoken publicly about four different ecologies that grain plants face, but here with his friends he describes four ecologies of the human heart. The third and fourth ecologies suggest a fatal choice. The choice seems unnervingly familiar, like one made in many congregations today. Soil and rocks cannot make choices, but human hearts can and must.

What choice? In the first two ecologies, the path and the rocky ground, the environment is too hostile. The seed is too vulnerable. It has no chance on the pathway. Grain will not grow on a pathway, where predators eat the seed before it can sprout. Rocky ground has nowhere for roots to mature and too little moisture and nutrients to yield grain. Seed might sprout, but it will never mature. In these ecologies, where the seed is doomed and grain can never grow, there seems to be little choice.

Both the third and fourth ecologies can sustain viable plant life. Here there might be a choice. The thorny environment has enough moisture and depth of soil to sustain vigorous plant life. There thorns grow so vigorous that they choke out young grain plants. The thorny plants discourage traffic and predators as much as they discourage grain. Some plants thrive in this ecology, but they will never yield grain.

However, this third ecology can be productive, even if unfruitful and unattractive. The Bible names

comes and takes away the word that is sown in them. ¹⁶And these are the ones sown on rocky ground: when they hear the word, they immediately receive it with joy. ¹⁷But they have no root, and endure only for a while; then, when trouble or persecution arises on account of the word, immediately they fall away. ¹⁸And others are those sown among the thorns: these are the ones who hear the word, ¹⁹but the cares of the world, and the lure of wealth, and the desire for other things come in and choke the word, and it yields nothing. ²⁰And these are the ones sown on the good soil: they hear the word and accept it and bear fruit, thirty and sixty and a hundredfold."

Exegetical Perspective

The Secret of the Kingdom (vv. 10–12). This passage is among the most problematic texts in the New Testament. It seems to say that Jesus taught in parables (understood as puzzles or riddles) in order to make sure that some people would not understand his message about the kingdom of God. That sounds perverse at best. Some scholars have argued that the passage comes not from Jesus but from early Christians who were frustrated by the failure of other Jews to accept the gospel (see John 12:40 and Acts 28:26–27). That is very likely so.

The first problem comes with the setting for this teaching in verse 10. The beautiful scene of Jesus teaching from the boat to the crowd on shore is quickly left behind. Now Jesus finds himself "alone" but with a small group that includes the Twelve (see 3:13–19). They ask him about the parables, even though thus far he has given them only one parable in Mark 4.

The problems continue in the first part of Jesus' answer (v. 11), when he claims that the "secret of the kingdom of God" has been given to them (insiders) but is presented to outsiders only in "parables" (presumably in the sense of puzzles or riddles). His response ("has been given") is cast in the "divine passive" construction; this is a pious way of saying

Homiletical Perspective

It does not take long in the reading of this text to be confronted with a disturbing statement by Jesus. Verse 10 suggests a new setting, a change from the previous nine verses. The public teaching is over. Jesus is now with a smaller group, the twelve disciples and an undetermined number of other people. Jesus is going to explain both why he uses parables and the meaning of the parable of the Sower. We are ready for the explanation, especially since we think we already know it. However, in verses 11 and 12 there is a surprise, a speed bump in the text. Jesus, of all people, seems to be saying there are those who will not understand his teaching, and that is how it is supposed to be.

The words used by Jesus referring to "those outside" are a shock. The words are harsh. The dilemma is deepened and driven home when Jesus explains in verse 12 that he speaks in parables "in order that" others will not understand. In Matthew's Gospel, Jesus explains his use of parables by saying it is because they do not understand. Luke's version of this teaching appears to support Mark's version of what Jesus said. Clearly Mark is suggesting God has determined that some people will not be able to understand what Jesus is saying.

Mark and the early church were struggling with the issue of why some people rejected the teachings

Mark 4:10–20

Theological Perspective

faithful discipleship. Jesus begins with an ironic statement that the disciples have been "given the secret of the kingdom of God" that has been hidden from others. They have indeed been given this secret; he is standing in their midst. However, they are confused and do not recognize that he is the secret that they already possess.

Following this somewhat ironic statement, Jesus issues a warning: "those outside" will not perceive the kingdom of God. For them, even if they look and listen, they will not see and hear. There is an ominous tone in Jesus' explanation of the parable. It immediately raises theological questions of divine foreknowledge and human free will that have been vigorously debated throughout the church's history. Theologians—from the apostle Paul in Romans to Augustine and Pelagius in the fifth century to Luther and Erasmus in the sixteenth—have pondered the questions of divine decision and human freedom. It is a debate that requires careful definitions of terms and nuanced philosophical categories, such as primary and secondary causation, future contingencies, and modalities of action.

Such conversations are often illuminating and clarifying but they are not the idiom of Scripture. The sobering warning of Jesus that those on the outside will not—indeed, cannot—see and hear is not a philosophical and theological theory. It is rather a description of what is empirically evident. Drawing from Isaiah 6:9, Jesus describes the human state of affairs: some have been given the mysteries of the kingdom of God and some are still in the dark. Those who are not within the kingdom of God simply cannot see and hear. Jesus is not blaming. He is not even explaining. He is stating. This is the way it works—some believe because they have been given the mysteries of the kingdom. Some do not believe.

From this observable fact, an additional theological theme emerges. There is an implicit theology of conversion in Jesus' account of the soil. In each type of soil, there is both the initiating act of the sower and the response of the soil. In the thin soil on the path, Satan interrupts and seizes the seed. For the rocky soul, the response is initial joy but subsequent withering away in the heat of trouble or persecution. The thorny weeds, which are the distractions of the world, choke out the germinating plant. In the good soil, the growth, although initially hidden, comes to full bloom. The central affirmation of Jesus' explanation of the parable is the call to the community of faith to hear and respond.

Pastoral Perspective

various thorny plants. Some are associated with pain and even torture and suffering; some are stalwarts and do good things. A thorny ecology can provide an ecosystem with shade and shelter for insects and bacteria and small animals. It can aggregate and preserve moisture in a scorching desert terrain. If you are a creepy crawly thing, these thorns might be your best friend. The infrastructure of a vigorous, wild thorny patch supports biodiversity and resists soil erosion. However, it will not produce grain to feed you. Jesus explained that thorns will choke out any grain plant whose seed had the misfortune of being tossed among the thorns to sprout. The earth needs vigorous, wild plant life, but people need cultivated good soil for growing food. The whole earth does not need to be planted with grain, but some soil must be protected for grain if we are to have bread.

It sounds like a message to many of our churches today. Recently I listened to a congregation talk about how they felt spiritually. They had vital signs, but they felt "choked." Participation declined. No new people came. They had a nice property and endowment funds to support their budget. They had expected young families from their preschool, but none joined them. There is some plant life, but where is the grain? I wonder if the members of that congregation allowed "the cares of the world, and the lure of wealth, and the desire for other things" (v. 19) to choke out the possibility of growing grain.

What if the members function as thorn plants? Thorn plants are generous volunteers. They happily move in to take up space not protected for grain. Thorn plants are happy to mature into hard and prickly things, unfriendly to outsiders, hospitable only to the creepy crawly things that grew up in their shelter. Such a stand of thorny plants might appear hearty, but it will never produce grain. It will never yield the bread that people need; grain that dares to sprout will never be allowed to bloom. Did that congregation choose to become a community of thorns when it once had been a fertile field for wholesome grain? Was it a choice to yield to the thorniest volunteers, because that was the path of least resistance, or was it the relentless tenacity of the ever encroaching thorns determined to prevail that made resistance futile? Did they choose for thorns, or did they simply default because they forgot their call to grow grain and eat and serve bread?

I served as pastor for a congregation that appeared to be dying on a rocky path. Not even thorns survived. When I arrived, the actual gardens and lawn were dead. Only tall weeds were in the

Exegetical Perspective

"God has given the secret." The "secret" (*mystērion* in Greek, *raz* in Hebrew and Aramaic) refers to the revelation of God's reign unfolding according to the divine plan, especially through the person and ministry of Jesus. The problem here is that Jesus seems to be deliberately hiding the "secret" from some people.

Bigger problems are ahead, however, and come in the form of a loose quotation (or better, a paraphrase) of Isaiah 6:9–10 in verse 12. The text does not correspond exactly with either the Hebrew (Masoretic) or Greek (Septuagint) version. The biblical text comes from the narrative in which Isaiah is called to be God's prophet and to preach repentance to the people of Judah in the face of an imminent attack from the Assyrian army. The passage encourages the prophet to proclaim God's message even if the people do not want to hear it.

The first problem in verse 12 comes with the Greek conjunction *hina*, which is translated as "in order that" by the NRSV. That suggests purpose. However, in koine Greek *hina* can designate result. The issue is whether *hina* refers to the cause (purpose) or the effect (result) of Jesus' teaching in parables. In Mark 4:12 the verbs are in the third person and the subjunctive mood ("they may indeed look"), while in the Hebrew of Isaiah 6:9 they are second-person imperatives ("keep listening but do not comprehend"). Still another problem is posed by the Greek word *mēpote* (NRSV "so that they may not"). It can be interpreted either as a negative conjunction of purpose ("lest they ever") or as an adverb ("perhaps"). Finally, at the end of the "quotation" Mark has "be forgiven" rather than the verb in the Hebrew text, "be healed."

Is the obtuseness of those "outside" the cause or the result of Jesus' teaching in parables? Neither interpretation seems much like good news for Christian preachers (or anyone else). In either interpretation Jesus seems to come off as promoting a deterministic and sectarian theology. That is, God has given revelation to insiders but consigned outsiders in advance to misunderstanding, whether on purpose or as a result of their not comprehending. This sounds like a proof text for the doctrine of double predestination.

Perhaps a way out of all these exegetical, historical, and theological problems is to look at the text from the perspective of Mark's special interest in the cross of Jesus as pivotal in the unfolding of the mystery of salvation. Throughout Mark's Gospel, what causes blindness and deafness is the paradox of God's will made manifest in Jesus' death on the cross

Homiletical Perspective

of Jesus and why others accepted. They were witnesses day by day to the rejection by the Jews and the acceptance by the Gentiles. As the resistance to the early church stiffened, the reality of rejection and the puzzling reasons for it became urgent matters. In perhaps a less urgent but still significant manner, we sometimes wonder why some people are responsive to the preaching and teaching of Jesus and others are resistant.

The scholarly community offers a wide diversity of interpretations of this dilemma. These interpretations range from the claim that the difficulty in hearing is self-created because of hostility to Jesus, to the claim that the text reveals a deliberate plan by God to prevent some people, those "outside," from hearing what Jesus has to say.

The belief that God would choose to have some people rendered incapable of understanding what God is saying and doing is expressed elsewhere in Scripture. It is hardly isolated to this text. For instance, God hardens the heart of Pharaoh. The apostle Paul struggles with this issue notably in Romans 9:18–26; 10:16–21; and 11:7–10. It also surfaces in John 12:37–41.

Of the various approaches to this text, the one by Joel Marcus is perhaps most promising. To begin, he asserts that either those who are "outside" are there because they have chosen their own blindness and hostility or because God has chosen that they be outside. Looking ahead to Mark 4:21–22, Marcus then asserts that blindness will not be the last word. Finally, he returns to the position that is both so evident and so challenging: in this text blindness is caused by God.[1]

It is all too easy to imagine the challenges in bringing this message from the text to a congregation. William Placher cites reactions to Jesus' words by various scholars who refer to them as "intolerable," "repellent," even "the most offensive words" in the Christian Bible.[2] One strategy for dealing with the offense of this text is to address the mysteries of God's sovereign freedom. There are texts—like God's answer in Job (Job 38–40:2) and Paul's struggle in Romans 9–11—that lead us toward a fundamental humility before God.

The issue of how some people will be prevented by God from hearing Jesus is not the only challenge in this text. Another dilemma concerns the difficulties encountered by those whom God allows

---

1. Joel Marcus, *Mark 1–8*, Anchor Bible (New York: Doubleday, 1999), 306–7.
2. William Placher, *Mark*, Belief, A Theological Commentary on the Bible (Louisville, KY: Westminster John Knox Press, 1996), 69.

Mark 4:10–20

Theological Perspective

Theologically, the ordering of divine initiative and human response is critical. The soil itself cannot generate and germinate. The seed of the word sown by the divine sower is a necessary condition, but the environment of the soil has direct impact on the success of the young plant. The soil can "receive" and "bear fruit," or it can "yield nothing" and "fall away." Conversion is a process; it has a pattern and a story just as surely as a seed falls into the ground, germinates, and then survives—or not.

In her novel *Horse Heaven,* author Jane Smiley tells the story of Buddy Crawford, who experiences a dramatic conversion. His zeal for the Lord is real, but it gradually encounters the doubts and frustrations of life. One night he prays, "Okay. Here's the deal. I thought I was saved. . . . But I find out all the time that I've got to keep getting saved."[1]

It is a theological challenge to understand Jesus' explanation of the parable of the Sower. He says that the ultimate harvest is in some sense determined; the sower sows the seed. In another sense, though, the harvest is open; the soil takes an active role of reception or rejection. To complicate the picture even further, demonic agency is involved as well. One commentator has said, "Just as the proclamation of the word is a complex process in which human and superhuman factors are confusingly intertwined, so the reception of the word is a fusion of the human, the demonic, and the divine."[2] Although most Christian traditions affirm a clear initiating divine gracious action, the role of the human persons and communities who receive the seed of the word is very strong. This means that patterns and embedded virtues of "getting saved" are important baptismal practices to be rehearsed over a lifetime of discipleship.

LEANNE VAN DYK

Pastoral Perspective

flowerbeds; the flowers were dead. Gang activity haunted the neighborhood; the ramshackle building was full of vermin and detritus. Crips-and-Bloods warfare was reaching its zenith on our streets. The church had about twenty-five older people a week in worship. The descant to hymns was provided by police sirens.

Nevertheless, it was a gift to be in that desolate patch where even the thorns were dying. We chose to resist the thorns. We chose to remove the dead wood. We mounted a resistance movement, and by God's grace, God's reign prevailed. As the word took root, as the shoots were nurtured and protected, as the grain became bread, the church came alive. We welcomed the homeless and laborers and professionals of many nationalities, young and old. It was much easier to have a laser focus on becoming grain for a hungry world, when the old thorny infrastructure became so overshadowed that it was no longer tempting as shelter. When we began, some thought we were rocky soil, forsaken by the sower, but they were wrong. We were in fact fertile soil that had been occupied by non-nourishing volunteer thorns. After years of good environmental choices that mitigated the thorns, the grain finally had space to grow. Our ground had been fertile all along, but the wrong plants had been getting fed.

Jesus seems to be warning the disciples about their need to resist the thorny plants. He names "the cares of the world, and the lure of wealth, and the desire for other things" as the things that "come in and choke the word" so that the word "yields nothing" (v. 19). The thorny structure might look as if it promises security and a future, but it is a breadless future. Disciples must resist the "cares . . . lures . . . and desires" that potentially call forth the thorns in each of us, lest the church fail to protect the shoots that will provide the grain for bread that feeds our hungry souls.

STEVEN TOSHIO YAMAGUCHI

---

1. Jane Smiley, *Horse Heaven* (New York: Alfred A. Knopf, 2000), 192.
2. Joel Marcus, *Mark 1–8,* Anchor Bible (New York: Doubleday & Co., 2000), 311.

Exegetical Perspective

(8:31–38; 10:45; 14:36). Mark insists that we do not really know Jesus or the kingdom of God unless we confront the mystery of the cross and the paradox of Jesus as the suffering Messiah. Perhaps this difficult passage makes its best sense when read in the broader context of Mark's theology, rather than in isolation.

The Interpretation of the Parable of the Sower (vv. 13–20). Many interpreters regard this as a sermon outline that was developed in early Christian circles on the basis of the parable of the Sower in 4:3–9. While it is not inconceivable that Jesus provided his own interpretation, there are several expressions in the interpretation that fit better with the experience of early Christians after Jesus' death and resurrection: "the word," "trouble or persecution," "the cares of the world," "the lure of wealth" and "the desire for other things."

The interpretation takes its starting point from the parable's insistence that the seeds (the message) and the sower (the preacher) are good, and explores the reasons for the failure and success of the various sowings. The allegory comes in assigning a theological or moral interpretation to each of the soils. As the vocabulary suggests, the reasons seem more appropriate as explanations for why some who embraced the gospel had fallen away and why others had thrived. So the seeds sown along the way were quickly seized by Satan. The seeds sown on rocky ground did well for a while but at the first hint of trouble or persecution fell away because they lacked strong roots. The growth of seeds sown among thorns was choked off by worldly cares and desires for wealth and other things. By contrast, the seeds sown in good soil heard the word, welcomed it, and acted upon it. In doing so, they produced a superabundant harvest.

While it may be tempting to dwell on the three failed sowings, the real point of the interpretation comes in what happens in the good soil (v. 20). Here in the "punch line" is the description of the ideal Christian: one who hears the word of God, welcomes it, and acts upon it. The conclusion suggests a balance between the power of God's word and the receptivity of the hearer.

DANIEL J. HARRINGTON

Homiletical Perspective

to listen. Listening to Jesus is not easy. Even the disciples do not seem to do a very good job. Ironically, even those on the inside evidently feel like outsiders. The people drawn close to Jesus ask him to explain what he has just said. Jesus explains the parable and the challenges to listening.

These challenges are not so hard to understand. The forces of evil and resistance to God are ever present. Initial enthusiasm for the good news, when not followed up with consistent practice and reinforcement, lead to a loss of faith. The cares of life can choke and eventually cut off faith. So the text leads the disciples, Mark's audience, and us to confront the challenges to listening and receiving what Jesus is saying. The real challenge in listening is not only letting the words of Jesus come into our hearts. It is also to choose the new life that is called for in the teaching of Jesus.[3]

Regarding the difficulties encountered by those who are allowed to hear, there are some themes the preacher can develop. The very function of a parable is to lead its listeners past easy conclusions and into deeper reflection. It can be acknowledged that whatever understanding God inspires in us is a cause for gratitude. The preacher can call for the community of faith to be supportive of the struggles to believe or to trust in God that are present in all of human experience.

In light of the challenges in the text, the preacher should not lose sight of the promise of listening and faithfulness. To those who are able to listen, who pay attention to the words of Jesus, who struggle patiently with their meaning, who are guided by God's Spirit, as well as by other teachings from Jesus, and who are supported by fellow disciples, the rewards are remarkable.

LAIRD J. STUART

---

3. Brian K. Blount and Gary W. Charles, *Preaching Mark in Two Voices* (Louisville, KY: Westminster John Knox Press, 2002), 64.

Mark 4:21–25

²¹He said to them, "Is a lamp brought in to be put under the bushel basket, or under the bed, and not on the lampstand? ²²For there is nothing hidden, except to be disclosed; nor is anything secret, except to come to light. ²³Let anyone with ears to hear listen!" ²⁴And he said to them, "Pay attention to what you hear; the measure you give will be the measure you get, and still more will be given you. ²⁵For to those who have, more will be given; and from those who have nothing, even what they have will be taken away."

Theological Perspective

One contemporary commentator on the Gospel of Mark identifies this passage as "one of the most formidable in the entire New Testament."[1] This short section on the lampstand and the measure presents significant challenges for the reader. It is not easy to grasp what Jesus means when he seems to suggest (v. 25) that the rich get richer and the poor get poorer. Nevertheless the imperatives of "Let anyone with ears to hear listen!" (v. 23) and "Pay attention to what you hear!" (v. 24) signal the urgency of these words. In spite of the hard saying of these parables, a theological perspective evokes a rich and nuanced understanding of the reign of God and the life of discipleship.

The kingdom of God is not explicitly mentioned in this section, but in the context of the surrounding parables, this pair of sayings gives further light to Mark's understanding of the kingdom of God. For Mark, the kingdom of God is a reality that is mysterious, even hidden, but unquestionably real. In all the parables of Mark 4, Jesus' point is that the kingdom of God is never quite what you might expect. The parable of the Sower makes the claim that although the seed of God's word is fruitful beyond

---
1. Joel Marcus, *Mark 1–8*, Anchor Bible 27 (New York: Doubleday, 2000), 301.

Pastoral Perspective

Jesus' reference to the bushel and the lampstand in Mark 4 may sound like images in the Sermon on the Mount, but these are two very different references to light. In the Sermon on the Mount (Matt. 5:14), Jesus declares that the disciples are "the light of the world," not to be hidden under a bushel; they are the source of illumination. In Mark 4 the disciples are not the illuminators; they are, rather, to be witnesses who look carefully at everything the light is illumining. "Shine brightly" was the message in Matthew 5. "Look! Pay attention to what God is doing!" is the message here. Jesus here is calling for visual attention to a world being illumined in a new way by the one who would declare in another Gospel, "I am the light of the world" (John 8:12).

Earlier, when Jesus introduced the parable of the Sower (Mark 4:3–9), he focused on auditory attention. The telling of the parable was opened and closed with an imperative "Listen!" while the parable itself distinguished four types of hearing. That auditory focus is now joined by a visual focus. "See! Look! Pay attention!" The disciples are given light to see everything clearly. It is a gift of illumination that comes from God.

Here in my well-illuminated, electronic, urban world of Los Angeles, where the ambient night light is so bright it is seen easily from outer space, one

Exegetical Perspective

Mark 4:21–25 consists of five loosely connected sayings about revelation and responses to it. In the structure of Mark's parables discourse (4:1–34) they parallel and modify somewhat the equally mysterious section on the rationale for Jesus' use of parables (4:10–12). The sayings may well have been put together in a little (oral or written) packet before Mark composed his Gospel. In their current form and context they seem to say that eventually the mysteries surrounding Jesus and his teachings will become clear to all, and that those who take hold of his teachings and act upon them will grow in wisdom.

The five sayings in Mark 4:21–25 have deep roots in the Synoptic Gospel tradition. They appear in the parables discourses in Matthew 13 and Luke 8, as well as in other contexts. The saying about the lamp (v. 21) occurs in the Sermon on the Mount (Matt. 5:15) and in Luke's parables discourse (Luke 8:16), while its Q form is in Luke 11:33. The saying on hiddenness and disclosure (v. 22) is placed by Matthew in his missionary discourse (Matt. 10:26) but appears also in Luke's parables discourse (Luke 8:17) and in a Q section (Luke 12:2). The call to hear (v. 23), already used in Mark 4:9, is found in Matthew 11:15 and in various forms in the letters to the seven churches in Revelation 2–3. While omitted in the

Homiletical Perspective

After the rigors of the previous two passages in Mark, this text is more hospitable to the preacher and the congregation, its intent and purpose more readily evident. It also addresses some of the challenges of the previous passages, especially the matter of hearing what Jesus has to say.

Here Jesus addresses the medium of his message about the kingdom of God. The message is not to be hidden or treated as a secret for insiders. Here, unlike in Mark 4:11–12, there is no suggestion of people being prevented from hearing. Jesus will still teach in parables. His message will still be mysterious at times. Yet the message is to be thrown out to all people, like so many seeds thrown from the swinging hand of a sower.

Beginning at verse 24 Jesus exhorts those who are with him to share in the teaching. Teaching is not to be restricted to Jesus. He also goes on to explain that there is both a promise and a warning for them to consider. Those who receive the teaching of Jesus are to give it away. The more they share and give it away, the more insight into the kingdom and the more faith will be given to them. Those who resist the teaching, who are unwilling to receive it, will understand even less than they did before. So the twin motifs of exhortation and encouragement, contained in prior parables, return.

Mark 4:21–25

Theological Perspective

any expectations, it is somehow also vulnerable. It can take root and grow, or it can be squeezed out by rocks or thorns and snatched away by birds.

This set of short parables makes a similar claim. The word of God is first imagined as a lamp which is brought into a house. The one carrying the lamp would certainly not hide it under a bushel basket or under a bed. The light would not then have a chance to illuminate the dark room, and the light itself would be extinguished. The word of God is next imagined as a measure, a unit of volume or perhaps money. This parable is the most formidable of all, for it seems to say, in effect, that the rich will inevitably flourish and the poor will just as inevitably fail. A difficult saying, indeed!

The two short parables about the lampstand and the measure resist easy interpretation. One possibility is that these parables explore the character of citizenship in the kingdom of God. Theological resources to explore this possibility include contemporary narrative theology. Narrative theology stresses the story-shaped nature of identity and rationality. Stanley Hauerwas reflects on how the church shares and embodies a common story: "A church [must] be a community of discourse and interpretation that endeavors to tell these stories and form its life in accordance with them."[2] Narrative theologians and ethicists stress that the truth and power of the kingdom of God is demonstrated in its ability to form a people. The story that is embodied by the community is not just any story. It is the story of Jesus, which then calls the community to participate in that story. It cannot be hidden because it will be disclosed, and it cannot stay secret because it will come to light. God's new age is arriving, despite all evidence to the contrary.

The kingdom of God, then, may seem hidden and secret, but it is in fact real and powerful. Apparently God would rather work behind the scenes, slowly and in small increments. The growth of the kingdom of God is more often quiet than noisy, more often concealed than revealed. Even though someday there will be "nothing hidden" nor "anything secret," for now, seeing the kingdom of God in all its tentative partiality requires the eyes of faith.

Narrative theology is also helpful in approaching the second small parable on the measure and its possibilities of increase or decrease. One of the streams that feed the rivers of narrative theology is

[2]. Stanley Hauerwas, *A Community of Character* (Notre Dame, IN: University of Notre Dame Press, 1981), 92.

Pastoral Perspective

can forget how dark the darkness can be. Even so, in California's mountains I can still find a deeper darkness when camping in the wilderness on a cloudy, starless, moonless night. Without an imported light source I see nothing in the darkness of the wilderness nighttime. When a lamp penetrates that wild darkness, the light is impossible to ignore. Even here in the city, when that rare widespread power outage strikes at night, the darkness is surprising and frightening. When the city's lights go out, people are drawn like moths to those with flashlights and batteries. In Jesus' preflashlight world, an oil lamp was a remarkable, life-changing gift to set on the lampstand. Not everyone could afford one. It was a privilege and comfort to have that extended ability to see in the darkness. Even today many around the world cannot afford a lamp at night.

Jesus' discussion of lamps, lampstands, and illumination (vv. 21–22) sets up the disciples for the big command in verse 24: "*Look* to what you hear" (my trans.). "Pay attention to what you hear" is how the NRSV renders this imperative form of the common verb (*blepō*), which is primarily about seeing or looking. This command to pay attention is in the language of seeing. It is meaningful only to those who have illumination. Those in the dark cannot see.

This is the first time in Mark's Gospel since calling the disciples that Jesus makes it very clear that the disciples are receiving the gift of special illumination. When Jesus was alone with "those who were around him along with the twelve," they asked him about the parables (v. 10). He answered them, "To you has been given the secret of the kingdom of God, but for those outside, everything comes in parables" (v. 11). They are privy to insider information. Later, in verse 33, Mark reports that Jesus "spoke the word" to the people "as they were able to hear it"; but "he did not speak to them except in parables" (4:34). In contrast, Mark spotlights the disciples' privilege, that Jesus "explained everything in private to his disciples" (4:34).

With that privilege come great possibilities from the God who multiplies the gift. "Listen if you have ears to hear, and *look* to what you hear!" (vv. 23–24a, my trans.). Jesus continues: "The measure you give will be the measure you get, and still more will be given you." He then concludes: "For to those who have, more will be given; and from those who have nothing, even what they have will be taken away" (vv. 24b–25) This marvelous gift comes with the disciples' privileged communication. Everything hidden is to be disclosed to them. Anything secret is to

Exegetical Perspective

other parables discourses, a saying about measures (v. 24) appears in the Sermons on the Mount and the Plain (Matt. 7:2 and Luke 6:38). The Markan form of the saying about giving and receiving (v. 25) occurs in the other two parables discourses (Matt. 13:12 and Luke 8:18), while the Q form comes at the ends of the parables of Talents (Matt. 25:29) and the Pounds (Luke 19:26).

These sayings most likely originated as individual proverbs or maxims. They probably circulated independently and were used and reused in various settings. So it is practically impossible to know their original referents and meanings. In their present context in Mark's Gospel, they constitute a short wisdom instruction, such as one finds in Proverbs 1–9, Sirach, and James. Here they are intended to shed some light on why Jesus characteristically taught in parables. Since these enigmatic sayings can be taken as puzzles or riddles, they also qualify as *meshalim* according to the wider Jewish concept of "parables." In this case there is a correlation between the medium and the message.

In what follows, the focus will be on what these sayings contribute to the Markan parables discourse in its present form. The audience for this short instruction is the same as that for the interpretation of the parable of the Sower—those "around him along with the twelve" (4:10). The saying about the lamp (v. 21) promises that Jesus' "secret" teachings about God's kingdom will be made clear for all to see. Their ultimate purpose is to reveal, not to conceal. Putting a lamp under a bushel basket or a bed would not only hide the light, but would also destroy both the basket and the bed. On the other hand, putting the lamp on a lampstand will allow it to achieve its purpose of giving abundant light. That day will come.

The saying about hiddenness and disclosure (v. 22) makes a similar point. In synonymous parallelism it affirms that the hiddenness is not permanent, and that the real purpose of Jesus' teaching in parables is revelation rather than concealment. Thus it modifies the impression given in the earlier private teaching in 4:10–12. It also points forward to the manifestation of Jesus as the glorious Son of Man (13:26; 14:62), to Jesus' identity as the suffering Messiah and the mystery of the cross, and to God's vindication of Jesus in the resurrection from the dead.

A form of the call to pay attention (v. 23) has already appeared in verse 9. Here it has the effect of affirming the importance of what has been said and what will be said in the instruction, and of shifting

Homiletical Perspective

In an intriguing interpretation, Pheme Perkins suggests that Jesus' saying about "those who have will be given more and those who do not have will end up with even less" was a saying about how the economic and social systems of his world worked. It was a world in which the rich usually got richer and the poor usually got poorer—a circumstance that is hardly unique to the first century. Jesus was taking common knowledge—and quite possibly resentment about how the world worked—and declaring that in this case God works along the same lines.[1]

The message that Jesus is bringing to his audience is also the message Mark is bringing to his audience. If they share in the proclamation of the gospel, they will receive the blessings of doing so. If they hide the light that is the news of the kingdom, more of their life will be taken from them. As the preacher's own proclamation of the gospel and teaching is a model of exhortation for the congregation, we may well be discouraged by what we perceive to be the lack of effectiveness in our preaching and teaching week after week. Where is the blessing? However, we also have to consider the latent impact on the congregation over time of our faithfulness to the tasks of both preaching and teaching.

This leads to the issue of enthusiasm. All the indications are that Jesus was enthusiastic and passionate about the message he had to proclaim. Part of being faithful to Christ and to the proclamation of Christ is to give evidence of our own enthusiasm. Enthusiasm is a difficult element in proclamation. Some of us are more outgoing than others; some of us are more naturally expressive than others. However, enthusiasm for the gospel does not need to be dependent on volume or emotive demonstrations. Preachers need to know that their own commitment to the gospel, their own faith in the gospel, their own joy and confidence in the gospel, should be evident in their sermons. Sermons become compelling not just when they are well organized and thoughtful, but also when they are given with an authentic enthusiasm for Christ.

The preacher is not only to model exhortation; the preacher is also to exhort brothers and sisters in faith to share in the exhortation. The preacher can be imaginative in describing how others can preach and teach. This can range from encouraging the congregation to share the teaching ministry of the congregation to inviting their witness to the gospel

---

1. Pheme Perkins, *The New Interpreter's Bible* (Nashville: Abingdon Press, 1995), 8:576.

Mark 4:21–25

Theological Perspective

the literature of virtue ethics. Virtue ethics has a long and distinguished history, including such eminent names as Aristotle and Thomas Aquinas. In recent decades, virtue ethicists have again explored character formation and the habits of faith. The storyline of a faithful Christian existence is one of countless small (and sometimes large) faithful decisions, actions, desires, and thoughts. It all adds up. Eugene Peterson expressed this in the title of one of his books: *A Long Obedience in the Same Direction*. The daunting challenge of persisting in the faith, day by day, is perhaps what prompted Peterson to comment, "Millions of people in our culture make decisions for Christ, but there is a dreadful attrition rate."[3]

This parable of the Measure illuminates the life of discipleship as a path with profound consequences. Faithful actions will grow more faithful actions. Those who squander their faith will lose even what they have. Fruitful hearers of the word are given to hear even more. Their ears and hearts and minds are tuned to the music of the gospel. Fruitless hearers of the word will gradually hear less and less. After a time, they will hear nothing at all.

This is not a threat; it is a description, a statement of what is. Although certainly there is an ominous tone of warning, this parable of the Measure intends to describe how discipleship happens. Practicing the virtues of hearing, obeying, and following will produce deeper virtues of hearing, obeying, and following. Ignoring those practices will lead to a complete loss of any ability at all. This is the life cycle of discipleship.

Both small parables speak to individuals and to communities. They illustrate the principle of small beginnings and great ends. The note of grace, even in the note of warning, is still unmistakable. God will disclose the hidden, shine light on the secret, and increase the measure. The believer is commanded to listen and follow.

LEANNE VAN DYK

Pastoral Perspective

be exposed to them. Through Jesus they were given access codes to the inner workings of the operating system, deeper insight into God's reign that the public did not yet perceive. With that deeper insight, a greater gift of opportunity and responsibility was also placed on the disciples: to work for the fruit of the harvest.

What opportunity does this present to a well-illuminated church today? What can those who are called to be disciples hope to see as they are given the insights and tools for an illuminating ministry? To what end do these parables point? In this sequence of Jesus' agricultural parables, all the planting and sprouting and growing of wheat point to one expectation: bearing fruit (*karpos*). The glory of the wheat comes when it bears fruit—"thirty and sixty and a hundredfold" (v. 20). The culmination of the plant's growth is when the wheat yields its fruit. For Jesus it is all about bearing fruit in the life of the disciples. These teachings are not simply agricultural advice; they shine a light on discipleship, and on the opportunity to bring forth the fruit that comes with the illumination.

God is in the multiplying business. To disciples who receive the gift of illumination, who pay attention well and receive the light, more will be given to them. That light is to be placed on the lampstand to dispel the darkness, to shine so that all can see. How sad it would be for the farmer if the farmer boasted of shiny shovels, maintained neatly furrowed rows, produced sturdy green plants, but produced no grain to feed the hungry people. Bearing fruit is the point. The gift of the light is given for sharing, to illuminate a world that hides in great darkness. What glory there can be when the harvest bears "fruit, thirty and sixty and a hundredfold."

STEVEN TOSHIO YAMAGUCHI

---

3. Eugene Peterson, *A Long Obedience in the Same Direction* (Downers Grove, IL: InterVarsity Press, 2000), 16.

Exegetical Perspective

the topic from the revelation itself to receiving (or not receiving) the revelation.

The saying about measures (v. 24) in the Markan context seems to suggest that the manner in which you "hear" the message will decide how much wisdom you will receive. There are "measure for measure" sayings in Matthew 7:2 and Luke 6:38, as part of the Sermons on the Mount and the Plain (and so probably from Q). There the context is warning against judging others too quickly and harshly; that is not the context here. Here the idea seems to be that those who truly "hear" the revelation—in the comprehensive sense of understanding it, welcoming and embracing it, and acting upon it (see 4:20)—will come to comprehend it even more. The promise of still more being "given" is another case of the divine passive construction; God is clearly the giver.

The final saying (v. 25) seems on the surface to be a version of our proverb "The rich get richer, and the poor get poorer." Here, of course, the context is not material goods or economics. Rather, it seems to be concerned with understanding the unfolding of the divine plan for the full coming of the kingdom of God. As in verse 24, the first part promises even greater wisdom to those who receive the revelation and act upon it. The second part ("from those who have nothing, even what they have will be taken away," v. 25) has been called the saddest line in the New Testament. The idea seems to be that those who pay little or no attention to the revelation of God's kingdom will eventually lose even what little knowledge they might have had.

A preacher might fashion a good sermon, or a teacher a good lesson, out of any one of these maxims, without paying much attention to the Markan context. However, if one wants to remain faithful to the Markan context, then these sayings encourage the hope that the day will come when the truth of Jesus' teachings about God's kingdom will be manifest to all. Our task now is to understand and act, as best we can, upon what he has already revealed to us.

DANIEL J. HARRINGTON

Homiletical Perspective

when opportunities arise in the world where they live and work. While the subject of evangelism can put people on the defensive, these verses in Mark leave us no option except to evangelize. Evangelism takes many forms. There is ample testimony to the compelling quality of a witness for Christ that happens when someone struggling hears the heartfelt witness of how Christ helped another navigate their own crisis. Such experiences suggest that evangelism as a winsome witness to Christ is far more useful than evangelism that is coercive.

The preacher can also embody the encouragement Jesus makes possible. As we are faithful in our proclamation, we live in hope that not only our own lives but also the life of the community of faith will be enriched. The question is what kind of enrichment will it be, especially in a congregation? So many congregations are small in numbers and seem almost trapped in their size. Some pastoral boldness is called for here. The promise of the text needs to be honored. The effective proclamation and practice of the news of the kingdom can draw other people into the life of a congregation. Working for the kingdom will hopefully bring others into that work. We need not be embarrassed by such a hope.

Yet the faithfulness of kingdom work is not determined simply by numbers of participants. In the end, the preacher needs to model and articulate the belief that our work for the kingdom is a form of devoted and intentional service, whatever the tangible results. At the heart of our ministry is the intent to be faithful to Christ and to the kingdom of God, not to the achievement of certain measurable results. The apostle Paul said some people will sow and others will reap. The image of a seed that grows mysteriously points to transformations that take time and are often not visible to the sower.

LAIRD J. STUART

Mark 4:26–29

²⁶He also said, "The kingdom of God is as if someone would scatter seed on the ground, ²⁷and would sleep and rise night and day, and the seed would sprout and grow, he does not know how. ²⁸The earth produces of itself, first the stalk, then the head, then the full grain in the head. ²⁹But when the grain is ripe, at once he goes in with his sickle, because the harvest has come."

Theological Perspective

The theology of God's reign weaves together strands of biblical teaching concerning creation, salvation, church, Christ, and final things, emerging as a theological tapestry all its own. The parables of the kingdom tease out some of these various theological threads, teaching us aggregately more than we would know about the kingdom from them individually.

With each of the "seed" parables, Jesus offers us a particular perspective on the nature of God's reign. Taken together, these parables help us comprehend important features of the kingdom landscape; yet each such parable also stands alone.

In our passage's brief parable of the harvest, several strands of kingdom theology's tapestry become evident upon reflection. The planting of the garden recalls the act of creation, involving both the preparation of a field and the sowing of a crop. There is a particular theater of action; seed is broadcast widely, but not infinitely. The creation story's night/day pattern echoes in the farmer's diurnal routine following the seeding process. A world of life is created that has a life of its own. It will realize its purpose in due time.

There is no hint in this parable that some of the grain is lost in the harvest—discarded as chaff according to the warning of John the Baptist in Matthew 3:12 and Luke 3:17 (a warning not voiced by the Baptist in Mark's Gospel). Nor does this parable

Pastoral Perspective

This little parable of "the seed growing secretly" is unique to the Gospel of Mark. It contains important lessons to affirm, instruct, and inspire the congregation in mission. In this parable we glimpse the internal logic of our individual and corporate witness. Our witness is integrally related to the nature of the kingdom of God. How the saving power of God has come into history and continues to be carried out in history is hidden from the natural eye. It seems foolish when compared with human wisdom. We who are beneficiaries of divine love have the wondrous privilege and responsibility to discern and join God's transforming work of grace that precedes us! Congregations in mission share faith through "*the process of spreading the gospel of the kingdom of God by word, deed, and sign in various contexts, through the power of the Holy Spirit*, and then waiting and watching in respectful humility and with expectant hope."[1]

"Scattering seed on the ground" is the responsibility of the church in mission. For there to be a harvest, we must establish relevant ministries that consistently express our love for God and neighbor. Furthermore, our missionary activities should be rooted in the conviction that God has taken the initiative to go before us to prepare the way for our witness. Our scattering

---

1. H. Eddie Fox and George Morris, *Faith Sharing*, rev. and expanded ed. (Nashville: Discipleship Resources, 2000), 55.

Exegetical Perspective

In these four verses, Mark continues his series of parables, returning to the seed imagery after a brief digression in verses 21–25 into lamp and measurement illustrations. Much like the main parable of this chapter, we have a seed, a planter, the process of growth discussed, and the final goal of ripening grain. Beyond those basic farming elements, however, this story has a very different shape. Unlike the story of verses 3–8, we are not presented with a variety of outcomes. In sharp contrast, we have the sense of a predestined outcome: the seed, once planted, will grow and give a harvest regardless of the farmer's understanding. We are given no sense that any outside factors affect the seed's growth: once scattered, it sprouts and grows, with no discussion of the farmer working on its behalf or the various soil types hindering that growth.

Actually, in a startling contrast to the initial parable of chapter 4, where certain soils hinder, here it is the soil *itself* that is said to cause the growth; *automatē*, "by itself" (v. 28), the soil brings forth fruit. So we have a very unusual parable where the soil and the seed do their work on their own, and the farmer is ignorant and seemingly irrelevant to much of the story. How do we read this ambiguous parable?[1]

---
1. See Claude N. Pavur, "The Grain Is Ripe: Parabolic Meaning in Mark 4:26–29," *Biblical Theology Bulletin* 18 (1987): 21–23, or David E. Garland, *Mark*, NIVAC (Grand Rapids: Zondervan, 1996), 177–79, for the diversity of interpretive options. Part of the difficulty is that this parable is unparalleled in the Synoptic tradition.

Homiletical Perspective

What a puzzle! Who scatters the seed? Is it God? Is it the disciples, is it the crowd—and by extension—is it *us*? Where is that part about going in with a sickle? These four vexing verses are in keeping with the literary, cultural, and christological context of Mark's Gospel. The *literary* setting is the little nest of parables in the fourth chapter, all of which use the metaphor of seeds and plants. This riddle is the parable in the middle. We must leap to chapter 12 to find another parable. The *cultural* context readily offers seeds as familiar details for a lesson about the kingdom of God. Jesus is speaking to an agrarian crowd. Just as the preacher today might reference popular television shows or issues with personal computers, Jesus is using an activity that most of his hearers would understand: planting a seed and watching it grow. Lastly, the Jesus in Mark's Gospel is keeping a *christological* secret: that he is the Messiah. It is in line with this secretiveness that Jesus teaches in parables so that hearers and readers may not understand at first. Likewise, we may not understand at first, especially in Mark's Gospel, where so much goes unsaid.

In the verses following the passage, Jesus talks about a specific kind of seed: a mustard seed. The multiple temptations may be to skip over the less familiar verses to get to the mustard seed; to read verses 26–29 only as a prelude to verses 30–34; or to

Mark 4:26–29

Theological Perspective

suggest that some parts of the field fail to produce appropriately, as does the previous parable at the beginning of Mark's fourth chapter. Here the issue is not final judgment but the mystery of growth.

The farmer presides over the entire process, from sowing until harvest. As both sower and reaper, the farmer harks to both Creator and Christ, the source and consummator of all things. The farmer also has the task of tending the field, watching and waiting while the life sown at creation comes to its place of fruition. Yet, in the story, the one tending the field has no idea how the crop grows. The story line has shifted the reference point from God to us, the parable's hearers, who do not know the secrets of the kingdom. The emergence of God's purposes is beyond both our understanding and our control.

Watching and waiting, we witness the inevitability of the Creator's purpose unfolding, until the field is ripe and the harvester comes to gather the grain and to separate it from hull and stalk. The dramatic arc of the parable has a specific beginning, a particular field of action, and it ends at a precise completion point. What we have here is not a general picture of things, but a story.

Here the kingdom of God is depicted as a story of God at work doing something—creating, watching, harvesting, saving. The action at any point along the way may be no more perceptible than the growth of flora—the text makes a point of underscoring the quotidian character of life as the kingdom emerges. Night and day, sleeping and rising, watching and waiting—this is the action line of God's reign progressing to its culmination.

The kingdom of God grows because of its inherent God-given nature, not because of the efforts of its custodians. We have here nothing like Paul's analogy where one servant plants and another waters. In the world of our parable, the church is in no position to determine the success of the kingdom. It simply looks for the fulfillment of what it receives as a field already sown. This relieves the church of an immense burden. It can do nothing to hasten the coming of the kingdom—its role is to await its consummation patiently, night and day.

This is no passive waiting. The church actively comes alongside the farmer—sowing seed, marking its progress, and preparing for its harvest. It also shares with the field the role of nourishing the life of the crop being grown for harvest. In addition, the church is surely at least part of the harvest. It turns out to be impossible to locate the church precisely in just one part of the story; the whole story is at one

Pastoral Perspective

of seed on the ground of human experience must bear witness to the gospel of peace.[2] We have not been commissioned to manipulate, dominate, or coerce people to join our fellowship of believers; neither is it necessary for new converts to accept a particular political perspective. Further, we must not reduce evangelistic efforts to culturally limited recruitment of members who "look like us."

Though it is true that we must scatter the seed by our words as well as our deeds, this parable also insists that we should be attentive to "the ground" on which the seed is scattered. Kingdom production is, in some sense, more about the earth than the seed. In our witness, we must pay attention to "the earth"—the personal and pastoral situation of our listeners and the social-cultural contexts that shape our congregants and our congregations. The famous dictum of the preacher having the Bible in one hand and the newspaper in the other is another way of expressing our need to pay attention to both "the seed" and "the ground." The ground of human experience is the arena of divine disclosure and of human response. People are free to accept, reject, or otherwise interpret our communication.

Christian servants who scatter seed on the ground of human experience "sleep and rise night and day" (v. 27). Our ministry involves inspection, evaluation, and assessment of the progress of the work that we share with the Triune God. On the other hand, it also suggests the need for us to take time for rest and engage in Sabbath practices of rest, renewal, reflection, and re-creation. As the farmer is aware of the dangers of soil erosion, we must guard against the erosion of our physical, mental, emotional, and spiritual capacities. We are admonished by the psalmist that "it is in vain that you rise up early and go late to rest, eating the bread of anxious toil; for he gives sleep to his beloved" (Ps. 127:2). Planning, implementation, and evaluation of our ministry are all important; however, the discipline of renewal combats our "eating the bread of anxious toil" in an age where people clamor for quick fixes and make ministers their scapegoats when specific and measurable results are not achieved on our timetables. Human efforts and achievements are in vain unless God is acknowledged as the ever-present source of help (Ps. 127:1–2).

The kingdom of God produces its fruit by its own internal power, a power that the sower does

---

2. Bryan B. Stone, *Evangelism after Christendom: The Theology and Practice of Christian Witness* (Grand Rapids: Brazos Press, 2007), 12.

Exegetical Perspective

First, it is worth noting the introductory statement to this parable. Verse 26 begins, "The kingdom of God is as follows." Given this very explicit parable setup, we immediately understand the rest of verses 26–29 as picturing *something* about the kingdom. No parable ever claims to tell the entirety of the story; instead, by teaching parable after parable, Jesus' hearers were given the opportunity to catch glimpses of different aspects of the kingdom. Having already issued in the first half of the chapter his stark warning to be good "hearers," now Jesus sharpens his focus to revealing the kingdom itself. No wonder the warning to be good hearers: if they misunderstand him now his audience risks missing the kingdom altogether. In Judea at the time of Jesus, between Zealots and Essenes, Pharisees and Romans, visions of the kingdom were diverse and often contradictory. Into this confused world, Jesus emerges with his own vision of the kingdom.

It may be worth considering this historical context for a moment longer. Ever since the Maccabees succeeded in ousting the Antiochenes from Israel, there was the sense among some other groups that they should *do* something to rid the land of the oppressors and that YHWH would support them in their endeavor. Some, like the bandits and later Zealots, sought to do this via violence, others, like the Essenes, through withdrawal and purity. Many of Jesus' listeners may have had some sense of what needed to be *done* in order to bring about the rule of God on earth.

In contrast, Jesus portrays the kingdom as coming without any effort or even knowledge on the part of the farmer. He goes through his daily life awaiting the seasons of the seed, sprout, stalk, and finally the head, waiting for the seed and soil to do their work. Perhaps Jesus was warning some of his hearers against presuming they knew how to bring about the kingdom on their time schedule and through their effort.

There is some confusion, of course, regarding the role of the farmer: in his scattering and harvesting roles he could be read in some divine fashion, but in his ignorance he cannot. The focus of the parable, however, is not on the relation of the sower to the seed, but on the seed itself and its growth *as the likeness to the kingdom*. The kingdom, Jesus seems to be emphasizing, will grow though it cannot be rushed or forced.

There is one more aspect to this parable. The first impulse when reading this parable today is to assume that the time of harvest is an exciting,

Homiletical Perspective

read them as a postlude to the parable of the Sower in verses 3–8. However, the Gospel of Mark never wastes a word; so let us consider what these agrarian words can say to a contemporary (probably urban) congregation.

One way to engage the text is to recognize the tension, to admit the mystery present here. Like many passages in the Bible, this parable is no simple users' manual for Christian life and practice: "Do this. Do not do that." As much as we might like a kind of *Discipleship for Dummies* unambiguous instruction, the written word and the Word incarnate do not always oblige. A faith statement of the former Presbyterian Church U.S. talks about it this way: "We need constantly to search out God's way in Scripture, not expecting detailed directions for every decision, but relying on the Word to tell us who God is, to press God's present claim on us, and to assure us of God's grace and comfort."[1]

First, what does this short parable tell us about who God is? It would be hard to believe that the one who scatters the seed is God. Verse 27 asserts that the one who scatters the seed watches it grow and sprout but "does not know how." How could the God who created all things not know how a seed grows? In Job, God asks: "Have you commanded the morning since your days began, and caused the dawn to know its place, so that it might take hold of the skirts of the earth?" (Job 38:12–13). So, if disciples, preachers, followers of Jesus—maybe you and me—are the ones who scatter the seed, God makes the seed grow. The Spirit brings the kingdom of God, not the farmer. So these verses tell us that God is powerful and in control.

Second, what is the present claim being made on us? Despite its puzzling nature, this parable can speak to us about how to nurture the Beloved Community. Two things shine through this little riddle: (1) we can scatter the seed and watch it grow, but it is not *our* work that makes it sprout and mature; (2) we will know when it is ready for harvest. In a roundabout way, Jesus seems to be saying that the seed will grow—we do not have to know how. There is a certainty in God's purpose, even if we do not understand it right now.

So what does this mean for us in the twenty-first century? In an age of decline for many mainline denominations, there is an anxiety that haunts congregations and denominational governing bodies.

---

1. *A Declaration of Faith*, the PCUS 1977, and reaffirmed as reliable by the PC(USA) in 1985, chap. 9, section 3, lines 47–51; available at https://www.pcusa.org/resource/declaration-faith/.

Mark 4:26–29

Theological Perspective

level the church's story, while it remains at a deeper level God's story of creation and salvation. Those two stories are inseparable.

While the entire story matters, the dramatic line lifts up two critical moments in the story, the daily wait and the final harvest. First, the daily wait. It is impossible to rush the kingdom. It will take its own time, and its advance is ordinarily imperceptible. Even when we do see real signs of its progress, like the first piercings of spring greenery through earth's crust, we cannot tell why it is growing, except that it is in its nature to do so. Its emergence is as irrepressible as it is unfathomable. The lesson is plain: God's kingdom is not ours to produce or to regulate. Our role is to wait, in that deeply biblical sense of waiting, that is, to pray unceasingly. The coming of the kingdom is something we participate most fully in by praying—by waiting on God.

Then finally comes the harvest. The important point here is that God—and God alone—determines the readiness of the crop and conducts its harvest. There is indeed a harvest, a climax and conclusion of the story; there is an *eschaton* toward which God's reign builds. The harvest is the ultimate reason for everything else in the story.

We can neither grow nor harvest the kingdom. As we watch and wait for its arrival by praying as our Savior taught us—*your kingdom come*—we do so with utter confidence that the harvest is indeed coming soon. The final force of the story for us is just this: keep good cheer, no matter our state or that of the world around us. The Lord reigns indeed!

SHELDON W. SORGE

Pastoral Perspective

not understand and does not control. The process is mysterious, hidden, ambiguous, and sometimes stressful and frustrating. Clergy (pastors, teachers, evangelists, missionaries) do not control how the kingdom grows. Specifically, this parable compares kingdom ministry with a farmer who is growing wheat. Farmers face many challenges related to the natural and social systems in which they operate. Just as soil erosion is the result of excessive plowing and must be avoided, so we must be aware of the erosion of people's receptivity to our witness that is a result of a shameful history of less than exemplary practices associated with missions and evangelism. Past and present practices of forced conversions, inquisitions, fraudulent television preachers, religious wars, crusades, genocide, colonization, and expansion of Western power throughout the world have contaminated the "ground" where we sow seeds. As a result, our context for ministry is a secular context that has rejected the church's ministry. Pastors must equip persons with the knowledge, skills, and motivation to inform, influence, convince, and invite persons who have been formed by a secular society to "be directly challenged by the gospel of explicit faith in Jesus Christ, with a view to embracing him as Savior, becoming a living member of his community, and being enlisted in his service of reconciliation, justice, and peace on earth."[3]

The final judgment is pictured in Revelation 14:14–20 as a reaping of the earth's harvest. At the culmination of the work of the people of God in the earth, God will be looking for justice and righteousness in the earth (Isa. 5:7). From our seemingly insignificant beginnings and sometimes meager results, we look for signs of God's kingdom, justice and righteousness, described metaphorically in the passage as "first the stalk, then the head, then the full grain in the head" (v. 28).

JEFFERY L. TRIBBLE SR.

---

3. David J. Bosch, "Evangelism: Theological Currents and Cross-Currents Today," in *The Study of Evangelism: Exploring a Missional Practice of the Church*, ed. Paul W. Chilcote and Laceye C. Warner (Grand Rapids: Eerdmans, 2008), 17.

Exegetical Perspective

positive time. In the Hebrew Bible and other parables, there is also a dark side. Most commentators agree that the final line in verse 29 is a reference to Joel 3:13, a text of judgment. Harvest is the time of separating the wheat from the chaff, the sheep from the goats, the righteous from the wicked. It is the time of decision in the kingdom. Joel warns, "Put in the sickle, for the harvest is ripe. Go in, tread, for the wine press is full. The vats overflow, for their wickedness is great" (Joel 3:13). There may well be a similar, implicit threat within this parable. The seed sprouts and grows, and it will bear fruit in accordance with its origin. If it is wickedness, that too is harvested, but destined for punishment. Harvest time is a time of sifting those who have borne the fruit they ought from those that have failed to attain maturity, or have failed to grow at all.

Alongside that warning, however, rests an equally great comfort: for those who hear, for those who receive the word (v. 20; cf. Jas. 1:21–25), this is not a parable of frantic work to somehow attain the kingdom. In contrast, for those who hear and receive, whether or not they understand how, the seed and the soil do their work, growing and bringing forth the full kernel. This is not simply personal piety, but the communal growth of God's word and kingdom throughout his people that brings them to fruition and enables a great harvest. For those who hear, the kingdom grows on its own in their midst. For those who close their ears, the kingdom will arrive as the time of judgment. Either way, the kingdom is not what they expect, for it begins with mere seeds and flourishes despite their not understanding how it happens, an apt illustration for a kingdom paradoxically confirmed in a crucifixion.

MARIAM J. KAMELL

Homiletical Perspective

We see it in ads for clergy: "Come grow our congregation. We are aging and want to attract young families. People do not get involved the way they used to." Denominational loyalty is a thing of the past.

This is where we come to that third way that Scripture is a gift to us. We are assured of "God's grace and comfort" in trusting that it is not we who make the seed grow. The kingdom of God—the Beloved Community—will be given. Jesus used this four-verse puzzle to reassure hearers that even if we do not understand or recognize it right now, the Spirit *will* bring fulfillment. God is sovereign.

The preacher can discern whether the congregation needs to rest in this assurance or whether they need to be challenged to go out and scatter more seed. Is the "present claim" of this text to stop fretting over changes in the congregation and denomination, trusting the Spirit to bring about the kingdom? Is its claim to call the congregation to scatter more seed, trusting the Spirit's work to bring folks into the faith—whether or not it turns out to be in our congregation or in our denomination?

In a time when faith sometimes gets equated with the certainty that "we" know God and are right and "they" do not know God and are wrong, the preacher can explore the role of mystery in our discipleship. The certainty glimpsed here is not one of clear dogma or ethics. It is a certainty that God is God, that we are called to play our part and let God do the rest.

In the worship service, hymns emphasizing the mystery of God, the work of the Spirit, the wonder of creation would all highlight important aspects of these verses. Possibilities are "All Good Gifts"; "For the Fruit of All Creation"; "God, You Spin the Whirling Planets"; and "God of the Sparrow."

LAURA S. SUGG

Mark 4:30–34

³⁰He also said, "With what can we compare the kingdom of God, or what parable will we use for it? ³¹It is like a mustard seed, which, when sown upon the ground, is the smallest of all the seeds on earth; ³²yet when it is sown it grows up and becomes the greatest of all shrubs, and puts forth large branches, so that the birds of the air can make nests in its shade."

³³With many such parables he spoke the word to them, as they were able to hear it; ³⁴he did not speak to them except in parables, but he explained everything in private to his disciples.

Theological Perspective

This triplet of seed parables continues with a final comparison between the kingdom of God and a tiny mustard seed that when sown grows into "the greatest of all the shrubs, and puts forth large branches, so that the birds of the air can make nests in its shade" (v. 32). Like the two parables that have preceded it, there are surprises lurking in the midst of this comparison between the kingdom, the seed, and its product.

William Placher reminds us that technically speaking, the mustard seed is not the smallest of the seeds. Botanists tell us this distinction belongs to the orchid.[1] Nevertheless, size matters. The great bush that rises out of the ground from the germination of the mustard seed will eventually produce a respectable shrub with branches that can support the nests of birds seeking shade. The tiny seed, one millimeter in diameter, produces a plant ten feet in height. It is a respectable bush but hardly a tree. To some extent, that is the point being made.

The parable can be interpreted as much by what it does not say as by what it does. What the tiny mustard seed does not produce is a mighty oak or a towering cedar. Ezekiel 17:23 has identified Israel's

---

1. William C. Placher, *Mark*, Belief: A Theological Commentary on the Bible, ed. Amy Plantiga Pauw and William C. Placher (Louisville, KY: Westminster John Knox Press, 2010), 73.

Pastoral Perspective

Recently, I received an unexpected message in my Facebook inbox that prompted reflection on pastoral experience that illustrates the parable of the Mustard Seed and the use of parables in the teaching of Jesus.

> Pastor Tribble, how are you? Did you used to pastor St. Andrews in Gary, Indiana? If you did, I know you most likely do not remember me. My family used to attend there under your leadership. James Hazel was my father. Brittany Francis was my aunt. I just want to say "Hi" and let you know [that] even as a child you encouraged me and I remember when you preached, "Do you know Jesus and have faith?" As a child, I didn't understand but I want you to know that in my adult life it has helped me get through a lot. Thank you.

At the time of this Facebook exchange, it had been fourteen years since I had served as pastor of St. Andrew African Methodist Episcopal Zion Church in Gary. It was my first pastoral charge. It was a humble beginning for a recent seminary graduate. On my first Sunday, there were only twenty worshipers in attendance. The pay was modest, but it was the best that the church could afford. The social problems were pervasive in a city with the reputation at that time of being "the murder capital of the nation." I was determined to give my best to the church and the community as a full-time pastor.

Exegetical Perspective

These five verses break into two sections: verses 30–32 give another parable of the kingdom, while verses 33–34 provide a conclusion to the entire series of parables in 4:3–32. The parable continues the seed imagery that has dominated the chapter, giving one final picture of the kingdom. It has the most elaborate introduction: "With what can we compare the kingdom of God, or what parable will we use for it?" (v. 30). From the brief "Listen" introducing the initial story of 4:3, Mark now provides a double introduction to emphasize this final parable's importance.

The verb *homoiōsōmen* ("be like"; "compare," v. 30 NRSV) appears only here in Mark, but it shows up repeatedly in the teaching sections of Matthew and Luke, including the parallels in Matthew 13:31–32 and Luke 13:18–19. While Matthew simplifies the introduction, Luke retains Mark's doubly emphatic prologue. With his question, Mark draws the hearer into the imaginative process of exploring the nature of the kingdom. Wright observes an echo here of Isaiah 40:18, which he explains is "not an accidental echo. [That] passage is all about a fresh vision of God."[1] Here also is a fresh vision of God's kingdom, come in the local ministry of an itinerant preacher

---

1. Tom Wright, *Mark for Everyone* (Louisville, KY: Westminster John Knox Press, 2004), 50.

Homiletical Perspective

Two different ideas jump from these five verses: big things can come from tiny beginnings, and Jesus chose to speak in parables to cloak his message.

The parable of the Mustard Seed is more accessible to us than some other parables. We see in creation that a small seed can grow into a large plant. Countless children's sermons have wee hands holding an acorn while talking about the mighty oak. People in areas where oaks do not grow might show the minute black seed that becomes the tall saguaro cactus, or twenty redwood seeds sitting on a dime. I still have a necklace that was my mother's—a little mustard seed in a marble-sized glass bubble. The preacher can focus on God's power to bring forth the beloved community from the acts of a few. The growth is not a personal thing. It is beneficial to many. The Gospels of Matthew and Luke have a second allusion to the mustard seed—this time about small faith doing great things. Mark has only this reference, and it emphasizes the development from a small beginning to a great thing that gives refuge to many. What small speck of hope will God turn into something beautiful for the world—in your life, in the life of your congregation, denomination, community?

Like the previous pericope, Mark's Jesus is reassuring the people that God's work *will* be done. The

Mark 4:30–34

Theological Perspective

expectation: "On the mountain height of Israel I will plant it, in order that it may produce boughs and bear fruit, and become a noble cedar. Under it every kind of bird will live; in the shade of its branches will nest winged creatures of every kind."

In light of that expectation, Luke and Matthew appear ill at ease with Mark's diminutive expectation. Luke forces the parable into Ezekiel's mold and says that the mustard seed grows into a tree (13:9). Matthew, on the other hand, combines Ezekiel and Mark, and explains that "when it has grown it is the greatest of shrubs and becomes a tree" (Matt. 13:32). Mark, the most spare, and the most botanically accurate, says the seed becomes a shrub.

Agnes Norfleet, in an unpublished paper on this text, notes that "by keeping it a shrub Mark is differentiating the kingdom Jesus proclaims from past prophetic dreams of glory and hope to be like the other nations."[2] In other words, the kingdom ushered in by Jesus is not the same as that which has been long awaited by Israel. The great and mighty cedar has given way in the gospel to a kingdom marked by a Messiah who is identified by lowliness, meekness, and humility. It may appear to his followers, who have held greater expectations for a Messiah than meekness, that if the kingdom is dawning in his life and work, it is indeed coming secretly.

The image of the nesting birds in the parable underscores the hospitality and inclusiveness of the kingdom that Jesus inaugurates. The spreading branches and leafy shade of the mustard shrub welcome those who wish to gather and nest there, providing shelter and invitation to all who would come. The sickle of the previous parable (4:29), the scorching heat (4:6) and thorny soil that choke the seedlings (4:7) are gone, so that this trilogy of parables ends on a positive note. The kingdom will not be a mighty cedar but a spreading shrub; not what we had expected as a symbol of power and strength, and yet a fitting image of a kingdom that will exceed the messianic expectations of Jesus' own people and welcome Gentile converts in due season.

The kingdom is like a mustard seed growing into a welcoming and hospitable shrub. That is the intentional description of the kingdom Jesus offers us. It is not what we expected, and yet there is a certain integrity to it that makes it irresistible, which is why the birds are attracted to it and make nests there.

Perhaps no parable has ever described so poignantly the dilemma faced by the church today.

---
2. Agnes Norfleet, "11th Sunday in Ordinary Time, Mark 4:26–34," privately published, The Moveable Feast Meeting. Decatur, GA (January 2012), 2.

Pastoral Perspective

The writer of this note is now a twenty-four-year-old confident Christian young woman who is active in her local church.

One of the gifts of social media is the communication that becomes possible when "old friends" unexpectedly "find" you. It is even more delightful when this communication is intergenerational and positive in nature. Years later, after leaving this pastoral charge, I was encouraged by the message that a Christian disciple can make a difference in a person's life in ways that they can scarcely imagine. The tiny seeds of ministry sown in this tough ministry context in urban America had not been in vain.

The lessons of Mark 4:30–34 resonate with these pastoral reflections. We should not judge the significance of the results of our ministries by the size of our beginnings. The mustard seed was proverbial for its smallness. Though it is not the smallest known seed, it was apparently the smallest seed with which Jesus' audience was familiar. Often, the focus of our interpretation of the parable of the Mustard Seed is the size of the tiny mustard seed. The central message is one of encouragement of disciples who become discouraged because of seemingly weak and significant beginnings. However, when we limit our focus to the size of the mustard seed, the interpretation of the parable becomes something like this: if a tiny mustard seed can become a great, hospitable, and protective plant for birds and other creatures of the earth, then know that in due time, your hard work for the kingdom will pay off!

A humorous Christian witness sweatshirt that I bought several years ago featured a picture of a "Salvation Express" card, designed to make obvious parallels with the American Express card and the benefits of having one. Playing off the American Express advertising message, "Membership Has Its Privileges," the sweatshirt conveyed an important message in a humorous way: "Keep working for the Lord. The pay isn't much, but the retirement plan is out of this world."

While this message of personal encouragement to keep an eternal perspective should not be discounted, we must be careful not to imply that the mustard seed grows into a great plant because of our hard work. The repetitions, of "sown" (vv. 31, 32) and of "upon the ground"/"on earth" in verse 31, suggest that the focus should not be on our hard work for God. The nature of the kingdom of God is mysterious. God's grace is at work within us, through us, and, often, despite us. God is at work in the world around us. The church is privileged to participate in

Exegetical Perspective

and carpenter. Those trained in hearing their Scriptures would recognize the similarly worded initial question (in the LXX, the verb *homoioō* is in the second-person plural rather than Mark's first-person plural), and would thus be engaged for new visions.

Mark's emphatic introduction to this parable is necessary because, more than any other parable so far, this one makes absolutely clear that the kingdom is not what the hearers might well want or anticipate. Rather, the nature of the kingdom is wholly unexpected. The mustard seed was possibly common in Jewish teaching as proverbially the smallest seed,[2] and verse 31 specifically highlights this diminutive state. So the mustard seed does not make a fitting analogy for the kingdom of God. To all expectation, God is already ruler of the world as well as its creator; so to compare it to something barely visible between thumb and forefinger makes no sense. Moreover, the mustard seed merely grows into a large shrub, not an imposing image by any stretch, although proportionally startling from the small size of its seed.

For people trained in the imagery of the proud cedar, this would be a shocking concluding parable. For instance, when he declared his faithfulness to Israel despite the king's rebellion, God promised in Ezekiel 17:23 regarding a branch from the king's tree: "On the mountain heights of Israel I will plant it; it will produce branches and bear fruit and become a splendid cedar. Birds of every kind will nest in it; they will find shelter in the shade of its branches" (NIV). It is the same imagery of safety, rest, and shade for the birds, except now instead of the proud cedar that dominates the landscape it is the wide-flung mustard shrub.

While his audience may look for the kingdom to come in ways that are recognizable and familiar (branch to cedar tree), a kingdom they can take pride in as noble and lofty, they are given a seed and a kitchen-garden shrub. Hence the necessity of the double introduction to the parable: "Listen closely, the kingdom is not what you expect. You may be looking for the branch of the righteous remnant to be vindicated by its full flourishing as a mighty tree that dominates everything around it. Instead I give you something smaller, a single seed that will grow far disproportionately to its size and provide the shelter you seek, but it will not be what you expect."

Jesus here uses the phrase "*kokkō sinapeōs*" for "seed of the mustard plant" ("mustard seed," v. 31 NRSV), narrowing the kingdom hope from a

2. See William L. Lane, *Mark*, NICNT (Grand Rapids: Eerdmans, 1974), 171.

Homiletical Perspective

gospel and God's kingdom will flourish. Right after this passage, Jesus stills the storm; then he goes on to heal the demoniac who is too strong for chains and shackles. This is a Messiah at peace in his surroundings—no matter how stormy, violent, or chaotic. He is, in family-systems parlance, a "nonanxious presence."[1] Does he speak to the crowds in parables to shield them from his unsettling call? Earlier in Mark, Jesus quotes Isaiah 6:9–11, saying everything comes in parables for outsiders so that "they may indeed look, but not perceive, and may indeed listen, but not understand" (4:12b). He has no need to be understood by the masses at this moment. He knows his purpose and the sacrificial path he will walk. For those he preaches to early in the Gospel, it is enough to speak in little stories. These stories make little sense in that immediate context, but he knows that when his earthly work is finished, they will be clearer.

Surely I am not the only one who bristles a bit at the idea of our Lord and Savior—God-with-us for the whole world—deciding to keep some things secret. Indeed, over the centuries some have understood this to mean that one needs special access to be a follower of Christ. The danger is to infer from these verses that there is some gnostic idea of "secret knowledge"—even now in the twenty-first century—possessed only by the lucky few. Some religious sects stress the need for a kind of password to obtain salvation. We often hear this kind of talk from a person who just happens to have access to the secret knowledge. All we need to do is buy this set of DVDs, contribute a percentage of our income, give up the ability to think for ourselves, and the locked gate will open. Preacher, beware of implying that you have all the answers.

The *good news* of the Gospel is that Mark does not end with chapter 4. We know the rest of the story. The first-century hearers of Mark's Gospel knew that Jesus healed, taught, was tried, crucified, died, and was buried. They and we have heard that when the two Marys and Salome went to the tomb, they found the stone rolled away and a man in white saying that Jesus was raised. Could that be why the earliest manuscript of Mark's Gospel ends with 16:8: "So they went out and fled from the tomb, for terror and amazement had seized them; and they said nothing to anyone, for they were afraid"? Is this Mark's typical taciturn way of saying only what is

1. For more on nonanxious presence and family systems in congregations, see Edwin H. Friedman, *Generation to Generation* (New York: Guilford Press, 2011).

Mark 4:30–34

Theological Perspective

Mainline denominations are in decline, hemorrhaging members on a yearly basis. "Success" in preaching the gospel is measured against megachurch models and prosperity-gospel standards. So perhaps it is time to rethink what it means to be faithful in sowing the seeds of the gospel. Is the faithfulness of the church to be measured against the North American model of corporate success, the Wal-Mart mold of undercutting the competition and putting everyone else out of business? Is there not something to be said for being faithful in preaching, teaching, and pastoral ministry, sowing the seeds of the kingdom in places and at times when the promise of a great harvest seems unlikely and the fields thorny? Perhaps it is not ours to know the eventual outcome of the seeds we sow; ours is simply to sow.

Surely this understanding of the gospel's secret growth is not that removed from the experience of those first disciples, whose dreams of seed planting imagined more cedars than shrubs. For those who went out to hear Jesus preach and teach, there was an expectation that he would usher in a new day of great change, and soon. How disappointing it must have been to hear instead a vision of a kingdom likened to a mustard seed's eventual growth into a shrub, or a seed, patiently planted and awaited day and night, growing to the harvest we know not when or how. Yet for those who could see such a promise in their mind's eye and hold such a promise in their heart's imagination, there would eventually be branches in which to nest and shade from the scorching heat.

JON M. WALTON

Pastoral Perspective

the mission of God. Thus a close reading of this parable suggests a need to place more attention on the transforming power of/in the earth. The tiny seed becomes a great bush only when it is sown upon the earth.[1] Though the church may be reluctant to engage popular culture and other "secular" spaces, these challenging sites of ministry may become "holy ground" where God's holy purposes are fulfilled.

We take our cue from the ministry of Jesus: "he spoke the word to them, *as they were able to hear* it" (v. 33, emphasis added). His approach to ministry and mission varied according to his audience. To "outsiders" as well as to children, he shared clear and compelling stories that revealed truths. Those truths invited each one to hear and act at the level of his or her understanding. To maturing disciples, who faithfully struggled to hear, understand, and respond to the messages of the kingdom of God inaugurated by Jesus, he devoted more time in private (v. 34). This implies his sharing with them not only the message of the good news of Jesus Christ (1:1), but also the depth of his life. The tiny mustard seed in this parable, when faithfully sown, will have transformative and productive results in the lives of persons, congregations, and communities. God can use our most meager seeds of ministry wondrously to accomplish God's rich and redemptive purpose. The kingdom of God may seem to have weak and insignificant beginnings, but a day will come when it will be great and powerful.

JEFFERY L. TRIBBLE SR.

---

1. Mary Ann Tolbert, notes on "The Gospel according to Mark," in *The New Interpreter's Bible, New Revised Standard Version with the Apocrypha* (Nashville: Abingdon Press, 2003), 1815.

Exegetical Perspective

remnant of the people to a singular seed, warning his audience not to be surprised or disappointed by the kingdom's seemingly insignificant beginning. The kingdom of God would not begin with conquest and glory, but a tiny seed. This beginning would be enough to fulfill the hopes expressed in Ezekiel of the birds being able to be housed, and to undo the damage expressed in Daniel 4:14, when the tree was destroyed and the birds scattered. Jesus' kingdom would fulfill all their expectations, but not in the way they expected.

Finally, what do we do with those final two verses of this passage, where Mark declares that Jesus taught only by parables? First, this clearly echoes back to the explanation of the initial parable of the chapter. In 4:11–12, Jesus makes clear that parables reveal the state of the hearers' hearts, whether they are blind like those in idolatry or they can perceive the truth being taught. His teaching was said to be "as much as they were able to hear or understand" ("as they were able to hear it," v. 33 NRSV), which indicates that Jesus did not do this spitefully to condemn those "outside," but rather as a wise teacher seeks to give his hearers what they need.

Moreover, there are clear indications in Mark that, even while he gave his disciples further instruction, they still did not fully understand. Jesus taught by parable so much for exactly the reasons given by the parables: his was not the kingdom his audience expected, and so ordinary teaching along common themes would not suffice to shock their imaginations awake to what was happening amid them.

Jesus taught "as they were able to hear," and thus Mark draws the sequence of parables to a close with another reminder that many who heard Jesus' words would refuse to understand, preferring instead a Messiah they could domesticate to their own visions of triumph, looking for the regal cedar tree. However, to the ones who responded to his call, the ones he called "his own," Jesus gave explanations to his illustrations. Despite their own lack of understanding (4:13), Jesus prepared them for the day they would comprehend and preach his unexpected kingdom to the world.

MARIAM J. KAMELL

Homiletical Perspective

needed—the messianic secret persisting, even after the first witnesses to the resurrection? One early manuscript adds this brief reassurance: "All that had been commanded them they told briefly to those around Peter. And afterward Jesus himself sent out through them, from east to west, the sacred and imperishable proclamation of eternal salvation."

Whether we are being charmed into understanding ourselves as "insiders," or the author believed Mark's Gospel to be sufficient without narratives about physical appearances by Jesus, the good news still lives in that metaphor of the tiny seed leading to a giant shrub that shelters the birds of the air. The "sacred and imperishable proclamation" goes out, even though only a handful of people were witnesses. In the twenty-first century, if we read our history, we know that this small group grew into a church of millions. Looking at the longer ending of Mark, they did as Jesus asked, proclaiming the good news "everywhere" (16:20).

One danger of latching onto the secrecy of parables is a hoarding of the good news of salvation. Reformers tried to change this by translating the Bible into the language of the people. They did this in part so that all could read (and pray, and confess) without clergy who monopolized some fictitious special knowledge or who tried to enforce one understanding or peddle salvation. Yes, many denominations still require specialized education for preachers and pastors, but the priesthood of all believers says that *all* of us can rest in the shade of the gospel. If we avoid the danger of secrecy, the gift is that all can know the gospel—Jesus' life, teachings, trial, crucifixion, *and* Christ's resurrection.

Suggested hymns about little things, the church, or the call to spread the gospel to the world include "Give Thanks, O Christian People," "All Things Bright and Beautiful," "Come Sing, O Church, in Joy!" "In Christ There Is No East or West," "O God of Earth and Space," "Called as Partners in Christ's Service."

LAURA S. SUGG

Mark 4:35–41

³⁵On that day, when evening had come, he said to them, "Let us go across to the other side." ³⁶And leaving the crowd behind, they took him with them in the boat, just as he was. Other boats were with him. ³⁷A great windstorm arose, and the waves beat into the boat, so that the boat was already being swamped. ³⁸But he was in the stern, asleep on the cushion; and they woke him up and said to him, "Teacher, do you not care that we are perishing?" ³⁹He woke up and rebuked the wind, and said to the sea, "Peace! Be still!" Then the wind ceased, and there was a dead calm. ⁴⁰He said to them, "Why are you afraid? Have you still no faith?" ⁴¹And they were filled with great awe and said to one another, "Who then is this, that even the wind and the sea obey him?"

Theological Perspective

This story is part of a carefully designed section of the Gospel that begins at 4:1 with the well-known parable of the Sower. After teaching that parable, Jesus draws his disciples aside and explains it to them line by line. He then tells a set of four more parables: the parable of a Lamp under a Bushel (4:21–23), the parable of the Measure (the one who has receives more; the one who has nothing loses even that; 4:24–25), the parable of the Low-maintenance Seed (4:26–29), and the parable of the Mustard Seed (4:30–32). After these parables are finished, Mark assures his readers that Jesus always explains everything to his disciples, setting us up to expect another line-by-line exegesis (4:33–34). Instead, there is a set of four stories describing four works of power. It seems clear that Mark intends us to hear these four events as the promised explanation for the four preceding parables.

The first of the four great works of power is found in this passage: the stilling of the storm. At the beginning of the story, Jesus is asleep. In Psalm 3, the psalmist says that he can lie down and sleep, even in the midst of his enemies, because God is his shield, his glory, and his sustainer. Similarly, Jesus is able to sleep here in the midst of a storm because of his abiding relationship with his Father through the Spirit.

Pastoral Perspective

When chaos threatens our lives and we are rendered helpless in its grip, fear and anxiety seize us. As people of faith, we cry out to the Jesus who promises to accompany us. Our cry sometimes reveals more about our fear than our faith. "Do you not care?" we shout. Jesus responds by asking us to choose faith over fear.

In this story, the long hours of a hot humid day are coming to a close. Jesus has spent the day teaching and tending to the needs of yet another large crowd gathered by the seashore. Settling into the quiet of the evening as the disciples row toward the opposite side of the Galilee, we can imagine the gentle waves rocking the exhausted Jesus into a deep slumber. He falls fast and soundly asleep, seemingly oblivious to the catastrophe that is about to unfold around him.

The disciples, like most of us, find the idea of Jesus *sleeping* through the moments of our lives when we are most in danger to be, frankly, astounding! Helpless and caught in the whirlwind, we want Jesus not only to be wide awake but at the helm taking control, ready to steer us through the difficult times. When we feel his absence, we become wracked with anxiety and fear.

Do you recall the first time you awoke at 3:00 a.m. gripped by worry? During a crisis we may lie awake

Exegetical Perspective

Mark links the dramatic story of Jesus' calming of the storm at sea with the preceding parables discourse (4:1–34) in several ways. The opening phrase, "On that day," refers to the same day on which Jesus taught the crowds about the kingdom of God. The antecedent of "them" in verse 35 is the disciples, who were just named as the recipients of privileged explanations of Jesus' teaching (4:34). The "boat" they now take to the other side is presumably the same boat that served as Jesus' pulpit when he taught in parables (4:2). Mark thereby suggests that the four mighty deeds that follow (4:35–5:43)—starting with the manifestation of Jesus' power over the stormy forces of chaos and darkness—are an integral part of his proclamation of the coming of God's kingdom (see 1:15).

The calming of the storm at sea follows the traditional form of a miracle story. After Mark establishes the setting, a problem emerges, in this case "a great windstorm" (v. 37) or powerful tempest. The details of the nighttime setting, of waves crashing and breaking into the boat, and of Jesus' deep sleep add to the calamity and terror of the disciples. Then the powerful word of the awakened Jesus intervenes (v. 39a) and produces "a great calm" (v. 39b, my trans.), which resolves the problem. The disciples' response (v. 41) verifies the miracle. These typical

Homiletical Perspective

The story that is Mark's Gospel unfolds like a classic tragedy, in which the main character is driven, inevitably, toward suffering and death. Each step in Jesus' journey establishes and reinforces this theme. To compound the tragedy, Mark depicts the disciples, Jesus' hand-chosen followers, as persistently dim, unable to grasp the significance of Jesus' teachings, actions, and ultimate end. At the same time, Mark also depicts Jesus as the mysterious bearer of the good news, the one who baptizes with the Holy Spirit, who performs signs and wonders, who heals and restores. In the midst of these signs of the arrival of the reign of God, only the demons and Jesus' executioner recognize him for who he is. Mark invites the readers to see to it that they do not follow in the faltering footsteps of Jesus' clueless disciples, but follow Jesus instead.

One challenge for the preacher lies in the fact that the Jesus of Mark's Gospel is mysterious and even distant as he leads his followers to suffering and death. This image of Jesus is not going to be terribly attractive to most congregations, and the preacher may be tempted to domesticate Mark's enigmatic Jesus. This temptation should be resisted, however, as the power of this Gospel lies in its complexity.

An example of Mark's complexity can be found in this account of Jesus calming the storm in the boat

Mark 4:35–41

Theological Perspective

He is awakened by his disciples, who ask, "Do you not care that we are perishing?" In response, Jesus opts to show rather than tell. He does not give a discourse on how he has taken the form of a servant for their sake, one that the disciples would have been ill equipped to understand. Instead, he demonstrates how much he cares about them and what he intends to do about it.

The storm is a time of chaos, the collapsing of the waters above and the waters below into one mass of water. It is an undoing of the first act of creation, which begins with the dividing of the waters (Gen. 1:6–8). When Jesus stills the storm, he is not only establishing himself as the Messiah who cares about the perishing of his disciples; he is also demonstrating that he is one with the Creator, who can divide the waters.

God's creative work is a call out of the chaos of nonbeing into real being. The trajectory for each creature is toward an increasingly real existence, in which we are more and more sharing in God's life, for God is the one who simply is Being, the one whose name is revealed to Moses as I AM (Exod. 3:14). The work of creation is a call from chaos into a life of fullness, of increased participation in God's own nature, in such a way that more and more of the creature's potential is realized.

We humans are made from both the dust of the earth and the breath of God, and therefore our calling is to stand as mediators between the natural and supernatural. We are to bring the rest of creation along on this trajectory into fullness of life: actualization, fruitfulness, and joy. That is our vocation. In the story of the fall, we reversed the trajectory; we turned around, deciding we liked it better back in chaos and nonbeing, and brought the creation down with us. Instead of exercising our priestly vocation to serve as "secretaries" of creation's praise,[1] we inserted our rebellion into the created world.

That rebellion ripples out in all sorts of ways, poisoning creation. The world now "groans" because of our sin (Rom. 8:22). The threatening storm over the sea, itself a biblical symbol for chaos, is a sign of creation's groaning collapse under the influence of human sin. When Jesus says, "Stop," he is reasserting his creative power and authority as Son of God. He is starting creation over again.

---

1. George Herbert, "Providence," in *The Temple*, 1633. http://www.ccel.org/h/herbert/temple/Providence.html ; accessed May 31, 2013: "Of all the creatures both in sea and land / Onely to Man thou hast made known thy wayes, / And put the penne alone into his hand, / And made him Secretarie of thy praise."

Pastoral Perspective

ruminating on our worst fears. At other times, what occupies our waking mind may be the list of many things waiting their turn for our attention. Underneath even these mundane worries lurks a deeper existential anxiety, one that asks, Am I enough? Strong enough? Good enough? Smart enough? These are the fears and anxieties we carry deep within us. We all have them, though they are closer to the surface at some times than at others. At the heart of all our anxious questions we are asking, Can I make it through life and all that threatens me?

While there is a distinction between anxiety and fear, often they become intertwined in ways that are difficult to separate. Fear may have an identifiable object of concern; the disciples fear being drowned when the boat breaks apart in the storm. Indeed, the question the disciples ask of Jesus—filled perhaps with equal measures indignation and bewilderment—conveys their *fear*: Do you not realize that we are about to die? However, the words the author chooses are steeped in *anxiety*: Do you not care that we are about to perish? The former is a question of survival; the latter is one of value. Jesus, are we not important enough for you to save us? Does God not care when our life is in chaos and the difficulty is more than we can bear?

"*Peace! Be still!*" With these words Jesus demonstrates his power to turn back the forces of nature. While this act might serve to confirm his role as the Son of God, it also, ironically, challenges the faith of many who are in the midst of their own raging storms when no such rebuke can yet be heard. Deep in our hearts we pray, perhaps expect, that God will intervene in the chaos unfolding around us. Sometimes the boat sinks anyway. Tragic loss ensues, slow degradation of the body or mind encroaches, the threshold of economic collapse moves ever closer, the faces of the hungry become our own. What do we do then? Where is Jesus then?

Jesus' answer is the same: *Peace, be still.* The object of Jesus' command is the disciples' fear as much as, perhaps more than, the elements of nature. What we learn to do with these words can shape our faith and our ability to embrace life in whatever situation we find ourselves. If we believe this story concerns only Jesus' ability to fix the chaos in our lives, then we will miss out on what it reveals about the deeper meaning of faith and so about a relationship of trust with God. Jesus asks us to have faith that whatever threatens us in the day or keeps us awake at night—even if our very life is under threat—cannot overcome the power of Jesus to bring peace and

Exegetical Perspective

elements of a miracle story are interrupted, however, by Jesus' challenge to his disciples, a point to which we will return below.

A number of scriptural passages lie in the background. One is Psalm 107:23–32, part of a psalm of deliverance. In this section, the psalmist recounts the experience of sea travelers who, in the midst of stormy winds, desperately cry out to God to save them. God responds by stilling the storm, hushing the waves, and bringing the travelers to safe haven. Mark 4:35–41 echoes several phrases and images from Psalm 107. The second passage is Jonah 1:4–15, where Jonah sleeps in a ship's hold during a tempest. The sailors' frantic plight is alleviated only after he is cast into the sea, which then ceases from raging.

While Jesus' sleeping during the storm recalls Jonah, there are significant differences between these two figures. Jesus' untroubled sleep (v. 38) shows forth his deep, abiding trust in God's power and protection. It also recalls the sleep of the farmer in the parable Jesus just told (4:26–29), the sleep that faithfully awaits God's creative work of nurturing the growth of the field and bringing it to harvest. This trust in God's power and protection contrasts with the panic and desperation of the disciples. However, the Markan passage reveals more than Jesus' trust in God.

Whereas Jonah is awakened and commanded to pray to his god for deliverance, upon being awakened, Jesus himself takes action. The verb translated "woke up" is intensive (*diegertheis* rather than the simple *egertheis*) and "conveys the image of Jesus rising to his full height on the stern of the boat in direct confrontation with the raging sea."[1] Raising himself against the storm, Jesus then rebukes the wind and sea: "Peace! Be still!" (v. 39). The verb "rebuke," the same verb used in connection with Jesus' casting out unclean spirits (e.g., 1:25; 9:25), connotes the belief that evil spirits were responsible for the tempest. In response to Jesus' command, the wind and sea obey (v. 41). Jesus reveals that he shares in God's power to still the storm-driven waters of chaos and to deliver those who cry out to him for deliverance. The episode therefore functions as a theophany, a manifestation of the divine presence and power in Jesus.

As is often the case in Mark's Gospel, Christology and discipleship are intricately intertwined here. Between the calming of the storm and its attestation by witnesses, Jesus asks two rhetorical questions of

Homiletical Perspective

with the disciples. It is one of two Markan stories that show Jesus as commander of natural forces (see 6:45–52, where Jesus appears walking on the water). In both stories, Jesus' demonstrations of great power fill the disciples with fear, but understanding eludes them.

The preacher may be tempted to assume a perspective superior to that of the disciples: "See: Jesus' own disciples misunderstand him, but we are not so stupid today!" While this may be satisfying to hear, it misses the complexity Mark has embedded in this story: that we too often fail to recognize the power of the gospel. Both Jesus' persistent demonstration of the mystery of God and Jesus' followers' persistent inability to grasp the mystery run like an undercurrent throughout Mark's Gospel.

This leads us to an even more challenging point: the mystery of the gospel is deliberately hidden from view. In the previous chapter, Jesus quotes Isaiah to explain his use of obscure parables: "they may look, but not perceive, and may indeed listen, but not understand; so that they may not turn again and be forgiven" (4:12). If the mystery of the gospel is purposefully hidden from the multitudes (itself a troubling idea), Jesus does attempt to explain to the disciples. Ironically, even then they fail to understand.

Again, this hidden gospel is difficult to preach. However, the power in Mark's perspective is to be found in his experience of the inscrutability of God. This is our experience as well. The human struggle to understand God is ongoing, and urgent. Mark provides a sympathetic, albeit not terribly encouraging, perspective on this struggle.

The account of the stilling of the storm is a case in point. This story is familiar to most hearers, having been included in countless children's Bibles and storybooks, and made the subject of innumerable artistic representations and musical interpretations. We instinctively identify with the frightened disciples in the boat: swamped, abandoned by the one who is expected to care for and protect them, even though they are finally saved by that same person. It seems to be a simple story with a happy conclusion. "Put your hand in the hand of the man who stilled the waters . . ."[1]

When we lean in closely, the story raises more questions than it answers. Jesus has just given a series of fairly disturbing parables to a crowd so large that he must take to a boat while the crowd gathers

---

1. John R. Donahue and Daniel J. Harrington, *The Gospel of Mark* (Collegeville, MN: Liturgical Press, 2002), 158.

1. Gene MacLellan, "Put Your Hand in the Hand," accessed March 9, 2014, http://www.youtube.com/watch?v-ZjS19m3vXsw.

Mark 4:35–41

Theological Perspective

This theme is continued in the remaining three works of power. The next work is the rescue of a man who has lost his humanity, who is surrounded by the symbols of sin and uncleanness—the old Adam personified. The third work is the healing of a woman who has a continual flow of blood, so that she has lost her power of fertility and is perpetually unclean, not allowed to approach her husband or her God. Finally, a child who has died is brought back to life. At the end of this series of four works, the new creation begun with the stilling of the storm has borne fruit in a new Adam, a new Eve, and a new promise for the generations that come after.

As it turns out, this is what the parables of chapter 4 are about. They all concern something that starts small and becomes great. This is the creation design, the trajectory that God intends for us, the potential that God—the Great Sower—has sown into creatures. Jesus is restoring this creation trajectory, starting a new creation with his coming, making it possible for us to be the people we were designed to be. Jesus himself is one who has become small, who has been sown into the world, and who is now fulfilling the trajectory of human creation, while also manifesting the fullness of God's glory.

No wonder Jesus chooses not to talk about the four parables to his disciples. They would never believe him, if he simply claimed to be the creating Logos. Even having witnessed his actions, the disciples are baffled, asking each other who he can be. The answer is pretty clear: he is the Son of God. This is a hard answer for them to accept. How can the Son of God be here in this boat, on this sea, telling us stories, and taking a nap? Of course, that is the good news: Jesus, the Son of God, is with us—right here in the boat.

LAURA A. SMIT

Pastoral Perspective

strength. The God who routinely upends all that we expect is able to transform our fear into courage.

A couple in their thirties rushed to the emergency room after receiving news that their teenage daughter had been injured while playing on a tire swing. The child arrived with a critical head injury sustained when the tree holding the swing fell on her. On his knees, the father prayed for God to heal his daughter from this crushing brain injury. A devout Christian, he asked, "Where are you, God? *Do you not care that our child is about to perish?*" The doctors came to say they had done everything within their power—she was not going to survive—and now was their chance to say good-bye. With faith-filled strength, they let go of their expectation that God would "fix" their daughter, that God would spare them from the heartbreaking chaos. Instead, they stepped into it and gathered her broken body in their arms, surrounded her with their love, and spoke the words she needed to hear: "Go to Jesus. He is waiting for you. *Peace, be still.*"

If our expectations of Jesus are elevated, his expectation of us clearly is even higher. It is reasonable to be afraid of that which causes harm to our physical bodies or creates mental anguish. Jesus is very aware that asking us to let go of those we love, to stand strong in the face of what threatens us, or to stave off the anxiety that consumes us, is hard. It may seem more than we can manage. Nonetheless Jesus boldly asks the disciples, "*Why are you afraid? Have you still no faith?*" (v. 40). Jesus is asking them, and us, to step into faith, even when we are afraid. Think about why you are afraid, he asks. Think and choose: fear or faith in me? Choose me, he says. It is not just a choice—it is an extraordinary choice.

M. JAN HOLTON

Exegetical Perspective

his disciples: "Why are you afraid? Have you still no faith?" (v. 40). Comparing two details of Mark's account with that of Matthew reveals the shortcomings of the disciples in the former. First, in Mark the disciples take Jesus into the boat (v. 36); in doing so, they are shown to fail in the primary task of discipleship, namely, to *follow* Jesus (cf. Matt. 8:23). Second, in Mark the disciples seem to doubt Jesus' care for them and his ability to save ("Teacher, do you not care that we are perishing?" v. 38), which differs from the prayer they utter in Matthew 8:25 ("Lord, save us!"). Jesus' questions in verse 40 thus challenge the disciples to place their trust in him. Indeed, the Markan Jesus often contrasts faith and fear (e.g., 5:36—"Do not fear, only believe"). The problem with fear is that it leads people to turn in on themselves and on their inadequacies. Jesus calls his disciples to keep their eyes fixed on him and to trust that he will protect them and provide what they need.

How do the disciples respond? The beginning of verse 41 reads, literally, "And they feared [with] a great fear"! (my trans.). Commentators have taken this in two ways. One way is to read the verse as signaling that the disciples remain entrapped in their fear. That is, they turn in on themselves and are unable to see and appreciate who Jesus reveals himself to be. In this way of reading, Jesus' action of producing "a great calm" (my trans.) from "a great windstorm" only results in "great fear"!

However, the noun *phobos* and the verb *phobeomai* can also refer to "awe" and "marvel." So another way to interpret the disciples' reaction is that they are in awe of what they witness. Even more, they marvel at the presence of the one who can quell the wind and sea with only a word of command. This is "fear of the Lord" in the salutary sense. In the biblical tradition, such fear is the beginning of wisdom. The ambiguity of the opening words of the final verse can function as a summons from Jesus today, one that calls us forth from paralyzing fear to liberating, awe-filled trust in him and the power of his word to save.

THOMAS D. STEGMAN, SJ

Homiletical Perspective

around the lakeshore: the parable of the Sower, only one-fourth of whose seed grows and increases; the parable of the Lamp that shines and exposes; the parable of the Mysterious Nature of Growth and Harvest; the parable of the Mustard Seed. Every one of these parables implies that the gospel is both mysterious and apparent, bearing both promise and judgment. At the conclusion of these sayings, Jesus proposes that they cross the sea in their boat. When, in the middle of the voyage, a storm arises, Jesus' ability to sleep through the violent storm seems to arouse the disciples' ire: "Do you not care that we are going to die?" (v. 38, my trans.).

Many classical commentators also seem troubled by Jesus' apparent indifference, and interpret it as a deliberate means of testing the faith of the disciples. Since the disciples' lack of faith and understanding is amply demonstrated throughout the Gospel, this interpretation seems strained. Even so, after the disciples wake him, Jesus rebukes first the storm and then the disciples: "Have you still no faith?" The answer, tragically, is no; they wonder (again) who he is.

The homiletical possibilities of this narrative, rich in complexity, narrative tension, and irony, are many. The preacher will want to make the most of the drama of the story, while drawing hearers into a deeper reflection on its challenges. The complex issues include these:

1. Mark, who writes self-consciously to the reader, is not simply retelling a history, but assuming that the readers are part of the story. What is our part then? Do we follow, and fail, like the disciples? Where and when do we risk missing the revelation of the mystery of the gospel?

2. One of the disciples' chief failings is their assumption that they deserve rewards for following Jesus. They clearly expect Jesus to protect them from suffering, but the entire movement of this Gospel demonstrates the inevitability of suffering. Do we share Mark's interpretation of Jesus as sufferer and the life of a follower of Jesus as a life of suffering?

3. Jesus charges the disciples for their fear as well as their lack of faith. How do we respond to fear? How does faith deal with fear? Can fear ever be overcome in this life?

MARJORIE PROCTER-SMITH

Mark 5:1–20

¹They came to the other side of the sea, to the country of the Gerasenes. ²And when he had stepped out of the boat, immediately a man out of the tombs with an unclean spirit met him. ³He lived among the tombs; and no one could restrain him any more, even with a chain; ⁴for he had often been restrained with shackles and chains, but the chains he wrenched apart, and the shackles he broke in pieces; and no one had the strength to subdue him. ⁵Night and day among the tombs and on the mountains he was always howling and bruising himself with stones. ⁶When he saw Jesus from a distance, he ran and bowed down before him; ⁷and he shouted at the top of his voice, "What have you to do with me, Jesus, Son of the Most High God? I adjure you by God, do not torment me." ⁸For he had said to him, "Come out of the man, you unclean spirit!" ⁹Then Jesus asked him, "What is your name?" He replied, "My name is Legion; for we are many." ¹⁰He begged him earnestly not to send them out of the country. ¹¹Now there on the hillside a great herd of swine was feeding; ¹²and the unclean spirits begged him, "Send us into the swine; let us enter them." ¹³So he

Theological Perspective

The book of Revelation tells us that there is no sea in the new creation (Rev. 21:1), because in the Bible the sea is a symbol of disorder, chaos, and nonbeing. As Jesus and the disciples emerge from the sea at the beginning of this passage, they discover a man with an unclean spirit living in an unclean place (the tombs, the place of the dead) in a Gentile (and therefore unclean) country. Jesus is visiting a place of comprehensive uncleanness. The man who lives there has been reduced to a state of self-destruction. Whereas the demons who are in the man speak to Jesus, the man himself is incapable of speech.

We see this man as a symbol of the fall, the undoing of creation's design for human beings. In the second story of creation in Genesis, the first thing that Adam does is speak. He names the world around him (Gen. 2:19–20). That is one way he reflects the image of God about which the first creation story speaks (Gen. 1:27). This man in Mark 5 cannot name anything. He can only howl. He has given his voice over to the demonic power inside him. When Adam was created, God breathed into him. This man has surrendered the spirit of God in him and instead is possessed by a spirit of uncleanness. This is a man who has lost his humanity.

The system of ritual cleanness and uncleanness in the Old Testament is about preserving ritual access

Pastoral Perspective

We cannot hide from Jesus. He searches for us whether we are shunned by the world or locked in isolation by actions of our own making. He will find us. No matter what we may have done, Jesus meets us with compassion and embraces the good within us.

Jesus chooses as his next port of call a graveyard—a ghastly, lonely place quite unlike the crowded villages along his journey thus far. Here Jesus' compassion draws him toward one man, isolated and alienated from family and community. The author tells us no less than three times that the man lives "among the tombs," a place marginalized by custom and culture. Perched atop the mountain, the man from afar sees Jesus coming. Bruised, bleeding, and nearly naked, he bounds down to meet the boat.

The author focuses these verses on the dialogue between Jesus and the demon, though we must remain aware of a third presence, the man himself. Separating the man from the demon creates a difficult tension. How does this story help us negotiate our understanding of the way forces beyond our control meet with our own actions to create suffering and despair? Subtle undertones of the text help remind us that ultimately the two are intimately bound.

Immediately Jesus knows the reason for the man's suffering and calls out the evil he recognizes. The

gave them permission. And the unclean spirits came out and entered the swine; and the herd, numbering about two thousand, rushed down the steep bank into the sea, and were drowned in the sea.

¹⁴The swineherds ran off and told it in the city and in the country. Then people came to see what it was that had happened. ¹⁵They came to Jesus and saw the demoniac sitting there, clothed and in his right mind, the very man who had had the legion; and they were afraid. ¹⁶Those who had seen what had happened to the demoniac and to the swine reported it. ¹⁷Then they began to beg Jesus to leave their neighborhood. ¹⁸As he was getting into the boat, the man who had been possessed by demons begged him that he might be with him. ¹⁹But Jesus refused, and said to him, "Go home to your friends, and tell them how much the Lord has done for you, and what mercy he has shown you." ²⁰And he went away and began to proclaim in the Decapolis how much Jesus had done for him; and everyone was amazed.

Exegetical Perspective

Mark's account of Jesus' casting out a legion of demons in Gentile territory is the second of a series of four powerful actions he performs in 4:35–5:43. Following the stilling of the chaotic forces of nature and sea (4:35–41), Jesus now manifests his authority over the demonic realm. He then goes on to reveal his power over incurable illness (5:25–34) and over death itself (5:21–24, 35–43). Through these mighty deeds Jesus continues his work of proclaiming and inaugurating the kingdom of God.

The present passage follows the standard pattern of an exorcism story: an introduction of the plight of the person possessed (vv. 1–5); a description of the encounter between exorcist and demon(s) (vv. 6–13); and a report of the healing and its verification (vv. 14–17). What distinguishes this particular exorcism story is that Mark offers several elaborate details that greatly heighten the drama of Jesus' manifestation of power. Mark also adds a brief commissioning scene at the end (vv. 18–20).

The introduction of the story links it to the preceding account. Arrival at "the other side" (v. 1) picks up the notice in 4:35; Jesus has safely guided the disciples across the Sea of Galilee. They now disembark in the country of the Gerasenes. For the first time in Mark's Gospel, Jesus is in Gentile territory (in the area of the Decapolis). He is suddenly

Homiletical Perspective

It would be difficult to invent a story with more drama, suspense, violence, and irony than the story of the man possessed by demons in Mark 5. For the preacher, especially the preacher who has a flair for the dramatic, this text is almost too rich in possibilities.

The enigmatic character of Jesus stands at the center of the story, but the demoniac has all the best lines, and certainly the most dramatic stage business. His character and behavior are clearly delineated by the author of Mark's Gospel: he lives among the tombs, which even in a modern-day context is a horrific place to be; he has superhuman strength, and is able to break shackles and evade all sorts of human restraints; he is dramatically self-destructive and demonstrative, "howling and bruising himself with stones," as the NRSV (v. 5) puts it. In short, he is like a character in a bloody horror flick, an object of both fear and fascination.

When Jesus enters the scene, the demoniac responds in what readers would already expect to be a dramatic manner. He shouts out, naming Jesus as Son of God, and demanding that Jesus leave him alone, although at this point in the narrative, the reader is not aware that Jesus is bothering him at all. Mark minimizes Jesus' presumably dramatic demand to come out of the man, addressed to the unclean

Mark 5:1–20

Theological Perspective

to God. Those who are unclean are not allowed to come into the presence of the holy God. They must first be rendered clean again. This man is not only consumed by uncleanness; he is possessed by demons, which means that he is utterly and completely alienated from God. He cannot come to God in worship. He seemingly cannot approach God or expect to hear from God. Nevertheless, this is the man whom Jesus approaches. Here Jesus demonstrates both that the man is not beyond God's reach and that Jesus himself cannot be polluted, harmed, or lessened by his uncleanness. This is the great classical doctrine of divine impassibility: we cannot harm God. Jesus can take whatever uncleanness he encounters, both to bear and to banish it. That is what he does in this story. He sends the unclean spirits into the unclean animals and then sends the whole mess into the watery chaos.

It is interesting that this man cannot be chained. In many ways he looks like the freest person imaginable, since nothing can confine him. However, the inability to be confined shows us that he is in fact enslaved, not free at all. He has lost all humanity, lost his voice, and lost his name—all defining qualities that include limits. The gift Jesus gives him is to restore him to his right mind. The result of that gift is an apparent curtailing of his freedom, since he is now under obedience to Jesus. He is constrained by the will of Jesus. He wants to come with Jesus, but Jesus tells him no, and he must obey. That obedience may look less free than his former state of being unchained, but in fact in obedience to Jesus he has found his freedom.

The ending of the story may at first seem rather sad, since Jesus sends the man away. Yet he is sent to be a missionary to the surrounding Greek cities. By the beginning of Mark 8, at the beginning of the Gentile outreach when Jesus comes back to the Decapolis, there are four thousand people gathered to hear him. Where do those four thousand people come from? Perhaps in part from this very man, who has been preaching, wandering about, and telling people what Jesus has done for him. This once-broken and now-healed man is the mustard seed sown out into the world.

Interestingly there are others who encounter Jesus in all his creative power and react quite differently. When the townspeople come out to see what is happening among the tombs, they ask Jesus to go away. There is something in each of us that is repelled by the work that Jesus does, rather than drawn to it. We say, "Please go away and leave us alone," instead

Pastoral Perspective

demon engages Jesus in a dialogue: "What have you to do with me?" Then, perhaps expecting Jesus to exact retribution for the years of torment inflicted upon the poor man, he begs, "Do not torment me." Fear drives the demoniac toward Jesus, but love and compassion for the man draws Jesus to confront the demons. The community no longer even attempts to see the human beneath the bizarre demonic behavior, while Jesus never loses sight of him.

Nothing in this encounter is subtle. The urgency, excitement, and panic are clear: the man *ran* and *bowed* and *shouted*. Why, he asks Jesus, am I the object of your attention? Jesus searches for us, sees us, and knows us—good, bad, ugly, and everything in between. There is nothing we can hide from Jesus, even if we are successful at hiding it from others and ourselves. We search for this depth of knowing that draws us intimately into relationship with one another and God, but we fear finding it, because it means revealing our true selves.

No longer able to live with those who once loved him, the man now roams among the dead. In an amazing feat of strength he has broken the shackles that perhaps were intended to keep him from hurting himself. A few years ago I had a National Public Radio (NPR) "driveway moment" while listening to the tragic story of a refugee family who had fled war in central Africa. They were forced to tie a beloved uncle who was suffering from mental illness to a tree during the day to prevent wandering that might lead to his becoming injured or lost. It is heartbreaking when loving care means confining another in his or her suffering. When we are lost, even from those who love us the most, it is Jesus who can reach through what binds us to offer comfort and hope.

Jesus, already aware of the answer, demands the demon surrender his name: "What is your name?" One must come to the point of naming—openly acknowledging—addiction, destructive behavior, or anything the keeps us alienated from living toward the full possibility of the flourishing for which we were created. Legion does not attempt to deceive Jesus. "I am not one but many," he says. When we finally come to a point of being as isolated and lonely as this man living among the tombs, there is rarely only one cause. Tragedy, especially of our own making, unfolds in layers and affects a large circle of people around us.

Many years ago I worked as the live-in crisis-intervention employee at a transitional living facility for women who were homeless due to some combination of incarceration, addiction, and mental

Exegetical Perspective

encountered by a man "with an unclean spirit" (v. 2), The possessed man's plight is the most fully depicted in all the Gospels. Three times we are told that he lives among the tombs (probably burial places cut into the mountains). He roams about like a wild animal, howling day and night. Attempts to shackle him with chains and fetters have failed. Feared and now avoided by all, he inflicts self-harm, bruising himself with stones. Mark thus makes abundantly clear that "the demons have stripped this man of every shred of humanity."[1]

As has been the case previously (1:24; 3:11), the unclean spirit recognizes who Jesus is, both his name and his true identity, "Son of the Most High God" (v. 7). In an ironic twist, the demoniac even attempts to take the role of exorcist by invoking God's name ("I adjure you by God," v. 7). Jesus wrests the initiative from the unclean spirit and takes control of the situation. Because knowledge of a demon's name gives one power over it, Jesus demands the unclean spirit to reveal its name. It immediately does so: "Legion." The term is a Latin loanword and refers to a large military unit of approximately six thousand soldiers. The name reveals why the man was so tormented: he was possessed by "many" demons (v. 9). Legion then tries to negotiate with Jesus, begging him not to destroy them but to send them into a herd of swine. The notice of swine in the area is another indication that the action takes place in Gentile territory (Jews were forbidden to keep pigs). Combined with the earlier references to "tombs," Mark not so subtly suggests that, from a purity perspective, the setting is unremittingly polluted.

Jesus permits the demons to enter the herd, which totals "about two thousand" (v. 13). The result is that they immediately thunder toward the sea and tumble into it. Both demons and swine are destroyed in the depths of the sea, over which Jesus has just shown mastery (4:35–41). The terrifying image thereby illustrates Jesus' power over formidable, death-dealing demonic forces. He is truly the "stronger one" who defeats Satan and his dominions (3:27). The removal of the demons and swine also conveys (at least from a Jewish perspective) that the coming of God's kingdom transforms *all* of creation.

The healing of the formerly possessed man is demonstrated by a point-by-point contrast with his prior condition (v. 15). Rather than running to and fro, he is now calmly seated; rather than

---

1. Pheme Perkins, "The Gospel of Mark: Introduction, Commentary, and Reflections," in *The New Interpreter's Bible*, ed. L. E. Keck et al. (Nashville: Abingdon Press, 1995), 8:583.

Homiletical Perspective

spirit, by adding, almost casually, that Jesus' demand prompted the demoniac's public naming of Jesus. At this point, the reader will notice that not only does the demoniac get all the most exciting stage business; he also holds the spotlight throughout the story. The dramatic climax comes when the invading spirits are sent out of the man and into a conveniently nearby herd of swine that thereupon races over the bank to be drowned in the sea.

Unlike a horror movie, this story has a happy ending (except for the swine, of course), when the formerly possessed man is later seen decently garbed and coherent. The whole event provokes fear in the observers, who beg Jesus to leave town, while the recovered demoniac begs to join Jesus' followers. Instead of accepting the man as a disciple or forbidding him to tell anyone about the healing, Jesus sends him home to tell of the wonders God has done for him. To the end, the demoniac is at center stage, and Jesus plays the supporting role. It is interesting to compare this story of the healing of a demoniac with a parallel story in Mark 1:21–28. This earlier story, which takes place in the synagogue, is considerably less dramatic and intense. It is also notable that those present in the first event react not with fear but with awe: they are impressed with Jesus' wonderworking skills, and the event bolsters his reputation in the region, keeping the readers' focus firmly on Jesus as the lead actor, so to speak.

The literary structure of this story raises some interesting possibilities for the preacher. For those trained in storytelling, this is a text well suited to a first-person dramatic sermon, in which the preacher could take on one of several roles: the lead role of the demoniac, the supporting character of Jesus (although, given the elusive and enigmatic character of Mark's Jesus, this would be tricky), a member of the town that responds to the demoniac's recovery, or even (for the very creative and daring preacher) one of the swine.

The dramatic tension of the story depends on several rhetorical strategies that the preacher would do well to keep in mind. First, the story depends on the notions of insider/outsider. The demoniac is the classical outsider, as indicated by his living among the tombs (abode of the dead and place that is ritually unclean), his antisocial behavior (his refusal to submit to human restraints), his self-destructive actions, and, most interestingly, his public announcement of Jesus' identity as "Son of the Most High." That this confession is made by one possessed by "unclean spirits" rather than by religious leaders or

Mark 5:1–20

Theological Perspective

of saying with the healed man, "Please let me come with you." We would often prefer for Jesus to love us and let us remain just as we are, in our unclean state of subhumanity, but Jesus does not offer grace alone; he also insists on offering healing.

It is very tempting to explain away the demonic presence in this story with a naturalistic explanation, speculating about medical conditions that might have been mysterious to first-century people and labeled as demon possession. That approach is a mistake. We ought not reduce the explanation of our sin and our misery to naturalistic forces. This man has given up the spirit of God, which is a supernatural spirit, and that spirit has been replaced by another supernatural spirit, a demonic spirit. There are two ways to misunderstand that. One way is to become obsessed with demons, see them everywhere, and think that demon possession is constant. The other way is to think that it is nowhere and that it does not happen at all. This second way is a particular temptation for most of us. While it may be true that demonic work in the world is more subtle and less dramatic today than it was in the time of Jesus, the book of Revelation suggests another reason that Satan is not as evident today. Just as in Mark Jesus sends the demons into the sea, so too the risen Christ binds Satan, limiting his power as it was not limited before. Even so, until the first heaven and the first earth are passed away and there is no more sea (Rev. 21:1), the limits of demonic power in the world will continue to be the work of those who would call people to freedom and fullness of life that is obedience to Jesus Christ.

LAURA A. SMIT

Pastoral Perspective

illness. One night, Sarah,[1] a beautiful young woman of deep faith and a much-beloved long-term resident who held the house record of twelve months' sobriety, relapsed. She returned to the house high on her drug of choice, crack cocaine. The effects of crack can be quite dramatic. It took two police officers to restrain this otherwise gentle woman from harming other residents. Handcuffed, she lay on the floor literally foaming at the mouth. With little else I could do to offer comfort, I gently stroked her hair and told her that everything was going to be all right.

It was a sad moment for the other residents, peering through the doorway. They had tears in their eyes as they watched the one person they believed was going to make it through recovery suddenly back in the chains of her addiction. If she relapsed, what hope did they have? Sarah was taken to jail and returned two days later with little memory of the event. I do not remember anything, she said, except a hand stroking my hair and someone telling me it will be all right. She was convinced that it was God who was able to use the hands of another to break through the harrowing effects of the cocaine and to bring hope when all felt lost. Jesus shows compassion by reaching through even the worst of what we do, while believing always in what we can become.

Jesus sees even the demons with a measure of mercy and compassion. For the second time Legion asks for mercy: "Do not banish us." Legion recognizes that they cannot live on their own. Demons, both those of the fanciful variety and the nagging ones that chase us through life, must feed like parasites off the spirit and flesh of another. "Let us enter into the herd of swine." Acknowledging Jesus' power, Legion asks, "Send us"; acknowledging that every act of surrender requires one's will, Jesus "gave them permission" (v. 13). Healing from what binds us requires both acknowledging God's power to save us and surrendering what holds us.

M. JAN HOLTON

---

1. All names have been changed for purposes of confidentiality.

Exegetical Perspective

bearing broken fetters, he is now fully clothed; rather than shrieking madly, he is now in his right mind. Moreover, he is now in the company of Jesus (and, presumably, the disciples), thereby ending his social alienation and isolation. Mark's word portrait powerfully conveys the restoration of the man's dignity and humanity.

Interestingly, the man's healing is not a cause of celebration for all. Swineherds who witnessed the strange events go to the city (i.e., Gerasa) and surrounding countryside to report what they have seen. A crowd gathers around Jesus and the healed man. The people's response is fear. Their fear prevents them from seeing and appreciating the implications of the newness of life Jesus has brought about in their midst. Indeed, after hearing the eyewitnesses' report about what happened to the demoniac and to the swine, the people "began to beg Jesus to leave" from their midst (v. 17). Jesus' first foray into Gentile territory is not welcomed. However, as the closing verses show, the gospel will be proclaimed and received there.

As Jesus gets into the boat to return to Galilee, the healed man wants to go along; he begs that he might "be with" Jesus (v. 18). In fact, "being with Jesus" is the distinguishing mark of those whom Jesus calls (3:14). However, Jesus refuses the man's request. This detail makes the point that it is only Jesus who initiates the call to discipleship. Nevertheless, Jesus *does* have a mission for the man: he is to go through the Decapolis and announce what the "Lord" (*kyrios*)—referring to God—has done for him (v. 19). The man does just that; notice, though, that he proclaims what *Jesus* has done. In making this proclamation, the man prepares the way for Jesus' later ministry in Gentile territory, a ministry that bears fruit (7:24–8:10, esp. 7:31). He also anticipates the time when good news will come forth from another tomb—namely, the empty tomb of the risen Jesus (16:1–7)—at which point the gospel is to be preached to all peoples (13:10). By bearing witness to the mercy shown to him by God through Christ, the healed man serves as a model for Christians of every time and place.

THOMAS D. STEGMAN, SJ

Homiletical Perspective

the disciples raises many interesting questions about the nature of faith and of religious inspiration. It also draws attention to Mark's use of irony throughout the Gospel. Jesus is consistently misunderstood by those closest to him and recognized by outsiders.

Another strong motif in the story is the use of fear. In this case, the townspeople, who might be expected to rejoice in the recovery and restoration of the demoniac to his right mind, instead react with fear and rejection. They beg Jesus to leave their neighborhood, ironically echoing the cry of the unclean spirits for Jesus to leave them alone. That Jesus' mighty acts provoke fear rather than awe and worship raises challenging questions about the nature of our own fears and rejections, and suggests that God may be found at work in events that we find frightening or even repellent. One might even consider the possibility that we, like the unclean spirits and the townspeople, might prefer that the Holy One leave us alone and not disturb us.

Liturgically, this text offers some interesting possibilities when connected with baptism. Water serves as the boundary that Jesus crosses ("the sea") to enter the territory of the Gerasenes (there are geographical problems with this part of the narrative, so it is best to understand Jesus' crossing of the sea in a poetic or narrative sense rather than as a strictly historical account). Water also serves as the receptacle of the unclean spirits in the form of the vast herd of swine. It is by means of water that Jesus comes to the demoniac among the tombs, and it is by means of water that Jesus restores the demoniac to life.

Finally, as a consequence of his restoration, the former demoniac, now relieved of his unclean spirits, is given (one might say) a new, clean spirit and charged to proclaim the mercy he has received to all who will hear him. In this movement from separation to restoration, from death to life, and from incoherence and self-destruction to an announcement of the good news of new life and grace, one might discern the baptismal pattern itself.

MARJORIE PROCTER-SMITH

Mark 5:21–24a, 35–43

²¹When Jesus had crossed again in the boat to the other side, a great crowd gathered around him; and he was by the sea. ²²Then one of the leaders of the synagogue named Jairus came and, when he saw him, fell at his feet ²³and begged him repeatedly, "My little daughter is at the point of death. Come and lay your hands on her, so that she may be made well, and live." ²⁴So he went with him. . . .

³⁵While he was still speaking, some people came from the leader's house to say, "Your daughter is dead. Why trouble the teacher any further?" ³⁶But overhearing what they said, Jesus said to the leader of the synagogue, "Do not fear, only believe." ³⁷He allowed no one to follow him except Peter, James, and John, the brother of James. ³⁸When they came to the house of the leader of the synagogue, he saw a commotion, people weeping and wailing loudly. ³⁹When he had entered, he said to them, "Why do you make a commotion and weep? The child is not dead but sleeping." ⁴⁰And they laughed at him. Then he put them all outside, and took the child's father and mother and those who were with him, and went in where the child was. ⁴¹He took her by the hand and said to her, "Talitha cum," which means, "Little girl, get up!" ⁴²And immediately the girl got up and began to walk about (she was twelve years of age). At this they were overcome with amazement. ⁴³He strictly ordered them that no one should know this, and told them to give her something to eat.

Theological Perspective

The stories of Jairus's daughter and the menstruating woman, joined by Mark's device of intercalation, should be read together, for they illumine one another theologically. Both stories are miracle stories, of course, and belong to Mark's proclamation of the power of God that will be finally confirmed by the resurrection of Jesus and the coming "kingdom of God." Jesus announced that kingdom, and he made its power felt, made the future present, in his miracles. In these two stories Jesus displayed already God's final triumph over death and over its power to threaten alienation from our own flesh, from our communities, and from God. So, "do not fear" (v. 36), but trust in the grace and power of God.

Both stories are also, of course, stories of women, and belong to Mark's focus on Jesus' regard for and attention to women. Most of the women in Mark's stories (e.g., the poor widow of 12:41–44, the Syrophoenician woman of 7:24–30) did not count for much as the world counted, but they counted with Jesus! He announced that in the good future of God "many who are first will be last, and the last will be first" (10:31), and he enacted that reversal in his treatment of these women. To remember Jesus and to follow him is still to put sexism aside.

The two stories are linked together, moreover, by the "twelve years" they share (vv. 25, 42). The woman

Pastoral Perspective

Mark uses the word "boat" eighteen times in his Gospel: three occurrences in chapter 5 and six in the next chapter. Every time Mark uses "boat," listen for lessons that prepare disciples to become the church.

The Bible's first physical symbol for the community of faith is the ark (Gen. 6–8). The ark was God's gift to carry God's people through the storms of life. Life on the ark was like life in the church: if the storm were not so fierce on the outside, people would refuse to endure the confusion on the inside.

Boats in Jesus' day were fragile vessels—and a common means of transportation. As this chapter opens, Jesus is calling and training disciples, and he is challenging entrenched religious leaders of the day. Boats and seacoasts, like the synagogue, are places where people meet God.

Pause for a moment. Ponder the scene; reflect on what Mark's words are saying to us. In chapter 5, Mark tells disjointed stories of people drawn to Jesus. One story tumbles on top of another. At the beginning, Jesus steps out of a boat and encounters the Gerasene demoniac. As our passage begins, he is back in a boat and off to the other side. Enter Jairus, leader of the synagogue. The Jairus story is interrupted by a hemorrhaging woman. Jesus encounters human crisis upon crisis. Mark is describing life in the church, is he not?

Exegetical Perspective

This episode contains motifs that are central to Mark's Gospel. As he does elsewhere (e.g., 11:12–22), Mark brackets one story (Jesus' healing of the bleeding woman) between the beginning and conclusion of another (the healing of Jairus's daughter) and invites us to interpret them in light of each other. Each episode features the healing of a girl/woman through physical touch.

Physical Touch and Ritual Impurity. Jesus heals the young girl by "taking her hand" (v. 41), an act of physical touch whose significance is illumined by Numbers 19:11–13:

> Those who *touch* the dead body of any human being shall be unclean seven days. They shall purify themselves with the water on the third day and on the seventh day, and so be clean; but if they do not purify themselves on the third day and on the seventh day, they will not become clean. All who *touch* a corpse, the body of a human being who has died, and do not purify themselves, defile the tabernacle of the Lord; such persons shall be cut off from Israel. Since water for cleansing was not dashed on them, they remain unclean; their uncleanness is still on them. (emphasis mine)

According to Numbers 19, the act of touching described in Mark 5 would transmit the ritual (not

Homiletical Perspective

Mark combines the story of Jairus and his daughter with that of the woman suffering from hemorrhages through intercalation, and what Mark has joined together the preacher should not put asunder. These stories ought to be read and interpreted together. Still, focusing this discussion (and perhaps the sermon) on the story of the synagogue leader is one good way into the concerns of the larger literary unit.

Evidently Jairus has not checked the official synagogue leader e-mail listserv recently, or he would know that Jesus is blacklisted (3:1–6). Maybe he did get the memo but has decided to risk his reputation on the chance that this traveling healer can save his sick daughter. If this is an act of desperation on Jairus's part, he is probably not in good practice. With the subtlety and economy that narrative affords, Mark lets us know what kind of person this is. Unlike most characters in the Gospel, he is important enough to have a name the reader might recognize. He is a man in a man's world, holds a respected position that implies both wealth and religious enfranchisement, and owns an unusually large house, with a separate room in which his daughter may convalesce. This is a person accustomed to getting what he wants. Transposing Jairus into our context we can make some educated guesses about

Mark 5:21–24a, 35–43

Theological Perspective

had been menstruating for as long as the girl had been alive. She had been ritually unclean, cut off ritually from the holy congregation of God's people by her flow of blood for all that time (Lev. 19–20). The "little girl" was twelve, the age Jewish girls become marriageable, the age they begin to menstruate. The good future Jesus made present in these miracles restored the woman to good health, to regular periods, and restored the little girl to life —and to embodied life *as a woman*. God's cause, the cause we are to serve, is not otherworldly; it reaches into our embodiment and includes the human flourishing we call "health," including women's health.

The stories are linked again by the threat of Jesus being rendered "unclean," first by the touch of the menstruating woman and then by his touching the corpse of Jairus's daughter. Here, as in the rest of Mark's Gospel (e.g., 1:40–42; 2:15–3:6; 7:1–23), Jesus shows himself to be carefree about ritual purity when a neighbor is in need. Jesus was ready to "get down and dirty" in order to exalt the humiliated and to restore the "unclean" to community.

Finally, the stories are linked by the audacious hope of Jairus and the woman. Both hope against hope that there is someone there who can hear a desperate cry and answer it, or feel an anguished touch and respond to it. There *is* someone. His name is Jesus. Here and throughout Mark, it is clear that faith comes before the miracle; but before faith, there is the promise of God to renew the creation—and us. God hears the lamenting cry and is touched by human anguish. In Jesus, God's promised future makes its love and power present. That is what faith looks toward, at first desperately, in the end confidently, but always audaciously.

For all that these stories have in common, however, the difference between Jairus's daughter and the menstruating woman is significant to Mark's intercalation and the theological import of the story. The little girl has a public advocate, her father Jairus, "one of the leaders of the synagogue" (v. 22). He is to be counted one of the "first" of the nation, and therefore he can come before Jesus. The menstruating woman, in contrast, has no advocate; she seems to be nobody's daughter. But on the way to Jairus's house, her anguished touch takes precedence over Jairus's desperate pleading. Jesus heals first the one who does not count for much; he makes the last first; he enacts God's preferential option for the poor.

Jesus makes the last first, but the first are not without hope. The grace of God is not a zero-sum game. The grace of God is more generous than that.

Pastoral Perspective

The passage brings to mind a day with two weddings, three hours apart. A few hours before the first wedding, word came that a friend was close to death. I raced to the hospital, spent time at my friend's bedside, and returned to church in time for the wedding—the wedding of the daughter of other good friends. I rejoiced in the celebration, explained why I would miss the reception, headed back to the hospital, just in time to be with the family as my friend died. I drove back for the second wedding, again skipping the reception in order to visit the family of the friend who had died and to make initial arrangements for the funeral.

Mark 5 understands that kind of day. Everybody wants a little bit of Jesus. Since pastors minister in Jesus' name, some days everybody seems to want a little bit of us! People look to church for many reasons. Help in crisis is often one of them; celebration is another. How church deals with people in the heights and the depths of human experience is crucial to ministry.

With this dynamic in mind, focus on Jairus. Jairus is drawn to Jesus because of deep need; Jairus is drawn by the crowd surrounding Jesus, drawn by this fellowship of inquirers and believers.

Note two great pastoral truths that Mark proclaims. First, the church of Jesus Christ is a ministry of presence: being with people amid the celebrations and the crises of life is at the heart of Christlike ministry.

Jairus wanted Jesus to heal his daughter, whom Jairus believed to be dying. Jesus wanted to lead Jairus to trust God's presence in Jairus's life and in the life of his daughter. Jesus went with Jairus. Pay attention to what Jesus wants for Jairus: faith in God's presence. The incarnation is not a miracle we believe; the incarnation is a presence we experience, a presence we grow to trust. The incarnation reveals God's commitment to be present with us in the world.

Humans are likely to ask, how? How did Jesus heal the daughter? Mark's question is, who? Who is this man, this Son of God, who orders Jairus to believe and not fear? This man Jesus travels by boat and on foot; he draws others to himself. He is the center and the power of the church's presence. When the community that bears witness to him enables people to "see" Jesus as Mark "sees" him, fear will diminish, healing will occur. People will trust and believe; people will become witnesses that create church.

Second, note that, though the faith of those drawn to Jesus is important, the faith of Jesus is

Exegetical Perspective

moral) impurity of the girl's corpse to Jesus. Mark regularly highlights the physical contact and transmission of ritual impurity between Jesus and those whom he heals. Jesus initiates physical touch with five of the twelve people he heals: the leper (1:41), Jairus's daughter (5:41), the deaf man with a speech impediment (7:33), a blind man—whom Jesus touches at least three times—(8:23, 25), and the child with an unclean spirit (9:27). Mark specifies four times that there is physical contact between the bleeding woman and Jesus (vv. 27, 28, 30, 31). Touching occurs between Jesus and large groups of people he heals (3:10; 6:56), and "touch" (*haptō*) functions as a synonym for Jesus' healing activity (8:22).

Such touching is significant because many of the characters whom Jesus heals are ritually impure and capable of transmitting such impurity through physical contact. The Torah classifies these Markan characters as ritually unclean: the leper (Mark 1:40–45; Lev. 13:45–46), paralytic (Mark 2:1–12; Lev. 21:16–20), man with a withered hand (Mark 3:1–6; Lev. 21:16–20), Jairus's daughter (Mark 5:22–24a, 35–43; Num. 19:11–13), the bleeding woman (Mark 5:24–34; Lev. 15:25–27), and two blind men (8:22–26; 10:46–52; Lev. 21:16–20). The demoniac (Mark 5:1–20) and the man with a hearing and speech impediment (7:32–37) are also associated with uncleanness (cf. Lev. 21:16–20).

The implication would be clear to readers/hearers familiar with Torah: Jesus is willing to become ritually unclean in order to heal people (in some cases thereby restoring social outcasts to community). In the Bible, ritual impurity can sometimes result in social exclusion, for religious prohibition—such as when people with physical disabilities are prevented from entering the sanctuary—can have a social dimension (Lev. 21:16–20; cf. 2 Sam. 5:8). In other cases, social exclusion is explicit. Lepers "shall live alone," and their dwelling "shall be outside the camp" (Lev. 13:46). People placed "outside the camp" also include those with a "discharge" and those who touch a corpse (Num. 5:1–4). Gentiles are sometimes expressly prohibited from marrying Jews (Ezra 9:1–6) and excluded from the Jewish community (Neh. 13:1–3). That some Jewish groups held to forms of exclusion (whether idealized or practiced) is evident in Dead Sea Scrolls texts that prohibit persons with physical disabilities from participating in a wide range of activities.[1]

Although Jesus demonstrates an ability to heal from a distance (7:29–30), he prefers to touch. Jesus is willing to become ritually impure and physically intimate,

1. See, e.g., 11QT^a 45:12–14; 1QS^a 2:3–10; 1QM 7:4–5; 4QMMT B 49–54.

Homiletical Perspective

his life. He has an advanced degree, a crossover SUV with excellent crash safety ratings, a nice house in the suburbs, and a 401(k) that has been showing signs of recovery lately. Gated community? Possibly. Health insurance? Certainly. He is chairman of the board at church. There is no judgment in any of it. Who would not be this insulated from chaos if they could manage it? However, chaos finds a way in eventually.

By the time we meet Jairus, the illusion of control has been dispelled. He has been urgently looking for Jesus ever since news came that the healer was back on the proper side of the sea. When Jairus gets his chance, we see signs of both desperation ("fell at his feet," "begged him repeatedly") and hints that this is still the guy who knows how to get what he wants in life. The request is both eloquent and detailed in its expectations: "My little daughter is at the point of death. Come and lay your hands on her, so that she may be made well, and live" (v. 23).

Jesus cooperates and for a brief moment it looks like things may go Jairus's way, as always. In the Hollywood version of this story, this is where the music swells and the camera pans and zooms out to show the grand parade: crowd and disciples press around the healer as he begins to follow after the worthy father, urging him toward a house in the distance, where a sick child awaits his healing touch. Things are looking good. We have seen this movie before.

There is, however, a wrinkle in this plot. The soaring orchestral strings give way to a sudden jolting needle-on-record scratch. There is some kind of disturbance in the crowd, and for the first time in the story Jesus is speaking: "Who touched my clothes?" (v. 30). It is a crazy thing to say. He is looking all around as if it might be difficult to find someone who has brushed against him in this crush of people. The disciples get the line here, but that may be because Mark was not allowed to print what Jairus said. "How can you say, 'Who touched you?'" they ask, "Who *didn't*?" (v. 31).

Jairus might be forgiven for wondering if this were really the time for such a debate. Even when it becomes clear just how extraordinary the touch is that grabs Jesus' attention, some impatience on Jairus's part would be understandable. After all, this woman is just as healed, whether Jesus stops everything to process the experience publicly or not. For that matter, she has been sick for twelve years. Why the big hurry to solve all of her problems now? There is an urgent matter at the house.

Mark 5:21–24a, 35–43

Theological Perspective

Jairus may be counted among the "first," but it was a good sign when he "fell at [Jesus'] feet" (v. 22) and humbled himself. To be sure, the situation suddenly looks hopeless when word comes that Jairus's daughter has died. Now Jesus rather than Jairus takes the initiative against that hopelessness. "Do not fear, only believe," he says (v. 36), and resumes the journey to Jairus's house, accompanied by Peter, James, and John. They are met at the house by the sounds of keening, and when he tells the mourners that the little girl is "not dead but sleeping" (v. 39), his words seem laughable (v. 40). She is not sleeping; she is dead. The dead are dead, and so they laugh.

As it turns out, this is the hilariously good news: God will not let death have the last word. Jesus takes the dead little girl by the hand and makes real and present the power of God that will raise him—and all of us—from the dead. He says, "Get up!" (v. 41). She does! The little girl "got up." It prompted "amazement" (v. 42), of course, for the dead are dead—unless God's love is stronger than death.

This little girl was raised from death to become a woman. It was not yet the final victory. She was raised to die again, but could live as one that knew death would not have the last word. She was raised to life as a woman, a position with its burdens in a patriarchal society, but now she knew something of a better "kin-dom." Suddenly a whole new world of kinship is opened to her—and to Jairus. She has brothers and sisters among those who would follow Jesus, among those who welcome "the kin-dom of God" that he promised, a community who would love and honor her as "sister," who would be the advocates for this poor child of God. The formation of a community of mutual love and care reveals the heart of Jesus and is at the heart of his message and performance of God's good future.

ALLEN VERHEY

Pastoral Perspective

more crucial. What Jesus believes about Jairus and his daughter outweighs what Jairus believes about Jesus or his daughter.

Friends come to Jairus, telling Jairus not to trouble Jesus anymore, because the daughter is dead. Jesus responds, "Do not fear; only believe" (v. 36). Off he goes to Jairus's home: faith in action.

No disciple can do what Jesus did with Jairus's daughter. Nevertheless, disciples are called to follow Jesus, to bear witness to Jesus, to be like Jesus. Discipleship is faith in action. As disciples, we believe God can use us, even us, whether we are ordained ministers, Stephen ministers, or faithful friends. God uses us when we touch the wounds of others in Christlike ways.

Mission trips to Haiti have created personal experiences of this truth. Recently, a friend about to go to Haiti for the first time asked for insights she might expect. I replied, "There is sacred joy in Haiti that defies explanation. Any illusion that we can help Haiti as a whole soon disappears; however, the gift of human presence is life-giving to those we visit. Even more amazing is the power of being in the presence of Haitians, of receiving their friendship and experiencing the ways their faith can transform our life."

Is that not the miracle of church as Mark proclaims it? In the midst of great need, Jesus shows up. He does not heal every sick person or reconcile every estranged relationship. However, in his presence church is born, people are transformed, disciples are trained. By Jesus' Spirit, the fragile boat called church sets sail and keeps sailing. The message painted on its sail is "Do not fear, only believe." Believe that God is with us. Believe that God is for us. Believe that God can use us—yes, even us—and others. As we go forth to be used by God, we will be changed, changed from people of fear to people of faith—Christlike faith.

Now, go and feed those brought to life by his presence. Do not talk about church. *Be* the church, God's vessel for a hurting, scared, and weary world.

ART ROSS

Exegetical Perspective

evidenced by putting his fingers into the ears of a deaf man, and touching the man's tongue (7:32–37).

Touching is a means by which Jesus acknowledges a person's humanity and validates his or her bodily existence.[2] This touching counteracts the isolation that some of these characters might have experienced, given their ritually unclean status. Such touching reflects a physical Jesus, whose healing activity brings him into contact with other human bodies and corrects perceptions—pervasive in the history of the church—of Jesus as a spiritual being. Foucault's quip ("the soul is the prison of the body")—an accurate characterization of much of the history of the church—is not true of Mark's Jesus.[3]

Secrecy Commands and Jesus' Identity. The story concludes with Jesus "strictly ordering" those who observe the healing that "no one should know" about it (v. 43). This order is one of eight secrecy commands Jesus gives in Mark. Such commands are always given in reference either to Jesus' identity (1:24–25, 34; 3:11–12; 8:29–30; 9:9) or his healings (1:43–44; 5:43; 7:36). The seriousness of the commands is underscored by the severe manner in which Jesus sometimes gives them; on three occasions Jesus "strictly orders" (*diastellomai*) people not to speak of what they witness (5:43; 7:36; 9:9).

The placement of every secrecy command in the first half of Mark's Gospel is a clue to their rhetorical intent. Jesus' healing activity culminates in Peter's confession of Jesus as the Christ (8:29), which elicits from Jesus yet another secrecy command (8:30). Immediately after commanding Peter not to tell anyone that he is the Christ, Jesus offers the first of three explicit predictions of his death and—in stark contrast to the secrecy commands—speaks about his death "quite openly" (8:31–32). Mark associates Jesus' identity as the Christ and Son of God with his suffering and death, not with his healings/miracles. The absence of secrecy commands in the second half of Mark corresponds with an elimination of healings/miracles (after 10:46–52) and a focus upon Jesus' future suffering and death. The centurion's confession of Jesus as Son of God (15:39) requires no secrecy command, because it occurs when he is suffering and dying.

MATTHEW S. RINDGE

Homiletical Perspective

For Mark's Jesus, the healing itself is not the only point, not the only urgent point, not even the main point. We saw this back in Capernaum with the paralytic lowered through the roof (2:1–12). "Your sins are forgiven," Jesus told him. What about the paralysis? "Okay, that too." From the beginning Jesus has understood his mission differently from those around him (1:32–39). This is one of the scariest things about Jesus: he does not always want exactly what we want. In our story, Jesus stops the parade to make a different kind of contact with the woman who has claimed physical healing through physical touch. Jesus wants to know who touched him because he has relational business with her, which is even more pressing than her disease, or even the little girl's deathly illness. He claims the woman as "daughter" and clarifies the cause of her healing: it is her faith in him, not magic, that has made this happen.

At just this moment, Jairus's worst fears are realized at last. News comes from the house that the girl is dead. Jesus overhears this verdict and turns from congratulating the woman's faith to challenging Jairus's: "Do not fear, only believe" (v. 36). Perhaps the disturbance caused by the woman was not a distraction from Jesus' main business with Jairus after all. What Jairus needs is not Jesus' immediate and undivided attention. What Jairus needs is the faith in Jesus this woman has just modeled.

By the story's end, things are back to normal at Jairus's house in the suburbs. The chaos has been averted. All is well that ends well. For now. Of course, even the ultrasafe SUV in the garage, the fence around the subdivision, and the premium health insurance will not be able to hold back the chaos forever. A day is surely coming when the illusion of control will be dispelled again. If Jairus has learned his lesson well, he will know what to do. He will remember what the main point is, whether or not Jesus can be persuaded to come around again and put everything back just the way it was: "Do not fear, only believe."

LANCE PAPE

---

2. For contemporary ethical implications of Jesus' healings in Mark, see Matthew S. Rindge, "Mark's Gospel, Social Outcasts, and Modern Slavery," *Journal of Lutheran Ethics* 10:6 (June 2010). http://www.elca.org/What-We-Believe/Social-Issues/Journal-of-Lutheran-Ethics/Issues/June-2010/Marks-Gospel-Social-Outcasts-and-Modern-Slavery.aspx.
3. Michel Foucault, *Surveiller et punir: Naissance de la Prison* (Paris: Gallimard, 1975), 34.

Mark 5:24b–34

24b And a large crowd followed him and pressed in on him. 25 Now there was a woman who had been suffering from hemorrhages for twelve years. 26 She had endured much under many physicians, and had spent all that she had; and she was no better, but rather grew worse. 27 She had heard about Jesus, and came up behind him in the crowd and touched his cloak, 28 for she said, "If I but touch his clothes, I will be made well." 29 Immediately her hemorrhage stopped; and she felt in her body that she was healed of her disease. 30 Immediately aware that power had gone forth from him, Jesus turned about in the crowd and said, "Who touched my clothes?" 31 And his disciples said to him, "You see the crowd pressing in on you; how can you say, 'Who touched me?'" 32 He looked all around to see who had done it. 33 But the woman, knowing what had happened to her, came in fear and trembling, fell down before him, and told him the whole truth. 34 He said to her, "Daughter, your faith has made you well; go in peace, and be healed of your disease."

Theological Perspective

As contemporary Christians, we would like to think that we have made significant strides in how we view the sick and infirm. However, we are more like Jesus' first-century companions than we would care to admit. Although few people today associate seizures with demon possession, individually and as a society we continue to isolate and ignore our ill and disabled. Sometimes out of necessity, sometimes for convenience, we warehouse our senior adults in increasing numbers. Not too many decades ago, we did the same with the mentally ill. As recently as the onset of the AIDS epidemic, some claimed disease was a punishment from God for immoral behavior and sought to quarantine sufferers like first-century lepers. In much of Africa, the stigma of AIDS is so great that many decline to be tested or to receive available treatments. The number of AIDS orphans on the continent continues to grow at an alarming rate. The Web site www.who.int reports that approximately 8.2 million children around the world have been orphaned by the HIV/AIDS epidemic. Ninety percent of the maternal orphans live in sub-Sahara Africa.

Today the World Health Organization defines health as complete physical, mental, and social well-being (note the absence of a spiritual well-being). While the lack of health in developing countries may be attributed to poverty and politics, in industrialized

Pastoral Perspective

A woman had been suffering. She had been suffering from hemorrhages. She had endured much under many physicians. She had spent all that she had. She was no better; rather, she grew worse. The woman had heard about Jesus.

Focus on this woman. Mark certainly does. In a series of short sentences and phrases, Mark shines a spotlight on her: her illness, her struggles, her courage. This unnamed woman slipped up from behind and touched Jesus' cloak.

Jesus was on the way to Jairus's home. Jesus was on a mission of compassion. Jesus was with an important man, a leader in the synagogue. An unnamed woman who had suffered from hemorrhages for twelve years, a poor person who had expended all her financial resources, interrupted Jesus.

Interruptions are the very nature of ministry. Some would say that interruptions often *are* ministry. The woman's touch not only interrupted Jesus' journey to Jairus's home. Her touch caught Jesus by surprise: "Who touched my clothes?" (v. 30). Ministry also involves openness to surprise and the asking of questions.

Notice that Jesus asked the question, not because he felt a tug upon his cloak, rather, he felt power go out of him.

Exegetical Perspective

Mark's story of the woman with a flow of blood, sandwiched in the middle of the story of Jairus's daughter (5:21–24a, 35–43), presents Jesus as a healer who integrates people more fully into community. Essential to understanding the woman's circumstance is the following Levitical instruction concerning menstruating women:

> If a woman has a discharge of blood [*rhysis haimatos*] for many days, not at the time of her impurity, or if she has a discharge beyond the time of her impurity, all the days of the discharge she shall continue in uncleanness; as in the days of her impurity, she shall be unclean. Every bed on which she lies during all the days of her discharge shall be treated as the bed of her impurity; and everything on which she sits shall be unclean, as in the uncleanness of her impurity. Whoever touches these things shall be unclean, and shall wash his clothes, and bathe in water, and be unclean until the evening. (Lev. 15:25–27)

Mark's use of the same precise term (*rhysis haimatos*, "blood flow," v. 25) found in Leviticus 15:25 (the term is used only once in the LXX) makes it likely that he is depicting a woman with a menstrual blood flow. Moreover, Mark uses a second term for the woman's hemorrhage (*pēgē*, v. 29) that is also used in the LXX to signal menstruation (Lev. 20:18).

Homiletical Perspective

Mark allows the story of the woman suffering from hemorrhages to interrupt the story of Jairus and his sick daughter. "Take a look at these two," he seems to be saying. "What do you see?" We see contrast. Jairus is a man with a name the reader might recognize; she is a woman designated only by her disease. He is a religious insider; she is a walking hazard to ritual purity. He has the financial resources implied by his position and multiroom house; she is flat broke. He approaches Jesus from the front and with eloquence; she reaches out to him silently from behind.

So perfect is her résumé of disenfranchisement that we may be in danger of mistaking her for a prop—a flat character who exists only passively to receive the surprising reversal of fortunes that Jesus offers the despised of this world. Look again. Like the Syrophoenician woman (7:24–30) whom she anticipates, she is down, but not out—still thinking on her feet, still searching for an angle, still trying to make something happen. This is remarkable. If she is still on a quest for wholeness after all this time, it is surely a quest that has carried her well beyond the borders of naiveté. She has filled out the endless SSI paperwork, endured the clumsy probings of interns at the free clinics, heard the excuses of those who do not want to take on the risk of her "preexisting condition." Mark's description needs no contemporizing

Mark 5:24b–34

Theological Perspective

nations the medical community has become so highly specialized that it may be difficult to find doctors who will work with other physicians across disciplines to optimize holistic health for a patient. Moreover, the cost of health care has continued to climb in industrialized countries, rendering care inaccessible for the underinsured and uninsured. In emerging countries where families struggle for clean water, sustainable agriculture, and basic medical care; and where life expectancy is not much higher now than in the first century, a holistic approach to health is unimaginable.

Christian interpretations of disease and health vary widely, as do Christian responses to world health issues. On one end of the spectrum, Pentecostal faith healers and Christian Scientists do not utilize modern medicine. Is this their right and/or choice? Are couples who elect not to utilize healthcare services on religious grounds required to seek medical treatment for their sick children? Legal battles are fought over these questions. The opposite end of the spectrum is home to those who trust their physical well-being to physicians and modern science and limit the role of God and clergy to matters of the spirit. The middle ground is inhabited by those who believe God answers prayers for healing, sometimes through physicians or medical mysteries in this life, sometimes not until the life to come.

As local theologians, pastors can help their congregations move toward both an informed understanding of health and disease, and compassionate action toward those who are in need of care. Drawing on the four areas of Wesley's quadrangle: Scripture, tradition, reason, and experience, congregational leaders can help their members struggle to balance faith and intellect, and work toward balanced positions that acknowledge the roles of the human and the divine in our overall health.

The insights of a number of theologians in this century and the last may inform our preaching and teaching about disease and health. Barth argued from a Christian perspective that health must be understood in terms of the goods and goals toward which human life is directed by God's good purposes made known in Christ.[1] In the early 1960s, and also from a Christian perspective, Paul Tillich argued that health must be understood as a "multi-dimensional unity" containing mechanical, chemical, biological, psychological, spiritual, and historical dimensions.[2]

---

1. Neil Messer, "Toward a Theological Understanding of Health and Disease," *Journal of the Society of Christian Ethics*, March 1, 2011: 161.
2. James Wind, "Health," in *A New Handbook of Christian of Christian Theology*, ed. Donald Musser and Joseph Price (Nashville: Abingdon Press, 1992), 215.

Pastoral Perspective

The woman had courage; Jesus had power. Courage to touch, power to heal: both are part of discipleship. Courage and touch are crucial elements of faith. A woman who goes to AA or Al-Anon for the first time has courage; the fellowship of those who follow the twelve steps of AA has power. The teenager who joins a Bible study has courage; the stories of the Bible have power. The man whose life or marriage is spiraling downward reaches out to a friend, a counselor, a pastor; that man has courage. If the friend, counselor, or pastor has wisdom, the wisdom that comes through grace, then the man who reaches out will receive healing—perhaps not the healing he expects, but healing will occur. Such is the witness of the Gospels; such is the promise of Christlike faith.

Perhaps the witness of this story—maybe even the witness of Mark's Gospel as a whole—is summed up in E. M. Forster's famous epigraph: "Only connect."[1] Those words are on the frontispiece of Forster's classic novel, *Howards End*. The novel explores the words in powerful ways. *Howards End* is about relationships and acceptance; the gospel of Jesus the Christ has the same themes.

Jesus' ministry is marked by connections created as he encounters and accepts people whose lives are hemorrhaging blood or guilt, hemorrhaging self-righteousness or blindness, hemorrhaging paralysis or greed. Sometimes he touches them; sometimes they first touch him. Sometimes the touch is with the hand; at other times the touch is through words—words that rest upon the heart and heal the soul. However the touch occurs, a connection is made.

Church, the body of Christ, comes into being through connections made, acceptance received, hemorrhaging healed. The woman did not need to touch Jesus' body; she only desired to connect in a way that allowed her to receive Jesus' power.

As is so often true in Mark, the connection does not require words of faith to be spoken, or acts of repentance to occur. Courage is the only sign of faith—courage tinged with desperation. Courage is enough for the connection to occur.

Pastor-preachers and teachers will find rich resources through this short interlude in Mark's Gospel. Women are drawn to this passage. Uncontrolled, sometimes unexpected, flows of blood are a part of women's lives. However, men's bodies also function in uncontrolled and sometimes unexpected ways. In both genders, these events are challenging reminders that our bodies, like our lives, are at times beyond

---

1. E. M. Forster, *Howards End* (New York: Vintage Books, 1954), frontispiece.

Exegetical Perspective

In light of Leviticus 15, the woman's menstrual status would classify her as ritually (not morally) unclean. The Levitical law implies that whatever the woman touches has the potential to transmit her uncleanness to anyone who touches the same items (Lev. 15:27). The woman in Mark 5 has endured a state of ritual impurity for twelve years, a condition which would have likely entailed significant caution on her part (and/or that of others) in order to prevent transmission of her ritual uncleanness. The woman's desperation to be freed from her condition is evident in two narrative details: she has exhausted her resources on physicians (v. 26) and she tries to touch Jesus' cloak (v. 27).

One of the primary consequences of this woman's healing would be the ability to participate again more fully in community. The woman is one of several figures in Mark whose healing by Jesus enables them to be (re)integrated into various dimensions of society. Nine of the twelve individuals whom Jesus heals in Mark have conditions that are potential cause for exclusion. Seven people have a condition that the Torah specifically labels as unclean or impure: the leper (Mark 1:40–45), paralytic (2:1–12), man with a withered hand (3:1–6), Jairus's daughter (5:22–24, 35–43), the bleeding woman, and two blind men (8:22–26; 10:46–52).

Because such impurity was sometimes deemed contagious, ritually unclean people faced potential social exclusion. Lepers, for example, were to wear torn clothes, sport disheveled hair, and cry out, "Unclean, unclean," so as to warn people of their proximity. The leper "shall live alone; his dwelling shall be outside the camp" (Lev. 13:45–46). Those with physical impairments, including the "*blind* or *lame*, or one who has a mutilated face or a limb too long, or one who has a broken foot or *a broken hand*, or a hunchback, or a dwarf, or a man *with a blemish in his eyes* or an itching disease or scabs or crushed testicles" (Lev. 21:16–20), were to be prohibited from making offerings to God.

Two other Markan characters, the demoniac (5:1–20) and the man with a hearing and speech impediment (7:32–37), may also be understood as "unclean." The former is associated with three "unclean" elements: an unclean spirit, tombs, and a great herd of swine (5:2, 3, 8, 11); the latter's hearing and speech problems might classify him among the physically disabled who were forbidden to give offerings to God (Lev. 21:16–20). When Jesus heals these characters, he removes their uncleanness and enables them to participate fully again in community. The

Homiletical Perspective

spin to resonate with the chronically ill in our context: "She had endured much under many physicians, and had spent all that she had; and she was no better, but rather grew worse" (v. 26). It has been a long twelve years; yet here she is, hatching another plot. Trying again.

Although Jairus and the woman are a study in contrasts, they share a common desperate need that leads them to the same conclusion: they both want a piece of Jesus. If desperation is the game, there can be little question that she is the better player. Nothing in Jairus's experience has prepared him for this moment; the woman knows exactly how to play when you have nothing to lose. Jairus may have Jesus' attention, but she has a plan.

"If I but touch his clothes, I will be made well" (v. 28). She has no intention of taking the direct approach. She has learned that people tend to get upset when she announces her condition in close quarters. There is no need to draw attention to herself. The healer is obviously very busy with more important matters. All she intends is to steal an anonymous touch. She is completely convinced that will be enough. What happens next happens all at once: "Immediately" the bleeding stops (v. 29). She feels it in her body. "Immediately" Jesus is aware "that power had gone forth from him" (v. 30). Immediately. It is Mark's favorite word, and here it seems to make perfect sense. Simultaneously it happens and she knows and he knows. In Mark's telling, the power gets away from Jesus and into the woman without so much as a nod of consent on his part.

All these healing miracles make us moderns squirm a bit, but this one is more bizarre than most. Jesus apparently walks around like a supercharged battery of power for life—a power with a mind of its own that can and will jump like a spark through his clothing and into the body of proximate, desperate need. The result is, amazingly enough, everything seems to go according to her plan. Let the parade to Jairus's house proceed on schedule; she has what she came for.

However, Jesus, completely passive up to now, does not have what *he* wants just yet. Now, for the first time in the story, he speaks up: "Who touched my clothes?" (v. 30). As Jesus begins looking "all around," it becomes clear that, for the moment at least, the parade is over. This was not part of her plan. Though others may be amused or annoyed by his peculiar behavior, one person in the crowd knows exactly what he is talking about. In her own

Mark 5:24b–34

Theological Perspective

More recently, James Wind has noted that the Christian tradition places discussions of health within a discussion of human finitude and fallenness. He asserts that health is a gift, not a right, and that we experience health in relation to disease, death, and human limitation. He further argues that we must resist the temptation to seek perfect and limitless health, which can quickly become an idol. Health must not be isolated as a solitary good or made private as only an individual concern.[3]

The themes described above are evident in the healings in Mark' fifth chapter. Although Jesus does raise Jairus's daughter from the dead and heal the woman from twelve years of hemorrhaging, neither act will last forever. The gift of mortal life is just that, mortal. Further, Jesus is concerned with total health, not just physical healing. In this chapter, Jesus' healing ministry extends to the daughter of a community leader and to a destitute woman, modeling that all members of society are worthy of care, blessing, and inclusion in the life in community.

How can we bear witness to the health and wholeness revealed in Jesus' healing ministries? The church is surrounded by health practitioners who are working for holistic models of health care, and the church would do well to continue to support such efforts locally and throughout the world. Politically, affordable and accessible health care is a hot-button issue. Whether we are supporters of government-sponsored health care initiatives or not, the reality is that there will always be those who "fall through the cracks." In our local faith communities, we can help members of our congregations be willing to cross social and economic boundaries to reach out to the infirm and disabled that we or others continue to ostracize, praying and working to restore them to be holistic members of vital faith communities.

TRACY L. HARTMAN

Pastoral Perspective

our control. For men and for women, such events can create vulnerability and stress. Regardless of gender, they are persistent reminders of finiteness and mortality. They create anxiety and confusion. When people have the courage to face these realities, when people have the courage to seek not only medical healing but also spiritual healing, often the result is a closer connection with Christ and with the church. Wise pastors come to know that words and actions shared in Christlike ways may lead to holy and healing connections.

Two major encounters with illness have reinforced this conviction. When deep depression stuck, during my early thirties, months went by before I had the courage to reach out to a counselor. When I eventually connected with a faith-based counselor, slow but steady healing transformed my life.

Years later, when I was diagnosed with an acoustic neuroma, courage enabled me to challenge the advice of one doctor, then continue to research options until my wife and I found a medical team we felt to be "in touch" with us.

In both instances, my soul needed to have the right touch, a holy connection, as much as my mind and body needed healing.

Both experiences proved to be powerful times for personal growth in prayer, in marriage and family relationships, and in maturing as a pastor to others in need of healing. Jesus' words to the woman—"your faith has made you well; go in peace, and be healed of your disease" (v. 34)—take on deep meaning as I reflect on these experiences.

Do I believe that faith alone heals? No! Does Mark teach that faith is a means of healing? Absolutely! In the journey of life, our minds, bodies, and souls endure much.

Humans seek relief in a variety of ways, many of which may cause us to spend all that we have in pursuit of healing that is elusive. When illness comes, and a cure seems beyond hope, Mark's Gospel calls forth the courage to touch Jesus' cloak and to receive from his body, the body of Christ, the church, power to be made whole.

ART ROSS

---

3. Ibid.

Exegetical Perspective

leper need no longer dwell "outside the camp." The bleeding woman can touch and be touched without fear of transmitting ritual impurity.

The primary effect of Jesus' healing is thus not personal but social. In restoring persons to full community, he restores the community as well. Jesus' words to the healed demoniac in Mark 5:18–19 ("Go home to your friends") capture this.[1] The salvation or wholeness that the bleeding woman experiences ("Your faith has saved [$s\bar{o}z\bar{o}$] you") is social and communal (v. 34; cf. v. 28). Jesus' healings are one of three strategies he employs to (re)integrate social outcasts into community. He also shares meals with tax collectors and sinners—an act that produces conflict with scribes of the Pharisees (2:15–17)—and he violently protests a temple system that excludes Gentiles (11:15–17).

Mark emphasizes the physical touching that occurs between Jesus and the woman by mentioning four times—in only five verses—a form of the word "touch" (*haptō*):

> She had heard about Jesus, and came up behind him in the crowd and *touched* his cloak, for she said, "If I but *touch* his clothes, I will be made well." . . . Jesus turned about in the crowd and said, "Who *touched* my clothes?" And his disciples said to him, "You see the crowd pressing in on you; how can you say, 'Who *touched* me?'" (Mark 5:27–31, emphasis added)

Mark's emphasis upon this physical contact is significant, given that touch is the primary vehicle by which the ritual impurity of a menstruating woman could be transmitted to others (Lev. 15:27). Touching the ritually unclean is Jesus' primary mode of healing. Mark explicitly notes that there is touch between Jesus and the leper (1:41), the bleeding woman (5:27–31), Jairus's daughter (5:41a), a deaf man (7:33), a blind man (8:23, 25), and a deaf and mute boy possessed by a demon (9:27). The woman's "faith" (*pistis*)—affirmed by Jesus as responsible for her healing—primarily consists in risking the social stigma and shame that could accompany her act of touching Jesus and transmitting ritual impurity to him (v. 34).

MATTHEW S. RINDGE

Homiletical Perspective

strange way, she has been in complete control up to now; but this is more than she bargained for.

So she comes "in fear and trembling" and tells "the whole truth" (v. 33). Mark does not say precisely what she is afraid of, though it is not that hard to figure out: the tables have turned. Jesus claims to have important business with her that only begins with the power transaction she has initiated. The power went out at her touch, yet he insists that what has happened between them is all about faith. Jesus stops the show in order to call her "daughter" (v. 34) and explain that she is well, and will be well, because she believes in him.

Faith is the main thing, according to Jesus. The good news in this for Jairus (and maybe for us) is that faith is not a finite resource. Relationship is not a zero-sum game. It turns out that desperation is not a contest after all, with winners and losers. Reading the Bible closely, those of us who have more in common with Jairus than with the woman may worry from time to time that God and Jesus like her kind better. However, in this story, the synagogue leader does not have to lose in order for the chronically ill woman to win. It seems for a moment as if this might be true when the news comes from Jairus's house that the delay on the road has taken its toll on the sick girl. Jesus assures Jairus that ultimately there is hope beyond death for everyone who follows the woman's lead. Her twelve years of brokenness have taught her how to trust in something other than herself. Though Jairus has not had nearly as much practice, the offer stands all the same: "Do not fear; only believe."

LANCE PAPE

---

1. For a more detailed examination of Jesus' treatment of social outcasts in Mark, see Matthew S. Rindge, "Mark's Gospel, Social Outcasts, and Modern Slavery," *Journal of Lutheran Ethics* 10:6 (June 2010). http://www.elca.org/What-We-Believe/Social-Issues/Journal-of-Lutheran-Ethics/Issues/June-2010/Marks-Gospel-Social-Outcasts-and-Modern-Slavery.aspx

Mark 6:1–6a

¹He left that place and came to his hometown, and his disciples followed him. ²On the sabbath he began to teach in the synagogue, and many who heard him were astounded. They said, "Where did this man get all this? What is this wisdom that has been given to him? What deeds of power are being done by his hands! ³Is not this the carpenter, the son of Mary and brother of James and Joses and Judas and Simon, and are not his sisters here with us?" And they took offense at him. ⁴Then Jesus said to them, "Prophets are not without honor, except in their hometown, and among their own kin, and in their own house." ⁵And he could do no deed of power there, except that he laid his hands on a few sick people and cured them. ⁶And he was amazed at their unbelief.

Theological Perspective

Attentive readers will have already noted that Mark believes there are many obstacles to hearing the gospel. By this point in his Gospel, for example, we know that some people fear that Jesus blasphemes by forgiving sins (2:7), some are suspicious because of the company Jesus keeps (2:16), some are scandalized because Jesus' disciples do not fast (2:18), some are outraged by the failure of Jesus' disciples to keep the Sabbath (2:23–24) and others by Jesus' healing on the Sabbath (3:4). Some in Jesus' own family think that he has "gone out of his mind" (3:21), and others say that he casts out demons by the power of Beelzebul. When Jesus announces that a young girl is asleep and not dead, he is laughed at for his foolishness (5:40). If we stay tuned, we will learn of still other obstacles. When Jesus tells the disciples—those on the inside—that he will be rejected and put to death, not even his closest disciples can understand this (8:31).

Could it be that Mark intended the parable of the Sower and Jesus' explanation of it (4:1–20) to serve as an interpretive guide for all of these problems of speaking and hearing about the kingdom of God? While biblical scholars and theologians have come to agree with Adolf Jülicher that the parables were not originally allegories, Mark seems to use the parable

Pastoral Perspective

In his spiritual memoir *Brother to a Dragonfly*, Will Campbell writes about the first sermon he preached for the hometown crowd. It was Youth Sunday, and Campbell was the designated teenaged preacher for the day.

"On that occasion," Campbell remembers, "I could have denounced Christianity as a capitalistic myth . . . and our youth choir could have sung Ukrainian folk songs and our Sunday School superintendent could have lectured on 'The Origin of the Species' and all the people would have said 'Amen.' Never had they been so proud of us."[1]

Most preachers who speak at a homecoming service or otherwise address the folks "back home" experience a welcome a lot more like Campbell's than the one Jesus received at his hometown synagogue in Nazareth. So why the difference? Why was Jesus received with such surprise (v. 2), offense (v. 3), and dismissal (v. 6)?

Perhaps because Jesus was not just a local boy or girl made good, returning to receive the accolades of his or her first-grade Sunday school teacher. Jesus was God's "prophet" (v. 4) speaking God's truth to power.

1. Will D. Campbell, *Brother to a Dragonfly* (New York: Continuum, 1977), 77.

Exegetical Perspective

This passage in Mark reminds me of a 1996 Hollywood movie entitled *Courage under Fire*. The movie is about a U.S. Army officer (played by Denzel Washington) who investigates a fallen female chopper commander (played by Meg Ryan) to see whether she should be the first woman found worthy of the Medal of Honor for valor in combat. The investigation unveils the hidden truth about the courage of the female commander who risked her life to save her male crew and then was intentionally left behind by the crew to cover up their cowardice. In this passage, Jesus was under fire not only by his friends and foes, but also by his own family members. Nevertheless he remained strong and was not discouraged by their misunderstanding and rejection.

The whole section of Mark 3:20–6:6a begins and ends with obvious conflict and tensions at "home" (3:19) or his "hometown" (6:1) among relatives and friends. While there is an absence of faith among Jesus' family members, in startling contrast there is tremendous faith shown by the synagogue official named Jairus (5:21–24a, 35–43) and the woman afflicted with hemorrhages for twelve years (5:24b–34). After performing a notable double miracle composed in the uniquely Markan sandwiched style (5:21–43), Jesus now returns home to Nazareth. The

Homiletical Perspective

There are at least six possible sermons in this brief text.

"He Came to His Hometown." This presentation could involve a very personal story of the preacher's experience of welcome far away, and then at home. Many of us, at some time, have to come home. The matrix of childhood is there. Expectations placed upon us, fulfilled or left hanging, are there. Parents present or absent are there, as are first loves and old rivals, roads not taken, and gratitude unexpressed. Sometimes we want to run away again, and sometimes we want to stay.

The question of home is important. Is it where our heart is? Does it still order the way we live? Does the Bible have it right when it suggests that, when God has not finished leading us, to settle down (as did Abram's father) is unfaithful? Is it the case that no matter where we are, "our true lives are hid with Christ in God"? A series of recollections about homecomings will allow our congregants to recall their own times at home and away. Conversations thus begun can flow into opportunities for pastoral care.

"His Disciples Followed Him." Here one might develop a sermon about leadership. In the simplest

Mark 6:1–6a

Theological Perspective

to provide a code for explaining why wisdom fails to take root in people's hearing.[1]

In Mark 6:1–6a we encounter a classic reason why people cannot hear real wisdom. The reason is not simply that a "prophet is without honor except in his native place"—how the text is often remembered. Mark's Jesus, in verse 4, drills down more deeply: "Prophets are not without honor, except in their hometown, and among their own kin, and in their own house." People cannot get beyond the shared assumptions and biases that stem from the most local of cultural institutions, the family and the village; one might as well be in Plato's cave, where people mistake for reality the shadows they have always been familiar with.

Here is a community that cannot acknowledge a criterion of dissimilarity, even when they experience one: "Where did this man get all this? What is this wisdom that has been given to him? What deeds of power are being done by his hands!" (v. 2). No sooner are these wonders raised than the rhetoric of familiarity takes the wind out of their sails: "Is not this the carpenter, the son of Mary and brother of James and Joses and Judas and Simon, and are not his sisters here with us?" Anyone from a large family knows where that line of argument is headed: "and they took offense at him" (v. 3).

The resistance to Jesus in this passage is not merely of individuals but of the group; there is a social dimension to the rejection of Jesus and his message. What is more disconcerting than the obtuseness and resentment of village life, however, is Mark's acknowledgment that such hostility actually undercuts Jesus' authority: "And he could do no deed of power there" (v. 5a). By this point in the Gospel, the hearer/reader is used to Mark's frequent mention that the unclean spirits recognize Jesus—a fine bit of irony. Here, however, at the beginning of chapter 6, what binds Jesus' hands is no unclean spirit per se. One almost wishes for the simplicity of an unclean spirit who would recognize Jesus and then skedaddle. The resentment of friends and family, by contrast, is a resistance far more entrenched and costly—rocky ground, indeed, for a sower.

According to Mark, word of Jesus' healings and exorcisms has drawn some large crowds, but these seem to dissipate as quickly as they gather, as though a good gust of wind could blow the seed to another field—"and the crowd came together again" (3:20).

---

1. See Bernard Brandon Scott, *Hear Then the Parable* (Minneapolis: Fortress Press, 1989), 42–43.

Pastoral Perspective

As a prophet, Jesus is already stirring up trouble in and around Galilee. He not only has a kind word for lepers, but he dares to touch and heal them (1:41). He heals the sick but, even more shockingly, also forgives their sin (2:7). He upsets the local etiquette police by eating with "tax collectors and sinners" (2:16). Jesus is an apostle of change, charging old wineskins are not adequate to hold the radical, effervescent grace of God (2:22). He is reading and interpreting Scripture in fresh new ways, suggesting pressing human need trumps religious ritual and rules every time (2:25–28). Is it any wonder the locals are worried Jesus is coming to town? Unlike most hometown preachers, he is not a guardian of the status quo but its most potent critic.

Luke's Gospel provides a second look at Jesus' rejection in Nazareth, an experience that baffled Jesus (v. 6) and seared its memory deep into the New Testament witness (see also Matt. 13:54–58). As Luke tells the tale (Luke 4:16–30), the crowd in Jesus' hometown synagogue initially warmed to his message (Luke 4:22); but when Jesus had the audacity to suggest God's love extends even to those outside the clan, namely, to ethnicities and social classes many thought were banned from the heart of God, the members of First Church of Nazareth quickly changed from a sleepy congregation to a killing mob (Luke 4:28–30).

Unlike Luke, Mark does not explain why Jesus met with such an unfriendly reception at his hometown synagogue. After five chapters of reporting the ruckus Jesus stirs up wherever he goes, Mark leaves the reader to connect the dots. Jesus' rejection at Nazareth turns on Jesus' fierce determination to be God's prophet, speaking painful, if liberating, truth, no matter the cost. Little wonder Jesus was an itinerant preacher, teacher, and healer. It is hard for a preacher to keep his or her day job if the preacher lingers too long at the prophetic end of the priestly-prophetic spectrum. As Saul Bellow reportedly said, "Being a prophet is a great job. The problem is finding *work*."

Besides Jesus' edgy prophetic vocation, there is a more mundane reason for his rejection by the hometown crowds: the offense of the familiar. The locals are *astounded* at the remarkable "wisdom" coming from *this* mouth (v. 2), *these* hands (v. 2), from Mary's boy (v. 3), from a working man with no formal education, from one whose brothers and sisters are quite ordinary (v. 3). The hometown crowd "takes offense" at Jesus—literally, *"stumbles"* over him—because like a misplaced toy one trips over in

Exegetical Perspective

passage begins with a very promising note of people being "astounded" (6:2) but ends with Jesus being "amazed" in the sense of being disappointed because of "their unbelief" (6:6a).

Mark 6:1–6a may be divided into three scenes. Verses 1–2a set the stage for a painful homecoming. Jesus is now in his "hometown," which is Nazareth. At his first homecoming (3:20), his relatives wanted "to restrain him," because they thought he had gone "out of his mind" (3:21). Since he had been away, his fame had spread. People in other towns and villages were amazed at him (5:20) and were "overcome with amazement" by what they witnessed (5:42). How, then, would his family welcome him after his having been away for some time?

Jesus' return was marked with great suspense. This homecoming was an important occasion for Jesus to reveal his true identity and mission to his homefolks and also to his disciples, who had accompanied him. The day was a Sabbath, and Jesus began to teach in the synagogue. Unlike Luke (4:16–30), who records what Jesus actually said and did, Mark keeps his readers completely in the dark. The reader is told only that those who heard him were "astounded" (v. 2a).

This leads to the second scene (vv. 2b–3), which describes the reaction of the crowd through a series of five questions. These questions are meant to undermine claims of his special origin, wisdom, and power. The questions belittle his identity. Being a *tektōn* ("carpenter," v. 3 NRSV), which referred to someone who worked with stone, metal, or wood, suggests that Jesus grew up and learned a simple trade like everyone else. Likewise, the mention of his brothers and sisters highlights his ordinariness. In a cultural context where one's geographical and genetic origins determine one's identity and status, Jesus' undistinguished and dubious origins kept his relatives from accepting him as anything but one like them. So they "took offense" at him (v. 3b NRSV, NAB). Other translations render the Greek word, *eskandalizonto*, more picturesquely ("they fell foul of him," NEB) or more plainly ("they rejected him," TEV).

The third and final scene (vv. 4–6a) describes Jesus' reaction. Jesus responded to the rejection by applying to himself an ancient aphorism: "Prophets are not without honor, except in their hometown, and among their own kin, and in their own house" (v. 4). This proverbial saying is recorded in the other Synoptics (Matt. 13:57; Luke 4:24) and also in John (4:44). It is also widely attested in Greco-Roman literature and is even found in the gnostic *Gospel of*

Homiletical Perspective

of actions, leaders are being watched and remembered. Likewise, we learn about leadership through every observation of those we admire. Upon reflection, who are the ones from whom the preacher has learned the most, and what lessons do we take from them? Whom do we try to teach, and whom do we really teach? Others follow us. Be careful with them. Be aware that not only our words and actions but our emotions come through loud and clear. It is often our emotional state that people will recall the longest.

The majesty of Christ and his gospel were constructed piece by piece, in little steps, little moments, little human touches we all have felt. The gift of faith comes from the ritual of good teaching and good learning day to day: in the house, on the street, on the job. The sermon might conclude with a litany of thanksgiving for those people we have "followed" and from whom we have learned much.

"He Began to Teach in the Synagogue, and Many Who Heard Him Were Astounded." Who is the preacher's "preaching hero"? Here is a one-line text to remind us of the possibility of people being moved by the words of a preacher or an experience in public worship. What, in particular, moves people? Is it scholarship, imagination, like-mindedness, clarity on issues, pastoral sensitivity, or experiences of friendship beyond the pulpit? Is it freshness that astounds, or daring, or tenderness, or nerve? Astounding moments are rare, even in our best efforts, and congregational resistance or disinterest can make their appearance even rarer.

Here the preacher could tell (maybe in an education hour) of her own experience of being astounded by the privilege and responsibility placed on those who preach and how that astonishment changed her practice and expectations. The preacher might even reiterate what he is trying to accomplish week by week, and where inspiration arises. The braver preacher may even name the issues that cannot be preached in the congregation, thereby letting the people know that she is well aware of them. Sometimes "astounding" is found in crossing a line just far enough to raise an eyebrow.

"Where Did This Man Get All This?" Herein lies a sermon about public resistance. Each preacher lives within a bubble of permission. The tradition of the congregation has limits. The popular mind-set of the people, or the community, or the town has limits too. Thus it is possible for the preacher to be silent to save his skin, or overly loud to try to break the

Mark 6:1–6a

Theological Perspective

Thus, while the presence of a crowd always gathers the reader's attention with the sense that something is afoot, the crowd in Mark is never the point. It is about the few: "except that he laid his hands on a few sick people and cured them" (v. 5b). Understatement is the secret trope of Mark's Gospel. While amazed at the unbelief of the many, Jesus continues to attend to the few: those who "hear the word and accept it and bear fruit, thirty and sixty and a hundredfold" (4:20).

Theologically, we are used to interpreting the Gospel of Mark through an eschatological lens—Jesus' proclaiming that the kingdom of God is near, confronting men and women with a radical decision for or against the gospel. Such a reading dominated the twentieth-century interpretation of Mark and of the Synoptics in general. Where and how this gospel will take root remains a genuine mystery. If it be successful at all, it will be so only insofar as it persists amid the thorns of a powerful set of institutional and traditional ways of thinking. In the passage like the one before us, there is no exaggerated confidence of success.

Instead, one finds a sober recognition that established habits of mind are powerful in resisting any gospel that would alter the balance of social power. Or do we think it is by coincidence that only those on the margins of society who have been healed by Jesus and the demons who have been expelled by him know who he is and proclaim him?

Still, for the hearer/reader of Mark—for one who is on the inside—the failure of Jesus' family and village to recognize him is an object lesson in discipleship and offers us a realistic wisdom about the realities of social and theological change: Do not be so sure that you are going to be successful; the forces arrayed against courage and compassion are significant, entrenched, and morally defended. In these passages of rejection, Mark's logic of the cross is beginning to unfold.

JOSEPH A. BESSLER

Pastoral Perspective

a dark room, they were not expecting it to be there. The locals in Nazareth were not expecting God to show up in a lowly carpenter who lived two doors down. Neither was anyone else.

The offense of the familiar is yet found in communities of faith where God is relegated to the spectacular side of life and the ordinary mercies of Christian living are devalued: the cup of water given in Jesus' name, the welcoming hug given "the least of these," the "two or three gathered in Jesus' name," daily bread, five loaves and two fish, a mustard seed, the leaven in the loaf, a widow's pittance, and wine and bread. All of these things so close to the heart of the kingdom Jesus preaches and lives, are so depressingly *familiar* (a word that shares the same root as "family"). Yet Jesus infuses the ordinary with an extraordinary presence and purpose and grace. The miracle is not that God is outside the ordinary but radiant with divine life and love *within* it.

Years ago as a freshly minted seminarian in the hunt for the "perfect church," I was blessed to run into a mentor from my childhood and youth. This former minister of music at my church had endeared himself to me with his honesty, zest for life, and progressive views. I shared with him my frustration about the congregations I was interviewing with—so plodding, so provincial, so imperfect. He listened patiently before speaking a truth that sounded as a depth charge in my soul: "To tell you the truth, I've always found church wherever I was." The message was clear: unless I was able to find church right where I was, I was not likely to find it anywhere else.

The life and faith we seek—the life and faith God wants for us—is not found someplace else. It is found right here, right now in the midst of the ordinary people and places where God lives. Little wonder Jesus—the Word made *flesh* (John 1:14)—was so disappointed that the people who knew and loved him best could not see or claim the divine so palpably present within him (vv. 5–6a).

The locals were *astounded* by Jesus the man (vv. 2–3) and *annoyed* by Jesus the prophet (vv. 4–5). What leads us to yet dismiss the miracle he was and is (v. 6)?

BOB SETZER JR.

Exegetical Perspective

Thomas: "Jesus said: No prophet is acceptable in his village; no physician works cures on those who know him" (*Gos. Thom.* 31). Notably, the latter part of the *Thomas* saying is a unique addition, which reflects what Mark says about Jesus, that "he could do no deed of power there" (v. 5). By this, Mark means that the townspeople's lack of faith prohibited the manifestation of Jesus' mighty works, not that Jesus was incapable of performing miracles per se. In response, Jesus was "amazed" (NRSV, NAB) or "marveled" (KJV) at the townspeople's "unbelief."

This "biographical story" of Jesus' rejection in his hometown and by his relatives is reported in the other Synoptics (Matt. 13:53–58; Luke 4:16–30) and seemingly even in John (John 1:11). This episode is attested multiple times and is deeply rooted in historical remembrance. Just as prophetic figures in the Old Testament were often rejected by their own people (2 Chr. 24:19; Isa. 52:13–53:12), Jesus, who is the prophet of God, was also not honored by those closest to him. If Jesus is the Messiah and yet was rejected, Christians who are called to a prophetic ministry should not be surprised or shocked that they too might encounter a similar fate.

In this passage, Mark shows that Jesus was under fire. His identity was put into question because he was too familiar and ordinary. The old saying is correct: "Familiarity breeds contempt!" People continue to evaluate people on the basis of old information and judge on the basis of their lineage and ethnicity. Consequently, the townspeople rejected Jesus. Nevertheless, he was not discouraged by their contempt but rather continued his ministry of teaching and healing, moving forward into other towns and villages. In the next verse, Mark writes, "Then he went about among the villages teaching" (v. 6b). Mark demonstrates that Jesus was truly courageous under fire. Jesus' failures and rejection are an important lesson for the disciples to witness and experience in preparation for their own mission (6:7–13), a mission Mark narrates immediately after Jesus' rejection at Nazareth.

VANTHANH NGUYEN

Homiletical Perspective

chains. It is worth pondering where Jesus' inspiration in the face of resistance came from. Where *did* he get all this? One could lead the congregation to go back in their imagination through Gospel stories and moments that broke their resistance. There were shepherds fearfully listening to angels; magi confronting a king for directions; Anna and Simeon waiting, wondering, and maintaining their faith. Good parents kept watch. Prophetic voices spoke across time. Political injustice and military atrocities left their scars. In all this, resistance gave way and the messianic expectation was sharpened. Our own voice raised above resistance may be heartened with a closing poem from Walt Whitman's "Leaves of Grass" (a great read for the preacher on a quiet night).

"He Could Do No Deed of Power There . . ." The sermon from this verse might address clergy burnout or congregational exhaustion. Even the Lord of life spent much of his ministry walking uphill and working at half speed. Ministers and congregations know that our work is mostly "sowing" and rarely "reaping." How do we know when we have done the job? How do we know that it was not our resigned refusal that made a difference, and our perceived failure that changed the game? Jesus may have walked uphill and worked at half speed, but we are still talking about him and finding life in his name.

It is good to acknowledge our sense of incompleteness and occasional frustration. Once we do, we can concentrate on all those good things we meet on that hill and at the speed we must travel. Often the friends we need to encounter are waiting for us just under the trees at the back of the roadside; those whom we may heal or even raise from the dead are lying just off the beaten track, out of the sight and mind of those who are racing from here to there.

". . . And He Was Amazed at Their Unbelief." Unbelief is like polluted air or like an uninvited force that overtakes us. Our life is diminished by it. We can even die from it. However, the bad air of unbelief and tough times are not all we know. Occasionally a crisp winter morning or a warm and sweetly scented hour in summer fills us with joy. Then, even in our hometown, we glimpse our true home that is Jesus, the Lord of life, who lives and breathes with us and in us.

G. MALCOLM SINCLAIR

Mark 6:6b–13

⁶ᵇThen he went about among the villages teaching. ⁷He called the twelve and began to send them out two by two, and gave them authority over the unclean spirits. ⁸He ordered them to take nothing for their journey except a staff; no bread, no bag, no money in their belts; ⁹but to wear sandals and not to put on two tunics. ¹⁰He said to them, "Wherever you enter a house, stay there until you leave the place. ¹¹If any place will not welcome you and they refuse to hear you, as you leave, shake off the dust that is on your feet as a testimony against them." ¹²So they went out and proclaimed that all should repent. ¹³They cast out many demons, and anointed with oil many who were sick and cured them.

Theological Perspective

On the heels of his hometown disappointment, our text begins with Jesus, who is "amazed at their unbelief," shaking the dust from his feet: "Then he went about among the villages teaching" (v. 6b). Having himself experienced both success and failure in reaching people with his message of the coming kingdom of God, Jesus gathers "the twelve" (first commissioned and named in 3:14–19) and proceeds to scatter them to the surrounding villages, giving "them authority over the unclean spirits" (v. 7).

As he sends them out, Jesus instructs the apostles to "take nothing for their journey except a staff; no bread, no bag, no money in their belts; but to wear sandals and not to put on two tunics" (vv. 8–9). The text here is reminiscent of Moses' instructions to the Israelites about preparation for the Passover as they readied themselves to flee from Egypt: "This is how you shall eat it [the Passover lamb]: your loins girded, your sandals on your feet, and your staff in your hand; and you shall eat it hurriedly. It is the passover of the LORD" (Exod. 12:11). The urgency in Mark is Jesus' proclamation: "The time is fulfilled, and the kingdom of God has come near" (1:15).

By inviting villagers to repent of their sins and to attend to the good news, the apostles are inviting the people into a new fellowship of God's reign, where God would heal their unclean spirits, cure them of

Pastoral Perspective

Franklin D. Duncan, PhD, is a pastoral counselor and clinical pastoral education supervisor who lives and works in Atlanta, Georgia. After practicing in the fields of chaplaincy, counseling, and supervision for thirty years, Franklin agreed to teach the introductory pastoral care course at a local divinity school. Doing so encouraged him to distill thirty years of pastoral experience into four rules of pastoral practice that he passed on to his students:

1. Show up.
2. Listen.
3. Speak the truth.
4. Do not take responsibility for the outcome.

Franklin's rules sound a lot like Jesus coaching the Twelve before sending them out on their first mission.

Jesus has launched his own ministry of preaching, teaching, healing, and exorcism (1:14–15), learned from the experience (6:6a), and continued and expanded his work (6:6b). Now the time has come to multiply the impact of his ministry by empowering others to preach, teach, and heal in his name and spirit ("gave them authority," v. 7). In this passage, we can see that Franklin's four rules of pastoral care are present in what Jesus tells the Twelve.

1. Show Up. The "showing up" is implicit in Jesus *sending* his disciples into action (v. 7). They are not

Exegetical Perspective

There are many challenges and difficulties in being a lone missionary. A lone missionary is more likely to be discouraged and at risk of danger and temptation. A pair of missionaries, however, can encourage and support one another, correct each other's mistakes, and overcome obstacles by praying and discerning together. In this passage, Jesus wisely sent out the apostles to participate in his teaching and healing ministry not as lone rangers but in pairs, "two by two" (v. 7).

In the previous passage, the apostles had just witnessed Jesus' rejection by his own family members and friends at Nazareth (6:1–6a). Not feeling discouraged by the incident, Jesus, accompanied by his disciples, continued to move from one village to another, teaching and healing (v. 6b). But here in this passage, the time has come for Jesus to send the Twelve out on their own to help advance his mission.

The "Mission of the Twelve" (6:7–13) is part of a larger intercalated literary construction (6:7–32). The sequence that begins with Jesus sending the apostles out two by two (vv. 7–13) later resumes with the report of their mission (vv. 30–32), after being interrupted by the story of the murder of John the Baptist (vv. 14–29). The famous Markan sandwich style creates the impression of the passing of time

Homiletical Perspective

Here is an opportunity to reflect on the church's evangelism and witness.

"He Went About among the Villages Teaching" (v. 6b). We may think of Jesus as Savior, Lamb of God, or Risen Lord. In this passage he is seen as a teacher. Does that seem too familiar for us? Over time, we have turned the teacher into the lesson. The messenger in the village has become the message to the world. Preachers might recall some of the great teachers in their lives and ponder what it was about them that hit home. What was the nature of their success? Content, zeal, charisma, timing, personal interest in the student?

Teaching is still a deeply valuable way of sharing the faith, even in the face of competing interests, with dwindling study groups and church-school attendance. When Jesus taught, what sort of teacher was he, and what did he teach? Traditional texts from the Scriptures, life lessons from the road, or visions of a God-engaging future? What do we teach in our churches, by our words and affect and style? How are the lessons going?

"He Called the Twelve and Began to Send Them Out Two by Two" (v. 7a). Who are being sent out as disciples today? Which ones in our congregations have

Mark 6:6b–13

Theological Perspective

illness, and call them to a profound level of commitment to Jesus' proclamation of the kingdom of God. It is that level of commitment that proved then, and still proves, the sticking point. For in the call to receive the good news is a call to open one's whole life to healing and to newness of life in response to God's initiative. A shift in one's fundamental loyalty is demanded in this new and urgent call. It is not difficult to imagine the felt tension these villagers would experience to embrace the kingdom of God Jesus proclaimed.[1]

If one imagines oneself in the company of the Twelve—as sent by Jesus into the world—one might learn several things from this text, three of which come immediately to mind. First, there is a sense of urgency. Among major theologians of the last forty years, the work of Johann Baptist Metz conveyed this sense of urgency better than others.[2] Any proclamation of the gospel must convey the profound importance of turning away from the world as we have ordered it and toward the world as God intends it to be, as disclosed in the profound ministry and message of Jesus. If theologians and ministers cannot articulate this sense of urgency—by interpreting anew what it means for Jesus to say, "The time is fulfilled; the kingdom of God is at hand"—they cannot be surprised when others fail to be moved. The work of seeing one's life in terms of the kingdom of God, instead of the conventional lenses of one's time and place, is enormously difficult—a constant theme in Mark's Gospel. Thus the challenge that the apostles take to these villages is a vast one.

A second thing to learn might be called "dress for success." Mark cares enough about the dress code Jesus demands of the Twelve that he spells it out: "take nothing for their journey except a staff; no bread, no bag, no money in their belts; but to wear sandals and not to put on two tunics" (vv. 8–9). Simplicity marks not only the figure of a sage, but a transparency of purpose. The Twelve come with open hands, neither offering wealth in exchange for receiving the good news nor asking for money. In announcing the kingdom of God, one must come with open hands, because the distinctiveness of the gospel must challenge the prevailing ways of appealing to self-interest and nativist impulses (remember Jesus' experience with his family), even as it holds open a new way of being in community.

---
1. It is not good news that Mark begins the next passage to be considered with the words: "King Herod heard of it" (6:14a).
2. See for example, Johann Baptist Metz, *Followers of Christ: Perspectives on the Religious Life*, trans. Thomas Linton (London: Burns & Oates Ltd., 1978).

Pastoral Perspective

to wait for those in need to knock on their study door or call or text for an appointment. Jesus' disciples are to take the lead from their Master—who went to the seashore, the marketplace, the synagogue—and to go wherever the people are and the need is. It is amazing how much hope and healing happens when a minister or lay leader from a local congregation simply "shows up" just as someone's world is falling apart.

Often when there is a death in the church family or the community at large, folks worry about what to say when paying their condolences. The truth is there are no words to make "everything better" in the wake of crushing loss. What matters is "showing up," armed with nothing more than a loving hug, sympathetic tears, and maybe a bowl of potato salad.

Ministering to others in the face of grief, dysfunction, addiction—or whatever the face of one's "unclean spirit" (v. 7, meaning an experience not sent by God)—is difficult, daunting work. Not surprisingly, Jesus sends his disciples out in pairs. The discouragement or ineptitude of the one will be countered by the wisdom and experience of the other. As the book of Ecclesiastes teaches, "Two are better than one.... For if they fall, one will lift up the other; but woe to one who is alone and falls and does not have another to help" (Eccl. 4:9–10).

2. Listen. The disciple sent in Jesus' name and spirit is not to impose his or her agenda on another. He or she is to travel light. Granted, Jesus' instructions about not taking excessive food, clothing, or money on the journey (vv. 8–9) are a call to live by faith; but these directions also demonstrate the need for Jesus' people not to show up so encumbered by their own "stuff" that they are not able to be truly present in the face of another's need.

Jesus always met people where they were, before trying to move them anyplace else. He always listened carefully to another's story—sometimes using questions to help clarify their need or expectation—before attempting to help (e.g., 1:40–41; 2:8–9; 2:19; 2:25).

Listening, really listening, is one of the highest forms of love. Before attempting to *share* the good news (1:1), Jesus' people first need to honor and love others with open ears and an attentive heart.

3. Speak the Truth. There is a "time to *keep silence*," but also a "time to *speak*" (Eccl. 3:7b). The time to speak comes only after one has so sufficiently lived with another in his or her pain (v. 10) that one comes to know the unique contours of his or her

Exegetical Perspective

and reminds the reader that in mission suffering and opposition are often unavoidable.

Mark 6:7–13 can be divided into three scenes. Scene one (v. 7) introduces the passage and sets the context of mission. The verb "to call" (NRSV) or "to summon" (NAB) often introduces a pronouncement of Jesus (3:23; 7:14; 8:1). Jesus' summoning and sending out of the Twelve recalls and fulfills an earlier prediction (3:14–15). The first task of an apostle is "to be with him" (3:14), which the apostles have been doing (see 6:1, 6b); the second is "to be sent out [*apostellō*] to proclaim the message" (3:14) and "to have authority to cast out demons" (3:15), which Jesus now bestows upon the Twelve in his commissioning of them (6:7). Jesus is able to share his power and authority with others without decreasing his own.

For practical purposes, Jesus wisely pairs them up. They can provide one another companionship, mutual protection, and moral support, and they can serve as reliable witnesses as they take on the mission that Jesus sets before them. The practice of Christian missionaries working in pairs or in teams was adopted by the early church (Acts 8:14; 9:38; 11:30).

In scene two (vv. 8–11), Jesus gives concrete instructions for the journey. The first set of instructions (vv. 8–9) deals with the apostles' traveling gear. These missionaries are directed to take a walking stick or staff and to wear sandals. Both of these items are practical instruments for travelers. Sandals protect one's feet, and a staff can be used to fend off enemies, snakes, or wild animals. However, in the Bible, wearing sandals also connotes dignity (Gen. 14:23; Exod. 12:11; Luke 15:22), and carrying a staff signals one's authority (Gen. 38:18; Exod. 4:17; Mic. 7:14).

The apostles' ministry clearly serves to extend Jesus' own. Besides these two items, the apostles were instructed to take no food, no sack, and no money in their belts, not even a second tunic. The mission charge suggested by Q (Matt. 10:9–10; Luke 9:3; 10:4) is even more austere, permitting neither sandals nor a staff. Jesus' instructions here in Mark seem to allude to the Israelites in Egypt, who were commanded to be ready with sandals on their feet and staff in hand (Exod. 12:11). By taking nothing else on the journey, the apostles demonstrate their complete dependence upon God and the hospitality of others.

This leads to the second set of instructions (vv. 10–11), which deals with missionary etiquette. The instruction to stay in one place and not move

Homiletical Perspective

been called to go out and for what purpose? In the early days of the church, enthusiasm marked those who were sent out to teach and heal. These days, evangelism is more about maintenance or survival. We are careful people who do not want to offend potential new members. What would be different if we were risk takers ready to lose our lives for the sake of the gospel?

The preacher may well ask what the present-day witness of the congregation is in the community. What form does the church's witness take? What would happen if members stepped out of their comfort zone: danced with the dancers or took the stage with the theatre company? What would making common cause with those across racial or ethnic divides do to change our lives, as well as the lives of those to whom we have been "sent"? What if we walked hand in hand with the one called "enemy"?

Compared with the Twelve, we act as though we were sent out to be tourists rather than disciples in the world. We plan, pack, and go. The cab driver, the airport attendant, the ship's crew are strangers—pleasant but separate. In every port, we are there solely for our own agenda. Hit the high spots, avoid the rubble, watch our backs, send pictures from the phone, and return to sea. No wonder tourists are often resented by the locals. No wonder Christians who seek to impose their agenda on the stranger are often rejected.

Might the witness we bear to the gospel at home also be touristlike? Our family wants and our business practices tend to be all about us, our church an institution that exists to meet our needs. To live as a tourist, even at home, is to live in a social bubble that negates our witness to the gospel. We were made to live in deep and abiding relation to one another and to order our corporate lives in relation to the common good. We glimpse this life when we choose to be vulnerable to the neighbor and the stranger, knowing the hurts, the needs, and the worth of the other. That is how disciples of Jesus Christ travel through life. Jesus sent his disciples out to be companions and friends, not tourists.

"*. . . And Gave Them Authority . . .*" *(v. 7b).* Mark recounts how Jesus gave his disciples authority. Do we have authority to knock on a door and to share, when appropriate, the truth of the gospel that has the power to make all things new? Do we have authority to name social evil, cultural blindness, and personal sin? A sermon might invite the congregation to

Mark 6:6b–13

Theological Perspective

A third thing we can take from this brief passage is its explicit advice about failure: shake the dust from your feet (v. 11). Years ago Langdon Gilkey was talking to a group of students at the University of Chicago Divinity School, telling them that they needed to develop a thicker skin when it came to theological debate. He said, in so many words, "You'll work for ten years on a book and once it is published, it will take your colleagues in the field about ten minutes to tell you everything you missed and got wrong." Chuckling, he added, "And you are supposed to learn from that." One has to learn to grow from adversity rather to fear it. Jesus did not wait, in Mark, until the very end of his life to send out the apostles; he knew it took time to grow the kind of courage that would produce fruit.

When Mark picks up the story again in verse 30, he writes that "the apostles gathered around Jesus, and told him all they had done and taught." This exercise in preaching and healing—their own experience of supervised ministry—had brought them closer to Jesus, closer to him not only by virtue of sharing in his power, but also by virtue of sharing in his message and in his suffering. If contemporary theology and ministry are to be persuasive as well as challenging, there must be a compelling sense of urgency to one's interpretation of the gospel and, more than urgent, it must be honest and direct, simple (not simplistic) in content. Finally, one must expect failure and learn to shake the dust from one's feet; it is part of the fieldwork of the gospel. Let those who have ears, hear.

JOSEPH A. BESSLER

Pastoral Perspective

broken heart. However, the good news of Jesus is not just about our empathy, or even God's empathy, but rather about what *God has done* to liberate us from the forces of bondage and brokenness (1:27, 31, 42; 2:5; 3:5; 5:15, 34, 42; 10:45).

The disciples of Jesus preach the good news of what God has done and is doing in and through God's Son (1:1, 14). This is a reprise of Jesus' own message that "the time is fulfilled, and the kingdom of God has come near; repent, and believe in the good news" (1:15). In light of this good news, change is required: "So they went out and proclaimed that all should *repent*" (6:12). It is not enough to *feel* better; Jesus has come to *make us better* by inviting us to know, love, and follow him (1:17, 20; 8:34).

4. Do Not Take Responsibility for the Outcome. Jesus' invitation for his disciples to shake the dust off their feet (v. 11) is a gracious, liberating word. Here is his blessed invitation to do our best and then leave the rest to God. No one, not even God, can (or will) control another's response (6:6a). The disciple's calling is faithfulness, not success.

This is the hardest lesson for many ministers and other Christian servants to learn. It is not our job to play God, let alone be God, but only to do what the Master asks. Thankfully what God makes of our efforts is in more able hands than ours (6:38–41).

In the end, Jesus' disciples were faithful in this, their first mission, not because they reached "everyone" but because "many" (v. 13) found liberation, hope, and healing. Jesus asked nothing more of his first disciples than this. Part of God's great good news is that God asks nothing more—and nothing less—of us.

Franklin's four rules of pastoral care are a good summation of what it takes to be fully present to another human being in a hopeful, healing way. That does not surprise me, since as Franklin's friend and former supervisee, I know Franklin to be a master practitioner of the pastoral art; and I happen to know he got his four rules, directly or indirectly, from Jesus.

BOB SETZER JR.

Exegetical Perspective

from house to house prevents missionaries from taking advantage of the hospitality they receive from their local hosts. Early Christian literature attests to the occasional abuse of hospitality perpetrated by some itinerant prophets and missionaries (*Didache* 11.4–6). The success of Christian missionary endeavors depended heavily on the cooperation of the missionaries and the local residents. Each needed to respect the other. Both were partners in mission (see Rom. 10:14–15). Consequently, being unreceptive to the message and hostile toward itinerant missionaries might make one liable for judgment and could have punitive consequences. Just as the Israelites did when returning from a foreign land, the disciples were to shake "off the dust" from their feet as a symbolic gesture of repudiation and solemn warning (Acts 13:51).

The final scene (vv. 12–13) describes the activities of the apostles. Besides preaching the message of repentance, they were also authorized to exorcise demons (v. 7) and to cure the sick by anointing them with oil. The apostles' mission, essentially the extension of Jesus' own mission, replicated what Jesus said and did. In so doing, the Twelve realized their vocation as "fishers of people" (1:17) and "apostles." Although the description of the mission is brief, their success provides a strong contrast to the unbelief that Jesus encountered in his hometown. Whereas Jesus there could heal only a few sick people (6:5), the disciples heal many.

In summary, Jesus had chosen an ordinary band of followers, who were often unperceptive and unbelieving and had many flaws, yet he conferred on them an extraordinary responsibility. Unencumbered by material things, they obediently went out with urgency to participate in Jesus' mission. Wearing sandals and carrying a staff, they relied completely on God and on the hospitality of others. They did not go out as lone missionaries but in pairs. Thus this Gospel passage offers us a glimmer of hope. Despite our flaws and sins, we are also charged with a mission, not as lone rangers but rather as partners in mission. Some may travel to distant lands, while others are local supporters. Both parties have an important role to play. Collaboration is crucial to the success of mission and ministry. Even when met with resistance, we ought not to be discouraged but we should obediently carry out the assignment with perseverance and determination together.

VANTHANH NGUYEN

Homiletical Perspective

reflect on the nature of Jesus' authority and how he shares that authority with the church today.

"Take Nothing for the Journey Except . . ." (v. 8). This text takes us first to the attic and then to the curb. It asks what we really need materially in order to be effective. In front of every preacher is a congregation full of stakeholders and relic rescuers. Churches have unraveled over new candlesticks on the communion table, and pews suddenly removed from the back two rows. The preacher might well compare herself to someone who is readying the church for its future occupants. In doing so she could lift up what is of real value in relation to the church's mission and what is superfluous, even wasteful. While we love our church furnishings, practices, and liturgies, in order to respond to the call of Christ to "go out," we must be light enough on our feet to leave the things that weigh us down behind. The preacher could also consider what he needs as basics for life and ministry, while asking what the congregation might need, and not need, to be effective.

"Wherever You Enter a House . . ." (v. 10). The Markan directive on church-canvassing etiquette acknowledges that our reception will vary from house to house. Some people will welcome us and show us hospitality; some will take our pamphlet through the crack in the door; some will slam that same door in our face. A sermon about the styles of sharing the gospel will help us ask why we go and how willing we are to let people respond as they will. If visitation is about building relationships, then the protocols of friendship must come into play. The neighbor is not prey, enemy, rival, or threat. He or she is a human life with a story to tell. The protocol of friendship begins with acquaintance, deepens with conversation, takes time, and may eventually lead to richer sharing and the revelation of one's most sacred treasures. This does not happen in five minutes at the door or two Sundays in the Beginners Class. It happens by God's grace and in God's time as the gospel transforms the lives of those sent out, as well as the lives of those who take them in.

G. MALCOLM SINCLAIR

Mark 6:14–29

¹⁴King Herod heard of it, for Jesus' name had become known. Some were saying, "John the baptizer has been raised from the dead; and for this reason these powers are at work in him." ¹⁵But others said, "It is Elijah." And others said, "It is a prophet, like one of the prophets of old." ¹⁶But when Herod heard of it, he said, "John, whom I beheaded, has been raised."

¹⁷For Herod himself had sent men who arrested John, bound him, and put him in prison on account of Herodias, his brother Philip's wife, because Herod had married her. ¹⁸For John had been telling Herod, "It is not lawful for you to have your brother's wife." ¹⁹And Herodias had a grudge against him, and wanted to kill him. But she could not, ²⁰for Herod feared John, knowing that he was a righteous and holy man, and he protected him. When he heard him, he was greatly perplexed; and yet he liked to listen to him. ²¹But an opportunity came when Herod on his birthday gave a banquet for his courtiers and offi-

Theological Perspective

The passage opens ominously as word has come to King Herod about the preaching and actions of Jesus and the apostles in the villages. Mark's report calls to mind Herod the Great's hearing of a child's birth in Matthew's Gospel. In Mark, however, this news about Jesus and the disciples prompts Herod Antipas to recall John the Baptist: "But when Herod heard of it, he said, 'John, whom I beheaded, has been raised'" (v. 16). Mark then recounts—as a virtual flashback—the events leading up to Herod's order to execute John.

In the flashback Mark portrays Herod as an ambiguous character. Herod is caught between his respect for John ("knowing that he was a righteous and holy man," v. 20) and his need to save face ("yet out of regard for his oaths and for the guests, he did not want to refuse her," v. 26). Indeed, Mark writes that Herod had sought to "protect John" from Herodias, that he "liked to listen" to John, even as John indicted him for marrying his brother's wife, and that he was "deeply grieved" to order John's execution. Mark insists on showing that Herod, despite his feelings for John, remained ultimately trapped by his own political ambitions. Later in the Gospel, Mark will portray Pilate as similarly caught between finding no guilt in Jesus and yet "wishing to satisfy the crowd" (15:14–15). In this way Mark undercuts

Pastoral Perspective

Some years ago, Rabbi Harold Kushner wrote a bestselling book entitled *When Bad Things Happen to Good People*. Despite the book's title, most people misstate the title as **Why Bad Things Happen to Good People**.

John Claypool, who finished his storied career as a pastor and author teaching at Atlanta's McAfee School of Theology, once spoke about a private conversation with Rabbi Kushner. Claypool asked Kushner why he did not title his book *Why Bad Things Happen to Good People*.

"Because," the rabbi answered softly, "that book would have been three words long: 'I don't know.'"

In the grisly tale of John the Baptist's murder, the *why* question thrusts itself upon us: How can one upon whom Jesus heaped the highest of praise (Matt. 11:9–11; Luke 7:26–28) meet such an unjust and diabolical end? Mark's Gospel does not address the *why* question. Indeed, Mark reports this unsettling story so matter-of-factly that many readers find his witness puzzling and even exasperating. It is as though Mark wants his readers to realize that despite high hopes for the ministry of Jesus and his disciples (6:6b–13) and the exciting things happening all around (6:14a, 30–56), sometimes bad things do happen to good people. These setbacks to God's best and brightest hopes for the world must not be allowed to derail

cers and for the leaders of Galilee. ²²When his daughter Herodias came in and danced, she pleased Herod and his guests; and the king said to the girl, "Ask me for whatever you wish, and I will give it." ²³And he solemnly swore to her, "Whatever you ask me, I will give you, even half of my kingdom." ²⁴She went out and said to her mother, "What should I ask for?" She replied, "The head of John the baptizer." ²⁵Immediately she rushed back to the king and requested, "I want you to give me at once the head of John the Baptist on a platter." ²⁶The king was deeply grieved; yet out of regard for his oaths and for the guests, he did not want to refuse her. ²⁷Immediately the king sent a soldier of the guard with orders to bring John's head. He went and beheaded him in the prison, ²⁸brought his head on a platter, and gave it to the girl. Then the girl gave it to her mother. ²⁹When his disciples heard about it, they came and took his body, and laid it in a tomb.

Exegetical Perspective

It is often easy to tell the truth or speak one's mind in safe environments. The real test is to speak up and set the record straight when the situation is dangerous and life threatening. In this passage, John the Baptist denounces the injustice that he sees and courageously speaks up for righteousness even in a hostile environment. Two noticeable characteristics shine brightly in the life of John the Baptist, namely, courage and honesty.

The account of John the Baptist's death found in Mark 6:14–30, which is often labeled as a "legend," is one of those famous stories that has often been portrayed in Christian art as well as in film and opera. While the story is also found in Matthew (14:1–13), it is significantly redacted and abbreviated from Mark. Luke, on the other hand, does not even record the event but only alludes to John's death (Luke 9:7–9). The Gospel of John tells nothing about John's death; furthermore, according to the Fourth Gospel, Jesus began his ministry (baptizing) even before John was arrested (John 3:22–24).

The Markan account of the death of John the Baptist is sandwiched between the sending of the Twelve (6:7–13) and the report of their return (6:30). The placement of this sordid story, which turns Herod's birthday party into a banquet of death, is by no means accidental. The account may be divided into

Homiletical Perspective

Like the two previous texts in Mark, this passage explores the threats and discouragements that can stifle the work of the faithful. The limits found in hometown expectations can do it, as can the various receptions at the door one meets when calling in a strange town. The threat of political power when in the grip of its own business or its obligation to the dance and demands of family can be lethal, even to the greatest of us.

"Some Were Saying . . ." (v. 14). In telling the details of any event, our recounting can be colored by our state of mind. The news that Jesus was among them was interpreted by some as evidence that the one who had been murdered had indeed returned to life; that is, John the Baptist was alive again. Some saw in Jesus an Elijah moment that signaled the long-promised day of reckoning finally at hand. Others took Jesus' presence as evidence of the power of prophets of old, a sign of the bedrock of God's purposes that always lie beneath any chaos. Those prophetic voices still sing a chorus of hope to us, Jesus singing a fresh verse in this enduring song.

When we tell stories of the Savior today, what is our state of mind? Are we smug, fearful, enthusiastic, unrealistic, or naive? A sermon might call upon hearers to reflect on the state of mind we bring to

Mark 6:14–29

Theological Perspective

the power of Herod and, later, of Pilate. Such figures appear powerful, suggests Mark, but they do not even have the character to do what they know to be right.

Following closely upon the story of Jesus' rejection by his own family, Mark's story of Herod provides the reader with yet another picture of how Jesus' message fails to find a receptive spirit. In Mark's telling of the story, Herod's belief that Jesus is John come back to life functions doubly: first, it links Jesus to John as a mighty prophet; second, it opens up Mark's flashback—a meditation really—on the limitations and dangers of political power. If Jesus' hometown remains unable to respond to Jesus because they remain caught in their own assumptions about Jesus' family and childhood, Herod is unable to respond to Jesus because he is also caught up in the past, in his guilt-ridden memories of John. In Mark 7:9, Jesus says to the Pharisees, "You have a fine way of rejecting the commandment of God in order to keep your tradition!" In each of these cases, people do not simply reject Jesus; Mark presents their rationales for doing so.

The rejection in these stories is more unsettling than Mark's stories of unclean spirits, because these human acts of rejection have more profound consequences. These human figures cannot simply be rebuked, and, unlike the unclean spirits, they do not even recognize Jesus. They are a more intractable obstacle to the gospel. Their inability to hear Jesus (4:9, 23), to be receptive to his message, has a kind of infectious, demonic power of its own. While Jesus has the power to forgive sins (2:3–12) and has, in fact, come "to call sinners" (2:17b), the power of this resistance will mean that Jesus' message of forgiveness and new life in the kingdom of God will be rejected. By Mark 8:31, Jesus tells his disciples that "the Son of Man must undergo great suffering, . . . be killed, and after three days rise again."

What one sees in the story of Herod and in Mark's other stories of rejection is the building of a confrontation between Jesus and the entrenched powers of conventionality and tradition that cannot see, and actively reject, the new kingdom of God taking root in their midst. In his construction of this confrontation, Mark defends the necessity of the cross and the apparent failure of Jesus' message. Mark suggests that such apparent failure, however, misses what God is doing in secret. Jesus, he argues, has been rejected from the beginning. That he should die for his message of transformation should come as no surprise; but along the way, his message has taken root in some, and his death will be like a

Pastoral Perspective

faithfulness to God's kingdom among Jesus' disciples, whether in first-century Jerusalem or Rome or twenty-first-century America.

Sad to say, if one stays in the ministry—or in social work, medicine, or law enforcement—long enough, one will eventually face the sort of diabolical evil depicted in this story. Consider the neglected or abused child who endures unspeakable atrocities; the battered wife whose bloodied nose, black eye, and broken heart say what she cannot or will not: that her violent, alcoholic husband often turns on her with a killing rage; the father who must go to the city morgue at three in the morning to identify his drug-addicted son, now dead at nineteen. To minister alongside such people at such times will likely send the battered, bewildered minister fleeing for the Psalms, praying and screeching the laments that were so thoughtfully left there for just a time such as this (e.g., Pss. 12:1, 8; 22:1–2; 35:20–23; 44:22–25).

There are certainly hints in the text about the disastrous chain of events that brings God's faithful servant John to such a violent end. There are the systemic evil and dysfunction in Herod and Herodias's own family histories that helped turn them into the monsters depicted in the story (see exegetical comments). There are Herod's lust and grasping for power and status (v. 17) and Herodias's consuming resentment (vv. 19, 25). There is the persistent refusal, at least on Herod's part, to heed the pangs of conscience (vv. 16, 20a) and his inclination to flirt with but not heed God's word (v. 20b). There is the strong suggestion of a wild party where intoxicants are flowing freely and compromise Herod's judgment (vv. 21–23). Finally, there is the moral vacuity of one who is more intent on pleasing his peers than God (v. 26, as distinguished from Jesus, Matt. 22:16b).

In short, this is a disturbing portrait of a severely dysfunctional family that rebuffs any and all attempts to break their terrifying descent into moral anarchy and madness. In the end, neither the good news of Jesus (1:1, 14) nor the bad news of John (v. 18) can save Herod from making a horrific mistake that will define him forever.

From there, the story plummets toward its terrifying conclusion. Herod appears to be exhibit A of Jesus' teaching about blasphemy of the Holy Spirit (3:28–30); namely, this is what happens when one so persistently rejects the wooing of God's Spirit that one becomes deaf to God's word and leading.

In the end, there is nothing John's disciples can do to stop the travesty that befalls their revered master. They have no answer to the *why* question: "Why

Exegetical Perspective

four sections: opinions regarding Jesus (vv. 14–16), the arrest and imprisonment of John the Baptist (vv. 17–20), Herod's birthday party (vv. 21–26), and John's death and burial (vv. 27–29).

The introductory scene (vv. 14–16) serves as a transition to this narrative interlude; it also gives various opinions regarding Jesus. The passage begins by stating, "King Herod heard of it." This is Herod Antipas, son of Herod the Great and Malthace, a Samaritan. He is actually a tetrarch, who is given authority to rule in the territory of Galilee and Perea. He never receives the title "king." In Luke, Jesus calls him "that fox" (Luke 13:32). At any rate, we are not told what Herod has heard. Presumably it has something to do with the mission of the disciples found in the preceding passage (6:6b–13), which must have also included making Jesus' name known (v. 14b). Mark gives three opinions regarding who people think Jesus is: John the Baptist raised from the dead, Elijah, one of the prophets of old. Interestingly these same three responses will be given by the disciples (8:28) when Jesus asks, "Who do people say that I am?" According to Herod, Jesus has to be John the Baptist, whom he had beheaded (v. 16).

The second scene (vv. 17–20) describes the arrest and imprisonment of John the Baptist. The Markan reader had already been told earlier about John's arrest (1:14); however, the cause and reason for his arrest have been withheld until now. John charged King Herod with an illegal marriage that was forbidden by the Law, namely, taking his brother's wife (Lev. 18:16). Consequently, Herodias wanted to kill John but could not, for Herod was afraid of him and wanted to protect him because he was "a righteous and holy man" (v. 20).

Mark's version of John the Baptist's arrest and death notably differs with Josephus's account (*Ant.* 18.5.2–4). There are two main differences. While the basis of John's arrest is personal in Mark, it is strictly political in Josephus; furthermore, while the place of imprisonment seems to be in Tiberias in the Gospel, Josephus situates it in Machaerus, a fortress located on the eastern side of the Dead Sea. Although the two versions differ slightly, they do not necessarily contradict each other. Rather, both versions add credibility to the historicity of the martyrdom of John the Baptist at the hand of a wicked ruler.

The third scene (vv. 21–26) shifts from John's prison to Herod's birthday party. Important guests from Galilee—political magistrates, military commanders, and prominent men—are invited to attend the banquet. The movement of the scene—entering,

Homiletical Perspective

our convictions about Jesus and the hope that is in us for God's people.

"But When Herod Heard of It, He Said, 'John, Whom I Beheaded, Has Been Raised'" (v. 16). This chilling tale, variations of which have doubtless been repeated in history across time, displays the ways in which we are dangerously vulnerable to each other. Herod, though king, is held in the grip of biting public criticism. He has broken a tribal taboo by marrying his brother's wife. Herod also knows the power and the reach of John the Baptist's popularity; he even senses John's spiritual authority.

Although he does not understand the depth of John's teaching, Herod "liked to listen to him." Herod is vulnerable to John but beware the ticking clock inside a conflicted king. When the alarm goes off, it can prove dangerous to one and all. Herodias, Herod's wife, is a woman scorned and offended by the public shame John has brought upon her. Her hatred knows no bounds. She wants John dead and wants Herod to give the order to have him killed. This cauldron of feelings, grudges, jealousies, and unfinished business is alive today in many a household, workplace, social institution, government department, and local congregation. Beneath high-sounding words and best intentions it plays a role in real lives. A sermon could examine the multiple voices, impulses, and fears that demand our attention and that threaten to undo us and undermine God's intentions for our world.

"But An Opportunity Came" (v. 21). Every plotter waits for the perfect moment. A young girl is the tempting apple of Herod's eye. For a variety of reasons, whether they are familial, sensual, or political, Herod promises her anything in gratitude for a single dance. The girl tells her mother, and the mother sets the trap. The daughter trips the snare, and the Baptist dies. The story is stark and startling in its violence, but if we are honest with ourselves, we may see how often part of our lives is lived at the level of sensuality and personal insecurity. Part of our lives is often driven by assumptions and fears that are poorly conceived and feelings that go unacknowledged.

The pastor and the church council are wise to ask the real and often mixed motivation that underlies any course of action. Life and death are involved in all that we do. A personal and vulnerable sermon that models the dark side beneath our choices could well be the needle that lances the boil that is slowing sickening many a soul.

Mark 6:14–29

Theological Perspective

seed that will become newness of life in the resurrection.

One aspect of this ultimate surprise and vindication can be glimpsed by returning to the very beginning of our passage. Herod has received word of Jesus and the speculation about his true identity: "Some were saying, 'John the baptizer has been raised from the dead; and for this reason these powers are at work in him.' But others said, 'It is Elijah.' And others said, 'It is a prophet, like one of the prophets of old'" (vv. 14b–15). A short two chapters later, similar speculation occurs, only this time with a definitive clarification. There, in Mark 8:27–30, Jesus first asks the disciples, "Who do people say that I am?" and the disciples say back to him, "John the Baptist; and others, Elijah; and still others, one of the prophets." Jesus then presses them, "But who do you say that I am?" It is at this point that Peter answers, "You are the Messiah."

This revelation is confirmed in chapter 9 with the story of the transfiguration, with the figures of Moses and Elijah in attendance, and the voice from the cloud saying, "This is my Son, the Beloved; listen to him!" (9:7). This indicates the extent to which leaders like Herod and the Pharisees, and even the people in Jesus' hometown, have not only failed to understand who Jesus is but have actually, if unwittingly, resisted the activity of God in their midst. Nevertheless the work of God's anointed—like the word that goes out from God's mouth and does not "return empty" (Isa. 55:11)—will prove fruitful, and it will multiply. Precisely because it was so strongly resisted and apparently defeated, will Jesus' message of the kingdom of God be yet more wondrous at the harvest.

JOSEPH A. BESSLER

Pastoral Perspective

would a good and just God let a good and just man die like this?" All they can do is answer the *when* question: *When bad things happen to good people*, God's people show up armed with nothing but their tears to minister to the grieving, bury the dead (v. 29), and pray—as Jesus taught us—that God's will might be done on earth as it is in heaven (Matt. 6:10).

In a sleepy seminary class years ago, my theology professor spoke words of truth that have steadied me when confronted by the apparent triumph of evil over good: "The affirmation 'God is love' cannot be sustained apart from a robust eschatology." In other words, unless someday God sets right what has gone so terribly wrong in this broken world, it is nonsensical to speak of God's love, let alone God's justice. There is just too much wickedness that goes unanswered, too much violence that carries the day, too much evil that runs roughshod over good.

What if Jesus is the Alpha *and* the Omega, the beginning *and* the End (Rev. 22:13)? What if Jesus is not just the shape of God's vulnerability and helplessness (as on Jesus' cross), but also the shape of God's future (as in Jesus' resurrection)? What if, as the twisted and gnarled John Merrick proclaims in the play *The Elephant Man*,[1] "The Bible promises that in heaven the crooked shall be made straight" (a phrase that recalls the ministry of John the Baptist, 1:3)? What then?

Then John's disciples, bewildered and brokenhearted, burying their master, are not the end of the story (6:29). For soon, other devastated disciples will fret about the body of their innocent Master, cruelly and viciously slain (15:43–47; 16:1–3). However, in the tomb of that One to whom John bore witness (1:7–8), God will be mysteriously present, plotting not only the resurrection of God's Son, but also the setting straight and re-creation of a whole new world (9:31; 10:34; 14:58).

Herod is right to fear a power, far greater than his own, about to be unleashed by the God who raised Jesus from the dead (6:14b).

BOB SETZER JR.

---

1. Christopher De Vore, Eric Bergren, and David Lynch, *The Elephant Man* (1980), directed by David Lynch, based on the story *The Elephant Man*, by Ashley Montagu.

Exegetical Perspective

exiting, and reentering—creates much drama and suspense. The point of view shifts from Herod and his guests to Herodias's daughter, from the young dancer to her mother, and back to the king. With each transition, the pace quickens. The narrative climaxes with Herodias getting exactly what she wants, the head of John the Baptizer. The king's contemptible oath and face-saving decision cause the death of an innocent and righteous man. Although he is "very sad," he does not hesitate to surrender to the foolish and gruesome request of a child.

The final scene (vv. 27–29) describes John's execution and burial. The king's command is swiftly carried out. The executioner beheads John. The head of Baptizer is given to the girl on a platter, and she in turn gives it to her mother. What begins as an ostentatious celebration turns into a banquet of death for a righteous prophet. John's role as the "forerunner" abruptly ends, but not before he is given an honorable burial by his own disciples. John's disciples bravely "took his body, and laid it in a tomb" (v. 29).

The dramatic interlude of the arrest and death of John the Baptist, which is artistically sandwiched between the accounts of the apostles going out on their mission and returning, is not a Markan literary accident. It functions as a sobering reminder to Christians, who might be under political or religious oppression or material allurement, to remain unwavering in God's mission and commitment. Like the prophets of old, John the Baptist was willing to risk his life for his message and not succumb to public pressure.

To have a share in the ministry and destiny of Jesus, discipleship will cost nothing less than everything. The question is now put to us: Are we willing to speak up or set the record straight under whatever conditions we find ourselves in? When we see injustice, suffering, or abuse, are we willing to call wrongdoing what it is? May we never sway from our role as disciples who are also being sent out (*apostellō*) to be messengers of the good news.

VANTHANH NGUYEN

Homiletical Perspective

"When His Disciples Heard About It, They Came and Took His Body, and Laid It in a Tomb" (v. 29). Here is courage. The scene is that of brave soldiers crossing a no-man's-land of snipers and razor wire. How far will we go to honor what a leader has envisioned, and to finish what a leader has begun? We are all handed incomplete work from other hands. Some go as far as they can, others as far as they dare. Some grow tired. Some can see no further ahead. Some need our fresh faces and insights to flesh out the dream. Cultural life is multigenerational. Each new age of life must mine for the gold among us.

To claim John's body and to bury him takes an intentional effort to know him and to understand his passion. How was he raised? What did he overcome? What was a great turning point in his life? What drew us to him? What did he ask us to do? What does that work look like now that he is dead? How do our gifts remain ours while honoring his?

Every congregation has its forebears and heroes. A sermon on this text could take the form of lifting up a name from a wall plaque or a photo from an old church yearbook. Tell of those times and compare them to these. Remember the issues facing the town and the people then. Trace the next steps taken in their honor; then pray for faithfulness and for a fresh link with them in our day.

This passage of threat and warning is surrounded by texts of miracles and wonders. The text could also give rise to a sermon about "placement," as we name the crises we know in our personal and social lives, acknowledging as well all the good things that call forth our faith and all the wondrous things that sustain it. Towns may bark at strangers, but homecoming brings joy. Officialdom may diminish life for its own reasons, but courage in the face of such diminishment is still the stuff of legend for those who follow on. Truth about the things that frighten us and enthusiasm about the things that save our lives have magnetic power for the human spirit.

G. MALCOLM SINCLAIR

Mark 6:30–44

³⁰The apostles gathered around Jesus, and told him all that they had done and taught. ³¹He said to them, "Come away to a deserted place all by yourselves and rest a while." For many were coming and going, and they had no leisure even to eat. ³²And they went away in the boat to a deserted place by themselves. ³³Now many saw them going and recognized them, and they hurried there on foot from all the towns and arrived ahead of them. ³⁴As he went ashore, he saw a great crowd; and he had compassion for them, because they were like sheep without a shepherd; and he began to teach them many things. ³⁵When it grew late, his disciples came to him and said, "This is a deserted place, and the hour is now very late; ³⁶send them away so that they may go into the surrounding country and villages and buy something for themselves to eat."

Theological Perspective

A theological vision of God's economy of plenty unfolds in this telling by Mark of the feeding of a multitude. Mark will tell a version of this story again in 8:1–10; in that case, as in this one, he is aiming to cast into bold relief the need of disciples to reunderstand core matters of material life from a divine and not merely human perspective. Mark perhaps cuts the disciples slack by opening the scene with an acknowledgment of their need to retreat from the constant pressures of the ministry in which they have been engaged. When unexpectedly confronted by a mass of needy people who have circled the shore and beat Jesus and the disciples (traveling by boat) to the place of retreat, the disciples may be forgiven for their slowness in responding to the crowd's needs.

Ever the good shepherd, Jesus is not put off, given this turn of events. Rather, he undertakes to fulfill their need, rather than seeking to avoid it—beginning "to teach them many things" (v. 34). Mark does not portray the disciples as assisting Jesus in this expression of concern for the people, but reintroduces them into the narrative when they come to counsel with Jesus about breaking up the gathering because the day is tilting toward evening. To be sure, their motivation arises from their perceptions of the crowd's need for sustenance. "This is a deserted

Pastoral Perspective

There is a strong echo in this passage, an abiding echo of a concern harbored by Moses and the prophets. It is this concern that rips out Jesus' guts as he sees the great crowd that is about to divert his plan to host a retreat for the disciples after a grueling missionary journey: "He had compassion for them" (v. 34). "Compassion" is a weak rendering of what was going on within Jesus. The Greek word (*splanchnizomai*) refers to a churning of the gut. Jesus was churning on his insides because those in the crowd "were like sheep without a shepherd."

Like sheep without a shepherd. That is an echo from various experiences of the people of God in the Old Testament. It is heard in Moses' yearning for a successor so that the people may not be bereft of leadership in the desolation of the wilderness, "like sheep without a shepherd" (Num. 27:17). It is heard in the Deutero-historian's reflection on life under the abominable reign of Ahab, as Ahab and Jezebel chased after idols rather than tending to the well-being of the people, leaving the people "scattered on the mountains, like sheep that have no shepherd" (1 Kgs. 22:17). It is heard in Ezekiel's eschatological oracle (Ezek. 34:8–23), offered to the people enduring exploitative leaders callously preying on the people for the leaders' own callous gain, namely, that the Lord will one day "set up over them one shepherd

³⁷But he answered them, "You give them something to eat." They said to him, "Are we to go and buy two hundred denarii worth of bread, and give it to them to eat?" ³⁸And he said to them, "How many loaves have you? Go and see." When they had found out, they said, "Five, and two fish." ³⁹Then he ordered them to get all the people to sit down in groups on the green grass. ⁴⁰So they sat down in groups of hundreds and of fifties. ⁴¹Taking the five loaves and the two fish, he looked up to heaven, and blessed and broke the loaves, and gave them to his disciples to set before the people; and he divided the two fish among them all. ⁴²And all ate and were filled; ⁴³and they took up twelve baskets full of broken pieces and of the fish. ⁴⁴Those who had eaten the loaves numbered five thousand men.

Exegetical Perspective

This portion of Mark's Gospel is the beginning of a literary unit, Mark 6:30 to 8:21, which is framed by boat trips on the Sea of Galilee (6:32, Jesus seeks a resting place for his disciples; 8:14–21, Jesus holds a quiet conversation with his disciples). The stories contained within these trips focus on Jesus the wonder worker. A more extensive discussion about the meaning and function of miracle stories in the first century and how they applied to Jesus can be found in the exegetical essay on Mark 6:53–56. In this essay we will enter into the thought world of Mark and his community, resisting attempts at twenty-first-century rationalizations about Jesus the wonder worker.

Mark offers his reader two stories in which Jesus feeds a multitude of people with a few loaves of bread and a couple of fish, here and in 8:1–9. The first story begins with the disciples reporting "all that they had done and taught" (v. 30). Jesus, sensing their excitement and exhaustion, invites them to "come away to a deserted place all by yourselves and rest a while" (v. 31). But their solitude is short lived. While Jesus is sensitive to the needs of his disciples, he also has compassion on the growing crowd "because they were like sheep without a shepherd" (v. 34). He speaks to their souls with his teaching, then turns to their physical needs. He will not let them leave spiritually or physically hungry.

Homiletical Perspective

Rest: we all need it, sometimes more than other times. Sometimes the rest we need is sleep; sometimes it is just solitude. The press of people can wear us out. Jesus needed rest too. He and his disciples had been busy. Mark emphasizes the rush of their lives with his repeated use of the word *euthys*, "immediately." Chapter 4 closes with Jesus sleeping in a boat until the disciples wake him to calm the waves. After that, they encounter the demoniac in Gerasa, cross over the Sea of Galilee, witness Jesus' healing of a hemorrhaging woman and his raising of Jairus's daughter. Then they travel on to Nazareth, where Jesus teaches and afterward sends them out two by two to other villages. About that time, King Herod has John the Baptist beheaded, adding grief to their exhaustion. As Mark tells it, this all happened without rest. Finally we find Jesus saying, "Come away to a deserted place all by yourselves and rest a while" (v. 31). Jesus needed to rest. His disciples needed to rest. Who cannot empathize with their need for rest?

Did they finally get to rest? Not yet! Perhaps the preacher can draw people into the story by reminding them of their own frustration with exhaustion, even as they continue to work. A litany in which the people confess their need of rest, even from the demands of the church, may also be a helpful way into the story.

Mark 6:30–44

Theological Perspective

place, and the hour is now very late; send them away so that they may go into the surrounding country and villages and buy something for themselves to eat" (vv. 35–36).

Now Mark's lesson for the disciples about God's economy of plenty can commence. Jesus' direct response to them is as terse as it is clear: "You give them something to eat" (v. 37). Jesus has invited the disciples to a deserted place for respite from the pressures of their work. Whatever hopes they have that this original intention would be renewed by their intervention are thus quickly dashed. Their response to his instruction displays how little they understand God's economy. Incredulously, they ask whether they should buy and distribute bread to the whole crowd, noting the considerable expense involved.

Again Jesus' response startles them by the turn it takes. Instead of sending them out on a shopping expedition, Jesus asks the disciples to take an inventory of the food at hand. "How many loaves have you? Go and see" (v. 38). Of course the report back was less than encouraging: five loaves and two fish. All of this leads to a pivotal moment in which Jesus sits the multitude down in groups and takes all the resources that the disciples have found among them. His first act is a blessing of the offering, followed by the presentation of the broken loaves and the divided fish to the disciples "to set before the people" (v. 41).

Two results of the action underscore Mark's understanding of God's economy of plenty. The first is that "all ate and were filled" (v. 42). The disciples see that, when the resources God has entrusted to his people are received in thanksgiving and shared with generosity, there is enough. No recourse is needed to increase the food supply in order to feed the hungry. Instead, the call to disciples is carefully to inventory what God has already provided, gratefully to acknowledge the provision to God, and generously to share with all who have need. The first step in understanding God's economy of plenty is to recognize that when this pattern is followed, all will eat and be filled.

The second result of Jesus' action depicted by Mark in this passage is that "they took up twelve baskets full of broken pieces and of the fish" (v. 43). In God's economy of plenty, there is more than just enough to go around. There is an overflowing abundance.

For disciples on our side of the text, this lesson about God's economy of abundance has a special relevance. Conventional economic wisdom in the

Pastoral Perspective

. . . [who] shall feed them and be their shepherd" (Ezek. 34:23).

Sheep without a shepherd. Sheep with faithless shepherds distracted by idols that do not save, that do not provide for the life and well-being of the sheep. Sheep with exploitative shepherds who use the sheep for their own gain. Having sustained suffering and deep wounds at the hands of such shepherds, some of these sheep remain in the pews of present-day congregations, but daring never to trust a shepherd again. Many others dwell beyond the bounds of our churches, determined never to expose themselves afresh to the risk of bad religion.

In one city a new form of a religious congregation has emerged, started by a one-time mainline pastor. The pastor declares that at the core this congregation is christocentric. However, he makes it clear the congregation is hesitant to declare it is "Christian" due to the baggage associated with that name. The congregation is, in his words, "for those who have been burned by the church." Burned by the church due to faithless or exploitative shepherds? Burned like the older man who sojourned in a contemporary megachurch only to return to his mainline congregation and with tears in his eyes ask its pastor, "Pastor, my son. Is he in hell? He moved to New York. He contracted AIDS and died. The pastor at the church I have been attending told me my son is in hell because he never repented of his lifestyle. Tell me, is my son in hell?"

There is a vast flock of sheep who have been burned by the church, by "shepherds" set on an agenda that feeds not the sheep but the egos, the self-interests, and the self-righteousness of the "shepherds." The evangelical writer Brian McLaren declares people are fleeing some popular expressions of the Christian church in the United States because they are tired of being told whom they must hate in order to be Christians.[1]

Jesus was confronted by a shepherdless crowd, a crowd lacking a true shepherd, a crowd whose leaders, Herod and the Pharisees (see 8:15), were not focused on the people's welfare but instead on their own agendas. These people chased after Jesus. Was it because of his many acts of healing and casting out demons? If so, he did not deliver what they expected. That is not the shepherd's job. As Karl Barth said, a good shepherd was one responsible for the sheep,

---

1. Brian McLaren, remarks at the Church Unbound conference, Montreat Conference Center, August 10–14, 2010.

Exegetical Perspective

There are several important interrelated items to consider in this passage. First, those who originally heard Mark's story might have recognized echoes from the Old Testament, in particular the Twenty-third Psalm, which begins:

> The LORD is my shepherd, I shall not want [I will not go hungry].
> He makes me lie down in green pastures;
> he leads me beside still waters;
> he restores my soul.

There are whispers of this psalm in Mark's story. "They were like sheep without a shepherd" (v. 34). Jesus feeds his sheep, restoring body and soul. Jesus has the crowd "sit down in groups on the *green* grass" by the waters of Galilee (v. 39). Mark's readers also might have thought about the scene in Exodus in which the hungry people of Israel are fed manna in the wilderness (Exod. 16; also Num. 11 and Ps. 78:23–25), a connection that John the evangelist makes explicit in his version of the story (John 6).

Now consider the geographical and cultural context. This story takes place near the northwest shore of the Sea of Galilee (v. 45), a largely *Jewish* territory not far from Jesus' home. Compare this context with Mark's second story about Jesus feeding a great crowd, this time in the "region of the Decapolis," a federation of ten *Gentile* cities (8:1–10). Note the lack of allusions to the Old Testament here.

Next think about the numbers Mark has used in his two feeding stories. For Mark's original readers, numbers did more than measure; they contained symbolic meaning. The first number, two hundred denarii, reveals how tired and grumpy the disciples are. They want Jesus to dismiss the crowd and let them fend for themselves, but Jesus will not be so inhospitable. "You give them something to eat," he tells them, and they respond with sarcasm: "Are we to go and buy two hundred denarii worth of bread, and give it to them to eat?" (v. 37). One denarius was about a day's wage for a laborer. Two hundred denarii might be enough money to feed the five thousand men, plus women and children, but it is unlikely that the disciples walk around with that much money.

They do, however, find *five* loaves of bread and *two* fish. After the crowd of *five* thousand men (plus women and children) is fed, the disciples take up *twelve* baskets of leftovers. Specific numbers provided a memory assist for those who passed along this story in its oral form. These numbers also connected the story to the Scriptures of Mark's

Homiletical Perspective

A big crowd found them, "and he had compassion for them . . . and he began to teach them many things" (v. 34). More work. Concentrating on people's emotional needs saps one's strength. Jesus must have been a strong man to do so much in just three years. Even though he needed rest, here he is again teaching them many things. You can almost hear the frustration in the voices of the disciples when they come to Jesus saying, "This is a deserted place, and the hour is now very late; send them away so that they may go into the surrounding country and villages and buy something for themselves to eat" (vv. 35–36). "Send them away, Jesus. They need food. Send them away." Release them. Dismiss them. Again, the preacher can touch on the universal experience of being tired while, at the same time, being needed.

But Jesus' compassion extended far beyond teaching. There are many examples of Jesus' compassion in our Gospels. Indeed, from the very first chapter until now, Mark tells about Jesus healing Peter's mother-in-law (1:30–31), "all who were sick or possessed with demons" (1:32), a leper (1:40), a paralyzed man (2:1–12), and a man with a withered hand (3:1), to mention a few. Luke also records Jesus in his parables pointing to the compassion of the good Samaritan (Luke 10:29–37) and of the father of the prodigal (Luke 15:11–32).

Compassion is a primary characteristic of Jesus. In fact, he is too compassionate to tell these people to leave and fend for themselves. Nor is he ready to let his disciples off the hook. He has already taught them what to say and do and has commissioned them to preach in the villages of Galilee. Having had good success with these things, now he has another assignment for them: "You give them something to eat" (v. 37).

We can almost hear their reaction: "Yeah, right. Like we have enough food for this crowd?" What they did say was that they did not have enough money to buy food for a multitude. This is beginning to sound like a church board meeting! One of the hardest lessons for believers to learn is that the Lord does provide. A sermon could encourage folks to step out in faith to serve the community, instead of checking the budget.

Judging from his other miracles, we assume that Jesus could have said the word and produced food out of nothing, but he asked the disciples to check the supplies. They counted five loaves of bread and two fish. One loaf and half a fish ordinarily are not going to feed more than a thousand people, but this was no ordinary day. When Jesus gives his blessing,

Mark 6:30–44

Theological Perspective

world's prevailing economy is that relentless economic growth (predicated on relentless growth in consumption) is the only mechanism available for achieving the just material aspirations of developing nations without restricting the accustomed material comforts of the developed world. Thus, the efforts of every government on earth, whatever the particular form of its economy, are aimed at economic growth. However, the too-often unacknowledged dilemma is that a finite planet cannot endure economies of infinite material growth. The growing recognition of the impact of our economic activity in adversely affecting the earth as creaturely habitat—not least through unleashing unsustainably high amounts of CO_2 into the atmosphere—suggests the pertinence of Mark's lesson about God's economy of plenty.

Instead of large-scale economies driven solely by a goal of growth, the story of the feeding of multitudes in Mark invites us to consider small-scale economies driven by a concrete awareness of what the needs are. In such economies, there can be a thoughtful accounting of what is already at hand without additional impacts on the environment, grateful acknowledgment of the bounty God has thus already entrusted to us, and generous acts of sharing these resources in resilient, face-to-face communities. Mark's insistence that there was not much stuff available (only five loaves and two fish) suggests an orientation away from growth fueled by the consumption of ever more stuff, to a recognition that God causes life to flourish in many ways that have little to do with more stuff.

The place where Mark's lesson about God's economy of plenty has been rooted most firmly in the Christian tradition is the Eucharist. It is no accident that the words and movement of this story vividly mirror the actions of the Eucharist: provisions are offered, thanks is given, and bread is shared. Just as in the Eucharist, what seems like so little turns out to supply abundantly the need. This lesson of Scripture and liturgy is a lesson that can point the way to sustainable flourishing in the present age.

D. CAMERON MURCHISON

Pastoral Perspective

one who acted on their behalf.[2] However, that is quite different from giving them what they want.

What does Jesus do when his guts are churning because of this encounter with shepherdless sheep? He teaches them many things. Perhaps these things are not what they want, but are they what the flock needs? Then, as the hour has grown late, with his disciples anxious about the continuing hunger of those sheep so burned by exploitative shepherds and bad religion, he calls on the disciples—dare we say the church?—to deliver: "You give them something to eat." Overwhelmed with inadequacy, the disciples object.

Jesus knows how this crowd's deepest need is to continue to be fed. It is through the resources of disciples, frail and untrusting as they are. Those resources, turned over to Jesus and blessed by Jesus, are more than adequate. Astonishingly, Jesus chooses to trust these disciples to be his undershepherds, through whom he continues to feed the people, rescuing them from their lostness due to being abandoned or used by unscrupulous shepherds.[3] So it is still with the church, among the vast horde of shepherdless folk within and around the church in this day.

Finally, two things should be noted. First, Jesus has the crowd sit down on "green grass." In the desert, green grass suddenly appears. This shepherd makes those who have been like sheep without a shepherd "lie down in green pastures" (Ps. 23:1–2). Second, "all ate and were filled." What is that but an echo of promised land, the place where people, seldom satisfied, are completely filled (Deut. 8:10).

Because Jesus has his guts ripped out by people who are like sheep without a shepherd, and has confidence that his bumbling disciples have what it takes to feed them, the resources of those disciples, the church itself, blessed by Jesus, are enough to transform the shepherdless crowd from being strangers and lost wanderers to being like children at home.

PETE PEERY

---

2. Karl Barth, *Church Dogmatics*, IV/2, ed. G. W. Bromiley and T. F. Torrance (Edinburgh: T. & T. Clark, 1936–1977), 186
3. Lamar Williamson, *Mark*, Interpretation series (Atlanta: John Knox Press, 1983), 126.

Exegetical Perspective

church—for example, the *five* books of Moses, the *twelve* tribes of Israel. Now recall the numbers Mark uses in his second feeding story: *seven* loaves and baskets, a number signifying the whole of creation that God called into being in seven days, and *four* thousand people, indicating the four cardinal points of a compass.[1] It looks as if Mark has expanded the scope of his narrative from the particular (a Jewish crowd) to the general (Jesus feeds both Jews and Gentiles). To reinforce this point, Mark has Jesus return to these numbers in his summary discussion with his students (8:18–21).[2]

Finally, note what Jesus does with the loaves and fish. He receives them, and like the host of a great banquet, he looks up to heaven, then *he blesses*, *he breaks*, and *he gives* them to his disciples to distribute to the people. The words in italics are a clue to the meaning of this story. We encounter this formula again in the second feeding narrative (8:6) and, most importantly, in Mark's account of Jesus' Last Supper (14:22). "He blessed . . . he broke . . . he gave" are words that resonated in the minds of those who heard this story, as they do in ours. These are the words we hear each time we share bread as a symbol of the body of Jesus.

Mark's story points the reader forward to that great messianic banquet in which Jesus welcomes all who attend—men, women, and children, Jew (Mark 6) and Gentile (Mark 8) alike. It will be a time of leisure with friends and family, and our gracious host will provide food sufficient for everyone, with leftovers for the journey home (see 8:3).

PAUL W. WALASKAY

Homiletical Perspective

nothing is ordinary, and that is what he does. He blesses the bread and breaks it, and then he gives the bread to them.

Does that sound familiar? Not long after this feeding, Jesus meets with his disciples in an upper room where, after eating a Passover meal, Jesus "took a loaf of bread, and after blessing it he broke it, gave it to them, and said, 'Take; this is my body'" (14:22). When Jesus blesses something we put at his disposal, great things happen. Not only is there enough for everybody, but there is an abundance left over. From either the communion table or the pulpit, believers need to be reminded that the blessing of Jesus is both refreshing and empowering.

The problem, of course, is that we do not very often put our resources at God's disposal. Our time, our talents, our wealth: too often individuals, families, and even churches hoard resources instead of putting them at God's disposal. A good sermon should help hearers recognize the resources available in the congregation and encourage them to bring those resources to Jesus for his blessing, breaking, and distributing. The Lord does provide, but the Lord usually does it with the help of his disciples.

How can our congregations live as disciples? Each congregation must find its own answer to that question. However we live out our faith, we need to balance rest and work. Sermons should point both to the compassion of Jesus, including compassion for us when we are weary, and to the command of Jesus telling us to get busy. "You give them something to eat." We sometimes fulfill that command literally, but more often we find people who need emotional nourishment or spiritual food. In one way or another, we welcome people to our table. Sermons can form people into active disciples of Jesus who, by feeding the hungry and performing other acts of kindness, become the means by which his divine compassion is extended to the world and his commandments are kept.

BRUCE E. SHIELDS

---

1. In this story some of the crowd "have come from a great distance" (Mark 8:3).
2. See the conclusion to the study of Mark 6:45–52.

Mark 6:45–52

⁴⁵Immediately he made his disciples get into the boat and go on ahead to the other side, to Bethsaida, while he dismissed the crowd. ⁴⁶After saying farewell to them, he went up on the mountain to pray.

⁴⁷When evening came, the boat was out on the sea, and he was alone on the land. ⁴⁸When he saw that they were straining at the oars against an adverse wind, he came towards them early in the morning, walking on the sea. He intended to pass them by. ⁴⁹But when they saw him walking on the sea, they thought it was a ghost and cried out; ⁵⁰for they all saw him and were terrified. But immediately he spoke to them and said, "Take heart, it is I; do not be afraid." ⁵¹Then he got into the boat with them and the wind ceased. And they were utterly astounded, ⁵²for they did not understand about the loaves, but their hearts were hardened.

Theological Perspective

A core theological issue in this passage has to do with the failure of Jesus' followers to comprehend the sustaining presence of God in the complex dynamics of their experience. The same lack of comprehension experienced in the preceding verses, when God's economy of plenty turned out to trump the disciples' assumptions of scarcity, reappears in this story of Jesus and a group of disciples who see a threat, not a miracle. It is important to understand that the consternation they expressed was not that of twenty-first-century skeptics dubious about the capacity of Jesus to walk on water. They were rather deeply anxious about what the mysterious figure passing them by might represent, fearing that it portended more harm than help.

Their failure of theological imagination is complete. Rather than understanding the epiphany of God-in-Christ represented by Jesus as he passed by, they feared a demonic attack of some sort. Having followed him more and less faithfully in the preceding days, they had grown accustomed to the "normal" form of his presence among them, teaching and healing the people. But in their own situation of distress, they were unable to "see" his encouraging manifestation of the divine presence on their behalf. The story includes the somewhat curious detail that as Jesus came toward them walking on the water, he

Pastoral Perspective

"Immediately he made his disciples get into the boat and go on ahead to the other side." The very first sentence of this pericope is loaded. It sets the stage for what is at stake in responding to the gospel of God. That gospel calls for going to "the other side."

Going to the other side in Mark's language means going to Gentile territory. It means going to the unknown, going to the foreign, going to the other side of humanity. No wonder the disciples were made, or as the Greek word more strongly suggests, *forced* to go. A deep motif of their religious community was the separation of Jew from Gentile. They knew that to make such a journey would only bring social hostility that could drown their little community. They certainly would not have chosen such a journey on their own, particularly without Jesus with them. Notice: Jesus sends them on their own. Could it be he trusted the disciples' capacity to make the journey?

Jesus' followers in the North American context today are being forced on a journey to the other side. Used to being culturally established in a predominately Protestant, primarily European heritage context, the Christian church in North America is being sent to places unknown. A church that has been very comfortable in its cultural context is finding the culture around it radically shifting. By 2042,

Exegetical Perspective

From the beginning of Mark's Gospel through the sixth chapter, note how often Jesus ventures by boat out onto the Sea of Galilee. This story provides a bit of a twist. This time Jesus makes his way to a boat by walking on the sea.

The narrative begins with one of Mark's frequently used words, "immediately." The pace of Mark's narrative seems to rush the reader headlong into the action, as if Mark wants to bring the reader to the final portion of his story quickly. As Mark raises the curtain on this scene, Jesus seems to be in a hurry to be rid of his disciples and dismiss the well-fed crowd. Perhaps he is ready for some "down time." Mark indicates Jesus wants to pray.

The story continues with time and location markers. It is evening. The boat filled with disciples is in the midst (Gk. *mesō*) of the sea, and Jesus is alone on the land. Jesus is able to see the disciples "straining at the oars against an adverse wind" (v. 48).

Mark now adds a second temporal marker. It was "early in the morning" (literally "the fourth watch of the night"—three to six a.m.) when Jesus began to make his way across the water in the dark. Mark includes another mystifying detail: "[Jesus] intended to pass them by" (v. 48). The Greek term, *ēthelen*, indicates volition; Jesus wanted to pass by the boat and continue to the far shore. Why, you

Homiletical Perspective

We fallible human beings should love this text for several reasons. For one thing, it shows the fallibility of the disciples: "they did not understand about the loaves" (v. 52). Is that not amazing and wonderful? Even the disciples did not understand what had happened when they brought five loaves and two fish to be blessed by Jesus and then fed a crowd with them. Were they overwhelmed or just plain dense? Perhaps their stupidity is not good news, but it sets the scene for the good news of God's grace in spite of our lack of understanding.

Mainly, though, we should love the text for what it shows us about Jesus. Having at last found some time to himself, praying up on the hilltop, he sees his friends in trouble. These grown men, some of them professional fishermen, are having trouble navigating the windy Sea of Galilee. Jesus walks across the water, a sight that is funny enough in relation to twelve men who are having trouble staying upright in a boat. Then he pretends to walk right past them!

When the disciples see him, instead of being relieved, they are "terrified" (v. 50). It is like the old story about a man hanging from a high cliff by a little branch. Calling for help he hears a voice saying, "Let go. I'll catch you." He looks up and says, "Who is that?" and hears the voice reply, "It is the Lord; let go, and I'll catch you." He looks to the bottom of the

Mark 6:45–52

Theological Perspective

intended to "pass them by" (v. 48). Since he came across the water in response to their distress on the sea, this cannot mean that he intended to ignore them. More likely, it represents Jesus' intention to go before them into any danger that might threaten. They thought they saw not a deliverer and sustainer in the midst of danger, but a ghost. So they shrank in fear.

Thereby, they pointed out how faithful followers of Jesus can be quick to mediate Jesus' healing presence to others while failing to receive it for themselves. As unusual as the physical features of this story are to contemporary readers, concentrating on the paranormal easily distracts from the theological point Mark is making for followers ancient and modern. In Jesus, God's presence passes by and abides with God's people, creating awareness of the divine reign that promises security, even in the midst of tumult. That is not just a message that disciples have to offer to others; it is emphatically a message that they have to hear for themselves.

Given the current state of the world, there is little that is producing as much tumult as the increasingly apparent consequences of climate change on the earth as habitat and home. Much of the immobility of the human family in the face of this great disruption has to do with an unconscious fear that there is little that can be done to obviate, mitigate, or otherwise avoid an unwelcome future. Rather than face the unsettling fear, it is far easier to pretend that the scientific claims are overstated alarms, if not outright falsifications.

Yet elsewhere in the New Testament, the same Jesus who addressed the disciples on the sea with a promise of comfort and hope is spoken of as the one in whom "all things hold together" and through whom "God was pleased to reconcile to himself all things" (Col. 1:17, 20). Thus arises the broader theological claim of the New Testament: that God-in-Christ continues to pass by the tumult and distress of God's beloved creation, manifesting the reign of God for the holding, healing, and reconciling of people, seas, and storms—indeed, of all things.

Perhaps for disciples of our era the challenge is whether we can trust the power and presence of God-in-Christ to quell the storms that have reached genuinely global proportions. The most urgent question for us is whether the power of God we have seen in Jesus is present to calm the watery chaos we face: the decreasing supplies of usable water, the inevitably higher tides along the world's coastlines, the correlative subsiding of the ice packs at the

Pastoral Perspective

non-Hispanic whites will no longer make up the majority of the population in the United States. By 2050 whites will compose only 46 percent of the population, whereas in 1960 they made up 85 percent of the population.[1] Since the 1960s, congregations in mainline, Protestant churches have talked a lot about diversity. Yet most of these congregations are just about as homogeneous and like-minded as they were fifty years ago.

Added to this unknown place for these congregations is another strange reality. The North American context is becoming a multireligious society in which one of the fastest-growing religious sectors is the "nones," those who claim no affiliation at all. Astoundingly for most "well-churched" people, these nones find no social pressure in the present culture to join a religious community.

The age of the culturally established Christian church is gone. The church is, again, sent by its Lord to cross over to the other side. There are adverse winds blowing against the church on this crossing, and the crossing is over "the sea"—"the deep," in biblical language—the symbol of threatening chaos.

Jesus leaves them all night struggling on this journey, straining at the oars. Clearly this is a wrenching experience for the disciples. However, Jesus is not about to abandon them to the wind and the chaos. He comes walking on the sea. That is what God does in the Old Testament (Job 9:8; Ps. 77:19). Strangely, he walks as if he intends to pass them. This is not an act of ignoring them. Instead, it is an act recalling Old Testament theophanies. It is a sign that the Divine is in the midst of the disconcerting chaos they are experiencing. God did this to Moses when Moses found it to be a hard thing to lead a "stiff-necked people" in the wilderness (Exod. 33). God did this to Elijah when Elijah's life was threatened by Jezebel and he had fled to the wilderness for refuge (1 Kgs. 19).

As the disciples see him, Jesus cries out to them, "*Egō eimi* [I AM]." That is indeed the divine name uttered to Moses at the burning bush (Exod. 3:14–15). Immediately upon uttering this name, Jesus commands, "Do not be afraid" (v. 50), the standard comment God makes throughout Scripture when God makes an appearance. As William Placher declared, all this is screaming, "Jesus is God!"[2] It is screaming, "God is with you!"

---

1. "Demographics of the United States"; http://en.wikipedia.org/wiki/Demographics_of_the_United_States; accessed May 10, 2013.
2. William C. Placher, *Mark*, Belief, A Theological Commentary on the Bible (Louisville, KY: Westminster John Knox Press, 2010), 100.

Exegetical Perspective

might ask? It could be the case that Mark indicates what he thought the disciples assumed, though that is an attempt to read the minds of Mark and the disciples. It might be best simply to hear Mark's text: Jesus really did intend to pass the boat, allowing his disciples to continue their struggle, both externally (straining at the oars) and internally (with their terror). Good teachers sometimes do this.

Good teachers also know when to step in and help. Jesus said to them, "Take heart, it is I" (*egō eimi*, "I am," v. 50). When he entered the boat, the wind ceased and "they were utterly astounded" (v. 51). The combination of wind, sea, passing by, fear, and "I am" might have evoked the notion of theophany in the hearers of Mark's story. The Old Testament is full of this kind of language to describe the presence of God, and the response of those who experienced this presence (Gen. 3, 15, 17, 18; Exod. 3:14 [God identifies himself to Moses as "*egō eimi*: I AM" {LXX}]; Job 9:8, 11; Ps. 77:19; Isa. 41:13 pulls it together nicely: "For I, the LORD your God, hold your right hand; it is I who say to you, 'Do not fear, I will help you'").

When Jesus entered the boat and the wind abated, the disciples "were utterly astounded" (v. 51), a natural response to what they had just witnessed. Had Mark ended this vignette here, the story might have retained coherence, but he continued: "for they did not understand about the loaves, but their hearts were hardened" (v. 52).

What are we to make of this? Why did Mark jump from Jesus walking on a stormy sea to the disciples thinking about bread?

In addition to portraying Jesus as a wonder worker, Mark has established that Jesus was an effective teacher. Moreover, Mark has emphasized Jesus' particular teaching style: "He did not speak to them except in parables" (4:34). Jesus was master of the parable in its many forms—aphorisms, metaphors, similes, and short stories. Some have described Jesus' parables as riddles, which makes sense in the context of this story. His parables were not intended solely to make an ethical point (though they sometimes did). Often they were open-ended riddles that invited students inside the parable in order to delve more deeply into their own souls. Parables were portals that opened into a new level of religious consciousness. Remember how many of Jesus' parables focused on the kingdom (reign, rule) of God. Jesus' disciples, including us, are invited to ponder the questions, "What does it mean for me to live a life of integrity under the rule of God? Is that possible for me? What will it require?"

Homiletical Perspective

cliff and then up again, and asks, "Is there anybody else up there?"

The disciples are not ready for help from a *phantasma* (Gk. for "apparition" or "ghost") walking on the water. Here we see the great patience of Jesus. He calms them, saying, "Take heart, it is I; do not be afraid" (v. 50). So often in the Gospels we hear the voice of Jesus calling, comforting, confronting, or convicting people; and that voice always changes the situation.

Jesus gets into the boat; immediately the wind dies down, and the sea is calm again. However, the disciples are not so calm. "They were utterly astounded" (v. 51). Although they were involved in the feeding of the five thousand, they do not understand. The preacher might wonder how they explained that miracle to each other. Did the disciples think people actually had brought extra bread and shared it? No. They must have recognized it as a miracle, but without understanding the implications of Jesus' divine power. So they were both afraid and astounded when he came to them walking on water, got into the boat, and calmed the wind. Power like that is attractive and fearsome at the same time. It is beyond our comprehension that something would happen that we cannot explain by natural causes. We are attracted to superhuman power, but we are also puzzled by it and more than a little afraid of it.

Whereas we have trouble dealing with the humanity of Jesus, a primary theme of Mark's Gospel is the failure of those closest to Jesus to catch on to his divinity. Mark tells the reader in the very first verse of the Gospel that the book is about the Messiah, the Son of God. Then he shows throughout the book how slow the disciples are to understand. He finishes the present pericope with a statement that is hardly an explanation: "Their hearts were hardened" (v. 52). The question of who did the hardening is left untouched, but the question of the purpose of the hardening is worth exploring in sermons and discussions. Mark's Gospel often shows the puzzlement of those closest to Jesus and the belief of some surprising people, especially the Roman centurion at the cross (15:39). The turning point of the Gospel is perhaps the cry of the father asking for healing of his son: "I believe; help my unbelief" (9:24b). We can all identify with the father's confession and confusion of faith.

One might wonder which is more troubling, the presence of Jesus or his absence. It is while Jesus and the disciples are separated that the contrary winds blow and the disciples have to strain at the oars. That

Mark 6:45–52

Theological Perspective

world's poles, and the consequent disturbance of the ocean currents that stabilize features of the climate around the world. In the midst of this global, contradictory complex of stresses on water everywhere, we have every reason to share the disciples' terror.

The more profound theological issue is whether we can share in the comfort Jesus offers in this text: "Take heart, it is I; do not be afraid" (v. 50). As noted earlier, our fear in the face of storms, not least the climate storms associated with water, leads us to denial and immobility. If the perfect love of God-in-Christ casts out our fear, then we are poised to be followers able to act with courage in a disrupted world that we believe holds together and is reconciled in Christ.

This passage ends with the cautionary note: the disciples in the boat still "did not understand about the loaves" (v. 52). While the incident of the loaves had shown that God's economy of plenty provides amply for all God's family when resources are received in thanksgiving and shared in generosity, the disciples still had to learn that lesson. Similarly, disciples in our time are challenged to believe that the resources of the earth as a whole are ample to supply the needs of God's family, human and other than human, sentient and nonsentient, when they are received in gratitude and shared in generosity.

To cultivate more fully our capacity for such gratitude and generosity, we need to attend more regularly and fully to the pattern of the Eucharist itself. In the Great Prayer we are retold the story of God's generosity, and in the offering of the elements we are summoned afresh to gratitude for the gifts that the earth has provided. Then, in receiving those same elements, we are astonished to understand once more how so little can embody so much. Small portions of bread and wine provide a bountiful share in the life of God hidden in Christ. Thus fortified with the communion in Christ, we are strengthened to face the challenges of a seemingly resource-limited world with the confidence that Christ passes by—and abides with—us.

He comes aboard, and the wind ceases.

D. CAMERON MURCHISON

Pastoral Perspective

The disciples do not get it. Mark tells us they are astounded for they do not understand about the loaves (v. 52). Just as they did not discern the Divine in Jesus' act of providing more than enough to satisfy the crowd, so they do not grasp the Divine in Jesus' presence with them in this journey to the other side. The wind has now ceased. The crossing is now possible. Yet Mark declares the disciples' hearts are hardened.

Remember, the Pharisees' hearts are also hardened. Mark describes what that hardening is about (3:1–6). The Pharisees with hardened hearts are sure they know where the boundaries of the community of God's kingdom lie—in their case, with those keeping the law, particularly the law of the Sabbath. Can it be that the disciples' hearts are also hardened because they are so sure they know where the boundaries of the kingdom lie? Certainly those boundaries cannot include folk on that other side in Bethsaida! Ched Myers declares that the sea stories in Mark, of which this is one, "intend to dramatize the difficulties facing the kingdom community as it tries to overcome the institutionalized social divisions between Jew and gentile."[3] Were the disciples convinced it could not be God's will that they go to that other side?

Does the church get God's demand to go to that other side? Does it see the presence of the Divine in the crossing to that other side? Is its heart hardened? Hardened in seeking to remain culturally homogeneous? Hardened in seeking to remain a community of the like-minded?

Interestingly, on this crossing, the disciples do not make it to the other side. They come ashore in Gennesaret, their side of the sea. The crossing fails. However, in Mark's telling, the story is not over. Jesus is determined that the community of the disciples will make the crossing. Ultimately they arrive in Bethsaida (8:22). Wondrously, even in its failure, the band of disciples is not cast off by Jesus. Through them, God's will is fulfilled. In all of its stumbling and failure, the church does well to take this to heart.

PETE PEERY

---

3. Ched Myers, *Binding the Strong Man* (Maryknoll, NY: Orbis Books, 1988), 197.

Exegetical Perspective

The sequence in 6:52 is important. The disciples did not understand (*synēkan*) about the loaves; their hearts were hardened. Perhaps the disciples were not yet able to comprehend the connection between Jesus and the loaves. They were not yet ready to move from miracle to metaphor, from the superficial to the substantial, in order to understand that there might be a riddle about Jesus as the "bread of life" hidden in the events they had just witnessed.

The careful reader of Mark's Gospel will discover a clue to the meaning of this riddle at the end of the next feeding story (8:14–21). There Jesus once again takes a postbanquet boat ride with his disciples. They are still kvetching about bread; there had been seven baskets of leftovers, and no one has remembered to bring any bread on board the boat. Jesus reminds them about their two experiences of sharing bread with thousands of people, with plenty of bread left over. Jesus pointedly has the disciples recall that there were *twelve* and *seven* baskets of leftover bread. Jesus was willing to feed all who came to him, both Jews (e.g., descendants of the twelve tribes of Israel) and Gentiles (seven is the number of all creation). Then he says to them, "Do you not *yet* understand?"[1] (8:21).

Throughout Mark's Gospel, Jesus is an enigma to his disciples. He is the ultimate riddle of Mark's story, the embodiment of a parable. The disciples never seem to have much insight about him, who he is. In this story the disciples do not understand that Jesus himself is the metaphorical key to the feeding miracle. He is the bread of life sitting in a boat with them.

PAUL W. WALASKAY

Homiletical Perspective

aspect of the text speaks directly to later generations of believers. Those who find the going rough get the feeling that they are alone, abandoned to the winds of fate. Mark reminds us that the Lord will find us. The assurance of the Lord's return is a great comfort when the going gets tough, even though most believers are in no hurry for that day. In fact we often feel uncomfortable when we think about being in the presence of the divine Son.

Like the first disciples, sometimes we overlook even the effects of God's presence in our lives. How often marvelous things happen in and around us, but we fail to credit the work to God. It is so easy to throw the word *coincidence* at things. The story is told about Archbishop William Temple reasoning with an atheist who insisted that "answers to prayer" were merely coincidences. The archbishop said, "That might well be, but I find that more coincidences happen when I pray."[1] Sometimes it is not so much our faith that is lacking as it is our perception. The power of God is at work all around us every day, but we rarely recognize it, even while claiming to believe.

Sometimes we find ourselves in a storm, buffeted by hard winds, and then things calm down a bit. Too often, we put the difference down to luck or changing circumstances, instead of giving God credit for stepping in and changing things. Do we think our troubles are too small for God to be bothered with? If so, then our concept of God is too small. God was concerned with the hunger of people. God was concerned with the fear of people. Why would God not be concerned with our everyday problems? After all, Jesus taught that God cares about sparrows and even the hairs of our heads. Why not trust God with everything?

BRUCE E. SHIELDS

---

1. *Syniete*, lit. "have insight," the same word used in 6:52.

1. David Watson, *Called and Committed* (Wheaton, IL: Harold Shaw Publishers, 1982), 83.

Mark 6:53–56

⁵³When they had crossed over, they came to land at Gennesaret and moored the boat. ⁵⁴When they got out of the boat, people at once recognized him, ⁵⁵and rushed about that whole region and began to bring the sick on mats to wherever they heard he was. ⁵⁶And wherever he went, into villages or cities or farms, they laid the sick in the marketplaces, and begged him that they might touch even the fringe of his cloak; and all who touched it were healed.

Theological Perspective

Whereas the disciples had been slow in the preceding verses to anticipate the presence of God to save and make whole when they were confronted by tumult, the people of the region have no such tardy response. These brief verses depict an intuitive theological awareness among people who have no established loyalty to Jesus that his presence can be trusted to provide healing. While it seems odd that the faithful are reluctant and the uninitiated enthusiastic, it also suggests that familiarity can, if not breed contempt, dull the spiritual senses.

The story makes clear that these enthusiastic newcomers to the Jesus phenomenon simply recognized him, presumably as the one about whom they had heard so much, the one who was said to embody the reign of God with its attendant health and wholeness. In light of their recognition, their hurried response was to rush around the entire area, rousting out the sick and lame. At each of Jesus' stops, they dragged them on their mats into his presence to make certain that these infirm members of the community were in reach of Jesus. They were confident that bringing the unhealthy into Jesus' presence would lead to restoration and healing.

It is noteworthy that they did not assume healing required that Jesus touch the sick, but only that the sick "might touch even the fringe of his cloak; and

Pastoral Perspective

The disciples were astounded (v. 51). Jesus was in the boat with them, and the fierce wind had ceased. God was with them! God was present in their midst, the same God who had been present through their gifts, those loaves, that fed the hungry crowd. Yet they did not understand.

Does that sound familiar? Does that sound like a normal congregation of the church of Jesus Christ?

This boat of disciples with Jesus in their midst is moored in Gennesaret. Gennesaret was not a particular town. It was a thickly populated plain between Tiberias and Capernaum in the midst of Galilee.[1] It not only was full of Jews, but also had a heavy population of Gentiles. Its people were predominantly poor and cut off from the center of commercial and political influence in Jerusalem.[2] When they got out of the boat, what happened? Mark tells us that the people, this motley population of poor, marginalized people, recognized Jesus. Maybe they did not recognize him as the Son of God, the One inaugurating the reign of God. Maybe they did not recognize him as the One calling them to turn from their patterns of life and follow him in whole new ways. Maybe

1. John R. Donahue and Daniel J. Harrington, *The Gospel of Mark*, Sacra Pagina (Collegeville, MN: Liturgical Press, 2002), 216.
2. Ched Myers, *Binding the Strong Man* (Maryknoll, NY: Orbis Books, 1988), 128.

Exegetical Perspective

In this brief episode, Mark shifts to another aspect of Jesus as a wonder worker. He reminds the reader that Jesus was a healer. With this vignette the Gospel writer also provides a subtle transition from the miracles performed by Jesus in Galilee (chaps. 1–6) to Jesus' interaction with legal experts from Jerusalem (7:1–23).

After a quick nighttime round trip to Bethsaida, Jesus and the disciples disembark from their boat at Gennesaret, probably not far from where they had left (6:45). Jesus has returned to his home territory near the northwest shore of the Sea of Galilee. It was here that Jesus gained fame as a healer of diseases. In Nazareth, Jesus' hometown, "the whole city was gathered around the door. And he cured many who were sick with various diseases, and cast out many demons" (1:33–34). At one point, Jesus felt so hemmed in by people in need that he instructed his disciples to plan an escape route. They were "to have a boat ready for him because of the crowd, so that they would not crush him; for he had cured many, so that all who had diseases pressed upon him to touch him" (3:9–10).

In this passage, Jesus again falls into the hands of the frenzied crowd that rushes at him to take advantage of his healing powers. In the midst of this frenetic scene, we will step aside to consider a few aspects of what is taking place.

Homiletical Perspective

Among the toughest kinds of text to preach is the summary, found in the Gospels and Acts. Summaries wrap up time spent by Jesus or the early evangelists in certain places or on certain issues. They tend to be very general, offering the preacher little local color and few names. They describe ongoing ministry, often giving statistics. Context is important for all biblical texts, but it is doubly important for the summaries. These four verses are no exception.

We have seen Jesus feeding more than five thousand people beginning with just five loaves of bread and two fish. We have seen him walking on the water and helping his disciples deal with a storm. We read that he set out in a boat for Bethsaida, about two miles west of Capernaum on the north side of the Sea of Galilee, but then are told that he landed on the east side of the sea, in the area of Gennesaret. Either the wind blew them off course, or the evangelist was not familiar with the geography of that part of the world. All in all, it had been a pretty exciting time for the twelve disciples. They had seen Jesus take command in several different situations, controlling evil spirits, multiplying food, stilling the wind, and even raising a dead girl to life, showing command over death itself (5:35–43). What will happen next?

We can learn something about preaching from this summary. Mark tells his story of Jesus so that

Mark 6:53–56

Theological Perspective

all who touched it were healed" (v. 56). This suggests that the reign of God manifest in Jesus does not have to be fully and uniquely focused on a particular person (usually us) to be powerfully at work in the situation. Just as there is collateral damage in human warfare, there appears to be collateral wholeness in God's restorative presence manifest in Jesus. To be near that presence is to experience its healing power.

One theological lesson to be learned from this vignette involves the global reach of Jesus' healing presence. To experience the power of God's presence most personally and powerfully does not require a kind of narcissistic "me and Jesus" relationship that is oblivious to the needs of the wider world. In the story, Jesus is not described as particularly attentive to the specific needs of these lame and halt ones. Jesus' embodiment of God's reign for the well-being of the whole world carries with it a healing balm for all who stand near and reach trustingly for its sustenance. A deeply personal life of faith is not at all in competition with a broadly social life of faith. The same saving power that heals the sick in our midst also binds up the wounds of injustice the world over. To say it the other way around, the saving power that binds up the wounds of injustice the world over also heals us in our most personal needs. So like those newcomers in this text, we may be moved to reach toward it in trusting faith on both personal and global levels.

Though these verses may seem to stand alone theologically in the sequence of verses that began with verse 30, there is more interconnectedness than appears at first glance. Already, allusion has been made to the contrast between the disciples' slowness to trust the calming presence of God in their experience on the sea (vv. 45–52) and the villagers' readiness to place the sick near Jesus. In this way, Mark reminds us that faithfulness is not always of the authorized sort. Sometimes it is more present among those who have not officially joined the Jesus movement, but who know their deep need and look beyond themselves to have it filled.

Contrariwise, among those of us who self-consciously intend to be followers of Jesus, there is often a slowness to trust the power of God's restorative work in the face of the dislocations and disruptions of our day. In this circumstance, it behooves us to attend to the witness of those who simply know they must reach out for the fringe of Jesus' cloak, since they have nothing else to sustain them. If, as suggested earlier, familiarity with things of faith sometimes dulls the spiritual senses, paying attention

Pastoral Perspective

they recognized him only as a healer, as someone who could do something for them or for their own people who were suffering.

Unlike the disciples, who did not understand the presence of the Divine in their midst, these people recognized something of that divine presence. So what did they do? They rushed throughout the whole region and brought the sick to wherever they heard he was, be it in the villages or the cities or the rural areas. In the public squares of these places they confronted him with their sick. There Mark tells us they "*begged* him that they might touch even the fringe of his cloak" (v. 56).

Begged. The Greek verb is *parakaleō*, "to call to the side of." It is the same verb used by the leper who interrupted Jesus' ministry (1:40). It is the same verb used by the Gerasene demoniac (5:10). It is the same verb used by Jairus, the synagogue leader whose daughter was at the point of death (5:23). It is the root of the word *paraklētos*, "Paraclete," "Advocate." the one that, in John's telling of the gospel, Jesus promises will be sent to the disciples (John 14:16). They came to wherever he was and called him to come to *their* side, to come along beside *them*, to be *their* advocate. What pastor of the church of Jesus Christ does not know this reality? The congregation of disciples the pastor serves likely is full of folk with a lack of understanding of who this Jesus is whom they are following. Nevertheless because that congregation bears Jesus' name, all sorts of people come: sick people, abused people, addicted people, mentally disturbed people, poor people, powerless people, socially and religiously unacceptable people.

Not only do people come, but in the public arenas and marketplaces of the cities and towns and hamlets in which congregations find themselves, the broken issues of the people are brought: school systems that fail to educate, social service structures that are overwhelmed and underfunded, prison systems that have become warehouses of dehumanization, political systems that are manipulated by special interests. "Come beside *us!*" "Be *our* advocate!" "Walk along with *us!*" "Identify with *us!*" "Be seen with *us!*" Every pastor knows of this call from the people throughout the territory surrounding the place where the church of Jesus Christ finds itself.

Every pastor also knows that those who are calling out to the church to come along beside them or beside their cause are not necessarily interested in being a part of the body of Christ. They are not interested in following. They are interested in getting: getting what they want, getting relief from

Exegetical Perspective

First, Mark indicates that "the people at once recognized [Jesus]" (v. 54) for what he could do for them, specifically in the realm of health care. That he is an effective teacher and compassionate human being is beside the point. Their plea is, "What can you *do for me*? Now!" By the end of the Gospel, the crowd will have forgotten his good deeds and will turn against him (15:11–15).

Second, this passage invites us to consider the etiology of disease and the mode of healing in antiquity.[1] Ordinary folks in Mark's world assumed that everyone had a personal demon, *daimonion*, that regulated his or her physical and mental health. One usually felt in "good spirits" and was not even aware of the demon inside. However, every so often that demon could turn (temporarily or permanently) on its host, or be forced out by the invasion of a bad demon. In that case, the demon's presence was acutely felt and the person became ill.[2] Poultices, herbs, drugs, and other folk remedies could be applied and were sometimes effective. The demon was soothed, and subsequently so was its human host. However, if that did not work, more drastic measures may have been needed. An exorcist could be summoned to apply his or her skills in casting out the evil demon and inviting a benevolent spirit to take its place. (See Jesus' story about the work of an exorcist in Matt. 12:43–45; also see the stories in Acts about exorcisms done by followers of Jesus, and others—Acts 8:9–24; 19:13–20.)

Third, careful readers of Mark have discerned a threefold pattern to the healing stories. First, information about the petitioner's *problem* is conveyed (in this episode, however, Mark offers only generalized information—lots of "sick people"). Second, Jesus offers words or actions that effect a healing—a *solution* to the problem. Third, the Gospel writer confirms that a healing has taken place, along with the reaction of the healed person and/or those looking on—*proof*.

Finally, modes of healing can vary greatly. Think about other healing stories in the Bible (including the Old Testament, e.g., 1 Kgs. 17; 2 Kgs. 5). Healing could be generated by a touch (either from the healer or the healed person), by a word, or vicariously (a person might intercede on behalf an ill loved one;

---

1. See the classic study by E. R. Dodds, *Pagan and Christian in an Age of Anxiety* (Cambridge: University Press, 1965). Also see P. W. Walaskay, "Biblical and Classical Foundations of the Healing Ministries," *Journal of Pastoral Care* 37 (September 1983): 195–206.
2. Remnants of this thought world are still in our quasi-medical vocabulary in such terms as "demented," "lunatic" (moon-struck), heart "attack," "stroke," and "seizure."

Homiletical Perspective

the reader/hearer leans forward, ready and eager for the next episode. A summary can be either dry information or vivid enough to have an audience wondering what comes next.

Mark does not give much detail in his text, but even a small detail such as the sick touching the fringe of Jesus' cloak helps us see the scene and feel the hope of the people. In a few short verses, the text shows clearly that Jesus is getting around. Jesus' reputation is growing. When Jesus shows up, it is not a normal day. As soon as people recognize him, they bring sick friends and relatives to him. His very presence causes excitement, and these excited people act on their own behalf. They want to be in his presence. They want to bring others into his presence, especially those with special needs. The strong carry the weak and find him in the marketplaces. This is no backdoor operation. This is out in the open, where everybody can see what is happening:

Healing is happening: "All who touched [the fringe of his cloak] were healed" (v. 56). Mark does not say that Jesus does anything. In fact, the touching appears to be done by the sick people themselves. Just touching the fringe of his cloak releases healing power. These people expect that Jesus can work wonders, a direct contrast with the fear and astonishment of the disciples in the previous passage. The faith of the crowds and the miracles that happen at Gennesaret are also a great contrast to what Jesus found in his hometown of Nazareth, where "he could do no deed of power" because of unbelief (6:1–6).

How can we understand the power of the presence of Jesus among people who believe in him? This is not just a question of biblical interpretation. It applies also to the experience of the church through the ages. When we read the Gospels, we should think not only of the activities of Jesus and the people he was present with during his lifetime. We should think also of the early church who first heard these accounts from the apostles and for whom the Gospels were written. What was happening in their lives that made the very presence of Jesus important to them? Were they under persecution, whether spiritual, political, or personal? They surely suffered from the same human ailments and grief that we all experience. How did they experience for themselves the touching of the fringe of Jesus' garment? There is always an element of mystery when somebody hears a report like this and becomes a believer.

How about us and the people we preach to? We all have times when we yearn to reach out and touch the fringe of Jesus' coat, times when we want some

Mark 6:53–56

Theological Perspective

to those who may not be "signed up" members of the faith community can sharpen them.

Therefore, one of the most important theological insights of verses 53–56 for the church in our day is the promise held out by those who reached for the fringe of Jesus' cloak. Their untutored act of faith reminds us that to know the restorative power of God's presence in Christ, we do not have to have some unique, personally and exquisitely tailored visitation of the Divine just for ourselves. Rather, we have only to reacquaint ourselves with the means of grace, the means of Christ's continuing presence entrusted to the church through the ages: word, prayer, and sacrament. However much these means of grace may undergo reexpression in the multitude of worldwide cultures where they have by now come to life, they are the fringe of Jesus' cloak with its restorative power for us. As we reach out to them in trust, we will experience again and again the grace of God's healing presence and power.

A twentieth-century communion hymn captures this sense of things, at least with respect to the Lord's Supper. "Draw Us in the Spirit's Tether" summons worshipers to the Eucharist. There two or three, being met together, will find Christ in their midst. Then, after singing the praise, "Alleluia," it uses the imagery of our text to describe what is taking place as it concludes the verse: "Touch we now your garment's hem."[1] What this hymn claims for the sacrament of the Lord's Supper may also be claimed for all the means of grace entrusted to the church through the ages: they are the regular and ordinary means by which the extraordinary grace of God's restorative and healing power is made present among us. Thanks be to those unauthorized, untutored enthusiastic villagers for reminding us!

D. CAMERON MURCHISON

Pastoral Perspective

their suffering, getting deliverance from their affliction. We do not know if those who sought Jesus out in Gennesaret for healing also intended to join his movement. We only know that they wanted something. That is what happens when the people all around sense there is a divine presence in their midst, even if those whom the Son of God has called to be his community do not understand who he is.

Mark tells us that those who called Jesus to come beside them, to be their advocate, begged to touch the fringe of his cloak. In the tradition of Israel, ones who were holy were to wear fringes or tassels on their garments (Num. 15:37–41). It was thought that an aura of power surrounded such holy persons.[3] Just to get close enough to touch the fringe of such a holy person's garment would be enough for those desperate people who sought out Jesus. They recognized Jesus was holy, full of divine presence in a way that would make a difference in their lives.

I wonder if that is the way it still is as the motley, marginalized, often rejected, clearly afflicted people come seeking out the place where they have heard Jesus is present. They come to the community that bears his name. They recognize holy power is present there, holy power they want on their side. The community may not understand that there is anything holy about it. It may not understand that God is present within it. Yet could it be that this community, the church, is the fringe of Jesus' garment? Touching it, are people healed, made whole, in ways we may not understand? Being touched by such people, does the church find itself embroiled in controversy and trouble? Just keep reading Mark (7:1–8:21)!

PETE PEERY

---

1. Percy Dearmer, "Draw Us in the Spirit's Tether," *The Presbyterian Hymnal: Hymns, Psalms and Spiritual Songs* (Louisville, KY: Westminster John Knox Press, 1993), #504.

3. Donahue and Harrington, *The Gospel of Mark*, 217.

Exegetical Perspective

e.g., Luke 7:1–10). In this passage Mark describes another way of healing. "They laid the sick in the marketplaces, and begged him that they might touch even the fringe of his cloak; and all who touched it were healed" (v. 56). Mark has already described this method of healing (the story of the woman who touched Jesus' clothing, 5:27–28).

The book of Acts also records an episode in which "God did extraordinary miracles through Paul, so that when the handkerchiefs or aprons that had touched his skin were brought to the sick, their diseases left them, and the evil spirits came out of them" (Acts 19:11–12; in Acts 5:15, even Peter's shadow has curative powers). The "fringe" on Jesus' garment probably refers to the blue tassel that Jewish males were expected to have on the corners of their cloaks (Num. 15:38–40), which would indicate Jesus' careful observance of Jewish law (a detail that provides a transition to the next episode in Mark's Gospel: a discussion about rabbinic legal traditions with Pharisees and scribes from Jerusalem, 7:1–23).

Mark concludes this portion of his Gospel with two generalizations that are in keeping with his portrait of Jesus. Those who were sick and their caretakers begged Jesus that they might just touch "*even*" the fringe of his garment; "and all who touched it were healed [Gk. *sōzō* has a wide range of meaning: "save," "rescue," "heal"]" (v. 56). Here in a nutshell is Mark's Christology: Wherever Jesus (the "body of Christ" in its fullest sense) is present—by the tranquil seaside (6:30–44), in the midst of a stormy sea (6:45–52), or in the bustling marketplace (6:53–56)—the deepest needs that sustain human life are met.

PAUL W. WALASKAY

Homiletical Perspective

tangible sign of the presence and healing power of the Lord. Too often fixated on the feeling that the Lord is absent, we overlook our own earlier experiences of his presence in our lives and dismiss the reports others give of his presence in theirs. Sometimes the Lord's presence comes to us in human form, as Christian friends walk into a hospital waiting room while a child is in surgery. Sometimes we sense his presence during a service of worship—perhaps at the Lord's Table or during a time of prayer. Often he draws near when we hear or read a passage of Scripture like Isaiah 6 or even our present text. For many, music—perhaps a song we find ourselves humming during the day—becomes the means of Christ's presence. For others, we sense his healing power in the beauty of God's creation, a sunset from a hilltop or beach.

However one might experience the movement of God's Spirit, when Jesus is present, the day is anything but ordinary. Whenever God's people gather in the name of Jesus, Jesus is present, as he promised (Matt. 18:20). This is the faith of the church, whether or not one feels that presence. In those times when we, like the disciples, do not understand the power of the present Lord, we would do well to lean in and listen for his "It is I" through the means of grace he has given us. Our regular worship times are extraordinary because, as we hear his address through texts like this one, we are given the assurance of his presence. Let us pray that we and the people to whom we preach this passage may know his powerful presence, every day and on into his promised future, when we will sing his praises and know his presence eternally.

BRUCE E. SHIELDS

Mark 7:1–23

¹Now when the Pharisees and some of the scribes who had come from Jerusalem gathered around him, ²they noticed that some of his disciples were eating with defiled hands, that is, without washing them. ³(For the Pharisees, and all the Jews, do not eat unless they thoroughly wash their hands, thus observing the tradition of the elders; ⁴and they do not eat anything from the market unless they wash it; and there are also many other traditions that they observe, the washing of cups, pots, and bronze kettles.) ⁵So the Pharisees and the scribes asked him, "Why do your disciples not live according to the tradition of the elders, but eat with defiled hands?" ⁶He said to them, "Isaiah prophesied rightly about you hypocrites, as it is written,

> 'This people honors me with their lips,
>   but their hearts are far from me;
> ⁷ in vain do they worship me,
>   teaching human precepts as doctrines.'

⁸You abandon the commandment of God and hold to human tradition."

⁹Then he said to them, "You have a fine way of rejecting the commandment of God in order to keep your tradition! ¹⁰For Moses said, 'Honor your father and your mother'; and, 'Whoever speaks evil of father or mother must surely die.'

Theological Perspective

This chapter falls right between Mark's twin stories of Jesus feeding the multitudes: the feeding of the five thousand (6:30–44) and the feeding of the four thousand (8:1–10). In chapter 7, Mark gives two portraits of Jesus engaged in arguments about food. This succession of stories shows just how significant—and how controversial—food and eating were in Jesus' ministry.

This first food story is the only one in chapter 7 that involves actual eating; his exchange with the Syrophoenician woman in verses 24–30 uses food as a metaphor. Here, in response to a charge of ritual defilement, Jesus rejects Pharisaic traditions about the purity required before coming to the table. The Pharisees and scribes ask, "Why do your disciples not live according to the tradition of the elders, but eat with defiled hands?" (v. 5). Jesus' response raises two classic theological questions, and bears directly on one more contemporary theological issue.

First, he accuses the Pharisees and scribes of attending to their own human traditions (vv. 3, 4, 5, 8, 9, 13) rather than God's commandment (vv. 8, 9). Mark presents "tradition" here as merely human invention, detracting from faithfulness to God's word (v. 13). This contrast has fed a variety of Christian condemnations of "others" who follow worship practices that seem to attend more to human custom

Pastoral Perspective

Not long after I had been installed as the first female head of staff of a 148-year-old congregation, I attended a welcome gathering hosted by the women's group in the church. During that gathering, one of the pillars of the organization stood up and made a welcome speech. She was so happy to have me, she said, and she knew that I would be as dear to them as "Debbie," a former minister's wife, who was "such a lady. The windows on *her* [emphasis hers, not mine] house were always spotless, a clear panel that the light of God could shine through. The windows of *her* house were like the windows into Debbie's soul." Debbie of the clean windows had been, in this pillar's words, a "saint."

I understood where this woman was coming from: she was coming from the same school that had shaped my own mother, the "Cleanliness Is Next to Godliness" School of Homemaking. My mother had lived by the same canon, the one with ordinances such as make the beds every morning, clear the counters and put away the dishes every night, take down the curtains and rotate the mattresses every spring and fall. This canon guided my mom as she created a warm, secure, inviting nest for the family over the years. It was a good collection of accumulated wisdom, and it offered guidelines for turning a house into a home.

¹¹But you say that if anyone tells father or mother, 'Whatever support you might have had from me is Corban' (that is, an offering to God)— ¹²then you no longer permit doing anything for a father or mother, ¹³thus making void the word of God through your tradition that you have handed on. And you do many things like this."

¹⁴Then he called the crowd again and said to them, "Listen to me, all of you, and understand: ¹⁵there is nothing outside a person that by going in can defile, but the things that come out are what defile."

¹⁷When he had left the crowd and entered the house, his disciples asked him about the parable. ¹⁸He said to them, "Then do you also fail to understand? Do you not see that whatever goes into a person from outside cannot defile, ¹⁹since it enters, not the heart but the stomach, and goes out into the sewer?" (Thus he declared all foods clean.) ²⁰And he said, "It is what comes out of a person that defiles. ²¹For it is from within, from the human heart, that evil intentions come: fornication, theft, murder, ²²adultery, avarice, wickedness, deceit, licentiousness, envy, slander, pride, folly. ²³All these evil things come from within, and they defile a person."

Exegetical Perspective

The main topic of Mark 7:1–23 is the Pharisaic purity code and Mark's community's difference from that code. This passage distinguishes "us" from "them." At points, the narrator intrusively draws a distinction between Jesus (and, by implication, the Markan community) and the Pharisees. The danger of falling into implicit anti-Semitism in a contemporary use of this passage is strong.

Seeing where a passage is situated, where the plot is going, and how a passage implements the plot is critical to understanding a narrative. Mark 6:6b to 8:26 is introduced with "Then he went about among the villages teaching" (6:6b), which can serve as a title for the section. Chapter 7 prepares an audience for the upcoming confrontation and crisis at Caesarea Philippi. Jesus engages on the one hand with the Pharisees and on the other hand with the disciples. The crisis comes to a head there and precipitates a turn toward Jerusalem, death, and resurrection. The transfiguration in Mark 9 calls upon the voice of God to resolve the conflict in Jesus' favor, hearkening back to the same voice at the baptism.

The passage has a clear rhythm: controversy with Pharisees (vv. 1–13), address to the crowd (vv. 14–15), instruction for the disciples (vv. 17–23). The author has structured the section to reinforce the conclusion, "For it is from within, from the

Homiletical Perspective

Chapter 7 opens on an extended confrontation with the Pharisees and scribes. This is by no means the first such scene; much of chapters 2 and 3 is already taken up with these episodes (2:6–12; 2:16–17; 2:24–27; 3:2–6; 3:22–27). Chapters 4 through 6 depict Jesus in other settings—teaching, healing, feeding multitudes, performing nature miracles, calling and sending the Twelve—and include a lengthy digression on the fate of John the Baptist.

With chapter 7, the Pharisees and scribes return, this time with reinforcements from Jerusalem. The chapter opens with an accusation (v. 5) and centers largely on themes of purity and impurity, the determination of what is to be deemed clean and unclean.

This passage describes Jesus' debate with the Pharisees over ritual hand washing. At issue are questions about purity and impurity that have proved vital ones for human societies from the earliest of times. Likewise, the so-called purification rites—from ritual baths and baptisms to the confessional—have played a continuing role in the quest for meaning and self-understanding. Such issues have often become entangled—even though not specifically in our text—with questions about sexuality and the place of women in society. Difficult as this may seem, perhaps attitudes toward the complex

Mark 7:1–23

Theological Perspective

than to the word of the gospel. Christians have used it against Jews, Protestants against Catholics, evangelicals against mainlines, emergents against evangelicals, and so on. John Calvin represents such a view in his commentary:

> This passage teaches us, first, that all modes of worship invented by men are displeasing to God, because he chooses that he alone shall be heard . . . ; secondly, that those who are not satisfied with the only law of God, and weary themselves by attending to the traditions of men, are uselessly employed; thirdly, that an outrage is committed against God, when the inventions of men are so highly extolled, that the majesty of his law is almost lowered, or at least the reverence for it is abated.[1]

Sixteenth-century Protestants found Roman Catholic Christians particularly guilty of this offense.

Preachers will do well to exercise caution here, so as not to play into such destructive anti-Catholic or anti-Jewish caricatures. Rather, Jesus invites us to reflect on the ways in which we ourselves carefully maintain familiar social customs—even in the church—that shield us from the more fundamental (and difficult) commandments to love God and neighbor.

In the second section of this passage (vv. 14–23), Jesus redefines what it means to be unclean or defiled. Again, he criticizes the Pharisees for their focus on clean hands and clean food, and focuses instead on "what comes out of a person": the intentions of the heart. Here, Jesus clearly places himself in the lineage of Israel's prophets, echoing not only Isaiah (as he does in vv. 6–7) but also Amos (who condemns ritual sacrifices in favor of justice and righteousness, Amos 5:21–24) and Jeremiah (who looks for the new covenant that will be written on people's "hearts," Jer. 31:31–34).

This argument is not, however, a spiritualized or disembodied appeal to interior heart over exterior actions. Notice that the list of "intentions" in verses 21–22 has everything to do with how we live out the law of God concretely in relation to one another. In other words, he is not teaching his disciples to disregard embodied practices. He is instead refocusing their attention on the most important embodied practices: those that display faithfulness, self-restraint, honesty, compassion.

---

1. John Calvin, commentary on Matt. 15:1, from *Commentary on a Harmony of the Evangelists, Matthew, Mark, and Luke*, trans. William Bringle (originally published for the Calvin Translation Society, Edinburgh, Scotland; repr., Grand Rapids: Baker Books, 2003), 1:246.

Pastoral Perspective

However, guidelines are one thing; measures of moral worth are another. From the lips of this pillar, the homemaker's guide sounded like the criteria used for the judgments of God. A bit stung, I smiled as saintly a smile as I could muster through clenched teeth.

I resisted the urge to cite this passage in Mark 7. Underlying this woman's words was the same issue lying behind this exchange between the Jewish pillars and Jesus: the authority of the tradition of the elders versus the authority of the commands of God. There is a difference between the human precepts developed and handed down to us by generations of earnest people, and the commands of the Holy One. No matter how much wisdom human precepts contain, no matter how they have shaped and defined a people, they are not to be equated with the word of God. When they are, ugly things happen.

This issue presents itself time and again in the life of people who are trying to be faithful. During the Protestant Reformation, the church wrestled with the distinction between tradition and Scripture. Across denominations today, the authority of tradition is tested by young clergy who view much of the polity and practice of the institutional church as "bureaucracy" devoutly to be dismissed. Congregations wrestle with the authority of tradition as they seek appropriate music and dress in worship. When do we continue to do things the way our elders did them, and when do we adapt and change?

Jesus gives some instruction in Mark 7: Make the distinction between human precepts and the commands of God. Do not invoke the authority of God to justify your human traditions and preferences. Do not hold onto empty practices, claiming they are holy things.

Most traditions arise out of some devout intent. Look for that original intention, and hold on to *that*, though its shape and form may change. If the goal of sacred music is to draw attention to God rather than the performer, then music of any style is sacred if it does that. If the motive behind the tradition of dressing up for worship has been to show respect, reverence, and modesty before the Lord, then the person who comes into the sanctuary of the Lord with respect, reverence, and modesty in his heart will be welcome. It is what lies at the heart of things that measures our moral disposition, says Jesus, and matters most to God.

Several years ago, during a service of the Lord's Day, I finished a sermon and stepped down from the pulpit, joining the congregation in a hymn. As

Exegetical Perspective

human heart, that evil intentions come" (v. 21). The issue is ritual purity, which we must distinguish from moral purity. Ritual purity marks off the sacred from the profane. Often the distinction is a matter of place. To use Mary Douglas's famous example, the difference between dirt and soil is place. Dirt is inside a house; soil is outside it. It is not intrinsically pure or impure; rather, place and situation determine its status.[1] We can confuse or conflate ritual and moral purity, making it hard to understand the point of the ancient text. For example, a menstruating woman is ritually impure, but not immoral.

The introduction sets up Jesus' controversy with the Pharisees and scribes. Jerusalem has been mentioned twice before in the Gospel. First, in 3:8, the crowds come from various places, including Jerusalem, to hear Jesus. The second reference, in 3:22, is more ominous: "And the scribes who came down from Jerusalem said, 'He has Beelzebul.'" The close parallel in wording indicates the continuing controversy. Pharisees, scribes, and Jerusalem are codes for the escalating conflict.

Pharisees and scribes are concerned about a violation of ritual purity, which the narrator explains to the readers in considerable detail (vv. 3–4), suggesting that the audience for this Gospel is Gentile.

While the Pharisees' question is neutral, Jesus' response is hostile. He calls them "hypocrites," that is, actors or pretenders. He quotes from Isaiah 29:13, a passage in which Isaiah attacked the temple rituals. Mark employs the quote in a similar way. By quoting Isaiah, Mark indicates that this issue is not unique to Jesus or to the Markan community, but has a history extending back to the prophets. In the context of debates with the Pharisees in the period after the destruction of the temple, this quotation from Isaiah says that Jesus and Mark's community are the true successors of the prophets.

In verse 9, Jesus ups the ante by accusing the Pharisees of not only abandoning God's commands but abolishing them. A sharp contrast is drawn between what "Moses said" (v. 10) and what "you say" (v. 11). The actual point of the debate, a prohibitive vow, is so arcane that one has to wonder if Mark's readers could understand what it is about. The point is not the prohibitive vow, but the debate itself and its conclusion. The Markan community is using Jesus' debate with the Pharisees as a model for their own debate with the Pharisees. The real debate

---

1. Mary Douglas, *Purity and Danger: An Analysis of Concepts of Pollution and Taboo* (London: Routledge & Kegan Paul, 1966), 3.

Homiletical Perspective

and sensitive topic of human sexuality in relation to purity and impurity could be addressed here.

The Pharisees, as is typical throughout the Gospels, are cast in a negative light. The preacher must handle such attitudes with care and a modicum of enlightenment. As contemporary scholarship has clarified the place of the scribes and Pharisees in Jesus' time, we have been compelled to move from a simplistic "Bad Guys versus Good Guys" scenario toward a more informed and nuanced understanding. Not only here, but throughout the New Testament, the preacher should avoid perpetuating the shameful portrayal of Pharisees and scribes, and even the Jewish people, as enemies of Jesus and his ministry.

Nevertheless, the weight of Gospel testimony cannot be ignored. The scribes and Pharisees, representing the official face of religion at that time, were deeply invested in matters having to do with purity and impurity, an investment that found them speaking in opposition to the message and ministry of Jesus. Still, today our congregations need to be reminded that Jesus himself, his disciples, and the earliest believers were also Jews, and that it was the religious authorities, not the Jewish people, who plotted and carried out Jesus' betrayal and execution.

Turning to the particular conflict concerning purity and impurity in these twenty-three verses, the preacher might consider taking a historical route, via a quick glance back at previous customs and attitudes toward "unclean" objects, habits, ideas, individuals, and groups. One might describe instances from one's own past in which things formerly viewed as unclean have since taken on neutral, or even at times positive, images. Attitudes toward other races and religions, other nations, other levels of society, or sexual orientations might provide such examples.

Closely aligned with conflicting views of purity and impurity is the manifestation of hypocrisy in religious communities that claim to be pure (vv. 6–13). This phenomenon occurs frequently in the Gospels and throughout the New Testament. Still today, hypocrisy is perhaps the most commonly despised of all our faults. The accusation is frequently leveled by nonbelievers against those who attend church and claim to follow Christ. To this taunt, the late William Sloane Coffin was heard on more than one occasion to suggest that those who would not join a church full of hypocrites should take heart because there was always room for one more. So too the famous twentieth-century evangelist Billy Sunday is quoted: "Don't hunt through the

Mark 7:1–23

Theological Perspective

Finally, some twenty-first-century North American Protestant readers of this text may see a connection between what Jesus says here and the question about whether people should be baptized before being invited to the Lord's Supper. The charge of the Pharisees, after all, is that Jesus' disciples do not wash their hands before eating. In our cultural context, this sounds like a challenge to the long-standing Christian assumption that people are to be baptized before coming to the Table of the Lord. Is such a requirement simply human convention? Does this practice have something to do with the word of the Lord?

Faithful Christians disagree on this matter. Two points, however, deserve attention: first, baptism is not simply a matter of ritual purity, which is what Jesus criticizes in this passage. Though baptism has long been associated with cleansing and forgiveness of sin, it has for just as long been associated with the deeply unclean death of Jesus. When we are baptized, we are joined to Jesus' death as well as his resurrection (Rom. 6:3–5). Thus, baptism does not remove us from the stains of the world, but joins us to blood, dirt, and anguish, and to all those whom the world regards as unclean.

Nevertheless a second point is in order: if our baptismal teaching and practice obscures this call, if it falls captive to the trivial teaching that we need to be clean before we can come to dinner, then it does indeed need to be challenged, and by Jesus' very words here. He cites Isaiah: "This people honors me with their lips, but their hearts are far from me; in vain do they worship me, teaching human precepts as doctrines" (vv. 6–7). After all, Jesus shows throughout chapters 6, 7, and 8 that he desires for all people to be fed, not because they are worthy, but because they are hungry. If we have made baptism into a rite of purity and the Table into a place where only the clean may approach, then we have misrepresented the gospel and made ourselves unfit to sit at the Table of the Lord.

MARTHA MOORE-KEISH

Pastoral Perspective

I sang, a man came forward to the pulpit and whispered, "I want to be baptized." Ed was well known to us. He had been married to a daughter of the church for nearly forty years. Ed had had his troubles over the years, having lost his business a time or two, and wrestled with alcohol addiction. We all knew Ed to be a guy who could be gruff; I also knew that his soul had been longing for God for many years, but he just could not find his way to accepting God's grace. "I want to be baptized," he said.

Now the polity of my denomination requires a vote of the elders to approve a baptism. It also calls for an elder to participate in the baptism. There are good reasons for these ordinances. On this Sunday, there was no vote and no official elder. Baptism in any denomination requires water. On this Sunday, there was no water in the font.

Several verses of the hymn gave me time to think—and pray. Perhaps the same Spirit that inspired this text in Mark prompted me that day. When the hymn came to an end, I spied under the pulpit the untouched glass of drinking water. I picked up the glass, led Ed over to the font, and began, "The promise is to you, and to your children, to all who are far off. . . . Ed, do you turn from the ways of sin and evil that would separate you and the whole world from the love of God? Do you turn toward Jesus Christ?" Though it was not according to the traditions of the elders, there was no doubt in anyone's mind when Ed answered, "I do," that his heart was in it. For that matter, so was the heart of every person in the sanctuary that morning. When the elders next met, they voted to approve Ed's baptism. They believed God's heart was in that moment too. Ed's windows might not have been very clean, but it had become evident that he was one of God's saints.

KAREN PIDCOCK-LESTER

Exegetical Perspective

concerns access to the sacred. For the Pharisees (in Mark's opinion of them), it is through ritual purity; for the Markan community it is through repentance and God's coming kingdom.

In the short second part of this passage (vv. 14–15), Jesus turns to the crowd. The artificiality of the setup is apparent in that suddenly the Pharisees disappear as suddenly as they appeared. Jesus turns to the crowd, making the important point that "there is nothing outside a person that by going in can defile, but the things that come out are what defile" (v. 15). This is the principle the Markan author wants to defend, and he has constructed this passage to reach this conclusion. This saying is almost surely from the historical Jesus. So radical was the passage in the early church that a later scribe added verse 16, "If anyone has ears to hear, let him hear," a saying often used as a warning about difficult sayings.

In the final section (vv. 17–23), Jesus turns to the disciples. The introduction echoes 4:10, when Jesus explains the "parables" to the disciples. In Mark, "parable" has about it the sense of riddle. So verse 15 should be understood as a riddle that the disciples themselves do not understand. Their lack of understanding, a major theme in Mark, will lead Jesus to call them hard-hearted (8:17), a grave insult. The issue is about heart, not ritual purity. The narrator, in an aside, interprets this to mean "Thus he declared all foods clean" (v. 19).

In this passage, Jesus and the author of Mark's Gospel throw down a radical challenge: defilement does not come from the outside but from the inside. This debate is with the Pharisees, not Judaism itself, and the disciples do not understand, thus indicating that, from Mark's point of view, it is also a debate *within* the Christian community. That debate is ongoing. We are still contesting issues of ritual purity, as can be seen in our debates over homosexuality, whom we welcome and exclude from our churches, and the way we evaluate people by the clothes they wear. The list is almost endless. Jesus and Mark remain radical even to this day.

In the next two readings, 7:24–30 and 31–37, Mark will elaborate on the theme "there is nothing outside a person that by going in can defile, but the things that come out are what defile" (v. 15).

BERNARD BRANDON SCOTT

Homiletical Perspective

church for a hypocrite. Go home and look in the glass."[1]

It might be helpful to investigate the extent to which, simply by aspiring to be a better person—more loving, more faithful, more generous, more active for justice and peace—one opens oneself to such accusations. To stand for high ideals and goals, even while falling short, may strike an unsympathetic bystander as a genuine example of hypocrisy. More often, it is the person who merely puts on the appearance of striving that truly deserves the label.

The tale is told of a very self-centered individual who became concerned about other people's negative image of him. Finally he spoke to his pastor, who proposed that he try, for one month, simply pretending to be a different person, one who cared deeply about the welfare of others. He was to live, in effect, as a hypocrite, pretending to be something he was not, to be a far better person than he actually was. By the end of those four weeks the generosity, concern, and selflessness had become so captivating that he found he was no longer pretending. Maybe hypocrisy has something to be said for it after all!

Finally, in verses 18–19, we come up against one of Jesus' most radical statements concerning purity: "Do you not see that whatever goes into a person from outside cannot defile?" With these words Jesus calls into question the rationale behind the entire Levitical structure of dietary laws and regulations. In so doing, he locates the roots of impurity, and hence of sin, where they belong: within the mind, the heart, and the soul. Appearances, he argues, external factors, conditions, and influences count for nothing. As Robert Burns once put it:

> The heart ay's the part ay
> That makes us right or wrang.[2]

Pure or impure? Clean or unclean? It is not a matter of ritual observance or of outward appearance, but of what is going on deep inside a person. Of that, in the last resort, only God can be the judge. Perhaps John Milton put it best of all:

> For neither man nor angel can discern
> Hypocrisy, the only evil that walks
> Invisible, except to God alone.[3]

J. BARRIE SHEPHERD

---

1. W. W. (Billy) Sunday as quoted by Frank S. Mead, ed., *The Encyclopedia of Religious Quotations* (Westwood, NJ: Fleming H. Revell Co., 1965), 242.
2. *Poems and Songs of Robert Burns*, ed. James Barke (London and Glasgow: Collins Classics. 1960), 114.
3. John Milton, *Paradise Lost*, Book III, l. 68.

Mark 7:24–30

²⁴From there he set out and went away to the region of Tyre. He entered a house and did not want anyone to know he was there. Yet he could not escape notice, ²⁵but a woman whose little daughter had an unclean spirit immediately heard about him, and she came and bowed down at his feet. ²⁶Now the woman was a Gentile, of Syrophoenician origin. She begged him to cast the demon out of her daughter. ²⁷He said to her, "Let the children be fed first, for it is not fair to take the children's food and throw it to the dogs." ²⁸But she answered him, "Sir, even the dogs under the table eat the children's crumbs." ²⁹Then he said to her, "For saying that, you may go—the demon has left your daughter." ³⁰So she went home, found the child lying on the bed, and the demon gone.

Theological Perspective

In this startling passage, Jesus again touches on the subject of food. Whereas he has just been rebuking the Pharisees and scribes for worrying about ritual cleanliness before eating (vv. 1–23), he now seems to protect the boundaries of the table, proclaiming that it is inappropriate to feed dogs before children. His conversation partner, the Syrophoenician woman, responds by turning his teaching around, arguing that even dogs eat the crumbs that fall from the children's table. Like the story before it, and the two feeding narratives in chapters 6 and 8, this passage suggests how central food issues were in Jesus' ministry.

Two painful ironies emerge in this text. First, Jesus has just been chiding the Pharisees for worrying too much about defilement, yet here he seems to state his own concern about those who are unclean. In implying that the woman and her daughter are like dogs rather than children, he groups them with the ritually unclean who are not welcome at the table. A second irony revolves around his use of the term "children." The woman begs Jesus to heal her daughter, her child. He agrees that children do need to be fed; yet her daughter does not even count as a child. She is nothing but a dog.

What are we to do with Jesus' apparent hostility, even rudeness, in this story? Interpreters through Christian history have taken a variety of approaches,

Pastoral Perspective

"Let the children be fed first, for it is not fair to take the children's food and throw it to the dogs." What possesses Jesus to speak to this woman in this way?

Whenever this passage is read, people wince, sometimes even gasp, as they hear Jesus' remarks. In this scene, without even touching or seeing the little girl with the demon, Jesus heals her. His power is staggering. This is his most astonishing miracle thus far, yet it is often overlooked. Jesus' power can be hard to see because of what we *hear*.

So, before the wincing faithful can see the miracle, they may need help hearing rightly Jesus' remark to this woman. They will need to understand that he is being a Jewish man of his time. Since the time of David and Goliath, we have heard Hebrew writers use the term "dog" to refer to opponents, enemies, or non-Jews in general. Paul will use this term in his letter to the Philippians, warning early Christians against opponents of the gospel (Phil. 3:2). In Revelation, John will refer to those outside the gates of the city of God as "dogs" (Rev. 22:15).

Hardly anyone in that house in Tyre would wince or gasp when they hear this Jewish teacher speak in this way to this woman. She is a Gentile. Centuries of bad blood, and probably a social caste or two, lie between this woman and her Jewish neighbors. When Jesus speaks in this way, he is standing

Exegetical Perspective

Chapter 7 in the Gospel of Mark forms a coherent unit with three parts. Mark 7:1–23, itself an elaborate triptych, sets the theme of which verse 15 can serve as a summary: "there is nothing outside a person that by going in can defile." The Syrophoenician woman (vv. 24–30) and healing of a deaf and mute man (7:31–37) elaborate and comment on that theme.

In verses 24–30, Jesus crosses the boundary into Gentile land and deals with a Gentile woman. Boundary breaking elaborates the unit's theme by showing from a different perspective what it means that things from the outside cannot defile a person.

The form or type of a story sets expectations, and this form is mixed. It is an exorcism story in which the woman goes on a quest. While exorcism stories focus on the contest between exorcist and demon, quest stories draw attention to the person on the quest.

Two considerations set up this story as a contrast between Jew and Gentile. First, the location is Tyre, Gentile country, while Jesus is from Galilee. Second, the woman is Greek (NRSV "Gentile") and Syrophoenician (v. 26), while Jesus is Jewish; all three terms denote boundaries that a pious Jewish male should not cross.

The woman's daughter had an unclean spirit, so she "came and bowed down at his feet" (v. 25), the

Homiletical Perspective

With a change in geography and the company he keeps, Mark creates a clear break between the contents of verses 1–23 and this passage. Jesus has traveled by himself to a radically different place, a peripheral area outside the territory of Israel proper. Jesus' encounter with a woman who is identified as a Gentile of Greek origin continues the preceding discussion about purity and impurity, about precisely what is to be regarded as clean and unclean. Here, the focus is no longer ritual acts of cleansing or prescribed and proscribed foods but living persons, namely, Gentiles. This is about the ancient and fundamental division between the Jewish people and Gentiles.

Given the setting of the scene in verse 24, it would seem that Jesus was seeking a brief respite from the crowds and the controversy: "He . . . did not want anyone to know that he was there." The Matthean version of this same incident (Matt. 15:21–28) makes no mention of such a desire for privacy. It even presents the disciples as the ones seeking peace and quiet, since they are bothered by the woman's incessant "shouting" at them. Mark's observation that Jesus just wants to be alone offers a more human, even vulnerable, picture of God's Son as one who can, and does, become weary and worn down by the constant pressure and demands of the clamoring crowds.

Mark 7:24–30

Theological Perspective

and the approach depends partly on whether the interpreter hears Jesus' words as a straightforward rebuke or as some sort of teaching device aimed at the woman herself or at those overhearing. For instance, in saying, "It is not fair to take the children's food and throw it to the dogs," Jesus may have been giving the woman an opportunity to show her faith, for which he then praises her. Thomas Aquinas quotes the earlier interpreter Theophylact, who offers this sort of interpretation: "The reason, therefore, why the Lord does not immediately hear, but delays His grace, is, that He may also shew that the faith of the woman was firm, and that we may learn not at once to grow weary in prayer, but to continue earnest till we obtain."[1] According to Theophylact, Jesus' response is a teaching moment about the nature of faith and the value of persistent prayer. Again, perhaps the Gospel writer here is offering a lesson to his audience about their own prejudices: Jesus may be articulating a belief he himself does not hold, and inviting the woman's response, in order that his listeners may be convicted by their own limited view of God's mercy. In either case, Jesus is portrayed as wise rabbi who knows exactly what he is doing in this troubling interaction.

Some more recent interpreters, however, have suggested that in this passage we glimpse the fully human Jesus, limited by his own culture with its prejudices. If we read the text as an account of a straightforward, unpremeditated exchange, Jesus seems to offer a condemnation of the Gentiles as dogs and then—because of the witty response of the woman—actually changes his mind. At stake, then, is how Jesus' human nature and divine wisdom interact in this passage. Does this rhetorical exchange show a brilliant glimpse of God's wisdom, or a deplorable moment of Jesus' own cultural captivity, redeemed not by his action, but by the wit of the woman herself?

Another theological issue that arises in this passage is the relation of Jews and Gentiles. Though it is a troubling text, it is one of the few that shows Jesus' own ministry beyond the bounds of the Jewish community. Jesus initially turns the woman away because she is not a Jew, and he is sent primarily to the children of Israel. However, in the end he does heal the woman's daughter (at a distance), honoring the mother's response to him. Some early interpreters have seen here a strong contrast between the faith of the Gentiles (embodied in the woman) and

---

1. Thomas Aquinas, *Catena Aurea* (London: J. G. F. and J. R. Ivington, 1842), 2:127.

Pastoral Perspective

squarely alongside the Jewish peasants; his instincts are to protect the poor and the weak.[1]

What is more, when Jesus answers this woman in this way he is sticking with God's agenda: salvation would come first to the Jews, then to the Gentiles. He is implementing policy, as if to say, "Their time will come."

However, this woman needs him *now*, and so she answers him: "Sir, even the dogs under the table eat the children's crumbs" (v. 28). She does not wince, gasp, or miss a beat when Jesus rebuffs her. She is respectful, humble, yet persistent, and even bold: she will not take no for an answer. Martin Luther thinks we should pay attention to this woman. She teaches us how to pray.[2]

What possesses her to speak in this way? What drives her to abandon her own pride, to set aside her own prejudice, to throw herself at the feet of this man who is almost certain to refuse her?

She is a mother, and her child is suffering. We can imagine that she has watched as her tormented daughter has become a stranger to her. We can picture this mother hearing her daughter's cries and holding her during fits and cleaning up her messes. Still, the woman is powerless to save her.

In the face of all that, what do the politics of a people matter? What does the race of a person matter, if that person can help you? What does it matter whether you are rich or poor? Though you risk rejection and ridicule, you throw yourselves at the feet of the one who can help and you hang on, sometimes for years, not taking no for an answer. You come like a dog, yes—but like a *bull*dog, tenacious, persistent, protective: "I may be a dog, but sir, even the dogs under the table eat the children's crumbs." Give us a crumb. A crumb from your table would be enough. A crumb from your table is all we need.

Sister Mary Scullion has hung on to Jesus' feet since 1976, pleading for homeless men and women in Philadelphia. She began Project H.O.M.E. in 1989, with the motto and mission "No one is home until all of us are home." That is the mission statement of a bulldog.[3]

Jesus commands us to love like a bulldog. "For saying that, you may go—the demon has left your daughter" (v. 29). Something changes here. Is it the woman? Has she passed some test? Perhaps. Her persistent hanging on, her continual intercession for

---

1. Joel Marcus, *Mark 1–8*, Anchor Bible (New York: Doubleday, 1999), 462.
2. Martin Luther, cited in Marcus, *Mark*, 469.
3. Sister Mary Scullion, http://www.projecthome.org/about/co-founders.php; accessed April 10, 2013.

Exegetical Perspective

normal posture for supplication. The parallel with the story of Jairus in 5:22 is clear. The contrast is also clear: Jairus is Jewish, male, and named (a rarity in Mark's narratives); she is pagan, female, and unnamed.

Jesus refuses to accede to her request, offering instead an aphorism: "Let the children be fed first, for it is not fair to take the children's food and throw it to the dogs" (v. 27). "First" indicates the priority of Jews, who are described as "the children," indicating their preferred status as heirs. The Gentiles are characterized with the insult "dogs." These are not pets but scavengers or mongrels. We find in 1 and 2 Kings a recurring curse in which "the dogs shall eat" the one who dies (1 Kgs. 14:11). Gentiles are often called dogs, as the well-known quote from Rabbi Eliezer indicates: "He who eats with an idolater is like unto one who eats with a dog."[1] The aphorism is dismissive. The woman's quest is denied, creating an obstacle.

She parries his aphorism with a clever play on words: "even the dogs under the table eat the children's crumbs" (v. 28). She turns mongrels into the house pets that eat the scraps under the table. Jesus has been bested in a Gospel in which he usually has the last word. He explicitly refers to her statement as the cause of his change of mind. Her riposte is the reason for his action, so he accedes to her request and tells her that the demon has left her daughter.

Some commentators note the woman's faith, but the word "faith" is conspicuously absent in the passage. By contrast, in the story of the woman who touches Jesus' garment (5:25–34), which is interlaced into the story of the healing of Jairus's daughter (5:21–43), Jesus explicitly comments on the woman's faith: "Daughter, your faith has made you well; go in peace, and be healed of your disease" (5:34). In Mark, faith does not mean "belief" but "trust" or "confidence." "Faith" is the expected word here, but Jesus says instead, "For this saying" (my trans.), signaling that the woman has bested him in the verbal dual. In that sense "this saying" is a sign of her confidence.

A major problem in early Christianity is that Jesus' mission was among Israel, as Matthew 15:24 has it, while early Christianity was rapidly expanding among the Gentiles. The legitimacy of the Gentile mission, a major theme in Paul's letters, evidently was an issue not easily solved. The evangelists too are on the lookout to signal by implication a Gentile

---

1. Vincent Taylor, *The Gospel according to Mark*, 2nd ed. (London: Macmillan, 1966), 350.

Homiletical Perspective

As the story unfolds, it is clear that the chief focus is not on Jesus' frustrated quest for solitude, or even on the act of healing (unusual in that it is performed "at a distance"), but on the fascinating verbal exchange between the Master and this Gentile woman, mother of a demon-possessed child.

My old New York colleague in ministry, Ernest Campbell, told me he had once preached a sermon series entitled "Things I Wish Jesus Had Never Said." The response recorded here to this distraught woman's plea must have been high on Campbell's list. The same one who is recorded as having issued the all-embracing invitation, "Anyone who comes to me I will never drive away" (John 6:37b), and who, in his parables of the Samaritan (Luke 10:29–37) and the Prodigal (Luke 15:11–32), opened the door wide to all of humanity, here contrasts Jewish "children" with Gentile "dogs." Considering all the words attributed to Jesus in the Gospels, this comment seems completely out of character. To make matters worse, most of the commentators note that in the East, still to this day, to call someone a dog is among the worst of conceivable insults.

Naturally many have attempted to get around this problem by seeking to ameliorate these apparently cruel and intolerant words. Some scholars have argued that our Lord was only pretending such hostility toward the woman in order to test her faith. While this may have some warrant in Matthew's Gospel, where Jesus commends her for her great faith, Mark's Jesus makes no reference whatsoever to her faith, only to her words: "For saying that, you may go" (v. 29).

Others have tried to make light of Jesus' name-calling. The actual Greek word used here for "dogs" is written in a diminutive form, signifying "little dogs" or "puppies" or "doggies," and could suggest that Jesus was being playful or only joshing. However, at the remove of two millennia and having only the text to work with, we cannot even make an educated guess about Jesus' tone or intention. Moreover, when translators and interpreters have attempted to erase the dissonance between the time of a text and our own time, the meaning has sometimes been missed. Therefore, we would do best to set aside all such well-intentioned attempts to reduce the harshness of Jesus' words and accept the text for what, to all appearances, it is: a stern, even insulting rebuke to the woman's plea of desperation.

Then how should we deal with Jesus' dehumanizing response to this woman? I have become convinced that the principal problem here is our

Mark 7:24–30

Theological Perspective

the "unfaith" of the Jews. This contrast may be even more starkly drawn when this passage is read against the indictment of the scribes and Pharisees in verses 1–23. Others have refrained from such judgment, though, and simply emphasized Jesus' response as a matter of timing: the gospel was first preached to the Jews and only then to the Gentiles; Jesus is rightly articulating that order.

In either case, however, this story anticipates the surprising reception of the gospel among the Gentiles in the decades following his resurrection. Those of us reading the story today might ask: who are the children now, and who are the dogs? Might this passage overturn our own cozy assumptions about who needs to be fed first, and about whom we regard as crazy, unclean dogs who do not deserve to come to the table?

Finally, this story prompts reflection on the role of women in Jesus' ministry, and thus the role of women in the Christian community today. Is this woman a model of persistent faith, or does she perpetuate harmful stereotypes of how women are to behave? Gentile that she is, and with a demon-possessed daughter, she is already marginal, and she lowers herself even further by first bowing down at Jesus' feet and then accepting his designation of her and her daughter as dogs.

Some interpreters have praised the woman for her humility, for her acceptance of her lowly role, as a symbol for the way all Christians are to relate to God. Though humility is indeed a virtue, there is also danger in this line of interpretation, if it reinforces self-abasing strategies of female behavior. However, the text does not clearly state that Jesus is rewarding her self-abasement. When Jesus says, "For saying that, you may go" (v. 29), he may be responding not to her self-designation as a dog, but to her creative, quick-witted rejoinder to his insult. In other words, this woman may well serve as a model of humility for the powerful, but for those without power, she models the courage and the cleverness to speak.

MARTHA MOORE-KEISH

Pastoral Perspective

her daughter, her refusal to give up, have shaped her into someone who is blind to race, wealth, and status, someone who sees clearly who Jesus is, and she trusts him.

Has something changed in Jesus too? At the beginning of the encounter, Jesus treats this woman as a Gentile, a non-Jew. Now Jesus looks upon this woman kneeling before him and no longer sees a type or a category or a demographic. He sees *her*—a mother who is putting her trust in him.

Try as he might to stick to the agenda, he heals the girl anyway. Because it is one thing to map out a strategy about a group or class or nation, one thing to have a policy about Gentiles, or the homeless, or immigrants, or gays, or women, or Muslims, or Jews, or Palestinians. It is quite another thing to see a *person* in front of us, to hear her cries, feel his pain, witness her faith. When we see the person—even an enemy—we often see something of ourselves in him, and compassion grows in us.

Does Jesus see something of himself in her? After all, he too loves his children with a tenacious, protective love. He too watches his children turn away, sees them suffer, hears their cries, cleans up their messes. He too will humble himself and submit to ridicule in order to save them.

Unlike the Gentile woman, he is not powerless to save his children. He can, he will, and he does. His compassion widens the circle of his mercy. His plan, his policy, will include anyone who comes to him. They will all be his children, fed from the table. It may be crumbs, but crumbs from the hand of Jesus work miracles.

One day, everyone who comes to him will be fed from the feast at the table. Until then, what is there to do but love like a bulldog and feed on the power of the crumbs from his table to make us whole?

KAREN PIDCOCK-LESTER

Exegetical Perspective

mission on Jesus' part. Mark has already signaled such a shift at the conclusion of the exorcism of the Gerasene demoniac. When the restored man, by place a Gentile, requests to remain with Jesus, Jesus tells him, "Go home to your friends, and tell them how much the Lord has done for you, and what mercy he has shown you" (5:19). The narrator remarks, "And he went away and began to proclaim in the Decapolis how much Jesus had done for him; and everyone was amazed" (5:20). In Greek, "to proclaim" is *kēryssein*, from which we get our word "kerygmatic."

Likewise, in this exorcism Mark uses a story set in the past to anticipate and justify the Gentile mission of the Gospel's community. In both cases, the stories are not complimentary to Gentiles. The first one concerns a healed demoniac, a demoniac of extreme proportions, a legion of demons. Furthermore, this Gentile woman is a dog. So while both of these stories anticipate and justify a Gentile mission, they both indicate the great boundary that had to be crossed to start that mission. Often forgetting that Jesus crossed that boundary for our sake, we Gentile Christians institute new boundaries between us and them. Mark intends the kingdom as radically inclusive; we often reconstitute it as exclusive.

The story of the Syrophoenician makes explicit one more boundary that had to be crossed: she was a woman. Twice in quick succession, the narrator reminds the reader that she is a woman (vv. 25, 26). The second explicit mention of "woman" could have been avoided in Greek with a pronoun or just a simple verb; but her femaleness is accented. Furthermore, she has a daughter, also twice mentioned. So the barrier of her femaleness is pointed out as yet another boundary Jesus will cross in Mark's effort to elucidate the meaning of 7:15. Even more, Jesus, as a Jewish male of honor, must give up some of that honor to meet the woman's request. The first must become the last and slave of all (9:35).

For Jesus and Mark, boundaries are inimical to the gospel. Mark even pictures Jesus being bested by a Gentile woman dog who forces him to cross the boundary—and he does.

BERNARD BRANDON SCOTT

Homiletical Perspective

persistent need to dehumanize Jesus, to insist that he was perfect in every sense, incapable of even the slightest human error or misjudgment. It is not difficult to infer here that Jesus was exhausted after the long and arduous ministry detailed in Mark's earlier chapters. Perhaps he responded initially to the woman out of his own deep-rooted Jewish tradition before being compelled, by the sheer audacity and sagacity of the woman's rejoinder, to think again, to come to himself, and to act according to the good news he had come to deliver and to embody. Applications of this passage might well explore in depth the humanity of Jesus, seeing this as a balance to Christianity's perennial tendency to focus exclusively on his divine nature. The entire paradox and power of the incarnation can be at stake here.

Resistance, and even more than that, boldness and creativity in prayer, as characterized by the mother's daring and astute response, is another potential theme to be developed. From the perspective of those who believe that Jesus manifests God's presence, this story stands in the long and worthy Jewish tradition of "arguing with God," which has deep roots in the Old Testament Scriptures. There we find Abraham resisting, even bargaining with, God over the fate of Sodom (Gen. 18:22–33); Moses confronting God, and actually changing God's mind, after the incident with the golden calf (Exod. 32:11–14); and the entire book of Job, as one drawn-out disputation between the Divine and the human.

Keep in mind, moreover, that in many Christian traditions, the Lord's Prayer is introduced in worship with the words "we are bold to say." After close to two thousand years of rote recitation, we often forget just how bold this prayer is. Perhaps this woman might act as a reminder of the radical boldness required of those who would petition God. How can our praying, in general, become more daring, more creative, or perhaps even—following those examples in the Old Testament and this woman—more argumentative? Again, the former theme of inclusiveness, of the breaking down of all barriers, might be picked up from verses 1–23 and further expanded upon.

J. BARRIE SHEPHERD

Mark 7:31–37

³¹Then he returned from the region of Tyre, and went by way of Sidon towards the Sea of Galilee, in the region of the Decapolis. ³²They brought to him a deaf man who had an impediment in his speech; and they begged him to lay his hand on him. ³³He took him aside in private, away from the crowd, and put his fingers into his ears, and he spat and touched his tongue. ³⁴Then looking up to heaven, he sighed and said to him, "Ephphatha," that is, "Be opened." ³⁵And immediately his ears were opened, his tongue was released, and he spoke plainly. ³⁶Then Jesus ordered them to tell no one; but the more he ordered them, the more zealously they proclaimed it. ³⁷They were astounded beyond measure, saying, "He has done everything well; he even makes the deaf to hear and the mute to speak."

Theological Perspective

After Jesus' troubling encounter with the Syrophoenician woman (7:24–30), he returns to more familiar territory, where he heals a deaf man with a speech impediment. This healing miracle is another event that shows Jesus as the one who inaugurates God's reign in the world. As promised in the book of Isaiah (Isa. 35:5; 43:8), the restoration of Israel would be marked by the blind receiving their sight and the deaf being able to hear. The sign that Jesus performs fulfills this promise in a way that people cannot miss. In him "the kingdom of God has come near" (1:15). The day of righteousness and peace has already begun. No wonder the people cannot stop proclaiming what he has done (v. 36).

Their proclamation, however, directly contravenes what Jesus asked. This is one of several passages in which Jesus tries to keep his presence and his power a secret: "He took him aside in private, away from the crowd" (v. 33) and "Jesus ordered them to tell no one" (v. 36). Why does Jesus seek such privacy? This has perplexed interpreters for centuries. Perhaps this is a sign of Jesus' humility, showing him as one who "did not regard equality with God as something to be exploited, but emptied himself" (Phil. 2:6–7). Perhaps his failed attempt at secrecy is Mark's narrative strategy to show that the kingdom of God cannot be hidden. Even when he tells them not to say

Pastoral Perspective

Convinced by recent publications about the need to encourage the practice of testimony in the life of the church, our congregation has been looking for opportunities for normally reticent Christians to speak personally about what God has done in their lives—to testify.

As a result, Pentecost Sunday will find two or three brave souls bearing witness to how and when they have seen the Holy Spirit at work in the world or in their lives. Several times a year at a Service for Wholeness, some earnest disciple will stand before the congregation with knees knocking to speak about how he or she has known God to be working for wholeness during an illness, unemployment, a significant transition, an addiction, an outreach endeavor, or a dark night of the soul.

These dear souls almost never volunteer for this. They are too shy, or too humble, or too awed to think they have anything to say that is worth hearing. They are inclined to think, "Who am *I* to talk about God? How can *I* put into words what God is up to?" Nevertheless we ask. Then after it is all over, they invariably are grateful for the opportunity to bear witness to what God has done. Invariably, the congregation is grateful too.

Sometimes people turn us down. Perhaps our timing is off, or our discernment is askew, and the

Exegetical Perspective

This healing story continues Jesus' journey in Gentile territory begun in 7:24 and so elaborates on the themes of the previous exorcism story. It further expands the commentary on 7:15: "there is nothing outside a person that by going in can defile."

This particular story is unusual in the tradition because it appears to employ magic. The Gospel's Greek-speaking audience would have viewed the Aramaic *Ephphatha* (v. 34) as a magical term (so also *Talitha cum* in 5:41). Since it has no parallel in Matthew or Luke, their copies of Mark may not have contained the story, or perhaps they both omitted the story because of its magical overtones.

Many commentators have noted the improbable geography of Jesus' movements, although the ancients did not have reliable maps and so may not have been aware of this improbability. More likely Mark's mention of "the region of Tyre, . . . by way of Sidon towards the Sea of Galilee, in the region of the Decapolis" (v. 31) signals the inclusiveness of Gentile territory. It is not meant to be a road map but a symbol of all this Gentile territory.

The man's exact ailments are unclear, although it would appear that he is deaf and unable to speak clearly. The cure in verse 35 mentions that his ears were opened and he began to speak correctly (*orthōs*, NRSV "plainly").

Homiletical Perspective

Once again, as in the previous section, the transition between these two healing narratives (v. 31) is indicated by a journey. Given the exceedingly lengthy and unlikely route Mark describes, scholarly consensus appears to be that Mark knew next to nothing of the actual geography of the Holy Land, and that geography was not important to him. Mark's traveling details are only there as punctuation, as devices to move the story along.

The individual brought to Jesus was deaf and suffered from some type of speech impediment (v. 32), perhaps a direct result of his deafness. The statement that Jesus "took the man away in private" could mean that Jesus was simply showing the utmost consideration for the man's feelings, not wishing to embarrass him with any public display. It also could indicate that Jesus wanted to gain the man's undivided attention, with no distractions from curious spectators. The move to a private place could even be connected with Mark's ongoing depiction of the messianic secret—Jesus' insistence throughout his early ministry on keeping his messianic identity under wraps. Such an explanation would fit with the instruction in verse 36 "to tell no one."

It is also hard not to wonder about Mark's reason for describing the long, drawn-out process of this miracle, especially when contrasted with the

Mark 7:31–37

Theological Perspective

anything, the people cannot control their proclamation of the good news. Finally, this "messianic secret" in Mark may be related to the unexpected nature of Jesus' messiahship. While many expected a messiah to bring in God's reign, no one expected that messiah to be crucified. In Mark's Gospel, Jesus is especially intent on showing that "the Son of Man must undergo great suffering . . . and be killed" (8:31). Jesus insists that no one can truly understand what it means to be Messiah apart from this suffering and death. So he seeks to keep his messianic powers quiet until his crucifixion and resurrection demonstrate the fullness of what "Messiah" means.

Many Christian interpreters of this passage have focused on deafness and speech impediments as metaphors for human inability to hear or speak the word of God properly. Only when we are touched by Jesus are we able to hear clearly; and hearing, we cannot help but proclaim the good news, as did the man and his companions in the story (vv. 36–37).

This interpretation led some medieval Christians in the West to develop an "ephphatha rite" (sometimes spelled "ephphetha rite") as part of preparation for baptism. A version of this is also practiced today in both Roman Catholic and Protestant churches that use a catechumenate model for preparation of baptismal candidates. According to this practice, on Holy Saturday, the day before Easter Sunday, candidates for baptism gather with their families and sponsors and other members of the congregation, to pray and to hear a reading of this very Gospel text. Then the priest or pastor touches the ears and lips of the candidates for baptism while saying these or similar words: "Ephphetha: that is, be opened, that you may profess the faith you hear, to the praise and glory of God."[1] This rite clearly signals that baptism, as entrance into the Christian community, enables people to hear and to proclaim the good news of Jesus Christ.

Some recent interpreters, however, have cautioned against reading this text as a metaphor for "spiritual deafness," calling attention instead to what this passage suggests about people who live with actual hearing loss. Does Jesus' healing of the man in the story mean that deaf people live in a deficient state, from which they need to be released? Is deafness a disability, or simply a difference in human experience to be honored rather than fixed? The story clearly portrays the man's hearing loss and speech impediment as issues that need to be addressed, and Jesus responds

Pastoral Perspective

people we ask to speak say, "No, I cannot." They have a "speech impediment."

Most often, they have a speech impediment because they have a hearing problem. The pain is too recent and raw for the woman who went through chemotherapy a year ago, and she has had a hard time hearing God since then. The anxiety and anger of the layoff have been overpowering for the family and have drowned out the voice of Jesus. Events in the headlines have hit too close to home, and the father of the soldier finds the Word of God garbled and incoherent.

Fair enough. When there is something wrong with our hearing, we cannot speak clearly, because what we cannot hear affects what we can say. The words the child absorbs at home, the music the teenager hears in the headphones, and the media outlets that claim our attention all affect our speech. If the woes of the world and the cares of daily routines drown out the voice of Jesus, it is understandable that a person would have a speech impediment when asked to share his or her faith.

That is when Jesus needs to mess with our ears. That is when Jesus needs to pull us aside, stick his fingers in our ears, spit, touch our tongues, look up to heaven and sigh, speak in some ancient language—do whatever he does to open the passageway and remove the blockage so that we who have grown deaf can hear again.

It may well be that things we have chosen to block out will become extremely loud again: the background of the world's hostilities, the cries of suffering, the wearying din. It also may be that, with a passageway opened, we will hear other things: the voice of Jesus whispering privately in our ears any instructions, guidance, wisdom, encouragement we need; the commands of Jesus authoritatively disarming the powers of evil; the lively testimony of others who have also seen God at work in astounding ways.

With an open passageway, we may hear more distinctly the stirrings of the realm of God coming into being, for that is what is happening here. When Jesus rummages around in this man's ears, he is inaugurating the opening act of a new order of existence, a new realm where things that have been unthinkable without Jesus are now not only possible, but becoming real in front of us. In the words of the old Shaker song, when Jesus opens our ears, we will hear "the clear, though far-off hymn that hails a new creation."[1]

---

1. International Commission on English in the Liturgy, *Rite of Christian Initiation of Adults* (National Conference of Catholic Bishops, 1985), #197.

1. Robert Lowry, "How Can I Keep From Singing?" *Bright Jewels for the Sunday School* (New York: Biglow & Main, 1869).

Exegetical Perspective

There are strong parallels to the story of raising Jairus's daughter (5:22–43). Both have a request that Jesus lay on hands to effect the cure; both take place in private; both employ an Aramaic phrase or word; those around are amazed; and Jesus enjoins them to tell no one. In a culture in which, rather than reading silently, one proclaims the gospel out loud and so hears, these parallels draw the stories together. The story of the healing of the Gentile man echoes the raising of Jairus's daughter.

The significance of the spittle is unclear. Some evidence indicates that the Greco-Roman culture viewed it as having curative effects,[1] while other evidence from Jewish texts indicates that it is an unclean discharge.[2] This would actually make a difference in how one views the healing act. Given that Mark has been picturing Jesus breaking boundaries, I would suggest that it is viewed in the Jewish fashion as unclean. By an unclean act Jesus heals; this makes the boundary breaking even stronger.

Following the healing, Jesus enjoins those around (who they are is unclear, since Mark says that "he took him aside in private, away from the crowd" [v. 33]) to tell no one, "but the more he ordered them, the more zealously they proclaimed it" (v. 36). To proclaim or preach (*kēryssō*) is an important word in Mark. John the Baptist proclaims a baptism of repentance (1:4); Jesus proclaims the good news of God (1:14); the Twelve are sent out to proclaim (3:14); the healed Gerasene proclaims to Decapolis (5:20), and now these Gentiles proclaim "more excessively" (NRSV "more zealously"; the KJV has the intriguing translation "so much the more a great deal they published it"). The good news of the kingdom is spreading further and further, crossing more and more boundaries.

A strong irony exists in that a deaf man who does not speak correctly is healed, and they (the Gentiles) proclaim the message. The healing matches the proclaiming. They hear and now speak correctly the good news of the kingdom.

The story's concluding exclamation explicitly draws this connection: "they" exclaim, "He has done everything well; he even makes the deaf to hear and the mute to speak" (v. 37). Mark's healing stories never end with a christological title. Only the centurion at Jesus' despairing death utters a title (15:39). The point of the exclamation is that the signs of the kingdom have come even to the Gentiles. The

---

1. Adela Yarbro Collins, *Mark: A Commentary*, Hermeneia (Minneapolis: Fortress Press, 2007), 372–73.
2. Ched Myers, *Binding the Strong Man: A Political Reading of Mark's Story of Jesus* (Maryknoll, NY: Orbis Books, 1992), 205.

Homiletical Perspective

"long distance," almost casual healing in the previous segment (7:24–30). If you imagine Jesus trying to communicate to this man who cannot hear, you might see his specific actions—placing fingers in the man's ears, spitting, touching his tongue, looking to heaven—as a form of sign language, a physical means of communication in place of words, to explain to the man what is happening. Seven distinct actions are listed, and each one is expanded upon at some length, often with considerable interpretive license. This is particularly the case with Jesus' glance heavenward, and the sigh (v. 34), the heavenly look representing the essential role of prayer in such matters, the sigh portending everything from sadness at the fallen state of the world to weariness at the never-ending demands of the populace.

The use of the Aramaic word *ephphatha* in verse 34 is highly unusual, although the Hebrew word *corban* appears earlier in this same chapter, and in Mark 5:41 we read *talitha cum*, Aramaic for "little girl, get up," in the raising of Jairus's daughter from the dead. The only other use of Aramaic in the Gospels, again by Mark, is seen in his account of the crucifixion when (15:34) Jesus cries out, *Eloi, Eloi, lama sabachthani*, "My God, my God, why have you forsaken me?"

The text offers no reason as to why Mark employs the original tongue, although its English translation, "Be opened," has lent itself to a harvest of homiletic fancy. As usual, it appears that Jesus' command to tell no one (v. 36) is immediately and flagrantly disobeyed, with the result that he is acclaimed as having "done all things well." The statement brings to mind Genesis 1:31 ("God saw everything that he had made, and indeed, it was very good") and is another instance in Mark's Gospel where Jesus is portrayed as inaugurating a new creation.

In terms of themes for homiletic development, one could explore the whole field of miracles and healing powers, considering not just their authenticity and factuality, but their role in religious belief. Can they serve as proofs, for example, of Christ's divinity, or do they simply provide signs, acted-out minidramas to illustrate what Jesus' ministry was all about—release, renewal, new life?

Related to this are the issues raised by the age-old, agonized question, "Why me?" or, much more typically in this case, "Why not me?" Why are some people cured and others condemned to continued suffering? Why are some prayers for deliverance answered and not others? These questions are by no means easy to answer, but they are posed repeatedly, and not only by persons seeking to attack the

Mark 7:31–37

Theological Perspective

by healing both. However, if we focus on the physical condition alone, we miss the larger significance of Jesus' healing power.

One recent interpreter, Thomas Reynolds, offers three general insights on Jesus' healing narratives that illuminate how this particular passage portrays disability and healing. First, "Jesus does not stigmatize persons with illnesses, diseases, and impairments." He enters into their presence, disregarding purity codes and seeking their good. This is amply clear in Jesus' gestures in this passage, which involve inserting his own fingers into the man's ears and spitting and touching his tongue. He does not flinch at the man's inability to hear or regard it as a sign of sin or impurity. Second, in the ancient world, sickness was not just an individual matter, but had an effect on the entire community. Thus, "sickness causes social isolation and alienation, interfering with a person's sense of being in community." In this passage, Jesus' act of healing does not simply restore the man's physical abilities; it restores him to community. He moves from being an isolated "he" in verse 35 to being part of "they" who proclaim the good news in verse 36. Third, the healing narratives are not primarily about "curing," which is restoration of physical function, but about "healing," which is a restoration of wholeness, a gift of abundant life. This healing points not to the one healed, but to the Healer himself: Jesus Christ. At the conclusion of this passage, after the restoration of the man's hearing and speech, the man does not call attention to himself, but he and his friends call attention to Jesus, who "makes the deaf to hear and the mute to speak" (v. 37).[2]

The point of this passage is not the disability of the man, but the identity of Jesus: as the Christ who heals and redeems, and who brings in a new creation of mercy and wholeness.

MARTHA MOORE-KEISH

Pastoral Perspective

How does Jesus get into our ears? How do we hear him speak to us? When he does, and we hear him clearly, we are able to speak plainly about what we have seen and heard God doing. No more speech impediment. In fact, if this story is any indication, we will not be able to hold back our testimony. Imagine that! Like the man with Jesus' fingers in his ear, we will not only have something to say, but we will also *want* to say it. We will be so astounded at what God has done, we will be eager to tell it.

Anne Lamott, in her book *Operating Instructions*, remembers an East Indian Jesuit named Tony de Mello "who used to tell this story about disciples gathered around their master, asking him endless questions about God. And the master said that anything we say about God is just words, because God is unknowable. One disciple asked, 'Then why do you speak of him at all?' and the master replied, 'Why does the bird sing? She sings not because she has a statement but because she has a song.'"[2]

Sometimes in the Christian life, almost inevitably we stumble upon times when we cannot hear God speaking to us, and so we ourselves cannot speak of God. In such times, we do not need an invitation to testify at a Service for Wholeness. Rather, we need someone like the friends of the deaf man, someone who will bring us to Jesus, perhaps even in that service, so that Jesus can get into our ears and do whatever he does to clear a passageway for his own voice.

KAREN PIDCOCK-LESTER

---

2. All citations from this paragraph are in Thomas E. Reynolds, *Vulnerable Communion: A Theology of Disability and Hospitality* (Grand Rapids: Brazos Press, 2008), 223–25.

2. Anne Lamott, quoted in Thomas G. Long, *Testimony: Talking Ourselves into Being Christian* (San Francisco: Jossey-Bass, 2004), 157.

Exegetical Perspective

acclamation may be echoing Isaiah 35:5–6: "Then the eyes of the blind shall be opened, and the ears of the deaf unstopped; then the lame shall leap like a deer, and the tongue of the speechless sing for joy. For waters shall break forth in the wilderness, and streams in the desert."

Chapter divisions often confuse and overly segment our view of Mark's narrative. This healing story serves as a pivot: it concludes a cycle of four healings and initiates a second cycle revolving around blindness or deafness. The first cycle deals with boundary breaking and enlarging the circle of the kingdom of God. The cycle begins with the raising of Jairus's daughter and the healing of the woman with a hemorrhage (5:22–43), continues with the healing of the daughter of the Syrophoenician woman (7:24–30), and concludes with the healing of the deaf and mute man. There are strong parallels between all four stories. There are also contrasts: the first two are situated within the sphere of Judaism, while the last two are among Gentiles. The prominence of women in three of the stories is notable.

In the second cycle, which this healing inaugurates, all the stories have a similar theme of blindness or deafness. Immediately before the so-called confession at Caesarea Philippi, Jesus heals a blind man at Bethsaida (8:22–26); immediately after the transfiguration he heals a boy with a deaf and speechless spirit (9:14–29); and before entering into Jerusalem he heals blind Bartimaeus (10:45–52). So this healing story plays a pivotal role in two cycles of miracle stories, one cycle concluding the Gospel's first half and the second helping structure the Gospel's second half. Since miracles virtually disappear in the second half of the Gospel, this cycle is especially significant.

The unit 7:1–37 radically expands the inclusiveness of the kingdom of God. It includes a redefinition of cleanliness, a major value in the Jewish and Greco-Roman worlds, breaks out of the boundary of Galilee into Gentile lands, and crosses boundaries between male and female, even showing Jesus' honor being challenged by a witty Syrophoenician woman. If we miss all this boundary breaking and the inclusiveness of the kingdom, we miss the gospel's essence.

BERNARD BRANDON SCOTT

Homiletical Perspective

faith. Sermons in this area, while not able to offer all the answers, should at least deal honestly with the often-painful realities involved and review the most promising of the answers offered by believers in the past. Harold Kushner's *When Bad Things Happen to Good People* (Norwell, MA: Anchor, 2004) is one example of a rabbi who has wrestled honestly with these questions.

Several commentators have linked Jesus' "sigh" of verse 34 with other displays of emotion in Mark's Gospel (1:41; 3:5; 6:6; 6:34; 8:12), demonstrating Christ's solidarity with human suffering and/or his distress at human stubbornness and refusal to believe. All of this might be helpful in reemphasizing the humanity of Jesus and his complete identification with our human condition.

The mysterious theme of the messianic secret could also be fruitfully developed. Given the never-ending popularity of mystery novels, one might consider the elements of mystery in the Gospel narratives: the enigmatic nature of many of Christ's sayings; the (at times admitted) hidden meanings of the parables; even the seeming hesitancy of Christ's claims to divine sonship in the earlier writings versus the full-blown announcements of the same in the Gospel of John.

In a similar vein, one might inquire as to the role of secrecy in the faith today. Is it ever appropriate to act as an "anonymous Christian"?[1] With so many unhelpful stereotypes attached to the title "Christian" in our times, might it be preferable to live a Christlike life without any label attached?[2] Certainly there are brief passages in the Sermon on the Mount (Matt. 6:3–6, 16–18) that would appear to advocate this kind of an approach. A series of popular novels in the last century by Lloyd C. Douglas sought to present example of lives lived in just this way. What would be the problems with such an approach? What might be the advantages? What would Jesus do?

J. BARRIE SHEPHERD

---

1. The phrase, though not the meaning displayed here, is Karl Rahner's. See Rahner, *Theological Investigations*, vol. 6 (London: Darton, Longman, & Todd, 1969).
2. See, for instance, Jonathan Malesic's book *Secret Faith in the Public Square: An Argument for the Concealment of Christian Identity* (Ada, MI: Brazos, 2009).

Mark 8:1–10

¹In those days when there was again a great crowd without anything to eat, he called his disciples and said to them, ²"I have compassion for the crowd, because they have been with me now for three days and have nothing to eat. ³If I send them away hungry to their homes, they will faint on the way—and some of them have come from a great distance." ⁴His disciples replied, "How can one feed these people with bread here in the desert?" ⁵He asked them, "How many loaves do you have?" They said, "Seven." ⁶Then he ordered the crowd to sit down on the ground; and he took the seven loaves, and after giving thanks he broke them and gave them to his disciples to distribute; and they distributed them to the crowd. ⁷They had also a few small fish; and after blessing them, he ordered that these too should be distributed. ⁸They ate and were filled; and they took up the broken pieces left over, seven baskets full. ⁹Now there were about four thousand people. And he sent them away. ¹⁰And immediately he got into the boat with his disciples and went to the district of Dalmanutha.

Theological Perspective

Theological paradoxes abound in this passage. Like its earlier parallel (6:30–44), the story invites disciples of every generation to question our assumptions about seeming contradictions in the life of faith.

Spiritual vs. Physical Hunger. The crowd gathered around Jesus has traveled from near and far, and now—three days later—they are hungry and weak. Their total spiritual engagement in listening to Jesus has put them at risk physically. It is hard to imagine Western Christians today devoting ourselves so completely to Jesus' instruction that we would endanger our material well-being—whether our literal physical security or, in a broader sense, our financial solvency.

Jesus resists the bifurcation between his followers' physical and spiritual interests. Indeed, his very reaction indicates an integration of body and soul: *splanchnizomai*, "have compassion or pity" (v. 2), is etymologically related to *splanchnon,* a word that is translated as both "one's inmost heart" and "entrails." Instead of disregarding the crowd's physical *or* spiritual hunger, Jesus cares about and attends to the needs of the whole of God's beloved people. The human body requires both bread and the bread of life. As God provided for Adam and Eve at creation, so also Christ provides nourishment for the sustaining of his people.

Pastoral Perspective

How are our people hungry? As we look out from the pulpit, or let the images of the members of our congregation roll through our thoughts, who comes to mind? How would we describe their hunger?

Perhaps their hungers are physical: they worry about putting food on the table. Perhaps their hungers are relational: they are lonely and seek companionship or the validation that long-term relationships provide. Perhaps their hunger is spiritual: they are desperately seeking meaning or purpose.

Then there is the hard-to-name hunger of those who have been with Jesus for a while, like the crowds in Mark 8. They are weak and depleted and need to be replenished. Perhaps we know disciples who have been pouring out what they have for others and suddenly find that they have nothing left to give. Perhaps we see church members who labor on behalf of their congregation's ministries but feel as if their labors are bearing little fruit.

Perhaps a depleted disciple stares at us from the mirror. Have we been with Jesus for a while and now feel depleted? Do we dare notice and name our own hungers—the places where we feel weak and have little to give others? Like the crowds who follow Jesus, we too may feel that it has been a long time since we have been fed and we have a long way to go before we can take time to be refilled.

Exegetical Perspective

Rerun or revision? Mark's audience surely remembers the feeding of the five thousand from chapter 6 (6:30–44). Why retell the story with some minor variations? The compassion element has been heightened. This crowd has spent three days in Jesus' presence without food; earlier it was the late hour in a deserted place that evoked concern. This time Jesus speaks first, calling the disciples to him; earlier the disciples had suggested dismissing the people because it was late. This time seven loaves and a few little fish are divided among four thousand; earlier, it was five loaves and two regular-size fish. Jesus' gestures in blessing the bread are more elaborately described in the first story than in this version, but identical verbs describe the result, "they (all) ate and were satisfied."

Of course, telling the same story more than once is a familiar feature of biblical narrative and oral story-telling cultures in general. Sometimes two versions just sit there side by side, as in the creation story (Gen. 1:1–2:4a; 2:4b–25). Sometimes they are interwoven, as in the flood story (Gen. 6:5–9:19). They may be separated by some narrative space, as in Abraham's attempts to pass off Sarah as his "sister" (Gen. 12:10–20; 20:1–18) or the giving of the Law at Sinai (Exod. 19:16–20:21; Deut. 5:1–27). Each time a story is told, the storyteller introduces changes.

Homiletical Perspective

What happens when four thousand break bread together? In this case, Mark's Gospel would seem to say that an act of justice occurs: all are brought to a table that is common ground where, in honoring small gifts, abundance is created for everyone without exception.

It can be a great lesson for many a modern congregation, composed of hearers faced with a world (no less than a local community) of vast human need, but having in hand a paucity of adequate resources to address it. How might preachers help them explore that dilemma through the lens of this text? We might begin with Jesus' enacted answer: in his compassion for the people, he does not work from a platform of scarcity. His ministry assumes—and models—abundance, even if it is abundance that begins with only a few fish and some half-dozen loaves. Mere sandwich materials, really, for a crowd of empty stomachs.

Jesus offered a different reason for the earlier feeding of the five thousand (6:34), who were "like sheep without a shepherd"; but his motive for feeding these four thousand comes solidly from concern for their hunger. Since Mark locates Jesus just prior to this event over in the region of Tyre and Sidon and in the Decapolis (that is, on the Gentile side of the sea), the crowd in question is likely a Gentile

Mark 8:1–10

Theological Perspective

Heartfelt Compassion vs. Practical Action. While it is easy to applaud Jesus' compassion, it remains difficult to imagine how the physical needs of the crowd will be met. It is interesting to note that the disciples, in contrast to their compassionate response in Mark 6, now accuse Jesus of "pie in the sky" thinking: "How can one feed these people with bread here in the desert?" (v. 4). It is not dissimilar to current political responses to collective need: those who cry for compassion for the masses are caricatured as naive socialists, and those who insist on practical solutions as coldhearted autocrats.

Jesus, however, resists the split between compassion and activity. Instead, he is the first to assess the very real need and immediately calls the disciples to action. Specifically, he has them take stock of what resources are available. Then he blesses the loaves and distributes them to the hungry crowd in a carefully planned way. Compassion does not begin and end with a feeling; it compels those who respond to take decisive action.

Human Independence vs. Divine Volition. It can be tempting to imagine that problem solving is either ultimately up to God, or ultimately up to us. When the need is overwhelming, we might well throw up our hands and ask God to provide; when we feel in control, we might give lip service to divine providence.

Jesus again resists the division between God's participation and our own. In the story of the feeding of the four thousand, Jesus does not simply pray that God will provide, and somehow enough food magically appears in front of them. Nor does Jesus rely only on human accomplishment, taking the seven loaves and a few fish and figuring out a way to feed the neediest. Instead, Jesus takes the food that the disciples have gathered from all of the resources of the people, puts those resources in God's hands, and then gives thanks for God's providence. Both human and divine resources are at work together.

The joke is apt about the farmer who has diligently worked the land, planting the seed, watering the fields, harvesting the crops. When a pastor says, "Look what God did for you!" the farmer replies, "Yes; and remember the land when God worked it alone." Jesus invites us to "work" our resources with God, neither relying on God alone nor assuming that the outcome is entirely up to our efforts alone. The very attempt to separate God's efforts from our own is futile, because God is far more intimately involved in our lives and actions than we can imagine.

Pastoral Perspective

The good news that Mark 8:1–10 offers is that Jesus responds to the needs of his followers with compassion and generosity. What Mark 8 affirms is that when we turn to Jesus, we find that he is always already turned to us, aware of our hungers and needs. Jesus wants to see that his people are fed and replenished, and he has the power to make that happen. As manna was given to the Israelites in the wilderness, so now Jesus feeds the four thousand.

Such an image of Jesus' compassion and generosity can give us confidence to make our needs known to God in prayer. As N. T. Wright observes in his commentary on Mark 8, our prayers receive "strong and warm encouragement from knowing that the risen Jesus certainly cares for his people at least as much, in his glorified state, as he had done when sharing our earthly existence."[1] In Mark's account of the feeding of the four thousand, we see in Jesus Christ that the God we turn to in prayer is not an aloof or stern taskmaster but a loving and merciful provider. Having this image of God can make all of the difference in our prayer life.

"How can one feed these people with bread here in the desert?" Jesus' response to the disciples' question not only shows us what he can do to meet our hungers and needs. His response also demonstrates the role that we are to play in feeding others. On the one hand, the disciples seem obtuse: have they not already witnessed the feeding of the five thousand in Mark 6? On the other hand, the question asked by the disciples is a natural one, one that might well be asked by many disciples today: "How can we feed these people?" The needs of the world can seem so great, and our resources as individuals and congregations so small. Mark 8 reminds flustered disciples then and now that what may seem improbable to us is possible with God. What we are called to do is both simple and difficult: to entrust the resources we have to Jesus, and then share them as he directs.

In Mark 8, we also see that Jesus wants to feed all of the people. Mark 8 takes place on the predominantly Gentile side of the Sea of Galilee, and we are told that some in the crowd "have come from a great distance." These clues suggest this crowd includes a significant number of Gentiles as well as Jews, perhaps in contrast to the crowds fed in Mark 6.[2] The implication is that Jesus has come to feed both Jew and Gentile, using the bread and fish that the crowds

---

1. N. T. Wright, *Mark for Everyone* (Louisville, KY: Westminster John Knox Press, 2004), 101.
2. For additional clues in the text, see William Placher, *Mark* (Louisville, KY: Westminster John Knox Press, 2010), 109–10.

Exegetical Perspective

Some of the differences may be due to the larger narrative in which a particular episode is found. Others may reflect an awareness that the audience has heard a version of the story already. Thus, on the second go-around, Mark can abbreviate the elaborate seating instructions given the crowd and the gestures Jesus makes in blessing the bread, but substitutes the Greek verb *eucharistein* ("give thanks") for *eulogein* ("bless"), underlining the link between the story and the Christian meal celebration. Listeners will use their imagination to add other details.

What about the placement of the "feeding of the four thousand" within the larger narrative sequence? This version opens with a rather vague temporal marker that sounds biblical: "in those days." When we last heard where Jesus was, he was outside the Jewish territory of Galilee in the largely Gentile cities of the Decapolis (7:31) and had attracted attention by healing a deaf and mute man (7:37). That sequence provides an important clue. We are not witnessing a simple rerun of the feeding story. Jesus has taken his healing and teaching to a new group of people who might not even be fellow Jews. That difference might also explain another shift. Earlier, Jesus expressed compassion for the crowd in the barren region as "like sheep without a shepherd" (6:34), an image from the Psalms and the prophets for the situation of God's people (Num. 27:17; Ezek. 34:8; Zech. 10:2). Here, that image has been replaced by concern for the physical danger faced by those who have been with Jesus for several days and must journey some distance home on empty stomachs.

Readers might even remember the dramatic miracle performed in Gentile territory, the healing of the Gerasene man who was possessed by a whole legion of demons (5:1–20). Jesus did not let that man follow him but sent him home to tell others what the Lord had done for him. Where did the man go? To the cities of the Decapolis (5:19–20). So it is not too great a literary stretch to envisage this crowd of four thousand as partial evidence that the Gerasene man's preaching about Jesus had achieved success. Now Jesus himself will feed them, just as God had done for the lost sheep of Israel earlier. Further support for this interpretation comes from the sequence that introduced the earlier feeding of the five thousand. There, Jesus' disciples have just returned from a triumphant mission in the towns and villages of Galilee. Jesus leads them apart to a deserted area hoping for some rest (6:30–32), but the crowd tracks them down. Our final clue to the Gentile setting of this feeding story should be the destination of Jesus

Homiletical Perspective

crowd. It is not who they are, though, but what they need—and what peril they face—that informs Jesus' motive here: "If I send them away hungry to their homes, they will faint on the way" (v. 3).

If "they [all] ate and were filled," it would have been miracle enough; but the incident suggests a further-reaching lesson. Given today's economic realities, many of our congregants hold a "scarcity" mind-set: "Since we have only a few little fish and seven loaves [read: a dwindling endowment, an aging membership, a changing neighborhood], we really cannot address the enormous needs around us." What are the resources your hearers have at hand, no matter how meager they perceive them to be? Could adopting a grateful attitude of abundance produce "leftovers," so to speak? Those leftovers in each case will be the preacher's to contextualize, but in memory of generations of our mothers who "made do" with what was on hand, the metaphor of "enough" invites both specificity and creativity. On the same afternoon that begins with Jesus' puzzled disciples—ourselves included—doubting that there could be any way to feed so many mouths, the seven baskets remaining when the picnic is over constitute an embarrassment of riches.

Once again the biblical story "reads us"[1]: the disciples' question regarding how one could feed so many "with bread here in the desert" (v. 4) points to our common failure to believe or rely upon the truth we have witnessed! So often, it is as if we have not seen what we have seen or have not heard what we have heard, and so we find ourselves asking the same old question: "Surely you do not think we have enough resources to heal the world—do you?"

It is significant that between the two mass feedings of chapters 6 and 8, a nameless Syrophoenician woman reminds us, as she contends with Jesus, that even the "dogs" who are not at the table—the marginalized, the poor, those others—eat the crumbs of the meal served to the family. There seems to be a Markan pattern, then, focusing our gaze and our longings upon "bread" for all, and our inescapable mandate to serve it: a dare that the pulpit not concede to the temptation to shrug with everyone else and bow to the popular supposition that, in the end, scarcity is our situation.

Here, as in the earlier feeding, nothing particularly extraordinary occurs, except that the crowds eat their fill, whether in bites or bits. Still, there is

---

1. Ched Myers, Marie Dennis, Joseph Nangle, OFM, Cynthia Moe-Lobeda, and Stuart Taylor, *Say to This Mountain: Mark's Story of Discipleship*, ed. Karen Lattea (Maryknoll, NY: Orbis Books, 1996), xi.

Mark 8:1–10

Theological Perspective

Scarce Resources vs. Vast Need. Still, Jesus' disciples are keenly aware of the inadequacy of their resources in comparison to the needs presented. A crowd of four thousand could never be fed with seven loaves and a few fish; moreover, they are situated in an unforgiving wilderness that holds no promise of yielding more. Many of us can relate: anyone who has sought to alleviate suffering, whether Africa's starving children or America's underprivileged families, knows the feeling of being overwhelmed and the temptation to give up.

Jesus resists the seeming conflict between immense need and limited resources. The crowd's hunger is not an insurmountable problem to be met with hand-wringing and resignation. It is not to be dismissed as a sign of human sinfulness or creation's finitude. Nor is it a sign of divine failure, as if the very presence of need indicates the absence of God. Instead, Jesus calls forth everything available, trusting that God has provided enough to meet the world's deep hunger. Indeed, more than enough is provided; vast amounts, with leftovers that surpass what was originally offered, remain.

The story of the feeding of the four thousand in the desert confronts our simple bifurcations between seemingly distinct and mutually exclusive choices. Jesus resists the disciples' inclination and ours to attend only to the spiritual needs of people at the expense of their physical hungers, or to substitute feeding stations for the nourishment of the Word. He resists our tendency to feel compassion without acting on it or to act without tenderness and love. He resists our propensity to trust for our well-being either human efforts alone or God's providence. He resists our zero-sum-game assessments of the world's vast needs and its apparent (but false) scarcity of resources, reminding us of the endless store of God's blessing.

It is no accident that this scene foreshadows the breaking of bread at the Last Supper at Passover: "he took a loaf of bread, and after blessing it he broke it, gave it to them, and said, 'Take; this is my body'" (14:22). Jesus continues to feed body and soul; to act with compassion; to provide far beyond what is apparently available to meet our deepest need; and to put into God's hands our very humanity, blessing it beyond our imagination.

CHRISTINE CHAKOIAN

Pastoral Perspective

have to share. The inclusive nature of the good news of Mark 8 gives us reason to ponder: Who are we being called to include, whom we might otherwise exclude? What are we being called to share, in our community and society, so that all may be fed?

Fred Craddock tells a story that might well illustrate the feeding of the four thousand. He was in Winnipeg, Canada, in mid-October when a freak storm dumped two feet of snow—an unusual storm even by Winnipeg standards. Travelers like Craddock were stranded, and restaurants were closed. The only place Craddock could find to eat was a bus depot café around the corner from his hotel, where the only thing on the menu was soup. Craddock describes the soup as "the awfulest. It was kind of gray looking."

A woman came into the restaurant seeking warmth from the cold. The owner refused to serve her when he found out that she did not even have the money for soup. So she got up to leave. "And almost as if rehearsed," Craddock recalls, "everybody in that little cafe stood up and started toward the door." Caught off guard by this showing of solidarity, the owner retreated, saying, "All right, all right . . . she can stay." Craddock then went back to eating the soup, which suddenly tasted much better. "I don't recall what was in it, but I do recall when I was eating it, it tasted a little bit like bread and wine. Like bread and wine."[3]

Like the feeding of that poor woman in a Winnipeg bus depot, the feeding of the four thousand is sacramental. We are reminded in these meals of the Lord's Supper, where all are equally welcomed and all are equally fed by our host and provider, our Lord and Savior.

W. CARTER LESTER JR.

---

3. Fred B. Craddock, *Craddock Stories*, ed. Mike Graves and Richard F. Ward (St. Louis: Chalice Press, 2001), 83–84.

Exegetical Perspective

and the disciples when they depart for "the district of Dalmanutha" (v. 10). Unfortunately neither we, nor ancient scribes who proposed substitutes, nor the evangelist Matthew, who retells the story (Matt. 15:32–39), have any idea where that is. Given Mark's usual literary pattern of sea crossing, it should be somewhere in the Jewish territory along the western shores of the Sea of Galilee.

In addition to Jesus and the crowd, the disciples are important actors in the feeding stories. They are not just along to pass out the bread and fish and to gather up the twelve or seven baskets respectively of leftovers. On the first go-around, they responded to Jesus' command to feed the crowd by protesting that not even two hundred denarii could buy enough (6:37). Surely their memories of that event would inform this episode! Apparently not. The disciples act as if this situation is the first feeding miracle ever: "How can one feed these people with bread here in the desert?" (v. 4). They do not recall that God once fed the Israelites in the desert for forty years (Exod. 16; Num. 11). They do not even remember what Jesus did for the crowd of five thousand men plus women and children a week or so earlier.

This exchange spotlights an important literary and theological theme in Mark's Gospel, the shaky faith of Jesus' closest disciples. On the one hand, Jesus chose them to follow him from the beginning of his ministry, and they have witnessed everything he did in public as well as received personal instruction. On the other hand, their faith still has weaknesses. By the end of chapter 8, Peter will be rebuked for rejecting Jesus' prediction of the suffering to come in Jerusalem (8:31–38). At the end of the Gospel, all Jesus' followers will flee in fear. Only the promise that the risen Jesus goes ahead of them to Galilee remains to light the way forward (14:28; 16:7).

PHEME PERKINS

Homiletical Perspective

something about this scene for preachers with ears to hear, a eucharistic nuance in Jesus' "having given thanks" (*eucharistēsas*, v. 6) before distribution of the food. Paul uses the term in his 1 Corinthians account of the Lord's Supper (1 Cor. 11:24); and the order of the verbs here—"took, [gave] thanks, broke, gave to them"—is also very similar to the Last Supper that Mark describes in 14:22–23.

It is the same connection made by Sara Miles, an atheist who became an unexpected convert to faith the day she wandered, on an impulse of mere curiosity, into St. Gregory of Nyssa Episcopal Church in San Francisco and was shocked by experiencing, suddenly, that "God, named 'Christ' or 'Jesus,' was real, and in my mouth,"[2] a story powerfully detailed in her memoir *Take This Bread*. Later, encountering in the Gospel stories a radically inclusive love embodied in ordinary actions like eating and drinking, she found a vast communion, "one I had sensed all my life could be expressed in the sharing of food, particularly with strangers."[3] When she subsequently envisioned and initiated the congregation's ministry of food distribution, it seemed to Miles that a program to feed needy, hungry bodies is appropriately centered at the same table where together we are welcomed to the joyful feast of the people of God, enacting that generous banquet to come.

In congregations large and small, whether or not involved in explicit ministries of justice, all of us entertain the disciples' hankering question in some niche of our corporate conscience: "How can one feed these people with bread here in the desert?" Indeed, what happens when we break bread together in soup kitchens, at church suppers, even in our desert places—using any small "loaves" we have and any few "fish" available—is that we have not only fed and been filled but mysteriously have begun already to do justice and prepare the way for jubilee.

GAIL A. RICCIUTI

---

2. Sara Miles, *Take This Bread: A Radical Conversion* (New York: Ballantine Books, 2007), 59.
3. Miles, *Take This Bread*, 93.

Mark 8:11–21

¹¹The Pharisees came and began to argue with him, asking him for a sign from heaven, to test him. ¹²And he sighed deeply in his spirit and said, "Why does this generation ask for a sign? Truly I tell you, no sign will be given to this generation." ¹³And he left them, and getting into the boat again, he went across to the other side.

¹⁴Now the disciples had forgotten to bring any bread; and they had only one loaf with them in the boat. ¹⁵And he cautioned them, saying, "Watch out—beware of the yeast of the Pharisees and the yeast of Herod." ¹⁶They said to one another, "It is because we have no bread." ¹⁷And becoming aware of it, Jesus said to them, "Why are you talking about having no bread? Do you still not perceive or understand? Are your hearts hardened? ¹⁸Do you have eyes, and fail to see? Do you have ears, and fail to hear? And do you not remember? ¹⁹When I broke the five loaves for the five thousand, how many baskets full of broken pieces did you collect?" They said to him, "Twelve." ²⁰"And the seven for the four thousand, how many baskets full of broken pieces did you collect?" And they said to him, "Seven." ²¹Then he said to them, "Do you not yet understand?"

Theological Perspective

The erratic faithfulness of the disciples in the Gospel of Mark frequently functions as fair warning of the temptations facing us as modern Christians. This passage is no exception.

The pericope opens with the Pharisees demanding a "sign" from Jesus. Given that Jesus has just performed miracle upon miracle—feeding the multitudes not once but twice, healing a deaf man in the Decapolis, curing the daughter of a Syrophoenician woman, healing the sick in Gennesaret, raising the daughter of Jairus, walking on water—their request feels ludicrous, cynical, disingenuous, and threatening. Only two chapters removed from the death of John the Baptist at the hands of Herod, the threat of the Pharisees foreshadows the very real danger Jesus will face.

Indeed, the encounter with the Pharisees seems an intentional interjection in a narrative that places Jesus and the disciples in a boat both before (8:10) and after (8:14). Back on the other side of the Sea of Galilee, the attention turns to the disciples, who have neglected to bring more than one loaf of bread to eat. Immediately Jesus warns them to "beware of the yeast" of the Pharisees and the Herodians. While the disciples concretize Jesus' teaching as a reference to physical bread, he is speaking metaphorically, and

Pastoral Perspective

"Do you not understand?" Jesus asks the disciples—not once but twice, in verses 17 and 21. The reason for Jesus' question is understandable to the reader of Mark's Gospel. Up to this point, hardly anyone is able to truly understand who Jesus is and what he is about. Jesus can make the blind see and the deaf hear, but he seems largely unable to help others really see what he is doing or hear what he is saying. As we encounter this passage again two thousand years later, we must ask ourselves: What about us? What gets in the way of our seeing, hearing, and understanding?

In the first scene, verses 11–13, Jesus' audience includes a group of Pharisees. They have not come with an open mind. Instead, they have come to argue with Jesus. They ask for "a sign from heaven, to test him" (v. 11). Jesus refuses to give them such a sign, although anyone who has spent any time with Jesus could not help but see one sign after another. He has fed four thousand and five thousand people with a few loaves and fishes on two separate occasions. He has cured the deaf, healed the sick, cast out demons, and taught with authority. Jesus refuses the Pharisees' request for a sign, "not because he is incapable of performing signs and miracles, but because the Pharisees' lack of

Exegetical Perspective

Missing signs or poor sight? The two episodes in this section of Mark's Gospel hardly distinguish the Pharisees from the disciples. Jesus rebuffs the former for demanding a divine sign (vv. 11–13) and castigates his disciples as blind and deaf (vv. 14–21). The action of the disciples anticipates Peter's protest against Jesus' words about his impending death (8:31–33). Mark strings these episodes together with notes about Jesus' journeys around the coast of the Sea of Galilee. His arrival back in Jewish territory at Dalmanutha (v. 10) is heralded by the Pharisees (v. 11). After that exchange, Jesus leaves by boat for Bethsaida (v. 22). Jesus and his disciples converse during that trip.

This scene is the third exchange while at sea. The first involved terrifying storms that Jesus quelled by his word, leaving the disciples in terrified fear (4:35–41), or that Jesus stilled by walking across the waters, an event that resulted in hard-hearted lack of comprehension by the disciples (6:45–52). The second voyage followed the feeding of the five thousand and was headed for Bethsaida, but the boat apparently was blown off course to Gennesaret. Thus this third boat trip, following the feeding of four thousand, also completes a sequence initiated earlier in the narrative. Both voyages toward Bethsaida include

Homiletical Perspective

It is an intriguing turn of events. First, the religious leaders of Jesus' day and, then, his hapless disciples hold up a mirror to our own hearts. Immediately following the impromptu picnic made up of a few loaves and fishes for four thousand hungry souls, two responses arise: "[But] give us a sign" (v. 11) and "We don't have enough bread" (v. 16). Mark notes that Jesus "sighed deeply in his spirit," (v. 12), but we may also imagine him rolling his eyes heavenward in exasperation at the dullness of human beings when we act like deep-sea creatures searching frantically for the water all around us.

Through his escalating questions to the disciples after overhearing their discussion about meager provisions, we hear Jesus' mounting frustration: "Do you still not perceive or understand? . . . Do you . . . fail to see? Do you . . . fail to hear? Do you not remember?" (vv. 17–18). With those words, he recalls God's instruction to Isaiah, when God commanded the prophet to dull the people's minds, stop their ears, and shut their eyes, "so that they may not look with their eyes, and listen with their ears, and comprehend with their minds, and turn and be healed" (Isa. 6:10).

What sign do we and the still-hungry disciples seek? The religious leaders missed—and the disciples

Mark 8:11–21

Theological Perspective

turns their attention to the two miracles of abundance he has recently performed in their presence: the feeding of the five thousand, which yielded twelve baskets full of broken pieces, and the feeding of the four thousand, which yielded seven baskets of pieces.

The theological question is this: what characterizes the yeast of the Pharisees and the yeast of the Herodians of which Jesus' disciples—then and now—must beware? Each group has its own unique leaven.

The yeast of these Pharisees is the insatiable need to defend their influence, a need that they and all religious authorities seem to have. Those who are in control of religious truths will always defend their position. Their threatened stance is revealed in their demand for more proof of Jesus' authority. No matter how often Jesus "performs," there will never be enough evidence, enough signs, enough miracles to convince them that he has authority to make the claims he does. Alongside the elders, chief priests, and scribes, the Pharisees accuse Jesus of insubordination and apostasy, recognizing Jesus' teaching as a threat to their own position (7:1–8; 11:27–33). Their accusation is not unfounded; he dismisses the legacy of scholarship that they have spent their lives defending. Now Jesus warns his disciples: beware of the endless thirst for maintaining your religious position. If you spend your lives defending what you think you know, you will overlook the signs of God's life-giving presence right in front of you.

The yeast of these Herodians—and their modern counterparts—is the insatiable desire for power. An influential party behind the Herodian dynasty, they favored the pro-Hellenistic policies of Herod Antipas (4 BCE–39 CE).[1] Like the Herodians, it is still the case that those who are rich in clout will often yearn for more, bending to whatever is politically expedient in order to defend their position and increase their influence. Already Herod had taken his own brother Philip's wife with apparent impunity; and while he respected John the Baptist as a righteous man and enjoyed listening to him, he remained unrepentant. Ultimately, Herod's careless promise and deference to his dinner guests cost John his life (6:14–29). Now Jesus warns his followers: beware of the addictive lust for authority. If you spend your lives defending the power you believe you have, you will abdicate real authority to popular opinion.

These warnings are particularly instructive to Western Christianity in this era. Many religious

---

1. http://www.britannica.com/EBchecked/topic/263495/Herodian; accessed February 8, 2013.

Pastoral Perspective

faith renders them unable to see the reign of God already present among them."[1]

In our time, we often hear people say, "Seeing is believing," when more often the opposite statement is true: "Believing is seeing." We think that if only God will make it obvious, either for ourselves or for some nonbeliever we care about, then faith will come naturally and easily. However, there is always a leap involved in faith, a trusting without seeing, because that is what faith is: "the conviction of things not seen" (Heb. 11:1). While what we see can affect what we believe, what we believe can also affect what we see. We see evidence of who Jesus is and what he is doing in the world that without the gift of faith we might otherwise overlook.

Consider these Pharisees. They want to test Jesus, which means that they want Jesus to fit within their preconceived notions of what the Messiah must look like and act like. They want Jesus to answer their beck and call, performing a sign when they demand it. Jesus is no genie in a bottle, who shows up whenever called upon, in order to fulfill the wishes of the one who summons him. Instead, Jesus shows up when and how he chooses, and his wish is intended to be our command. He resists our efforts to test and control him.

C. S. Lewis captures this holiness, this resistance of Jesus to our control, in his book *The Lion, the Witch, and the Wardrobe*. In the book, Susan is nervous about meeting Aslan, the lion and Christ figure of Lewis's imaginative story. She asks her companions, Mr. and Mrs. Beaver, if Aslan is safe. "'Safe?' said Mr. Beaver. 'Don't you hear what Mrs. Beaver tells you? Who said anything about safe? 'Course he isn't safe. But he's good. He's the King, I tell you.'"[2]

In the second scene, verses 14–21, the disciples are not trying to test Jesus, as these Pharisees want to do, but the disciples are almost as blind. The disciples' problems are their lack of trust and their focus on the wrong things. Jesus wants to warn the disciples about "the yeast" of the Pharisees and Herod, which is in danger of corrupting them and leading them astray. All that the disciples can focus on is that they have only one loaf of bread on board.

The dullness of the disciples is almost comical. Did they not just see Jesus feed four thousand and five thousand with a few loaves and fishes? This is the third time that the disciples have been in the

---

1. Dawn Ottoni Wilhelm, *Preaching the Gospel of Mark: Proclaiming the Power of God* (Louisville, KY: Westminster John Knox Press, 2008), 137.
2. C. S. Lewis, *The Chronicles of Narnia: The Lion, the Witch, and the Wardrobe* (New York: HarperCollins, 2004), 81.

Exegetical Perspective

ominous words of judgment about the disciples. Mark 6:52, "their hearts were hardened," recalls Pharaoh's heart in Exodus 7:3 as well as Israel's stubbornness (Deut. 29:18; Ezek. 11:19). Mark 8:17 picks up that verse as a question posed by Jesus: "Do you have a heart that has been hardened?" which is followed by a quote from the prophets: "Do you have eyes, and fail to see? Do you have ears, and fail to hear?" (from Jer. 5:21; Ezek. 12:2).

The evangelist crafts the incident in the boat as an illustration of how deficient the interpreters are in reading the signs Jesus gave in feeding first five thousand and then four thousand. Although a few loaves had been more than sufficient in those settings, as soon as they embark, the disciples are concerned over having only one loaf for thirteen people (v. 14). After the prophetic challenge, Jesus jump-starts the memory of his disciples (and the Gospel's audience) with a quiz on both of the earlier feeding miracles (vv. 19–20).

Returning to the brief exchange with the Pharisees that preceded the boat trip raises another puzzling question: do the disciples belong to "this generation" that seeks a sign but will not receive it (v. 12)? The verbs that Mark employs in that episode heighten tensions in the scene. The Pharisees are picking an argument (*syzētein*) and testing or tempting (*peirazein*) him (v. 11). The verb *peirazein*, "tempt," has a particularly ominous tone, since it was used of Satan's attack on Jesus during the forty days in the wilderness (1:12–13). Consequently, the challenge to produce a "sign from heaven" is not the demand to perform yet another dramatic miracle. Nor has this group shown up to take Jesus on concerning items of Sabbath observance (2:24) or purification (7:3–5). This situation calls for a more ominous understanding of the demand. Mark's readers may remember that Jesus himself received such a sign at his baptism. The divine voice acclaimed him God's beloved Son (1:11). The wilderness testing followed immediately.

Possibly Jesus is being tempted a second time. The challengers may even expect that he will attempt to call forth nothing less than the divine voice in confirmation of his own teaching. Perhaps they hope for some dramatic rebuttal comparable to the prophet Elijah's defeat of the Baal prophets (1 Kgs. 18:20–40). As Jesus dies on the cross, bystanders even suggest that perhaps Elijah will come to carry Jesus into heaven (15:34–36). If the goal of this engagement was to counteract Jesus' growing influence with the people, then pressing him for a "sign from heaven"

Homiletical Perspective

never noticed—the meaning of the baskets of bread collected after community suppers on both the western (Jewish) and eastern (Gentile) sides of the sea. Surely the "sign from heaven" and the lesson to be learned from it are both deeply associated with nourishment as mundane and glorious as everyday bread, the stuff of life that leaves no one hungry. Yet the disciples are still framing their reality as scarcity-based. Could it be that even as the one who is the living bread rides the waves with us, we fail to perceive the most important "sign" of all?

We too swim in a sea of signs, living our lives with quotidian glories surrounding us. How often do we fail to perceive them? During that brief time in a week when our hearers truly pause and become quiet in spirit for a few rare moments, might our words from the pulpit serve as a brush with which to paint or portray some of the powerful signs available to those who search for them? For congregations used to telling themselves, "We have no bread," reflection on this text might effect a subtle redirection of their gaze to the feast of vivid resources taken for granted.

In a culture much too committed to argumentation and testing, preaching in response to this demand for a sign can also be a fraught and delicate operation. Preachers may find themselves challenged, not only to resist preaching judgment on Pharisees and early disciples for blind hard-heartedness without seeing ourselves in them, but also to deal tenderly with the human difficulty of achieving insight. In response to Jesus' prophetic questions, it is humbling to realize that we do fail to see, we do fail to hear, and we seldom remember of our own accord our spiritual citizenship.

After all, the tendency of biblical characters to measure Jesus' teaching against their own preconceived criteria resides in us as well. While bread had a positive connotation in the Hebrew thought of Mark's time, leaven did not necessarily carry such connotations: it was seen, sometimes, as the substance of malice and evil (1 Cor. 5:6–8). If those of us preaching this text were to project such bias against ancient Jewish leaders, when Jesus' warning is to look into our own hearts, we would be practicing the same literalism that caused him to sigh in his spirit. (Indeed, this first half of Mark 8 closes with his question, "Do you not yet understand?") In his challenge to the disciples' slowness, he uses two different terms for basket (vv. 19, 20) that clearly refer to different contexts: for the "larger" feeding, *kophino*, a distinctly Jewish term (6:43); and for the feeding of four

Mark 8:11–21

Theological Perspective

leaders—including this author—have grown accustomed to possessing authority. The academic stamp of seminary training and the denominational imprimatur of a well-positioned assignment still count in many minds as signals that our voices should be taken seriously. Indeed, in spite of the slide of importance of the mainline churches in North America, many Christian leaders of all stripes enjoy a place at the civic table as arbiters of personal morality and, to a lesser extent, social ethics. If our generation is looking for a sign that we are the true "defenders of the faith," we may be in for some uncomfortable surprises.

Similarly, many Americans—again, including the author—have taken for granted our nation's position on the global stage. Furthermore, those who hold positions of public authority or corporate power on that stage are even more likely to defend their place. It is easy to presume our worthiness or wisdom, and it is easier still to find ourselves—often unknowingly—cutting ethical corners to consolidate control. The abdication of moral responsibility in the face of threatened power repeats itself again and again. If it was true of the capitulation of the German church to National Socialism during Hitler's rise, and of the silent complicity of most (Christian?) Afrikaners to apartheid, where might such abdication of moral responsibility be at work today?

To beware of the yeast of the Pharisees and Herodians begins with being aware of it. Yeast, of course, is very small grained, and it is hard to see its presence without a magnifying glass. However, it is easy to see the effect of its presence when the dough begins to rise.

Perhaps the most important theological work, then, is to examine our personal and institutional life very carefully for evidence of the effects of yeast. When the insatiable desire for religious authority and political power rises—as both will continue to do throughout human history—then disciples of any age would do well to heed Jesus' invitation to turn our gaze. Jesus urges us to look to *other* places—perhaps unexpected places—that testify instead to God's presence: places where multitudes are being fed with precious little, places where abundance impossibly overflows, places where disciples are privileged not to defend power, but to share the wealth of the good news, the abundance of the gospel.

CHRISTINE CHAKOIAN

Pastoral Perspective

boat with Jesus. On the two earlier trips, they saw him still the storm (4:35–41) and walk on the water (6:45–52). Despite all these encounters, they cannot understand what Jesus is talking about, because they are too busy worrying about where their next meal will come from.

We may laugh at the disciples' obtuseness, but where are we equally dull? How often do we focus on the size of the problems that we face, or the meagerness of the resources we have to meet those problems, and forget that Jesus is in the boat with us? How often do we, as individuals and as congregations, look at present obstacles and future uncertainties with fear and trembling, and forget how God has provided for us in the past? Mark 8 reminds us that when Jesus is in the boat with us, we need not worry. Instead of being distracted by our fears, we should be paying attention to Jesus, so that we might better understand and be prepared for the challenges we have yet to face.

In the face of his own challenges, the Pharisees' resistance, and the disciples' dullness, Jesus is understandably angry and frustrated. Nevertheless he does not give up on any of them. He will continue to speak with his opponents, and he will continue to teach his disciples, all the way to the cross. "Do you not yet understand?" Jesus' question in verse 21, functions not just as a reproach for the incomprehension of disciples then and now. It also functions as an invitation—to disciples of Jesus' day and our day—"an invitation to read on in the Gospel, and in our lives to stay with Jesus till we do understand."[3]

W. CARTER LESTER JR.

---

3. Lamar Williamson, *Mark* (Atlanta: John Knox Press, 1983), 146.

Exegetical Perspective

could be to provoke either words or actions that would fail. Because Mark's narrative does not specify either the subject of the debate or the nature of the sign, just as he did not specify the nature of Satan's tempting, readers may fill in various possibilities.

What of Jesus' response? Before he speaks, Mark describes him as emitting a tortured groan (*anastenazein*, v. 12). Why? The underlying malice of his challengers? However, his words are not addressed simply to this group of Pharisees. Instead, Jesus addresses "this generation" as the subject seeking such a sign. Then, with the solemn punctuation provided by the word "Amen," Jesus' pronouncement terminates the episode as Mark's readers have learned to expect in such stories. The wording of Jesus' reply is a truncated Semitic idiom, "If a sign will be given." The idiom calls for a curse on the speaker (or some other party) if X happens. "Over my dead body" can function that way for English speakers. The variant to this episode in the other Gospels lacks the idiom but captures its meaning: "No sign will be given" (Matt. 12:39//Luke 11:29).

This response is picked up in the conversation between Jesus and the disciples that follows. Jesus breaks into their concern over insufficient bread with a warning to watch out for the leaven of the Pharisees and of Herod (v. 15). The disciples do not hear him; they treat it as an observation about their failure to bring bread (v. 16). Presumably Mark's readers are not so inattentive. The evangelist attributed deadly malice to the unlikely alliance of "Pharisees and Herodians" after Jesus healed the man with a crippled hand on the Sabbath (3:1–6). He also included the tale of how Herod was manipulated into executing John the Baptist (6:17–29).

Since leaven was thought to work by causing a kind of invisible "rotting," the metaphor need not refer to cleansing out leaven before Passover. Jesus is making an observation about the significance of the brief episode that just occurred. Three episodes later in Mark's narrative, the tone becomes even more somber. The only sign provided Jesus' generation will be his rejection, suffering, and death (Mark 8:31). As they follow Jesus along his path to that destiny, the disciples will fail to understand repeatedly.

PHEME PERKINS

Homiletical Perspective

thousand reported earlier in this chapter (8:8), *spyridas*, a Greek term with Gentile affinities. It is as if to remind us that he feeds without regard to border, on both sides of the sea. Where we find ourselves spending too much energy differentiating our own tradition from that of others, what he seems to be saying with such precise care in his ancient context speaks just as vividly to our generation: the abundant feast of life in God's realm is open, not just to some but to all, whether it is gathered in Jewish or Gentile baskets!

Whether we reach clear back to the exodus, where manna is provided daily, or step back only slightly to the scene preceding this chapter, the imagery is rich and available for use in preaching a message of abundance. Intervening between the first feeding story and this text are three healing episodes, the second of which (7:24–30) is the healing of a Syrophoenician woman's little daughter. She is a Gentile who receives only the crumbs that fall from the master's table—prefacing Mark 8, where not just crumbs but loaves are offered to all who respond in hungry faith with perceiving hearts and eyes to see.

What is "the meaning of the loaves" that is essential for contemporary disciples to understand if we are to remain faithful? We could occupy ourselves with distinctions between the leavened and unleavened, or the ratio of mouths fed to baskets left over. We might continue looking to heaven in search of another mannalike portent for our own age. In the end, if we hearken deeply to Jesus' words, what we get is bread—simple, fortifying, and "enough." We get the eucharistic stuff that must be thankfully broken, nourishment that draws on both memory and promise, strengthening us to continue journeying with the One who feeds multitudes abundantly.

GAIL A. RICCIUTI

Mark 8:22–26

²²They came to Bethsaida. Some people brought a blind man to him and begged him to touch him. ²³He took the blind man by the hand and led him out of the village; and when he had put saliva on his eyes and laid his hands on him, he asked him, "Can you see anything?" ²⁴And the man looked up and said, "I can see people, but they look like trees, walking." ²⁵Then Jesus laid his hands on his eyes again; and he looked intently and his sight was restored, and he saw everything clearly. ²⁶Then he sent him away to his home, saying, "Do not even go into the village."

Theological Perspective

Mark is a Gospel of miracles. In 8:22–26 we have one of Jesus' more unusual and important miracles, with several vital theological issues to reflect upon.

The healing at Bethsaida highlights the relationship between miraculous healing and the person of Jesus. Throughout his Gospel, Mark uses miraculous healings to frame his understanding of Jesus as the messianic Son of God. In themselves they are not the proof of Jesus' identity, but rather point to the central miracle of the cross and resurrection. The "works of power" (*dynameis*) demonstrate that Jesus is the stronger one—mightier than John the Baptist, and stronger than Satan—yet the ultimate demonstration of his power will be the cross and the resurrection. For Mark, Jesus is the king who "stoops to conquer," whose greatest act of healing comes through the deep humiliation of the cross and the astounding vindication of the resurrection.

This becomes clearer when we see the role of miraculous healing in Jesus' ministry with his disciples. Mark 8:22–26 fits in a larger narrative about the gradual lifting of the disciples' blindness that runs from chapter 8 through chapter 10. "Do you still not see or understand? Are your hearts hardened? Do you have eyes but fail to see, and ears but fail to hear?" (8:17–18 NIV). Here the blind man of

Pastoral Perspective

With this story of the healing of the blind man, the narrative of Mark's Gospel reaches its midpoint. As if to signal this, Jesus and his disciples leave the sea and their boat for the last time and begin a land journey that will take them from the north of Israel all the way to Jerusalem. Thus far, the narrative has repeatedly lifted up the fact that though the disciples have been constantly with Jesus, they do not understand who he is, where he is going, or what his destiny will be. As a result, they have no sense at all of what it will mean to follow him and to be his disciples. It is as if they are all blind!

The story resumes in a place called Bethsaida, the bridge to the second half of the Gospel. This is not the first time that Mark has referred to Bethsaida, for it was the destination of an earlier sea voyage (6:45) that ended unsuccessfully and included Mark's first indictment of the disciple's blindness. Now the community of blind men arrives at last in Bethsaida, a place where it turns out blindness is healed.

Once a sleepy fishing village at the mouth of the Jordan River, the town has been rebuilt, enlarged, hellenized, and given the name Bethsaida Julius by Herod the Great. Living in the town is a blind man whose friends bring him to Jesus and ask Jesus to touch him. Perhaps it is Mark's antipathy to this

Exegetical Perspective

A Blind Man . . . and Blind Disciples. With this passage the Gospel of Mark makes a significant transition in the narrative. It is a transition that looks both back and ahead. This story of the healing of the blind man, found only in Mark, looks back to two significant features of the Gospel narrative to this point. The first concerns a clear parallel with a previous miracle story, in which Jesus heals a deaf, mute man (7:32–37). In both stories Jesus spits and touches the part of the body in need of healing (the tongue for the mute man, the eyes for the blind man). Immediately after the healing of the deaf and mute man Jesus multiplies the loaves and the fishes in 8:1–9. However, the disciples are without understanding.

The second parallel comes in 8:18, where we find a quote from Jeremiah 5:21, which serves as a commentary on the failure of the disciples to comprehend the meaning of Jesus' ministry. Even though they have eyes and ears, they neither see nor hear. Precisely in the context of Jesus healing a physically deaf man and then a physically blind man, we see Mark's Jesus making a crucial comment about the spiritual deafness and blindness of the disciples. Their misunderstanding will become even more manifest throughout the rest of Mark 8, 9, and 10.

Homiletical Perspective

By this point in Mark's Gospel, an attentive reader may be used to the unexpected turns that challenge the theological assumptions typically brought to these texts. Mark regularly takes such risks. He portrays a Jesus with anger-management issues (1:41; 1:43; 3:5; 3:12; 10:14; 11:14; 11:15–17). He exposes an impatient and ridiculing Messiah (7:6–13; 8:14–21; 9:19; 12:24). At home Jesus is thought to be insane by his family, and he summarily disrespects them in public (3:21, 32–34). Jesus is even cast as ethnocentric in his response to the Syrophoenician woman. (7:24–27). In this episode of the healing of the blind man, Mark makes Jesus appear weak, in order to say something important about who Jesus is, who the disciples are, and what Jesus is doing to form them into the kind of followers and leaders they need to be.

Jesus' apparent weakness is a vehicle for Mark to convey something that is at the heart of true discipleship. In the initial call narrative (1:16–20) Mark alone of the Gospel writers uses the expression, "Come on after me, and I will make you become [*ginesthai*] fishers of people!"[1] (my trans.). The extra

---

1. Joel Marcus, *Mark 1–8: A New Translation with Introduction and Commentary*, Anchor Yale Bible 27 (New Haven, CT: Yale University Press, 2000), 3.

Mark 8:22–26

Theological Perspective

Bethsaida is healed, which leads to Peter's confession. Finally, Mark 10 recounts the healing of Bartimaeus, who then follows Jesus "on the way" (10:52)—meaning toward Jerusalem and the cross. At the end, however, it is the Roman centurion who acknowledges in 15:39 (NIV), "Surely this man was the Son of God." Peter and the disciples, by contrast, can only muster an accurate though incomplete confession in 8:29.

Mark's miraculous healings, especially this one, are central to the way Jesus evokes faith. Leonard Goppelt observes, "In every case people came to faith only in the immediacy of individual encounter with Jesus' person."[1] Commentators in every age have noted the importance of Jesus' touch. It is not the healings themselves that evoke faith, but rather the person of Jesus who performs the healing. He heals physically so that he may be seen spiritually.

From this perspective, faith is not the precondition of miracles; rather, faith itself is the result of God's healing work upon us. The blind man in Bethsaida demonstrates this dramatically. Others bring him to Jesus; he does not ask to be healed and says nothing at all about who he believes Jesus to be. Yet Jesus honors the faith of his friends, and leads the man to a place where he can receive healing and begin to demonstrate trust in him. Faith and trust in Jesus require a work of healing in us. T. F. Torrance writes, "Man is existentially severed from the Truth, as Kierkegaard once put it, and needs to be reconciled to the Truth. Therefore reconciliation and healing have to take place if real communication is to be achieved."[2]

Miraculous healings are the work of the creative and dynamic Triune God who created the universe as the context for an encounter with persons through God's Word and Spirit. Unfortunately, the discussion of miraculous healing often veers off into abstract debates about the possibility of miracles in general. Many think of miracles generically as interferences with the natural order by supernatural power, which suggests that God is not normally part of space and time, and must set it aside in order to act directly.

Recently, some scientists and theologians have pointed out the need for a more nuanced view of the way God interacts with creation. Space and time are contingent upon God—created and upheld by God. They are not independent or autonomous from God. The universe may seem "closed" to God from our

---

1. Leonard Goppelt, *Theology of the New Testament*, vol. 1, *The Ministry of Jesus in Its Theological Significance* (Grand Rapids: Eerdmans, 1981), 151.
2. T. F. Torrance, introduction to *The School of Faith* (Edinburgh: James Clarke, 1959), xxxvii.

Pastoral Perspective

Hellenistic place that causes him to have Jesus lead the man by the hand outside the town.

Once there, Jesus applies his own saliva to the man's eyes and lays his hands on him. "Do you see anything?" Jesus asks. "I see people that look like trees walking," is the blind man's response. Jesus then places his hands on the man's eyes and his blurred vision is transformed. The blind man sees everything clearly. The story concludes with Jesus instructing the man to go home and not to return to the village.

This is not the only story of the healing of a blind man in Mark's Gospel. The other that immediately comes to mind is that of blind Bartimaeus (10:46–52). Mark uses these two stories, which only he of all the Gospel writers tells, to bracket everything that takes place between them. This includes such things as Peter's confession of who Jesus is, with its accompanying rebuke by Jesus; the statements of Jesus concerning his suffering, his death, and his resurrection; the discussion about discipleship and its cost; and the transfiguration. The last of these is of particular significance, since it involves light and sight and seeing Jesus as he truly is. Interestingly enough, in the Eastern Orthodox celebration of the feast of the Transfiguration, it is not Jesus who is transfigured but the three disciples, who see him for the first time as he has always been.

Mark uses the first healing story to indicate that at the end of the first half of the narrative the disciples are blind. They have learned nothing about who Jesus really is, and they do not see where he is going or what it will mean to follow him. They still desire to have important places in the kingdom over which they think Jesus will reign. They are also like the man who is deaf and has a speech impediment whom Jesus heals (7:32–35). They neither see nor hear. The picture of the disciples is sad and seemingly hopeless.

Mark's narrative does not leave things there, however. If the man from Bethsaida does not see clearly at first, Jesus' perseverance brings him clarity of sight. The difference, of course, is that this man goes home and does not become a follower. Bartimaeus, on the other hand, is healed immediately and immediately follows Jesus. The Bethsaida healing is, in the end, a sign of encouragement and hope because of Jesus' continuing effort to bring healing. The healing of Bartimaeus is qualitatively different.

What is the difference? It comes with seeing who Jesus is and what it means to follow him. Peter's confession is on the face of things correct, but it leads to a life of true discipleship only as he sees it in light of the crucifixion and resurrection.

Exegetical Perspective

A Tale of Two Blind Men. The story of healing the blind man in 8:22–26 also looks ahead to another story about the healing of a blind man, in 10:46–52, the story of Jesus healing blind Bartimaeus. The two stories form an effective frame for all the material in this middle section of the Gospel, which focuses on Jesus' passion predictions and the continued failure of the disciples to understand. The contrasts between the two stories are also quite instructive. In 8:22–26 a crowd brings the blind man to Jesus, whereupon Jesus takes him by the hand and leads him outside the town; in 10:46–52 Bartimaeus hears that Jesus is there and shouts out for "Jesus, Son of David," to have mercy upon him. The crowd attempts to silence him, but he shouts even louder. When Jesus calls him, the blind man throws off his cloak, springs up, and comes to Jesus. This blind man sees who Jesus is. His spiritual sight will soon be matched by physical sight, which comes to him immediately after Jesus tells him that his faith has made him well (10:52).

In contrast, the healing story from 8:22–26 is much more elaborate and much less successful. The healing takes place in two stages. Jesus puts saliva on the man's eyes and lays his hands on him. We expect that the man will be healed, that he will recover his sight in a miraculous manner, but that is not what happens. Jesus asks the man, "Can you see anything?" (v. 23), and the man responds with a puzzling remark: "I can see people, but they look like trees, walking" (v. 24). Even after Jesus has performed an act of healing, the man is not healed. He sees, but he does not *really* see. What he sees is distorted. Nothing is said about the faith of the man or the faith of the people who bring him. This healing will take an extra effort by Jesus. The second stage of the healing simply has Jesus laying his hands on the man's eyes again. After this, we are told that the man's sight is restored, and that he sees clearly.

Then Jesus sends him away to his home, charging him not to go into the village. This command reminds us of Mark's theme of the messianic secret, where Jesus tells those he has healed to say nothing about their healing. Again, by contrast with the healing story in chapter 10, we find that upon regaining his sight Bartimaeus follows Jesus. Bartimaeus recognizes Jesus twice as the Son of David and as "my teacher" (10:51); he is healed immediately; he follows Jesus; he is a disciple who understands. He is a blind man who seems to have spiritual sight, even before he has his physical sight restored to him, because of his faith. He is a model of a faithful disciple, in contrast to Jesus' other disciples. They have physical

Homiletical Perspective

word "become" implies that, for Mark, following Jesus is a process of becoming something that only Jesus can bring about in the disciple's life. In our story the blind man concretizes the process. He does not see clearly all at once. It takes time and repeated hands-on action from Jesus before the man sees "everything clearly" (v. 25).

The blind man can be read as a metaphor for the disciples. The disciples are in the process of becoming just who it is that Jesus is leading them to be, the persons God has destined them to be. At this midpoint in Mark's narrative what we know about discipleship is this: (1) disciples immediately follow when Jesus calls; (2) they go wherever Jesus leads; (3) they listen to his teaching and proclamation of the gospel; (4) they observe his healing, exorcisms, and miracles; (5) they become conduits for Jesus' own work, going out and proclaiming repentance, exorcising, and curing the sick.

However, they are not perfect. They are flawed, and in Mark they are especially, seriously flawed. Even when they appear to understand who Jesus is and what that means for them, in the next instant they fail miserably. Such missteps illustrate their partial sight. Peter confesses, "You are the Messiah!" (8:29), but when Jesus begins to lay out just what kind of Messiah he is—a Suffering Servant, cruciform Messiah—Peter takes Jesus aside to rebuke him for his misinformed Christology.

Jesus, not as pastorally sensitive as Peter, outs Peter in front of them all: "Get behind me, Satan!" (8:33). Peter's apparently correct confession turns out to be demonic. Later Peter exclaims, "Look, we have left everything and followed you!" (10:28), but it becomes very clear that "everything" did not include their greed for power or their desire for Jesus to be a Messiah in their image. Surreptitiously, James and John corner Jesus: "We want you to do for us whatever we ask. . . . Grant us to sit, one at your right hand and one at your left, in your glory" (10:35–37). Later still, Peter exclaims again, "Even though all become deserters, I will not" (14:29). Shortly thereafter we see him in the flickering campfire light, shaking his head and swearing, "I do not know this man you are talking about" (14:71). Is that a denial, or the deeper, ironic truth?

Jesus is the Messiah that to these disciples looks like a tree walking around. Even more disturbing is the fact that they never achieve clear sight or understanding—not in Mark's narrative. Commentators like to say that the resurrection was the moment that full sight came for the disciples—but not in Mark.

Mark 8:22–26

Theological Perspective

side, but it is actually open to God. T. F. Torrance observes, "We are to think of the miraculous acts of Jesus within the limits, conditions, and objectivities of our world, not as involving in any way the suspension of the space-time structures which we call 'natural law,' far less implying the abrogation of the God-given order in nature they express, but rather as the re-creating and deepening of that order in the face of all that threatens to break it down through sin, disease, violence, death, or evil of any kind."[3] In this sense, miraculous healings do not break natural laws, but are rather instances of the creation becoming healed.

All miracles—including miraculous healing—serve God's purposes, not ours. Miraculous healings are exceptional; they happen, but not as frequently as we would like. While Jesus heals many, he does not heal all. Yet his ministry of healing provides the foundation for our hope of healing today. Unfortunately, Christians who overemphasize healing often wind up disconnecting the act of healing from its purpose and from the person of Jesus. When miraculous healing becomes the point, we lose sight of how it helps us understand Jesus and the gospel of God's ultimate victory over suffering, disease, and even death itself through his cross and resurrection.

Miraculous healings are also provisional; that is, health and wholeness are restored only for the time being. Every person that Jesus heals later dies, including Lazarus, whom Jesus raises from the dead (John 11:1–44). So while the acts of healing Jesus performs on earth do not provide ultimate healing from death, they do succeed in pointing to his ultimate victory through the crucifixion and resurrection. We should continue to pray for and celebrate miraculous healings today, but in ways that reflect the purpose of God in Jesus Christ. Our hope of healing rests in the healing hands of our faithful Savior.

ROBB REDMAN

Pastoral Perspective

It is now evident that for Mark the mission of Jesus is that the blind should see, the deaf should hear, and the dumb should speak. For Mark, sight has emerged as the principal metaphor for faith—to "see things clearly"; in the healing of blind Bartimaeus there is new hope for Jesus' disciples then and now.

What implications does Mark's way of presenting the meaning of faith and discipleship have for our efforts to teach the Christian faith to the members of our congregations? Clearly it is not sufficient simply to teach our children and young people the answers to formal catechetical questions, though we may often give that impression. Peter had to learn that Jesus was going to Jerusalem to die, and that being his disciple would involve self-denial and bearing one's cross—in short, living life for others. Moreover, Peter had to witness these terrible events in Jerusalem for himself.

If it takes a village to raise a child, it seems to me that it takes a church to nurture and sustain a Christian. That must involve the church in listening to all sorts of people in all sorts of places, in order to hear the truth, even when the truth is painful and difficult. The church must open its eyes, to see what God is up to in the world around it, and it must have the courage to speak the truth, whatever the cost or the consequences. That would perhaps be too much to expect from the church, were it not that the way of the cross is also paradoxically the way of joy.

V. BRUCE RIGDON

---

3. T. F. Torrance, *Divine and Contingent Order* (Grand Rapids: Eerdmans, 1981), 24.

Exegetical Perspective

sight, but they do not have spiritual sight. They have eyes, but they do not see.

Significantly, the story of blind Bartimaeus occurs only after the three dramatic passion predictions in Mark (8:31–33; 9:30–32; 10:32–34), for only in light of the passion of Jesus can the disciples truly see and understand the meaning of Jesus' ministry.

Progressive Discipleship: From Blindness to Sight. The disciples cling to their own understanding of Jesus' ministry, an understanding that will not tolerate Jesus' suffering and death. Indeed, as will become evident in their responses to the passion predictions, the disciples' plan is to follow a glorious and powerful Messiah into the triumphant coming of the kingdom of God. That is the ministry in which they wish to share, not a ministry that involves suffering on behalf of others, certainly not a ministry that risks death. Theirs is a desire for power *over*, not power *for*. They have, to this point, witnessed Jesus demonstrating power *over*: over demons, over illness, over physical handicaps, over nature, over scribes and Pharisees. They have witnessed triumph after triumph. Only in Nazareth did they see that Jesus could do no mighty works because of their unbelief (6:5–6).

Now once again Jesus' power to heal seems to come into question. Nothing is said in this case about belief or unbelief. Rather, the passage seems to be a clear commentary on the failed perceptions of the disciples. They do not yet see or understand that the ultimate triumph will come only through Jesus' suffering and death, and likewise only through their own embrace of human suffering, all to be redeemed by God in resurrection to new life. Even Peter's seemingly correct confession of Jesus as the Christ in 8:27–30 will prove to be only a shallow understanding that must be corrected. As yet the disciples see only fuzzy people, like trees walking.

JEFFREY S. SIKER

Homiletical Perspective

The resurrection message in Mark, proclaimed by the man in white in the Jesus-less tomb, compounds the disciples' failure. Those entrusted with the news—with special instruction to tell Peter about it—flee in fear and silence.

This inability of the disciples in Mark to achieve sight is a source tension. It is the same tension that Mark's nonending creates. The rhetorical function of Mark's ending forces the reader to exclaim in horror, "No! It cannot end that way! The good news of Jesus Christ, the Son of God, cannot, must not end in fleeing, fear, and silence!"

Mark's strategy worked. The Markan manuscript tradition, the other canonical Gospels, and Paul (1 Cor. 15:1–8) confirm that the church decided that the resurrection proclamation had to be told again and again.

The nonmanifestation of true discipleship among those closest to Jesus creates the same tension, and has a similar rhetorical effect. The reader is supposed to become frustrated with these bumbling idiots. "How can they not get it? How do they make the same mistakes over and over? Someone has to do it better than this!" Exactly. That is the ongoing claim these texts make on those who read in faith. The blind man achieving sight—albeit not all at once—gives disciples of every age hope.

Although we do not now see all things clearly (1 Cor. 13:12), we can take solace in the process. Jesus calls and then puts in place the time for "becoming" the people he wants us to be. It takes time and sometimes multiple actions of Jesus on us for us to become who we are destined to be in him. Jesus' gift of sight to the blind men gives subsequent disciples hope that sight is possible, and ultimately something that only Jesus can accomplish.

In all probability, as Paul alludes to in 1 Corinthians, complete, clear sight of everything will be achieved only as an eschatological reality. In the meantime, in this journey of discipleship, the literally blind (the unnamed man and Bartimaeus) lead the figuratively blind (Peter and the disciples and, by extension, disciples of every age).

ANDRÉ RESNER

Mark 8:27–30

^{27}Jesus went on with his disciples to the villages of Caesarea Philippi; and on the way he asked his disciples, "Who do people say that I am?" ^{28}And they answered him, "John the Baptist; and others, Elijah; and still others, one of the prophets." ^{29}He asked them, "But who do you say that I am?" Peter answered him, "You are the Messiah." ^{30}And he sternly ordered them not to tell anyone about him.

Theological Perspective

Peter's confession in 8:29 and Jesus' response in 8:30 have kept scholars and preachers busy for generations. In Mark's narrative, Peter's confession represents a pivotal moment in the disciples' growing awareness of who Jesus is. By this point, others—including demons—have acknowledged Jesus (1:24; 5:7). Later passages hearken back to 8:29, most notably the question of the high priest at Jesus' trial, "Are you the Christ, the Son of the Blessed One?" (14:61). Jesus' response in both cases leaves little room to doubt his messianic self-understanding; but it also appears his understanding of Messiah diverged sharply from the popular messianic expectations. His view seems to be rooted in the expectation of the appearance of the Son of Man found in Jewish eschatology (14:62), not the political understanding of the Messiah as a successor to the Davidic throne and the overthrower of Judah's enemies. It is thus reasonable to assume that Jesus sought to avoid a messianic misunderstanding in verse 30 rather than to reject a messianic identification altogether.

While the exact meaning of the term "messiah" and the intention behind Jesus' instructions to keep quiet are important, it is important not to limit ourselves to these matters and miss other, equally important christological issues.

Pastoral Perspective

Mark is a remarkable storyteller. He addresses his Gospel to readers who already know about the crucifixion, resurrection, and ascension of Jesus. The stories that Mark tells are therefore directed over the heads of the participants to those who hear or read them in another time and place, including our contemporary congregations. The narratives invite us in, and the text is therefore interactive. We are expected to react, respond, and participate.

The principle question of Mark's Gospel concerns who Jesus is and what it means to call him the Christ. Only as that becomes clear is it possible to understand what it means to follow him and to be his disciples. The first verse of Mark's Gospel reads, "The beginning of the good news of Jesus Christ, the Son of God." That word "Christ" does not appear again until it is used by Peter in his confession concerning the identity of Jesus, in the eighth chapter of the Gospel.

Virtually all commentators agree that that chapter and this story mark the midpoint in the structure of the Gospel. The context is important for the significance of the stories themselves. If Mark's Gospel is understood to be an account of a journey, the first half of that journey has taken place on the sea in small boats and in the wilderness. Now the disciples

Exegetical Perspective

This passage comprises the first part of the literary and theological hinge of Mark's Gospel. Everything in the Gospel leads up to the question about Jesus' identity. After Peter's confession (vv. 27–30) the response of Jesus in 8:31–33 governs everything that follows in the Gospel. Indeed, the entire hinge (8:27–33) is arguably the single most important passage in the whole Gospel, for it reveals Jesus' true identity and the ultimate meaning of that identity. Jesus is the Messiah, but not the Messiah they had imagined. Rather, as 8:31–33 will reveal, the messianic identity is completely wrapped up in Jesus' eventual suffering, death, and resurrection. This is *not* what Peter had in mind when he made his famous confession.

An Imperial Context. The geographic context for this story is significant. Jesus had just been in Bethsaida, the northeast fishing town on the Sea of Galilee that belonged to Philip's tetrarchy. Caesarea Philippi was further north in this territory and was to be distinguished from the much larger coastal city of Caesarea Maritima. Herod the Great had named this inland Caesarea in honor of Augustus. He also had a temple of white marble built and dedicated to Augustus in the city (Josephus, *Jewish Antiquities* 15.10.3). The imperial overtones underlying

Homiletical Perspective

Two questions can be seen to drive all of Mark's concerns: Who is Jesus? Who are those who would follow this Jesus? For Mark, everything is about identity disclosure and the tensions created by identity confusion.

Two stories about Jesus healing blind men frame 8:22–10:52. We might think of this part of Mark's Gospel as Intensive Discipleship Training. The blind men are symbolic of disciples who are on the way to seeing Jesus' identity, yet not quite there. It turns out that these followers of Jesus are more like the first, fuzzy-seeing blind man (8:22–26).

The first cured blind man's clear-seeing self never materializes in the Markan characterization of the disciples. Neither does Bartimaeus (10:46–52), who represents the ideal disciple in Mark. Blind Bartimaeus correctly confesses Jesus' Davidic lineage. He leaves all behind to get close to Jesus. When Jesus asks Bartimaeus what he wants, he does not selfishly exploit the situation as James and John do (10:35–37), but humbly asks just to see. Then, when given his sight and the opportunity to go away, he instead shows that he does indeed see, because he follows Jesus on "the way" (10:52). In the next episode, the way leads to Jerusalem, the city where Jesus' suffering messiahship will be fully manifest.

Mark 8:27–30

Theological Perspective

The Christological Question. Jesus was not fishing for information or conducting an opinion survey in verse 27. Instead, he carefully chose the time and the place to ask the "who question," as Dietrich Bonhoeffer famously put it, beginning with the "word on the street" about Jesus. Not surprisingly, then as now, everybody has an opinion about Jesus. The continuing interest in Jesus in our culture should remind us that Jesus is not the intellectual property of the church. Here Jesus used it as a springboard into a deeper discussion with his followers about who he is.

In theological reflection, much depends on asking the right questions. Often Jesus' teaching started with probing questions to the disciples and others. For Bonhoeffer, the crucial question of Christology is not the *how* question (as in how is it possible for Jesus to be both divine and human) but, rather, the *who* question.

In the church, where Christ has revealed himself as the Word of God, the human question is: Who are you, Jesus Christ? The church receives God's address every day anew. It is up to the human community to understand God's word as it is given, and to reflect upon it and analyze it as it exists. It remains always the question, "Who?"[1]

While the how question seeks to explain Jesus from our frame of reference (effectively "killing the Word," as Bonhoeffer puts it), the who question allows Jesus to disclose his identity to us through his Word and Spirit.

The shift from "how" to "who" questions thus places us in a different relationship to Jesus. As an artifact of human history, Jesus can be analyzed and categorized. As the risen Lord, Jesus turns the tables on us and makes it impossible for us to remain noncommittal, hiding behind our dispassionate investigation. Instead of passing judgment on Jesus, we find ourselves severely though mercifully judged by him.

The Old Testament and the Gospel of Jesus the Messiah. The term "messiah" roots Jesus inescapably in the history of God's covenant relationship with Israel. As Messiah, Jesus fulfills God's covenant promises recorded in the Old Testament. The proclamation of Jesus Christ is not another covenant alongside a previous one, much less a replacement of it. The tumultuous history of God's engagement with Israel is the context of the appearance of the messiah. T. F. Torrance used to say that Jesus was born from

---

1. Dietrich Bonhoeffer, "Lectures on Christology," in *Dietrich Bonhoeffer Works*, vol. 12: *Berlin 1932–1933* (Minneapolis: Fortress Press, 2009), 304.

Pastoral Perspective

find themselves with Jesus in the northernmost territories of Israel, areas with a much heavier Gentile population and a more profound presence of Hellenism. The journey will now lead southward, from the margins of Israel to its heartland and finally to Jerusalem itself.

The disciples have been "on the way" as the text says (v. 27), but the implicit question addressed to them and to us is, "Do you not yet understand?" If the first half of "the way" has been about learning what discipleship means, it appears to have been a very discouraging failure. The disciples remain as deaf and blind as the people in the stories that Mark tells about Jesus' healing miracles.

The question for the second half of the Gospel is Jesus' own question to Peter: "Who do you say that I am?" That question, it turns out, is the hinge that holds the two parts together.

Jesus and his disciples are "on the way" in the district of Caesarea Philippi, located about twenty-four miles north of the Sea of Galilee. Jesus inquires of his disciples concerning who people say that he is. The answers include John the Baptist, Elijah, and one of the prophets. Each suggests a very different perspective on who Jesus is and how his mission might be perceived.

Then Jesus intensifies the question. "Who do *you* say that I am?" Peter is the first to speak. "You are the *Christos*," he exclaims. "You are the Messiah." Immediately Jesus tells them that they must tell no one. Thus the messianic secret of Mark's Gospel is created.

This exchange is fascinating. It indicates that those who have seen Jesus have apparently concluded that he is a pivotal figure in signaling the soon-to-appear Messiah of Israel. In his preaching about the kingdom, people have begun to anticipate the appearance of Israel's Messiah, but they have not identified Jesus himself as that Messiah. He is the forerunner, the preparation for what is to come. Of course, all of them have different ideas about what this Messiah will be like and what he will do. It is easier to believe that a Messiah will come than it is to believe that one has already arrived. Common to their notions about a Messiah is that he would be strong, courageous, powerful, and that above all he would destroy Israel's enemies and set the nation free from its oppressors. No doubt this has also been what the disciples themselves have believed until this moment when Peter affirms the astonishing conviction that this very Jesus is himself the Christ, the Messiah.

Exegetical Perspective

the geographic location of the story are clear. Mark has Jesus identified as the Christ, the anointed one, the Messiah, indeed a royal figure, precisely here in a city dedicated to another king, and from Mark's perspective a lesser, earthly king. The eventual irony of the charges against Jesus, that he was the "King of the Jews" (15:26), is already anticipated in 8:27–30.

Who Is Jesus? The question about the identity of Jesus provides the cohesive power of these few verses. This question had been asked several times before in Mark's Gospel. The crowds had already been amazed in 1:27, after Jesus had cast out an unclean spirit: "What is this? A new teaching—with authority! He commands even the unclean spirits, and they obey him." The implicit question here is, "Who is Jesus and where does he get this power?" In 2:1–12 Jesus told a paralytic that his sins were forgiven. This pronouncement resulted in a conflict, as the scribes questioned in their hearts, "Why does this fellow speak in this way? It is blasphemy! Who can forgive sins but God alone?" Again the question revolved around the identity of Jesus. In order to prove that as the Son of Man he indeed had the authority to forgive sins, Jesus then healed the man. In 4:35–41, when Jesus calmed the storm on the Sea of Galilee, the response of the disciples again raised the question about the identity of Jesus: "Who then is this, that even the wind and the sea obey him?" (4:41).

Finally, now that the crowds, the scribes, and the disciples had all wondered about the identity of Jesus, Mark has Jesus ask the same question, but this time addressed to his disciples: "Who do people say that I am?" (v. 27). The disciples gave several answers, all of them centered on well-known prophetic figures, starting with John the Baptist. The notion that Jesus was John the Baptist raised from the dead had already been broached in 6:14: "Some were saying, 'John the baptizer has been raised from the dead; and for this reason these powers are at work in him [Jesus].'" Mark tells us that Herod Antipas was convinced that Jesus was John the Baptist, whom he had beheaded (6:16). Similarly, some had the idea that perhaps Jesus was Elijah, having returned from his assumption into the heavens in a fiery chariot. This notion is also found in 6:15. Speculation about the identity of Jesus and the source of his powerful teachings and deeds was something that exercised the minds of those who encountered Jesus, friend and foe alike. At the very least, people concluded that he stood squarely in the prophetic tradition of Elijah and John the Baptist.

Homiletical Perspective

Mark 8:27–30 is the disciples' midterm exam in their Christology course, and it has only two questions: (1) "Who do people say that I am?" and (2) "Who do you say that I am?" Question one is a relatively safe exercise. Christology done this way asks the student to report on what *others* think about Jesus, whether the others be scribes, Pharisees, the general public, or theologians such as Karl Barth, Rudolf Bultmann, Edward Schillebeeckx, James Cone, Rosemary Ruether, and Martin Luther King Jr.

According to the first respondents, like Herod, Jesus might be John the Baptist raised from the dead, a situation that, if true, would strike fear into his paranoid heart. If he were Elijah, that would conjure hope in Jewish hearts aching for God's promised Messiah, since many expected Elijah to be the necessary prerequisite to messianic appearance. If he were a prophet like those of old, that would give reassurance and raise trust that God had not abandoned them, even though they were still occupied by the Romans and did not have their own Davidic king.

All such talk is eventually hearsay. The midterm exam ramps into high gear with the second question: "Who do you say that I am?"

This is the existential question, a direct address of Jesus to his followers, and it demands that they answer from their core. They cannot rely on hearsay—gossip theology—from politicians or theologians. They must take a personal stand. The answer may or may not reveal who Jesus is, but it will certainly reveal who the disciple is. Here the preacher must begin to pay very close attention to what Mark is trying to do and say in Peter's response. His purpose is subversive.

Peter's exclamation that Jesus is the Messiah appears to give us hope that the disciples are starting to understand who Jesus is. Unfortunately it is a false hope. Peter's "correct confession" is deceptive. It points out an important reality: we can have what appears to be everything in order—words, actions, and so on—and still have it very wrong.

Correct confession can be deceptive. It can mask false discipleship, idolatry, and even a perspective that Jesus attributes to Satan. A perfectly correct mission statement does not reveal the true discipleship of either the pastoral staff or the congregation that appears to follow it to a tee.

Verse 30 helps the preacher to stay on Mark's track, because in the face of Peter's confession Jesus does not give approval or praise. Rather, he rebukes the disciples: "He sternly ordered them not to tell anyone about him." The word translated "sternly

Mark 8:27–30

Theological Perspective

"the womb of Israel": "It is in the history of Israel, in the Old Testament revelation with its covenant and liturgy and law that the lineaments of the face of God begin to be seen, until the face of God is fully seen in the face of Jesus Christ himself in whom God and man meet face to face."[2]

The history of Israel is specifically a messianic history, rather than a more abstract and vague "salvation history," because both the fulfillment and outworking of revelation and reconciliation are focused firmly on Jesus. First, this messianic history shapes our understanding of Jesus' crucifixion and resurrection as the fulfillment of the promises and commands of the covenant. Two key passages in Mark's Gospel in particular—his pledge "to give his life a ransom for many" (10:45) and his declaration of "my blood of the new covenant" (14:24)—are rooted in the establishment of the covenant at Sinai (Exod. 19–20; 24). Jesus offers himself on God's behalf to us and on our behalf to God, and in that atoning life, death, resurrection, and ascension reestablishes communion between God and humanity in himself.

Again, this messianic history also shapes the outworking of Jesus' mediatorial ministry, its impact on persons and the world. Hans-Joachim Kraus observes, "The messianic history is the path of God's coming into the world of the nations, the establishment and implementation of Christ's rule upon the earth, the transformation of unjust conditions, the infiltration of justice and righteousness, freedom and peace in every sphere of life and community."[3] Our prayer is always, "Thy kingdom come," for only Jesus can bring the kingdom he proclaims and reigns over; but the ministry of Jesus the Messiah continues through the Holy Spirit in and among the church. By uniting us with the risen and ascended Jesus, the Spirit places us in the flow of his messianic history and makes us partners with him in his ongoing ministry of revelation and reconciliation.

ROBB REDMAN

Pastoral Perspective

This is the moment when we might expect Jesus to affirm Peter, to indicate that Peter has not come to this conviction on his own, but that it has been revealed to him by God. We expect that because Matthew presents it in exactly that way in his Gospel (Matt. 16:13–20). Matthew then has Jesus bless Simon, give him the name Peter (the Rock), and speak about the role of Peter's faith in the life of the church.

Is it not the case that we stand in the same place with the disciples? Like them, we may believe that Jesus is the Christ, but we may be even more confused than they about what that actually means. We are surrounded by two thousand years of the church's very diverse expectations, claims, and explanations about who Jesus is and what he does as God's anointed one. He has been used as a sponsor for conquests, crusades, inquisitions, empires, revolutions, wars, and all sorts of causes, noble and demonic. So what can we teach our children about who Jesus is, and what it means to follow him and to live as his disciples?

In contrast to Matthew, Mark has Jesus silence Peter and the disciples. Over and against their notions of what his messiahship will be like, he tells them that the Messiah must suffer and die. When Peter objects, he is sternly rebuked by Jesus. It is clear that whatever it means to be "Christos" will be defined by Jesus himself, not by the preconceptions and self-interests of others.

Mark gives extraordinarily important clues as the conversation continues. Those who wish to follow Jesus must walk the way of the cross, which involves self-denial and giving one's life for others. Is Jesus also telling us that, like him, we must surrender thoughts of destroying our enemies and the powers that threaten us, since ultimately our worst enemy is violence itself? Does Jesus' witness of active, nonviolent love epitomize what it means to deny oneself and to bear the cross?

Does this require the church to teach nonviolence as essential to being a disciple of Jesus? Is it central to the gospel itself? Mark's Jesus would seem to require this. What would that mean for the church's teaching, witness, and ministry?

V. BRUCE RIGDON

---

2. T. F. Torrance, *Incarnation: the Person and Life of Christ* (Downers Grove, IL: InterVarsity Press, 2008), 44.
3. H.-J. Kraus, "Perspektiven eines messianischen Christus-glaubens," in *Rückkehr zu Israel* (Neukirchen-Vluyn: Neukirchener, 1991), 152 (author's trans.).

Exegetical Perspective

Peter's Confession. Then Jesus turned directly to the disciples and asked the same question: "Who do you say that I am?" The "you" here is plural (*hymeis*), so the question was truly addressed to all of the disciples. Peter's response, therefore, was on behalf of the group as a whole: "You are the Messiah." This is the first time the term "messiah" has appeared in Mark's Gospel since the very first verse, 1:1, where Mark tells the reader that this is "the beginning of the good news of Jesus Christ, the Son of God." Mark has saved repetition of the term for this climactic moment within the narrative, for this hinge that will lead to the revelation of the suffering, death, and resurrection of Jesus, against all expectations. The term translated as "messiah" is *christos* in the Greek, from which we derive the word "Christ." It literally means "one who is anointed" and most clearly has connections with the anointing of kings in ancient Israel (1 Sam. 15:1; 16:13; Ps. 2:2). We still find an echo of the root meaning of the association with anointing in the English term "christening."

The meaning of the term *christos* is clear enough on one level. God's Messiah would come in the line of the greatest of kings, King David (see 10:47–48). He would exercise great power and lead to the restoration of Israel, both nationally and religiously. We find this expectation echoed in the Emmaus story from Luke's Gospel (Luke 24:21) and the Acts of the Apostles (Acts 1:6). Thus far in Mark's Gospel, Peter has witnessed Jesus demonstrating tremendous power in every way. Peter has the right term, *christos*, but not the right meaning.

Perhaps this is why Jesus commands the disciples not to say anything about this confession of his identity (v. 30). Jesus will redefine the meaning of this title by virtue of his suffering and death. In this regard Jesus will become the crucified Messiah, folly to the Gentiles and a stumbling block to traditional Jewish sensibilities (so Paul in 1 Cor. 1:23). In the very next scene in Mark's Gospel, 8:31–33, Peter will demonstrate just what a stumbling block the message of the cross was.

JEFFREY S. SIKER

Homiletical Perspective

warned" (*epitimaō*) is an important word in Mark. The word is used to describe Jesus' rebuke of the unclean spirits (1:25; 3:12; 9:25) and the storm on the sea (4:39). As Ethelbert Stauffer points out, typically, humans rebuke the wrong people. Mark illustrates this by having Peter wrongly rebuke Jesus (8:32), the disciples wrongly rebuke those who brought children to Jesus (10:13), and the crowd wrongly rebuke Bartimaeus, who cried out for Jesus (10:48). "Again and again human threatening and reproof is shown to be presumptuous and overhasty. *Epitimao* is not for man [sic], but for God."[1]

When Peter here takes Jesus aside to rebuke him, he makes the ultimate presumption, for only the Divine has the power to discern when a demonic force is present and needs to be quashed. To have in mind "the things of God" rather than "human things" means relinquishing our human definition of who God is and who Jesus is. It is the ultimate idolatry to make God in our own image, and that is what is at stake in Peter's confession.

The preacher might identify ways that we make Peter's mistake today. As we hand Jesus his job description, we impose our own expectations. Whether we fashion him according to a prosperity gospel, a social gospel, a spirituality gospel, or a psychotherapeutic gospel, we make him into the savior we had in mind. However, it is a false God and gospel that I create, one that feeds my greed. This practice of fashioning a God that does what we want is ongoing and multifaceted. Calvin claimed that "man's [sic] nature, so to speak, is a perpetual factory of idols."[2] Jesus' stern ordering of the disciples in 8:30 is his signal to them—they will not understand what it means to confess him as Messiah until they stand beneath his cross.

ANDRÉ RESNER

---

1. Ethelbert Stauffer, "*Epitimaō*," in Gerhard Kittel, ed., *Theological Dictionary of the New Testament*, trans. Geoffrey W. Bromiley (Grand Rapids: Eerdmans, 1964), 2:624.
2. John Calvin, *Institutes of the Christian Religion* (Philadelphia: Westminster Press, 1960), 1.11.8.

Mark 8:31–33

³¹Then he began to teach them that the Son of Man must undergo great suffering, and be rejected by the elders, the chief priests, and the scribes, and be killed, and after three days rise again. ³²He said all this quite openly. And Peter took him aside and began to rebuke him. ³³But turning and looking at his disciples, he rebuked Peter and said, "Get behind me, Satan! For you are setting your mind not on divine things but on human things."

Theological Perspective

This small passage raises theological issues that connect messianic expectations and the meaning of true discipleship. First, there is the enigmatic Son of Man saying (v. 31) that appears to defy popular messianic expectations of the day. Second, there is openness to suffering as a distinctive mark of discipleship for those who would follow Jesus.

What does the phrase "the son of man" mean? The Greek actually reads "the son of the man." First and foremost, "the son of the man" is spoken by Jesus only in the Synoptic Gospels. Second, it carried messianic meaning for the Gospel writers. Third, it should not be confused with the generic expressions "son of man/sons of men."

By placing the expression "the son of the man" only on the lips of Jesus, the evangelists elevate the term to a special status. This action conveyed to the original reader that this term reveals in some way who Jesus is. Indeed, Mark 8:29 reads, "You are the Christ." Moreover, "the son of the man" functions as Jesus' own way of referring to himself in the Synoptics. It separates him from the crowd and functions as distinctive self-reference, similar to the way persons often refer to themselves in the third person. Scholars continue to debate whether or not the phrase was a messianic title for Jesus; however, its role as a significant self-reference should not be

Pastoral Perspective

It is noteworthy that the first ten chapters of the Gospel of Mark are dedicated to the description of three years of the ministry of Jesus, while the remaining six chapters describe his final week of life. Mark 8:31–33 is particularly significant because this is the first passage where Jesus foresees the passion. Whereas the earlier ministry of Jesus was marked by healing, teaching in parables, and the working of miracles, the emphasis now is on his role as teacher, one who speaks with clarity about his identity as God's appointed Messiah (8:29). This message would have struck a chord with the original hearers, Gentile believers who were also facing suffering, oppression, and persecution at the hands of the Roman Empire. They were familiar with the ability of oppressive systems to crush people, spiritually, psychologically, emotionally, and physically. This Gospel was written to encourage them in and through their persecutions and to call on them to serve Christ faithfully, even as they shared in his sufferings.

A Suffering Messiah? The idea that the Son of Man was to suffer was in complete contrast to the Jewish expectations of the day. Likewise, the disciples could not associate belief in resurrection with the Son of Man. Son of Man was a self-designated title that Jesus used to refer to himself. Though he never fully

Exegetical Perspective

Mark's lean Gospel pivots on these verses, which turn the narrative decisively toward its climactic events. Jerusalem will not actually be named as the destination of their solemn pilgrimage until Jesus' third explanation of what awaits them there: "See, we are going up to Jerusalem," he says (10:33), pointedly walking *ahead* of his companions, who are by then "amazed" and "afraid" (10:32). It is clear from this first prediction onward that the meaning of the entire ministry hinges on what will happen there.

To emphasize the destination, though, is not to diminish the significance of the journey. It is, after all, while they are "on the way" (8:27) that Peter first identifies Jesus as the Messiah. Ched Myers calls this "the true narrative site for discipleship."[1] Their location at this moment adds other layers of meaning: not only is Caesarea Philippi named for two rulers whose claims to sovereignty Peter implicitly rejects in naming Jesus (not the Roman Augustus or the Herodian Philip) as the anointed one; it also stands near the site of an ancient temple of Pan, a place associated with revelation.

---

1. Ched Myers, *Binding the Strong Main: A Political Reading of Mark's Story of Jesus* (Maryknoll, NY: Orbis Books, 1988), 241. Both of Mark's subsequent passion predictions (9:33; 10:32) find the disciples "on the way."

Homiletical Perspective

This three-verse paragraph is the meat, as it were, of a Gospel sandwich, slapped between the hard crusts of the disciples' confession at Caesarea and Jesus' invitation to "anyone who wants to be my disciple" (8:34).

Is Jesus teaching the disciples (then and now) what it means for him to *be* the Christ? That is a typical interpretation of this text, undergirded by the motif of the messianic secret: the disciples, in the person of Peter, have recognized and confessed Jesus as the Messiah; he tells them to keep it quiet for now, but begins teaching the definition of the word they have blurted out. They understand that Jesus *is* the Christ, though not what it means for him to *be* the Christ. Nor does Jesus want it announced until after the crucifixion.

Yes, Mark the evangelist tells us, at the beginning of his Gospel, that Jesus is the Christ, even though he knows and evangelizes from a postcrucifixion vantage. He is at pains to show us the suffering and death of Jesus, and in a sense also the vulnerability of Jesus.

Yes, Jesus does have power—to exorcise demons, cure the sick, still violent storms, walk on water, and multiply loaves. Yet all of those miracles, no matter how powerful, cannot create faith as evidenced in Jesus' visit to his hometown (6:1–6). When it comes

Mark 8:31–33

Theological Perspective

in question. Furthermore, it is definitely a messianic self-reference for the evangelists (Matt. 16:13). Biblical scholar Adela Yarbro Collins notes similar developments in Jewish writers roughly contemporaneous with Mark's Gospel.[1]

That leads to our third point on this topic: "the son of the man" should not be confused with the generic expressions "son of man" and "sons of men." The Hebrew Bible consistently uses "son of man" and "sons of men" to denote humans. These were never used as messianic titles. In light of this, it is noteworthy that the Gospel of Mark distinguishes between Jesus' self-references and generic expressions. For example, Mark 3:28–29 (NASB) reads, "Truly I say to you, all sins will be forgiven the sons of men ... but whoever might blaspheme against the Holy Spirit ... is guilty of an everlasting sin." This is not a self-reference by Jesus but a means of referring to potential human culpability.

Some would argue that Daniel 7:13 is the definitive text for our understanding of "the son of the man" in the Jesus tradition. Therein lies the problem. Daniel 7:13 reads neither "son of man" nor "the son of the man." It reads, "one *like* a son of man" (NASB, emphasis added). This is one of many descriptions of heavenly beings in human likeness throughout the Christian canon.

In this passage, Jesus, the son of man, shall win the ultimate victory through suffering in the immediate context, implying that his true disciples must be willing to do the same. This went against the grain of contemporary political messianic expectations of the military overthrow of the Romans and the establishment of God's unending kingdom.

The passages also speak to a contemporary theological problem in Christianity: the so-called prosperity gospel and the nature of true discipleship. The prosperity gospel constitutes the abuse of the true good news. Jesus states plainly in verses 31–33 that he must suffer but later be resurrected. Peter, however, has other plans and begins to chastise Jesus. A disciple correcting the teacher was a cultural faux pas in this first-century context. Jesus' response, therefore, is most understandable, given the social conventions. He calls Peter the Rock "Satan" because Peter, who earlier confessed him as the Christ (8:29), has quickly betrayed his confession, setting his mind on human things, and this is not a good thing.

---

1. Adela Yarbro Collins, *Mark: A Commentary*, Hermeneia (Minneapolis: Fortress Press, 2007), 403.

Pastoral Perspective

disclosed his own understanding of the term, the disciples linked it with it the figure in Daniel 7:13–14 and regarded Jesus as the coming Messiah.

This first prediction (see also 9:31; 10:32–34) by Jesus—that he, the Son of Man, must undergo great suffering, be rejected (by elders, the chief priest, and scribes), be killed, and then be raised after three days—was met with awe and wonderment toward Jesus, the Messiah who claimed this path of faithfulness, and toward the God in whose will and way Jesus was totally and wholeheartedly aligned. Mark tells us that, in response to Jesus' words, only Peter rebuked him, leaving readers and hearers of this Gospel to wonder about the reaction of the other disciples and inviting us to reflect on our own reaction today. A further question has to do with Jesus' reaction to the suffering and rejection he faced and was about to face: were these the words of one who willingly followed the path God had laid before him, or did he have a choice?

Listening vs. Hearing. In response to this self-disclosure, Peter rebuked Jesus. Why did Peter respond as he did? Was it that Peter could not understand this new teaching concerning the Son of Man (due to his cultural, religious, or traditional upbringing)? Did he clearly understand, but choose to reject an idea so new, so radical? After all, Jewish expectations about the Messiah were in complete contrast to what Jesus was describing. Even with good intentions, was it possible that he thought he could influence, manipulate, or compromise what Jesus was saying?

This was an important listening and learning period in the lives of the disciples' spiritual formation. Perhaps that is why Jesus had told them earlier not to tell anyone who he was; they themselves were not ready—mentally, theologically, or spiritually. Perhaps they could not be ready to understand until after Jesus' death and resurrection.

Jesus in turn, and in plain sight of the disciples, rebuked Peter. He was not calling Peter Satan, but rather was acknowledging that the influence and inspiration behind what Peter was saying was from Satan. In other words, Peter was encouraging Jesus to take another route to messiahship, one that was easier, more comfortable, and possibly less demanding. It is in that spirit that Jesus rebuked Peter, as a public witness to his steady faith in God's way and will for his life. Jesus looked beyond the suffering, the rejection, and even death—to the resurrection, to the glory. We must look through the suffering and pain that cannot be removed from a life of faithful

Exegetical Perspective

The mainspring of this portentous journey is being wound by several key tensions as it passes this turning point.

First, there is the matter of the messianic secret: Jesus' strict instruction, freshly reiterated, that the disciples "not . . . tell anyone about him" (v. 30). This ban is consistent with the silence he imposed following healings: of demon possession (1:25), of deafness (7:36), and of blindness (8:26). It reinforces the parabolic strategy (4:10–12) that intentionally leaves those outside his inner circle at a loss to understand the full significance of his ministry. It prefigures this Gospel's ultimate silence, when the Easter witnesses to the fulfillment of all that Jesus here predicts flee in mute terror from the empty tomb (16:8). The guarding of secrets in itself foments tension. It also contradicts the frankness with which Jesus now proceeds to explain "quite openly" (*parrēsia*—frequently used in the NT, although Mark alone applies it here) the ominous significance of what Peter has affirmed. By the end of this exchange, having described explicitly the necessary fate of the Son of Man and his followers' collateral experience, the only connection that will for now remain *implicit* is the one between the suffering Son of Man and the person Jesus, who continues to use the third person in evoking the archetypal figure from Daniel 7. Adela Yarbro Collins hears advice to the persecuted church in this volatile mix of secrecy and candor: "They may keep their identity secret with a good conscience. But they are warned that it will be impossible to do so in the long run. When they are discovered, they must confess their identity bravely, as Jesus did, and risk conflict that may lead to death."[2]

At the most overt narrative level, the tension is fed by the ensuing conflict between Jesus and his closest deputy. Peter's challenge to the one whom he has just named Messiah may seem a blot on his piety. However, his temerity is at least comprehensible: scarcely four chapters earlier he and his companions had wondered, "Who then is this, that even the wind and the sea obey him?" (4:41). Is God's Anointed One now saying he cannot control the mere earthly powers that might oppose him?

The tone of rebuke is fresh in the air since Jesus' dressing-down of his bewildered disciples (8:17–21) for their failures to grasp the significance of two miraculous feedings (chaps. 6 and 8). The tone echoes back all the way to Mark's first chapter (1:25),

---
2. Adela Yarbro Collins, *Mark*, Hermeneia (Minneapolis: Fortress Press, 2007), 171.

Homiletical Perspective

to *people*—human beings and their institutions, whether political or religious—Jesus has little if any power at all.

Yes, he can invite people to follow him, but some will not. Even among those who do, Jesus has no power to create faith. He *cannot* heal in the face of unfaith (6:5). It is no surprise then that he will be powerless before political and religious leaders of his day, so much so that he will "undergo great suffering, and be rejected, . . . and be killed" (v. 31).

For Mark, ironically, it is Jesus' weakness that proves his lasting strength. By means of the cross Mark tells us who Jesus is and what resurrection might mean.

Yes, we readers know that Jesus is the Christ—have known since verse 1 of chapter 1. However, we see him from this side of the cross. In the Gospel itself, only the centurion sees and speaks the truth, and that only when Jesus breathes his last: "truly this man was God's Son" (15:39).

A customary interpretation of this text, then, is that Jesus' rebuke of Peter in verse 33 is aimed not at Peter's confession per se, but at Peter's unwillingness to receive Jesus' teaching in terms of the suffering it portends. Peter is horrified and rebukes Jesus! Jesus is angry and rebukes back!

It is interesting that the same Greek verb is used in verse 30 (there most often translated into English as "strictly charged" or "sternly ordered") and in verses 32 and 33 ("rebuked"). In each instance, a colloquial rendering of the verb could be, "Shut your mouth!" or "Don't say that!" In verse 30, is Jesus preemptively zipping the secret-letting lips of the disciples?

Contrary to the traditional interpretation, is he perhaps muting the confession itself, disavowing the very title or benediction? In verse 31, Jesus self-identifies as "Son of Man." Is Mark's Jesus telling us that the disciples are just as mistaken in *their* "guess" as to his identity ("You are the Christ!") as the "people" are with theirs? Is Mark teaching us that Jesus will suffer and die, not as a divine agent but as a representative human?

Be that as it may, there is power to and support for the customary interpretation: in sum, that the disciples may know the title Messiah but in applying it to Jesus they do not know what it means. In Matthew 16:17, we are told that *the word* is a matter of revelation; here in Mark, Jesus is *revealing* the word's content. It is, then, to this radical teaching that Peter reacts, revolts, and even rebukes Jesus: "Shut your mouth! Don't say that!"

Mark 8:31–33

Theological Perspective

In other words, Peter had a prosperity gospel of his own, based upon worldly standards, not heavenly ones. He associated righteousness with power and privilege. He believed wealth and social status were synonymous with piety and sanctification. Unfortunately, Peter failed to see the inconsistency between his personal political theology and his personal social situation: if he were a true disciple, why was he poor? This is a very human error even today.

Furthermore, Peter was selfish. He focus was on what might accrue to him as a disciple of Jesus when Jesus came into power. Peter possessed an insight about Jesus' true identity, but he failed to place his own hubris in check. As Christians, it is not enough to have a sound theology or spiritual insight. Theology and insight must manifest themselves through the lives of true disciples. This is also a very human error; however, true Christian discipleship demands fidelity, regardless of the immediate consequences.

Selfish ambition has its own open-door policy. Selfish ambition is not bound by ethnicity, nationality, physical disability, social location, gender, or physical proximity to the Master. It is a liability of human nature. Peter had bought into the popular messianic expectation of the day: the complete religious, political, and military restoration of God's people. This restoration meant the political overthrow of Roman imperial powers. However, God had planned a different type of revolution, one in which ultimate victory comes through suffering, turning the standards of the world on its head.

Among the major social movements of the twentieth century, India's fight for independence from Britain, the civil rights movement in the United States, and the struggles to end communism in eastern Europe and apartheid in South Africa had one thing in common. The prevailing leadership in each case sought change through nonviolence. In each instance, innocent people gave their lives to end senseless, arrogant oppression. It was not a shallow promise of prosperity that fueled these movements. Rather, it was the fervent belief that the evil would not last always. It was hope in the midst of a seemingly hopeless situation.

The true gospel is not about material gain or economic power or political power, but about the power to survive in a powerless situation. It is about the miniresurrections that sustain us through life until the final resurrection enables us to step from mortality into immortality.

THOMAS B. SLATER

Pastoral Perspective

discipleship, as we journey through life with the God of the Bible. Perhaps it is to this reality of daily living that Jesus' rebuke of Peter draws attention, for contemporary readers as well as those enduring trial in the early communities of Jesus followers.

How Can Life Be Meaningful in the Face of Injustice and Death? How do our congregations witness to the Jesus of this text? In his book *The Cross and the Lynching Tree* (New York: Orbis Press, 2011), James H. Cone, Charles A. Briggs Distinguished Professor of Systematic Theology at Union Theological Seminary, presents a different perspective on the meaning of the cross. Highly regarded as one of the most influential theologians in North America, Cone explores the symbols of the cross and the lynching tree. These are two of the most emotionally charged symbols in the history of the African American community. Cone traces their interconnectedness in the history and theology of African Africans. Through the witness of men and women, both the known and those whose names are unknown to us, he contemplates the greatest challenge of any Christian theology: to explain how life can be made meaningful in the face of death and injustice. While both symbols represent the worst in human nature, they also represent the refusal to let the worst determine our final meaning.

For African Americans, the image of Jesus, hung on a tree to die, powerfully grounded their faith that God was with them, even in the suffering of the lynching era. Throughout the world people try to make sense of violence: violence between nations that leads to countless tragic deaths, violence within urban neighborhoods across the nation that tears the fabric of our contemporary relationships, and domestic violence that is hidden in the homes of every congregation. In response, the church is challenged to articulate publicly a witness to God and to the meaning of life in the midst of chaos and injustice.

MARSHA SNULLIGAN HANEY

Exegetical Perspective

when Jesus rebukes the first of several demons he will encounter—demons who, like Peter, recognize Jesus for precisely who he is. The verb in these exchanges (*epitimaō*), suitably strong for exorcism, is shocking when applied to the disciple-teacher relationship. Jesus' rejoinder raises the stakes even higher: "Get behind me, Satan," he says—the very command with which, in Matthew's telling (Matt. 4:10), he dismissed the tempter to end their wilderness encounter. Mark's Gospel, of course, does not include a full narration of the temptation story as it appears in the other Synoptic Gospels. Perhaps Mark's version is embedded here instead—as Jesus faces down, not an archetype or a manifestation of his own inner demons, but a compatriot.

Peter, even in his distress, had apparently tried to be discreet in challenging Jesus' dire prediction, "taking him aside" (v. 32) to express his objections. Jesus, instead, seizes this moment as a teaching opportunity. Widening the audience with an intense gaze, he says, "You are setting your mind not on divine things but on human things" (v. 33). This is Mark's only appeal to the stark dualism connoted by *phronein*, more characteristic of Pauline writings (e.g., Rom. 8:5, Col. 3:2). "By rejecting the plan of God that involves a suffering messiah/Son of Man," write Donahue and Harrington, "Peter puts himself on the wrong side of . . . the cosmic struggle that shapes human history until the *eschaton*."[3]

One other form of tension pervades this episode: irony—the layered tension between what the characters understand, what the narrator knows, and what the reader's perspective adds. Jesus knows what Peter is unwilling, yet, to know: that their journey leads to death's door. Mark, as narrator and witness to the resurrection, knows that the story, although it includes unspeakable suffering, continues beyond the grave. Jesus too may grasp this. Nevertheless, before the end he himself, in Gethsemane (14:32–39), will plead for a different outcome, in tones perhaps as anguished as Peter's, if less presumptuous. Although the reader cannot be sure whether this Gospel's sober clarity about the fate of the Son of Man is refracted through the lens of Mark's hindsight or Jesus' prescience, the reader at least knows with utter certainty that, although Mark's Easter witnesses fled in silent terror, the story has nevertheless found its way to us who are still "on the way."

RICHARD E. SPALDING

Homiletical Perspective

Why the horror on Peter's part? Rebuke occurs in verses 30, 32, and 33, evoking images of both Peter and Jesus as the speakers spitting, expectorating, and coughing out their agitation. The obvious exposition is that Peter cannot imagine this end for God's anointed. Moreover, Peter cannot imagine this happening to his friend. Peter has answered Jesus' call to follow, and whether or not Peter has come to believe in Jesus and his mission in more than nominal ways, it seems that Peter is devoted to him.

Derivatively, perhaps Peter realizes that if he is with Jesus, and this is what is going to happen to Jesus, this is what will happen to him. Jesus will say something of the sort not many verses hence. This particular end is not what Peter had in mind when he left his nets on the shore in Capernaum. Yes, Jesus says quite openly, resurrection will come, but on this side of the cross resurrection may seem too little reward for such suffering.

I suspect that the horror Peter feels is deeper even than that. Jesus says that he will be rejected by the *religious leaders*, the very men (and their institutions) Peter has been taught to trust and in fact does trust. That Jesus, the "representative human," will suffer at the hands of the religious and political authorities is a horrifying revelation about these institutions: about religious leaders, rolling over the poor, perverting the will and purpose of God in favor of their own purposes; and about the Roman Empire, allegedly guaranteeing the common good through its imposed peace that brought oppression through violence.

All Peter's certainties crash! Only when Peter relinquishes his preconceptions of what the Messiah can and cannot do is he ready for true discipleship. This reading makes for powerful preaching. Perhaps we too would muzzle and mute Jesus, inasmuch as we too have in mind seemingly inviolate images of what it means for Jesus to be the Christ. Only when we understand our expectations to be illusions does real discipleship become possible, because then we are in a position to learn what Jesus is actually teaching.

THOMAS R. STEAGALD

---

3. John R. Donahue and Daniel J. Harrington, *The Gospel of Mark*, Sacra Pagina (Collegeville, MN: Liturgical Press, 2002), 262.

Mark 8:34–9:1

³⁴He called the crowd with his disciples, and said to them, "If any want to become my followers, let them deny themselves and take up their cross and follow me. ³⁵For those who want to save their life will lose it, and those who lose their life for my sake, and for the sake of the gospel, will save it. ³⁶For what will it profit them to gain the whole world and forfeit their life? ³⁷Indeed, what can they give in return for their life? ³⁸Those who are ashamed of me and of my words in this adulterous and sinful generation, of them the Son of Man will also be ashamed when he comes in the glory of his Father with the holy angels." ⁹:¹And he said to them, "Truly I tell you, there are some standing here who will not taste death until they see that the kingdom of God has come with power."

Theological Perspective

While some scholars believe that the verses in this passage are a collection of isolated sayings, the eschatological and ethical dimensions can also be seen as distinctive yet interrelated. In other words, one's ethics in this life will determine one's fate in the next, and one's eschatological vision shapes one's ethical stances and practices in the now. This relationship is key to our understanding of the demands of discipleship.

Mark 8:34 continues the thought of the preceding section by defining in more detail what it means to be a Christian disciple. Linking his own fate to that of his disciples, Jesus says clearly that Christian discipleship involves denying oneself and living a life that shares in his suffering. New Testament scholar Adela Yarbro Collins points out that the Greek phrase translated "deny himself" (NRSV "deny themselves," *aparnēsasthō heauton*, v. 34) "means that such a person must refuse to recognize or must ignore oneself."[1] African American ministers often use the imagery of an empty pitcher before a full and overflowing fountain to convey that Christians are empty vessels that must be filled by the overflowing and abundant Spirit of God.

Pastoral Perspective

One of the most often-heard critiques of the Christian faith, both within the church and outside of it, is that it is too other-world oriented. By this, critics mean that the church does a good job preparing people for life after death, for life eternal, but is not very helpful when it comes to helping people live life today. The voice of Tashi, a character in Alice Walker's book *Possessing the Secret of Joy*, helps us to understand this perspective:

> I began to see how the constant focus on the suffering of Jesus alone excludes the suffering of others from one's view.... I knew I wanted my own suffering, the suffering of women and little girls, still cringing before the overwhelming might and weapons of the torturers, to be the subject of a sermon. Was woman herself not the tree of life? And was she not crucified? Not in some age no one even remembers, but right now, daily, in many lands on the earth?[1]

Tashi's life had been defined by female genital mutilation. While this particular social issue may not be one that many persons face in our North American societies, there are many other issues in our neighborhoods and societies that cause people

---

1. Adela Yarbro Collins, *Mark: A Commentary*, Hermeneia (Minneapolis: Fortress Press, 2007), 408.

1. Alice Walker, *Possessing the Secret of Joy* (New York: Pocket Star Books, 1992), 275–76.

Exegetical Perspective

Jesus now widens the circle to take in a crowd for a moment of urgent and public teaching—evidently to demonstrate that the standards of costly discipleship apply to "any [who] want to become my followers" (v. 34). This invitation apparently reverses his earlier dismissal of those uncomprehending "outsiders" for whom "everything comes in parables" (4:10–12). Now his clear evocation of what lies ahead "on the way" (8:27) for those who choose to follow is anything but parabolic. At this turning point, Jesus and Mark collaborate to extend the choice to the widest possible audience.

Discipleship, says Jesus, is first and always a matter of following—not a matter of thinking or even of speaking. (Peter may have correctly understood and expressed Jesus' identity; but when he disputes the trajectory of the path they must follow, he earns some of the harshest words Jesus ever uttered.) It is an act of choice—compelling but not compelled. It is an act of faithful self-denial (*aparneisthai*): a way of dislocating oneself, displacing self-interest, knocking oneself off-center for the sake of the way.

That Jesus sets the criterion of self-denial for discipleship is perhaps as startling to our culture, which exalts the value of "self-care," as his insistence that each one "take up his [NRSV "their"] cross and

Homiletical Perspective

There were times Jesus explained things to his disciples away from the crowds. Early in Mark, after Jesus had told the parables of the Sower, the Lamp, the Growing Seed, and the Mustard Seed, Jesus "explained everything in private to his disciples" (4:34). In the (parabolic) lesson before us, Jesus offers an explanation not in private, but in public: "He called the crowd with his disciples, and said to them, 'If any want to become my followers . . .'" (v. 34).

The implications of these few words are many and stark. On one hand, just because a person is a *disciple* of Jesus does not necessarily mean that person is a *follower*. The literal meaning of "disciple" is student: a student may learn from the teacher but demur or, indeed, "fall away" (see 4:17; 14:27) when it comes to fulfilling the course's requirements—especially outside of the classroom.

On the other hand, a follower of Jesus may not be a self-identified or formally recognized disciple. In 9:38, John says, "Teacher, we saw someone casting out demons in your name, and we tried to stop him, because he was not following us." Jesus tells John and the others to cease their desisting efforts, and he blesses anyone "who does a deed of power in my name" (9:39). Sadly, in many quarters there are those faithful ones who may, with good intentions

Mark 8:34–9:1

Theological Perspective

Although the reference to the cross may be a prophetic prediction of Jesus' own death, crucifixion was also a well-known Roman form of capital punishment. Convicted criminals normally carried their own crosses to the place of crucifixion and died a slow, miserable death. The message was evident: following Jesus would not lead to prosperity but to pain, suffering, and persecution. As New Testament scholar Morna Hooker persuasively argues, this saying and those around it in Mark do not address those who acknowledge Jesus as Messiah and those who do not; rather, they point to a "crucial divide" between "those disciples who are prepared to follow him on the way of suffering and those who are not."[2] True discipleship is defined not by what one might receive, but by what one is willing to give.

The summons to discipleship is not only to those within the story, but extends to readers as well. In first-century Roman society, disciples were expected to emulate their teachers. This was also true within rabbinical schools and in Greco-Roman philosophical schools. The expectations of the followers of Jesus are particularly demanding. Furthermore, the call to discipleship is not a special call to the preacher but a call to everyone: the demands of Christian discipleship are no less for laypersons than for clergypersons.

The teaching on saving and losing in verse 35 was as countercultural in that day as it is today. Most persons expected exaltation, not demise. The context is eschatological. Roman society expected persons to strive for success in every social endeavor; however, in light of the preceding verse, verse 35 would mean that Christians must be prepared to give their lives for the sake of the gospel and for the sake of Jesus.

Verses 36 and 37 continue the theme found in the two preceding verses. Many argue that these verses constitute a proverbial teaching on the importance of attaining life at the eschatological judgment. The point of these two verses is that honor, glory, and financial success in this world are not indicators of blessedness or righteousness. Rather, true discipleship requires faithfully following Jesus in this world, regardless of the outcome. Steadfastness in this way alone leads to living in the next age/world. This is the opposite of the so-called prosperity gospel. It is, however, the heart of the true gospel: the God of the universe loves and cherishes the faithful regardless of their social status in this life.

The next two verses are prophetic sayings. Verse 38 warns that present behavior has future,

2. Morna D. Hooker, *The Gospel according to Mark* (Peabody, MA: Hendrickson Publishers, 2009), 209.

Pastoral Perspective

to wonder if God is concerned, and if the church cares. No doubt the issues that impact the human spirit will vary from community to community, as will the response of each congregation. Nevertheless, in every community the question remains: are those who suffer today not crucified as Jesus was crucified on the cross?

While it may be true in some social and cultural contexts that Christianity has ignored the pain and suffering of people, this is not a correct understanding of this gospel message. Mark 8:34–9:1 serves as evidence that the call to Christian discipleship is a call to follow Christ *into* the world rather than *away from* the world. This radical clarion call to discipleship as presented by Jesus, the Son of God, identifies an invaluable four-part lesson on how to live life meaningfully in a world where suffering and death are inevitable. The first lesson reveals discipleship as a call to an alternative way of living life meaningfully based on self-denial and the renunciation of self-centeredness (v. 34). The second invites us to examine God's paradoxical perspective on life, one that has implications for reaching full human potential: if you want to save your life, you will lose it; if you are willing to lose it, you will save it (v. 35). The third lesson speaks to the seriousness of the theological consequences of choices we make, the values of reciprocity and accountability in light of our faith stance (vv. 36–38). The fourth lesson presented is one that points to the coming signs and wonders, evidences of the power and reign of God (9:1), as glimpsed later at the transfiguration (9:2–8).

What, then, is the meaning of the cross for us who are not the Messiah? The New Testament uses two words to describe the cross: *stauros* (cross) and *xylon* (tree). The cross that Jesus references in this passage (*stauros*) has a more personal and individual meaning as a symbol or an image for choosing a life marked by a close, intimate, and transformative relationship with God (as demonstrated by Jesus). It is a sign that stands for a conscious and deliberate choice and journey of life in obedience to God's way and God's will. It is also a symbol of a God-inspired transformation that leads to a new identity, new awareness, and a new way of being and doing.

Each time I reflect on the meaning of the cross, what comes to mind are familiar words I heard sung by Christians in southern Sudan, where I served as a mission coworker in Juba from 1979 to 1981. "With the cross before me and the world behind me, I will follow wherever he [Jesus] leads me, I will follow wherever he leads. There's no turning back, no

Exegetical Perspective

follow" (v. 34) was to the crowd in Caesarea Philippi.[1] Although this is the first reference in this Gospel to the cross, it was a familiar image among Jesus' audience, and Mark's. Josephus (*Antiquities* 13) reminds us that crucifixion was a common sight, a highly public Roman technique of intimidation. Ched Myers says that the cross "had only one connotation in the Roman Empire: upon it dissidents were executed."[2]

In all probability Mark was writing from the midst of some of the most gruesome persecution the church has ever endured. Having himself perhaps seen scores of condemned prisoners lugging the horizontal bar, as Jesus had, toward their own execution, Mark would have had every reason to hear this hard teaching in a most literal way. Luke's addition of the word "daily" to the end of the phrase "take up his cross" (Luke 9:23) bends it toward metaphorical interpretation: a regular discipline of self-giving, rather than a once-and-for-all sacrifice. How much more pointed is the teaching Jesus unpacks here; its closer parallel is John 15:13 where, now in the looming shadow of his own cross, Jesus observes that "no one has greater love than this: to lay down one's life for one's friends." Mark will eventually add another layer of irony when Jesus is ridiculed during his agony by those who provoked it because "he saved others but he cannot save himself" (15:31).

The appearance of substantially similar renditions of verses 35–37 in the other Synoptics heightens the sense that these teachings may have circulated independently, perhaps as part of a collection of sayings. The word "life" (*psyche*) is richer even than the sense of "safety" or "mortality" that might be connoted by the shadow of the cross. The equivalent Hebrew word *nephesh* (as in the LXX) suggests the breadth and depth of the idea: "what is at stake is the inner core of the person, what constitutes the self."[3] Verses 36 and 37 add a heightened sense of indelibility to the sacrifices being described, as Jesus asks his audience rhetorically, what price can you pay that will enable you to buy back your inmost self, your soul, once you have sold it cheaply?

Jesus' warning about the consequences of being "ashamed" of him or his teaching (v. 38) is

---

1. The NRSV, in its laudable attempt to render v. 34 (and vv. 36–37) inclusively, blurs its individual focus: in the Greek, the requirement is that any would-be follower take up [his or her] cross—not that they all somehow adopt an ethos of communal humility and collectively take up "their" [singular] burden together. Jesus is setting a standard of courageous personal commitment, not describing a shared mission project.
2. Ched Myers, *Binding the Strong Man: A Political Reading of Mark's Story of Jesus* (Maryknoll, NY: Orbis Books, 1988), 245.
3. John R. Donahue, SJ, and Daniel J. Harrington, SJ, *The Gospel of Mark*, Sacra Pagina (Collegeville, MN: Liturgical Press, 2002), 263.

Homiletical Perspective

like the disciple John, seek to obstruct the good that others do, because they are not of "our" company of followers. While they are certainly following Jesus and doing mighty deeds of power in his name—even perhaps taking up their crosses and giving their lives—they are not "following *us*" (9:38, emphasis added).

Again Jesus says, "If any *want* to become my followers," which tells us that not everyone, even among the called, will want to follow Jesus in this way. His own chosen, those he has called, flee into the shadows before the cross, while Bartimaeus, who called to Jesus and received his sight, "*followed him on the way*" (10:52). Many may know what that way is, but few will follow as Bartimaeus followed.

The most chilling question remains: Who, in fact, is "ashamed of [Jesus] and of [his] words in this adulterous and sinful generation"? (8:38). How often, throughout history, has the answer been the church itself? If the tendency to universalize (or relativize) the "message" leads some disciples to blush at the thought of confessing the man Jesus to be the Christ, those who *do* confess him as Savior may be ashamed of (or rationalize) the costly demands of his actual *words*. In either case, it seems that the church is the object of Jesus' warning in verse 38.

Shame manifests itself, not only in what we say we believe about him, but also in what we do and where we stand in relation to him. We see in the Gospels compelling evidence that when it might have mattered most, the disciples turned away in order to save their lives: they were ashamed. Ched Meyers suggests that the young man in Gethsemane who flees the scene of Jesus' arrest (14:51) is not a *person* at all but a personification of the *church*. The young man escapes, but he is "naked"; he saves his life but loses it; under the form of a "linen garment" he forsakes his witness and identity. That garment becomes, in effect, the "burial garment" of Jesus.[1]

The choice for self-preservation is ironic, tragic, and ultimately self-destructive. However, some interpreters claim, the same young man reappears Easter morning to the women who come to anoint Jesus' body. In this is a sign that the church's witness can be rehabilitated, even as the instruction to "follow" Jesus, who has gone ahead into Galilee (16:7), presumes Peter's redemption after his denial and the others' restoration to discipleship after they had fled in fear for their lives.

---

1. Ched Myers, *Binding the Strong Man: A Political Reading of Mark's Story of Jesus* (Maryknoll, NY: Orbis Books, 2008), 368–69.

Mark 8:34–9:1

Theological Perspective

eschatological consequences. This "adulterous and sinful age" (NRSV ". . . generation") is a typical Jewish expression that uses the image of improper sexual ethics to denote religious infidelity. This reference was also typical of many contemporary Jewish texts that spoke of an evil age followed by a pure age/world. Coupled with verses 34–35, these verses suggest a context where Christians are oppressed.

At present, there is no evidence that Christians enjoyed a measure of respect in Roman society. The ease with which Nero persuaded Roman citizens of Christian culpability in the burning of Rome suggests the opposite. Indeed, Christian writings normally depict Christian suffering. Some Christians developed a rationale for suffering (e.g., Phil. 1:12–14; Jas. 1:2–3). Others related Jesus' trials with their own (e.g., John 15:18; 1 Pet. 4:13; Rev. 5:9–10), while still others placed their individual situations on a cosmic scale (e.g., Eph. 6:12; 1 John 5:1–5). Some also sought vindication for their suffering (e.g., Matt. 24:9–35; 2 Cor. 4:17; 1 Pet. 1:6–12). Mark 8:34–9:1 is not an anomaly, but a reflection of daily Christian existence.

It is difficult for many twenty-first-century Christians in the United States to imagine situations where hardship and discipleship might be interchangeable terms, but this was the case in the early church.

The early Christian community identified Jesus as the messianic Son of Man. Scholars have identified three basic types of Son of Man sayings in the synoptic Gospels: (1) present sayings, which function as self-references (e.g., Luke 9:58); (2) future sayings, which depict the Son of Man as an eschatological divine agent (e.g., Mark 13:26); (3) suffering sayings, which predict the passion, death, and resurrection of Jesus (e.g., Mark 8:31). Mark 8:38 falls into the second category. Those who stand with Jesus in this life shall also stand with Jesus in the next life.

Mark 9:1 contains the second prophecy "apparently unfulfilled . . . , since, almost twenty centuries after the words were spoken, there is little sign of the Kingdom of God being established in the world."[3] There have been many attempts to explain this passage. Some suggest that this prophecy refers to the transfiguration, or the resurrection, or Pentecost, and/or the destruction of Jerusalem in 70 CE. Others propose that Jesus was mistaken about the time frame; still others argue that this saying belongs to the early church, not to Jesus.

THOMAS B. SLATER

Pastoral Perspective

turning back."[2] When sung by the Sudanese Christians, the words of this passage affirm the cross as a symbol of life and are a reminder of their obedience and commitment to Christ in a predominately Muslim country where they are the religious minority.

This reflection began with an introduction to Tashi, a committed Christian who is trying to understand how the Christian faith, specifically the suffering of Jesus, is supposed to impact her life and the suffering she is forced to experience simply because she is a woman. Her voice is a challenge to congregations to engage in a critical theological self-examination, to see if in fact our devotion to Jesus and his suffering prevents us from seeing and responding to those who are suffering in our midst.

Theologically, as we reflect on and respond to those who today suffer like Jesus and are being crucified on a variety of crosses, she challenges us to be courageous and bold in the living and proclamation of our faith. Hers is the challenge for the community of faith to become a bold, fresh expression of the church that is capable of responding to the sufferings and crucifixions around us. In other words, those like Tashi in our world challenge us to connect the suffering of Christ in history to the developing story of God's work in the church, especially as the church encounters persons who are suffering and are being crucified daily. Our passage reminds those who follow Christ that the church is also called to be a missional church that follows Christ by focusing on God's purposes and that lets God's action shape our worship in the world and witness to the world.

MARSHA SNULLIGAN HANEY

2. S. Sundar Singh, "I Have Decided to Follow Jesus," *Timeless Truths Free Online Library*, public domain, http://library.timelesstruths.org/music/I_Have_Decided_to_Follow_Jesus; accessed June 1, 2013.

3. Hooker, *Mark*, 211.

Exegetical Perspective

distinctive to this passage and its parallels. In effect, he has already accused Peter of this egregious attitude—and shamed him in return. Paul, on the other hand, seems to have taken this particular warning very much to heart, so careful is he to affirm that he is *not* ashamed and does not intend to shame others (e.g., Rom. 1:16; 1 Cor. 4:14; 2 Cor. 10:8). Jesus addresses this warning rather generically to the "generation" around him—which he indicts as "godless" or "adulterous" and "sinful" (v. 38; also Mark 8:12; cf. Matt. 12:38–42 and esp. Luke 11:29, where their clamoring for a sign is equivalent to a temptation). The desire of the prevailing culture for some definitive (magical) sign-on-demand that will exempt them from the public risks of standing with him and the gospel is reminiscent of the faithlessness of another "generation": those whose grumbling and testing in the Sinai wilderness cost years of time wasted in wandering (Deut. 32).

The first verse of chapter 9 is now generally seen as the conclusion to this sobering and tumultuous exchange—rather than as a preamble to the transfiguration story. For one thing, the words of Jesus are evidently addressed to a large group of people, only some of whom will see the fruition of this final piece of his prediction. For another, notwithstanding the sobriety and the criticism that Jesus has heaped on his listeners in these few intense verses, these closing words hold out hope that the final, transcendent resolution of his prediction is as real as all the risk and suffering that precede it. As we will see in the ensuing episode, there are indeed a few who will experience the Son of Man clothed in power. Perhaps what we see and hear in the vicinity of Caesarea Philippi and on the mountain of transfiguration stands in for a wilderness temptation story and for a resurrection appearance, in the lean Markan evocation of the tribulation and triumph of the Son of Man.

RICHARD E. SPALDING

Homiletical Perspective

This passage offers an obvious challenge and invitation to those who live and believe in a context of persecution, as indeed the original audience of Mark may have. To these believers, Jesus' warning is literal: following him will look like a cross, death. Jesus says, "Do not flee. Stand fast and embrace the suffering ahead. Take up your cross and follow me."

What might these words mean for those of us who do not live in a context of persecution, where violent death is part and parcel of faithfulness? What are we to make of this text in terms of its parabolic consequence? Is Jesus teaching "many things" here (4:2)? Will the meaning of discipleship change as our context changes, here and there, now and then? In *Falling Upward: A Spirituality for the Two Halves of Life,* Richard Rohr contends that for the first half of life each of us is busy about the business of self-created identity. We make a life and world, we craft an identity; we pour enormous time, energy, and resources into creating ourselves. There comes a time, however, of "necessary suffering"[2] that causes us to realize how the life we have made for ourselves is insufficient and shallow. At that point, we can double back and try to replicate or save the life we have created—a futile exercise that leaves us exhausted and bitter. On the other hand, we can embrace the loss, take up the cross, let go of what is gone, and open our hands to receive the self God intended us to be from the beginning.

Everyone suffers. Some will attempt to flee. Those who are willing to interpret their necessary suffering as the *spiritual* task of relinquishment, who are willing to lose *their* lives (as they have made them) for Jesus' sake, will receive a new, better, and—dare we say—resurrected life. The way through suffering is the way taken by any who would *become* a follower of Jesus.

THOMAS R. STEAGALD

---

2. See Richard Rohr, *Falling Upward: A Spirituality for the Two Halves of Life* (San Francisco: Jossey-Bass, a Wiley Imprint, 2011), 73.

Mark 9:2–8

²Six days later, Jesus took with him Peter and James and John, and led them up a high mountain apart, by themselves. And he was transfigured before them, ³and his clothes became dazzling white, such as no one on earth could bleach them. ⁴And there appeared to them Elijah with Moses, who were talking with Jesus. ⁵Then Peter said to Jesus, "Rabbi, it is good for us to be here; let us make three dwellings, one for you, one for Moses, and one for Elijah." ⁶He did not know what to say, for they were terrified. ⁷Then a cloud overshadowed them, and from the cloud there came a voice, "This is my Son, the Beloved; listen to him!" ⁸Suddenly when they looked around, they saw no one with them any more, but only Jesus.

Theological Perspective

At the beginning and again at the end of Mark's Gospel, readers witness moments of revelation. At both points, someone gets a glimpse of what lies beyond the curtain that separates heaven and earth. Here in the middle of the story, the reader—along with Peter, James, and John—gets high enough to see, if not into heaven, then at least beyond the boundary of space and time. On each occasion, a voice makes the same assertion. This one, Jesus, is "Son of God."

Mark's metaphor for revelation comes from the book of Isaiah. The exilic Isaiah had sought to comfort the battered, exiled remnant of Judah by declaring the heavens God's tent (Isa. 40:21–23). No matter how far removed from Jerusalem and the rubble of the temple, the people of Israel still dwelled in God's tabernacle. By the next generation, however, the curtain seemed a barrier behind which God hid from the people. Hence, the postexilic Isaiah called on God to rend the heavens and come down (Isa. 64:1–4, my summary): "Show yourself, God! Come out of hiding. Make some noise. Shake things up."

In Mark, God takes the dare, but in the strangest way. In the one who stands silent before councils and kings and then dies in darkness, God comes out of hiding. The curtain that conceals God rips wide open. A centurion, of all people, finally sees the truth, not in some noisy cataclysm, but in the way

Pastoral Perspective

Jesus and his disciples have recently begun the journey toward Jerusalem; they are "on the way" (8:22–10:52). On this journey Jesus teaches about discipleship: denying one's self (8:34–37), becoming least, being a servant, becoming like a little child (9:33–37). Some might imagine the disciples are expecting this trip up the mountain to be a kind of time-out, an interlude, when Jesus takes a break from his teaching on discipleship. Instead the scene offers the disciples a glimpse of God's glory in the face of Jesus. There are also two dynamics in this scene that speak to the life of faith and the practice of prayer: the dynamics of seeing/not-seeing and of speaking/listening.

The first dynamic is the dynamic of seeing/not-seeing. The convention of calling this scene the transfiguration suggests its highly visual character. Jesus is transfigured in front of the disciples, and his "clothes became dazzling white" (v. 3). This vision must have appeared stunning. To add to the impressive quality of the scene, two central figures from the Hebrew Bible make an appearance, an added visual treat. Peter, James, and John are sufficiently awed by what they see, and Peter suggests they stay.

This visual display and the disciples' awe can be reminders of how, in an increasingly visual culture, we long for our lives of faith to be fueled by sensory

Exegetical Perspective

The transfiguration lifts the veil between one reality and another, plunging us into the world of mystery. The passage begins, "Six days later" (v. 2). Six days later than what? It is unusual for Mark to be so specific in identifying an itinerary. Only here and in 14:1 ("It was two days before the Passover") does he do this. This is a sign that we need to pay attention, and read this event in the light of six days earlier at Caesarea Philippi, when Jesus demands, "Who do you say that I am?" (8:29). Peter's response that Jesus is the Messiah evokes a sharp reprimand and a warning that Jesus is not the Messiah they might imagine, that he will indeed suffer, die, and rise from the dead.

What then happens on this mountaintop has led some to ask if the transfiguration is a misplaced resurrection appearance. Moses and Elijah, figures who have defined Israel's past, appear, and Jesus himself is changed. It is as if the earthly Jesus is stripped away and we see him in all his postresurrection glory. Mark ends his Gospel so abruptly—frightened disciples fleeing an empty tomb—that one wonders if this does indeed belong to that end that we find missing. It would be more satisfying to have the risen Christ appear; yet Mark is very intentional in the way he arranges his material. Placed here, this event gives a glimpse into that glorious future at the very time

Homiletical Perspective

Mark's account of the transfiguration of Jesus is found at the heart of the Gospel in a series of passages dealing with questions of identity: Who is Jesus? Who are his followers? Until this point, Mark's Gospel has moved at a frenetic pace, shifting "immediately" from one event to another. Now Mark records the timeline with unusual specificity: "Six days later" Jesus and his closest disciples went up the mountain. With these words, Mark points back to Peter's confession that Jesus is Messiah (8:27-30) and to Jesus' first passion prediction (8:31). Peter's attempt to rebuke Jesus for suggesting the Messiah must suffer reveals that Peter got the title right but not the meaning. He does not understand that suffering, death, and resurrection are central to Jesus' mission, nor does he understand the implications of following Jesus.

The transfiguration account directly follows, and like the preceding passage, speaks to Jesus' identity and to the meaning of discipleship. On the mountain, Jesus is revealed to the inner circle of disciples as the Son of God, the one who is greater even than the spiritual giants Moses and Elijah, the one who will come in glory in the fullness of time. Discipleship means heeding his difficult teachings.

"Listen to him!" the voice commands (v. 7). At Jesus' baptism in Mark, the voice from the heavens

Mark 9:2–8

Theological Perspective

this man died, praying a Hebrew psalm of lament, instead of cursing and taunting like everyone else at the scene.

This is the Son of God, God's Messiah, and this is how he reigns. "The kingdom of God has come near," Jesus had said earlier (1:15). Now, in this bizarre enthronement, God's rule has come.

From our vantage point on the mount of transfiguration, readers can see beyond that moment. We peer into the "place" where, at least according to the apocryphal *Assumption of Moses*, the great lawgiver dwelled with God along with Elijah, the prophet "taken up" in a whirlwind some generations after Moses' time (2 Kgs. 2:1–11). Jesus, who appears with these two, wears garments that shine as Moses once did after one of his mountaintop sojourns (Exod. 34:29–35). As we eventually learn, these garments are also resurrection garb.

What did these three discuss? The manifold revelations Moses received atop the mountain? The last peak from which Moses peered into the land of promise he would never enter? The mountaintop where Elijah learned that God did not show up in wind, or earthquake, or fire, but in the sound of sheer silence (1 Kgs. 19:11–12)? All these things and more, Mark would doubtless have us imagine, as we ponder the various ways in which these two representatives of the Law and the Prophets prefigure and anticipate the great revelation of God in the darkness and silence of Golgotha.

In Mark's Gospel, this scene serves another theological purpose that the reader only vaguely anticipates prior to the last scene in the story (16:1–8). The young man at the empty tomb tells the women that they will not find Jesus there, but in Galilee, just as he told them. "He has been raised," the young man says (16:6), but no one in Mark's story sees him. For precisely this moment, however, Jesus has warned the disciples (9:9–10), and the reader, to save the story of their having seen Jesus' meeting with Moses and Elijah.

Each Gospel in its own way teaches readers how to answer the questions, "Where is this risen Jesus you Christians proclaim? What is he doing? Can we see him?" One way Mark answers is to have readers recall Jesus' instructions about the transfiguration scene, and at the end of the Gospel recall and rehearse it. We have seen Jesus among those who have gone to be with God—with Moses, the great teacher, and with Elijah, the prophet upon whom folks in Jesus' day still called for help in times of need. Some have said that in this way Mark teaches

Pastoral Perspective

stimulation. I think of the new, growing church near the very old church I pastor; it has the technological sophistication to produce rock-concert-quality graphic displays every Sunday morning. Thousands worship there each week. I think of the added hundreds who worship with us on Easter Sunday, when our sanctuary is more visually alluring than any other Sunday of the year. In an increasingly visual culture, it is easy to think faith comes by *seeing*; but this sensory stimulation, which we easily confuse with what God intends to reveal, is often fleeting.

Similarly, the vision that Peter, James, and John are given is quickly taken away: "Then a cloud overshadowed them" (v. 7). The cloud is a powerful metaphor, an image to which most people of faith can relate. Meditating on the image of the cloud can open the door to a conversation about how, even though we long for visual stimulation, living the life of faith is more like traveling in a cloud. For many sitting in the pews, this image of the cloud will help them to name how there is significantly less clarity in their own lives of faith than one might like. If mystics like the anonymous author of the *The Cloud of Unknowing* and John of the Cross are right, we should expect the experience of being overshadowed by a cloud to be normative for the life of faith. The life of faith is a life of becoming increasingly at home with God's hiddenness.

The second dynamic is the dynamic of speaking/listening. When Moses and Elijah join Jesus, they engage in conversation. Peter, dazzled by the transfiguration and witnessing the conversation, speaks as well. However, Peter's speaking is not part of a conversation; it is an impetuous blurting out, because "he did not know what to say" (v. 6). This is not the first time Peter has done this. Only a few verses earlier (8:29) Peter declared that Jesus is the Messiah (he was technically right, but he still did not know what he was talking about), and then he rebuked Jesus for suggesting that the Son of Man will suffer and die (8:32). In this context, God's speaking from the cloud sounds like a very pointed rebuke to Peter's speaking-without-knowing: "Listen to him."

While this could be reduced to the simple and good advice that we should listen before we speak ("God gave us two ears and one mouth," as the old cliché goes), such moralizing would avoid the deeper implication. This is an invitation to examine how we fundamentally relate to God: not primarily by speaking but by listening. Furthermore, it can serve as a chastening to Christians who speak too easily for God, who assume they know what God wants for

Exegetical Perspective

when the reality of Jesus' death is coming closer. Not only does the transfiguration point forward, it also points back to the preincarnated Jesus. We see him as he will be, and we see him as he was. We see the glory that he set aside to become one of us.

Why does Jesus include his disciples in this event? Is it meant to expand their understanding of who he is? While the disciples do not want to hear what Jesus says about suffering, it is also clear that they do not hear what he says about resurrection. How could they? This mystery lies outside normal experience. Peter's response to such an extraordinary event is understandable. He has no context that can explain it.

Why does Peter address Jesus as Rabbi here (v. 5)? It is a title that appears later at another moment, when the disciples misunderstand who Jesus is and what he is doing, when Peter sees the fig tree Jesus cursed before he had rid the temple of the merchants (11:12–22). Would Peter find it easier to erect booths than to follow the man who is headed to Jerusalem and a cross?[1]

Why do Moses and Elijah appear? Unlike Luke, who tells us they are talking about Jesus' "exodus" (NRSV "departure," Luke 9:31), Mark gives no explanation for their appearance or for the content of their conversation. One interpretation is that they represent the Law and the Prophets, two great traditions in Israel's faith. Another is that both Moses and Elijah have mysterious deaths. Moses climbs Mount Nebo, sees the promised land, and dies, "but no one knows his burial place to this day" (Deut. 34:6). Elijah "ascended in a whirlwind into heaven" (2 Kgs. 2:11). Jesus' own experience with death will be yet more extraordinary. Another interpretation is that both Moses and Elijah have experienced theophanies at their own times of danger and discouragement. Moses came down from the mountain to find his people cavorting before the golden calf, then returned to the mountain and a second confrontation with God (Exod. 32:9–35). Elijah was a hunted man on the run, whose journey to the mountain brought him into the fire and storm and the "sound of sheer silence" (1 Kgs. 19:11–13).

References have already been made in Mark's Gospel to these two towering figures of Israel's faith. John the Baptist, appearing in the wilderness with his diet of locusts and his wild clothing, is a kind of Elijah figure. As giver of the law, Moses is

---

1. The irony is that if you go to the mountain identified as the place where this happened, there is a very beautiful church where the main altar is dedicated to Jesus Christ and the two side chapels are dedicated, one to Moses and the other to Elijah. Peter got his booths after all!

Homiletical Perspective

speaks to him alone; now the revelation of his identity is shared with the disciples closest to him. The narrative is full of striking visual imagery: the dazzling white clothes, the appearance of Moses and Elijah, the overshadowing cloud; yet the command is not to see but to listen. Jesus offers no new revelation on the mountain. Rather, the command to listen points back to what they have already heard and what Jesus will tell them again: the prediction of Jesus' passion and resurrection and the extended teaching on the necessity of suffering and "taking up the cross."

These passages juxtapose suffering and glory and show that both are essential parts of Jesus' identity and mission. Beverly Gaventa writes,

> What the disciples (and Mark's audience) need to understand is that Jesus is both the Son of God, powerful agent of healing and subject of dazzling glory, and the Son of Man, who will be betrayed and persecuted and crucified. The disciples, in common with many Christians throughout the church's life, want to have the glory that they can see without the message that they must hear, but the two cannot be separated.[1]

The preacher might explore ways in which Christians continue to resist the idea of a suffering Messiah and its implications for discipleship.

In a memoir, Donald Miller, a writer on Christian spirituality, describes traveling to Peru with friends to hike the Inca Trail. The trek began along a river in the Sacred Valley, and their guide pointed out that if they followed the trail that ran along the river, they would reach Machu Picchu in just six hours. In ancient times, the river was a commercial route, but those going to Machu Picchu on pilgrimage had to take the Inca Trail across the snow-covered Andes Mountains. "Why would the Incas make people take the long route?" one of the hikers asked. "Because the emperor knew," their guide answered, "the more painful the journey to Machu Picchu, the more the traveler would appreciate the city, once he got there." Four days later, after climbing summits of nearly fourteen thousand feet and descending back into the valley, Miller and his group arrived at Machu Picchu. He recalls running the last mile to the Sun Gate on blistered feet and sore legs. Weary as they were, the pilgrims knew that the guide was right: "You can take a train and then a bus, and then hike a mile to the Sun Gate. But the people who took the bus didn't

---

1. Beverly Gaventa, *Texts for Preaching Year B* (Louisville, KY: Westminster/John Knox Press, 1993), 180–81.

Mark 9:2–8

Theological Perspective

that Jesus has joined this "committee" and for the fledgling church he becomes the teacher and protector, present with the community in the same way God has for centuries made Moses and Elijah available to bring God's people gifts they need to sustain their faith and trust. Some, who could be said to veer into supersessionism, say that the eventual disappearance of Moses and Elijah at the end of the scene means Jesus has replaced them, and perhaps also the Law and the Prophets they represent.

We also find theology, albeit impoverished, in the words and actions of Peter as he and the other disciples witness this meeting of the great ones. First, Peter calls Jesus "Rabbi," the same title he will give Jesus later in Mark when he sees the accursed fig tree withered and cannot understand what has happened (11:21). The only other use of this title in Mark comes on the lips of Judas as he kisses Jesus in betrayal (14:45).

Peter's suggestion for preserving the moment serves as commentary on this respectful but pedestrian title he gives Jesus. "Let us build three dwellings [*skēnas*]," he says, "one for each of you." Commentators suggest a connection here to the Feast of Booths and humankind's penchant for reducing holy things to festive commemorations. Others point to the tabernacle of Israel's wilderness sojourn, since *skēnē* is the Septuagint's word for God's old wilderness tent. However, *skēnē* is also Isaiah's word for the heavens themselves, the curtain that envelops the world and must be rent somehow if God is to "come down" to do some moving and shaking.

Peter, like the women at the empty tomb, does not have adequate words. He too is afraid. Like subsequent generations, which also struggle to make sense of Jesus' life, death, and resurrection, Peter needs plenty of time to study what Moses and the prophets have to say about the ways God does, and does not, rend the heavens and come down.

FREDERICK NIEDNER

Pastoral Perspective

our neighbors, and who fail to recognize how much they do not know.

This word from God to people longing to be dazzled and eager to speak suggests a reorientation of both our individual lives of prayer and our congregational lives of faith by opening wonderful possibilities for reflection and conversation on the question, what does it mean for disciples today to listen to the Son? This passage does not answer that question. Rather, it creates space to consider ways of listening to God through various spiritual disciplines. For example, we might consider attending to the words of Scripture through Bible study and the practice of *lectio divina*. We might listen through means of silent prayer, like meditation or centering prayer. We might focus on God by paying attention to and offering up the shape of our own lives and desires. We might hear God's voice by listening to the voice of our neighbors.

Furthermore, reflection on this story provides an opportunity to consider the experience of an ever-increasing segment of the population that identifies itself as "spiritual but not religious." Such reflection allows one to explore forms of spiritual practice that aim at focusing attention and opening awareness (yoga, meditation), while also honoring the fundamentally christocentric focus of Christian spiritual practices. The voice from the cloud does not invite the church to listen in general, but to listen to the Son, without giving a recipe for how that is to be done. How do practices of attentiveness relate to the Christian call to be attentive to Jesus?

None of these questions has easy answers. As the cloud descends, the vision is taken away; when Peter speaks, he speaks because he does not know what to say. Listening to God—no matter what form that listening takes in practice—marks a life of faith that in humility and with patience can navigate the uncertainty that at times marks true faith.

L. ROGER OWENS

Exegetical Perspective

the authority to whom the Pharisees look. Jesus has dared to rebuke these critics, not with arguments, but by his own authority. It is ironic that the one whom the law keepers would cite against Jesus comes to affirm him in this perilous time.

While we do not know what is said between Jesus, Moses, and Elijah, we do hear the voice that affirms Jesus' own role and challenges the disciples. Echoing the voice that speaks at Jesus' baptism ("You are my Son, the Beloved," 1:11), this time the voice addresses the disciples, rather than Jesus himself. "This is my Son, the Beloved; listen to him!" (v. 7). We listen, but Jesus is silent. What is it that we are to hear? Has it already been said? If indeed this story is to be read in the light of the passion predictions, then what we are to hear is what Jesus has already said about his suffering and dying and his rising from the dead.

What do we make of the white robes? Every Gospel text has three audiences: the folk who lived it, the church for whom it was written, and the present reader. Mark's focus on suffering and dying leads us to speculate that either his church, so taken with the resurrection, was paying little attention to the suffering that had preceded it, or that Mark wishes to prepare his church for persecution and suffering. After all, in addition to warning the disciples about his own suffering, Jesus has also warned those who would be disciples that following him will mean they too must pick up their cross. They too must choose a path that may well lead to suffering. This story, set within the framework of the passion predictions, warns them, and us, that God's glory comes not by going around the dark valley, but through it.

NETA LINDSAY PRINGLE

Homiletical Perspective

experience the city as we experienced the city. The pain made the city more beautiful. The story made us different characters than we would have been if we had skipped the story and showed up at the ending an easier way."[2]

An easier way? Perhaps that is what the disciples wanted when Peter offered to build tents and stay up on that mountain. The disciples caught a glimpse of Christ's glory, a preview of the fullness to come, and perhaps all they wanted was to take the shorter route, just go ahead, and get to that glorious ending an easier way. It turns out that there is no easier way to get there—not for Jesus, not for his disciples, and not for those who follow him today.

The life of faith means taking the longer route—an often arduous journey, full of grueling climbs and treacherous valleys and sometimes stunning vistas, a journey traveled in the hopes of encountering God's glory. Along the way, there are times when we would give anything for a shorter route, to be able to take the bus around the weariness of grief, or the radiation treatments, or the couples counseling, or the 12-step meetings, or the unemployment line. We just wish there were a way to skip ahead, to show up at the ending an easier way.

When Jesus appeared in his glory on that mountaintop, he stood with Moses and Elijah, the greatest of the prophets. Tradition says that they did not die, that God raised them up to heaven before they ever tasted death. Yet Jesus, greater than these, the very Son of God, took the longer route, the one that sent him through a garden of agony, and only then to the cross.

The disciples stand on that mountaintop hoping for an easier way. They do not realize this: that even as they glimpsed God's glory on the mountaintop, God's glory will also be revealed to them in the long and painful journey. That is the mystery of God's glory. God chooses to be made known not only on mountaintops, but also in the valley of the shadow of death.

LEANNE PEARCE REED

---

2. Donald Miller: *A Million Miles in a Thousand Years: How I Learned to Live a Better Story* (Nashville: Thomas Nelson, 2009), 139–43.

Mark 9:9–13

⁹As they were coming down the mountain, he ordered them to tell no one about what they had seen, until after the Son of Man had risen from the dead. ¹⁰So they kept the matter to themselves, questioning what this rising from the dead could mean. ¹¹Then they asked him, "Why do the scribes say that Elijah must come first?" ¹²He said to them, "Elijah is indeed coming first to restore all things. How then is it written about the Son of Man, that he is to go through many sufferings and be treated with contempt? ¹³But I tell you that Elijah has come, and they did to him whatever they pleased, as it is written about him."

Theological Perspective

These few verses in Mark attest to the vast amount of theological work the early church had to do before it could tell the story of the crucified Jesus as good news and have any hope that others might understand and believe it. Both the secret that Peter, James, and John could not share until later and the question about Elijah's coming point to matters of mystery and contention that insiders and outsiders alike raised in response to the church's proclamation.

The first portion of this reading properly belongs with the immediately preceding account of the transfiguration. Verse 9 addresses Mark's readers, not merely the trio of disciples to whom Jesus explains the appropriate time for recounting what they have witnessed. When the Son of Man is raised from the dead, questions will arise that the story of the transfiguration will help answer. As if in response, the young man at the tomb in Mark 16:1–8 speaks for the whole community that declares, "Jesus has been raised. You will not find him in the tomb. If you want to see him, go to Galilee, even as he told you."

Mark's readers have no way to "go to Galilee" except to return to the beginning of the story, which begins in Galilee, and then follow Jesus through his journey. This trek takes readers through his baptism into a world where Jesus lives and behaves already as a resurrected one amid all the ills and threats

Pastoral Perspective

Once I sat with an older couple as the husband was preparing for knee-replacement surgery. Out of the blue his wife told me, "I am waiting for the sermon on the resurrection of the body. I do not understand what that means." I was momentarily confused, because I had been planning a sermon series on the Apostles' Creed but had not told anyone. How did she know I would soon be preaching on the resurrection of the body? Obviously she did not know. The resurrection was something she had long wondered about and wanted her preacher to address in a sermon. Two months after I preached on the resurrection of the body, she told me, "I am still waiting for an answer about the resurrection of the body." Apparently my sermon raised more questions than it gave answers.

The three unanswered questions in this passage from Mark's Gospel suggest that our failure to answer questions and our inclination to raise questions about the resurrection are faithful responses to Scripture.

Peter, James, and John ask the first question among themselves. Walking down the mountain after the transfiguration, Jesus tells them not to tell anyone what happened until "after the Son of Man had risen from the dead" (v. 9). This perplexes the disciples, but they do not question him about it: "They kept the matter to themselves, questioning

Exegetical Perspective

This text serves the practical purpose of getting Jesus, Peter, James, and John down from the mountain and on to the problem facing the disciples who have stayed below, namely, that of the boy filled with a spirit that makes him unable to speak or hear. In addition, it is the locus of some important theological reflection on the transfiguration that took place on the mountain. What the three disciples have seen there continues to dominate the discussion. What are they to do with what has happened? "Tell no one," says Jesus. How many other times has he given that instruction to his disciples? The leper cleansed of his disease is told to tell no one (1:44), as are those who witness the healing of the deaf man with a speech impediment whom Jesus and his disciples meet in the Decapolis (7:36). When the young daughter of Jairus wakes from death, "He strictly ordered them that no one should know" (5:43). When Peter confesses, "You are the Messiah," he is sternly ordered not to tell anyone (8:29–30). Now, after the deep mystery of the transfiguration, the disciples are again told not to tell—at least not now. Why?

Each of these "do not tell" events points to Jesus as someone with extraordinary power who is able to do what others cannot. That Peter's confession of Jesus as Messiah is immediately followed by predictions of his suffering and death would indicate that

Homiletical Perspective

This passage depicts the conversation between Jesus and his inner circle of disciples on their way down the mountain following the transfiguration (9:2–8). It serves as a transition from mountaintop glory to on-the-ground ministry, it demonstrates the disciples' continued confusion, and it helps interpret the extraordinary event they had just witnessed. In order to understand this brief passage, listeners must be oriented to its context, particularly the preceding transfiguration account.

The preacher might provide the needed context and explore the misunderstanding of the disciples by inviting listeners to imagine the memories and questions that troubled the disciples as they made their way down the mountain. Perhaps the disciples recalled how they left behind their work and their homes to follow Jesus. Maybe they remembered the dramatic scenes of healing they had witnessed as Jesus cast out demons, healed leprosy, gave sight to the blind, and even restored a young girl to life. Perhaps they thought back to the crowds that flocked around Jesus, his puzzling teachings on the kingdom of God, the way even the storms and the waves obeyed his command.

When Jesus called, they had followed; yet no matter how hard they tried to keep up, Jesus was always ahead of them. They never quite understood what he

Mark 9:9–13

Theological Perspective

that only those who already have death behind them need not fear. Jesus touches the unclean, but instead of becoming unclean, everything around him becomes clean (e.g., 5:1–43). He walks on water, and just as in Luke's and John's postresurrection appearance stories, disciples can look right at Jesus and not recognize him (6:47–56). Where is the risen Jesus? He remains unrecognized and at large, loose with his healing powers in a world overrun with threats against life and wholeness.

The saved-for-later story of the mountaintop meeting also serves as part of Mark's answer to the question of Jesus' post-empty-tomb whereabouts. In one of those rare moments when humankind is granted a glimpse of what lies beyond the boundaries of space and time, we have seen Jesus in the company of Moses and Elijah, who dwell somewhere beyond the curtain of the heavens and still serve God. Luke, John, the letter to the Ephesians, and eventually the creeds of the church borrow the language of Elijah's story and say Jesus "ascended" or "was taken up" (Luke 24:51; John 20:17; Eph. 4:10),but it may be that the theological groundwork for such talk is found in Mark.

Skeptics inside and outside the church also wanted to know how to answer the argument that Jesus could not have been the Messiah of Israel, because Elijah had not yet come to prepare Israel for such a moment. The widely known tradition that underlies this assertion appears in the last chapter of Malachi (Mal. 4:5–6). There the prophet foresees a day when the Lord will scorch the earth and whatever arrogant evildoers walk on it. In that day, those who revere God will tread upon the wicked and walk on the ashes of the incinerated. To get the faithful ready for such a day, the prophet reminds them to study the precepts of Moses and look for the coming of Elijah, whose teaching will work repentance among God's people.

"Why do the scribes say Elijah must come first?" Because they have read Malachi. Much earlier in the story, Mark has let readers know that Elijah has come to prepare the way by preaching repentance, and John the Baptist, he of the camel-hair coat, leather belt, and diet of locusts and wild honey (Mark 1:4–7 and 2 Kgs. 1:8), is Elijah redivivus.

Jesus' response to the disciples' question is more complex than necessary. He asks his own question about a writing that predicts the suffering of the Son of Man, and then compares that figure's treatment with the newly appeared Elijah, aka John the Baptist. Commentators universally agree on the difficulty of

Pastoral Perspective

what this rising from the dead could mean" (v. 10). Long after the resurrection of Jesus, people are still asking this same question. For some, the answer is no clearer now than it was to the three disciples.

The disciples' question about the meaning of the resurrection is at the very heart of the Christian faith. Was it fear that kept them from asking Jesus about his rising? Specifically, were they afraid to voice their doubts? Do our own doubts keep us from openly asking our questions about matters at the heart of the Christian faith, because we are afraid we will lose our faith? Have we internalized the unspoken message that questioning these matters is out of bounds?

Mark's report of the disciples questioning among themselves also gives preachers and teachers permission *not* to "answer" the deep questions at the heart of the Christian mystery. Rather, they may make room for perplexity and assure people that questions need not be asked on the fringes of church life. In fact, questions sometimes belong at the center of our faith. We proclaim boldly that God raised Jesus from the dead; we can also create the space for people to ask, without fear of reproach, what this could possibly mean.

Perhaps it is the belief that only certain questions belong that leads us to notice the second kind of question in this passage, the one the disciples *are* willing to ask, namely, a question of interpretation: "Why do the scribes say that Elijah must come first?" (v. 11). Too much focus on the *content* of this question can distract from a more significant conversation about the *kind* of question it is. Compared to the first question about the resurrection, this question is safe. It reminds me of a Bible study I led once where the members loved to bombard me with questions about details in the Bible: Why does it say this? What does this mean? Did Adam really live 930 years? How long did Noah and the animals stay on the ark? Instead of these safe questions, I longed for them to risk asking the substantive questions that engaged their lives, questions like "What is this passage saying to me?" and "How should this text shape my life?"

Why do people ask the questions they do of Scripture? What questions are they allowed to ask, and what questions are they encouraged to dare? As preachers and teachers we would do well to ask ourselves: Do our sermons and lessons open possibilities for genuine questions to be asked in the face of the Christian mystery? Do we preach and teach in ways that drive inquiry out to the margins of church life, signaling that certain questions do not belong?

Exegetical Perspective

the extraordinary events witnessed by the disciples need to be understood in the light of what is yet to come: Jesus' own death and resurrection. After that, the disciples can "tell." Until that time it is clear the disciples are at a loss to understand. What does rising from the dead mean? They will not know until it happens, and even then it will instill terror in them.

Jesus commands the disciples to keep silent about his messiahship, but even more significantly, he does not use that term to describe himself. Instead, he uses the title "Son of Man," often substituting it for the first-person pronoun. Used in various ways throughout the Old Testament, Son of Man did not carry the same political and institutional weight as did Messiah (or the Greek translation, *Christos*). Jesus himself, however, has earlier referred to the Son of Man coming "in the glory of his Father with the holy angels" (8:38) and will later use it to describe "coming in clouds with great power and glory" (13:26).

This points Mark's readers back to Daniel's vision of the Son of Man in dazzling white robes who comes forth from the very throne of God to be given power over the beastly and destructive empires that have for so long ruled the world (Dan. 7). The book of *Enoch*, written around 70 BCE, is part of the intertestamental literature that perhaps was known to many of Jesus' listeners. It develops Daniel's Son of Man into a figure who is both superhuman and divine. In *1 Enoch* 46:1-2 we see an apocalyptic Son of Man who will destroy the enemies of God and the enemies of the people of God:

> There I beheld the Ancient of Days whose head was like white wool, and with him another, whose countenance resembled that of a man. His countenance was full of grace, like that of one of the holy angels. Then I inquired of one of the angels, who went with me, and who showed me every secret thing, concerning this Son of Man; who he was; whence he was; and why he accompanied the Ancient of Days. He answered and said to me, This is the Son of Man, to whom righteousness belongs; with whom righteousness has dwelt; and who will reveal all the treasures of that which is concealed: for the Lord of spirits has chosen him; and his portion has surpassed all before the Lord of spirits in everlasting uprightness.

Jesus addresses the disciples' puzzlement about the events on the mountain with Son of Man references. If the disciples have any familiarity with the visions of Daniel or of *Enoch*, the shining white robes, the presence of the two heroic figures of Israel's past,

Homiletical Perspective

was doing or what he meant or even who he really was. Just six days earlier, Jesus had finally put the question to them directly: "Who do you say that I am?" Only Peter was bold enough to answer: "You are the Messiah" (8:29). Just when they thought they were beginning to understand, Jesus dismayed them with talk of suffering and death and rising again (8:31). This was not the Messiah they had expected. Surely, as they walked down that mountain, the disciples pondered their astonishing and terrifying experience on the mountaintop—the way Jesus' clothes became dazzling white, the appearance of Moses and Elijah, the cloud that overcame them, and the voice that commanded, "This is my Son, the beloved; listen to him!" (9:7). Perhaps the disciples, more confused than ever, wished that Jesus could give them understanding as easily as he gave sight to the blind.

While the baffled disciples walked down the mountain with Jesus, he commanded them to keep silence about the glorious vision they had just experienced. The true nature of Jesus' identity, kept secret until this point in the Gospel, must remain a secret a while longer. For the first time, Jesus explained that his true identity may be shared only after his death and resurrection. Now the reason for silence became clear: the glory manifest on the mountaintop does not reveal the full identity of Jesus. His glory and his suffering could not be separated; the glory of the mountaintop must be understood in light of his suffering, death, and resurrection to come.

Jesus' imminent suffering was foreshadowed in the fate of the great prophet Elijah. As they tried to make sense of all they had seen and heard, the disciples asked Jesus, "Why do the scribes say that Elijah must come first?" Jesus told them, "Elijah has come, and they did to him whatever they pleased." Jesus seemed to speak of John the Baptist, who preached and baptized in the Jordan (1:3-8) and was later imprisoned and executed, with his head served on a platter at Herod's banquet (6:17-29). The return of Elijah in the person of John the Baptist served to fulfill the prophetic expectations of Scripture, such as Malachi 4:5. More importantly, the suffering and death of John the Baptist anticipated the fate of the Messiah. Lamar Williamson writes,

> Reflection on the fate of John the Baptist should help disciples to understand that the suffering and death of Jesus as Christ, Son of God, and Son of man is in accord with the will of God. Reflection on the transfiguration of Jesus in light of his death and resurrection should enable disciples to accept

Mark 9:9–13

Theological Perspective

interpreting Jesus' words here. To what writing about the Son of Man might Jesus refer? Where does any text inside or outside the canon say the newly come Elijah will meet with contempt or abuse?

While these questions may go unanswered, it seems obvious that Mark's Gospel, like the other Gospels, finds the meaning of Jesus' life and death partly in the ancient stories of Israel. Accounts of the miraculous feedings in Mark 6 and 8, for example, recall the Torah's stories of manna in the wilderness and show God acting once again in a well-known pattern.

The only "son of man" in the Bible who suffers abuse and contempt is one whose name in Hebrew would be *abel ben adam*: Abel, son of Man, the first martyr, or at least the first to die amid bitterness over who enjoyed God's favor and who did not (Gen. 4:1–16). By juxtaposing Elijah and the Son of Man as figures destined for suffering and contempt, Mark's Gospel offers a hint about a piece of Scripture the church might see occurring again, not only in Jesus' life, but also in their own.

Into the mix of images helpful for understanding Jesus' story, insert the very first Son of Man, come again to walk among humankind. Then picture him as the one who will come to judge the world. Jesus promises those who judge and condemn him that they will see this judge in session (14:62). Chances are, however, they did not recognize the judge on his rough-hewn bench, the cross.

Jesus, like Abel, seems to have lived only to die. The same fate has befallen Mark's first readers, presuming they are Christians of Nero's Rome after the debacle of 64 CE. In the chaos of that time, their lives made no sense—unless, of course, they could find the meaning somehow in the ancient patterns of God's dealings with humankind. They would go the way of the Son of Man, to the cross, where they would, like their Lord, hang as silent judges of the world that treats kindness and inclusion with contempt. As we witness one day on the holy mountain, however, that will not be the end of the story.

FREDERICK NIEDNER

Pastoral Perspective

Are we personally willing to ask the questions at the heart of the Christian mystery that shapes our Christian existence? Do we avoid those more threatening questions in favor of safe questions? The types of questions permitted in the life of a congregation are a pastoral concern.

Jesus' answer is enigmatic at best. Again, although it is worth exploring exegetically what his answer means, it is just as significant to notice the form his answer takes, because in his answer to their question we find this passage's third question. Jesus himself asks the disciples, if Elijah is coming to restore all things, how is the Son of Man's suffering possible? (v. 12). He does not answer this question for them; instead, implicit in his question of the disciples is the question most often asked in churches, the question of suffering. If all things are being restored, how could there be suffering in general, and the Son of Man's suffering in particular?

The key pastoral point is that the question is *not* answered. Jesus does not answer it, which suggests that perhaps neither should we. If Jesus asks a deep and perplexing question like this, then in his questioning there is surely an invitation for us to ask such questions without fear of reproach.

The questions asked in this passage of Mark's Gospel, a passage that is rich in teaching about discipleship, remind us that faithfulness to Christ does not mean getting answers to all of our questions and having our faith neatly figured out intellectually. If there are answers to be discovered—and for some questions there may not be answers—we discover them as we become participants with Jesus on this journey to the cross, a journey that leads us to wrestle with the meaning of his rising again. The questions of Mark's Jesus invite us to be open and willing to ask risky questions about what his suffering and his rising again could possibly mean for us in the context of our lives and at the hour of our death.

L. ROGER OWENS

Exegetical Perspective

the sense of having broken through the boundaries between heaven and earth all contribute to their seeing Jesus in that light. Here, in the face of opposition from leaders of his own people and from Rome, Jesus claims to be the one to whom God has given the kingdoms of the earth. He claims power over the very forces that would destroy him. The defendant in the court of Rome will become the judge in the heavenly court. The very use of Son of Man becomes a message of hope in the face of despair.

Mark has told us that Elijah appeared on the mountain "with Moses." His wording is different from that of Matthew and Luke, who both use the wording "Moses and Elijah." As Jesus and the disciples come down from the mountain, in Mark Moses disappears from the conversation, but Elijah continues to be a topic of interest. The prophet Malachi ends with the warning that his listeners remember the teaching of Moses, but that Elijah himself will come to bring a day of judgment (Mal. 4:4–6). When the disciples ask, "If we are to expect the Messiah, what about Elijah? Isn't he to come first?" (v. 11), they are drawing on that tradition. Jesus replies that Elijah has indeed come. With his rough clothes, his diet of locusts, and his words of judgment, John lives out the Elijah role. In glaring contrast to the disciples' expectations of triumph, Jesus reminds them that despite John's status as Elijah, he was put to death by Herod and that the same fate awaits Jesus himself.

NETA LINDSAY PRINGLE

Homiletical Perspective

the path of suffering as the way of true glory for Jesus, and for themselves as well.[1]

Discipleship, then, invites followers to participate in the suffering of the Son of Man, or as Jesus put it, to "take up their cross and follow me" (8:34).

Like the first disciples, listeners today may find this kind of discipleship difficult to embrace. Peddlers of prosperity theology teach that those who follow Jesus will be richly rewarded in this lifetime. They suggest that God will bestow professional success, financial reward, and even lucrative real-estate deals on the faithful believer. This passage offers quite a different perspective on discipleship. Here Jesus did not promise that followers would receive "the good life" as a sign of God's favor. Instead, he described how those who come in God's name would meet with suffering. When Elijah returned in the person of John the Baptist, he was not showered with praise and privilege; "they did to him whatever they pleased" (v. 13). In the same way, the Son of Man "is to go through many sufferings and be treated with contempt" (v. 12). As Eduard Schweizer points out, "No reason for the suffering is given which might make it easier to endure; no, there is only the statement that the suffering is imposed by God and is necessary, as was the fate of John the Baptist-Elijah."[2]

This challenging teaching also offers comfort. It reminds listeners that suffering does not indicate the absence of God, for the most faithful servants face suffering. It reassures them that the Son of Man who suffers with them is also the Son of God who reigns in glory. The disciples got a brief glimpse of this glory on the mountaintop; Jesus' post-Easter followers know the glory of the resurrection. The knowledge of the resurrection and the promise it contains may sustain believers through times of suffering. Suffering may be part of the story, but it is not the final word.

LEANNE PEARCE REED

---

1. Lamar A. Williamson, *Mark*, Interpretation series (Atlanta: John Knox Press, 1983), 161.
2. Eduard Schweizer, *The Good News according to Mark*, trans. Donald H. Madvig (Atlanta: John Knox Press, 1970), 186.

Mark 9:14–29

¹⁴When they came to the disciples, they saw a great crowd around them, and some scribes arguing with them. ¹⁵When the whole crowd saw him, they were immediately overcome with awe, and they ran forward to greet him. ¹⁶He asked them, "What are you arguing about with them?" ¹⁷Someone from the crowd answered him, "Teacher, I brought you my son; he has a spirit that makes him unable to speak; ¹⁸and whenever it seizes him, it dashes him down; and he foams and grinds his teeth and becomes rigid; and I asked your disciples to cast it out, but they could not do so." ¹⁹He answered them, "You faithless generation, how much longer must I be among you? How much longer must I put up with you? Bring him to me." ²⁰And they brought the boy to him. When the spirit saw him, immediately it convulsed the boy, and he fell on the ground and rolled about, foaming at the mouth. ²¹Jesus asked the father, "How long has this been

Theological Perspective

At first glance, the element of the human condition this story diagnoses is susceptibility to such things as epileptic seizures. These mysterious "powers" dash us to the ground or, as the father's description in this story says literally, they "break us in pieces." They keep us from living productive lives.

A second look reveals a deeper malady, namely, a lack of faith. Mark's often prickly Jesus, sounding here like an angry prophet of old, upbraids the disciples, who could not help the epileptic boy. He accuses them of faithlessness. Jesus then proceeds to mock whatever tentative faith the boy's father might have in Jesus' potential as one who might heal the child.

Elsewhere, Mark's Gospel teaches that in the absence of faith, the suffering receive no healing. They may find their symptoms relieved, as did the faithless people of Jesus' hometown; but there, because of their unbelief, Jesus could do no actual deeds of power (6:1–6). Genuine healing, as described by Mark with forms of the Greek verb *sōzō* (also the word for saving and being saved), comes only in the presence of faith (2:5; 5:34; 10:52).

In this instance, despite Jesus' rebukes concerning the community's obvious faithlessness, the boy receives healing. What accounts for this? The answer appears in the last verses of this episode. When Jesus and the disciples are alone and the disciples ask why

Pastoral Perspective

The situation that Jesus, Peter, James, and John discover when they return from their trip up the mountain is dramatically rich: argument, conflict, frustration, hope, fear. Because this situation is not unlike our own lives, this scene is pastorally prolific as well. By paying special attention to the role the central characters play in the drama, we will see the potential for this passage to speak to people's lives today.

We begin with the disciples. The disciples are in the middle of a dispute with some scribes. A crowd has gathered. Apparently the argument is about why the disciples could not cast the spirit out of a child. When Jesus learns the details of the situation, he rebukes his disciples, along with the rest, for their failure in the middle of this complicated situation. Certainly disciples of Jesus today can relate to the disciples then and their sense of failure.

For years I have been involved with a ministry in my community that pairs people coming out of prison with care teams made up of church members. The purpose is to support and encourage the ex-convicts as they try to reenter society and become productive citizens again. In one case, a man was arrested several times while a care team worked with him. Finally, he was sent to prison again, too far away for the team to visit him. I remember the despair of one care partner, who through tears

happening to him?" And he said, "From childhood. ²²It has often cast him into the fire and into the water, to destroy him; but if you are able to do anything, have pity on us and help us." ²³Jesus said to him, "If you are able!—All things can be done for the one who believes." ²⁴Immediately the father of the child cried out, "I believe; help my unbelief!" ²⁵When Jesus saw that a crowd came running together, he rebuked the unclean spirit, saying to it, "You spirit that keeps this boy from speaking and hearing, I command you, come out of him, and never enter him again!" ²⁶After crying out and convulsing him terribly, it came out, and the boy was like a corpse, so that most of them said, "He is dead." ²⁷But Jesus took him by the hand and lifted him up, and he was able to stand. ²⁸When he had entered the house, his disciples asked him privately, "Why could we not cast it out?" ²⁹He said to them, "This kind can come out only through prayer."

Exegetical Perspective

As Jesus, Peter, James, and John descend from the mountain where these three disciples have witnessed Jesus' transfiguration, they are greeted by the other disciples and a crowd of onlookers. Some sort of argument has been going on with the scribes; however, we are not told just what it is. Neither are we told what it is that inspires them with awe as they rush to meet Jesus. Does some of the glory from that earlier experience cling to him?

Jesus plunges into the controversy with the scribes: "What are you arguing about?" (v. 16). Before anyone can answer, the father of a troubled boy breaks in. His son is in need of healing and the disciples are incapable of dealing with it.

Our temptation at this point is to look for a twenty-first-century medical diagnosis. It rather sounds as if the boy is epileptic. However, that is not the issue for Jesus. While Jesus in no way negated human responsibility for our own lives, he certainly understood that one goal of his ministry was to free humanity from the grip of evil. "Jesus regards his healings and exorcisms as an assault on the kingdom of Satan and an indication that the kingdom of God is breaking in. The gospel is very much a cosmic battle in which Jesus rescues humanity from the dominion of evil powers."[1]

[1]. Walter Wink, *Naming the Powers, the Language of Power in the New Testament* (Philadelphia: Fortress Press, 1984), 27.

Homiletical Perspective

At the beginning of his ministry in the Gospel of Mark, Jesus proclaims, "Repent, and believe in the good news" (1:15). This story gives insight into the nature of belief in a life of discipleship. The passage immediately follows the account of the transfiguration of Jesus and offers a striking contrast. On the mountaintop, Peter, James, and John experience the power and glory of Jesus. Down the mountain, Jesus confronts the powerlessness and frustration of his disciples. A father comes to them seeking help for his son, who has experienced life-threatening seizures since his childhood. The preacher may want to orient listeners to the first-century understanding of illness reflected in the text. While many readers today interpret the boy's symptoms as signs of epilepsy, this word is never used in the passage. From the viewpoint of the text, the boy is the victim of a hostile spiritual force. This spirit is beyond the control of the disciples, who fail to cast it out and heal the boy.

The father then turns to Jesus for help. When Jesus tells him, "All things can be done for the one who believes," the father cries out, "I believe; help my unbelief!" (vv. 23–24). His plea, one of the most famous lines in Scripture, will be familiar to many listeners, even if they are not aware of its origin. Many will share the father's perspective. From first-time visitors to longtime church members,

Mark 9:14–29

Theological Perspective

their ministrations had failed, Jesus does not repeat his charge that their lack of faith rendered them powerless. Rather, he says, "This kind can come out only through prayer" (v. 29).

So whose prayer succeeded in casting out the debilitating spirit in this story? Mark does not describe Jesus as praying. Instead, Jesus screams at the spirit in the same rough language he used on the wind when the frightened, faithless disciples woke Jesus from his nap amid the life-threatening storm on the Sea of Galilee (4:37–41).

The prayer in this story comes on the lips of the stricken boy's father, who prays for faith in words that Mark's readers of every generation have used in their own paradoxical moments of simultaneously believing and not believing: "I believe; help my unbelief." Whatever faith this man needs, for himself or for his son, comes not from the depths of his own being, but from the God who answers prayers like this and who gives faith and trust to frightened souls and doubting hearts.

This story does not teach that if one has enough faith, one can cure epilepsy. The story does not claim that those with enough faith will never have a debilitating condition in the first place, or if they do, they can will it away themselves. Rather, it teaches that people are safe, and saved, in the company of those who throw themselves on God's compassion. This is where the father put himself and his son with his half-believing prayer, which actually began a few lines earlier: "If you are able to do anything, have pity on us and help us" (v. 22). At this point readers familiar with the New Testament easily enough hear Paul's comforting promise to the Romans: "In our weakness, . . . we do not know how to pray as we ought, but [the] . . . Spirit intercedes with sighs too deep for words" (Rom. 8:26).

Even when we do know how to pray, and even when we pray confidently, often enough the one for whom we pray does not recover from illness or injury. Every veteran of the "prayer chain" phenomenon today can tell stories of those who perished despite the prayers of hundreds, even thousands, of petitioners banging on God's door. No cure was granted, not even temporary relief, in some cases. Was there no healing of the kind Jesus seems to guarantee the faithful? Does healing, if not a cure, come perhaps when one dies not alone, but in the arms of hundreds, or thousands, whose acts of praying carry one faithfully through the valley of the shadow of death?

Later in Mark's Gospel, a troubling spirit will throw Jesus, sorrowful even to death, to the ground,

Pastoral Perspective

announced that the team had failed. I imagine this scene is repeated in church after church: disciples facing difficult situations discover that they do not have the power to effect the changes they had hoped to make.

This pericope in Mark provides the opportunity to consider failure and to ask: What does it mean to succeed? What does it mean to fail? When Jesus calls the disciples, the crowd and the scribes a "faithless generation" (v. 19), is this reproach a judgment on the failure of the disciples to cast the spirit out of the child? Since the crowds and scribes are clearly included in the denunciation, is it possible that Jesus is not rebuking the disciples for their failure, but rather reprimanding the whole lot of them for their arguing? Perhaps Jesus' chastisement is not a rebuke of their failure per se but of their faithless and divisive response to failure.

If the disciples provide an opportunity for us to explore the place of failure in the Christian life, the response of the father allows us to explore the interplay of faith and doubt, belief and unbelief. While it is nice to imagine that we ourselves are full of faith, and that our churches are filled with people who never experience doubt, the reality is that most of us have the tentative faith of this father. Our faith begins with "if." Yet this father is celebrated for acknowledging the admixture of belief and doubt in his own life. Standing in front of Jesus, with his own child suffering from possession by a spirit, this man is willing to announce both his belief and unbelief all at once, comingled.

How, we might ask, does the church relate to this father? "I believe; help my unbelief!" (9:24): is this bold declaration a response to the sense of failure and powerlessness experienced by the disciples earlier? Comparing and contrasting the failure of the disciples with the belief/unbelief of the father could prompt a discussion of the freighted relationship between faith and healing.

Finally, we come to the child. This child's possession, in many ways, reflects the difficult situations and evil circumstances faced by disciples of Jesus, who long to make a difference. His circumstance also invites us to consider the many injustices and oppressions people face in our communities and around the globe. Symbolically, the child's suffering could stand for other forms of injustice and oppression, and so remind us to pay particular attention to the varied injustices that affect children disproportionately: hunger, war, discrimination, modern-day slavery, sexual exploitation.

Exegetical Perspective

Although this text is often read through the lens of the transfiguration event—Jesus coming down from the spiritual high of the mountain into the needs of ordinary human life—an alternative reading sees this text in the light of Jesus' confrontation with the power of evil. It is a battle that we find throughout Mark. The confrontation begins with Jesus' time in the wilderness. Mark's description, unlike the extensive stories of Matthew and Luke (Matt. 4:1–11 and Luke 4:1–13), is brief and does not identify the nature of the temptations. Mark simply tells us that following his baptism, the Holy Spirit drives Jesus out into the wilderness, where he is tempted by Satan and lives among the wild beasts—both a literal and a figurative description (1:12–13). Returning from the wilderness, Jesus calls his first disciples, goes into the synagogue in Capernaum, and immediately performs an exorcism. The unclean spirit in the man in the synagogue is the first one to recognize Jesus as the Holy One of God, and cries out, "Have you come to destroy us?" (1:21–28).

The battle is joined and continues throughout his ministry. In yet another confrontation with the scribes, Jesus' answer to their accusation is to ask if he is able to cast out demons because he himself is possessed by Satan. That, he tells them, makes no sense: "No one can enter a strong man's house and plunder his property without first tying up the strong man" (3:27). A related event in this battle with evil occurs in 4:35–41, where the word Jesus uses to calm the storm is *epetimēsen*, "be muzzled" (4:39). It is the same word he uses to exorcise demons, although in the next scene the demons are of the sea.[2] Having crossed the sea, Jesus releases the Gerasene demoniac from the power of the evil spirits that have destroyed his life (5:1–20). In Mark's next chapter, when the disciples are sent out two by two, Jesus gives them authority over the unclean spirits (6:7). Like Jesus, they are empowered to plunder Satan's house even as he does. Throughout his Gospel, Mark shows that part of Jesus' mission is to bind evil in its many forms. The healing of a troubled boy in this text is the last of several such challenges.

Although earlier the disciples were given the power to drive out evil spirits, and were successful in their ability to do so (6:6–13), at this point they are powerless to drive out this particular spirit. Jesus loses patience with them: "How much longer do I have to put up with you?" (v. 19).

---

2. William Barclay, *The Gospel of Mark* (Philadelphia: Westminster Press, 1976), 27.

Homiletical Perspective

the preacher will face listeners who grapple with questions of belief and doubt. These listeners may question what they must believe to call themselves Christian or to join a particular church. They may feel guilty for experiencing times of doubt. They may wonder if it is okay to say a creed in worship if they are not certain of every word.

This text provides an opportunity to assure such listeners that they are not alone in their questions. The father's poignant cry, "I believe; help my unbelief!" has resonated through the centuries with those who struggle with their faith. John Calvin wrote, "These two statements may appear to contradict each other, but there is none of us that does not experience both of them in himself."[1] The father experiences belief and unbelief together, and both are manifest in his actions. He brings his son to Jesus, but only in desperation after all other options have failed. He asks for healing, but hedges his request with "if you are able."

Perfect faith is not required. The father does not permit his doubt to paralyze him. Instead, he moves closer to Jesus. He acknowledges the limits of his own power and asks Jesus to do the rest. Jesus responds with compassion. Jesus may have rebuked the disciples and crowd, calling them a "faithless generation" (v. 19), but he has no harsh words for the father. As William Placher observes, "In our story, Jesus does not say to the father, 'Well, you'll have to try harder.' The father having begged for faith, Jesus simply cures his son. So we take our fragile, half-broken faith to God, and in God's grace it suffices."[2]

The portrait of the faith of this father invites listeners to a richer understanding of belief. In contemporary Christianity, belief is often understood as intellectual assent to a set of doctrines. In this story, however, the question is not whether the father can affirm a specific creed or statement, or whether he follows a particular faith community. In this story, belief is portrayed as a matter of trust: trust in the power of God to transform situations that are hopeless by human standards.

How do followers cultivate this kind of faith? According to Mark, the answer is prayer. When Jesus' disciples question him privately about the reason for their failure to cast out the spirit, he explains, "This kind can come out only through prayer" (v. 29). Indeed, the father's plea to Jesus for healing

---

1. John Calvin, *Commentary on a Harmony of the Evangelists, Matthew, Mark, and Luke*, trans. William Pringle (Edinburgh: Calvin Translation Society, 1845), 2:325.
2. William Placher, *Mark*, Belief, a Theological Commentary on the Bible (Louisville, KY: Westminster John Knox Press, 2010), 133.

Mark 9:14–29

Theological Perspective

and Jesus will pray much as the epileptic boy's father did. Jesus will ask to have some other fate than the one that seems nearly certain, now that a traitor has done his work, but he will take whatever fate, drink whatever cup, the Father wills (14:32–36). An evening and a morning later, when all the thrashing about has ended in Jerusalem, Jesus lies dead, but God raises him.

In Mark 9, this is precisely what happens to the boy. After the prayer that finally saves him from the convulsing spirit, the boy lies on the ground like a corpse. "He is dead," say the bystanders. Then, in words reminiscent of several earlier "raisings" in Mark, Jesus takes the boy by the hand, raises him, and the boy stands (cf. 1:31; 5:41).

This two-stage sequence, seen also in the story of the blind man in 8:22–26, does more than foreshadow Jesus' own fate in the story. It also teaches something about the theology of healing. The first stage involves the end of presenting symptoms—blindness in the earlier story, convulsions in this one—but the sufferer has not yet become whole. The blind man's sight remains confused. The boy with seizures cannot yet stand. However, Jesus is not yet finished with those whom he heals. He sticks close to them, and through his faithfulness to them performs a second, less immediately obvious act of healing.

The healing that Jesus works becomes complete on the cross. In the way Jesus dies, the centurion will finally see what no one else could see, and he at last will pronounce Jesus "Son of God" (15:39). When Jesus lies dead as the boy, then God will raise him—and the boy. Together they will stand. You will see them in Galilee, even as he told you.

FREDERICK NIEDNER

Pastoral Perspective

Significantly, the phrase "Jesus took him by the hand and lifted him up, and he was able to stand" (v. 27) points to the shape of the church's engagement with these issues. First, if at all possible, such engagement should not be at a distance. If the church lives as the continuation of the incarnation, the body of Christ on earth, then it will not keep safe distances from injustice by only making pronouncements, signing petitions, and lobbying for legislation. The church will take victims by the hand and build relationships. Might it be that the failure to do this—the failure to touch the child—was the beginning of the disciples' inability to cast out the spirit?

The end result of Jesus' intervention is that the child is "able to stand." This beautiful, affirming phrase might give us an imagination for the effect of God working through our own working for justice: that the oppressed might be freed to stand on their own, no longer bound, but neither dependent on systems of charity. The outcome is the full freedom and dignity of God's children.

At the end Jesus tells the disciples that this kind of evil can be cast out only by prayer. He does not tell them to use a specific prayer, nor does he offer them a formula. His own habit of prayer in Mark's Gospel is to withdraw and spend time alone with the one he calls Father. Jesus' own practice is a reminder to his disciples today and to the church that there is no easy formula for facing evil and injustice. However, the people who can walk into situations like this—situations of chaos, oppression, despair—and have a salutary influence, are those whose lives are shaped by prayer, by their participation in the conversation between Jesus and the one he called Father in the Spirit.

L. ROGER OWENS

Exegetical Perspective

The ability to drive out the evil spirit is connected with the ability to believe. The Greek word is *pisteuō* (v. 23), here translated as "believe" but also sometimes translated as "have faith." Rather than a concern for knowledge, the word has to do with relationship, specifically the relationship between human beings and God. To borrow a phrase from Kathleen Norris, the question is, where do we give our heart?[3] To believe is to have confidence in God's ability to act. Jesus has a relationship with God that gives him the power to drive out the spirit. By contrast, the disciples do not. Perhaps because of their earlier success, they think that they do have confidence in God; their inability to heal the boy bears witness that they do not. When Jesus says that such things are possible only by prayer, he is telling them that to pray is to trust that God is capable of effecting change.

In verse 28 there is a change of scene. Jesus leaves the crowd that has met him in the out-of-doors. Now he and his disciples are "in the house," a location that Mark employs for private discussions with those who are already followers and, by implication, with those who are in the house of the church.

As the evil spirit departs, the boy seems to be dead. Jesus knows better and lifts him up to life. Is this a hint of the soon-to-come death and resurrection of Jesus? The related events of the transfiguration and this healing are sandwiched between two predictions of Jesus' own suffering, death, and resurrection. Because Mark is very careful in the way he arranges his material, we are led to see the connection; however, there will be a significant difference between the recovery of this boy, who will certainly die again, and the resurrection of Jesus, which will defy the power of death.

NETA LINDSAY PRINGLE

Homiletical Perspective

is much like a prayer. Of course, Jesus' response to the disciples does not mean that if only they had remembered to pray first, then they could have expelled the demon. Prayer does not function as a magic formula, always yielding the desired result.

In exploring the connection between faith and prayer, the preacher will need to be attentive to how this passage may be heard by listeners experiencing illness themselves or facing the illness of a loved one. How will it be heard by those who have prayed mightily for healing, and yet healing has not occurred? Some listeners may hear Jesus' statement, "All things can be done for the one who believes," and infer that unanswered prayers must result from lack of faith. Jesus says all things "can be done" (v. 23), but listeners know that, for inscrutable reasons, all things are not done. Sometimes healing does not occur. Sometimes prayers seem to go unanswered.

The difficult reality is that belief, no matter how strong, and prayer, no matter how fervent, do not guarantee a particular outcome. Even Jesus experienced a prayer that was not answered, at least the way he prayed it, when he asked in the Garden of Gethsemane for the cup to be taken from him (14:35). Rather, prayer points us back to the God who is the source of all power and all healing. Prayer is an expression of faith, giving voice to our dependence on God and our need for God. In prayer, we cease looking at ourselves and look instead to God. In this, the father proves himself a model of faithful discipleship, and his story brings good news to those who struggle to believe: faltering, fumbling faith is enough, for God carries us the rest of the way.

LEANNE PEARCE REED

---

3. Kathleen Norris, *Amazing Grace, A Vocabulary of Faith* (New York: Riverhead Books, Penguin Putnam, 1998), 62.

Mark 9:30–32

³⁰They went on from there and passed through Galilee. He did not want anyone to know it; ³¹for he was teaching his disciples, saying to them, "The Son of Man is to be betrayed into human hands, and they will kill him, and three days after being killed, he will rise again." ³²But they did not understand what he was saying and were afraid to ask him.

Theological Perspective

We live in an age in which people want to know what the future holds for their world and for their lives. One popular cultural meme in 2012 surrounded the Mayan calendar. According to some, the world was supposed to end that year. Most of us were not worried, however, as we did not have confidence in a media-induced crisis. Yet we do have our fears about what the future will bring.

As we reflect on this passage, we find disciples who do not want to know what Jesus is trying to teach them about the future (v. 32). Mark tells us that Jesus has returned to Galilee to teach his disciples about what was ahead and why he must suffer. He has returned to the place where his ministry began to speak about how it will end. Yet Jesus' teaching is not a prediction of what will happen to the empire or the world. Jesus wants his disciples to understand the death he would die and what is imminent for them.

He is the Messiah, and as the Messiah he is to be betrayed, physically defeated, and killed. Yet he insists that he will rise. Although disturbing, the message is not completely negative; after all he will rise again. Jesus' message is nevertheless inherently challenging. No wonder the disciples are afraid to ask him about it. If the master must die, what is

Pastoral Perspective

Here is a text that offers preachers an opportunity to massage the "balm of Gilead" into the sore muscles and weary bones of a polarized church and a fractured, angry nation. The word is an unexpected word, which says, in effect: the church lives always under the cross, under the shadow of suffering.[1] Yes, there is resurrection, but in Mark the resurrection frightens rather than comforts. (In the other Gospels, the risen Christ frightens some and brings others to skepticism or scorn, even as the women and most of the disciples receive him with wonder and gratitude.)

We know this text as the "second prediction of the passion." In the Synoptics, it follows Jesus' transfiguration and his healing of an epileptic boy. In Mark's account we are told that Jesus is teaching his disciples alone about the way of the cross. We then learn from their reaction that they do not understand what he is saying and are afraid to ask him what it means. Can this be good news? Yes, for three reasons.

First, it brings us to reality about the church, past, present, and for all time—until the kingdom

---

1. See F. Dale Bruner, *Matthew: A Commentary*, vol. 2, *The Churchbook: Matthew 13–28* (Grand Rapids: Eerdmans, 2004), 200–201.

Exegetical Perspective

The Gospel of Mark is famous for its characterization of the disciples as utter failures to understand. They never seem to grasp what Jesus teaches or does. His twelve closest disciples, including women who follow him (15:40–41), are privileged students who receive all the secrets of the kingdom (4:1–12); yet instead of becoming believers they increasingly become incapable of understanding Jesus' teaching and the meaning of his miracles (4:35–41; 6:30–44; 6:45–52; 8:1–21; 9:31–32; 10:13–14). In this passage, Jesus shares with his disciples the most profound suffering he will encounter—death. The text tells us, though, that instead of being in empathy or solidarity with him, "they did not understand." He shares a message of hope with them, namely, that he will rise from the dead, but they are afraid to ask him for clarification (v. 32). This is not even the first time Jesus has predicted his death and resurrection (see 8:31–33), and still they do not understand.

In Mark, Jesus "chooses twelve disciples who in the end betray, flee, and deny him; he preaches a message of service, sacrifice, and humility that even his own disciples never seem to understand; he is put to death . . . and his resurrection is announced to women followers at an empty tomb who respond by saying nothing to anyone, for they

Homiletical Perspective

This text is addressed to the disciples of Jesus, that is, to a select group of insiders (v. 31). So it may strike contemporary readers as odd, for much of the church's energy in recent decades has been focused on preaching the gospel to those outside the church. Who can deny the validity of that emphasis? Nevertheless, this text presents a different dynamic. The evangelist is addressing this insider teaching to his first-century audience, and we overhear it along with them.

What is Jesus teaching us? For the second of three times in Mark, Jesus predicts his violent suffering and death at human hands, to be followed by his rising again (v. 31; see also 8:31; 10:32–34). Like the first disciples who heard it once, then twice, and would hear it again, we may wonder if we will ever move past this persistent refrain about the suffering of Jesus—albeit followed by his promise of rising again. The answer, of course, is no. The passion narrative itself (chaps. 14–15), along with the odd empty-tomb story that awaits those who read to the end of Mark (16:8), is not an ending in the strictest sense, for resurrection is no "they lived happily ever after" conclusion. This structure is no surprise to those of us who have read Mark many times, to those of us who observe Good Friday and Easter every year. Suffering and promise remain difficult for

Mark 9:30–32

Theological Perspective

going to happen to them, his disciples? The disciples are afraid to ask. They would rather live in fear than learn more from Jesus. Here is where we must compare their theology to our own.

As those who live in the light of the resurrection, we believe Jesus is not just some remarkable miracle-making rabbi. We embrace his resurrection. We follow a living Lord. We are encouraged by the witnesses to the gospel who have gone before us over the last two thousand years in the church. We have the advantage of the church's reflections on the teachings of Jesus and their meaning for our witness today. We live without the fear of the disciples, for we know that God raised Jesus from the dead, do we not? Our clearest understanding of Jesus is that he is the Christ, the Messiah, and the One who has saved and is saving us as well as the world. This being so, what is there to fear? If our redemption is complete, why should we be anxious?

Mark reveals that the resurrected Christ will not change the future as the disciples had hoped he would. He will not overthrow the Romans and set up a new Jerusalem. He will not reign politically and therefore will not be able to delegate to them prime posts for service. Since Jesus is not to reign and rule (at least as the disciples hoped), what will he do, and therefore what will he give them to do? In the world the disciples knew, where the strong oppressed the weak, what service is proper for disciples, and what roles and status can be assigned to them? They had mistakenly believed that their following Jesus would set them up well in the world with power and privilege. Thus Jesus' words to them in Galilee challenged their expectations and caused them to be anxious about a future that was not in their control. This is also our challenge.

Jesus rose from the dead, and still death seems to have dominion and to be what we fear most about the future. Even though Christianity spread and grew by the blood of the saints, it became, over time, a religion of the powerful. Perhaps this is why the church as we now know it is not living as though death has been defeated. In this wealthy and powerful country, where millions suffer hunger and homelessness, the church seems to be more intent on saving its life rather than risking its life to follow a living Lord.

What are Jesus' disciples to do? How are we to do it? Although Christians are no longer routinely martyred in the West and although the gospel has spread internationally, what is the work of modern disciples? Perhaps our fear is not of persecution,

Pastoral Perspective

comes and the new heaven and earth appear. We glorify the past and think, oh, if only we could have lived when people were close to Jesus and rejoiced in the power of the gospel. They often did, but they also knew conflict and division, apostasy and falling away. These conditions are well recorded in the epistles; they are hinted at in the Gospels. This text demonstrates that there will always be a refusal to understand the way of suffering, and a hankering after spiritual peace beside still waters as the path that leads us home. No, it is the way of the cross.

Second, as night follows day, so the gospel brings not only approval but also misunderstanding and rejection—and sometimes a cross. A witness for justice or peace is often met with violence, rejection, or death. We think of Archbishop Oscar Romero in El Salvador, those who resisted apartheid in South Africa, or even our own Ruby Bridges. As a six-year-old African American when the schools in New Orleans were being integrated in the 1960s, she was cursed and spat upon, even as she was guarded by the police on her way to school. When asked why she did not hate her tormentors, she said that her preacher said that Jesus said to love her enemies, and she put her faith in Jesus.

How often do we hear that if we will only preach the gospel, people will flock to the church, hungry for baptism and church membership? When we see the beginnings of the church in Acts we are told, right enough, that the Holy Spirit added (often thousands) to their number day after day. There's the rub: the Holy Spirit added to their number. The true gospel has about it the reality of the cross, as Paul declared in 1 Corinthians 2:2: "For I decided to know nothing among you except Jesus Christ, and him crucified." When the cross is preached faithfully, even if misunderstood, even if the hearers shut their ears, it is the power and wisdom of God for bleeding, broken lives and torn hearts. The Holy Spirit makes it plain, and turns those who have not believed into followers and disciples.

Third, and most important, what Jesus is teaching his disciples is an eternal word that stands over against the church and against the kingdoms of the world. Who is not discouraged by denominations that are fracturing, schismatic, and bleeding members? Who cannot be disheartened by the "success" of the prosperity gospel, or the growth of a fundamentalism linked to national sovereignty? Who cannot be appalled by the use of biblical literalism to attack Muslims and gays with hatred? What we need in our discouragement about the church is the sound

Exegetical Perspective

were afraid."[1] The Markan Jesus and his disciples thus seem to be traveling on parallel roads. The Gospel of Mark also characterizes Jesus as a secret Messiah who does not wish explicitly to expose his identity, activities, and teaching; he repeatedly requests some form of secrecy (1:34, 44; 5:39–43; 8:30). In this passage Jesus "did not want anyone to know" (v. 30) his movements and what he was teaching his disciples.

The historical context of the Roman Empire means that Jesus' status as a Messiah politically challenges the colonial powers to set the oppressed free. It also means that his associates could face the same accusation. His secret messiahship and the ignorance of his disciples possibly articulate an underground language for a resistance movement, and provide teachable moments as well. This short, terse, and intense passage captures these Markan themes.

Exegetically the passage is instructive to contemporary pastors, leaders, and activists as well as to the disciples. As a teacher of disciples who increasingly become ignorant and fearful, Jesus highlights the challenges that sometimes confront transformational leaders. One may give the best to one's work, but it is not a guarantee that the best will be heard, seen, understood, or received. The passage underlines that you may not always reap what you sow! We may not judge the work by its fruits—at least for a while. Many hard workers do not reap the equivalent results. Many poor people work very hard and remain poor. This is because there are many structural and ideological forces in between them and their goals that prevent understanding, courage, and transformation. There will no doubt be many lonely moments for preachers, leaders, activists, and workers who seek transformation.

Despite what may appear to be the dismal status and outlook for those who are disenfranchised and marginalized, there lies a brighter day ahead. There is hope that such suffering does not have the last word, for Jesus assures his disciples that there will be resurrection. Jesus, who will suffer and die at the hands of the Roman Empire, will rise against his colonially induced death. Resurrection thus becomes the power of God in solidarity with the oppressed and exploited. Many times the subordinated may seem too weak against the dominant powers. The dominant powers may seem destined to prevail forever. The dominated may seem destined to suffer, die, and disappear. So

---

1. Mary Ann Tolbert, "Mark," in Carol Newsom and Sharon Ringe, eds., *Women's Bible Commentary* (Louisville, KY: Westminster John Knox Press, 1992), 263.

Homiletical Perspective

readers of the Gospel to understand. The challenge for preachers and their congregations is to see the reality of this text all around us.

One can see glimpses of the passion in many places. We see it among victims of the persecution suffered by both Christians and other religious groups, a dynamic that Mark's first readers understood quite well. We can discern the suffering of Christ among victims of abuse, among starving children, and among those who suffer from lack of adequate medical care. We hear echoes of Christ's passion on the world's many battlefields, as well as among those who battle less visible foes such as loneliness, depression, and suicidal impulses.

One can even find it on death row, where Jesus himself spent time. Arguments in favor of executing murderers often speak of closure for victims and just punishment for offenders, yet as particularly notorious criminals approach execution, the stories of crimes committed years ago are often retold in grisly detail. Media pursue the families of victims, looking for new material, and the new chapter ends with a detailed account of another violent death. Closure?[1]

Indeed, the persistent gospel refrain about suffering is consistent with the life that we know. Preachers must come to terms with this hard reality, and can help their congregants do the same. The growing number of churches that name local murder victims in their weekly prayers of the people have begun this journey. They can work at comprehending more and more within such prayers.

What should the preacher do with the so-called messianic secret, which we find echoed in this text (v. 30, "He did not want anyone to know it")? Earlier in chapter 9, as he came down from the mountain of the transfiguration along with Peter, James, and John, Jesus told them to tell no one "until after the Son of Man had risen from the dead" (9:9). These are odd sayings that have mystified many students of the text. In part, one needs to accept it as part of the weirdness of the text. Whatever the evangelist may have intended to convey through the secret, as one reads through Mark, one must realize that there is no way to know anything about Jesus apart from this dynamic of dying and rising.[2] Therefore, when it comes time for others to know the gospel—that is, catechumens,

---

1. For example, see the article by Jennifer Emily, "Mastermind of Texas Seven prison break executed in slaying of Irving officer," *Dallas Morning News*, February 29, 2012; http://www.dallasnews.com/news/crime/headlines/20120229-mastermind-of-texas-seven-prison-break-executed-in-slaying-of-irving-officer.ece?ssimg=486750#ssStory486438; accessed March 10, 2012.
2. Eric F. Mason. "Secret, Messianic," in Katharine Doob Sakenfeld, ed., *New Interpreter's Dictionary of the Bible* (Nashville: Abingdon Press, 2009), 5:150–51.

Mark 9:30–32

Theological Perspective

but of having to make further and more rigorous sacrifices, to give up the privileges that pretend to secure our future. The disciples of Jesus were simple peasants who had never experienced wealth and had, until they met Jesus, no expectations of wealth, prestige, or power.

In contrast to them we now live in an age in which even common Christians believe that they can secure the future only by success and money in the bank. Accordingly our fear is tied to our affluence. While we desire to serve God, we do not want to jeopardize our enjoyment of all the so-called good things of life. This way of being in the world is antithetical to serving Christ. We shall see in the following passage that the disciples are similarly concerned with their stations in life. If we know that people are suffering here in America and abroad, yet do not devote ourselves to serving others because we are afraid for the future, we live as though God did not raise Jesus from the dead. Historically this question was the source of fear for the disciples; it is also a source of fear for us.

Jesus did not live a life of prosperity, of affluence. He did not die in bed peacefully and comfortably of old age. We confess that he is risen, but we live as if such a reality is exceptional and that taking up his yoke is not a life appropriate for present-day disciples. Accordingly, we have our faith and we have our fear. Our faith is handicapped by our fear. If we, like the disciples, cannot even ask the hard questions about how we should serve him, then we are left with a troubled world in need of our witness to the gospel, but with no real possibility of following Jesus. Jesus calls us to do more. He calls us, as he called the disciples that day in Galilee, to go with him to the cross.

DARRYL TRIMIEW

Pastoral Perspective

of eternity breaking in upon those places where we are stuck, lost, and at a seeming dead end.

This teaching of Jesus about his destiny (this word of grace and truth) is conceivable only as an invasion of eternity, a divine word. Nothing this extraordinary could have come from human understanding or human ingenuity. Only God could be the author of such a plan of salvation, of rescue, of deliverance. The NRSV translation leads us astray. The Son of Man is not "betrayed" but "handed over." The Son of Humanity is handed over into human hands. This we will do to the Holy One in whom God is well pleased, to whom God instructed his disciples to listen on the mount of transfiguration. We will do what we please. We will kill him, but that does not defeat the purposes of God, who will raise Jesus up.

So here, in the preaching of the cross is a word of rejoicing. It is the good news of the gospel. Even when not understood by disciples, even when they are afraid to ask Jesus what it means, that word prevails—all the way through Mark's curious telling of the Jesus story, even through the fleeing of the disciples, the betrayal of Peter, and the trembling of the women who, when told of the resurrection, run away in fear and say nothing to anyone. This word will not be defeated. It cannot be stopped by apostasy or schism, by fractiousness and division, or by national ineptitude or mendacity. It will not be defeated by religious hatred and violence. Because this is God's word—the same yesterday, today, and forever. God's word not only prevails; it breathes into aching muscles and weary bones the energy of new life. As we often sing, it is "a balm in Gilead, to make the wounded whole."[2] It is the good news of the gospel.

O. BENJAMIN SPARKS

---

2. "There Is a Balm in Gilead," *The Presbyterian Hymnal* (Louisville, KY: Westminster John Knox Press, 1990), #393.

Exegetical Perspective

Jesus will also suffer and die. Yet that is not the end of the story, for him or for the oppressed. Jesus will suffer and die, but promises to rise on the third day. Resurrection is thus the power of the oppressed to prevail. It is transformation from death.

It is therefore notable that Jesus is on a journey with his disciples, and he invites them to transformative journeys. These are at once physical, spiritual, bodily, and political journeys, within and through their hometowns, the nation, and the world. The Markan Jesus keeps his messianic identity a secret, but he knows that the time is coming when he must openly face the Roman Empire. So he foretells that he will suffer and be put to death. The Roman Empire did not want any Messiah, for it did not wish to give freedom and justice to the oppressed Jews and other colonized subjects. He thus appears before Pilate, the Roman governor, who asks him, "Are you the King of the Jews?" (15:2). The king of the Jews is the Messiah, the anointed one, who comes to liberate them from colonial oppression. Jesus dies on the cross for the salvation of his people and other colonized subjects—for taking a stand for liberation.

Now we realize that the characterization of disciples as those incapable of understanding Jesus may be a subtle resistance strategy that protects them from physical death at the hands of dominant powers. In each context there are journeys toward liberation to free the oppressed among us. There are various strategies to be adopted at different stages of the journey, including secrecy and playing ignorant. Each generation can take its particular journey and come out of its secret silence and fears and voice out that the oppressed among us must be liberated. Although such speaking out can have deadly consequences, resurrection lies ahead. Resurrection is the expression of God's power in solidarity with those confronting the forces of oppression. Living in the resurrection power of God is thus the act of living in the inevitable hope that liberation and justice must, and will, prevail.

MUSA W. DUBE

Homiletical Perspective

seekers, and any others who may hear the call to become disciples under our care—they also will learn to know Jesus according to this way of dying and rising.

Preachers must come to terms with the fact that we have no easier word to offer them, no docetic seeker's message (or children's message) that we hope they will then one day trade in for a more mature gospel. Making this assertion does not mean that we must confront our listeners with overly dramatic stories of physical suffering, either that endured by Jesus or endured by others. Nor should we encourage persons to court suffering as a dramatic expression of piety. Suffering will find our listeners soon enough. Ours is to repent of denial and to walk with those who suffer.

This text ends with the expressed bewilderment of the disciples. They did not understand Jesus, and they "were afraid to ask him" (v. 32). Perhaps we also are afraid to ask, to pursue deep questions of discipleship, because we know the paschal dynamic of the gospel all too well. Nevertheless, there is no avoiding it. The promise of rising again is the key, not just for the end of Jesus' story, but for ours as well. Simply hearing that promise may speak little to us, however. We can proclaim the resurrection of Jesus in our creeds and perhaps hear it as a comforting word to those who face death, but can we see it working in our discipleship, as a word of resistance to a violent world?

Here note that the word translated to "rise again" (*anistēmi*) occurs elsewhere in Mark. It is the same word used in the previous passage to describe what Jesus did when he came down from the mountain and freed a boy from an unclean spirit. In that case Jesus "lifted him up" (9:27). Although the disciples had failed in that case, Jesus implied that subsequent disciples could, in fact, do similar work "through prayer" (v. 29), perhaps through intercession both spoken and enacted.

MARK W. STAMM

Mark 9:33–37

³³Then they came to Capernaum; and when he was in the house he asked them, "What were you arguing about on the way?" ³⁴But they were silent, for on the way they had argued with one another who was the greatest. ³⁵He sat down, called the twelve, and said to them, "Whoever wants to be first must be last of all and servant of all." ³⁶Then he took a little child and put it among them; and taking it in his arms, he said to them, ³⁷"Whoever welcomes one such child in my name welcomes me, and whoever welcomes me welcomes not me but the one who sent me."

Theological Perspective

When in doubt, fight it out. Right? Too frequently our approach to uncertainty is to engage in a fight-or-flight response. Here Mark depicts disciples who have been fighting about who is to be the greatest among them. Further, when asked about their discussion, they are unwilling to be honest with Jesus. What is God saying to us in this passage?

We must look closely at what Jesus does, for he is our role model. Jesus' teaching for the disciples is as unsettling as they had anticipated. Jesus rejects their theology of standard human power and privilege. Worse, for them, Jesus leads by first being a servant himself. His welcoming the most vulnerable and least valued person in his community—a small child—is his paradigmatic act of leadership. If we are properly to serve God, we too must welcome children. When we do so properly, then we are true disciples of Jesus.

In contrast to Jesus' servanthood, let us consider a popular TV show. *Supernanny* is a current show in which a family is distressed.[1] Kids are out of control, and parents do not know what to do. Enter the supernanny. She talks with the family, watches the interactions, the dysfunction, and then tells the parents what to do. Sometimes the parents are a bit

1. *Supernanny*; http://www.supernanny.co.uk/; accessed May 22, 2012.

Pastoral Perspective

Jesus' teaching of his disciples continues. Now they have left the road and are in Capernaum in the house. He asks them what they were discussing on the road, which is where he was telling them about his suffering, death, and resurrection. They are silent. On the way to Jerusalem and to the cross they have been arguing about who among them is the greatest. No wonder they are silent. Jesus' teaching appears to have made little impact on them. Even after Peter's great confession, even after Jesus has rebuked Peter for denying that he would be crucified, and even after Jesus has told them that anyone who comes after him must take up a cross and follow him (8:34)—even then they were impervious to his teaching, for they were arguing about who would be the greatest. Had these obstinate blockheads learned anything? Apparently not.

Rather than upbraiding them, Jesus tells them the true measure of greatness for his disciples: they are not to seek greatness by welcoming the great and powerful; they are to seek not to be the greatest or to be the first, but to be last and to become the servant of all. Then he illustrates his teaching by taking a child and saying, "Whoever welcomes one such child in my name welcomes me" and in such an act of generosity and hospitality welcomes the One who sent me (v. 37). The way of Jesus is not only the way

Exegetical Perspective

The key issues in this passage include journey, misunderstanding, and correction. To begin with the journey, Setswana culture holds that "Go tsamaya ke go bona." It means that to undertake a journey is to receive sight, revelation, or growth from one's previous stand. The framework of journey is central to this passage, for while the Markan Jesus carries out his ministry largely in and around Galilee (1:9–8:21), he begins a journey toward Jerusalem while he instructs his disciples about suffering (8:22–10:52). Our passage is situated in the latter literary context. In the passage Jesus journeys with his disciples and brings them to a specific place: Capernaum.

Yet a journey is more than just a physical undertaking; it also involves mental and spiritual traveling. A positive journey includes willingness on the part of the traveler, not only to embrace a new place and new perspective, but also to allow oneself to begin to see home, or that which is familiar, as strange. Such a journey becomes gainful, allowing travelers to rethink home or the status quo.

This passage is consistent with the Markan portrayal of the disciples as people without understanding. While on the road to a new place, the disciples do not embody a new understanding of status and the use of power. They do not understand that Jesus defines his power in relation to suffering and death.

Homiletical Perspective

In this text, Jesus continues his conversation with his disciples. In the previous pericope (9:30–32), we heard again the evangelist's emphasis on the impending death and resurrection of Jesus; then we were reminded that the disciples simply did not understand this teaching. In the conversation reported here, we see just how badly they misunderstood Jesus. We must continually remind ourselves, however, that the evangelist is not only reporting a first-century conversation. He is also allowing Jesus to address similar conversations among those of us who hear the text proclaimed today. Jesus asks his disciples, "What were you arguing about on the way?" (v. 33). We should ask, "On the way to where?" On the surface, their argument occurs on the way through Galilee to a house in Capernaum. However, knowing the structure of this Gospel, we know that Jesus and his disciples are traveling the way of discipleship, on the way to Jerusalem and the cross. The evangelist's community is on a similar journey. His question silences what appears to have been a spirited discussion. Whereas in the previous pericope the disciples are afraid to ask Jesus a question, here, ironically, they are afraid to answer him. Their silence is appropriate, even if a bit late, "for . . . they had argued with one another who was the greatest" (v. 34). The silence does not remain, however.

Mark 9:33–37

Theological Perspective

slow to change their parenting, and she disciplines the children. The children properly disciplined and controlled act better, and the crisis seems to be averted. The parents now appear to have a blueprint of how to act. What is theologically interesting about the show is the never-changing fact that the primary problem in the family is that the parents do not know how to raise their children. Supernanny, on the other hand, knows what the best child-raising practices are and how they should be instituted. And even though Supernanny does not love the children as much as the parents do, her approaches are always the correct ones.

Supernanny's power and genius do not come from above, though. If she is trying to do the will of God and trying to get the family to do likewise, such serving and orientation are not evident in the show. This is not to say that Supernanny is against God or Jesus Christ. Rather, her modeling of service simply is not divinely generated. What is so artificial about the show is that the deep social, economic, and political problems of families are never addressed. The family is always two-parented, at least middle-class, with no obvious problems with money, security, or health issues. The problems dealt with are real, but very limited, compared to the problems that most families in the real world face. Real life-and-death issues simply do not fit into the show's format and therefore are never addressed.

Too frequently we serve God as if we were supernannies. First, like the disciples, we desire to be in charge, to have the authority, power, recognition, honor, and prestige. We are willing to serve, but only from a position of power. We are willing to minister, as long as we are in charge and serving in our comfort zone. We viewers identify with the supernanny, but not with the children. The oppressed and suffering in our world are in some respects like children, in that they are extremely vulnerable and are usually struggling for survival.

At the same time, they are not children, even though they may have been treated as such. Our troubled world is filled with the broken and lost, and some of them are innocent, but some of them are not. Most have their own understandings of the good life and how they should behave in the world. Here we must not take the child metaphor too literally. Many of our homeless have had homes, some that were better than ours but were lost in the recent mortgage meltdown.

Jesus in his instructive act of both service and pedagogy welcomes a small child. According to René

Pastoral Perspective

of the cross. Under that sign, normal human values are reversed. The child is not only a literal child, but stands for the weaker members of the Christian community.[1]

It is devilishly difficult for the church in any age to comprehend, much less to follow, such teaching. Mark does his readers a favor by showing that Jesus' disciples, far from progressing in learning and obeying his teaching, are going from bad to worse. They do not improve—in insight or faithfulness—and the last time we see them on the night of Jesus' arrest, they run away in fear.

What, then, does the church need to hear? It needs to hear this text for the sake of its leadership, especially now that the secular world has taken up similar themes. In church and community, in evangelical, Catholic, Orthodox, and progressive circles, we do not see servant leadership; we are instead engaged in bids for power and control. Granted many congregations have become expert in welcoming the least and the lost, but often these are the people to whom we minister, people who are outside the community of faith. Churches keep their hierarchical structures. Even in representative and congregational churches, they keep the same conflicts on the front burner, neither welcoming nor providing for the weaker members of the community. We seem, like the disciples, to be going from bad to worse.

Is it getting better among us, by the providence of God? Is God glorified by the failure of the church to live up to the teaching of Jesus, to fail to welcome among and within our own fellowship the "weak ones" rather than the strong? Where is the church that takes the time, and has the patience, and practices the long suffering genuinely to appreciate and encourage and support those among us who are weak in faith, weak in Christian practice, weak in theology? In truth are we not more likely to silence their voices and exclude them from our presence by neglect, avoidance, or rejection? How many churches, small and large, have established patterns of leadership and control that undermine rather than exalt genuine servanthood?

This text begs to be preached on ordination, installation, and consecration Sundays, and on anniversary celebrations of long pastorates. This text begs to be used at church leadership retreats; this is a text of grace, nestled in the shadow of judgment, repentance, and new life. This text is best exposed for the

---

1. M. Eugene Boring, *Mark: A Commentary* (Louisville, KY: Westminster John Knox Press, 2000), 281.

Exegetical Perspective

The irony lies in that while the disciples are physically traveling to towns and places of great familiarity, their spiritual astuteness—or lack thereof—makes them appear lost at best.

The passage does not explicitly tell the reader the details of their argument, save that "they had argued with one another who was the greatest" (v. 34). Mark 10 gives us a hint into the desired status: "James and John, the sons of Zebedee, came forward to him and said to him, . . . 'Grant us to sit, one at your right hand and one at your left, in your glory'" (10:35, 37). Apparently "when the ten heard this, they began to be angry with James and John" (10:41). The disciples' preoccupation with status and power is disappointing to Jesus, for it is not consistent with the type of power they should yearn for. Again, such a polemic reveals the degree of spiritual displacement the disciples, at least in this case James and John, are undergoing.

Upon arrival in a new place, Capernaum, Jesus brings up the subject again, asking, "What were you arguing about on the way?" (v. 33). The disciples remain notably silent about Jesus' question, denoting perhaps that it is their time to listen and hear from Jesus. They may be silent because they know that their position is problematic. Jesus begins to introduce a new way of understanding greatness, using the images of servants and children.

First, Jesus points out that "Whoever wants to be first must be last of all and servant of all" (v. 35). In the Greco-Roman context, households were stratified according to gender, class, and age (cf. Eph. 5:21–6:9; Col. 3:18–4:1; 1 Pet. 2:18–3:7). There were masters and servants, husbands and wives, parents and children. The masters, husbands, and fathers had power, while servants, wives, and children were to be obedient to those in power. Servants were at the very bottom of this hierarchy of power, closely followed by children. More often than not, the powerful oppressed the subordinate groups. This hierarchical and dualistic model supported the ideology of colonizing the other. Thus Jesus points out, "among Gentiles those whom they recognize as their rulers lord it over them, and their great ones are tyrants over them. But it is not so among you" (10:42–43).

The disciples of Jesus crave power. Jesus does not discourage such desires but redefines the understanding of greatness for his disciples. His followers must not understand greatness as the art of occupying a seat of power that allows them to be served. He redefines greatness as servanthood to others and allowing others to define themselves first, before

Homiletical Perspective

Arguments such as theirs have persisted among the disciples of Jesus, occurring in small churches and large ones, from diocesan conventions to the faculties of theological seminaries, sometimes occurring under a veil of pious self-justification or intellectual gamesmanship. Often they occur off to the side, where we think Jesus cannot hear us. The wise preacher will suggest places where this distracting argument continues in the church, and he should be willing to implicate himself in the process.

As he has done, Jesus addresses the argument through his ongoing rhetoric of reversal, in a sense applying the dynamic of dying and rising to the question at hand: "Whoever wants to be first must be last of all and servant of all" (v. 35). So we hear that Jesus puts a child in their midst and takes it into his arms (v. 36). We may well ask where the child has come from, and we will be hard pressed to answer, perhaps as hard pressed as the disciples were when Jesus posed his earlier question about their argument.

In first-century Roman society children were viewed as socially inferior and thus could be largely invisible, if not endangered.[1] Why would anyone have noticed them? Here, Jesus makes them visible, just as he made lepers and women visible. One might spiritualize this statement about children, softening it by treating it as a mere analogy, but one should be reminded that Jesus made it while holding a real child in his arms (see also 10:15).

Those who hear this text proclaimed today must not allow themselves to escape the scandal of its particularity. The call to embody the servant ways of Jesus through receiving children remains remarkably contemporary, not to mention culturally challenging. Children remain among the most vulnerable among us, perhaps with more rights than they held in the first century, but such rights are notoriously difficult to defend, especially against domestic abuse, dysfunction, and outright parental incompetence, not to mention predators of all types. Opting for parenthood can still be perceived as a bad career move. In the main, church positions dedicated to the teaching of youth and children are not among the most highly coveted and esteemed. Day-care workers are in high demand, but often poorly paid. Some exclusive residential settings have attempted to exclude children altogether. Some of the clothing sold in our department stores has been produced by child labor. Many children have

---

1. Judith M. Gundry-Volf, "Child, Children," in Katharine Doob Sakenfeld, ed., *New Interpreter's Dictionary of the Bible* (Nashville: Abingdon Press, 2006), 1:588–90.

Mark 9:33–37

Theological Perspective

Girard, Jesus led by serving as a role model.[2] He combined his model of service with his theology. His way of being in the world was to serve God and to serve God best by first serving the most vulnerable and needy persons in his society. This modeling by Jesus was intended, according to Girard, to encourage his disciples to do likewise. Further they were to understand theologically that this action by Jesus was a modeling of the action of God, whom Jesus sought first and foremost to imitate.

Jesus was no supernanny. He served the most vulnerable because this was the will of God. In welcoming a child, we are welcoming the God who has first welcomed us. Whatever else service in the reign of God may entail, it begins in participating in the ministry and service that God initiated. We are called to imitate Jesus, not his disciples. They argue over who is to be greatest, rather than compete to be the most serving.

In Girardian terms, they model mimetic rivalry with each other rather than a mimetic desire to imitate Jesus. Jesus is right in front of them, but they do not really understand him or his ministry. Jesus calls us not to rivalry for status, but for service to the world. Our commitment to Christ is best evidenced not by talking about Jesus or God but by welcoming children. Welcoming the most vulnerable members of our society is itself sacrificial, demanding, and sometimes dangerous. Of course, in doing so, Jesus gets in trouble, is arrested, and finally is killed. This is the service to which we are called, and it is this perilousness that made the disciples slow to learn, slow to grasp, slow to act, and afraid to ask Jesus. We do not want to serve others first, especially those who cannot reciprocate, but this is what Jesus wants us to do.

DARRYL TRIMIEW

Pastoral Perspective

life of the congregation by recalling the church in Corinth, in controversy over whether to eat meat that has been sacrificed to idols (1 Cor. 8:1–11:1). In his discussion Paul understands, even applauds, those who are strong, for whom idols do not really exist. He is one of them, he writes. He has no difficulty with his stomach or his conscience when he eats meat that has been sacrificed to idols, especially when he is a guest in the home of a pagan. However, he concludes that if his own confidence and strength should cause his weaker brothers and sisters to stumble or fall, he will not eat meat. This is true servant leadership, which welcomes and makes provision for the weak. So in Mark Jesus "took a little child [a weaker sister or brother] and put it among them" (v. 36). How often do we welcome, without judgment, the weaker ones among us?

Eugene Boring writes of the seriousness of the admonition: "Mark is greatly concerned that the character of church leadership correspond to the cross-centered character of Christian faith."[2] Therefore, let preaching and teaching admonish and encourage church members, governing councils, and assemblies to heed with humility and seriousness, with faith and repentance, in joy and in sorrow, in good times and in bad, the truth of Jesus' teaching. The Gospel of Mark proclaims the same reality from beginning to end: that the one who is introduced to the readers as one with authority, even Jesus the Messiah, preaches and teaches, invites, exorcises, and heals, lives and dies and is raised from death as a servant who walks in the way of the cross.

We can talk the talk. When will we Christians begin to walk the talk?

O. BENJAMIN SPARKS

---

2. An excerpt from René Girard, *I See Satan Fall Like Lightning* (Maryknoll, NY: Orbis Books, 2001); chap. 1, "Scandal Must Come," is at http://girardianlectionary.net/res/iss_1-scandal.htm; accessed May 22, 2012.

2. Ibid.

Exegetical Perspective

exerting power over them. Greatness should be about occupying the space of serving others to realize fully their potential by taking the position of being last—servanthood.

Jesus continues to elaborate on the new model of greatness, using the image of welcoming children. He takes a child in his arms, saying, "Whoever welcomes one such child in my name welcomes me, and whoever welcomes me welcomes not me but the one who sent me" (v. 37). The image of Jesus, an ancient man, holding a child in his arms and talking to twelve men is awesome and highly subversive. He challenges dominant masculinities that disassociate child minding from men. He challenges violent masculinities by underlining the importance of welcoming children as the Christian duty to worship God. He challenges the Roman imperial culture that hardly celebrated children's empowerment. More specifically, children during this time were not valued and often were treated as slaves and outcasts, if they did not have the protection of family. Here Jesus employs social reversal that welcomes, not discounts, even the littlest of humankind. It is therefore important to dwell on the act and the meaning of the word "welcoming" (v. 37).

When we welcome people—visitors and friends—in our homes, we make efforts to make them comfortable and to give them the best, as well as to ensure that they are safe. In Setswana they say, "Dintsa dibogilwe" ("all dogs are tied up"), which means no harm will come to you as a visitor; you are truly welcome and safe. Jesus challenges males to welcome children as an important part of their worship. His teaching brings them to a new place about understanding hospitality and how to welcome God. Overall, Jesus' model for greatness invites the disciples to journey into a new place and new understanding of relating and exercising power.

MUSA W. DUBE

Homiletical Perspective

been enslaved within the sex industry. If we are willing to hear it, this pericope can help us come face to face with such difficult realities, leading us to active repentance (*metanoia*) and the resistance of evil.

To receive children is to receive the One who sent Jesus (*apostellein*, v. 37), and thus it is apostolic ministry in the fullest sense, although it is a different form of greatness than that espoused by the contentious disciples. The faithful preacher will point to such reversals, but then what does she do? How does one assist this work of *metanoia*, this turning to a new way of living? Besides sermons, regular intercessions for children like those named above would help congregations engage the spiritual dynamics of this pericope, as would singing contemporary hymns like "Star-Child," a Christmas hymn by Shirley Erena Murray that compares the Christ child to various children at risk.[2]

Holy imagination can play an important role within a sermon. Like the first disciples, many times we find ourselves captive to a narrative that is rooted somewhere other than in the reign of God. Competition is deeply ingrained in many of our communities, with adults working harder and harder to be the greatest, and children being urged to imitate them, lest they fail to gain admission to the college of their choice. Are such children and youth happy, much less healthy? What about their adults?

Without resorting to complete naiveté regarding economic viability within contemporary contexts, the preacher might ask her congregation about the times that have been most fulfilling for them. Was attaining the promotion really the blessing that was perceived from afar, or did it lead primarily to more work and further alienation from loved ones and the earth itself? Pastors and academicians might well ask themselves the same question. In many instances, the most spiritually and emotionally fulfilling times in one's life occur quite apart from matters related to measuring one's rank.

What does this teach us? What if we lived our lives as if we believed that greatness comes through the exercise of servanthood, even to the receiving of little children? What would that look like?

MARK W. STAMM

---

2. Shirley Erena Murray, "Star-Child," ©1994 Hope Publishing Company, in *The Faith We Sing* (Nashville: Abingdon Press, 2000), 2095.

Mark 9:38–41

³⁸John said to him, "Teacher, we saw someone casting out demons in your name, and we tried to stop him, because he was not following us." ³⁹But Jesus said, "Do not stop him; for no one who does a deed of power in my name will be able soon afterward to speak evil of me. ⁴⁰Whoever is not against us is for us. ⁴¹For truly I tell you, whoever gives you a cup of water to drink because you bear the name of Christ will by no means lose the reward."

Theological Perspective

"The church of Jesus Christ on earth is essentially, intentionally, and constitutionally one," claimed Thomas Campbell.[1] Campbell (1763–1854) was one of the founders of the Christian Church (Disciples of Christ), and this theological maxim is a part of its foundation. With this ecclesiology Campbell hoped to encourage greater cooperation of all Christians in the service of Jesus Christ in the evangelization of the world. He rejected the schismatic divisiveness of his era. His total commitment to ecumenism was right for his generation and is also right for ours.

What we see in this passage of Mark is the foundational theology for such a doctrine. Campbell understood that those who truly follow Jesus will all perform basically the same tasks and in so doing will be Jesus' servants to the world. Christians thereby become cooperative players all on the same team. True disciples, faithful Christians, all have the same master, the same call, the same challenges and tasks.

Our text depicts a stranger, an unknown person who nevertheless calls upon the name of Jesus in exorcising a demon. This one is not, of course, recognized by Jesus' historical disciples. This lack of recognition of coworkers in the faith once again

Pastoral Perspective

In this short narrative Jesus is responding to John's claim that he and the other disciples are "purifying" the community of those who are not followers, but who nonetheless use the power of Jesus' name to cast out demons. Here is another example of the disciples' inability to understand or accept the fact that the kingdom inaugurated by the suffering and death of the Messiah challenges the thinking of this world. Jesus' instruction turns their worldly thinking upside down.[1]

As these stories have proceeded in chapter 9, we do well to remind ourselves that they are shadowed by and blossom alongside the second prediction of the passion of our Lord. They are incomprehensible apart from that prediction.

If ever the church needed to hear such a word, it is now. Not only the American church—evangelical, Catholic, and mainstream Protestant—but also world Christianity, has long since broken apart. One body of Christians says to another body of Christians: "Be gone; we neither know you nor any longer want to be associated with you. You are not one of us." Such attitudes are underscored by the imperial claims and positions of first-world Christians over against

---

1. Thomas Campbell, *Declaration and Address* (Washington, PA: Brown & Sample, 1809), 17.

1. Douglas R. A. Hare, *Mark*, Westminster Bible Companion (Louisville, KY: Westminster John Knox Press, 1996), 114–15.

Exegetical Perspective

Jesus continues to teach his disciples within the literary context of the journey to Jerusalem. The preceding themes were on suffering, resurrection, and the proper understanding of greatness. This passage continues the motif of misunderstanding among the disciples, which prompts Jesus' teaching. In these verses Jesus teaches them about recognizing and welcoming possible supporters and friends, after John reports their attempt to stop a man who is casting out demons in the name of Jesus. Some key aspects to this passage therefore are using the name of Jesus, how to recognize potential supporters, good reasons for encouraging supporters, and welcoming those who speak in the name of Jesus.

Biblical literature, especially the Gospel of Mark, was composed for oral presentation. Mark was written to be heard by an audience that did not necessarily have their own copies of the Gospel. Consequently, repetition was an important device for emphasizing and verbally reiterating key concepts. To repeat something served as a verbal red light to indicate relevance, urgency, and importance. Repetition could be in the form of single words, phrases, sentences, concepts, or typologies. For example, the Gospel of Mark is notoriously known for repeating the word "immediately" forty-two times, in order to call the attention of the listener.

Homiletical Perspective

Notice that even the disciple John did not dispute the effectiveness of the ministry conducted by this unauthorized exorcist, whoever he may have been: "Teacher, we saw someone casting out demons in your name" (v. 38). At least one person's life had been changed for the better, perhaps radically so, yet John offered no word of thanksgiving or celebration for that work of deliverance. The preacher can help her congregation notice this odd response. If the preacher has not helped her congregation think through first-century perceptions regarding demon possession, then she should do so.[1] That said, with this passage one should focus on the exchange between John and Jesus.

John was preoccupied with another concern, that this person who was casting out demons in Jesus' name "was not following us" (v. 38). Indeed, he and the other disciples had tried to stop him. Enthusiastic people who believe they are doing God's work can be hard to dissuade. Notice the word "follow" (*akoloutheō*), and the subtle way it is used in verse 38, especially in contrast to a key saying from the previous chapter. There Jesus said that true disciples must "deny themselves and take up their cross and

---

[1]. For an excellent discussion of this topic, see Kathy Black, *A Healing Homiletic: Preaching and Disability* (Nashville: Abingdon Press, 1996).

Mark 9:38–41

Theological Perspective

demonstrates that these disciples do not fully understand the ministry of Jesus. Jesus is task oriented; he is always about doing the business God calls him to do and always involved in the process of relieving the suffering of humanity. Thus the stranger who is observed by Jesus' disciples performing an exorcism is faithful, even as the disciples do not fully understand the ministry of service that Jesus is calling them to do. Here the irony of the passage is monumental. The stranger, perhaps even unknown by the historical Jesus, understands nevertheless better than Jesus' own disciples that which Jesus wants all of us to do. However, while the stranger is serving Jesus, he is being criticized by Jesus' closest followers—his personally called disciples.

The successful exorcism depicted in Mark done in the name of Jesus by the stranger is not, however, based upon camaraderie or cronyism with Jesus. The power of God is available to this unknown exorcist by his acting in faith to invoke Jesus' name. He is not wasting time arguing over who will be the greatest among them in the future when Jesus will reign as Messiah. The mimetic rivalry that is exhibited by the disciples (who have, as we may recall, argued over who will be preeminent in the reign of the Messiah) is absent from this unknown follower of Jesus.[2] His identity is never given in Mark. This anonymity is important to note. What is important for true disciples of Jesus is not their pedigree, not their genealogy, not their connections, not even their personal familiarity with Jesus. What is important is their devotion to Jesus' devotion to God and to their conjoined service to humanity.

So who should serve Jesus? Who are our coworkers in the faith? This passage of Scripture makes it clear that what binds Christians together is not first and foremost our coordinated activities to advance ourselves, such as our congregations or denominations, but rather our service to the world in the name of and at the command of God. Ecumenism is of little importance if it is merely the celebration of a variety of Christians who have forgotten that faith without works is dead (Jas. 2:20).

Jesus corrects his disciples' self-righteous antagonism as Mark makes it clear to us that we are all called to serve Christ, rather than to evaluate or vet each other's credentials. A reading of this Scripture would not be complete without taking seriously the work of Jacqueline Grant. Grant, a womanist

Pastoral Perspective

developing-world Christians, as well as by those who resist reformation, and by those who scurry forward to embrace every new "doctrine" under the sun. It is now predicted that Roman Catholicism will divide, that much of American and Western European Catholicism will break away (either officially or de facto) from Catholicism in the rest of the world over issues of celibacy and the ordination of women to the priesthood.

Jesus wisely shows how dangerous and destructive are the attitudes of the disciples. John almost brags to Jesus about excluding the exorcist. The text reads as if he is expecting approbation. Instead, Jesus rebukes him and says not to stop the man, because "no one who does a deed of power in my name will be able soon afterward to speak evil of me" (v. 39). It is no coincidence that the one the disciples are worried about is an exorcist as Jesus is. Jesus goes on to say that "whoever is not against us is for us" (v. 40).

This story and Jesus' response to John are especially evocative of the underlying themes of Mark's Gospel, where the notion of approaching cosmic conflict is woven into the story from the beginning. As early as chapter 3 we learn that the Pharisees and Herodians are hatching a plot to destroy Jesus. By chapter 5 we learn of Jesus' encounter with the Gerasene demoniac. That story in Mark's telling is so powerful and detailed that it led one biblical scholar to name his commentary on Mark *Binding the Strong Man*.[2]

The implication is that these disciples and the church (early and late) have always to guard against "the wiles of the devil. For our struggle is not against enemies of blood and flesh, but against . . . the spiritual forces of evil in the heavenly places" (Eph. 6:11–12). If that is the situation of disciples and the church, it is far more important to stand with everyone who calls on the name of Jesus and does "works of power" in his name than to spend energy and waste resources wondering if we are all on the same team, and trying to exclude, denigrate, or excommunicate those who in our judgment encroach on our turf.

The tendency to drive from the community and punish those who are "not one of us" has ancient origins. Church conflict over leadership and inclusion has been there from the beginning, and what a sorry mess we have made of things over the centuries.

This gives the church a lens through which to observe with sadness and gratitude these present

---

2. For more on mimetic rivalry, see René Girard, *I See Satan Fall Like Lightning* (Maryknoll, NY: Orbis Books, 2001).

2. Ched Myers, *Binding the Strong Man: A Political Reading of Mark's Gospel* (Maryknoll, NY: Orbis Books, 1988).

Exegetical Perspective

Acting in the name of Jesus is a central concept in these verses, for it is mentioned repeatedly, to substantiate both views—the disciples' and Jesus' perspectives. Thus, when the Gospel writer repeats the name "Jesus," the author wants the reader to stand with full attention to what is about to happen in the text. When the disciples act or speak in the name of Jesus, it is to recognize his God-given power, his authority, and his status as the Son of God, the Christ. People should pay attention to Jesus! To employ his name to restore health or exorcise evil spirits is therefore an act of faith in Jesus on the part of the actor. It is an acknowledgment of the potency of such a name, to the extent that invoking it brings about transformation in the lives of people. In the early church the use of the name of Jesus played an important part, attested by several passages (Acts 3:6, 16; 4:7, 10, 30).

The disciples' attempt to stop a man from performing exorcism in the name of their teacher brings Jesus to talk to them about recognizing potential supporters. The way Mark's Jesus perceives the matter is that there is no harm done. One who uses his name to do good deeds is unlikely to speak evil against him, for such a person openly attests his faith in the goodness and power of Jesus. Given that during his ministry Jesus had his share of supporters and dissenters, he underlines that "whoever is not against us is for us" (v. 40). In short, potential supporters must be welcomed and encouraged. This follows previous passages in which Jesus engages in social reversal in order to affirm and welcome the least likely (9:33–37).

As a Messiah, Jesus is automatically an enemy of the Roman Empire and the collaborating ruling elites, hence his adoption of a secretive identity. In fact the Markan Jesus sometimes uses casting out demons as a symbolic resistance to the Roman Empire and demonstration of his power as a liberator—a Messiah. The symbolism behind the exorcism is to rid the world of the demonic political and imperialistic structure of the *Pax Romana*, the much-vaunted "Roman peace." This is attested in Mark 5:1–20, where he liberates a man who lives in the graves, apparently possessed by a legion of demons. The term "legion" is used to describe a unit of a thousand Roman soldiers. Entered by demonic imperial spirits, the man has lost his sanity and lived at the grave sites, tearing himself, thus highlighting the tragic wound of colonized subjects.

Jesus, acting out his messianic power as a liberator, casts out the legion and drives the thousand evil

Homiletical Perspective

follow me" (8:34). There one finds a clear demand for full commitment. The text before us brings a subtle but telling change. Where Jesus had spoken of following *me*, now the disciples were speaking of following *us* (v. 38).

Once again, the preacher should locate contemporary disciples within this text. Of the three who accompanied Jesus at the transfiguration—Peter, James, and John—all took turns at misunderstanding Jesus' intentions for disciples. Peter resisted the call to the cross (8:32). In this pericope, John saw spiritual authority not as means to participate in God's liberating work, but as a possession to be guarded. Later, James (and John) saw God's promise as opportunity for promotion (10:35–37). In each case we see enthusiasm focused on the wrong goals, but it does not help us if we merely talk about first-century disciples who missed the mark.

For many of us, commitment to Christ takes the shape of doing what the church does, and well it should, but this text should make us wary of positing direct correspondence between Christ and his church. Faithful reading of Scripture holds a prophetic tension between following Christ and following church.

Such talk can make pastors nervous—not to mention bishops. We are, after all, trying to follow Jesus within the ecumenical body of Christ, and so we proclaim belief in the "holy catholic Church."[2] Many of our churches require seminary training for clergy, and with good reason. Those who complete a seminary education are better equipped to talk publicly about God and are less likely to do harm in God's name—although some may find cause to argue with this assertion. To acknowledge that God is at work outside of our faithfully discerned structures opens the door to ecclesiastical anarchy, the thought of which distresses my decently ordered heart.

Nevertheless, God's work is messy and Jesus makes no apology for that reality. Those who hear God's word must repent of all notions that we control it, and this includes those of us who hear it while preaching. Such an assertion does not mean that the ordained should forsake their credentials and join an independent company of exorcists. For better or worse, those who organize such fellowships must develop their own ecclesiastical forms soon enough. The problem is not the formation of such disciplines, and so the solution to the various problems that we face within the contemporary church is not rejection of the church itself. Rather, we should acknowledge that God's work

---

2. See the Nicene Creed and the Apostles' Creed.

Mark 9:38–41

Theological Perspective

theologian, rejects the assumed subservience that has been traditionally imposed upon black women. Grant boldly declares that black women have faced a triple imposition of oppression: subjugation by race, class, and gender. Such a devaluation of their humanity automatically presupposes that black women should serve immediately and automatically, for this is their calling to their supposed "lowly station." Further, she is correct in locating this oppressive theology in the Christian tradition.[3]

While Grant is insightful in this criticism, we are nevertheless called to serve and to serve first by welcoming children (the most vulnerable people in society). What should be rejected in our tradition is the demeaning of servanthood and disrespect of black women. Our service to Christ is our joint calling, and it is a responsibility of all Christians, starting with the most privileged. We see this point in the modeling of Jesus, who serves first, serves the lowliest, and insists that this welcoming of little children is a welcoming of God. Given American history, black women are not of course presumed to be the first to serve. We who would follow Christ are all called to serve and to be the last in seeking favor, rather than the first. It is only in so doing that we imitate Jesus rather than the worst sentiments of his disciples.

In today's world we must all work together with other Christians without regard to minor doctrinal differences or mere ethnic diversity. Ecumenism in the service of Christ is a modern manifestation of Pentecost. Different Christians are blessed with the opportunity to work for Christ without rivalry, competition, or self-regard. Our oneness is in Jesus Christ and in the blessed ministry of the gospel that we can render to a hurting and marginalized world. This is the deepest teaching of Jesus of Nazareth, and it is as accessible to us as it was to his disciples. To be part of the blessing, however, we must not be afraid to ask—or afraid to follow and serve.

DARRYL TRIMIEW

Pastoral Perspective

conflicted times: sadness for how little we have learned over the centuries, and how often we have so rampantly disobeyed and continue to do so. There is nevertheless also cause for gratitude. In every age God's Spirit raises up congregations, societies of Christians (the Benedictines and the Franciscans, for instance), leaders, theologians, and movements within the church to fight for causes like the abolition of slavery. All of these challenge our complacency, correct or reform our corruption and apostasy, and lead us toward more authentic obedience. In practical terms, the waves in the sea of darkness are so high and dangerous that we need all hands on deck to bail without ceasing. We dare not risk losing anyone.

Further, this text underscores the mandates against violence of Christian toward Christian, and of Christians toward persons from other religious traditions. Every time we strike back, and return evil for evil—even when we are violently attacked because we bear Christ's name—we deny the gospel and make a mockery of the saving power of the cross. Those who want to become followers of mine, said Jesus, must deny themselves and take up their crosses and follow me. This was his response to Peter's rebuke, after Jesus first predicted that he would go up to Jerusalem where he would be handed over, experience great suffering, be rejected by the elders, chief priests, and the scribes, be killed, and after three days rise again.

When Christ said all this openly to his disciples, Peter, who had just named Jesus the Messiah, took him aside and rebuked him. After rebuking Peter in return, Jesus, according to Mark, told him he was measuring reality according to human thinking, not according to divine reality. Then Jesus continued: "those who want to save their life will lose it, and those who lose their life for my sake, and for the sake of the gospel, will save it" (8:35). What would we give in exchange for our lives?

The history of the church demonstrates that we will give many things, even good and noble things, in exchange for obedient witness. The grace of God, in every age, overcomes our sin. Thanks be to God.

O. BENJAMIN SPARKS

---

3. Jacqueline Grant, *White Women's Christ and Black Women's Jesus: Feminist Christology and Womanist Response* (Atlanta: Scholars Press, 1989), 6.

Exegetical Perspective

spirits into the sea, leaving behind a free man. This stranger, who acts in the name of Jesus to cast out demons, might be in the resistance movement of casting out the evil spirits of the Roman Empire that possess people; in so doing he expresses hope that liberation must surely come to the oppressed. Jesus says such a man is in their camp and should not be stopped. Anyone who wants to cast out the demons of the emperor and his cohorts is welcome to follow Jesus.

Jesus turns the conversation back to his disciples, who will also work and be sent in his name. He informs them that "whoever gives you a cup of water to drink because you bear the name of Christ will by no means lose the reward" (v. 41). Giving "a cup of water to drink" to visitors, travelers, and strangers in desert countries symbolizes a welcoming spirit. In John 4:9, Jesus sits at a well, tired and thirsty, and a Samaritan woman at first refuses to give him a drink, due to the tension between Samaritans and Jews. Welcoming strangers also sometimes includes washing their feet (Luke 7:44; 1 Tim. 5:10).

In this teaching, Jesus reconnects with his earlier teaching about hospitality (9:37). While he has encouraged his disciples to express their greatness by welcoming children, because in so doing they are welcoming both Jesus and the one who sent him, in this teaching Jesus says that those who welcome his disciples will be recognized for their hospitality (cf. Matt. 10:40–42; Luke 10:16). Jesus' teaching serves to encourage the disciples also to welcome others who work or come in the name of Jesus, for such people are likely to remain valuable supporters. Thus, the disciples must be careful and not too quick to discard anyone who they think is not like them. As they will travel to various places and rely on the grace of strangers, they must be careful not to discount persons whose actions appear strange to them. Jesus says to welcome everyone.

MUSA W. DUBE

Homiletical Perspective

does not stop at the walls of the church as we know it, nor does that work subsist entirely within the outreach programs that we sponsor.

Generally, the work done within such church programs is beneficial, liberating at best and benign at the least, but when the rhetoric of church leaders—especially pastors—is overly focused on programs, that can be discouraging to those whose work and other responsibilities make it difficult to participate in them. What about those who work in hospitals most of the day, or care for young children either in schools or at home, or repair automobiles so that others can arrive at work safely and on time? These persons and those engaged in many other vocations may have neither the leisure nor the energy for such church work, yet the messages often spoken by their pastoral leaders may cause them to believe that they are poor disciples.

In like manner, pastors of small churches sometimes unfavorably compare their congregations to larger ones with well-organized outreach programs. Have they noticed what their parishioners are actually doing on a daily basis? Have they asked them about their work or given them the theological tools to reconsider the meaning of that work? Preachers can bring a liberating word by shifting their rhetoric away from the work of the church, institutionally perceived, toward the daily work of the baptized. Liturgists can support this shift through specific intercessions offered for persons in their various vocations. Such a shift calls church leaders to *metanoia*, that is, to turn toward God, just as John and the other disciples described in this pericope were called to conversion. This refocusing does come with a cost, however, for the daily work of the baptized may not show up as well on reports submitted to bishops and other judicatory offices. Will such denominational officials become more discerning in understanding the work of the faithful?

Those who serve in Jesus' name will be drawn into deeper friendship with him, and the standards are clear: those who give the cup of cold water find their reward. Those who are not against Jesus are for him. This claim makes for a large set of disciples that cannot be easily tracked, but we should pray that this company increase all the more. What would the church's life together look like if we defined the boundaries of God's ministry in this more generous manner?

MARK W. STAMM

Mark 9:42–50

⁴²"If any of you put a stumbling block before one of these little ones who believe in me, it would be better for you if a great millstone were hung around your neck and you were thrown into the sea. ⁴³If your hand causes you to stumble, cut it off; it is better for you to enter life maimed than to have two hands and to go to hell, to the unquenchable fire. ⁴⁵And if your foot causes you to stumble, cut it off; it is better for you to enter life lame than to have two feet and to be thrown into hell. ⁴⁷And if your eye causes you to stumble, tear it out; it is better for you to enter the kingdom of God with one eye than to have two eyes and to be thrown into hell, ⁴⁸where their worm never dies, and the fire is never quenched.

⁴⁹"For everyone will be salted with fire. ⁵⁰Salt is good; but if salt has lost its saltiness, how can you season it? Have salt in yourselves, and be at peace with one another."

Theological Perspective

In his 2011 book *Love Wins*, Rob Bell rocked the evangelical Christian world with his claim that "at the center of the Christian tradition since the first church have been a number who insist that history is not tragic, hell is not forever, and love, in the end, wins and all will be reconciled to God."[1] The ensuing controversy underscored the extent to which the idea of hell as depicted in Mark 9:42–50 continues to occupy an important place in the theological imaginations of many North American Christians. Clearly a judgment text, this passage is full of warning as it portrays in dire terms the consequence of the disciples' causing their brothers and sisters to "stumble" or "be scandalized."

Fondness for God's loving-kindness and not divine judgment toward all people may make this passage's tone and imagery appear startlingly harsh. Using a body metaphor for the community, the writer portrays Jesus interrupting the disciples' argument about rank with talk about their being drowned in the sea, thrown into hell, and salted with fire. Gruesome verbal portraits of bodily self-mutilation hardly comprise the most familiar type of speech placed in the mouth of Jesus by New Testament Gospel writers.

Pastoral Perspective

Images of cutting off hands and feet, gouging out eyes, and hell as a place of raging fires may make twenty-first-century American Christians more inclined to cast these verses into the sea than to see them as admonitions about how disciples actually are supposed to live. The pastoral task is to help people move away from the literal images and to take these words of Jesus seriously. What are metaphorical stumbling blocks today that cause separation from God, a separation that could be considered an existential hell?

Pastoral issues in this text are both personal and corporate. The warnings in verses 43–47, which emphasize the self-judging aspect of the text, appear to focus primarily on the personal dimension. Most mainline Christians will not be tempted to self-mutilation, so the challenge is to help people identify the metaphorical "hand," "foot," or "eye" in their own lives that may be keeping them from faithfully following Jesus.

For example, "hand" conjures up images of one's handiwork, that is, what one does or produces, or how one makes a living. Especially in a time of rampant unemployment, there are profound economic consequences to "cutting off" the hand that feeds you, and this admonition addresses the question of ethical issues regarding one's work. Potential whistleblowers wondering whether to expose wrongdoing,

---
1. Rob Bell, *Love Wins: A Book About Heaven, Hell, and the Fate of Every Person Who Ever Lived* (New York: HarperCollins, 2011), 109.

Exegetical Perspective

Discipleship requires being least of all and servant of all (10:43–44). Dramatically illustrating this lesson, Jesus has just taken a child in his arms and said that anyone who receives such a child "in my name receives [NRSV "welcomes"] me" (9:37). A series of sayings with the phrase "in [my] name" follows (vv. 38, 39, 41). At this point the narrative pauses, and the evangelist inserts a collection of Jesus' sayings that are loosely related to the context.

At first reading, the sayings may seem random and their placement arbitrary. The "hook," however, is the reference to "one of the least of these" (NRSV "one of these little ones") in verse 42, which ties the saying to this context. The evangelist then continues the organizational pattern he used in verses 37–41, where a series of sayings contains the same phrase.

A parenthesis is in order here. The evangelists drew on oral tradition, and the Gospels themselves were probably recited or performed orally. Only something like 10 percent of the population was literate, so in their original setting more people heard the Gospels performed orally than could have read them. Material meant for retention in memory could be related in a story, clustered topically, or organized by what we may call "catchword linkage." This latter technique strings together sayings in which each saying picks up a key word or phrase in the previous

Homiletical Perspective

"Jesus couldn't possibly mean that, could he?"

It is tempting when reading this passage to default quickly to the assumption that Jesus is employing hyperbole merely to capture his audience's attention. Various commentators reinforce this response. Lest the force of Jesus' radical claims be diluted, however, one dare not automatically and carelessly dismiss the shocking words Jesus pronounces as mere exaggeration. Of course, as a preacher, it could be catastrophic to take these as unexamined, literal claims straight into the pulpit. Think of the outcry. Think of the potential for litigation! Imagine the courtroom exclamations of accused preachers: "But the Bible says . . ."

Wherever one ends up on this matter, it is altogether clear that readers better take Jesus seriously and not slide into mealy-mouthed, easily swallowed encouragement to good behavior and responsible stewardship, or to a limp list of moral imperatives. If Jesus did not intend his words to be taken literally, he most certainly intended that they be taken seriously. If it is not a matter of death or dismemberment, it surely is a matter of eternal life or eternal condemnation. Any consideration that waters down the severity of the choice does an injustice to the nature of the claims Jesus presents.

One does not have to look for very long to find examples of the "stumbling blocks" (the Greek word

Mark 9:42–50

Theological Perspective

Yet here vivid and horrifying pictures conjure a world in which these elective amputations are somehow preferable to the terror of the unquenchable fires of hell and worms that never die.

Mark's explanatory gloss on hell or gehenna (or the valley of the sons of Hinnom) as a place of fire and suffering provides fuel for traditional depictions of hell used across the centuries by artists such as Hieronymus Bosch (*The Garden of Earthly Delights*) and by contemporary fear-based evangelists. The theme of hell as a place (literal or otherwise) where sinners experience the wrath of God's judgment stands prominently in Christian theology across time: Jonathan Edwards's sermon "Sinners in the Hands of an Angry God" comes immediately to mind, as does Thomas Aquinas's assertion that "the fire of hell is not called so metaphorically, not an imaginary fire, but a real corporeal fire."[2]

John Calvin, by contrast, considered all such descriptions of hell's fire to be figurative, a means by which the Holy Spirit can invite a transformed life by inspiring a sense of dread in believers about the possibility of separation from divine love. Even now, at the dawn of the twenty-first century, when many Christians do not share a worldview that includes a literal hell, images such as those in this passage from Mark still operate to help many people make sense of the universe as morally cohesive, that is, a place in which evil and wrongdoing ultimately meet punishment in hell, while goodness and righteousness are rewarded in heaven.

The theological challenge for church leaders today concerns the task of separating ancient cosmologies of a literal, physical hell from theological understandings about God and human nature. Equally challenging to some readers of Mark, though, is the recognition in this text that the Christian tradition insists that God's judgment is always gracious judgment. Grace is present in Jesus' concern for those at risk of stumbling, as well as in the text's warning role in the lives of disciples. Theologian Daniel Migliore writes about hell paradoxically as a "symbol of Christian hope." It functions this way, says Migliore, because "the fire of God is the fire of a loving judgment and a judging love that we know in the cross of Christ to be for our salvation rather than our destruction." He goes on to define hell as "the terrible weariness and incredible boredom of a life focused entirely on itself."[3]

---

2. Thomas Aquinas, *Summa Theologica*, sup.70.3, trans. Fathers of the English Dominican Province (Westminster, MD: Christian Classics, 1981), 2829.
3. Daniel L. Migliore, *Faith Seeking Understanding: An Introduction to Christian Theology* (Grand Rapids: Eerdmans, 2004), 246.

Pastoral Perspective

employers considering expending profits to improve working conditions instead of increasing stock dividends, employees pondering whether to resign a position that demands they sacrifice family life, unemployed persons tempted to accept a job that conflicts with their moral values: these are all individuals who hold the knife in their hands, and wonder if they will have the courage to cut.

"Feet" move us toward a destination, thus raising the ethical issue of whether our goals in life are in keeping with the goals of being citizens of God's realm. Christians pondering this text may include college students choosing a major, persons wondering about a career change, retirees considering how to spend leisure hours, church officers determining the annual budget, parents grappling with how to help their children make choices. They all struggle with issues about whether their feet are stumbling, rather than carrying them in the direction Jesus is leading.

The "eye" implies what attracts our attention. The moral implications of this stumbling are wide ranging. Internet sites are replete with advertisements seeking to draw our attention. Wandering eyes include far more than sexual attraction. Decisions about how one uses time, spends money, and establishes priorities are based on where the eye is focused. Is attraction to Christ being impeded by all that is competing for attention and affection?

Jesus admonished disciples to temper their own behavior because of how it may affect other people. In an age where ethical individualism reigns, this concept of one person's actions having a moral consequence for another person is becoming more countercultural. The text calls Christians to consider the influence their individual decisions and behavior have on others. What one person does, says, or thinks may be acceptable—or even without sin—for that individual, but could have a negative impact because of how it inspires another person to behave.

The Interrupters, a documentary film by Steve James and Alex Kotlowitz about the Violence Interrupters program of CeaseFire, depicts how former gang members intervene to stop violence in their Chicago neighborhoods.[1] The film illustrates how an individual's actions can have an effect, positively or negatively, upon others. It is a reminder of how grave might be the unintended consequences of our actions. Those who take Jesus' words seriously will have to deal with the awful, awe-filled truth that how

---

1. PBS Online, *Frontline: The Interrupters*, http://www.pbs.org/wgbh/pages/frontline/interrupters/; accessed February 22, 2012.

Exegetical Perspective

saying (e.g., Jas. 1:2–8). The sayings may not have any topical or thematic continuity, but the catchwords serve as mnemonic aids. In Mark 9:42–50 the evangelist offers a series of sayings (vv. 42, 43, 45, and 47) that all feature the verb *skandalizē* ("cause to stumble"). The latter three are structurally the same: "If your hand/foot/eye causes you to stumble, cut it off/pluck it out; it is better for you to enter life maimed/lame/with one eye than to have two hands/two feet/two eyes and go to/be thrown into hell." The references to gehenna (hell) then attract the saying on being salted with fire (v. 49), and "salt" serves as a catchword for the two sayings that follow in verse 50.

One other introductory comment is necessary. Did you notice that verse 44 or 46 is missing from modern translations? Several early manuscripts (notably Alexandrinus and Bezae, both fifth century) insert here the words of verse 48 verbatim, but these verses do not appear in other early manuscripts (notably Sinaiticus and Vaticanus, both fourth century).

Verse 42 offers both protection and a warning for Jesus' disciples. To cause someone to stumble is vivid metaphorical language for causing another to lose faith. The stumbling block in this instance means in the first place to dismiss as unimportant (the child in v. 36), to hinder or forbid (the exorcist in v. 38), or to refuse hospitality (see v. 41). If Mark wrote for a persecuted community of believers (see 4:17; 10:30; 13:9–13), this saying pronounces judgment on their persecutors, while warning them not to follow the ways of the persecutors.

Visitors to Capernaum today can see millstones that were originally shared by neighbors in courtyards. The lower millstone is shaped like an inverted ice cream cone. The upper millstone is like a doughnut that sits on the lower millstone, with a funnel-shaped opening on the top side. A handle or lever would fit in a square opening on the side of the upper millstone so that the upper millstone could be rotated around the lower millstone. Grain was poured into the funnel-shaped opening and ground between the two stones. The milled grain or meal would drop to the ground around the stones, ready to be collected for the day's baking.

Jesus' language is descriptive. Literally, he says that it would be better for one who causes the least of his followers to stumble if "a millstone of a donkey" (v. 42), meaning a large millstone turned by a donkey, were hung around his neck and that person were thrown into the sea. Smaller millstones could be turned by women grinding the grain. Donkeys were used for the larger ones. One can imagine such

Homiletical Perspective

is *skandalon*, from which we derive the word "scandal") that have been thrown before "these little ones." News stories and reports of various sorts of abuse, compounded by attempts at cover-up, continue to erode trust in church leaders. Preachers have been removed from their pulpits because of unethical use of other people's materials. Lack of accountability persists in too many quarters.

In the verses leading up to this passage, Jesus trudges through and tromps on cherished notions, reversing long-held beliefs, standards, and procedures. He could easily be perceived as unnecessarily brutal in his demands. He seems to have no concern to modify his message to make it more palatable. In earlier verses, Jesus employs the image of a child to evoke the attitude the disciples should take toward those to whom they are to minister. In 9:38, the disciples express concern about what they perceive as competition. Jesus turns the matter right around and puts the spotlight on the disciples' behavior. He says, in effect, "Do not worry about them. Make sure your own house is in order."

Being a follower of the Christ is not a competition with others. The disciples must have experienced a painful cognitive whiplash in the sudden and dramatic change in the direction of their conversation. They were summarily put in their place. Jesus has already referred to his audience as a "faithless generation" (9:19). Now he calls the disciples on their myopic sense of values in regard to others who are healing in Jesus' name (9:39). There is no mincing of words here. Face it, belief in Christ, becoming a follower of Christ, is far more than we ever reckoned on, more than we are capable of understanding.

Jesus' demands take priority over everything else. They are not a convenient, cozy, self-affirming add-on to whatever else we may hold dear. They replace everything else we hold dear, no matter the cost to us. I occasionally suggest that adults coming to be baptized or parents bringing their children to be baptized sign a "hold harmless" waiver in order that they recognize what it is they are getting involved in, what they are committing themselves to. We may be saved by grace, but that does not mean a free lunch. This is no happy, feel-good prosperity gospel. This is about ultimate, all-or-nothing commitments.

If the passage seems to offer only dire warnings to disciples about proper priorities and their myopic vision of the kingdom of God, the last two verses offer a glimmer of hope. They speak of the benefits of such discipline: peace. The outcome of this radical re-visioning of the nature of the kingdom

Mark 9:42–50

Theological Perspective

Jesus' warning speech to his disciples addresses this very situation, as their preoccupation with self-positioning and power threaten their ability to attend to the well-being of the faith community, especially its "little ones," for whom their conflict might become a "stumbling block" or scandal. Mark's use of the phrase "little ones who believe in me" (v. 42) is at once a reference to children, already established by Jesus in 9:30–37 as exemplary of real discipleship, but also a reference to others in the community whose circumstances or resources situate them as "little" in contrast to disciples who want to be big (powerful, important, and influential). Out of such assertions about children's value to Jesus come theological claims concerning the care of children and the church's call to protect them from harm and abuse. So also the metaphorical "little ones" in the church, those who wield no power or influence or whose needs lay claim to the community's care, invite us to pay attention to whatever stumbling blocks may litter their paths.

A well-traveled theological road taken by some interpreters of this passage sees good disciples as those who would rather sacrifice their own wholeness than threaten the well-being of the community, people like Coptic Christians who stand in the doorways of Egyptian churches to protect them. With this focus on the community's well-being, rather than on individual morality per se, the text's emphasis on leadership that willingly empties itself of power and prestige in order to care for the community's vulnerable members can contribute much to a contemporary theology of leadership. Taken to excess, however, such an emphasis can end up glorifying self-abnegation, including various forms of victimization, as sought-after marks of discipleship—a move strongly criticized by feminist theologians in light of sexist societies' peculiar willingness to position women in roles requiring sacrificial subordination of their needs and well-being to those of others.

JOYCE ANN MERCER

Pastoral Perspective

they live has an impact on people they know and love, as well as on those who "hear" the gospel by observing their behavior. What Christian would not rather cut off, figuratively or literally, a hand or foot that was leading a beloved sister, brother, or child to sin? The alternative may be living with the guilt of causing another's downfall, a guilt that could indeed feel like hell on earth.

The admonition against setting up stumbling blocks before others has corporate dimensions, challenging a congregation or denomination to consider how its actions and reactions may hinder "little ones" (e.g., children in the congregation, young people who consider themselves "spiritual but not religious," or new Christians) from becoming part of the church, or from living as faithful followers of Jesus Christ. Such consideration might give rise to issues regarding the peace, unity, and purity of the church as they relate to biblical interpretation.

For example, should one group "cut off" others from a congregation or from ordination because it is right to keep the purity of the church? Does strictly adhering to a particular biblical interpretation mean creating a stumbling block for those whose interpretation differs? The tendency is to see one's opponents as those erecting the barriers. Either side could use this text to bolster the argument that they are seeking to prevent others from embarking on a path of destruction. The challenge is to recognize that one's own position, whatever it may be, could too narrowly define God's truth, and that narrow point of view could be causing others to stumble.

This text calls the church to consider seriously how it engages in ministry and mission. In light of the warning about erecting stumbling blocks, the church must consider how everything that it does or fails to do—from worship to Web sites to mission projects—has the potential either to enhance faith or to be a stumbling block to faith. Could some of what is done in the church's name be damaging? Could lack of action be equally damaging?

Perhaps the enigmatic sayings about saltiness (vv. 49–50) relate to the opposite of causing another to stumble. Christians are called not only to refrain from actions that lead others to stray, but also to bring a distinctive flavor to the world. Being salty may not be popular. It is easier to conform to the crowd, but disciples seek to join in God's transforming work. How are Christians making positive impacts? Is the church's saltiness demonstrating God's grace in a world needing good news?

MARY JANE KERR CORNELL

Exegetical Perspective

a large stone tied to a person's neck, but the image may be even more dramatic: the offender is wearing the large stone with a hole in the middle of it around his or her neck like a giant collar! For those in Capernaum, a fishing village on the Sea of Galilee, the sea was just a few yards away.

Some thought that the body would be raised as it was at one's death (*2 Bar.* 50:2). As a result, without affirming such thinking, Jesus could say that it would be better to be raised with one hand, foot, or eye, than to be whole in body but be cast into gehenna.

Gehenna was the garbage dump in the Hinnom Valley, south of Jerusalem, where fires smoldered day and night. Jesus pointed to it as an image of unending torment, "the unquenchable fire" (v. 43). Following the last of this series of sayings, Jesus appended a quotation of Isaiah 66:24, which also has the verb "to quench" (v. 48).

Salt in a wound burns; hence the attraction of the sayings on salt to the preceding sayings. Salt was used for preservation as well as seasoning. Fish, for example, was salted for export. Perhaps persecution, or the testing of one's faith, was viewed as salting "with fire." The two sayings in verse 50 also feature salt, although they have nothing to do with persecution. Elsewhere Jesus said that his followers were to be like salt (Matt. 5:13; cf. Col. 4:6), but if they lose their saltiness (something that does not happen with pure salt but happened with other mixtures of minerals), how could it be restored? In other words, if disciples of Jesus cease to be distinctive, like salt that seasons, preserves, and burns, how can they be restored?

Finally, he admonished them, "Have salt in yourselves, and be at peace with one another" (v. 50). How are salt and peace related? Perhaps the sense is that those who are genuinely Jesus' disciples, serving the least among them and causing no offense to others, will show they are disciples by living in peace. Pass the salt, please!

R. ALAN CULPEPPER

Homiletical Perspective

of God that Jesus calls for is peace. When all the impurities in our lives have been removed (burned off or salted), that is, all of the distractions, all of the lies and misplaced priorities, all of the greed and guilty pleasures, have been removed, what remains is peace. That is what Jesus wants for us: peace. The question persists, however: Are we willing to pay the price? Is peace worth the cost? Will we simply settle for a false and ultimately unsatisfying alternative?

The sheer volume of the discussion on the dire consequences for malfeasance as a disciple would seem to swamp the brief mention of the proposed benefit, provided almost in passing, "Be at peace with one another." That is the promise and that is what the world is clamoring for, however: peace, after seemingly endless rounds of conflict among world and regional powers, the exhausting demands of economic uncertainty, mindless political haggling, and the relentless conflict of competing claims. Too often, however, the search for peace devolves into escape, escape from the fractured, complicated world of false promises. Try to image for your hearers some concrete examples of this desire for escape as a faint substitute for peace.

Peace here need not be seen as a reward for dogged persistence or mere obedience, but as the natural outcome of a life lived in accordance with the discipline outlined by Jesus. It is more than a matter of moral imperative; it is a matter of understanding who we are as Christ's followers. We are freed from using others to achieve our own ends and freed for building them up. While the Bible passage spends little time teasing out the specifics of this peace, the preacher will need carefully to image and witness to the essential nature of this peace, or it will simply disappear in the tsunami of harsh images left in the minds of the hearers from the bulk of the passage (vv. 42–48). Be specific; be concrete. Look around. Where do you see this peace? When have you experienced it?

RICHARD STERN

Mark 10:1–12

¹He left that place and went to the region of Judea and beyond the Jordan. And crowds again gathered around him; and, as was his custom, he again taught them.
²Some Pharisees came, and to test him they asked, "Is it lawful for a man to divorce his wife?" ³He answered them, "What did Moses command you?" ⁴They said, "Moses allowed a man to write a certificate of dismissal and to divorce her." ⁵But Jesus said to them, "Because of your hardness of heart he wrote this commandment for you. ⁶But from the beginning of creation, 'God made them male and female.' ⁷'For this reason a man shall leave his father and mother and be joined to his wife, ⁸and the two shall become one flesh.' So they are no longer two, but one flesh. ⁹Therefore what God has joined together, let no one separate."
¹⁰Then in the house the disciples asked him again about this matter. ¹¹He said to them, "Whoever divorces his wife and marries another commits adultery against her; ¹²and if she divorces her husband and marries another, she commits adultery."

Theological Perspective

Mark's Gospel gets personal. This passage sticks its nose right into the most personal of matters, intimate relationships. Believers today still want to know, along with the religious authorities of Jesus' time, whether divorce is permissible among the faithful. Some branches of the church answer, "No, never!" Others regard divorce as an unfortunate but taken-for-granted reality, and move on to other relationship questions such as same-sex marriage (and divorce) among Christians.

However, reading Mark merely as a manual for individual discipleship misses the boat. Jesus' teachings concern the nature of community life and of just relations between persons, with particular attention to those who are vulnerable to abuses of power. Since intimate relationships of marriage, family, and children lie at the heart of a community's life, this passage holds both personal and deeply social implications.

The Pharisees' question invites Jesus to choose sides in an ongoing debate between rabbinical schools. Jesus refuses, explaining instead why the Mosaic law allowing divorce came into being, namely, as a concession to human frailty. Jesus draws upon Genesis 1:27 and 2:24 from the creation stories as the proper way to understand marriage, rendering a deeper reading of God's intentions for human intimate partnership in which both men and women

Pastoral Perspective

Marriage begins with promises. The bride and groom join hands before God, family, and friends and promise, in the traditional vows, to be loving and faithful "in plenty and in want, in joy and in sorrow, in sickness and in health, so long as we both shall live."[1] As a preacher's child I became familiar with these vows at an early age. My father performed the ceremony without notes, so prior to a wedding he walked around the house reciting the ritual. By the time I was ten years old I could repeat the vows—at least what I thought were the vows. It was only years later that I discovered the promise was not "in sickness and in hell."

Marriage begins with promises meant to be kept. On the day of the wedding most couples truly intend to keep their vows. However, the following years will bring times and seasons when a couple's life together may feel more like hell than a match made in heaven, and sometimes promises are broken. Christians pondering this text will include many whose lives have been touched by divorce. In addition to those whose marriages have ended, are their parents, siblings, children, relatives, and friends. For all of these people divorce is a personal issue, and for

---

1. *The Book of Common Worship* (Louisville, KY: Westminster/John Knox Press, 1993), 845.

Exegetical Perspective

This text bristles with difficulties. It is a field of land mines for interpreters and an unavoidable danger zone for ministers, in a culture in which adultery and divorce are common. Divorce was also a contested issue in ancient Judaism. The Pharisees debated the circumstances and procedure by which a man could divorce his wife (*m. Gittin* 9.3, 10). The Essenes forbade a man from remarrying as long as his wife was alive (11Q19 57.17–19), and priests could not marry divorced women (Lev. 21:7). Roman law allowed a woman to divorce her husband, a right Jewish women did not have under Jewish law. There were exceptions, however. Among the Herodians, Salome and Herodias divorced their husbands (Josephus, *Ant.* 15.259–60; 18.136).

While the Pharisees may have been trying to get Jesus to support one side or another (Hillel or Shammai) regarding divorce, it is more likely that they were trying to trap him into taking a position critical of Herod Antipas, as John the Baptist had done (6:18).

Jesus adroitly opens a trap for the Pharisees in return. He asks them what Moses said, knowing that they would appeal to the Mosaic commands and he would dismiss them. As he expected, the Pharisees affirmed that Moses allowed a man "to write a certificate of divorce and to release" (my trans.) his wife. The essential formula in the bill of divorce was "Lo,

Homiletical Perspective

This pericope has a nearly cinematic feel and structure. The author guides the attention of the listener or reader by means of scene change and altered focus. There is an evident zooming in of the hermeneutic lens from a wide-angle, establishing shot in verse 1, where Jesus is again teaching the crowds, to a medium shot of the conspiratorial Pharisees engaging Jesus (vv. 2–9). The scene then cuts to the intimate setting of the house interior, where Jesus and the disciples have gathered to hear Jesus explain his just-proclaimed view on divorce (vv. 10–12). As with the analysis or dissection of any good movie, after the initial viewing we will want to go back and look more closely at the business conducted in each scene. How does the author/narrator direct our attention and to what purpose? This series of scenes could well become the architecture for the sermon.

These verses interrupt a longer discussion crafted around the images of children and other "little ones," in order to explore the nature of the kingdom of God, a passage that in turn is sandwiched between two of Jesus' three predictions of his death and resurrection. Scenes and contexts change frequently and abruptly in the Gospel of Mark, which has, at points, a certain hurried, even breathless quality that is easily missed when examining short passages isolated from the larger flow of material, a situation that

Mark 10:1–12

Theological Perspective

participate. He thereby grounds marriage in God's intentions for humanity, embodied in creation itself. Marriage is not so easily cast aside, as anyone who has experienced the brokenness of an intimate partnership knows. When two people join to "become one flesh," both are changed. Jesus' method of interpreting the law by reading one part of Scripture (Deut. 24:1–4) in terms of another part (Gen. 1:27; 2:24) gets underneath the surface question about divorce, to address instead the meaning of marriage as the central theological issue at stake.

Even more controversial, though, are Jesus' subsequent private conversations with his disciples because of the hard word concerning remarriage. Novel in Jesus' remarks is not the connection he makes between divorce and adultery, but rather his assertion that the woman is wronged when a man divorces his wife and marries another: the man "commits adultery against her" (v. 11). Instead of seeing the woman as an object in a transaction between men, she becomes subject and agent. Of course, the concomitant reality is that she also becomes ethically responsible (v. 12). The passage thus makes a significant theological claim about human personhood and how gender differences work out in social arrangements, leaving no room for objectification or the erasure of agency.

Feminist theologian Hisako Kinukawa suggests that the key target of Jesus' critique is a particular kind of termination to marriage, in which a husband "throws away" his marriage partner without that person's consent, in order to marry another:

> In Deut. 24:1, a husband writes his wife "a certificate of divorce." "Certificate" is in Greek *apostasion*, which means "abandonment" or "alienation," and the word may be used because there is no reciprocity in this kind of divorce. It also implies that the dissolution of marriage could be done without reciprocal consent at all.[1]

Since women were far more likely than men to be tossed aside without their consent, Jesus spoke against unilateral setting aside of one partner by another. Biblical scholar Elisabeth Schüssler Fiorenza similarly focuses on the patriarchal context of divorce in the time of Jesus, in which only men could initiate an end to marriage and in which adultery was, legally speaking, an infraction of one man against another: "God did not intend patriarchy, but

---

[1]. Hisako Kinukawa, "Sexuality and Household: When 'Cultural Reading' Supersedes and Skews the Meaning of Texts," in Nicole Duran, Teresa Okure Wilkinson, and Daniel Patte, *Mark*, Texts @ Contexts (Minneapolis: Fortress Press, 2011), 147–70; quote from 165.

Pastoral Perspective

some of them Jesus' words sting with judgment or condemnation.

Marriage is a different institution today from what it was in first-century Palestine, and taking the text seriously in the twenty-first century means considering the modern audience. Modern readers may hear Jesus' words in the context of questions about the "sanctity of marriage." The pastor must consider not only the issues hidden in this code phrase, but also the counterpoint to those issues. For instance, are people outraged over laws allowing gay marriage? The counterpoint is that same-sex couples in long-term relationships may wonder why their commitment should not be included when discussing the bond of marriage. Are people mourning a nostalgic 1950s image of a working husband with a homemaker wife baking brownies for the children's after-school snack? The reality of today's economy makes such a scenario the luxury of the wealthy. Are people distressed by society's acceptance of unmarried couples living together? Children of broken marriages may be wary of commitment, and for some senior citizens marriage would have serious economic consequences. A pastoral approach is to consider the fear underlying these questions and issues, and explore whether or not the text provides guidance for addressing them.

While Jesus was not focusing on such contemporary questions, his words do address the "sanctity of marriage" in the sense of condemning a casual attitude toward the marriage relationship. By challenging the notion that divorce may be taken lightly, the text raises a parallel issue: marriage should not be a careless, blasé act. Celebrity marriages that end before the honeymoon is over, reality television shows (e.g., *The Bachelor*), and a 2011 proposal in the Mexican legislature to allow renewable two-year marriage contracts are but a few extreme illustrations of how modern marriage is no longer regarded as a "till death do us part" institution.

Perhaps the sanctity of marriage is threatened by our society's disregard for the difficulty of maintaining healthy, faithful relationships. Good marriages do not just happen; they take work. This work is not limited to the spouses. It takes a village, not only to raise a child, but also to sustain a marriage. Married couples need the support of family and friends beyond the wedding day. The church frequently fails in lending support to marriages. A strict focus on the sinful nature of divorce can lead to preserving marriages at the expense of human beings, in essence destroying the couple to save the marriage.

Exegetical Perspective

thou art free to marry any man" (*m. Gittin* 9.3),[1] but the schools of Hillel and Shammai differed on the interpretation of the phrase in Deuteronomy 24:1 regarding permissible grounds for a divorce:

> The School of Shammai say: A man may not divorce his wife unless he has found unchastity in her, for it is written, Because he hath found in her indecency in anything. And the School of Hillel say: [He may divorce her] even if she spoiled a dish for him, for it is written, Because he hath found in her indecency in anything. R. Akiba says: Even if he found another fairer than she, for it is written, And it shall be if she find no favour in his eyes. (*m. Gittin* 9.10)[2]

Jesus' response is breathtaking. He dismisses this entire debate, and by implication the Mosaic law on divorce, as evidence of their "hardness of heart," a term that evokes the resistance of both the Pharaoh and the recalcitrant Israelites to God's instructions (Exod. 7:13–14; Ezek. 3:7). The implication is that the law was framed with the waywardness of the Israelites in mind, but the Mosaic law was not the sole authority for God's will for the covenant people. God's will was also revealed in the creation.

As a result there is a universal standard for ethics in relation to fellow human beings created in God's image, and in particular in God's intention for marriage. Jesus quotes Genesis 1:27 and 2:24. The earliest manuscripts of Mark (Codex Sinaiticus and Codex Vaticanus, both fourth century) lack the continuation of Genesis 2:24, "and be joined to his wife," and the Nestle-Aland *Novum Testamentum Graece*, twenty-seventh edition, puts the phrase in brackets, indicating that it is doubtful (cf. Matt. 19:5). Jesus quotes from the creation account in Genesis 1 and 2 (he never refers to the subordination of women to men in Gen. 3:16), and he sets God's original intention for the creation above God's response to human sinfulness in the Mosaic law. God's will is that "the two become one flesh." Therefore, Jesus forbids divorce.

Mark offers the most stringent, and possibly the earliest, tradition of Jesus' teaching on divorce, but the New Testament itself gives evidence of alternate traditions and pastoral interpretations. In Matthew Jesus allows divorce in cases of *porneia*—adultery, unchastity, or perhaps polygamy or marriage within forbidden degrees of relationship (5:32; 19:9; cf. Acts 15:20, 29; 1 Cor. 7:2; 1 Thess. 4:3), and Paul allows divorce if the unbelieving partner demands it (1 Cor.

---
1. Herbert Danby, trans., *The Mishnah* (Oxford: Oxford University Press, 1933), 319.
2. Ibid., 321.

Homiletical Perspective

is difficult to avoid in liturgical preaching, unless one conscientiously attends to the *lectio continua* nature of portions of the liturgical year.

Following the transfiguration, readers join Jesus as members of a southbound caravan made up of disciples, curious crowds, and antagonistic enemies. Jesus has been teaching his way through Galilee and Judea. The subject of his teaching has ranged from predictions of his betrayal and death, to what it means to be the greatest, to an exhortation on responsible discipleship with its promise of peace, and now, catechesis on divorce.

Those looking for wiggle room on divorce—under what conditions it is permissible, for example—may be frustrated by this passage. There does not seem to be any room to maneuver. In a culture in which fewer people get married at all and some get married later in life, in which some half of the couples getting married eventually get divorced, and furthermore in which parenthood does not need the institution of marriage, these verses must seem outrageously outdated and simply irrelevant. Marriage becomes a quaint but vestigial enterprise. Still, people continue to get married and remarried. What can these verses possibly say to our time? What is your judgment?

On the flip side of the hermeneutical circle, however, how do these verses judge us? While the immediate context is the discussion of divorce and remarriage, the larger context recalls the concern of the disciples in 9:38–41 about who belongs to the in-group and who does not. Jesus reorients the matter by refocusing on a proper attitude for the disciples, that is, not to be stumbling blocks for "these little ones." Here too Jesus reorients the discussion, away from what those involved in the discussion might hope for, to a proclamation of what God wants. In terms of these verses, God hopes that marriage be a once-and-forever commitment.

What is it that we hope for in marriage, or in any other relationship? It is too easy to dismiss this passage because it embodies values that, as a culture, we do not seem to uphold. The passage asks us to take an even larger look at the whole complex of what we value and how it squares with the way we believe God created things to be. When there is divorce and possibly remarriage, there should at least be the recognition that harm has been done to all those involved. No one escapes unscathed. Promises made have been broken. Commitments may have become betrayals. Marriage here is not simply a legal or sociological matter, but an ontological matter of God's

Mark 10:1–12

Theological Perspective

created persons as male and female human beings [who] enter into a common human life and social relationship because they are created as equals."[2]

Embedded within Mark's larger theme of empowerment of the "disinherited" of the earth within the reign of God is the economics of divorce. In Jesus' time, women depended upon kinship and marriage ties for livelihood, as still is the case in some societies. In contemporary North American social contexts, while women have greater economic independence, divorce still has a greater negative economic impact upon women and those who depend upon them, namely, children.

One urgent theological issue in interpreting this passage concerns the church's damaging history of complicity in legitimating violence against women by requiring them to stay in dangerous marriages. This clearly is not an appropriate understanding of Jesus' words as a theological claim about the meaning of marriage. Unarguably, with intimate-partner abuse, the joining and companionship meanings of the relationship are already breached. Reading the larger trajectory of Mark's Gospel, with its focus upon relational justice and the upending of status hierarchies, it becomes impossible faithfully to interpret this text as requiring the subjugation of women to violent partnerships.

At the same time, though, the passage speaks against casual treatments of marriage that threaten to trivialize its significance by a series of actions in which persons glide in and out of relationships. The pastoral theological claim embedded in Jesus' teachings is the assertion that in the wake of discord that leads to separation, the problems and the people are not mended merely by ending the marriage contracts. Andrew Root's recent work on children of divorce makes the parallel claim that while for parents divorce often represents a liberating move to seek new, differently meaningful relationships, for children it problematically involves a "loss of being." What children of divorce need, Root says, is "a place to belong, a community in which their humanity is upheld."[3] The idea that the faith community might be a place of stability, being, and belonging seems entirely in line with this Gospel writer's larger trajectory of the renewal of family, children, and economic relations under the reign of God.

JOYCE ANN MERCER

Pastoral Perspective

Buying into society's myth of individualism can cause the church to neglect offering couples and families the guidance and support of the community. Close-knit congregations may ostracize one or both of the partners following a divorce. The text challenges Christians, individually and as congregations, to explore how to be more faithful in caring for marriages, and more proactive in supporting families.

When the Pharisees questioned whether divorce was lawful, Jesus answered that his followers are to demonstrate a radical faithfulness that supersedes legality. Divorce is allowed because of "hardness of heart," that is, because humans are sinful. However, that is not the way it is supposed to be; God's intention is for loving relationships, not broken ones. Anyone suffering the agony of divorce knows the legal act of dissolving a marriage does not negate the fact that once there was a relationship.

In its broadest sense the text addresses the issue of relationships. Jesus' words emphasize that God intends marriage to be one of the strongest of human relationships, if not the strongest. Modern society focuses a great deal on the relationship between parent and child, but this text says clearly that a child leaves parents for the spouse. It takes a toll on marriage when children come first for one or both of the parents. It takes a toll on children when they sense responsibility for keeping their parents together. Divorce also takes a toll on children, even when it occurs after they have left home. This Scripture underscores that the bond between spouses is the glue of family life, and breaking this bond has consequences for all who are part of the extended family.

The text calls individuals and communities to a serious consideration of radical faithfulness. Promises are not to be taken lightly, and to enter into and maintain a marriage relationship requires radical commitment that must rely on God as well as the faith community. For Christians, marriage is not simply an agreement between two people; it is a covenant that includes God as a partner. Recognizing and cultivating God's presence in a marriage can enhance joy and give hope in sorrow. However, no human relationship is without sin, and sometimes promises are broken. While living with this reality, Christians can hold fast to the promise that God is always radically faithful, and there is nothing that will divorce us from God's love.

MARY JANE KERR CORNELL

---

2. Elisabeth Schüssler Fiorenza, *In Memory of Her: A Feminist Theological Reconstruction of Christian Origins* (New York: Crossroads, 1985), 143.
3. Andrew Root, *Children of Divorce: The Loss of Family as the Loss of Being* (Grand Rapids: Baker Academic, 2010), 121.

Exegetical Perspective

7:10–15). The early church adapted the absolute prohibition of divorce to pastoral situations, while retaining Jesus' teaching that marriage should be indissoluble.

Questions naturally arose regarding remarriage (which is also forbidden in the *Damascus Document* 4:21–5:2). Mark often reports that Jesus gave private teaching to his disciples (4:10, 33–34; 7:17; 9:33), so the disciples continued the discussion with Jesus (10:10). The purpose of a certificate of divorce was to make it legal for a divorced woman to marry (see *m. Gittin* 9.3 above), but she could remarry only with her former husband's consent (Josephus, *Ant.* 15.259). It is possible that verse 11 means that a man who divorces and marries again commits adultery with the second wife, but the more widely accepted view is that it means that he commits adultery against his first wife. The same is true for the woman; if she marries another, she commits adultery. These verses extend the logic of Jesus' view of marriage as creating a union that cannot be broken. In Mark, Jesus offers no provision for remarriage.

Questions of marriage and divorce were (and remain) central for Judaism because they were connected to membership in the covenant community. Jesus' teachings on this subject appear to be closer to those of the Essenes and the House of Shammai than to the more lenient view of Hillel. For scriptural support, he turned not to the Mosaic law but to Eden, the order of creation—the ideal, not the accommodated ethic. As categorical as the Markan tradition on divorce and remarriage is, it is equally significant that the church embraced the provisions allowed by Matthew (*porneia*) and Paul (an unbelieving spouse). The New Testament therefore holds forth the ideal for marriage (that it is a union between husband and wife that cannot be dissolved), while recognizing circumstances in which the ideal is not attainable. However, maintaining the balance of this polarity has been a challenge for the church from its very beginning.

R. ALAN CULPEPPER

Homiletical Perspective

hope or design. The preacher can call the assembly to a greater or larger understanding of what marriage is in the church's theological understanding; it is more than a mere rite of passage, which can be done and redone as the need or desire arises.

A sermon structured on the movement of these verses might begin by speaking of Jesus teaching the crowds about the life of the disciple, about how the crowds followed him around hoping for enlightenment, for insight and inspiration. Many today are calling for preachers to lay down the law, to tell them what the Bible teaches, so that they can have clarity about what to expect from God, from others, and from themselves.

Then the preaching perspective might move in a little closer to the Pharisees, who attempt to trap Jesus but then step into the trap themselves. As usual, Jesus sidesteps the Pharisees' attack, as they unwitting become victims of their own treachery. This calls attention to the need to examine the agenda one may bring to Jesus' teaching. In order that the teaching to the crowds might become even clearer to the disciples, the scene finally cuts to the house scene, where Jesus explains the teaching in simple and certain terms: divorce and remarriage equal adultery. What about cases of extramarital affairs, spouse and child abuse, and other such matters? Is a spouse obligated to stay in a dangerous relationship? In such instances, it is even clearer that these situations are not what God hopes for in any relationship. All parties suffer, no matter how faultless any of them may be. It might well be better to divorce and perhaps remarry, but this does not deny or mitigate that God's hope for the marriage was not fulfilled, and possibly not respected. In each of the above sections, the preacher will need to image the idea with concrete examples, and to avoid becoming moralistic. This is not a passage that intends to condemn but to reorient, exhort, and empower.

RICHARD STERN

Mark 10:13–16

¹³People were bringing little children to him in order that he might touch them; and the disciples spoke sternly to them. ¹⁴But when Jesus saw this, he was indignant and said to them, "Let the little children come to me; do not stop them; for it is to such as these that the kingdom of God belongs. ¹⁵Truly I tell you, whoever does not receive the kingdom of God as a little child will never enter it." ¹⁶And he took them up in his arms, laid his hands on them, and blessed them.

Theological Perspective

These four verses tell what probably is the best-known story about children in all the Gospels. Children hold special significance in the narrative of Mark's Gospel. On the one hand their presence across the Gospel indicates that Jesus interacted with children throughout his ministry. Behind these stories are actual children in need of the healing, feeding, caring, blessing, and welcome of Jesus. On the other hand, children in the Gospel of Mark also play an important symbolic narrative role, standing as avatars for all those who were without power, status, or security. In the sociopolitical context of Mark's writing, there were many such people, because agrarian village life under the terms of the *Pax Romana*, the "peace of Rome," was life in a state of political and economic subjugation that followed military conquest and occupation. Rebellion was promptly squashed by state-sponsored terrorism through mass slaughter and enslavement.

Alongside this program of violent subjugation were Rome's economic policies involving heavy taxation of people in occupied lands to pay for the empire's building programs and feed its armies. Together, these policies of taxation and terrorism created a climate of scarcity and fear. Against this oppressive form of imperial rule, Mark's Gospel tells of a different kind of rule—one premised not on

Pastoral Perspective

Where do children belong? That question is as pertinent today as it was for Jesus and his disciples. The disciples did not think children belonged with Jesus, who could have been rubbing shoulders with the rich and powerful, instead of touching the heads of infants. Twenty-first-century Christians, on the other hand, may be quick to proclaim that of course children belong with Jesus! Actions and attitudes may speak louder than words, though. Jesus' admonition, "Let the little children come to me; do not stop them" (v. 14) calls Christians to ponder how children are hindered from encountering Jesus.

Contrary to first-century attitudes, life in many modern families revolves around children. Calendars and clocks are programmed according to school and sports schedules. Parents agonize over financial decisions related to the costs (necessary or perceived) of providing for their offspring. Do families devote the same amount of time, energy, and emotional capital to ensuring that children are not hindered from being blessed by Jesus? Is family prayer time sacrificed for study time, because getting into the best college seems more important than getting into the best relationship with God? Does participating in a faith community assume as high a priority as participation on an athletic team? Will parents choose to send children to confirmation class or to soccer

Exegetical Perspective

Jesus' relationship with the disciples has its stormy moments, but Jesus uses even these confrontations as teaching moments. This section of the Gospel develops the teaching that to follow Jesus his disciples must lay aside their own self-absorption and self-interest and be servants of all (9:35; 10:43–45). To illustrate this lesson, Jesus blesses a child (9:36) and tells the disciples that anyone who receives such a child receives him (9:37). That scene becomes the basis for further teachings on not stopping the unauthorized exorcist (9:38–39), hospitality (9:41), forbidding husbands to divorce their wives (10:1–12), renouncing possessions (10:17–31), and granting a beggar's request (10:46–52).

Throughout, Jesus overturns prevailing assumptions about the place of children in society, the role of brokers and patrons, male prerogatives with regard to divorce, the status of the wealthy and powerful, and the disciples' right to control ministry in Jesus' name. The disciples assume that it is their duty to keep people from coming to Jesus. They seek to prevent the exorcist from invoking Jesus' name; they seek to prevent parents from bringing their children to Jesus; and they (or some in the crowd) seek to silence Bartimaeus when he calls out to Jesus. In other words, they seek to broker access to Jesus and his power to bless and heal.

Homiletical Perspective

There is no overt indication that this scene has shifted from the previous pericope. The intimate feel of the scene has changed, however, as people intrude into Jesus' private moment with the disciples. Jesus continues in the teaching mode, returning to the discussion of children and their status and role in the kingdom of God. There are at least two levels from which one could preach these verses, levels that are not mutually exclusive. Indeed, in combination they suggest a possible sermon structure, moving from particular to universal, from obedience and moral norms to transformation or conversion of the heart. The first or surface level is the presenting matter of what it means to receive the kingdom as a little child. The second is the overarching concern that ties this and the previous two passages together: what it means to live as a disciple.

Unfathomably, the disciples seem already to have forgotten Jesus' words about children from a few verses earlier (9:36–37). Is this the author's attempt at reinforcing the idea of the disciples as witless and bumbling buffoons? Maybe no one has really understood the full implications of this image. Children would appear to be in the top ten of our culture's list of concerns. Doting parents insist on only the best for their cherished offspring: clothes, toys, schools, friends, and so forth. As Garrison Keillor has noted

Mark 10:13–16

Theological Perspective

subjugation, scarcity, and fear, but on the kingdom of God as proclaimed in the life and ministry of Jesus. Under God's reign, this Gospel announces, even the lowliest persons find welcome and empowerment into the abundant life of God, and power and significance are measured in very different terms than those of the imperial regime. Mark thus offers a counternarrative to the dominant story of empire.

As if to reiterate elements of a previously told story involving children (9:33–41), the Gospel writer here offers another vignette featuring an action between Jesus and his disciples in which Jesus takes children in his arms. New Testament scholar Judith Gundry-Volf notes parallels in Hellenistic texts of the same period that also use the same term (*enankalizomai*) to depict children being taken into the arms of women. She holds that Jesus, by acting in a manner commonly associated with the work of women, made care for children into "a sign of greatness for all disciples. What appeared to be an undistinguished activity—care for children, belonging to the domain of women—becomes a prime way for all disciples to demonstrate the greatness that corresponds to the reign of God."[1] Jesus' action thus underscores the continuing theological theme in Mark of the kingdom of God's continual overturning of hierarchies and expectations about power.

Jesus embraces the children on the heels of the disciples' rebuke (*epetimēsan*, v. 13) to those bringing children to him for his touch. He responds to his disciples with anger, telling them not to stop the children for "it is to such as these that the kingdom of God belongs" (v. 14). He tells them that whoever does not receive (or welcome) the kingdom of God as a child cannot enter into it (v. 15). Then he takes the children in his arms (as in 9:36), places his hands on them, and blesses them. The passage thus ends with Jesus blessing those whom the disciples would have turned away, and defining access to the *basileia tou theou*, the reign of God, in terms of them. The disciples, appointing themselves gatekeepers, instead find themselves rebuked by Jesus for their efforts. Once again Jesus overturns expectations about who matters and who is welcomed, by welcoming these children from the crowd, while also suggesting that those who would be gatekeepers of God would do well not to make assumptions about those whom Jesus would welcome.

The theological question upon which this text hinges is, what does it mean to receive the kingdom

---

1. Judith M. Gundry-Volf, "The Least and the Greatest: Children in the New Testament," in *The Child in Christian Thought*, ed. Marcia J. Bunge (Grand Rapids: Eerdmans, 2001), 44.

Pastoral Perspective

practice? Parents may hinder their children's access to Jesus by failing to demonstrate that active involvement in the community of faith is one of the most important priorities in their own lives.

The question of the role of children is also pertinent for churches. Are children viewed as an integral part of the worshiping community? Do congregations welcome children in worship or see them as a distraction? Does the worship experience engage all the senses? Do the architecture and order of service say that worship is a spectator sport or a participatory event? Are children asked to be worship leaders on dates other than Youth Sunday? Is intellect or education a prerequisite for encountering Jesus in the sanctuary, with complex theological language masking the truth of the good news? Welcoming children in worship does not mean trying to assure that children totally understand worship, or that all of it is relevant to their lives. Even adults do not have to comprehend everything or expect all that happens in worship will address their specific circumstances. More than "getting something out of it," people of all ages come to worship to "put something into it"—giving praise and thanksgiving to God. This text can push congregations to consider practical ways to welcome children beyond simply inserting a children's sermon into the order of worship.

Jesus claims that children are the sermon: "It is to such as these that the kingdom of God belongs. . . . Whoever does not receive the kingdom of God as a little child will never enter it" (vv. 14–15). These words raise the issue of what it means to be "like a child." Certainly it does not mean to be "innocent" or "good." Any parent who has experienced the tantrum of a toddler or the rebellion of an adolescent will refute that notion. One key to understanding what it means to be like a child is to consider how children are designated on the IRS income-tax form: dependents. Children are powerless, needy, and totally dependent on others. By this definition, who are the children in today's world? They are not only the sweet-faced youngsters whose antics are depicted on YouTube videos, but may include people of all ages who stand in lines at soup kitchens, redeem food stamps in the grocery checkout, rely on Medicaid for health care, or sleep in homeless shelters.

The call to become like children, a call to radical dependence, is countercultural in today's society. The pastoral task is to challenge the concept that dependency is negative. A first step to overcoming this prejudiced attitude may be to open one's eyes. We are reluctant to acknowledge the reality of

Exegetical Perspective

That is the way power and kingdoms work. Position is maintained by brokering or dispensing power, wealth, and privilege to others in quid pro quo arrangements. The exorcist has not contracted to exercise the power of Jesus' name. Women, children, and beggars have nothing to give in return. Although Jesus is on his way to his death, the disciples are focused on securing positions of privilege and power for themselves (9:34; 10:35–45).

Social perspectives seem to have moderated in the Hellenistic period, but society in antiquity had a very low, unenlightened attitude toward children. Children were generally thought to be willful, lacking in understanding, and in need of stern discipline (Isa. 3:4; Eccl. 10:16; Wis. 12:24; 15:14), and rabbis did not waste their time with children: "Morning sleep, mid-day wine, chattering with children, and tarrying in places where men of the common people assemble destroy a man" (*m. Aboth* 3.11). The disciples are therefore acting in accord with prevailing norms in regard to the exercise of power, their role as brokers, and the common understanding of children.

Jesus is incensed! *Aganakteō* is a strong word meaning to "be aroused, indignant, angry" (10:41; 14:4). Both Matthew and Luke omit the term in their accounts (Matt. 19:13; Luke 18:15), editing out Mark's freer references to Jesus' anger (3:5; cf. variant in 1:41). We are left to interpret Jesus' anger from the context and what Jesus says in response to the disciples: (1) he loves children and wants to bless them; (2) he is angry and frustrated that the disciples still do not understand (4:13; 6:52; 7:18; 8:17, 21); and (3) their lack of understanding strikes at the core of what the kingdom of God is about, as the references to the kingdom in verses 14 and 15 show.

Jesus condemns every effort to keep people from coming to him, regardless of what he is doing at the time or who they are. In contrast, "hinder" (*kōlyō*) is the New Testament word for the church's misguided efforts to keep people away from Jesus. In addition to the children and the unauthorized exorcist, it is used in reference to the Ethiopian eunuch (Acts 8:36), the house of Cornelius (Acts 10:47; 11:17), speaking in tongues (1 Cor. 14:39), Gentiles (1 Thess. 2:16), those who want to marry (1 Tim. 4:3), and those sent by the elder John (3 John 10). Luke, on the other hand, chronicles "the struggle for an unhindered gospel," declaring the triumph in Rome when Paul is able to preach the gospel "openly and unhindered" (Acts 28:31 RSV).[1] Children are not a nuisance or an

---
1. See Frank Stagg, *The Book of Acts: The Early Struggle for an Unhindered Gospel* (Nashville: Broadman Press, 1955).

Homiletical Perspective

about the residents in Lake Wobegon, "All of the children are above average."

Advertisers use images of overly precious and precocious children (as well as dogs and cats) to sell products that may have nothing to do with children (or dogs or cats). We all love our children, do we not? Several states offer license plates that promote proper care for children, for example, "Kids first" or "Keep kids safe." If everything were so perfect, would states have any reason to offer these license plates, which in fact serve as reminders that we have fallen far short of our ideal? Nightly news programs report the latest arrests of parents whose children are living in homes that also function as meth labs, with the attendant toxic chemicals all about. Mug shots of child abusers all too frequently grace the front pages of the daily newspaper. Churches adopt policies of "No child left alone," that is, with only one adult present. Windows are installed in classroom and office doors.

In Jesus' day, of course, there would have been no such noble sentiments adorning the license plates of chariots and donkey carts making their way through the streets of Jerusalem. Children were well ensconced at the bottom of the social ladder. So why Jesus' persistent reference to children? It cannot be their innocence or sweet character. Children can be as mean and nasty as any embittered, maladjusted adult. Is it their complete dependence on the goodwill of others? Maybe the focus is not really on the children.

In this pericope, as in 9:42–50, Jesus fleshes out the motives or predispositions of the disciples, who are all too inclined to make judgments about the worthiness of others. The disciples are concerned about status in relationship to Jesus, but they again have misread the situation and display their dull-witted lack of understanding of even the most blatant clues to the nature of Jesus' messiahship. Jesus summarily upends their pretensions. Discipleship is defined not by status but by relationship, in particular, by one's service to others less fortunate. A theological term for this is "kenosis," or "self-emptying." This is not an exclusively religious ideal; it can have civil dimensions. John F. Kennedy referred to it in his inaugural address when he exhorted us, "Ask not what your country can do for you; ask what you can do for your country."[1] This self-emptying is most powerfully exemplified, though, in the life and

---
1. John F. Kennedy, January 20, 1961. Manuscript available at http://www.jfklibrary.org/Search.aspx?nav=Ntk:SearchAll%7cinaugural%7c1%7c,N:16; accessed January 17, 2013.

Mark 10:13–16

Theological Perspective

of God as a child? Many interpreters equate this with a romantic vision of a child as one who simply, joyously, and spontaneously accepts the teachings of Jesus. There is also a temptation to understand Jesus' statement in terms of the need for persons seeking to enter the kingdom of God to act in humility or innocence. Reading Mark's Gospel as a counternarrative to the oppressive imperial policies suggests a different theological agenda at work here. It would be entirely understandable for those in occupied territories like Galilee in Palestine, as people laboring under the oppressive economic policies of Roman occupation, to focus on securing resources for themselves and their own families in the face of scarcity.

From all indications, however, the children who come to be touched by Jesus are not just children from nuclear families brought by their parents, but, rather, the casualties of imperial policies of economic oppression and terrorism that kept families from functioning as economic units and sent children into destitution. As was the case when he refused to restrict his own family to a narrow kinship network of mother and brothers (3:31–35), here also his action of welcoming children involves opening up the boundaries of membership among God's people. In Mark's context, then, entering the kingdom of God comes from solidarity with those most vulnerable to the hardships of imperial oppression.

Also of significance, Jesus speaks to his disciples—the ones arguing about their status and positions of power—these words about the necessity of receiving the kingdom of God like a child. The narrative thereby underscores another important theological theme in Mark, one that would not have been lost on the emerging leadership of the church at the time this text was written, a generation after the events it describes. Jesus' preaching of a new kingdom is not a message about replacing one power hierarchy with another. Rather, as this passage stresses, receiving the kingdom of God as a child constitutes, in the words of biblical scholar Elisabeth Schüssler Fiorenza, "a challenge to relinquish all claims of power and domination over others. . . . The child/slave who occupies the lowest place within patriarchal structures becomes the primary paradigm of true discipleship."[2]

JOYCE ANN MERCER

Pastoral Perspective

powerlessness. Some people will counter the call to awareness with arguments about individual responsibility. Such arguments may arise from a desire to claim sole credit for one's personal success. Someone able to admit his or her own dependence is more likely to recognize a kinship with these other dependent children of God.

Members of Alcoholics Anonymous and other 12-step programs understand the importance of acknowledging their dependence. The first steps—admitting one's powerlessness and trusting in a power greater than oneself—are a modern-day example of childlike behavior. Pastors and teachers studying this text might gain a greater insight by visiting an open meeting of AA, where conversation is likely to revolve around issues of faith and dependence.

Children are those who do not worry about tomorrow but who trust their lives and their well-being to a power beyond themselves. Such trusting does not mean children are unquestioning. Little children always ask questions, especially "why?" Childlike trust does not dispel doubts, but enables honest questioning without fear. Receiving the kingdom of God as a child may mean that one's doubts, questions, and even protests can be voiced to a loving Parent without fear that doing so will threaten the continuing gift of divine love and grace.

Parallel to the question, where do children belong? is the question, where do children *not* belong? Children do not belong with abusive parents or guardians. They do not belong in sickbeds without access to health care. They do not belong in underfunded schools or inadequate day-care centers. They do not belong in prisons, having been lured into crime while living in poverty or despair. They do not belong on the street as prostitutes, victims of commercial sexual exploitation.[1] This text challenges Christians to recognize that although much of our culture seems to revolve around children, in fact many children are still marginalized in our society, as much as they were in the first century. Jesus demonstrated a radical acceptance of these little ones. As followers of Jesus, Christians are called not only to keep from hindering children, but also to engage in action, advocating for programs and policies that address children's issues.

MARY JANE KERR CORNELL

---

2. Elisabeth Schüssler Fiorenza, *In Memory of Her: A Feminist Theological Reconstruction of Christian Origins* (New York: Crossroad, 1985), 148.

1. Street GRACE is an example of how churches in Atlanta, GA, are working to end commercial sexual exploitation of children. See www.streetGrace.org; accessed November 15, 2012.

Exegetical Perspective

interruption of Jesus' work; they are as important as the rich man in the next scene. Blessing the powerless and insignificant in society is what Jesus' kingdom work is all about.

The common translation of verse 14, "to such as these . . . the kingdom of God belongs" (NASB, RSV, NIV, NRSV), is really a paraphrase. The verb in this verse is not "belongs to" but "is." The meaning may therefore be a more sweeping assertion about the nature of the kingdom: the kingdom of God is "of" such as these; it is defined by, or will be recognized by, the fact that it embraces those who are as unassuming, unpretentious, and insignificant in the eyes of society as children. We can therefore recognize the kingdom today when we see "such as these" being embraced, accepted, and cared for.

Verse 15 is attested in various forms in several strands of the Gospel tradition (Matt. 18:3; Luke 18:17; John 3:3), but always with the same elements: (1) "amen" (doubled in John 3:3); (2) "I say to you"; (3) a condition, related to receiving the kingdom of God as a child would (Mark 10:15), becoming like children (Matt. 18:3), or being born again ("from above," John 3:3); and (4) "you will never enter it." The kingdom is defined by those who can receive it. The proud, arrogant, self-sufficient—not to say the calculating, ambitious, and self-absorbed—cannot enter the kingdom of God. Paradoxically, the kingdom is open to everyone, but only those who can receive it as joyfully and spontaneously as a child can enter.

Dramatically overturning the social conventions of the day and the disciples' understanding of what he is about, Jesus wraps his arms around the children, blesses them, and lays his hands on them. One verb will not do to convey Jesus' joy and delight in the children.

Look again at the traditional picture in the church's nursery—the one of Jesus surrounded by children beaming with his love. It is not a nursery picture. It is a picture of the kingdom of God.

R. ALAN CULPEPPER

Homiletical Perspective

death of Jesus, who did it not just for a nation but for all creation. Are there others you can identify who exemplify this ideal in ways large or small?

This passage, though, along with the preceding 9:42–50 and 10:1–12, is about more than the particulars that it addresses. It points to a larger scale of judgment. We exist in the tension of living between two competing poles: the world's values and the values of God. We are ambivalent, pulled this way and that. The lure and demands of the immediate, however, too often trump the call of the eternal.

On the basis of these passages, we will most certainly need to recalibrate our systemic priorities. Instead of a measure of status, we are called to a measure of inclusive service. How can we be of ever more service to others? The standards by which we typically make judgments are inverted so that disciples are now on the bottom of the scale, emptying themselves in humble service to God's invitation to discipleship. This, of course, is completely contrary to the values of the culture in which we live, where we are called to get more and more, not give more and more. Save the nation; go to the mall!

I suppose the tendency is to water down the demands of passages like this one and, in the process, dismiss their claim on us. They ask too much. That response, however, is a sure indication that conversion has not yet taken place, that the demands are still a list of dos and don'ts, moral imperatives without sufficient attention to the empowerment of God to make the demands possible. Most of us join the myopic disciples, who fail to notice or understand that Jesus is the model for this service, the one who calls us to join him, and the one who empowers us to live into that calling. This self-emptying is not a matter of the oppression of external forces demanding our compliance with a set of rules. It is a statement of identity. The more one lives out of and into that identity, the more one sees the deep, abiding value of it as a force for good.

RICHARD STERN

Mark 10:17–22

¹⁷As he was setting out on a journey, a man ran up and knelt before him, and asked him, "Good Teacher, what must I do to inherit eternal life?" ¹⁸Jesus said to him, "Why do you call me good? No one is good but God alone. ¹⁹You know the commandments: 'You shall not murder; You shall not commit adultery; You shall not steal; You shall not bear false witness; You shall not defraud; Honor your father and mother.'" ²⁰He said to him, "Teacher, I have kept all these since my youth." ²¹Jesus, looking at him, loved him and said, "You lack one thing; go, sell what you own, and give the money to the poor, and you will have treasure in heaven; then come, follow me." ²²When he heard this, he was shocked and went away grieving, for he had many possessions.

Theological Perspective

The man who stops and questions Jesus in this passage introduces two key terms for the discussion that follows: "good" and "inherit." The question of the "good" is interesting because Jesus' response both questions the man's statement ("Why do you call me good?") and directs the man to the source of all good ("No one is good but God alone," v. 18). Jesus is not trying to deny his own goodness; rather, he is asking the man if he knows what he is saying and why he is saying it. Jesus refuses any empty flattery (if that is what it is) and takes the opportunity to challenge his interlocutor with a deeper question, "Do you even know what it means to call something or someone good?" Jesus seems to think the man is confused about what is good. We might say he is confused about the grammar of the good, unable to distinguish good from goods.

"Good" or "the good" (as the philosophers say) is that attribute of God that names God's moral perfection. Anything that is good in this world is such because it participates in the goodness of God. So, on the one hand, our economic language of goods (as in "goods and services") implies that the material things we buy and sell are good because they are drawn from God's good creation. On the other hand, the language can be used to mean simply riches, material possessions, that are treasured, not

Pastoral Perspective

Notice first that this story begins with an interruption. The initiative is this man's, not that of Jesus. Jesus' agenda is the journey on which he is now setting out—the journey that he has begun toward the cross. Before he has gone more than a few steps down the road, however, this fellow runs up, kneels down, and poses a question. The road forward is blocked, perhaps literally by the kneeling form of this man, but in any case decidedly by the decent regard that is owed any supplicant. Jesus stops, takes time, responds, listens, and responds again. He lets himself be interrupted.

So much of life—not least, so much of pastoral ministry—is like this, carried on in interruptions and detours from what we think we should be doing or what we set out to do. There is an often-told story about a professor about to retire who speaks of how he has resented the constant interruptions of his career by needy students and extraneous tasks. Only now, he says, he realizes that the interruptions have been his career. So perhaps we take a bit of comfort and solidarity from this image of the interrupted and responsive Jesus; or perhaps, instead, we resent his holy example, finding it of little help in our own attempts to balance the claims upon us. Whatever our response, Jesus' interruption does seem worth noticing.

Exegetical Perspective

As Jesus proceeds on his journey through Judea toward Jerusalem, his message regarding the kingdom of God and discipleship becomes increasingly relevant, critical, and challenging. Crowds gather around him as he teaches. Pharisees continue to test his knowledge. Strangers bring their children for blessings. Strange men solicit his counsel. Here, a man stops Jesus along the way, asking him about the kingdom of God. Human relations is an important component to discipleship and life in the kingdom of God. The story of the rich man, the third human relations story in Mark 10, continues to illustrate this point. The first story (10:1–12) deals with the issue of marriage and divorce; the second (10:13–16) affirms the presence of children in the kingdom; and this story confronts class.

Mark's terse storytelling directs the reader's attention to the man's wealth. The narrator describes the man simply as one who has many possessions, that is, he is rich (v. 22). Unlike Mark, the parallel Gospel stories describe the rich man in more detail. Matthew describes him as young (Matt. 19:20), whereas Luke describes him as a certain ruler (Luke 18:18). Mark's simple description of the man makes economic class easily identifiable as the central concern of this story, without the trappings of naiveté or politics. Through this story, Mark demonstrates that

Homiletical Perspective

The pericope starts with a direct and simple question that a number of Christians today may think is *the* question with regard to the religious life: "What must I do to inherit eternal life?" or variations like "How do I get into heaven?" "How can I be sure that death is not the end?" "How do I know for certain that I am saved?"

However, the answer that the Markan Jesus gives to this question is anything but direct. First, before the answer there is a scolding, which includes a self-deprecatory implication that is somewhat surprising, coming from the lips of Jesus: "Why do you call me good? No one is good but God alone" (v. 18). Then comes the initial answer: "You know the commandments"; but readers discover almost immediately that this is apparently not the real answer, or at least not the answer in its totality. As soon as the man responds that he has done this for all of his life, he is told he still lacks one thing. (The question might be raised: if the man had responded, "Thank you, Lord, for the insight; I'll go home and work on practicing the commandments more faithfully," and then walked away, would the pericope have ended there? Would Jesus have pressed further with a more humble inquirer, or does the question of lack get raised only because the man insists that he does not lack?)

Mark 10:17–22

Theological Perspective

because they reflect God's artistic glory or are put to divine use, but because they satisfy our unchecked desire to possess and consume. We discover at the end of the story that the rich man cannot relinquish his "goods" because he cannot recognize where "the good" resides.

The second theme introduced in this opening question is inheritance. The man rightly thinks of God's rewards as something to be inherited; yet he acts as if they are something to be possessed. The language of inheritance suggests waiting and receiving—a posture of receptivity—while this man shows himself to be saturated with stuff and thus unable to receive. The language of inheritance also suggests relationship. An inheritance carries with it history and kinship (and thus responsibility), whereas abstract wealth severs such ties in favor of detached and unaccountable possession. The rich man thinks he wants inheritance, but what he wants is an eternal form of abstract wealth. He soon discovers that God does not give gifts that are detached from God's own self (for if they were, how could they be good?). The gift of inheritance that God offers arises out of a life in relationship with God—hence, Jesus' invitation to "come, follow me."

So we have a man who calls Jesus good, but does not know how to identify the good, and therefore does not know what he is saying. We have a man who wants an inheritance, but who does not understand that inheritance cannot be reduced to abstract wealth. Therefore the man does not understand what he wants. We have someone who is lost, even though he keeps the commandments and has been rewarded with wealth. Nevertheless Jesus, looking at this man, "love[s] him" (v. 21).

Here we find the third central theme of this passage: love. Jesus' call and challenge to the rich man arise from love and invite the man into love ("give the money to the poor"). Jesus' invitation is not a command or a judgment, not an attempt to exact justice; it is, rather, an attempt to enact gratuity. To love the man, Jesus must tell him the hard truth, that his wealth is in his way. So Jesus invites him, as an act of love, to unload his burden, to give away his wealth, to free himself from that which has come to bind him, even though he has no idea he is so bound. This is love. This is the truth—and it is hard to hear.

"You lack one thing," Jesus tells him, and in so doing turns this man's self-understanding on its head. He, of all people, does not lack, for he is rich. Paradoxically his abundance has created a lack, and

Pastoral Perspective

Such notice, moreover, may remind us that interruptions are not just occasional problems in Mark's description of the ministry of Jesus. They happen almost constantly, from the preaching in the synagogue at Capernaum onward. It is not only the necessity of arguing with critics and trying to correct those who misunderstand. In the Markan narrative, the ministry of Jesus is itself a series of distractions and detours that frustrate his mission. Those countless exorcisms and healings, which both compassion and faithfulness compel him to perform, are also interruptions that get in his way.

Mark 1:14–15 describes the mission of Jesus as proclamation of the realm of God in the lives of those addressed; but immediately his work seems understood by others in terms of his stature and authority, of what he can do, and of how powerfully he speaks. He becomes the object of messianic expectations, and what was meant to empower others becomes, instead, his power and fame. No wonder the unclean spirits seek to "out" him as the Messiah; no wonder he seeks to silence the stories about him; and no wonder he sometimes has to withdraw. After eight chapters of that, he has now taken up a new description of his mission, one that will bring him to disappoint the expectations that all those holy interruptions have created.

Thus the outset of this pericope may serve as yet another reminder of the problem with which many of us live: on the one hand, the experience of such interruptions that display grace and faithfulness and, on the other hand, the danger that such ministry of our own may replace the gospel that we are called to make known in the lives of others.

With all that acknowledged, let us turn to the man who comes with his plea to Jesus: "Good Teacher, what must I do to inherit eternal life?" (v. 17). Whatever we understand by "eternal life," it is evident that he wants some assurance about it, some confidence that he does not now feel. Is there something he can do? This does not sound like one of those academic questions or hostile tests aimed at Jesus by the scribes. It appears that the man really wants to know. Many of us may have encountered people with a similar yearning.

In line with what was noted above, Jesus first responds by seeking to deflect the invocation of his own virtue: "Why do you call me good? No one is good but God alone" (v. 18). Then he puts forward a very simple response, pointing to the basics of the law. Is the issue of abiding life no more complex than doing right and avoiding wrong? Is that really

Exegetical Perspective

the kingdom of God requires sacrifice, self-denial, and sharing as components of response to the call of discipleship.

The story begins with a man who runs out and kneels before Jesus, asking him the critical question, "Good Teacher, what must I do to inherit eternal life?" (v. 17). Unlike the Pharisees in 10:2 (see also 8:11 and 12:15) who come to Jesus to test him, this man asks a sincere question, as indicated by his greeting of and posture toward Jesus. Although the man's formal greeting and prostrating himself seem excessive, Jesus affirms his sincerity through his later response (v. 21).

Before Jesus answers the man's question, he establishes that his teaching regarding the kingdom of God comes from God and not himself. The man's greeting suggests that he comes to Jesus because he perceives him as a good teacher. Although the text does not explain how or why the man calls Jesus good, Jesus is clear that God alone is good. Jesus' declaration is not self-deprecating; rather it is reorienting the man to recognize that God is the source of all that is good, including Jesus' teachings and humanity's faithfulness to the law.

As a starting place, Jesus responds to the rich man's question by reviewing some of the Ten Commandments. The commandments demonstrate that God is the giver of eternal life, as God is the one who lays out the journey. However, reviewing the commandments, Jesus focuses on the second tablet, which contains directives regarding human relationships. Omitting commands from the first tablet, the text suggests that Jesus assumes that the man is already devoted to God, honoring God's name, and worshiping God. Jesus includes do not murder, do not commit adultery, do not steal, do not bear false witness, and do not defraud, and honor your parents (v. 19). The commandment "do not defraud" may strike the reader as strange, as it is not listed in either Exodus 20 or Deuteronomy 5, although it is very similar to Leviticus 19:13. "Do not defraud" could be associated with "do not covet." However, this language seems to be distinctively related to the possible actions a wealthy person may commit in order to maintain or increase his wealth through injustice and oppression. Neither Matthew nor Luke includes "do not defraud" in their versions. Mark's inclusion reflects his attention to economic injustice.

The rich man declares that he has followed all of the commandments. His response demonstrates that obedience to the Torah is not enough for inheriting the kingdom of God. The sincerity of his question

Homiletical Perspective

Even here, the answer is not a perfect fit for the question that is asked. The answer is not, "Sell what you own and give the money to the poor, and then you will inherit eternal life," but rather, "Sell what you own and give to the poor, and you will have treasure in heaven" (v. 21). The shift may appear subtle at first glance, but still, a congregation might benefit from reflecting on how Jesus' answer changes the question. What happens to our understanding of the spiritual quest if, rather than asking, "How do I live forever?" or "How can I be certain that I am saved?" we ask instead, "How do I store treasure in heaven?" "How do I become rich in the things that pertain to the divine realm?"

Jesus' exhortation to strive to be rich in heavenly things is different from the man's expressed desire to know the secret of attaining eternal life. Moving from the man's question to Jesus' answer shifts the goal of the religious life from getting oneself into heaven to expanding the self one will have when one reaches the end of life's journey, from saving one's soul to making one's soul. Anxiety about saving one's soul can lead to an unhealthy obsession with one's self-preservation. Making a soul is a different project altogether, a lifelong task of cultivating wisdom, humility, righteous anger, loving-kindness, mercy, and hospitality, among other virtues. This is the path down which Jesus attempts to send the seeker.

What is the direction Jesus gives as the means to storing up treasure in heaven, to becoming rich according to divine measure? "Sell what you own, and give . . . to the poor" (v. 21). Here, as in so many passages of Scripture, earthly possessions are regarded as obstacles on the path to true enrichment. As paradoxical as it might seem in a culture that embraces economic prosperity as the highest measure of a person, Jesus sees such prosperity as an encumbrance, something that a true religious seeker should renounce entirely.

How far to press this point in a sermon in a middle- or upper-class congregation in North America, where accumulations of personal wealth far exceed any measure that would have been used by Jesus' first audience in assessing their own economic standing, is difficult to know. No less tricky is selling this ethic of abandoning goods to a congregation that is already feeling economically pinched. One might, at least, remind that gospel standards of ethics are higher than anything we normally embody in our own lifestyles, as a means of calling a congregation to a measure of humility when they assess their practice of Christian ethics. One might also persuade

Mark 10:17–22

Theological Perspective

he can fill the lack only if he divests himself of abundance. Interestingly, though, Jesus promises him a return and retrieval of abundance: "you will have treasure in heaven" (v. 21). Dispossession is not an end in itself; it is part of this man's path to an end that offers true plenitude. Commenting on the lavish rewards Jesus promises in Scripture, C. S. Lewis has written:

> If we consider the unblushing promises of reward and the staggering nature of the rewards promised in the Gospels, it would seem that Our Lord finds our desires not too strong, but too weak. We are half-hearted creatures, fooling about with drink and sex and ambition when infinite joy is offered us, like an ignorant child who wants to go on making mud pies in a slum because he cannot imagine what is meant by the offer of a holiday at the sea. We are far too easily pleased.[1]

In light of Lewis's insight, we might suggest that the rich man in Mark's story has been too content with his riches. His riches are "goods" but fail to be "good," and so they fail to mediate the infinite joy God offers us. Instead, they become for him a hindrance, restricting his gaze and making him settle for less, because they look like the best offer around. Jesus bestows a different kind of abundance, a different kind of reward, in which goods become good by being circulated, both given and received, so that neither poverty nor self-denial becomes the final word for anyone's life. Instead, all are offered "treasure in heaven," even as all participate in the flow of goods in this life—a participation that transforms our weak desires into a robust appetite for God's kingdom.

SCOTT BADER-SAYE

Pastoral Perspective

enough? Jesus does not say otherwise, and when the man says that he has kept the commandments since his youth, Jesus does not criticize him for naiveté or shallowness. What the text does say is that Jesus looks on him with love and says to him, "You lack one thing; go, sell what you own, and give the money to the poor, and you will have treasure in heaven; then come, follow me" (v. 21).

These words speak a universal mandate in which Jesus expresses a heightened and deepened requirement beyond the commandments already mentioned. Perhaps they are more to be heard as the particular response evoked by this man's own yearning for something more. They may more simply say that if the commandments have been kept and there is still this unease or incompleteness, then this is the next step to be taken. The radical challenge is to the man who may be ready for, and in need of, such a move. Perceiving his anxiety and entrapment in his possessions, Jesus calls him onward to the freedom to be found in divestment and discipleship.

To hear the story this way—as an intensely personal exchange with a particular challenge to a particular person, that is, to read it as Socratic or Kierkegaardian rhetoric rather than as dominical command—can possibly be used to evade or defuse it. That is a danger, whether we are considering the meaning of the text for the stewardship of our own lives or are interpreting it for others. Nevertheless, such a sense of the text can also sharpen it and drive it more deeply into us as a challenge and invitation. The story speaks more powerfully than a commandment. It speaks of anxiety, of yearning, of love, of invitation, and then, finally, of the difficulty of responding and letting go, and of sadness in the failure to do so.

In the sorrow of the ending, however, is the stirring of hope for some better ending or some new beginning: for this man (who now disappears from our sight), for those we meet who are like him, and perhaps also for us.

JOHN K. STENDAHL

---

1. C. S. Lewis, "The Weight of Glory," in *The Weight of Glory and Other Addresses* (New York: Macmillan, 1949), 3–4.

Exegetical Perspective

suggests that the inquirer is not simply seeking Jesus' affirmation but, rather, entreating information about inheriting eternal life. Therefore, Jesus responds to him with love. Actually, the rich man is the only person whom Mark tells us explicitly that Jesus loved. Therefore, Jesus pushes the man's concept of discipleship and interpretation of the commandments by asserting that he lacks one thing, abandoning his wealth and distributing it among the poor.

Mark's story requires the man to sell as much of his possessions as he has, which is different from requiring him to sell all of his possessions as described in Luke 18:22. Although the difference between these versions is subtle, Mark's narrative does not convey that the rich man has to forsake everything he owns. Jesus teaches that discipleship requires sacrifice, self-denial, and sharing. By requesting that the man give his abundance to the poor, Jesus is not advocating that he enter poverty himself. Jesus is not glamorizing or encouraging a life of poverty. Instead, Jesus wants to alleviate poverty and prevent systemic economic injustice.

By selling and giving away his wealth, the rich man will receive treasure in heaven. Although Jesus invites the man to follow him, joining in his nomadic ministry is not a requirement for receiving heavenly treasure. The sequence of Jesus' command suggests that the man would receive treasure in heaven by focusing on relationships with the community, particularly those who are not as fortunate.

Jesus' command is too much for the man, who leaves dismayed and grieving. He is unwilling to receive Jesus' word, because the sacrifice would be extremely great. Walking away from Jesus, the man walks away from participation in the kingdom of God. The man's response is in stark contrast to the children's response to Jesus in verses 13–16. Jesus glorifies the children's openness to be received and blessed by him. The children's response is the model for how one should receive the kingdom. The rich man's response is the antithesis.

The kingdom of God is a not a place, but a way of life that requires sacrifice, self-denial, and sharing, in exchange for treasures of heaven as given by God.

BRIDGETT A. GREEN

Homiletical Perspective

one's listeners that if it seems impossible to follow the exhortation to sell all of one's possession, it might be possible, at least, to learn to hold on to them less tightly, to set acquisition and maintenance of wealth as lower priority than they currently are.

Notice also that the exhortation to sell all is not singly focused on enriching the one who sells. The exhortation is dual: "sell, give." The commands, first to liquidate those possessions and then to use the proceeds as a means to alleviate the earthly misery of the poor, are understood as closely related commands. Through giving this command Jesus stands in a long tradition of Israelite prophets and teachers. Biblical authors understand economic resources as finite, so that, if one has too many resources, this inevitably means that others have too few. Therefore, selling one's possessions is not merely for the purpose of freeing oneself; it is also an act of justice for the sake of the poor.

Finally, notice that for a pericope of such brevity, in which narrative details are spare and characterization is slight, the passage does provide some details concerning the emotions of the characters as they interact. In a rare attribution of emotion to Jesus, he is said to look upon and love the man who doggedly inquires after eternal life. What about this encounter prompts the narrator to include the response of Jesus' love for the man? Does he love because, even though the man has asked the wrong question, he has at least asked? Because he is Torah observant? For no reason whatsoever? Furthermore, the man with great accumulated wealth, on walking away from the invitation to sell, give, and follow, is said to be both shocked and grieving. This man has greater insight than many who are rich, for he registers through his grief that he is aware of how much he is losing by not being able to let go of his accumulated material wealth.

SHELLY MATTHEWS

Mark 10:23–31

²³Then Jesus looked around and said to his disciples, "How hard it will be for those who have wealth to enter the kingdom of God!" ²⁴And the disciples were perplexed at these words. But Jesus said to them again, "Children, how hard it is to enter the kingdom of God! ²⁵It is easier for a camel to go through the eye of a needle than for someone who is rich to enter the kingdom of God." ²⁶They were greatly astounded and said to one another, "Then who can be saved?" ²⁷Jesus looked at them and said, "For mortals it is impossible, but not for God; for God all things are possible."
²⁸Peter began to say to him, "Look, we have left everything and followed you." ²⁹Jesus said, "Truly I tell you, there is no one who has left house or brothers or sisters or mother or father or children or fields, for my sake and for the sake of the good news, ³⁰who will not receive a hundredfold now in this age—houses, brothers and sisters, mothers and children, and fields, with persecutions—and in the age to come eternal life. ³¹But many who are first will be last, and the last will be first."

Theological Perspective

After having spoken hard words to the rich man in the preceding verses and having seen him walk away from the call to follow, Jesus turns to his disciples and generalizes his words about wealth. In so doing, he refuses them (and us) the consolation of believing that his words to the rich man were specific to a single case. Rather, Jesus says, this is about all of you, all of us.

The first generalization, "How hard it will be for those who have wealth to enter the kingdom of God!" (v. 23), is followed by a second, even broader, generalization, "Children, how hard it is to enter the kingdom of God!" (v. 24). However, lest we start to take refuge in the idea that it is equally hard for all of us, and that therefore the particular words about wealth are relativized before our generic sinful state, Jesus returns to the issues of riches by noting, "It is easier for a camel to go through the eye of a needle than for someone who is rich to enter the kingdom of God" (v. 25). When the disciples express dismay—"Then who can be saved?" (v. 26)—Jesus reassures them, "For mortals it is impossible, but not for God; for God all things are possible" (v. 27).

Again, we might mistakenly assume that these words relativize all moral differences; if salvation is a general impossibility that requires God's miraculous intervention, does it really matter whether we

Pastoral Perspective

Jesus' words in Mark 10:23 follow the departure of the man Jesus told to divest himself of his possessions. The challenge appeared to be more than the man could bear. How hard it is when there is so much to lose! One could imagine condemnation in Jesus' words, but in context one senses more a quality of pity and sadness, the note often heard as the conclusion to that story.

It is, however, the disciples' perplexity at those words that now drives the text onward and leads to a slightly altered repetition of the thought and to the ensuing conversation. Why were they confused? It might be imagined that they believed that the wealthy were favored by God and/or that money and possessions entailed a greater freedom for virtue and faithfulness. Such privileging of the rich, often accompanied by a sense of relative moral powerlessness for common folk, is certainly a familiar phenomenon, and it may be that such was the source of the disciples' perplexity. We are called to vigilance against such foolish adulation of the wealthy and the consequent warping of our own norms and expectations. Neither should we excuse from full ethical and political agency those who can define themselves either as poor or "middle class," the preferred American identifier.

It might also be that such was not the problem for the disciples. There was certainly no lack of text and

Exegetical Perspective

Discipleship is difficult. The cost is great—too great for the rich man in Mark 10:17-22. The cost is not impossible, however. Immediately after his encounter with the rich man who refuses the path of discipleship (10:17-22), Jesus discusses with his disciples his previous conversation. Jesus' exchange with the rich man becomes public discourse and a teaching moment that further describes the challenge of discipleship.

The Scripture lesson begins with Jesus' analysis of the difficulty for a wealthy person to join the kingdom of God. Twice he says, "How hard it will be for those who have wealth to enter the kingdom of God!" (v. 23-24). The duplication of Jesus' statement suggests that issues of wealth and poverty are important to him, so much so that he expands on his pronouncement with an exaggerated metaphor. Jesus announces, "It is easier for a camel to go through the eye of a needle than for someone who is rich to enter the kingdom of God" (v. 25). This pronouncement seems as harsh as it is comical. For such a large animal as a camel to squeeze through the tiny aperture of a needle is inconceivable, let alone impossible. However, as an analogy, the metaphor illustrates the impossibility for a wealthy person to inherit eternal life.

On the surface, Jesus' message seems to condemn the wealthy. However, condemnation of the wealthy is not Mark's objective. As demonstrated in 10:21,

Homiletical Perspective

This text is an anxious one. It is hard to imagine anyone hearing it who would not feel that anxiety. The text presses toward the embrace of loss as the means of entering the kingdom of God. First, we confront the fantastic image of the impossibility of those with wealth entering at all—like a camel passing through the eye of a needle. Then, we find the frightening affirmation that this journey into the reign of God can also mean abandoning ties even more precious than those held to material things: leaving home and family, our sense of place and belonging. The text is so anxious that, even in the midst of an affirmation, that loss will be followed by gain: those who leave everything for the sake of the gospel are promised new home and family, but persecution is added to the list of things one should expect to acquire. What are we to do with a text containing such anxious images?

It is important to note, first, that entering the kingdom of God is a larger concept in Mark than merely "getting into heaven after one dies." The Greek term often translated as kingdom (*basileia*) of God has verbal as well as substantive connotations, and thus in many early Jesus sayings it signals a way of being in community in this world, more than a place in the hereafter. One way to tone down the anxious rhetoric of the passage is to shift focus, from

Mark 10:23–31

Theological Perspective

share our wealth or hoard it? Such a reading would founder on the shoals of antinomianism and "cheap grace." For, as Sondra Wheeler observes, "There is nothing to suggest that God's call or its demands will be somehow softened or made more 'reasonable' and more compatible with ordinary life: only that God can make possible—even for the rich—the wholehearted response that the kingdom requires."[1]

Peter reminds Jesus that he and the other disciples have already left everything to follow him. In response, Jesus surprisingly promises not just a reward in heaven (what he had promised to the rich man in the previous verses) but a hundredfold return of goods "in this age." We might be surprised by such a promise, since we have come to imagine that giving should not be caught up in a web of reciprocity. We worry that any return on the gift simply negates its giftedness. If we get something back, then have we really done anything virtuous in giving?

Behind these worries lies a prevalent (though problematic) way of thinking about Christian love, *agapē*, and divine grace. We say, for instance, that grace (and by extension Christian love) is radically free, meaning that it is offered in a way that is utterly indifferent to return. It comes with no strings attached. There is truth in these statements, insofar as they distinguish loving generosity from the logic of contracted return—a logic in which the given and the received must be equal and balance the scales, leaving the parties free to depart without need for ongoing relationship. True love, true giving, avoids the limitations of contract—or better, exceeds contract in the direction of gratuity.

What, though, if utterly indifferent giving and contractual demand were not the only two options? What if Christian love is always about response and reciprocity, though not in the mode of contract? True gift, for it not to be a paternalistic act of the disengaged and the powerful, needs to be open to return and indeed desirous of return, since the gift of love seeks relationship, and relationship is sustained through the reciprocity of gifts given, received, returned, and accepted. Love can never be a unilateral act, indifferent to response, since what it seeks is the forming and sustaining of true relationship. Indeed, a gift that was utterly indifferent to return might fail to be an act of love. John Milbank drives this point home with an example from family life. He writes: "Giving within families would seem not

---

1. Sondra Wheeler, *Wealth as Peril and Obligation* (Grand Rapids: Eerdmans, 1995), 47.

Pastoral Perspective

discourse that spoke sharply against the privileges of the rich, not just in the mighty words of the prophets, but also in contemporary critiques of oppression and exploitation. Could it be that the shock of Jesus' words lay in his *not* dismissing the rich as excluded from the kingdom, but speaking compassionately about their difficulty in entering that realm? They were not just a foil for his argument or an object for his condemnation. A curse on the wealthy would perhaps have been the disciples' expectation, but Jesus spoke in a different key. It is striking that when he repeated his thought, he mitigated the language and addressed the disciples as his children, without any specific reference to the rich. He went on to speak about the problem of wealth, but first he exclaimed more inclusively: "How hard it is to enter the kingdom of God!" (v. 24).

Then again, even if at the risk of anachronism, we might also hear the disciples' difficulty with Jesus' words as reflective of yet another problem in our culture and churches, the notion that the realm of God has nothing to do with issues of wealth and possessions, or class and economic power. There can of course be great discomfort in confronting such issues, and we can frequently be secretive and ashamed around matters of personal finance, consumption, debt, and affluence. Churches conduct "campaigns" to support their missions, but fairly seldom do they force confrontation with the issue of the power of money over our lives. So it may be that discomfort with Jesus' words derived from the expectation of a wall between spirituality and economics.

Jesus continued with the famous saying about the camel and the eye of the needle. That metaphor's hyperbole can send us looking for extenuations and exemptions, but it would seem unfaithful to rush off without honoring the words as forceful elaboration of what Jesus was saying just before: it is hard, really hard, damned hard, to enter into the realm of God when one has so much to lose. The familiar explanation of the needle's eye as an actual gate too narrow to allow a baggage-laden camel to enter is a useful homiletical trope (especially since most of us are laden with far more than we need), but it suffers not only from dubious factuality but from the way it domesticates and moralizes the pungent saying of Jesus.

The disciples now ask a question that may be on our minds also: "Then who can be saved?" (v. 26). Jesus does not give a comprehensive or systematic answer; he just makes it clear that with God the door can always be open. The teaching still stands, a reminder that if one is never to despair, neither is

Exegetical Perspective

Jesus loves the rich man who comes to him. The problem is not wealth itself but, rather, the behavior and attitudes that wealth and privilege may evoke. In first-century-CE Roman Palestine, the wealthy elite had the political power, along with their economic status, to direct others' behavior.[1] Often, the elite would hoard their power, privilege, and prestige. Therefore, to renounce controlling power, to share economic resources, and to forsake privilege (or use it differently) would have been a difficult task, even for the sake of God's kingdom. Following Jesus includes sacrifice, selflessness, and sharing. Hence, to sacrifice the comforts of privilege and to share economic and social power are elements of a life of discipleship.

Surprisingly, the disciples respond to Jesus with shock. Expected reactions are relief and rejoicing, since some of the disciples were not wealthy, but known fishers and subsistence laborers. Their reactions (vv. 24, 26) suggest a twofold assumption: (1) obedience to the Torah alone should provide salvation and (2) a wealthy person would enter the kingdom of God with ease, or at least with no more difficulty than the average person. The response of Jesus questions both of these.

First, following the commandments alone is not enough to ensure a way of life (i.e., the kingdom of God) that protects the poor and provides justice for the oppressed. Although this interpretation is valid, it does not speak to Jesus' emphasis on the difficulty of a wealthy person's entering into the kingdom. Second, Jesus disabuses the disciples of the perception that having economic wealth is a demonstration of God's grace. At the time, many of the socioreligious elites, including the Sadducees and chief priests, were wealthy and held dominant roles in the priesthood and temple. Seeing wealthy elites as leaders of religious and political communities, Jesus' disciples and the general populace probably believed that God's hand was upon the elite group called by God to lead the people. Hence, the disciples' question, "Who is able to be saved?" For Jesus, the answer is everyone!

Responding to the disciples' cry, Jesus offers a reassuring word for all hearers: what is impossible for humans is possible for God (v. 27). As all things are possible for God, God is able to do that which is difficult, including empowering a wealthy person to sacrifice and to share for the sake of gospel in order

---

1. Pheme Perkins, "The Gospel of Mark," in *The New Interpreter's Bible*, ed. Leander E. Keck (Nashville: Abingdon Press, 1995), 8:651.

Homiletical Perspective

whether receiving this passage allows one entrance to the afterlife, to what insight this passage can offer into fuller life here and now.

If one has already explored biblical exhortations to detach from wealth that were central to the preceding pericope (10:17–22), taking up the camel aphorism may mean repeating messages already delivered. An alternative strategy would be to focus on the saying concerning the family abandoned and the family reconstituted.

In order to understand Jesus' words here, perplexed listeners might welcome reflection on how the ancient family structure differed from family structures in some modern contexts. Family systems in this historical place and time were much more rigidly fixed than they are for many today, owing especially to the privilege conferred on the male head of household. The father of the ancient household held legal and social power over the women, children, and (if present) slaves of any family. Though it is difficult to say how often it was exercised in practice, this power of the patriarchal head of household included, at least theoretically, power over questions of life and death. Thus, for the first hearers of this saying, to leave family for the sake of the gospel might be understood as true release, possibly even literal salvation.

The composition of the newly constituted family in verse 30 suggests that Jesus is questioning excessive patriarchal power. While Jesus acknowledges that among his followers are those who have left brothers, sisters, mothers, fathers, or children, he promises to those who have left everything for the sake of the gospel a new family that is constituted only of brothers, sisters, mothers, and children. No patriarchal fathers appear in this vision of new family in the reign of God. The thrust of this pericope that promises a family without fathers is not antimale. Formulated in the historical context of the heavy-handed patriarchal head of household, it is, rather, antiauthoritarian (this saying matches the exhortation in Matt. 23:8–10 to call no one father, which has a similar egalitarian thrust).

Underscoring this fact might lead to further reflection on what it would mean for men and women in any church community to live out these particular family roles for each other—brothers and sisters, mothers and children. Biblical scholar Jane Schaberg, reflecting on the place of the "private brother" in the writings of Virginia Woolf, remarks that she herself understands both the historical figure of Jesus and women's participation in the early

Mark 10:23–31

Theological Perspective

freedom but folly were it too unilateral: the parents who showered gifts on their children expecting absolutely nothing in return by way of gratitude, a good use of their possessions, opportunities and education, would indeed give an entirely poisoned gift, a 'gift' of spoliation."[2]

Perhaps, then, we can no longer think about Jesus' promise of reward "in this age" as a problematic undermining of a so-called pure gift, but rather as a description of the proper reciprocal relations that God desires for us, in which all needs can be met by the ongoing circulation of goods, which not only enacts the minimum standard of justice but exceeds that standard in the direction of gratuity.

Lest we assume that this promise of reward "in this age" aids and abets the prosperity gospel of get-rich-quick Christianity, Mark reminds us that alongside the many goods that will be received—"houses, brothers and sisters, mothers and children, and fields"—we must also expect to receive "persecutions" (v. 30). Furthermore, the list of restored goods promises neither a life of leisure nor a life of abstract wealth. What is received back is a wide set of relationships, the economic means to produce plenitude (fields), and the conditions for making a common life together (houses). In other words, Jesus promises fullness of life, real life, not just in the age to come but here and now. To those who would characterize Christianity as a promise of "pie in the sky," we need but refer to this passage to see that the Christian life is one of shared abundance here and now, as a foretaste of the eternal abundance of God's reign.

SCOTT BADER-SAYE

Pastoral Perspective

one to presume. Strikingly, a similar concern about the forbidding stringency of the kingdom comes from the disciples in Matthew's parallel to the teaching about divorce (Matt. 19:11–12). There the disciples exclaim that it would be best not to marry at all in that case, and Jesus responds, rather strangely, about some becoming eunuchs. He then says, "Not everyone can accept this teaching, but only those to whom it is given." There, as in Mark 10, there is a call for sacrifice and arduous discipleship, but also the kindly recognition that not everyone is capable. The gate is both so narrow and so very wide open. That paradox may frustrate consistent people, and it also demands of us skill and wisdom, lest we get the timing wrong and swing the door the wrong way, merely comforting the comfortable or further afflicting the afflicted.

When Peter, typically uncircumspect, pointed out that (unlike the man in vv. 17–22) he and the others had left everything to follow Jesus, his teacher did not upbraid him for his self-congratulation but, rather, affirmed him and all those who have discarded possessions and belongings to set out on this journey. Jesus' response rings quite movingly as words not so much to Peter as to the Christian community. Believers in this time would have known about loss, material and familial and social, for the gospel's sake; they knew about persecution and martyrdom. They knew it was happening to their communities, even if not to them personally. Jesus himself was reminding them of what they had gained, a wider world of freedom and belonging and connection on the other side of the door from their narrow allegiances and purely private possessions. They had a worldwide family now, and in that larger, freer realm even persecutions could be swallowed up in blessings and, somehow, even being killed would not harm them.

Can we imagine envisioning our church and thinking about our identity in that way?

JOHN K. STENDAHL

---

2. John Milbank, "Can a Gift Be Given? Prolegomena to a Future Trinitarian Metaphysic," *Modern Theology* 11:1 (January 1995):124–25.

Exegetical Perspective

to join in God's kingdom. Who can be saved? With God, anyone can be saved.

Speaking on behalf of the group, Peter looks to Jesus for reassurance as he recounts that he and the disciples have sacrificed everything for a life of discipleship. In contrast to the rich man in verses 17–22, the disciples have given up their lives, families, and homes to follow Jesus. Jesus lifts up two major features of their sacrifice. First, the disciples left everything because of their response to and belief in the gospel. When Jesus called the disciples to follow him, he did not offer them a material reward but, rather, a different life. The disciples followed Jesus as response to their witness of Jesus' works and teachings (1:34–39; 2:13–14; 3:13–19). Second, for all they have lost, the disciples will gain one hundred times over (v. 30). The new community does not replicate their old life, including social and political standing. Rather, the community is family reimagined (cf. 3:31–35), with new friendships and resources. Although the new community reflects the present reward for Jesus' immediate disciples (v. 30), it also reflects the reward given to Jesus' disciples hearing the Markan story. For this new community, the kingdom of God is not constrained by the rules of status, power, privilege, prestige, and human expectations; it is a community where the first will be last and the last will be first (v. 31).

The early hearers and readers of Mark's story would take solace in this message as well. The phrase "with persecutions" (v. 30) seems to speak of persecutions that Jesus' followers endure due to their decision to follow (cf. 13:9–11). Similarly, Mark is probably referring to the persecutions his community endured during the time he created the Gospel in 65–70 CE in the midst of the Jewish revolt against Roman oppression. During the same period, Nero was persecuting known movement leaders, such as Peter and Paul in Rome. Persecution was acute for Mark, and one of the highest costs of discipleship. The cost of discipleship is surprisingly high; through God, however, discipleship can be achieved.

BRIDGETT A. GREEN

Homiletical Perspective

Christian movement in terms of sibling relations. In her historical reconstruction, she imagines Jesus

> reconceived as a brother: a male who is not a father, not a lover, a male who might be a guide to the limited male world, or who might even be guided into women's spheres, thus confusing private and public. Who might use the power and privilege he has to defend and foster, to open doors. Not hero or leader or God, but companion, "comrade-twin," moving toward an early pointless death.[1]

While those coming to the text with different christological convictions might protest Schaberg's very low Christology here, her description of what the sibling relationship among men and women could be, both then and now, is still compelling—the idea that in one's Christian family, those with power and privilege might use these resources "to defend and foster, to open doors" and to walk with another as a "comrade-twin."

Julia Kristeva, a Freudian philosopher writing from a very different perspective, suggests how the example of maternal love for children can foster deeper human relationships. While acknowledging that in practice mother-child relations can have their own destructive tendencies, she proposes that ideally maternal love, in contrast to erotic love, consists of "love-tenderness," which strives to care for and to nourish: "I like to think that, in our human adventure, we can encounter 'the other'—sometimes, rarely—if, and only if, we, men and women, are capable of that maternal experience, which defers eroticism into tenderness and makes an 'object' an 'other me.'"[2]

The text today presses anxiously for followers of Jesus to embrace loss for the sake of the gospel. By reflecting more deeply on the family relationships offered by Jesus in the newly constituted community, one sees how much could also be gained. In living out with each other the family roles of brothers and sisters, mothers and children, we deepen our human connections, honing our abilities to extend to one another practices of camaraderie, nurture, and tenderness.

SHELLY MATTHEWS

---

1. Jane Schaberg, *The Resurrection of Mary Magdalene: Legends, Apocrypha, and the Christian Testament* (New York: Continuum, 2004), 43.
2. Catherine Clément and Julia Kristeva, *The Feminine and the Sacred*, trans. Jane Marie Todd (New York: Columbia University Press, 2001), 56–57.

Mark 10:32–34

³²They were on the road, going up to Jerusalem, and Jesus was walking ahead of them; they were amazed, and those who followed were afraid. He took the twelve aside again and began to tell them what was to happen to him, ³³saying, "See, we are going up to Jerusalem, and the Son of Man will be handed over to the chief priests and the scribes, and they will condemn him to death; then they will hand him over to the Gentiles; ³⁴they will mock him, and spit upon him, and flog him, and kill him; and after three days he will rise again."

Theological Perspective

Mark's third passion prediction inextricably links theology and ethics.

Jesus' way to Jerusalem entails a moral purpose. As Joel Marcus demonstrates in his commentary on Mark, Jesus is not exclusively the "divine man" come to free individuals from sin and for resurrection.[1] Jesus' way requires the courage to suffer ignominious public disdain, torture, and death for an end to which Jesus held steadfastly. The suffering service is also ultimately prudent. Jesus does not fatuously disregard long-term consequences. The way of suffering produces moral consequences; it helps bring resurrection and an eschatological renewal for the "last ones" (10:31, Marcus's trans.).

Jesus' moral purpose is religiously informed. Courage, prudence, and consequences must be understood in an eschatological framework that engenders hope for a long-term triumphant outcome, although not an outcome defined by currently dominant values. Neither Jesus nor his disciples are destined to become powerful in the usual sense. Jesus sets his face toward Jerusalem and certain suffering, because God's providence necessitates it as the means for the new kingdom to come. The moral

1. Joel Marcus, *Mark*, Anchor Bible 27 (New Haven and London: Yale University Press, 2000), 75–79.

Pastoral Perspective

Many of us love to travel. The thought of experiencing a new destination, the thrill of preparing, packing: all of it can be exciting. My own love of travel only grew when I was in college, because the football team on which I played traveled to a new city for at least six out of the eleven games we played each season. The road trips were exciting because they revealed to us a whole new world, good and bad, that was out there. It was during these road trips, over the four-year course of my football career, that I learned many valuable lessons.

One of the lessons I learned was the importance of teamwork and togetherness. The football team grew together as a family because of these road trips. The all-night bus rides and the countless airplane flights, staying in hotels, and eating in restaurants built bonds that are not easily broken. Even though some twenty years have passed since the last road trip I took with that football team, the relationships I made then have been maintained even to this day.

Mark 10:32–34 finds Jesus on a road trip of sorts to Jerusalem, with his own team of disciples. Mark indicates in verse 32 that, unlike the enjoyable road trips of my youth, this road trip will instead bring great challenge to these disciples. This will not be an easy road trip, even though this is familiar terrain they are traveling up to Jerusalem. There will be

Exegetical Perspective

Jesus' third passion prediction in Mark weaves the threat of conflict, suffering, and death together with the promise of divine power, manifested in the resurrection, as the way to liberation from the deathly powers that rule this world. Throughout this section, threat is mingled with promise and astonishment with fear. As this passage begins, Jesus resumes the journey begun in 10:17, a journey that was immediately interrupted by a rich man on a quest for eternal life (10:17–31). That story culminates with a series of teachings that reverse the disciples' assumptions about the relationship between wealth and the kingdom of God. If not the rich, "then who can be saved?" they wonder (10:26). Jesus turns from his warnings against the dangers of wealth, however, to the promise of abundance for those who leave all in order to follow him. The episode that follows this final passion prediction also includes a series of teachings that challenge the disciples' assumptions, this time about status and power, especially the ways divine power is manifested through service in the community of disciples (10:35–45).

As Jesus' journey now resumes, Mark tells us the destination: Jesus is on the way up to Jerusalem, where he will give up, not only his possessions, but his life, for the sake of the kingdom of God. This, the third of Jesus' predictions of his impending suffering,

Homiletical Perspective

With these verses, we have come to the third and final passion prediction in Mark's Gospel. This longest and most detailed prediction serves as a kind of table of contents for what will unfold in chapters 14–16. Most sermons would likely combine verses 32–34 with 10:35–45, since all three passion predictions move from Jesus' announcement of his suffering, death, and resurrection to an incident that clearly shows that his disciples do not get it (see 8:31–38; 9:31–37). What value might there be, then, in forming a sermon around these three verses as a distinct unit?

A sermon focused on verses 32–34 causes us to walk with Jesus on this uncomfortable road longer than we might otherwise choose to do. Frankly, we would prefer the distraction of James and John's request to share in Jesus' glory, or we would prefer exploring Jesus' familiar teaching about discipleship as service, to dealing with the untamed emotions of amazement and fear that can accompany us as we accompany Jesus. Focusing on these three verses compels us to explore why we are amazed and afraid in his presence.

Is it because of the very hard thing Jesus has just said—that it is easier for a camel to walk through a needle's eye than for a rich person to squeeze, much less swagger, into God's kingdom? Are Jesus'

Mark 10:32–34

Theological Perspective

action becomes intelligible in light of the eschatological theology.

Mark's third passion prediction evinces what James M. Gustafson describes as Jesus' incarnation of "theocentric piety."[2] The passion prediction cannot be fully understood as an abstract cosmic transaction between God and evil forces to save individuals from sin and death, or as proclaiming a morally laudable way of life comprehensible independent of devotion to God. It foretells actions that challenge religious and government authorities who do not exhibit care for the sick, the poor, and the vulnerable, that is, the last ones (10:31). Jesus' actions, which bring him suffering, cannot be understood or justified apart from the eschatological reversal foreseen in the risen one (v. 34) and the formation of the Christian community. Jesus' hope in God's providence and Jesus' courage and prudence in following the way inform each other. Without the theological virtue of hope, the moral virtue of courage becomes foolhardy and prudence evaporates.

Much of contemporary culture and many Christians fail to comprehend this connection between religion and morality. Television news pundits recently quipped that the early Barack Obama took a religious stance on gay marriage, while his evolved position is based on respect for the dignity of each person. The observation implies that religion resolves moral matters by citing specific biblical texts or church teachings and that respect for human dignity is uninformed by religious beliefs. This erroneous separation of religion from morality is, unfortunately, commonplace. Christian or religiously informed conceptions of dignity are not necessarily unique or even radically different from secular conceptions. However, respect for dignity is for Christians informed by the "theocentric piety" Jesus incarnated. Respect for dignity should also be informed by contemporary science and appeals to experience, but Jesus' beliefs regarding an eschatological reversal shape our understanding of this principle.

This link between religion and the moral life neither requires nor permits using Mark's text as a precise command to challenge religious or governing authorities. It does not require following the literal, or even the same type of, actions that Jesus undertook in challenging the authorities in Jerusalem. However, the one who was devoted to God's purposes, although eschewing violence and pursuit of military, political, and economic power for their own sake, actively challenged and exposed the lack of concern for the

---

2. James M. Gustafson, *Ethics from a Theocentric Perspective* (Chicago: University of Chicago Press, 1981), 1:275–77.

Pastoral Perspective

something different about this road trip, as Jesus tells the disciples. In verses 32–34, he tells them the itinerary, graphically detailing what is to come.

Jesus predicts that the chief priests and scribes will turn against him. The crowds will have nothing to do with him. The disciples will abandon him. The Roman justice system will convict him on trumped-up charges and execute him, and this violence will make the disciples even more afraid.

The record states that they whipped him and beat him that night (15:15, 19). The accusers disrespected his humanity and dignity. The horrific events Jesus would face would be so intense that the Romans would compel an African, Simon of Cyrene, to assist Jesus in carrying the cross that he would suffer and die upon, through the streets of Jerusalem out to an old hill on Calvary. Yet Jesus, according to Mark 10:32–34, not only accepted this road trip but went resolutely, purposefully, and boldly.

The itinerary confirms that Jesus went ahead of the disciples; Jesus led the way with confidence and calm, even though he was about to suffer a horrific outcome. Mark points out for us that while the disciples were afraid of what they were hearing, Jesus was intent on completing the road trip to Jerusalem. The writer tells us that the disciples were both amazed and afraid at what awaited them at their destination (v. 32). This most specific of the three passion predictions in Mark's Gospel highlights the specific moment in that story. Jesus is indeed to be handed over to the chief priests and the scribes (10:33; 14:1–2, 10–11, 43–46); condemned to death (10:33; 14:53–65); handed over to the Gentiles (10:33; 15:1–15); mocked (10:34; 15:16–20); spit upon (10:34; 15:19); flogged (10:34; 15:15); and killed (10:34; 15:22–39). Jesus' final prediction, that he would rise again in three days (10:34), also took place (16:1–8), although the women who were witnesses to the fact that he had been raised were too frightened to say anything (16:8).

Our service is often mixed with fear that way. The opportunity to make an impact on the world with the good news is amazing. Then the challenge of balancing a church budget in this troubled economy is frightening. The joy of welcoming new members into the church family is a beautiful duty, but the frustration of losing members because of conflict is heartbreaking. Like these disciples, we sometimes allow worry and fear to overrule our peace and calm.

Mark's Gospel, however, captures the right message of Jesus and gives us a wonderful example to follow in times of trial and tribulation. The message of Mark's Gospel is that Jesus has come to liberate

Exegetical Perspective

death, and resurrection (cf. 8:31; 9:31), is the most detailed and graphic of the three, but the only one for which Mark does not record either direct resistance or confusion as the response of Jesus' disciples. It will immediately become clear, however, that their misunderstanding persists. At least some of the disciples are now making the transition not to acceptance of Jesus' messianic fate, but to an expectation of status and power in his coming messianic rule (10:35–37). No longer is Jesus' suffering and death the dominant theme that attracts their attention, but rather the glory in which they hope to participate. As Jesus' prediction again makes clear, though, there is no resurrection glory apart from suffering and death.

Mark sets the scene with Jesus walking ahead of his band of followers, who are both amazed and afraid. Jesus is not merely on the road from Capernaum to Jerusalem, but on "the way"—the way of obedience, conflict, suffering, and hope that will liberate from bondage, oppression, and death not only his followers, nor even only faithful Israel, but all the peoples of the earth (10:52; Acts 9:2). While his disciples may not yet know clearly what lies ahead of them as they follow on this way, their responses of both amazement and fear (v. 32) are equally appropriate. Twice already in the Gospel Mark has used the word for amazement in association with an event or saying in which Jesus stretches the bounds of credulity (1:27; 10:24).

What is it about his leading them now onto the way to Jerusalem that provokes this response? The answer may lie in part with the disciples' dawning awareness of where Jesus is leading them. Mark's reference to amazement and fear also casts this scene in a divine hue. Throughout the Gospel, both amazement and fear (4:41; 5:15, 33; 6:50; 16:8) accompany manifestations of Jesus' God-given power. Here amazement and fear seem more to anticipate what is to come than respond to anything Jesus is doing at the moment. By mentioning amazement and fear Mark makes clear that the simple act of Jesus' leading the disciples out onto the road to Jerusalem—the way to death and vindication—already bears the shadow of divine power.

Jesus "goes before." On its face, this verb suggests a sense of resolve and decisiveness about Jesus' vision and vocation. Jesus knows what lies before him, apparently in great detail, but shows no reluctance to proceed. To "go before" here also anticipates the way the crucified and resurrected Jesus will go before his disciples to Galilee (14:28; 16:7), where they will once again take up their own journey

Homiletical Perspective

followers amazed and afraid because, with this decisive mention of Jerusalem, we now know where we are headed with him—into the heart of established religious life and authority and into the political, public fray, with all of the promise and danger inherent in such encounters? The details Jesus lays out, what will happen to him as a result of challenging the powers of this world, do not make us feel any better about the potential cost to us as we follow him farther down this road!

A sermon with the courage to stick with these three verses prevents us from hurrying past such questions. We follow One who sets before us radical sacrifice and leads us into risky confrontation with unjust powers, armed with nothing but faith. If we are not amazed and afraid by such a path, by such a claim on our lives, then perhaps we are not really on the same road Jesus is walking after all.

At this point in the sermon, it is important to show that the text does not begin (nor will it end) with our faltering faith, clumsy with amazement and fear. Instead, the text begins with a resolute Jesus "walking ahead" (v. 32) of us, walking purposefully or, as the new Common English Bible puts it, "with Jesus in the lead." The passage ends with the same confidence. First, we hear an extensive and devastating listing of all the violence others will do to Jesus: *they* will hand him over to the chief priest and scribes; *they* will condemn him to death; *they* will hand him over to the Gentiles; *they* will mock, spit, flog, kill. Then, after these relentless two verses comes this: *he* will rise again. "They" (we) will do the worst that humans are capable of doing . . . *and he will rise again*. That is the last word of this passage. Mark 10:32–34 begins and ends with the assurance that Jesus is "in the lead." This same verb, Jesus "walking/going ahead," shows up twice more when disciples need buoying most. In 14:27 Jesus tells his disciples, "You will all be deserters," but adds, "I will go before you to Galilee" (14:28). At the end of Mark's Gospel, in 16:7, just before "terror and amazement" seize us again, the young man beside the empty tomb delivers the unstoppable Easter message: "He has been raised. . . . he is going ahead of you."

The young church to which Mark's Gospel was addressed was beset by persecution and uncertainties more difficult than Christians in North America face today. It is no wonder that costly discipleship leads to amazement and fear. So imagine the good news offered in these few verses: legal proceedings, condemnation, mocking, beatings, and even death do not have the last word. There is a power beyond such

Mark 10:32–34

Theological Perspective

vulnerable and poor. Jesus went "ahead of them" (v. 32)—those following him, including the Twelve— and told them the things that would happen.

Far from being quiescent, Jesus led and provoked. He did not rule out violence or prescribe passive patience for all times and places, nor did he preclude service as a religious or political authority. He did not require that we seek to be mocked, spit on, scourged, and condemned to death (v. 34). The theocentric piety Jesus manifested in predicting and enacting the passion requires that those claiming faithfulness to him have the courage to look beyond standards of contemporary morality and beyond personal ambition for authority. Jesus called for the courage to accept opprobrium and persecution and the prudence to know when effective exposure of wrongdoing, even if it brings suffering, promotes the good for a new era.

Looking beyond the current unjust configuration of power and justice to a new era transcending condemnation and death, Jesus' theocentric piety compelled him to take the precise actions he took. These actions were demanded, even though they astonished his followers and struck fear in the hearts of those who might share his destiny. The pericope does not specify actions, but it clarifies dispositions and general principles of action that demand specific acts, warranted by particular circumstances. Religion does not eclipse the moral; it informs and requires it.

We do not have to affirm God's providence over particular events or claim that Mark was historically accurate in describing Jesus' predicting the exact events of the passion. Jesus' piety and courage are more astonishing if he did not foreknow particular future events. However, Jesus' facing toward Jerusalem and the inevitable suffering that he and others anticipated is inexplicable apart from hope in God's ordering and the eschatological reversal of the current broken order. This hope justified the provocation that led to Jesus' condemnation and death.

Moral principles such as respect for the dignity of the last ones and virtues such as courage entail different actions when they are informed by eschatological hope. Jesus' "astonishing" (v. 32, Marcus trans.) actions even become prudent. We do not have to share Mark's cosmic apocalypticism in order to understand that he was right about Jesus' suffering serving to reverse the old order. Courage, prudence, and respect for the last ones exist without religion, but they are not identical with moral virtues, and they are actions informed by Jesus' theocentric piety.

HARLAN BECKLEY

Pastoral Perspective

the people from the power of evil and from the structures that permit evil in the world. Specifically, Jesus has come to set people free from the spiritual bondage of the Romans' rule. Even though ministry is difficult and sometimes overwhelming, we have an exemplary model to follow: we too can embrace the journey and assignments of ministry with boldness and purpose.

I began this reflection talking about my love for travel, especially football road trips. When I was asked what made the road trip most enjoyable, my answers would include: "The trip back home after we won the game." We loved the means of travel, whether it was a jetliner or a spacious bus. We loved the accommodations, because the hotels were always five-star. We loved the food; we always ate at the best restaurants. However, what made the road trip was after we completed our business on the field, wrapping it all up with a big win. We always had a ball on the return trip home. We laughed. We celebrated. We sang the latest hit songs. It was a party all the way back to Wilberforce, Ohio. We always talked about the game and the significant plays that won the game on the field. We cheered whoever had a big play, a great catch, an amazing tackle, or a great block. We replayed the game at some point on the road trip back home.

As Mark closes his story, he does something similar, even if his tone is more subdued. Mark tells us that in spite of how tough the road trip is, in the end, Jesus wins. Jesus wins the biggest victory of all, which is the defeat of death and the overcoming of the grave. Because Jesus wins, you and I can win now.

WILLIAM E. CROWDER JR.

Exegetical Perspective

toward liberation. As the one who now "goes before" his disciples, Jesus adopts the role of the forerunner. John had gone before Jesus in both proclamation and death; Jesus now prepares his disciples not only for his death and resurrection, but also for the new life that follows the empty tomb. As the teachings that precede and follow this section make clear, this new life is no mere disembodied, spiritualized abstraction, no simplistic removal from this world to another, glorified realm; rather, it entails a foundational re-formation of power, politics, and social and economic relationships.

The level of detail that distinguishes this final passion prediction suggests that Mark intentionally tells this story in a way that emphasizes divine purpose. How does Jesus know already that "the Son of Man will be handed over to the chief priests and scribes" (cf. 14:1, 44, 53; 15:1), or that he will then "be handed over . . . to the Gentiles" (v. 33; cf. 15:1, 15), or that he will be mocked, spat upon, flogged, and then killed (v. 34; cf. 15:16–20)? This is not Jesus' rough, educated guess about what might go wrong as he confronts the powers in Jerusalem. Nor is this merely Mark's way of confirming Jesus' divine foreknowledge as he begins this final journey, as if an epistemological claim about Jesus' divinity were the key point.

Rather, in this brief, superficially humble scene we can discern the contours of a sacred moment, where divine will and human activity converge as one, where time is redirected from its ordinary pattern, and where God's purpose and power are manifested even in the apparently ordinary act of going farther up the road. The two earlier passion predictions followed closely on the heels of revelatory moments (Peter's confession, the transfiguration). Here the moment of revelation occurs as Jesus steps onto the road that leads up to Jerusalem. The way to Jerusalem is "the way" to eternal life, "the way" to liberation from the powers of this world, and "the way" toward the conquest of death itself, not only for Jesus but also for his disciples. For disciples, this "way" is not merely the means (suffering) to an end (salvation), but the space where suffering and redemption continue to meet.

STANLEY P. SAUNDERS

Homiletical Perspective

earthly powers, made known to us through Christ's rising from the dead. The good news is that wherever we are called to go as his disciples, whatever circumstances we are called upon to endure, Jesus is already out there, always before us, in the lead.

Many years ago, Tom Long, noted preacher and professor of homiletics at Candler School of Theology, met a South Korean pastor who had been imprisoned for preaching and teaching the Christian faith. He related that "conditions in the prison were so grim that he began to lose hope. Day after day, he found his faith ebbing away. He stopped studying the Bible and praying; he stopped hoping and believing. Every few weeks, the government would march him into the courtroom, demanding that he renounce his political and theological views. After months of deprivation, he decided to give in—to recant.

Entering the court, he was surprised to see his wife and several members of his church in the gallery. He had not seen her for months. His eyes welled up with tears. The judge told him to stand and renounce his "traitorous" views. He stood wearily, ready to recant, when suddenly he heard his wife and his Christian friends saying with one voice, "God is alive! God is alive!" It was all they could utter before being removed from the court; but it was enough. He sat down without betraying his faith, renewed in his confidence that God is, indeed, alive.[1]

The risen Christ goes before us. As we continue in our commitment to follow him, the sermon might end by asking: On our road of discipleship, what amazes us? What makes us afraid? If nothing comes to mind, we might consider whether or not we have lost sight of his lead.

KIMBERLY L. CLAYTON

---

1. See Thomas G. Long, "When the Church Is the Church," *Pulpit Resource* 28, no. 3 (2000): 13.

Mark 10:35–45

³⁵James and John, the sons of Zebedee, came forward to him and said to him, "Teacher, we want you to do for us whatever we ask of you." ³⁶And he said to them, "What is it you want me to do for you?" ³⁷And they said to him, "Grant us to sit, one at your right hand and one at your left, in your glory." ³⁸But Jesus said to them, "You do not know what you are asking. Are you able to drink the cup that I drink, or be baptized with the baptism that I am baptized with?" ³⁹They replied, "We are able." Then Jesus said to them, "The cup that I drink you will drink; and with the baptism with which I am baptized, you will be baptized;

Theological Perspective

Some might read this pericope as mere history: Jesus coping with the recalcitrant obtuseness of James and John and the other ten disciples because they misunderstood the passion prediction. Others might read it as timeless specific demands for all Christians. Joel Marcus provides us with a context for understanding this pericope differently. Instead of recounting a historical event or proclaiming a timeless command, Mark built on the passion prediction preceding this pericope to proclaim a moral message within "the liturgy of Mark's Christian community,"[1] a community that was persecuted in specific circumstances. We live in differently situated Christian communities; hence reading this passage as a liturgical message to Mark's particular Christian community sheds light on the contemporary significance of Jesus' instruction and admonition to his disciples.

First, Jesus' teachings to the disciples pertain to current Christians, as they did to the community Mark addressed. They are not historical accounts relevant only for the disciples, nor are they general moral principles or religious promises for all times. They should be interpreted for faith communities that confront different circumstances and probably

1. Joel Marcus, *Mark 1–8: A New Translation with Introduction and Commentary*, Anchor Bible (New York: Doubleday, 2000), 67–68.

Pastoral Perspective

On February 4, 1968, the Rev. Dr. Martin Luther King Jr. preached his last sermon, "The Drum Major Instinct," exactly two months to the day before his death. The sermon, based on this text from Mark, speaks powerfully and perceptively about the human desire to be out in front leading the parade. In our case it may be desiring the limelight, the front page of the newspaper, the lead story on MSNBC, or the position as lead pastor of one of the largest congregations in town. Few of us are immune to this "drum major instinct."[1]

This same desire appears to drive James and John, the sons of Zebedee, in this text from Mark. The brothers have the nerve to ask Jesus for special seating in glory. These two brothers request special seats, not in the back of the room but in the front of the room, to the right and the left of Jesus in glory (vv. 35–37).

It is interesting that James and John think to request such a thing. Instead of their mother asking on their behalf, as she does in Matthew 20:20, James and John are bold enough to ask the favor of Jesus themselves. Where I come from, this is called "getting a big head" or "being full of oneself." My

1. The sermon is available at http://mlk-kpp01.stanford.edu/index.php/encyclopedia/documentsentry/doc_the_drum_major_instinct/; accessed May 24, 2013.

⁴⁰but to sit at my right hand or at my left is not mine to grant, but it is for those for whom it has been prepared."

⁴¹When the ten heard this, they began to be angry with James and John. ⁴²So Jesus called them and said to them, "You know that among the Gentiles those whom they recognize as their rulers lord it over them, and their great ones are tyrants over them. ⁴³But it is not so among you; but whoever wishes to become great among you must be your servant, ⁴⁴and whoever wishes to be first among you must be slave of all. ⁴⁵For the Son of Man came not to be served but to serve, and to give his life a ransom for many."

Exegetical Perspective

What has the politics of life within the Christian community to do with the world's politics? Does the goal of Jesus' mission, "to give his life a ransom for many" (v. 45), ultimately entail our removal from this world and thereby render politics—whether within the church or beyond—of secondary importance to the saved on their way to heaven? In this passage, Jesus asserts that the community of disciples must in fact focus on the disciplined practice of the politics and power of servanthood and that this practice is crucial to the movement of Jesus' disciples with him on "the way."

Jesus, resuming the journey that had been interrupted by the rich man (10:17–22), "goes before" (NRSV "walking ahead of") his disciples, leading them onto "the way" (NRSV "the road") up to Jerusalem (10:32). No sooner does he resume the journey than his own disciples interrupt him. The brothers Zebedee "come forward" (v. 35), joining Jesus at the front of the tour and leaving the other disciples behind. Their entreaty makes James and John sound like kids in the messianic candy store: "We want you to grant whatever wish we ask for!" Their request for the places of greatest honor and power when Jesus comes in glory is no less an immature fantasy for all its focus on grown-up aspirations. James and John demonstrate that they are

Homiletical Perspective

After each of the three passion predictions, Mark demonstrates how Jesus' disciples fail to understand the true nature of discipleship. This text offers a particularly detailed opportunity to roll our collective eyes at them, especially the power-grabbing, tone-deaf James and John. Is this the best way to read the text?

Notice that Jesus does not criticize James and John for asking to sit at his right and left hands in glory. He simply states a fact: they do not know what they are asking. Jesus, in turn, asks them a question: Are you able . . . to drink this cup, to bear this baptism? In their pre–Good Friday confidence, they are sure they are able. We have the benefit of knowing what James and John do not yet know: that Jesus' "glory" will be the cross, that at his right and left hands will be two criminals who will die with him. Notice too that the other ten are angry, perhaps not that James and John ask Jesus for this place of honor, but that they ask it only for themselves, and before the rest of them thought of it!

The sermon, instead of ridiculing James and John, might explore our own struggle to understand and practice the sacrificial discipleship Jesus taught and modeled. Roman society thrived on the exercise of power—enforced by threat and intimidation, by bribery and currying favor. Our culture uses similar tactics; and the access to power and status we

Mark 10:35–45

Theological Perspective

hold different cosmic beliefs from those embraced by the early church Mark addressed.

Second, when we participate in baptism and drink from the eucharistic cup, we are not merely enacting a ritualistic propitiation for our sins, in order to receive the benefits of Jesus' sacrifice. By drinking from the cup Jesus drank from and being baptized into the life Jesus led, we commit to a moral life in the way of Jesus. We are linking ritual and morality, as Jesus required of his disciples who would reap the blessings of his glory. This pericope joins worship and the moral life.

Third, the message does not demand that contemporary Christians seek persecution or embrace beliefs about an imminent and cosmic *eschaton*. Mark's historically bound message was a challenge and comfort to a particular community, a church confronting persecution. The admonition to accept service that often entails suffering obtains, but that is not a universal call to seek martyrdom. Moreover, the message of hope persists, but not in the form of a cosmic apocalypse to reverse the fortunes of martyrs.

In sum, understanding this encounter between Jesus and the disciples as addressed to worshipers in a particular early church enables a more perceptive interpretation of its theological and ethical significance for our particularly situated faith communities. Understanding the pericope in this context reminds us of our tendency to ask with James and John for a special place of glory for our faithfulness to Jesus; or perhaps, like the other ten, we are jealously irritated by those who preempt our petitions for a place of honor. Our situation differs from Mark's addressees; we are not called to seek persecution by religious or governmental authorities. However, we are called to service that may entail suffering, opprobrium, and even physical harm at the hands of oppressive powers.

Service as a "ransom" for others (v. 45) is action that liberates particular people—not Jesus' sacrifice in order to pay for human sins for all times. This ransom that liberates is not sheer capitulation and subordination to current dominating mores and powers. We know from the passion predictions that Jesus' admonition to drink from his cup means actively challenging those who neglect or oppress the vulnerable "last ones" (10:31).[2] To be the "slave of all" (v. 44) cannot mean subordination and servitude to powers that impede God's purposes. The noted Mennonite theologian John Howard Yoder never

---

2. The translation is Joel Marcus's, in Marcus, *Mark 8–16*, Anchor Bible 27A (New Haven and London: Yale University Press, 2009), 576.

Pastoral Perspective

grandfather would have said James and John were "getting too big for their britches." In any case, this request is problematic because it profoundly misunderstands what Jesus has just said about himself in 10:32–34 and what he says in this passage, 10:35–45.

Jesus says, "The Son of Man came not to be served but to serve, and to give his life a ransom for many" (v. 45). James and John have misunderstood the purpose of Jesus' life and ministry. Their request is for a political or governmental appointment in a presidential administration. The brothers' request of Jesus to sit at his right hand and his left is a political move, a request for positions of power. Sadly, they miss the mission that Jesus was sent to fulfill. Jesus was not sent to establish a government that would attack its enemies to maintain its power. On the contrary, Jesus was sent to bring about a nonviolent movement that would halt the evil systems and structures of the day. Jesus was sent to bring in a new order with the real possibility of peace, joy, and love for those who would choose to follow him.

Mark paints a picture of James and John being so caught up in popularity and power that they cannot see reality. James and John are observing the popularity of Jesus and not the harsh political reality that Jesus is about to be handed over to those who hate his life and want to see it brought to a humiliating end. James and John have no earthly idea what they are asking. This is due in part to the perspective that they have on Jesus.

Yet Jesus does not ignore James and John's strange request; he answers their request with a question. Jesus asks James and John if they are able to drink the cup he is about to drink and be baptized with the baptism that he is about to undergo (v. 38). In the structure of the story, Jesus clearly is referring to his passion. That is confirmed in Gethsemane when Jesus prays, "Take this cup from me" (14:36). It is the cup of suffering that Jesus is describing to James and John, and the baptism is the baptism of death. It is vitally important to understand the symbolism of both the cup and baptism. When we understand the seriousness of both the cup and baptism, it should cause us to stop, think, and pray about our Christian vocation.

The cup means, in a very real sense, that Jesus is going to experience unimaginable pain and ultimately death. The baptism means, in a very real way, that Jesus will feel as though he is drowning in sorrow and suffering (v. 39). James and John are oblivious to the reality of what the cup and baptism mean; they desire to sit on the right and the left hands of Jesus, not pick up their own crosses and follow him

Exegetical Perspective

readying themselves, not for the mission that Jesus envisions, but for a world much like the one they already inhabit, with all the attendant consequences. The community of disciples is now splintering at the very moment when Jesus most needs their support and solidarity.

Jesus' reply sounds at first like a father chiding his children: "you do not know what you are asking" (v. 38). Do they understand that his cup and his baptism refer to power realized in suffering for others? His question, "Are you able?" does not just mean, "Are you capable of this?" The Greek word *dynamai* often connotes legal authorization and empowerment, as an agent of the emperor would be granted authority to carry out certain actions. This sense fits with James and John's imperial ambitions (see also 10:42). Their easy answer, "We are able" (v. 39), suggests that they are either claiming such authority of their own accord or presuming that Jesus will grant it to them. In either case, they are mistaken.

They do not yet understand what drinking his cup and being baptized with his baptism mean. They do not yet realize that the authority to which they are laying claim will be earned in service and suffering, not by an executive order granting them the chief seats in his empire (vv. 43–44). Despite their lack of understanding, Jesus proceeds to authorize their participation in his cup and his baptism (v. 39), thereby granting them the right to suffer as he will and to give their lives for the sake of many. However, the rewards of power and honor at his right and left hand are not his to grant. When Jesus manifests his divine power, two thieves, not his own disciples, will be at his right and left hands. James and John thus get both less and more than they bargain for.

In the process, James and John also ignite the indignation of their fellow disciples. Self-interest and the quest for power have fractured the community. While the ten are upset at James and John, it is not clear whether they hold fundamentally different values or are just upset that the sons of Zebedee have beaten them to the punch. Jesus' response (vv. 42–45) suggests that the whole group needs to be reminded of the differing foundation upon which the distinctive politics of the community of disciples is built. Jesus uses the very model his disciples presuppose and apparently idealize—the so-called "rulers" (v. 42), who subdue and lord it over the nations—as a foil for the politics of servanthood. "But it is not so among you!" (v. 43) rings ironically, since division, domination, and the exercise of exclusive power is precisely what the disciples have been

Homiletical Perspective

enjoy through educational, economic, political, and military advantages makes it difficult for us to take our "rightful place"—not in seats of glory, but in the posture of humble service. Cultural standards, however accepted and entrenched, should not determine how Jesus' followers live before God and others. Jesus is shaping an alternative community in the world, forming disciples who will embody a different definition of "greatness"; people who follow Jesus exercise power on behalf of others, not over against them.

In this chapter Jesus upends acceptable norms and practices in regard to marriage and divorce (10:2–12), the status of children (10:13–16), and possessions and wealth (10:17–30). Despite society's legal permission to "set aside" a spouse, leaving her vulnerable, Jesus upholds covenantal responsibility for one another. Jesus lifts up devalued children as examples of those who welcome the kingdom. A man worth a fortune turns away, dragging behind him the weight of many possessions.

From the position of privilege, we often cannot see—or we refuse to see—what the gospel makes plain. In the next (and last) story of chapter 10, Jesus asks the same question of blind Bartimaeus (10:51) that he asked of "insiders" James and John (10:36): "What do you want me to do for you?" Guess which one sees clearly enough to follow Jesus "on the way" (v. 52)?

This question is the heart of the sermon. What *do* we want Jesus to do for us? If we are following him comfortably, without much disruption or cost, if we have some measure of power and status and use it for good purposes, then an honest answer might be that we want Jesus to keep things as they are, or even increase our sphere of influence so that we can do even more good in his name.

Can you see? If we are a woman left economically and socially devastated, a child powerless against neglect or abuse, a person left by the side of the road in a society that values those who are able bodied and gainfully employed, if we are victims of prejudice or hate, then we are likely to ask Jesus to make the world radically different. We may ask him to make the world more fair, just, and loving by making disciples who will be fair, just, and loving. We may ask Jesus how together a whole community of disciples can change things if we give up our power over others in order to give ourselves away on their behalf. We may ask Jesus to help us see how to do that and then to give us enough love and courage to live this way.

Mark 10:35–45

Theological Perspective

tired of reminding us that even nonviolent service does not entail or permit passive nonresistance to powers that challenge God's purposes for the last ones.[3]

Yoder also repeatedly reminded us that prudent actions that challenge evil powers without directly seeking power and glory through conventional means require eschatological hope. Jesus does not deny to James and John that there will be "glory" (v. 38), and he tells the ten that some can be "great" by becoming a "servant" and some will be "first" by being a "slave of all" (vv. 43–44). We cannot know the precise nature of the glory, but we are assured that God has "prepared" a place for some, which even Jesus cannot "grant" (v. 40). This "glory" is not the riches of the man who "had many possessions" (10:17–22) or the lording it over the Gentiles by their "great" rulers (v. 42). We know that the glory is often associated with suffering in order to serve the vulnerable and the "least ones." The glory is not contained in the suffering itself, but in the reversal of fortunes wrought by God through the suffering service. No iron-tight linear logic allows the disciples or us to see the triumph emerging from suffering, but Jesus assures them, Mark's church, and us that hope for triumph through and beyond service to God's purposes is justified.

This hope identifies neither an exact eschatological process nor the precise thing hoped for. Many contemporary Christians, for good reason, doubt Mark's view of an imminent cosmic *eschaton*. However, evidence abounds that the suffering of Jesus and even the reticent suffering of the disciples triumphed in the empty tomb and the rise of the church. We have also witnessed success in consonant, if not equally paradigmatic, suffering service at several points in history, for example, in the American civil rights movement. We do not have to share every aspect of Mark's eschatology to justify hope that courageous advocacy for the vulnerable, challenging the present order, issues in a related future reversal that depends on God's ordering, not merely on the foreseen direct consequences of our service.

This passage does not offer timeless instruction; it does remind us that when we participate in baptism and drink from the cup, we commit ourselves to the way of Jesus that brings new possibilities.

HARLAN BECKLEY

Pastoral Perspective

(8:34). Their quick response implies that James and John do not give it much prayer, thought, or reflection; they both quickly answer yes (v. 39). We who follow Christ are not assigned seats of honor, but we are given sometimes very difficult assignments of sorrow and suffering to complete. Thus we should always take time to reflect and pray before accepting. We are called upon to walk with parishioners, friends, and family who face life challenges, storms, and the valley of the shadow of death.

Now there is the problem of offended disciples to resolve. Mark reports that the other ten disciples are quite offended and angry about the request made by James and John for special seating (v. 41). The question becomes, "Are the other disciples offended and angry because James and John asked first, or are they offended and angry because they thought that it was inappropriate to ask such a thing?" In either case, Jesus uses James and John's request and the disciples' offense and anger as a teachable moment. The writer captures Jesus explaining to the twelve disciples that real ministry is never about where you sit; rather, it is ultimately about how you serve. Jesus articulates a new paradigm of ministry: whoever is great among us must be willing to serve those who are least among us (v. 43). Jesus instructs us through this text to worry less about leading the parade and work more to improve the lives of the poor and the disenfranchised of society.

WILLIAM E. CROWDER JR.

---

3. John Howard Yoder, *The Politics of Jesus* (Grand Rapids: Eerdmans, 1972, 1994), passim, esp. 89–92.

Exegetical Perspective

seeking. The "great ones" among the "Gentiles"—whether ancient Rome or peoples today—practice tyranny, but those who wish to be great in the community of disciples are slaves of all.

Servanthood is too often a platitude in congregations, or a mantle thrust upon some to the advantage of others, rather than a defining, shared practice. Where service is valued only by a few and consumed by others, the church merely replicates the politics of the Gentiles. Distrust and division, displayed here by the disciples, are sure symptoms of communal life disrupted by the quest for personal power. For disciples following Jesus "on the way" to the cross, mutual service is both an essential sustaining practice and a light to the nations. Only in this way will disciples make it to Jerusalem with Jesus, and beyond.

Jesus' final statement (v. 45) confirms the link between servanthood and the mission of the Son of Man, whom Jesus last mentioned while offering the final prediction of his passion and resurrection (10:33–34), as he was beginning the journey up to Jerusalem. Jesus calls himself the Son of Man whenever he speaks of his passion; in Mark the title designates his vocations of service, redemptive suffering, and messianic judgment and deliverance, as well as his common humanity. Here he reminds the disciples that the Son of Man's power lies not in being served but in serving. His mission heretofore and to come in Jerusalem are both defined by service for others.

When heard merely as another way of saying that Jesus saves us, the assertion that the Son of Man came "to give his life a ransom for many" may occlude Jesus' focus throughout this passage on the political life of his disciples. "Ransom," however, refers to the price required to redeem Israelites and their land from debt slavery. Jesus accomplishes this by his death at the hands of the Gentile overlords and tyrants. Liberation from the power of death is at the same time liberation from the power of debt. Ransom by the Son of Man is not another way to talk about salvation in the world to come, but a dramatic assertion that the way of redemption is service and suffering (10:21, 45!).

STANLEY P. SAUNDERS

Homiletical Perspective

I hope Mark is right, that Jesus did not scold or judge James and John for preferring glory to self-sacrifice, but continued patiently to teach them, again, his alternative way, seeing in them a possibility they could not yet imagine for themselves. There is some evidence that James and John were eventually martyred for radically living the way of Jesus for the sake of others.

Perhaps Jesus still has such patience and forbearance with us. Jesus came as a "ransom" for many, a ransom freeing us from whatever enslaves us and turns us away from the kingdom God intends. As the Common English Bible puts it, he came to serve "and to give his life to liberate many people" (v. 45).

Mark implies that we too can live in ways that ransom others; Jesus frees us well-intentioned disciples struggling with a desire for safety and glory over sacrifice and service. Still, such Christlike service does not come to us easily. While pastoring an urban church, I saw dozens of homeless people come daily seeking help. Our Outreach Center offered many services. One day, a man leaving the Center asked me if he could borrow a stapler. He made this request from the hallway while I stood behind the safety of our office wall and glass window. I am ashamed to admit it, but I hesitated. He held no papers in need of stapling. Behind the wall of my office and "wall" of privilege, I held a stapler.

In that momentary hesitation, Christ came to teach me, again, the nature of discipleship. By God's grace, I went out and gave him the stapler. He bent down and began to staple his torn pants leg from his ankle to his knee. He had only wanted to shield himself from the bitter cold —and I had almost refused to serve in even that simple way. It did not cost me anything, yet it might have cost me my soul. I understand all too well James and John's wrongheaded request. The sermon might help Jesus' disciples explore how, with God's help, they may drink from his cup, bear this baptism, however modestly, today.

KIMBERLY L. CLAYTON

Mark 10:46–52

⁴⁶They came to Jericho. As he and his disciples and a large crowd were leaving Jericho, Bartimaeus son of Timaeus, a blind beggar, was sitting by the roadside. ⁴⁷When he heard that it was Jesus of Nazareth, he began to shout out and say, "Jesus, Son of David, have mercy on me!" ⁴⁸Many sternly ordered him to be quiet, but he cried out even more loudly, "Son of David, have mercy on me!" ⁴⁹Jesus stood still and said, "Call him here." And they called the blind man, saying to him, "Take heart; get up, he is calling you." ⁵⁰So throwing off his cloak, he sprang up and came to Jesus. ⁵¹Then Jesus said to him, "What do you want me to do for you?" The blind man said to him, "My teacher, let me see again." ⁵²Jesus said to him, "Go; your faith has made you well." Immediately he regained his sight and followed him on the way.

Theological Perspective

The story of the blind man known only as "son of Timaeus" raises intriguing theological questions regarding the role of human agency, perhaps even of human initiative, in our dealings with God as revealed in Jesus Christ. On the one hand, the Gospel of Mark proclaims Jesus as the emissary, indeed the very embodiment, of the reign, rule, and presence of God in the world. Thus, the person and ministry of Jesus the Anointed One is the sign par excellence of divine initiative. In Christ, God has moved lovingly and compassionately toward creation, toward this world so wracked and rent by the power of sin. Jesus, we confess and believe, is the movement of God toward us in redeeming love.

On the other hand, we ought to acknowledge that Bartimaeus demonstrates a gutsy perseverance in his response to the divine initiative in the person of Jesus. The text fairly shouts the loud persistence of this marginalized human being. He will not be silenced.

Noteworthy too is the man's addressing Jesus as "Son of David"—clearly a title of messianic implication. In his own desperate way, he recognizes this divine initiative in the Messiah's approach. It is God who draws near through Jesus to reclaim Israel, a people who remember the past glories of King David: "Jesus, Son of David, have mercy on me!" (v. 47).

Pastoral Perspective

Jesus and his friends have come to the last leg of their journey from the Galilee to Jerusalem, the center of religion, power, and wealth. As happened at the beginning of their journey (8:22–26), the travelers encounter a blind person. Mark tells us that the blind man has probably heard rumors about Jesus, that he was able to heal the sick and that he was possibly the Anointed One, descended from the line of King David. In the story the blind man runs up to Jesus and is very excited, until Jesus' surprising question stops him in his tracks: "What do you want?" (v. 51). The answer seems so obvious. The man is blind and Jesus is a healer. Put one and one together, Jesus!

How often are we as congregational leaders in comparable situations? To us everything seems to be totally clear; of course we need this staff position, no doubt we have to renovate the sanctuary, clearly we will join the Habitat for Humanity project. Then somebody on the board or on the evangelism or social justice committee asks the question, "What is the connection here with our mission?" Everyone is stunned, begins to backtrack, to rethink and reword, to emphasize differently how she wants to approach the task at hand. The blind man in our story does not hesitate to say the obvious, because it is the most important to him: "I am blind, I wish to see."

Exegetical Perspective

Our passage represents a significant turning point in the Gospel of Mark. On the one hand, it is the culminating moment in Jesus' Galilean ministry (1:39–10:52). The miracle story about blind Bartimaeus recapitulates portrayals of Jesus as a miracle-working healer and teacher found throughout the first part of Mark. The miraculous healing of Bartimaeus parallels stories such as the healings of the leper (1:40–45), Jairus's daughter (5:21–24, 35–43), the woman with the hemorrhage (5:25–34), and the blind man at Bethsaida (8:22–26). Moreover, Bartimaeus's address to Jesus as "teacher" (v. 51) underscores his numerous teachings scattered throughout the Gospel (2:18–22; 3:20–30; 4:2–32; 7:1–23, 8:4–21, 34–38). *Rabbi*, the Greek root word for "my teacher" (v. 51), occurs four times in Mark (9:5; 10:51; 11:21; 14:45). The only instance of its Aramaic form, *rhabbouni*, in Mark occurs in the story of Jesus and Bartimaeus (see John 20:16). The attribution indicates Jesus' authority as an interpreter of Scripture and his peculiar practice of selecting his own disciples.

On the other hand, our passage foreshadows Jesus' Jerusalem ministry and the events found in the latter portion of the Gospel. Immediately preceding our passage is the last of Jesus' three passion predictions (8:31–33; 9:30–32; 10:32–34). Here, Jesus explicitly names Jerusalem as the site of his suffering

Homiletical Perspective

I have heard that there is a bronze statue somewhere in the heart of Texas depicting this scene. The blind man is crouching, starting to spring up, one hand extending out to Jesus, the other holding his cane and cape, ready to drop them in the dust. The statue captures so much of this story: it is as much about discipleship as about healing, as much about following as about seeing.

In Mark, Bartimaeus is the last person to be healed and called. Immediately after this healing, Jesus enters Jerusalem on his march toward the cross. Curiously, in Mark, Bartimaeus is the only healed person who is named. Others are identified only by their infirmities: the woman with the hemorrhage (5:25–34), the demoniac (5:1-19), the blind man at Bethsaida (8:22–30). Mark even reiterates the name, in case we do not catch it the first time: Bartimaeus, son of Timaeus.

As others have noted, the name Timaeus would have been familiar among Mark's readers because of Plato's popular essay, "Timaeus."[1] In it Plato writes:

---

1. See Gordon W. Lathrop, *Holy Ground: A Liturgical Cosmology* (Minneapolis: Augsburg Press, 2003), 25–38; and Earle Hilgert, "The Son of Timaeus: Blindness, Sight, Ascent, Vision in Mark," in Elizabeth A Cestelli and Hal Taussig, eds., *Reimagining Christian Origins: A Colloquium Honoring Burton L. Mack* (Harrisburg, PA: Trinity Press International, 1996), 190–91.

Mark 10:46–52

Theological Perspective

What if this blind man had not cried out for mercy? Presumably Jesus and his disciples, along with the large, enthusiastic crowd tramping along behind, would have strode on, unhindered, toward Jerusalem.

We find in this story, then, the rich and complex intertwinings of divine mercy and human misery—but also human determination. We might be tempted to say that it was the Holy Spirit that moved Bartimaeus to cry out to Jesus for mercy. That might even be true. We should acknowledge, however, that the text makes no such claim. Instead, we encounter here an otherwise forgettable figure who stubbornly persists in begging for mercy and is rewarded accordingly. Thus, while some in the crowd tell Bartimaeus that "[Jesus] is calling you" (v. 49), this blind man first calls to Jesus.

We might even note that the text informs us that Jesus, hearing the man's cries, "stood still" (v. 49). He has set his face toward Jerusalem; he knows that political and religious tensions are mounting; he is about to be "baptized" (10:38) in deep suffering and death. Indeed, he feels the divine "must" (*dei*, 8:31) upon him as he strides for Jerusalem. Yet here, at this poor beggar's insistence, Jesus stood still. The Gospels often portray Jesus' agenda being interrupted by unanticipated human need, unscripted cries of misery. One begins to surmise that such actually is Jesus' (and therefore God's) true agenda.

In any case, this story insists that we take quite seriously the real agency of Bartimaeus. Jesus does not simply hear the man's cries and, in royal majesty, solve all his woes with a mere wave of his hand. Instead, Jesus asks him, "What do you want me to do for you?" If nothing else, the question Jesus poses implies that divine grace evokes and encourages our human voice and human will. Jesus the Anointed One of God, the very mercy of God incarnate, does not blissfully stride past this beggar, nor does he run roughshod over him, nor does he wave a magic wand. Instead, he gives the man room, a space in which to speak. Accordingly, Chrysostom observed that God promises deliverance on the condition of "cooperation from [us]," for God's promise is not offered to "sticks and stones, being inactive," but to human beings.[1]

There is yet another layer of the narrative to embolden our own voice, our own initiative vis-à-vis God as readers of this text. "Go," Jesus says, "your

---

1. Chrysostom, *Homilies on Thessalonians*, Homily V: 2 Thess. 3:3–5, in *Nicene and Post-Nicene Fathers*, first series, ed. Philip Schaff (repr., Peabody, MA: Hendrickson, 1995), 13:393.

Pastoral Perspective

Often it is not easy for us to see or say the obvious. We may not dare to admit that we have a completely different perspective or simply lack a convincing one. I am thinking of the well-known story of a group of blind men who are asked to determine what an elephant looks like by feeling different parts of the elephant's body. Each of them comes up with an image of the elephant, depending on which part he has felt. For example, the one who has felt a leg says the elephant is like a pillar; the one who has felt the tail says the elephant is like a rope. Each has a different perspective, and they all are right. However, none of the blind men has the whole perspective and a realistic image of an elephant.

The story of the blind men and the elephant can be an example of our own "blind spots." For any developing process we need to broaden our perspective: to know where the starting point is, what the framework looks like, and what the goal for the process is. Perhaps the most important question is how well we can see the whole picture. As an example, I have friends in Europe who have the impression that all Christians in the United States are creationists and fundamentalists. We know that this is not the case. Here is another example: what of those who are against abortion but have no problems with capital punishment or sending soldiers to war; and what of those who are against war and capital punishment but have no problem with abortion? What is the overall perspective behind these opinions?

Like many other stories in the Bible, this Markan pericope has a metaphorical framework. It reminds me of a situation from my time as a youth minister. On the second day of summer camp, a fourteen-year-old girl who was terribly homesick complained about a strong headache, and soon she was not able to see. I was not sure what was happening. I took her to the hospital, but the examination did not show anything physically wrong. The doctor kept her overnight in the hospital for observation. The girl fell asleep, and I left the hospital pondering whether to inform her parents immediately. I decided against it. When I came back the next morning, the girl had regained her eyesight, and I called her parents. This anecdote may suggest different approaches to interpreting Mark's first-century story for twenty-first-century people. For instance, Mark's narrative may apply to spiritual blindness as much as physical blindness. Jesus really sees Bartimaeus. He is touched by the blindness, the poverty, and the social isolation of this man. Through Jesus' act of compassionate inclusion, the man is healed, his whole life

Exegetical Perspective

and death. Furthermore, the story's use of the honorific title "Son of David" (v. 47) highlights the Gospel's geographical turn to Jerusalem. As the first occurrence in Mark, the title underscores the imminent event: the Son of David's entrance into Jerusalem, the city of David. Thus the story of Bartimaeus both reviews and previews Jesus' various acts and the various responses to him.

While functioning as a story bridge, our passage also highlights genuine discipleship as a central theme of the Gospel of Mark. The verb for following Jesus (*akoloutheō*) appears eighteen times in Mark (1:18; 2:14–15; 3:7; 5:24; 6:1; 8:34; 9:38; 10:21, 28, 32, 52; 11:9; 14:13, 54; 15:41). In particular, the reference in verse 52 is reminiscent of 1:17, when Jesus calls Peter and Andrew to "follow him." Even more interesting is the way this passage depicts the actual practice of true discipleship, as prescribed by Jesus in Mark 8:34: "If any want to become my followers, let them deny themselves and take up their cross and follow me." In verse 52 Bartimaeus disobeys Jesus' explicit command to "go." Nevertheless he obeys Jesus' consistent mandate to "follow me" by following Jesus "on the way" to Jerusalem (10:32, 52). True disciples of Jesus do not go away from Jesus, but follow him without promise of self-advantage and convenience. Thus the features of true discipleship are defined at the juncture between Jesus' itinerant ministry through Galilee and his entrance into Jerusalem.

The particular significance and meaning of discipleship in Mark is further illuminated when Mark's version is compared to the other Synoptic Gospels' telling of the Bartimaeus story (Matt. 20:29–34; Luke 18:35–43). Mark's version of the blind man is unique in several aspects. First, Mark's Gospel is the only one explicitly to name the blind man Bartimaeus. *Bar* is the Hebrew word for "son of"; Bartimaeus, therefore, literally means "Son of Timaeus." Luke sticks to a general description, naming him "a blind man" who begs. Matthew doubles the number, making the story about the healing of two blind men, rather than just one. Second, Mark's Gospel is the only one in which the blind man calls Jesus "teacher." Both Luke and Matthew select "Lord" as the proper address to Jesus when the blind man (or men) requests to be healed. Lastly, most of Mark 10:49–50 is entirely absent from Luke and Matthew. In this section in Mark, Jesus' act of calling the blind man is explicitly stated. Additionally, Bartimaeus's response, which includes "throwing off his cloak" and approaching Jesus, is accented. At the moment

Homiletical Perspective

The sight in my opinion is the source of the greatest benefit to us, for had we never seen the stars and the sun and the heaven, none of the words which we have spoken about the universe would ever have been uttered.... And from this source we have derived philosophy, than which no greater good ever was or will be given by the gods to mortal men. This is the greatest boon of sight, and of the lesser benefits why should I speak? Even the ordinary man [if he were deprived of them] would bewail his loss, but in vain.... God invented and gave us sight that we might behold the courses of intelligence in the heaven, and apply them to the courses of our own intelligence which are akin to them. (47a–c)

For Platonists, philosophy is the greatest good and philosophers are the greatest people. Sight for them eventuates in philosophy; for ordinary people, sight remains only a sense. Pity those who do not have this rare and wonderful gift of superior insight.

Bartimaeus is no philosopher or even an ordinary person, but even less: a beggar. Perhaps he is even a caricature of all the sons-of-philosophy who not only lack insight but are completely blind. Their supposedly superior, learned path has led nowhere but to emptiness. His "insight" is that he knows he is blind, what he lacks, and he knows where to seek healing. Bartimaeus cries out to Bar-David for mercy. "Son of David, have mercy on me!" he repeats (v. 48), persistent though many try to hush him. "What do you want me to do for you?" Jesus asks him. "My teacher," he says, "let me see again" (v. 51).

The preacher might do well simply to focus the question on the competing worldviews we confront. Where does the world look for the greatest truth or the highest good? What power or leaders does the world revere most? Whence do we expect our salvation to come? If we do call out to Jesus, son of David, what do we want Jesus to do for us? If it is to make us superior, successful, sophisticated people, we had better go back to Plato. If it is to see, really see—that he can help with.

First, we have to know that we are blind.

The late Malcolm Muggeridge was, by all accounts, quite sophisticated, a "British intellectual, gadfly, editor of *Punch* magazine, with opinions about everything."[2] Meeting Mother Teresa changed his life. He wrote of this profound discovery:

> Suddenly, almost with a click, like a film coming into sync, everything has meaning, everything is

---

[2]. John Buchanan, "Sight Restored," sermon preached at Fourth Presbyterian Church in Chicago, October 26, 1997.

Mark 10:46–52

Theological Perspective

faith has made you well" (v. 52). It is striking how often Jesus is described in the Gospels as having said things like this—things that make us wonder just how much power for healing God has entrusted to us, to our wills, to our imaginations, to our persistence through misery and suffering (see Mark 5:34; Matt. 9:22; Luke 17:19).

While a story like this will probably not make Pelagians of us, it may nonetheless help inspire a newfound appreciation for Pelagius's insistence, against Augustine, upon the divinely mandated role of the human mind and human will in salvation. We do not save ourselves, certainly; again, Jesus Christ is always already the ultimate sign and promise of God's gracious initiative. Nevertheless, Jesus' coming among us invokes, invites, empowers a truly human reply, a crying out for mercy, a persistence in faith that may yet make us well—well enough to follow Jesus.

Interestingly, even in this matter of following Jesus, we find a final note of human initiative, human will. Jesus instructs the man, "Go, your faith has made you well" (v. 52); but the man does not "go"; instead, he "comes" with Jesus, following him "on the way" to Jerusalem. This fascinating vignette forces us to reconsider our often terribly glib pronouncements celebrating divine grace at the expense of human will. Nothing in this story hints at a crippling helplessness in this man, even given his disability. Yes, we can insist once more that Jesus is the very presence of God moving mercifully in the midst of weak and wayward humans, and all that is true. Still, Bartimaeus also instructs us about the dignity God has granted human beings: the dignity to speak, to cry out to God, to specify what we need, and to exercise faith in God, who in Jesus Christ has come to salve us with deep mercy. Of course, even Pelagius's persistent critic, the sainted bishop of Hippo, could insist that "the God who made you without you, does not justify you without you," without our "willing consent."[2]

MICHAEL LODAHL

Pastoral Perspective

is transformed, and as a result of that process he follows Jesus. The compassion of Jesus is paired with Bartimaeus's own strong wish for change. Just imagine for a second that he actually runs (!) to get to Jesus; after all, he is still blind!

Jesus heals by revealing a new perspective. In Mark's Gospel, the disciples seldom understand what is going on and why. However, the formerly blind Bartimaeus "gets it" and changes not only his perspective but also the direction of his whole life: he follows Jesus. He is transformed and begins to see life around him differently. The perspective of Jesus and his friends changes Bartimaeus's outlook on life, as they together continue their journey to Jerusalem.

Healing transformation is a life-giving event in the here and now. Bartimaeus is ready for God's call, and he answers promptly. The few words in Mark's narrative describe a total transformation, just as the former slave trader John Newton did when he wrote the hymn "Amazing Grace" and talked about the changing power of grace that turned his blindness into sight.[1] Transformation is liberation from being stuck, change from being self-centered to being God-centered. It is the giving way of blind eyes and a closed heart to the freeing perspective of compassion and hope.

What are some of our own "blind spots"? Could it be hubris that makes us believe that Christianity is the only possible path to God? Could it be ignorance that lets us think that our own country is the best in the world and cannot do wrong? Could it be complacency that makes us give a dollar to the homeless person at the traffic light and forget about systemic poverty and injustice in our society and the world? Could it be piety that makes us create God in our own image, instead of letting the living God fill the core of our being?

Jesus can heal our blindness if we, like Bartimaeus, are ready for the call and willing to follow him.

WOLFGANG H. STAHLBERG

---

2. *The Works of St. Augustine: A Translation for the 21st Century*, vol. III/5, Sermon 169, ed. John E. Rotelle, OSM, trans. and notes Edmund Hill, OP (New Rochelle, NY: New City, 1992), 231.

1. John Newton, "Amazing Grace," 1779.

Exegetical Perspective

of Jesus' direct call to him, Bartimaeus abandons his garment.

The experience of personal loss and a realignment of personal values in response to Jesus' call are not new ideas in Mark. The controversy and teaching material of Mark 2:18–22 suggest the need to separate the old situation from the new. Just as new cloth cannot be attached to old, so too Bartimaeus cannot bring the remnants of his blind and beggarly lifestyle to Jesus in pursuit of a new situation. Bartimaeus's intentional disregard for his cloak is a counterimage to Jesus' loss of his clothes at the crucifixion. Whereas Bartimaeus has the luxury of choosing to leave his garment in pursuit of a new life situation, Jesus' clothes are forcibly taken from him at the loss of his life (15:20, 24).

Jesus' activities as a miracle-working healer and authoritative teacher underscore the teacher-student dynamic, in which Jesus calls disciples to follow him "on the way." Mark maintains that following Jesus comes with both benefits and sacrifice, but the sacrifices of Jesus' followers continue to pale in comparison to the ultimate sacrifice Jesus made at the cross. While Jesus' followers forfeit social standing, material resources, and family relationships, Jesus forfeits his life on behalf of many (10:45).

What remains unresolved in the story is just how much Bartimaeus's social situation is reversed at the moment of his encounter with Jesus. Following his healing, Bartimaeus fades into the background, much like other recipients of Jesus' miraculous power. While the readers are assured that Bartimaeus can now see, his social standing as a beggar or one without resources is open to question. Does Bartimaeus's decision to join Jesus on his journey result in automatic care and provision for his needs? Does following Jesus mean there is no need to "go" and with one's newfound wellness improve his or her life situation? While the story of Bartimaeus certainly highlights discipleship as an act of true faith in Jesus, it neglects entirely the social implications and challenges to such a call. Thus Mark's emphasis on the theme of discipleship says more about Jesus' identity as the Christ and the Son of God (1:1) than about his followers' identity and actions as responsible social agents in the world. As such, we should not mistake Bartimaeus's immediate reaction of abandonment and pursuit as normative for daily Christian living.

SHIVELY T. J. SMITH

Homiletical Perspective

real: and the meaning, the reality, shines out in every shape and sound and movement, in each and every manifestation of life.... How, I ask myself, could I have missed it before? How could I not have understood that the grey-silver light across the water, the cry of the sea gulls and the sweep of their wings, everything on which my eyes rest and my ears hear, is telling me about God?[3]

Some things have not changed since Jesus' day; or perhaps they have come full circle. We live in an era steeped in a thousand philosophies and schools of thought, each competing for our allegiance. Most of our churches are filled with would-be sophisticates, and if not sophisticated in the well-read, cultured sense, people who are tracking the latest trends, buying the latest gadgets, seeking the greatest good through greater "goods." We are raising our children in hopes that they will be successful; and by "successful" we do not mean Mother Teresa, we mean "employable." No one wants to think their sons or daughters are ordinary, needy, weak, or deficient. No one wants them to be poor. We are more like Timaeus than blind Bartimaeus, not even knowing we are blind.

This is not a rant against our present-day philosophers. This is a challenge to see more clearly the world and our place in it, and to consider what the gospel allows us to see that others miss. Perhaps we will even see the ones our "success" has left by the side of the road. This is an invitation to consider what we really want from Jesus. He offers his help, a hand reaching down to clasp ours and to lift us up, an offer of a different way of life. This Way will not lead to superiority or sophistication, but into a world in which everything has meaning and is real and belongs. Our teacher wants us to be well and to see again.

KAREN CHAKOIAN

---

3. Malcolm Muggeridge, *Seeing through the Eye: Malcolm Muggeridge on Faith*, ed. Cecil Kuhne (San Francisco: Ignatius Press, 2005), 10–11.

Mark 11:1–10

¹When they were approaching Jerusalem, at Bethphage and Bethany, near the Mount of Olives, he sent two of his disciples ²and said to them, "Go into the village ahead of you, and immediately as you enter it, you will find tied there a colt that has never been ridden; untie it and bring it. ³If anyone says to you, 'Why are you doing this?' just say this, 'The Lord needs it and will send it back here immediately.'" ⁴They went away and found a colt tied near a door, outside in the street. As they were untying it, ⁵some of the bystanders said to them, "What are you doing, untying the colt?" ⁶They told them what Jesus had said; and they allowed them to take it. ⁷Then they brought the colt to Jesus and threw their cloaks on it; and he sat on it. ⁸ Many people spread their cloaks on the road, and others spread leafy branches that they had cut in the fields. ⁹Then those who went ahead and those who followed were shouting,
   "Hosanna!
      Blessed is the one who comes in the name of the Lord!
¹⁰ Blessed is the coming kingdom of our ancestor David!
   Hosanna in the highest heaven!"

Theological Perspective

Mark's story of Jesus' "triumphal entry" into Jerusalem is a masterpiece of brevity and understatement, leaving a host of theological questions both unasked and unanswered. It thereby invites its readers to wrestle not only with the text itself, but also with the mystery of God's ways in the world.

How did Jesus know his disciples would find a colt upon which he would ride into the city? Mark does not tell us. Was it a matter of a divine knowledge in which Jesus shared? In the history of Christian tradition, those who have emphasized Jesus' divine nature—perhaps in this case to the dangerous extreme of Apollinarianism, the heresy that Jesus had no human mind but instead was a body possessed of the divine Logos—have tended to read Jesus' instructions for his disciples as signifying such an omniscience.

Did Jesus simply know the colt's owner and make arrangements for the animal's use ahead of time? If that is the case, was the sentence "The Lord needs it and will send it back here immediately" (v. 3) an agreed-upon password? Again, Mark does not tell us. Those who have been anxious to protect Jesus' authentic sharing in human nature have tended, understandably, to favor this interpretation.

Was it some third possibility? Perhaps something more like a first-century version of a "Jedi mind

Pastoral Perspective

This narrative is often called the "triumphal entry" to Jerusalem. Is that really a good description? I cannot find anything triumphant about this demonstration. Instead, I see it as an "Occupy Jerusalem" event—in some ways similar to the worldwide "Occupy" protest movement of 2011–2012 that spread from New York's Wall Street around the world, criticizing the financial and corporate control of the world by a few.

It is the time of the annual Passover celebration. The city of Jerusalem is filled to capacity with Jewish pilgrims and tourists who have arrived from all over the Roman Empire. The Roman governor, who otherwise resides in Caesarea on the shore of the Mediterranean Sea, comes up to Jerusalem for this occasion every year. He does not make the trip because he is interested in the holy days, but because he is in charge of crowd control. In the past, more than once the huge gatherings of people have shown their anger and frustration against the Roman occupation, and the military power has come in to restore order. After all, Passover is the Jewish celebration of liberation from the unjust and cruel domination system of pharaonic Egypt.

When the governor Pilate comes into Jerusalem, he enters the city from the west with an excessive show of military pomp and circumstance. He leads a large group of cavalry and foot soldiers, and rides

Exegetical Perspective

By the time we reach today's passage about Jesus' entrance into Jerusalem, readers of Mark's account anticipate both triumph and conflict. Up to this point in the Gospel, Mark has depicted Jerusalem as the home of some of Jesus' greatest opponents, the scribes and Pharisees (3:22; 7:1). In the preceding chapter, Jesus identified Jerusalem as the site of great suffering and persecution for the Son of Man (10:32–33). Readers should feel some gratification and great apprehension at the grand entrance of Jesus into the city of David. How will Jesus be received and treated in Jerusalem? According to Jesus' three predictions in the previous section (8:31–33; 9:30–32; 10:32–34), suffering and persecution, not victory and triumph, await him.

At first glance, the form of Jesus' entrance into Jerusalem and his predictions of pending suffering and death appear incompatible. Jesus' authority as a teacher is on display as he sends two disciples to bring him a colt (v. 2). Jesus' entrance into Jerusalem on a colt and the people's celebratory response to him through the use of their cloaks and "leafy branches," and shouts of "Hosanna!" imitate a royal coronation (vv. 7–10). Jesus enters Jerusalem like a Messiah-king leading a royal procession in celebration of divine deliverance. It is reminiscent of the Jewish pilgrimage festivals, such as the festival of

Homiletical Perspective

If preaching this text in a series on Mark, the tension of Jesus' entrance into Jerusalem will be clear. However, preaching on Palm Sunday presents challenges. For one, even our most faithful worshipers often skip the services of Holy Week and jump straight from here to Easter. One solution is to read the passion narrative on Palm Sunday. The entrance into Jerusalem comes early in the service, with at least a celebratory hymn and perhaps with a happy children's anthem about Jesus' coming. Then the mood shifts, the journey to the cross is read, chapter after chapter, laying out that awful week, drawing us into the drama and pathos of the road to the crucifixion.

A second challenge in preaching Jesus' entrance to Jerusalem is to set the stage enough for people to get the sense of the story without bogging down in historical and exegetical explanations. The religious, cultural, and nationalistic contexts are certainly inseparably intertwined, yet many of our members are so biblically illiterate that they know almost nothing of the back-story. One must explain something of the import of Jesus' leaving Galilee to enter Jerusalem, the center of Jewish power and commerce, historic identity and religious meaning. One must mention the echoes of Psalm 118, sung as the faithful entered the temple; the temple's profound meaning as the symbolic and real heart of Judaism;

Mark 11:1–10

Theological Perspective

trick" that left the disciples' questioners speechless? Mark simply does not let us in on the secret.

The fact that Jesus is portrayed as carefully describing the colt as never having been ridden seems to suggest the special, even transcendent, identity and mission of "the Lord" who would be its first rider. He is indeed the Lord—and yet a Lord who "needs" this beast of burden to accomplish his task of entering the Holy City. This is, at the very least, a mild paradox.

Then there is the glaring fact that Mark makes no mention of the prophecy of Zechariah 9:9–10, addressed to "O daughter Jerusalem," regarding "your king" who arrives triumphantly and yet "humble and riding on a donkey." Granted, fulfilled prophecies are not nearly the priority for Mark that they are for Matthew (see Matt. 21:4–5), but this would seem to have been a golden opportunity. On the other hand, the fact that neither Mark nor Luke, in his account of Jesus' entry into Jerusalem, makes any mention of Zechariah's pronouncement may serve as a proper restraint of the popular logic of prophecy-fulfillment.

Jesus would have known the words of Zechariah. He was not a puppet in some divinely scripted drama whose text was written from eternity. In Marcus Borg's estimation, Jesus' entry into Jerusalem was a staged "political demonstration" serving as an "indictment of the Temple as a center of nationalist resistance"[1] against Roman occupation. A "king" making his procession on such a slow and lowly beast can hardly be understood to be inspiring violent resistance. In this reading, Jesus seized the opportunity to enact a prophetic parable, clearly rooted in Zechariah's promise, proclaiming his ironic but true kingship. This kingship is humble, nonviolent, even noncoercive—so that if in fact this king "will cut off the chariot from Ephraim and the warhorse from Jerusalem; and the battle bow shall be cut off, and he shall command peace to the nations" (Zech. 9:10), the divine work of disarmament shall not be accomplished with force or coercion. To exercise divine violence in order to establish peace would undercut the very nature and logic of this humble king's rule. This is a "triumphal" entry? Certainly not triumphalist.

This perspective on the story of Palm Sunday may actually create a new appreciation for Mark's detailed description of how Jesus and the disciples

---

1. Marcus Borg, *Conflict, Holiness and Politics in the Teachings of Jesus* (Harrisburg, PA: Trinity Press International, 1988), 188, 189.

Pastoral Perspective

an impressive stallion. He is the highest representative of the imperial power of Rome in the area. One imagines that the inhabitants of the city stand motionless and silent at the street corners; only a few of the tourists are overly excited. One can hear short military commands together with drum beats and the clop-clop of horseshoes. Pilate represents the emperor himself, the "son of god," "lord of all," and "savior of the world." His entry into Jerusalem is clearly a demonstration of the ever-present Roman power.

On the east side of town, Jesus and his friends enter the city. Jesus has organized some things in advance. Two disciples get the young donkey that Jesus has arranged for them to use. Jesus has planned a demonstration that is as different as it can possibly be from Pilate's power demonstration on the other side of town. The donkey Jesus rides mocks Pilate's powerful horse. Instead of weapons, there are hastily written posters that quote the prophet Zechariah (9:9–10). In the narrow streets, the band of friends from Galilee, men and women, is joined by a handful of other people. They are a joyful group of people; they cheer and laugh. More people join in when they understand the demonstration's message about a peaceful king. This is guerrilla theatre, poking fun at the Romans, who would not have understood, even if they had seen it. At the end of the day, Jesus is checking out the temple, already thinking of the demonstration there the next day.

In our time, congregations join the Pride Parade and the MLK Parade and march in demonstrations against war or for a homeless shelter. Clergy and parishioners take part in the demonstrations of the Occupy movement. Churches work together with other NGOs to advocate for the rights of the marginalized, the hungry, and the homeless. All of this demonstrates what it means to live in the world, but not of the world. We Christians raise our voices for the voiceless, and we use these opportunities to show the world that Christianity is so much more than right-wing evangelical television preachers. As active witnessing communities of believers, we sometimes dare to communicate and demonstrate our convictions. This could be revealed on our church signs, on our Web sites, in our newspaper ads, or through our teaching and preaching.

Did Jesus have to go into Jerusalem? I believe that this organized demonstration, right at the beginning of his stay in the city, shows that Jesus obviously felt that he had to take his alternative message of the kingdom, of the reign of God, into Jerusalem,

Exegetical Perspective

Booths (Lev. 23:40; 2 Kgs. 9:13; Neh. 8:15; 1 Macc. 13:51). However, Jesus' transportation into the city, in the form of riding on a colt, raises questions regarding Jesus' identity. Is Jesus destined to rule as the Davidic king in the way the larger populace envisions?

The word *hosanna* carries the Israelite expectation of divine vindication, victory, and deliverance. The Greek form of the title is a transliteration of its Hebrew form. It symbolizes a type of praise that means "help now" or "save now." It became a liturgical formula of praise associated with the collection of Jewish psalms known as the Hallel (Pss. 113–118). Mark 11:9–10 paraphrases Psalm 118:25–26, which describes the procession of the king and his people into the gates of the temple. Within the gates, the king moves forward to place branches on the sacrificial altar (Lev. 23:40). The word *hosanna* and its image of the victorious king delivered by God occur four times within the Gospel tradition (Matt. 21:9, 15; Mark 11:9–10; John 12:13). The connection between Jesus' identity and the messianic hopes of Israel and the Davidic lineage is a recurring image in Mark's account (2:25; 10:47–48; 11:10; 12:35–37).

Jesus' entrance into Jerusalem on a colt does not solely symbolize his authority and victory as a teacher and king. Indeed, the Greek term used for "colt" in our passage, *pōlos*, is ambiguous. It is unclear whether it is a type of donkey or a horse.[1] When the term appears alone, it is usually understood to refer to a horse. A colt or young donkey was known as a burden-packing animal.[2] There are various examples of such animals in the Old Testament, and they usually carry supplies (Gen. 44:13) or food (Gen. 42:26) or pull chariots (Isa. 21:7). The image of Jesus sitting on a colt reflects his role as one destined to serve and suffer, rather than a king destined to reign. This is in contrast to the explicit and dual image of Jesus as both the Davidic king and Suffering Servant found in Matthew 21:2–7 (see Zech. 9:9).

Our passage represents a definitive shift in the identity of Jesus. Outside Jerusalem, in and around Galilee, Jesus is the miracle-working healer and preacher. Upon his entry into Jerusalem, Jesus is received as the divinely sent savior who is expected to usher in the kingdom of David (11:10). The form of Jesus' entrance extends his identity to include persecution. Jesus has entered Jerusalem to suffer at the

---

1. "*Pōlos*," in W. Bauer, F. W. Danker, F. Arndt, and F. W. Gingrich, eds., *Greek-English Lexicon of the New Testament and Other Early Christian Literature*, 3rd ed. (Chicago: University of Chicago Press, 2001), 900.
2. Lisa Michelle Wolfe, "Ass," *Eerdmans Dictionary of the Bible* (Grand Rapids: Eerdmans, 2000), 117.

Homiletical Perspective

the colt as a kingly symbol; and the timing of the Passover and its reenactment of liberation. Attention should also be given to the huge crowds who would have thronged there on pilgrimage with their cries of "Hosanna!" as a call to "save us."

Even if we do not give a history lesson, it is important that our people understand how highly charged the scene was. Jesus was neither the first nor the last to raise the messianic hopes of the people gathered in Jerusalem. As Joel Marcus notes, when Simon Maccabeus entered Jerusalem, he was similarly accompanied by "praise and palm branches." Marcus notes that "this passage [about Simon Maccabeus] is just one of a series of ancient Jewish texts that conjoin triumphal entry into Jerusalem, popular acclaim, and cultic activity in the temple, often with some sort of royal nuance."[1]

Perhaps few other passages require this kind of background to be provided, but if we leave the passage as a happy-sweet children's story about boys and girls welcoming Jesus with their loud "Hosannas" waving palms, we will have grossly misused Mark's Gospel. The electricity of this moment must be understood in order to preach this passage faithfully. Dynamics of hope and expectation, politics and power, must be understood.

Contemporary analogies might be both necessary and useful, but with caveats. Ancient Jerusalem might be analogous to a conglomerate of Washington, D.C., and New York City, that is, of politics and commerce; the crowds might be like a political rally or sporting event with all of their energy; and the threat to authority might be similar to the prophetic, rallying power of the Rev. Dr. Martin Luther King or, more recently, the Arab Spring. We must be careful, though. What has it really to do with us? We cannot simply assume a parallel with our own context. Washington is not Jerusalem; we are not a country under oppression from another empire; there is no religious center that unites us as a nation; and even the great Dr. King is not the Messiah.

Perhaps the most important move is to awaken longing for the promised reign of God that generated the electricity that coursed through the city when Jesus came riding in, the deep and abiding hope that the prophetic promises would be fulfilled, and the kingdom would be restored. They were waiting for a Messiah to save them; they were hoping against

---

1. Joel Marcus, *Mark 8–16: A New Translation with Introduction and Commentary*, Anchor Bible 27A (New Haven and London: Yale University Press, 2009), 779.

Mark 11:1–10

Theological Perspective

procured the beast of burden. Ched Myers points out that "well over half of the episode concerns the instructions given by Jesus" to a pair of his disciples in anticipation of his "grand entrance" into the Holy City (vv. 1–7). "This gives the distinct impression that all is being deliberately planned and choreographed" in the interests of what Myers calls "political street theater"[2] that parodies earthly rulers' delusions of grandeur.

The irony here, of course, is that even as Jesus intentionally enacts this dramatic proclamation of a peace far more radically peaceful than the *Pax Romana*, he is welcomed into Jerusalem by a crowd that, while undoubtedly characterized by a host of mixed expectations, is clearly hoping for a decisive change in Jerusalem's political climate: "Hosanna!" . . . "Blessed is the coming kingdom of our ancestor David!" (vv. 9–10). No reader should miss the implication: David's great kingdom was built on bloodshed (1 Chr. 28:3) and military might. This new king, in contrast, enters humbly, on a colt, and will very soon shed no blood but his own. Perhaps the colt's never having been ridden is less a commentary on Jesus' unprecedented purity as its rider, and more on the colt's complete unsuitability to lead a charge into battle.

Such hopes as at least many in the crowd held on that Palm Sunday die hard. Consider how often and how consistently throughout church history Christians have longed and prayed for an apocalyptic inbreaking of God's mighty rule in Jesus Christ to right all wrongs. While this hope springs from an understandable desire to see the end of suffering, warfare, hunger, abuse, and violence, one might wonder if Jesus, on that first Palm Sunday, very intentionally proclaimed in prophetic act that such is not the way that God brings healing our way. God's rule comes not by force, but gently and humbly, enthroned on a lowly beast of burden.

MICHAEL LODAHL

Pastoral Perspective

which was the center of power and wealth in first-century Palestine. Jesus was aware of the risks, but he definitely believed in his message and did not want to hide it. This included a subversive criticism of the powers that be. Jesus stood up with his life for the integrity of God's message of justice, peace, and love. Just as Martin Luther King Jr. in 1963 needed to take the civil rights movement from Selma and Montgomery in Alabama to the nation's capital in the March on Washington, Jesus in the year 30 had to take his alternative-empire movement from the Galilee to Jerusalem.

In his 2004 movie *The Passion of the Christ* Mel Gibson got it all wrong. In the film he did not include Jesus' demonstrations and discussions at the beginning of what we now call Holy Week. Instead, he focused exclusively on the pain and bloodshed of Jesus before and at the crucifixion.[1] Certainly, crucifixion was a terrible and violent event. The Romans used it to get across their message: do not mess with us! However, the crucifixion was neither Jesus' goal nor God's plan! It was a consequence of Jesus' courageous message of God's dream of an alternative empire built on justice, not military violence. In our pericope, the eventful last week of Jesus' life begins with an "antitriumphant" demonstration.[2]

The question for us, as followers of Jesus, and for our communities is which kind of demonstration we want to support or even be part of. Are we on the side of the powers that be, supporting the status quo with its injustice and inequality, its results of war, poverty, and destruction of creation? Are we, rather, on the side of God's rule with its nonviolent, creative movement of peace, justice, and love for all of God's children and for the whole cosmos? Do we shout a welcoming "Hosanna" to Jesus or a hostile "Crucify"?

WOLFGANG H. STAHLBERG

---

2. Ched Myers, *Binding the Strong Man: A Political Reading of Mark's Story of Jesus* (Maryknoll, NY: Orbis Books, 1988), 295.

1. *The Passion of the Christ*, dir. Mel Gibson (20th Century Fox, 2004 DVD).
2. Useful reading for this whole context is Marcus Borg and John Dominic Crossan, *The Last Week: The Day-by-Day Account of Jesus' Final Week in Jerusalem* (San Francisco: Harper, 2006).

Exegetical Perspective

hands of the Romans, rather than to reign as the conquering king against them. Again, Mark's readers are confronted with the question, "Who is Jesus?" (1:1; 8:27–30). Mark 11:1–10 provides a tentative answer. Jesus is the divinely appointed Davidic heir and savior of God's people who must die before he reigns.

In Mark 11:1–10, readers encounter what seems to be a moment of revelation and great expectation among Jesus' disciples and the people around him. It appears the general populace finally understands who Jesus is and accepts what Jesus is ultimately destined to accomplish. However, the repeated acclamations of *hosanna* carry hints of misunderstanding. Jesus is destined to be more than just the savior of the earthly kingdom of David. Like Peter, the Jerusalem crowd correctly identifies Jesus as the Messiah, but misunderstands his role as Son of Man (8:29–33). He is more than just a political reformer who has come to Jerusalem to overthrow the Roman Empire. Jesus is the savior who saves through his death and resurrection (8:31–33; 9:30–32; 10:32–34; 15:6–39). While the crowd celebrates Jesus' triumphal entry, it is not clear they truly understand how their salvation and deliverance will come about. After all, in Mark 15:13, the crowd turns against Jesus, their *hosanna*.

As readers of Mark's account, we are caught between a moment of celebration and a moment of apprehension for the suffering to come. In the last section of Mark, during Jesus' final days in Jerusalem, we are confronted with a challenging paradox (11:1–16:8). Do we celebrate human suffering? Do we, rather, suffer in order to celebrate human perseverance? According to Mark, Jesus' public suffering happens at the hands of humans (14:1–2, 10–11, 26–31; 15:6–15, 16–20, 21–32, 33–41). Yet the final victory and exaltation actually occur by the work of God, who remains the prime mover and power working in the background of Jesus' ministry, movements, and final days (1:1, 9–11; 8:38; 9:2–8; 13:32; 14:36; 15:34; 16:1–8).

SHIVELY T. J. SMITH

Homiletical Perspective

hope that the world would be turned upside down and God would right what was wrong. Whether by armed insurrection or by divine intervention, something had to change.

Do our people dare to hope now? Leader after leader disappoints us. Even if we do not hold them personally responsible, we understand the odds against real change are great. What hope do we have that the poor will really be fed, that the unemployed will have good, decent jobs, that children will not be used to manufacture our cheap, wonderful trinkets or, worse, to work the appalling sex trade? What hope do we have that climate change will be reversed, when every year the situation gets worse and yet nothing changes, even though the repercussions will be terrible? What hope does the gospel offer against the nihilistic despair that grips so many of our youth?

What if we could offer a word of hope in spite of all the evidence?

What if we proclaimed that God will be present in the city and in the countryside, and understands full well our desperate hopes and aspirations; that the vision we have of what could be, while painful, may very well be the heart of God speaking into our midst; that our holy imagination, our very realization of what is wrong and what is right, is a gift from God? What if we could offer a word of hope that this crazy planet is going not nowhere, but somewhere, that there is a *telos,* an end, a destination, and that it is the fullness and completeness of God's good creation?

I am convinced that as preachers of the Word, the one true thing we can offer is a vision of the world that is the kingdom of heaven. Jesus' kingdom is not what the people expected or hoped for when he rode in to their whoops and shouts. Jesus' kingdom does not magically undo the tragedy or pain or injustice of the world in which we live. Still, it does exist, even on the streets of the city or on the cross of a condemned man. The kingdom exists because God exists, and we have witnessed the depth of God's love for the world in the daring courage of his Son, riding in to face his death—and resurrection.

KAREN CHAKOIAN

Mark 11:11–26

¹¹Then he entered Jerusalem and went into the temple; and when he had looked around at everything, as it was already late, he went out to Bethany with the twelve.
¹²On the following day, when they came from Bethany, he was hungry. ¹³Seeing in the distance a fig tree in leaf, he went to see whether perhaps he would find anything on it. When he came to it, he found nothing but leaves, for it was not the season for figs. ¹⁴He said to it, "May no one ever eat fruit from you again." And his disciples heard it.
¹⁵Then they came to Jerusalem. And he entered the temple and began to drive out those who were selling and those who were buying in the temple, and he overturned the tables of the money changers and the seats of those who sold doves; ¹⁶and he would not allow anyone to carry anything through the temple. ¹⁷He was teaching and saying, "Is it not written,
 'My house shall be called a house of prayer for all the nations'?
 But you have made it a den of robbers."

Theological Perspective

The writing style of the author of the Gospel of Mark is characterized by clarity and terseness. The author uses his distinct style to bring out different shades of meaning. He must have been familiar with the Greek language. He was probably an interpreter of the message of Jesus to the people of the city of Rome.

In this linguistic and historical context Mark places the story of the fig tree before and after the incident at the temple. For Mark, the fig tree is a metaphor for the dwindling of the teaching and authority of the priests. Just as Jesus wants to find fruit on the fig tree, Jesus wishes to witness "fruit," the fruit of faith, at the temple. However, the temple is no different from the withering fig tree.

This story does not mean to convey a moralistic reading of the exclusive authority of Jesus. Rather, it is intended to show Jesus' reading of the particular time and the possible consequences of the values, religious or otherwise, that were prevalent in the Roman world. Why did Jesus curse a fig tree? Fig trees were a common and important source of food for the people. The withering fig tree pointed to spiritual decay of the day. The prophets of the Hebrew Bible depicted the languishing fig tree as pointing to the decline of Israel (see Joel 1:7, 12; Hab. 3:17; and Jer. 8:13). Jesus' act of cursing a fig tree pointed to his prophetic action against the worldviews and the

Pastoral Perspective

"Rabbi, look!" Peter exclaims. "The fig tree that you cursed has withered" (v. 21).

What pastoral word could this bizarre account of a shriveled fig tree possibly offer? The story is violent. The tree is withered to its roots. It is unjust. Spring is not the season for figs. It seems like a gross misuse of Jesus' power. If he was hungry, the one who could restore sight to the blind and heal the lame could certainly call forth fruit from the tree. Instead, he destroys it.

No wonder Luke omits this story from his Gospel, and commentator Halford Luccock calls it the "least attractive of all the narratives about Jesus."[1]

Maybe Jesus could be excused for not knowing it was not time for figs. He was a carpenter by trade, not an arborist. Later, Jesus tells Peter and three other disciples to learn the lesson of the fig tree (13:28). As the tree's leaves herald a new season, so too the apocalyptic events of chapter 13 will herald the coming of the Son of Man. He may not be a tree specialist, but Jesus knows the seasons of a fig tree's life.

At least in Mark's Gospel, the object of Jesus' ire is only a fig tree, not a small child. In the noncanonical *Infancy Gospel of Thomas*, Jesus curses a

---

1. Halford Luccock, "The Gospel According to St. Mark: Exposition," *The Interpreter's Bible*, ed. Nolan B. Harmon (Nashville: Abingdon Press, 1955), 7:828.

¹⁸And when the chief priests and the scribes heard it, they kept looking for a way to kill him; for they were afraid of him, because the whole crowd was spellbound by his teaching. ¹⁹And when evening came, Jesus and his disciples went out of the city.

²⁰In the morning as they passed by, they saw the fig tree withered away to its roots. ²¹Then Peter remembered and said to him, "Rabbi, look! The fig tree that you cursed has withered." ²²Jesus answered them, "Have faith in God. ²³Truly I tell you, if you say to this mountain, 'Be taken up and thrown into the sea,' and if you do not doubt in your heart, but believe that what you say will come to pass, it will be done for you. ²⁴So I tell you, whatever you ask for in prayer, believe that you have received it, and it will be yours.

²⁵"Whenever you stand praying, forgive, if you have anything against anyone; so that your Father in heaven may also forgive you your trespasses. ²⁶But if you do not forgive, neither will your Father in heaven forgive your trespasses."

Exegetical Perspective

In the wake of the triumphal entry, it is striking that Mark now weaves together a pair of stories about judgment. The close alignment of triumph and tragedy provide a fascinating glimpse into Mark's theology. In our passage, a fig tree morphs into a symbolic representative of the city that has just welcomed Jesus with shouts of acclamation, a city where a temple intended to bring glory to God has, according to Mark, become a site of exploitation. Narratively, the triumph of Jesus' arrival in Jerusalem is short lived. Jesus' prediction that he will be betrayed and condemned to death by the local Jerusalem leadership is certain (10:32–34).

Our verses contain two stories. In the first, Jesus curses a fig tree. In the second, he "cleanses" the temple. Mark's literary ingenuity is evident as he brings these two seemingly disparate tales together in what scholars call an intercalation. Basically, Mark has taken one story, sliced it in half and inserted an additional story between these two halves; it is a "Markan sandwich," if you will.[1] Why write this way? By joining these two stories, Mark makes clear that they are mutually interpreting; we understand one in the light of the other. For Mark, these are not two stories but one.

1. Compare, for example, 5:21–43 and 6:7–30.

Homiletical Perspective

As we ponder a cursed and consequently withered fig tree whose parabolic bookends encase a dramatic act of cleansing judgment issued by Jesus at the front end of Holy Week, we imagine that what happened in the Jerusalem temple centuries ago could actually provide a mirror for our own lives and times. Recalling Reinhold Niebuhr's haunting contention that "the worst corruption is a corrupt religion,"[1] we sense that this story is both old and contemporary. We perceive that the incensed Savior who boldly confronts and upends ancient persons and their institutions is also the strangely caring, jarring, curing judge of our present times and systems.

We are intrigued, if not ill at ease, that the fig tree is adorned with leaves that mask a condition laced with deception and deterioration, a state of being that threatens the very soul of a people. Mark's worrisome passage constitutes a sober warning about the temple, which embodies the historic visions, traditions, and values of Israel. What has happened to this cherished institution that causes our angry Savior to lash out with such passionate and critical actions? What does it mean for human communities to become fruitless, or even practically dead, before it is obvious to most observers?

1. See Arthur Schlesinger Jr., "Forgetting Reinhold Niebuhr," *The New York Times Book Review*, September 18, 2005, 13.

Mark 11:11–26

Theological Perspective

associated values of the day that profaned the Sacred through patterns of economic inequality and social injustice.

Jesus' cleansing of the temple was an action calling for the institution of equality and justice. In this incident we see Jesus' somewhat surprising action in cleansing the temple of those who used it to exploit the worshipers of God. Jesus saw the money changers taking advantage of the poor and other disfranchised people by driving them to pay many times what should be paid. Their exploitation of those who were socially and economically disadvantaged not only dishonored God but was unjust toward their neighbors. By his rather surprising behavior, Jesus both shows his indignation toward the money changers' act of profaning the Sacred and his goal of building a just world in his time. The harshness of Mark's style and tone reflects Jesus' own intention.

The "gentle Jesus" so familiar to many does not appear in this story. His demeanor is very different. In this passage the tone and tenor of the story change. The message here is that such societal issues as injustice, poverty, and inequality are no less than religious in nature. The religious, political, and economic leaders have become complicit. Their complicity dishonors God, the very Sacred to whom they are accountable, the Sacred who exhibits a "preferential option for the poor."[1] After all, the Sacred is the accurate witness to what is going on in life, collectively as well as individually.

The Sacred becomes profaned in a variety of ways. The societal frameworks of culture, laws, and religions exist in order to shape public protection from social evils arising from the excess of those who possess power. A healthy and just society needs fair and equitable access to public resources. What we see in this passage is the religious authorities of Jesus' day siding with the economic, social, and political establishments that augmented their own power deriving from material wealth. The religious authorities had became the voice for the few at the expense of the vast majority of the society.

"'My house shall be called a house of prayer for all the nations' . . . But you have made it a den of robbers" (v. 17). The salt, the prophetic faith, has lost its flavor. The religious authorities of the day have lost credibility. This was the struggle facing the people of faith then. This also is the struggle facing us today. The struggle of faith does not take sides, conservative

Pastoral Perspective

playmate who has displeased him: "'Behold, now also thou shalt be withered like a tree, and shalt not bear leaves, neither root nor fruit.' And straightway, the lad withered up wholly." Later when another boy bumps into him, Jesus' curse causes a child to die.[2]

Jesus' zapping the fig tree has often been interpreted theologically as a metaphor for the temple incident it brackets. Like the figless fig tree, a traditional Christian argument goes, the temple system bore no fruit for the soul. According to this interpretation, sacrificing pigeons and other rituals did not feed the people's spiritual hunger any more than the barren tree could feed Jesus' physical hunger.

Such an interpretation can not only support anti-Semitism; it also misses the point of the temple cleansing. Jesus was not railing against ritual. He was, after all, a Jew who knew his Torah. He was angry at the misuse of ritual for the economic gain of merchants and money changers. If the story of Jesus destroying the fig tree is not a metaphor for Christianity superseding Judaism, what purpose does it serve?

First, it confirms Jesus' humanity. Both Mark and Matthew affirm that Jesus was hungry. However, Mark underscores just how hungry he was. In Matthew's account, the fig tree is by the side of the road. In Mark, Jesus has to go out of his way to get to the tree. He is not just hungry; he is very hungry. He also has to be tired, frustrated, and anxious. In the preceding chapter, Jesus predicts his suffering and death for a third time. Once again, the disciples prove they are clueless. Two disciples ask to be seated with him in glory, and dissension breaks out among the others (10:35–45). Moreover, the story occurs as Jesus proceeds to Jerusalem and the confrontation in the temple. Given all that he is facing, it is not surprising he might lose his temper when in his hunger he finds no figs.

If the incarnation is to be believed and Jesus was truly human, then he must have had truly human feelings. When he takes out his frustration on the fig tree, there can be no denying that Jesus knows the exhaustion, depletion, and even anger that come with being human. The story of Jesus and the fig tree offers proof positive that we do in fact have "a high priest who is able to sympathize" (Heb. 4:15)—and empathize—with our humanity.

Second, the story proves Jesus' power and displays the choices he makes about using that power.

---

1. The expression "the preferential option for the poor" was first articulated by Gustavo Gutiérrez in his book *A Theology of Liberation: History, Politics, and Salvation* (Maryknoll, NY: Orbis Books, 1973).

2. *The Apocryphal New Testament*, ed. M. R. James (Oxford: Oxford University Press, 1924), 50.

Exegetical Perspective

The narrative frame of this story is the only miracle found in Mark's passion week.[2] Also striking is that it is, in a sense, a negative miracle. We are left not with a healed person but a withered tree. Moreover, Jesus' frustration that the tree cannot sate his appetite stands in tension with the miraculous sustenance he provides in 6:30–44 and 8:1–10. Finally, Mark specifically notes that the season is not right for the tree to produce figs (v. 13); only leaves and mere buds of fruit are growing at this time. Why curse the tree then?

By splitting the story of the fig tree, Mark makes it clear that the fig tree points to the next scene, when Jesus arrives in the temple. There he finds merchants providing important services to worshipers at the temple. The money changers were necessary as they exchanged coins with graven images, which could not be used in the temple. The merchants made animals available for sacrifice for the temple's many pilgrims. So, in many ways these merchants were providing necessary services for the worshipers who streamed into the temple grounds.

Mark's Jesus is troubled not by the temple itself, but by what has gone amiss on the temple grounds. This is evident in verse 17, where Mark joins citations from Isaiah 56:7 and Jeremiah 7:11. The surrounding passage in the original context of Isaiah 56 details how God has promised to make a place of worship open and inviting to all the peoples of the earth. Thus Isaiah imagines a place of worship that opens its doors to all who would worship the God of Israel. The Jeremiah citation then specifies the problem: "But you have made it a den of robbers."

What has gone wrong, then? What is the object of Jesus' condemnation? It may be that these merchants and money changers have gone beyond providing vital services to exploiting their position as gatekeepers in the temple. Anyone who wished to worship God had to deal with them and become their customer. One can imagine how they quickly could become enamored of the profitability of their profession. Instead of enabling pilgrims to worship, these merchants may have become corrupt guardians of a truly holy place, a place meant to be open to all the peoples of the world. Therefore, Jesus' radical actions were meant to criticize a temple closed off to those who sought to draw near to God, a temple open only to those able to pay their way in.

Verse 18 sounds an ominous tone, but this is a sense of foreboding that begins as early as 3:6, when

---

2. Pheme Perkins, "The Gospel of Mark," in *The New Interpreter's Bible*, ed. Leander E. Keck (Nashville: Abingdon Press, 1995), 8:660.

Homiletical Perspective

Something has gone terribly wrong and is out of joint inside this sacred space where trusted leaders have degenerated into the nonreforming protectors of business as usual. The business of the temple is no longer the business of pouring oneself out and into an intense service of God, world, and neighbor. As the sacred is desacralized and as servant ministry is deemphasized, an opposite tack appears to rule the day—puffing up oneself and one's interest groups. Established to serve as "a house of prayer for all nations" (v. 17), the temple now operates as a closed house of exclusivism. The focus of its leadership is inward and self-serving, rather than outward, inclusive, and self-giving. Jesus' daring act of judgment seems appropriate and necessary when leveled against the fruitless religious and national life of those whose given mission and calling now founder in the grips of neglect and prideful misdirection.

Do we fit into this scary biblical picture? A sermon on this passage should struggle with this eerie question. Although G. K. Chesterton, a distinguished British visitor, once referred to America as "a nation with the soul of a church,"[2] surely our ongoing and somewhat insatiable cultural quests for self-fulfillment and personal freedom could lead to our own loss of soul, by enticing us to believe that self-realization is the chief end of human life. Working, playing, and worshiping in self-promotional environments, we are deeply tempted to cherish individualism more than community, to play down the substantive and reflective, and to prefer the trivial over the transcendent.

Therefore, let us be grateful for the pushback we sometimes receive from the Protestant principle, that is, from Protestantism's historic commitment to the ongoing nature of reformation itself. Ironically, perhaps among the more important contributions of the "withering" ecumenical Protestant churches are their institutionalization of self-criticism and their passion for present and future reform. The Protestant principle appreciates reformation as a process, a continual action. It is not an accomplished goal; it is an active and dynamic prophetic encounter and movement, whereby our interest groups, our institutions, and we are "reformed and always being reformed." It provides a persistent prophetic judgment of our religious and secular arrogance.

Verse 25 offers a gateway for our hopeful movement toward personal and communal reformation. The text calls us to subject ourselves to God as the

---

2. This memorable phrase appears in the first chapter of Chesterton's *What I Saw in America*, 1922. See *The Collected Works of G. K. Chesterton* (San Francisco: Ignatius Press, 1990), v. 21, 45.

Mark 11:11–26

Theological Perspective

or liberal. God favors the disfranchised—the widow and the orphan, the stranger and the poor, people who are homeless and languishing in prison. Caring, kindness, and mercy that prove the power of faith and justice are the true measure and the worth of the authority.

The government leaders and temple priests are accountable for how the disadvantaged fare under their watch. Jesus is the one who lives among the disinherited. Mark's story of Jesus challenges the complacency of the civic, political, and religious leaders. Jesus does so because "my house shall be called a house of prayer for all the nations" (v. 17). He teaches that the caring for our less fortunate neighbors is the very source of the power of faith and justice.

We are confronted with an awful truth in this passage: "Whenever you stand praying, forgive, if you have anything against anyone; so that your Father in heaven may also forgive you your trespasses" (v. 25). This comment of Jesus is somewhat puzzling, given what transpired immediately before; his outrage expressed in this day regarding poverty, religious leaders' hypocrisy, and the trustworthiness of those who are in power all pointed to the profaning of the Sacred. Translated into our situation, Jesus' outrage points to income inequality between the well-to-do and the poor, government collusion with corporate interest, overcrowded prisons, and the neglect of the vulnerable. We steal the future of our children and grandchildren in our self-preoccupation. Where is our capacity for outrage? Where is our ability to sustain indignation at injustice that comes from our own complacency? Have we forgotten that the real antidote to despair is indeed the will to face up to injustice and fight it?

FUMITAKA MATSUOKA

Pastoral Perspective

With mere words, Jesus withers the tree to its roots. Just as the disciples have seen Jesus' power to heal, they—and we—now witness his power to destroy. That witness is crucial. In the passion story that follows, Jesus destroys neither the religious leaders nor the Roman authorities. Without the fig tree's proof that he has such power, his choice not to annihilate his adversaries can be interpreted as his lacking the power to do so.

At any point along the torturous path to Golgotha, Jesus could do to his tormentors what he does to the fig tree. The money changers, the religious leaders, the armed crowd who arrest him, Pilate who condemns him, the Roman soldiers who beat him and crucify him: all of them could suffer that same fate. They do not, not because Jesus lacks the power to destroy them, but because he chooses not to use it. The fig tree's demise offers undeniable proof of Jesus' decision not to match violence with violence, death with death.

Finally, Jesus uses his encounter with the fig tree to underscore the disciples' power. Just as he has empowered them earlier in the Gospel to heal the sick and cast out demons, he now affirms that through faith in God they have the ability to destroy even the temple. With prayer, they could command the very mountain on which it stands to be thrown into the sea.

Then Jesus takes the discussion in a surprising direction. He ends not with a call to arms, but with the commandment to forgive. A passage that starts with the destruction of a fig tree concludes with a treatise on prayer and forgiveness. Jesus affirms that, like him, the disciples have the power to destroy and seek vengeance. He also affirms that, like him, they have the power to make a different choice. So do we.

Given the power unleashed on the fig tree, the passion story that followed could have led to the carnage of battle. Instead it led to the cross. That was the choice he made. What is ours?

TALITHA ARNOLD

Exegetical Perspective

the Pharisees and Herodians start to conspire against Jesus. In our passage, this conspiracy is stoked once again as "the chief priests and the scribes" hear of Jesus' actions in the temple, and their ire is raised anew. People of power and privilege sense the threat of radical openness. For the moment, Jesus is protected from a murderous conspiracy by the adoring crowds, crowds that have just welcomed him into the city but that will soon call for his death (15:13).

The next day, Jesus and his disciples pass the fig tree once again and find it withered. The Markan interpolation demands we read the fig tree in light of Jesus' actions in the temple. Written shortly after the destruction of the temple, the Gospel of Mark must grapple with this catastrophic moment. How does Mark understand the fall of God's abode on earth? According to Mark, the destruction of the temple is the result not just of the military might of Rome, but also of God's condemnation of the temple's corrupt leadership and workings. Jesus' condemnation is not of the temple itself or of a whole people, but of the walls of obstruction some have built around its perimeter. This was a true temple, ordained by God, but it had also become a holy place for a few who were privileged and powerful, while it morphed into a site of oppression for everyone else.

Our passage ends with some bold assertions. Such is the power of prayer that the faithful can call a mountain to be cast into the sea. In the wake of the disaster of the temple's destruction, faith would be fleeting for many. Mark's Jesus calls for a bold faith, a faith that gazes into the rubble of a once glorious city and still believes. Even as we grieve, we trust. Even as we mourn, we look for God's new day.

ERIC D. BARRETO

Homiletical Perspective

vital center of our gratitude, instead of anxiously pretending that we are the center of life, that we are the heart of life's picture, instead of a part of life's picture. The text also beckons us to a renewed commitment to Christ's amazing miracle of grace, which, according to ethicist Donald Shriver, is to live and love as "a company of forgiven forgivers."[3] Shriver stresses the interdependent nature of repentance and forgiveness. He affirms that forgiveness loses its moral integrity apart from repentance; and repentance, apart from forgiveness, will remain fruitless in our human relations. Throughout life we discover that we need forgiveness and we need to forgive. We also find that the practice of prayer opens and prepares us for these experiences of grace. We are also prepared to clothe our visions and leadership in a cloak of humility. We who live by forgiving also live by being forgiven. These two Spirit-filled streams, which deeply relate the mystery of our human selfhood with the mystery of God, are meant to flow generatively into and out of one another.

The miracle of grace and the possibility of reformation just could lead us to a parable quite different from the story of the fruitless fig tree, which sandwiches Christ's severe judgment issued in a worship center whose practices had become self-centered. Thus we continue to be inspired by the picture of a woman who enters a Quaker meeting. She is puzzled because the people are sitting in prayerful silence. She waits and waits, but nothing happens. "When does the service begin?" she asks the person next to her. "When does the service begin?" "When we leave," the person answers. "When we leave." As Professor George Dewey Carter once preached powerfully and prophetically in a sermon now memorialized on a plaque on a great wall outside Caldwell Chapel at Louisville Presbyterian Theological Seminary,

> It is not enough to profess.
> We have to practice.
> It is not enough to talk.
> We have to do.
> It is not enough to promise.
> We have to embody the promise.
> It is not enough to say, "Ain't it awful."
> We have got to get close enough to get hurt.

DEAN K. THOMPSON

---

3. Donald W. Shriver Jr., "Politics: The Mismaligned Calling," *The Living Pulpit* 5 (April-June 1996): 10; see also Shriver, *An Ethic for Enemies: Forgiveness in Politics* (New York: Oxford University Press, 1995).

Mark 11:27–33

²⁷Again they came to Jerusalem. As he was walking in the temple, the chief priests, the scribes, and the elders came to him ²⁸and said, "By what authority are you doing these things? Who gave you this authority to do them?" ²⁹Jesus said to them, "I will ask you one question; answer me, and I will tell you by what authority I do these things. ³⁰Did the baptism of John come from heaven, or was it of human origin? Answer me." ³¹They argued with one another, "If we say, 'From heaven,' he will say, 'Why then did you not believe him?' ³²But shall we say, 'Of human origin'?"—they were afraid of the crowd, for all regarded John as truly a prophet. ³³So they answered Jesus, "We do not know." And Jesus said to them, "Neither will I tell you by what authority I am doing these things."

Theological Perspective

The subject of this passage is the question of authority, which is treated in compelling and yet somewhat subtle ways. The questions that the chief priests, scribes, and elders ask Jesus, "By what authority are you doing these things? Who gave you this authority to do them?" (v. 28) expose the implicit assumptions that these religious and societal leaders of Jesus' time bring to their understanding of authority. These leaders crave an authority that protects their own power; this fact is instructive for us today.

One of the pervasive assumptions behind the notion of authority that exists in America today is the myth of meritocracy coupled with plutocracy. Merito-plutocrats, people who have achieved both great success and great wealth, are convinced that their intelligence, skills, and wealth are equal to any task or challenge; they are likely to embark on prideful projects. They become infatuated with measurable strategic models that appeal to a modern world. "We know better." When this assumption is coupled with accumulated wealth, elitist merito-plutocrats become the ruling authority. They proclaim: "We are rich because we are smart."

For some decades, the United States has accorded privilege to its brightest, wealthiest, and most socially popular people by placing them in positions of power. In 1890, in the wake of the revolt that swept across

Pastoral Perspective

"By what authority are you doing these things?" More than two thousand years separate us from the Sanhedrin's question to Jesus. Nevertheless their challenge to his authority, along with his response to that challenge, is as relevant today as it was that day in the Jerusalem temple.

Recent surveys document that most church conflicts have less to do with doctrine and belief than with leadership and decision making. In a word, with authority. The phenomenon is not limited to clergy or churches. "Who gave you the right?" is a question members of our congregations also face in their work settings, regardless of the profession or the content of the dispute.

Jesus heard that same question throughout his ministry. From the beginning of Mark's Gospel, the people are amazed by Jesus' authority, and the religious leaders terrified by it. Throughout the Gospel, they focus less on the content of his teaching or the miracle of his healings than on his right to teach and heal. Jesus tells a paralyzed man his sins are forgiven, and the leaders call it blasphemy, because only God has the authority to forgive (2:7). He heals a man on the Sabbath, and the Pharisees watch him "so that they might accuse him" (3:2). He casts out demons, and the scribes proclaim he is possessed by Beelzebul, the ruler of the demons (3:22).

Exegetical Perspective

Mark once again brings us into Jerusalem, a city that has both received Jesus with accolades and been the recipient of his judgment. This is yet another step in an inexorable path leading straight to the cross. Jesus' actions in Mark are consistently audacious. He stills roiling waters. He heals. He teaches with authority. Just verses earlier, he has entered the temple courts and disrupted the commerce and worship occurring there. All along, local leaders have grown increasingly alarmed by Jesus' audacity and been troubled by his bold claims.

A cabal of conspirators confronts Jesus with a loaded question: "By what authority are you doing these things?" (v. 28). Remember that the conspiracy against Jesus was first hatched in Mark 3:6. Now, in these closing chapters, this conspiracy is reaching full flower as more and more individuals of power pit themselves against Jesus. The question they pose therefore is not innocuous. In the first-century world, authority rests in Rome and its representatives in Judea. To these powerful individuals, Jesus has no legitimate authority. Their inquiries are fundamentally dishonest and intended only to put Jesus to the test.

However, as Jesus is wont to do, he answers a question with yet another question. Mark's Jesus recalls the ministry of John the Baptist with which

Homiletical Perspective

Where does Jesus get the authority to act as a cleansing royal judge? Who does he think he is, as he steps forward with this startling prophetic move in the temple? As the religious authorities confront Jesus about the problem of his own authority, both they and we are aware that these concerns have smoldered since the beginning of his ministry. In 2:1–12, when Jesus healed and forgave a bedridden paralytic, angry leaders called him a blasphemer, while an enthusiastic crowd praised God. Across the centuries of human history, true prophets have both inspired their observers and also made them angry.

To the demanding question rendered by the religious authorities, "Who gave you this authority?" Jesus responds with a rabbinic counterquestion. According to historian Jaroslav Pelikan, Jesus answers "by standing the question on its head." Pelikan recalls a humorous "old story about a rabbi who was asked by one of his pupils: 'Why is it that you rabbis so often put your teaching in the form of a question?' To which the rabbi answered: 'So what's wrong with a question?'"[1]

Is John's authority undergirded by divine power or by human power? Jesus asks his would-be interrogators. Rabbi Jesus' questioners are temporarily

---

1. Jaroslav Pelikan, *Jesus through the Centuries* (New Haven and London: Yale University Press, 1985), 13.

Mark 11:27–33

Theological Perspective

the Great Plains, populist orator Mary Elizabeth Lease said, "Wall Street owns the country. Money rules. . . . Our laws are the output of a system which clothes rascals in robes and honesty in rags. The [political] parties lie to us and the political speakers mislead us."[1] Her words still speak to us today. Political leaders and powerful bankers provide favors for one another, while few helpful laws that support the poor get enacted in the Congress. Merito-plutocracy leads to hypocrisy for the gradual deterioration of democracy. Many authority figures launder money in their attempt to acquire power and position.

The Industrial Revolution of the last few centuries greatly expanded the gulf between extraordinary wealth at the top and horrible misery at the bottom. In the United States, wise and perceptive citizens analyzed what was really going on in the society and organized people to educate them about this disturbing trend. The movers of democracy are these wise and observant citizens. They together helped to enact minimum wage and child labor laws in the Congress, sought to guarantee workers' safety and adequate compensation, and ensured nontoxic foods and safe drugs. Ordinary citizens succeeded in establishing Social Security and Medicare programs. Today ordinary citizens are doing the same. What this long road of struggle of Americans says is that democracy begins among ordinary citizens when they struggle to realize their dreams. Democracy does not begin at the top.

The message learned here is clear: selfishness, arrogance, and pride do not result in success. The "whiz kids" who led this nation during the Vietnam era made war according to a mathematical formula. The economic prodigies of recent years thought that they understood the complexity of global economics. The political and military geniuses of the Iraq war thought that they would be able to create a lasting peace in the Middle East. Over and over again, the geniuses are proven wrong. Ordinary people who are really outsiders with wisdom, compassion, and good instincts are the ones who see through the follies of merito-plutocrats and revolt against them. What is needed is not to replace the arrogant with the ignorant, the genius with the incompetent. In place of the reckless self-love of meritocrats and plutocrats, we need wise and intelligent leaders in positions of authority who have a sense of humility and awareness of their own limits, mature people whose lives have taught them

---

1. Mary Elizabeth Lease, "Wall Street Owns the Country," circa 1890, Kansas Historical Society, www.kshs.org/kansapedia/mary-elizabeth-lease/12128; accessed April 2, 2013.

Pastoral Perspective

The pattern of direct confrontation by the Pharisees, scribes, and elders continues the day after Jesus has driven the money changers out of the temple. They seek him out and demand to know, "By what authority are you doing these things?" (v. 28). Jesus demonstrates his skill as a leader by the way he answers their question—namely, with a question of his own: "Did the baptism of John come from heaven, or was it of human origin?" (v. 30). By answering a question with a question, Jesus is not simply paying homage to his rabbinic tradition. Instead, he is refusing to be hooked into his interrogators' agenda. He puts the focus back on the religious leaders and makes them responsible for the answer.

Jesus' response to the Pharisees and scribes offers a good model for leadership, including pastoral leadership. Clergy are often questioned about their right to speak or lead, be it in the church or the wider culture. Faced with such questions, it can be tempting to think our job is to provide answers and prove our legitimacy as spiritual leaders. Jesus offers a different approach, one that gives the responsibility for the answer back to the inquisitors. In so doing, he demonstrates the self-differentiation necessary for good leadership.

As family therapist and rabbi Edwin Friedman affirms, such self-differentiation includes "the capacity to maintain a (relatively) non-anxious presence in the midst of anxious systems."[1] Jesus definitely has a lot to be anxious about in his confrontation with the chief priests, scribes, and elders: they are the very leaders who he predicted, three chapters earlier, would reject him and instigate his execution. They are the same leaders who, three chapters later, will come with clubs and swords to arrest him. Because he does not take their bait and instead turns the question of authority back to them, though, Jesus does not let their fear and anxiety become his. That is a good leadership practice, whatever the situation or century.

Jesus' spotlight on John the Baptist also offers a plumb line for authentic spiritual leadership. Like Jesus, John was a powerful and charismatic leader. "People from the whole Judean countryside and all the people of Jerusalem were going out to him" (1:5). John did not let such adulation go to his head. Instead, he pointed to an authority beyond himself: "The one who is more powerful than I is coming after me" (1:7). By directing the attention away from his own leadership to the one who would follow

---

1. Edwin Friedman, *Generation to Generation: Family Process in Church and Synagogue* (New York: Guilford, 1985), 27.

Exegetical Perspective

the narrative begins. In Mark, John's active ministry takes up all of eleven verses (1:2–11, 14). We learn only later, in 6:14–29, of John's tragic demise at the hand of Herod and his dysfunctional and power-hungry family. In Mark, John becomes a victim not just of Herod but of a profoundly corrupt sense of authority. After all, Herod is the active hand of Rome in these conquered lands. What authority could possibly execute a prophet like John? The real questions that Jesus asks might be, "With what authority does Herod do these things? With what authority did he imprison and execute a prophet of God?" The subtext of these questions is, "With what authority will these conspirators soon deem Jesus worthy of death?"

Thus, Jesus' query is politically loaded. Was the source of John's ministry divine or human? Was it a work inspired by God, or merely the laughable delusion of a wild-eyed man? Was his execution a justified act, or a vivid symbol of Rome's broken reign? Of course, Mark's readers know exactly how to answer the question.

In contrast, Jesus' interrogators quickly realize that their attempts to trap him have backfired. Neither response is politically palatable. If they point to the divine origin of John's work, then their faithlessness, their inability to hear God's call, becomes evident. Moreover, the raw and cruel exercise of Roman power is once again made evident in a restive land. If they point to a human origin, the crowds will react with hostility, as they correctly perceive John's important status in the work of God in the world. After all, John was a true prophet.

They eventually find themselves unable to negotiate two untenable responses and merely claim ignorance. "We do not know," they respond in verse 33. They claim not to know how to answer this politically problematic but rather simple question. As they struggle to find the right political spin, Mark's audience can easily answer the question. John's mission was God-ordained. The crowd is right to call him a prophet. In contrast, Jesus' politically powerful opponents know the answer to Jesus' question, but they do not know how to answer the question without implicating themselves in John's cruel and unjustified execution.

Thus Jesus can escape the trap they seek to set. He challenges the very premise of the question posed by pointing to the unjust ways that authority was and will be exercised. He refuses to identify the source of his authority. However, as informed readers, we are not left in the dark. We know who Jesus is; Mark

Homiletical Perspective

silenced by his difficult riddle, which appears to throw them off balance. "Answer me," he demands. By not answering Jesus' counterquestion, the religious leaders seem unwilling to open themselves to the possibility of his true authority. It is not that Jesus does not know and even embody the answer to their demand and to his counterdemand; but it will be necessary for them and for us to wait for fullness in time. Ultimately, the resurrection will provide the answer.

Had Jesus been anointed at his baptism by John, and through the ministry of the Holy Spirit, to behave in such a kinglike way as the one who cleanses and saves with the power and authority of God's own Son? With Jesus' reverberating command, "Answer me," this dramatic encounter with Jerusalem's religious leaders is thrust beyond its original setting and into ours as well. It is both old and new. This encounter about the authority of Jesus belongs to the dynamic historical context in which it first happened; it also belongs to the ages. This story is not over, and we are part of it. This story is ours. We too must decide. We too must answer. Is Jesus a crafty teacher and would-be authority, or is Jesus the God-life on earth?

Once, on a mystical mountaintop, the disciples who made the climb with Jesus suddenly heard a voice, which said, "This is my Son, the Beloved; listen to him" (9:7). As we listen to Jesus, giving our undivided attention, as we search the heart of our own experiences of his authority in the days and years of our lives, and as we drink from a cup of noteworthy testimonies offered by other pilgrims who have deeply felt and believed in his powerful and life-saving presence, we are moved by a spiritual conviction that the authority of Christ comes to us not so much as argument or debate, but rather as self-authenticating mystery. As we wrestle with a sermon on this demanding text about authentic authority, hymn writer Huub Oosterhuis moves us to the core of belief with his captivating and prayerlike confession of faith:

> He did not want to be far,
> Nearness he intended,
> Therefore into what we are
> Christ the Lord descended.
> Among you is standing
> He whom you don't know.
> God of God and Light of Light,
> Keeper of creation,
> He assumed the human plight,
> Joined our generation.

Mark 11:27–33

Theological Perspective

caution. We need leaders who are to be "wise as serpents and innocent as doves" (Matt. 10:16).

The challenge facing us today is humbly to realize that the human drama of history is played out in a larger frame of significance that is beyond our self-serving comprehension or imagination. Jesus' response to the chief priests, the scribes, and the elders, "Neither will I tell you by what authority I am doing these things" (v. 33), points to the challenge of acquiring awareness of one's own limits and a sense of humility. It begs for the honest confession that we are not that honest after all. Jesus' refusal to give an easy answer to the merito-plutocratic leaders of his day points to the lack of openness on their part even to consider the different realm whence comes the sense of wisdom and humility that overcome the belief in human mastery.[2]

By self-preoccupation we become focused on our own goodness and power that often results in the false sense of human mastery that we can achieve goodness on our own. We come to the dangerous and destructive notion that we can indeed prove our absolute authority over our own life and world. Along with our frustration about our limitations, we lust for destructive power. In our world history we have witnessed repeatedly these crises and judgments which we bring on ourselves. The gospel message, in contrast to this human arrogance and pride, insists that God reveals Godself in history, personified in Jesus Christ, as self-giving love that overcomes the human temptation to self-deification and makes possible constructive human history.

In this story of Mark, the authorities answer in the only way left open: pleading ignorance. This leads to Jesus' not giving any direct answer to them as well. Those with faith in Jesus will recognize him for who he is. On the other hand, those without faith will not be able to do so, no matter what they are told. A person blinded by arrogance, pride, and self-love cannot hear the message. Mark has thus identified an inconsistency between their portrayal of their purpose and their actual methods. The argument is against them. He still has not answered their question, but he has shown that they have no right to expect an answer from him until they can perform the job required of those who can ask such questions.

FUMITAKA MATSUOKA

Pastoral Perspective

him, John underscored the most essential element of spiritual authority: God is the focus, not the leader.

When Jesus asks the temple leaders, "Did the baptism of John come from heaven, or was it of human origin?" (v. 30), he reminds them what true spiritual authority looks like, namely, that it comes from God, not human authority. He also reminds them how far they are from John's standard—that the focus is on God, not the earthly leader (1:7). Had faith in God been the source of their own spiritual authority, they might not have been so undone by Jesus' question.

In this encounter with Jesus, as in many that precede it, the religious leaders seem far more concerned with their reputation and the crowd's response than they do with anything having to do with God. Indeed, their fear of the crowds is the driving force behind their actions throughout the Gospel. As the chief priests, scribes, and elders try to answer Jesus' question, their focus is not on what they actually believe about John's baptism. Instead, they are afraid of what the crowd will think.

Jesus' reference to John further exposes their fear-driven leadership. John had shown no such fear, not even of Herod. His willingness to speak the truth to Rome's toady king—and face the consequences—stood in sharp contrast to the temple leaders' constant worry about the crowds (e.g., 11:18, 32; 12:12; 14:1–2). Both Jesus and the chief priests, scribes, and elders also know that John's commitment to the truth and to God had cost him his life. John's acceptance of that cost was yet another affirmation of the authenticity of his spiritual authority. Before and after this confrontation about Jesus' authority, the religious leaders continue to look for a way to kill Jesus. He knows that and, like John, is willing to make that sacrifice. As was true with John's leadership, Jesus' authority is rooted in his willingness to go the distance, even if it means his death.

"By what authority are you doing these things?" the religious leaders ask Jesus (v. 28). Part of the answer is that authority comes from his being willing to face what they in their fear will do to him.

One wonders if any of them saw the irony.

TALITHA ARNOLD

---

2. Bob Tostevin, *The Promethean Illusion: The Western Belief in Human Mastery of Nature* (Jefferson, NC: McFarland & Co., 2010).

Exegetical Perspective

identifies Jesus in the very first sentence he writes: "Christ, the Son of God" (1:1)!

Of course, this is not the first time in Mark's narrative that the source of Jesus' authority has come under scrutiny. Very early in the narrative, a group of faithful individuals bring their paralyzed friend to Jesus, hoping for his healing (2:1–12). Seeing the faithfulness of his friends, Jesus forgives the man's sins. This leads to the scribes questioning in their hearts from what source Jesus derives such authority. In order to demonstrate the depth of the authority granted to him by God, Jesus commands the paralyzed man to rise. Jesus has the power both to forgive and to heal.

Let us return to the question posed: By what authority does Jesus do these things? That the questioners cannot answer Jesus' question bespeaks their duplicity. At the same time, Mark expects the reader to fill in the gap, to answer the question. Jesus' response is both telling and mysterious: "Neither will I tell you by what authority I am doing these things" (v. 33). Jesus refuses to tell them because theirs is not a true question. Nothing he says can persuade them, for his actions, especially his healings and exorcisms, have been visible markers of Jesus' authority. Moreover, in 6:7, Jesus grants his followers this very same authority. What additional evidence could they possibly seek? What could persuade powerful individuals concerned less with truth than the maintenance of their authority?

By what authority? The answer lies before them, and the answer is given by Mark in his very first sentence. Jesus is God's Messiah. This evident truth is fleeting and an open secret throughout Mark. What is most obvious is apparently most difficult to grasp.

In Mark, this is true not only of Jesus' opponents but even of Jesus' closest followers. As Jesus takes these final steps on the way to the cross, this brief exchange is a poignant reminder of both Jesus' unquestionable authority and also the difficulty even the faithful face in embracing the truth that Jesus embodies and teaches.

ERIC D. BARRETO

Homiletical Perspective

Among you is standing
He whom you don't know.[2]

We are moved to the core of belief by Reinhold Niebuhr's profound confession of faith:

> For the Christian, the event of Christ—which is not only the person of Christ, not merely the teachings of Christ, but the whole drama of his life, death, and resurrection—is the luminous point at which the mystery of the Divine is revealed, and we apprehend this by faith. . . . History is brought to its final pinnacle and the Divine mystery is brought down into history.

We are moved to the core of belief by Jaroslav Pelikan's exquisite confession of faith:

> [A]s respect for the organized church has declined, reverence for Jesus has grown. For the unity and variety of the portraits of "Jesus through the centuries" has demonstrated that there is more in him than is dreamt of in the philosophy and Christology of the theologians. Within the church, but also far beyond its walls, his person and message are, in the phrase of Augustine, a "beauty ever ancient, ever new," and now he belongs to the world.

We are moved to the core of belief by an older Hindu woman who offered this incredible confession of faith to a missionary from whom she first heard the gospel of Jesus Christ: "Thank you! I have always loved him, and now you have told me his name."[3]

Yes, true authority comes to us as a self-authenticating mystery that graciously gifts us with faithful eyes to behold and opened ears to hear. In temporarily refusing to answer the authority issue raised by his challengers, perhaps Jesus' implied response is, "Wait and see; you will know my answer when the time is right." On the day of resurrection, we will confess our faith that the Spirit of Jesus Christ is alive in this world, where we are and where we are going, and in the midst of our conflicts, joys, hopes, and fears. We will bear grateful witness to the One whose living authority bonds us to the very heart of God.

DEAN K. THOMPSON

---

2. Huub Oosterhuis, "He Did Not Want to Be Far," *The Worshipbook* (Philadelphia: Westminster Press, 1975), #412, stanzas 1, 3.
3. Reinhold Niebuhr, in *Justice and Mercy*, ed. Ursula Niebuhr (New York: HarperCollins, 1974), 8; Jaroslav Pelikan, *Jesus through the Centuries*, 232–33; R. Maurice Boyd, *A Lover's Quarrel with the World* (Philadelphia: Westminster Press, 1985), 48.

Mark 12:1–12

¹Then he began to speak to them in parables. "A man planted a vineyard, put a fence around it, dug a pit for the wine press, and built a watchtower; then he leased it to tenants and went to another country. ²When the season came, he sent a slave to the tenants to collect from them his share of the produce of the vineyard. ³But they seized him, and beat him, and sent him away empty-handed. ⁴And again he sent another slave to them; this one they beat over the head and insulted. ⁵Then he sent another, and that one they killed. And so it was with many others; some they beat, and others they killed. ⁶He had still one other, a beloved son. Finally he sent him to them, saying, 'They will respect my son.' ⁷But those tenants said to one another, 'This is the heir; come, let us kill

Theological Perspective

"True peace is not merely the absence of tension: it is the presence of justice."[1] These words of Martin Luther King Jr. capture the spirit of the words of Jesus in this passage of Mark. Jesus told this familiar parable with additional meaning: the use of status to protect honor does not accomplish its intended purpose; on the other hand, refraining from the use of violence leads to honor in the sight of God. In this passage Jesus thus challenges status as the protection of honor and also violence as a means to peace. Jesus' life and impending death on the cross are foretold in this passage of Mark.

The Gospel of Mark was probably written in Rome for Christians and those who contemplated becoming Christian. For this purpose, the Gospel of Mark conveys messianic claims regarding the authority of Jesus as the Son of God. This particular passage places the central position of Jesus' ministry in Jerusalem. Mark alludes to a large number of Old Testament passages that must have been familiar to his audience, early Christian Jews. At the end of chapter 11, Jesus challenges the highest authorities of the temple: the chief priests, the scribes, and the elders. Jesus' audience probably was made up of

---

1. Martin Luther King Jr., during the Montgomery bus boycott in 1955, as quoted by Stephen B. Oates, *Let the Trumpet Sound: A Life of Martin Luther King, Jr.* (New York: Harper & Row, 1982), 82.

Pastoral Perspective

This is a dangerous story. For centuries, Jesus' last parable in Mark's Gospel has been one of the Christian texts used to justify all manner of prejudice and violence, particularly against Jews, but also against persons of other faiths, and even other Christians labeled as heretics. Commonly titled the "Parable of the Wicked Tenants," the story could as easily be named for "The Vengeful Landowner" who retaliates for his son's death by annihilating the tenants. Given that the landowner is a stand-in for God, another title could be "The Least Pastoral Parable in the Bible."

This parable of retribution is also problematic because it contradicts other teachings of Jesus. Its message of "a life for a life" is a far cry from Jesus' injunction in Matthew to turn the other cheek. Just a few paragraphs earlier in Mark's Gospel, Jesus tells his disciples: "Whenever you stand praying, forgive, if you have anything against anyone" (11:25). That is not the theme of this parable.

With its violence and vengeful portrayal of God, some have argued that the parable should be disregarded. Both Thomas Jefferson and Leo Tolstoy left it out of their "Bibles." Yet the parable cannot be ignored. Versions of it are found in all three Synoptic Gospels, which means it was important to the self-understanding of the earliest Christians. Ignoring the

him, and the inheritance will be ours.' ⁸So they seized him, killed him, and threw him out of the vineyard. ⁹What then will the owner of the vineyard do? He will come and destroy the tenants and give the vineyard to others. ¹⁰Have you not read this scripture:

'The stone that the builders rejected
  has become the cornerstone;
¹¹ this was the Lord's doing,
  and it is amazing in our eyes'?"

¹²When they realized that he had told this parable against them, they wanted to arrest him, but they feared the crowd. So they left him and went away.

Exegetical Perspective

This story about a wealthy landowner and his tenants will surely strike many of today's readers as strange, for it evokes an economic system foreign to many Westerners. To Mark's audience, however, this parable would have been familiar. Though foreign to us, the economic assumptions of the parable point to a world in which such cruelty was alarmingly common.

This parable follows several critical moments on the road to the cross. After Jesus' triumphal entry, his cleansing of the temple, and finally the first of a number of confrontations with the local leadership, he turns to speaking in parables. The parable is the third word of judgment to follow in the wake of the acclamation found at the beginning of chapter 11. Here, once again, it is a word of judgment that Jesus speaks: something is fundamentally amiss in the ways religious and political power is being exerted.

Initially, it may be helpful to reflect a bit on how we read parables. At first glance, parables often seem to be straightforward, simple stories. However, their simplicity belies the complexity of their teaching. I often tell my students that if they think the meaning of a parable is evident, then they have probably already missed its point. In one sense, parables are simple, for they typically refer to the quotidian experiences of the audience. Shepherds, unjust judges, the dangers of travel on deserted roads: most if not

Homiletical Perspective

To make a very strong point: that is the initial intention of Jesus' parable about our persistent corruption as human beings and about God's amazing patience, serious judgment, and promise of restoration. To the religious authorities Jesus is saying: "Just in case you are personally blind to the ongoing, arrogant, and even violent nature of your own institutional life and leadership, let me put things in the starkest of contexts. Here is my take regarding the depths of your personal and systemic pride and sinfulness."

Surely this stark parabolic picture, painted by Jesus in light of his own journey of sacrificial leadership, can be applied to countless religious, political, and cultural situations across the ages of our human history of immoral defiance and disobedience. For centuries, God's called and commissioned prophets of judgment, justice, and hope have been rejected, abused, and even destroyed by those to whom their prophetic messages have been directed. Indeed, is there any era that has not been seeded with the sacrificial bravery and blood of God's prophetic visionaries and bold voices? We remember them and the pain they have sacrificed; we lift up their names in gratitude; and we weep. In the book of Esther, brave Queen Vashti speaks out against dehumanizing power and loses everything but her integrity. Centuries later, in El Salvador, brave Archbishop Oscar

Mark 12:1–12

Theological Perspective

these folks, some gathering of people in the temple, and his disciples. This is important to remember as we see what Jesus has to say to them.

Mark's message to his audience was that the abuse of power embedded within the old order needed to be critiqued—and that this was a necessary step in God's plan for the establishment of God's own reign. The authorities must have recognized that Jesus was challenging them in his allegorical statements. They could not counter Jesus, however, because of his popularity and also his genuine authority.

What is the vineyard? Isaiah uses this image to describe the house of Israel in Isaiah 5:1–2. Who are the tenants in Mark's parable? They likely refer to the Jewish leaders of Israel. However, if the "house of Israel" points to God's promised relationship with humanity, then the tenants could refer also to those who mismanaged their status as the chosen people of God. Who are the servants sent one after another by the owner, even though they were repeatedly killed? They represent the prophets whom God continually sent to Israel who, like the servants in this passage, consistently dismissed and persecuted them. Finally, the owner sent his son, whom the tenants killed because they were jealous of his authentic power and real authority. This anticipates Jesus' death on the cross; that would have been obvious to Mark's audience. The son here represents Jesus, since the words "beloved son" are the same words used in the first chapter of the Gospel when a voice from heaven announces at Jesus' baptism, "You are my Son, the Beloved; with you I am well pleased" (1:11). This also points to the source of Jesus' authority that is given by God in his visit to the vineyard. To Mark's audience, this parable equally points to a sign that they are meant by God to take control of the vineyard, that is, the inheritance of Jesus as being the chosen one of God.

The use of violence does not lead to its intended purpose, as Mark points out. In the story the tenants beat two slaves and kill the owner's son. The result of these violent acts, however, is neither the legal obtaining of the vineyard nor the protection of their honor. They probably lost the very honor they wanted to protect for themselves. Jesus here challenges both status as the protection of honor as well as the use of violence. Resorting to violence does not necessarily lead to honor; similarly, the use of violence does not achieve honor for the perpetrator.

This passage illustrates the significance of the way that we treat people. It matters to our humanity that we treat offenders according to standards that we

Pastoral Perspective

parable does not make the parable or its historical impact go away. If we want to counter the religious violence the parable has been used to justify, we need to deal with it, not dismiss it.

Acknowledging the parable's role in sanctifying Christian anti-Semitism and other prejudice is the first step. Setting the parable in its original context is the next. Despite its common Christian interpretation as a story about Christianity replacing Judaism, the parable's actual setting—and the conflict it addressed—was thoroughly Jewish. A rabbi (Jesus) tells the parable to the Jewish rulers (priests, elders, and scribes) of the Jerusalem temple. Moreover, its central image of the vineyard in Judaism is a common metaphor for Israel. Jesus' description of the landowner's care for the vineyard—he sets a hedge, digs a pit for the wine press, and builds a watchtower—echoes Isaiah's song of the vineyard (Isa. 5:1–7) and how God has cared for Israel. This is a Jewish story to its core.

The parable's denunciation of the unfaithful and unjust tenants also illustrates its Jewish roots. The prophets often used the health of the vineyard as a mark of Israel's faithfulness. Hosea proclaimed to the people: "you have plowed wickedness, you have reaped injustice, you have eaten the fruit of lies" (Hos. 10:13). In Isaiah, God "expected justice, but saw bloodshed; righteousness, but heard a cry!" (Isa. 5:7). Isaiah was particularly concerned about the unjust practice of land consolidation whereby the wealthy elite bought up the small farms of the peasants to create great estates. When they joined "house to house" and added "field to field" (Isa. 5:8), self-sufficient farmers became sharecroppers on their own land. Such practices violated God's covenant with its commandment to care for the poor and ensure a just distribution of land and resources. Therefore Isaiah predicted the hedges around the vineyard (Israel) would be taken down and the vineyard overrun.

As dire as their warnings were about the vineyard's (aka Israel's) fate, the prophets' goal was not to replace Judaism, but to reform it. "Sow for yourselves righteousness," Hosea proclaims, "reap steadfast love; break up your fallow ground; for it is time to seek the LORD, that he may come and rain righteousness upon you" (Hos. 10:12). Jesus' parable of the vineyard is in that same tradition. It needs to be read not as a mandate to displace Judaism, but as a call for the religious rulers to repent and return to a just and right relationship with God and the people. Such a reading of the parable is supported later in the same

Exegetical Perspective

all the parables speak about the stuff of everyday life. This simplicity, however, masks the radical and subversive theological insights contained within these brief but powerful stories. The proper response to one of Jesus' parable should not be a simple nod of approval but a shocked conscience. One temptation to avoid in interpreting most parables is facile allegorization, in which every character and scenario points to a specific individual or community in the world. Allegorization is not always the best option for interpretation, although it seems to work for this parable for a number of reasons.

The image of the vineyard in verse 1 would likely have drawn Mark's audience to the poetic comparison that Isaiah 5:1–7 draws between Israel and a vineyard planted by God. Isaiah narrates the care with which God prepares and preserves the vineyard, but then the image turns to a moment of judgment. God interrogates Israel, asking why God's people have not produced the fruits of a well-tended land. In the end, God "expected justice, but saw bloodshed; righteousness, but heard a cry!" (Isa. 5:7b). In the wake of Jesus' previous critiques, this condemnation rings true when applied to the political and religious leaders of his own day.

As in Isaiah, the landowner in Jesus' parable carefully prepares a vineyard. In Mark, however, he turns it over to tenants who are to care for it and pay the owner a set amount of the produce of the land. When the time comes for the season's harvest and the owner's due payment, however, the tenants respond with violence, beating and even killing a number of the owner's servants. Finally, the owner reckons that these tenants will not treat his own "beloved son" (v. 6) with such disdain. The landowner, however, miscalculates the reasoning of his tenants. In the arrival of this son, they do not see a reflection of their guilt but an opportunity to enrich themselves: "This is the heir; come, let us kill him, and the inheritance will be ours" (12:7b).

If we are listening carefully, we might wonder about the credulity and naiveté of this landowner. We might wonder what drove the tenants toward such violence. This story is often called the parable of the Wicked Tenants, but Mark never directly calls them "wicked." Certainly their actions are ruthless, but are they merely wicked, or are their motives more complex? Might their resistance to a distant and powerful landowner who demands a share of the produce he did not help harvest reflect the imperial realities of Mark's days? How exactly are we to understand these tenants?

Homiletical Perspective

Romero speaks out against dehumanizing power and loses his life. The stories are legion.

We also do more than weep, as we digest this difficult teaching from Mark's Gospel, for the strange movements of God's prophetic Spirit are tinged with irony and hope. The God of this parable is extraordinarily patient, long-suffering, and filled with pathos in reaching out to the unfaithful vineyard stewards. The tension in this story builds and builds in an almost unbelievably dramatic manner. As our violent disobedience, deceit, fickleness, and betrayal extend and extend, God patiently sends us caring prophets, again and again, who challenge us and charge us to change our ways and to claim our better angels.

As the tenant trustees murder the "beloved son," this parable points to an apparent victory of violent humanity over the Creator of life. It is a terrible mirror of our human history of violence and disobedience, our history of perverting our intended life situation through our failure to remember that God is God. We have not been given our privileges, principles, and stewardship responsibilities in order to replace God as the center of our existence. In this sober teaching, God chooses to confront us as we boast of our own ultimate power and self-sufficiency. Life's vineyard is not ours; it is ours to care for. Their Creator has richly blessed the vinedressers/tenants with freedom and responsibility, with privileges and principles.

However, they vaingloriously abuse their freedom and defy the essential meaning of responsible selfhood, the integrity of nonviolence, and the sanctity of life. They ignore and blatantly defy the Source of their freedom and responsibility; and, in doing so, they call forth Dwight Eisenhower's wise admonition near the end of his first inaugural address, January 20, 1953. Calling for sacrificial citizenship and leadership, the new president warned: "A people that values its privileges above its principles soon loses both."[1]

This parable ends in dark judgment on all of us, as we choose to love ourselves, our privileges, and our violent abandonment of the creation more than we love God and other persons. Mark offers this passage from the decisive vantage point of Easter, which is our final angle of vision into the depth of Mark's message of restoration by way of God's own relentless and sacrificial abidingness. Thus, the ultimate word from this judgment parable is a vision of the rejected One who restores. This judgment

---

1. *The Chief Executive: Inaugural Addresses of the Presidents of the United States from George Washington to Lyndon B. Johnson*, ed. Fred L. Israel (New York: Crown Publishers, 1965), 294.

Mark 12:1–12

Theological Perspective

recognize as just. Justice is not revenge; it is paving the way for a solution that is oriented toward peace, peace being the harder but more humane way of reacting to injury. That is the very basis of the idea of rights.

Martin Luther King Jr. wrote:

> It is not enough to say, "We must not wage war." It is necessary to love peace and sacrifice for it. We must concentrate not merely on the negative expulsion of war, but on the positive affirmation of peace.... We must see that peace represents a sweeter music, a cosmic melody that is far superior to the discords of war. Somehow we must transform the dynamics of the world power struggle from the negative nuclear arms race which no one can win to a positive contest to harness man's [sic] creative genius for the purpose of making peace and prosperity a reality for all of the nations of the world. In short, we must shift the arms race into a "peace race." If we have the will and determination to mount such a peace offensive, we will unlock hitherto tightly sealed doors of hope and transform our imminent cosmic elegy into a psalm of creative fulfillment.[2]

Indeed, these words of Judith Butler echo the words of Martin Luther King Jr. pointing to true peace as the presence of justice: "Peace is a resistance to the terrible satisfactions of war."[3]

FUMITAKA MATSUOKA

Pastoral Perspective

chapter by Jesus' praises for the wise scribe who understands that love of God and neighbor is far more important than ritual sacrifice (12:28–34).

As in Isaiah's time, Jesus had ample reason to call for repentance among the religious elite. Recent archaeological evidence confirms that the Jerusalem priests and other leaders had joined their Roman counterparts in buying up multiple tracts of land, joining field to field.[1] A parable about the overthrow of unjust tenants by a righteous God (aka landowner) would have found fertile ground among the impoverished farmers. It would have also made the religious rulers very nervous. As the prophet Nathan did with King David (2 Sam. 12:1–7), Jesus aimed his parable directly at the Jerusalem elite and said, "You are the men." No wonder they wanted to kill him, just as the tenants wished to kill the landowner's beloved son.

Understanding the parable's context can open our eyes to the social and economic issues of our time that parallel those in Jesus' day. Displaced farmers and homeowners facing foreclosure have a lot in common. In addition, if we can hear the parable as a call to repent and reform—not as a mandate for Christianity to replace Judaism—then we can also hear its challenge to us. In the church and the wider culture, how have we done as tenants and stewards of God's estate? What good fruits, if any, do our religious institutions—our vineyards—bear?

There is still the problem of the landowner's vengeance. Did Jesus advocate revenge in the name of God? Is violent retribution a cornerstone of the Christian faith? While the parable's finale has certainly been seen as a justification of religious warfare, one can argue for a different reading. As a Jewish teacher, Jesus often used the technique of hyperbole—exaggerating a story or lesson to the point of absurdity. Earlier in Mark's Gospel, he tells the disciples to cut off their hands or gouge out their eyes if these body parts cause them to sin (9:43–47). We seldom encourage our congregations to go and do likewise. If this parable were read with the same eye for exaggeration, Christians might have talked about war, violence, and God's intention in a very different way. We still can.

TALITHA ARNOLD

---

2. Martin Luther King Jr., "The Quest for Peace and Justice"; see http://www.nobelprize.org/nobel_prizes/peace/laureates/1964/king-lecture.html.
3. Judith Butler, interview in *The Believer Magazine* 2 (May 2003): 2; http://www.believermag.com/issues/200305/?read=interview_butler.

1. Richard A. Horsley, *Jesus and Empire* (Minneapolis: Fortress Press, 2003), 94.

Exegetical Perspective

Mark, however, seems little interested in such queries and complexities. Instead, he turns quickly to the conclusion of the parable, which promises the landowner-father's harsh judgment against the tenants. They will be destroyed, but in Mark, unlike Isaiah 5, the vineyard is left intact and placed in the care of others. The vineyard is preserved while its stewards are condemned. In the end, the vineyard is preserved for the sake of those who will inherit it.

Verse 12 makes the target of the parable clear. However, we would be mistaken to read the "they" of verse 12 as referring to Israel as a whole or some other large swath of people. The focus of the judgment of Mark's Jesus is strictly on those individuals in power who see in Jesus a threat to be quashed, rather than God's Messiah. Jesus' condemnation is narrow but unswerving, specific but part of a larger tradition of prophetic hope in God's graceful response and lament over the stumbling of God's people.

Moreover, the condemnation of these corrupt leaders is a word of hope to the great masses struggling to worship God despite the many obstacles that they face from both imperial and religious powers. Psalm 118 clinches Jesus' point: the rejected stone bears the weight of the building. This radical reversal is "the Lord's doing, and it is amazing in our eyes" (v. 11, quoting Ps. 118:23). The eventual execution of Jesus on the cross under the watchful eye of these leaders will be the means by which he is lifted up and by which the people will see God's good work.

In the end, these words of judgment are the greatest of good news. Pheme Perkins suggests, "By drawing our attention to the larger pattern of social violence, the parable explains how it is that allegedly religious people came to oppose Jesus. . . . People became blinded by their own desires, concepts of what constitutes the future, and attachment to particular authorities."[1] In short, Jesus here promises to set a twisted world aright.

ERIC D. BARRETO

Homiletical Perspective

parable looks through the lens of Easter at the God who yearns for our restoration through the rejected, suffering, and crucified Son whose resurrection overcomes our self-centered and destructive violence and arrogance, and who promises to serve as the cornerstone of our true humanity. In the words of theologian Donald G. Dawe, Jesus dies "our death so that we may live his life." Here theologian Shirley Guthrie is also helpful as he urges us to find God's providence in the midst of evil and suffering. He urges us to look "to the self-giving, suffering love of God" and to expect to recognize God's presence "in the depths of tragedy and suffering." For "God's sovereign power is not only God's willingness to save us from the hurts and hardships of life; it is God's willingness to share them with us. It is God's willingness to take our deserved and undeserved suffering into God's own life."[2]

This is a word almost impossible to believe, as Mark points us to the possibility of God's own completion and fulfillment of what we cannot possibly complete and fulfill: life itself. Although the God who comes to us in love is treated cruelly and rejected, again and again, this parable is grounded in the suffering and restoring death of Jesus Christ the "beloved son" who is the judging and restoring cornerstone of our existence, whether we like it or not! The rejected One will be lifted up. The rejected stone will become the cornerstone. God's power will be greater than the power of evil, violence, crucifixion, and death itself. As Mark records this teaching, looking through the lens of Easter, rejection and crucifixion have become preludes to resurrection, renewal, and what theologian H. Richard Niebuhr has profoundly called "the final prevailing love of God."[3]

DEAN K. THOMPSON

---

1. Pheme Perkins, "The Gospel of Mark," in *The New Interpreter's Bible*, ed. Leander E. Keck (Nashville: Abingdon Press, 1995), 8:672.

2. Donald G. Dawe, *Jesus: Lord for All Times* (Atlanta: John Knox Press, 1975), 51; Shirley C. Guthrie, *Christian Doctrine*, rev. ed. (Louisville, KY: Westminster John Knox Press, 1994), 187.

3. William Stacy Johnson, ed., *H. Richard Niebuhr* (New Haven and London: Yale University Press, 1996), 206.

Mark 12:13–17

¹³Then they sent to him some Pharisees and some Herodians to trap him in what he said. ¹⁴And they came and said to him, "Teacher, we know that you are sincere, and show deference to no one; for you do not regard people with partiality, but teach the way of God in accordance with truth. Is it lawful to pay taxes to the emperor, or not? ¹⁵Should we pay them, or should we not?" But knowing their hypocrisy, he said to them, "Why are you putting me to the test? Bring me a denarius and let me see it." ¹⁶And they brought one. Then he said to them, "Whose head is this, and whose title?" They answered, "The emperor's." ¹⁷Jesus said to them, "Give to the emperor the things that are the emperor's, and to God the things that are God's." And they were utterly amazed at him.

Theological Perspective

These words of Jesus are received in amazement, as they challenge dominant understandings of Roman rule and Jewish messianic expectation. Messianic expectations have a long and diverse history. Three messianic visions popular in Jesus' time include an earthly ruler who would reign justly, a Son of Man coming from heaven to transform creation itself, and a Suffering Servant (Isa. 53). Jesus, having resisted the temptation of earthly rule (see Luke 4:5–8 or Matt. 4:8–10), combines the two other traditions and proclaims, "The Son of Man is to be betrayed into human hands, and they will kill him" (9:31). The amazement in verse 17 is at the claim that this suffering Messiah, who declines to wield earthly political power, will yet somehow change everything, and even remain a savior.

It is precisely the political power—rejected by Jesus—over which many groups found themselves in competition. The Pharisees were members of a reform movement that sought to influence social, political, and legal spheres in support of their vision of community. A sign of their growing influence was their political alliance with the Herodians, supporters of Herod Antipas, during whose reign Jesus was born. Herodians supported paying taxes to the Roman Empire, to whom they owed their political fortune. The words of Jesus revealed the tensions in

Pastoral Perspective

Our world is in a state of flux. Shifts due to globalization and technological innovation suggest the birth pangs of a new age. Social and political changes, seismic in scope, trigger anxiety, conflict, and division as we grapple for new stability and order.

In this era of postmodernity, with life's "new normal" seemingly recalibrated daily and with dizzying effect, William Butler Yeats's famous poem of the modern age, "The Second Coming," seems prescient. Written at the end of World War I, the poem depicts the world breaking apart, as it envisions a falcon frantically flying in ever-widening circles to the extent that it has lost contact with and can no longer hear its falconer. "Things fall apart," writes Yeats, "The center cannot hold."[1]

Yeats's depiction of the chaotic overlap of two historical eras describes a polarized people where "the best lack conviction" and the worst "are full of passionate intensity." The poet's message of opposing forces in conflict brings to mind not only our current historical landscape, but also the last days of Jesus' life and his struggle with authorities, both political and religious, as found in this passage from Mark.

1. W. B. Yeats, "The Second Coming," in *The Collected Works of W. B. Yeats*, vol. 1, *The Poems*, 2nd ed., ed. Richard J. Finneran (New York: Scribner, 1997), 189.

Exegetical Perspective

Mark depicts an extended series of conversations (12:13–17, 18–27, 28–34) between Jesus and various religious authorities, including some Pharisees (v. 13), Herodians (v. 13), Sadducees (v. 18), and scribes (v. 28). Together with those whom Mark identifies as elders, these characters tend to function collectively throughout the narrative as religious authorities, specifically those based in Jerusalem (cf. 7:1–3). The latter detail is significant, for in Roman-occupied Judea the chief priests at the temple in Jerusalem were appointed by the Roman governor.

In Mark's apocalyptic narrative, Jerusalem and the temple are emblematic of the difficult, tangled relationship between Roman and Jewish authorities. Mark's Jesus often stands in tension with occupied Jerusalem, not with Judaism. As the ones who are placed in the position of upholding and defending conventional authority, in a Gospel that champions a radical recasting of the status quo as the way of God, the religious authorities function more like stock characters, or even caricatures, than as wholly reliable representations of what historians know about first-century Pharisees and other Jewish authorities.

In keeping with the apocalyptic contestation between the ruling of God and the way of the world that frames the entire Gospel, Mark 12 is driven by building tension, in its steady movement toward the

Homiletical Perspective

Preaching is a visual medium whose images are painted with words. Each text either portrays or evokes an image for the congregation that organizes and grounds the sermon in reality. At the center of Mark 12:13–17 is the simple yet profound vision of Jesus Christ looking at a coin emblazoned with the image of Caesar. Whether they know this pericope or not, this image has cultural cachet for contemporary listeners. The phrase "Render unto Caesar . . ." from the King James Version remains in the lexicon of the English-speaking world. This opens clear avenues for the preacher to reflect theologically upon numerous socially significant issues in the life of the congregation.

However, the movement to meditate on topics such as the empire, the relationship between church and state, government power, taxation, and wealth (to name a few) is not without risk. In our zeal to inform and convict the hearts of church people, we risk moving too quickly from the person of Jesus in the text to the implications of his statement "Give to the emperor the things that are the emperor's, and to God the things that are God's." Without clearly establishing who Jesus is, the preacher risks rendering exegesis and contextual analysis as mere trivia. We can bury Jesus at the center of this text in a mountain of facts and figures describing first-century

Mark 12:13–17

Theological Perspective

their alliance: Herodian political interests would not affirm the Jewish messianic hopes of not paying tributes to Rome. Jewish messianic interests would not affirm a communal identity in which God was not owed everything. Thus the words of Jesus may have appeared both surprising and provocative, given the religious and political climate.

What then is saving about a Messiah who will not wield earthly political power? If all things are not owed to God, what then is the good news of the gospel? Good news in Greek is *euangelion*, a word used by the Romans to proclaim military victory. This may indeed be the mystery at the heart of the messianic secret of the Gospel of Mark, where Jesus asks people not to tell anyone after he healed them. In Mark's narrative structure, the community of faith is privy to something that those being healed are not: the crucifixion, resurrection, and ascension of Jesus Christ. Thus one speaks of personal healing only after being put within historical, political, global, and cosmic understandings.

Reinhold Niebuhr, a twentieth-century American theologian, contributed significantly to our thinking about the proclamation of kingdom of God by Jesus and its relevance for contemporary social, cultural, and political affairs. Niebuhr's insights are prescient for these verses, as they do not reveal clear distinctions between "two kingdoms," "two cities," or easy admonitions for Christian understandings of citizenship. Niebuhr challenged the popular idea in liberal Protestant churches that the kingdom of God could be brought about by human effort grounded in a love ethic. Rather, it is the crucifixion of Christ that continues to stand in judgment on Christian efforts to use political power in Christ's name.[1] The ambiguity of discerning what is owed to Caesar and to God lies within each individual Christian. Thus the words of Jesus in verse 16 are striking, in that we are presented with deeply complex imagery that symbolizes the challenges facing believers: a human image inscribed upon the coin, while God's image is inscribed in humanity (Gen. 1:27).

In "The Suffering Servant and the Son of Man" Niebuhr argues, "The contradictions of human existence which prevent power from ever being good enough to belong to the Kingdom and which equally prevent pure love from being powerful enough to establish itself in the world, must be finally overcome; but they can only be overcome by divine

Pastoral Perspective

Jesus' opponents create an unholy alliance, a coalition of the religious and the political: Pharisees and followers of Herod intent on trapping Jesus. His opponents pose a leading question, "Are we to pay the tax, or not?" in effect asking to whom are we to pledge allegiance (v. 15). Their aim is to bait and catch him in his speech. Although they miss their mark, Jesus' aim is sure. He asks his opponents to produce the tribute coin with its image and inscription ascribing divinity to the emperor. They fish for a coin and promptly present one. Jesus, however, eludes their question by asking one himself: "Whose head is this, and whose title is stamped on this coin?" Their answer, of course, is, "The emperor's" (v. 16). In a startling, decisive moment, Jesus teaches the way to God. It is not to pretend that one lives only in the spiritual realm; instead, one is called to maintain ultimate fidelity to God, while living in the world and among its powers. However—and most crucially—it is not to subjugate oneself to Caesar at the expense of one's lifeline to God.

Jesus sees straight into their souls—and into ours. The tacit question for them and for us is, "Whose image is stamped on us? Whose name is written upon our hearts?"

For us, and for the disciples, the answer is that we are coins minted in the image of God.[2] With all that competes for our allegiance in this age, how can we remember that we are icons with God's name written on our hearts? How can we remember to whom are hearts are given?

We can dedicate ourselves to communal and embodied spiritual practices that focus our fears and allay our anxieties. As example, the pastor might reflect on practices that orient us toward God and that engender transformation, such as labyrinth walking, a prayer shawl knitting ministry, or chopping vegetables for the local soup kitchen.

A pastor might also explore the way in which all that we give and offer ultimately comes from God as a gift, using examples of what giving means. When we acknowledge the gifts and benefits we derive in a life that is given to us by God, we transform discontent. Conversely, when we fail to acknowledge life as gift and begin to believe that we are the sole source of our well-being, then our Godward orientation becomes skewed.

Given the polarization and discontent in our political sphere, an interesting parallel might be

---

1. Reinhold Niebuhr, *An Interpretation of Christian Ethics* (1935; repr., New York: Meridian, 1956).

2. George Buttrick, exposition of Mark, in *The Interpreter's Bible* (New York: Abingdon Press, 1951), 7:519.

Exegetical Perspective

crucifixion that Jesus predicts three times (8:31; 9:31; 10:33–34). Having observed that "the chief priests, the scribes, and the elders" (11:27) had been unsuccessful in their quest to undermine Jesus' authority, Mark sets the stage for the Pharisees and the Herodians to try their hand at eroding Jesus' influence.

His reference to the priests' fear of the crowd (12:12) is a succinct reminder of the politically difficult role that the chief priests had to play during the first century, when the land promised to Abraham was under Roman subjugation. The priests' authority was an important means of maintaining order among the crowds in the temple precincts, which were monitored by a strategically placed Roman garrison, especially during the politically and religiously charged Jewish Passover. Any temple priest would be keenly aware of Rome's record of using force to address perceived disturbance anywhere in the empire. The priests' effort to assert their power over that of Jesus was likely fueled, at least in part, by the desire to prevent potential unrest and subsequent Roman intervention. Historically, the chief priests were viewed by some Jews as protectors of the people and by others as collaborators with the empire.

Mark 12:13–34 details debates centering on the interpretation of Scripture. The Pharisees and Herodians seem at first to express positive regard for Jesus: "Teacher, we know that you are sincere, and show deference to no one; for you do not regard people with partiality, but teach the way of God in accordance with truth" (v. 14). However, their follow-up question reveals their true intention to lay a trap for him (v. 13): "Is it lawful to pay taxes to the emperor, or not? Should we pay them, or should we not?" (vv. 14–15). Posing a no-win question about the law, just as they did in 10:2–4, the Pharisees raise the ante by setting before Jesus a politically dangerous challenge.

The issue is not at all akin to that of paying taxes in a democratic society. Rather, the question alludes to a politically and religiously sensitive subject, namely, the payment of tribute imposed upon the people by Rome, a concrete expression of their subjection to the empire. The aim of the question seems to be that of forcing Jesus either to answer affirmatively and risk alienating the crowd, or to answer negatively and offend the Roman authorities. From the perspective of the Pharisees and Herodians, Jesus is in a lose-lose situation. Either scenario could trigger events that would hasten his arrest.

As he did in 10:5–9, Jesus meets the challenge by redefining the grounds of the debate. After exposing

Homiletical Perspective

Palestine and/or our current age, and thereby fail to relate how this information illuminates the person of God portrayed in the text.

An effective way to draw the image of Jesus in Mark 12:13–17 is to retell the narrative with an eye for details that make its characters recognizably human. This both assists in telling an interesting story and creates points of resonance for the preacher to claim for the present day through the text. This pericope is a familiar "trap text"; one sees these throughout the Gospels. In this case, the Pharisees and Herodians evoke a painful and controversial subject among Jews—their relationship to Rome—in an attempt to push Jesus into saying something unfaithful or illegal. For Jews, the issue of taxation created enormous religious tension, because Roman currency was emblazoned with the image of the Caesar, who was understood to be divine. This meant that every coin was an idol.

In explaining this context to a congregation, the preacher risks conveying this information in a manner that presents the Pharisees and Herodians as proverbial cartoon villains, one-dimensional characters engaged in evil for evil's sake. Far more honest and profound preaching will result if the preacher takes the time to humanize Jesus' opponents. Ask yourself questions such as: "What is at stake for them?" or "What good are they trying to accomplish?" "What are they trying to protect?" or "Why is Jesus a threat to them?" Everyone is a hero in his or her own story. How are the Pharisees and Herodians attempting to be heroic? Within the boundary of the text, there is enormous room to explore meaning and purpose through the richness of the details we provide.

Once the preacher establishes the characters within the text, it is time to push forward with the narrative. The Pharisees and Herodians exhibit a formal politeness and deference in framing their question to Jesus regarding taxation. This is a clear signal that they are setting a verbal trap for Jesus; they have used this same style of speech in previous attempts to ensnare him. However, many of the people who hear the sermon may not recognize this pattern. Preaching this text well ensures that the irony of this moment is clear to the congregation.

The Pharisees and Herodians may be disingenuous in stating that Jesus speaks sincerely with deference to no one, regards people without partiality, and teaches the way of God in accordance with the truth. Nevertheless, they are accurately describing him. The ironic contrast may be heard in the way

Mark 12:13–17

Theological Perspective

actions."[2] In a world that is not the kingdom of God, says Niebuhr, love, pure goodness, always ends up on the cross. Pure goodness without power is crucified, and pure goodness with power is corrupted.

Niebuhr's reading of the Gospels confronts the contemporary church with the insight that Jewish messianic hopes and Roman imperial rule both represent the "first Adam" that crucifies the "second Adam" in the name of keeping order and building up society. The inability of the Pharisees and the Herodians to realize their respective visions shows that "every morality which begins by counting on the success of a pure action must end by reducing the purity of the action in the interest of its success."[3] The words of Jesus in verses 15–17 reveal the mutual corruption of their moral visions when they conspired to kill him after a healing in the synagogue (3:6).

This form of realism should not be confused with pessimism or resignation. Rather, the perennial message of the crucifixion reveals the reality by which Jesus can be said to be "sincere, and show deference to no one; for you do not regard people with partiality, but teach the way of God in accordance with truth" (12:14). In the crucifixion of Jesus, the world judges the kingdom of God, and the kingdom of God judges the kingdoms of the world. This judgment saves humanity from the idolatry of identifying any given government or political movement with God or the kingdom of God. Humanity is always tempted to believe that once a given leader is elected, an unjust law repealed, a social wrong rectified, a moment of justice achieved, the kingdom of God will have arrived in its fullness.

It is a temptation that besets all communities that yearn for justice and release from oppression. To misread a singular moment in time, secured by human effort, as having achieved the kingdom of God, free from further conflict and injustice, is to court profound despair. The history of Christian thought has long maintained an intimate and constitutive relationship between revelation and salvation. A Messiah whose life revealed divine love rejected earthly power to save humanity from the idolatrous hope in its own institutions. The saving power of the crucified Messiah is that hope can safely be placed in God and God alone.

CHRISTOPHE D. RINGER

Pastoral Perspective

drawn by exploring our appreciation of government's role in the well-being of our society. A sensitive pastor serving an affluent congregation could raise up the way in which many besides those who are poor benefit from government programs. Cornell professor Suzanne Mettler, for instance, explains that we often scapegoat the poor, yet those with home-mortgage deductions receive more financially from the government than those on food stamps. In other words, the vast majority of American citizens have at some point relied on government programs but often fail to recognize that government is the source of this assistance. In failing to acknowledge the benefits derived by social programs that aid people of privilege, it becomes easier to scapegoat those who are impoverished and reliant upon the more visible social-welfare programs.[3]

Such awareness-building—along with the spiritual practices outlined above—constitutes time spent with God in which we once again discover how close we are to God, how God is inscribed upon our souls. This counters spiritual disorientation and promotes wholeness in the body—in the body physical, the body social, the body politic, and the body of Christ. These kinds of ministries also bolster informed citizenship, increasing our gratitude not only for God, but also for the world God so loves. Such gratitude has a positive effect on diffusing political polarization.

Such work reminds us that God's seal is upon our hearts, and in dedicating ourselves to these practices, we are drawn ever nearer to the heart of God that resides at the center of all realities. As we navigate the changes of life, we experience a center that holds us eternally as we regain our true north in our Godward journey. When we are grounded in God, God can use us for the healing of the world.

In times of conflict and transition, it is easy to lose our way, like the falcon that loses contact with the falconer. When we strive to be loyal to the One in whom all life holds together, we will find ourselves grounded in God, whose mark is upon our hearts, and able to do God's transformative work in the world.

CAROL L. WADE

---

2. Reinhold Niebuhr, *Beyond Tragedy: Essays on the Christian Interpretation of History* (New York: Charles Scribner's Sons, 1937), 178.
3. Ibid., 185.

3. Suzanne Mettler, *The Submerged State: How Invisible Government Policies Undermine American Democracy* (Chicago: University of Chicago Press, 2011), 5, 13, 22, 38.

Exegetical Perspective

the hypocrisy of their false flattery, he tells his opponents to bring him a denarius, a silver coin imbued with political significance. Not only did it serve as an example of Roman propaganda, with its engraved image of Caesar's wreathed head and the declaration of his divinity on the obverse side; it was the coinage in which tribute was to be paid. As the primary means of disseminating Caesar's image throughout the empire, the denarius functioned as a sure reminder of Roman domination. For pious Jews, the coin also stood in violation of biblical teaching against graven images (Lev. 19:4; 26:1; Deut. 7:25) and idolatry. The repugnance generated by Jesus' request for a denarius would have only been intensified by what he next asks: "Whose head is this, and whose title?" (v. 16b). Forced to acknowledge what was already painfully obvious, the Pharisees and Herodians answer, "The emperor's" (v. 16c), thus underscoring their collective subjugation.

Shifting the focus, from a debate about what is lawful according to Torah, to the undeniable and unresolvable conflict between God and Caesar and between divine and human things, Jesus declares, "Give to the emperor the things that are the emperor's, and to God the things that are God's" (v. 17a). Give to Caesar *only* what belongs to Caesar. The things of God—creation and humankind made in God's own image (Gen. 1:26–27)—are of ultimate significance. Jesus disarms his interlocutors and redefines the terms of the conversation, so that he can underscore the Gospel's central theme, the dawning of the kingdom that Jesus proclaims and its calibration of what is truly of God.

It is to distinguish the ways of the kingdom that Mark casts the religious authorities in such harsh light. His concern is not to write history, but to share a gospel that exposes and judges the corrupt and oppressive powers of the current age, one that is to be eclipsed by the inbreaking ruling of God (1:15). No wonder, then, that beginning in 1:27, Mark weaves throughout the Gospel narrative a stark and persistent contrast between Jesus' true authority and the counterfeit authority exerted by Rome and, by extension, the religious leaders, who, willingly or unwillingly, are placed in the position of serving its interests.

MARY F. FOSKETT

Homiletical Perspective

we read the text and how we present the narrative. If congregations can view the Pharisees and Herodians as complex and fully formed human beings who are acting in accordance with what they think is right and righteous, then Jesus' repudiation of them will have far greater meaning. It is difficult to claim the complicated and difficult struggles of the contemporary world with a biblical text if the congregation cannot view the tensions in the Bible as equally complicated and difficult.

At the center of this narrative is a calm and reflective Jesus. His first question, "Why are you putting me to the test?" evokes the admonition in Deuteronomy 6:16 that Israel is not to put the Lord their God to the test. The implicit claim of divinity produced by this phrasing shapes the context of the pericope. The image of Jesus grasping a coin with an image of Caesar upon it is one of divinity holding the power of empire in the palm of his hand. As contemporary readers of the text, we know that the claims of the Roman Empire and its leader to be eternal proved false. The coin, which could purchase goods and services throughout an unprecedented portion of the world in the first century, is now a museum piece.

As the preacher stands before the congregation and proclaims this pericope, the very act of preaching testifies to the eternity and power of Christ. By organizing our proclamation of this text around the image of Jesus holding the coin, the context of the Scripture's claim upon the present becomes Jesus' relationship to this world, rather than a division of power and resources between God and empire. On this basis, the questions the text raises about the present situation of our congregation and the broader world are rooted in God's relationship to the power of this world, rather than a determination regarding the proper division of resources.

MATTHEW FLEMMING

Mark 12:18–27

18Some Sadducees, who say there is no resurrection, came to him and asked him a question, saying, 19"Teacher, Moses wrote for us that if a man's brother dies, leaving a wife but no child, the man shall marry the widow and raise up children for his brother. 20There were seven brothers; the first married and, when he died, left no children; 21and the second married the widow and died, leaving no children; and the third likewise; 22none of the seven left children. Last of all the woman herself died. 23In the resurrection whose wife will she be? For the seven had married her."

24Jesus said to them, "Is not this the reason you are wrong, that you know neither the scriptures nor the power of God? 25For when they rise from the dead, they neither marry nor are given in marriage, but are like angels in heaven. 26And as for the dead being raised, have you not read in the book of Moses, in the story about the bush, how God said to him, 'I am the God of Abraham, the God of Isaac, and the God of Jacob'? 27He is God not of the dead, but of the living; you are quite wrong."

Theological Perspective

Contained within a seemingly theological conundrum are important themes for understanding human communities and the nature of God. More specifically, these verses underscore our deepest concerns about the flourishing and preservation of human communities, as well as how our best intentions often threaten them.

This passage opens with a clear statement about the denial of the resurrection by the Sadducees. The Sadducees, another movement competing for social and political influence at the time of Jesus, interestingly rejected the resurrection for what would become a key tenet of Christian orthodoxy: God is not the author of evil. The Sadducees were uncomfortable with the assertion made by other movements that, in spite of the good or evil actions of persons, God was still active in human affairs. The belief in God's providence in spite of human action thus potentially involved God in evil or immoral acts. Such beliefs appeared to violate free will as well as the goodness and justice of God. Thus, they rejected the entire theological discussion of what lies beyond death, including the immortality of the soul, rewards, and punishments.

It would be inaccurate to consider the Sadducees as not being concerned with the future or faithfulness to a received tradition of the past. In verse 19

Pastoral Perspective

Jesus comes to announce the kingdom of God, a new world that promises to be rightly ordered as God intends, both in this age and the next. In Jesus' pivotal last days in Jerusalem, his proclamation of God's kingdom mission is under attack: the chief priests, scribes, and elders publicly question Jesus' authority and then send a coalition of Pharisees and Herodians to entrap him. By deftly reframing their questions, Jesus eludes their snare. In this passage, a third offense is now underway as the Sadducees come to discredit Jesus.

The Sadducees' worldview was essentially shaped by the Pentateuch, the first five books of Moses, Genesis through Deuteronomy. In contrast to the Pharisees, the Sadducees did not believe in revelation beyond these five books, and neither did they accept oral interpretation of Torah. Moreover, the Sadducees, members of an elite and priestly class who benefited from the temple system, did not believe in the resurrection. Perhaps they were wary of such a hope-infused promise that ran the risk of upending the powers that be, filling the lowly with the power of God to rise to new and greater life. This passage makes clear that the kingdom message can be unsettling for those, in both Jesus' day and ours, who derive power and privilege from existing structures and whose worldview is dependent upon maintaining the status quo.

Exegetical Perspective

Mark 12:18–27 depicts another debate between Jesus and a group of religious authorities. When the Sadducees approach Jesus, they confront him with an absurd scenario, one that centers on the concept of resurrection. Mark's opening line, "Some Sadducees, who say there is no resurrection" (v. 18), depicts Jesus' interlocutors as hypocrites who engage him only in the hope of ensnaring him.

Verse 18 reminds the reader that resurrection was a contested concept in first-century Judaism, one to which the Sadducees did not adhere and which also raised questions in the minds of others (see 9:10). The Jesus movement developed, but did not invent, the notion of resurrection. We know from Paul (1 Cor. 15:12–58) that the Pharisees held that at some point in God's plan for the future, God would raise from death all those who had died, at which time they would be returned to a bodily experience, constituted either by their own restored bodies, by new bodies, or perhaps by new kinds of bodies. What was key to the notion of resurrection was the valuation of the human body and God's creation. To separate the created order from God's plan for the future was inconceivable to those who believed in the resurrection of the dead. Furthermore, the resurrection was believed to be a collective phenomenon, something that in the fullness of time would happen to all who had died.

Homiletical Perspective

For many preachers, proclaiming the creeds and theological beliefs that founded their traditions casts them into treacherous waters, rather than providing sanctuary. In an age that struggles with paradox, to preach on the Trinity or the dual nature of Christ or the resurrection seems to many to be overly didactic or irrelevant to daily living (or even an affront to science). However, to elide or recast the creedal pronouncements about the person of God as metaphor bears a significant theological cost. In the case of Mark 12:18–27, the price of failing to proclaim resurrection is to lose a lens into the person of God and how God relates to humanity.

The pericope begins with the Sadducees (who do not believe in the resurrection of the body) attempting to render Jesus' proclamation of the resurrection as false by applying the internal logic of the Hebrew Scriptures to his claims. The nature of their hypothetical scenario is to render the concept of resurrection as a farce through the classical rhetorical technique of reductio ad absurdum. The law of Moses commanded that when a man's brother died he was to marry the widow if she were childless (Deut. 25:5–6). This was an act of compassion, as it prevented the widow, who could not inherit property, from becoming destitute; at the same time it opened the possibility that the

Mark 12:18–27

Theological Perspective

the question of levirate marriage, in which a widow is forbidden to marry outside the family if a son has not been produced, stands as representative of their commitment to the teachings of Moses. If indeed the soul perishes with the body and the actions of divine providence have no bearing on human actions, then marriage as an institution bears significant meaning. Moreover, the Sadducees take the practice of levirate marriage and project it into the resurrection so as to render both concepts absurd. If the Sadducees can appear to make an absurdity of the teachings of Moses, the social and political consequences are significant.

Elisabeth Schüssler Fiorenza's pioneering work *In Memory of Her* helps to illuminate what is a stake. She argues that levirate marriage "served the purpose of continuing the patriarchal family, by securing its wealth and the inheritance within it, a concern important to the Sadducees, many of whom were upper middle class priests, rich landowners living in Jerusalem—thus profiting doubly from the fees due them as priests and those due them from the tenants who worked the land."[1] The response of Jesus in verse 25 reveals that in the resurrection we inherit a relationship with God in eternity that is not bound by the interests of marriage in time. This is consistent with Jesus' astounding claim, within earshot of his mother and brothers, that those who do the will of God are his mother and brothers (3:35). Thus Jesus simultaneously articulates two powerful ideas in response to this rhetorical trap. The first is that the resurrection is not merely a continuation of this life, endless time. The second is that human relationships that exist by the power of an eternal God may not conform to the standards our time.

The relationship of God, humanity, and time is a perennial mystery that every generation struggles to understand. There are, however, consistent themes in Christian thought that shed light on these verses. The first is that God alone is eternal, and time belongs to creation itself. Creation is that which is subject to change, growth, and decay. Thus humanity is able to mark its passing and create various calendars to organize time for a particular culture. Because time belongs to creation, time can become meaningful for us. Jesus in several passages attempts to make it known that he speaks from eternity in the midst of time. Jesus describes himself as the Alpha and the Omega (Rev. 21:6), and says that before

Pastoral Perspective

Jesus' opponents seem to be more motivated to prove him wrong than to live in right relationship to others. Jesus extends an invitation to receive new life, to open themselves to the power of God through the gift of a living word. However, the Sadducees have received the word laid down by Moses as inerrant; furthermore, for them, its meaning is forever etched in stone. Jesus calls them out on this and tells them that they are misinformed. Jesus, in citing the Sadducees' honored canon, creatively draws on both tradition and interpretation, and makes clear that if God is a God of the living, then God's word is indeed still alive. In truth, the word laid down is dead unless it has the power to raise us up into new and resurrected life.

The worldview of the Sadducees with its immutable traditions enables the subjugation of the marginalized in harmful ways and allows for the abuse of power. The absurd example of a woman passed along to seven brothers, meant to demean Jesus and his teaching, also denigrates the woman. As we read this text in our context, it asks us to consider where the vulnerable and disenfranchised still experience subjugation, and it challenges us to be Jesus' prophetic voice.

The extreme example of levirate marriage offered in the text, as described in Deuteronomy 25:5–10, is concerned with ensuring a family's lineage, so that the deceased man's "name may not be blotted out of Israel" (Deut. 25:6). Levirate marriage, a term derived from the Latin word *levir,* meaning "husband's brother," was considered a protection for a widow and orphan. However, treating the woman as property, as the Sadducees' hypothetical story does, blots out the woman's dignity and agency. It can only be seen as positive in a patriarchal society where the woman is under the possession and servitude of her husband or his brothers. In too many places, this is still the case.

Today, levirate marriage remains a common practice in many developing countries throughout the world, such as in regions of Africa and Asia. Collaborating with God's family on behalf of the vulnerable is Jesus' mandate to us. Even the smallest mission grants in some programs enable women in developing countries to gain the freedom hard won by the cross. A small grant or microloan for the purchase of seeds for food crops unleashes the transformational power of God available to each of us. Enabling communities to develop the means to help themselves is crucial to the work of human fulfillment. In many villages, the women work together to create farming

---

1. Elisabeth Schüssler Fiorenza, *In Memory of Her: A Feminist Theological Reconstruction of Christian Origins,* 10th ed. (New York: Crossroad, 1994), 144.

Exegetical Perspective

It is this notion of resurrection that serves as the framework for the Sadducees' query. Drawing on biblical legislation regarding levirate marriage (Deut. 25:5–6), the Sadducees present Jesus with the hypothetical (and decidedly hyperbolic) case of a widow who marries her deceased husband's six brothers in a series of successive marriages, each of which ends with the husband's death and none of which produces a child. Given this scenario, the Sadducees ask, "In the resurrection, whose wife will she be? For the seven had married her" (v. 23). The question assumes that at the resurrection, the dead will be returned to a bodily existence and the restoration of all their human relationships. Surely the Sadducees know it is a laughable scenario. Perhaps they pose the question precisely in order to belittle the concept of resurrection.

Rather than trying to adjudicate between the seven husbands in the ludicrous scenario, Jesus changes the terms of the debate. He pulls no punches in responding to both the question the Sadducees pose and what he knows to be their refutation of the resurrection: "Is not this the reason you are wrong, that you know neither the scriptures nor the power of God?" (v. 24). In verse 25 Jesus asserts that resurrection entails the transformation, not merely the restoration, of the body. To envision the resurrection as simply a recapitulation of the way things are now is far too limiting. Neither the hypothetical widow nor the priests need be concerned about human conventions like marriage in the postresurrection future. To maintain such a small view of God's future for humankind is to underestimate the vision and power of God.

Jesus continues by taking up the Sadducees' refutation of the resurrection of the dead, a position they have conveniently neglected to admit but of which he is nonetheless aware. On this point, Jesus criticizes the Sadducees' interpretation of Scripture by drawing on Exodus 3:6: "As for the dead being raised, have you not read in the book of Moses, in the story about the bush, how God said to him, 'I am the God of Abraham, the God of Isaac, and the God of Jacob'? He is God not of the dead, but of the living; you are quite wrong" (vv. 26–27). Jesus cites the Exodus story first to remind the Sadducees of God's infinite power, and then to make a scriptural argument that favors belief in a future resurrection.

Some scholars see in Jesus' citation of Exodus 3:6 (*eimi*, "I am") the suggestion that he perceives the patriarchs to be alive in some real and meaningful way. Perhaps readers can interpret Jesus' reference

Homiletical Perspective

deceased brother's line would continue through his sibling.

The Sadducees twist this compassionate commandment into an intellectual trap. They ask Jesus what would happen if a childless widow were married by seven brothers, each of whom died without a son after their union. The logical trap within this narrative is this question: to whom will this woman be married after she and all the brothers have died and are resurrected? Of course, the basic dilemma would exist with two brothers; but seven brothers render the situation, and thus the concept of resurrection, totally ludicrous.

Jesus responds with a rebuke for their attempt to trivialize a compassionate commandment by reducing it to grist for the mill in a continuing argument over the afterlife. In stating, "You know neither the scriptures nor the power of God," he is not speaking of scriptural illiteracy. Rather, he is claiming that they are missing the point. For all the knowledge a Sadducee may have of the Hebrew Scriptures, Jesus does not believe they understand what they have read. An imagination that produces the scenario of the widow and the seven brothers is malformed. It fails to comprehend the person of God revealed to them in their sacred texts and that God's relationship to humanity.

In proclaiming Mark 12:18–27, the preacher risks falling into a similar trap by presenting resurrection as a theological concept to be argued for or against, rather than a condition of humanity's relationship to God. When preachers limit this text to support for an argument about the possibility of resurrection, they may not be condensing this central element of our faith to absurdity as the Sadducees did; but they are being reductive nonetheless. Resurrection is not simply another box to mark on the checklist of orthodox doctrines; it is a claim about who God is and how God relates to us.

The statement that God "is the God not of the dead, but of the living" speaks of a God who is in relationship with us in life and in death. Though the social order of life after death may change, Jesus does not make a distinction between God's connection with people in this world and after death; they are the living. Jesus' interpretation of God's revelation to Moses through the burning bush speaks to the eternality of God among the great cloud of witnesses. The use of "I AM," God's self-designation in naming God's relationship with Abraham, Isaac, and Jacob, defines their relationship in the present tense. This understanding of the affiliation of God's people in former

Mark 12:18–27

Theological Perspective

Abraham was, he is (John 8:58). It is not that Jesus is hundreds of years old, which would be to misunderstand his point. Rather, he is from eternity, which is the starting point, the ground, the foundation, and the reality by which time exists. Eternity is that from which something can be born and to which something can return.

Jesus articulates this understanding of time and eternity, not only in reference to himself, but also as the basis for his rebuttal of the Sadducees' interpretation of the law. In recalling God's words to Moses, Jesus reminds us that God is still the God of Abraham, Isaac, and Jacob (vv. 26–27). Moreover, God is the God of the living, not the dead. The point is not that Abraham, Isaac, and Jacob did not experience death. Rather, they now have their life in the eternal realm of God. The Gospels themselves reveal the ambiguity of expressing such ideas within the limits of human speech and images taken from time, and then projecting them beyond the boundaries of our lives. The words of Jesus here find expression in the transfiguration (9:2–8). Moses and Elijah are not merely remembered; rather, they are present and talking with Jesus. They exist in the eternal life of God, which is not time without meaning, that is, timelessness. Nor it is endless time, the repetition of a single life without end, without change, which could describe hell.

The challenge of Jesus to the Sadducees continues today as the church continues to discern the meaning of God, time, and the creation through the lenses of our various cultural traditions. How often in culture wars do we appeal to the Scriptures, as if the past can easily settle the question of our future? The church has often kept tradition at the expense of advancing the kingdom. This is in part due to our inability to discern the difference between being in communion with the saints of the past and attempting to repeat their moment. The communion of the saints is a doctrine based on discerning the eternal, the very life of God, which occasions our experience of the past, the present, and the future.

CHRISTOPHE D. RINGER

Pastoral Perspective

cooperatives, as they plant the crops of new possibility. Excess harvest proceeds gleaned and given to other widows or orphans enables additional women to cultivate and harvest food, and the circle of new life grows. Proceeds from such endeavors also help pay for the education of girls. Most schools in Africa, for instance, require tuition past the primary level, and a girl child is often denied funds in favor of educating a boy.

Low levels of girls' education lead to economic instability, higher infant mortality rates, and greater hunger and poverty; so when we look at working to alleviate global poverty, women and girls matter. A popular saying in Africa is, "If you educate a man, you educate an individual. When you educate a woman, you educate a nation." The girls want to be liberated to choose life, to exercise their agency as children of a good and loving God. Education provides access for girls to accomplish their dreams and to know the power of God to shape the lives they wish to live.

We are called to be agents of hope and resurrection with and for the disenfranchised and marginalized. The possibility of new life, new vision, and an empowered people challenged the status quo in Jesus' day, just as it does in our own. Jesus uses the tradition to show that God is at work, challenging structures and transforming our world. Although Jesus' opponents are intent on discrediting him, Jesus does not return the ill treatment of his antagonists, but rather responds in truth and love to open their eyes to God's new world. This passage encourages us to work for and with others on behalf of God's liberating justice that transforms the world. We have not only Scripture but also the resurrected Christ and his Spirit to show us how to live God's word for the life of the world.

CAROL L. WADE

Exegetical Perspective

to Abraham, Isaac, and Jacob in light of Mark 9:4–5, where Peter, James, and John witness Elijah and Moses appearing in the company of the transfigured Jesus (see 9:9). Read in this way, Jesus seems to be calling the Sadducees to envision the forebears of Israel as "living patriarchs" and to acknowledge the possibility of future resurrection.

On the other hand, Jesus' citation of the story of the burning bush suggests another way to understand his reference to Exodus: God's identity and activity throughout Exodus 1–3 reveal that God is indeed "God not of the dead, but of the living" (v. 27). Exodus 1–3 illustrates several instances where God or God's agents act to preserve and restore life when death seems imminent: the Hebrew midwives act to keep newborn boys alive (Exod. 1:17); Pharaoh's daughter rescues Moses from the Nile, and Moses' sister sees to it that he will be nursed by his Hebrew birthmother (Exod. 2:5–10); Moses finds refuge in Midian (Exod. 2:15); God heeds the cries of the Hebrew people, remembers the covenant with Abraham, Isaac, and Jacob, and takes notice of the plight of the Israelites (Exod. 2:23–25); and finally, Moses encounters a blazing bush that remains unconsumed by the flames (Exod. 3:2–3). Each of these turning points in the early chapters of Exodus illustrates the power of God, who sees to it that life will overcome death.

Recalling the context and content of Exodus 3:6, Jesus' declaration that God "is God not of the dead, but of the living" (v. 27) is comprehensible. The Sadducees are wrong in failing to believe in the reach of God's life-giving power. The concept of the resurrection of the dead is consistent with the activity of God revealed in Scripture. Thus the key difference between Jesus' religious vision and that of the Sadducees pertains to their respective notions of the power and capaciousness of God's own vision and will for humankind. Belief in resurrection acknowledges God's unlimited affirmation of life and divine creation.

MARY F. FOSKETT

Homiletical Perspective

times to those of the present day is reminiscent of the cloud of witnesses in Hebrews 12:1 whose lives are a source of perseverance for Christians running the race God has placed before them. As Jesus says, God is "God not of the dead, but of the living." Although people may one day be "like angels in heaven," the fundamental nature of life remains the same as it is now: all life is lived in the presence of God.

From this perspective, resurrection defines the relationship of the church to the world. It is the basis of Christian hope, the promise that humanity's relationship with the eternal God will never be broken, not even by death. Thus, preaching this text illuminates the work of the church. It is the basis of our mission and a foundation for our call to work for social justice; for wherever there is life, God is present. To share the gospel is to make others aware of the presence of God in their lives; to help the least of God's children is to work to bring about the kingdom in God's cherished world.

Great comfort is found in proclaiming the resurrection in the context of funerals, but Jesus' explanation of resurrection in this pericope means that it is a comfort in life as well as in death. For victims of injustice or abuse or those who find themselves trapped in the struggles of life, the resurrection offers a clear sign that the order of this world is not the enduring definition of life. Amid the pain of our existence, the resurrection may provide strength and courage to act to throw off the chains that bind us. Not only do we know that death is not the final word, but because God is the God of the living, we have comfort in knowing that the presence of God sustains each moment of our existence. Life in God is not reserved for the time when we shuffle off this mortal coil. It breaks the bonds of death in all its forms. For this reason, texts that provide a narrative extension of creedal proclamation demonstrate not only the basis for our theology but the manner in which it illuminates God's presence in all of creation.

MATTHEW FLEMMING

Mark 12:28–34

²⁸One of the scribes came near and heard them disputing with one another, and seeing that he answered them well, he asked him, "Which commandment is the first of all?" ²⁹Jesus answered, "The first is, 'Hear, O Israel: the Lord our God, the Lord is one; ³⁰you shall love the Lord your God with all your heart, and with all your soul, and with all your mind, and with all your strength.' ³¹The second is this, 'You shall love your neighbor as yourself.' There is no other commandment greater than these." ³²Then the scribe said to him, "You are right, Teacher; you have truly said that 'he is one, and besides him there is no other'; ³³and 'to love him with all the heart, and with all the understanding, and with all the strength,' and 'to love one's neighbor as oneself,'—this is much more important than all whole burnt offerings and sacrifices." ³⁴When Jesus saw that he answered wisely, he said to him, "You are not far from the kingdom of God." After that no one dared to ask him any question.

Theological Perspective

Jesus' response to the question posed to him by the scribe about the greatest commandment, which combines Deuteronomy 6:4–5 and Leviticus 19:18b, invites the reader to think about the way these verses interpret not only the Torah but also the gospel. To whom exactly is the imperative verse 29 addressed? It is addressed to a people, Israel, who are in a covenant relationship with God. This very particular identity is inseparable from a more general designation, the neighbor, whom Israel is commanded also to love. This blend of particularity and universality establishes one's identity through those within Israel and without. The neighbor provides the ongoing challenge, as the neighbor might be one's enemy (Luke 6:27) or the socially outcast and vulnerable (Luke 10:25–37).

In addition, the focus in Mark 12:29 on the oneness of God resonated deeply within the early Christian movement as it attempted to distinguish itself within a Greco-Roman culture of religious diversity. Indeed, the scribe is praised for affirming that "he is one, and besides him there is no other" (v. 32). However, within the broader currents of the New Testament, God is also love (1 John 4:8). If God is love, the indivisibility of God occasions what many have called the hard sayings of Jesus. These include verses such as, "If you love those who love you, what credit

Pastoral Perspective

Finally, an opportunity to speak about the essence of faith! Following three controversial encounters with opponents who wield questions as weapons, how grateful Jesus must have been for a genuine inquiry from the scribe! How grateful the scribe must have been for Jesus' attentiveness to his question, "Which commandment is the first of all?" The scribe's question is an important one, its primacy foundational to a life grounded in God.

The dialogue between Jesus and the scribe seems to create instant rapport. In his teaching to the scribe, Jesus affirms that the twofold commandment—to love God and neighbor—is the ground of our prayer and action, the law made plain yet dynamic. For the scribe, perhaps what once was complex now seems simple, what was heavy is now light.

Likewise, beset with the complexities of twenty-first-century life, how grateful contemporary listeners are to have their faith articulated in plain sense too: love is the essence of the Christian life. Simplification is everything! Simple does not mean easy, though. There would be no need for the commandment if it were. Therefore, this passage affords an opportunity to teach about the nature and purpose of self-giving love as the ground of Christian faith. Jesus' summary of the law creates a helpful three-point focus: love of God, neighbor, and self. If Jesus'

Exegetical Perspective

In Mark 12:28–34, the series of debates between Jesus and an assortment of religious authorities sees a shift in tone. A certain scribe, upon witnessing the dispute between Jesus and the Sadducees over the interpretation of Torah, sees that Jesus has answered the Sadducees admirably. That the scribe is drawn to the discussion is not at all surprising. Whereas Christian readers, taken aback by the bold line apocalyptic writing uses to distinguish between characters, may read deep antagonism into any intense religious exchange, the scribe is attuned to debate over scriptural interpretation as an expression of genuine and earnest piety. Rigorous study and discussion of Torah has ancient and important roots in Judaism. While the strength of one interpretation of Torah over another could certainly be cause for contention in first-century Judaism, that interpretation mattered was not.

Thus Mark casts the scribe in 12:28–34 as one who is sincerely interested in engaging Jesus in further discussion. The narrative neither attributes negative motives to the scribe nor characterizes his positive approach to Jesus as unusual. Even in a Gospel prone to depicting the scribes, Pharisees, Sadducees, and others in a decidedly negative light, there is room for what is probably more realistic variety in the response that Jesus evokes.

Homiletical Perspective

It takes great discipline to know how to get out of the way of the text. Often preachers feel the need to embroider and embellish upon Scripture when it stands beautifully on its own. The need to trust God and the text is important whenever we preach—but sometimes the wonder of the biblical text emanates so brightly that the task of preaching is to hold the text up and look at the world through the warmth of its light. Such is the case with Mark 12:28–34. "The Lord our God, the Lord is one; you shall love the Lord your God with all your heart, and with all your soul, and with all your mind, and with all your strength" and "You shall love your neighbor as yourself": this is the essential command of Scripture. As Jesus says in verse 31, "There is no other commandment greater than these."

A great temptation in proclaiming these words is to try to explain them. However, the risk of lessening the power in the ears of the listener, by becoming pedantic or by offering metaphors that fail to uphold the weight of the text, is great. Trusting that the text does not need the preacher's assistance to make an impact upon a congregation frees the preacher to illuminate the presence of such love in the world. Changing the question from "What is love of God and neighbor?" to "Where is love of God and neighbor present?" offers the preacher a chance to name

Mark 12:28–34

Theological Perspective

is that to you? For even sinners love those who love them" (Luke 6:32).

In an effort to untangle Christian love from mere sentimentality, Paul Tillich argues that love is the moving power of life. Love is the drive to unify that which has been separated, divided, or estranged. Love is not merely an abstract principle animating life devoid of emotion; rather, it encompasses all of the qualities in verse 30: heart, soul, mind, and strength. Thus the relationship between the particular found in Jewish identity and the generality of neighbor is grounded in the very nature of God, who is love, spirit, and the source of life itself (1 John 4:16; John 4:24; Eph. 4:6).

The scribe rightly discerned that this is precisely why love and justice are always intertwined. No general law can ever do justice if the demands of the concrete situation are not met. Thus love is not something that is added to justice. Rather, it is already a part of the experience of justice, and injustice is the very denial of love. The commandment to love one's enemies or those who are socially outcast is not a request for something to be done. Rather, it reveals the personal transgression already experienced, the cultural fabric that segregates, and the political power that dominates. Thus the unity of love, power, and justice constitutes God as the power of life and the structure of human relationships.[1]

There is a recurring theme in contemporary discussion of these passages that would have been both curious and scandalous to the early Christian thinkers: self-love. The concept of self-love is not explicitly stated in the Great Commandment. Oneself is not the *object* of love but is the *quality* ("as oneself") of love by which one loves the neighbor. To make oneself the object of love in the classical Christian tradition is to commit the sin of pride or rebellion against God. This is illustrated by Augustine, the early Christian bishop, in a bitter controversy with the Donatists, Christians who broke communion after surviving persecution. Their steadfastness in not giving up the Scriptures or renouncing Christ led them to hold themselves in higher esteem than other Christians. Augustine pleaded with them, as he genuinely believed their souls were in mortal danger. The danger, as Augustine saw it, was not that they believed wrongly but, rather, that they held their right belief in pride. Thus they were in jeopardy of damnation due to their rebellion against God. A

---
1. Paul Tillich, *Love, Power, and Justice* (New York: Oxford University Press, 1960), 109.

Pastoral Perspective

prior teaching on taxes underscored the primacy of loving God alone (12:13–17), then this reading extends that teaching to emphasize that love shared with God's people is love shared with God.

Jesus tells the scribe that the greatest commandments are love of God, as articulated in Deuteronomy 6:4–5, and love of neighbor, as expressed in Leviticus 19:18, and that indeed the two are one, as God is one. The scribe affirms this dynamic teaching as he repeats the Scriptures back to Jesus. Significantly, though, he adds, "This is much more important than all whole burnt offerings and sacrifices" (v. 33). It is as though this scribe has been paying attention to the whole of Mark's story and understands that Jesus' judgment on the temple establishment is about to cost Jesus his life. This noteworthy exchange reminds us that not all scribes were hostile to Jesus' teaching; moreover, it suggests that this particular scribe apprehended what Jesus' closest followers failed to grasp, or needed to deny—the true costliness of entering the kingdom.

It is, however, Jesus' praise of the scribe in verse 34 that is the clincher of the story: he is "not far from the kingdom." Jesus' assessment of the scribe's predicament is striking. Knowledge of God's love brings us close to the kingdom, but to enter the kingdom requires something more. Loving God entails loving others and upholding justice and dignity for all. One such as the scribe, who derives benefit from existing structures, may be hard pressed to accept the kingdom's call.

The scribe is not alone in this dilemma. We too know the kingdom's cost, but are often fearful of paying the price. To follow Jesus is to share his passion for living the kingdom in concrete ways that inevitably challenge the status quo. Yet it is supremely his example of self-giving love that enables us to reach out courageously in sacrificial love of neighbor. As we grow in grace, commitment, and will, we grow in our capacity to love and serve as Jesus commands, and we do so far beyond the walls of our churches. Love turns prayer into action and action into living prayer because, above all, it is love made real that reveals the kingdom.

The concept of the kingdom of God, or God's reign, permeates the Bible. The Hebrew Scriptures envision God's reign as a world sheltered in God's love, justice, and peace, which engender the wholeness of *shalom*. In the New Testament, descriptions of the reign appear some one hundred times in the Synoptic Gospels. Thus we understand the reign of God as central to Jesus' life and mission of

Exegetical Perspective

The scribe enters the conversation by posing a question of his own to Jesus. In a manner reminiscent of the wealthy man who approaches Jesus in 10:17, he asks Jesus a worthy question: "Which commandment is the first of all?" (v. 28). Jesus' apt response is rooted in Torah. First, he cites the Shema, the biblical prayer that pious Jews throughout history have recited during their morning and evening prayers (Deut. 6:4), adding the verse in Deuteronomy that follows: "'Hear, O Israel: the Lord our God, the Lord is one; you shall love the Lord your God with all your heart, and with all your soul, and with all your mind, and with all your strength'" (Mark 12:29–30; Deut. 6:4–5). Jesus' citation in Mark, aimed at capturing the full meaning of Deuteronomy 6:5, includes reference to loving God not only with all one's heart (*kardia*, "will" or "intention"), soul (*psychē*, "self"), and strength (*ischys*), but with all of one's mind or intelligence (*dianoia*), as well. As in the other Synoptic Gospels, Jesus' citation aims to convey the fullness of Deuteronomy. (Matt. 22:37 omits reference to "strength"; Luke 10:27 retains both "mind" and "strength," but in reverse order from what appears in Mark.)

The point is to love God completely and comprehensively, with all of one's being. Thus Israel is to live and breathe the directives that Moses shares with the people in Deuteronomy 6:4–5: "Keep these words that I am commanding you today in your heart. Recite them to your children and talk about them when you are at home and when you are away, when you lie down and when you rise. Bind them as a sign on your hand, fix them as an emblem on your forehead, and write them on the doorposts of your house and on your gates" (Deut. 6:6–9).

Jesus expands his answer to the scribe by citing Leviticus 19:18 as a second commandment that the question did not originally solicit: "'You shall love your neighbor as yourself.' There is no other commandment greater than these" (12:31). Jesus reminds the scribe that love of God and love of neighbor together capture the essence and express the greatest concern of God's commandments. Taken together, these texts from Deuteronomy and Leviticus underscore the interconnected relationships between self, God, and neighbor that permeate the biblical tradition. It is these tenets on which Jesus builds his gospel proclamation and that serve, in turn, as the foundation of Jesus' vision of the kingdom of God.

Just as Deuteronomy underscores how the unfettered and unyielding love of God is key to human flourishing, so Leviticus 19 recounts the origin and

Homiletical Perspective

such love in a manner that shows congregants that the love of God and neighbor is not simply a wonderful idea but a present reality practiced by the church every day.

The pericope itself demonstrates the potential power of these words to the listener. When the scribe hears Jesus' answer to the question, "Which commandment is the first of all?" he states that the love of God and neighbor is more important "than all whole burnt offerings and sacrifices," to which Jesus replies, "You are not far from the kingdom" (vv. 33–34). After this exchange, Mark states that "no one dared to ask him any question" (v. 34). The sense of awe that this scene portrays is unlikely to be shared upon the hearing of the text today, for the simple reason that, for many congregants, this image of love is foreign or merely conceptual.

An effective way to promote an atmosphere where awe may be rediscovered is to recontextualize what the congregation may think they know about this passage. Few congregants will miss the beauty of the idea of loving God with all your heart, soul, mind, and strength and your neighbor as yourself. However, many in the church have heard the words repeated over and again without applying them to life. Mark 12:28–34 provides the preacher with an opportunity to rectify this issue. The text can serve as a lantern that illuminates the presence of the love of God and neighbor in the congregation and beyond.

A preacher can never preach about the saints of his or her congregation too frequently. We often speak in the church of clergy burnout due to stress and overwork. This is a pressing issue, one of the great challenges of the twenty-first-century church. Of equal importance, though, is the number of congregants who are experiencing similar mental, physical, and spiritual exhaustion. They work, raise a family, and serve their community. They also find time to serve God's kingdom within the church and beyond, typically without expectation of reward. In any context, lifting up the woman in her congregation who quietly volunteers every Tuesday morning for years at a soup kitchen, or the young couple who works with the youth group, or the elderly gentleman who is always on call for the maintenance and repair of the church building is an important acknowledgment of service.

To claim that those actions represent obedience to the greatest commandments is to give theological weight to their actions. It is a gift from the preacher to the congregation as the simple act of affirmation is not only an encouragement but also a window into

Mark 12:28–34

Theological Perspective

positive regard for oneself was an outgrowth of the love of God as the soul is rooted in God.[2]

The question of self-love takes on additional urgency in our time, as one's identity and sense of self are considered a lifelong project, not predetermined by social caste or culture. Within the context of African American religion and culture, the problem of self-love emerges as a fruit of racism, which consistently assaults and denigrates one's sense of self. Cultural critic and social activist bell hooks sees self-love as a critical issue. In *Salvation: Black People and Love*, she notes the priority love held in the civil rights movement of the 1960s, which included the injunction to love one's enemies as well as loving oneself and one's community. Her concern is that the "abandonment of a discourse on love, of strategies to create a foundation of self-esteem and self-worth that would undergird struggles for self-determination, laid the groundwork for the undermining of all our efforts to create a society where blackness could be loved, by black folks, by everyone."[3]

The relationship hooks establishes between the particular experience of blacks and its general relevance for the society reveals the ongoing relevance of the Great Commandment for the cultural issues of our time. Moreover, the problem of self-love reveals the social and political injustices occasioned by the stigmatizing of entire groups of people. It is the "as oneself," the quality of love within the Great Commandment, that is disfigured. It is this disfigurement in the quality of love that affects our ability to love our neighbor. The radical love of God, disclosed in the gospel, supplies the critical affirmation of oneself. Thus the quality of love by which we love our neighbor is rooted in God's love for us (1 John 4:19).

CHRISTOPHE D. RINGER

Pastoral Perspective

reconciling the world to God and foundational to his ethic of neighbor love. When we practice love of neighbor by participating with God in mending a broken world, Jesus comes near.

This mended world is God's dream for creation and is nothing less than a world rightly ordered according to God's good purposes. It is a world where all are fed and housed, with access to clean water, health care, adequate education, and meaningful work; where none is excluded for reasons of race, gender, ethnicity, or sexual orientation; and where young and old alike are cherished, as God's family endeavors to sustain the precious resources of this fragile earth.

The majesty and mystery of God's reign, nearly unfathomable in scope and proportion, can seem daunting to us, even heartbreakingly out of reach. When we participate in God's dream, God's reign manifests itself through small gestures made by every global citizen. By saying bedside prayers at a hospital visit, helping someone search for a new job, equipping a young person to live out a social justice ministry, bringing dinner to a grieving friend, or serving in a literacy program, humans choose to be one with and for God in their daily lives and help alleviate suffering and redeem injustice. They manifest the kind of change that our world so desperately needs.

While much of this work happens outside the church, its seeds are sowed within it. Through education, outreach, worship, preaching, feeding, and tending to the life, growth, and health of God's wondrously diverse family, the church creates roots that grow deep and strong from generation to generation. The gospel message sustains members of the church who proclaim and practice it in community so that all can be sent into the world and do the work that enables us to recognize God's reign. Accordingly, the good news of that reign is not reliant on human progress, but on God's love, taking root deep within our souls—for it is by love made real that we know Christ and enter the kingdom.

CAROL L. WADE

---

2. Oliver O'Donovan, *The Problem of Self-Love in St. Augustine* (Eugene, OR: Wipf & Stock, 2006), 37.
3. bell hooks, *Salvation: Black People and Love* (New York: William Morrow, 2001), xxiii.

Exegetical Perspective

purpose of humankind, a theme first sounded in the biblical story of divine creation. Humankind, made in the divine image (Gen. 1:27), is to reflect God's own being. A repeated refrain that runs throughout Leviticus 19:1–18 hearkens back to Genesis: "Speak to all the congregation of the people of Israel and say to them: You shall be holy, for I the LORD your God am holy. . . . I am the LORD your God" (Lev. 19:2, 4). Israel is to embody holiness, largely defined here in terms of social justice, in order to reflect God's own holiness.

Each of the directives that follow, a majority of which illustrate in detailed fashion the love of neighbor that 19:18 elevates, culminates in the divine reminder that such holiness reflects God's own being. The refrain, "I am the LORD" or "I am the LORD your God," occurs repeatedly in Leviticus 19:10, 12, 14, 16, 18 and lends coherence and cohesion to the entire passage. Israel is to live in ways that reflect the holiness of God and express the purpose for which humankind was created in the first place.

By drawing on both Deuteronomy and Leviticus as he does here in Mark 12, Jesus points to the ways in which love of God and love of neighbor summarize human purpose and the meaning of what it is to be human. The scribe demonstrates the depth of his grasp of Torah by genuinely affirming Jesus' response (vv. 32–33). The contrast he draws between the value of keeping these scriptural commandments and the practice of offering burnt offerings and sacrifices reminds the reader of the divide between Jesus and the religious authorities in Jerusalem that frames the chapter. As Jesus' intent is to point beyond the divide to his central proclamation of the nearness of the kingdom of God (1:15), he affirms the scribe by telling him, "You are not far from the kingdom of God" (v. 34). This is Jesus' vision of the reign of God—one that affirms and recapitulates Torah teaching—that lies at the heart of his ministry and mission.

MARY F. FOSKETT

Homiletical Perspective

the manner in which a congregant's life is faithfully participating in the kingdom of God.

In an increasingly secularized world, even lifetime Christians can struggle to name the presence of God outside of the walls of the church or see their actions as those of the kingdom: the elderly man who unflaggingly cares for his dementia-ridden wife; the CEO who weighs tough decisions about layoffs against the command to love God and neighbor; the child on the bus who defends a special-needs kid who is being taunted. The language of faith can easily become isolated.

Without social reinforcement, it can be difficult to bear witness to daily acts of love and service as examples of loving God and neighbor because the meaning of language is derived from the use and context of words. If words of faith remain only within the church, then that is the only place they will be comprehensible. When a preacher reinforces the presence of the love of God and others in all areas of the listener's life in a sermon about the greatest commandments of God, the imagination of the listener may be inspired to reappraise moments of life outside the traditional activities of the church as expressions of faith and service to God through one's neighbor.

For a congregation to grow to see that their entire existence is an offering to God is a great gift a preacher can facilitate in a church. This text provides language for people to name their lives in this way. Paired with the faithful engagement of God and others, Mark 12:28–34 can serve not only as a window into an ethic of living but also as a description of the Christian life of love. This education in awe is a lens into a view of life lived in the presence of God—when we love our neighbor as self and love God with all of our being—which is valued by God more than all whole burnt offerings and sacrifices.

MATTHEW FLEMMING

Mark 12:35-37

> [35]While Jesus was teaching in the temple, he said, "How can the scribes say that the Messiah is the son of David? [36]David himself, by the Holy Spirit, declared,
>
>> 'The Lord said to my Lord,
>> "Sit at my right hand,
>> until I put your enemies under your feet."'
>
> [37]David himself calls him Lord; so how can he be his son?" And the large crowd was listening to him with delight.

Theological Perspective

All disagreements are founded on agreements. We disagree when we share enough in common to recognize in the other's statements a conclusion or perspective we do not share and think those conclusions or perspectives are worth challenging, because we might sway them or, perhaps, even be shaped by them. That is, disagreeing is what we do when we are neither talking past each other nor ignoring each other. Jesus' engagements with the scribes in Mark 12 constitute just such a disagreement.

Having spent a fair amount of time playing defense by answering their questions, Jesus goes on offense: "How can the scribes say . . . ?" (v. 35). He begins by tacitly pointing out the things that he and the scribes apparently agree about: The Hebrew Scriptures are authoritative. David wrote the Psalms. The Messiah will come from David's line. The meaning of this text from David is not self-evident: short a peculiar warp in the space-time continuum, there is no easy way to make sense of David's calling one of his descendants "lord" because he, David, initiates that regal line. "So," Jesus seems to argue, "if you agree with me about all these things, why won't you agree with the conclusion that the Messiah is going to be different than you anticipate—and that I might be he?" It is a clever bit of rhetorical jujitsu

Pastoral Perspective

This passage begins in the middle of Jesus' temple rebuke. He had already attacked the religious authorities, vandalized their sacred space, publicly refuted every challenge they made to his deeds and teaching. They clashed frequently. There was one break, however, in this series of heated debates. At one point it appeared as though Jesus and the scribes finally agreed. That was on the subject of the nature of God and the essence of God's will for human beings. They concurred: God is one, and the essence of the law is about loving (12:28–33).

Had Jesus let it go at that point, he might have ended the debate. So long as they agreed on the heart of the matter, he could have concluded that the rest was optional. Had he been willing to flex, history might have turned out differently. Jesus and the scribes might have parted as friends, or at least not enemies. Jesus might not have been condemned. There might never have developed a split between Christianity and Judaism. We might have become heirs of a great and unified religious tradition.

This is a very timely subject. In our post-9/11 world the stakes are high and the tensions grave between the three great monotheistic faiths: Christianity, Judaism, and Islam. Peacemakers hope to find a way to alleviate the friction. The most common way of attempting this is by emphasizing the

Feasting on the Gospels

Exegetical Perspective

From the beginning of Mark's Gospel, the readers know what the characters do not know: Jesus is the Son of God (Mark 1:1). When Jesus first appears in Mark, the divine voice says at his baptism, "You are my beloved Son" (1:11; cf. 9:7). From that moment on, he speaks and acts with authority.

Jesus' authority is divisive from the beginning. Crowds follow him (2:13; 3:20, 32; 5:21, 24, 27); disciples even leave their occupations behind (1:16–20; 2:14). Still, neither the crowds nor the disciples recognize his identity until Peter finally says, "You are the Christ" (8:29). Even those who accept him are often confused (4:12; 8:31–33), for he does not fit into any existing categories.

While the crowds and disciples follow him, the Jewish leaders see him as a threat. Although Jewish leaders are divided into several factions, they are united in their rejection of Jesus. Mark describes their animosity toward Jesus in five conflict stories in 2:1–3:6, which result in the rare agreement between the Pharisees and the Herodians, who from that moment conspire to destroy him (3:6). The conflict reaches a culmination in chapter 11, when Jesus enters Jerusalem like a king, with the acclaim of the crowds, and then cleanses the temple. Now the chief priests and the scribes unite to seek to destroy him (11:18). Once more the leaders of the various

Homiletical Perspective

"And the large crowd was listening to him with delight" (v. 37). How easy it is to presume that delight means acceptance, agreement, or, even more fundamentally, understanding. It may signify mere entertainment or distraction. This preacher was once greeted at the end of worship by a delighted listener (O rapture!) who had fixated on one word from the sermon he could use in his next game of Scrabble! Mark's Gospel rehearses the repertoire of the crowd's moods and responses to Jesus.

Here the reaction may be a reflection, actually, of a provocative observation by Jesus that is meant to encourage and challenge the listener to think and hope "outside the box" about how God will renew the world and fulfill covenanted promises. Jesus does not so much ask a question as propose a riddle. If David speaks of the Messiah in the present tense and as his Lord (Ps. 110:1), how can the scribes refer to him as an eschatological descendant of David? Maybe there is more at stake in the promise of a Messiah than the renewal of a golden age, the restoration of an ancient complex of political, cultic, cultural realities, which is neither to ignore nor to diminish the extremities of the present situation.

For at least two days since entering Jerusalem, Jesus has been engaged in a running encounter with the religious powers that be, sometimes in

Mark 12:35–37

Theological Perspective

Jesus employs and, to judge from verse 37, the crowd appreciates his deft verbal sparring style.

However, Jesus' disagreement with this group of scribes (Jesus did not see all the scribes as opponents, as v. 34 reveals) is about more than winning a point. Jesus is no sophist. Instead, he is shaping a larger argument about how a Messiah behaves and what it means to follow one. That argument begins chapters earlier—perhaps in 8:31—and will go on, both in word and deed, all the way to the cross. In this regard, Jesus implies that while the Messiah may not come as a military leader and will certainly come as a servant, the Messiah will, nonetheless, be a political figure of the type that will shape the lives of those who follow.

"Lord" is a political term, though not one that those of us who live in representative democracies often think about in political ways. After all, most such democracies fought revolutions in order to get out from under the authority of lords. So unless we live in parliamentary democracies that retain a House of Lords—though even there, lords are appointed or elected rather than birthed—we do not come across the term in political discourse. During Jesus' day, though, the term carried a great deal of religious and political authority (especially in a culture that did not really differentiate religious and political authority). It is no accident that Psalm 110:1, the verse that Jesus cites, is the single verse of Hebrew Scripture most frequently quoted in the New Testament. It carries the weight of both a claim about Jesus' significance and the recognition that his significance has political implications.

The peculiar political fit of the term "lord" today may be part of the reason that it has come under criticism. Feminist theologians since Sally McFague have pointed out that monarchical models of God (of which "Lord" certainly is one) have had the effect of reinforcing hierarchical understandings of the universe that were then carried over into the structures of human relationships such as those in the family. Moreover, they have advanced a vision of God as separated and distant from the world God has created.[1] This is an important concern and one worth taking note of, lest we too blithely sail into the churning waters of unacknowledged metaphors, uttering phrases like "Jesus is Lord" without an awareness of the way such language has been weaponized, as when monarchical models are used to justify oppression.

---

1. See Sally McFague, *Models of God: Theology for an Ecological, Nuclear Age* (Philadelphia: Fortress Press, 1987), esp. 63–69.

Pastoral Perspective

commonalities and downplaying the differences. The commonalities are striking. We can all agree that God is one and that God's law is about loving. If we can focus on this, the theory goes, the world will know peace. All we need to do is refrain from mentioning Jesus. Jesus Christ can graciously just be kept out of the way.

This is not very difficult for the average North American Christian to accept today. We have become accustomed to mentioning God and Jesus separately as if they are completely separate entities. We also harbor a general aversion to "Lord" language. "Lord" to us sounds anti-American. We do not have lords. "Lord" sounds medieval. "Lord" sounds chauvinistic. "Lord" sounds compulsory and controlling. We believe in equality. Until we get into trouble, we will to be masters of our own fate. While many claim Jesus as their "personal Savior," other saviors are in the realm of possibility. Most prefer to relate to Jesus as a role model and a friend. Then he is neither offensive nor threatening to those who hold different beliefs. Peace may seem attainable if we keep Jesus as an option of faith.

The temple authorities were clearly tired of arguing. After agreeing on what they perceived as the crux of the faith, they seemed willing to stop bickering. However, Jesus would not stop talking. Instead, he questioned: "How can the scribes say that the Messiah is the Son of David?" To be the Son of David implied that the Messiah was to be a royal-blooded human being, but human nonetheless. The Messiah will be sent by God—but certainly not Lord, not equal to God, and not meant to be worshiped.

In rebuttal of this view of the Messiah, Jesus quoted from a psalm, commonly assumed at that time to have been authored by David himself. The section ("The Lord said to my Lord," etc.) seems nonsensical at first hearing, or like a riddle that eludes interpreting. However, if we go to the source (Ps. 110) and read a more complete section (Ps. 109:26–111:2), we find a clear messianic prophesy. David in his distress appeals to his God for help. He affirms his belief that God will stand at the right hand of the needy and save them (Ps. 109:31). Then, as if David is privy to a heavenly conversation, he overhears God's plan for salvation. David hears the Lord God telling another who is also referred to as Lord to sit at his right hand. The Lord God then tells this mysterious someone that he will lead a mighty battle out from Zion, execute judgment among the nations, and remain as a priest forever according to the order of Melchizedek. This is the Messiah, the

Exegetical Perspective

groups—often in conflict with one another—agree on one thing: Jesus has to be stopped.

Before they conspire to arrest Jesus, they bombard him with questions in the hope that his answers will incriminate him. All of the factions come together—chief priests, elders, Pharisees, scribes, and Herodians—unlikely allies joined in their interrogation. They ask politically explosive questions ("shall we pay taxes to Caesar?") and arcane questions of law, but his answers leave them speechless; they can ask no more questions (12:34).

Jesus asks the final question. Rather than ask his antagonists, he poses the question of his audience, "How can the scribes say that the Messiah is the son of David?" (12:35). It was a peculiar question. Undoubtedly everyone agreed that the Messiah would be a descendant of David, and the scribes could have appealed to numerous passages to make that case. Many Jewish writers remembered God's words to David, "Your house and your kingdom shall be made sure forever before me; your throne shall be established forever" (2 Sam. 7:16). Apocalyptic writers promised the coming of the son of David to restore Israel. Even Jesus accepted the crowds' acclamation as he entered the city, "Blessed is the coming kingdom of our ancestor David" (11:10). Indeed, he himself was a descendant of David, as the united witness of the New Testament indicates. He could hardly disagree with the scribes in calling the Messiah the son of David.

The problem is this: Jesus does not fit the scribes' expectation for the son of David. The scribes probably shared the common understanding of the son of David as the political ruler who would liberate Israel from the oppressors. According to the *Psalms of Solomon*, the son of David would "shatter the unrighteous rulers" (*Pss. Sol.* 17:21) and "purge Jerusalem from nations that trample her" (*Pss. Sol.* 17:25).

In Mark, Jesus appeals instead to a passage spoken by David himself. The scribes will agree with him that David is the author of the Psalms, and that he spoke "in the Holy Spirit" (12:36). David himself said, "The LORD says to my lord, 'Sit at my right hand until I make your enemies your footstool'" (Ps. 110:1).

Psalm 110:1 was originally a royal psalm. Its first word, "The LORD," refers to YHWH, Israel's God. This "LORD" speaks to "my lord," the Davidic king, who will defeat all enemies. He is metaphorically "at God's right hand" as he executes God's judgments over Israel's enemies. Jesus sees a new dimension to the psalm that the scribes have not seen. The

Homiletical Perspective

the presence of the general populace. Whatever religious or theological significance may have been ascribed by anyone to his arrival in the city, it could have seemed as problematic as a hostile corporate takeover. Given his actions in cleansing the temple (11:15), it must have felt like a personal assault on its precincts. Where would this lead? What did he want? What was his agenda?

By the time we get to this passage about the mystery and identity of the son of David, the Messiah, Jesus has engaged all of the recognized members of the religious and temple system at least once. They all take turns having a go at him, but all are stymied either by his responses or by their assessment of the possible reactions of the crowd. The situation is tense.

There is a subversive playfulness to Jesus' question. The crowd hears it as a challenge to the scribes' stewardship of the Scripture. So everyone (except the scribes?) is delighted. Good one, Jesus! The delight is more of a manifestation of the distance and disregard that is felt toward the institution of the scribes. That is different from the substantive question Jesus is asking. If David, before he is the king, the dreamer of the temple, the divinely chosen champion, is no more (nor less) than a humble believer, then the hope and fate of every individual in the crowd begins with their willingness to acknowledge "my Lord." The God who calls David from tending the sheep (his circumstances), who calls him out of the household of Jesse (his family and background), who calls him in and through the conflict with the Philistines (his historical moment), is present to everyone in the fearful and hopeful identity of "the Lord." Whatever God may be preparing for just over the historical horizon cannot mitigate the hope that is incumbent in faithfulness toward the present moment. God wants and deserves disciples, not believers.

In its delight with Jesus' remark about the scribes, the crowd believes that Jesus has drawn near to it. That is very different from what it will take for the individuals of this aggregate to draw near to him, the way the individual scribe drew near to him in verse 28 and then in verse 34. The scribe was moving beyond being a student of the Scripture, the law, to being one who submitted to being studied by the Scripture. The scribe knew that all the temple apparatus could be abused, becoming a way of evading life before God and avoiding the requirements and rewards of love (v. 33). Whatever else a crowd is, it is a place to hide. For this crowd, the first way that it hides from the double form of love is an easy

Mark 12:35–37

Theological Perspective

Reinforced hierarchies, though, are not the only dangers of Lord language. In the absence of any political context in which lords are an experienced reality—but aware that in other times or in other places, lords have ruled—the term may carry for many of us the qualities of the archaic, the passé, or the nostalgic. To judge from the American fascination with English royalty and their marriages, monarchies may not represent expressions of power to be feared so much as sources of romantic entertainment to be consumed. Where feminist criticisms of Lord language revolve around concerns about the unjust concentration and use of power, this concern revolves around the degree to which a primary metaphor for God and God's relationship to us has been drained of any significant political significance.

The utterance "Jesus is my personal Lord and Savior" becomes not so much a confession that shapes a kind of public political engagement, but a password that lets its users recognize each other and revel in their in-crowd distinctiveness. It is subjective, private, and possessive. Rather than weaponizing the metaphor, such an approach enfeebles it by draining it of its scandalous and, to judge from the larger Markan context, counterculturel political implications.[2]

Perhaps rather than weaponizing or enfeebling the metaphor, we might reclaim its power by exploring its original context. How was Jesus using the term? How do Jesus' words and actions reveal what his lordship is like? What might it mean to treat our confessions about Jesus' lordship as freighted with political implications about how we are to behave when we live in Western liberal democracies? Might claiming that Jesus is Lord actually help us resist both hierarchies (by not allowing anyone or anything else to usurp that role) and privatization (by remembering that what we say and how we live implicate each other)?

We may disagree about the answers to these questions, but exploring them may lead us in provocative, fertile, and sanctifying new directions of thought and action. Disagreements, after all, are founded on agreements—and the argument over how a Messiah behaves and what it means to follow one is as pertinent as it was in Jesus' day.

MARK DOUGLAS

Pastoral Perspective

one to come as David's Son, who exists eternally. This Messiah who is David's Son, fully human, is also Lord, *Adonai*, fully God.

The early apostles certainly understood this to be true. In Peter's Pentecost sermon the apostle affirms King David's faith in the Messiah's resurrection. As Peter declared, David understood that the Messiah was both his God and his descendant (Acts 2:29–36). The author of Hebrews also attests the Messiah's divine preexistence, earthly incarnation, and victorious ascension by using the very same passage (Heb. 1:5–13).

What can all this mean to the average Christian? It means Christ is not expendable. It means the essence of God necessarily includes him. Jesus is *Adonai*, Lord. As Lord, we owe him full obedience. We are commanded to love the Lord with all our heart, all our understanding, all our strength. As Lord he rules. We follow him. He holds the power of life and death. He owns the estate; we are simply caretakers of his land. We do a very poor job without his leadership. This Lord is also the Messiah, the Son of David, fully human, who knows all our needs. As Messiah he comes to us in our crisis. He successfully fights the battle over evil on our behalf. He rescues us from sin. He is savior, model, and friend.

Had Jesus bent a little, compromised, allowed the authorities to settle with him their differences, his love and our love for the one true God would be fraudulent. An imposter would have compromised to hold on to his share of the religious market. Jesus did not need to worry about that. If Jesus is the only Christ of God, no politically correct language or polite hush can ever change that fact. Christ is who he is. He does not need our protection. He is not harmed by neglect or offense. He has nothing to lose. We have everything to gain as he takes his rightful place at the Father's right hand. We owe him our full allegiance.

DEBORAH RAHN CLEMENS

---

2. See Mark Douglas, *Confessing Christ in the 21st Century* (Lanham, MD: Rowman & Littlefield, 2005), esp. chap. 3.

Exegetical Perspective

Messiah is not only son, but Lord. That is, David expected more than a descendant—someone who would be not an earthly ruler, but one who is confessed as Lord. The expectation of the scribes is too ordinary. Perhaps their inadequate view explains why they have rejected Jesus all along.

The passage anticipates the final verdict against Jesus. At his trial, the high priest asks, "Are you the Messiah, the Son of the Blessed One?" (14:61). Jesus answers, "I am, and 'you will see the Son of Man seated at the right hand of the Power,' and 'coming with the clouds of heaven'" (14:62). According to Mark's Gospel, that answer was the decisive evidence leading to Jesus' conviction and execution. Only with the resurrection do the participants in the story understand that the Son of God is not the Messiah of popular expectation.

Psalm 110 is the most frequently cited passage in the New Testament.[1] The early Christians appealed to it to express their most basic confession: Jesus Christ is Lord (cf. Phil. 2:11). The confession that "Jesus is Lord" was a challenge to those who looked for an ordinary man to rule Jerusalem and even to have imperial power. As Jesus' response to the high priest indicates, to say that Jesus is Lord is to say that he is the exalted one who will come again. To say that he is Lord is to claim that he is not one among others but the one before whom "every knee should bend" (Phil. 2:10). The large crowd is "listening to him with delight" (12:37), but the leaders plan to destroy him.

Jesus has been a divisive figure from the beginning. Mark has shown all along that the crowds follow Jesus, while others reject him. This scene reflects not only one episode in the ministry, but the experience of Mark's church as well. Many accepted the claim that "Jesus is Lord," and others greeted it with hostility. This Christian confession transformed the lives of some, and evoked hostility among others. No one was neutral to the claim that God has made him "Lord and Christ" (Acts 2:36).

JAMES W. THOMPSON

Homiletical Perspective

derision of and distance from the figure of the scribe and what he represents.

Even though Jesus' questioning remark is about the scribes, it is actually his way of searching for the individual in the crowd. He is also calling forth his reader, his listener, from the multitude. The crowd is as much a system as is the temple with its routine and machinery. One does not belong to the crowd; rather, one becomes submerged in it. At the end of this Holy Week the crowd will have become the mob. There is a world of difference between a crowd and a community, especially the "beloved community." Even the disciples are part of the crowd.

Many congregations in the process of seeking new pastoral leadership develop a profile that enumerates the values, skills, and commitments desired of candidates for placement. One such profile listed preaching as a high priority, stipulating that it be spiritually inspiring and intellectually challenging. However, the quotation from the parish survey used to sum up the desired capacity insisted that preaching from the Bible leave politics and any social agenda out of it.

Thus even a congregation can be the crowd, a place to hide; even a Bible study can be a place to hide from the individuality that says with David, "my Lord." Yet the congregation can also be a place to grapple with the hard questions Jesus raises. It ends up being someone within the system, a scribe, who rehearses the truth that is larger than the system, the routine, the massive machinery of the temple life. It is the truth that takes you "outside the box": the love of God and neighbor is "more important than all whole burnt offerings and sacrifices" (12:33). He has come near to Jesus in more ways than one.

DWIGHT M. LUNDGREN

---

1. See David M. Hay, *Glory at the Right Hand: Psalm 110 in Early Christianity*, SBLMS 18 (Nashville: Abingdon Press, 1973).

Mark 12:38-40

³⁸As he taught, he said, "Beware of the scribes, who like to walk around in long robes, and to be greeted with respect in the marketplaces, ³⁹and to have the best seats in the synagogues and places of honor at banquets! ⁴⁰They devour widows' houses and for the sake of appearance say long prayers. They will receive the greater condemnation."

Theological Perspective

Though regularly divided into separate pericopes, Mark 12:38–40 and Mark 12:41–44 need to be read against each other. In the former, Jesus condemns religious leaders for taking everything from widows; in the latter, he seems to commend a widow for giving everything to religious leaders! Not only do they mirror each other—though, as mirrors do, by reversing the objects they reflect—but attention to their mirroring can lead to new insights that grow out of both passages. In this essay, I will focus more on Mark 12:38–40, but inflections from this essay will show up in the succeeding essay. Vice versa, in the following essay, I will focus more on Mark 12:41–44, but thoughts from this essay will show up there.

It is important to begin by recognizing that standard English translations insert grammatical markings into the text that are not present in the Greek, and that these markings have the effect of significantly changing the meaning of the passage. Thus the NRSV has Jesus say, "Beware of the scribes, who like to walk around in long robes, and to be greeted with respect in marketplaces, and to have the best seats in the synagogues and places of honor at banquets!" (vv. 38–39). The effect of all those commas is to claim that scribes, as a category of persons, are preening and self-absorbed leaders who use their positions of prominence for their own ends. Other

Pastoral Perspective

Jesus' words come alive for our time. "Beware of politicians who like to walk around in fancy clothes and to be greeted with respect in the marketplaces and to receive the best seats in the assemblies and places of honor at the banquets. They devour widows' houses and for the sake of appearances make far too many speeches. They will be held accountable in the end" (vv. 38–40, my wording). Granted, I changed a few words. Jesus was talking about scribes. I inserted the word "politicians." The truth of the matter is that in his time the scribes were the politicians.

They were the people with the power and clout who often negotiated their way into office through playing dirty tricks. They came up through the ranks by making lots of promises to the constituents and loyally holding party affiliations. They were theoretically the advocates for the people. They were supposed to be the trusted leaders, worthy representatives, and hardworking civil servants. Theoretically they worked for the masses. In reality, however, they sponged off the poor, buying luxuries with the ancient equivalent of middle-class taxes. Today they would be chauffeured around in limousines, wearing designer suits, and living in mansions. While devouring widows' homes, Jesus said, they are worrying about keeping up appearances.

Exegetical Perspective

Because of the emphasis on the written word in the Judaism of Jesus' time, the scribes played an indispensable role. Ezra, the paradigmatic scribe, was "skilled in the law of Moses" (Ezra 7:6). The scribes studied the law and taught "the statutes and ordinances in Israel" (Ezra 7:10). In the second century before Christ, Sirach lauded the scribe as the one who sought divine guidance in Scripture and sought out the wisdom from the past (Sir. 39:1).

In the New Testament, however, the scribes receive bad press, for these teachers of the law are among Jesus' primary antagonists. They criticize Jesus for breaking with the scribal interpretation of the law, for forgiving a paralyzed man's sins (2:6) and eating with sinners (2:16). They accuse him of collusion with demonic power, even as he exorcises demons (3:22). Finally, they join with the chief priests to destroy Jesus (11:18) and collude with others in challenging Jesus with provocative questions (11:27).

After portraying the scribes' constant antagonism to Jesus throughout the narrative, Mark comes to the end of his story with Jesus' challenge to them. After criticizing the scribes' interpretation of Scripture (12:35–37), he launches into warnings about their conduct (12:38–40). In his admonition to "beware," which is reminiscent of an earlier warning about the

Homiletical Perspective

Clearly people were paying attention to the scribes, listening to their teachings of the law and traditions. Jesus' warning in this passage is not about the content of the teaching but, rather, about some scribes' behavior in society. Whatever truth there may be in their teaching is compromised by practices that subvert the power and authenticity of the teaching as divinely authored.

There is an implied, more comprehensive warning here. This is not about the character of any particular scribe (or Pharisee or preacher or minister, etc.). It is about the temptations inherent under our humanity in being a steward of the spiritual life or the offices and practices of a particular spiritual tradition. These temptations are accompanied by dangers to the soul at least as catastrophic as a blatant disregard for the recognized expressions of God's will.

The passage suggests three types of temptations. First, there is the premature and misleading evaluation of one's calling and character in the mirror of other peoples' reactions. Second, there is the acceptance, if not solicitation and expectation, of preferments that serve as expressions of gratitude and status. Third, there is the vicious and voracious behavior of using one's calling to prey upon others for all kinds of material gain, taking advantage of someone's vulnerability, trust, and neediness. In

Mark 12:38–40

Theological Perspective

translations treat the scribes (or "teachers of the law" [NIV]) in the same way.

The better reading, then, is "Beware of the scribes who like to walk around in long robes and to be greeted with respect in the marketplaces and to have the best seats in the synagogues and places of honor at banquets!" Beware of the scribes *who behave in this way*, not *beware of the scribes,* who behave in this way.

These commas in most translations are problematic in at least three ways. Exegetically, they undermine Jesus' commendation of a scribe—one who would fall into the very category of persons that the commas suggest—a short four verses earlier: "When Jesus saw that he answered wisely, he said to him, 'You are not far from the kingdom of God'" (12:34). In a set of passages so critical of hypocrisy, it makes little sense for Jesus to speak out of both sides of his mouth. Morally, they sustain and perpetuate the kind of anti-Semitism that has so stained the church's history of engagements with Judaism, by treating a category of people as worthy of condemnation—suggesting that all scribes act the same, are driven by the same motives, and share the same fate. In a set of passages so concerned with justice, it makes little sense for Jesus to speak in stereotypes.

Theologically, by blurring the behavior of some individuals with an entire group of people, the commas undermine one of the basic points that Mark is making in the second half of his Gospel: that followers of Jesus will behave in ways that follow from his behavior. In a Gospel in which questions about how the Messiah behaves and how that Messiah's followers behave are so tightly related—and related so tightly in order to press his audience to ask of themselves, "How are we behaving?"—such blurring not only makes little sense; it also justifies dangerous (and ultimately condemned) comfort to us, Mark's readers. We need to think about the length of our own robes, not laugh behind our sleeves at the hard fate that awaits "the scribes."

The traditional translations with commas actually become a provocative instance of the very sin that the passage would warn us against: offering false and flowery words that presuppose our own righteousness while at the same time perpetrating injustice. (Ah, the pleasures of all the dependent clauses shaped by those lovely commas! Perhaps they are the secular equivalent of the long prayers of verse 40.) The commas give us readers an "out"—a way of avoiding asking hard questions of ourselves—rather than exploring our own complicities in injustice

Pastoral Perspective

This is an easy text for contemporary discussion. The issues are thoroughly current. The poor are getting poorer, and the rich are filthy rich. Far too many politicians are in bed with billionaires and profitable corporations. We have an inane desire to admire them, to give them our respect, to push through the crowds simply to get to shake their hands, so that we may become wealthy and privileged just like them. Pastors must beware. We should not want to encourage false admiration of the rich and famous. This is a human problem. This was a problem identified by Jesus. He knew that the glamour and glitz associated with privilege attract people like a magnet. We must hold on to a certain amount of skepticism when showing loyalty to any earthly government. The prosperity promises made to us almost always get actualized at someone else's expense. The polished speeches and expensive dress are often but illusions. Behind the facade are flawed and finite human beings. Beware the politicians.

The vast majority of citizens have no concept about the disparity between the average Joe and the upper 1 percent. The challenges of day-to-day living cannot be compared. For many, the struggle to keep food on the table, to pay bills and taxes, to keep homes from foreclosure, and to have decent health insurance is constant. The rich are unaffected. The burden of government cutbacks falls hardest on the poor. It affects mostly the people who are hidden and voiceless. The burden settles on widows, as observed by Jesus, who work all their lives for next to nothing and get punished in old age for not having pension plans. When they lose their homes because they cannot pay their taxes, who speaks for them? The burden rests on impoverished inner-city children. They have nowhere to go to play in safe environments. Their parents or guardians are strapped and working minimal jobs at best. Early intervention and after-school enrichment programs are being slashed. This is to prevent new taxes on the rich. Who speaks for those children? The burden rests on minorities, the handicapped, the homeless, the addicts, and the working poor. Who speaks for them?

The answer is Jesus does; and it should also be those of us who follow him. He said, beware of the privileged.

It is tempting for the masses to enjoy vilifying those who have the advantages. It is not hard to drum up hatred and resentment anytime anyone has more than we do and we take notice. In the name of the poor, Christian communities may be called to rally around issues of social justice. The danger is in

Exegetical Perspective

"yeast of the Pharisees" (8:15), Jesus calls attention to the conduct that serves as a negative example for his followers. He does not object to Jewish practices, but to the self-centered distortions that can accompany religious practices. The scribes like to wear long, flowing robes that announce their high status. The same word (*stolē*) was used for the vestments of the priest and for the "white robe" of the angel at the tomb (16:5). They love the greetings in the marketplace; to be greeted first was a sign of their importance. They love the seats of honor in the synagogue reserved for those of special rank. In a world where mealtime could be an occasion for seats arranged according to rank, they insisted on the best places.

Jesus' description of the scribes may be an occasion for addressing the abuses that were temptations among his own followers. He has already pointed to negative models of conduct in the stories of James and John, who ask to sit at his right and left hand in his kingdom (10:37). This desire for power angers the other disciples (10:41) and undermines the harmony of the community. Jesus' reply to the disciples anticipates his warning about the scribes. He says, "You know that among the Gentiles those whom they recognize as their rulers lord it over them, and their great ones are tyrants over them." He adds, "But it is not so among you; but whoever wishes to become great among you must be your servant, and whoever wishes to be first among you must be slave of all" (10:42–44).

As is true everywhere, all of the models of leadership in the culture emphasize the desire for power and prestige. The responsibilities of leadership carry the temptation to exercise power (see 1 Pet. 5:1–5). Paul consistently encourages his own communities to "do nothing from selfish ambition" (Phil. 2:3), because he knows of the persistent temptation within all communities for ambition to destroy cohesion. Jesus envisions a countercultural community that rejects the desire for prestige that was common both among the scribes and among the Gentiles. As he makes his way to the cross, he provides the model for the conduct that is suitable for his own community, describing himself as the one who came to serve and give his life for others (10:45).

Jesus' critique of the scribes culminates in his pointing to the very problem that desire for prestige engenders: despite outer signs of piety, they violate the call to give of oneself for others, especially those in need, which is one of the most basic statutes of the Torah. They pray long prayers, and still they "eat up widows' houses." The Old Testament portrays

Homiletical Perspective

the current discourse on the ethics of professional behavior, Jesus is talking about boundary crossings and boundary violations. They are dangers to the soul (of the scribes); they are temptations to the crowd to dismiss the task of the scribe's calling. They compromise everyone's relation to God's will.

When I was in the parish ministry, which included four parishes over a span of thirty-five years, I received the usual invitations to pray at public events (I gradually gave those up) and to sit at the head table of meal events, public and parochial. I even once received tickets from the mayor's office to a concert he was not going to attend. I was always wary of such interactions for the way they enacted a network of social performance and roles that was secondary, if not tertiary, to the pastoral call. However, they were easy to enjoy because of the acceptance and recognition they offered and the social importance they conferred.

How easy also it is for the community to feel and believe that because we have invited the minister to the wedding reception . . . we have invited the pastor to bless the football game . . . we have invited the clergy to sit at the head table when the senator is addressing a luncheon of the local business association, therefore, of course religious faith is valued within our community. The challenge on both sides is not to confuse opportunities and relationships with rewards or payoffs.

It is appropriate to remember that this passage occurs after Jesus' Palm Sunday entry into Jerusalem and is an element in the accelerating movement toward Good Friday. The robe will be stripped off Jesus, replaced by a wreath of thorns; the respect of the crowd will be replaced by the spit in the face of the soldiers; and the prominence of a place in the marketplace of society will be replaced by Pilate's courtroom and the literal lifting up of crucifixion.

If there are religious or spiritual leaders out there who are no more than wolves, preying financially on the vulnerability and credulity of believers, there are also lay folk who use the appearance of their involvement in the life and community of faith to augment their prospects for economic and social success. Over the years, in different parishes, I had people join and then leave because their anticipation of meeting the right people and making the right contacts was disappointed. They moved on to congregations that improved their contact and prospect lists. So it fundamentally raises the question of how any of us uses our spiritual profession and participation in a community of faith for more mundane, self-serving ends.

Mark 12:38–40

Theological Perspective

and moral failure. They invite us to evade charges of hypocrisy, rather than wonder whether we are behaving in hypocritical ways. While there are many kinds of hypocrisy (including those more innocuous instances of trying but failing to live up to the patterns of behavior we think should be normative), surely the most insidious and destructive is the kind that uses the speech and structures of establishmentarian religion (or traditional translations) to justify ignoring the aspirations and actions of radical faith.

In the middle of all this, biblical exegetes have helped us see how these scribes—undoubtedly superior interpreters of the very law that condemns mistreating widows, given their very proximity to the temple in Jerusalem—could "devour" the houses of widows. Since widows of the time were more likely to lack recourse to the courts and, in many instances, to the marketplace (due to the absence of a male relative to speak for or support them), they were comparatively easy to victimize. For example, high-interest loans to cover the costs of living and lawsuits over debts incurred by their deceased spouses might lead to foreclosures. As leading legal minds in the area, such exploitative scribes might not only be the first to find out about such matters, but might persuade those involved in such foreclosures to include the temple in their settlement, thereby providing a veneer of religious respectability to a corrupt practice.

We are, perhaps, a long way from a time when some religious leaders could so obviously and directly benefit from a housing system that favored the powerful. However, in a time in which the dramatic growth of subprime loans led to an explosion of toxic assets, all bundled and hidden from investors by leading banks and mortgage companies, which eventually set off a global economic crisis, our hands might not be quite so clean as we wish. To the degree that we participate in modern global economic systems (and make no mistake: we all participate), we too are implicated in a system that devours the houses of the vulnerable.

What are we to do? Jesus' words in verses 41–44 are an instructive place to start.

MARK DOUGLAS

Pastoral Perspective

justifying hatred in the name of Jesus, while possibly masking our unhappiness at not being similarly rich. Pastors must help congregants remember that wealth is relative. We too are often privileged. Sometimes we get so used to our privileges that (like the super-rich) we feel entitled to them. It is just normal. We do not notice what we have. We rarely turn down honors when they are given. If offered a high-priced seat, we take it. If able to buy an expensive dress, we buy and wear it. If someone will take the time to listen to us go on about our personal virtues, we will speak to them, feigning humility. We do not mind that others take notice of our church attendance and Christian service. However, we do not take notice of the poor that we pass while driving in to worship. Beware of being religious.

Most of the abuses and injustices done to the poor and the voiceless are not done with overt evil intention. They are not personal. No one expressly wants to hurt little old ladies and innocent children. No politician would speak out against them. Likewise, the scribes were not hateful. They were not criminally bad. They warmly greeted widows and showed pastoral concern when they saw them. That is why Jesus needed to draw the people's attention to them. Their abuse was not only personal. The abuse was corporate. They were part of a system that was being perpetuated from generation to generation. They did not create it. The system ran almost on its own. It would not be stopped unless there was a corporate, systemic, and institutional desire to stop it.

We too are part of a great system that perpetuates our advantages over the vast majority of the world's citizens. For the most part, we do not even notice. Our cars, our homes, our clothes, the price of our gas, our medical benefits are ours at someone else's expense. There are people working in sweatshops. There are people risking their lives laboring in unsafe conditions. There are children working. There are citizens dying in wars fought over gasoline. This is all so that we can hold on to our privileges. Beware, Jesus says. Who will receive the greater condemnation?

DEBORAH RAHN CLEMENS

Exegetical Perspective

God as the special helper of widows, along with strangers, orphans, and the poor (Deut. 10:18). Job includes his treatment of widows as an example of his righteousness (Job 29:13). Special provisions were made to ensure that widows could glean in the fields (Deut. 24:19–22; Ruth 2:21–23). The early church gave special attention to provide for widows (Acts 6:1–7; 1 Tim. 5:3–16).

Perhaps Mark is suggesting that widows have placed their trust in their religious leaders to protect their belongings. Religious leaders sometimes acted as guardians for widows' property, but demanded so much in return that the widows were impoverished. The signs of piety among the scribes have led the widows to trust them with their few possessions. This combination of piety with exploitation of the poor is especially egregious. Whereas the Torah gave special attention to the care for poor widows, the scribes robbed them. Mark uses the graphic term "devour" (*katesthiein*), which was commonly used for the ravenous eating by animals. He undoubtedly knew the temptations in his own community for leaders to misuse their positions of trust and the management of the sacrificial gifts of others for personal gain. As a countercultural community, the church is called to provide for the most vulnerable in society.

In their greed, the scribes are the negative foil for all that Jesus calls his disciples to be. He calls the rich young man to sell his goods, give to the poor, and to follow him (10:21). When the young man will not pay the price, Peter says, "We have left everything and followed you" (10:28).

The concluding words of the story indicate the gravity of the offense of exploiting piety for personal gain: "They will receive the greater condemnation" (v. 40). The epistle of James contains a similar comment in cautioning teachers that they will be judged "with greater strictness" (Jas. 3:1). Religious leaders receive the greater condemnation when (a) they know the law and (b) they abuse their responsibility.

JAMES W. THOMPSON

Homiletical Perspective

Given religious television programming these days, it is easy to read this passage and immediately think of the religious personalities that pray loudly, if not in a prolonged manner, for the financial well-being of their listeners and then harangue the listeners to fork over their "seed faith" contribution to their ministry, which it turns out is the required key to activate God's attention and mercy. Talk about devouring widows' houses. Obviously, there are multitudes who are suffering the actuality and anxiety of want, and even outright impoverishment. Those who offer the almost immediate fix of offering a miraculous prayer are either blind to or careless of the conditions of life that cause and perpetuate that impoverishment. For the whole community of faith, prayer is intercession for and solidarity with the needs of those around us. It is a counterfeit practice if it does not emulate the voice that spoke to Moses from the burning bush: "I have observed the misery of my people. . . . I have heard their cry. . . . I know their sufferings. . . . I have come down" (Exod. 3:7–8).

For Jesus, the behaviors of the scribes that drew his attention were object lessons to call attention to dangers that individuals in the crowd also faced. The goal is not to discredit the scribes' calling but rather to ask: "How does each of us compromise the stewardship of God's will, both its demand and its promise?"

Jesus is seeking in the crowd the individual who—like the scribe earlier in the chapter—comes to the place where they confess that the daily drama of our life before and with God is described by the call of the double command of love (12:32–34). We all have ways of qualifying, compromising, even using it for secondary gain. Institutions, rituals, programs, and practices serve our awareness and attention to it, but they are not the drama itself. Faithful preaching always strives to call us, preacher and listener alike, to the moment Jesus notes by saying: "You are not far from the kingdom of God" (12:34).

DWIGHT M. LUNDGREN

Mark 12:41–44

⁴¹He sat down opposite the treasury, and watched the crowd putting money into the treasury. Many rich people put in large sums. ⁴²A poor widow came and put in two small copper coins, which are worth a penny. ⁴³Then he called his disciples and said to them, "Truly I tell you, this poor widow has put in more than all those who are contributing to the treasury. ⁴⁴For all of them have contributed out of their abundance; but she out of her poverty has put in everything she had, all she had to live on."

Theological Perspective

Mark 12:38–40 ends with Jesus' denunciation of those scribes who "devour widows' houses" while saying long prayers; Mark 12:41–44 begins at the scene of the crime: the treasury of the temple. At the start, Jesus sits down "opposite the treasury." One wonders at his choice of location. Not only does this give him an excellent vantage point from which to watch the goings-on across the way; it also marks him as someone who is not participating in the systems of money collection he is observing.

Having watched rich person after rich person contribute large sums of money to the temple coffers, he notices a poor widow add her own two cents. Jesus, in his distinctive way, treats the event as the occasion for an object lesson for his disciples: "This poor widow has put in more than all those who are contributing to the treasury. For all of them have contributed out of their abundance; but she out of her poverty has put in everything she had, all she had to live on" (vv. 43b–44).

Usually the object lesson is taken to mean something like, "See how she gave everything she had? You should do the same." However, a number of clues in the text suggest that things are not quite so simple. First, Jesus has just finished criticizing those who, under the guise of religious significance, take from widows. So why would he then commend a

Pastoral Perspective

Why are most churches struggling financially? There are two places we can place the blame. The first is on Jesus. He himself is responsible for at least one-half of church budgetary aches and pains. Jesus did not take an economics course in college. Even if he had, it would not have made any difference. None of his principles would have changed. His standards for stewardship would have stayed exactly the same. This passage proves Jesus' unorthodox ideas about economics.

The Jewish temple had no problem getting funding, even though the institution was massive, the property expansive, and the accoutrements lavish. There were solid economic reasons for this. It was a monopoly. Jewish law allowed only one temple, one place to make sacrifices to the Lord, one place to house the Holy of Holies. Therefore there was no other place for people to run off to if things did not go their way. Everybody who was anybody in Jewish society had to pay their temple tax, an obligatory levy placed on every Jewish family. The tax was a mandatory assessment to be paid to the temple coffers each year. It was due, like it or not, use the temple services or not, worship or stay away.

Then there were also the sales. Lining the entire complex were hundreds of little booths of vendors selling animals to be sacrificed, officially authorized

Exegetical Perspective

The cleansing of the temple, according to Mark, sets in motion the final conflict that leads to the crucifixion of Jesus (11:18). Mark then records an extended day of teaching in the temple, presumably in the outer court. After answering the provocative questions of his adversaries (11:27–33; 12:13–34), Jesus offers his final instruction to the crowds about the nature of discipleship. As the last scene in Jesus' public ministry (before the speech in chap. 13 and the passion narrative in chaps. 14–15), it makes a special impression. First, Jesus offers the negative example of religious leaders who exploit the widows (12:38–40), the most vulnerable people in the society. Then, in the final scene (12:41–44), he offers the positive example of a widow, whose conduct is a model for others. While widows were the vulnerable ones in that society, they were not only the objects of charity. This episode is distinctive in portraying the widow as an example to emulate.

Jesus apparently sits in the outer court that was accessible to women as he watches the people put money (literally copper) into the treasury. According to the Mishnah (*Shek.* 6:5), there were thirteen such receptacles in the form of trumpets. As the crowd puts money into the treasury, Jesus focuses on the sharp contrast (a) between the many rich people and the one widow and (b) between the large sums given

Homiletical Perspective

There is a significant slice of American church life where the faithful are strenuously exhorted to contribute financially as a way of impelling God to rescue them from a variety of impoverishments that afflict their lives. (We shall not name names!) Although I have never heard it so used, it would not be surprising if this passage were misused to support those exhortations. An even greater number of preachers and teachers have turned to this passage during the annual stewardship period in the congregation to build commitment to the fundraising goals. Jesus was not the last person, clergy or lay, to look out at fellow congregants and wonder about the meaning and extent of their financial participation.

It would seem useful if not important to pause and enlarge attention to the entire moment and scene. This scene ends the chapter, and this chapter ends the narrative of the Gospel before the events of the passion proper commence in chapter 14. Separating the accounts of Jesus' ministry and his passion is chapter 13, the little apocalypse, which begins with the prediction and warning of the destruction of the temple. The temple! In the passage about the poor widow, both her offering and the offerings of the prosperous go for the upkeep of the temple and the maintenance of its services. These offerings and the services they make possible cannot guarantee the

Mark 12:41–44

Theological Perspective

widow for giving everything? Were this the only clue that things are more complicated, we might chalk the difference up to one of agency: it is wrong to take something from another, but it is not wrong to give something to another. Yet this is not the only clue.

The second clue is that the widow puts in two small copper coins. These may indeed be everything she has, but that does not necessarily mean she is behaving in an especially sacrificial way. Two such small coins would not buy her anything else, either. Giving two pennies when one has only two pennies simply does not make that much difference, as there is nothing two pennies will buy anyway. Perhaps the widow is trying to buy a bit of divine (or at least religious) favor by giving her last coins—as if such favor is fungible. Perhaps, but that would hardly justify commendation from Jesus, who in Mark shows no real support for such negotiations.

The third clue is that immediately following this passage, Jesus foretells the destruction of the temple (13:2). It makes little sense to give anything—let alone everything—to something that is on the verge of destruction anyway. Might the point of the example of the widow be that we should give heedless of the consequences of our giving? While such a moral might make sense in another context, it hardly fits here: the rich people are also giving without giving heed to the consequences of their giving. The temple is coming down, no matter who gives, no matter how much they give.

So what are we to do with these clues and their implications? Some feminist theologians have challenged the claim that the widow is being treated as someone to emulate, and with good reason. Since Valerie Saiving's landmark essay, "The Human Situation: A Feminine View,"[1] such theologians have taught us about the damaging consequences that come with asking those who give most—usually women—to give more. Jesus never actually commends the woman or her behavior in the text; he merely comments on it. Of course, other feminist theologians have pointed out that by giving everything she had, the widow foreshadows Jesus, who gives everything he has on the cross in chapter 15. There is something provocative and noteworthy in having a woman—and a widow, at that—prefigure Jesus' actions. In any case, it is at the very least worth noting that Jesus attends to—and points us toward—the widow in the midst of all the others who are

---

1. Valerie Saiving (Goldstein), "The Human Situation: A Feminine View," *The Journal of Religion* 40 (April 1960): 100–112.

Pastoral Perspective

grains for offerings, souvenirs to be taken home after a pilgrimage, and the infamous money exchange. The commission generated enormous profits. There were also the fees that the temple administrators took for acting as trustees over widows' and orphans' estates. There were also the nepotism, graft, and politicking by which the chief priests, administrators, and scribes acquired their unchallenged authority. The system profited nicely through these power plays. If we would follow this New Testament example and run our churches like the temple business, no congregation would have another deficit.

As he proved when he turned over the money changers' tables, Jesus was unquestionably bad news for the temple's economic well-being. He is also bad news for any churches that depend on market principles to stay solvent today. Market principles tell us, give people what they want, and the money will keep flowing. We could set the price for our goods and services and minister on a pay-as-you-go basis. We could charge $25 per person per worship service, $75 for counseling, $10 per Sunday school lesson, and $5 for every social and youth event. People would be getting a bargain. It would work—except for Jesus.

We could hire a collection agency to go after those who are delinquent. We could start a club for the biggest contributors, put their pictures in the newspaper, publicize the amount of their checks, and smother them with special pastoral attention so that they keep on giving. It would work—except for Jesus.

We could hold raffles, play bingo, give door prizes. We could hoard large sums, out of fear that tomorrow might be a rainy day. We could set a policy that we will not give any money away until we have paid our own expenses. It would work—except for Jesus.

Our worries would be over. We could send the stewardship committee into retirement. Except Jesus keeps managing to get in the way. "My house shall be called house of prayer for all the nations, but you have made it a den of robbers," he raged (11:17). Maybe, if Jesus had taken an economics course or two, his opinion about money would have changed. However, it was not out of ignorance that he spoke. It was out of love for God and neighbor. It was because of his faith.

Jesus got so angry at the abuses because he so desperately wanted his Father's house to be the place where all people are treated equally regardless of their wealth or their ability to pay. There, indigents get handouts and inactives are ministered to with no judgment and no penalty. There, persons who

Exegetical Perspective

by the rich and the two copper coins given by the widow. Jesus does not criticize the gifts of the rich, which were probably tithes given in accordance with the law. Inasmuch as the rich were known for giving ostentatiously in some instances (Matt. 6:2), the comparison with the widow may suggest that this is the case here.

The focus is not, however, on the many rich people, but on the one poor widow. Her attire would have identified her as a widow. In contrast to the large sums given by the rich, she gives two *lepta* (NRSV "copper coins"). Since Mark is writing for a distant audience, he converts the sum into Roman currency; two *lepta* are the equivalent of one *kodrantēs* (NRSV "a penny," v. 42). The *lepton* is the smallest Greek (and Jewish), coin, while the *kodrantēs* is the smallest Roman coin. The *kodrantēs* was a small fraction of a denarius, the pay for a day's work by a laborer. Thus Mark has called attention to the vast difference in the amounts given by the rich people and the widow.

This remarkable scene is the occasion for a lesson on discipleship, for Jesus calls his disciples (v. 43), as he has earlier when he wanted to make an important pronouncement (6:7; 8:1, 34; 10:42). Despite the vast difference between the sums given, Jesus makes the paradoxical statement: "This poor widow has put in more than all those who are contributing to the treasury" (v. 43). She is neither the object of charity nor a victim, but the model of discipleship. She stands in contrast both to the rich and the scribes who "devour widows' houses" (12:40).

The rich are reminiscent of another man in Mark's Gospel who has great possessions (10:22). He has kept all of the commandments (10:20), probably including the giving of alms to the poor. Indeed, he probably would have felt comfortable putting large sums into the treasury. Like the rich people who gave to the treasury, he undoubtedly is willing to give from his surplus, but not to risk the loss of his possessions.

While the widow does not give a large sum, she gives all that she has. Indeed, she could have dropped in one *lepton* rather than two, but she "gave her whole life" (NRSV "all she had to live on," v. 44). Those who give from their surplus do not deeply affect their existence. In giving from her need, she gives her life.

Appearing at the end of Mark's story, this poor widow has a special significance. First, she epitomizes what Jesus has taught about discipleship. At the beginning of the story (1:16–20), four disciples

Homiletical Perspective

permanence of the temple as an institution. The relativity of the institution has already been confessed earlier in chapter 12 by the scribe who affirms that the double commandment to love God and neighbor is more important than "offerings and sacrifices" (12:33).

As Jesus sits here within the precincts of the temple, on the threshold of the unfolding passion events, his attention to this unknown, impoverished widow gives insight into how he might have been thinking about faith, hope, and love—about the surrender of one's life out of both its abundance and poverty. In the mind of the writer of the Gospel, Jesus already knows that the days of the temple are numbered. The monetary value of the gifts of the rich and the poor is practically meaningless. It is even more meaningless if the act of giving serves as either a distraction from, or a denial of the living into, the double love commandment. It certainly says something about the tenor of the moment that one of the proposed elements in the indictment against Jesus is his alleged claim to sovereignty over the existence of the temple (14:58).

One possible way to think with Jesus about the widow's offering is to look at Psalm 4, specifically verses 6–7. After referring to those who implore God to bless their lives (materially?), the writer says in verse 7: "You have put gladness in my heart more than when their grain and wine abound." Jesus points out the woman's poverty. But her offering is an expression not of her neediness, as great as that might be, but rather of her gratitude and trust.

Her life, its gratitude and trust, is the real treasury! Out of that treasury comes a life of abundance that cannot be measured by a balance sheet. We could certainly wish we knew more about her—and about the unknown woman who anoints Jesus in the home of Simon the leper (14:3) and becomes through her extravagance a witness to the gospel. The actions of both of these women—one acting unaware of Jesus, the other directly enacting a comment on his fate—suggest that their actions are reflections of the holy, abundant generosity that will be the drama of the cross.

The drama of the cross highlights the mystery of this gracious abundance as it enlarges the mystery of love. As Paul reminds us in 1 Corinthians 13:1–3, love can be either present or absent from gifts, acts, powers, or commitments. Love is an act of loyalty to the gratitude and trust that is humbly amazed at the gift of existence and treasures it with and for others. Paul actually makes the same point in 2 Corinthians

Mark 12:41–44

Theological Perspective

coming and going from the temple treasury. Now that he has pointed her out to us, we need to ask, what is the sign that she is for us?

Perhaps, following from his comments in 12:38–40, Jesus might be signaling something about the nature of integrity in the face of hypocrisy. Giving from their abundance, the wealthy may or may not be acting out of integrity: perhaps their concern really is for the welfare of the temple and the faith; perhaps, though, it is to reinforce their images as important and generous people. Any number of conclusions—some laudatory, some less so—can be drawn about the motives of the wealthy. Behavior without clear costs or consequences is hard to evaluate. As a result, the integrity of the person performing those actions is all but impossible to ascertain.

The widow, though, gives out of her poverty. While her actions too are open to a range of interpretations, that range is significantly more constrained. Maybe she is committed to the good of the temple and the faith; but if so, that commitment almost certainly includes the recognition that she relies on the temple and the faith for her own welfare. Maybe she is trying to buy divine relief. In either case, her actions and her commitment to pursuing them reveal something basic about her: that she is in need. While not wanting to romanticize poverty, it is still the case that poverty—and, for that matter, any significant weakness, whether economic, political, physical, or spiritual—is clarifying. Whatever else is driving the widow, it is not hypocrisy.

The widow is not necessarily a model to be emulated. Lacking the ability to display even the illusion of self-sufficiency, the widow stands in contrast to those who hide behind their wealth (v. 41) or their long robes (v. 38). Thus she is a signal to the rest of us about what an integrated (or at least a non-hypocritical) life will look like: it will mean going all in—and, for that matter, doing so because we cannot hide our need.

MARK DOUGLAS

Pastoral Perspective

are sick, hungry, and poor become the church's first priority; bills are paid out of sheer gratitude; money is given simply so that God's name continues to be praised. There, we learn that living hand to mouth might be spiritually healthier, as we plead for our ration of bread each and every day. Follow Jesus' advice, and there is a good chance we could end up impoverished. The truth is, however, that Jesus' economic principles are not the reason churches struggle financially. The real reason is our own perspective on giving.

Jesus walked over and situated himself opposite the temple treasury. He watched people come, making contributions freely and faithfully. They were not buying anything there. They were not paying the tax and were not out to bribe or influence anybody. These were anonymous gifts. Lots of people stopped by, including plenty of people who were wealthy. Jesus just kept on watching. Then a widow moved in. From her hand she dropped two copper coins worth a penny. "There," Jesus exclaimed. "See that? That is the kind of contribution I have been waiting for. That is my idea of giving." One penny would not eliminate the deficit, pay a salary, buy fuel oil, or even help the needy. Her offering made no difference to anybody. The temple would function just as well without it. No one would miss her sacrifice. No one would care if she had kept the money, except for Jesus.

He celebrated it because she modeled true charity and real stewardship. She gave without even thinking of herself, how she would get fed, where she would sleep that night, what she would keep in reserve to bargain with, how she would be buried. She gave because she loved God more than stuff. She believed in compassion and helping. That for her was enough. If we could give as this widow gave, because we had a heart for sharing, we would meet the church budget year after year. There would be abundant surplus—and widows like her would never again be homeless.

DEBORAH RAHN CLEMENS

Exegetical Perspective

leave their nets—their means of livelihood—to follow Jesus. In the middle of the story, Jesus says to his disciples, "If any want to become my followers, let them deny themselves and take up their cross and follow me" (8:34). The widow stands in sharp contrast to the rich man who has great wealth (10:22) and the scribes who devour widows' houses (12:40). She is also a reminder that those who follow Jesus are not people of position and rank, but the poor, the lame, and the deaf. Even a blind beggar (10:46–52) follows him to Jerusalem, where he will die. The widow is a reminder that Jesus brings good news for the poor.

Second, the story of this widow anticipates another account of an unnamed woman in Mark's Gospel. After the discourse in Mark 13, Mark describes another woman who will not be forgotten. The woman comes with an alabaster jar of costly ointment of nard, breaks it, and pours the ointment on the head of Jesus (14:3–9). Those who criticize her wasteful act say that the ointment could have been sold for three hundred denarii—an astronomical sum in comparison with the widow's two *lepta*. This sum was almost the equivalent of a day laborer's pay for a full year. Despite the difference between the amounts given, the two unnamed women have something in common. While the widow gives all that she has to live on, the woman with the jar of ointment does "what she could" (14:8). Both women are reckless in giving what they have, placing their trust in God.

Finally, of course, the widow's story also anticipates the path of Jesus himself, for in the days ahead he will give his life for the sake of others. In anticipation of his act of self-sacrifice, he teaches his disciples not to limit their commitment by keeping the law's demands, but to give their whole being to God.

JAMES W. THOMPSON

Homiletical Perspective

using explicit economic imagery: "For you know the generous act of our Lord Jesus Christ, that though he was rich, yet for your sakes he became poor, so that by his poverty you might become rich" (2 Cor. 8:9).

We know this sometimes poignantly when we hear stories of the self-sacrifice that saves lives. One or two weeks before September 11, 2001, I was standing across the street from the World Trade Center in New York. As I waited for the stoplight to change, I looked up and mumbled to myself: "These are incredible achievements; they'll never come down." I was echoing the words of the disciples after they left the temple where they had observed this widow's offering. What continue to move me are the stories of the fire, police, and service personnel, on duty and otherwise, who rushed up into the chaos knowing that despite their training and skills, this might be the end for them.

Day in and day out, our lives are enhanced and undergirded by myriads of small, less dramatic acts of self-giving. They are sacrifices only to the observer, not to the agent of the act. The double commandment of love, which is the coordinate for proximity to the kingdom of God, may sound too formal (or religious!). Another way to imagine it is as the call to create in our engagements, exchanges, and initiatives "neighborhoods of grace," the stewardship of the divine extravagance of our lives.

Our rituals of worship are meant to remind us of this and to draw us more deeply into its reality. They do so authentically only when we honor each person's contribution as issuing from the same divine treasury.

DWIGHT M. LUNDGREN

Mark 13:1–8

¹As he came out of the temple, one of his disciples said to him, "Look, Teacher, what large stones and what large buildings!" ²Then Jesus asked him, "Do you see these great buildings? Not one stone will be left here upon another; all will be thrown down."

³When he was sitting on the Mount of Olives opposite the temple, Peter, James, John, and Andrew asked him privately, ⁴"Tell us, when will this be, and what will be the sign that all these things are about to be accomplished?" ⁵Then Jesus began to say to them, "Beware that no one leads you astray. ⁶Many will come in my name and say, 'I am he!' and they will lead many astray. ⁷When you hear of wars and rumors of wars, do not be alarmed; this must take place, but the end is still to come. ⁸For nation will rise against nation, and kingdom against kingdom; there will be earthquakes in various places; there will be famines. This is but the beginning of the birth pangs."

Theological Perspective

"Things are not always what they seem," writes Phaedrus, the early-first-century fabulist. "First appearances deceive many: few minds understand what skill has hidden in an inmost corner."[1]

Jesus warns his disciples that things are not how they may appear when it comes to the coming of the kingdom of God. That which seems most stable and reliable will not necessarily endure: the large stones and buildings that comprise the temple and its courts present themselves as monumental, for example, but will one day be destroyed. That which will seem most surely to frame the final chapter of human history will actually be only an introduction to what is to come. There will be false prophets, "wars and rumors of wars" (v. 7), political upheavals, earthquakes, and famines, but these things will not, in fact, mean the reign of God has yet arrived. Jesus warns the disciples they should guard against being distracted by how things seem. While many will be led astray (v. 6) because they are swayed by false prophets and deceptive first appearances, the disciples are to remain faithful to Christ and the work of proclaiming the good news.

Most scholars agree Mark was written soon after the destruction of the temple in 70 CE. The

1. From Book IV, Fable 2 of Phaedrus's *Fables*, in *The Comedies of Terence and the Fables of Phaedrus*, trans. Christopher Smart (London: George Bell & Sons, 1887), 410.

Pastoral Perspective

Chapter 13 in the Gospel of Mark has often been referred to as the little apocalypse, because of all the frightening specters and dire language. Oft-quoted texts like "wars and rumors of wars," of earthquakes and famines, have been used by Christian alarmists throughout the history of the church. This is ironic, not only because Jesus says, "Do not be alarmed" (v. 7), but because his striking imagery is intended to do just the opposite. Its purpose is to divert attention from the spectacular to the morning-by-morning faithfulness of a people caught between the ages. This is the private instruction of Jesus for his beloved followers, giving them the perspective they will need to sustain them as they engage in discipleship after he is gone. This is pedagogy for a transitional time.

In this way, Jesus' conversation with his disciples can be seen as Mark's version of the famous farewell discourses in the Gospel of John. However, while John emphasizes love and unity, here Jesus is concerned with another poignant, all-too-relevant pastoral question: knowing what lies ahead for his followers, how should they witness to hope when surrounded by fear, violence, demagoguery, and (potentially most damaging) indifference?

The question is masterfully set against the backdrop of the disciples' visit to the temple, where they say with mouths agape, "Look, Teacher, what

Exegetical Perspective

Chapter 13 is distinct from the rest of Mark's Gospel in style, content, and form. It forms a bookend to Jesus' revelatory teaching in chapter 4, but unlike that chapter it focuses on a single topic, the events leading to the coming of the Son of Man. Mark pauses the narration of Jesus' life to focus on events surrounding the Jewish war with Rome (66–70 CE) and their connection to final judgment. Mark's goal is to warn readers about false interpretations (vv. 5–6, 7–8, 21–23) and to encourage endurance through present traumas (vv. 9–23) and future ordeals (vv. 24–27).

The discourse is composed of sayings of Jesus, early Christian prophecies, elaborations on biblical texts, and Jewish and Christian apocalyptic materials, which Mark has distinctively edited.[1] Because it contains apocalyptic motifs, this chapter is often referred to as the Markan apocalypse, although it lacks many features of that literary genre. In a sense the chapter is an antiapocalypse. Rather than revealing future events, it insists that these cannot be

---

1. The chapter may be based on a pre-Markan written or oral collection of these materials, but the redaction of the source makes its exact contours hard to discern. Full discussions of the sources, genre, and history of the chapter's construction can be found in Adela Yarbro Collins, "The Apocalyptic Rhetoric of Mark 13 in Historical Context," *Biblical Research* 41 (1996): 5–36; and George Beasley-Murray, *Jesus and the Last Days: The Interpretation of the Olivet Discourse* (Peabody, MA: Hendrickson, 1993).

Homiletical Perspective

You do not have to go to the boardwalk in Atlantic City to find a fortune-teller these days. A growing number of people have opened up shop in big cities and in small towns to read palms or tarot cards. Many people read their daily horoscope at the kitchen table while sipping their first cup of morning coffee. Daytime television commercials encourage viewers to pick up the phone and call a "psychic friend." You can buy an app for your Blackberry or iPad that will provide you with your very own personal numerology reading.

We human beings seem to be hardwired to want to know the future. What will tomorrow bring? Thoughts of the future can unnerve us. Often just below the surface of musing about the future is fear. The uncertainty of the future can leave us feeling nervous and out of control. Will I be able to afford to retire? Will I come down with an incurable disease that causes me great suffering? Will my children grow up to be happy and healthy adults? Will our country be prey to terrorists? Will global warming cause irreversible damage to our world?

Those experiencing good times in the present may fear loss in the future. Those at the other end of the spectrum, the ones facing difficulties now, may fear that the future will simply bring more of the same, with no relief in sight. Is there any hope for a preacher to proclaim?

Mark 13:1–8

Theological Perspective

first scene of chapter 13 (vv. 1–2) is meant to guide troubled readers in making sense of this event by positing that Jesus has prophesied and interpreted it. Theologians have long suggested Mark is reorienting the early Christian community, decentering it in relation to the temple rituals and recentering it in relation to Jesus Christ. Textual evidence includes Jesus' claim of authority to clear the money changers out of the temple (11:27–33) and his critique of the hypocrisy of the scribes who "say long prayers," in contrast to the authenticity of the widow who gives everything she has (12:38–44). While on the one hand Jesus himself teaches in the temple, on the other he represents some temple teachers as precursors to the false prophets who are to come, warning the disciples to beware of them. The risk of being led astray from participation in the emerging kingdom of God is not only a future hazard, Jesus suggests, but also a present one (vv. 5–6).

The second scene of the passage (vv. 3–8) shifts the location of Jesus and the disciples' continued exchange from the temple courtyard to the Mount of Olives. While before they were close up and marveling at the stature of the buildings, now the disciples are sitting across the way from the temple, privy to a panoramic view. In the narration of the story, they are literally able to see, in better perspective, what deceived them when they were only at arm's length.

One interesting detail, from a theological perspective, is that the Mount of Olives is a place where the bodies of Jewish people have been buried for more than three thousand years. Looking across at the temple site from the vantage point of the cemetery where victims of the persecution and destruction of 70 CE were almost surely lain suggests that all God's people—those who have died, as well as those who are still alive—will be included in God's coming reign. Connections can readily be made here to the ancient confession of "the communion of saints," in the Apostles' Creed and to our own experience of the church healed and made whole through the work of the Spirit.

This two-part conversation between Jesus and the disciples is driven by concrete historical claims, yet it refuses to settle itself into any singular space or period of time. There is a sense in which it nudges the watchful, wary disciple of Christ into a maddening position: we are to be continuously reading the signs of God's working, but we are at the same time not to get overly exercised about them. Our goal is not to be experts at determining when the end of the world will come, but to be faithful disciples of Christ

Pastoral Perspective

large stones and what large buildings!" (v. 1). For these Galilean fishermen, the daunting power of the temple, the Holy City, and the Roman forces may have seemed irresistible. Jesus, sensing a pastoral moment, reacts in ways later seen in the apostle Paul to the Corinthians, when he declares that "the present form of this world is passing away" (1 Cor. 7:31). In other words, the world we experience in times of hardship is not an expression of the way God intends for the world to be. The powers of the present age are transient. Because of this reality, the witness of the church should not be understood as primarily fear based. It is countercultural, transcendent, impatient, hopeful, and justice seeking. It is focused not on separating insiders and outsiders, but on breaking down the walls that divide.

In sharing this, Mark is not denying that crises exist, or that there are times when present suffering calls for urgent action, or even that some of Jesus' dire prophecies may have already happened at the time of his writing. Instead, he clearly presents such cataclysms as the "birth pangs" (v. 8) of God's transformation of the world. Because of this, any voices that seek aggrandizement by ascribing disaster experienced by others to God's judgment are inherently suspect (vv. 6–7). It is not clear whether Mark wrote this with the knowledge that the temple would be destroyed; regardless, the message would be the same: earthly disasters are not necessarily an indication that judgment is near.

Then as now, there may be those who claim calamities as divine sanction for judgments against others (e.g., religious leaders who claimed Hurricane Katrina and other disasters were evidence of divine wrath). Jesus here denies that God is necessarily the agent of coming destruction. In light of what must inevitably arise as his followers seek to be faithful in an often-hostile world, Jesus recognizes that they could easily lapse into a fear of great catastrophe that would render them incapable of doing what is necessary to witness to God's coming kingdom. More often than not, it is not God but humanity who has been the cause of its own threat of extinction, whether by nuclear holocaust, environmental degradation, or one of the myriad other ways we are capable of bringing God's good creation to the brink of disaster.

Jesus is aware of the human tendency to lock in on more powerful forces and to become cowering and paralyzed by fear due to threats, violence, war, the tenuous standing of the church, the finitude of our existence, or lured by all those enticing voices

Exegetical Perspective

known (vv. 32–33) and warns against the deceptions of those eager to provide them (vv. 5–6, 22–23).

Moreover, Mark insists that faithful anticipation of the end is not a matter of calculating when the Son of Man will appear (vv. 7, 8, 14, 20–22, 29), but of witnessing to the gospel (v. 10) and vigilant waiting (vv. 34–35). Jesus' instructions oscillate between warning against false interpreters and expectations (vv. 5–6) and informing the disciples about the real indicators of the end (vv. 7–8). Natural catastrophes and human conflicts, Jesus insists, are not reliable signs of the end times, only their precursors. Only cosmic phenomena, beyond human control, point to God's imminent entrance into history. The discourse shifts attention from speculative chronology to matters of vigilance and discernment (vv. 5, 9, 23, 33), heightening the audience's eschatological expectations.

The section has four parts: the setting and pronouncement (vv. 1–2), the disciples' questions, "when will this be, and what will be the sign that all these things are about to be accomplished?" (v. 4), Jesus' warning against impostors (vv. 5–6), and his warning against misinterpreting the events of the war with Rome (vv. 7–8). The private audience (Peter, James, John, and Andrew; cf. 1:16–20 and 9:2), Jesus sitting as an authoritative teacher (v. 3; cf. 4:1), and the Mount of Olives setting underscore the discourse's importance, not only for the disciples but also for Mark's audience (cf. v. 14 and v. 37, "What I say to you, I say to all").

Verses 1–2 close Jesus' prophetic actions about the temple and introduce his explanations about its destruction (13:5–32). Prompted by an anonymous disciple's exclamations about the temple structure, Jesus prophesies its utter ruin (cf. Mic. 3:12; Mark 14:57–58; 15:29). The emphatic negative *ou mē* (v. 2) emphasizes the obliteration: "Not one stone will be left here upon another." The phrase "stone upon stone" mimics, yet inverts the promissory language of Haggai 2:15 (LXX). At the narrative level, this concludes Jesus' criticisms of the temple activities (11:12–12:44). At a symbolic level, it anticipates the divine presence's departure from the temple, echoing oracles found in Ezekiel 11:22–23 (cf. Mark 15:38).

The setting shifts in verses 3–4 to the Mount of Olives, directly across from the temple. Mark's language recalls Zechariah 14:4–5, which connects the Mount with an assault on Israel. The disciples now ask when the destruction ("these things" [*tauta*], v. 4) will occur and what sign will indicate that the events before the return of the Lord ("all these things" [*tauta panta*]) are about to be accomplished

Homiletical Perspective

At first glance, in this text from Mark, the Gospel writer seems to answer that question with a resounding no. Will the future be bright? Not a chance. Terrible things are on the way.

Jesus and his disciples are coming out of the temple in Jerusalem when one of the disciples comments on the beauty of those sacred buildings. Immediately Jesus bursts the disciple's aesthetic bubble and tells of a future when "not one stone will be left here upon another; all will be thrown down" (v. 2). This special and beautiful place, the very dwelling place of God, will be destroyed. The disciples are eager to know more about this ominous future. When will this take place? What will be a sign for us? They may even hope that this would take place as part of a military coup led by Jesus himself.

Jesus does not give them a direct answer to their when and what questions. Instead, he offers them what they need: sage advice about how to think about the present and live into the future. The first piece of advice is to be wise and to use caution when interpreting events. Jesus warns that many will come in his name and lead people astray. Some individuals will misuse their power and influence in ways that prey upon the fears of the masses and cause them great harm. Followers of Jesus Christ cannot afford to be naive or gullible.

The second part of Jesus' advice is for his followers to pay attention to the crises of their times. Political battles will be waged, and the weapons of warfare will lead to bloodshed. Calamities of nature will be experienced as famine sweeps across the land and as the earth trembles and quakes. A significant question to ponder within the Christian community may be, "Where is God in all of this?" In 1 Kings 19 the prophet Elijah wondered if God was at work in the power of nature, but the readers are told that the Lord was not in the wind, earthquake, and fire. Jesus' disciples tried to make sense of the headline news of their own day when the tower of Siloam fell and killed eighteen people. Jesus taught that those who died were no worse offenders than all the others living in Jerusalem (Luke 13:4).

What then shall we say about the tragedies of our day? People want desperately to make sense of natural disasters. Many a survivor of a tornado or hurricane looks into the television camera and asserts that they were saved by God. When a young person dies in an automobile accident, some well-meaning person is likely to say that they hope Sally's death will teach other youth to wear their seatbelts and drive the speed limit. People of faith often search

Mark 13:1–8

Theological Perspective

in the here and now, even as we keep an eye on what is going on around us.

It is significant, along these lines, that Jesus eventually declares Peter, James, John, and Andrew's question, "when will this be?" unanswerable, even by him (v. 4, then v. 32). The great danger to Christ's disciples is not that we will underread the signs of the times, but that we will overread or overreact to them and be "led astray." Certainly overreading has been a problem in Christendom from Jesus' day until the present. One example of a Christian who intentionally avoided such temptation is John Calvin, who opted not to write a commentary trying to elucidate the book of Revelation, because he did not want to waste energy that could be devoted to proclaiming the majesty of God on idle speculation.

Finally, Mark here presents Jesus as wanting his disciples to participate in the reign of God as it is being realized in time and space, without imagining it could be in any way governed or confined by time and space. To ignore the birth pangs altogether is, on the one hand, to resist participation in the kingdom. It is to give up the hope that what God promises is not ethereal, but real and concrete. To think one has pinpointed the coming of God's reign is, on the other hand, also to have missed it.

This is because the purpose of the watching, the waiting, and the observing is to experience and be changed by something altogether different from what we have known. It is to be transformed by something beyond ourselves that we can neither understand nor manage. Jesus desires for us ever to be open to God's kingdom breaking into our own historical reality, challenging our understandings of what will endure and what will not. Jesus desires us to expand our perception of how and when God's Spirit is at work in bringing the good news to all nations (13:10), even in the face of sufferings and devastations, even from the perspective of the cemetery.

CYNTHIA L. RIGBY

Pastoral Perspective

promising the false security of other idols, quick fixes, and scapegoats. To respond to this inevitable reaction to powerful forces, Jesus provides three important spiritual disciplines for navigating transitional times.

First, believers must engage in discernment in the face of threats from both without and within—not simply overt threats, but more subtle ones such as allowing the false security of a cultural, consumer-driven theology to creep into the community. In today's culture, this can often take shape in the assumption that a church that is growing, vibrant, and happy is "filled with the Spirit," as though these are visible indications of being spiritually dressed for success, or that a church in decline has necessarily lost the moorings of the more steadfast faithfulness of bygone years.

Second, believers must be patient. Birthing a new heaven and new earth takes time. There are many evils to eradicate, many hopes to realize. These are the birth pangs of a new age. God's transformation and the witness of believers must compete with many forces, biases, demons, and appetites. Working out God's promises occurs during the life of the world as well as in and for the world. Being patient requires cognizance of the truth that, while the powers of this world are imposing, they are not indomitable.

Trusting that God is transforming the world, and that believers are called to participate in God's saving work, is fundamental to Mark's conception of the Christian life. In that task, believers are sustained by the third important reminder: for the Christian, there is always hope. There will be times when believers feel beleaguered and vulnerable. Growth, change, and the coming of new life are a painful process, but in suffering there are always hope and the promise of a new day. Hope sustains us through the birth pangs of change and the necessary struggle that leads to growth. It is Mark's prescription for the church in transition: discernment, patience, and hope, a provisional sign to stand in the midst of tension in a passing world.

JOHN E. COLE

Exegetical Perspective

by God (*synteleisthai* is a divine passive). Jesus' initial response clarifies that the temple's destruction and the end are connected but not identical. The end will come, but it is not yet (v. 8).

Jesus warns that many (*polloi*) false interpreters will lead many (*polloi*) disciples and others astray (vv. 5–6). The phrases "those who will come in my name" and who say "I am" (v. 6) are ambiguous. Commentators offer four possible historical references: (1) followers of Jesus who invoke his authority (cf. 9:37–39); (2) false Christian prophets who claim to speak for the Lord; (3) Jewish messianic pretenders (13:21–23; cf. Matt. 24:5); and (4) Christians who present themselves as the returning Jesus. None of these historical explanations is entirely satisfactory.[2] Mark might have intended any of these possibilities, but given the apocalyptic tenor of the discourse, specificity may not have been his aim. The formulaic language enabled him to warn against any false interpreters and to remind the readers that their future appearance was to be expected (cf. 2 Thess. 2:1–12).

Verses 7–8 turn from false prophets to miscomprehensions about the war and rumors. Jesus warns the disciples not to be disturbed (*throeisthe*) by reports and rumors of war for two reasons. First, since wars are a tragic recurrence in human history, such reports are commonplace. Second, the wars and reports are not incidental, but part of God's plan (cf. the divine passive *dei genesthai*, "must take place," v. 7). Jesus' language recalls Old Testament prophecies of wars (Jer. 4:16; Dan. 9:26) and nations made to fight one another (Isa. 19:2). In verse 8 the conflicts are connected to the terrors of earthquakes and famine (cf. Isa. 13:13; 14:30).

The pericope concludes by repeating the theme of the discourse. These horrors are not the end, only its harbinger, "the beginning of the birth pangs" (cf. 4 Ezra 13:31–32).

STEVEN J. KRAFTCHICK

Homiletical Perspective

desperately for the fingerprints of God in the midst of the rubble of life's tragedies. Others may not look for God's involvement at all. Instead, they interpret human and natural disasters as simply a matter of chance. Perhaps there is some cosmic force at work.

In Christian terms, the larger question is about how we think about the providence of God when the world is turned upside down. Mark's Gospel does not explain how God is involved in these unsettling experiences, but it asserts that God is not far removed from them. Christians living on this side of the resurrection can recall Jesus' promise to his disciples that he would not leave them stranded after his ascension into heaven. God the Holy Spirit is present with us always, even—or perhaps most importantly—in times of suffering. The Holy Spirit is with us offering consolation and courage, hope and wholeness.

Mark urges the readers of his Gospel to interpret wars, rumors of wars, and natural disasters as the contractions that lead to a new birth. Just what is God birthing? God is bringing about a new reality, a new creation in Jesus Christ. The Son of Man will come again in glory to heal the nations and transform the world. Temples built with human hands will be replaced by the presence of God in Jesus Christ.

The faithful presence of the Holy Spirit today and the promise of God's restoration of creation in the future enable us to join our voices to sing,

> Jesus, the name that charms our fears,
> That bids our sorrows cease;
> 'Tis music in the sinner's ears,
> 'Tis life, and health, and peace.[1]

NANCY MIKOSKI

---

[2]. The options are discussed in Eugene Boring, *Mark: A Commentary* (Louisville, KY: Westminster John Knox Press, 2006), 362–63; Adela Y. Collins, *Mark: A Commentary* (Minneapolis: Fortress Press, 2007), 603–5; Morna Hooker, *The Gospel according to Saint Mark* (Peabody, MA: Hendrickson, 1991), 306–9; and Joel Marcus, *Mark 8–16* (New Haven, CT: Yale University Press, 2009), 875.

[1]. Charles Wesley, "O for a Thousand Tongues to Sing," 1738.

Mark 13:9–13

⁹"As for yourselves, beware; for they will hand you over to councils; and you will be beaten in synagogues; and you will stand before governors and kings because of me, as a testimony to them. ¹⁰And the good news must first be proclaimed to all nations. ¹¹When they bring you to trial and hand you over, do not worry beforehand about what you are to say; but say whatever is given you at that time, for it is not you who speak, but the Holy Spirit. ¹²Brother will betray brother to death, and a father his child, and children will rise against parents and have them put to death; ¹³and you will be hated by all because of my name. But the one who endures to the end will be saved."

Theological Perspective

Persecution for religious beliefs is all too prevalent in our twenty-first-century world. Estimates for the number of countries in which persecution is a reality range from about twelve to fifty. One reliable study suggests religious persecution actually increased from 2006 to 2009 in about a third of the world's countries.

For Christians who have experienced or who live with clear threat of persecution, Jesus' words here offer some consolation. Persecution is not a faith-testing challenge, but a sign that the faithful have indeed not been led astray (v. 5). Believers are not expected to outwit their persecutors, devoting precious life energy to the advance preparation of trial-trumping comebacks. They can trust, rather, that God will be with them, that the Spirit will give them the right words to say when they need to say them. They can stick to the work of proclaiming the coming of God's kingdom, knowing their efforts will not be in vain. The good news will, it is certain, eventually reach all nations!

Christians living in countries that uphold freedom of religion will likely have greater difficulty resonating with this text. Many Christians in the world today have never been beaten or dragged before councils, or experienced life-threatening betrayals as people of faith. For this they should be thankful, although

Pastoral Perspective

After beginning chapter 13 with instruction for spiritual discernment in the midst of transition, Jesus now turns to the more specific forms of persecution and resulting problems his disciples will face. In these verses, as in the first eight verses, the reader should not be distracted by the apocalyptic language. The language is prophetic, but its purpose is pastoral. Ralph Martin has referred to the "trifocal lens" of this chapter, which begins with contemporary issues (vv. 1–13) before moving on to the near future (vv. 14–23) and, finally, the end of the age (vv. 24–37).[1] Here Jesus prepares the disciples for the daunting challenge that awaits them as they proclaim the gospel. Their mission will provoke opposition—even hatred—despite their best intentions.

It is hardly a great prophetic leap for Jesus to raise the specter of persecution. Jesus' knowledge of what happened to John the Baptist and what was, by this time in the Gospel, certain to happen to himself is sufficient to predict that his followers will also undergo persecution. The issue in this passage is not the possibility of persecution, but what form it will take and how to respond when trouble comes. Suffering is a common theme in Mark, but here it is depicted in terms of conflict with religious and civil

---

1. Ralph Martin, *Mark* (Atlanta: John Knox Press, 1981), 76.

Exegetical Perspective

In this section Mark's goal to connect the temple's destruction with events of the end time while maintaining a distinction between them, and thus to exhort his readers to vigilance, continues. The repetition of "beware" (*blepete*, 13:5, 9, 33) signals the shift to a new aspect of the tribulations: personal sufferings brought on by religious prosecutions and family betrayals. The disciples must heed "yourselves." The use of the personal and reflexive pronouns (*hymeis*, *heautous*) directs the disciples (both those of the narrative and of Mark's audience) to appraise their capacity and willingness to experience personal sufferings as part of the end-time woes (v. 8). Just as they must guard against deception by false prophets (vv. 5–6) or misdirection by rumors (v. 7), they should not misunderstand the trials and family tribulations they are experiencing or permit them to overwhelm their faith. Jesus now calls for perseverance in their personal misfortunes through admonition (v. 9a), predictions (vv. 9b, 11, 12, 13b), a mandate (v. 10), and a promise (v. 13a).[1]

Mark's audience is depicted as participating in Jewish thought and belief, and so under the authority of local Jewish councils (*synedria*) and

---
1. Adela Yarbro Collins, *Mark: A Commentary* (Minneapolis: Fortress Press, 2007), 606–7.

Homiletical Perspective

Most Christians in North America today will never have the kind of experience described in this passage from the book of Mark, and thankfully so. Most commentators agree that these words in chapter 13 are words of instruction and encouragement for first-century Christians who were experiencing persecution for being followers of Jesus Christ. Some of our earliest forebears in faith paid a great price for their commitment to Jesus. They found themselves in trouble with civil authorities and alienated and despised within religious circles. Some were abused and some were martyred for being Christian.

This passage presumes two things: that Christians will live in such a way that others will take notice, and that when challenged, they will be able to proclaim the good news. These two presumptions, and the words of instruction and encouragement that accompany them, open the door for the preacher who stands before a contemporary North American congregation with little experience of persecution for their faith.

"If you were on trial for being a Christian, would there be enough evidence to convict?" This was the question posed to a few hundred teens attending a Christian summer camp. The room was silent, except for the whir of a large overhead fan. The speaker let that question hang in the air for what felt like an

Mark 13:9–13

Theological Perspective

Christians who stand at a distance from the threat of persecution commonly err toward assuming such experiences will never come to them, or are even irrelevant to their lives. In contrast to this assumption, Jesus speaks of persecution as something all faithful disciples will inevitably face. How should we who have never been persecuted interpret this?

Some Christians read Jesus' statement and search for the ways they are currently being persecuted or that persecution seems to be coming, just around the corner. They study the news, examine culture, and argue vehemently that Christians are being marginalized, even if not explicitly attacked. Dispensationalist Christians are among those who analyze the signs of the times, preparing themselves to suffer for the faith as the end of the age draws closer.

Christians who do not expect ever to be persecuted sometimes worry they lack commitment to the faith. What sense can be made, they wonder, of Jesus' statement that "the one who endures to the end will be saved" (v. 13)? Does this mean endurance in the face of persecution is necessary to right relationship with God? If so, does this mean those who live with no threat of persecution should seek to be persecuted, or at least to live lives of faith that could draw persecution?

Christian theologians vary considerably both in how they understand persecution and in whether they think a believing Christian should aspire to it. John Calvin (sixteenth century) advises that persecution should be avoided, if possible, or else faithfully endured. Simone Weil (twentieth century) argues that persecution is easier to bear than affliction, given that the persecuted understand they are suffering for the sake of the gospel, while the afflicted, faced with the absence of God, experience a sense of purposelessness and hopelessness. James Cone (twenty-first century) holds that there is nothing at all redemptive about persecution and that Jesus' persecution on the cross calls out and condemns the United States' disgraceful use of the lynching tree.

Whether we understand persecution as something to be avoided, a spiritual good to be embraced, or an atrocity that must be actively condemned, one thing is clear both in this text and in our world: persecution is a reality with which believers must contend. Perhaps enduring to the end, for those Christians who engage in faith practices in places that protect religious freedom, involves deepening an awareness of how and where Christians are currently being persecuted, what they have to teach those of us who have not been persecuted, and how we can

Pastoral Perspective

authorities (vv. 9–11) and disruption within families (v. 12).

While much of the pressure from these anticipated threats comes from outside forces, the tenor in this section tends toward internal conflict brought on by these outside tensions. There is a sense that the greater threat to the continuing witness of the church will involve anxiety that arises from persecution and other threats to the health of the body. This anxiety, in turn, will give rise to internal conflicts: family disintegration, false claims, and false leaders (vv. 12–13).

In preparation, Jesus lays out several important considerations for the disciples to remember when these times arrive: trust in the Holy Spirit (v. 11), awareness of how anxiety operates within family systems (v. 12), and the experience of salvation through endurance (v. 13). Believers can count on the Spirit to bring hope in their struggles.

First, the Spirit brings insight and discernment, enabling the faithful to judge between the Word of God and a world of charlatans, false claims, and the fear-laden tyranny of the urgent. In times when the church finds itself chasing after the latest hot-button social issue, locked into whatever false choice the world serves up, the Spirit provides believers with healing words for a world in distress, a nonanxious presence to navigate often distorted and distressed systems.

Second, the Spirit provides courage and boldness for meeting those challenges, even when under direct threat. Here Mark's Gospel is reminiscent of the apostle Paul, locked in a Roman prison and awaiting trial, declaring to his beloved Philippian congregation his "eager expectation and hope that I will not be put to shame in any way," but that he will speak with all boldness (Phil. 1:20). Believers need not fear that they will be swallowed up by cowardice when the time comes. The Spirit will be there to strengthen and embolden them.

Last, the Spirit will bring perseverance and sustenance in the midst of hardship. There will certainly be days when the world's constant barrage bears down upon and wears away at the resolve of those seeking to witness to the gospel, days when the powers of this world appear overwhelming. The Spirit will give the faithful the strength to endure, persist, and advance the gospel simply by the power of their daily commitment.

Jesus anticipates contemporary family-systems theory with his prophetic word in Mark 13:12, where he raises the important issue of family tension in

Exegetical Perspective

synagogues (v. 9) before whom they must account for their claims concerning Jesus. In verses 9 and 11 Jesus predicts that his disciples will be "handed over" (*paradidōmi*) to the councils, subjected to disciplinary beatings (cf. 2 Cor. 11:24), and tried before secular rulers (cf. Acts 23:33; 25:23) because of their belief in Jesus as Messiah.[2] The phrase "for my sake" (NRSV "because of me") in verse 9 carries a double meaning. At the most obvious level, the disciples are persecuted because of their allegiance to Jesus as the Christ (10:29). On a more pertinent level, their experience of suffering at the hands of religious leaders follows Jesus' own suffering (8:34–38). Their suffering is a form of discipleship and an opportunity to express their faithfulness. The language predicting the trials confirms this, as *paradidōmi* ("to hand over" or "betray") is also used to depict the arrest of John the Baptist (1:14; 6:17–29), Jesus' own betrayal (10: 33–34; 14:10–21), his trial before the Sanhedrin (14:55; 15:1), and his death (15:1, 15).

Despite the trepidation these trials could produce, disciples should not be anxious. Their witness to the gospel will occur not through their skill or initiative but through the power of the Spirit (v. 11). The trials are redefined once more as part of a disciple's calling and proof that these events are not accidental but under God's control.

Verse 10, which mandates preaching the good news to all the nations/Gentiles, interrupts Jesus' exhortation in verses 9 and 11 (the use of *paradidōmi* linking vv. 9 and 11). The verse's distinctive Markan language (e.g., the use of *euangelion*, "the good news"; cf. 1:1, 14, 15; 8:35; 10:29; 14:9; and the use of *prōton*, "first") suggests that the sentence was inserted to provide another reason for the hiatus between the destruction of the temple and the return of the Son of Man. The phrase "must be preached" (*dei kērychthēnai*, NRSV "must . . . be proclaimed," v. 10) is a divine passive (cf. 13:7, 14 for the same use, as well as 8:31 with reference to Jesus' death), meaning that God requires the gospel message to be announced to all peoples before the final consummation. The destruction of the temple, the war with Rome, the trials before judiciaries, and the preaching of the gospel are not random events but a connected complex of activity under God's providential control.

---

2. Eugene Boring notes, "That they are subject to such punishment means that they still are considered insiders to the Jewish community, and consider themselves to be such; it is not a case of one religion, 'Judaism,' persecuting adherents of another religion, 'Christianity,' but of discipline of dissidents within the Jewish community" (Eugene Boring, *Mark: A Commentary* [Louisville, KY: Westminster John Knox Press, 2006], 364).

Homiletical Perspective

eternity. What kind of evidence could there be? Was going to church enough? Was being nice evidence of being a Christian?

For decades many Americans would have agreed with the statement that the United States is a Christian nation. The distinctives of Christianity blurred with the ideals of patriotism and the American way. As our country has become more pluralistic, the notion of our country being called a "Christian nation" has come under scrutiny. Mainline Protestant Christians no longer have the power and influence in government and in society that they once did. Today not a single Supreme Court justice is a Protestant. While some grieve the changes in our nation and debates about politics and religion are far from over, the twenty-first-century church in America has an opportunity to break free from our cultural captivity and become a contrast community. It will require much more from us than simply going to church on Sundays and being nice.

Who is Jesus Christ? What role does he play in our lives? Is he at the center of our lives? Does he shape our values, our hopes, our beliefs, and our behaviors? Is he, instead, out on the periphery? Research by Christian Smith cited by Kenda Dean suggests that the majority of American youth today are not atheists or unbelievers. They have not rejected God or the idea of a supernatural being. God just is not very important for their day-to-day lives. Their faith can best be described as "moralistic therapeutic deism."[1] When asked the more particular question about Jesus (and not God), they have very little to say.

Before we start pointing our fingers at today's youth, we should let another part of Smith and Dean's research sink in. Where did our young people get their theology? Where did "moralistic therapeutic deism" come from? They learned it from us. It is what they have received from the pulpit, in the youth room at church, and in their own homes. We must ask ourselves the primary question: Who is Jesus Christ for me? Once we have an answer to this, it is time to think creatively about how to bear witness to him.

Martha Grace Reese has conducted research on evangelism in mainline Protestant churches. The research can be very depressing, but she also has good news. Reese has found that there are mainline churches—they vary in size and location and

---

1. Christian Smith and Melinda Lundquist Denton, *Soul-Searching: The Religious and Spiritual Lives of American Teenagers* (New York: Oxford University Press, 2005), cited in Kenda Creasy Dean, *Almost Christian: What the Faith of Our Teenagers Is Telling the American Church* (New York: Oxford University Press, 2010), 7.

Mark 13:9–13

Theological Perspective

work as brothers and sisters in Christ to support one another in our common ministry of sharing the good news.

Enduring to the end might also include hard reflection on and confession of the ways in which Christians have contributed, and continue to contribute, to the persecution of people of other faiths. Unfortunately, we do not have to go back to the age of Constantine or to the Crusades to see examples of our own persecuting acts. Christian persecution of Jews during World War II (not only by Nazis but also by their collaborators), and of Muslims post-9/11, makes a mockery of the good news we claim to believe.

Living and proclaiming the truth of this good news is to be the focus of all Christian disciples. As Jesus reoriented the disciples away from their fixation on the temple and back on himself—as he advised them to keep watch, but not to be distracted from their work by the threat of persecution—so he challenges all of us to hold steadfastly to who we are and what we believe.

Enduring to the end entails not being lured into overinterpreting the signs of the times or overplanning ways to manage persecution. This does not mean we are to be passive. On the contrary, it means holding fast to the strongest defense we have against oppression, namely, the good news itself. For the good news, according to Mark, is that the reign of God is coming and that this reign will transform the world by supplanting all oppressive powers, bringing persecution to an end.

I close with a personal example of what it might look like for Christians today to proclaim the coming of God in the face of persecution. Recently, I (who have never been persecuted) taught a group of Laotian Christians (most of whom had been jailed multiple times for their faith). At one point I confessed to them that I did not know whether or not I would have their courage if faced with the same circumstances. They responded with off-putting clarity, refusing either to disarm my cowardice or to offer the persecution-surviving advice I apparently anticipated. Instead, they exhorted me simply to keep on proclaiming the good news, every day, as best I can. It is only in the hope that drives that task, they said, that we Christians are all united in resisting the destructive powers of this world.

CYNTHIA L. RIGBY

Pastoral Perspective

matters of faith. In the early church this was serious business, often pitting faithful Christian living against both Jewish and pagan family traditions, community norms, and social advancement. These tensions could impact careers and damage the social standing of entire families and communities. Familial terms like "brother," "sister," "father," "mother," and "child" are all used in the New Testament to refer to a broad spectrum of relationships—beyond biological connections to religious and community settings. Archaeological evidence exists throughout the Middle East of Greco-Roman households hedging their bets by offering sacrifices and possessing idols to various gods as an ordinary part of political and social life. Throughout the Gospel of Mark, there are plenty of examples of family tension, from intervention early in Jesus' ministry (3:31–35) to his return to his hometown (6:1–6), to his promise of a new family (10:30).

Today believers are more likely to experience this tension in non-Christian or nominally Christian families, where there are embarrassed glances or awkward silences if the subject of faith arises or if a family member wholeheartedly strives to embrace life according to his or her Christian calling. In a culture that fosters compartmentalization of faith and life, the idea of moving faithful living beyond weddings, funerals, baptisms, and polite networking can cause disruption within family systems. By identifying this subtle, destructive result of pressure on the faith community, Jesus lays a foundation for recognition when such anxieties inevitably arise.

Despite such a disconcerting prophecy, Jesus promises that, by the power of the Holy Spirit, the endurance of the faithful will be rewarded. This is not to suggest a salvation by works, but the truth that faithfulness is a necessary condition for the experience of salvation. Perseverance assures the salvific presence of the Holy Spirit. It is the cost of discipleship.

Jesus foresees a world where faithful Christians are consigned to outsider status, viewed in polite society as an embarrassing disruption. Even for well-meaning believers who want only to spread the good news, following Christ is a difficult path, one that may lead to conflict and even death. Authentic Christian living offers not a prosperity gospel, but a challenge to the prevailing culture to such a degree that it seeps beyond external opposition into the subtle, institutional, and familial relationships that make up our personal worlds. Thankfully, this dire prophecy is accompanied by the reassurance of the Holy Spirit, who brings insight, courage, and sustenance for our walk of faith.

JOHN E. COLE

Exegetical Perspective

Just as these events serve God's purposes, so also will the misfortune of familial dissent and disintegration. Mark employs prophetic motifs and apocalyptic scenarios (cf. *1 Enoch* 100:2) to portray human conditions prior to final judgment (cf. Mic. 7:5–7). The word "betray" (*paradidōmi*) is repeated in verse 12, connecting this suffering with the religious and secular trials just mentioned (vv. 9, 11). Now the tragedy is more personal; one brother hands over another for execution, a father delivers a child into the hands of prosecutors, and children abandon their elders. The escalation of events—appearing before tribunals, experiencing discipline, execution, and the utter disintegration of the family—show how devastating the end-time woes will be.

Allegiance to Jesus as Messiah will disrupt personal relationships, especially the intimate relationships among siblings and with parents. Mark foreshadows this disruption with the story of James and John's leaving their father to follow Jesus' call (1:19–20) and with Jesus' rejoinder to Peter's inquiry about a heavenly reward (10:28–30). A disciple's family might consider him or her a heretic or "out of his mind," as Jesus' family had done (3:21, 31–34). In the days before the return of the Messiah this rejection will escalate into betrayal, but as Jesus' exhortation shows, even this devastating experience should not deter the follower from continuing to be faithful.

The pericope concludes by warning that the disciples "will be hated by all" on account of Jesus' name (v. 13), repeating and expanding the sentiment of verse 8. The phrase *eis telos* ("to the end," v. 13) is nuanced, referring both to persevering through the trials and to the end of history. If one endures (*hypomeinas*) the trials, then one will be prepared for the end because God will save (*sōthēsetai*) the follower through the present trials and betrayals and ultimately, at the coming of the Son of Man. Mark's language in this verse echoes Micah 7:6b–7: "your enemies are members of your own household, but as for me, I will look [*epiblepsomai*] to the LORD, I will wait [*hypomenō*] for the God of my salvation [*sōtēr mou*]." Preparation for the end is not achieved by calculation or by deciphering the events of history, but through steady, faithful endurance of the sufferings that will accompany belief in Jesus as Messiah.

STEVEN J. KRAFTCHICK

Homiletical Perspective

theological perspective—that are doing a great job of sharing the good news with people who have never been Christian or who have been away from God and the church for a long time. "Evangelistic churches, like many good churches, concentrate on helping people grow in their faith lives through spiritual practices. But the evangelistic churches also hone in, with laser-like focus, on helping their members articulate and share their growing faith."[2]

A common aphorism attributed to Francis of Assisi says, "Preach the gospel always and if necessary, use words." The church has become so comfortable relying on our good deeds to share the good news of Christ that we have become mute to preaching or sharing the gospel with our words. We have adopted a kind of "Don't ask, Don't tell" policy, and it is not working. It has failed our children and our members, and it is failing to be effective in bearing testimony to Christ beyond the walls of the church.

Mark 13 offers us some very good news. We are given the gift of the Holy Spirit to help us talk about our faith in Jesus, to answer the questions that come at us from a place of hostility or a place of curiosity. Fear and anxiety about what to say in sharing our faith story is not unexpected, but it can be overcome with the help of God the Holy Spirit. It is God's great desire that the good news be proclaimed to all nations. We timid Christians need help in order that this might happen. Reese suggests that the best way to become comfortable with putting our faith into words is to practice doing just that within our own faith communities. In such moments we can trust the Holy Spirit to use our clumsy and inadequate words to help others come to faith or grow in faith.

Earlier I said that most Christians in North America today will never have the kind of experience described in this passage from the book of Mark. I wonder what would happen if they did.

NANCY MIKOSKI

---

2. Martha Grace Reese, *Unbinding the Gospel: Real Life Evangelism* (St. Louis: Chalice Press, 2008), 97.

Mark 13:14–23

¹⁴"But when you see the desolating sacrilege set up where it ought not to be (let the reader understand), then those in Judea must flee to the mountains; ¹⁵the one on the housetop must not go down or enter the house to take anything away; ¹⁶the one in the field must not turn back to get a coat. ¹⁷Woe to those who are pregnant and to those who are nursing infants in those days! ¹⁸Pray that it may not be in winter. ¹⁹For in those days there will be suffering, such as has not been from the beginning of the creation that God created until now, no, and never will be. ²⁰And if the Lord had not cut short those days, no one would be saved; but for the sake of the elect, whom he chose, he has cut short those days. ²¹And if anyone says to you at that time, 'Look! Here is the Messiah!' or 'Look! There he is!'—do not believe it. ²²False messiahs and false prophets will appear and produce signs and omens, to lead astray, if possible, the elect. ²³But be alert; I have already told you everything."

Theological Perspective

This passage, like others sometimes labeled "difficult texts," is not included in the Revised Common Lectionary. Whatever the reason for its exclusion, a quick look at its contents might easily lead the preacher or teacher to give thanks for the omission and feel justified in ignoring the verses. It is, however, worth a more careful look.

Mark 13 contains Jesus' final private instructions to his disciples before his passion (Mark 14–16). That instruction consists of at least two dominant elements: a double-edged exhortation to vigilance in turbulent times and encouragement that, despite all appearances, God is in control. What we have here is instruction in discipleship in a fraught context.

A double-edged exhortation to vigilance runs throughout the passage. It begins with an apocalyptic image from Daniel: "desolating sacrilege" (v. 14). While Jesus (or Mark) would seem to have expected his audience to recognize the reference, scholars today are reduced to speculation on a range of events that might have constituted the sacrilege. In contrast, there appears to be considerable scholarly agreement regarding the devastation to which the sacrilege would point: the destruction of Jerusalem and its temple.

Jesus was warning his followers to be vigilant in the face of a twofold threat. First, the occurrence of the sacrilege would signal the onset of immense

Pastoral Perspective

Jesus speaks such wild words in the thirteenth chapter of Mark that the whole section feels otherworldly, foreign. The images pile up, layering disaster upon disaster, suffering upon suffering, until we are overwhelmed by the intensity of the passage: the temple destroyed, wars and rumors of wars, earthquakes, labor pains, persecution before councils, beatings, desolating sacrileges, fleeing believers, woes to new mothers, sun and moon darkened, stars falling from heaven. Surely such excesses would mean the end of the world. Surely no one would experience such pain until the end comes, until the Son of Man comes to set all wrongs to the right.

Reading this text for the first time, I wonder whether it is so extreme that it cannot actually speak to my congregation at all.

Nevertheless, every time I peer out over the congregation and begin to note the turmoil that roils within the lives of those sitting in the pews, I am reminded of Henry David Thoreau's observation in *Walden*: "The mass of men [sic] lead lives of quiet desperation. What is called resignation is confirmed desperation. . . . A stereotyped but unconscious despair is concealed even under what are called the games and amusements of mankind. There is no play in them."[1]

1. Henry David Thoreau, *Walden* (1854; repr., Rockville, MD: Manor, 2007), 10.

Exegetical Perspective

In response to Jesus' prediction of the destruction of the temple, the disciples ask about timing and indication (13:2–4). They view the temple's demise as one among a series of eschatological events leading to the end of the world (cf. Matt. 24:3); hence the large scope of events covered in Jesus' response is not surprising. Not only does Jesus anticipate the fall of the temple; he also warns the disciples of all that will happen until the coming of the Son of Man (13:24–27).

Jesus begins with general but ominous signs of the beginning of the end: deception, wars, earthquakes, famines, and persecution (13:5–13). There will be terrible and escalating suffering, for sure, but the followers of Jesus must persevere in order to be saved. This dual emphasis on suffering and salvation continues in verses 14–23.

With the announcement of "the desolating sacrilege" or "an abomination of desolation" (NKJV v. 14), Jesus homes in on the fate of the temple. The term "desolation" has been used elsewhere to refer to the destruction of the temple (Jer. 2:2; Tob. 14:4), but this particular phrase comes from the book of Daniel. It alludes to the atrocities of Antiochus IV Epiphanes, the Syrian king who placed an altar of a pagan idol on top of YHWH's altar, defiling the temple and leaving it desolate (Dan. 9:27; 11:31;

Homiletical Perspective

"Woe unto the preacher who draweth Mark's little apocalypse as her Sunday text! Pray that it cometh neither during a stewardship campaign nor upon a new member Sunday. If anyone doth enquire, 'When shall these things be?' or 'What is the desolating sacrilege?' or 'Believest thou this with thine own heart?!' descend thou not from thy chancel, nor even shake any hand at the sanctuary's back door . . ."

Mark 13 is not an easy text to preach. You know that, and more than a few customarily courageous clergy have dodged it. The Revised Common Lectionary actually omits it. Preachers flee it, and for reasons we can understand.

Apocalyptic can be a theological asset, surely. Ernst Käsemann famously called apocalypticism the "mother of all Christian theology."[1] The vigor and intensity of an expectant, trusting faith gave passion and power to the early Christians who embraced it and have continued to do so for Christians who have embraced it through the centuries. Theologians and preachers can celebrate the way "the already" and "the not yet" of apocalyptic living collaborate to supply the faithful with hope. Accordingly, some who reconstruct the life and teaching of Jesus locate apocalyptic eschatology at the center of his prophetic

---

1. Ernst Käsemann, "The Beginnings of Christian Theology," *Journal for Theology and Church* 6 (1969; orig., 1960): 40.

Mark 13:14–23

Theological Perspective

suffering and chaos, greater than anything previously endured. Jesus' audience should be ready to flee at a moment's notice. Delay could be deadly. Second, even as Jesus warned his disciples of the anguish to come, he also warned them against making more of these events than was justified. As cataclysmic as the destruction of Jerusalem and the temple would be for Jews, including Christian Jews, the event would not mark the end of the world. In reality, these foci of Jews' identity, which played so heavily in their relationship to God, lacked ultimate significance; however, in the chaos that would attend their destruction, charlatans, false messiahs, and false prophets would claim that the devastation signaled the *eschaton*.

It is always tempting to read one's own meaning into catastrophe. When life is fundamentally disrupted, when one's identity is challenged, when cherished religious symbols come under attack, when presumably invulnerable markers of community life fall apart, people do not just seek meaning. In their disorientation they seek to impose meaning on the bewildering circumstances.

Jesus acknowledged the precariousness of faith on such occasions and warned his disciples against letting anyone lead them astray. He knew that many would come forward with manufactured answers, with scapegoats, with claims that the end is near; yet their interpretation of events, however compelling, would be based on unreality, a dangerous lie.

The reality would be the loss of Jerusalem and the temple, the loss of the institutions to which the disciples had committed themselves, the loss of religious symbols that they believed essential and thus indestructible. These losses, however, would be evidence, not of the end of the world, but only of the transience of the world and all that is within it. They would expose the falsehood of believing that anything other than God is ultimate.

Although nothing created can be ultimate, created things do have value. That value is demonstrated by a second element in this passage: divine providence. "Providence" is the term that Christians use to refer to God's care for, activity within, and even control over, the creation. The word itself is not found in Scripture, but Christians employ it to designate what is claimed and described in Scripture: God's care over peoples, such as Israel and the church, and over individuals, such as Abraham, Joseph, and Ruth, as well as over the earth itself.

In the Gospel, Jesus was teaching his followers that in the turmoil and disaster that lay ahead, God's

Pastoral Perspective

It may seem extraordinary to us, but nearly every line in this litany of prophetic curses in Mark 13 is welcomed by the quiet, desperate lives in our congregation with a familiar nod. When we read these words from the pulpit, "those in Judea must flee to the mountains" (v. 14), we might think first of refugees, and many of our congregations have obvious examples. We also have a runaway in our pews, though, a man who left home thirty years ago because his mother drank too much, and it was not safe for him. He will nod in silence when he hears these words, words that describe the end of his old life and the terror of a new one.

When we say, "the one on the housetop must not go down or enter the house to take anything away" (v. 15), the woman who had to flee from her husband in the middle of the day with her children will remember the day vividly. "Take only what you need," someone told her, and she will remember the albums she left behind—of her parents' wedding photographs, of her children's first report cards, of her past that cannot be reclaimed.

When a young couple in the congregation hears, "Woe to those who are pregnant and to those who are nursing infants in those days!" (v. 17), they will wonder how they are going to manage to raise their expected child, now that their jobs have been eliminated to improve the company's earnings per share. How they will afford the hospital bills, now that their health insurance is gone? Behind them, of course, is a couple who cannot conceive a child and who find it hard to sit there and consider any words that start, "Woe to those who are pregnant."

"Pray that it may not be in winter" (v. 18) needs no interpretation for a worshiper who lives on the street—nor anyone with a child who lives on the street. Someone in our congregation probably fits that description.

These lines of discourse, which at first seem so foreign to the tidily dressed congregant, are actually so pertinent and pointed that they will cause our congregation to draw in deep breaths and wonder if they can make it through the day's service. For they know it is true: "there will be suffering, such as has not been from the beginning of the creation" (v. 19).

These congregants need something of value to meet this pain. As Christians and as readers of the next passage, we claim that "'the Son of Man coming in clouds' with great power and glory" (v. 26) can meet that pain, that he will gather his people from the four winds and all will be well.

Exegetical Perspective

12:11; 1 Macc. 1:54, 59). Soon after that, the temple was renamed the temple of Olympian Zeus (2 Macc. 6:2). Recalling that incident in 167 BCE, Jesus now warns that the temple will again be defiled and abandoned, so that "not one stone will be left here upon another" (13:2).

Mark's parenthetical statement "let the reader understand" (v. 14) brings the warning close to home for his readers. It suggests that Jesus' prediction is coming to pass as Mark pens this narrative in the years leading up to the fall of Jerusalem in 70 CE. The exhortation to "flee to the mountains" implies that there is still time to do so. Once the Romans have laid siege to the city and closed it off entirely, no one can escape.

It is not easy to pinpoint the exact nature of the desolating sacrilege. In the Greek, the word rendered in English as "sacrilege" or "abomination" (*bdelygma*) is a neuter noun, yet the participle to denote its position, translated as "[being] set up" or "standing" (*hestēkota*), is masculine. Could the grammatical ambiguity refer to an idol representing a pagan god or a deified emperor? According to Josephus's account of the Jewish War, in 67/8 CE John of Gischala led the Zealots to occupy the temple. They converted the temple into a fortress and illegitimately appointed a high priest to perform temple rituals. These actions angered the populace and resulted in bloodshed within the temple among the Jews themselves.[1] Although exactly who or what is on Mark's mind may be hard to determine with certainty, the overall direction of his thought is clear: the temple is doomed for destruction, and time is running out.

Likewise, during this tumultuous period there is no shortage of candidates for the false prophets and messianic pretenders about whom Jesus warns in verses 21–22. Josephus describes these characters as ambitious and self-promoting, purporting to perform works of wonder and offering their compatriots false hopes of deliverance from the Romans. For example, Menahem rebelled against the Romans and entered Jerusalem dressed in royal garb, pretending to be a king. Most prominent of all was the despotic but charismatic leader Simon, son of Gioras, who defeated the Zealots in Jerusalem and was hailed as savior and protector by his followers.[2] In times of dire distress, it is tempting to grasp at straws. Even the faithful are not immune to deception. Watchfulness, therefore, entails discernment, the ability

---

1. Flavius Josephus, *The Jewish War*, trans. H. St. J. Thackeray, Loeb Classical Library (Cambridge: Harvard University Press, 1926–1927), 4.150–57, 196–207.
2. Ibid., 2.433–48; 4.503–44; 6.285–300; cf. Deut. 13:1–3.

Homiletical Perspective

message and draw strength from it for the living of these days.

Apocalyptic texts can also be confusing, though. Some suggest that, because of its persistent apocalypticism, the New Testament lacks a long view of mundane history. For some, this lack makes justice work tantamount to rearranging deck furniture on the *Titanic*. For these, the afterlife that will be ushered in by the *eschaton* is the true life, to which the present is a mere prequel. Imminent eternal salvation eliminates any call to social justice. Possibly as a response to this otherworldly voice, some recent scholars of the historical Jesus have jettisoned these sayings as early Christian accretions, offering an emphatically this-worldly picture of Jesus in its place. In this embattled theological context, it is no wonder that Mark 13 leaves people in our pews confused—and not a little scared.

Another current debate can challenge the preacher of Mark 13. Our people wonder what God and creature suffering have to do with one another. Is God altogether good? Then God is not all-powerful. Is God all-powerful? Then God must not be altogether good. If God is both all-powerful and all-good, whence suffering? People flock to hear speakers who ask these questions, so we hope Mark's Jesus will answer them here. Does God inflict the suffering Jesus describes, or simply allow it? Is God powerless to change it? Is there a force of evil that wins battles but finally loses the war?

As much as we might wish for a Rabbi-Kushner-esque discussion of *When Bad Things Happen to Good People*,[2] in Mark 13 Jesus does not trace out the agency behind wars, famines, earthquakes, persecutions, and family strife. He simply exhorts the faithful to pray that their plight will be brief (v. 18). Jesus knows the future, but he does not claim to be guiding it or to have any control over it at all. In fact, even God is the subject of only one verb here: *kyrios* cuts short the suffering (v. 20).

Though Jesus (and Mark) brings comfort rather than answering our philosophical questions, we preachers so badly want to find those answers here that we are tempted to demythologize and explain: "What the good Teacher is trying to say is . . ." We want to answer our congregation's intellectual questions about the origin of suffering, even though Mark's Jesus does not.

In this embattled context, what shall we preach? Surely Jesus here offers reassurance. In this passage

---

2. Harold Kushner, *When Bad Things Happen to Good People* (1981; repr., New York: Anchor, 2004).

Mark 13:14–23

Theological Perspective

providence would be exercised both in judgment and in mercy. The destruction of Jerusalem and the temple would be an act of judgment, but that judgment would not be all consuming. God's mercy would cut short the suffering; otherwise, not even the chosen would remain steadfast.

Jesus reassured the faithful that he had told them all that they needed to know: terrible suffering was about to take place; the end of the world was not at hand; God was in control. The events that were to take place were the necessary outworking of the divine will; thus, whatever suffering the faithful might undergo, they were not to fear.

Jesus' double-edged warning, in combination with his reassurance of God's providential care, carries a message for us today. In the midst of bewildering change, we are often tempted to make claims about God's activity in historical events. We would do well to heed the warning of Augustine of Hippo (d. 430), a theologian of enormous influence in the West. Augustine was convinced that we simply have not been given the inspiration or the authority to know and to declare what God is doing in particular historical events.[1]

Scripture provides its own inspired interpretation of the events recounted there. The Holy Spirit assures us of the divine will and work on these occasions. In contrast, there is no such authoritative, inspired interpretation for events that have occurred and will occur outside the canon. Recklessly declaring the hand of God in these events can be not only futile but also detrimental to faith. For example, declaring that the attacks on September 11, 2001, were God's punishment on a particular group suggests that God is both malevolent and subject to the limitations of human prejudice.

In this life, in which the goodness and justice of God are so often hidden, claims about God's purpose in specific historical events reveal little but the biases of the persons making the declarations. Even in those events and circumstances that prove to be beneficial to the church, Christians should not indulge the temptation to declare God's purposes. Jesus reassures us: it is God and God alone who is in control, and God's judgment has been and will be tempered by mercy for the sake of the faithful.

REBECCA H. WEAVER

Pastoral Perspective

If we are not careful, though, our rush to meet that pain with a word of hope can feel like a denial of the pain itself. As William Sloane Coffin said in a sermon he preached ten days after the death of his son, "In my intense grief I felt some of my fellow reverends . . . were using comforting words of Scripture for self-protection, to pretty up a situation whose bleakness they simply couldn't face. But like God herself, Scripture is not around for anyone's protection, just for everyone's unending support."[2]

The impulse to protect ourselves from the enormity of the pain that is in the pews sometimes means we will cop out and try to pretty up the situation, rather than offering something that is hard won and true about suffering. Protecting yourself from the interior work necessary for preaching a text like this is offering them a false Messiah, one who comes with only enough power to pacify, not enough strength to save.

Instead, this text offers the preacher a chance for honest testimony about how God has saved us when we have fled for safety, were in danger, grieving, lost, or worrying over our children. If it is true that people will grasp for any Messiah during their times of enormous trial, then one of the greatest gifts we can give them is to offer them a genuine one, the one who knows what sort of pain awaits us, has experienced it himself, sticks through it with us, and has promised that his people will share in his ultimate triumph over it. Use this text for honest testimony.

This passage is what it feels like to lose your way, and the woe spoken over the believer seems extreme, but only in the aggregate. Individually, they make up the hidden pain of our congregants, and individually they allow us to offer a real hope for those who are suffering.

L. CASEY THOMPSON

---

1. R. A. Markus, *Saeculum: History and Society in the Theology of St Augustine* (Cambridge: Cambridge University Press, 1970), 17, 20–21, 187–96. See *City of God*, 20.2; 18.36.

2. William Sloane Coffin, "Alex's Death," in Thomas G. Long and Cornelius Plantinga Jr., eds., *A Chorus of Witnesses: Model Sermons for Today's Preacher* (Grand Rapids: Eerdmans, 1994), 264–65.

Exegetical Perspective

to distinguish truth from falsehood (vv. 21–22; cf. 13:5–6).

The entire scenario painted by Jesus is shot through with irony and urgency. First, the Jews are as culpable as the Gentiles in desecrating God's temple. At least Antiochus IV Epiphanes was a pagan, but then, during the Jewish War, the temple suffers defilement not only by the Romans, but also by Jewish Zealots, messianic pretenders, and corrupt priests. Second, the temple no longer attracts but repels. Instead of being a place of prayer and worship (11:17), it has become desolate, as the Jews flee from Jerusalem and nearby cities to hide in the hill country of Judea (cf. Jer. 16:16; 1 Macc. 2:27–30). Third, there is no time to retrieve any belongings (vv. 15–16). Those already vulnerable—pregnant women, nursing mothers, and infants—are even more vulnerable (v. 17). What a dreadful plight this would be if the flight had to take place in the cold and stormy winter months (v. 18)!

On one level, this text clearly speaks of Israel's national catastrophe of 66–70 CE, for the temple is deserving of judgment. Once again, God allows the temple to be destroyed at the hands of Israel's enemies. On another level, history will repeat itself. The suffering during the First Jewish War, though described as having unprecedented intensity, is not yet the final tribulation. It is but one among many more sufferings, each greater than the one preceding, that are yet to afflict the world as it careens towards God's ordained denouement (v. 19).

Where there is judgment, there is also grace. By divine sovereignty and power, the God of creation will limit the suffering of the elect (v. 20). In fact, the final siege of Jerusalem in 70 CE lasted only five months, and the war was over by the summer of that year. In the midst of tribulation, God remains sovereign and mindful of those who stand firm in faithfulness. God's elect, both Jewish and Gentile followers of Jesus, will be saved—not from but through tribulation. In the following section, verses 24–27, Jesus gives the assuring promise of his return in glory to gather the faithful to himself. Meanwhile, vigilance, watchfulness, and perseverance are the order of the day (13:5, 9, 23, 29, 33, and 37).

DIANE G. CHEN

Homiletical Perspective

about trauma to come, Jesus resolutely proclaims that suffering is not the last word—even in the cataclysmic drama that culminates history. The future looks dark in this passage: "There will be suffering, such as has not been from the beginning of the creation" (v. 19). In fact, the fearful circumstances Jesus anticipates for his disciples would be devastating if not for God's decision to "cut short those days" (v. 20).

Whether Mark has in mind the early stages of Jerusalem's destruction or some other threat, most commentators sense that Jesus' words are meant to describe a reality Mark's audience will recognize from their own experience—and to comfort the afflicted more than to afflict the comfortable. Apocalypse does that. It maps current difficulties in a way that gives context to suffering and acknowledges God's ultimate say in what will be ultimate. A preacher need not identify a present-day desolating sacrilege in order to speak this word powerfully to real lived lives. The message of hope amid our present suffering resounds through this text, and can resound through our sanctuaries when we hear it together.

Formally, Mark's drama offers an opportunity for the preacher to abandon the didactic sermon in favor of the apocalypse as genre. Casey Thompson's pastoral essay on this passage brilliantly narrates his own path from seeing Mark's apocalypse as exotic to letting it describe specific present suffering that surrounds him and us. Could this fit your congregation's experience?

My opening paragraph here facetiously mimics the tone of apocalypse in order to address preachers' homiletical fear of Mark 13. Could your sermon employ the genre more seriously, collating the ancient examples with contemporary ones that your people know all too well, in order to address your congregation's life fears? Mark's audience were suffering terribly, we imagine. Mark chose to bring an apocalyptic Jesus into their midst. Your people are suffering too. With your help, they might just experience a pulpit apocalypse as the healing balm that Mark hoped it would be to his fearful faithful.

However you preach them, Jesus' scary and reassuring words of Mark 13 need preaching. They offer hope to faithful sufferers. They name horrors that preachers are tempted to avoid but parishioners know by name. Apocalypse as opportunity? Who would have thought it?! Imagine yourself actually hoping to draw the short straw the next time this passage is assigned.

ALLEN R. HILTON

Mark 13:24–27

> ^{24} "But in those days, after that suffering,
>   the sun will be darkened,
>   and the moon will not give its light,
> ^{25} and the stars will be falling from heaven,
>   and the powers in the heavens will be shaken.
> ^{26}Then they will see 'the Son of Man coming in clouds' with great power and glory. ^{27}Then he will send out the angels, and gather his elect from the four winds, from the ends of the earth to the ends of heaven."

Theological Perspective

These four verses employ metaphorical biblical language to describe the indescribable: the end time, the *eschaton*. This cosmic event will follow closely on the tribulations to be suffered by Jesus' followers, as described in the preceding verses (vv. 14–23). Sun, moon, and stars, seeming constants, will fail. The Son of Man will come in clouds of glory for the sake of gathering the widely scattered elect.

The Gospel has borrowed dramatic imagery from elsewhere in Scripture (e.g., Isa. 13:10; Ezek. 32:7–8; Joel 2:10, 31; 3:15; Dan. 7:13–14) to signal the Parousia or second coming of Christ. In contrast to the incarnation, when the Savior came in the helplessness of an infant, and in contrast to the crucifixion, in which the Savior suffered the humiliation of the cross, this second coming is one of power and glory. Descending from his throne at the right hand of God, the Savior eliminates any remaining doubts about his identity or purpose. God has intervened in history to vindicate the elect. The passage reassures them that the return of Jesus will be to their benefit.

The passage tells us that the end of time will be dramatic; yet anxiety about the future and misgivings occasioned by the previous tribulations are misplaced. God is in control. The events described are not to be an outgrowth of history but the interruption, even elimination, of history, of time itself.

Pastoral Perspective

Harold Camping, the man in charge of things at Family Radio, had a bad day on May 21, 2011. Mr. Camping had gleefully spent millions of other people's dollars announcing that day as the world's expiration date, but May 21 passed without incident.[1]

It is not surprising that Mr. Camping was wrong. He had been wrong before: in 1994, when he predicted the end of the world three times, and in 1995, when he predicted it once. Backtracking on 0 for 5, he claimed that May 21 was just a prelude to the real end. October 21, 2011, would be the real date. Harold Camping is not the only one who has failed in his predictions. He just did it with the greatest number of billboards and RVs.

Bishop Clement of Rome predicted it would happen around the year 90. Hilary of Poitiers predicted the end of the year in 365. His student, the more famous Martin of Tours, revised that estimate to sometime before the year 400. The German emperor Otis III thought an eclipse in the year 968 was the harbinger of the close of the age. Then, during the lesser known Y1K crisis,[2] accounts of the end created such panic in Christian nations that they dumped

---

1. All historical references in this essay can be found at http://en.wikipedia.org/wiki/List_of_dates_predicted_for_apocalyptic_events; accessed January 24, 2013.
2. Y2K was popular shorthand for the year 2000. See Warren H. Chaney, *Y2K—A World in Crisis* (New York: Swan, 2007). Y1K refers to the year 1000 CE.

Exegetical Perspective

In this chapter, the eschatological events Jesus cites are linked by the catchphrase "in those days" (13:17, 19, 20, 24), which is common parlance in the Old Testament for describing what will happen at the final consummation. "In those days," YHWH will deal evil a definitive blow, banish the wicked to eternal punishment, gather the righteous, and establish the new age of salvation (Jer. 33:15–16; Zech. 8:22–23; Joel 3:1).

Jesus' predictions point to an ominous crescendo toward the end, when things of this present world get increasingly worse as they approach their final denouement. Natural disasters and collapse of relationships between people and nations now give way to destruction on a cosmic scale. These verses depict the final stage—"in those days, *after* that suffering" (13:24, cf. 13:19)—when even the heavens, the sun, the moon, and the stars disintegrate into nothingness.

The issue is not whether these cosmic phenomena ought to be taken literally, since that will become clear when the actual time arrives. The more pertinent question is this: what theological and symbolic messages are conveyed through these horrific images of the celestial bodies, where even heaven is reverting to its primordial state of darkness and chaos?

The language of verses 24–25 is reminiscent of the oracles of judgment by the Old Testament prophets.

Homiletical Perspective

Sun, moon, and stars darkened, the heavenly powers shaken, the Son of Man riding the clouds, and the elect finally gathered in from everywhere. With language drawn from the Hebrew prophets, this passage traces a temporal trajectory from the fourth day of creation (when sun, moon, and stars began, Gen. 1:14–19) through to history's culmination. It also spans the spatial expanse of the universe, as angels go to the four corners of earth and heaven to gather the faithful. In four verses, Mark's Jesus takes us through the entirety of time and space.

With all the size and drama in this passage, the homiletical challenge of the day will be to imagine with our congregations where this fits in our lives. The pictures are the stuff of scary movies. The imagery can seem remote, and we can slip into the role of an audience in a gigantic outdoor theatre. The cataclysmic interruption seems far from our workaday, play-a-day world. Is this our story? If it is, how is it our story?

The bridge between the cosmic and the close is the speaker himself, Jesus, who connects our present to the coming *eschaton* through his two-stage vocation as Son of Man. Mark quotes Daniel 7 in the middle of this passage, when he pictures "the Son of Man coming in the clouds" (Dan. 7:13; Mark 13:26). Much scholarly ink has been spilled through the

Mark 13:24–27

Theological Perspective

Habitual assumptions about the workings of the world no longer apply. Ordinary categories of thought are rendered useless.

So how might the teacher or preacher communicate the message? More pointedly, is there here any message for today? The Revised Common Lectionary, in scheduling the passage for the First Sunday of Advent, gives some indication of what that message might be. In awaiting the nativity, Christians are also awaiting Christ's return. They are to be vigilant but also filled with hope.

There are several elements to that vigilant yet hopeful posture. Perhaps chief among them is humility, a recognition of our limitations. Christians simply do not know—because we have not been given—a neat explanation of what is being described. It lies outside the boundaries of our experience. The Bible offers us imagery rather than definition, suggestion rather than declaration. As in the case of the incarnation and resurrection, we are invited to stretch our imaginations, to ruminate upon the meaning, to trust the abundant mercy of God, but we are not promised comprehension. It is as Paul tells us: "now we see in a mirror, dimly" (1 Cor. 13:12). Yet the claim of Christ's return is in the creed. We believe.

On the other hand, the passage allows for more than humble acknowledgment of our ignorance. It does make some theological claims that have become fundamental elements of Christian faith. One of these is its presentation of Jesus as the Son of Man. The figure of the Son of Man, already familiar in Mark, here becomes the central figure in the events of the end time in which God's purposes will be fully revealed and accomplished. Jesus is essential to the fulfillment of the divine will for all creation.

The Christology is stunning. It makes inescapably clear that there is only one sign of the end of all things: Jesus himself, the Jesus who is and is to come. In contrast to the "desolating sacrilege" (13:14), which was to be the sign of horrific temporal events, the destruction of Jerusalem and the temple, Jesus is the sign of the end of time. As such, he is the only trustworthy bridge from time to eternity, from a world in dissolution to a reality that is indissoluble. Jesus is the only sign that points unfailingly to God, because in him alone are creature and Creator indivisibly joined. Those who preach another gospel, that is, the false prophets and false Messiahs (v. 22), preach unreality, a lie.

There is another element of Christology that demands attention. Mark has put the claims of these

Pastoral Perspective

the entirety of Christ's teachings about nonviolence and tried to beat the love of Christ into pagans so they might be saved.

In 1284, Pope Innocent III expected it all to end. He came to this conclusion by adding 666 to the year Islam was founded, 618. Of course, we usually date Islam to 622, which means he made two mistakes. Innocent was anything but innocent. He started the Fourth Crusade and sent its army to Constantinople, expecting that the large force of Christians would repel Turkish threats to that beleaguered city. However, when the Christian troops got there, they scared off the Turks by sacking the city themselves.

Many Shakers suggested 1792. Charles Wesley preferred 1794. He probably wrote a hymn about it somewhere. His brother John preferred the mid-nineteenth century. It was 1914 for Jehovah's Witnesses—also 1915, 1918, 1920, 1925, 1941, 1975, and 1994. By the way, this makes an excellent conversation starter if they knock on your door.

Christians of every flavor have consistently predicted that the end was near—and consistently been wrong.

I suspect we inherit this tendency from Jesus and the early church. Every person of note whose words survive to us from that era—Jesus, John the Baptist, Paul—expected the rapid arrival of the kingdom of God. Within the generation. Soon, they said. Soon. Hold on. We will make it.

Which is what the people sending money to Harold Camping were saying too. "Hold on. Soon," they said. "Christ will come again. And when he does . . . Oh to be here when he does. Because when Christ is with us, we will not suffer anymore. Even more: Blessed am I if people revile me and persecute me and utter all kinds of evil against me falsely on the Lord's account—for my reward will be great. Come, Lord Jesus. We will be at peace. That fight with my sister, it may have kept us apart for the last two years, but when Christ comes . . . The lymphoma that is cracking my mom right now, when Christ comes . . . My depression, the one that handcuffs me to the bed, maybe the captives can go free when Christ comes? This job, the one that eats at me, when Christ comes . . . My debt, all debts, the constant phone calls that treat me like dirt, that lecture me like a child, when Christ comes . . . Soon," they said.

Soon, we hope. Soon, we will not watch children die in Africa from dirty water. Soon, we will not watch soldiers travel back in bandages, terrified of their lives back home. Soon, we will not watch students pepper-sprayed for protests. Soon, we will

Exegetical Perspective

Speaking of God's punishment of the wicked, Isaiah writes, "The stars of the heavens and their constellations will not give their light; the sun will be dark at its rising, and the moon will not shed its light.... Therefore [God] will make the heavens tremble, and the earth will be shaken out of its place, at the wrath of the LORD of hosts in the day of [God's] fierce anger" (Isa. 13:10, 13; see also 24:21, 23). Similarly, Joel warns that on the day of the Lord "the earth quakes before them, the heavens tremble. The sun and the moon are darkened, and the stars withdraw their shining" (Joel 2:10; cf. Ezek. 32:7–8; Isa. 34:4; Amos 5:18–20). These passages, as well as Mark 13:24–25, indicate that God is infinitely more powerful than all other powers, whether earthly or heavenly. When God comes, Satan and his minions are doomed. The darkening of the celestial bodies denotes their darkness and their depletion. Likewise, the image of stars falling from the sky graphically anticipates the ultimate annihilation of evil (cf. Isa. 14:11–15; Luke 10:18; Rev. 6:13).

In the next two verses, Jesus injects a surprising reconfiguration of the traditional eschatological anticipation found in the Old Testament. Instead of God coming in glory in the clouds with the angelic hosts, a typical scene of end-time theophany (Hab. 3:3; Isa. 59:19; 66:18–19; Zech. 14:5), Jesus announces that "they will see 'the Son of Man coming in clouds' with great power and glory" (v. 26). What a sight for the defeated powers and principalities to behold! Seeing the Son of Man in his glory is tantamount to seeing God in full revelatory radiance.

Just as "the desolating sacrilege" in verse 14 calls attention to events alluded to in the book of Daniel, the title "Son of Man," which Jesus uses often of himself, brings to mind Daniel's vision of "one like a son of man" appearing before the Ancient of Days to receive dominion and glory (Dan. 7:13–14). In Daniel's context, this heavenly figure is connected with the saints of the Most High, functioning as a representative of the faithful people of God, who receive vindication after having endured much persecution (Dan. 7:15–28). The twin themes of glory and suffering characterize the path on which Jesus himself will shortly embark, a way that his disciples and Mark's readers will likely follow.

Nevertheless, several differences remain between Daniel 7 and the return of the Son of Man in Mark 13. First, at the Parousia, Jesus the Son of Man will come from God, rather than be presented to God. Second, in Daniel the appearance of the "son of man" occurs after the heavenly court has completed

Homiletical Perspective

years on Mark's references to the Son of Man—especially because, as the first of the four Gospel writers, Mark is the first to use this term in our canonical New Testament. Daniel famously describes "one like a son of man," or a humanish figure (NRSV "one like a human being"), who comes from the heavens to rule earth in place of the recently destroyed beast (Dan. 7:13). The Ancient of Days gives this "son of man" dominion (Dan. 7:14).

Mark's picture is more complex. Daniel's "one like a son of man" comes with the clouds and reigns victorious over all peoples, and all people serve him. He ends the terror of the faithful and ushers in a new epoch. This image of power and reign is not altogether absent from Mark, of course. The term "Son of Man" appears thirteen times in this Gospel, and five of those feature his power. In 2:10 Jesus has the authority to forgive sins, and in 2:28 he is lord of the Sabbath, both of which are Godlike prerogatives. Here in 13:24–27 and again in Jesus' words at the trial in 14:62, he will come powerfully with the clouds at some future time, in the fashion of Daniel's depiction. Jesus imagines a future time when the Son of Man (in the company of God and the angels) will be ashamed of those who were ashamed of him on earth (8:38). Daniel's powerful "one like a son of man" is no stranger to Mark.

What Mark adds to Daniel's drama is the humble and suffering "Son of Man," the one who is most frequent in the latter half of the Gospel. Jesus first alludes to this role in the pivotal scene at Caesarea Philippi, with his first passion prediction: "He began to teach them that the Son of Man must undergo great suffering" (8:31). In fact, all three passion predictions are stated in terms of what will happen to "the Son of Man" (8:31; 9:31; 10:33). Daniel's humanish one comes in to clear up the mess humanity has made; but Mark's Son of Man suffers the mess himself first: "they will mock him, and spit upon him, and flog him, and kill him" (10:34).

When we lay Daniel and Mark side by side, the most striking difference is in the relationship of the Son of Man to all people. Mark's specific vocabulary can hardly be accidental. The prophet pictures dominion and power, during which "all peoples, nations, and languages should serve [the one like a son of man]" (Dan. 7:14). Mark turns this obeisance on its head during the earthly life of Jesus, using the same language that Daniel uses, when Jesus tells his disciples, "The Son of Man came not to be served but to serve, and to give his life a ransom for many" (10:45). The Son of Man came to serve. We are far

Mark 13:24–27

Theological Perspective

astonishing events in the mouth of Jesus. There is much scholarly debate over the source or sources of the material in this chapter, but as it stands, Mark's Jesus is the one making the eschatological, even apocalyptic, claims. Albert Schweitzer, in *The Quest of the Historical Jesus*, written at the beginning of the twentieth century, claimed that Jesus understood himself in eschatological terms. He sought "to bring all ordinary history to a close" and was "crushed" by his own efforts.[1] Schweitzer was warning against a domestication of Jesus. He condemned our tendency to make Jesus someone with whom we are comfortable, rather than the thoroughly eschatological figure that Schweitzer believed him to be. To follow this alien one might well mean rejecting the world that we inhabit. Whether or not we agree with Schweitzer's depiction of Jesus, we, like all Christians, always stand in danger of preaching and teaching a Jesus who conforms to, rather than challenges, our beliefs and biases. In other words, we stand in danger of preaching unreality, a lie.

At least one further point should be noted. The final verse speaks of Jesus sending angels to "gather his elect from the four winds, from the ends of the earth to the ends of heaven" (v. 27). The use of the word "elect" points to gracious divine prerogative. In the present context it would seem to refer to those who were faithful to Jesus. (The question of whether they were faithful because they had been elected to the grace of perseverance is not addressed and likely was not even considered.) The expansiveness of the arenas from which the elect were to be gathered (all of earth and heaven) leaves open the possibility that on the last day not only the elect followers of Jesus but also the elect of Israel, living and dead, were to be brought together by the angels. Again we encounter the suggestiveness of imagery rather than precision. What is clear is that the last day belongs to the Son of Man. Those who await him can but pray for the grace to remain faithful.

REBECCA H. WEAVER

Pastoral Perspective

not watch the poor of our cities waste away without health insurance. Soon, we will not watch a tenth of this country's young, male, African American population get thrown in lockup. Soon, we will not have to hear the awful statistics of sexual predators and children and pretend that it is really a rare circumstance. Of course, it does not stop there.

Is it any wonder our people cry out for Christ's immediate return, crave it with their entire hearts? Christ will come again, and when he does, we will not suffer anymore. That is why, over and over, Christians have tried to predict the end of the world. Because we want to manifest it, we want the suffering to end.

The thirteenth chapter of Mark provides an excellent opportunity for the preacher to identify the heartaches sitting in the pew, the pains that create this desire in us for an entirely new world, and then answer it with a hopeful word from Christ: "Then he will send out the angels, and gather his elect from the four winds, from the ends of the earth to the ends of heaven."

The Son of Man who comes with great power and glory is a figure our congregants still urgently need, an icon for whom they desperately long. The difficult task of a preacher as she travels through this chapter is to offer this word of hope, that Christ will come again and remake the world, while also offering some balm for their suffering that is not reliant on Christ's immediate return. There are a number of options, of course: the acts of bearing one another's burdens, engaging in prayer, the offering of ourselves in service, participating in the sacraments, learning the art of generosity, reflecting on the already of the already-and-not-yet. Each of these practices can offer a congregation some solace as we wait for the final gathering of God's people "from the ends of the earth to the ends of heaven."

L. CASEY THOMPSON

---

1. Albert Schweitzer, *The Quest of the Historical Jesus: A Critical Study of Its Progress from Reimarus to Wrede*, trans. William Robinson (1906; repr., New York: Macmillan, 1968), 370–71.

Exegetical Perspective

its judgment, whereas Jesus' future return will precede the final judgment. Third, the Danielic figure is given glory on that occasion, but Jesus will come in glory that he already possesses.

Instead of forcing Jesus' description of his return to conform exactly to the vision in Daniel, it is conceivable that Jesus is making use of ideas associated with the son of man tradition to express something else about his own person and mission without adopting the context in Daniel in its entirety. In *4 Ezra* (dated between the first century BCE and the first century CE) and *1 Enoch* (dated around 100 CE), Daniel's "son of man" is identified as the Messiah who is to come (*4 Ezra* 13:25–58, *1 En.* 48:10; 52:4). Calling himself Son of Man seems to be Jesus' way of hinting at his messianic identity without declaring plainly that he is the Messiah.

Aside from the background from Daniel, two other passages in Mark support the reading of 13:26 as pointing to the Parousia. In Mark 8:38, Jesus warns his followers against apostasy, lest they be rejected in the future "when [the Son of Man] comes in the glory of his Father with the holy angels." Later, standing trial before the Sanhedrin, Jesus predicts his vindication when he tells the high priest that the latter "'will see the Son of Man seated at the right hand of the Power,' and 'coming with the clouds of heaven'" (14:62). Thrice in this Gospel, therefore, the Markan Jesus calls himself Son of Man, not only to claim messianic identity, but also to speak of his future return.

Seen in this light, verse 27 confirms the idea that God's coming on the last day will be executed through the agency of Jesus, the messianic Son of Man. Just as God promises to gather the faithful for eternal salvation, here the Son of Man is said to "gather his elect from the four winds, from the ends of the earth to the ends of heaven" (13:27; cf. Deut. 30:4–5; Isa. 11:11; 27:12–13; 43:5–7). The Son of Man thus takes on the function of judgment and salvation, bringing the unity between Jesus and God to its highest expression.

DIANE G. CHEN

Homiletical Perspective

from Daniel's world. Clouds and power will come later, of course, but this Son of Man came first to serve. It is no wonder the disciples did not catch on right away!

We return to Mark's apocalypse. The day is coming when the second phase of Mark's Son of Man story will begin, when the cosmos will change and the powerful One will reign. However, the story is changed by the suffering. This is no untouched heavenly emissary. This is the one who has suffered all that humanity could throw at him and all that humanity has suffered. It is he who will shorten the time of tribulation. It is he who will halt the suffering of the faithful. It is he who will send angels in all directions to gather them all to himself.

The image of sun and moon losing their light comes from Isaiah 13:10, where the specter announces salvation for the exiles. Cosmic interruption signals an interruption in dreadful history for a captive people.

Mark's Jesus has endured the suffering of the faithful, and he will ultimately call that suffering to a close for them. It is worth noting that Mark's Jesus does not avenge the faithful. We do not hear lurid tales of retribution on the oppressor (another difference between Mark and Daniel, and certainly a difference between Mark and Revelation). Mark's Jesus also does not picture the future in detail. No one knows the time of redemption, and he is not telling what it will look like. All he needs the faithful ones to know is that suffering will not be the last word—that the one who stands at the end of history is the same one who stood at its beginning. Maybe that is all our faithful ones need to know too.

ALLEN R. HILTON

Mark 13:28–31

²⁸"From the fig tree learn its lesson: as soon as its branch becomes tender and puts forth its leaves, you know that summer is near. ²⁹So also, when you see these things taking place, you know that he is near, at the very gates. ³⁰Truly I tell you, this generation will not pass away until all these things have taken place. ³¹Heaven and earth will pass away, but my words will not pass away."

Theological Perspective

Each of the Gospels contains statements from Jesus about the end of history as we know it. Mark 13, sometimes referred to as the little apocalypse, includes a number of Jesus' sayings, woven together because of the end-time theme. These statements are presented as Jesus' longest single discourse in the Gospel of Mark. The chapter is not a full-blown apocalypse with a detailed account of final things, though, as much as it is a farewell exhortation for the disciples. Jesus is preparing them for an uncertain future. Over and over, Jesus refers to what life will be like "in those days" (13:17, 19, 20, 24), but his descriptions repeatedly include encouragements.

Underlying the entire chapter is the understanding that God is finally in control of all of life and all of history. There is a firm foundation that undergirds our entire experience of the shifting sands of human events, including what may happen at the end. Jesus speaks with authority about how things really are, if we could only pull back the curtain and see behind the events.

God is neither impressed by human efforts to control destiny nor surprised by the unfolding of what seems unexpected or disruptive. Mark 13 is introduced by Jesus' observation that even the great temple of Jerusalem, which was seen by many as a clear example of the ability of human beings to create

Pastoral Perspective

From a very young age, I have known that the point of any hike was to get to the destination. Whenever we went hiking, I, the second-born among four boys, competed with my brothers to see who could take the lead and hold it. Dad would keep up with us to be sure we followed the trail and did not get hurt. We hiked through forest lands in the Pacific Northwest, where we grew up. We scrambled up trails making all kinds of noise, trying to hold each other back and chiding younger brothers for not keeping up with those of us who were older and stronger. When we got to the end of the trail, we would collapse and wait . . . and we would wait . . . and wait.

It was a rule that we could not eat our snacks or lunch until Mom joined us. The problem was Mom was so slow. We would end up complaining to Dad about having to wait, but we knew the rule. We always ate together as a family. Eventually, to our relief, Mom would show up. She had made her way steadily up the trail. We would sit down together, pray, and then eat.

While eating, the conversation always ended the same way. At some point, Mom would look at us and ask, "Did you boys see the marmot?" "No. There was a marmot? Where?" we would ask, perplexed. "Along the trail," Mom would say. We would be quiet, thinking about how cool it would be to see a marmot.

Exegetical Perspective

The clear majority of scholarship places the writing of Mark sometime between the late 60s and the late 70s CE. Mark was therefore likely written during the tumultuous decade that saw Israel's successful revolt against Rome, Rome's ensuing recapture of Israel, and the punishing sacking of Jerusalem and destruction of its temple. This military defeat and the sight of Jerusalem in ruins eviscerated traditions of Israel for all those devoted to them around the Mediterranean.

All of Mark pulses with people living with pain, excruciating loss, and haunting trauma. All kinds of bodies writhe. The Gerasene demoniac smashes himself with stones (5:5); the woman with the flow of blood experiences it for a seemingly interminable period (5:25). The pivotal call of Jesus is to pick up one's cross and follow him toward suffering and death (8:34–35). Jesus himself dies shouting an angry protest to God (15:34). His resurrection is never proclaimed by anyone (16:1–8). Mark 13:28–31 itself envisions the destruction of the earth and sky, and it appeals to those following Jesus to pay attention to this devastation.

Readers need to see the stories and teachings of Mark within the misery of the people of Israel during this violent decade. It is important to remember that none of the communities within the legacy of Jesus at this time had any notion of "Christianity"; they simply

Homiletical Perspective

Apocalyptic warnings in the Bible usually appear when people are afraid. Beneath the fear is hurt, for such warnings always address a threatened, marginal community. Daniel addressed the nation of Israel in exile; John of Patmos wrote from exile to the persecuted Christians in Asia Minor; and here Mark's listeners were a tiny band of Jesus' followers whose very lives were at risk and whose hopes for the return of the Son of Man were dimming daily. Thus the task of the preacher in this text, or any other apocalyptic text, is to be both pastoral and prophetic.

The pastoral dimension involves helping our listeners move from fear to hope. The movement begins by putting ourselves in the shoes of those on the margins, beginning with Mark's community. The preacher could begin by describing the social upheaval in Jerusalem when Mark wrote his Gospel, which was one of the worst eras of Jewish history. Poverty was increasing, especially among the Jews, many of whom were becoming destitute. Violence abounded during the Jewish revolt, as crosses lined the highways from Rome to Jerusalem.

Where is the good news here? Let the preacher trace how, in Mark, God empowered Jesus through the Spirit to announce that God's kingdom *(basileia)* has drawn near (1:9–15). Mark reminds us that under the reign of God, people are freed from

Mark 13:28–31

Theological Perspective

something enduring, would be completely destroyed. This observation provoked a logical question, "Tell us, when this will be?" (13:4). Jesus responded by saying that there will be plenty of signs, but no exact timetable. Only God knows the exact timing (13:32). God understands the suffering of humankind that will accompany these events. God is in control and will provide prophets to point the way and a Messiah—a Savior—to gather "the elect."

Throughout the chapter there is a growing momentum and sense of tension. Destruction, war, persecution, and disasters mount, but these are all offset by Jesus' assurance of God's awesome power and unquestioned authority. The great climactic moment of God's action is described in verses 26–27, when God's people "will see 'the Son of Man coming in clouds' with great power and glory. Then he will send out the angels, and gather his elect from the four winds, from the ends of the earth to the ends of heaven."

Intertwined among these threads of prophecy and encouragement is Jesus' pastoral care to his followers, based on key theological assumptions. He understands the all-too-human responses to the struggles of life and the unfolding crises of history; so he reminds his followers to "be alert" (13:5, 9, 23, 33) and to stay focused on the truth that he has revealed (13:23).

In Mark 13:28–31 Jesus summarizes what he has already said about knowing the "signs of the times" (see 13:4–8, 12–25) with an analogy to peoples' everyday observations of things in nature. When you see a fig tree beginning to sprout leaves, you know that summer is coming. Likewise there are indications in history that life as we know it is moving into a new season. Jesus' point is not that history is cyclical, but rather that there are indications of the future written into the unfolding events of the present.

There is a destiny to human existence toward which history is headed and to which our experiences point. The key element of that destiny is that God will finally be experienced as "near." One of the most difficult claims of people of faith is that "God is with us." "How can God be with us," those of every generation have justifiably asked, "if all these terrible things have happened to us?" (See, e.g., Judg. 6:13.) Certainly it is a fair question. Our experience many times seems to indicate the absence of God, rather than God's loving and gracious interaction or involvement with us. Does God see what is happening? Does God care? In Mark 13, Jesus turns this reasoning right around and indicates that the

Pastoral Perspective

Then Mom would speak again. "Did you boys see the family of beavers and their house?" "Beavers!?" we would exclaim. "Where?" "In the middle of the lake we passed a couple of miles into the hike. They were so busy. I enjoyed sitting and watching them," Mom would reply. "What lake? There was a lake?" we would ask. "You missed the whole lake?" Mom would ask incredulously. Then she would smile and say, "Perhaps we could stop by the lake on the way back down and see if the beavers are still working." Of course, on the way down we would make so much noise that any beaver or marmot sighting would be impossible. Disappointed, we never doubted that our mother had seen those things. We just wondered why it was that time and again we could never see those things. They were there. We just never looked for them.

In this reading in Mark about the coming of the end of the age, Jesus uses the ubiquitous fig tree as an object lesson for the disciples. The disciples have learned to read the signs of the natural world around them. They know that when the fig tree sends out its tender new branches and sprouts its first fresh leaves, then summer is on its way. A new season is coming. This is common knowledge to all who are able to recognize the signs. This is common knowledge to all who pay attention to what is happening around them.

Jesus then assures the disciples with the cryptic phrase that the "current generation" will not pass away until all "these things" have taken place. Scholars continue to debate the meaning of this verse, and while it is interesting to do so, some wonder if too much attention has been paid to these words so that, once again, we have missed the clear message of the entire passage: that followers are simply supposed to pay attention—not only to the destination, to what will happen in the end, but also, more importantly, to what is happening now around them. We spend so much time focusing on the destination that we miss the journey itself. We miss the signs of life shown to us by the fig tree and the marmot and the family of beavers.

Nelle Morton was born soon after the turn of the twentieth century in the hills of East Tennessee. She was fifteen years old when women were given the right to vote, forty-nine years old when the United States Supreme Court declared school segregation to be unequal and therefore unjust, and sixty years old when her denomination, the Presbyterian Church in the United States, ordained its first clergywoman. She was the first female tenured faculty member (and for many years, the only female tenured faculty

Exegetical Perspective

identified themselves as belonging to the (devastated) traditions of Israel. Indeed, Jewish historian Josephus's description of Jerusalem's fall to Rome in 70 CE in the following passage is reminiscent of "all these things" of destruction mentioned in Mark 13:30:

> While the temple was on fire, everything was plundered.... nor was there pity for any age.... but children, old men, profane persons and priests were all slain in the same manner.... The flames also spread a long way and roared in unison with the groans of those that were slain, and because ... the size of the burning pile [was] so great, one would have thought the whole city had been on fire; nor could one imagine anything either greater or more terrible than the noise. (*Jewish War* 6.5)[1]

How does this passage relate to the larger literary structure of Mark? Scholars have often assumed that Mark 13:28–31 fits within the rest of chapter 13, and in particular with verses 24–27's description of the darkening of sun and moon, the falling of stars from the skies, and the coming of the Son of Man. Although attention to Mark 13 as a literary unit is helpful, close attention to verses 28–31 demonstrates a distinction between these verses and the rest of Mark 13, as well as significant links to larger themes of Mark as a whole. In three particular ways, these particular verses help reorient all of Mark 13 away from interpretation of the chapter as a prediction of the end of the world.

First, there is a strong emphasis in this passage that counters interpreting Mark 13 as a picture of the end time. The assurance that "my words will not pass away" (v. 31) concludes the unit and blunts the sense of disaster in verses 24 and 25 with its reassurance. This does not mean that the reassurance overcomes the presence of disaster in these verses, but simply that they exist alongside one another.

Second, as noted above, verses 28–31, along with the rest of chapter 13, attend directly to the trauma and loss of Israel during the Roman invasion of 68–70 CE. Interpretations of chapter 13 as a picture of the end of the world tend to miss the way Mark, along with other first- and second-century writers, comments quite directly on the destructiveness of the Roman Empire. For instance, Revelation 17–18 refers to the destruction of and by Rome with its reference to the seven hills on which the great prostitute and beast sit. *Fourth Ezra* makes a similar connection:

---

1. Josephus, *Jewish War*, trans. H. St. J. Thackeray, Loeb Classical Library 210 (Cambridge: Harvard University Press, 1927).

Homiletical Perspective

whatever binds them by Jesus' teachings and miracles. All people—regardless of class, gender, race, age, or physical condition—are received and valued by God and taught to include all in a new, inclusive community.

In that context, then, we can begin to see how these verses bring good news to those who find themselves in bondage of any kind. We are to "learn" from the fig tree, whose first buds give an unerring sign that spring is about to arrive and the dead of winter is over. We are to "know" that, just as the harshness of winter is over and summer is approaching, in our own sufferings for God's reign there are signs of the approach of the Son of Man, who is near, even at the gates.

The preacher could note how Mark makes use of the poetry of apocalyptic language, which is designed to open up possibilities rather than limit them, to evoke rather than define meanings. As Mitzi Minor suggests, while many things make us look, poetry, along with other artistic expressions, enables us to "see." "The evocative power of apocalyptic's poetic descriptions invites readers' imaginative participation so that they can 'see' the vision that is narrated."[1] Here Mark's poetry does not lock the reader into a specific date for the coming of the Son of Man, for Jesus goes on to say that the exact time is not known, except by the Father. Nevertheless the language conveys a sense of urgency regarding his return. Know that he is near, Jesus teaches, and because he is near, even suffering for his sake and persevering as his listeners proclaim the gospel is vital.

How might the preacher now move to the pastoral/prophetic word of hope in the midst of such bewildering poetic apocalyptic language? After all, after hearing these words in Mark 13 many of our listeners might assume that God is simply a vengeful destroyer. The movement is made by looking to the margins of our own culture in our own time, by "learning" from and "seeing" with them.

This is made clear in Bill Moyers's remarkable book *Genesis*, in which he engages a number of scholars from a variety of faith perspectives to discuss the stories of the first book of the Bible. Among those engaging the story of the flood are two feminists, Karen Armstrong and Carol Gilligan, and an African American pastor and theologian, Samuel Proctor. The women try to convince Proctor that the God of Noah is vengeful, angry, vindictive, and

---

1. Mitzi Minor, *The Spirituality of Mark: Responding to God* (Louisville, KY: Westminster John Knox Press, 1996), 66.

Mark 13:28–31

Theological Perspective

examples of increasing pain, suffering, and crisis in the world are actually sure signs that God's unquestionable presence will soon be made known. When these things happen, you will know "that he is near, at the very gates" (v. 29).

Jesus characterizes the tragic suffering of this world as "birth pangs" (13:8), which are short-lived, but intense, harbingers of a glorious future that yet awaits. Verse 30 is one of those enigmatic and often discussed statements about the when of all of this. Was Jesus simply mistaken in his statement that all these things would be accomplished in the lifetime of his followers? It is a problem only if Jesus' hearers assumed that "all" included the dropping of the final curtain on this age and the complete revealing of the glory of the Son of Man. However, if "all" simply refers to what the disciples have already experienced and the additional historical undulations that they could see coming if they would only be more observant, then what Jesus said is more straightforward. All of this—including his own death, the agony of the disciples, various natural disasters, the destruction of the temple, and so forth—would indeed take place within the generation. All of it would be a sign that God is standing at the very gates.

In looking back at our lives, a common experience of believers who have gone through the most intense times of persecution, suffering, or grieving is that they never felt God's nearness more than through these places of pain. Where some complain of God's seeming abandonment, others see God's presence more clearly than ever before.

This was certainly the case with the first disciples. Life would become gravely more difficult in the days that would soon follow Jesus' words, but God's presence would become more and more immanent as well.

Jesus closes this text with the resounding reminder that underlying all of life are those things that will not change. Jesus' words, Jesus' promises, Jesus' assurances would not pass away. no matter what the unraveling of human history might produce. God is a sure foundation. God is near. God's Word will never fail us.

STEPHEN A. HAYNER

Pastoral Perspective

member) at the Theological School of Drew University in Madison, New Jersey, where she taught Christian education.

Recognized for her important scholarship as a feminist working for the rights of women in the church and society and for the civil rights of African Americans and eventually all persons throughout the globe, her most important work was published in 1985, two years before her death. Titled *The Journey Is Home*, the work is a collection of essays woven with her own autobiography. The book's title comes from her consistent use of the "journey" as metaphor. Morton muses, "Maybe journey is not so much a journey ahead, or a journey into space, but a journey into presence."[1]

In a taped interview after Morton's work had been published and a year before her death, an interviewer sought to juxtapose Morton's understanding of journey with the metaphor of home. "I think I understand why this metaphor of journey is so important to you," said the interviewer. "But honestly, is there not a point where you get weary of the journey? Is there not a point where you want the journey to end and you want to be home?" Morton was quiet in the interview for a few moments and then she spoke slowly but surely in response: "Home? Home? But don't you understand? For me, the journey *is* home."[2]

Pay attention, Jesus says to his followers. Look not only to the destination, to the end, to home, for that will surely come. For now, for these days, pay attention to the signs that are all around you. Pay attention to the journey, because, for now, the journey is your home.

RODGER Y. NISHIOKA

---

1. Nelle Morton, *The Journey Is Home* (Boston: Beacon, 1985), 227.
2. Presbyterian Church (U.S.A.), *Nelle Morton: The Journey Is Home*, VHS (Louisville, KY: Education and Nurture Unit, 1989).

Exegetical Perspective

And I said, "Oh sovereign Lord . . . from all the lands of the worlds you have chosen for yourself one region . . . and from all the multitude of people you have gotten for yourself one people. . . . And now, oh Lord, why have you . . . scattered your only one among the many? And those who opposed your promises have trampled on those who believed your covenants. If you really hate your people, they should be punished at your own hands." (4 *Ezra* 5:23–30)

The idea of this text as a prediction of an end time unhooks it from its historical situation and hijacks it to function as a generalized prediction about the world's future.

Instead of understanding this passage as an independent picture of the destruction at the end of the world, we do well to read it in the context of Mark's larger struggle with the searing Roman violence experienced by all those associated with spiritual Israel. Mark 13:28–31 in its agony and consolation fits with the rest of Mark's insistent and complicated joining of loss, healing, trauma, and incomplete resurrection.

Third, the relationship of this passage to the one following it (13:32–37) fits with the larger tensive portraits in Mark of uncertainty, rather than a triumphant and determined prediction of a general end time. Just as Mark mixes Jesus' healing many and failing to heal others (6:5) with his steely resolve to be crucified (8:31–37; 9:30–32; 10:32–34), even while afraid and angry about it (14:32–42; 15:34), and resurrected (16:6) but never proclaimed (16:8); so the joining of 13:28–31 with 13:32–37 present a complex mix of assurance, fear, certainty, and contradiction. Both in verses 28–37 and in the whole of Mark, the reader is invited into an inscrutable mix of healing rescue, violence, and destruction, and offered the possibility of living boldly and expressively in a volatile present.

Verses 28–31 as such form a nugget at the heart of Mark's message. Far from an abstracted prediction about another time, it mixes the certain freshness of summer, the certainty of violence and loss, and the power of Jesus' words in the middle of it all. Freed from the notion of an end-time prediction, these verses (and Mark in general) hold out the gift of fresh aliveness in a devastating context.

HAL TAUSSIG

Homiletical Perspective

murderous. There is nothing hopeful or compassionate about a God who simply in a fit of pique brings on a great flood and destroys most of humanity.

In response Proctor asserts the black experience: "Black people identified themselves with Daniel in the lion's den, the Hebrew boys in the furnace, the Israelites coming out of the Flood. They saw the Bible in the context of their own experience, and they kept it alive, . . . They took the Hebrew Bible saga, and made it their own story." The women see nothing but a false reassurance in the rainbow as the flood ends, but Proctor insists that "it's not just a rainbow," but a sign of hope for oppressed people. "Black people could have put God on trial," he says, "but instead we put white supremacy on trial. . . . People had gunpowder and ships, and they used their freedom [to] enslave others. But . . . in time, we can correct these things. I'm living with that bow in the cloud right now. And if I'm the last optimist left, I don't mind that at all."[2]

It is easy to despair these days when we see the hurt and suffering of those who remain marginalized in our society and even in our communities of faith. We get discouraged at the injustices that remain, and sometimes even feel that hard-fought victories of the past are being whittled away. Women still struggle for equality and suffer an inordinate degree of poverty, as do people of color. Jim Crow laws are being resurrected, aimed this time at immigrants. However, we learn from the fig tree, and we see that summer is near. The kingdom, the *basileia*, is closer than we think. We therefore live without fear. We await the Son of Man with hearts full of compassion for those who suffer, and we do so with hope, for he is near—very near.

STEPHEN R. MONTGOMERY

---

2. Bill Moyers, *Genesis: A Living Conversation* (New York: Doubleday, 1996), 118–28.

Mark 13:32–37

³²"But about that day or hour no one knows, neither the angels in heaven, nor the Son, but only the Father. ³³Beware, keep alert; for you do not know when the time will come. ³⁴It is like a man going on a journey, when he leaves home and puts his slaves in charge, each with his work, and commands the doorkeeper to be on the watch. ³⁵Therefore, keep awake—for you do not know when the master of the house will come, in the evening, or at midnight, or at cockcrow, or at dawn, ³⁶or else he may find you asleep when he comes suddenly. ³⁷And what I say to you I say to all: Keep awake."

Theological Perspective

Mark 13 serves as a bridge from Jesus' three years of ministry to the story of his passion. In this sense, Mark 13 is a kind of farewell message. The chapter underlines Jesus' assertion that history is moving toward a time when God will enter human experience in a definitive way and make all things right. God is fully in control, even though there are daily illustrations all around that seem to indicate otherwise.

Rather than focusing on how his followers could calculate when the final curtain would fall, Jesus' message throughout Mark 13 is how they should prepare for their immediate future, which would include both mission and suffering. There are nineteen imperatives in this one chapter—commands about what faithful behavior looks like in a time of unprecedented catastrophe. What Jesus envisioned for his followers was not some sort of fervor for or questioning about the eschatological events to come, but rather a determined and single-minded obedience to cross bearing (8:34–38) and sharing in Jesus' ministry to the world.

Here in verses 32–37 Jesus brings his message about the end times to a conclusion by underlining again that what will be needed in the future is faith and vigilance.

The paragraph opens with the words "about that day" (v. 32), which evoke a whole list of references

Pastoral Perspective

Fasten your seat belts. That is the current message of the Rapture Ready Index. You can view it online.[1] It is an index provided for Christians to indicate how near we are to the second coming of Christ, which according to some will surely begin with the rapture of all righteous believers from the face of the earth. In case you were wondering, "fasten your seat belts" is the ultimate category, just above "high prophetic activity." According to the index, we are scoring currently well above the 160–point mark, which is the threshold for when Christians need to "fasten your seat belts" because of all that is happening in the world. The index quantifies a series of events (wars, famine, disasters, immorality, false prophets) to reach its current number.

What is more, the Rapture Ready Index is just one of hundreds of sites available to give Christians more information about when Jesus is coming again. A search on Amazon.com reveals nearly 300,000 books and movies that relate somehow to Christ's return and the end of the world. All of these sites, books, and movies have a ready audience. They would not exist if people were not logging on to them and reading the books and viewing the movies.

---

1. Rapture Ready Index, http://www.raptureready.com/rap2.html; accessed January 20, 2013.

Exegetical Perspective

It seems likely (although not unmuddled) that the event to which this passage refers—about whose "day or hour no one knows" and for which the disciples are to be "on your guard"—is the coming of "the Son of Man . . . in clouds with great power and glory" in 13:26. This is an event associated with much destruction, including "the desolating sacrilege set up where it ought not to be" (13:14) and the darkening of the sun, the falling of stars, the shaking of the powers in the heavens, and the gathering by the Son of Man of his chosen (13:24–27).

When Will These Things Happen? Although much of chapter 13 places emphasis on the dramatic character of the predicted disasters and gathering of the chosen, the confusion about when exactly these things are to happen is not clarified in this final portion of the chapter. Indeed, this conclusion of the chapter insists that the timing of the predicted events is unknown: "about that day or hour no one knows, neither the angels in heaven, nor the Son. . . . [Y]ou do not know when the time will come. . . . [K]eep awake—for you do not know when the master of the house will come" (vv. 32–35).

This question regarding when these events will happen is complicated by the preceding paragraph (13:28–30), which both guarantees that everything

Homiletical Perspective

As Mark's little apocalypse draws to a close, several homiletical themes can be gleaned from these final six verses.

What We Do Not Know and What We Do Know. It is hard for many of us to admit the limits of our knowledge, but that has not kept us from offering sure and certain predictions about the future through the centuries. Such predictions are not limited to the days of old in ancient Israel or the early church. Nor are they limited to medieval warnings from the likes of Melchior Hoffmann in 1533, who preached so passionately about the coming end of time that the leaders of the city of Strasburg arrested him and he spent the next ten years until his death in prison pondering his calculations. There was William Miller, who identified October 22, 1844, as the final judgment day. More recently, many will remember Harold Camping, an 89-year-old California evangelist and radio broadcaster who whipped people into a frenzy with his prediction that May 21, 2011, would be the date of the Rapture. People sold their possessions and liquidated their pension funds to advertise the warning.[1]

---

1. Jon M. Walton, "The Rembrandt in the Living Room" (sermon, First Presbyterian Church, New York City, June 5, 2011).

Mark 13:32–37

Theological Perspective

to Old Testament predictions about the future. For example, Amos 8 speaks of "that day" when the sovereign Lord will bring catastrophe on the disobedient and neglectful; Zephaniah 1:15 pictures the warrior Lord avenging himself on "that day." "That day" was a shorthand way of talking about God's radical intervention in human history—a time when both judgment and promise would be realized and a new heaven and earth would appear.

While Jesus affirms the expectation and hope regarding the fulfillment of God's future plan, he makes it clear that no one knows when the end will come. No one. Not the angels who dwell in the very presence of God. Not even the Son. This is the same point that the resurrected Jesus makes when the disciples ask him before his ascension if he is about to bring a great political restoration: "It is not for you to know the times or periods that the Father has set by his own authority" (Acts 1:7). In this instance too, Jesus turns their attention toward their responsibility in the interim.

For some, Jesus' assertion that even he does not know the timetable may create a theological conundrum. How is it that Jesus, being in his very nature God, would not know what the Father knows? How is it that the Bible can describe the Son and the Father as "one" and yet Jesus would not know what God is planning? Can Jesus be divine without being omniscient? Here it is important to consider what it means that Jesus "emptied himself" (Phil. 2:6–8) when he took on human flesh. There are certain areas of knowledge and authority that belong only to God the Father and cannot be known by the incarnated Jesus. When the moment comes, God will send the Son with the holy angels (8:38; 13:26–27), but until that moment the timing will remain a mystery even to Jesus.

So what are the disciples to do in the interim? Since they do "not know" (13:32, 33, 35) when God will finally intervene, they are to "be aware," "alert," and "awake" (13:5, 9, 23, 33, 35, 37). They are to be attentive and watchful.

Jesus punctuates this point with a final short parable about a homeowner who goes away and leaves his servants in charge of the household. Each of the servants has assigned tasks, including watching at the door for their master's return. Because the master could come at any time, even at night, faithful servants are to be ready and watchful. They are to be obedient in their assigned tasks, and not distracted or prone to falling asleep.

Jesus' last command in his message is "Keep awake!" Only a short time later, these words would

Pastoral Perspective

It seems to be in our nature to want to know. For some, it is simple curiosity and amusement. For others, it is complete silliness and absurdity. For yet others, it is very, very serious.

In practically every generation, some believers have reached the conclusion that Christ's return was imminent. There is much evidence that the early Christians thought this and were certain of it. They were ready and waiting, and when their expectations did not pan out, many were confused and some left the church. After every disaster, be it the plague of the fourteenth century or the world wars of the twentieth century, word arises that surely Christ is coming again soon. Tragically, whenever these voices reach a certain level of hysteria, people get swept along with them. There are stories of persons quitting jobs and selling homes and huddling together in clusters waiting for that expected moment. Even more sadly, there are some even more misguided who, when the predicted moment passes, end up so disillusioned and despairing that they take their own lives.

For all, the words of Jesus in Mark's Gospel serve both as a warning and as a comfort. Jesus tells the believers clearly that of the moment he is to return, no one knows except the Father. It is striking that Jesus himself, the one who is to return, does not know. Only God knows. No Rapture Ready Index or biblical scholar or eloquent preacher or persuasive teacher knows. Only God knows. These words are a warning to all those who hear or read of anyone who says they have somehow been given a special revelation about Christ's return. This is a warning. Do not be deceived. These persons are claiming that they alone, more than the angels in heaven and Jesus himself, have been chosen by God to know the particular time of the second coming. Jesus is clear. It is not so. No one knows.

While these words serve as a warning, they also serve as a comfort. They serve as a comfort because ultimately, while Christ is surely coming again, when he is coming is not our concern. We need not fret about when Christ is to return. All we need to do is keep awake. This keeping awake is a comfort, because even in the midst of tragedy, Christ is coming to redeem us all and to bring hope out of despair. Even when all may seem lost, we know how the world is going to end. Our task is to keep awake. This image of keeping awake is not one of passivity. The image is a potent one. Jesus compares this wakefulness to servants who know their master is to return but do not know when. These servants are not sitting around; rather, they are anticipating the

Exegetical Perspective

will happen within a generation and asserts that there are already clear signs—as clear as the presummer signs of a tree before it produces fruit—about when these things will occur. Although verses 32–37 insist that no one can tell, the immediately preceding verses pointedly emphasize that it is easy to know, if one just looks at the signs.

It would be easy to conclude that Jesus' discussion of the predicted devastation in Mark is simply contradictory and confusing. However, there are two trajectories of Markan scholarship that may make the apparent contradiction of chapter 13 more intelligible.

The first trajectory of scholarship that helps unmuddle this confusion reads the ending of Mark 13 in light of other passages in Mark in which Jesus' teachings are framed by ambiguous parables regarding the kingdom of God. The "nearness" of the kingdom of God is beautifully uncertain with regard to its timing. Jesus' announcement in 1:15 emphasizes the nearness of the kingdom: "The time is fulfilled, and the kingdom of God has come near; repent, and believe in the good news." What does it mean for the kingdom to be "near"? To complicate the nearness of God's kingdom, a number of Jesus' parables actively compare the kingdom of God to ordinary yet strange happenings in everyday life. As he says, "The kingdom of God is as if someone would scatter seed on the ground, and would sleep and rise night and day, and the seed would sprout and grow, he does not know how" (4:26). (See also his comparison of the kingdom of God to a mustard seed in 4:30–32.)

These parables suggest that the kingdom of God is present in ordinary processes of labor and nature, but in both cases as something curious and unpredictable. So the present, but complicated, reality of the kingdom in the parables helps us interpret the apparent contradiction in the timing of events in Mark 13:28–37 by underlining the ironic nature of the kingdom's presence. Mark clearly intends verses 32–37 to be understood in conjunction with these earlier parables, since the text itself includes a kind of parable (v. 34) regarding the coming of the Son of Man: "[The coming of the Son of Man] is like a man going on a journey, when he leaves home and puts his slaves in charge, each with his work, and commands the doorkeeper to be on the watch." This similarity between Jesus' view of the kingdom's nearness in daily life and the haunting predictions of chapter 13 and their frustratingly ambiguous temporal character lies in their mutual ambiguity and proximity. Rather than point to a way of grasping the kingdom

Homiletical Perspective

Mark reminds us that we do not know a great many things. "About that day or hour no one knows, neither the angels in heaven, nor the Son, but only the Father" (v. 32). Jesus says he does not know. Only God knows, and there is grace in not knowing. Jesus calms the frenzy and fears caused by those who come saying, "We know."

We do know, however, that we have hope, because whatever we may expect, history is in God's hands. The world is not chaos but the creation of one who seeks to relate to us as a loving parent. The real power in the world is not brute force or the weapons of violence but the goodness of Christ, who is calling all the world to its final destination in his mercy. To believe this world is ultimately and finally Christ's requires no little courage.

Keep Alert. Because we do not know when the time will come, we are to keep alert, says Jesus (v. 33). Pay attention. What does this mean? For some, this means watching for the literal end of the world. Jesus dispels this line of thinking, admitting that even the Son does not know the day or the hour.

However, that does not leave us spiritually paralyzed. On the contrary, we are told that there is work to do. Just as each servant is given a particular task in this parable, we know we have work to do, and our work is given shape and meaning by our hope of Christ's coming in victory. Though we do not know when or how the master will finally come, we are assured throughout Scripture that Christ's kingdom will be a kingdom of justice for all people. This hope encourages us and gives us strength as we stand with Christ against everything that betrays and destroys human life.

The story is told of a meeting of state legislators in colonial New England that rapidly descended into darkness because of a solar eclipse that no one predicted. Some panicked and sought to adjourn the meeting. Then one of them said, "Mr. Speaker, if it is not the end of the world and we adjourn, we shall appear to be fools. If it is the end of the world, I should choose to be found doing my duty. I move you, sir, that candles be brought."[2]

Being alert calls us to work, but it also calls us to worship. In worship we watch and wait and tune our ears for good news. In some sense, worship is an elaborate dress rehearsal, where we practice and get our cues right for the day when the Son of Man returns. We watch for that. With Christians around

---

2. Lamar Williamson Jr., *Mark* (Atlanta: John Knox Press, 1983), 242.

Mark 13:32–37

Theological Perspective

echo once more in the Garden of Gethsemane (14:34, 37, 38), when the disciples could not stay awake for even a short hour. Once again, Jesus would say to them, "Keep awake and pray that you may not come into the time of trial; the spirit indeed is willing, but the flesh is weak" (14:38).

Throughout Mark 13, the message is clear. No matter what persecution might come, and no matter what apparent delay in God's salvation might be experienced, followers of Jesus are to live faithful and vigilant lives, in the certainty that the Son will finally be sent in a definitive victory over the chaos. Because Jesus does not know when the end will come, even he has to live by this same faith and make attentiveness and obedience the hallmarks of his walk with God. This is an important recognition of Jesus' real humanity. As the author of Hebrews says, "he had to become like his brothers and sisters in every respect" (Heb. 2:17).

There is an interesting footnote hidden in the last lines of Jesus' message. As Mark tells the parable of the Journeying Homeowner, Jesus makes the point that the homeowner comes at night. On the one hand, this detail connects this discourse with the other critical moments in these last chapters that occur at night (14:17, 43, 72). The shadows of night are about to give way to the glories of dawn (16:1). On the other hand, Mark's formulation here includes *four* watches at night (evening, midnight, cockcrow, and dawn). This was the Roman division of time. The Jews reckoned only three watches in the night. This detail, and Jesus' extension of his final exhortation to include "all" (v. 37), is an indication that this message was intended not only for the current followers of Jesus, but also for the Christians who were listening to Mark's Gospel throughout the Roman Empire. "All" includes not only Jewish disciples, but everyone who would hear this teaching and follow him. Jesus' command to "stay awake!" should ring in every ear: vigilance in time of trial; faithfulness to the mission!

STEPHEN A. HAYNER

Pastoral Perspective

master's return and keeping up the house so that when the master returns, all will be ready and as it should be. This is a kind of comfort that demands our response and attention.

I made plans to visit with some friends of mine at their home for dinner. We had set a time for me to arrive but it was an "ish" time, such as five-ish. There was no particular time, just a general understanding. When I pulled up to the home, I saw the face of Catherine, the nine-year-old, in the window. She was jumping up and down as I got out of my car. I waved to her and she waved back at me. When I got in the door, Catherine hugged me and quickly dragged me off to show me her latest artwork from school. Later, her mom Lynn said she was grateful I arrived when I did, because Catherine was driving her crazy. Knowing that I was going to come for dinner, Catherine had worked with her mom to clean up her room and be sure she was dressed in her favorite outfit. Ever the planner, she had even written out an agenda of things she wanted to show me and games we were to play. "Thank goodness you arrived when you did," Lynn said. "Catherine was making us all crazy preparing and waiting for you to arrive."

No one knows exactly when Jesus is to come back, even Jesus himself. We know he is coming, but we do not know when. Frankly, *when* Jesus is coming back should not be the focus of our attention. What should be the focus of our attention is, like Catherine, doing all that we can to prepare and anticipate his coming, so that our lives are in order. These are words of both warning and comfort. Keep awake, for Christ is coming back. Keep awake and make all ready, so that our lives and all of creation will show our anticipation of his coming again.

RODGER Y. NISHIOKA

Exegetical Perspective

or the coming of the Son of Man, both the parables and chapter 13 create a persistent, yet unsteady, expectancy. The overall Markan tactic, so pointedly and caustically expressed in both the parables and chapter 13, keeps the reader off guard, countering tendencies to give up, to flee, or to claim vengeance or triumph.

The second scholarly trajectory that helps interpret the apparent contradiction in Mark 13 is that the Markan Jesus' predictions were likely not written before the events of the late 60s and early 70s CE, in which Jerusalem was devastated and the temple destroyed by the Romans. The Markan Jesus' "predictions" of the devastation, then, may have been written by a community that was processing the devastation. Seen in this way, the lack of explicit information from Jesus and his double and triple takes on whether one can know when devastation will actually happen reflect the experience of living in the middle of destruction. This text engages what living with destruction is like, rather than giving a clear picture of what will happen.

Stay Awake. This passage repeats the injunction to "keep alert" or "keep awake" three times (vv. 33, 35–36, 37). The backdrop for keeping awake is also repeated; that is, neither you nor anyone knows "when the time will come." This concluding section of chapter 13's larger address to the violence that will overcome Israel in the early 70s CE has few answers about how to address this destruction. It simply presses for consciousness (keeping awake) over against the most persistent human responses to violence and desolation: denial, depression, anxiety, and inevitability.

Like the parables about the kingdom in ordinary life, it calls for an alert response in the middle of a disaster. Mark artfully and forcefully disappoints the reader who expects a clear strategy for how to proceed in life in the wake of such destruction and violence. Instead of instructions for what to do, Mark keeps the reader in the tension of the situation, refusing to conclude either triumphantly or tragically. Wakefulness—consciousness, instead of denial or flight of fancy—is the mark of faith.

HAL TAUSSIG

Homiletical Perspective

the world we sing *maranatha,* "come, Lord Jesus" (1 Cor. 16:22). Come and heal this world.

In the Absence, There Is Presence. Verses 34–37 present a parable of absence, and Mark's listeners who were without the physical presence of Jesus could well identify with the servants put in charge while the master was away. In the absence, we do Christ's work of healing the sick and feeding the hungry and working for justice. In so doing, we become servants of Christ to others. We are entrusted now with his work to do, and we live each day accountable and thankful to the God who has given us life. We look after others as if the Son of Man himself were serving. We light a candle on a darkened path so that others who follow may find their way home. We build a home where sometimes a stranger and always a friend may enter in and get warm by the fire, finding nourishment for soul and spirit.

This parable reminds us that we have more than enough gifts to work Christ's healing and hope in the world, even in a world filled with global and national tumult. "When we're down and out, instead of coming to God to look for a pick-me-up, as though God were a spiritual drugstore and we'd written out for ourselves a prayer prescription," writes Brian Blount, "perhaps we ought to come looking for ways to identify with someone in trouble, and give of ourselves, even when we feel given out. Perhaps it's in the giving to others that we get the peace we seek."[3]

Indeed, the very peace of Christ.

STEPHEN R. MONTGOMERY

---

3. Brian Blount and Gary Charles, *Preaching Mark in Two Voices* (Louisville, KY: Westminster John Knox Press, 2003), 227.

Mark 14:1–2, 10–11

¹It was two days before the Passover and the festival of Unleavened Bread. The chief priests and the scribes were looking for a way to arrest Jesus by stealth and kill him; ²for they said, "Not during the festival, or there may be a riot among the people.". . .

¹⁰Then Judas Iscariot, who was one of the twelve, went to the chief priests in order to betray him to them. ¹¹When they heard it, they were greatly pleased, and promised to give him money. So he began to look for an opportunity to betray him.

Theological Perspective

There are passages in Scripture that are almost too painful to read. This is one of them. Like so many stories depicting the deceit and faithlessness of God's elect—one thinks here of the simple words in 2 Samuel 11:2, when we are told that "it happened, late one afternoon," as David espied Bathsheba bathing—so here, with little fanfare, we read that Judas, "who was one of the twelve," sought out the chief priests "in order to betray him to them" (v. 10). So simple. So apparently motiveless. Unlike John or Matthew, Mark offers no avaricious or demonic motive for this betrayal. He simply notes that Judas took the initiative to betray Jesus to those who were looking for a way to arrest him by stealth and kill him.

What are we to make of this story of deadly betrayal, of the complicity of one of Jesus' chosen band, of the ease with which the whole sad business is carried off?

The church has often debated the relative weight of responsibility for Jesus' death, sometimes assigning the burden more to the religious authorities (the chief priests and the scribes) and at other times to the political powers. Mark, though, makes it clear this was an inside job, that "the chief priests and scribes," for all their stealthy plotting, were hamstrung, unable to move against Jesus on their own. What was needed was one of his own, someone

Pastoral Perspective

One of the most enigmatic figures in the Gospels is Judas Iscariot. Instrumental to the arrest of Jesus, he is found in all four Gospels, though the portrayals vary. His act of betrayal has baffled the faithful for generations, so much so that possible motivations have been suggested, in part drawn on Gospel accounts. In contemporary popular culture, Judas has been presented in literature, film, and on the stage in ways that seek to rehabilitate his reputation or at least refashion him into a more sympathetic character.[1] He has become, for example, an idealistic revolutionary, a pragmatist concerned for the poor, a tragic hero, and a disillusioned disciple.

The depictions of Judas from the early centuries of the Jesus movement are not monolithic either. The Gospels of Luke and John attribute his treachery to possession by Satan (Luke 22:3; John 13:27). John also insinuates that Judas was a thief (John 12:6), who resented the anointing of Jesus with expensive perfume because it would cut into his pilfering of the funds used to support their ministry. Matthew too introduces greed as a factor in Judas's duplicity (Matt. 26:15), though he adds an element of remorse that ends in Judas's death by his own hand (Matt.

---

1. See for example Kim Paffenroth, "Film Depictions of Judas," *Journal of Religion and Film* 5 (2001); http://www.unomaha.edu/jrf/judas.htm; accessed January 17, 2013.

Exegetical Perspective

This passage marks a crucial point in the Gospel. Jesus has completed his Galilean ministry, entered Jerusalem to tumultuous popular acclaim (11:1–10), publicly debated the religious authorities there (11:15–12:40), and summoned his disciples to eschatological watchfulness (chap. 13). Now the events that were foretold in the three passion predictions—betrayal, condemnation, and death (8:31; 9:31; 10:33–34)—begin to unfold. Throughout chapters 14–16, days, times, and places are noted with new precision, the narrative is more unified, and time seems to pass more slowly. Only three days are covered in these three chapters. All of this serves to signal the importance of the events narrated here and to heighten their drama.

The episode is recounted in two parts, separated by the story of Jesus' anointing by an unnamed woman (vv. 3–9). Mark often uses this "sandwiching" of one story within another, a technique called intercalation, to imply that the events related in the two stories occurred simultaneously; that is, the woman's generous act of love occurred at the very moment that the chief priests and scribes were plotting Jesus' death. Intercalation also increases the ironic tension by suggesting that two very different stories, the frame and the insertion, should be interpreted in light of each other.

Homiletical Perspective

Betrayal is not one of the first things that comes to mind when thinking about preaching the good news in worship. However, in the Gospel story in general, and in this pericope in particular, one cannot avoid it. Betrayal is front and center in this passage recounting Judas Iscariot's duplicity in the arrest of Jesus—his leader, teacher, and friend—by Jewish authorities in exchange for money (vv. 10–11). The preacher is literally forced to confront the issue head-on in this pericope. There is no escaping the reality of betrayal, as it leads the Gospel story on to the arrest, trial, beating, crucifixion, death, and resurrection of Jesus. Additionally, this act by Judas Iscariot invites the reader or listener to enter into an experience of trying to understand why one might betray another, especially a friend.

When we address this text from the pulpit, we are also led to examine the motivations of those who sought to arrest Jesus by stealth (v. 2). The chief priests and scribes were looking to arrest and kill Jesus, but they also knew there were obstacles to doing that during the festival of the Unleavened Bread prior to the Passover (v. 1). This is a holy time in Jewish tradition, and they did not want to stir up trouble. Many had come to respect and follow Jesus. Arresting and killing him would potentially cause a riot among his followers. However, the religious

Mark 14:1–2, 10–11

Theological Perspective

who could sell Jesus out from the inside, subverting thereby any claim that this itinerant rabbi was in fact the Lord's anointed.

Of course, that is what hurts. The heaviness of the passion narrative does not derive from the bad guys who do Jesus in. Strangely, the story, while not overlooking them, does not focus on them at all. No, the story is not about them, but about us. Judas's very name identifies him as representative of Judah, one of God's elect people. He was not someone on the outside, threatened by Jesus' fame or suspicious of Jesus' ministry. No, he was "one of the twelve" (v. 10), one whom Jesus had chosen, one of Jesus' own.

Of course, that is the history of God's people, the history of Israel, the history of God's elect, who have always found a reason—it really does not matter which one—for selling God out. Sin really is not what "they" do. That hardly describes the true horror of human perfidy before God. Sin is what *we* do, we who have been chosen by God, protected and loved by God, nourished and fed by God, claimed and forgiven by God. Precisely then, as the recipients of God's grace, we find something that is more valuable to us than God's grace; we find a reason to barter, negotiate, manage a better solution. The resulting violation comes then not from those who actively oppose Jesus and his ministry, but from those within, who have eaten his bread and shared his lot. Then the real hurt is done. Betrayal is what kills, not the evil hosts surrounding us, not the great odds against the Christian message, not the "world" or "unbelievers" or skeptics of various sorts.

Karl Barth notes that knowledge of sin is always a function of our knowledge of Jesus Christ.[1] We would like to think that sin is something more obvious, something more manageable, something that we can discern on our own and judge for ourselves. That is just another way we attempt to render sin harmless. Only in the light of the revelation of Jesus Christ do we see the truth, the horrible truth of what sin is, of what happens when we seek to be our own judge, rejecting the love and faithfulness of him who calls us into his life. We "win." That is the sad and yet utterly amazing result. We sell the gift out for "money," as in Judas's case, and what we are left with is "money," the devastating, soul-destroying, emptiness of getting what we want.

Mark makes only two other mentions of Judas in his Gospel, when he introduces Judas at 3:19 as the

---

1. Karl Barth, *Church Dogmatics*, IV/1, *The Doctrine of Reconciliation* (Edinburgh: T. &T. Clark, 1956), 389.

Pastoral Perspective

27:3–5). In Acts, Luke communicates another tradition about Judas whereby he dies a gruesome death, disemboweled in a fatal fall in a field purchased with his blood money (Acts 1:18).

Curiously, the Gospel of Mark contains none of these elements, nor does it attempt to ascribe motivations to Judas's act of betrayal. On the one hand, Judas's actions remain inconceivable and inexplicable; on the other hand, this is one more instance in the Gospel of Mark where one of the Twelve, the inner circle of disciples, behaves poorly. In this sense, Judas's action is consistent with Peter's denials (14:66–72), the disciples' inability to comprehend who Jesus was or where his actions were leading, and their failure to stay awake and accompany him in his darkest hours (14:37–41).

In preaching and teaching about Judas, it is tempting to construct a harmonized character by mixing and matching details from across the Gospels. For example, in reading Mark, in which the betrayal follows the anointing of Jesus with expensive perfume, interpreters read avarice into the text with evidence gleaned from John's aspersions on Judas as a thief. In the hope of unraveling Judas's motive, other interpreters create psychological profiles of him, treating as fact his self-inflicted death, even though this is found only in Matthew.

Collateral pastoral damage results from these undifferentiated portraits of Judas, which fail to account for the significance of each Gospel context. For example, in the popular Christian imagination Judas is sometimes synonymous with betrayal and suicide, even though only Matthew's narrative mentions his hanging himself. Some theological interpretations of him have contributed to negative responses of churches toward people who commit suicide. These responses have produced painful consequences for their communities, for those who loved them, and for the reputations of the deceased.

In his influential *City of God*, Augustine addresses the issue of voluntary death out of pastoral concern. He is seeking to dissuade some Christians of his time from their unhealthy attraction to a cult of martyrdom. In the course of his discussion (book 1, section 17), Augustine briefly singles out Judas, yet he does not identify that this interpretation is based solely on Matthew's version of the passion narrative. Augustine sees Judas's self-inflicted death as aggravating and not expiating the guilt of his betrayal. For him, the irreversibility of Judas's action demonstrated a despair that left no room for God's mercy or healing

Exegetical Perspective

A Passover Plot (vv. 1–2). The Passover context of Jesus' passion is a firm part of the tradition and adds layers of meaning to the events. This feast was (and is) the central observance of Jewish faith, a time of remembrance and hope that celebrates God's love and saving acts toward Israel (Exod. 12:1–28). As such, it is an appropriate context for the climax of God's new saving event. While Mark does not go so far as to identify Jesus with the Passover lamb (cf. John 1:29, 36; 19:14, 36), the Passover meal provides an evocative occasion for Jesus to interpret the significance of his imminent death (14:22–25). Though Passover was originally celebrated in private homes (Exod. 12:46), at an early date it had been joined with the Festival of Unleavened Bread and transformed into a pilgrimage event (Deut. 16:1–8). These conjoined festivals drew huge crowds to Jerusalem, which contributed to the atmosphere of expectation among the people and the nervousness of the religious and political leaders that pervade the passion narrative.

During Jesus' Galilean ministry, the Pharisees were his primary antagonists (e.g., 2:15–3:6; 7:1–13; 8:11–13). With his entry into Jerusalem, however, the chief priests (the leading men among the temple officials) assume this role (11:15–18, 27–33). Scribes (authoritative teachers) appear with both groups (2:16; 7:1; 11:27; 14:1). The chief priests' animosity was provoked by Jesus' attack on corrupt practices in the temple (11:15–18) and exacerbated by his humiliation of them in public debate (11:27–12:12). At a deeper level, though, their animosity was rooted in fear.

Throughout the Gospel, fear has been a frequent response to Jesus' words and deeds. The disciples responded with fear to Jesus' stilling of the storm and to his walking on the water (4:41 NRSV "awe"; 6:50 NRSV "were terrified"), and they responded to Jesus' words about his death and resurrection in the same way (9:32 and 10:32 NRSV "afraid"). The townspeople responded to Jesus' healing of the Gerasene demoniac with fear (5:15); and the hemorrhaging woman, when summoned by Jesus, came "in fear and trembling" (5:33). Mark has emphasized that fear signals lack of faith and understanding (5:36; 9:32), and certainly this was true of the chief priests. Their fear, however, may have had a political component as well: fear that the messianic enthusiasm that Jesus generated in the crowds could lead to Roman reprisals. The Gospel suggests, however, that the priests' primary fear was that Jesus' words and deeds were eroding their status and authority in the eyes of the people (11:18, 27–33; 12:12).

Homiletical Perspective

leaders of the day knew this and sought to do their work by subterfuge and secrecy. The betrayal of Jesus by Judas Iscariot provided the opportunity for that stealthy arrest. Often, it seems, this is the place where betrayal occurs—under the cover of secrecy and darkness.

This text reminds us that Judas, after striking the deal with the religious leaders, "began to look for an opportunity to betray him" (v. 11). In our own lives we can at times feel as if others are looking for an opening by which to exploit our weaknesses and to betray our trust. This kind of living in fear of betrayal is known by many. It never feels good. The act of betrayal is ugly in so many ways and can come in a variety of forms, but few have not experienced it in one way or another. A profound example of this occurs in the novel and various film adaptations of *The Count of Monte Cristo* by Alexandre Dumas.[1] In it a man is betrayed by his very best friend and is imprisoned for a crime he did not commit. He escapes and then seeks revenge against that friend. The feelings of anger and hurt are palpable in the text and on the screen. In this instance, betrayal surprisingly came from a dear friend, just as it did with Judas and Jesus.

In preaching about betrayal, the preacher should attend to feelings of vulnerability and fear that may be present for individuals or in a congregation (for instance, marital betrayal, fear of change or pastoral transition, or recovery from clergy misconduct—all of which can result in feelings of anger and hurt). At the same time, it is important to offer grace in moments when we too betray others. Judgment from the pulpit that is too cut and dried can be detrimental to those working on getting past moments of betrayal in their lives. For example, to preach a sermon condemning all divorces without grace could be very detrimental to someone in the congregation going through a divorce. Additionally, you may also have both betrayer and betrayed in the pews at the same time.

According to John, Judas had not only become a disciple of Jesus, but he was also in charge of the finances of the followers of the Way (John 13:29). In John's Gospel, it is greed that motivates betrayal. Mark, however, does not name a motivation for Judas's betrayal. More important for Mark is that betrayal is a necessary part of the path to the cross. The preceding passage reminds readers that this path

---

1. Alexandre Dumas, *Count of Monte Cristo* (1846; repr., New York: Signet Classics, 2005).

Mark 14:1–2, 10–11

Theological Perspective

one "who betrayed him," and when he describes the act of betrayal itself (14:43–45). Unlike Matthew or Luke, Mark shows no interest in Judas's future. Having done his work, Judas simply disappears. Perhaps this is because Judas has no future. When we seek to become our own judge, when we get our own way, the nothingness we have worked so hard to obtain becomes our own in full.

What then can one say about Judas or, perhaps more to the point, about all of us who have in large and small ways sold Jesus out, sometimes for much less than Judas ever did? Does Mark have something to tell us, some word for Judas and the rest of us?

In his description of the crucifixion, Mark notes that the inscription of the charge against Jesus reads: "The King of the Jews" (15:26). Thank God. This one, the crucified, is Judas's judge and Lord. This one is in truth the King of the Jews, which means for honorary Jews like you and me and other Gentiles. He is our King also, having engrafted us into Israel's life and mission through his body and blood. We may not like that, any more than Israel always liked being chosen as God's elect.

Precisely there, in his company, we learn the good news of this king and this kingdom. When we betray this king in things large and small, he absorbs the poison of our betrayals and refuses to let us be stuck with our "winnings," even when that is what we prefer. We cannot remove this One from being our judge and Lord and king. We cannot make our lies the truth, despite our most fervent efforts. Our sin, for all its devastating hurt to ourselves and others and to God, cannot unseat the one who is in truth the king of all God's elect who have betrayed him again and again. That is good news—for Judas and for us, Jesus Christ the Crucified is Lord. Can there be a better word?

THOMAS W. CURRIE

Pastoral Perspective

penitence.[2] Such theological stances fostered views that suicide was among the worst of sins and raised concerns about the salvation of the ones driven to such desperate acts. The stigma of Judas thus passed to those who for any number of reasons took their own lives. While the field of psychology has greatly reshaped attitudes in pastoral care, it has not eliminated the specter of these positions in the popular imagination or in popular culture.

In an effort to make sense of his own brother's suicide, theologian Aaron Maurice Saari wrote his master's thesis on the entanglement of Judas with Christian teachings and attitudes on suicide. This scholarship became the basis for his book *The Many Deaths of Judas Iscariot: A Meditation on Suicide*. While biblical scholars may certainly question his controversial interpretations, Saari's study of these New Testament narratives, intertwined with the poignant story of his brother, provides a powerful example of intertextual interpretation. His sorting through the connections between long-accepted assumptions about Judas and responses to those who commit suicide illuminates the dangerous move whereby "people who voluntarily die are regarded as betrayers of God."[3]

Very little is written about Judas in each Gospel, yet a composite narrative has emerged over the centuries, communicated by countless preachers, teachers, and various media of the day and assumed by many Christians. Focused attention on Judas in the New Testament reveals several fleeting images, but no developed portraits and few if any clear motives for his handing over of Jesus. Among the challenges in teaching and preaching this Gospel is keeping Mark's Judas in perspective.

In Mark's Gospel, Judas is emblematic of the dysfunction in the inner circle of the disciples. There is a pattern of ineptitude among the Twelve, a stinging indictment in the Gospel that also raises questions about Jesus' selection of his inner circle. Whatever his motives might have been (and Mark remains silent on the matter), Judas participated in an act of unspeakable violence. Wrestling with the figure of Judas is risky business, considering the baggage that has accrued to him over the centuries. It obliges interpreters to be ever mindful of the collateral damage caused by perpetuating uncritically a harmonized narrative and calling it "gospel."

CARMEN NANKO-FERNÁNDEZ

---

2. Augustine, *City of God*, trans. Marcus Dods (Peabody, MA: Hendrickson, 2009), 21.
3. Aaron Maurice Saari, *The Many Deaths of Judas Iscariot: A Meditation on Suicide* (New York: Routledge, 2006), 119.

Exegetical Perspective

Jesus' popularity with the people motivates the priests to proceed "by stealth" (14:1–2). The Greek word *dolos* means "deceit" or "treachery," which suggests even greater malice than "stealth." Earlier, Jesus mentioned deceit and other traits like murder, avarice, wickedness, envy, slander, and pride in a list of "evil things [that] come from within, and . . . defile a person" (7:21–23). Many of these traits are here illustrated by the actions of the chief priests.

The Betrayer Appears (vv. 10–11). The chief priests' need for deceit is answered by Judas's decision to betray Jesus. The threat of betrayal (*paradidōmi*, also translated "arrest," "hand over," or "hand on" in the NRSV) has been hovering over the narrative since the beginning of the Gospel (3:19; 9:31; 10:33; 13:9–12), but it moves to the forefront in this chapter (seven references) and the next (three references). At Judas's first appearance in the Gospel (3:19), when Jesus chose him as one of the Twelve, he was identified as the future betrayer. Now, when he initiates the betrayal (v. 10) and again when he executes it (v. 43), he is identified as one of the Twelve. Certainly with these cross-references Mark intends to highlight the pathos of the situation: Jesus is betrayed by a member of his most intimate circle of disciples. However, as the passion narrative unfolds, Judas is not presented as a tragic exception, the one bad apple in the group. Rather, as the other disciples misunderstand (8:31–33; 9:30–34), abandon (14:50–52), and deny Jesus (14:66–72), it is clear that Judas stands for the group, the most monstrous example of the failure of them all (see also 16:8).

Why did Judas betray Jesus? The chief priests promised to pay him, but unlike Matthew, Mark does not explicitly identify greed as his motive (cf. Matt. 26:15). There is no mention in Mark of a falling-out between Judas and Jesus (cf. John 12:1–8), no explicit link posited between Judas and Satan (cf. Luke 22:3; John 13:21–30). Nor is there a word about Judas's ultimate fate (cf. Matt. 27:3–10; Acts 1:18–19). Judas, marked from the beginning for his fateful role, fulfills it and vanishes, leaving the stage to others.

JOUETTE M. BASSLER

Homiletical Perspective

for Jesus is foretold (13:24–25). This chapter of Mark leads readers to encounter the cross, examine the transformative gift of God through the life and death of Jesus, and consider their own faith response to this good news. How will we respond when we turn our backs on the Lord or run away from the mission to which we are called? How will we respond when others betray our trust or lead us to betray another person in our life?

In preaching this passage, one might consider the varying experiences of the people in the pews in regard to betrayal and failure to act on one's mission. In regard to betrayal, the preacher is likely to have both the betrayer and the betrayed sitting in the same pew. A word of redemption for those who have inflicted the pain of betrayal is in order, as is a word of grace and comfort for those who have felt that sting. The preacher should be cautious not to lose sight of the human frailty to which we all fall victim.

This passage is a place for grace to be encountered in the preaching moment, even though it is less evident in the text itself. Jesus was indeed betrayed, but his mission for humanity was completed. Judas Iscariot was led to betray a friend, but we are offered an opportunity he did not experience in the text—a word of grace that we are forgiven, even when we fall short of who we are called to be. In this story we do not get to a grace-filled resolution. We get a man who betrays his friend and receives money in exchange. So where is the good news? The good news is about to be fulfilled in the death and resurrection of Jesus, but we must start this journey as it was foretold, and that starts with betrayal.

KARYN L. WISEMAN

Mark 14:3–9

³While he was at Bethany in the house of Simon the leper, as he sat at the table, a woman came with an alabaster jar of very costly ointment of nard, and she broke open the jar and poured the ointment on his head. ⁴But some were there who said to one another in anger, "Why was the ointment wasted in this way? ⁵For this ointment could have been sold for more than three hundred denarii, and the money given to the poor." And they scolded her. ⁶But Jesus said, "Let her alone; why do you trouble her? She has performed a good service for me. ⁷For you always have the poor with you, and you can show kindness to them whenever you wish; but you will not always have me. ⁸She has done what she could; she has anointed my body beforehand for its burial. ⁹Truly I tell you, wherever the good news is proclaimed in the whole world, what she has done will be told in remembrance of her."

Theological Perspective

This story is told in one form or another in all four Gospels (Matt. 26:6–13; Luke 7:36–38; John 12:1–8). Each evangelist places it in a slightly different context, sometimes with different characters, but there is something about this story that is so deeply true, so revelatory of the Jesus story, that none of the Gospel writers could ignore it.

So what is it about this story that made it so unforgettable?

The story is about a woman. She is nameless, and in Mark's Gospel, she appears without any particular context (i.e., she is not termed a "sinner" or even a disciple). She just appears as Jesus is sitting at his host's table, and she brings with her "an alabaster jar of very costly ointment," which she proceeds to pour onto Jesus' head. Those gathered in the room may well have seen her act of pouring ointment on Jesus' head as a messianic sign, though "some were there," we read, who missed the significance of this act altogether. They saw only the expense and the waste, framing their scolding judgment of this woman in terms of their righteous concern for the poor. Jesus rebukes them and interprets the sign for them and for the others in the room, making it clear that what she has done defines the path the Messiah will take, the way of the cross. "She has done what she could; she has anointed my body beforehand for its burial" (v. 8).

Pastoral Perspective

The last line of this passage is not lacking in irony. "Truly I tell you, wherever the good news is proclaimed in the whole world, what she has done will be told in remembrance of her" (v. 9). The fact that the Synoptic Gospels, in this case Mark, seem incapable of naming this woman betrays an incongruity between words and reality. Feminist biblical scholar Elisabeth Schüssler Fiorenza observes, "Wherever the gospel is proclaimed and the eucharist celebrated another story is told: the story of the apostle who betrayed Jesus. The name of the betrayer is remembered, but the name of the faithful disciple is forgotten because she was a woman."[1] Chapter 14 records the names of Judas, Peter, James, John, and even the host in Bethany, Simon the leper; yet the one whose actions are to be remembered and proclaimed globally remains unnamed and slips from collective memory. In the midst of the bungling Twelve, the one who seems to "get" Jesus, his message, and its inevitable consequence is an unknown woman whose actions demonstrate the proper response from a disciple.

In Mark's Gospel, the denseness of the Twelve and the inappropriateness of their actions in Jesus' time

---

1. Elisabeth Schüssler Fiorenza, "In Search of Women's Heritage," in Judith Plaskow and Carol P. Christ, eds., *Weaving the Visions: New Patterns in Feminist Spirituality* (New York: HarperCollins, 1989), 29. See also Schüssler Fiorenza, *In Memory of Her: A Feminist Theological Reconstruction of Christian Origins* (New York: Crossroads, 1994).

Exegetical Perspective

This is a remarkable story. A woman pours oil over Jesus' head, a generous gesture of hospitality, but also the gesture by which a king was prophetically and publicly identified. Those with Jesus react angrily to the expense, while Jesus himself praises the woman and adds yet another layer of meaning to her action. The setting for this puzzling but portentous event is the house of a leper!

The passage begins by locating the action in a house in Bethany, a small village a few miles east of Jerusalem. From that village Jesus made his triumphant entry into Jerusalem (11:1–10) and to that village he then returned, apparently finding refuge there while making daily journeys into the increasingly hostile environment of the city (11:11, 12, 15, 27). All Mark tells us about Jesus' host is that his name was Simon and that he was a leper. Mark says nothing to suggest that Simon is the leper healed in 1:40–45, or even that Simon's leprosy had been healed. "Leprosy" was used to refer to a variety of skin diseases, some more serious than others, but all considered dangerously polluting and contagious. Lepers were rigorously avoided, and extensive purification rites were required for them (Lev. 13:45–46; 14:1–57; Mark 1:44). To eat in a leper's home would have been socially unthinkable, but it was utterly in keeping with Jesus' association with outcasts.

Homiletical Perspective

This biblical passage presents two different issues at the same time. On the one hand, it is a story about elegantly displayed devotion from the woman who anoints Jesus with the costly container of nard (v. 3). On the other hand, we see hard realities in the anger of some at the use of the costly item in such a way (v. 4) and in the problematic words of Jesus as he proclaims that the poor will always be part of our lives (v. 7). This second statement leaves those who advocate for an end to poverty scratching their heads and wondering what he really meant.

Dealing with such diversity in one sermon can be difficult in the best of circumstances. Yet the text implores the preacher to attend to the totality of this episode and to share the good news that being devoted to Jesus is our task, one that the disciples would soon not be able to do any longer (v. 7).

Being in the home of Simon the leper, Jesus and the others with him were eating at a table (v. 3). This Gospel account states that "a woman" anointed his head with perfume. It is both simple and astonishing. She gives all she has with her in a gesture of devotion, but some respond to this action with derision and complaint (vv. 4–5). The reaction of those present at this act is somewhat confusing, since anointing a guest with perfume was a fairly common practice during this period, but it shows their

Mark 14:3–9

Theological Perspective

Elisabeth Schüssler Fiorenza notes that this woman, whose act of anointing Jesus so offended those gathered around him, serves in fact as "the paradigm for the true disciple."[1] Peter's earlier triumphant confession of Jesus as the "anointed one [*Christos*]" (8:29) is here given its true meaning, as this nameless woman acknowledges what Peter could not bring himself to admit, namely, that this anointed one is bound for death on the cross. "Truly I tell you," Jesus concludes, "wherever the good news is proclaimed in the whole world, what she has done will be told in remembrance of her" (v. 9). What she has done. Not her name, not her background, not her relationship to Jesus—none of that is emphasized in this story. Only what she has done.

This story of what this woman has done is sandwiched between the stories of Judas and what he has done (14:1–2) and what he will do (14:10–11), and it is meant to serve as a contrast to his act of betrayal. What this woman has done is such an extravagant gesture, such an all-in acknowledgment of Jesus' lordship, that it is meant to get our attention. She knows something. In contrast to Judas and in contrast to those who have been scolding her, she knows the cost of discipleship, or more to the point, the cruciform shape of the gospel. Nevertheless, she is utterly committed to this "anointed one." She will not sell him out. She will not let the virtues of good stewardship or caring for the poor distract her from the one thing that is needful: to bear witness to her Lord as he prepares to walk this final part of his journey.

We should not miss the lavish nature of her act of devotion. Mark emphasizes the fact that the alabaster jar of nard is "very costly." Not just costly, but very costly. The extravagance of this woman's act of faith, its sheer wasteful uselessness, reflects the extravagance of what Jesus is about to do, the lavish giving of himself poured out on the cross for sinners. It is so useless. Such love is such poor stewardship. It is wastefully poured out on folk who do not deserve it. It receives so little in return. It does not increase our efficiency or enable us to master the habits of highly successful people or secure our social status. This love does not make us richer or more powerful or more successful. All it does is embrace us. All it does is draw us out of our self-absorbed ways, lifting us into God's own life. All it does is grant us the gift, the marvelous gift that this woman knows so well, of

Pastoral Perspective

of profound suffering stand in contrast to the actions of the unnamed woman. Judas betrays, Peter denies and, with James and John, continues to fall asleep, seemingly unaware of proximate danger. Schüssler Fiorenza finds in this woman, as in the other women mentioned in Mark's passion narrative, a model of true discipleship. These women recognize that Jesus' ministry was about service (*diakonia*), not earthly power or kingly glory.[2] Understanding this reality requires a posture of willingness to accompany others in suffering.

In many ways this unnamed woman emerges as a model for pastoral ministry. In her actions she goes about tending the necessary business of care. In this case she treats with dignity the body of one who would be executed as a criminal. She prepares for burial one whose body would typically be denied such attention by virtue of the circumstances of his death. She reads a painful context accurately and responds accordingly with what is available to her. In the words of Jesus, "She has done what she could" (v. 8).

In ministry, one is hard pressed to avoid death and suffering. In some pastoral contexts, it is part of the daily rhythm of ministry; funerals are, for example, an integral part of parish or congregational life. Burying the dead is an expectation associated with ministry. Precisely because of its ordinariness, one can easily become complacent in the presence of such loss, especially when it does not personally make an impact on the minister.

Several years ago a family in the congregation suffered the death of a parent on Monday of Holy Week, and the funeral was set for Holy (Maundy) Thursday. The days from Palm Sunday through Easter can be hectic in many churches, with increased activity, greater attendance, and more worship services. These holy days demand a significant investment of time and resources. In other words, it is hardly the most convenient time for a funeral. While the parish had an abundance of ministers, the bustle of these days and their incumbent responsibilities resulted in less care than usual in this family's time of intense grief. The funeral service seemed rushed, the children's names were forgotten, and the family was informed that no minister was available to lead the prayers at the grave.

In the time of this family's great suffering and loss, the parish was busy instead preparing for its liturgical remembrance of the suffering, death, burial, and resurrection of Jesus. What got lost in

---

1. Elisabeth Schüssler Fiorenza, *In Memory of Her: A Feminist Reconstruction of Christian Origins* (New York: Crossroad, 1994), xliv.

2. Schüssler Fiorenza, "In Search of Women's Heritage," 30.

Exegetical Perspective

We are told even less about the woman: not her name, her social status, or even her purpose in pouring the oil on Jesus' head. The cost of the unguent (nearly a laborer's yearly wage) implies wealth, and her presence at a male banquet without a male escort implies considerable boldness. Her gesture could be read as an act of generous welcome for an esteemed visitor (see Ps. 133:2; Luke 7:44–46), but it resonates most forcefully with Mark's proclamation of Jesus as Messiah, God's Anointed (1:1). In Israel, the king of God's choice was publicly identified when a prophet anointed his head with oil (1 Sam. 10:1; 1 Kgs. 19:16; 2 Kgs. 9:3), and in Mark it is only after this episode that Jesus is hailed—mockingly but accurately—as king of the Jews (15:2, 9, 12, 18, 26, 32). Was the woman consciously assuming the role of prophet? We read nothing of her intent.

To her act of hospitality and recognizing royalty, Jesus adds a third layer of meaning: he defines her action as anointing his body (not head!) for burial— and his definition carries more weight than the other narrative possibilities. It is likely that Mark intends for all three to resonate with the reader. The woman's extravagant welcome is sandwiched dramatically between episodes of extreme rejection (14:1–2, 10–11). The messianic implications of the action are also unavoidable, yet in this Gospel Jesus emphasizes that his messiahship is defined not by power, but in and through his death (8:27–33; 10:41–45). Thus Jesus' interpretation of the woman's act is meant to supplement, not supplant, the implications of welcome and royal anointment.

Others at the meal focus on yet another aspect of the anointing: they scold her (literally "snort in anger," *embrimasthai*, v. 5) because of its cost, and the value of the ointment (oil scented with spikenard) is indeed emphasized. The ointment is also described as *pistikos*, meaning "faithful" (v. 3). This is an odd description of oil—the NRSV omits it—yet it brings faithfulness into the ambit of the woman's action. On the other hand, while the others' putative concern for the poor matches Jesus' message and ministry, in this setting their rebuke of the woman implies that they have missed the point of her action and thus have missed the essence of Jesus' identity. Who are these people? Unlike Matthew, who identifies them as disciples (Matt. 26:8), Mark simply refers to them as "some" (*tines*, v. 4), and their querulous rebuke is similar to earlier actions of both the Pharisees (7:5) and the disciples (10:13). Perhaps the ambiguity is deliberate, for in their growing faithlessness the disciples are becoming indistinguishable from Jesus' opponents.

Homiletical Perspective

clear objection to her extravagant devotion. One of the stunning points in the text is that the woman literally breaks open or smashes the alabaster jar to anoint Jesus in preparation for his burial (vv. 3, 8). This description might lead many to wonder why she would risk damaging the costly perfume by having alabaster fragments fall into it. However, archeologists have discovered some small, long-necked bottles that might have required the snapping of the bottle's neck to pour out the contents without shards of glass or pottery spoiling the ointment.[1] When I was young, my father preached that she broke the container because she was so honored to be in the presence of Jesus that she never wanted to use either the costly ointment or the container again. She broke it to use it all out of joy at being in the presence of Jesus. It is an image that has stuck with me.

The tradition of saving the best for guests is still part of cultural expectations in many places. Some have towels that they reserve for special guests. Some prepare the best meals of the year for guests who visit for special occasions. Some have a room set aside that no one uses except for guests. This type of radical hospitality and generosity is evident in this passage.

However, one is left to ask what it means to save the best for a guest and then listen to criticism for being too extravagant. She is blessed by the presence of Jesus and acts to show her devotion, an act that also ritually prepares his body for burial. This kind of extravagance should be encouraged. By her example we are reminded that we too should give our best to Jesus. We should pour out our lives in devotion and love for the One who transformed the world through his life, death, and resurrection. Jesus affirms this in his response to her.

One of the most interesting elements of the story is that the woman with the nard is unnamed and does not speak in the entire pericope. Jesus' words help us understand what her intent might be.[2] However, we are left to wonder if she was a servant (although the cost of the oil suggests otherwise), a guest (also unlikely, since women were not invited to dine with male guests), or a woman who heard of his presence and came to bestow this act of generosity upon him. She is one of a number of unnamed women in the Gospels, but one thing is immensely clear: she is remembered by her extravagant act of

---

1. Graham N. Stanton. *The Gospels and Jesus* (New York: Oxford University Press, 1989), 147.
2. Mary Ann Tolbert, "Mark," in Carol A. Newsom and Sharon H. Ringe, eds., *The Women's Bible Commentary* (Louisville, KY: Westminster John Knox Press, 1992), 270.

Mark 14:3–9

Theological Perspective

being able to forget self in order to share in the outlandish joy of Christ's extravagant gift of himself.

In preaching or teaching or studying this text, one should note that Jesus does not recommend ignoring the poor or dismissing their very real needs for the sake of a more "spiritual" version of the gospel. On the contrary, he calls us to "show kindness" to the poor whenever we can. The temptation he cautions against is not the moralistic one of "neglecting the poor," so much as it is the theological one of considering ourselves so rich as not to think we are in great need. Only the very rich can be so full of themselves as to afford the luxury of worrying about the stewardship of "costly ointment" when the abundance of God's love is placed right before them. To paraphrase Oscar Wilde, only they know the price of everything and the value of nothing.[2] Only they are so well insulated as to be blind to their own neediness and to miss the extravagance of God's forgiveness that includes even them and beggars all our attempts to limit it.

A final note: just as it is possible to make too little out of this woman—as the church seems to have done over the centuries—so it is also possible to make too much. Like Calvin, like Moses, like Mozart, she disappears from the scene without a shrine to be worshiped or a grave to be kept. She is one of those nameless saints who so richly populate the Christian faith. Jesus remembers her not by celebrating her name but by drawing our attention to "what she has done." That is her gift to us that simply cannot be forgotten.

THOMAS W. CURRIE

Pastoral Perspective

all their busyness was the urgent attention owed to the suffering members of the body of Christ in their midst. The ministers were by no means ill intentioned, nor were they deliberately uncaring or insensitive; yet, like the disciples in Mark's Gospel, they were clueless. They neglected to see what was in front of them, and so they failed to respond in a manner that reflected an authentic understanding of the ministry of Jesus. In a place where the good news is proclaimed, the lessons of "what she has done" were neither remembered nor emulated.

Consider too this story of a home health-care worker. A young Nigerian, she lovingly tended to the daily needs of another woman under hospice care. In many ways these women were strangers to each other, drawn together only by the circumstances of preparing for death. They were separated by generations and by geography. While both were immigrants, one hailed from Nigeria and the other from Belgium. They were both committed Christians, but one was Pentecostal and the other Roman Catholic. Their time together was all too brief, yet the intensity of their shared experience bound them as mother to daughter, a union forged in a prayerful relationship of mutual care and concern. In the early hours before dawn, a quiet passing occurred: the mother returned home. Upon learning the news from the woman's grieving sons, her new daughter raced to the house on her day off. Tearfully she had one request, "May I bathe and prepare our mother's body as I would my own mother, as is traditional among my people?" In a place where the good news was lived, the lessons of "what she has done" were remembered.

God among us, as one of us, is mediated concretely in relevant ways that open our imaginations to encounter and grapple with the obligations of the mystery of the incarnation, a mystery that does not exclude suffering or death. Sacred obligations call us forth to accompany each other, especially in times of suffering, to recognize the dignity of each life, and to respond to the impact of each loss—to do so "in remembrance of her."

CARMEN NANKO-FERNÁNDEZ

---

2. Oscar Wilde, *Lady Windermere's Fan: A Play about a Good Woman*, Act 3 (London: Elkin Matthews & John Lane, 1893), 95.

Exegetical Perspective

The passage focuses, however, on the woman, not the complainers. First, Jesus stops the verbal abuse of the woman and then describes her action as a "good service" (NRSV) or "beautiful deed [*kalon ergon*]" (my trans.)—words of high praise. There follows a remarkable promise, unlike any other in this Gospel, one that looks beyond the Gospel's narrative: "Truly I tell you, wherever the good news is proclaimed in the whole world, what she has done will be told in remembrance of her" (v. 9). There is irony here: the story is to be told in memory of the woman, but her name has not been remembered—and Luke and John have forgotten the story itself or modified it beyond recognition.

In Luke the woman is a sinner seeking forgiveness; she anoints Jesus' feet, so that the action is without messianic overtones; and the event occurs early in Jesus' ministry, not on the threshold of his death (Luke 7:36–50). In John the woman is named: she is Mary the sister of Martha and Lazarus. Her gesture is thankful, not prophetic, an anointing of Jesus' feet offered in gratitude for the raising to life of her brother (John 11:1–6, 17–44; 12:1–8). As in Mark, Jesus reinterprets it as preparation for his burial, but in John it carries no messianic overtones.

The anonymous woman in Mark's version does not appear again in the narrative. It is easy to connect her with stories of other faithful women: the widow who gave "everything she had" (12:41–44); the hemorrhaging woman who trusted Jesus to heal her (5:25–34); the Syrophoenician woman who challenged Jesus to heal her daughter (7:24–30); the women followers of Jesus who went to the tomb to anoint Jesus' body (16:1–8). However, her significance eclipses them all. She is presented as the loving counterpoint to the hatred and fear of the authorities and the blindness of others at the meal, as the faithful counterpoint to the women who failed in their task of providing Jesus with proper burial anointing, and as the prophet who anointed Israel's messianic king. Small wonder that she is to be remembered, although without a name.

JOUETTE M. BASSLER

Homiletical Perspective

devotion, just as Jesus says she will be (v. 9). We may not know her name, but we know her story of devotion.

This is in contrast to the men in the scene, who do not respond exactly as one might hope. They seem to be scolding her in their conversation for using her nard to anoint Jesus, and they are generally gruff about the whole incident. Additionally, this scene is placed in the midst of a story of betrayal. This setting makes this story of extravagance even more powerful. She does not choose to use the nard ointment for herself, though she obviously could have. She uses it on the Lord. The ones who objected do not suggest that she should use it for herself. Instead, they suggest she should have sold it to give the proceeds to the poor (v. 5).

So what do we do with the statement Jesus makes about having the poor with us always? Some hear a callous disregard for the poor and marginalized, but Jesus' words do not have to be heard as dismissive of the poor. They are a reminder that we should never forget their presence and should show extravagance to them just as it was shown to Jesus.

Jesus is teaching the people at dinner with him that now is the moment. It appears that he is letting them know, once again, that his time on earth is coming to an end. The moment to pour out our extravagant devotion on Jesus is at hand.

KARYN L. WISEMAN

Mark 14:12–16

¹²On the first day of Unleavened Bread, when the Passover lamb is sacrificed, his disciples said to him, "Where do you want us to go and make the preparations for you to eat the Passover?" ¹³So he sent two of his disciples, saying to them, "Go into the city, and a man carrying a jar of water will meet you; follow him, ¹⁴and wherever he enters, say to the owner of the house, 'The Teacher asks, Where is my guest room where I may eat the Passover with my disciples?' ¹⁵He will show you a large room upstairs, furnished and ready. Make preparations for us there." ¹⁶So the disciples set out and went to the city, and found everything as he had told them; and they prepared the Passover meal.

Theological Perspective

This sliver of the passion narrative hardly seems substantial enough to form a text from which the gospel can be proclaimed. What is in this little story about the disciples' questions, Jesus' explicit but somewhat strange directions, and the preparation for a meal that tells us something that we need to hear?

In Mark's Gospel, Jesus' Last Supper with his disciples takes place as the Passover meal that he bids them to prepare. The text suggests that Mark discerns a connection between the celebration of Passover, recalling God's deliverance of Israel, and the impending deliverance that Jesus will bring about through his death on the cross. What is clear about this passage is that the disciples, like other pilgrims in Jerusalem, are anxious to secure a place to prepare the Passover meal, yet they seem quite unaware of the storm that is about to break upon them. It is the logistics that bother them, the where and how questions that pilgrims often ask. It is equally clear that Jesus, as an observant Jew, intends to eat the Passover meal with his chosen disciples.

The disciples have a hard time in Mark's Gospel. They often seem clueless or vacillating or simply baffled by Jesus' words and actions; but here, though they are the ones asking the questions, they are not depicted as failures. They are simply asking for directions. Jesus, in giving what seems to us to be a set

Pastoral Perspective

The ubiquitous letters WWJD are familiar to many people. They refer to a perennial Christian question: "What would Jesus do?" A correlative question arises when preachers, teachers, and ministers engage the texts from the Synoptic Gospels that recount what is portrayed as Jesus' last meal with his disciples: "What did Jesus do?"

This question is driven by a search for authenticity, an effort to retrieve, and in some cases re-create and even restore, what has often been overlooked in Christian circles, namely, the Jewishness of Jesus. Toward this end, the relationship between the Last Supper and Passover has received particular attention. The Synoptic Gospels, Mark included, situate this meal and the subsequent arrest, passion, and execution of Jesus on the first night of Passover. John's Gospel, on the other hand, does not mention a meal, and the crucifixion occurs on the preparation day, the occasion for the sacrificing of the Passover lambs in the temple in Jerusalem (John 19).

This juxtaposition of Passover and the passion in the Gospels leads to curiosity among Christians about the nature of that last meal. Some posit that indeed Jesus and his disciples prepared for and participated in a Seder meal. This interpretation has led to the development of a practice among some Christian communities, across denominations, to

Exegetical Perspective

This passage, though seemingly straightforward, is filled with subtle oddities. The first concerns the dating of events. Though Passover and the festival of Unleavened Bread had long been linked together (Exod. 12:1–20; Lev. 23:5–6; Num. 28:16–17), the exact timing of their overlap seems muddled in Mark. Here, for example, the day the Passover lambs were sacrificed, which occurred on 14 Nisan (Exod. 12:6; Lev. 23:5; Num. 28:16), is identified with the beginning of the festival of Unleavened Bread; but that festival traditionally began the next day on 15 Nisan (Lev. 23:6; Num. 28:17). Moreover, in Mark 14:1, the first day of Unleavened Bread is identified with the Passover feast itself, not with the sacrifice of the lambs. Loose terminology, compounded by the Jewish custom of using sunset to mark the beginning of a new day, probably account for the apparent discrepancy. Mark's reference here to the sacrifice of the Passover lambs (v. 12) does not seem to be intended to equate Jesus' imminent crucifixion with that sacrifice (cf. John 1:29; 19:14, 36); however, it does anticipate indirectly Jesus' later identification of the Passover wine with his blood (14:24).

There are other oddities as well. The disciples, usually placid, uncomprehending, or fearful followers (4:35–41; 6:45–52; 10:32), here initiate the preparations for Passover. They do seek—and

Homiletical Perspective

The details provided by the author of this passage lead us to understand who Jesus is and how he endeavored to prepare his followers for the coming time of trial. We see the depth of his insight and the height of his awareness of all things around him. When his disciples ask where the meal should occur, he sends out two of them to prepare a place for the Passover meal (vv. 12–13). He tells them, "Go into the city, and a man carrying a jar of water will meet you; follow him, and wherever he enters, say to the owner of the house, 'The Teacher asks, Where is my guest room where I may eat the Passover with my disciples?' He will show you a large room upstairs, furnished and ready. Make preparations for us there" (vv. 14–15). The details are vital to the story, because through them we see the wisdom of Jesus and his prophetic knowledge of what is to come.

John Wesley writes that this passage provides us with proof of Jesus "knowing all things and of his influence over the minds of men [sic]."[1] It is also reminiscent of Jesus' prescient statement that upon entering Jerusalem for his final days, the disciples would find a young colt tied up that had never before been ridden (11:2). Details, details.

---

1. G. Roger Schoenhals, ed., *John Wesley's Commentary on the Bible: A One Volume Condensation of His Explanatory Notes* (Grand Rapids: Francis Asbury, 1990), 432.

Mark 14:12–16

Theological Perspective

of strange directions, makes it plain that he intends to be with his disciples on this particular night, gathered with them in an upper room, eating and remembering the deliverance of God's people.

After the rather strange and complicated directions are given, and after the two disciples are sent into the city, the task of securing a place and preparing the meal is the work not of Jesus but of his disciples. They serve. In this little vignette, it is the disciples who take the initiative, who prepare the meal, who obey and find everything just "as he had told them." When so much has happened to Jesus on this day and so much will happen later, when Jesus is so clearly the center of this whole passion narrative, here, strangely, in this little story, it is the disciples who occupy center stage.

Jesus, even on the night when he is betrayed, does not play the role of the tragic figure who bravely stands alone against a harsh and indifferent world. No, at this moment of great (if not supreme) significance, Mark depicts Jesus as willing to be with his disciples, giving them clear directions for their work, allowing them space to do what they are able to do, and sharing with them in the task and the gift of remembrance and hope. The picture here is of a band or group, not of an individual. The occasion is a communal event, a shared memory and shared celebration. Here is a life together.

Why should that be so noteworthy? Why must we be told of the role of the disciples in preparing the meal for all, even Jesus? This little slice of a story frames the passion of Jesus Christ in terms of the life together he shares with his own, the life together that is Israel's history, the life together that is God's mission in the world. The disciples ask, and though they may be unsure as to the way they are to go, they nevertheless obey and find it all as Jesus has told them. From their standpoint, their life together with Christ is formed through this obedience rendered in small things to their Lord. From his standpoint, their life together is constituted by his solidarity with them, the same solidarity manifest in the love of the God of Israel for a people called to serve.

Jesus exercises his lordship in this strange yet utterly faithful way. He does not act alone, but always in the company of those whom he has called. So many meals are recorded in the Gospel accounts, so many stories of banquets to which folk are invited, so many conversations with others along the way. The salvation Jesus offers is relentlessly and even uncomfortably social. This "last supper," prepared for him by those whom he has commissioned, will be

Pastoral Perspective

commemorate the Last Supper as a Seder and/or to host a so-called Christian Seder, in some places on Holy (Maundy) Thursday.

These practices may be well intentioned, but they are fraught with troubling implications. They are not to be confused with the interfaith Seders that arose in the latter half of the twentieth century, which reflected a growing appreciation of Jesus as a faithful Jew of his time, as well as of the intertwined roots of Judaism and Christianity. The interreligious dialogues of these decades motivated theologians and pastors to think creatively and carefully about concrete ways to communicate these new Christian perspectives about Jews and Judaism. In light of almost two millennia of destructive anti-Judaism and anti-Semitism, these motivations reflected movement in more positive directions. These interreligious relations reached new levels of intimacy and trust, which fostered mutual knowledge and a maturing respect and concern for preserving the integrity of each faith tradition in all its richness. In these contexts Seder meals were prepared either by Jews and Christians together or by Jewish hosts who invited their Christian dialogue partners to the table to experience a communal Seder which functioned as a teaching moment.

Both Jewish and Christian scholars have questioned whether the meal referred to in the Synoptic Gospels was even a Seder, let alone a Seder that would be familiar to contemporary Jews. The Seder as most know it today developed after the destruction of the Jerusalem temple in 70 CE and does not include the serving of lamb. Without the temple, animal sacrifice eventually ceased. Little is known about the preparation that is alluded to in the Gospel. "Presumably, Jesus and his disciples would have visited the Temple to slaughter their Passover sacrifice. Then they would have consumed it along with unleavened bread and bitter herbs, as required by the Book of Exodus. And presumably they would have engaged in conversation pertinent to the occasion. But we cannot know for sure."[1]

Therefore Christian attempts "to do what Jesus did" are not historical and may even be inappropriate. As mentioned earlier, initially Christian participation in Seders was in interfaith settings, teaching moments not typically during Passover, led usually by rabbis at tables where Christians could learn from their Jewish companions about their shared roots and experience Judaism as a living tradition. The Christianized

---

1. Jonathan Klawans, "Was Jesus' Last Supper a Seder?" *Biblical Archaeology Review*, http://www.bib-arch.org/e-features/jesus-last-supper.asp; accessed January 23, 2013.

Exegetical Perspective

follow—Jesus' advice on the matter, yet it is *their* question that seems to set events in motion. However, the disciples' initiative here may not represent a radical break with their past incomprehension. In fact, it may suggest a business-as-usual response to Jesus' alarming words about his imminent death (14:8).

The wording of their question to Jesus contains another oddity: they inquire about making "preparations for *you* [not "*us*"] to eat the Passover" (v. 12). Did they presume that Jesus would eat this inherently communal meal alone? If so, Jesus corrects this misconception: they were to make preparations "for us" (v. 15). Jesus' full response is in the form of an odd, minutely detailed prediction: a mysterious stranger with a water jug will meet them, and they will follow him to a house whose owner has apparently already prepared a room for them. There they are to prepare the Passover meal. Then, Mark concludes, it happens just as Jesus says!

Characteristically, Matthew and Luke smooth out many of Mark's odd features. Matthew, for example, avoids potential confusion over the date by mentioning only the festival of Unleavened Bread (Matt. 26:17–19). More significantly, he eliminates the entire prediction-fulfillment structure of Mark's passage. There is no prediction of encountering and following a man with a water jar, no reference to a room already prepared, and, significantly, no summarizing comment that they "found everything as he had told them" (v. 16). Matthew's focus is instead on Jesus' statement that his time (*kairos*) was near, the last of a series of statements in his Gospel about portentous times (Matt. 8:29; 13:30; 14:1; 16:3; 21:34, 41). Luke's alterations move in a different direction. This evangelist retains the prediction-fulfillment motif, but Jesus and the disciples play their customary roles: the former takes the initiative, and the latter follow his instructions (Luke 22:7–13). There is no suggestion by anyone in Luke that the Passover is for Jesus alone.

Matthew and Luke have thus tamed many of the eccentricities of this passage and tuned it to their own concerns. So what message does Mark's version communicate? For all its emphasis on the need to prepare the Passover meal (vv. 12, 15, 16), there is no description of the actual preparations. There is no reference to the purchase, sacrifice, or roasting of the Passover lamb or to the acquisition of the other elements of the meal—the unleavened bread, the wine, the bitter herbs. The focus of the passage is on the lengthy description of events that would transpire

Homiletical Perspective

This power of perception and seeing all things is a powerful part of who Jesus is. It displays to the disciples then and to the reader now Jesus' knowledge of the journey set before him and his determination to follow it to the end. The two sent in this passage, like the two sent to retrieve the colt, were to see a man carrying an earthen vessel and follow him to a house where they would meet. Clearly, Jesus is one who knows what is to come, leads his followers from that vision, and faithfully follows the path laid before him.

When I was a young child I sometimes thought of Jesus as a "magic man," because he could perform miracles and know things he could not possibly know. This is one of the passages that led me to have this concept of him. One day I described Jesus as a "magic man" to my Sunday school teacher. She was a wise and wonderful woman who explained to me that my idea, while interesting, was a misreading of who Jesus actually was. She wanted me to understand the miraculous things Jesus was doing in the Scriptures were well beyond magic—that they were holy acts empowered by God. She wanted me to understand the power of God in the person of Jesus the Christ. She wanted me to comprehend the faith it takes to accept Jesus' power as a reality in my life as well. A magician uses power to entertain, but Jesus' profound miracles were a sign of God's power in the world.

It took many years for me to understand the point in verse 16 of this text: "So the disciples set out and went to the city, and found everything as he had told them; and they prepared the Passover meal." They go in search of what Jesus has foretold—and they find it just as he predicted. They trust his words. They believe he will not lead them astray. We are called to believe and to do the same, although we rarely go as willingly into the task as these two disciples.

A preacher might draw attention to the fact that this event and the instructions for the disciples are about preparation. It is about making ready a Passover feast for Jesus and his disciples in the upper room of a house. We know that this particular meal is going to be of enormous import. During this meal Jesus announces that one of his followers is about to betray him (v. 18). We cannot be certain what makes up the meal for a Jewish rabbi and friends, although it likely includes unleavened bread, bitter herbs, wine, and salt. The disciples would be particular about making the preparations complete. They know the details are important. Jesus gives them guidance to do what is required.

As we read and hear this text, we are reminded that doing all we can to prepare ourselves for our

Mark 14:12–16

Theological Perspective

the means by which he exercises his final act of lordship with his own, pouring out his own body and blood in a liturgy of table fellowship with them and with a sinful and broken world.

In the Presbyterian Church (U.S.A.)'s *Book of Common Worship*, one of the concluding collects for Morning Prayer reads as follows: "Eternal God, you call us to ventures of which we cannot see the ending, by paths as yet untrodden, through perils unknown. Give us faith to go out with courage, not knowing where we go, but only that your hand is leading us and your love supporting us; through Jesus Christ our Lord."[1] This prayer faithfully traces the arc of this passage: we are not alone, and even when "we cannot see the ending" of things and are walking "through perils unknown," there is One whose hand is leading us and whose love will not be without us. He gives us tasks to do and space to undertake those tasks.

The question before us, just as it was before the disciples in this text, is one of obedience. That was the question with which Israel struggled throughout its history, and it is the question that Jesus, in solidarity with Israel and his own disciples, takes up in his own faithful walk to the cross. It is not the heroic obedience of an isolated individual, but that gracious obedience that wills to be with others. It is not the obedience that educated, well-informed, civilized people fear as oppressive, but the strange freedom that knows the gift of clear direction and shared life together that accompanies those who seek to follow Jesus Christ.

THOMAS W. CURRIE

Pastoral Perspective

Seders that have become increasingly popular lack any interfaith dimension, let alone Jewish participation. Sadly this absence neglects to account for the value of a most powerful teaching and learning tool, interreligious table conversation. In creating Christian Seders, congregations shift the focus from remembering the exodus together to imposing Christian meaning on Jewish practice. They shift the locus from the home to the church hall, a move that also changes the ritual's meaning and impact. The celebrations of Seder are domestic practices; family and friends gather around table at home, not at a synagogue. These efforts do indeed risk "trampling on the other's holy ground," a caution even for interfaith Seders.[2]

The Gospel of Mark depicts the disciples going about the business of preparation for the Passover meal. Situated within the passion narrative, this text raises for Christians opportunities to reflect on how we might ourselves prepare to learn about the richness of Judaism, about Jews as they identify themselves and as they understand their rituals and stories. In other words, these texts invite Christians to explore Passover more deeply on Jewish terms and to prepare ourselves to be good guests, not hosts, at Seder tables not of our own making. Toward this end, over the years, varying Christian-Jewish dialogues have prepared resources to aid congregations. One helpful example, "About Jewish-Christian or Interfaith Seders," reminds all parties that "such events as the Jewish-Christian Seder are occasions for us not to lose our respective identities through some sort of blending, but rather to deepen who we are as Jews and Christians by appreciating the distinctive though related ways in which we covenant with God."[3]

In preparation for Passover, perhaps it is better for Christians to prepare to be good neighbors, to cultivate genuine friendships with Jewish neighbors and colleagues individually and across congregations. As these relationships mature, then it is best to prepare ourselves to be good guests at a Seder table in a Jewish home, if we are blessed to be invited. Such gracious invitations provide opportunities to participate in a lived spiritual heritage rather than Christian reenactments of the Last Supper.

CARMEN NANKO-FERNÁNDEZ

---

1. *Book of Common Worship* (Louisville, KY: Westminster John Knox Press, 1993), 501.

2. ELCA Church Council, "Guidelines for Lutheran-Jewish Relations," *Dialogika* (November 16, 1998): #9 http://www.ccjr.us/dialogika-resources/documents-and-statements/protestant-churches/na/lutheran/677–elca98nov16; accessed January 23, 2013.

3. "About Jewish-Christian or Interfaith Seders," *Dialogika*, http://www.ccjr.us/dialogika-resources/educational-and-liturgical-materials/liturgical-resources/passover/784–interfaith-seders; accessed January 23, 2013.

Exegetical Perspective

and then confirmation that everything happens as predicted. Mark does not intend to suggest by this that Jesus has made prior arrangements for the water carrier to meet the disciples and for the homeowner to prepare the room. Rather, he is dramatically conveying that Jesus knows how the future will unfold, including the mundane details. The account of Jesus' entry into Jerusalem (11:1–7) has a similar structure and a similar message. Jesus sends two disciples ahead into a village with the information (prediction) that they will find a colt tied there, which they are to bring back to Jesus. It happens just as he says; even the response of the bystanders corresponds to his prediction.

Each of these stories conveys a message about Jesus' divine omniscience, and together they form a powerful framework for a section of the Gospel that is filled with Jesus' prophecies of his death and resurrection (12:6–8, 36), of the calamities that will befall the earth (13:8, 14–25), and of the gathering and salvation of the faithful (13:26–27). Of these predictions, only that of his death is fulfilled within the Gospel's narrative. However, the vivid stories of Jesus' omniscience in the two framing passages provide strong reassurance that in these larger prophecies as well readers will eventually find "everything as he had told them" (v. 16).

That, it seems, is the dominant message of this odd passage, especially in conjunction with its twin passage in chapter 11. There are, however, some subsidiary messages as well. Insofar as Jesus is showing profound knowledge of how the future has been ordered by God, he is also showing that here and throughout his life he is following the way set down for him by God. Primarily omniscience, but also obedience, is conveyed by this passage. There are also echoes of older stories that add depth to this brief episode. Elijah, the prophet with whom Jesus is often linked in Mark (1:13; 6:15; 8:28; 9:2–13), and Elijah's successor Elisha resided for a time in upper rooms. Indeed, it was there that both performed their most spectacular miracles, the raising to life of the dead sons of their hostesses (1 Kgs. 17:17–24; 2 Kgs. 4:8–37). In a similar upper room Jesus will announce his death to his disciples and point to new life in the kingdom of God (14:17–25).

JOUETTE M. BASSLER

Homiletical Perspective

own journeys of faith is essential. There are elements of preparation many Christians undertake in Lent or during other pivotal spiritual journeys. The persons who sit in our worship services are likely in a variety of places on their paths to faithfulness. Some present will still be questioning the path before them; others will be further along their journey of faith, but still have concerns or doubts; while still others will be quite mature in their beliefs. In preaching this text, one must be aware that all of those present are called to grow in faith, to prepare over and over again to encounter Christ, and must strive to follow the teachings of Jesus in daily living, even when they are not as clear as the instructions in this text.

In preparing for this meal, the disciples have a number of tasks to complete. We too make preparations. Some of them are simple, like placing items at the ready for the next day's activities. For extended international travel, some persons pack an array of items, including electrical adapters, accessories for our myriad gadget needs, and clothing for various occasions. Some are preparing for health procedures or for family transitions. We follow the pre-op instructions to get the best from the procedure. We do all we can to prepare our kids for a new addition to the family. Whatever the reason, preparations are necessary.

Being part of a tradition that prepares—a tradition of faith that implores us to be alert and make ready for the return of the Lord—leaves us with a commission. It is a commission to follow and be obedient, even when we do not see what the Lord sees before us.

KARYN L. WISEMAN

Mark 14:17–21

¹⁷When it was evening, he came with the twelve. ¹⁸And when they had taken their places and were eating, Jesus said, "Truly I tell you, one of you will betray me, one who is eating with me." ¹⁹They began to be distressed and to say to him one after another, "Surely, not I?" ²⁰He said to them, "It is one of the twelve, one who is dipping bread into the bowl with me. ²¹For the Son of Man goes as it is written of him, but woe to that one by whom the Son of Man is betrayed! It would have been better for that one not to have been born."

Theological Perspective

Viewed in comparison to the other Gospels (Matt. 26:24–25; Luke 22:21–23; John 13:21–30), this passage in Mark appears perfunctory; the dialogue is brief and there are no gestures to intensify Jesus' knowledge about his betrayer and what that betrayal meant in the context of the intimate act of breaking bread together.

By simplifying the connection between this betrayal and the Lord's Supper, however, Mark highlights the vulnerability that pervades the event. On a personal level, this vulnerability is displayed in the fact that Jesus' betrayer has been one of his chosen apostles, a member from the leadership of this community. There is also the vulnerability that comes from political betrayal; the intimacy and safety of the community itself has been breached by one regarded as a trusted friend but who is actually an enemy. Most significantly, there is the eschatological vulnerability evident in the meal itself. As a celebration of the Passover, this meal ritually expressed not only the deliverance from oppression in Egypt but also hope for the Messiah's coming. Mark's account of Jesus' messianic coming, though, is one in which vulnerability is unavoidable. Jesus is not a mighty deliverer impervious to wounds, but a suffering servant whose victory will be revealed in the power to

Pastoral Perspective

Difficult words, distress, denial—this passage has it all. As the disciples encounter difficult words of truth from Jesus, they respond with distress and denial. Their all-too-human response invites us to recognize that difficult truths spoken in love might instead be for us an occasion for discernment and deepening discipleship.

Difficult Truths. "Truly I tell you . . ." "Truly," in Greek *amēn*, prefaces some of Jesus' statements telling his followers something about themselves that is especially hard to hear. It is as if he anticipates resistance or reluctance to hear and believe what follows. In this passage, Jesus begins, "Truly," because what comes next—the truth of the betrayal to come from among his closest followers—is painful to hear.

"Truly" is also how Jesus underscores for his followers important insights about others. Not long before, after a poor widow contributed two small copper coins, Jesus had called his disciples together as he affirmed, "Truly I tell you, this poor widow has put in more than all those who are contributing to the treasury," because she gave generously out of her poverty (12:43). Then, after a woman had anointed Jesus at Bethany, Jesus had chided the disapproving disciples and asserted, "Truly I tell you, wherever the

Exegetical Perspective

In the Gospel of Mark's chronology, this momentous "evening" marks the beginning of the Passover festival and the first scene in Jesus' last meal with his disciples (14:17). Later scenes in the passion narrative will have wider scope, with crowds, Jewish leaders, and Roman authorities. Here, however, the focus is intimate—on Jesus and his nearest followers. The tone is heavy, full of foreboding, as spare, carefully crafted sentences convey a complex flow of meaning.

In the preceding passage describing meal preparations (14:12–16), both Jesus and the narrator spoke of his disciples (*mathētai*, vv. 12, 13, 14, 16). With the meal scene, however, reference narrows to the Twelve (vv. 17, 20), the special, symbolically numbered inner circle. They recline and eat with Jesus (v. 18), thus evoking broadly shared ancient values associated with formal and festive meals—leisure, friendship, trust, conversation. At a Passover meal, the bond at table also includes a shared memory of the divine deliverance of Israel from slavery in Egypt (Exod. 12:14–20). Yet at this meal, when Jesus initiates conversation—using an *amēn* expression ("truly I say") to intensify his words—he starkly predicts a violation of such values and memories. One who is sharing this table will hand Jesus over.

Homiletical Perspective

Jesus acknowledges the blunt realities of discipleship in this intimate setting with his inner circle. The path to the cross is one that compels nothing less than complete transparency from Jesus. This passage helps us to acknowledge the truth about which Jesus spoke regarding Judas: there are forces at work which would lead us to trade on our loyalties to Christ for our personal advantage.

These realities are no less real for us today. When this passage comes along for those of us who preach, we are reminded how the path of following Jesus is filled with temptations to compromise for an easier way. The promise of money to Judas comes in a wider array of contextual possibilities for us and for those to whom we preach. It is worth exploring in a sermon what these compromises might look like in each preacher's unique context, naming them as they occur to us in a wide variety of settings: as individuals; as congregations and communities of faith; as denominations; as citizens of cities, states, and nations; and even as global citizens.

If we were to preach this passage highlighting those temptations to trade our commitment to the mission (and person) of Jesus for other temptations, we might find that we are beginning to work with a

Mark 14:17–21

Theological Perspective

transform—rather than banish—violence, suffering, and death. These personal, political, and eschatological layers of vulnerability are reflected in the psalm alluded to in this narrative: "Even my bosom friend in whom I trusted, who ate of my bread, has lifted the heel against me" (Ps. 41:9).

Although there has been much debate about the personal status of Judas—whether he can finally be redeemed or not—the theological implications of Judas's betrayal receive little attention. When theologians discuss the "primal sin" of humanity, it is usually that of violence or the reckless desire for domination and conquest (*libido dominandi*). However, this passage suggests an even deeper sin—betrayal. By placing Judas's betrayal right alongside the institution of the Lord's Supper, Mark lifts up not only the fundamental means by which we are healed but the fundamental sin that this sacrament addresses. Moving along these lines, Origen notes the larger fabric of salvation that is woven into this act: "There was another by whom he was betrayed, namely, the devil, of whom Judas was the instrument. The 'woe' is not only for Judas but for all who betray Christ."[1] At the same time, as Karl Barth also notes, it is precisely because of the grace established by Jesus that Judas's ultimate fate is an "open question," for in the figure of Judas the "reality of human wickedness" stands in tension with "the overwhelming power of grace."[2]

Every betrayal involves the violation of trust and the repudiation of relationship. However, betrayal alters the identity of the agent as well. As Elaine Scarry notes in her study of torture, the intention behind a coerced betrayal is not to extract secret information, for the information gained in these circumstances is often useless. Rather, the purpose of forcing a betrayal through torture is to destroy the victim's own identity: "one betrays oneself and all those aspects of the world—friend, family, country, cause—that the self is made up of."[3] In the act of betrayal, the betrayer is betrayed as well.

In this passage from Mark, Judas's decision to betray Jesus is uncoerced and he suffers the same world-destroying effects that Scarry describes: he loses his friends, his mission, his faith, and his Lord. By contrast, Jesus is steadfast and refuses to have

---
1. Origen, *Commentary on Matthew*, 50, in *Ancient Christian Commentary on Scripture: New Testament II Mark*, ed. T. C. Oden and C. A. Hall (Downers Grove, IL: InterVarsity, 1998), 194.
2. Karl Barth, *Church Dogmatics*, II/2, *The Doctrine of God* (Edinburgh: T. & T. Clark, 1957), 466, 476.
3. Elaine Scarry, *The Body in Pain: The Making and Unmaking of the World* (New York: Oxford University Press, 1985), 29.

Pastoral Perspective

good news is proclaimed in the whole world, what she has done will be told in remembrance of her" (14:9). After the crucifixion, the task of saying what is true fell to others, as in the centurion who affirms, "Truly this man was God's Son" (15:39).

"Truly" announces a teachable moment, an opportunity for insight about ourselves, others, and God that we might otherwise miss or ignore. How do we open our ears and hearts to hard truths about ourselves? How do we tell the difficult truth in love? How do we hear or speak surprising truths? Do we see with Jesus' eyes and honor the generosity of those who give much of what little they have? When some disparage self-righteously, do we offer a different perspective about the faithful actions of others? How do we tell the good news about God? Do we hear the truth when it comes from an unlikely source, or do we discount it because of the speaker?

Distress. The disciples' reaction to hearing this difficult truth is to be "distressed." Mark uses the same word to describe the reaction of the wealthy person who asked what he had to do to inherit the kingdom and heard Jesus' difficult answer: sell all you have and follow me. The privileged one went away "distressed" because of his many possessions (10:22). He had sought comfort and affirmation, and instead heard challenge. The disciples, enjoying such closeness with Jesus, must have anticipated an evening that affirmed their special relationship with Jesus.

Distress: instead of interpreting it as a problem, perhaps we might regard it as a positive opportunity for growth that moves us beyond our comfort zones. How might we use our experience of being distressed to focus our attention on important challenges to familiar faith? How might we embrace a feeling of distress as a prod to let go of easy assumptions about ourselves and our faith, and as an invitation to face what is difficult but necessary and true?

Denial. For the disciples, distress gives rise to defensive denial. The disciples reply one after the other, "Surely, not I?" (v. 19). Rather than a genuine, open, wondering, "Is it I?" they ask in a way that expects a comforting answer of, "No, no, of course it is not you." Instead of reassuring some of them that it is not they, Jesus simply affirms the truth that he will be betrayed by one who shares table fellowship with him. Without Jesus' hasty reassurance, they are left to wonder in their hearts, "Is it I?"

How often do we leap to the easy "Surely, not I"? Rather than asking uncomfortable questions,

Exegetical Perspective

The verb *paradidōmi* ("turn over," "hand over," or "betray") has already been used in two of Jesus' predictions of his death (9:31; 10:33). The verb appears with unusual density in chapter 14: in Judas's collusion with the chief priests (vv. 10–11), in this meal scene (vv. 18, 21), and in the later arrest scene (vv. 41–42, 44). The crisis of betrayal is imminent. Jesus' prediction, "One of you who is eating with me will hand me over," seems also to echo a line from a psalm (particularly in its Greek version) in which a righteous sufferer laments an offense against table fellowship: "For even the man of my peace, upon whom I hoped, the one who eats my bread, has magnified his deception against me" (Ps. 40:10 LXX, my trans.; Ps. 41:9 NRSV). For those who hear the scriptural echo, the events now unfolding resonate with old precedents and prophetic purpose.

The singularity of this betrayal seems reinforced by the individuality of the anxious protestations that come from the Twelve. Grieving, they reply "one by one" (*heis kata heis*) or "one after another, 'Surely, not I?'" (v. 19 NRSV). As Jesus reiterates the prediction, he repeats the key numbers, "*one* of the *twelve*," then offers a vivid, tactile image of intermingled hands dipping food into sauces or condiments, heightening the sense of the betrayer's closeness and broken trust: "one who is dipping with me into the bowl" (v. 20, my trans.).[1]

In his final statement of this subsection, Jesus warns that the betrayer will face an unspecified but dreadful outcome. The statement is crafted with a tight, twice-repeated alternation between what will happen to "the Son of Man" and to "that man." Here (and elsewhere) Jesus uses "Son of Man" as a term of self-reference. As a title, it may also recall the eschatological judge of Daniel (Dan. 7:13; NRSV one like a "human being"), or a prophetic figure with a particular commission from God (e.g., Ezek. 2:1, 3, 6, 8; NRSV "mortal"). Both the "Son of Man" and "that man" face dire futures, but one will be purposeful, the other's so tragic that, "It would be better for that man not to have been born" (14:21). Jesus' exclamation of "woe to that man" seems more predictive than vindictive, with its tone of warning and lament.

In Mark's account of the last meal, then, Jesus does not specify Judas as the betrayer, either by word or gesture. In Matthew's telling, Judas specifically says, "Surely not I, Rabbi," and Jesus replies, "You have said so" (Matt. 26:25). In John, the

---

1. The NRSV adds "dipping *bread*" to clarify the meal practice, although "bread" is not in the Greek.

Homiletical Perspective

homiletic pattern of trouble/grace.[1] This is indeed the bad news of sinful humanity: we are tempted to seek our own advantage rather than maintain our fidelity to Christ, especially when that loyalty might prove to be costly to us. The disciples' distress and disbelief are also reminders that we can all too quickly dismiss (or believe that we are immune to) our own weaknesses as disciples.

There is, of course, the other side of this dynamic: the side of grace. Jesus knows that this is going to happen, and knows that it is a part of the way to the cross. Jesus' assessment of his betrayer's birth as woeful does not strike us like a word of grace. This essay is not the place to wrestle with how Jesus consigns his betrayer. The grace, however, and one that needs to be proclaimed loudly, is that Mark invites his readers into this story to help would-be disciples. We are invited to hear and see ourselves in this story. Mark warns us gracefully through an example, like a loving parent, and invites us into the kind of discipleship that owns up to our own frailty, admitting that a discipleship too self-confident, overly assured, and inflexible is indeed a recipe for deluded discipleship and a sure path to betraying the gospel message.

Another preaching possibility in this text is the focus on the word "betrayal." This is an awfully sharp word in our vocabulary, usually reserved for books and television and movie dramas (Can you hear the movie preview voice? "A story of betrayal . . ."). In movies, television shows, and books we watch betrayal from a safe distance. Unfortunately, this is an experience with which many people in our pews are all too familiar. Betrayals happen in friendships, in supposedly loving and committed relationships, in the workplace, in families, in our own bodies, and yes, even in our congregations and communities of faith. When we are betrayed, the conditions that once provided stability and a context of love and trust in our lives are thrust into an anchorless chaos. Anyone who has been betrayed knows the disappointment, the broken trust, and the emotional pain that results from this experience. Betrayal leaves open wounds that take tremendous amounts of time to heal. Many sermon listeners will be able to identify with this kind of experience, and it is wise to create identification in the sermon, although with sensitivity.

In some of the most critical moments Jesus has on earth, he encounters the most destructive dynamics that can happen in a relationship of trust. When

---

1. Paul Scott Wilson, *The Practice of Preaching* (Nashville: Abingdon Press, 2007), 157–83.

Mark 14:17–21

Theological Perspective

his world closed down, even though he has been betrayed and is about to suffer incredible violence. Jesus remains true to himself and his calling.

Viewed from this perspective, it is possible to see the whole sweep of human alienation and sin in the Scriptures falling under the category of betrayal: the serpent betrays Adam and Eve, Cain betrays Abel, Jacob betrays Esau, Joseph's brothers betray him, Delilah betrays Samson, Saul betrays Samuel, David betrays Uriah, Absalom betrays David, and Gomer betrays Hosea. These interpersonal betrayals take place within a larger relationship with God, and, in each betrayal, God is also betrayed. However, none of these betrayals stands as the final word in the narrative. Faced with these betrayals, God's infinite power is expressed as his ability to bring about reconciliation so that the covenants that these betrayals have violated are reestablished on a foundation of mercy and forgiveness.

Therefore, the betrayal of Jesus highlights a central teaching about the institution of the Lord's Supper: it represents God's merciful reestablishment of the covenant that is strong enough to counteract the betrayals that have wrecked humanity. In establishing this sacrament, Jesus joins us to his body so that our identities and relations might be remade through his death and resurrection. The Lord's Supper joins us to God at a deeper level of intimacy than the betrayals that have taken place. In this passage, the intimacy of the meal, which the betrayal has destroyed, is recreated nearly at the same moment by the revelation that the bread and wine the disciples are sharing is a participation in Jesus' own body and blood.

Finally, within the Gospel of Mark, Judas's betrayal stands in line with other rejections during Jesus' earthly ministry. The sacred history of the betrayals noted in the Scriptures above is present in Jesus' own life, beginning with his own family thinking he is out of his mind (3:20–21) and his rejection by the people in his hometown (6:1–6). Jesus' prediction that the Son of Man "is to go through many sufferings and be treated with contempt" (9:12b) indicates that his response is found in his patient determination to refrain from entering into the cycles of betrayal found in his and every life. Rather, he will place his trust in the transformation provided through his cross and resurrection.

WILLIAM J. DANAHER JR.

Pastoral Perspective

do we ask questions intended to elicit reassurance? What insights into ourselves and our relationship with God do we lose when we are so eager to defend our faithfulness that we do not contemplate our human struggles and shortcomings? How much richer might our faith be if we allowed ourselves to linger in the question, instead of leaping to our own defense and denial?

Discipline and Discernment. What would happen if each of us practiced, as a spiritual discipline, using distress as a prompt for discernment, for asking questions that do not seek comfort but clarity?

What situations in our world today would we be called to see truly? What calls us to put aside distress and denial? Is it the painful truth that millions of children die each year of largely preventable causes? Is our culpability in that ongoing tragedy one that distresses us so much that we deny it rather than ponder and act on it? Is the painful truth the ways that we betray Christ in our worship life, failing to welcome those unlike ourselves? Is it that we profess our faith and loyalty and love of God with our lips but not our lives? Do we leap to the "surely, not I," rather than reflecting on what might be so and seeking to deepen our discipleship?

Not long ago, in a board meeting of a nonprofit organization, board members and staff gathered anticipating an evening of comfortable collaboration that affirmed their mutual devotion to the cause. Then one board member asked challenging questions about how the earlier actions of another who was present had undercut the board's collective work revising the mission statement. The one whose actions were criticized responded with distress and denial, rather than experiencing the uncomfortable words as an opportunity for discernment.

It offered a glimpse of how hard it is to hear difficult words "truly" spoken and to use distress as an opportunity for seeking clarity rather than comfort. Using difficult truths and distress as opportunities for discernment and deepening discipleship is easier said than done, to be sure, but a spiritual practice that might help us hear God's word for us. After Jesus' difficult words, he shared bread at table with all gathered. We too may find in the Lord's Supper strength and sustenance to face challenging truths with discernment.

SHANNON DALEY-HARRIS

Exegetical Perspective

identification of Judas is even clearer (John 13:25–27). Mark, however, keeps the identification at the meal oblique, at least to the other diners. Their dismay prompts each of them not to guess about others, but to ask about himself, "Surely, not I?" Mark's reader, however, already knows who the betrayer will be. Not only has Judas's plot just been set in motion (14:10–11), but very early in the Gospel, a list of the Twelve introduces this disciple as "Judas Iscariot, who betrayed him" (3:19). For Mark's reader contemplating the betrayal of Jesus from the circle of his closest followers, the question of "who" generates no suspense. Questions of "how" and "when" will be answered as the plot unfolds (14:43–45). Questions of "why" linger through the history of interpretation.

Unlike other New Testament writers, Mark offers no account of what became of Judas after his betrayal (i.e., Matt. 27:3–10; Acts 1:18–19). Yet in Jesus' prediction that the one who will hand him over will meet a dire fate, Judas is represented as culpable for his choice. Divine purpose does not negate personal responsibility. The Gospel of Mark treats this breach of trust as voluntary, not inevitable. Mark scholar Joel Marcus remarks, "Our text is a classical expression of the mysterious interpenetration between divine sovereignty and human responsibility."[2]

Mark's representation of Jesus is also marked by an interplay of divine purpose and human agency. Jesus' control of the situation, whether as foreknowledge or prearrangement, was evident in the preceding passage as he directed his disciples' preparation for the meal. Now, at the meal, his knowledge of Judas's treachery, his allusion to Scripture, and his use of the title "Son of Man" all suggest divine mission and prophetic insight. Jesus knows, chooses, and is not passive. What is happening and will happen was and is prophesied, yet is also chosen by each person involved. Yet the pain and pathos of betrayal are not mitigated by divine purpose. The first scene of Mark's last supper is tinged with shock and sorrow.

B. DIANE LIPSETT

Homiletical Perspective

he knew that the world was about to turn against him in a physically threatening way, one of those in whom he had placed trust to carry out the work of God's love and justice was prepared to hand him over, dispensing with the bonds of friendship. Preaching that takes the word "betrayal" from this passage as its focal point will help listeners find in Jesus one who has experienced the kind of betrayal that led to an arrest, trial, and crucifixion.

It is in Jesus' own betrayal that we find comfort and the resources for healing and transformation. As the King James Version says of Jesus: "For we have not an high priest which cannot be touched with the feeling of our infirmities" (Heb. 4:15). For those who have been wounded by betrayal, Jesus presents a sympathizing character who quite literally bears the scars of betrayal. Preaching this passage from the perspective of betrayal offers a potential pastoral, healing moment for many (if not all) of those who hear us preach on this passage

Of course we cannot preach this without recognition of the effect that the act of betrayal has on the betrayer. Betrayal takes a toll on the offender as well. Perhaps Jesus' exclamation of woe upon the betrayer is not so much a condemnation of his life as anticipation of how the betrayer will feel about himself when he follows through. Indeed, other evangelists know this to be true in Judas's own actions after the crucifixion. Jesus' words declare the effect of the betrayal on the betrayer: guilt, shame, self-loathing (see Matt. 27:3–5; Acts 1:18–19). The effects of betrayal run deep, and we do well to acknowledge this in our preaching. Still. behind this knowledge of the deep effects of betrayal on the betrayer lie the hope for and possibility of reconciliation. We know well Peter's reconciliation with Jesus after his denial, although Mark only hints at it (16:7). In all cases of betrayal, we know there is substantial work required for healing on behalf of all parties involved, but the possibilities for reconciliation and forgiveness are part of the work to which Christ calls us. Leading people toward that difficult work in our preaching is part of the joy and burden of what we do each week.

RICHARD W. VOELZ

---

2. Joel Marcus, *Mark 8–16: A New Translation with Introduction and Commentary*, Anchor Bible (New Haven, CT: Yale University Press, 2009), 955.

Mark 14:22-25

²²While they were eating, he took a loaf of bread, and after blessing it he broke it, gave it to them, and said, "Take; this is my body." ²³Then he took a cup, and after giving thanks he gave it to them, and all of them drank from it. ²⁴He said to them, "This is my blood of the covenant, which is poured out for many. ²⁵Truly I tell you, I will never again drink of the fruit of the vine until that day when I drink it new in the kingdom of God."

Theological Perspective

In Mark's institution of the Lord's Supper, Jewish sacrificial traditions are echoed and amplified within the context of Jesus' impending crucifixion and death. The clearest instance of this complex engagement is the relation between the Passover tradition (Exod. 12) and the Last Supper. The Passover remembered the deliverance of the Hebrews from oppression, but it also expressed the hope for the coming Messiah who would gather Israel into one nation again (Isa. 11:11). Therefore, the setting of the Last Supper at the Passover meal presented the opportunity for the disciples to understand better the revelation of Jesus as Messiah, which they been quietly puzzling over since Peter's proclamation (8:27–30).

At the meal, however, Jesus not only implicitly presents himself as the messianic answer to these Passover prayers; he also compares himself to the lamb customarily sacrificed (14:12). Jesus' identification of the bread and wine as his "body" and "blood" broadens the traditional sacrificial nexus of the bread, wine, and lamb beyond the Passover tradition to include his own pending sacrifice on the cross. The implication is this: just as Passover remembered God's surprising deliverance of Israel, so would this meal of his body and blood remember Jesus' crucifixion as an event that released the world from oppression.

Pastoral Perspective

In the Picture. The 1594 painting *The Last Supper*, by the Italian Renaissance artist Jacopo Tintoretto, bursts with images and seems to bustle with activity. Angels swoop from the ceiling signaling God's presence. Jesus' head is encircled by a bright gleaming halo, the age-old artist's neon sign blinking "divinity." Muted light encircles the heads of eleven of the disciples, although those junior halos would not keep them from falling away not long after the scene depicted. Some of the disciples watch Jesus attentively while others engage intently in conversation with each other. Judas, the lone disciple to cast no glow, perches awkwardly on the side of the table opposite all the others. The table runs at an angle from bottom left to top right of the painting, creating a more dynamic scene than depictions with a neatly centered table with poised and posed disciples symmetrically flanking Jesus. What I love most about the painting, though, is all of the additional activity in the room. Serving people busy themselves—some are immersed in their tasks, while others look over to the table where there is no place set for them. A cat pokes her nose into a basket of dishes. One servant is talking to a disciple who holds up his hands to halt the servant's speech, presumably so the disciple can catch what Jesus is saying.

Exegetical Perspective

With the phrase "while they were eating," Mark opens the second scene of Jesus' last meal with the Twelve (v. 22, echoing v. 18). Jesus continues to anticipate his death, but the associations shift away from the heaviness of betrayal toward symbols of redemptive self-giving drawn from the meal. The passage moves through three moments: Jesus blesses (*eulogeō*), breaks, distributes, and interprets the bread (v. 22); he gives thanks for (*eucharisteō*), distributes, and interprets the cup (vv. 23–24); and he looks forward, anticipating both his approaching death and the ultimate reign of God (v. 25). While the Gospel of John understands Jesus to have celebrated his last meal the evening before Passover, Mark, like Matthew and Luke, makes it a Passover meal commemorating the exodus of the ancient Israelites from enslavement in Egypt (Deut. 16:1–15). Whichever chronology is more historically plausible, the symbols and meanings of Passover clearly shaped Christian memories of the meal.

As Jesus distributes bread, his actions echo the Gospel's earlier miraculous feeding stories: blessing, breaking, and giving (6:41; 8:6). The bread also gains significance as part of a Passover Seder, although there is little detailed evidence for how the meal was celebrated at the time of Jesus or of Mark's Gospel. Nevertheless, offering a blessing of bread in

Homiletical Perspective

This reflection must begin with a confession: I am a member of the Christian Church (Disciples of Christ). Like our Roman Catholic, Orthodox, Episcopal, and Lutheran sisters and brothers, part of our liturgical heritage is that we meet around the Lord's Table each week. There is no week off from this liturgical act. For those of us who make our homes in these traditions, preaching in the context of the Eucharist is familiar territory. Some version of our text here, what is traditionally called the "words of institution," is present each week in the churches I know, and always in close proximity to the preaching moment. For some of us, however, preaching in the context of the Eucharist might not be such familiar territory. For both groups, the ground for preaching this passage is certainly fertile when all roads lead to the Table—whether we hear these words every single week or less frequently.

This text presents the perfect opportunity to help listeners dig deep into their understanding of what happens when we share in the meal. We might properly call this kind of preaching liturgical preaching and doctrinal preaching at the same time. That is, when we preach this text, we will likely preach it in the context of liturgical action (some formally so, others less formally), but we will also try to add depth and complexity to what congregants believe

Mark 14:22–25

Theological Perspective

In addition to the Passover, Mark engages the sacrificial tradition as a whole, particularly as portrayed in Leviticus. Jesus' identification of the "bread" as his "body" recalls the detailed instructions in Leviticus about the "unleavened bread" consumed at Passover (Lev. 23:6). Jesus also refers more generally, though, to the priests' consumption of animals offered in sacrifice. The priests are commanded to eat the "sin offering" that is offered with the assurance that "whatever touches" the offering "shall become holy" (Lev. 6:27). Analogously, the bread Jesus offers as his "body" is also a sacrificial offering for sin that must be consumed. Likewise, the blood of the sacrificial animals sprinkled on the altar of the temple (Lev. 1:5) is echoed and amplified in the wine Jesus gives his disciples, which represents the "blood of the covenant, which is poured out for many" (v. 24).

Finally, Jesus recalls and reinterprets the traditional roles and identities of the priests who presided at sacrifices. Although he compares himself to the Passover lamb and sacrificial victim, he presides at the Lord's Supper as a priest. Just as Moses instructs Aaron and his sons to "drink no wine or strong drink" when they "enter the tent of meeting" (Lev. 10:8), so Jesus states that he "will never again drink of the fruit of the vine" until his work is complete (v. 25).

At the same time, Jesus also draws the circle of priesthood wider than its traditional limits. In the sacrificial tradition, consuming the offering is restricted to priests, those chosen to determine between "the holy and the common, and between the unclean and the clean" (Lev. 10:10) and to offer sacrifices on behalf of the people. In the context of the Last Supper, however, Jesus' sharing of the sacrifice of his body and blood symbolically admits his disciples into the circle of this priesthood. Not only are the disciples made "holy" by partaking in the meal as noted above, but by sharing the bread and cup with his disciples, Jesus reinforces the fact that his kingdom welcomes all; the former line between "holy and common" and "unclean and clean" has been redrawn by his grace and forgiveness.

Viewed retrospectively in light of his wider mission in Mark, this admission to the priesthood includes not only the disciples present, but all those Jesus has met and healed during his earthly ministry who would normally be considered ritually unclean, such as the man with a withered hand (3:1–6) and the woman with a flow of blood (5:25–34). At the institution of the Lord's Supper, then, Jesus expands the ranks of this new priesthood of

Pastoral Perspective

Despite the distance from us in millennia from the original event and centuries from the creation of the painting, it is easy to find one's place in Tintoretto's picture. Perhaps our experience of identification is different each time we ourselves approach the Lord's Table. Sometimes we might experience the Lord's Supper feeling aglow with the inner warmth of welcome and attentiveness to the moment. Even then, of course, like the disciples our faith is never perfect or complete, and we will fail the ones we love, despite our best intentions or most fervent protestations of loyalty and love. Surely there are times we find ourselves at the Lord's Table not with a glow but with Judas's glower, feeling guilty or inadequate or isolated from those around us. Sometimes we are the disciple who has to halt the distractions of others to attend to what Jesus would say to us, and other times we may be the ones doing the distracting. Some of us never feel as if we have a place at the Table and are looking on wistfully or immersed in tasks that keep us away from connection and communion with our loved ones or our Lord.

The painting is a reminder for us that even though our current administration of the sacrament of Communion may be neatly ordered, more akin to those symmetrical depictions of the Last Supper than Tintoretto's lively scene, those currents of emotion, distraction, and different points of view swirl under the surface for those who approach the table or await Communion in the pews.

In the Moment. One is struck by a sense of immediacy in the painting. Each person present seems to be gripped by their experience of the moment. In our passage from Mark, there are no words institutionalizing Communion, "Do this in remembrance of me." Those words come from elsewhere, in Matthew, Luke, and 1 Corinthians. In our passage, Jesus' words have an immediacy, an urgency, an attentiveness to what each disciple is called to do right then, at that moment.

Theologically, of course, the sacrament of Communion will always bind together past and present and future in the name of the one who was and is and will come again. Pastorally, what might it mean to receive Communion attentive to the moment, not bound by betrayals past and to come, by flaws and failures, sins and shortcomings? Just to receive it as it was first given, after thanks and blessing, with the simplest instruction: take. Could we allow ourselves to be nourished so simply? It was attentiveness to the moment that had guided the woman with the

Exegetical Perspective

the middle of a meal is unusual and may suggest a Passover practice. Bread at a Seder would have been unleavened, symbolizing both "the bread of affliction" associated with slaves and the poor, and the Israelites' speed of departure as they escaped Egypt (Deut. 16:3). Affliction, vindication, and redemption symbolically link the unleavened bread of Passover with Jesus' body.

Jesus' words concerning the bread in Mark are offered in similar form in Matthew and Luke, as well as in 1 Corinthians (the earliest of the texts, although not necessarily the most primitive version of the saying):

> "Take; this is my body." (Mark 14:22)

> "Take, eat; this is my body." (Matt. 26:26)

> "This is my body that is for you." (1 Cor. 11:24)

> "This is my body, which is given for you." (Luke 22:19)

Comparing the sayings highlights Mark's stark simplicity, and the strength of his unelaborated statement. The theological question of whether Jesus offers a metaphor or a more literal presence of his body in the bread cannot be answered from Mark alone. However, in urging the disciples to take the broken bread-body, Jesus seems to invite them to identify with both the affliction and the redemption that lie ahead.

As Jesus gives the cup to the disciples, Mark reports that they all drank—Judas too, it seems. Matthew and Luke omit that detail, perhaps to avoid showing the disciples drinking before Jesus' interpretation of the cup (Matt. 26:27; Luke 22:20; note that in Luke, there is also an earlier cup, 22:17). In Mark, the disciples drink simply because Jesus has given them the cup, not because he has explained its significance.

Mark's version of Jesus' word over the cup carries complex scriptural echoes and also invites comparison to its New Testament parallels:

> "This is my blood of the covenant, which is poured out for many." (Mark 14:24)

> "Drink from it, all of you; for this is my blood of the covenant, which is poured out for many for the forgiveness of sins." (Matt. 26:27–28)

> "This cup is the new covenant in my blood." (1 Cor. 11:25)

> "This cup that is poured out for you is the new covenant in my blood." (Luke 22:20)

All four variations mention blood and covenant, language that recalls Moses performing covenant ratification ceremonies at Sinai (Exod. 24). Moses

Homiletical Perspective

they are doing and how they live in accordance with those beliefs. This kind of preaching need not be boring, dry, or stiff. On the contrary, on the occasion that this text comes up for preaching, we are at an opportune moment to link ritual action to homiletic action. How does the preacher's particular tradition or theological heritage understand what Jesus does here, and how might she bring that into vibrant preaching? Well-told stories from denominational histories as well as wider histories of the church are especially appropriate here. Sermon listeners consistently desire to learn something in preaching, so a lively connection to how your community of faith has conceptualized the Lord's Supper helps listeners to increase their appreciation of that ritual action.

Another sermon possibility focuses on the literary nature of the text. In the midst of talk of betrayal (14:17–21) and desertion (14:26–31) before and after this passage, Jesus pauses for the ritual meal and the institution of a new covenant. Sandwiched in between the reminders of our proclivity to betrayal and denial is the reminder that Christ extends the covenant to his disciples—and to us—through this ritual meal. It might be a worthy homiletical goal to reproduce the rhetorical force of this passage. In other words, if we choose to develop a sermon that imitates the rhetorical force of the text, then we will seek to craft one that helps listeners identify and feel the force of the covenant-making, covenant-affirming Christ in the midst of our own tendencies to betray and desert our faith. The Latin phrase is true: *simul iustus et peccator*, simultaneously justified and a sinner.[1] This is part of what the meal does for us: in the midst of our lives as people who cause fragmentation, injustice, and brokenness, we pause regularly at a table to which we are invited, to remember how God's covenant with us is extended through the work that Jesus foreshadows in the meal.

This leads us to an equally important doctrinal sermon possibility: what about covenant? The idea of covenant is not one we take with us much outside church walls. In denominations and in theological study we are certainly familiar with the idea of covenant. Outside the confines of the life of faith, though, we are much more comfortable talking about contracts or expectations or obligations. We have little facility working with the idea of covenant in daily life. A sermon interested in mining our own theological and liturgical language will do some

---

1. Martin Luther, "Lectures on Romans," in *Luther's Works* (St. Louis: Concordia, 1972), 25:260.

Mark 14:22–25

Theological Perspective

the kingdom to include Judas his betrayer and Peter who will deny him.

These resonances with the sacrificial tradition help illuminate what is at stake theologically in this passage. In the history of Christian thought, the Lord's Supper has been more a topic of common disagreement than agreement, chiefly regarding three debates: its status as a symbol of the church's unity, the doctrinal expression of what happens to the bread and wine, and the worthiness of communicants. Although these concerns are not addressed directly, it is possible to draw some lessons regarding each in this passage.

Like the Passover, Jesus' passion, death, and resurrection liberate the people of God from the oppression of sin and death. The source, then, of the church's unity is our common identity as those gathered by Jesus' grace and redeemed for God's sake. As a ritual, the Lord's Supper reveals the power of God in a way that is not only remembered but somehow reenacted. Therefore, what is at stake is not what happens to the bread and wine in terms of their materiality as much as what they represent. Through them, Jesus binds believers to his body in such a way that their lives will be remade through his crucifixion and resurrection. Concerning worthiness, that Judas and Peter participate in the Lord's Supper suggests that all are worthy and welcome to participate in this sacrifice. The disciples represent not merely followers but a "priesthood of all believers" (cf. 1 Pet. 2:5–9) that will be gathered from all nations.

Most importantly, like the traditional celebration of the Passover, the Lord's Supper is, as Robert Jenson argues, a "sacrifice" in the sense of being a prayer composed of "language ... objects and gestures" in which there is "a giving-over of oneself out of love." In offering this sacrifice, Jesus "obliterates a common distinction between the offerer and what is offered" by portraying himself as both priest and sacrificial offering, and by portraying the disciples as both priests and penitents. However, it is also clear that here, as he does on the cross, Jesus offers a "sacrifice" of prayer for us that we could not make, so that our divisions and differences are overcome by his infinite power in not only the church but the world.[1]

WILLIAM J. DANAHER JR.

Pastoral Perspective

alabaster jar to know what was right and needed in the moment (14:3–8). Did Jesus yearn for his followers to be present to the moment of taking bread and cup as well? Are we?

In Community. Jesus "took" the bread and instructed the disciples: "take." Both Greek forms come from the verb *lambanō*. What associations might the Gospel writer have us make when we read that Jesus took the bread? Earlier in Mark we read, "And He took the five loaves and the two fish" (6:41 NASB); "Then he ordered the crowd to sit down on the ground; and he took the seven loaves" (8:6 NRSV); and finally "Jesus took a little child and put it among them" (9:36). Bread and fish for the hungry, a child with no power or social standing, bread and cup in a Passover meal commemorating the flight from slavery to freedom: all were sign and symbol of God's reign, a foretaste of the realm in which all are fed, children are welcomed, and all are free.

Today, when we leave the institutionalized, sacramental administration of Communion, how might we be attentive to other kinds of communion, opportunities to participate in God's reign and invite others to experience God's reign? Will we connect our Communion with the communion we experience when we work to see that those who are hungry are fed? Will we experience more deeply Communion when we recognize that children—even without power or social standing—point the way to God's reign, and that whenever we welcome the child we welcome Christ and the one who sent him? Will we look for situations today where God's power and the courageous leadership of God's people are needed to bring others out of bondage into freedom, and be nourished for that work in community by our Communion?

Wherever we are in the picture, wherever we are in our faith journeys, Jesus invites us to be in the moment, present to the foretaste of God's reign in which none is hungry and all receive as a child, with the simplest of instructions, of invitations: take.

SHANNON DALEY-HARRIS

---

1. Robert W. Jenson, *Systematic Theology,* vol. 1, *The Triune God* (New York: Oxford University Press, 1997), 192.

Exegetical Perspective

sprinkles or splashes on the people blood from the "offerings of well-being," declaring, "See the blood of the covenant that the LORD has made with you in accordance with all these words" (Exod. 24:5, 8). Jesus' language also recalls Zechariah's prophecy that the covenant between God and Israel assures liberation and renewal for Jerusalem: "As for you also, because of the blood of my covenant with you, I will set your prisoners free from the waterless pit" (Zech. 9:11). In Mark (and Matthew) Jesus speaks of "my blood of the covenant," suggesting that his death will effect or open something more in covenantal relations between God and humanity.

Each of the Synoptic Gospels also includes a phrase about "poured out" for others—for "many" in Matthew and Mark, for "you" in Luke. "Pouring out" is another term found in sacrificial contexts. In this saying, then, Mark may speak of Jesus' death "for many" as a sacrifice that atones for sin. Matthew's addition, "for the forgiveness of sins," suggests that Matthew, at least, understood Mark this way (Matt. 26:28). The "pouring out" language also, however, recalls Isaiah's depiction of the Suffering Servant—a righteous person who "poured out himself to death, . . . yet he bore the sin of many, and made intercession for the transgressors" (Isa. 53:12). Such a form of atonement is vicarious, but not necessarily sacrificial.[1] The vicarious and liberating effect of Jesus' death is also suggested in an earlier saying, "the Son of Man came not to be served but to serve, and to give his life a ransom for many" (10:45). Mark's Gospel invites more than one way to find meaning in the death of Jesus: as sacrificial, as vicarious, as new exodus, and more.

In Jesus' final saying at the meal, he looks ahead. The nearness of his death is suggested by his prediction that he will not drink the fruit of the vine again "until that day when I drink it new in the kingdom of God" (v. 25). Grammatically, "new" could modify either what Jesus will drink—new wine—or the new manner in which he will drink at an anticipated eschatological meal in the realm of God (drawing on banquet imagery such as Isa. 25:6–8).

Mark's narrative of the Last Supper offers imaginative participation in the redemptive events of the past, while renewing hope for a fuller, future consummation—a ritual and storied melding of past, present, and future similar to that of the Passover Seder.[2]

B. DIANE LIPSETT

Homiletical Perspective

work with this term. How is it that listeners actualize covenant in their daily lives, even if they do not recognize it as such? How might a sermon identify the ways that sermon hearers break covenant or twist covenant to their own advantage? For those who preach creation-care themes, this might be an appropriate place to highlight the reciprocal covenant we make with the earth.

An important set of questions to answer in a sermon on this passage might be these: What exactly is this covenant Jesus describes? How is it different, if at all, from the covenant with the patriarchs in the Hebrew Bible? Preachers will also do well to identify their own definition of covenant, making sure to understand carefully how Christianity relates to Judaism when talking about this term. This may be an appropriate place to help listeners clarify their own understanding of Jewish-Christian relations through the idea of covenant.

Finally, we must also not forget that Jesus' word choices make this an eschatological meal. Those of us who follow the Revised Common Lectionary in our preaching run into eschatological thought most notably around those first couple of weeks in Advent. This passage provides an opportunity to preach eschatological themes at different times and with a different focus. Eschatological themes in the sermon on this passage are tuned to a hopeful key of the great banquet feast with Christ in the *basileia* (NRSV "kingdom") of God. In the *basileia* of God, death is not allowed to have the final say. So, in preaching this text, we are reminded that hope is a central theme of what normally constitutes a somber ritual action in many of our churches. The hope we have (and preach!) takes shape in the form of robust communion with God and with each other. A sermon identifying God's hopeful future of communion with humanity does justice to this text as well.

RICHARD W. VOELZ

---

1. Adela Yarbro Collins, *Mark*, Hermeneia (Minneapolis: Fortress Press, 2007), 656–57.
2. Joel Marcus, *Mark 8–16: A New Translation with Introduction and Commentary*, Anchor Bible (New Haven, CT: Yale University Press, 2009), 965.

Mark 14:26–31

²⁶When they had sung the hymn, they went out to the Mount of Olives. ²⁷And Jesus said to them, "You will all become deserters; for it is written,
 'I will strike the shepherd,
  and the sheep will be scattered.'
²⁸But after I am raised up, I will go before you to Galilee." ²⁹Peter said to him, "Even though all become deserters, I will not." ³⁰Jesus said to him, "Truly I tell you, this day, this very night, before the cock crows twice, you will deny me three times." ³¹But he said vehemently, "Even though I must die with you, I will not deny you." And all of them said the same.

Theological Perspective

Like the passage concerning betrayal that immediately precedes Mark's telling of the institution of the Lord's Supper (14:17–21), the focus in this passage is on desertion, another expression of disloyalty. Where Judas remains largely offstage in Jesus' prediction of his betrayal, here Peter boasts of his own steadfastness in the face of Jesus' prediction that his disciples will fall away. Further, unlike his prediction of his betrayal, here Jesus' prediction of desertion is framed by explicit reference to a messianic prophecy from Zechariah 13:7 of a servant whose suffering opens the way for the salvation and purification of God's people.

These distinctive moments bring to the surface of the narrative the fact that everything then happening to Jesus operates on a level that lies beyond the reach of human agency or power. Although many voices in the Christian tradition criticize Peter for his hubris, his boasting highlights the fact that the redemption brought by Jesus through the crucifixion is achieved not only apart from but also in spite of our best knowledge or efforts. Jesus' retort, then, responds not merely to Peter's personal character flaws, but to all human attempts to discern the actual shape of the transformation God will bring about through him. Our limited human resources are no match for God's infinite divine resources, which remain in deep

Pastoral Perspective

The instructor of the test preparation course announced one of her surefire tips for finding the correct multiple-choice answer: look for the answers including the words "all" or "none" and rule them out, because very rarely is such a sweeping statement true. In our passage, however, the opposite is true: Jesus predicts that all will fall away, and they all do. Peter wants to believe that he will be the exception, "even though all" of the others will desert Jesus. He was not. "All of them said the same" as they protested their loyalty, yet not one of them was right. "All of them deserted him and fled" (14:50). So much for easy shortcuts to the right answer when we are tested in ways that really matter.

We read this passage and know what the disciples did not know in the moment: that they all would fail and flee. From that perspective, the protestations sound at best heartfelt and naive, at worst foolish or cocksure. We can also read this passage and look still further down the road to where the disciples' faith journeys would take them as described in the Gospels—to meet again the one they had fled, to break bread with the one they had denied, to embrace the one they loved with their full but flawed human hearts. Poet Rainer Maria Rilke wrote, "It is also good to love: because love is difficult. For one human being to love another human being: that is perhaps

Exegetical Perspective

Jesus and his disciples close their Passover meal by singing a hymn (*hymneō*). Indeed, only here do the evangelists picture Jesus singing (14:26; Matt. 26:30). Perhaps at Passover, as at other festivals, the group would have sung the Hallel, consisting of Psalms 113–118, or perhaps another psalm.

Their singing marks the transition out of the city to the Mount of Olives, the ridge east of Jerusalem across the Kidron valley. In Mark, the Mount of Olives has been mentioned in Jesus' triumphal entry (11:1) and as the site of his apocalyptic discourse (13:3). In the Old Testament, the Mount of Olives is explicitly named only twice, but both may have resonance for the events unfolding in Mark 14. There David, fleeing Jerusalem at the revolt of his son Absalom, weeps and learns of the betrayal of a close counselor (2 Sam. 15:30–37). In Zechariah, in a prophetic description of the Day of YHWH, the Mount of Olives is the place where YHWH will decisively intervene in an eschatological last battle (Zech. 14:4–5). In Mark, this ridge, with its varied associations of kingship, betrayal, and eschatological expectation, now becomes the scene of crucial events, beginning with predictions for and about the disciples.

Jesus has already made plain that one of the Twelve will hand him over (14:18–21); now he declares that they will all "become deserters"

Homiletical Perspective

As a preacher who often visualizes biblical texts as movie scenes, I find that the final line in this Markan pericope composes a haunting episode by virtue of one line of dialogue: "And all of them said the same." In my imagination, I hear a great many voices saying this all at once to Jesus, falling in line behind Peter's leadership. One of those voices is my own; and then there is an uncomfortably long silence. What does anyone say after this?

It is perhaps too easy for us to focus on Peter and his up-and-down status as chief disciple. So it is that here the final line of Jesus' words deflects the attention away from Peter alone, to all of those who are with him. Because none of the disciples is off the hook, it is simultaneously frustrating and helpful to hear Jesus admit the inevitability of the disciples' failure. A sermon on this passage might help listeners give voice to this frustration and give them the opportunity to realize that Jesus recognizes our limits. Both of these ideas are homiletical moves that express pastoral sensitivity.

On the one hand, the sermon could help listeners hear Jesus tell us just how difficult it will be to follow him. Why does Jesus make discipleship so hard? He knows the inevitability of our denial; with our words and actions we will deny our knowledge of and relationship with him. Jesus knows that, like Peter and

Mark 14:26–31

Theological Perspective

control, even in moments when God appears absent and powerless.

His protestations aside (v. 29), in this passage Peter is a representative figure for the disciples as a group, which intensifies a role Peter plays throughout Mark. Indeed, there is a sense in which the Peter portrayed in Mark rhetorically embodies the emerging witness of the early church. Among other defining moments, Peter is called and renamed by Jesus as one of the Twelve (3:16), present at the raising of the young girl from the dead (5:37), delivers the proclamation of Jesus as the Messiah (8:29), and is witness to the transfiguration of Jesus on the mountain (9:2). In all of these passages, Peter serves as the mouthpiece of the early witness about Jesus.

At the same time, Peter also reveals that Jesus' message has been misunderstood and imperfectly delivered. Peter tries to rebuke Jesus when he predicts his betrayal and death (8:32–33), and he misunderstands the implications of the transfiguration, which is to establish continuity, rather than equality, between Jesus, Moses, and Elijah (9:5). Finally, Peter's explicit and repeated denials of Jesus (14:66–72) reinforce the fact that, like the other disciples, he is all too human when it comes to following the crucified one faithfully.

Taken as a whole, then, the complex discipleship of Peter creates the impression that the gospel revealed in Mark is one that rests entirely on God's mysterious power revealed in Jesus through his cross and resurrection. Particularly in light of Peter's boasting and eventual denial of Jesus (14:66–72), the postresurrection directive to "tell his disciples and Peter that he is going ahead of you to Galilee; there you shall see him, just as he told you" (16:7), represents a vindication of Jesus' faithfulness despite the disciples' denial. The explicit naming of Peter indicates that one aspect of Jesus' postresurrection ministry is gracefully to confront those who have deserted him, so that they may be judged, forgiven, and reconciled. Viewed in this light, Calvin's reflections on Peter's denial are appropriate: "Peter's fall . . . brilliantly mirrors our own infirmity. His repentance in turn is a memorable demonstration for us of God's goodness and mercy. The story told of one man contains teaching of general, and indeed prime, benefit for the whole church; it teaches those who stand to take care and caution; it encourages the fallen to trust in pardon."[1]

---

1. D. W. and T. F. Torrance, eds., *Calvin's Commentaries: A Harmony of the Gospels: Matthew, Mark and Luke and the Epistles of James and Jude*, trans. A. W. Morrison (Grand Rapids: Eerdmans, 1972), 3:172.

Pastoral Perspective

the most difficult task that has been entrusted to us, the ultimate task, the final test and proof, the work for which all other work is merely preparation."[1]

In our culture, we like to think we will be extraordinary, special, one of a kind, a standout. The passage, however, reminds us that despite everything that makes each person unique, what we all share is human finitude and sinfulness. Try as we might, much as we wish, perfection will always elude us. That is why we need to seek to stay close to God, through personal spiritual disciplines and participating in the life of a faith community—not because we are perfectly faithful, but precisely because we are not. Our failures—which Jesus knew so well—are what call us into the forgiving embrace of our gracious God. Our mistake is not our failure to achieve perfection; our mistake is protesting that it is possible.

Our culture also celebrates confidence. Confidence can lift us up, but wrongly placed, it can let us down. We know that Peter's confidence in his own faithfulness was misplaced. Not once but twice Jesus had to tell him the truth. Even after the second time, when Jesus began with the underscoring, "Truly I tell you," Peter held fast to his confidence in himself rather than in the word of the one he claimed to follow. Peter spoke "vehemently"—the only time the Markan author uses the word—so supremely confident was he in himself. What if our confidence, instead, lay in the sure knowledge that win or lose, succeed or fail, measure up or fall short, we are known and loved by God? What relief it would be to lay down the insupportable burden of trying to be—or seem—perfect, and rest instead in those everlasting arms that support us!

How can we nurture faith in our children and accept faith in ourselves that is not perfect but affirms that our imperfection is what will draw us and keep us close to the only one who was without sin? How can we foster comfort and confidence in being known by God better than we know ourselves, and accepted just as we are? How might our faith increase when we stop posing as perfect and start listening to the word that God has for us to hear?

In the course of this conversation with his disciples, Jesus said, "After I am raised up, I will go before you to Galilee" (v. 28). Not one of the disciples paused to really hear and understand what Jesus had just said. After you are raised up? What do you mean? Tell us more. Instead, Peter is leaping in to

---

1. Rainer Maria Rilke, *Letters to a Young Poet*, trans. Stephen Mitchell (1903; repr., New York: Random House, 1984), 68.

Exegetical Perspective

(NRSV), or "fall away" (NJB, NIV, RSV), or, more literally, "be tripped up"[1] (*skandalisthēnai*) (v. 27). To confirm the prediction, he cites Zechariah 13:7 (slightly modified), describing sheep scattered after the striking of their shepherd. The image suggests confusion and distress, but Jesus continues: "after I am raised up, I will go before you to Galilee" (v. 28). Like Jesus' earlier passion predictions in Mark (8:31; 9:31; 10:33–34), this one offers a sketch in small of key events, but in this case they are events particularly significant for the disciples: crisis of leadership, scattering, Jesus' resurrection, then an implied reunion. Jesus promises that he will "go before" (*proagō*) the disciples. The same verb was used earlier to describe their journey to Jerusalem: "They were on the road, going up to Jerusalem, and Jesus was walking ahead [*proagō*] of them; they were amazed, and those who followed were afraid" (10:32). The parallel suggests that, much as Jesus went before them into these fearful experiences in Jerusalem, so he will go ahead of them toward a postresurrection encounter in Galilee.[2] At the end of the Gospel, this promise underlies the message for the disciples that the young man in Jesus' tomb entrusts to Mary Magdalene, Mary, and Salome: "But go, tell his disciples and Peter that he is going ahead [*proagō*] of you to Galilee; there you will see him, just as he told you" (16:7).

Now, on the Mount of Olives, however, Peter is gripped not by the intimation of reunion, but by the prediction of desertion. He protests emphatically, "I will not" or "But not I" (*all' ouk egō*, v. 29). Jesus' reply begins with an intensifying *amēn* formula, "Truly I tell you," then moves through three progressively more specific indicators of time that heighten suspense and emphasis: "this day, this very night, before the cock crows twice." He concludes with the devastating prediction—Peter will deny or disown Jesus three times (v. 30). All four Gospels use numerical specifics to predict Peter's disloyalty before dawn, although the precise number of crows and denials varies. In Matthew, the rooster crows three times and Peter denies three times (Matt. 26:33–35, 75); in Luke and John, the rooster crows, and Peter denies thrice (Luke 22:31–34; John 13:36–38). Mark's is the most numerically complex and vivid prediction. The symmetries of some of Mark's patterns of threes also reinforce the sense of

---
1. Joel Marcus, *Mark 8–16: A New Translation with Introduction and Commentary*, Anchor Yale Bible (New Haven, CT: Yale University Press, 2009), 968–69.
2. Pheme Perkins, "The Gospel of Mark," in *The New Interpreter's Bible* (Nashville: Abingdon Press, 1995), 8:705.

Homiletical Perspective

the rest of the disciples, not even our best intentions can keep us from denial. So why ask us to do something that is impossibly hard to accomplish?

On the other hand, there is a freedom in Jesus' telling the disciples what he knows. If Jesus knows that his disciples will deny him, there must be a graceful note to be played on this tune of inevitability. If Jesus knows it, and expects it, then in some sense he must be willing to forgive and anticipate restored relationships (and here we cannot hide the fact that we know the end to Peter's story). A sermon that explores both the frustration of the difficulty of discipleship and the grace of discipleship in our failure helps listeners to navigate the inevitable places in our lives where we will stand witness to the arrest, trial, and crucifixion, and are pressed with the possibility of denial.

Another sermon possibility begins with a wonderful treasure of Christian history in the account of the pilgrim Egeria (or Etheria). Egeria brings into vivid detail her visit to Jerusalem during one Holy Week in the late fourth century.[1] She catalogs the pilgrims' activities on the Mount of Olives to commemorate each moment in the life of Christ during Holy Week. At the Mount of Olives, the pilgrims pray, read the Scriptures, sing hymns, and contemplate the activity of Jesus and the disciples. Her account of pilgrim activity in Jerusalem shows a strenuous, vigilant commemoration of Jesus' final week.

The historical accounts of gathering in Jerusalem by ancient pilgrims, and perhaps the preacher's or congregants' own contemporary pilgrimages, provide a stark contrast to Jesus' statement that all will desert. A sermon that places Mark's text in parallel to Egeria's account or other pilgrimage accounts makes a profound statement about the Christian life: We are still here. Although at times we may live in denial of our status as disciples of Christ, through God's power we still show up. The life of discipleship involves revisiting the places of our failure and pledging to follow more closely in the future. We gather in churches, at camps, at retreat centers, and in other places, in order to renew our commitment as disciples. We confess our sins, we put our hands in baptismal waters, and we say the creed one more time, but not simply to prove Jesus wrong. On the contrary, we know all too well our tendencies to live in denial of our discipleship.

The question for a preacher here, then, is how might a sermon help people to identify the places

---
1. *The Pilgrimage of Etheria*, trans. M. L. McClure and C. L. Feltoe, http://www.ccel.org/m/mcclure/etheria/etheria.htm; accessed March 12, 2012.

Mark 14:26–31

Theological Perspective

In the early Christian interpretive tradition, it is said that Peter is the primary source for Mark, which shaped the particular points stressed in his Gospel. Eusebius wrote that "Mark, who had been Peter's interpreter, wrote down carefully as much as he remembered, recording both sayings and doings of Christ, not however in order." For Mark was, Eusebius noted, "not a hearer of the Lord" but a "follower of Peter," and Peter had "adopted his teachings to the needs of his hearers as one who is engaged in making a compendium of the Lord's precepts."[2] Whether or not this is historically accurate, many within the Christian tradition read Mark, and the depiction of Peter in particular, as bearing important moral lessons for the church. Chiefly, interpreters use Peter's boasting as counsel to engage in soul searching to further the process of what has been traditionally called the "mortification of the flesh." The vice of Peter's hubris presents believers with an opportunity to cultivate the virtue of humility.

Such moral readings have continued in contemporary interpretations. However, the emphasis is now less on the individual process of sanctification and more on how one might live a redeemed life in community. On this, Mark's passage lacks closure, and this lack provides imaginative space for reflecting on what our own lives of faith might look like. As David Rhoads and Donald Michie note, viewed within the "larger Markan framework," the story of Peter's boasting and denial therefore serves the purpose of presenting "a character with whom the reader could identify and empathize, but whose actions" he or she "should not emulate." Although Peter's reconciliation with Jesus "is strongly implied," it is not "actualized," and this is "because the action of the reader in the future story world becomes more important than the action of any one character, including Peter."[3]

WILLIAM J. DANAHER JR.

Pastoral Perspective

talk about himself. Imagine what a different conversation might have unfolded if Peter had understood that this was ultimately about Jesus and not him.

The passage begins with Jesus drawing on prophecy from Zechariah, saying that all of his followers like sheep will "desert" or "fall away." The Greek verb translated "desert" or "fall away" is *skandalizō*, from which we get our modern English word "scandal." However, forms of the same Greek word elsewhere in Mark and other Gospels have different translations: "cause to stumble" or "be caused to stumble" (e.g., Mark 9:43). It offers us a different perspective on what Jesus was saying lay ahead for the disciples. Rather than the volitional, intentional act of "desertion," what his disciples would experience was more akin to stumbling, to losing their way, getting off the path they had been following. Would we be gentler with ourselves if we understood our losing our way as stumbling rather than desertion? Would we be less judgmental and feel more kinship with others whom we see stumbling too?

Although in this passage we are reminded that "all" the disciples were not there for Jesus, Jesus was sent by God to be there for all of them, "poured out for many" (14:24). In the passage preceding this one, Jesus extended the cup to all—even the one who would betray him, even to the one who would deny him, even to all who would fall away and flee. Bread and cup are offered to all, that we may be sustained in our journey—after all of our stumbling and fleeing—back to the one who knows and loves all of us, back to God in whose image all of us have been made.

SHANNON DALEY-HARRIS

---

2. Eusebius, *Ecclesiastical History*, III, 39.15. This translation from H. E. W. Turner, "The Tradition of Mark's Dependence upon Peter," *Expository Times* 71 (1960): 260, quoted by Robert W. Herron Jr., *Mark's Account of Peter's Denial of Jesus: A History of its Interpretation* (Lanham, MD: University Press of America, 1991), 16.

3. David Rhoads and Donald Michie, *Mark as Story* (Philadelphia: Fortress Press, 1982), 97.

Exegetical Perspective

crisis among the disciples. Mark's three central passion predictions (8:31; 9:31; 10:33–34) are now followed by three varying predictions that Jesus' closest followers will turn away: one will betray (14:18–20), all will desert (v. 27), Peter will deny (v. 30). Peter's denial itself will be threefold.

Peter's reply to Jesus is insistent. Comparing English translations of the introductory verb and adverb (*ekperissōs elalei*) helps catch the intensity: "he said vehemently" (v. 31 RSV, NRSV); "he repeated still more earnestly" (NJB); "he kept saying insistently" (NASB); "he insisted emphatically" (NIV). Earlier in the Gospel, Peter famously rejected Jesus' revelation that the Son of Man would suffer and die (8:31–33). Now, however, Peter seems to understand that Jesus will die and to think that he is ready to embrace the possibility of dying with Jesus. If Mark's early readers knew that Peter had been martyred by the time the Gospel was composed, they might have heard his avowed willingness to die as doubly poignant—wrong in the near term, but eventually true.

As is often the case in the Gospels, the portrait of Peter helps reveal something about the whole group of disciples. According to Mark, "And all of them said the same" (v. 31). Throughout this section of the story, Mark has repeated the term "all" (*pantes*) at key junctures: all the disciples drank of the cup at the Passover meal (v. 23); Jesus predicts that all will fall away (v. 27); all now speak as Peter does (v. 31). Very soon, at Jesus' arrest, Mark will note, "All of them deserted him and fled" (14:50). For Peter, the disavowals that fulfill Jesus' prediction and culminate at the second cock's crow will be narrated more slowly, with confusion and sorrow (14:54, 66–72).

This close exchange between Jesus and the disciples offers more evidence of Jesus' control, knowledge, and choice in the events that are unfolding. However, Mark's narrative joins that sense of control together with the sharp perception that the cohesive group of Jesus' nearest followers is about to come apart, and that he is facing abandonment, distress, and suffering.

B. DIANE LIPSETT

Homiletical Perspective

where their commitment to faithfulness is renewed, in full view of the knowledge of betrayal? How might a sermon rally people around the determined exclamation: "Despite our moments of desertion, we have returned! Through God's grace, we are still here!"? A sermon that culminates in a collective act that expresses this sentiment could be a part of the preacher's sermon and worship planning process.

Finally, a sermon on this text might tread some well-worn ground. Singing the hymns and traveling with Jesus in an intimate way do not serve as inoculation from denial. This speech from Jesus is hardly the pep talk the disciples needed in an already tense atmosphere, but this was the reality of their discipleship, and ours as well. Our mountaintop experiences of faith, our successes as disciples, and our close walk with Jesus do not prevent us from stepping off the path and joining the crowd of deserters. The pleasant memories and close-knit feeling we may have with God and those in our faith community do not provide a warrant for losing vigilance in our attempts to remain faithful disciples.

A sermon that takes this route might celebrate the many wonderful things that have gone on in the life of a church: works of justice, baptisms, ministries established, buildings built or paid for, programs added, lives changed, prayers answered, reconciliations achieved, conflicts resolved. All of this the disciples had experienced and more. And as with the disciples, a sermon might turn on the hinge of a kind of "and yet . . ." statement. Despite our high spots as disciples, despite the moments of flight we achieve, a kind of healthy memory should accompany us that warns of the possibility for us to end up as deserters. While John's Gospel was written "so that you might believe," Mark's Gospel continually alerts us to our humanity as disciples, helping us avoid the pitfalls of our ancestors in faith. A sermon that points to Mark's portrayal of the disciples in this way gives to contemporary listeners gospel companions for the journey ahead.

RICHARD W. VOELZ

Mark 14:32–42

32They went to a place called Gethsemane; and he said to his disciples, "Sit here while I pray." 33He took with him Peter and James and John, and began to be distressed and agitated. 34And he said to them, "I am deeply grieved, even to death; remain here, and keep awake." 35And going a little farther, he threw himself on the ground and prayed that, if it were possible, the hour might pass from him. 36He said, "Abba, Father, for you all things are possible; remove this cup from me; yet, not what I want, but what you want." 37He came and found them sleeping; and he said to Peter, "Simon, are you asleep? Could you not keep awake one hour? 38Keep awake and pray that you may not come into the time of trial; the spirit indeed is willing, but the flesh is weak." 39And again he went away and prayed, saying the same words. 40And once more he came and found them sleeping, for their eyes were very heavy; and they did not know what to say to him. 41He came a third time and said to them, "Are you still sleeping and taking your rest? Enough! The hour has come; the Son of Man is betrayed into the hands of sinners. 42Get up, let us be going. See, my betrayer is at hand."

Theological Perspective

Jesus' prayer in Gethsemane is notable for many reasons, not the least of which is the raw Christology that Mark invites the readers to witness. Long before church councils negotiated doctrines that defined the relationship between Jesus and God, Mark's story marks a genuine, honest struggle between what Jesus wills and what God wills. This text will not address christological questions that arise later in the tradition. It will only insist that those questions respect the gritty reality of two relationships: between Jesus and God, and between Jesus and the disciples.

Jesus concludes his prayer with the heroic words, "Yet, not what I want, but what you want." However, before Jesus reaches this conclusion, Mark invites us to witness an enormous struggle. It is not just an emotional struggle for Jesus, in the face of an agonizing death. Mark describes it as a struggle between Jesus and God. As Mark tells the story, Jesus "began to be distressed and agitated," professing to the disciples, "I am deeply grieved, even to death." The suffering that culminates on the cross has begun. Then Mark describes Jesus' prayer as a struggle between Jesus' will and God's will. Narratively, Mark says that the point of Jesus' prayer was "that, if it were possible, the hour might pass from him." In an earlier story, Jesus had responded forcefully to the phrase "if it is possible," arguing that with God, all things are

Pastoral Perspective

In the church where I grew up, there was a huge round window over the choir loft with a picture of Jesus praying in the Garden of Gethsemane. Wearing a robe of incandescent white, he is splayed out upon a rock, with his bare feet touching the ground and his hands clasped tightly in front of him. James Weldon Johnson, in a poem entitled "The Crucifixion," uses these words to describe this scene of Jesus' praying in Gethsemane: "my sorrowing Jesus, the sweat like great drops of blood upon his brow."[1] I recall walking down to the front of the church one Sunday morning to get a closer look. Indeed, the artist had included sweat and tears falling from the well-lit face of a beatific Jesus. Even a six-year-old could get the message: here is a man filled with sadness. What has happened to make him sad, and why is he facing upward toward heaven?

Following their last meal together, Jesus and his disciples walk out of the city walls to the Mount of Olives and a garden that is probably simply an olive press. Here, in the evening hours, they will enact a drama of intense sorrow and, for Jesus, agonizing loneliness. True to form, the disciples fall asleep and cannot watch and pray even on this last night.

1. James Weldon Johnson, *God's Trombones: Seven Negro Sermons in Verse* (New York: Viking, 1927), 40.

Exegetical Perspective

Mark's "theological geography" may be at work in the name of the place where Jesus experiences intense isolation and terror shortly before his arrest. The name "Gethsemane," unknown in other ancient Jewish sources, means "oil press," as in the device where one wooden wheel turning within another crushes olives, forcing the liquid oil into a trough. To produce olive oil, intense pressure is placed on the olive. There may have been an olive press or the memory of one at Gethsemane, but it also seems likely that Mark is adding another, deeply ironic level to the story by mentioning its name. Here God's "anointed-with-oil one," hailed twice by Bartimaeus (10:47–48) as "Son of David," and greeted during his triumphal entry into Jerusalem by crowds expecting the coming reign of King David (11:10, though see also 12:35–37), prepares not to be crowned but to be crucified.

Mark's readers will remember another place name that Mark seems to have created or chosen deliberately for theological purposes: as Jesus approaches Jerusalem he passes well-known Bethany and completely unknown Bethphage, a name that means "house of unripe figs" (11:1), hinting at the intercalated fig tree and temple incident story of 11:12–25. That story, while clearly related to Jeremiah's prophetic judgment against the Jerusalem temple (Jer. 7:1–15; see 8:13), is also a reminder that just as it is

Homiletical Perspective

The choice to preach on Jesus' prayer in Gethsemane might be right for the Sunday of Holy Week (Passion/Palm Sunday). John Calvin chose it for the Sunday before Easter as one of nine texts he preached on throughout the week, preparing his congregation in Geneva for the Lord's Supper on the following Easter Sunday.[1] When Calvin spoke to his congregation about the disciples who fell asleep while Jesus prayed throughout the night before his crucifixion, he urged the people in Geneva to recognize how even the best of us are prone to miss the urgency of Jesus' struggle, and yet to realize even more deeply that Jesus saves us even when we nod off. The care with which Calvin chose the passage reminds us how important it is for us to select carefully Bible readings and preach sermons on them throughout the year—whether or not it is the Sunday before Easter—so that we help people live by the gospel in its fullness.

The choice of a text from the passion of Christ for the Sunday before Easter has its hazards. Once when a minister did so and reminded his people that Jesus entered Jerusalem in order to take up his cross and die for us, an older woman approached the preacher

---

1. Hughes Oliphant Old, "Calvin as Evangelist: A Study of the Reformer's Sermons in Preparation for the Christian Celebration of Passover," in John H. Leith, ed., *Calvin Studies VII, Papers Presented at a Colloquium on Calvin Studies, Davidson College Presbyterian Church, Davidson, North Carolina* (January 28–29, 1994), 52.

Mark 14:32–42

Theological Perspective

possible (9:21–24). Likewise, Jesus begins this prayer with the words, "Abba, Father, for you all things are possible" (v. 36). When Jesus gets to the petition, "Remove this cup from me," it is not a question of whether God can, but whether God will.

The words "Yet, not what I want, but what you want" (v. 36) are predicated on the difference between what Jesus wants—for the hour to pass from him—and what God wants—for Jesus to accept the cup. In the end, Jesus accepts what God wills, but prior to that, the difference is stated quite simply. As such, this prayer is reminiscent of many lament psalms, perhaps even imprecatory psalms, which express honestly one's immediate feelings and desires as the genuine matter of prayer, regardless of whether or not they are reflective of proper theology. They are genuine and authentic expression, even if, in the end and upon reflection, one accepts a different path of faithfulness. The turning point is the word "yet." Even with the honest expression of what Jesus wants, the final word of this prayer—like so many lament or imprecatory psalms—is an embrace of God's will.[1]

As Karl Barth describes it, the "riddle" that confronts Jesus in the garden and evokes his horror is that the "answer of God was identical to the action of Satan."[2] The agony of Jesus' prayer lies not simply in the human will to live, but in the irony that what God wills is what Jesus' own enemies are conspiring. They have set out to destroy the one sent from God. In their success, God's will is done.

Between the petition, "let this cup pass from me," and the final concession, "yet, not what I want, but what you want," lies a volume of Christology. Jesus recognizes and accepts that the salvation that God wills is going to be accomplished through his subjection to those who reject him as the one sent from God. Within that riddle, Jesus prays an agonizing prayer.

Another relationship that animates this text is between Jesus and the disciples. Most of the disciples are instructed to sit at the entrance to Gethsemane while Jesus prays. Three of the disciples are instructed to remain nearby and to "watch"—a word that could refer to the work of sentries anticipating an attack or a porter keeping an eye out for thieves— and to pray. Significantly, Jesus is not in the garden

Pastoral Perspective

It seems that they have a talent for drifting off at the most demanding moments. Mark underscores it three times. Jesus asks them, "Watch and pray with me," only to head off into the heart of darkness alone.

The inner circle of Jesus cannot sustain him through this distress of his prayer in the garden. Mark's Jesus is not approaching this last night of his life with detachment or resignation. He is shaken to the core, terrified by his inner struggle and the night demons at play. Peter, James, and John cannot keep their eyes open, not even for this last act in the drama of their life with Jesus. Mark underscores the miserable followership of those who would be leaders into the new day. The flesh is scared and weak, even if the spirit could declare a willingness to wake up and move ahead. All, it would seem, is darkness; even those who could see light cannot lift the heaviness of their eyes to see.

How many times have we fallen asleep in the midst of a crisis, either in our own lives or in the community or the world? I have watched as dedicated and lively folks have basically sleepwalked through the illness of a spouse or the death of a parent. President Bill Clinton will always bear the sorrow of not being immediately responsive to the slaughter in Rwanda, and Hurricane Katrina was a classic case of the leadership's being asleep at the wheel, unable to comprehend or believe that something so enormously tragic could actually happen in New Orleans. The agonies of the world, whether personal or political, demand our spirit's watchfulness and a lifetime of physical presence; but too often we cannot bear the freight of the pain of the world. Recently, after a death in the family, a young seminarian wrote, "Grief is exhausting."[2]

Too often, we are just not up to it. Peter, James, and John stand in for us as we make our often feeble attempts to minister in the tragic gap of a broken world. When Jesus prays that the cup of suffering be removed from him, he also has the presence of mind and spirit to turn himself over to the will of God. It is a total surrender and who among us wants that kind of suffering? We would rather fall asleep and face the criticism that we are lazy or just plain too exhausted to take on that kind of a life.

As the old song reminds us, though, "what a friend we have in Jesus, all our sins and griefs to bear."[3] When Jesus prays into the depths of the vast darkness of that awful night, somehow he is renewed

---

1. John Calvin describes Jesus' petition as his way of committing to God what troubles him, which he "corrected" with his embrace of God's will (John Calvin, *Harmony of the Evangelists, Matthew, Mark, and Luke* [Grand Rapids: Eerdmans, 1949], 3:231).
2. Karl Barth, *Church Dogmatics*, IV/1, §59 (Edinburgh: T. & T. Clark, 1961), 268.

2. Samuel Rennebohm, personal text, 2012.
3. Joseph M. Scriven, "What a Friend We Have in Jesus" (1855).

Exegetical Perspective

not God's appointed time for figs, so also it is not God's appointed time for Jesus to be crowned king in the Davidic tradition. These two apparently constructed place names are in exegetical conversation.

Once in Gethsemane, Jesus takes with him the inner circle of disciples (Peter, James, John) whom he had called first (1:16–20; 3:16–17) and whom he privileged to be with him at the raising of Jairus's daughter (5:37) and at his transfiguration (9:2), but who had also misunderstood his mission and threatened to derail it (8:31–33; 10:35–45). Borrowing language from the Psalms, Jesus tells them that he is "deeply grieved, even to death" (v. 34) and requests their support as he prays for his life: "remain here, and keep awake," using words he had pointedly repeated at the end of chapter 13 (13:33, 35, 37). That chapter ended with Jesus' words ringing in our ears: "what I say to you I say to all: Keep awake." Prior chapters have prepared us and we are not surprised when Jesus' closest disciples promptly fall asleep in response to his plea to "remain here and keep awake" (v. 34). The first task of the Twelve is "to be with him" (3:14). Now when it matters most, even his closest disciples fail him, falling asleep and leaving him terribly alone.

Mark delays telling us about the failure of Peter, James, and John, presumably to focus our attention on the terror-filled agony of Jesus. Instead of the split screen (Jesus here, disciples there), the narrative camera moves in for a close-up shot of Jesus under intense pressure. "Going forward a bit" (v. 35, my trans.), he moves some distance from the disciples and falls on the ground. The action is ambiguous: it could refer to the self-abasement or prostration of one begging for mercy from a sovereign ruler; but, as Joel Marcus has suggested, it may also be evidence of divine judgment. Marcus notes the intriguing parallel in the story of King Saul collapsing on the ground upon hearing of his own approaching violent death. Once "the Lord's anointed," he has now been rejected by God, who refuses to hear his prayer and allows him to be handed over to his enemies to be killed (1 Sam. 28).[1]

Jesus prays that "if it were possible, the hour might pass from him" (v. 35). Some narrative tension exists between this indirect description of his prayer and the direct discourse of the prayer itself, where God is described as the One for whom "all things are possible" (v. 36). Many have seen a connection between Mark's passion narrative and the apparent

---

1. Joel Marcus, *Mark 8–16*, Anchor Yale Bible (New Haven, CT: Yale University Press, 2009), 977.

Homiletical Perspective

after the service and said she was really disappointed that the sermon neglected the joyous theme of the triumphal entry. Perhaps the sermon did omit the gospel joy. However, as cognitive psychologists and common sense tell us, we often do not want to face loss. Sometimes we do not want to face the harder lessons of Jesus' ministry, the depths to which he was finally willing to go for our good. Something in us all wants to jump from an imagined Palm Sunday triumph to Jesus' resurrection and empty tomb, skipping his cross in between.

The passion story challenges us in deep ways. When we refer to Jesus' passion, we mean the particular willing suffering that he accepted as the requirement of the Scriptures and the will of God for his service and ministry to all people. Passion in this special biblical sense is not our usual meaning. In common parlance the word has a psychological sense, referring to emotion, particularly the emotions of fear, hate, love, sexual desire, or joy. On the Mount of Olives, Jesus said the disciples would all reject him, and he repeated the teaching about the Scripture's requirement that he suffer, die, and then be raised and go before them into Galilee where they would meet him. Jesus' passion was that he willingly relinquished his power to act as he has done before in preaching, healing, casting out demons, feeding, and teaching in parables. The time for these parts of his ministry has passed. Now, outside events take over.

In Jesus' prayer, "Abba, Father, for you all things are possible; remove this cup from me; yet, not what I want, but what you want" (v. 36), Jesus accepts God's plan. His prayer leads us to ask, "In what sense was it God's will that Jesus suffer and die on the cross? How could God want the death of his own Son?" We confront a mystery here that we cannot resolve. The first thing God wants is for us to love God and our neighbor as ourselves, just as Jesus taught us. God wants us to give up everything and follow Jesus in his feeding, healing, and proclamation that God is the sovereign ruler of the world. Only Jesus did fully these things that God wants.

The suffering of Jesus shows us that even without faithful human responses, God still will have things his way. So we believe that in the passion of Christ, in his prayer and acceptance of God's will, he did show what God truly desires for the whole world. In his deep agony and his humiliation he did what nobody else could do. In that very human weakness and vulnerability, Jesus was most truly like God. Jesus taught that he would suffer because of human failures to love God and neighbor. Through the

Mark 14:32–42

Theological Perspective

alone. A short distance away are those whom Jesus invited to be part of the struggle that he must face. A little farther along are those who were invited to sit in waiting. While Jesus must take the cup of suffering, the disciples are invited to be part of the moment by sitting, watching, or praying.

Instead of struggling with Jesus, the disciples sleep. Even Simon Peter is unable to stay awake, unable to watch and pray, unable to articulate a response when Jesus finds him sleeping three successive times. The disciples' slumber is part of the picture of the utter failure of the church, right in the moment of Christ's decisive struggle with the prospect of the cross as God's means of overcoming sin.

The slumber of the disciples is more failure than fatigue. It takes on pernicious meaning when we see the depth of the struggle that is taking place just a stone's throw away from the slumber. Christ faces death. Meanwhile, the church sleeps. Christ is "distressed and agitated" (v. 33). Meanwhile, the church sleeps. Christ is horrified at the awful prospect that God's will is performed through the actions of those who reject God's chosen one. Meanwhile, the church sleeps. Even in that critical moment, when Christ embraces the will of God by accepting the cup of suffering, the church sleeps. The profound contrast between the struggle and the slumber might be a way of understanding a common expression of human sinfulness. John Calvin claimed that our knowledge of God's glory is inherently connected with our knowledge of human sinfulness.[3] The depth of human sin might not be expressed in vile acts of utter evil as much as in the act of sleeping when the fate of the world hangs in the balance a mere stone's throw away.

D. MARK DAVIS

Pastoral Perspective

and given strength for the journey to the cross. Jesus faces up to his death through the privilege of prayer uttered into the void of holy terror. This is not a Sunday school utterance, but a soul-shaking, earth-moving, direct request for the power of *Abba* God to be present in life and in death. The difference between Jesus and his followers is not that the flesh is weak or the spirit willing; it is that the demons of night and the day to come are directly met through the summons of the Spirit of the living God.

"Sit here while I pray," Jesus invites us. Can we comprehend the power of staying awake through the discipline of fervent and frequent prayer that will enable us to face whatever cup of life is given us? There will be times when we will be asked to leave the city of comfort to enter the garden beyond the walls to pray—times of grief, distress, terror, and demand. Can we stay awake all on our own? Will we remain alert, even vigilant, to all that the world asks of us? Will we submit to the strength and courage of the One who waits for us and asks only that we be present and stay awake? Such is the demand and the promise of the Holy One.

As we enter into our own cities and gardens, whatever they may be, let us have the strength to stay awake, even for one hour. Perhaps in these powerful seasons, we will use that sacred hour to return to the Holy a prayer for courage and strength in the midst of a violent world, asking for love that outshines our propensity toward fondness and with a wide-eyed commitment to outlast our inclination to fall asleep when the going gets toughest and most terrifying.

PATRICIA E. DE JONG

---

3. John Calvin, *Institutes of the Christian Religion*, 1.1.1–3, ed. John T. McNeill, trans. Ford Lewis Battles (Philadelphia: Westminster Press, 1960), 35–39.

Exegetical Perspective

reference to Gethsemane in Hebrews 5:7 ("In the days of his flesh, he offered up prayers and supplications, with loud cries and tears, to the one who was able to save him from death, and he was heard because of his reverent submission"). It is important to see that Jesus' prayer consists of two parts: in the first, he begs for his life ("remove this cup from me") while in the second, he submits to God's will ("yet, not what I want, but what you want," v. 36). The image of the cup of suffering and death that one must drink is common in Scripture and is usually related to God's judgment. Mark's readers have been introduced to it previously at 10:38–39 (the request of James and John) and immediately before this passage at 14:23–24 (the cup identified with Jesus' blood of the covenant, which is poured out for many).

The word Jesus uses for God, *Abba* ("father," v. 36), reminds us of the words spoken by the voice from heaven at Jesus' baptism (1:11): "You are my Son, the Beloved; with you I am well pleased," and again at the transfiguration (9:7): "This is my Son, the Beloved; listen to him!" Isaac typology is almost certainly in the background here; we are meant to recall that Abraham was told to sacrifice "your son, your only son, Isaac, whom you love" (Gen. 22:2). The divine rescue of Isaac reminds us that, by contrast, at the hour of the death of the beloved Son of God, the voice from heaven will remain silent, and the Son will imagine that he has been abandoned (15:34). So the lonely intensity of Jesus' prayer in Gethsemane subtly foreshadows the horror of the death to come.

There is no need for concern about how the disciples learned the content of Jesus' prayer when he was some distance away and they were asleep. Mark's omniscient narrator has, throughout the Gospel, discerned matters of the heart and mind. Similarly Jesus' threefold rebuke to his disciples suggests oral transmission patterns. What matters most at this point is the announcement that the dreaded hour has not passed from him; it has come: the threefold passion prophecy (8:31; 9:31; 10:33) is being fulfilled: "the Son of Man is betrayed into the hands of sinners."

A. KATHERINE GRIEB

Homiletical Perspective

events of cross and resurrection, the church would come to believe that God was in Christ for reconciliation and justice in the world.

Jesus' prayer in Gethsemane is the last offering he makes to God before his arrest. It falls at the crucial turning point from his action to his passion. He prays earnestly for God to take the bitter cup away from him. This is the cup that only he can drink (see 10:38). If it is a cup of God's fury and wrath, a cup whose drink causes staggering and falling, God will call his servant to stand up again (see Isa. 51:17, 22). God answers Jesus' prayer, lasting until the early hours of the day of his crucifixion, by giving him the clarity and courage to get up, wake his sleeping disciples, and face the hour that has come. In his prayer and submission, Jesus himself becomes the sermon, the miracle, the parable, the bread and the wine, offering us his death for our life in the kingdom of God. The deep resonances of Jesus' suffering with our human questions about the way God deals with evil in the world, with our questions about how God answers our prayers, and with our discipleship of offering real comfort and help to those who experience oppression, whatever its nature, are some of the many issues of faithful living that this text offers us. The interpreter can return to it again and again throughout the year.

CHARLES RAYNAL

Mark 14:43–52

⁴³Immediately, while he was still speaking, Judas, one of the twelve, arrived; and with him there was a crowd with swords and clubs, from the chief priests, the scribes, and the elders. ⁴⁴Now the betrayer had given them a sign, saying, "The one I will kiss is the man; arrest him and lead him away under guard." ⁴⁵So when he came, he went up to him at once and said, "Rabbi!" and kissed him. ⁴⁶Then they laid hands on him and arrested him. ⁴⁷But one of those who stood near drew his sword and struck the slave of the high priest, cutting off his ear. ⁴⁸Then Jesus said to them, "Have you come out with swords and clubs to arrest me as though I were a bandit? ⁴⁹Day after day I was with you in the temple teaching, and you did not arrest me. But let the scriptures be fulfilled." ⁵⁰All of them deserted him and fled.

⁵¹A certain young man was following him, wearing nothing but a linen cloth. They caught hold of him, ⁵²but he left the linen cloth and ran off naked.

Theological Perspective

Mark 14:43–52 is an account of Jesus' arrest and the actions of those who surround him. Unlike the earlier seclusion of the garden, there is quite a crowd at the arrest: those who set out to arrest Jesus (a posse sent from the chief priests, the scribes, and elders, whom we will collectively call the "enemies" of Jesus), the deserters (whom we presume to be disciples), Judas, Jesus, and the strange cameo appearance of a young man loosely dressed. To explore the theological dimensions of this text, we will turn first to the disciples and their varied initial reactions, then to Jesus' proclamation that everything happening in this dark hour is necessary to fulfill the Scriptures (v. 49).

In the previous pericope, the disciples were noted chiefly for their slumber. In our present pericope, the slumber becomes desertion, the very thing Jesus predicted (14:26–27). However, the disciples' journeys toward desertion were varied. One of those who were standing nearby grabbed a sword and initiated a violent response. Next we hear that all fled. Then the young man who had followed was also seized, but by leaving behind his garment, he too fled. Of course one disciple is still standing there, as far as we can tell: Judas, the betrayer who betrays with an affectionate kiss.

What a curious portrait of discipleship! Disciples act in concert with Jesus' enemies, they exhibit

Pastoral Perspective

Have you ever been arrested? I have not been, but I can recall a time when I was speeding down a highway in my parents' 1998 Oldsmobile. It was a hot summer night and I was singing to the music on the radio and, just barely above the notes, I heard a siren. Looking in the rearview mirror, I saw the red lights of a cop's car spinning in rapid circles behind me. I glanced at the speedometer. I was traveling at a cool 92 miles per hour! I thought I would be thrown in jail and sentenced right then and there, so getting a ticket for speeding felt like a relief to me.

Most of us cannot begin to imagine the kind of arrest Jesus went through in the garden on that spiritually hot night. He had already been through so much leading up to this moment, but the worst was yet to come. We say it every time we break bread together: "on the night of Jesus' arrest and betrayal," but this first time actually initiates the everlasting ritual of our faith, seeing in the bread and cup the broken body and lifeblood of Jesus. Rather than squad cars and spinning red lights, the guards enter the garden on stealthy feet, led by Judas, who, no matter how quiet the night, screams betrayal. He walks straight to Jesus and kisses him, making sure that there is no mistaking the rabbi for anyone else. We marvel that Jesus shows no resistance at all; neither does he attempt to run away. He is nonviolent in the

Exegetical Perspective

Jesus awakens his sluggish disciples a third time with the news that they have managed to miss the entire ordeal that has preoccupied him for the last several hours. The famously difficult word translated "it is enough" (*apechei*, 14:41) concretizes an economic metaphor suggesting that something has been bought and paid for. In this context, the word is less likely to refer to the money paid to Judas the betrayer (promised at 14:10–11) than to suggest the missed opportunity of the disciples. It is as if they are at an auction where Jesus has warned them that the only item he cares about is coming up and they should be alert, ready to bid on it. Instead, they fail to pay attention and let it go by. The economic language portrays a spiritual reality: the disciples' opportunity to assist Jesus in his agony is now lost; that window has been closed; the hour he has prayed would pass from him has now come.

The sign that the interval of opportunity has ended is the imminent arrival of Judas: "Get up, let us be going. See, my betrayer is at hand" (14:42). Although some interpreters read "while he was still speaking" as evidence that Jesus saw the crowd approaching and reported his observations to the disciples, Mark probably intends a prophecy on the part of Jesus, which is then immediately fulfilled. Mark's readers recognize this pattern from the very

Homiletical Perspective

Judas is fascinating. In the rock opera *Jesus Christ Superstar*,[1] Judas is motivated by disappointment in Jesus. Better to force Jesus' hand or at least get him out of public view before he gets them all killed! Judas clears his conscience with his own agenda before events get the better of him. However, Mark does not give us a clue about Judas's motivation. The Gospel says directly that Jesus chose Judas to be one of his twelve faithful followers. Judas did not remain loyal. He handed him over for arrest by the guards, and so does what is necessary to fulfill the Scriptures. The first time he is introduced in Mark's book he is described as "Judas Iscariot, who betrayed him" (3:19).

Can Judas, in spite of himself, help us come to a better understanding of how we are to respond to the passion of Jesus, to find a deeper trust in the forgiveness and power of God for living more fully in faith, love, and hope?[2] This discovery would be a real treasure!

First, Judas is one of the Twelve, partaking with them all of the intimate company and blessing of Jesus' Last Supper. At the Seder, while they were

---

[1]. *Jesus Christ Superstar*, directed by Norman Jewison (Universal City, CA: Universal Pictures: 1973).
[2]. See Karl Barth, *Church Dogmatics*, II/2 (Edinburgh: T. & T. Clark, 1957), 458–507.

Mark 14:43–52

Theological Perspective

inordinate violence, and they change from being followers one moment to being deserters the next. If Mark's story ends with what is called the "shorter ending" (16:8), Werner Kelber's conclusion that the church ultimately fails in Mark's Gospel would be hard to avoid.[1] It is a portrait of utter failure in a variety of ways. The call to discipleship was not to consort with those who were opposed to Jesus, nor to run away from the danger, nor to resist the moment in armed struggle. The call had been, from the beginning, to follow, even at this point of taking up one's cross as the means of following.

The kiss of Judas particularly has become a rich symbol of betrayal in its worst form—under the guise of affection. As disturbing as it is, Mark consistently sets Judas's betrayal within the larger context of the disciples' failure in general. We may be tempted to cast our strongest aspersions at Judas, or even to find Judas to be a sympathetic figure acting out of impatience and confusion. Such reactions might be compelling, but Mark invites us to regard Judas within the disciples' failure in all of its forms. In that respect, this text offers a wide portrayal of human failure—not only as one might point to it outside of the church among Jesus' enemies, but also as it is experienced among disciples, the deserting followers of Christ.

While this text is indeed a story of utter failure on the disciples' part, it is not only a story of failure. Something else is afoot in this story, which Jesus discloses in verse 49 with the pronouncement, "But in order that the scriptures may be fulfilled" (my trans.). This pronouncement is a dependent clause, grammatically connected to the act of arresting Jesus in stealth and immediately followed by the act of desertion. It is theology in life, not speculative conjecture or ivory-tower deduction. This theology says that, somehow—between the betrayer's kiss, the enemies' stealth, the violence real or threatened, and the disciples' failure—the will of God made known in the Scriptures is being fulfilled. In this sense, Jesus' pronouncement marks the victorious outcome of the struggle in the garden and its conclusion, "Not my will, but yours."

It is one thing to say that the Scriptures are ultimately fulfilled by the death and resurrection of Jesus. It is quite another to look at each actor in this story and to say it. In Judas, the Scriptures are being fulfilled. In the chief priests, the scribes, and the

---

1. Werner H. Kelber, *Mark's Story of Jesus* (Minneapolis: Fortress Press, 1979). See esp. chap. 3, "The Suffering of the Son of Man," 43–56.

Pastoral Perspective

face of violent arrest. Mark does not report what will happen to Judas after that terrible kiss. One wonders what will become of Judas after he betrays his leader and friend and hands him over to the authorities.

Betrayal is one of the greatest of human sins, because it severs the bonds of trust and love in a relationship in a way that is rarely reparable. The act of betrayal leaves a permanent injury in the lives of both parties. Without confession and forgiveness, there is no future and no real life to be had. We recall the work of Archbishop Desmond Tutu in postapartheid South Africa with the Truth and Reconciliation Commission, reminding all of us that there is "no future without forgiveness."[1]

Throughout human history and in recent times, we have seen dictators betray the will of their people by resisting their desire for freedom and involvement with their destinies. Often there is very little remorse. In the Christian story, however, we watch as the leader holds on to his truth and a nonviolent relationship with his tormentors, even as he is arrested, betrayed, and sentenced to death on a cross. Even his own followers cannot comprehend his strength and humility. They fold like a flimsy deck of cards in the wake of the arrest in the garden.

They leave Jesus to face his arrest alone and without any support. As Ched Meyers has written, "They flee for their lives. The sheep have scattered. The discipleship narrative has collapsed."[2] In addition to arrest and betrayal, Jesus must endure the loneliness of being without friends or allies. He is forsaken and alone. We cannot imagine how it is done, but there are those in the world who are pulled from their families and homes, arrested, tortured, and stuffed into prisons for protesting the evil of totalitarian regimes. Sarah Shourd, an American hiker who was found in Iranian territory after she mistakenly crossed the border, spoke of being removed from community and being put into solitary confinement in prison as the loneliest and most difficult of all fates. There was no one who was with her, and it felt as if no one cared about her or what happened to her.[3] Jesus faces another moment of betrayal in the garden as he watches his friends run away and he stands alone before the guards. Later he will be stripped of his clothing, but now he is stripped bare of his community and his life as he has lived it. It is

---

1. Desmond Tutu, *No Future Without Forgiveness* (New York: Doubleday, 1999).
2. Ched Myers, *Binding the Strong Man: A Political Reading of Mark's Story of Jesus* (Maryknoll, NY: Orbis Books, 1988), 364.
3. Sarah Shourd, "Tortured by Solitude," *New York Times*, November 5, 2011, SR4.

Exegetical Perspective

beginning of the Gospel (see the deliberate sequence of fulfilled prophecies in 1:2–9). During most of his narrative, the prophecy-fulfillment pattern has surfaced only occasionally, but here it reappears with an intensity that contributes to the sense of impending danger.

Jesus has just predicted (14:41) that the Son of Man would be "betrayed into the hands of sinners." This word clearly describes Gentiles hostile to the God and the people of Israel, as elsewhere in both biblical testaments, but Mark has also prepared us for "sinners" in Jerusalem collaborating with the Romans to effect Jesus' death. (See the double "betrayal" and "handing over" of 10:33–34, where the same Greek word is used to prophesy both Judas's betrayal of Jesus to the chief priests and scribes and their subsequent delivery of Jesus to [the Gentile] Pontius Pilate [15:1].) When Judas Iscariot is introduced (3:19), his name is tightly linked to the betrayal. Here Mark highlights the scandal that Jesus was betrayed by "one of the twelve" (v. 43; also 14:10, 20), that is, one of the disciples whom he had chosen "to be with him" (3:14).

Mark employs the literary device of flashback to explain that Judas's kiss was a prearranged signal. When Mark wrote his Gospel about 66–70 CE, Christians almost certainly greeted one another with the kiss of peace as if they were family, and probably also exchanged the kiss of peace in liturgical settings. Paul, writing almost two decades earlier, referred to the "holy kiss" (Rom. 16:16) as if it were well known (see also 1 Thess. 5:26; 1 Cor. 16:20; 2 Cor. 13:12). This sign of affection was already practiced within Israel.

Here the kiss is deceptively dangerous, the proverbial "kiss of death" of Proverbs 27:6 and 2 Samuel 20:9–10. The betrayer had urged his confederates to seize and lead away "securely" whomever he would kiss. The Greek word *asphalōs* (note the English cognate "asphalt") is better translated "securely" than "safely," to clarify that there should be no possibility of escape (thus the NRSV's "under guard," v. 44). Judas addresses Jesus as "rabbi," a term of respectful affection used by disciples of the teacher they follow. Its use here is painfully ironic: the deceptive greeting and kiss result in the immediate arrest of Jesus.

The Isaac-Jesus typology continues (see my commentary on Mark 14:36) as Mark reports that "they laid hands on him." At Genesis 22:12, God's messenger intervenes in the near-sacrifice of Isaac, instructing Abraham not to lay his hand on his beloved son Isaac. Here, by contrast, no heavenly intervention

Homiletical Perspective

eating, Jesus told them that one of them would betray him, and they began to be distressed, saying, "Surely not I!" (14:19). Even though none of the others betrayed Jesus, any one of them could have done it. They were all affected by Judas, and they wondered out loud which of them it would be. Judas revealed some flaw and fear in them all.

Second, Judas did something evil. Jesus says what Judas did was necessary to fulfill the Scriptures, but "it would have been even better for that one not to have been born" (14:21). Judas did his work at night. He enabled the guards to take Jesus when the crowds were off the streets, as the chief priests wanted it. They offered Judas money (14:11). Judas counted Jesus for sale. He had his own life, and he would keep it. Other traditions about Judas say how his choice led him to a bitter end. According to one, he repented, threw the money down in the temple, and hanged himself (Matt. 27:3–10). According to another tradition, he bought a field with the money and fell down to a horrible death, bursting open on the Field of Blood (Acts 1:18–19). These traditions are not in Mark. Mark simply shows that Judas is in the wrong: he rejected the message of Jesus; he claimed his own independence and freedom from Jesus. It is a horrible choice. Jesus said of him, "Woe to that one by whom the Son of Man is betrayed" (14:21).

Is there any grace for Judas? This is a difficult question. Since Judas was one of the disciples, received the Lord's Supper for the forgiveness of sins, and was one for whom Jesus died, was the promise denied to Judas? How different were the other disciples from Judas? Although none of them conspired with Judas, they all forsook Jesus and fled at his arrest. Judas's deed caused the breakup of their fellowship. Simon Peter, the last and bravest holdout, emphatically denied he knew Jesus at his trial. Though they did not betray him, they all were weak. They would all require a new gospel from beyond Judas's betrayal and all these events leading to Jesus' crucifixion. They shared much with him, but Judas was gone forever before Jesus died. The answer to whether Judas could claim God's grace is beyond our knowing. We should leave it at that and say no more about it.

We do affirm that Peter, James, John, and the others did live beyond the day Jesus died. Because Mary Magdalene, Mary the mother of James and Joses, and Salome knew where he was buried, they took spices to the grave and heard a message from God on the other side of Jesus' death (16:1–8). Beyond all of their fears at the dawn of the day of resurrection, they did tell the others and Peter that Jesus was

Mark 14:43–52

Theological Perspective

elders the Scriptures are being fulfilled. Even in the disciples' failure, the Scriptures are being fulfilled. It is a stunning profession of God's providence to say that in the midst of human schemes and sinfulness, the Scriptures are being fulfilled.

Robert Scharlemann provides a profound way of understanding how acts of evil, malice, and cowardice can still be nonetheless a way that God's will is done.[2] The location for this paradoxical possibility is the cross. According to Scharlemann, because the cross is a symbol of self-negation that Christ willingly accepts, it has dialectical power. As such, the cross fulfills its meaning when one accepts Jesus as the Christ, as well as when one rejects Jesus as the Christ. To reject Christ—as all of the players in this scene do, from conniving enemies to deserting disciples—is to fulfill the purpose of the cross, since it is a symbol of rejection. To accept Christ, as disciples are called to do, is to embrace the meaning of the cross. What Scharlemann presents is not a verbal sleight of hand, but a profound way of understanding why God wills that Jesus would take this awful journey to the cross. In Jesus' willful embrace of this journey, the cross has become a powerful symbol whereby God's will is done, among disciples and deserters alike.

Scharlemann's argument, however, reflects a postresurrection perspective, when God has transformed the rejection of Christ with decisive power. For the moment in Mark's dramatic journey to the cross, the questions regarding the disciples' failure, and particularly Judas's betraying kiss, remain profoundly disconcerting. Nevertheless, even in the midst of malice, betrayal, and failure, Jesus' post-Gethsemane assurance guides the story: these things are happening "in order that the scriptures may be fulfilled."

D. MARK DAVIS

Pastoral Perspective

a moment of such singular and profound loneliness, and yet Jesus faces this too with the integrity of his true identity as the Son of God.

There is an odd image at the end of the story that serves to remind us of what is about to happen. A young man wrapped in a linen cloth is grabbed, but all that is caught is the sheet. He runs off into the darkness, a spirit, a freed and naked being, untethered by the prison of earth and the violence of arrest and betrayal. It is as if Mark is reminding us that all is not lost, that there are some who cannot be captured and held against their will. Perhaps we would see Jesus breaking free, running through the hills outside the city gates, running on and on into a new time and a new world. Perhaps this image of the young man and the linen cloth is a foretaste of the young man in white at the mouth of the tomb who carries the message of future generations, "he is not here" (16:6).

It is too early to speculate or know for sure. The young man is a mystery in the dark story of Jesus' arrest and betrayal. For now, Jesus stands alone; the discipleship community has failed to stand strong for the vision of a new world. They have scattered into the night, leaving their friend and leader to face whatever lies ahead with no certain hope that justice will prevail or love survive. On this dark night, we can only watch and wait as the conflict with the powers that be is played out before us.

PATRICIA E. DE JONG

---

2. Robert P. Scharlemann, *Reflection and Doubt in the Thought of Paul Tillich* (New Haven, CT: Yale University Press, 1969), 23.

Exegetical Perspective

occurs. As if to stress its absence, Mark mentions the futile gesture of a bystander who draws his sword and cuts off the ear of the high priest's slave. Mark's curious expression *heis . . . tis* ("one" or "someone") has long puzzled readers, both ancient scribes and contemporary text critics. It may refer to someone whose anonymity the author wishes to protect or whose identity the audience already knows, as in "you know who tried to prevent the arrest," although neither of these is necessary, and an interpreter may or may not choose to follow later tradition identifying this "certain one" with Peter. Although a disciple would be the most logical source of resistance, the "bystander," a word Mark uses nowhere else of a disciple, could be anyone in the crowd. At any rate, Mark's point probably is that the gesture achieves nothing.

Mark's Jesus either does not notice the incident or chooses not to comment on it, either favorably or unfavorably. Instead, he directly confronts those arresting him as though he were someone violent. He contrasts their nocturnal action with his own teaching "during the day," or better, "day after day" (v. 49 NRSV), implying multiple opportunities to arrest him publicly.

The sentence that follows is best read as an anacoluthon, an unfinished idea left hanging in the air: "But so that the Scriptures might be fulfilled . . ." This literary device both stops the action and points to divine control over it.

The desertion of the terrified disciples (prophesied by Jesus earlier at 14:27; see also 4:17) is engraved on the minds of Mark's readers by the detail of the unidentified "young man" (Gk. *neaniskos*; see 16:5) who leaves behind his "linen cloth" (Gk. *sindona*; see also 15:46) and runs away naked (vv. 51–52). The rich interpretive tradition concerning him suggests that historical and metaphorical readings need not be in tension here: any disciple who could escape did so, leaving Jesus to face his death alone.

A. KATHERINE GRIEB

Homiletical Perspective

raised and they would meet him in Galilee. The disciples came again to the gospel on the other side of Jesus' death, and they handed Jesus on to us in their proclamation and teaching. The same technical term for Judas's betrayal in this new and rehabilitated sense refers to the handing on of the tradition of the gospel of God (1:14), which the early church under the power of the Holy Spirit handed on to us.

Finally then, we come to examine ourselves in the light of the betrayal of Jesus by Judas. Because the betrayer was one of the Twelve, we should take warning that Judas's action is not so different from what may be hidden in our own temptation to give Jesus only a part of ourselves. We are tempted to keep a lot of our time and freedom for ourselves at the expense of loving God with all our heart and mind and soul, and loving our neighbor as ourselves. When John Calvin preached on this passage, he urged his congregation to prepare for the Lord's Supper: "So then let each one prepare himself, knowing for what he has been called of God and what responsibility [we have] been given." Then referring to Judas's betrayal, Calvin adds, "But in coming to him let us be well advised never to call him master with the tip of the tongue when we are nevertheless his enemies."[3] Instead, we have received the gospel of God and have the Lord's commission to hand it on faithfully so others may enjoy it.

CHARLES RAYNAL

---

3. Hughes Oliphant Old, "Calvin as Evangelist: A Study of the Reformer's Sermons in Preparation for the Christian Celebration of Passover," in John H. Leith, ed., *Calvin Studies VII, Papers Presented at a Colloquium on Calvin Studies, Davidson College Presbyterian Church, Davidson, North Carolina* (January 28–29, 1994), 52.

Mark 14:53–65

⁵³They took Jesus to the high priest; and all the chief priests, the elders, and the scribes were assembled. ⁵⁴Peter had followed him at a distance, right into the courtyard of the high priest; and he was sitting with the guards, warming himself at the fire. ⁵⁵Now the chief priests and the whole council were looking for testimony against Jesus to put him to death; but they found none. ⁵⁶For many gave false testimony against him, and their testimony did not agree. ⁵⁷Some stood up and gave false testimony against him, saying, ⁵⁸"We heard him say, 'I will destroy this temple that is made with hands, and in three days I will build another, not made with hands.'" ⁵⁹But even on this point their testimony did not agree. ⁶⁰Then the high priest stood up before them and asked Jesus, "Have you no answer? What is it that they testify against you?" ⁶¹But he

Theological Perspective

The story of Jesus' appearance before the Sanhedrin pulls together three ongoing theological conversations throughout Mark's Gospel, namely, the question of Jesus' identity, the charge of blasphemy, and the call to follow. Our text discloses a paradox at the heart of each of these topics.

Jesus' Identity. The primary theological issue of this text is the identification of who Jesus is. While Mark's Gospel begins plainly, "The beginning of the gospel of Jesus Christ, the Son of God,"[1] it is peppered throughout with questions, declarations, apprehensions, and misapprehensions about who Jesus is. In our text, the chief priest puts the question this way, "Are you the Christ, the Son of the Blessed One?" (v. 61). Jesus answers, "I am," and follows with an allusion to Daniel 7:13, identifying himself as "'the Son of Man seated at the right hand of the Power' and 'coming with the clouds of heaven'" (v. 62). This intertextual reference, already invoked in 13:26, is Mark's way of identifying Jesus with a familiar figure of hope from the Hebrew Bible.

The paradox of Jesus' identity is evident in the way our story progresses. Jesus, the "Son of the Blessed One" and/or the "Son of Man," whom the

[1] In the Greek text there is no definite article modifying the word "gospel."

Pastoral Perspective

Years ago, when I was a campus pastor, I took a small group of students to San Francisco for spring break. Along with a trip across the Golden Gate Bridge, we also visited San Quentin Prison, a large, foreboding structure that rises out of the waters of the bay like a concrete fortress. While there, we visited an older part of the prison and were led into a room with an electric chair. It was old and the leather seat was worn; it had not been used for a long time. I can still recall the terrible chill of being a witness to the very place where death-row inmates had spoken their last words and been led into the chair to die. We were invited one by one to sit in the chair. As each student sat in that chair for a brief moment, they reckoned with the force of being condemned to die in the electric chair.

To be condemned to death is to have everything in life come to a screeching halt. Your life story now contains the time of your death; so the story of your life is no longer wide open to possibility, change, or hope. The death penalty is a cruel way for a society to control its members, especially when many of those condemned to death row are poor, of color, or without the means to afford a fair trial. For Jesus to face his accusers in the middle of the night, without representation or support, was cruel and starkly unjust.

was silent and did not answer. Again the high priest asked him, "Are you the Messiah, the Son of the Blessed One?" [62]Jesus said, "I am; and

> 'you will see the Son of Man
> seated at the right hand of the Power,'
> and 'coming with the clouds of heaven.'"

[63]Then the high priest tore his clothes and said, "Why do we still need witnesses? [64]You have heard his blasphemy! What is your decision?" All of them condemned him as deserving death. [65]Some began to spit on him, to blindfold him, and to strike him, saying to him, "Prophesy!" The guards also took him over and beat him.

Exegetical Perspective

Jesus is brought to the house of Caiaphas the high priest, which several scholars have identified with an imposing Herodian building in the upper city overlooking the Temple Mount. Caiaphas's long term in office (18–37 CE) suggests strong political skills of collaboration with the Romans, especially his patron, Pontius Pilate. Indeed, Josephus (*Ant.* 18.58–59, 95) says Caiaphas lost his high priesthood only after Pilate was sacked following Samaritan uprisings in 36 CE, which explains the actions of both Caiaphas and Pilate after Jesus' arrest. Mark reports that all the chief priests, elders, and scribes were present (14:53; "the whole Sanhedrin" in 14:55, my trans.), suggesting formal legal procedures arranged for the sole purpose of putting Jesus to death (14:55, cf. Ps. 37:32) using the testimony of false witnesses (14:56).

In recent years, Jewish and Christian scholars have cooperated to reconstruct probable historical events by attempting to reconcile various layers of Jesus tradition reflected in the somewhat conflicting Gospel accounts, written decades afterward, with even later sources of relevant Jewish and Roman legal material. Clearly no historically accurate reconstruction of these important events is possible, although John's Gospel, describing a less formal interrogation by the high priest and others, is suggestive.

Homiletical Perspective

Good preaching about the passion of Christ in Mark will grow out of careful attention to Mark's dramatization of the events that follow from Jesus' teaching his disciples. The handing over of Jesus—by Judas in the night to the armed guard, by the guard to the interrogators, by the interrogators to the full council, by the council to Pilate, and by Pilate to the executioners—is an inexorable chain of events, necessary for Jesus' accomplishment of his office as the Messiah of Israel. In relating these events Mark reaches the climax of the Gospel.

Dramatic irony in Mark's narrative, especially in the trial scenes, provides richness for good homiletic use and gives the interpreter a good edge with listeners. Irony means that a hidden meaning lies beneath the literal meaning of the spoken words. The characters in the plot miss the true meaning. The real truth is in the hidden meaning. As David Bartlett puts it, "through gospel irony we know that what appears to be bad news is good news."[1] So the preacher can lead the congregation to discover the surprise of good news that waits beneath the surface.

---

1. David L. Bartlett, *What's Good about This News? Preaching from the Gospels and Galatians* (Louisville, KY: Westminster John Knox Press, 2003), 39–49; Donald H. Juel, *The Gospel of Mark* (Nashville: Abingdon Press, 1999), 35–37, 139–52.

Mark 14:53–65

Theological Perspective

Sanhedrin will see seated at the right hand of power, is spit upon, blindfolded, beaten, and slapped—hardly a portrayal of blessedness or power. This paradox is consistent with the baptism story, where Jesus is declared God's Son and then immediately thrown out into the wilderness to be tempted. It is consistent with the moment of Peter's confession, which is immediately followed by the first disclosure that Jesus is heading to Jerusalem to be handed over and killed. At the heart of Jesus' identity is a paradoxical understanding of what it means to be God's beloved, the Christ, the Son of the Blessed One, the Son of Man. These honorific titles are fraught with suffering and death.

Blasphemy. The second theological issue in this text surrounds the charge of blasphemy. Jesus had already been accused of blasphemy in Mark 2, after saying to a paralytic, "Your sins are forgiven." Adela Yarbro Collins describes the charge of blasphemy as "an encroachment upon divine prerogatives and a usurpation of a role not appropriate to [Jesus'] status."[2] In our text, the Sanhedrin attempts to establish the charge of blasphemy against Jesus by means of false witnesses, whose testimonies prove to be laughably inconsistent. In the end, the chief priest argues that Jesus' own words are reason enough for condemnation.

The paradox here lies in the purpose of Mark's Gospel: Jesus' identification as "the Son of Man seated at the right hand of the Power" is regarded by the Sanhedrin as a damnable act of presumption, yet it is the very thing that Mark's readers are called to embrace. One of Søren Kierkegaard's critiques of Christendom is that it has taken away the offense of embracing Jesus, by relegating him to oblivion as a historical figure who has since been made heroic by the church, rather than seeing him as a "contemporaneous" figure whose actual humanity carries with it the offense of calling him the Christ.[3] The paradox of Mark's story is that embracing Jesus as the Christ is to embrace this blasphemy as truth.

Discipleship. The final theological paradox in our text pertains to discipleship. The disciples fail miserably at the time of Jesus' arrest, demonstrating the truth of Zechariah 13:7: "I will strike the shepherd, and the sheep will be scattered" (14:27).

2. Adela Yarbro Collins, "The Charge of Blasphemy in Mark 14.64," *Journal for the Study of the New Testament* 26, no. 4 (2004): 379–401.
3. Søren Kierkegaard, *Training in Christianity*, trans. Walter Lowrie (1850; repr., New York: Vintage, 2004), 30–31.

Pastoral Perspective

As Jesus is led away into the dock, the Sanhedrin has to struggle to come up with charges against him. Oddly, their goal is not justice, but putting him to death as quickly as possible. They need to move this along quickly, while everyone is in the mood. You would be surprised by how powerful it makes a person feel to judge another life as unworthy. No one seems to be able to come up with a story that sticks; each charge becomes more trumped up than the last one. Mark states twice that the witnesses give false testimony.

The central piece of their accusation is built upon a literal reading of Jesus' declaration that the temple would be destroyed and rebuilt in three days. In those days, the temple played the most vital role in the spiritual and economic life of Israel. It was threatening for anyone, let alone a minor rabbi, to make disparaging remarks about the sanctity of the temple (13:2). False testimony, built upon angry emotion and justifying lies, culminates with the high priest asking a single question: "Have you no answer?" (v. 60).

Jesus does not plead the Fifth; he goes the council one better. He remains silent. There probably is not anything more annoying in a kangaroo court than a defendant who is silent. Jesus refuses to play the game and to recognize the charges against him as legal or binding. This political trial is designed to embarrass the defendant and do away with him as soon as possible. As he responds with silence to the trumped-up charges, he only exposes the trial for what it is: a political sham, a street theater of injustice.

In our congregation, on Sunday mornings we often sit in silence as a response to the Prayer of Confession. Silence at that moment can be full or empty, depending on the mood in the congregation. There have been times when silence has been deeply emotional and full—as if God is coming alive in the empty spaces between all the noise and words. As Jesus held the silence of that space, God was alive to him and present in him in ways that those around him could not begin to imagine. Sometimes silence does speak volumes, as the old saying goes, and this is one of them. Jesus embodies the spiritual power of the moment and gains the upper hand of integrity, even though he is the one standing before a line of accusers, all of whom are "worthy."

Silence is broken only when he is questioned about something he believes is just and deserves an answer. "Are you the Messiah, Son of the Blessed One?" asks the high priest, most likely a snarky

Exegetical Perspective

After describing the total abandonment of Jesus by his disciples ("all" in 14:50), Mark makes a qualified exception for Peter, who follows Jesus "at a distance" (14:54) into the courtyard of the high priest's house. Mark's literary device of intercalation contrasts Peter, warming himself "below" at the servants' fire (14:54 and 14:66–72), with Jesus, on trial inside the high priest's house (14:55–65). Mark's implied critique of Peter's discipleship at a (safe) distance (cf. Ps. 38:11) prepares us for the threefold denial that follows (cf. 15:40, the women's distance from the cross). Yet both the women and Peter (16:7), together with the disciples who flee, are recognized by the "young man" at Jesus' tomb as continuing to be disciples of the risen crucified one.

At the intercalation's center is the "trial" of Jesus by the high priest and the Sanhedrin. Mark reports that, in spite of multiple attempts, the project of gathering false testimony to convict Jesus and engineer his death was floundering, since the witnesses' testimony did not agree. This general description is followed by a tightly focused close-up view of one part of the evidence given against Jesus, his prophecy of the Jerusalem temple's destruction. Earlier (13:2), in preparation for this passage, what Jesus had actually said about the temple was directly quoted. Jesus had prophesied that no stone "would be left" upon another: the temple would be completely destroyed. In Mark, Jesus' use of the divine passive (meaning that God would destroy the temple) contradicts the testimony of the false witnesses who testify that Jesus threatened to destroy this temple "made with hands" himself and in three days build another "not made with hands" (14:58).

Mistakes (e.g., 6:17; 15:35) and falsehoods (14:58; 14:64) are usually theologically loaded in Mark's Gospel, especially here. The contrast between the two humanly constructed Jerusalem temples (both of which God had allowed or would allow Israel's enemies to destroy) and the divinely conceived heavenly temple, on which the humanly constructed buildings were modeled, was well known in Jewish messianic eschatology. The end times would bring the destruction and reconstruction of the temple, according to Qumran texts (e.g., 4QFlor 1:1–13), suggesting the present Jerusalem temple would be replaced by a sanctuary built by God's hands alone. This action of God would coincide with two other eschatological events: the beginning of God's reign on earth and the revealing of God's Son, the descendant of David mentioned in the oracle of Nathan (2 Sam. 7:13–14) and "the Branch" oracle (Zech. 6:12–13).

Homiletical Perspective

A good example of dramatic irony in the trial scene is when someone says to Jesus, "Prophesy!" (v. 65). He intends to humiliate and mock Jesus. However, in truth the soldiers and the religious authorities are caught up in Jesus' prophecy. For one thing, he repeatedly has told his disciples about the necessity that he be handed over to the chief priests and the scribes, and be condemned to death. For another thing, just as Jesus is on trial, so is Peter. Jesus has already prophesied that Peter would deny him three times before the rooster crows twice. While Jesus is telling the truth about his identity at the cost of his life, Peter is telling a lie to save his own skin. Peter's denial forms the framework within which Mark recounts the interrogation before the council. So Jesus' prophecy is coming true at the same time that his interrogator mocks him as a prophet. This irony in Mark's dramatization of Jesus' trial is the literary means by which he makes the trial show that Jesus is the Messiah, the sovereign ruler of the kingdom of God.

In thinking about the trial of Jesus, consider the purpose of a trial. A criminal trial is intended to establish the truth about the alleged crime and recommend a just punishment. Jesus' trial on the surface is a mockery of the truth about him and results in the miscarriage of justice in his being sent to the cross. The quick arrangement of the interrogation at night is to hide the religious leaders' previous determination to do away with Jesus. The failure to find witnesses to warrant the charge and the contradictions among the witnesses whom they do find constitutes contempt of court. Furthermore, the duress of the examination under torture throughout the night is a really extraordinary rendition. So everything on the surface looks like a travesty of what is true and just.

Nevertheless, the emphasis of the teacher or preacher should not be on the betrayal and falsehood leading to the verdict against Jesus. Instead, it should proclaim more clearly the discovery of the real gospel in the apparent travesty of Jesus' trial. The two charges against Jesus are that he threatened the temple and that he was alleged to be the Messiah, the king of Israel. The temple authorities were defensive of their prerogatives in the religious life of the people, especially of those who were flocking to the Jerusalem temple for the Passover celebration. The religious officials were angry with Jesus for his teaching that the law of God stood above their law. The chief priests resented that Jesus turned over the fund-raising for their worship and were furious at

Mark 14:53–65

Theological Perspective

The disciples, called to follow, are scattered. In this story, Peter follows Jesus tragically—from a distance and alongside Jesus' enemies. The narrative makes Peter's action stark by bracketing Peter's following within a description of the Sanhedrin. The chief priests, elders, and scribes "assemble themselves" in judgment of Jesus; meanwhile, Peter is "seated together" outside with the guards who arrested Jesus (vv. 53–54, my trans.).

Peter's fellowship with the guards makes stark the failure of the disciples in Mark's Gospel. The paradox, however, lies with the fact that they are disciples, the ones who left everything to follow Jesus; they are the "sheep" of the shepherd. To read the disciples' failure as a singular event among just a few miserable folk is to miss the meaning of the call to discipleship. The disciples scatter when Jesus is arrested because they have thrown their lot in with him entirely. They are not independent of his fate; they have not held a respectful distance from him. They have followed him because they believed that he was the Christ. Now they are scattered because the Shepherd whom they have followed has been struck.

Kierkegaard's critique against relegating the "contemporaneous" Christ to being a hero of the past is also applicable to the question of discipleship in Mark's Gospel. In vain we imagine that, had we been there, we would have acted differently. Mark says no, none of them acted differently—no, not one. So Mark invites us to reckon with the paradoxical call to discipleship. To follow Christ is to risk everything by aligning oneself with the rejected, the despised, the battered and bruised. When we see the disciples scattered and Peter following from a safe distance, then sitting with the guards, we see a very contemporaneous portrayal of the church, safely distancing itself from the victims and sitting among the oppressors.

When Peter sits with the guards, we see the full implications of the call to follow. To follow is to follow Jesus to the cross; any other response is to align oneself with the powers that oppose him. While it is easy to despise Peter's cowardice, we would do well to see Peter's dilemma as an ongoing challenge to the church. We too have been called to follow. To hear that call as anything but the call to take up the cross is to miss the point altogether and to seat oneself with those who set out to destroy Jesus.

D. MARK DAVIS

Pastoral Perspective

remark. "I am," is the simple answer (vv. 61–62). The words that follow confirm the relationship with the Father, but also offer an opening to the high priest.

We hear it now as a statement of truth and as a reminder of YHWH's name ("I AM WHO I AM," Exod. 3:14). Jesus claims his authority and his spiritual lineage with those two simple words. It is this confession that gives the high priest the edge he is seeking. Jesus is charged with blasphemy and condemned to death. Permission is given for violence and abuse; the eager crowd gets into the act and the guards also beat him. As is usually the case, violence begets only more violence. It is stunning to see Jesus standing in the midst of all this, neither meek nor mild. He is fully present to all that is taking place around him, but he refuses to participate in the charade.

Recently I heard a Christian pastor say that he feels uncomfortable wearing a cross around his neck. He views the cross as a symbol of violence and suffering, and the world is already full of it. Rather than seeing Christianity as being preoccupied with violence at Jesus' death, we might embrace this moment in Jesus' life as one that helps us reclaim the integrity of nonviolence in a violent world. Jesus' powerful relationship to the Spirit of God in the midst of a terrifying moment gives us hope for the world. Instead of viewing ourselves as helpless in response to violence, may we be empowered to claim a weighty silence that speaks loudly of our identity as those who embrace God's promise to overthrow terror, to hold us in life and death, and to grant us courage and wisdom for the living of difficult days.

PATRICIA E. DE JONG

Exegetical Perspective

What was wrong with the Jerusalem temple? The "made with hands" language suggests the critique of idolatry by Israel's prophets (e.g., Isa. 44:9–20). Mark had also intercalated the stories of the fig tree and Jesus' prophetic temple action (11:12–22) to recall Jeremiah's antitemple sermon (Jer. 7:1–20, note Jer. 7:11 and 8:13), suggesting the corruption of the temple leadership (11:17). Moreover, Mark may have shared either the conviction of the author of Revelation 21:22 that the temple would be redundant at the end because of God's direct and abiding presence on earth, or the conviction of Paul (1 Cor. 3:16–17) and others (Eph. 2:21; 1 Pet. 2:5) that the community of the Messiah would itself become "the temple."

Mark reports that since the testimony of the false witnesses (cf. Ps. 27:12) about Jesus' temple saying did not agree, the high priest takes charge: first, by inviting Jesus' response to their accusations and, when that fails because Jesus remains silent (cf. Ps. 38:13–14), by interrogating Jesus directly: "Are you the Messiah, the Son of the Blessed?" (v. 61). The question as reported by Mark must be hostile, even sarcastic, but Caiaphas unwittingly speaks the truth. Perhaps Mark is following a tradition where the high priest speaks prophetically while in office (cf. John 11:49–51).

Both the high priest and Jesus speak of God using pious circumlocutions ("the Blessed" [v. 61] and "the Power" [v. 62]), and Jesus' "I am" (or "You say that I am" if the textual variant is correct) probably ought not to be read as the divine Name of Exodus 3:14. The charge of "blasphemy" (v. 64, cf. 2:7) probably results from Jesus' Son of Man saying, which combines allusions to Psalm 110:1 and Daniel 7:13 to suggest that God will vindicate him with heavenly royal power. The high priest promptly tears his robes, and "they all" condemn Jesus to death. Covering his face, they strike him, asking him mockingly to "prophesy!" (probably which of them would strike him next, cf. Matt. 26:68, Luke 22:64). Jesus' prophetic power is at once reestablished in the next section, when Peter denies him three times (14:66–70), just as Jesus has foretold (14:30).

A. KATHERINE GRIEB

Homiletical Perspective

his charge that its rituals were not worth the sacrifices of the money changers in the courtyard. To the chief priests. the freedom from the Sabbath and ritual law that they saw in Jesus and his followers made them renegade libertines. In response to the first testimony that he would destroy the temple built with hands and build another in three days, Jesus was only silent. No "You say–I say" answer for this question. To this charge, "he never said a mumbalin' word."[2] His silence, like that of the African American slaves who sang the spiritual, was his only available subversion of the pretext for the charge.

The second charge was more serious: "Are you the Messiah, the Son of the Blessed One?" (v. 61). Jesus affirmed that he was. His interrogator thought it was preposterous, and so considered Jesus' testimony about himself to be sufficient for the capital sentence of blasphemy and execution under Jewish law. Mark shows that the trial, even though full of lies, is true concerning the testimony of Jesus about his own identity as the Son of God. This strange irony shows that even the treachery and injustice of the trial cannot snuff out the real truth of the gospel that Jesus is the sovereign Lord of the kingdom of God. The trial confirms God's true servant Messiah. God has sway over the treachery.

To develop an effective sermon on the trial of Jesus in Mark, the interpreter should look carefully at the details of the narrative in the Gospel, reflect on the use the author makes of irony, and help the listeners hear and receive, in words that seem only to convey bad news, the true and good news of the gospel of Jesus Christ, the Son of God.

CHARLES RAYNAL

---

2. *The Presbyterian Hymnal* (Louisville, KY: Westminster John Knox Press, 1990), #95.

Mark 14:66–72

⁶⁶While Peter was below in the courtyard, one of the servant-girls of the high priest came by. ⁶⁷When she saw Peter warming himself, she stared at him and said, "You also were with Jesus, the man from Nazareth." ⁶⁸But he denied it, saying, "I do not know or understand what you are talking about." And he went out into the forecourt. Then the cock crowed. ⁶⁹And the servant-girl, on seeing him, began again to say to the bystanders, "This man is one of them." ⁷⁰But again he denied it. Then after a little while the bystanders again said to Peter, "Certainly you are one of them; for you are a Galilean." ⁷¹But he began to curse, and he swore an oath, "I do not know this man you are talking about." ⁷²At that moment the cock crowed for the second time. Then Peter remembered that Jesus had said to him, "Before the cock crows twice, you will deny me three times." And he broke down and wept.

Theological Perspective

This familiar passage reflects a profound examination of human nature and consciousness, and Christ's understanding of it. The story of Peter's denial cannot be considered apart from the earlier passage where Jesus predicts that all of his disciples will desert him (14:26–31). In that intimate conversation on the Mount of Olives, Peter protests that he is different from the rest—more loyal, more courageous, more faithful. Jesus speaks with specificity about the denial: "Before the cock crows twice, you will deny me three times" (14:30). Peter is vehement in denying his denial. Even if he has to die, he will never deny Jesus, his friend and mentor! Yet here is a promise made in the abstract, not yet tested by reality.

That reality comes soon enough. As Jesus is being interrogated and tortured, Peter is close by in the courtyard. A servant girl recognizes him, and his denial that he in fact was with Jesus comes instinctively, smoothly, off his lips. Peter hears the cock crowing in the background, but his ears are drawn more keenly to the girl's conversations with others in the courtyard. Perhaps a small crowd is gathering. Again, Peter denies ever having known Jesus. Someone else hears his Galilean accent and also challenges him. His earlier, effortless white lie now becomes a passionate denial as he curses and swears "an oath" (v. 71). The vehemence coming

Pastoral Perspective

When encountering the biblical narratives that tell of the Savior's last hours, the followers of Jesus quickly find themselves at the foot of the cross. Christ's suffering on the cross dominates the church's theological reflection on the text as betrayal, desertion, and denial rise up at various points along the way. The familiarity of this journey that is the way of the cross makes it much easier for the reader to look ahead toward Christ's sacrifice. Such a forward look makes it more difficult for the hearers of the Word to find a place in the story. The fast read allows the congregation to become merely spectators at the crucifixion rather than participants along the way. With a slower read and intentional stops, the power of the narrative invites, even demands a role for those followers who find themselves walking this way with Jesus again. Remember, the story is not only about him; it is about us too.

Peter's encounter with the servant girl in the courtyard is one stop along the way that is far too easy to gloss over. Peter's threefold denials are often seen as foreshadowing of the breakfast scene with the risen Christ in the Gospel of John. There on the shore of the Sea of Galilee Jesus allows Peter the chance to revisit the denial by asking him three times to affirm his love. Resurrection hope trumps denial. The risen Christ's charge to "feed my sheep"

Exegetical Perspective

Mark tells the story of Peter's denial in two parts, so that they bracket the account of Jesus before the Sanhedrin, thus providing both a setting for Jesus' arraignment, and a contrast to it. Earlier, immediately after Jesus' arrest (14:43–53), we heard how Peter followed Jesus "at a distance" (presumably a safe distance) into the high priest's courtyard, and so came to be "sitting with the guards, warming himself at the fire" (14:54). Then followed the account of Jesus' examination and condemnation by the Sanhedrin (14:53–65). Now, completing the bracket, we return to the courtyard and to Peter, who is also about to be put on trial, though he does not know it.[1]

First a slave girl (*paidiskē*)[2] says to him, "You also were with Jesus, the man from Nazareth!" Peter denies it, feigning ignorance (vv. 67–68), even though being "with" Jesus was what had enabled him and his fellow disciples to share in Jesus' ministry (3:14; 6:7–13) and was, indeed, a basic element in Jesus' institution of him and others as "the Twelve" (3:14). Next, after Peter has moved to the

---

1. This way of speaking is sometimes known by the Latin word *inclusio* ("confinement"). It is effective orally, and hence is common in ancient literature, which is generally designed to be listened to—as is Mark's Gospel: see Christopher Bryan, *A Preface to Mark* (Oxford: Oxford University Press, 1991), 76–77 and throughout.
2. NRSV's "servant-girl" is inaccurate. In the New Testament *paidiskē* invariably refers to a slave.

Homiletical Perspective

Here again in these verses is Peter denying Jesus, a memory so indelible for early Christians that all four Gospels capture it with essentially the same details. Jesus predicts it; Peter denies Jesus' prediction; Peter denies Jesus; a cock crows. For more than two thousand years we Christians have been putting ourselves in the place of Peter as he stood in the courtyard that night that Jesus was enduring his humiliations at the hands of the chief priests, elders, scribes, and guards. Every year during Holy Week we say that we are just like Peter, who in each denial takes a step further away from Jesus as he moves from courtyard to forecourt and finally as far away as he can get. Remember, Peter disappears at this point in the story until after the resurrection (16:7). Even then, he does not appear but is only mentioned.

Often missing in all this self-flagellation is the recognition that Peter's actions that night might be considered fairly rational, even honorable. Biblical scholars Richard Rohrbaugh and Bruce Malina say, "Quite consonant with Mediterranean values, Peter practices deception to maintain his honor and independence in face of challenges. Lying to others about his relationship to Jesus would not have been considered wrong."[1]

---

1. Bruce J. Malina and Richard L. Rohrbaugh, *Social-Scientific Commentary on the Synoptic Gospels*, 2nd ed. (Minneapolis: Fortress Press, 2003), 216.

Mark 14:66–72

Theological Perspective

from self-preservation is stronger even than the force of his earlier pledge of self-sacrifice. The cock crows a second time, punctuating his moral journey from high-minded idealism and commitment to sniveling cowardice. The sound of the rooster pierces through whatever remaining sense of self-righteousness this follower of Jesus might have. In despair, he breaks down and weeps.

Mark's structure focuses us on the two bookends of this drama within a drama. It would be easy to frame an interpretation of Peter's story as evidence of Jesus' supernatural ability to predict events, but that would reduce the meaning of this story to magical thinking. A psychological reading might interpret this as an example of self-fulfilled prophecy. Both are reductionist and attribute to Jesus the power (whether magical or manipulative) to create what is clearly an emotionally devastating experience for Peter—and for what purpose? Is Jesus intent on creating pain for someone he loves, in order to make a point about his own power? Certainly that does not fit the tenor of the narrative in which Jesus is divesting power, "empty[ing] himself of all but love."[1]

As much as Jesus, at some level, might want to believe Peter and allow himself to be reassured that not everyone would desert him, he knows human nature all too well. Humans are created with freedom to choose and to act; we are not creatures of a cosmic puppeteer. Human freedom enables us to choose to embrace the laws and gifts of the Creator, or not to. Jesus understood the gravitational pull of self-promotion and self-preservation as a strong force within that freedom. It is present from our waking moment, or before the cock crows twice. Despite our resolve, we cave in to our selfishness, to put what we think are our own interests first.

Reinhold Niebuhr labels this the "will to power," inevitably present not only in individuals but in organized interest groups in wider society. He concludes, in his classic work *Moral Man and Immoral Society*, "This insinuation of the interests of the self into even the most ideal enterprises and most universal objectives, envisaged in moments of highest rationality, makes hypocrisy an inevitable by-product of all virtuous endeavor."[2] In this passage, Peter becomes the poster child for hypocrisy.

We also have a window into the workings of the human conscience. Peter has publicly declared his moral standard in relationship to Jesus: to remain

---

1. Charles Wesley, "And Can It Be That I Should Gain" (1738).
2. Reinhold Niebuhr, *Moral Man and Immoral Society* (New York: Charles Scribner's Sons, 1932), 45.

Pastoral Perspective

implies forgiveness. Before reaching, though, for the less than subtle symbolism of the number three that takes us to resurrection, why not linger for awhile there in the courtyard with Peter? After all, in light of Mark's Easter morning brevity, he never tells of that postresurrection conversation between Jesus and Peter. So the reader should not rush past Peter and the slave girl.

Preachers and commentators have labeled the denial as "the trial of Peter." Such a title draws the comparison to the trial of Jesus before Caiaphas and Pilate. Peter's interrogation at the hands of the servant girl is nestled here in Mark between those two gripping scenes. As false testimony is offered against Jesus, the high priest demands an answer from Jesus. Jesus is blindfolded and beaten by guards. The appearance before Pilate includes similar accusations and repeated questioning. Through it all Jesus says remarkably little.

In stark contrast, Peter's questioning comes from a nameless, powerless servant girl who begins the confrontation with a stare. When she acknowledges recognition and says, "You also were with Jesus, the man from Nazareth" (v. 67), Peter first pretends he does not understand her comment. In moving to the forecourt, he tries to get away from her. The servant girl either follows him or keeps looking. This time she says something to the others standing around; "This man is one of them!" (v. 69). Peter's next move is flat-out denial. The crowd joins the interrogation, and Peter's denial elevates from feigned confusion to a rooftop shout: "I do not know this man you are talking about" (v. 71). Jesus responds so little at his trial. Peter says way too much at his. The trial of Jesus includes physical abuse. Peter's night in the courtyard starts with him warming himself by the fire.

Interestingly, as Mark tracks Peter's responses, location cues are also provided. From following Jesus at a distance, to standing below in the courtyard, to moving out into the forecourt, it is as if Peter's increased distance from Jesus underscores his denial. The infamous cockcrow, combined with the denial predicted by Jesus at the Passover meal, results in Peter's weeping. Those tears have come to symbolize Peter's broken soul. Yet the progressive distance and the gradual heightening of denial also point to a part of Peter's humanity that resonates with the reader. Broken trust and failed relationships begin with the smallest of behaviors and disappointments.

Failed relationship, brokenness, and a whole lot of tears; now there is an entry point to the Gospel narrative that takes us on the road to the cross.

Exegetical Perspective

gateway—perhaps to a place where he will be less conspicuous, surely to a place where it will be easier for him to make a quick getaway if he needs to—he overhears the same girl, now not only persisting in what she has said about him, but also passing it on to bystanders. So the threat level increases! That moves him from feigned ignorance to outright denial (vv. 69–70a). Finally, the bystanders as a group start to challenge him, "Certainly you are one of them, for you are a Galilean!" (v. 70b). Peter's Galilean accent has, presumably, given him away (*b. Erub* 53a, 53b). This time Peter reinforces his denial with an oath, invoking on himself a curse (v. 71). At that moment, the cock crows. Peter, realizing what he has done and remembering what Jesus said to him, breaks down and weeps (v. 72).

It has been suggested that the form of this narrative, with its threefold question, is intended to reflect courtroom procedure. Certainly it reminds us of other legal proceedings against Christians wherein the accused were given three chances to deny their membership in the illicit group (Pliny the Younger, *Letters* 10.96). Peter is questioned three times, and each time the question, and what it implies, increases in seriousness, as does the level of his denial. On the other hand, the rule of three is a fairly common feature of oral narratives (three bears, three wishes, and so on), so the similarity may be accidental.

So Peter, who had sworn he would die with Jesus if necessary, fails his test, just as his Lord told him he would (14:29–31). Yet the scene is not without hope. Peter grieves bitterly for what he has done, but this is a godly grief that leads to repentance and salvation (cf. 2 Cor. 7:10); and of course Mark's hearers as they listen to the story would know perfectly well that Peter subsequently died a martyr. Mark's account at this point has, moreover, another effect. Peter fails his test, just as his Lord has told him he would—and that is the point. The story of Peter's denial is also a story of the fulfillment of Jesus' prophecy. Thus Mark subtly reminds us—all appearances to the contrary notwithstanding—that it is Jesus who is in charge here, not Caiaphas, and only Jesus really knows what is going on. Those who scorn Jesus and presume to judge him understand nothing. This is situational irony of a high order: indeed, it is the first in a series of such ironies that will mark the entire narrative of Jesus' passion and death.

We may assume that Peter's own reminiscence is the basis of this story. Of course each of the four evangelists has reflected on the story and tells it in his own way, but all who try to write history must

Homiletical Perspective

After all, Peter's very reputation was at stake. Not just his personal honor but his entire family's status and loyalty to both the Jewish and the Roman authorities were on the line. It was not just his own life and livelihood that were at risk if he admitted an association with the now-disgraced Jesus. It was also that of his wife, his children, his parents, siblings, aunts and uncles, cousins. They all had something to lose if he were officially linked with a known criminal.

This deepens my appreciation for the position of Peter, who now really does seem just like me. I too am also caught between various "goods." Do I offer my child the best education I can by moving to the suburbs so she can attend a well-regarded public school or by sending her to private school? Do I, instead, educate her in accordance with my own commitments, rooted in Jesus' own inclusivity, to the betterment of public education in urban areas? Do I spend my money on renovating and updating our home, thereby making it more hospitable and welcoming to others, not to mention increasing the property values of all the houses in our neighborhood? Do I, instead, give that same amount of money to the food bank across town, or various worthy projects around the globe? Do I ask for a raise as my own pastoral responsibility and experience have grown? Do I, instead, push for budget increases for equally worthy areas—like the salaries of other staff members, worship improvements, or communal outreach? The opportunities for denying one good in favor of another multiply exponentially in modern North American society, and our choices are legion.

However, the true rub of Peter's dilemma does not lie in the complexity of competing goods. No, the problem is that he sets himself up several verses back. Jesus says, "Truly I tell you, this day, this very night, before the cock crows twice, you will deny me three times" (14:32). "No, not me," Peter says vehemently. Malina and Rohrbaugh note, "It is the fact that he did not fulfill his word of honor given to Jesus in the presence of others that is shameful."[2]

So, what if, in that moment of Jesus' prediction of denial, Peter had said, "Yeah, you are probably right, Jesus. I will follow along behind you when they pick you up, but if someone notices me, I will say I just happened to be in the area minding my own business, when I heard the commotion and ran over to see what was happening. I have never seen that man before. He is nothing to me." Would he have then been more honorable in the eyes of his community

2. Ibid.

Mark 14:66–72

Theological Perspective

loyal, even to death. Although his transgression of his own standard seems at first so effortless and unconscious, there is a growing sense of awareness of his guilt with each challenge from the crowd. Perhaps the cock's crowing provides a trigger to that self-awareness. The ubiquitous cry of the chanticleer redirects his consciousness. Upon hearing the familiar sound, Peter reconnects with Jesus and sees himself acting in contradiction to that relationship. This cognitive dissonance between belief about himself and observing his own behavior creates a growing anxiety in Peter. Finally he implodes into despair.

Ironically, the perspective on oneself that the conscience provides is finally a gift. John Calvin had this to say about the conscience: "Therefore this awareness which hales man before God's judgment is a sort of guardian appointed for man to note and spy out all his secrets that nothing may be buried in darkness."[3] This capacity for self-examination and critique, while often painful as we confront our truest selves, acts as a "guardian," leading us to confess our sinfulness into the arms of our forgiving God. Without the gift of the conscience, born in our freedom, we would not ever be aware that we are in need of God's love and forgiveness.

Most of us have mental files of cringe-worthy moments in our lives, when we have acted in contradiction to how we see ourselves, or at least to how we want others to see us. We can laugh at embarrassing moments, but we hope that our more egregious displays of imperfection never see the light of day. It is remarkable, therefore, that at some point Peter was obviously able to share this incident with the community of faith. Enough people could identify with Peter's humanity that it became a chestnut within the oral tradition of the early church and eventually made it into the canon. Peter's gift to us is, in the end, hope: even in our pitiful failures of moral courage, God in Christ remains ready to forgive us. In any given moment we are free to choose to follow Jesus or not. However, our conscience will awaken and, like a guardian, lead us back to where we need to be. These lessons can be excruciating, but not easily forgotten.

KATIE DAY

Pastoral Perspective

Peter's weeping places him in a pretty small crowd in the Gospels. Weeping points to the most common denominator of the human condition. Peter does not weep because he hears the cock crow. His weeping may be touched off by remembering what Jesus said, but it is not the teaching of Jesus that makes him weep. Peter breaks down and weeps because of his own denial of Jesus. Peter's tears come with the recognition of the devastating consequences of his own feeble and sinful self.

All hearers of the Word can attest to the frailty of our relationships and the role we play in keeping them fragile. To stick with such a general witness to our brokenness, however, does a disservice to the ways we deny Christ and his lordship in our lives. When we find ourselves standing with Peter warming ourselves by the fire, a more robust gospel encounter will challenge us to confront how we deny Christ and his lordship in our lives in both big and little ways. For some, such reflection may be the start of a fresh devotional life. Others may find themselves at such a distance from Christ that it leads to repentance and transformation. Still others may be overwhelmed by the notion of the church's collective participation in behavior that denies rather than affirms Christ and his kingdom in our midst.

If one mistakenly thinks such corporate denial is a matter of doctrine rather than justice, piety rather than righteousness, creed and song rather than life and action, then think again of the nameless servant girl. She is the powerless, almost invisible one who chooses to take on a man she knew to be a follower of Jesus. Remember her and her opening argument in Peter's courtyard trial. Her indictment of Peter started with one long stare.

Whenever the church gathers to walk the way of the cross with Jesus, the powerless, the invisible, the voiceless, the outcasts, they still stare at us, waiting to see if the witness of our life together in the world will be an affirmation or a denial of Christ the Lord.

DAVID A. DAVIS

---

3. John Calvin, *Institutes of the Christian Religion*, ed. John T. McNeill (Philadelphia: Westminster Press, 1973), 1.848.

Exegetical Perspective

to some extent combine fact with imaginative construction, and that is what the evangelists have done. What is incredible is the notion that the church would have *invented* a story that reflected so poorly on one of its most significant early leaders.

Viewed superficially, this is a simple tale of a police action involving people from the humblest possible background—a slave girl, soldiers, casual bystanders, and a fisherman who gives way under pressure. A hero so weak does not at all fit with the sublime style of high classical literature, and normal literary convention of the day would have seen Peter's story as either scurrilous or comic. Yet in Mark—as, indeed, in all four Gospels, for all their individual differences—the story of Peter's denial is neither scurrilous nor comic. On the contrary, in his very weakness Peter has for two thousand years roused men and women to profound and serious sympathy.

How can this be? The German philologist and critic Erich Auerbach was surely right: it is because Peter's story as told in the Gospels

> portrays something which neither the poets nor the historians of antiquity ever set out to portray: the birth of a spiritual movement in the depths of the common people, from within the everyday occurrences of common life, which thus assumes an importance it could never have assumed in antique literature. What we witness is the awakening of "a new heart and a new spirit." All this applies not only to Peter's denial but also to every other occurrence related in the New Testament.[3]

CHRISTOPHER BRYAN

Homiletical Perspective

when those things actually happened? The answer, I think, is yes. He would at least have been more honest about himself in front of everyone else. He would not have had to face the painful shattering of his illusions about himself as Jesus' faithful, steady, right-hand man.

Which leaves us with this choice: is it better to have no misconceptions about oneself, to know fully the dimensions of our constant, distracted, casual perfidies in the face of the least prodding? That seems to be the preferred postmodern stance: we make no commitments, so that we never have to disappoint ourselves, and others, when we cannot live up to them. Is it better to pledge ourselves brashly to a great cause, fully determined to live out that pledge with all our heart, and soul, and mind, and strength? To believe in the moment of such a pledge that we really can keep it? Then, when we discover inevitably that we cannot carry through, to face the crushing disenchantment with our own abilities? This latter choice is certainly more painful.

If Peter had made the first choice, I doubt that the earliest Christians would have even remembered him later—but he made the second choice. So we tell his story over and over to one another, reminding ourselves that in fact Peter in these moments is a mirror of our own tendencies—rushing to make promises we cannot or will not keep, backing off from those commitments as soon as we are challenged, running away in shame, guilt, and horror from our broken vows in the heat of the moment—and discovering again that the love Jesus offered to Peter, and to us, is not dependent upon our ability to keep promises we should not have made in the first place, if we only cared about honor.

NANCY CLAIRE PITTMAN

---

3. Erich Auerbach, *Mimesis: The Representation of Reality in Western Literature*, trans. William R. Trask (Princeton, NJ: Princeton University Press, 1953), 42–43.

Mark 15:1–5

¹As soon as it was morning, the chief priests held a consultation with the elders and scribes and the whole council. They bound Jesus, led him away, and handed him over to Pilate. ²Pilate asked him, "Are you the King of the Jews?" He answered him, "You say so." ³Then the chief priests accused him of many things. ⁴Pilate asked him again, "Have you no answer? See how many charges they bring against you." ⁵But Jesus made no further reply, so that Pilate was amazed.

Theological Perspective

Mark's narrative of Jesus' persecution, trials, torture, and death draws us into the pathos of a very real drama. This is not a mythical story of a cosmic transaction within the Trinity that leads to the atonement of sin. Rather, we enter into a gritty political tableau, complete with blood, sweat, and tears, enacted squarely in the context of human experience.

As with the parallel accounts of Peter's pledge of loyalty and then betrayal of Jesus, Mark structures the plot symmetrically. This appearance before Pilate is the second trial of Jesus, echoing his appearance before the Jewish council (14:53–65). There is a resonant rhythm to the two trials. Jesus is forcibly taken to the authorities and confronted with charges about his public claims regarding his identity, claims that challenge the authoritarian structures. In the first trial, the high priest asks if he is "the Messiah, the Son of the Blessed One" (14:61). Here, Pilate's interest is solely in his allegedly political claims: "Are you the King of the Jews?" (15:2). In both the religious and the civil trials, accusations are met with cryptic affirmation and silence. Jesus does not try to defend himself or engage in argument. The two trials end in the same way: Jesus is condemned for blasphemy or insurrection, beaten, and ridiculed.

In the dialogue with Pilate, Jesus proves to be a frustratingly unpredictable enemy of the state, not

Pastoral Perspective

Attentive readers of Mark's Gospel will remember how often the term "immediately" appears. Just here, in the passion narrative that surrounds Jesus appearing before Pilate, "immediately" abounds. Judas arrives at the garden "immediately" (14:43). Judas goes up to Jesus at once, or "immediately," and kisses him (14:45). In the courtyard drama of Peter's denial, Mark records that when the cock crows a second time, it happens "immediately" (14:72). So at the beginning of chapter 15, when Mark writes "as soon as it was morning," what the reader ought to realize is that the morning dawn comes "immediately" (v. 1, in Greek).

Immediate morning. The dawn breaking. A new day comes. The broad witness of Scripture testifies to the promise of each new day. The steadfast love and mercy of the Lord are fresh every morning (Lam. 3:23). Weeping lingers for the night, but joy comes in the morning (Ps. 30:5) Morning is the time when God's people offer praise and adoration. The rising sun is creation's testimony to the faithfulness of God. Each new day offers a witness to the promise of the gospel and the hope of the resurrection. After the dark night, the bright morning light shall surely come.

One would expect that an "immediate dawn" in Scripture would offer a breath of goodness and new

Feasting on the Gospels

Exegetical Perspective

Following Peter's denial, the scene changes again. "As soon as it is morning," the Sanhedrin, having determined that God's honor requires the death of the blasphemer, takes Jesus before Pilate the Roman governor, evidently intending him to ratify their decision and carry out the execution (15:1). Early morning was the time normally set aside under Roman custom for hearing legal cases,[1] so this was not a matter, as preachers sometimes suggest, of the Sanhedrin's interrupting Pilate at his breakfast, but rather of their being anxious to fit into his schedule!

Why, if the Sanhedrin was satisfied that Jesus deserved death, did they take him before the governor? Neither Mark nor either of the other Synoptic evangelists offers a reason, but the Fourth Evangelist does: "Pilate said to them, 'Take him yourselves and judge him by your own law.' The Jews said to him, 'It is not lawful for us to put any man to death'" (John 18:31–32 RSV). The law of which they speak is Roman, not Jewish. Rome, according to John and

---

1. See A. N. Sherwin-Wright, *Roman Society and Roman Law in the New Testament* (Oxford: Oxford University Press, 1963), 45–46.
2. Specialists in Roman law and history generally agree this was the case. Some biblical scholars have attempted to question the evidence, but their arguments are implausible, and evidently weighted by concerns other than historical. For discussion, see Christopher Bryan, *Render to Caesar: Jesus, the Early Church, and the Roman Superpower* (Oxford: Oxford University Press, 2005), 59–65, esp. 71–75; also Sherwin-Wright, *Roman Society and Roman Law*, 46–47.

Homiletical Perspective

What is the purpose of court trials? In North America we share a ready answer: the establishment of truth and the dispensation of justice, of course. After decades of watching televised fascination with all kinds of trials—trials of celebrities accused of murder, politicians charged with scandal, financiers indicted for corruption—this simple answer seems less clear. Indeed, the purpose of such trials may be to embarrass the defendant, to vent frustration over long-neglected wounds in our society, to provide entertainment, to avenge wrongs, to provide satisfaction of some sort to the victims of crimes. It is much harder to say that our modern trials are only about truth, justice, and the American way.

Jesus' trial before Pilate was certainly not about those things either, although we have often presumed that the Roman prelate was at least supposed to be interested in truth, justice, and orderly procedure. In the first half of the twentieth century, Walter M. Chandler published a two-volume set of books, *The Trial of Jesus from a Lawyer's Standpoint*.[1] In these weighty tomes he argued that the Roman system of justice was based on an orderly determination of the facts in accordance with strict procedure

---

1. Walter M. Chandler, *The Trial of Jesus from a Lawyer's Standpoint*, 2 vols. (New York: Empire, 1908).

Mark 15:1–5

Theological Perspective

playing his expected role. Pilate challenges him and Jesus does not defend himself or deny that he is King of Jews, but ironically ascribes the authorship of the title to Pilate: "You say so." This is not the designation of royalty Jesus would choose for himself, shaped in a political context. He brings a very different understanding of kingship. His threat to the state is as neither a political or nor a military leader, but is much more fundamental. When Pilate confronts him with the plethora of charges, Jesus does not take the bait. He will not engage the empire; his reign is of a deeper substance that finally calls into question the very foundations and nature of the Roman Empire.

The kingdom he has spoken about is not reactionary or incendiary, but it is at its heart revolutionary. He has preached liberation to those on whose backs the empire was built—the poor, the broken, the marginalized. In his kingdom, those considered insignificant by the state are loved and honored by God, and free to follow another way. His kingdom undermines the very premises of the *Pax Romana*, dependent as it was on the worship of a centralized human hierarchy, enforced militarily. The peace he preaches about is not the absence of military conflict, but reconciliation with God, with community, and with self. So, by his silence, Jesus indicts the empire. To participate in its structures and processes would be to validate them. Nonviolent, nonverbal, nonparticipatory is a language the empire does not speak. Pilate is amazed.

The moral power of silence has been employed by others who have confronted principalities and powers—we think of Gandhi's resistance to the British Empire, Dietrich Bonhoeffer's to the Third Reich, and that of Dr. Martin Luther King Jr. and so many of those in the civil rights movement who confronted the structures of Jim Crow and racist laws. Their courageous witness in the face of truncheons, dogs, fire hoses, and the gallows exposed the invalidity of the empires they confronted. Sometimes silence is louder than speech in exposing and transforming injustice.

The philosopher G. W. F. Hegel wrote about the freedom that those who are dominated can have over their oppressors. In his famous passage on "Lordship and Bondage,"[1] he argues that the dominators cannot think of themselves apart from the one(s) they oppress. The empire cannot exist without the subjects it controls, but those who are dominated do not need their oppressor to tell them who they

1. G. W. F. Hegel, *Phenomenology of Mind* (New York: Harper & Row, 1967), 228–40.

Pastoral Perspective

life. Clearly that is not the case here as the trial of Jesus continues with his interrogation before Pilate. Any promise of the new day is stomped on by the chief priests, the elders, the scribes, and the whole council, who hold an early morning meeting. To call it a "consultation" makes it sound businesslike, matter of fact, consensus building. Interestingly, this instance in Mark is the only use of the English word "consultation" (v. 1) in either the New Revised Standard Version or the King James translation of the New Testament. A more appropriate connotation here has to do with hatching a plan or launching a conspiracy. The only consultation in all of the New Testament is the one meeting called to plot the arrest and death of Jesus.

Creation's witness to the fresh promise of God is overmatched by a dark side of humanity that works destruction and plots death. At this point in the story of Jesus, with the inevitability of his death coming now into view, it is difficult not to conclude that the forces of darkness will win. On that early morning when Jesus is hauled before Pilate, it is very clear which side in the cosmic drama is pulling ahead. The consultation trumps the sunrise.

It is not the first, nor will it be the last, instance where powers and principalities seem to carry the day. Who among us has not had the experience of being overwhelmed by the world news of the day? A beautiful spring morning can quickly be trampled by the twenty-four-hour news cycle. When the days are full of treatments and tests and doctor visits, the longing for just a little bit of good news lingers into the night. As the ruthless power of poverty or violence or hatred only escalates, how many wonder if things are getting worse as dreams and visions of the kingdom of God seem to fade? It is like rising to greet the new day, only to learn that death and destruction have a head start. Like starting to sing a morning hymn of praise and realizing that Jesus is well on his way to Calvary.

Of course the agonizing reality and the piercing truth of the good news is that Christ keeps going. The passion narrative plays on beyond that breaking of day. Yes, Pilate's questions arise. Yes, Jesus' abuse and suffering is next. Yes, the crucifixion is carried out. Yes, the third day comes. Christ is risen! He is risen indeed! God's faithfulness triumphs with resurrection power. That great new day is coming. For now, though, all we have is what looks like a losing battle and the screaming silence of Jesus.

Pilate is amazed that Jesus makes no further reply. Pilate marvels that Jesus says nothing. Of all

Feasting on the Gospels

Exegetical Perspective

numerous other sources, reserved the right of execution to itself.[2]

So Jesus is brought before the governor. Mark evidently expects us to understand what he does not actually say, namely, that in order to increase their chances of success with Pilate, the Sanhedrin has redefined the charge. Naturally they cannot expect Roman officials to be as sensitive as they are about blasphemy against the God of Israel. However, Jesus' messianic claim—claiming to be Israel's true king, to which he has clearly assented—surely has a political aspect. So for Pilate's benefit they have restated the charge in terms that the Romans would recognize as *laesa maiestas*—treason. Hence Pilate's initial question to Jesus: "Are you the King of the Jews?" (v. 2a). This is not, as some have suggested, mockery, as if he thinks the whole thing a joke—"Is someone as pathetic as *you* claiming to be a king?" The question is serious. Indeed, it is deadly serious: for if the prisoner answers in the wrong way, he will have shown that the Sanhedrin's charge is justified. The phrase itself is a Gentile way of expressing the matter—possibly, again, adapted by the Sanhedrin for Pilate's benefit. A Jew would more naturally have said, "the king of Israel."

The idea of Jesus as king is, however, also one of the threads that bind together Mark's narrative of Jesus' passion. He is referred to as king six times in thirty-one verses, and he is called so by virtually everyone involved: by Pilate (three times: 15:2, 9, 12–13), by the Roman soldiers (15:18), by the official *titulum* over his cross (15:26), and by the chief priests and scribes, who also speak of him as "the Christ" (15:32). For Pilate, the title is possible grounds for a charge of treason. For the priests, it will be mockery. Whatever the characters in the story think, for Mark it is the truth. Jesus *is* the Christ, the king of Israel. Hence irony surrounds the entire proceeding. All these people think they understand what is going on—but they do not.

Jesus' response to Pilate, "You say so [*sy legeis*]" (v. 2b) is just as ambivalent in Greek as in English. It contrasts sharply with his forthright answer to the high priest (14:62). Jesus cannot give a forthright answer to Pilate's question, because in Pilate's sense it is a question about treason, and in that sense Jesus is *not* "king"; he is not interested in rebellion against Rome, nor is he concerned to abolish one human polity (Roman) in order to set up another human polity

3. Some New Testament scholars have recently asserted that Jesus *was* a political rebel making joint cause with Zealots, and that the early Christian movement was anti-Roman. This is implausible. It misrepresents early Christian history and distorts the history of Jewish-Roman relations, projecting into the 30s CE a situation that did not evolve until the 60s CE. See Bryan, *Render to Caesar*, 39–111; on Jewish-Roman relationships before 66 CE, see Martin Goodman, *Jerusalem and Rome: The Clash of Ancient Civilizations* (New York: Knopf, 2007).

Homiletical Perspective

and a well-defined practice of law—in other words, due process of some sort. So the trial before Pilate, he presumed, was a methodical affair in which justice could have been meted out fairly—if only the Jews had not been trying to rid themselves of Jesus in such an unfair way. We should note carefully here Mr. Chandler's shift of blame away from the orderly Romans and toward the Jewish authorities of the day who are presumed guilty with no effort to establish innocence. It is unfortunate that Mark himself places blame on the Jews by simply omitting mention of a spoken guilty verdict from the lips of Pilate. It is even more unfortunate that we perpetuate this too-often unconscious assumption that only the Jewish leaders of Jerusalem stood to benefit from Jesus' death, conveniently forgetting that all the powers in Rome, Gentile and Jewish, had something to gain by getting rid of the imminent threat to order and the status quo that Jesus represented.

When we admit our too-convenient bias we come a bit closer to understanding the purpose of this particular trial as it is recorded by Mark. It was not to discover truth and establish justice but to get rid of Jesus, and to get rid of him in such a humiliating and publicly shaming way that not only would his person be destroyed, so would his reputation, his honor, and his memory. The people of Jerusalem who stood against Jesus were participating in a "status degradation ritual," say Bruce Malina and Richard Rohrbaugh.[2] This is "a process of publicly recasting, relabeling, humiliating, and thus recategorizing a person as a social deviant."[3] A public trial in which accusations are bandied about while the accused stands silent and bound by ropes and chains is indeed mortifying. An offer to swap Jesus for a known criminal escalates the degradation. A crown of thorns here and a derisive comment there about some outlandish pretense of being the king of the Jews completes the disgrace. And once such a complete revision of Jesus' identity is accomplished, it is just a few short steps to the cross, the tomb, and then home for dinner.

If only we could say that such rituals are just something those bad old ancient Mediterranean societies invented for their own purposes! But we have our own versions of status degradation here in twenty-first-century North America. Jesus would not have fared much better with them. Whenever anyone speaks out against the commonly accepted order

2. Bruce J. Malina and Richard L. Rohrbaugh, *Social-Scientific Commentary on the Synoptic Gospels*, 2nd ed. (Minneapolis: Fortress Press, 2003), 216.
3. Ibid., 413.

Mark 15:1–5

Theological Perspective

are. Rome, and even Pilate, needed all its subjects to be intimidated so that they could stay in power. Only raw power could tell these rulers who they were. They were therefore dependent on those they oppressed. Jesus, in contrast, even though he will be put to death by the empire, has the freedom not to be defined by it. His silence unmasks where the power really lies; not with the infrastructure of a human empire but with the One who came to be known as the Word.

Not all the followers of Jesus are courageously silent, of course. Mark's narrative contrasts his response, or nonresponse, to Pilate with Peter's vociferous denial of his association with Jesus. In the passage immediately preceding, Peter is increasingly verbal (to the point of being abusive) in his self-defense before those in the courtyard outside of the legal proceedings who ask about his relationship with Jesus. In the same moment of time we see self-preservation in stark contrast to self-sacrifice; lying and deceit in contradiction to guilelessness; a frantic attempt to survive against a measured and grounded acceptance of unjust execution. Even as Peter is lying his way out of identification with the One to whom he has sworn allegiance not so long ago, Jesus is identifying with human sinfulness.

In framing the story in such a way, the writer is highlighting the purity of God's action in the context of our sordid experience. Dietrich Bonhoeffer wrote, "What is good in history is God's action alone; human historical action is good only insofar as God draws it into God's own action."[2] Good is being accomplished through this historical moment through God's action alone. In spite of the fickle crowd, the political intrigue, the betrayal of friends, and the self-serving kangaroo court, the spotlight is focused on the goodness of God, which convicts and redeems it all.

KATIE DAY

Pastoral Perspective

the reasons to stand in awe of Jesus, his silence is what gets to Pilate. There are so many possibilities that could cause wonder when it comes to Jesus: all those miracles, all those healings, all that teaching, every parable, the meals with sinners, hanging with the outcasts. There is so much that could astound the Gospel crowds, the church, you and me—but it is the silence that leaves Pilate in awe. The silence offers no defense. The silence claims no identity for Jesus. The silence shows no anger or resentment. This is not Jesus claiming the right to keep silent. Jesus is not invoking the silent treatment here in order to teach Pilate, or anyone else, a lesson. Pilate has to be wondering why Jesus will not defend himself. Pilate wonders, and so do we. Perhaps the silence simply speaks to Christ's determination to move on toward the cross.

His lack of a reply here is a unique silence. Of course the importance of the passion narrative in salvation history sets apart every aspect of the story the church knows so well. However, being in awe of the few words of Jesus does not necessary imply that silence in the face of suffering and abuse is a virtue. To affirm the uniqueness of his muted response is to honor the church's voice in the face of violence and suffering and the expectation that the church's faith-filled response will be to use it.

Religiously justified silence in the face of sinful abuse is unacceptable. Jesus' choice not to respond should never be touted as an example or an excuse for our failure to speak. Any implication that the silence of Jesus here is a pious sampling of turning the other cheek underestimates the power of the unfolding drama. His silence pushes salvation's story forward.

Pilate must have been taken with Jesus' own refusal to defend himself. It is the silence, however, that reveals the Lord's intention to keep going to Calvary and willingly to empty himself on the cross. In his silence, Jesus claims, announces, and lives his servanthood. The silence proclaims the Suffering Servant. That is amazing.

DAVID A. DAVIS

---

2. Dietrich Bonhoeffer, *Works*, vol. 6, *Ethics* (Minneapolis: Augsburg Fortress, 2008), 227.

Exegetical Perspective

(Israelite). As the Fourth Evangelist will have him say, "My kingdom is not from this world" (John 18:36).[3]

Clearly the priests realize that Jesus' reply to Pilate is from their viewpoint unsatisfactory—which is to say, he has not condemned himself out of his own mouth, as he did before the Sanhedrin (14:61–63); but then neither has he said anything that would indicate he does *not* now make the claim he made there. So they press the charge: they accuse him "of many things" (v. 3). The exact force of "many things" (Gk. *polla*) is disputed. It could be adverbial, meaning "vehemently," or it could be substantive, as the NRSV takes it. In any case, the sense is the same: the Sanhedrin is not producing against Jesus a list of misdemeanors, but supporting one fundamental charge that carries the death penalty.

So Pilate gives Jesus another opportunity to defend himself: "Have you no answer? See how many charges they bring against you!" (v. 4). Roman officials involved in a legal proceeding were expected to try to determine the facts of the case and to provide the defendant with a chance to reply to the charges (cf. Acts 25:16!). Jesus says nothing more, "so that Pilate was amazed" (v. 5). Since it was obviously in the prisoner's interest to defend himself, especially on a capital charge, Pilate's surprise is understandable. For Mark, however, Jesus' silence before his accusers is the silence of the righteous sufferer of the Psalms (Ps. 38:13–14), and perhaps of Isaiah's Suffering Servant of the Lord (Isa. 53:7).

CHRISTOPHER BRYAN

Homiletical Perspective

on behalf of the dispossessed and the trampled, our media crank up the background-check machinery to find a little dirt on that someone. Whenever anyone reminds us that God is not particularly interested in amassing wealth or pursuing war or dividing society into haves and have-nots, we race to the blogosphere to find out what is wrong with that person. Whenever anyone makes a claim about understanding more fully the purposes of God for our communities, the gossip, the innuendo, the accusations spread quickly in an effort to undermine credibility and redefine that person's status among us.

So Jesus faces Pilate in the clear light of morning after a night full of threat, physical and verbal. His accusers continue to hurl charges at him. Pilate asks a couple of questions, the purpose of which is not so much to find out the facts but to pursue a way out of this mess. And after a few half-hearted attempts to reply, Jesus at last stops responding with the enigmatic phrase, "you say so," to Pilate's question about whether or not he is the king of the Jews. He says not another word, according to this Gospel, until he is on the cross. Even then he utters only a lament over God's forsaking him.

In this version of the trial before Pilate, however, as in all the canonical Gospel versions, irony saves the day. Pilate and the crowds inside the story think they have degraded Jesus' status so fully that they will never hear another word from him or about him. But the readers know better. The trial of Jesus, at which all the wrong accusations are made and all the wrong conclusions drawn, at which the search for truth and justice is eclipsed by the religious and political motives of all the leaders, Roman and Jewish, in Jerusalem, signals the veracity of this claim: Jesus has come to turn the world upside down (cf. Acts 17:6). And like Pilate at the end of this text, the whole world will be amazed.

NANCY CLAIRE PITTMAN

Mark 15:6–15

⁶Now at the festival he used to release a prisoner for them, anyone for whom they asked. ⁷Now a man called Barabbas was in prison with the rebels who had committed murder during the insurrection. ⁸So the crowd came and began to ask Pilate to do for them according to his custom. ⁹Then he answered them, "Do you want me to release for you the King of the Jews?" ¹⁰For he realized that it was out of jealousy that the chief priests had handed him over. ¹¹But the chief priests stirred up the crowd to have him release Barabbas for them instead. ¹²Pilate spoke to them again, "Then what do you wish me to do with the man you call the King of the Jews?" ¹³They shouted back, "Crucify him!" ¹⁴Pilate asked them, "Why, what evil has he done?" But they shouted all the more, "Crucify him!" ¹⁵So Pilate, wishing to satisfy the crowd, released Barabbas for them; and after flogging Jesus, he handed him over to be crucified.

Theological Perspective

A long history of biblical and theological interpretation emphasizes that Mark's depiction of Jesus' trial before Pilate represents the exchange of Jesus' life for a presumed criminal named Barabbas—a symbolic exchange of Jesus' life paid as a ransom for all sinners. This interpretation resonates with the well-known satisfaction theory of atonement, identified with Anselm of Canterbury (1033–1109). Humans owed a debt to God so great that it could be satisfied only by the One who was both fully God and fully human. Contemporary theologians recognize that interpreting the account of this story as it is told in Mark's Gospel is a complex task for several reasons.

Mark's narrative blends historical realism and theological imagination. The trial's details are interwoven with legend and allusions to imagery drawn from psalms of lament and the Suffering Servant passages in Isaiah. Additionally, contemporary views of suffering as God's intended purpose for Jesus or other human beings stand in contrast to earlier interpretations. The experience of peoples carrying the burden of economic and social suffering in the world enables feminist, womanist, and postcolonial theorists to make powerful arguments against the characterization of suffering as God's intended condition for Jesus' ministry and for the lives of Christ's followers.

Pastoral Perspective

The haunting spiritual asks, "Were you there when they crucified my Lord?" Mark answers, drawing us into the drama of Jesus' passion, so that we are not merely spectators but participants. In the scene of Jesus before Pilate and the crowd, issues emerge that resonate with the demands of faith in both the life of the church and the life of the soul. Even as we locate ourselves among the actors in the passion, though, it is crucial to remember: God is there, directing the drama and playing the leading role. Hold that thought.

From the beginning of his "gospel of Jesus Christ, the Son of God" (1:1), Mark would have us understand that in Jesus we have to do with the very presence, power, and purpose of God. Straightway Mark reports Jesus' confrontation with the powers of evil, sin, and death: his temptation in the desert (1:12–13), his announcement of God's kingdom come, casting out demons, healing the sick, forgiving sins (who but God can do that? See 2:1–12), raising the dead daughter of Jairus, disputing with religious leaders, standing with equanimity before the civil authorities.

The passion narrative continues the confrontation of kingdoms. Pilate, representing Rome's rule of intimidation, comes face to face with Jesus, representing the rule of grace that marks the kingdom of God.

Exegetical Perspective

Jesus' appearance before Pilate continues in these verses, culminating with Jesus being sentenced to death. A new character is introduced: Barabbas, another prisoner awaiting his fate. This episode is full of powerful melodrama; unfortunately, it is also full of a host of historical problems, the first of which arises in the opening verse with its claim that at every festival Pilate used to release a prisoner of the people's choice (presumably meaning every Passover, although the noun lacks a definite article; cf. John 18:39, which ties the custom specifically to Passover but describes the practice as a custom of the Jews, rather than Pilate's own custom). There is no historical evidence to support this practice as having occurred.

Furthermore, Pilate is presented as reluctantly yielding to the demands of the religious leaders and the crowd in ordering the crucifixion of a man he considers innocent of the charges leveled against him. Would Pilate, whose tenure as prefect depends upon his ability to keep the peace in Judea, likely release an individual like Barabbas who is accused of being an insurrectionist? This portrayal of Pilate has been questioned, based on the depictions of Pilate in Josephus and Philo, both of whom present him as at times decisive, ruthless, and quick to rid himself of troublemakers or agitators.

Homiletical Perspective

The passion narrative is reaching its climax. The triumph of Christ's resurrection and his defeat of death still loom before us, but we must tread a cadence of sorrow to reach that victory. The story's original characters are still in play, but they have dropped by the wayside of the action: Peter has denied his Lord, the religious council has manipulated the judicial process, Pilate has been politically expedient, and the crowd has chosen someone else. Foreboding builds with every scene. We know how this will end, and it will not end well.

The passion narrative takes up a significant portion of Mark's Gospel. The story is rendered through a series of difficult texts whose depths are not easily plumbed. These texts display a dismal, dismaying parade of events of human failings through which the preacher gives witness to the gospel claim that is not yet apparent, but is nevertheless present in the narrative.

The preacher must lead listeners in a way Scripture invites them to be moved. The dreary spirit that overshadows the passion narrative can keep listeners from recognizing that grace and salvation have entered the world through Jesus Christ. By following the movement of the text, preachers will not diminish the grimness of the drama, nor will they allow injustice to be the final word.

Mark 15:6–15

Theological Perspective

Within the context of Mark's narrative, Jesus' suffering and execution are the outcome of his trial before Pilate and best understood as the result of struggles for power amid social, economic, and political strains caused by colonization. Jesus' own silence before Pilate symbolizes his resistance to colonial rule.

The story of testimony given against Jesus before temple authorities precedes his trial before Pilate. Chief priests, who represented a religious minority, did not possess the political authority within the Roman Empire to sentence Jesus to death. The action in Mark's account of the trial focuses on the Roman prefect, the chief priests who hand Jesus over, and the crowd.

Mark refers to the prefect's custom of releasing a prisoner during a festival. There is no historical evidence outside the Gospels to verify such a custom. Pilate, however, did possess Caesar's *imperium* (commanding power) and the right to render decisions related to unrest within his territory. Pilate never renders a judgment of guilt against him. Rather, Pilate speaks to the crowd asking: "Do you want me to release for you the King of the Jews?" (v. 9). Realistically, it is unlikely that Pilate spoke Jesus' native language of Aramaic, so speaking directly to him would not have been possible. Pilate also would have known that no Jew could claim the title of "king" in the Roman Empire. Pilate may have been mocking Jesus by calling him king.

Many commentators emphasize that Mark offers a positive depiction of Pilate, because he seems to believe in Jesus' innocence and tries to make a way to free Jesus. At best, however, Pilate's actions can be interpreted as taking a stance of neutrality in Jesus' case. Remember, Pilate possesses the power to dispose of the cases brought before him in any way that he sees fit, but he defers to the crowd.

The roles played by Barabbas and the crowd also need attention. The name Barabbas, Bar Abba, literally means "Son of the Father." *The Gospel of the Hebrews* referred to him as *filius magistri eorum*, "son of their teacher."[1] Origen in his *Commentary on Matthew* observed that the name included in some very old manuscripts was Jesus Barabbas (cf. Matt. 27:16). Postcolonial theorists describe Barabbas as a "native insurrectionist."[2] The vast majority of people in the ancient world lived at the subsistence level. Roman imperial taxes and unplanned events could

---

1. Samuel Tobias Lachs, *Rabbinic Commentary on the New Testament: The Gospels of Matthew, Mark, and Luke* (Hoboken, NJ: KTAV, 1987), 427.
2. Simon Samuel, *A Postcolonial Reading of Mark's Story of Jesus* (New York: T. & T. Clark, 2007), 149–50.

Pastoral Perspective

Jesus' refusal to discuss sovereignty on Pilate's terms and his confident silence before his priestly accusers leave the governor amazed, perplexed, possibly wondering just who is on trial here. Could this be Pilate's first inkling that the power of Rome is not "eternal" and thus open to challenge and critique by another sovereignty, secure enough not to have to defend itself with force? It is enough to give one pause.

Down the ages the tension between Christ and Caesar has been ongoing. Always there are other powers, causes, or movements that covet the approbation of religion and to which it may seem harmless enough, or even a "good thing," to link the gospel: God and country, church and state, Christ and culture, Christianity and capitalism/socialism. The most dangerous word in all of that is the little word "and"! Just so are the gospel's truth and otherness subordinated, compromised, even sacrificed, in favor of its usefulness to the kingdoms of this world. The kingdom of God accepts no coregents.

Pilate's duty to maintain order brings him quickly back from perplexity to matters at hand—to his role as politician, bureaucrat, decision maker. As we join him, he is facing a dilemma. The customary release of a political prisoner during Passover offers a way to set Jesus free. Already Pilate realize that Jesus is no threat to start a riot, the charges against him being bogus. Furthermore, Jesus is not without a certain following. Some call him "King of the Jews" or Messiah ("Son of the Most High"). His release would be popular with some people. On the other hand, political tension always runs high during this festival, and Jesus' accusers are stirring up the crowd to demand the release of the rebel Barabbas, "son of the Father." (Some manuscripts [see Matt. 27:16] call him "Jesus Barabbas," which offers a striking parallel.) Is one man's freedom worth risking a riot sure to provoke counterviolence, which would result in increased resentment and lingering unrest, not to mention how Pilate's superiors in Rome would view matters when word reached them?

As is so often the case with unexceptional politicians, expedience wins out in Pilate's decision to release Barabbas. In his subsequent treatment of Jesus, Pilate turns feckless. Presumably he could release Jesus as well. Does he not have that authority? In any case, he effectively lets a lynch mob decide Jesus' fate: "What should I do with the man you call King of the Jews?" (v. 12).

It is easy to make Pilate the villain here, but if we are looking to assign blame, there is more than enough to go around. Consider the crowd under

Exegetical Perspective

The text describes Barabbas as being "in prison with the rebels who had committed murder during the insurrection" (v. 7). Mark apparently assumes his readers know to which insurrection he is referring ("the" insurrection). None of our historical sources mentions an armed uprising in the years immediately preceding this scene. This period is framed, however, by violent episodes following the death of Herod the Great in 4 BCE and in the years leading up to the First Jewish Revolt, which began in 66 CE. Richard Horsley and John Hanson have argued that even though no specific uprisings are recorded during this period, it was still a time when civil unrest and banditry were present.[1] Perhaps "the insurrection" should be understood in a more general sense, meaning the disturbances or troubles that were occurring in Palestine.

Even the name of this rebel is not explicit. "Barabbas" was likely not his given name, but a patronymic, that is, a term identifying him by means of his father—the son of Abba. (Some ancient texts of Matt. 27:16 include a given name for this character, Jesus Barabbas, which most textual critics consider likely to be original. On that basis, some scholars have suggested that the Markan text originally included the name Jesus, but that it was omitted by scribes out of reverence for the "true" Jesus.)

Since *abba* is Aramaic for "father," some scholars have suggested that Mark intends his readers to understand the term Barabbas ("son of the father") as irony. Jesus, the true "son of the Father," is falsely accused of being a political threat ("King of the Jews") and executed on that basis. Barabbas, an actual revolutionary and false "son of the Father," is released. Whereas such a reading of the text is appealing, it is perhaps too subtle. Mark gives no clues to his readers that such a meaning is his intent. Even without the contrast of the names, however, Jesus and Barabbas stand as opposing figures in this scene: one innocent of the charge, yet crucified; the other guilty, yet set free.

The historical problems do not necessitate the conclusion that the story of Barabbas is completely unhistorical. More plausible is the suggestion that a man named Barabbas had been arrested, perhaps even around the time of Jesus' arrest, during a disturbance in Jerusalem in which some people died. Pilate, in Jerusalem at Passover to make sure public order was maintained, released Barabbas because

Homiletical Perspective

We know the scene: Jesus has been brought before the religious council, then before Pilate's court, and now before the crowd gathered outside. The council wants Jesus dead. Pilate may not agree with the council, but he still leaves Jesus to the fate of an unruly, politically manipulated mob. Hackles raised, the crowd chooses life for someone else and condemns Jesus to death. As the action swirls around him, Jesus meets Pilate's questioning with resolute silence. He does not have a chance.

Who is at fault for condemning Jesus to death? The religious council? Pilate? The crowd? All of them. It is far too easy for us to point out the culprits without considering our own complicity. Our present resistance to the text denies our participation in the very forces that sent Christ to the cross. Why, when people are confronted with someone who calls them to their higher selves, should they try to kill him? Motives may differ, but the primary response of the religious council, Pilate, and the crowd is fear. It is astonishing how easily injustice occurs when fear is allowed to thrive. Any time we are manipulated by fear, or manipulate others out of fear, we condemn the one who came to cast out fear. In this sense, we were there when they condemned Jesus to death: "Were you there when they crucified my Lord?"[1]

The realization of our own complicity in the narrative opens us to a growing awareness of our propensity to distort or destroy God's priorities for love and justice. A preaching emphasis on daily living through this text may seem to give the narrative short shrift, considering its incredible importance. Yet the text lends itself to the consideration of Christian ethics: we are in the crowd, and we are complicit. The goal of this recognition is not an end in itself. It is only the beginning of a journey to the cross that is ultimately good news for the listener. This journey of spiritual discovery, from the fear of the crowd to the redemption of the cross, has several movements, each one fruitful territory for the preacher. There is no need to cover all the ground in explicating the homiletical possibilities of the passage.

The first stage of the journey of spiritual discovery is to locate ourselves in the crowd. This is where we begin—with our humanity. It is imperative to recognize the complexity of the situation and our own complicity in the narrative. Whatever the reason, the motive, or the circumstance, we are there in the crowd. Perhaps we live with constant anxiety and

---

1. Richard A. Horsley and John S. Hanson, *Bandits, Prophets, and Messiahs: Popular Movements at the Time of Jesus* (San Francisco: Harper & Row, 1985), 48–87.

1. "Were You There?" *The Presbyterian Hymnal: Hymns, Psalms and Spiritual Songs* (Louisville, KY: Westminster/John Knox Press, 1990), #102.

Mark 15:6–15

Theological Perspective

easily threaten their livelihood. It seems reasonable to speculate that chief priests would have had little trouble "stirring up" the crowd who must have needed a leader to advocate for them. These observations shift the meaning of Pilate's question: Which Jesus will you choose? Do you want the violent revolutionary or the nonviolent "king"?

Jesus remains hauntingly silent. Can you imagine standing before those with the power to torture you and condemn you to death while remaining silent? Biblical scholars point out that Jesus' silence may be an allusion to the Suffering Servant of Isaiah (see Isa. 52:13–15; 53:7). On the surface, Jesus' silence seems to disrupt Mark's earlier depiction of Jesus' public ministry embodied in acts of healing and reconciliation. Is Jesus' silence symbolic of his awareness that God has already predetermined his fate? Does Jesus' silence, rather, represent his resistance to Roman authority and imperial rule? How much of a threat was Jesus' ministry of healing and feeding to leaders comfortably sitting in places of political or religious authority? In the political, social, and economic context, did Jesus really have any hope of being acquitted?

Womanist and postcolonial theologians offer interpretations of Jesus' trial before Pilate relevant to our contemporary context. Three-fourths of the people around the globe live in cultures shaped by colonialism. Womanist theologian Raquel St. Clair says that Jesus' suffering and death result from "socially constructed evil at the hands of particular social groups."[3] Postcolonial theologians cast the power dynamics represented in Jesus' trial before Pilate in light of the imperialism of the Roman Empire and the impact of colonization on the identities and cultures of those living under colonial rule.

Historically, women and men were stolen from their homes in West Africa, chained, branded with hot irons, and stowed skin to skin aboard slave ships bound for the plantations of the Western Hemisphere. Slaves were expected to "suffer in silence." Slavery remains a reality. Hundreds of thousands of women and children trafficked around the world silently endure their suffering in contemporary slave-like conditions. In this context, viewing Jesus' silence in the face of his impending suffering and execution as God's ultimate purpose for his life and ministry becomes problematic. Jesus' suffering and execution are the result of faulty choices made by people struggling for power in a culture crafted by colonization.

3. Raquel St. Clair, *Call and Consequences: A Womanist Perspective on Mark* (Minneapolis: Fortress Press, 2008), 162.

ELIZABETH L. HINSON-HASTY

Pastoral Perspective

whatever influence. Why choose one "son of the Father" over the other? Is it because Barabbas comes closer to satisfying the popular idea of a messianic hero who will drive out the Romans—a man of action and violence versus the prince of peace? Often the Jesus we are given is not the Jesus we prefer. Simon Peter has already had to learn painfully (8:27–38) that when one says to Jesus, "You are the Christ," the subject of that confession must control the predicate. You, Jesus, define the Christ of God—and not a Messiah who will sanction our preferences, baptize our agendas, and meet our expectations. Age after age we have to decide which Jesus to follow, and it is no easy choice. It never has been.

For all the blame and guilt that, in this shameful scene, might be assigned to Pilate, Jesus' accusers, and the crowd (including ourselves as Mark's participating readers), this is but one part in an event of infinitely greater significance and purpose. The passion narrative is not primarily about the world's great failure, much less about the failing and malice of individuals. It is about God's great act of love on the world's behalf. The passion describes the Father's handing over of the Son to death for the sins of the world, including those whose decisions and actions played a part in it: Judas, Caiaphas and his council of priests, elders, and scribes, Pilate, the crowd. Note specifically the words "handed him over" in verses 1 and 15.

They and we may be forgiven the choices and actions that take Jesus to the cross. We are not excused; there is no excuse! We are not puppets, but participants: conscious, willing, unwitting, ambivalent! However, we may be—are!—forgiven by One who goes to any length—to hell and back—and whose love reaches into every life and any circumstance to accomplish God's redeeming purpose. "Who delivered up Jesus to die? Not Judas, for money; not Pilate, for fear; not the Jews, for envy—but the Father, for love!"[1]

JOHN B. ROGERS

1. Octavius Winslow, *No Condemnation in Christ Jesus* (London, 1857), 358, quoted in Brian K. Peterson, "What Happened on 'The Night'? Judas, God and the Importance of Liturgical Ambiguity," *Pro Ecclesia* 20, no. 4 (Fall 2011): 363–64.

Exegetical Perspective

he was not convinced of his guilt. (Even the Markan story never explicitly says Barabbas is guilty of the crimes with which he is charged.) Either Mark or the tradition before him was intrigued by the similarities and ironies of the stories of Jesus and Barabbas and reworked them, so that an incident about Barabbas that had a factual basis was used to dramatize the evil and ironic choice that was made in the condemnation of Jesus.[2]

This scene in Mark of Jesus before Pilate leaves no one blameless—except the innocent victim sentenced to die. The religious leaders take the lead in pushing for the death of Jesus. They are the ones who hand him over to Pilate and who incite the crowd to call for Jesus' crucifixion. Among the crowd, no one calls for the release of Jesus; rather, they prefer the release of a violent agitator (Barabbas is, at the very least, guilty by association—he is imprisoned with "the rebels who had committed murder," v. 7). Not only do they call for the release of Barabbas; with reference to Jesus they twice shout insistently, "Crucify him!" (vv. 13, 14).

Pilate, who seems unconvinced of Jesus' guilt (Mark tells us that Pilate "realized that it was out of jealousy that the chief priests had handed him over," v. 10), is ultimately culpable as well. Despite the efforts of some strands of later Christian tradition to present Pilate as a sympathetic character (and even as a saint!), Pilate shares the blame in the Markan account. He has the power to do the right thing, to see that justice is served, and he fails. Ultimately it is his decision to hand Jesus over to be crucified after flogging him (additional, gruesome punishment whose effect would have been to weaken the victim and hasten his death when crucified). The question of Pilate to the crowd concerning Jesus is filled with irony: "Why, what evil has he done?" (v. 14). Of all the characters in the story, Jesus is the only one who has not done evil. All the others have become complicit in the triumph of evil.

MITCHELL G. REDDISH

Homiletical Perspective

fear. Perhaps we have been manipulated and played to our fear. Perhaps we have been the manipulator. We are in the crowd.

Recognizing our own complicity in the woundedness of the world can bring a greater awareness of others' complicity. Fear and injustice wield tragic consequences in families, communities, and nations. What role does fear play in our lives, in our local and national communities, in our global context? Locating ourselves in the crowd, recognizing our own complicity, and gaining an awareness of the greater abuses of fear and power in the world bring us back to our own life. We can consider the choices we have made in the crowd. The intent is not to condemn ourselves; rather, it is to recognize how much too easy it is for us to condemn others.

This journey of spiritual discovery begins in the crowd and ends in the believer's heart. It is not meant to end with a moral code: you should do this or should not do that. Rather, the listener is invited to engage a "what if?" kind of spiritual experience. What if Christ is alive and active in the world? What if the gospel makes a claim on my everyday living? What if I have a choice to make, rather than being swayed by the crowd? If I do, what choice serves the kingdom of God?

Liturgically, this text cries out for a prayer of confession, or some type of simple penitential rite, even when the text is preached on some other day than Good Friday. The point is to experience conviction, both in the negative and positive sense: to be convicted of our complicity and to be convicted with a renewed sense of the gospel for our everyday living.

KRISTIN SALDINE

---

2. See Raymond E. Brown, *The Death of the Messiah: From Gethsemane to the Grave: A Commentary on the Passion Narratives in the Four Gospels* (1994; repr., New Haven, CT: Yale University Press, 2008), 1:819–20.

Mark 15:16–20

¹⁶Then the soldiers led him into the courtyard of the palace (that is, the governor's headquarters); and they called together the whole cohort. ¹⁷And they clothed him in a purple cloak; and after twisting some thorns into a crown, they put it on him. ¹⁸And they began saluting him, "Hail, King of the Jews!" ¹⁹They struck his head with a reed, spat upon him, and knelt down in homage to him. ²⁰After mocking him, they stripped him of the purple cloak and put his own clothes on him. Then they led him out to crucify him.

Theological Perspective

Jesus' silence in his trial before Pilate bears witness to his active resistance to oppressive Roman rule. To remain silent in the face of Pilate was to refuse to give authority to an official of the Roman Empire. If Jesus' resistance to Pilate's authority is not enough to clarify the role that a colonial power played in his execution, then the story that follows makes inescapable the flagrant abuse of imperial power and systematic exploitation of a religious and ethnic minority.

Two important observations should be made about the story of the imperial soldiers' mocking coronation of Jesus. First, Jesus' active nonviolent resistance in the face of soldiers' abuse renders their claim to superiority on any level completely absurd. Second, the soldiers' actions illustrate the damage that violence causes even to its perpetrators.

Mark focuses on the actions of the soldiers who were trained to protect and defend the empire, without making any specific mention of Jesus' response to their abuse. Readers of Mark's story are left to imagine Jesus' reaction. However, the picture of the soldiers' actions is quite clear. A few soldiers lead Jesus to the courtyard of the governor's palace and then help a "whole cohort" (v. 16) gather there so that many would witness their display of power as they force Jesus to don a purple cloak (the color of

Pastoral Perspective

A scene from W. H. Auden's "Christmas Oratorio" pictures King Herod in a dither over having heard from the magi about the birth of God. Full of self-pity, Herod complains:

> One needn't be much of a psychologist to realize that if this rumor is not stamped out now, in a few years it is capable of diseasing the whole Empire.[1]

Auden describes Herod imagining a world turned upside down: "Reason will be replaced by Revelation.... Idealism will be replaced by Materialism.... Justice will be replaced by Pity as the cardinal human virtue."

Herod continues:

> Naturally this cannot be allowed to happen. Civilisation must be saved, even if it means sending for the army as I suppose it does. How dreary. Why is it that in the end civilisation always has to call in these professional tidiers to whom it is all one whether it be Pythagoras or a homicidal lunatic that they are instructed to exterminate?

Herod argues the absurdity of God incarnate, which would mean among other things, he says, "that God

---

1. W. H. Auden, "For the Time Being: A Christmas Oratorio" in *Religious Drama I*, ed. Marvin Halverson (New York: Meridian, 1957), 60.

Exegetical Perspective

Mark places the account of the Roman soldiers' mocking of Jesus at the conclusion of the interrogation by Pilate, an arrangement followed by Matthew. Luke has a different account. In his version, the mocking is done not by the soldiers of Pilate, but by the soldiers of Herod Antipas when Pilate sends Jesus to Herod for examination (a story unique to Luke). John has the soldiers of Pilate ridicule Jesus in the middle of Pilate's multifaceted interrogation of Jesus, not afterward. Although the historical discrepancies cannot be untangled, all the Gospel writers concur that Jesus endured taunts and ridicule as a part of his final ordeal. Not surprisingly, the early church used the Suffering Servant figure of the book of Isaiah, one who "was despised and rejected by others" (Isa. 53:3), to help them interpret the life and death of Jesus.

After Jesus is flogged, Pilate hands him over to his soldiers, who lead him into the praetorium, a term for the residence of the governor. In this case, it most likely refers to the palace built by Herod the Great along the western wall of the city (not the Fortress Antonia, as sometimes claimed). Pilate, whose official residence was in Caesarea, would likely have stayed at the Herodian palace when in Jerusalem. (Mark thus implies that the interrogation by Pilate, as well as the flogging of Jesus, took place outside

Homiletical Perspective

This is a text is about suffering: Jesus' suffering and by homiletical implication, our own suffering and the suffering of the world. It is a topic preachers are wary to speak about, in part because the theological territory is difficult. Was God redemptively present in the suffering of Jesus? If so, how? What difference does that make in a world full of suffering? What difference does it make, since suffering continues? The questions cannot be avoided. The cross looms ahead and grows larger with every rejection, injustice, insult, and humiliation. Making theological sense of Jesus' suffering is crucial to shaping a claim for the sermon.

Jesus did not suffer the most heinous death in human history. Crucifixion is an evil end, to be sure, but human history is littered with atrocities that destroy bodies and minds. Jesus' suffering is of paramount importance because of who he was as savior of the world. In this text, the Gospel is as surprising as it is dramatically forceful. Jesus' true identity as Messiah is revealed through the very powers of cruelty and inhumanity that seek to destroy him.

The text can be approached with a two-part preaching strategy. First, preachers can speak honestly about the suffering of Jesus. There is no need to shy away from the pain and humiliation in the text. It preaches itself! Listeners need very little prompting

Mark 15:16–20

Theological Perspective

royalty) and a thorny crown. Simon Samuel, a postcolonial theorist, argues that this macabre ceremony represents the soldiers' attitude toward a "native anticolonial" figure.[1] Attributing authority to Jesus with a title like "King of the Jews" must have seemed completely absurd to the soldiers.

More recent examples of mocking easily come to mind. Public humiliation is a common strategy employed by colonial powers to prove their authority and superiority over victims of their conquest. For example, England secured the unity of the British Empire by establishing English as the official language of its colonies. The 1536 Act of Union, which established the political and legal union between England and Wales, included a "language clause." One of the ways colonial powers commonly reshape cultural identities is by forcing victims of their conquest to stop speaking in their native languages and humiliating those who fail to adopt the new language.

The true story of Sandra Laing that is so powerfully depicted in Anthony Fabian's film *Skin* offers another potent example.[2] Laing's story obviates the social construction of race used as a tool to differentiate, subordinate, submerge, and control the black majority of South Africa. The Afrikaner National Party implemented apartheid laws between 1948 and 1954. In 1955 Sandra was born with brown skin to two white-skinned parents. The government at the time provided documentation of the "official" race of its citizens, and being white carried with it special privileges. Laing's father went to great lengths to ensure that Sandra was officially classified by the government as white. In one of the most horrific scenes, Sandra goes before a committee to be examined by a doctor. The doctor looks at her teeth, touches her hair, and considers the size of her frame. Even science was used as a tool to support the Afrikaners' racist ideology. In this scene the doctor, along with the committee, mocks the young girl, brown in body, who dared to try to claim for herself the trappings of white privilege.

Many other examples could be used to underscore this point: Jewish people being required to wear a yellow Star of David by the Nazis; Native American peoples being forced to adopt Western dress, forcibly removed from their lands, and forbidden to speak their own languages; and the mocking and torture of prisoners at Abu Ghraib Prison. The

1. Simon Samuel, *A Postcolonial Reading of Mark's Story of Jesus* (New York: T. & T. Clark, 2007), 151.
2. *Skin*, dir. by Anthony Fabian (BBC Films DVD, 2008).

Pastoral Perspective

had given me the power to destroy Himself."[2] Might Pilate have appreciated Herod's discomfort when, to satisfy the crowd, he handed Jesus over to be crucified?

In any case, Pilate orders the soldiers to tidy up this mess, and they decide to have a little fun at their prisoner's expense. After all, it is not every day they get to execute a king. The whole cohort joins in the cruel irony of the robe and the crown and the mocking tribute. Rather than a purple robe, some passages mention a scarlet or crimson cloak, a military garment worn by Roman generals (see Matt. 27:28).

Could any ridicule have been more humiliating? The savior in the regalia of the oppressor; the Prince of Peace clothed in the trappings of military might; the Suffering Servant dressed in the robe of pampered royalty? Although Jesus suffers this indignity at the hand of his enemies, there are times, even in the Gospels, when consciously or unconsciously his friends are the perpetrators: Simon Peter on the road to Caesarea Philippi: "No, Lord! Messiahs do not suffer; Messiahs conquer" (Mark 8:31–33). At the final meal, as John tells it: "No, Lord; you will never wash my feet! Messiahs do not do the work of houseboys" (John 13:2–8). James and John on the way to Jerusalem: "Lord, in your glory [when you have conquered] let us sit on your left hand and your right" (Mark 10:35–40).

Still today Jesus is mocked whenever he is made to play some role or sanction some viewpoint foreign to his nature. It happens when politicians or parties, ideologies or special interests, churches or governments find Jesus useful in promoting their own agendas. It happens wherever Christ is so overlaid with one nation's point of view or one economic theory, one cultural perspective or one political strategy, one method of evangelism or one denominational emphasis that he ceases to question, challenge, and judge us.

Far more is going on here than the soldiers'—and our own—cruel mockery. The task of interpretation is still before us after we have stated the obvious. Consequently, the most significant pastoral aspect of this passage is that it marks God's own self-surrender in Jesus Christ for us. For all the "handing over" of Jesus that takes place in the passion narrative—Judas's handing him over to the religious authorities, who hand him over to Pilate, who effectively hands him over to the crowd and then, doing their bidding, hands him over to the soldiers for crucifixion—it is

2. Ibid., 61.

Exegetical Perspective

the praetorium in a more public setting.) The soldiers call together the entire cohort (10 percent of a Roman legion, or usually six hundred men). In order to accommodate such a large number, the setting for this scene as envisaged by Mark is probably the courtyard of the palace, rather than inside the palace building proper.

Just as the religious leaders during the previous night had mocked Jesus, now the Roman soldiers taunt and mock him. Their abuse of Jesus is both physical and verbal. They begin by dressing him up like a king, placing on him a purple garment and a crown they have woven out of thorny branches, both makeshift objects to resemble royal attire. Purple dye, made from shellfish, was expensive and a symbol of royalty. Mark does not explain where they would have been able to obtain a purple garment. (Matt. 27:28, perhaps to alleviate this difficulty, changes the color of the garment to scarlet, suggesting the cape sometimes worn by Roman soldiers.) The crown of thorns would have resembled a laurel wreath worn by the emperor. Despite later artistic depictions, as well as popular imaginings, Mark gives no indication that the crown of thorns was intended as an instrument of pain or torture. The soldiers simply gather materials available to them to create a mock crown.

Not content with their visual mockery, the soldiers begin to taunt Jesus by proclaiming, "Hail, King of the Jews!" a parody of the greeting addressed to the emperor, "Hail, Caesar!" The soldiers become physically violent, as they strike Jesus on the head with a reed and spit on him, actions that demonstrate their true evaluation of this "king" who stands before them. Their treatment of Jesus fulfills the third passion prediction of the Markan Jesus, who said that the Son of Man would be handed over to the Gentiles; "they will mock him, and spit upon him, and flog him, and kill him" (10:33–34). Matthew's account enhances the mockery, adding the detail that the soldiers place a reed (for a scepter) in Jesus' right hand (Matt. 27:29), which is then the reed with which they strike him. The soldiers next mockingly kneel in homage to Jesus, assuming the same subservient posture one would take when coming before the emperor, other dignitaries, or a divine figure. (Matthew, apparently sensing the awkwardness of Mark's arrangement, rearranges the order of these actions, placing the kneeling and worship immediately after the soldiers' taunting acclamation of Jesus as king.)

Finished with their cruel bullying of Jesus, the soldiers remove the purple garment and place Jesus'

Homiletical Perspective

to identify their own sufferings and those of others, so preachers can name the suffering of individuals, of our communities, of the world, indeed, of the whole of creation. In a digital age of constant news, we live in a world painfully aware of its own sorrow. Second, preachers can proclaim boldly the redeeming love of God and can encourage listeners to seek God's redeeming love in action in a world in pain.

A word of caution here: preachers need to be clear about how they make theological meaning from Jesus' suffering. We need to be mindful of how those who suffer experience this text. Jesus' suffering has sometimes been exploited for suffering's sake. In other words, his suffering has been overemphasized to the extent that it overshadows the power of God's redeeming work. The danger of this approach is that it perpetuates the notion that suffering is divinely motivated and is salvific in itself. As Sally Brown observes, "when sufferers and abuse victims believe that Jesus' death was divinely orchestrated violence and that the suffering of Jesus was intrinsically redemptive, the results can be disastrous."[1] Suffering is not the primary theological focus of the passage. Rather, the narrative is telling us something about Jesus as Christ.

At the same time, preachers should not avoid Jesus' suffering. His abuse at the hands of his accusers and their deputies is central to this Gospel narrative. From beginning to end, the physicality of his entire passion, not just his crucifixion, is substantial. The crowd that arrests him is armed with swords and clubs. He is led away under guard. He is spit upon, blindfolded, struck, beaten, bound, and flogged. His emotional torment is significant as well. He endures betrayal, desertion, false testimony, condemnation, public humiliation, derision, taunts, and mockery.

There is a social justice claim to be made. Jesus' physical suffering is in part politically motivated and is so intense that it amounts to torture. Torture can be defined as the infliction of intense pain to punish, coerce, or afford sadistic pleasure. There are at least three instances in the narrative that include features of punishment or sadistic pleasure that fit this definition. The first occurs at the religious council. After members spit on him and strike him in punishment for his self-identification as the Messiah, Jesus is turned over to the guards and beaten. The second act of torture occurs when Jesus is brutalized at the hands of Pilate's soldiers, indeed, from the entire

---

1. Sally Brown, *Cross Talk: Redemption Here and Now* (Louisville, KY: Westminster John Knox Press, 2008), 2.

Mark 15:16–20

Theological Perspective

list of exclusionary practices could go on and on. Unfortunately, the list of stories of nonviolent resistance is shorter.

Now imagine in your mind Jesus' response to the taunting, torture, and humiliation he suffered at the hands of the soldiers. The temptation to respond to such abuse with violence was great. In Mark's narrative, though, the choice between the violent revolutionary (Barabbas) and the nonviolent king (Jesus) has already been made. It is reasonable to speculate that the soldiers would hope for Jesus to respond with violence, thereby enabling them to give a more convincing display of their own power. As Jesus resists, he refuses to accept their power over him and the empire's appraisal of his value and worth.

Nonviolent activists in the civil rights movement adopted a similar approach in response to aggressive police. When protestors were threatened with water hoses, dogs, billy clubs, or electric rods they were taught to resist without resorting to violence. They were trained to allow their bodies to go limp if police tried to drag them away from a sit-in or other line of protest. Their avoidance of violence ultimately won over the crowds and highlighted the absurdity of the physical force used by police to maintain "civility" and "peace."

Feminist ethicist Sharon Welch makes an astute observation about the corrosive effects of imperialism on both the colonized and colonizer. She writes that "with violence to others comes a cost to us: we become brutal in the doing and callous in the disregard. To emphasize as a fair calculus their death and humiliation for our gain reflects a tragic lack of empathy and imagination."[3] Welch directs her discussion toward our contemporary context, but her observations are easily applied to Mark's story of the soldiers' mocking of Jesus. Jesus refuses to match violence with violence. His nonviolent resistance represents the depth of Jesus' understanding of shared humanity; he matches the soldier's taunting and torture with what Welch calls "empathy and imagination." Jesus avoids being complicit with the destruction and devastation associated with imperial rule, either in life or in death.

ELIZABETH L. HINSON-HASTY

Pastoral Perspective

the Father who hands the Son over on our behalf and on behalf of the world.

In Jesus Christ, God takes into God's own life the human condition—its brokenness, its mortality, its estrangement from God. God enters into our need. The extent to which God is who God is and does what God does is that for us, in Jesus Christ, God becomes the substitute, taking our place, enduring the fullness of divine wrath and judgment. The crucifixion, death, and burial of the Son take place within God's own life. Jesus' passion is neither a symbol of, nor a theory about, God's way with the world. It is the very enacted reality of God's reconciling love for the world and those who dwell therein.

The church has sought in creed, doctrine, and metaphor to declare what is finally beyond its capacity to express. What is crucial in any reference to this unspeakable event that anchors our faith and life is that it says these words: for us! For us Jesus was crucified (rejected); for us he died (knew the last possible experience in human life); for us he was buried (he made our end his own); for us he descended into hell (he knew God-forsakenness).

Because God alone is the Substitute—because God became the Rejected One—the work of salvation is complete, perfect, and accomplished once, for all, and forever. In Christ's passion God has taken into the divine, triune life the estrangement, the punishment, and the ultimate consequences of evil, has borne them to the fullest, and has borne them away. Separation from God can no longer be our destiny. God has not merely given us a chance, offered us a deal, increased our options. God has determined to give us life—God's own life. In the words of the familiar communion hymn, God's love "has broken every barrier down."[3] God has gathered all of us into the reconciliation accomplished in Christ. There is, truly, now "no condemnation for those who [through the self-surrender of God] are in Christ Jesus" (Rom. 8:1). We have no life now, nor have we a future destiny, as anything other than God's redeemed children.

After mocking him, they stripped him of the purple cloak and put his own clothes on him. Then they led him out to crucify him (v. 20)—for us!

JOHN B. ROGERS

---

3. Sharon D. Welch, *After Empire: The Art and Ethos of Enduring Peace* (Minneapolis: Fortress Press, 2004), 174.

3. Charlotte Elliott, "Just As I Am, without One Plea" (1834).

Exegetical Perspective

own clothes back on him. Nothing is said about the crown being removed, suggesting that Jesus was forced to wear it while carrying the cross and then being crucified, which is a typical artistic depiction. (Matthew follows Mark here, while John does not mention removal of the purple garment or the crown. Luke does not include the mocking by Pilate's soldiers.) This passage ends with the chilling statement, "Then they led him out to crucify him" (v. 20).

Whereas Jesus' interrogation by the religious authorities dealt with whether Jesus was "the Messiah, the Son of the Blessed One" (14:61), his appearance before Pilate and his ridicule by the soldiers focus on whether he is "the King of the Jews." Three times Pilate uses this title for Jesus (the third time he attributes it to the crowd), and the soldiers mercilessly deride him as a pseudoking. Modern readers who are familiar with certain Hollywood presentations of the flogging and mocking of Jesus may be surprised by the reserved way in which Mark presents these scenes (as well as the later crucifixion scene). Mark gives more details of the mocking of Jesus than he does of either the flogging or the crucifixion, but even here he does not dwell on the mocking for emotional effect.

The ridicule by the soldiers serves to highlight the irony at the center of this episode. Neither Pilate nor the soldiers believe that Jesus is a king. At most, they may think he foolishly (and perhaps dangerously) has political aspirations to reestablish the kingship over Judea (the phrase *ho basileus tōn Ioudaiōn* can also be translated as "the King of the Judeans"). Yet by their words and actions, Pilate and the soldiers say more than they intend and more than they know. Whereas Jesus is not a king in the way they understand the term, for Mark he is indeed king in another sense. He is the anointed king of the people of God who will reign over God's coming kingdom. In the words of another ironic taunt later in this chapter, he is "the Messiah, the King of Israel" (v. 32).

MITCHELL G. REDDISH

Homiletical Perspective

cohort. The third instance is the crucifixion itself. If we remember that Jesus was condemned for sedition, a political crime, we can make a fluid connection to the atrocious stories of political torture in our contemporary world and speak against them.

We can make these connections because, in the end, Jesus' suffering points not only to his extreme vulnerability and powerlessness, but also to his divine kingship in the midst of the tragedy. Pilate's soldiers take sadistic pleasure in the elaborate, ironic ritual of paying homage to "the king of the Jews" through physical humiliation and abuse. Jesus is vested with the trappings of kingship: robe, crown, and scepter. Soldiers bow before him to pay mock homage. What they could hardly realize is that, in their mockery, the soldiers give witness to a greater truth. As Donald Juel observes, "Jesus is most consistently depicted as king when he looks least like a king." What religious and political authorities mock as absurd and ridiculous, believers who hear the Gospel narrative know as testimony to the truth: Jesus is king of the Jews.[2] The suffering of Jesus was not what rendered him king of the Jews. The truth of Jesus' kingship is revealed in his suffering, but it is not bound by it.

Herman Waetjen suggests that, given the probable illiteracy of the intended audience, the Gospel of Mark was probably read publicly.[3] As a dramatic narrative, its aurality is a strong point. This passage deserves to be read well in worship, with practiced and thoughtful interpretation. As preachers, we sometimes forget to give sufficient attention to our reading voices, cadence, and rhythms. Hymns, prayers, and litanies chosen for a Sunday when this text is preached need thoughtful consideration as well. The repertoire of music and liturgy for the passion story, both traditional and contemporary, contains a wide theological range. Care should be taken to design worship in a way that supports the claim of the sermon. Acts of worship that insinuate the "divinely orchestrated violence" of Jesus' suffering undermine the prophetic witness of the text.

KRISTIN SALDINE

---

2. Donald H. Juel, *The Gospel of Mark* (Nashville: Abingdon Press, 1999), 154.
3. Herman C. Waetjen, *A Reordering of Power: A Socio-Political Reading of Mark's Gospel* (Minneapolis: Fortress Press, 1989), 2.

Mark 15:21–32

²¹They compelled a passer-by, who was coming in from the country, to carry his cross; it was Simon of Cyrene, the father of Alexander and Rufus. ²²Then they brought Jesus to the place called Golgotha (which means the place of a skull). ²³And they offered him wine mixed with myrrh; but he did not take it. ²⁴And they crucified him, and divided his clothes among them, casting lots to decide what each should take.

²⁵It was nine o'clock in the morning when they crucified him. ²⁶The inscription of the charge against him read, "The King of the Jews." ²⁷And with him they crucified two bandits, one on his right and one on his left. ²⁹Those who passed by derided him, shaking their heads and saying, "Aha! You who would destroy the temple and build it in three days, ³⁰save yourself, and come down from the cross!" ³¹In the same way the chief priests, along with the scribes, were also mocking him among themselves and saying, "He saved others; he cannot save himself. ³²Let the Messiah, the King of Israel, come down from the cross now, so that we may see and believe." Those who were crucified with him also taunted him.

Theological Perspective

The narration of Jesus' death creates its emphasis through direct quotations, beginning with the sign over the cross (v. 26), including derisive words from passersby (vv. 29–30) and from the religious authorities (vv. 31–32), Jesus' speaking Psalm 22:1 (v. 34), the bystanders' mistaken response (vv. 35–36), and finally the centurion's witness (v. 39). In verses 21–32 each quotation engages different ways in which being "saved" was and is still understood. Kings (v. 26) save by creating order and protecting subjects. The temple (v. 29) saves by creating space in which appropriate worship may be safely performed. The Messiah, King of Israel (v. 32), closely relates these two understandings. "Save yourself, and come down from the cross!" and "he cannot save himself" (vv. 30–31) both specifically refer to protecting and continuing physical life. Whether "he saved others," spoken by the high priests and scribes, refers to earlier healings performed by Jesus or to some other form of saving act is left unclear in the text.

What is clear is that Mark pushes readers to clarify how we understand Jesus' power to save in relation to his crucifixion. The narrative moves readers to "see and believe" and eventually to bear witness to what has happened, as the centurion does. This portion of the Gospel points toward different expectations of what it means to be saved and yet

Pastoral Perspective

In biblical times, it was customary for a condemned man to carry his own cross, and indeed John 19:17 assumes Jesus did so. We do not know why Jesus was relieved of that obligation. Perhaps he was too weak from the ordeals of the trial, the mockery of the soldiers, and the flogging. Because they had been ruthless in their treatment of Jesus, we can assume that compelling Simon of Cyrene to carry the cross for Jesus was not an act of compassion by the soldiers. They were determined that Jesus would not die before he was crucified. We do not know why the soldiers picked Simon. We can only imagine, again in the interest of getting to Golgotha, that Simon appeared strong enough to bear the beams.

Although the writer of Mark gives the cross-bearer a name, we know nothing about Simon except that he had come from the country. We do not know whether he resisted the soldier's choice or what it cost him to bear the cross of Christ. Was Simon resentful or even bitter about being seized by the soldiers, as Luke reports (Luke 23:26), to carry the cross for Jesus? Was Simon changed in the moment, so that later his sons Alexander and Rufus were known to the Christian community in Rome, for whom the Gospel of Mark was written (15:21)?

This moment when Simon of Cyrene begins to carry the cross for Jesus is the fifth station in the

Exegetical Perspective

The execution of Jesus in Mark 15 should come as no surprise to the reader of Mark's Gospel, even though it does surprise Jesus' obtuse disciples. Mark has punctuated his narrative with indications throughout of where the story is heading. This begins in 1:14, where Mark notes that Jesus commences his public ministry in Galilee after the arrest of John, whose gruesome beheading he recounts in 6:14–29. John's arrest and murder by Herod Antipas foreshadows Jesus' eventual execution by another political authority, the Roman governor Pilate. Already in chapter 2, opposition to Jesus by the religious authorities emerges and grows in a series of critical questions concerning Jesus' authority to forgive sins (v. 7), his eating with tax collectors and sinners (v. 16), his not fasting (v. 18), his disciples' "careless" Sabbath observance (v. 24), and his own healing on the Sabbath (3:2). As early as 3:6, the reader is informed that Jesus' life is threatened, for "the Pharisees went out and immediately conspired with the Herodians against him, how to destroy him."

That he faces "great suffering," rejection, betrayal, and execution is made explicit by Jesus himself in a series of three passion predictions (8:31; 9:31; 10:33–34). The third provides a concise summary of what will take place in chapters 14–16: "See, we are going up to Jerusalem, and the Son of Man will be handed

Homiletical Perspective

This scene is not easy to preach. It describes Jesus' crucifixion but not yet his death. To preach this text leaves a congregation hanging a bit. On the other hand, to rush to Jesus' death robs Mark's passion story of its pathos. Whatever homiletical approach is taken, preachers will want to make room in the sermon to rehearse the whole scene slowly enough to help the congregation experience this pathos. Three homiletical strategies rise to the top of potential approaches for finding an entry into the scene.

First, preachers could ask their congregations to identify with and view the scene through the eyes of Simon of Cyrene, who is mentioned in verse 21. As with the fishermen who become Jesus' first disciples and follow him obediently without having any foreknowledge of him (1:16–20), Mark presents Simon as having no previous connection with Jesus. He acts not out of devotion but simply because he is required to do so by the powers that be. However, the details naming his sons indicate that he (and they) must have become important to Mark's community of faith (cf. the way Simon is named in Matt. 27:32 and Luke 23:26). In other words, the notice of the names of Simon's sons indicates that he came to be known as a follower of Jesus after the fact.

In some sense, then, this event functions as a call or conversion experience for Simon. Identification

Mark 15:21–32

Theological Perspective

does not specify one meaning. As readers living in faith, we are challenged by the text to articulate our own understanding of salvation in response to the whole narrative.

The activity of "saving" involves an old condition, a new condition, and an action that transforms the old and makes the new possible. The passersby and the priests, when they taunt Jesus with "save yourself and come down from the cross," are portrayed as expecting that the new condition after coming down from the cross will be the same kind of life that Jesus had before being hung to die. This expectation for what constitutes being saved is made impossible by the actual death of Jesus. The new, saved condition that follows his death will not be the same as what had come before. All of the various Christian understandings of what constitutes salvation follow Mark's narrative lead and describe the new condition as something that was not previously possible.

Six main theological themes interpreting salvation have emerged in Christian tradition as resources for our thinking through our own response to the text's challenge. Each identifies the fundamental problem with the old condition, the gift and possibility of the new condition, and how Christ's action responds to the old and inaugurates the new in human history. Particular expressions of soteriology often blend more than one theme.

1. The early church, for example, Athanasius and the Cappadocians, thought of salvation as a process of deification, becoming perfected in love in the way that God loves. The crucifixion involved removing a barrier to sanctification; thus we die and rise with Christ. Old condition: not holy. New condition: becoming holy as God is holy. Christ's act removes the barrier to becoming holy.

2. Reformation period theologians such as Luther emphasized the enormity of the barrier between humans and God and so focused on the human need to be made righteous before God. In the old condition human sin makes us unrighteous and deserving punishment. Christ's sacrifice on the cross imputes righteousness to those who have faith in him. This righteousness resolves the punishment that would otherwise rightfully come to humans. Thus in the new, saved condition we are restored to relationship with a righteous God.

3. Union with Christ emphasizes the other side of what occurred when the barrier to relationship with God was removed. Humans have personal access to the new condition of being one with our creator through union with Christ. Here the old condition is

Pastoral Perspective

Roman Catholic devotional discipline of fourteen stations of the cross. This practice dates from at least the fourth century, and the pattern of fourteen stations was fixed in the fifteenth century. There are variations of this practice in Protestant churches, some of which follow the biblical narrative more closely. When Simon is compelled to carry the cross, those who follow this devotional practice of walking the way of Jesus to his death are invited to pray for those who follow in the steps of Jesus, that they follow him in service.

It is the model of burden bearing and the invitation to service that intrigues me most about the reference to Simon of Cyrene, both in the biblical texts and in Christian devotional practice. Jesus is clear about discipleship in his name: we are to bear one another's burdens. At the end of his own life, Jesus could not carry his own burden. It was too heavy and he was too weak. For anyone near death or for anyone in good health who fears dying, this is a remarkable gift from Jesus. At the end of his life, Jesus had to trust the kindness of a stranger to carry a burden he could no longer bear. He needed help with his mortality as he was dying; and so do we all, both in our living and our dying.

More remarkable still, handing over his cross to Simon continues the passivity of Jesus in his journey to death. British theologian William Vanstone has proposed that when Jesus is handed over to his captors in the garden of Gethsemane, "the ultimate dimension of the divine glory becomes manifest in Jesus and evident to humankind."[1]

Conditions of passivity—weakness, vulnerability, waiting, receptivity, dependence, and need—are not alien to God, but rather partake of the very being of God. Human passivity, no less than human activity, expresses the divine image mirrored in the dying of Jesus. Lying in a hospital bed, we are no less Godlike than the extraordinarily skilled medical specialist at the peak of her powers who tends to our treatment. The dying of Jesus invites us to embrace a new vision of active passivity.

Without knowing, Simon embodies the life Jesus has lived to his death. The life we receive in one moment, we give away in the next. We do not have our life as a possession. When a life is lived in and for God, it is constantly received, then expended for others. While we cannot know the impact on Simon of this action, we are aware that being compelled to carry another's burden may be costly and

---

1. William H. Vanstone, *The Stature of Waiting* (New York: Seabury, 1982), 75.

Exegetical Perspective

over to the chief priests and the scribes, and they will condemn him to death; then they will hand him over to the Gentiles; they will mock him, and spit upon him, and flog him, and kill him; and after three days he will rise again." Betrayal, arrest, a hearing before the Jewish religious authorities, a trial before Pilate, mockery, torture, and execution await Jesus in Jerusalem. Still, he goes there.

Mark continues to build the dramatic tension once Jesus enters Jerusalem, first through his cleansing the temple of the money changers, then through a series of debates in the temple between Jesus and his opponents (chaps. 11–12). One by one Jesus bests in debate representatives of the various factions in Judaism, and their anger and frustration grow. Mark tells us repeatedly that the chief priests and the scribes keep "looking for a way to kill him" (11:18; also 12:12; 14:1). Finally, Jesus predicts the destruction of the temple itself (13:2) and his future vindication (13:26–27). This twofold prediction is later cited as the grounds for his condemnation by the chief priests at his trial before the council (14:58-64).

On the human, social, and political level, Mark's plot develops inexorably through this series of increasingly hostile conflicts between Jesus and his opponents toward Jesus' execution. For Mark, however, the suffering of Jesus, Messiah, Son of God (1:1), is not simply a historical tragedy but also a divine necessity, and so is in accord with Scripture. "The Son of Man *must* [Gk. *dei*] undergo great suffering" (8:31), Jesus himself tells his disciples at Caesarea Philippi after Peter first confesses him as the Messiah. At the Last Supper and during his arrest Jesus announces that his passion is in fulfillment of Scriptures: "for the Son of Man goes as it is written of him" (14:21); "it is written, 'I will strike the shepherd, and the sheep will be scattered'" (14:27); "let the scriptures be fulfilled" (14:49). Jesus' prayer in Gethsemane, "Abba, Father, for you all things are possible; remove this cup from me; yet, not what I want, but what you want" (14:36) affirms his reluctant, yet willing acceptance of his suffering as God's will.[1]

Mark's brief account of the execution of Jesus is stark and unrelentingly bleak. His disciples have all deserted him (14:50). His cross needs to be carried to the execution site, Golgotha, the Skull

---

1. The notion that suffering may be God's will raises many important theological and pastoral issues that Mark's Gospel does not address. It needs to be held in tension with God's clear intention to bring healing and alleviate suffering through the ministry of Jesus. Mark's Gospel does not explain why Jesus' suffering is God's will, only that it is. The closest to an explanation is Mark 10:45: "For the Son of Man came not to be served but to serve, and to give his life a ransom for many."

Homiletical Perspective

with Simon can be important, given that he is from Cyrene, part of current-day Libya. The New Testament is primarily focused on the Mediterranean world, from Jerusalem north and northeast to Syria, Asia Minor, Greece, and Rome. Thus New Testament role models that are African are significant, which is why Simon has been an important biblical figure for the Black Church.

We must be careful, however, not to draw too strong a focus upon Simon; he is not the main character of the scene. A different (and perhaps better) homiletical use of Simon here is as a lens through which to view the scene christologically. Mark's presentation of Jesus' needing someone to carry his cross (cf. John 19:17, where Jesus is explicitly described as carrying his own cross) presents him as weakened by the arrest, trials, and mocking he has willingly endured. A way to show the significance of this depiction of Jesus' vulnerability is to contrast it with the images of God's sovereignty and strength in other parts of the canon.

Creating a litany of such images will effectively set up the contrast: God as creator who simply speaks the universe into being (Gen. 1); God who liberates the Israelite slaves (Exod. 1–15); God as the only one truly able to provide and redeem (over and over again in the Psalms). An especially provocative contrast is the story of Uzzah in 2 Samuel 6. David and his men are escorting the ark of the covenant on an ox cart. When the cart shakes, Uzzah reaches out his hand to keep the ark from tipping over but is struck down for daring to imagine that God needs Uzzah to steady God. Jesus, on the other hand, needs Simon to carry his cross. The almighty God is made known through the vulnerability and weakness of Christ.

A second homiletical path into this passage is through the reference to the two thieves crucified with Jesus, "one on his right and one on his left" (v. 27). This is less a case of asking the congregation to identify with the characters and more one of zooming in on their appearance as a starting point, and then zooming out to get the whole of the scene in perspective. For Mark, their appearance in this scene is not coincidental; it is theological. The language used to describe the thieves at the crucifixion echoes an earlier scene in the Gospel (10:35–40). After Jesus predicts his passion and death for the third and final time (10:32–34), James and John make a request of him: "Grant us to sit, one at your right hand and one at your left, in your glory" (10:37). Jesus responds by saying, "To sit at my right hand or at my left is not mine to grant, but it is for those for whom it has been prepared" (10:40).

Mark 15:21–32

Theological Perspective

estrangement from God as a result of sin. The action of Christ allows humans to recognize our guilt for sin, repent, and receive forgiveness; thereby the barrier to relationship is removed.

4. Using distinctions made by Kant, some late-nineteenth-century theologians conceived salvation as a kind of moral perfection. The old condition involves being subject to physical and emotional impediments to right action. Christ teaches and demonstrates the moral law, even in the face of death. This action makes possible the new condition of growth in the moral life.

5. Without limiting human life to morality, other theologies express salvation as the recognition and power to begin living in the way that humans were created to live, before the effects of sin began to distort genuine humanity. These theologies engage the life and death of Jesus as salvific, placing the crucifixion into the larger context of an entire life of self-giving love. The old condition is a truncated version of human life; the new condition involves the fullness of head, heart, and action relationally engaged directly with God.

6. Liberation theologies of the twentieth century identify the old condition as estrangement from other human beings and God, which results from the misdistribution of resources and power, which is sinful and evil. Salvation, the new condition, is an economic, social, and political human community that supports the flourishing of all persons, particularly previously marginalized persons. God's identification, through Jesus Christ, with the marginalized makes possible joint effort to challenge and transform patterns of sin that are larger than individuals and locales.

All six of these themes can be read, in one way or another, onto the narrative Mark provides. It is striking, however, that the text does not support an understanding of salvation that conceives of it as a ticket to one's place in heaven after one's death. Jesus' promise from the cross, "Today you will be with me in Paradise" (Luke 23:43), is not included in Mark's account. Perhaps this omission has occurred because a "ticket to heaven" delays the new condition, placing it outside of human history, and does not change relationships with God or neighbor in the present. The various meanings of "save" in Mark's account emphasize immediacy, whether in the mouths of those who do not believe, or in the centurion's witness. Mark's narrative invites the reader to join that witness.

CATHERINE L. KELSEY

Pastoral Perspective

have unintended consequences. You may have been compelled—perhaps even against your will or best judgment—to pick up another's responsibility or suffering, and you were changed by carrying their burden. Whenever we have volunteered to pick up a heavy load someone is carrying in the workplace or in the family, we are at minimum reminded that our life is not something we possess.

Those who follow Jesus live as he did; they live in constant awareness of need or what Arthur McGill calls "resting-in-neediness." We are related to God as receivers, that is, in terms of our neediness. Jesus does not promise to eliminate our neediness, but following him will entail an intensification of need as we learn, with Simon of Cyrene, what it means to take up his cross. "The condition to which we are led by Jesus is a condition of *utter dependence* on God and *relative dependence* on one another."[2]

A year after my friend Mark had surgery for a malignant brain tumor, it was determined that the lesion on the left temporal lobe had continued to grow. In that year, he had learned the difference between surrender and resignation. Surrender was not giving up, but giving over in trust. He remembered the words from the cross as Jesus was dying: "Into your hands I commend my spirit" (Luke 23:46). Even before he spoke those words, Jesus had handed over his burden to Simon to carry. Because Mark trusted deeply the promise of God's faithfulness in his life, he was able to trust others to care for him. Like Jesus on the path to Golgotha, Mark knew well the work of dying that he needed to do, but the journey belonged to God and depended on trusting others along the way.

HERBERT ANDERSON

---

2. Arthur McGill, *Death and Life: An American Theology* (Philadelphia: Fortress Press, 1987), 90.

Exegetical Perspective

Place, by a conscript (v. 21), probably due to Jesus' severely weakened condition from the flogging he has received.[2] The crucifixion itself is described in just three words, "they crucified him" (v. 24). The charge over him reads, "The King of the Jews" (v. 26), ironically true despite the repeated mocking of Jesus' Roman executioners (15:2, 9, 12, 18; see 15:32). Then, as he hangs on the cross, Jesus is derided, mocked, and taunted by those passing by, by the chief priests and scribes, and finally even by the two bandits being crucified on either side. His only words are, "My God, my God, why have you forsaken me?" (15:34), before he gives a loud cry and breaths his last (15:37). Mark has described nothing that mitigates the depth of Jesus' suffering.

Nevertheless, what are we to make of the way that Mark has woven the language of Scripture into the specific details of his account of Jesus' death? The offer of wine in verse 23 echoes Proverbs 31:6; the dividing of his clothes and casting lots in verse 24, Psalm 22:18; the mocking and shaking the heads in verse 29, Psalm 22:7; the offer of sour wine in verse 36, Psalm 69:21. Most significant of all, Jesus' cry of abandonment in verse 34 is a direct quotation of Psalm 22:1. Psalms 22 and 69 are both "passion psalms" that tell of one who suffers undeserved terrible violence at the hands of others, but in the end receives God's help and vindication. Does Mark intend for us to see that the suffering of Jesus will also be vindicated by God?

ERNEST HESS

Homiletical Perspective

These linguistic connections make it clear that, within Mark's narrative world, the thieves are those for whom the right-hand and left-hand places have been prepared. What this signifies theologically, therefore, is that Mark understands the cross (instead of the resurrection) as Jesus' moment of glory. Preachers can offer congregations a new perspective on the meaning of the cross by exploring the irony of calling this tragic moment of vulnerability and suffering the time of Jesus' glory and what it means to "see" Christ's glory in contemporary experience.

Finally, preachers might want to lift out of the text the way Mark narrates the actual crucifixion itself. Since the first hanging of a crucifix in a sanctuary or the first passion play, preachers have loved to dwell homiletically on the details of Jesus' crucifixion: the nails piercing his skin, the echo of the hammer, the blood dripping down his arms, the pressure on his lungs and heart, and on and on. Describing the gruesome elements of Jesus' suffering in as much detail as possible has been used by preachers to show the level of Christ's sacrifice, and thus to evoke deeper emotional response on the part of the hearers.

Even though it is commonly recognized that Mark's Gospel presents the cross as the climax of the good news, the evangelist does not give details of Jesus' being placed on the cross. He narrates the actual crucifixion in the simplest terms: "And they crucified him" (v. 24). It is the fact of Jesus' crucifixion and death that is theologically important for Mark, not the description of it. Noting Mark's direct and sparse description gives congregants the opportunity to critique the bloody and grotesque images and interpretations of the crucifixion in art and the media that are meant to create an intense emotional response; instead, Mark's account offers them room to explore the significance of the cross for contemporary theology in new ways.

O. WESLEY ALLEN JR.

---

2. So Raymond E. Brown, *The Death of the Messiah: From Gethsemane to the Grave. A Commentary on the Passion Narratives in the Four Gospels* (Garden City, NY: Doubleday, 1994), 2:914–15. This severe weakness would also account for the quickness of his death, which surprised Pilate (Mark 15:44).

Mark 15:33–41

³³When it was noon, darkness came over the whole land until three in the afternoon. ³⁴At three o'clock Jesus cried out with a loud voice, "Eloi, Eloi, lema sabachthani?" which means, "My God, my God, why have you forsaken me?" ³⁵When some of the bystanders heard it, they said, "Listen, he is calling for Elijah." ³⁶And someone ran, filled a sponge with sour wine, put it on a stick, and gave it to him to drink, saying, "Wait, let us see whether Elijah will come to take him down." ³⁷Then Jesus gave a loud cry and breathed his last. ³⁸And the curtain of the temple was torn in two, from top to bottom. ³⁹Now when the centurion, who stood facing him, saw that in this way he breathed his last, he said, "Truly this man was God's Son!"

⁴⁰There were also women looking on from a distance; among them were Mary Magdalene, and Mary the mother of James the younger and of Joses, and Salome. ⁴¹These used to follow him and provided for him when he was in Galilee; and there were many other women who had come up with him to Jerusalem.

Theological Perspective

The death of Jesus is at the center of soteriology. In many theologies it is how Christ saves human beings and the whole creation. Noticing how Mark's account relates to each major line of interpretation invites the reader to notice how much one is reading into this sparse text. Four images form the basis for the main theological trajectories of interpretation: (1) sacrifice, (2) victory, (3) legal transaction, and (4) example. What follows connects this text's details to each trajectory.

1. Religious sacrifice can be offered as penance, that is, as a mediating act that offers surplus value that spills over and benefits persons associated with the offering. Sacrifice may also be offered to God simply because God is God. In the theological tradition that emphasizes the three "offices" of Christ—prophet, priest, and king—the priestly office is associated with sacrifice. Christ as priest became the offering itself. Mark's account, however, does not offer many details that suggest this interpretation. The tearing of the temple curtain is a clear reference to a location where sacrifice is made, although the text leaves ambiguous what meaning to ascribe to its destruction. More distant allusions might also be found in the presence of the women, seen as beneficiaries of the sacrifice, and the centurion, seen as the priestlike presider over the sacrifice.

Pastoral Perspective

Some years ago, when our grandson Jonah was about two and a half, his parents left him in the care of grandparents for two days. To make it easy for everybody, they left while he was napping. When Jonah awoke from his nap in a strange house to discover that his parents were *gone*, he sobbed for the better part of a day with the same lament: "*mommydaddygone.*" It was a futile lament, even if it was necessary. His parents *were* absent, and his protesting would not bring them back. In that moment, Jonah had no assurance of their return. Sometimes, of course, the child's lament of protest will bring the parents back from the theater or a romantic dinner. It is always a struggle for parents to know how long to let the protest go, especially when an infant's cries penetrate a parent's heart.

From infancy to the end of a life, lament over the absence of someone we love is a common occurrence. Children who become homesick at summer camp or in the first year of college may have found absence from home intolerable, even though some might argue that such pain is necessary to foster full maturity. The dread of abandonment for those who are dying or the anguish of separation after a death are other instances in human life when the pain of absence is particularly acute. Martin Marty's reflections after the death of his wife, aptly called *The Cry*

Exegetical Perspective

Mark's spare account of the death of Jesus is dark, both literally and metaphorically. As he tells it, "when it was noon, darkness came over the whole land" (v. 33). According to Raymond Brown,

> The intervening three hours since the soldiers crucified Jesus at 9 A.M. (15:25) have been filled with the mocking of Jesus on the cross by the passersby, by the chief priests, and by the co-crucified. No human beings have shown mercy to God's Son, and now at noon in the realm of nature the whole earth goes into darkness. . . . Even on the most obvious level of symbolism, the darkness adds to Mark's dour description of the crucifixion. . . . However, there is a deeper level of reference.[1]

This deeper, theological level of reference is revealed through the Old Testament parallels. Unnatural darkness appears as a heavenly sign of God's judgment in the exodus story (Exod. 10:21–23) and the Hebrew prophets (Isa. 13:10; 50:3; Ezek. 32:7–8; Joel 2:10, 31; and esp. Amos 8:9). Toward whom is the divine judgment signaled by the uncanny darkness at noon directed? Is it directed toward those who are crucifying and mocking Jesus? Is it directed at the one who hangs on the cross in

---
1. Raymond E. Brown, *The Death of the Messiah: From Gethsemane to the Grave. A Commentary on the Passion Narratives in the Four Gospels* (Garden City, NY: Doubleday, 1994), 2:1035.

Homiletical Perspective

The previous passage (15:21–32) narrated the morning of Jesus' crucifixion. This passage picks up at noon but moves (in darkness) to midafternoon in a glance. Were the author interested in emphasizing the details of Jesus' suffering, this would not be the case. On the other hand, whereas the previous passage focused on details around Jesus' crucifixion, this one does not allow the readers to take their eyes off Jesus as he dies. We look through the eyes of the narrator, the centurion, and the women.

The death of Jesus is difficult to preach because of the central and much debated role it plays in Christian theology. Mark's version of the story of Jesus' death, however, is especially difficult to preach, because it (and not the resurrection) is the climax of the story, the point to which the whole of the narrative has been leading. Mark offers a corrective Christology that lifts up the cross to a community of faith, a community that has in some way been deemphasizing the cross inappropriately in their understanding of and devotion to Jesus as the Christ. To preach this passage, then, is in some sense to preach the whole of the Gospel of Mark.

To do so, a preacher must rehearse stretches of Mark's narrative in a few sentences. One way to do this is to focus on the disciples and their developing characterization. The fishermen follow when Jesus

Mark 15:33–41

Theological Perspective

Another interpretation using the image of sacrifice focuses specifically on the suffering of Jesus as the sacrifice that he offered. More details in Mark's account support this interpretation, particularly the fact that Jesus died through crucifixion, the appeal to Elijah for help in distress that was not answered, and Jesus' use of the opening words of Psalm 22 expressing forsakenness. Even though the bystanders misunderstand Jesus when they think they hear him appeal to Elijah, both the mention of such an appeal and the absence of a response heighten the narrative's expression of distress. The previous pericope in Mark adds to the list of suffering both the refusal of the sedative sour wine and the mocking by passersby, priests, and scribes, and even the other two persons crucified with him.

Jesus not only suffers pain and death; he is abandoned and isolated emotionally and socially throughout the experience. The text does not explain why Jesus' suffering is necessary, nor is the physical suffering described in graphic detail. In contrast, his relational isolation is highlighted by the details in the account of those who deride him, his speaking Psalm 22, the unresponsiveness of Elijah when called upon by bystanders, and the women who have been so close to him in Galilee "looking on from a distance." Jesus very clearly suffers abandonment in Mark's account.

2. A second line of interpretation works with the image of victory: Christ's victory over Satan, sin, and death (objective use), or victory over the existential forces that threaten authentic human existence (subjective use). Both interpretations are supported primarily by the miraculous events narrated in verses 33–41. Darkness covers the land for three hours while Jesus is hanging on the cross; at his death there are two unexpected "witnesses": the temple curtain, tearing apart from top to bottom, and the centurion responsible for the killing, exclaiming, "Truly this man was God's Son!" Additional witnesses are at a distance and are women, yet their testimony to unwelcome death is received and transmitted—a miracle of sorts. The repeated references to Psalm 22 in the account also suggest miraculous fulfillment of prophecy.

Subjective use of the victory image is supported by the darkness, Jesus' experience of forsakenness, and the surprising faith response of the centurion after witnessing the manner of his death—although the precise details of what changes the centurion's perception remain unclarified in the text. Perhaps this ambiguity itself supports a subjective, internal, individualized interpretation of the victory.

Pastoral Perspective

of Absence, include a poem by John Crowe Ransom that describes absence in the heart as a "furious winter blowing."[1]

Martin Marty describes the Roman Catholic theologian Karl Rahner as a "wintry sort." One of the consequences of experiencing the absence of God, Marty suggests, is that it creates a wintry sort of spirituality that is in "solidarity with those whose horizon excludes God."[2] At the least, a "wintry spirituality" might include the cry of Jesus from the cross, because we understand absence as consequence of presence in life and faith.

While we cannot know the mind of Jesus, we do know the psalm he quotes. It is a lament psalm in the rich tradition of protesting God's seeming absence from the center of our lives. The lament psalms are filled with terror and hurt and bewilderment and confusion about the absence of God when life is not going well, or with anger that life is not going well because God is absent. While a lament protests against God's absence, it eventuates in a renewed sense of God's presence. "Where have you been, God? If there was ever a time I needed you, this was it. Where were you? I have been calling and calling, and I have left messages, but there was no response. I needed you to be there for me. Where are you?"

C. S. Lewis gave this experience of God's absence a powerful image in the little notebook *A Grief Observed*, which he wrote after the death of his wife Joy. "Go to God when your need is desperate, when all other help is vain, and what do you find? A door slammed in your face, and the sound of bolting and double bolting on the inside. After that, silence. You may as well turn away. The longer you wait, the more emphatic the silence will become."[3]

Some people of faith have been offended by the vividness of Lewis's anger toward God in the midst of his grief. However, because the protest of C. S. Lewis occurs in the same covenant with God as the lament psalms, it does not and cannot end with absence. God repents. God comes back. God hears the argument and returns. There is trust in the promised presence of God again—until the next time of absence. The psalms of lament are possible because of the promised covenant with God, who will not be absent permanently. Our deep conviction that God is present and active in our lives includes the possibility of absence. It is precisely in those

---

1. "Winter Remembered," from *Selected Poems by John Crowe Ransom* (New York: Alfred A. Knopf, 1924), quoted in Martin E. Marty, *A Cry of Absence: Reflections for the Winter of the Heart* (Grand Rapids: Eerdmans, 1997), 1.
2. Ibid., 56.
3. C. S. Lewis, *A Grief Observed* (New York: Seabury, 1961), 9.

Exegetical Perspective

the darkness? Simply noting the darkness, the narrator does not give an explanation.

Instead, Mark records a loud cry spoken by Jesus in his native tongue of Aramaic: "'*Eloi Eloi, lema sabachthani?*' which means, 'My God, my God, why have you forsaken me?'" (v. 34). What are we to make of this heart-rending cry of abandonment? In Mark's account, these are the only words Jesus speaks as he dies on the cross. They are, however, a direct quotation from Scripture, from the opening line of Psalm 22, details of which have infused Mark's description of the crucifixion (vv. 24, 29). This psalm vividly expresses the lament of a person crying out to God in the midst of terrible, unjust suffering. This goes on for twenty-two verses before it ends with praise to God for deliverance in the last eight verses. There is no praise spoken by Jesus on the cross; there is only the agony of feeling forsaken in the midst of suffering. Still, the vindication of the psalm lies hidden, beneath the surface, as a possibility.

The last time Mark's readers heard Jesus pray was in Gethsemane, when he also addressed God in Aramaic, as *Abba,* Father (14:36). On the cross, now that Jesus is drinking the cup he had asked his *Abba,* Father, to remove from him, the cup of his blood "poured out for many" (14:24), the more intimate form of address has been replaced by the more distanced and generic *Eloi, Eloi,* "My God, my God," of the psalm.

The bystanders misunderstand what Jesus has said, and wonder aloud if Elijah will come rescue Jesus. The popular Jewish expectation was that the prophet Elijah, who had been taken up to heaven alive (2 Kgs. 2:9–12) would return at the "end of the age" (Mal. 4:5). The offer of sour wine (v. 36) creates a moment of heightened expectation among the bystanders, even as it weaves into the passion story another allusion to the Scriptures (Ps. 69:21). Mark's readers, however, know that Elijah has already come in the person of John the Baptist and been killed (9:13; 6:15); so there will be no rescue by Elijah.

Instead, having let go a "loud cry" (v. 37), Jesus expires (*exepneusen*). It is not clear from Mark's use of the aorist participle ("after he gave a loud cry") if this is a second cry or if it refers back to the anguished cry of verse 34. Either way, Mark's unrelentingly bleak passion narrative seems to have reached its grim conclusion. Having been betrayed, arrested, interrogated, condemned, denied, mocked, tortured, and crucified, Jesus expires with a pain-filled cry of abandonment by God as the last words from his lips. There is nothing in Mark's account to

Homiletical Perspective

calls them, even though Mark does not describe them as having any prior knowledge of Jesus' teaching or healings (1:16–20). Such obedience draws us (the reader, the congregation) into identifying with them. All seems well until the parables discourse in chapter 4. Jesus makes clear that the parables divide those who hear him into insiders (those who understand) and outsiders (those who do not). The problem is that the disciples do not understand the parables, and Jesus must explain the teachings to them (4:10–13, 34). The ultimate insiders are starting to look like outsiders. Immediately after the parables scene, Jesus stills a storm because of the disciples' fear. He accuses them of having no faith, and they end up asking who this person is they have been following (4:35–41). Mark is slowly turning the tables on the reader. Having identified with the disciples when they seemed to "get it," the author makes us question our understanding of Jesus when our representatives are confused.

Skip ahead to Jesus' three passion predictions. Each time the disciples respond inappropriately. The first time (8:27–33), Peter rebukes Jesus. This shows that in his prior claim that Jesus is the Messiah, Peter knew the right words to speak but not the content that filled out that language. The second time Jesus tells the disciples of his impending death, they begin arguing about who is the greatest (9:30–37). In other words, they are arguing about who will be his successor. After the third and final prediction, James and John ask to sit on Jesus' right and left when he comes into his glory (10:32–45). Clearly, they fail to understand fully who Jesus is as the Son of God.

This progression of misunderstanding leads us back to our passage and Jesus' death. The disciples have denied and deserted him (14:27–31, 50, 66–72). Standing there "facing him" is only the centurion, the symbol of Roman oppression, an unclean Gentile—indeed, the very man who killed Jesus. This man is the only human in the entire Gospel of Mark to recognize and proclaim Jesus as God's Son (v. 39). This dynamic could be seen as an indictment of the disciples (and the readers) for misunderstanding who Jesus is, but the message is really more of an invitation than a condemnation. The readers are invited to see Jesus anew through his death.

In terms of homiletic potential, this dynamic today allows the congregation to consider that their status as "insiders" may not mean they really understand who Jesus, the Christ, the Son of Humanity, the Son of God is. Sometimes being too familiar can lead us to see Christ as we want to see Christ, to

Mark 15:33–41

Theological Perspective

3. The image of a legal transaction, in which merit is transferred from Christ to those who have not earned it, is the basis for the most familiar atonement theories, in which Christ (a) represents humans in species solidarity or (b) makes it possible for us to participate with him in his death and resurrection or (c) in substitution for us takes on the punishment due to sinners. None of the details in Mark's account of Jesus' death clearly points to the transfer of merit, in contrast, for instance, with Jesus' words of forgiveness from the cross found in Luke 23:34. A representative role for Christ (theory a) is alluded to in the ascription "The King of the Jews" but is not elaborated. Mark's account undermines the proclamation of our participation in dying and rising with Christ (theory b) by describing social distance between Jesus and everyone around him rather than identification. The details related to suffering noted above may be interpreted as Christ's accepting the punishment earned by sinners (theory c). This acceptance without protest may then be interpreted as obedience unto death, which is necessary if his merit is to be exchanged for rightful punishment of others. The text allows this interpretation of the suffering but does not require it.

4. The image of an example is ambiguously supported by the text. The derision of the priests and scribes is explicitly based on the *inadequacy* of Christ's example: "let the Messiah, the King of Israel, come down from the cross now, so that we may see and believe" (15:32); but he does not come down, and they do not believe. The centurion's witness, in contrast, does demonstrate the immediate impact of the way Jesus dies and the revelatory power of his example. Exemplarily, all of Jesus' attention in Mark's account is directed toward God alone; he is not distracted by the passersby, religious leaders, the bandits, or even the persons trying to offer him sour wine.

Mark adds a detail that is curious in all four lines of interpretation: "Jesus gave a loud cry and breathed his last." Cry of victory? Cry of defeat? Mark leaves both options open. The Gospel text puts a stark series of events before us. The text might have made those events easier to hear if it had narrated them using a fully formed theological explanation of what God has done. Mark chooses not to do that.

CATHERINE L. KELSEY

Pastoral Perspective

moments when God seems most absent that God is paradoxically present in hidden and unexpected ways, bringing life and hope from death.

Many people today face agonizing struggles with the absence and presence of those they love. Parents of a young adult child who boarded a bus and has not been heard from since live with the ambiguous grief of physical absence and yet psychological presence. Children or a spouse of someone whose obsessive work life or lingering depression make him or her physically present but psychologically absent know this pain. When someone we love is afflicted with the disease of Alzheimer's, we know well the struggle of physical presence and psychological absence. It is the permanent presence of absence.

The disciples' lapse into sleep in Gethsemane was already a moment of absent presence on the journey of Jesus to his death. Whether God had abandoned Jesus as well as he hung on the cross is immaterial. Jesus felt enough alone to invoke a lament psalm protesting God's absence. That cry of Jesus is a liberating word for anyone living with absence or grieving ambiguous and complicated loss.

Ironically, our lamenting the absence of God may also be our best witness. Consider the centurion who heard the fully human cry of Jesus and decided that this was truly the Son of God. The centurion's words emerge solely from his witnessing the passivity of the suffering Christ. When our laments have a ring of authenticity because they come from deep anguish, they may also become an invitation to faith in God, particularly for those who live with the presence of absence.

HERBERT ANDERSON

Exegetical Perspective

mitigate the depth of Jesus' suffering. In the darkness Jesus hears no affirming voice from heaven (cf. 1:11; 9:7). Elijah does not come and take Jesus down from the cross. It is not the temple (13:2), but Jesus who has been destroyed.

At this point Mark's narrative takes a surprising, dramatic twist: "the curtain of the temple [*to katapetasma tou naou*] was torn [*eschisthē*] in two, from top to bottom" (v. 38). This symbolic act of God rending the temple curtain (God's agency is implied by the use of the passive voice) is a heavenly sign of judgment against the temple and chief priests who condemned Jesus (14:58–64). It vindicates Jesus by signaling the eventual destruction of the temple as he has predicted (13:2).

Apparently, it is seeing God's sign of tearing the temple curtain at the death of Jesus that evokes from the Roman centurion the unexpected confession, "Truly this man was God's Son!" (or "a son of God," v. 39). This Gentile is the first person in Mark's Gospel to name Jesus as God's Son. Up to this point, only the heavenly voice of God at Jesus' baptism and transfiguration (1:11; 9:7) and the demons (3:11; 5:7) have called him God's Son. Mark's Gospel insists that human beings cannot fully understand Jesus as God's Son before the Son of Man has suffered (9:30–32).

Mark closes this section with another group of unexpected witnesses to these events. "There were also women looking on from a distance" (v. 40). According to Ched Myers, Mark describes this group of women "in a manner that virtually epitomizes them as model disciples. Not only did they 'follow' (*ēkolouthoun*), but they 'served' Jesus throughout the Galilean ministry.... The women have done the two things the males in the community found impossible: they have been servants, and they continued to follow Jesus even *after* he was arrested and executed."[2] Disciples such as these will recognize in the crucified one God's Son.

ERNEST HESS

Homiletical Perspective

create God in our image. What might a new perspective on Jesus' death today help us to see about Christ that we have missed, beyond the clichés we use to describe that death? Who might the centurions of today be who can proclaim Christ anew to us from outside our Christian household?

A radically different route to preaching this text is to focus on Jesus' cry of lament at the moment before he breathes his last (vv. 34–36). Jesus' utterance comes from Psalm 22:1, "My God, my God, why have you forsaken me?" At first glance, it looks as though Mark presents Jesus as ending his life in doubt. This has been a difficult biblical pill to swallow for many who believe that doubt is the opposite of faith. How could Jesus, the Son of God, who knew in advance he was going to die, experience such anguish?

What Jesus' lament does for the contemporary church is to legitimate lament as an important element of the Christian faith. In his last moment, Jesus does not deny God. Indeed, his words acknowledge the silence of God as God at his moment of death. It is an incredible act of faith to trust God enough to question God concerning why we are suffering, or why (more broadly) evil is at work in the world. Preachers who lift up Jesus' cry as a positive model for being faithful and connect his lament with the much-attested tradition in the Hebrew Bible of naming our pain to God and asking, "How long?" offer permission and absolution to those in the pews who feel this sort of angst and anguish at times, but feel they must repress it.

Indeed, to follow such a sermon with a prayer of communal lament for the many forms of meaningless suffering, hatred, discrimination, oppression, violence, and death will give congregants words to use in their individual prayers. Of course, following the model of Psalm 22, the lament can lead to expressions of trust in God's steadfast love. Thus the bad news of the world is answered by the good news of God's providential and merciful care for us.

O. WESLEY ALLEN JR.

---

2. Ched Myers, *Binding the Strong Man: A Political Reading of Mark's Story of Jesus* (Maryknoll, NY: Orbis Books, 1988), 396.

Mark 15:42–47

⁴²When evening had come, and since it was the day of Preparation, that is, the day before the sabbath, ⁴³Joseph of Arimathea, a respected member of the council, who was also himself waiting expectantly for the kingdom of God, went boldly to Pilate and asked for the body of Jesus. ⁴⁴Then Pilate wondered if he were already dead; and summoning the centurion, he asked him whether he had been dead for some time. ⁴⁵When he learned from the centurion that he was dead, he granted the body to Joseph. ⁴⁶Then Joseph bought a linen cloth, and taking down the body, wrapped it in the linen cloth, and laid it in a tomb that had been hewn out of the rock. He then rolled a stone against the door of the tomb. ⁴⁷Mary Magdalene and Mary the mother of Joses saw where the body was laid.

Theological Perspective

This story presents Joseph of Arimathea claiming the body of Jesus from Pilate. Some commentators have deemed it as containing probable historical accuracy while some details, e.g., that the disciples have fled, have "no detectable theological motive."[1] Besides the introduction of characters seemingly marginal to the narrative of Mark's Gospel as a whole, here we find interesting references to Jesus' body, through which the evangelist and his community may be trying to tell us something of theological significance.

Not much is left of the "Jesus movement" by the time we get to this point in the story. Most of his followers, as well as his close associates (the disciples), have fled. The exception, besides this Joseph of Arimathea, is a small group of women, those who were "watching" (NRSV "saw," v. 47) where the body of Jesus was put to rest. This part of the narrative begins in the evening of the day of Jesus' crucifixion. The Sabbath day is about to commence, and the body of Jesus needs to be removed from the cross. Joseph is described as a "respected member of the council" (v. 43; maybe the Sanhedrin, though we are not really given details), apparently an affluent

[1]. See, for example, Eduard Schweizer, *The Good News according to Mark*, trans. Donald H. Madvig (Richmond: John Knox Press, 1970), 361.

Pastoral Perspective

The memory of Jesus' death is a somber one with cosmic salvific significance for believers. The liturgy of Good Friday evokes profound sorrow for sin and high resolve to work for an end to its consequences in injustice, violence, and estrangement. Sometimes overlooked in this weighty set of considerations, however, are smaller, quieter dimensions of the Lord's death that evoke emotions less dramatic but equally converting. One such emotion is simple human tenderness; for after all else is said and done, ethically and soteriologically, Jesus' saving death remains the death of someone we loved. This is the reason that Joseph, who saw to it that this beloved body received a modicum of respect, became an object of grateful affection in Christian tradition. All four canonical Gospels record this deed of his (and no other), all four want us to know his name, all four want us to know where he hailed from, an obscure village called Arimathea.

Listeners can easily relate to the tradition's regard for Joseph. The indignation aroused when unscrupulous undertakers improperly handle or dispose of bodies; the anguish of 9/11 families upon learning that unidentified remains recovered from the rubble were discarded in the trash; the furor over whether to allow photographs of flag-draped caskets arriving

Exegetical Perspective

In the Gospel of Mark the closest followers of Jesus fail to comprehend the suffering that awaits him in Jerusalem. From their early misunderstandings (e.g., 4:13, 40, 41; 6:37, 51, 52), to their inability to comprehend his explanations (8:31–33; 9:30–32; 10:32–34), all the way to the Passover meal they share with Jesus on the night before he is handed over to the Romans (14:17–25), they remain clueless. In the closing chapters of Mark's Gospel, their failure to grasp the meaning of his ministry intensifies, resulting in denial and abandonment (14:32–52, 66–72). As darkness covers the whole land, the cry from the cross in 15:34 is a powerful portrait of this forsaken Jesus. In the distance, however, Mark tells us there are women looking on, women who used to follow him.

The next six verses (15:42–47) contain a brief description of the burial of Jesus. At the request of Joseph of Arimathea, Pilate gives him the body of Jesus, which Joseph wraps in a linen cloth and places in a tomb hewn out of the rock. A stone is then placed over the opening. This is fairly typical of Jewish burials in Roman Palestine, where often bodies were placed in a long narrow chamber cut out of the rock, and a stone (sometimes round, sometimes rectangular) was placed at the mouth of the tomb. After

Homiletical Perspective

When read as part of the Liturgy of the Word on the Sunday of the Passion/Palm Sunday, Mark 15:42–47 is easily lost in the larger story. Indeed, in the short version of the Gospel for the day, it is bracketed as an optional part of the lesson, pointedly making the centurion's declaration "Truly this man was God's Son" (15:39) the last words of the readings. Similarly, the tendency to meld all the versions of the passion into one makes it easy to miss the poignancy of Mark's story, since the "information" from other Gospels smoothes out the difficulties. In preparing to preach on Mark 15:42–47, therefore, the first task is to read it carefully in its own terms and then within the context of Mark's larger story.

As the conclusion to the passion narrative of 14:1–15:41 and in anticipation of the resurrection in 16:1–8, Mark's story of the burial establishes the reality of Jesus' death, which some groups in the early church questioned (like those addressed in the epistles of John). The centurion, who was summoned from the scene of the crucifixion, serves as the chief witness (vv. 44–45). While Pilate's "wondering" if Jesus was already dead adds tension to the scene, his acceptance of the centurion's report confirms the death; his release of Jesus' corpse (*ptōma*) makes

Mark 15:42–47

Theological Perspective

or wealthy man, someone with some standing, "respected" (by whom? by the community? by the authorities?), who goes to Pilate to ask for the body of Jesus.

According to the narrator, Joseph's petition was considered a bold move, a daring act, since he went directly to Pilate himself. Why he did it remains obscure except for the narrator's declaration that Joseph "was himself waiting expectantly for the kingdom of God." As is well known, the message about the "kingdom of God" occupied much of Jesus' own proclamation, as testified by Mark and the other Synoptic Gospels. In order to be understood, this "kingdom message" and hope ought to have been understood by many of Jesus' own listeners, because it was part of the religious ethos of Palestine in Jesus' times.

Joseph of Arimathea may have been a pious man, even a secret admirer of Jesus. We might assume that Joseph, like others, sympathized with Jesus from a safe distance and, also like a few others, had a belief, desire, and expectation for the coming rule of God in the Jewish people's lives. In any case, what matters to the narrator is the fact that Joseph made a bold move, a courageous and pious deed, that was worth reporting.

Joseph claims Jesus' body (Gk. *sōma*, v. 43). After a procedural assurance to Pilate that Jesus was already dead, Pilate grants Jesus' corpse (as the text says, using the Gk. *ptōma*, v. 45) to Joseph. It seems likely that the writer wants to point his readers in the direction of a different perception of the same reality. Jesus is dead, a corpse, and there is no more to it—at least in Pilate's understanding. There is also the writer's—and his community's—respectful treatment of and belief about Jesus' body (*sōma*), not merely a corpse (*ptōma*), because he is the one who, as they had come to believe, would not remain in the tomb. They know of the Lord's body, which is a living body for the community of believers who worship and celebrate Jesus.

Because of what we know of the early Christian witness, the possibility is strong that Mark the evangelist is trying to tell us something. On the one hand, these references to body (*sōma*) and corpse (*ptōma*) emphasize the reality of Jesus' physical or material existence: his real body, his life as a human being in flesh and blood, his true humanity, with all that goes with being a body. This is an emphasis that Christian writers and communities would insist on: the reality of Jesus' fleshly humanity, his being like one of us. On the other hand, we have the distinction between Pilate's naming of Jesus' corpse and the narrator's

Pastoral Perspective

at Andrews Air Force Base: these and other instances point to the strong sense of obligation people feel toward their dead. For all our modern haste to be quit of the sights, smells, sounds, and residue of death, when such outrages occur, we find that we still care deeply about the body; we still identify the life and love of a person with even the smallest relics of the physical self; we are still filled with gratitude for everyone whose ministrations to our dead are marked by the respectful intentionality that befits the dignity of every human life.

Few listeners in the congregation will never have had to deal with postmortem decisions. Cremation or burial, open casket or closed, whether to dress the body in dark colors or bright, whether to remove a wedding band worn for more than sixty years: these are the "nuts and bolts" of human grief, the last loving services the bonds of affection require; and we want to get them right. Weaving together the story of Joseph's care for the body of Jesus with stories of our own care for the dead, the preacher might help the congregation appreciate more deeply the full humanity of Christ.

To be sure, we believe that his death was an unjust martyrdom of world-changing importance, but it was also, in the end, "just" a death, a death like all the deaths we ourselves have known. Faith in Jesus' resurrection does not entitle us to regard his death as somehow different; it was as final, lamentable, and unfathomable as any other. Its character as the death of a Savior does not obscure its character as the death of a man. That he was "buried" is the tradition's way of making the point.

Exegetes quarrel about whether this passage describes an honorable burial carried out by a secret disciple risking his considerable reputation, or a dishonorable burial for a shamed Jew carried out by a dutiful councilor (not necessarily a disciple) seeking only to close a chapter opened when he cast his vote to condemn. Some think Mark may subtly be shifting blame for Jesus' death away from the Romans and onto the religious leaders by hinting that the council itself, represented by Joseph, is having guilty second thoughts. Others think Mark has invented the entire episode as a cover story for the probability that Jesus was not buried at all, but left on the cross to be pecked to bone by birds, or tossed out along with the bodies of other miscreants to be picked over by dogs. We are well within our devotional rights to sidestep these debates from time to time, take Joseph and his pious deed at face value, and be moved as human beings by the human care he shows for the mortal remains of our brother and friend.

Exegetical Perspective

the body decomposed in the chamber for one year, the bones were collected and placed in an ossuary.[1] A closer look at the characters Mark has included in this story provides a useful lens for addressing this passage as a whole.

Joseph of Arimathea. It is difficult to ascertain exactly who Joseph is and why he is requesting the body of Jesus for burial. He is described as "Joseph of Arimathea," leaving the reader to determine whether he is a resident of Arimathea and serves on the council there (Mark uses *boulē* rather than *synedrion* [cf. 15:1], possibly to distance Joseph, a positive character, from the recent decision of the Sanhedrin to seek the execution of Jesus) or someone who is on the Jerusalem council and has come from Arimathea. Joseph is described as one who "also himself" (v. 43) anticipated the kingdom of God. One reasonable interpretation of this description is that Joseph's eschatological view is in sympathy with the apocalyptic teaching of Jesus. This does not, however, explain whether he is actually a follower of Jesus.

Regardless, it is noteworthy that Mark describes Joseph as "daring" or "plucking up his courage" (NRSV "went boldly," v. 43) to request the body of Jesus directly from Pilate. Why a member of the council would need to be courageous to request the body raises several questions. Is it because of how any association with this crucified one might be viewed by Pilate, or is it Mark's way of contrasting the courage of this stranger with the cowardice of Jesus' own disciples or family—both of whom are conspicuously absent? (Or both?)

Once he receives the body, Joseph procures a linen shroud, wraps the body, and buries it. As stated earlier, this is fairly typical of Jewish burial, and it includes most of the usual elements of burial—with the obvious exception of anointing. Perhaps Mark expects the reader to remember the anointing of Jesus in Bethany (14:8), or perhaps the author is anticipating the anointing by the women in 16:1. The reader is left wondering if the absence of the anointing is due to Jesus' dishonorable burial (as argued by Raymond Brown in his *Death of the Messiah*)[2] or is simply due to lack of time, as evening on the day of Preparation is approaching.

---

1. For more on death and burial in first-century Palestine, see Byron R. McCane, *Roll Back the Stone: Death and Burial in the World of Jesus* (New York: T. & T. Clark, 2003).
2. Raymond E. Brown, *The Death of the Messiah: From Gethsemane to the Grave. A Commentary on the Passion Narratives in the Four Gospels* (New York: Doubleday, 1994).

Homiletical Perspective

it unambiguous.[1] Mary Magdalene and Mary the mother of Joses, who had looked on the crucifixion from afar (15:40), serve as corroborating witnesses, in that "they saw where he was laid" (v. 47).

A surprise witness to the reality of Jesus' death is Joseph of Arimathea, whose role is so poignant in Mark. For it is Joseph, and Joseph alone, who attends to Jesus' burial. Not only does he ask for the body, but he also buys a linen cloth, takes the body down from the cross, wraps it in the cloth, lays it in the tomb, and rolls a stone against the door. This is quite remarkable for someone who had been part of the council that condemned Jesus for blasphemy and delivered him over to Pilate (14:64 and 15:1).

Indeed, Joseph's actions are so striking that preparing to preach on this passage cannot stop with the simple observation that Jesus was well and truly dead—however important that may be theologically or historically. Mark is pointing in other directions, which opens interesting ways to explore the passage for use in preaching. Here are three:

1. Though we can never know why Joseph buried Jesus, we can ask why the writers of the Gospels tell his story as they do. Matthew (27:57) and John (19:38) refer to him as "a disciple of Jesus," suggesting that he acts from real devotion. Mark, however, does not call Joseph a disciple. In fact, reporting that Joseph buries Jesus may be Mark's way of emphasizing yet again how the disciples fail. Earlier in the Gospel of Mark, they do not understand Jesus (8:21), rebuke him (8:32), abandon him (14:50), and deny him (14:68, 70, 71). Now they do not even show up to bury him. So whatever motives we might attribute to Joseph, Mark puts him in sharp contrast to the disciples, all the more so in that he describes him as "a respected member" of the opposition (15:43).

Also, earlier in this Gospel Jesus chastised the disciples for trying to stop an outsider from casting out demons in Jesus' name (9:38–41). By referring to Joseph as one "waiting expectantly for the kingdom of God" and acting on it, therefore, Mark may be including Joseph in the wider circle of the kingdom. If so, Mark's story of Joseph invites openness to "outsiders," among whom the sermon might include other churches, synagogues, mosques, and any other person or group that might prove to be an unexpected ally in the work of the kingdom.

---

1. The NRSV reads "body" (*sōma*) here, as do some ancient manuscripts. The starker term "corpse" appears in a number of important manuscripts, however, and is to be preferred, since it is more difficult and since its directness reflects Mark's style.

Mark 15:42–47

Theological Perspective

own assertion that this is no longer any corpse, but the body of the one Jesus Christ, the one who is proclaimed throughout Mark's Gospel as Lord and Messiah. Moreover, Jesus' body is a present reality in the worship of the earliest community, first of all through the subsequent witness to a risen Jesus, and then also through the experience of the sacramental meal in those earliest Christian assemblies.

Joseph wraps the body of Jesus in linen and puts it in a tomb. For all of Joseph's interest and care, this is no doubt a hurried burial, given the fact of the Sabbath eve, but also given the fact that Joseph has to "gather courage" to ask Pilate for Jesus' body after he has been crucified as an enemy of the state for sedition, executed as a criminal. None of the proper rites and anointing of the body are performed. The one who claimed to be lord even of the Sabbath (2:28) cannot be given a proper burial for the sake of following Sabbath rules and order. Once the stone of the tomb is rolled in place, the story is basically over.

However, is it really the end? On the one hand, this looks like a logical conclusion to the story of Jesus, following the flow of the events that lead to his death by crucifixion. On the other hand, there is one element in this story that seems to try to alert us to what is to come next. Some women are mentioned at the end of the narrative (v. 47). They have been mentioned before this text, in 15:40, where they watch from afar as Jesus dies. In both these instances, these women are ever "watching," and they also see where the body of Jesus is laid. As we know, the witness of the women is to become more significant in the passages that follow.

NELSON RIVERA

Pastoral Perspective

At the end of this passage, Mark tells us that "[the women] saw where the body was laid" (v. 47). Whether the women accompanied the body openly or watched what became of it from afar, the text does not say; but it wants us to know that Joseph was not the only one who cared about what happened to Jesus' body. There were witnesses. Mark may have added this line as part of an overall polemic against the claim that Jesus did not die, or was not buried, and thus did not rise from a tomb. Whatever the evangelist's intention, it is a poignant detail. Those who loved him "saw." They took note. They will remember and tell.

By means of this final line, the preacher might lead listeners from a consideration of Jesus' death as the death of a loved one whose departure from this life was indeed cruel, but at least noticed, marked, and mourned, to a consideration of the deaths of countless human beings whose cruel departures are made all the more cruel for being unnoticed and unmourned. These are the expendable refuse of many indifferent empires. No one sees where their bodies are laid. They are deprived of the loving obsequies of dutiful friends. No one can find them. If anyone tells their stories, they tell them in fear, hushed and hastily, looking over their shoulders.

The preacher may wish, therefore, to have listeners dwell for a while, like the women at Jesus' burial, taking careful note of bodies interred not under mounds of love and in tenderness, but under mounds of hatred and greed, power and pride. If they dwell there for a while, watching—if they "see"—they will be able to find their way back to that place, time and again, bringing others with them to notice too. Then, enlisting the Power that once burst from a rock-hewn grave, they will raise the forgotten also from the dead.

MARY LUTI

Exegetical Perspective

Having wrapped the body, Joseph places it in an unspecified tomb and closes it with a stone. How does he put the stone in place? What is the shape of this stone? Whether round or rectangular, it is unlikely that one person could secure the stone at the opening of the tomb. (Mark does perhaps offer a clue in 16:6 as the young man tells the women, "See the place where *they* [emphasis mine] laid him.")

Pilate and the Roman Centurion. The brief appearance of Pilate and the centurion in this burial narrative serves to validate the death of Jesus and thereby remove any doubt about the resurrection. This is further underscored by the use in verse 45 of *ptōma* ("dead body"), a harsh term designating a body killed by violent death. This is in contrast with the use of the word *sōma* in verse 43. After the roles they played in the death of Jesus, the brief appearance by these two is quickly followed by their disappearance from the story. In his commentary on the Gospel of Mark, Joel Marcus suggests the disappearance of these imperial powers is indicative perhaps of Mark's opinion that imperial powers only seem to rule.[3]

The Women. With one simple statement (v. 47) Mark brings two of the women previously mentioned back into the story line. We met these women in 15:40, where they were described as watching from afar. In verse 40 Mark lists "Mary of Magdala, Mary the mother of James the younger and Joses, and Salome" as women who had followed and served Jesus. With the exception of Simon Peter's mother-in-law (1:29–31), Mark has not mentioned women serving Jesus. The mention of two of these three women here in verse 47 keeps them fresh in the reader's mind and sets the stage for the women's discovery (16:5) of the empty tomb. Had they not been present to see where Joseph buried Jesus, they would not have known where to go to anoint the body. Their appearance, though brief, alerts us to the fact that there is more to come.

JUDY YATES SIKER

Homiletical Perspective

2. In the NRSV, Joseph "went boldly to Pilate" to ask for Jesus' body (v. 43). The RSV says that Joseph "took courage and went to Pilate." We might even translate the phrase as "Joseph dared to go to Pilate." Each has a slightly different nuance, though all imply that a conscious decision was involved in asking for the body of Jesus and that it required overcoming fear. Because none of the other Gospels alludes to Joseph's courage, Mark's attention to it is noteworthy.[2] Here again, therefore, Mark finds a way to put Joseph in contrast to the disciples, so that, without calling him a disciple, Mark offers Joseph as a model for those who want to be disciples.

Exploring this aspect of the text could be an occasion for recognizing and giving thanks for Christians whose faith requires boldness and courage in the face of opposition and danger, whether from officials in power or from mobs. It could also recognize the quiet courage of those who face other threats—terminal illness, depression, or addiction. More daringly, the preacher might include, as an extension of Joseph's boldness, Christians and others who stand up against oppression in the workplace, in the voting booth, or even in churches and other houses of worship where people are denied justice. As the Gospel of Mark shows again and again, being a disciple has its costs. Boldness, courage, and daring will be required—sometimes openly, sometimes quietly.

3. Another point of entry into Mark 15:42–47 is Joseph's attending to the body of Jesus as ministry in the face of death and dying. Among the various ways of envisioning this story is to contemplate one of the many Orthodox icons of the deposition of from the cross. One can also imagine it by observing the tenderness of a nurse or hospice volunteer arranging the sheets of someone who has just died after a long illness or when viewing news videos of a soldier carrying the body of fallen comrade. These too can be acts of discipleship.

OLIVER LARRY YARBROUGH

---

3. Joel Marcus, *Mark 8–16* (New Haven, CT: Yale University Press, 2009), 1076.

2. John develops the story differently. Though Joseph is a disciple of Jesus, he goes to Pilate "secretly, for fear of the Jews" (John 19:38).

Mark 16:1–8

¹When the sabbath was over, Mary Magdalene, and Mary the mother of James, and Salome bought spices, so that they might go and anoint him. ²And very early on the first day of the week, when the sun had risen, they went to the tomb. ³They had been saying to one another, "Who will roll away the stone for us from the entrance to the tomb?" ⁴When they looked up, they saw that the stone, which was very large, had already been rolled back. ⁵As they entered the tomb, they saw a young man, dressed in a white robe, sitting on the right side; and they were alarmed. ⁶But he said to them, "Do not be alarmed; you are looking for Jesus of Nazareth, who was crucified. He has been raised; he is not here. Look, there is the place they laid him. ⁷But go, tell his disciples and Peter that he is going ahead of you to Galilee; there you will see him, just as he told you." ⁸So they went out and fled from the tomb, for terror and amazement had seized them; and they said nothing to anyone, for they were afraid.

Theological Perspective

The Sabbath is over. Life returns to its routine, except for those women followers of Jesus, the ones who were left "watching" in the previous passage. There is one thing they still need to do: to offer a proper burial to Jesus, including the anointing of the body, as was the custom. They may be forgetting, or did not know, that another woman, the one that Jesus declared would be remembered by her deed, had already anointed Jesus with oil (14:3–9).

Early in the morning the women went to the tomb, wondering who would help them to roll the stone away (although it is strange that they had not thought about it before). However, by the time that they got to the tomb, the stone had been already rolled aside. Inside the tomb they encountered "a young man dressed in a white robe," a messenger who told them that Jesus had been raised from the dead and was not to be found in the tomb any longer. The young man had a word for them all, the disciples and the women: to go to Galilee, where they would see Jesus. In Greek, the meaning of "appearance" is "to be seen." Moreover, to "see" Jesus may refer to an encounter with him, or even to his next (or second) coming.

The mandate to go to Galilee also makes sense in this way: they were going back to the place where everything had begun for Jesus and his disciples.

Pastoral Perspective

This text is thought to be the original ending of Mark's resurrection story. Commentators never fail to note that unsatisfied scribes later appended a longer, happier ending, bringing Mark's tentativeness into line with the largely affirmative mood of the other canonical accounts. The elusive character of this ending may not have pleased our ancestors, but it is well suited to the spiritual lives of many modern Christians—especially young adults—who do not seek propositional truth so much as wisdom, nor the anchor of clarity so much as the steady companionship of an inquiring community. For them, the joyous ancient Christian greeting, "*Christ is risen! Risen indeed!*" is best uttered hesitantly—not because they doubt or deny it, but because, like Mary pondering the salutation of Gabriel, they have no idea what such a mysterious greeting might mean.

Neither, apparently, do the women at the tomb. The two Marys and Salome flee from it, traumatized and unwilling to speak, despite the young man's instruction (v. 8). We are not told the reason for their reaction, but we should be glad Mark does not overexplain. His reticence clears a space for us to feel whatever we feel when confronted with the Easter proclamation, without having to shoehorn our response into the usual template of triumphant exuberance. Easter is neither a documentable historical

Exegetical Perspective

Mark 16:1–8 has long been thought to be the original ending of Mark's Gospel, even though it is not a particularly satisfying ending, and even though the passage has garnered much scholarly debate. Most scholars have maintained that Mark originally ended with 16:8, but there are some (e.g., Robert Gundry, Rudolf Bultmann) who argue differently. Gundry, for example, says verse 8 is the beginning of the next section—which has been lost. Gundry and others base their conjecture in part on what they think is the improbability of a sentence's ending with the particle *gar* ("for").

More scholars, however, argue that verse 8 as the final sentence better explains the additional endings for Mark's Gospel (the so-called "shorter ending" and the "longer ending"). Even if we can come to terms with this somewhat unsatisfying ending to Mark's Gospel, the history of tradition demonstrates that others were not able to do so, and we have twelve additional verses that have been added to the Gospel (16:9–20). Although we remain bothered by the absence of fully developed resurrection appearances, clearly more important to Mark is the stark, bold testimony that "he has been raised" (v. 6).

In turning directly to 16:1–8, we meet the women first introduced to us in Mark 15:40, two of whom are mentioned again in 15:47, coming to the tomb

Homiletical Perspective

Mark 16:1–8 is the most challenging of the resurrection stories in the Gospels, largely because of verse 8. The NRSV renders it: "So they went out and fled from the tomb, for terror and amazement had seized them; and they said nothing to anyone, for they were afraid." Most readers find this an unsettling conclusion to the story. That is precisely where the preacher's task begins: Do I work with the text as it is, or look to other versions that are more satisfying?

Looking for another ending is a time-honored approach to the Gospel of Mark, for while some very important manuscripts end with 16:8, others add a "short ending" (usually attached without verse numbering) that indicates the women did in fact give a brief report to the disciples and that Jesus later appeared to the disciples and sent them out to proclaim eternal salvation. Still other manuscripts have a "longer ending" (usually numbered vv. 9–20) in which Jesus appears to Mary Magdalene, who then "told those who had been with him." Both the shorter and longer endings indicate that many scribes who copied from versions of Mark that ended with verse 8 thought the story needed a better conclusion.[1] Whether or not Matthew and Luke were

---

1. Most Bibles have footnotes explaining the history of the various endings of Mark. See also the exegetical commentary in this volume.

Mark 16:1–8

Theological Perspective

Galilee has theological meaning. Galilee was the land of a marginal people, a different people, known to many by their accents, clothing, and probably by their demeanor. The women were too afraid or shocked to say anything to anyone. As the Markan story ends, we are left to ponder the true meaning of Jesus' rising and of these instructions.

Surely there are different ways to end a story. One way is to offer a neat conclusion, leaving no loose ends. Another way is an open-ended narrative, where the reader can be said to finish the story from her or his own point of view and incorporate her or his own experience. Probably nothing will speak more powerfully to an individual than this latter possibility. What about a story with clues as to what follows, the kind a committed reader, one with some stake in the story, would probably pursue? This is how I see Mark's ending of his Gospel. This ending is not so much an accident, the result of clumsy editing, or necessarily one that demands later additions. This seems to be a message inspired by theological convictions. The problem is that we may not be in a situation to perceive or understand all the clues left for the anticipated or assumed readers.

Yes, many readers and commentators—not the least Matthew and Luke—have found incompleteness at the end of this Gospel. However, it may have been intended this way, and the reasons are probably theological as well as literary. The story of Jesus does not end with his death. God has done something new, something unheard of to this point. The crucified is now the risen one, but risen to a new life, rather than simply to more of the same life. This is a better ending to the story than where it was left in the previous chapter. In this sense there is completion, a kind of open-ended closure.

Nevertheless and at the same time, there is no final and conclusive end in sight, since the life of the risen one continues. It is time to dig, to struggle in order to understand what this Jesus is all about. The immediate need and command is to go back to Galilee, the place and context where everything began for Jesus and the disciples. Galilee was a beginning without clear boundaries. The same can be said of the return to Galilee now. It is equally open ended.

This points to a deep truth about Jesus and Jesus' God. Their future is ever open, and yet trustingly inviting. The God who did a new thing in Jesus is the one who is working a future for the disciples in Jesus.

A sense of incompleteness to the story clearly reflects the trust that it is God who is at work. God is

Pastoral Perspective

event nor a poetic metaphor for renewal; it is a great mystery of faith. As such, it addresses us in sovereign freedom and in multiple complex and inexplicable ways. No matter how much glorious light it sheds, at its core is the darkness of unknowing. If over time a preacher succeeds in guiding a congregation down into those depths, it may not be only the pious women who flee, impelled by a fear that is the beginning of wisdom.

Because this would be a good thing—anytime we get real, it is a good thing—the pastoral preacher will be a restrained preacher, offering little more than Mark does: a tomb empty of Jesus, and a promise that we will be met by him, if we go where he has gone. If we say much more, eschewing a necessary modesty and too cleverly overexplaining the Easter texts, we may not leave room for the disciples who are our listeners to write their own endings, and we may end up domesticating Easter's fearsomeness.

Among other things, Mark's honesty about the traumatic character of Easter stands as a counterpoint to the relentlessly sunny, unwrinkled religiosity that characterizes American religion, especially the religion that has taken center stage in American politics. The brave preacher may wish to note the way candidates speak of Christian faith as if it were as plain as a thirty-second spot or as neat as a set of talking points.

That there is something obscure and even scary about this faith messes with the message: Christianity is the cornerstone of American exceptionalism; God's realm is aligned with American empire; Jesus is a founding father. No one seems to appreciate the irony, for example, of tipping our patriotic hats to a savior who was tortured by legitimate state authority. No one seems to feel queasy about proclaiming allegiance to a man who was judicially executed, even though innocent. No one seems to think it could be dangerous, or even just embarrassing, that he now lives fully everywhere, including in states where legal murders are a dime a dozen. No one seems the least bit worried that it could be payback time.

That it is not payback time may be more the Easter miracle than the resurrection itself. Mark's young man is explicit about it. The women are to tell the disciples and Peter (or as other translations have it, *even* Peter) that Jesus is waiting in Galilee (v. 7). The deliberate inclusion of Peter should take our pastoral breath away. In this and other Easter accounts, there is not a single recriminating word about the past, no demands for an explanation, nothing that would settle the score. The risen Christ upbraids the disciples

Exegetical Perspective

with spices for preparation of the body—preparation rendered impossible by the rush to bury Jesus before the onset of Sabbath (see exegetical commentary on 15:42–47). This is the third of three appearances in Mark (see also 15:40 and 15:42). Now, with the ending of the Sabbath, the action can resume and the women return to the place where they saw him laid (15:47).

In Mark 16:3 the reader is given a window into their thinking. After the Sabbath they bought the spices and were prepared to anoint their teacher's body; but how, they wondered, would they be able to get to him? The stone that was rolled to cover the entrance of the tomb was very large, and they could surely not move it. This preoccupied them right to the point of arrival. When they arrived, they looked up and were amazed. The stone was gone! Entering the tomb, the women were alarmed to see, not the body of their beloved teacher, but a young man dressed in white, a young man who addressed their fear and both explained where Jesus was and instructed them about what they were to do next. Not surprisingly, this unexpected encounter filled them with fear. Even though this apparently angelic figure told the women not to be alarmed, they fled and said nothing to anyone. (How could they not be alarmed?!)

As Mark sets the stage for this story, one notes a typical Markan doubling: very early in the morning, when the sun had just risen. The metaphor of the sun is important here, as the darkness of the crucifixion now gives way to the morning light. One is reminded of the words of Psalm 30:5: "weeping may linger for the night, but joy comes with the morning." Although the reader may be prepared for the "joy in the morning" as he or she is drawn into Mark's story, in narrative time the women were concerned with the practicalities of anointing this body as, with recently purchased spices in hand, they arrived at the tomb.

Indeed, the women in the story were preoccupied with the task at hand. Their realization that the stone had been removed from the entrance to the tomb was preceded by their looking up (*anablepō*). The action captured in this Greek word is associated three times in Mark with an impending miracle or revelation of divine power (6:41; 7:34; 16:4).[1] Here, the manifestation of divine power, the removal of such a large obstacle, results in overwhelming fear.

---

1. Joel Marcus, *Mark 8–16* (New Haven, CT: Yale University Press, 2009), 1084.

Homiletical Perspective

based on the Gospel of Mark, they too end the story with the women reporting to the disciples what they had seen (Matt. 28:8 and Luke 24:9). So too does the Gospel of John (20:1–13), though it differs considerably from Mark in other details. It is clear, therefore, that the other Gospels in the New Testament and most manuscripts of Mark make the preacher's task easier, at least with regard to moving beyond the women's fear. Even if one concludes that a sermon focusing on this passage needs to move beyond verse 8, however, it is worth spending time with the story as it is.

Attention focuses on the women who come to anoint Jesus' body (v. 1). Mary Magdalene, Mary the mother of Joses, and Salome had also been present at the crucifixion (15:40). Mary Magdalene and Mary the mother of Joses appear in 15:47 as witnesses to where Jesus' body was laid. So, on first reading, we are drawn to them as ones who care for Jesus, but Mark's treatment of them is not so simple. At the crucifixion, they look on "from a distance." When they see where the body was laid, they take no part in taking it down from the cross, wrapping it in the cloth, or laying it in the tomb (15:46). Then when they see the young man in the tomb "they [are] alarmed" (v. 5). Finally, verse 8 raises the tension even more: when the young man commands them to tell the disciples he will see them in Galilee, "they went out and fled from the tomb, for terror and amazement had seized them; and they said nothing to anyone, for they were afraid." The words now are jolting, or at least should be. They are not what we expect or want to happen. We might even add that it is *not* what happened, since the gospel was in fact proclaimed and the church is evidence of it. Nonetheless, this is how Mark reads. But why?

It is not to denigrate women, for the disciples are no better. We expect more than Mark credits to them. They never seem to understand Jesus' teaching. Even when Peter confesses Jesus is the Messiah, he rebukes Jesus when Jesus announces he must suffer and die. Then in the end they forsake him in the Garden of Gethsemane, leaving him to die alone. Again and again, therefore, we are disappointed—at the disciples whom Jesus called and at the women who followed him.

How might we invite a congregation to respond to this way of reading Mark's story of the empty tomb? One way is to suggest that our disappointment in the disciples and the women is just the response the author of this Gospel wants from us. For the moment we see they are wrong is the

Mark 16:1–8

Theological Perspective

not done with the Christian community yet. Is God ever done? Surely not short of the kingdom of God coming in fullness—as in the expectation of Joseph of Arimathea and others. It says that God was at work in Jesus, is still working through Jesus; therefore, any sense of completion, any expectation that all things must and will come to fruition, lies in God and God alone. "Go to Galilee" and wait!

The best of the Christian faith and message is forward looking, and forward moving. The future is God's; God does things from the future that burst into our present. Just so in Jesus' resurrection: God working in the present moment from the vantage point of the future. God raised Jesus, as God will do with all the dead in Christ. This is prolepsis, showing in advance what God has in store, what God is able to do, as the promise and guarantee of the expected and believed future for us. Jesus has his future secured, thanks to God's action in the here and now, and we are promised that very same future in Jesus Christ. This word becomes the foundation of Christian hope in the here and now.

It is important to see that hope is not founded on human capacities to "finish the story" or "finish the project" that Jesus began. It is not necessarily about finding our own way from now on. All hope is founded on God—Jesus' God—who can finish the job for and with Jesus, whom God raised from the dead. Despite a seemingly truncated ending to the Gospel, the story of Jesus continues, its significance continuous with and through us.

NELSON RIVERA

Pastoral Perspective

for being slow to believe he is living, but he never holds them accountable for having been cowards while he was dying. That someone would withhold judgment is hard enough for the guilty to accept; but that he would show singular affection to the one who failed most spectacularly is almost unbearable. The Living One, it appears, is not content to forgive: he really does forget. It is as if nothing ever happened. This is the painful way he drives us deep.

In our human experience there is no such thing as a world free of revenge. Both our inner and outer worlds are structured for blame. It makes satisfactory sense of life. Yet the Christian tradition claims that Easter inaugurates a world free of reprisal. It is the down payment on a world structured for mercy, according to a new pattern laid down by an innocent who returns without blame for the guilty, who does not require satisfaction or scapegoats, and whose love for us pours from the empty tomb.

If Easter is true in this way, it carries a potent ethical and political charge. It posits a way of relationship, intimate and global, that is a far cry from the age-old, score-settling way of mayhem. It changes everything. No wonder it inspired fear, and even revulsion, in the first disciples. We would all feel better if we got punished. We would all feel better if we could keep on punishing. The charge, though, in this text is otherwise; and sooner or later, as the women in Mark's account eventually did, we will stop being traumatized by such love and begin to speak of it boldly, delivering the awful good news of reconciliation to every Peter out there who believes things cannot be helped and will never change; that memories and politics and families cannot be healed; that a cowardly screwup can never again be worthy of love; and that we are doomed to die in our sins as God looks on with righteous satisfaction. Not so, says Easter, not so. The pastoral preacher will make sure people know it.

MARY LUTI

Exegetical Perspective

Their fear and amazement are compounded when they encounter a living being inside the tomb. The description of this figure, "a young man, dressed in a white robe, sitting on the right side," calls to mind for the reader the expected figure, Jesus, as well as the transfigured Jesus (9:3) and the enthroned Jesus (12:35–37).[2] Perhaps they encountered this one as an angel. Although Mark does not call him an angel, the encounter fits the literary trope of fear and reassurance. The admonition, "do not be afraid [NRSV "alarmed"]" is a familiar one for the reader and echoes the words to a frightened Joseph in Matthew 1:20, to a perplexed Mary in Luke 1:30, and to terrified shepherds in Luke 2:9, 10. Clearly the women were astonished, not only by the very presence of this young man, but also by his declaration. This heavenly being knew not only whom they sought, but also where to find him. Although he instructed them to go and tell the disciples what they had learned, they fled in terror and told no one.

It is certainly understandable that their reaction to this angelophany and this news would leave them fearful and mute, but it is a less than satisfying ending for our Gospel story. (The Gospels of Matthew and Luke, who use Mark as a written source, have also found this ending unsatisfying.) Here the characters were maintaining that messianic secret they were encouraged to keep earlier; now that they were told to go and tell, they were silent. The women were not silent in the parallel passages in the Gospels of Matthew and Luke. In Matthew 28:8, they ran to tell the disciples, with fear and great joy. In Luke 24:9 they shared the message with the eleven and all the rest.

This is not the resurrection story we anticipate for our bold Easter proclamations. However, there is more here than meets the eye. In the messenger's admonition to the women we hear that Jesus "has been raised; he is not here. . . . He is going ahead of you to Galilee; there you will see him, just as he told you" (vv. 6–7). So the believer steps beyond this Gospel ending, going to see Jesus in Galilee.

JUDY YATES SIKER

Homiletical Perspective

moment we begin to recognize what the author wants us to understand: that the call to discipleship is serious and engages us deeply. By responding to the ending of Mark's Gospel by saying, "No, this is not the way it should end," we have begun to see what a better end might be—and to develop a strategy for bringing it to completion.

To take this further, the sermon might address the deep emotions that run through the text: alarm, terror, amazement, and fear. These are not emotions the preacher can or should try to evoke in a sermon. That would lead to trivialization. However, to acknowledge that most of us experience such emotions from time to time (even if we have not had the kinds of encounters Mark describes) is to open new ways to explore faith where people really live. Looking back at Jesus in the Garden of Gethsemane is one way to explore how Mark treats Jesus' being "distressed and agitated" in the face of death (14:33), as would his cry "My God, my God, why have you forsaken me?" (15:34). Might these stories change the way we look at the women's fear—and at our own?

Going further still, a sermon could ask what the women might have feared. Ridicule? Failure? Rejection? If these are possibilities, how might the announcement "he has been raised" and "he is going ahead of you" help address them?

From quite another direction, preparing for a sermon on Mark 16:1–8 could involve looking at responses to Jesus throughout this Gospel. The NRSV uses forms of "amaze" in 5:20; 5:42; 10:32; 12:11 (a quotation from Ps. 118:23, which might be a key to understanding Mark's usage); 12:17; and 15:5. "Fear" or "afraid" appears in 5:15; 6:50; 10:32; 11:18 and 32. The disciples are "terrified" of Jesus in 6:50 and 9:6. Such reactions surprise many of us, but are central to Mark's story. Are there ways to recapture a sense of awe in a technological age?

OLIVER LARRY YARBROUGH

---

2. Adela Yarbro Collins, *Mark: A Commentary* (Minneapolis: Fortress Press, 2007), 795.

Mark 16:9–20

⁹[[Now after he rose early on the first day of the week, he appeared first to Mary Magdalene, from whom he had cast out seven demons. ¹⁰She went out and told those who had been with him, while they were mourning and weeping. ¹¹But when they heard that he was alive and had been seen by her, they would not believe it.

¹²After this he appeared in another form to two of them, as they were walking into the country. ¹³And they went back and told the rest, but they did not believe them.

¹⁴Later he appeared to the eleven themselves as they were sitting at the table; and he upbraided them for their lack of faith and stubbornness, because they had not believed those who saw him after he had risen. ¹⁵And he said to

Theological Perspective

It is common in scholarly circles to speak of this passage as a later addition to the text, as an attempt to provide a proper ending or conclusion to this Gospel. This passage is usually referred to as the "longer ending." This addition to Mark was probably put together by drawing from the other canonical Gospels, including passages from Matthew (chap. 28) and especially from Luke (chap. 24) and John (chap. 20). In any case, as we have it, this passage has been part of the received text and treated as such for centuries now. It has a place in the history of interpretation as well as in the imagination of the Christian people.

Unlike the passages leading to this one, here only one of the women is named, Mary Magdalene, with an interest in her personal witness as the one from whom Jesus "had cast out seven demons" during his ministry (Mark 16:9; Luke 8:2). Details matter, and they matter for a reason. Among those details, signs performed by Jesus have peculiar importance. The signs lend validity to the view of Jesus as a miracle worker. Miracles are signs from God for those who believe. However, and despite Mary's witness, we are told that the other disciples did not believe her word about the risen Jesus (Mark 16:13; Luke 24:11). As it had happened before during the life of Jesus, the disciples did not believe the report of witnesses.

Pastoral Perspective

In these final verses of Mark's Gospel, the risen Lord makes an almost comical effort to get noticed. He appears first to Mary. She reports her sighting, but no one believes that "he had been seen by her" (v. 11). (The "her" in this verse is fascinatingly specific. Is it general disdain for women's testimony, or a hint that she—that is, a person like "her"—was in some way especially unworthy of belief?) When Mary's testimony fails to persuade her weepy brothers, Jesus appears again, this time to two disciples on the road. Their witness also fails to sway "the rest" (vv. 12–13). Exasperated, Jesus goes to them himself, "upbraiding" them for their stubborn unbelief (v. 14). The text does not record their reaction to this dressing down, but some Christians in our pews would be happy to supply one: "Give them a break, Jesus! Give me one too. I'm pretty sure I wouldn't have believed it back then, and I'm not at all sure I believe it now."

It was not easy to "believe in the resurrection" in the first century; it is not any easier in the twenty-first. Many of the Gospels' postresurrection stories are frank about this vexed nature of Easter faith. The pastoral preacher will reassure us that if we have trouble believing, we are in good company. Some preachers may exhort their listeners to master doubt. Others may explain that doubt is a necessary

them, "Go into all the world and proclaim the good news to the whole creation. ⁱ⁶The one who believes and is baptized will be saved; but the one who does not believe will be condemned. ¹⁷And these signs will accompany those who believe: by using my name they will cast out demons; they will speak in new tongues; ¹⁸they will pick up snakes in their hands, and if they drink any deadly thing, it will not hurt them; they will lay their hands on the sick, and they will recover."

¹⁹So then the Lord Jesus, after he had spoken to them, was taken up into heaven and sat down at the right hand of God. ²⁰And they went out and proclaimed the good news everywhere, while the Lord worked with them and confirmed the message by the signs that accompanied it.]]

Exegetical Perspective

English readers of Mark's Gospel may notice unusual notations within the text of the last chapter of Mark. While the two oldest complete manuscripts of Mark end with 16:8, there are other early manuscripts that include additional verses. In many translations two sentences are included between 16:8 and 16:9. This is referred to as "The Shorter Ending of Mark" and is followed by verses 9–20, often called "The Longer Ending of Mark." While most scholars agree that the original ending of the Gospel is verse 8 (see exegetical commentary on Mark 16:1–8), scholars do not agree on why the Gospel ends so abruptly or on the origin or authorship of verses 9–20. If Mark 16:1–8 is the original ending of Mark, many questions remain for the reader. Not only does this mysterious, enigmatic ending offer no resurrection appearances, but the first witnesses to the empty tomb flee in fear and say nothing to anyone. Readers of the biblical text, however, may not even notice that there is a problem, because our English Bibles include twenty verses in the final chapter of Mark's Gospel and verses 9–20 are replete with resurrection appearances. Jesus comes to Mary Magdalene, then to two of his disciples, and later to the rest of the followers.

Close reading, however, suggests that the verses beyond 16:1–8 are even more enigmatic that the first eight. Here the reader learns that signs will

Homiletical Perspective

Mark 16:9–20 is a collection of postresurrection stories that brings the narrative of the Gospel of Mark to a close. Found in both the Vulgate and the Received Text on which the King James Version was based, these verses have been part of the traditional text of Mark from very early and continue to be included in whole or in part in most lectionaries today. Questions about these verses began to arise, however, with the discovery of important biblical manuscripts that do not have them. Taking these discoveries into account and acknowledging the serious questions they raise concerning the original shape of Mark, the editors of most modern Bibles set 16:9–20 apart from the rest of the text and add footnotes to inform readers of the various ways ancient manuscripts bring the Gospel of Mark to a conclusion.

Sermons are not the best occasion to treat questions of the canon, of course, though the preacher need not avoid them completely. In this case it may be especially appropriate to acknowledge the questions about a text, since at least some in the congregation will be curious about the way they appear in their Bible. However one treats canonical questions in the sermon, attending to them will inform and enrich preparation for preaching on this passage.

We begin with the challenge of reading 16:8 as the end of Mark's story. To put it bluntly, how could

Mark 16:9–20

Theological Perspective

The unbelief of disciples and others plays a crucial, albeit complex, role in Mark. Unbelief can become an opportunity to clarify who this Jesus actually is. It may be the occasion for public witness through interrogation and dialogue on the part of Jesus with an interlocutor, a literary device to keep the reader's interest in the story. It can also have theological significance, as in the contrast between belief and unbelief, in the subtle dynamic between these two almost simultaneous moments of a single person's mind—for instance, in the public confession of a man who struggled with both belief and unbelief. After having declared to Jesus himself his own belief, he immediately asked for Jesus' help: "I believe; help my unbelief!" (Mark 9:24). The addition of an ending to the Gospel gathers this motif in an interesting way: this time the disciples do not believe the report of witnesses to Jesus' resurrection and appearances.

Unbelief is responded to here with a list of signs and wonders that would follow the disciples as they engage the proclamation in continuity with the mission of Jesus. Emphasis is on the disciples' mission to many, across national boundaries. Moreover, the disciples themselves will be able to perform these signs, almost on demand. A ministry of healing will be part of their mission.

As we can expect from a narrative summary that has been put together by relying heavily on materials provided by and copied from other written Gospels, this ending lacks some of the distinctiveness of Mark. Ambiguity and messianic secrets are gone, although the disciples' stubbornness remains—witness the risen Jesus scolding them for this very thing (v. 14). The late editor of Mark adds consistency and a sense of completion to this ending for the sake of clarity of message, but also for harmony with the other Gospels. This is more than a matter of changed theological views after the resurrection. This ending actually introduces new theological elements to Mark's presentation of Jesus.

The problem is that this ending tinkers with the open-ended nature of Jesus' story according to Mark. It wants to impose completeness upon what is unfinished, conclusiveness upon what is provisional, definitive belief upon searching faith in the future of Jesus' message and life. This ending tries to make the disciples and all followers into spectators rather than active participants in Jesus' story, introducing a conditional note into Jesus' message. In this ending, to believe clearly brings salvation, and not to believe brings condemnation for everyone. The latter

Pastoral Perspective

dimension of faith. Both messages are commendable. However, in either case, if the preacher frames "believing" as a matter of individual effort to acquire personal conviction about the credibility of doctrinal affirmations, she will have missed something crucial.

In this text, as in other postresurrection stories, disbelieving disciples are not scolded solely for having personally refused to accept the "fact" that Jesus lives. There is also an ecclesial dimension involved, and it may be pastorally important to dwell on it. The Lord upbraids the eleven, we are told, because "they had not believed *those who saw him*" (v. 14). In other words, in order to disbelieve the mystery of the resurrection, each disciple first had to mistrust and dismiss the sister or brother who brought the testimony. The failure was not so much dogmatic as communal, the resistance not so much to a belief as to the experience of fellow believers. The "growing edge" was not assenting intellectually to a proposition but opening themselves to the revelatory character of the spiritual lives of other disciples.

Belief looks different—and more possible—in the context of a community of disciples. It could help people who struggle with creedal affirmations to hear that believing, although important, is not the goal; rather (as John says in his story about Thomas), believing is ordered toward life, and that life is found most richly through insertion in a fellowship of faith. It is instructive that when the eleven finally believe that day, they are together, sitting at the table (v. 14). As in the Emmaus story, Christ is known (and thus believed) when disciples gather, sit, break bread, and rehearse the story of love. Believing is not a private accomplishment, but a shared project of trust and mutual traditioning in the fellowship of believers of all times and places who, by the power of the Spirit, edify one another in strength and supply one another in lack.

We might learn from this and other postresurrection stories to speak of the church as a company of disciples who pool the gift of faith, inquiring into, testing, grounding, and trusting each other's experiences of God, thereby building a great storehouse of faith small and great, new and seasoned, questioning and serene, from which we all borrow and to which we all lend, generation to generation, until we see him together, until he comes again. To this end, pastors might encourage the revival of the practice of testimony in congregations where public faith sharing is unknown. Often what people lack is not faith, but language, practice, a sincere welcome of their insights, and a safe space in which to declare to "the

Exegetical Perspective

accompany those who believe, and these signs include exorcisms, speaking in tongues, snake handling, and immunity from poison drinks. Indeed, a reading of verses 9–20 provides the reader not only with resurrection appearances, signs, and portents accompanying believers, but also an ascension story. Whatever questions are left by 16:1–8 are addressed and answered in 16:9–20.

Close reading also suggests that the longer ending reflects knowledge of the other Gospel resurrection and postresurrection stories. For example, verse 9 seems to echo elements from John 20:1–18 and the description of Jesus coming first to Mary Magdalene, and also the description in Luke 8:2 of Mary Magdalene as the one from whom seven demons had been cast out (as if it is the first time readers would have met her). This apparent knowledge of or dependence on the other Gospels continues through the next several verses of 9–20. In verse 11 we hear echoes of Luke 24:11 and the disciples' unbelief upon hearing the news that Jesus is alive. Similarly, Mark 16:12 seems to be an encapsulation of the Emmaus story of Luke 24:13–31 and almost presumes knowledge of the longer story. Mark 16:12–13 is parallel to 16:9–11, another proclamation of the news of Jesus' appearance met again with disbelief (again echoing Luke 24:13–31).

Next we find yet a third telling of a resurrection appearance. Verse 14 describes Jesus reprimanding those who refused to believe the ones to whom he had appeared. Thus we move from no resurrection appearances in 16:1–8 to three in this longer ending. While the text does not explicitly name the location of any of these appearances, 16:14 reflects the appearance in Galilee as described in Matthew 28:16. Similarly, Mark 16:15 is reminiscent of the commissioning of the disciples in Matthew 28:19.

The tone shifts from reprimand to promise as we move to the latter portion of this longer ending. Verses 16–20 describe the powers available to those who believe, as well as the judgment coming to those who do not. In addition to the promise of salvation, those who believe will be accompanied by signs (*semeia*).[1] These signs appear to be available to any who believe as they go out, not simply to the disciples. Casting out demons and speaking in tongues are attested in other places in the New Testament (Mark 6:7, 13; Acts 2:1–11), but neither snake handling nor immunity from poisonous drinks has

---
1. This is the word used by John, but not by Mark for miracles or mighty works.

Homiletical Perspective

a Gospel end so indecisively? Though some scholars see verse 8 as an appropriate end to Mark's deeply ironic narrative, many argue that it could not have ended this way and that the last page(s) must have been lost. Either way, it is almost certain that 16:9–20 was not the original ending, but was added later to provide a more satisfying conclusion. Wrestling with just how satisfying a conclusion it is will be one of the preacher's primary tasks.

Mark 16:9–20 is in fact a series of vignettes that allude to resurrection appearances in the Gospels of Luke and John and to miracles stories recounted in the Acts of the Apostles.[1] The first two scenes recount Jesus' appearances to Mary Magdalene (based on John 20) and to the two disciples on the road to Emmaus (based on Luke 24). In both, the witnesses report what they have seen to "those who had been with him" and are met with unbelief. In the third scene, Jesus himself appears to the eleven and "upbraid[s] them for their lack of faith and stubbornness, because they had not believed those who saw him after he had risen" (v. 14).

The key theme in these three scenes is "faith/belief/trust,"[2] which is an obvious entry into the passage. The ways the passage treats "faith" provides opportunity to explore less familiar ways of understanding it. For while the content of faith in these three scenes is the proclamation "he is alive," the real focus is on believing those who proclaim it. Jesus' words to the eleven make this clear. When he upbraids them for "their lack of faith and stubbornness," he directly ties it to their not believing those who saw him. Thus a sermon might explore the relation between faith in the gospel and trust in those who proclaim it. Approaching the passage with this question should not be limited to the clergy, as the story of Mary Magdalene makes clear. Indeed, her place in this story invites serious consideration of what it takes to trust those on the margins. As the commissions in verses 15 and 20 show, exploring what it might take to win the world's trust is also a theme to consider.

The second part of Jesus' address to the eleven deals with "signs" that confirm the proclamation of the gospel: casting out demons, speaking in tongues, picking up snakes, drinking deadly things, and laying hands on the sick (vv. 17–18). Faith and belief are central to this section also, though it is not

---
1. The exegetical commentary in this volume and notes in most study Bibles identify the various sources.
2. The NRSV uses "faith" and "belief" to translate *pistis* and the various forms of this Greek term. "Trust" may be used to good effect in some instances, as we shall see.

Mark 16:9–20

Theological Perspective

introduces a change to the theological character of this Gospel.

What I know of Mark's theology seems to be mirrored in the well-known words of the martyred archbishop of El Salvador, Oscar Romero, who said,

> Nothing that we do is complete, . . . No statement says all that can be said. No prayer fully expresses our faith. No confession brings perfection. No pastoral visit brings wholeness. No program accomplishes the church's mission. No set of goals and objectives includes everything. . . . We cannot do everything, and there is a sense of liberation in realizing that.[1]

This "longer" ending to Mark's Gospel loses some of that open-endedness, the invitation to participate trustingly in God's future.

This ending to the Gospel also does something right, however. It puts the presence of the risen one in a different light or perspective. Jesus is now present in the disciples' proclamation. This implies at least some continuation with Jesus' own ministry, as well as the rest of Mark's Gospel. However, it does so against the background of Jesus being taken up to heaven. Thus it also takes away some of the impact of Jesus' new presence, and makes it seemingly dependent on signs and wonders in the disciples' lives. Because of the editor's uneasiness with inconclusiveness and the contradictions that are part of the Gospel narrative, some of that wonder about Jesus' true identity and character is missing as well.

Another element that gets introduced into this ending is the proverbial happy ending. In this one, the disciples—once clueless, helpless, and unbelieving—have become the prototypes of a new courageous, faithful, and powerful group There is no indication of suffering as inevitably part of the life of those who would minister to others in the way that Jesus did. Suffering in the form of rejection, persecution, and sacrifice is out of the picture. There is no mention of opposition or risk but, rather, a definite stress on being unharmed and in control. The perception seems to be that that the vulnerability of discipleship is a thing of the past, a different perspective from what we gain through even a general reading of Mark as a whole.

NELSON RIVERA

Pastoral Perspective

rest" what they have seen and heard of the Lord in the course of their daily lives.

A second brief point might be made on another piece of this text: not that disconcerting bit about handling snakes and drinking poisons, but something more dangerous: the Great Commission (vv. 15–16). Just as testimony has fallen out of use in some quarters of the church, evangelism—not the sort that encourages us to "invite people to our friendly church," but the commending of the faith to people who do not know the grace of Jesus Christ—seems largely confined to evangelical circles. As long as the evangelistic offer of faith to "all the world" (v. 15) is accompanied by the threat of eternal damnation, we might wish those circles would become even smaller. Jesus upbraids his disciples for their unbelief; he does not damn them to hell. Although all Christians must take seriously the commission to evangelize, we need not scruple to disbelieve this part (v. 16) of the charge.

Of course, in "mainline" circles, disbelieving this part is not hard. The challenge in this wing of the church is not to get people to stop condemning, but to get them up, out, and commending. To invite someone to consider embracing a way of life after the pattern of the crucified and risen Jesus presupposes that the inviters love that way of life and can articulate an appealing case for it. It also presupposes that if the invitation is accepted, they are prepared to welcome, enfold, and ground the neophyte in the community of pooled faith described above. We have not acquitted ourselves of the charge to evangelize when someone says yes. If belief as such is not the goal, and if fullness of life among the brothers and sisters is, then the Easter challenge is not so much convincing people to believe that Jesus rose from the dead as it is shaping communities in which his new life is so palpable that everyone who enters can actually meet him as he lives and reigns in its worship, learning, mission, justice making, and mutual care.

MARY LUTI

---

1. Romero's prayer, "Prophets of a Future Not Our Own," is reproduced at http://bogners.typepad.com/church/2004/03/the_prayer_of_o.html; accessed August 24, 2012.

Exegetical Perspective

New Testament precedents. The concluding verses of this ending echo the language of the ascension of Jesus in Acts 1:1–2, 9, and the seating of Jesus on the right hand of God is reminiscent of the references to Psalm 110:1 in Mark 12:35–37 and throughout the New Testament. All is neatly summarized and completed in verse 20 as the disciples go out and proclaim the good news.

Overall, the proclamation of this longer ending reflects the interests of the early church. Our English translations include several of the "additional" endings, including verses between 16:8 and 16:9 as well as the longer ending, 16:9–20. Another interpolation, known as the Freer Logion, attested in a fourth-century manuscript, Codex Washingtonianus, expands this longer ending ever further. This apocalyptic passage appears in Codex W between 16:14 and 16:15:

> And they defended themselves saying, "This age of lawlessness and unbelief is under Satan, who does not allow the truth and power of God to prevail over the unclean things of the spirits. And so, reveal your righteousness now." They were speaking to Christ. And Christ foretold to them, "The term for the years of Satan's authority has been fulfilled; but other terrible things draw near. And I was handed over to death for those who have sinned, in order that they might return to the truth and sin no longer, that they might inherit the spiritual and imperishable glory of righteousness that is in heaven."[2]

The additions of these various endings to Mark's Gospel in the early centuries of the church reflect the ongoing questions about and reflections on the resurrection of Jesus.

While the content reflects elements of the resurrection and ascension stories in other parts of the New Testament, the style and content of this longer ending of Mark do not match that of the evangelist in the rest of his Gospel. Even in the English translation the longer ending reads quite differently. One should note, however, that while these verses most likely are not Markan in origin, they are attested quite early, reflecting the desire early in the history of the church to provide a more satisfying ending to this Gospel.

JUDY YATES SIKER

Homiletical Perspective

altogether clear how we should understand the purpose of these signs. To some extent the author of this passage may see them as "proofs" of the message. It is important to note, however, that in verse 17 signs "accompany" belief; they are not the object of belief, a point made again in verse 20. So here too a sermon might explore signs as a way of establishing trust in the one who proclaims the message rather than being part of the message itself.

Either approach to treating the signs will likely be challenging, since for some in the congregation, the list in verses 17 and 18 will be disturbing. For most people, talk about handling snakes and drinking deadly things strains credibility. Many will also find casting out demons and speaking in tongues just as hard to take. For some, even laying hands on the sick will be a challenge. So should a sermon dismiss the notion of signs completely? Probably not, for signs that the Lord is working with us and confirming our message are important for establishing trust, both within the church and for its mission to the world.

A sermon therefore might well seek to develop another list of signs, one more appropriate for contemporary preaching. The preacher will want to exercise care, however, lest one set of incredible signs be replaced by another. Since the sermon will be working from Mark, its exploration of true discipleship in 8:34–38; 9:35–37; and 10:42–45 is a good place to start.

Before giving up the list of signs in Mark 16:17–18, however, consider this: Many will find language of serpents, demons, and deadly things appropriate to describe their deepest fears. Laying hands on the sick may not cure a disease, but it can still be healing. Speaking in new tongues need not be limited to ecstatic speech. It can also apply to learning new languages that allow more productive work with immigrants or opportunities to engage in mission in other parts of the world.

OLIVER LARRY YARBROUGH

---

2. Bart D. Ehrman and Zlatko Plese, *The Apocryphal Gospels, Texts and Translations* (New York: Oxford University Press, 2011), 357.

Contributors

O. Wesley Allen Jr., Associate Professor of Homiletics and Worship, Lexington Theological Seminary, Lexington, Kentucky

Herbert Anderson, Research Professor in Practical Theology, Pacific Lutheran Theological Seminary, Berkeley, California

Kathryn E. Anderson, Executive Director, John Knox Ranch, Fischer, Texas

Talitha Arnold, Pastor, The United Church of Santa Fe, Santa Fe, New Mexico

Scott Bader-Saye, Academic Dean and Professor of Christian Ethics and Moral Theology, Seminary of the Southwest, Austin, Texas

Eric D. Barreto, Assistant Professor of New Testament, Luther Seminary, St. Paul, Minnesota

Jouette M. Bassler, Professor of New Testament Emerita, Perkins School of Theology, Southern Methodist University, Saugerties, New York

Harlan Beckley, Fletcher Otey Thomas Professor of Religion, Washington and Lee University, Lexington, Virginia

David Michael Bender, Pastor, Faith Presbyterian Church, Indian Land, South Carolina

Joseph A. Bessler, Robert Travis Peake Associate Professor of Theology, Phillips Theological Seminary, Tulsa, Oklahoma

Marianne Blickenstaff, Independent biblical scholar, Louisville, Kentucky

M. Eugene Boring, Professor Emeritus of New Testament, Brite Divinity School of Texas Christian University, Fort Worth, Texas

Richard N. Boyce, Associate Professor of Preaching and Pastoral Leadership, Union Presbyterian Seminary, Charlotte Campus, Charlotte, North Carolina

Robert W. Brewer, Campus Chaplain and Assistant Professor of Religion, Greensboro College, Greensboro, North Carolina

William Brosend, Professor of Homiletics, Sewanee School of Theology, Sewanee, Tennessee

Christopher Bryan, C. K. Benedict Professor of New Testament Emeritus and Editor, *Sewanee Theological Review*, The School of Theology of the University of the South, Sewanee, Tennessee

Christine Chakoian, Pastor, First Presbyterian Church of Lake Forest, Lake Forest, Illinois

Karen Chakoian, Pastor, First Presbyterian Church, Granville, Ohio

Gary W. Charles, Pastor, Central Presbyterian Church, Atlanta, Georgia

Diane G. Chen, Associate Professor of New Testament, Palmer Theological Seminary of Eastern University, King of Prussia, Pennsylvania

Kimberly L. Clayton, Director of Contextual Education, Columbia Theological Seminary, Decatur, Georgia

Deborah Rahn Clemens, Pastor, New Goshenhoppen United Church of Christ, East Greenville, Pennsylvania

John E. Cole, Pastor, First Presbyterian Church, Rock Hill, South Carolina

Brant S. Copeland, Pastor, First Presbyterian Church, Tallahassee, Florida

Mary Jane Kerr Cornell, Pastor–Interim/Transitional Ministry, Presbyterian Church (U.S.A.), Decatur, Georgia

Stephanie Buckhanon Crowder, Adjunct Faculty, New Testament Studies, McCormick Theological Seminary, Chicago, Illinois

William E. Crowder Jr., Pastor, Park Manor Christian Church, Chicago, Illinois

R. Alan Culpepper, Dean and Professor of New Testament, McAfee School of Theology, Mercer University, Atlanta, Georgia

Thomas W. Currie, Dean of Union Presbyterian Seminary, Charlotte Campus, and Professor of

Theology, Union Presbyterian Seminary, Charlotte, North Carolina

Shannon Daley-Harris, Director, Proctor Institute, Childrens Defense Fund, Princeton, New Jersey

William J. Danaher Jr., Dean of Theology, Huron University College School of Theology, London, Ontario, Canada

David A. Davis, Pastor, Nassau Presbyterian Church, Princeton, New Jersey

D. Mark Davis, Pastor, Heartland Presbyterian Church, Clive, Iowa

Katie Day, Charles A. Schieren Professor of Church and Society, and Director, Metropolitan/Urban Concentration, Lutheran Theological Seminary of Philadelphia, Philadelphia, Pennsylvania

Patricia E. de Jong, Pastor, First Congregational Church, Berkeley, California

Mark Douglas, Professor of Christian Ethics and Director, Master of Arts in Theological Studies Program, Columbia Theological Seminary, Decatur, Georgia

Musa W. Dube, Professor of New Testament, University of Botswana, Theology and Religious Studies, Gaborone, Botswana

Matthew Flemming, PhD student at Emory Graduate Division of Religion, Decatur, Georgia

Mary F. Foskett, Professor of Religion and Director of WFU Humanities Institute, Wake Forest University, Winston-Salem, North Carolina

Bridgett A. Green, Doctoral Candidate in New Testament, The Divinity School, Vanderbilt University, Nashville, Tennessee; and Acquisitions Editor, Westminster John Knox Press, Louisville, Kentucky

A. Katherine Grieb, Professor of New Testament, Virginia Theological Seminary, Alexandria, Virginia

Marsha Snulligan Haney, Professor of Missiology and World Religions, Interdenominational Theological Center, Atlanta, Georgia

Daniel J. Harrington, Professor of New Testament, Boston College School of Theology and Ministry, Chestnut Hill, Massachusetts

Tracy L. Hartman, Professor of Homiletics and Practical Theology and Director, Doctor of Ministry Program, Baptist Theological Seminary at Richmond, Richmond, Virginia

Stephen A. Hayner, President and Professor of Christian Leadership Development, Columbia Theological Seminary, Decatur, Georgia

William R. Herzog II, Professor Emeritus of New Testament Interpretation, Andover Newton Theological School, Newton Centre, Massachusetts

Ernest Hess, Pastor, Covenant Presbyterian Church, Atlanta, Georgia

Allen R. Hilton, Minister for Faith and Learning, Wayzata Community Church United Church of Christ, Wayzata, Minnesota

Elizabeth L. Hinson-Hasty, Associate Professor and Chair of the Department of Theology, Bellarmine University, Louisville, Kentucky

M. Jan Holton, Associate Professor of Pastoral Care and Counseling, Yale Divinity School, New Haven, Connecticut

Paul K. Hooker, Associate Dean for Ministerial Formation and Advanced Studies, Austin Presbyterian Theological Seminary, Austin, Texas

Leah McKell Horton, Acting Associate Pastor, Pilgrim Church of Duxbury, Duxbury, Massachusetts

Paul Junggap Huh, Assistant Professor of Worship and Director of Korean American Ministries, Columbia Theological Seminary, Decatur, Georgia

E. Elizabeth Johnson, J. Davison Philips Professor of New Testament, Columbia Theological Seminary, Decatur, Georgia

Mariam J. Kamell, Assistant Professor of New Testament, Regent College, Vancouver, British Columbia, Canada

Catherine L. Kelsey, Dean of the Chapel and Spiritual Formation, Visiting Assistant Professor of Theology, Iliff School of Theology, Denver, Colorado

Steven J. Kraftchick, Professor of the Practice of New Testament Interpretation, Candler School of Theology, Emory University, Atlanta, Georgia

Timothy Andrew Leitzke, Pastor, Tree of Life Lutheran Church, Odessa, Delaware

Bill J. Leonard, Professor of Baptist Studies and Professor of Church History, Wake Forest University School of Divinity, Winston-Salem, North Carolina

W. Carter Lester Jr., Co-Pastor, First Presbyterian Church, Pottstown, Pennsylvania

B. Diane Lipsett, Professor of Religious Studies, University of North Carolina at Greensboro, Greensboro, North Carolina

Michael Lodahl, Professor of Theology and World Religions, Point Loma Nazarene University, San Diego, California

Dwight M. Lundgren, Manager, American Baptist Personnel Services, American Baptist Home Mission Societies, King of Prussia, Pennsylvania

Mary Luti, Visiting Professor of Christian History and Worship, Andover Newton Theological School, Newton Centre, Massachusetts

Fumitaka Matsuoka, Robert Gordon Sproul Professor of Theology Emeritus, Pacific School of Religion, Berkeley, California

Shelly Matthews, Associate Professor of New Testament, Brite Divinity School of Texas Christian University, Fort Worth, Texas

Donald K. McKim, Editor, *These Days*; *Joining the Feast*; and *Being Reformed: Faith Seeking Understanding*, Germantown, Tennessee

Joyce Ann Mercer, Professor of Practical Theology, Virginia Theological Seminary, Alexandria, Virginia

Nancy Mikoski, Pastor, Pennington Presbyterian Church, Pennington, New Jersey

Stephen R. Montgomery, Pastor, Idlewild Presbyterian Church, Memphis, Tennessee

Martha Moore-Keish, Associate Professor of Theology, Columbia Theological Seminary, Decatur, Georgia

D. Cameron Murchison, Professor Emeritus of Ministry, Columbia Theological Seminary, Decatur, Georgia

Carmen Nanko-Fernández, Associate Professor of Hispanic Theology and Ministry, Catholic Theological Union, Chicago, Illinois

vanThanh Nguyen, Associate Professor of New Testament Studies, Catholic Theological Union, Chicago, Illinois

Frederick Niedner, Professor of Theology, Valparaiso University, Valparaiso, Indiana

Rodger Y. Nishioka, Benton Family Associate Professor of Christian Education, Columbia Theological Seminary, Decatur, Georgia

L. Roger Owens, Associate Professor of Leadership and Ministry, Pittsburgh Theological Seminary, Pittsburgh, Pennsylvania

Lance Pape, Granville and Erline Walker Assistant Professor of Homiletics, Brite Divinity School, Fort Worth, Texas

Julie Peeples, Pastor, Congregational United Church of Christ, Greensboro, North Carolina

Pete Peery, President, Montreat Conference Center, Montreat, North Carolina

Pheme Perkins, Professor of New Testament, Boston College School of Theology and Ministry, Chestnut Hill, Massachusetts

Karen Pidcock-Lester, Co-Pastor, First Presbyterian Church, Pottstown, Pennsylvania

Nancy Claire Pittman, Vice President of Academic Affairs and Dean; Associate Professor of the Practice of Ministry, Phillips Theological Seminary, Tulsa, Oklahoma

Neta Lindsay Pringle, Interim Pastor, Calvary Presbyterian Church, Willmington, Delaware

Marjorie Procter-Smith, Professor Emerita of Preaching and Worship, Perkins School of Theology, Southern Methodist University, Dallas, Texas

Charles Raynal, Associate Professor of Theology Emeritus, Columbia Theological Seminary, Decatur, Georgia

Mitchell G. Reddish, O. L. Walker Professor of Christian Studies and Chair, Department of Religious Studies, Stetson University, DeLand, Florida

Robb Redman, Vice President, Dean of the Seminary, and Associate Professor of Theology and Ministry, Multnomah Biblical Seminary, Multnomah University, Portland, Oregon

Leanne Pearce Reed, Pastor, Montevallo Presbyterian Church, Montevallo, Alabama

André Resner, Professor of Homiletics and Church Worship, Hood Theological Seminary, Salisbury, North Carolina

Gail A. Ricciuti, Associate Professor of Homiletics, Colgate Rochester Crozer Divinity School, Rochester, New York

Cynthia L. Rigby, W. C. Brown Professor of Theology, Austin Presbyterian Theological Seminary, Austin, Texas

V. Bruce Rigdon, President Emeritus, Ecumenical Theological Seminary, Chicago, Illinois

Matthew S. Rindge, Associate Professor of Religious Studies, Gonzaga University, Spokane, Washington

Christophe D. Ringer, PhD Candidate in Graduate Department of Religion, Vanderbilt University, Nashville, Tennessee

Nelson Rivera, Associate Professor of Systematic Theology, Lutheran Theological Seminary at Philadelphia, Philadelphia, Pennsylvania

John B. Rogers, Pastor, Retired, Presbyterian Church (U.S.A.), Montreat, North Carolina

Art Ross, Pastor, Retired, Presbyterian Church (U.S.A.), Raleigh, North Carolina

Kristin Saldine, Associate Professor of Homiletics, Austin Presbyterian Theological Seminary, Austin, Texas

Stanley P. Saunders, Associate Professor of New Testament, Columbia Theological Seminary, Decatur, Georgia

Bernard Brandon Scott, Professor of New Testament, Phillips Theological Seminary, Tulsa, Oklahoma

Bob Setzer Jr., Pastor, Knollwood Baptist Church, Winston-Salem, North Carolina

J. Barrie Shepherd, Pastor, Retired, Presbyterian Church (U.S.A.), Wallingford, Pennsylvania

Bruce E. Shields, Professor of Christian Ministries Emeritus, Emmanuel Christian Seminary, Johnson City, Tennessee

Jeffrey S. Siker, Professor of Theological Studies, Loyola Marymount University, Los Angeles, California

Judy Yates Siker, Research Professor, San Francisco Theological Seminary, San Anselmo, California

G. Malcolm Sinclair, Pastor, Metropolitan United Church, Toronto, Ontario, Canada

Thomas B. Slater, Professor of New Testament, McAfee School of Theology, Mercer University, Atlanta, Georgia

Laura A. Smit, Associate Professor of Religion, Calvin College, Grand Rapids, Michigan

Shively T. J. Smith, Doctoral Candidate, New Testament Program, Emory University, Atlanta, Georgia

Sheldon W. Sorge, General Minister to Pittsburgh Presbytery, Pittsburgh, Pennsylvania

Richard E. Spalding, Chaplain to the College, Williams College, Williamstown, Massachusetts

O. Benjamin Sparks, Pastor, Retired, Presbyterian Church (U.S.A.), Richmond, Virginia

Wolfgang H. Stahlberg, Pastor, Messiah Community Church, Evangelical Lutheran Church in America, Denver, Colorado

Mark W. Stamm, Professor of Christian Worship, Perkins School of Theology, Southern Methodist University, Dallas, Texas

Thomas R. Steagald, Pastor, Hawthorne Lane United Methodist Church, Charlotte, North Carolina

Thomas D. Stegman, SJ, Associate Professor of New Testament, Boston College School of Theology and Ministry, Chestnut Hill, Massachusetts

John K. Stendahl, Pastor, Lutheran Church of the Newtons, Newton, Massachusetts

Richard Stern, Professor of Homiletics, St. Meinrad School of Theology, St. Meinrad, Indiana

Laird J. Stuart, Pastor, Retired, Presbyterian Church (U.S.A.), Saugatuck, Michigan

Laura S. Sugg, Associate Pastor and Presbyterian Campus Minister, Westminster Presbyterian Church, Charlottesville, Virginia

Hal Taussig, Visiting Professor of New Testament, Union Theological Seminary in the City of New York, New York, New York

Dean K. Thompson, President and Professor of Ministry Emeritus, Louisville Presbyterian Theological Seminary, Black Mountain, North Carolina

James W. Thompson, Professor of New Testament, Onstead Chair of Biblical Studies, Graduate School of Theology, Abilene Christian University, Abilene, Texas

L. Casey Thompson, Pastor, Wayne Presbyterian Church, Wayne, Pennsylvania

Leonora Tubbs Tisdale, Clement-Muehl Professor of Homiletics, Yale Divinity School, New Haven, Connecticut

Jeffery L. Tribble Sr., Associate Professor of Ministry, Columbia Theological Seminary, Decatur, Georgia

Darryl Trimiew, Professor of Philosophy and Religious Studies, Medgar Evers College, The City University of New York, Brooklyn, New York

Thomas H. Troeger, J. Edward and Ruth Cox Lantz Professor of Christian Communication, Yale Divinity School, New Haven, Connecticut

Leanne Van Dyk, Dean and Vice President of Academic Affairs, Professor of Reformed Theology, Western Theological Seminary, Holland, Michigan

Allen Verhey, Robert Earl Cushman Professor of Christian Ethics, Duke Divinity School, Durham, North Carolina

Richard W. Voelz, Senior Minister, Johns Creek Christian Church (Disciples of Christ), Johns Creek, Georgia

Carol L. Wade, Dean and Rector, Christ Church Cathedral, Lexington, Kentucky

Paul W. Walaskay, Professor Emeritus of Biblical Studies, Union Presbyterian Seminary, Richmond, Virginia

Jon M. Walton, Pastor, The First Presbyterian Church in the City of New York, New York, New York

Richard F. Ward, Fred B. Craddock Professor of Homiletics and Worship, Phillips Theological Seminary, Tulsa, Oklahoma

Rebecca H. Weaver, Professor Emerita of Church History, Union Presbyterian Seminary, Richmond, Virginia

Annette Weissenrieder, Associate Professor of New Testament, San Francisco Theological Seminary and the Graduate Theological Union, Berkeley, San Anselmo, California

Wain Wesberry, Pastor, First Presbyterian Church, Fernandina Beach, Florida

John Wilkinson, Pastor, Third Presbyterian Church, Rochester, New York

Dena L. Williams, Pastor, Evangelical Lutheran Church in America, Denver, Colorado

Karyn L. Wiseman, Associate Professor of Homiletics and Director of United Methodist Studies, Lutheran Theological Seminary at Philadelphia, Philadelphia, Pennsylvania

Steven Toshio Yamaguchi, Presbytery Pastor, Los Ranchos Presbytery, Anaheim, California

Oliver Larry Yarbrough, Professor of Religion, Middlebury College, Middlebury, Vermont

Mark E. Yurs, Pastor, Salem United Church of Christ, Verona, Wisconsin

Randall C. Zachman, Professor of Reformation Studies, University of Notre Dame, Notre Dame, Indiana

Author Index

Abbreviations
EP Exegetical Perspective
HP Homiletical Perspective
PP Pastoral Perspective
TP Theological Perspective

Contributors and entries

O. Wesley Allen Jr.	Mark 15:21–32 HP; 15:33–41 HP
Herbert Anderson	Mark 15:21–32 PP; 15:33–41 PP
Kathryn E. Anderson	Mark 2:13–17 EP; 2:18–22 EP
Talitha Arnold	Mark 11:11–26 PP; 11:27–33 PP; 12:1–12 PP
Scott Bader-Saye	Mark 10:17–22 TP; 10:23–31 TP
Eric D. Barreto	Mark 11:11–26 EP; 11:27–33 EP; 12:1–12 EP
Jouette M. Bassler	Mark 14:1–2, 10–11 EP; 14:3–9 EP; 14:12–16 EP
Harlan Beckley	Mark 10:32–34 TP; 10:35–45 TP
David Michael Bender	Mark 1:29–34 PP; 1:35–39 PP
Joseph A. Bessler	Mark 6:1–6a TP; 6:6b–13 TP; 6:14–29 TP
Marianne Blickenstaff	Mark 1:29–34 TP; 1:35–39 TP
M. Eugene Boring	Mark 1:1–8 EP; 1:9–11 EP; 1:12–13 EP
Richard N. Boyce	Mark 1:1–8 TP; 1:9–11 TP; 1:12–13 TP
Robert W. Brewer	Mark 1:29–34 HP; 1:35–39 HP
William Brosend	Mark 2:23–28 HP; 3:1–6 HP; 3:7–12 HP
Christopher Bryan	Mark 14:66–72 EP; 15:1–5 EP
Christine Chakoian	Mark 8:1–10 TP; 8:11–21 TP
Karen Chakoian	Mark 10:46–52 HP; 11:1–10 HP
Gary W. Charles	Mark 1:14–15 HP; 1:16–20 HP; 1:21–28 HP
Diane G. Chen	Mark 13:14–23 EP; 13:24–27 EP
Kimberly L. Clayton	Mark 10:32–34 HP; 10:35–45 HP
Deborah Rahn Clemens	Mark 12:35–37 PP; 12:38–40 PP; 12:41–44 PP
John E. Cole	Mark 13:1–8 PP; 13:9–13 PP
Brant S. Copeland	Mark 3:13–19a PP; 3:19b–30 PP; 3:31–35 PP
Mary Jane Kerr Cornell	Mark 9:42–50 PP; 10:1–12 PP; 10:13–16 PP
Stephanie Buckhanon Crowder	Mark 3:13–19a EP; 3:19b–30 EP; 3:31–35 EP
William E. Crowder Jr.	Mark 10:32–34 PP; 10:35–45 PP

R. Alan Culpepper	Mark 9:42–50 EP; 10:1–12 EP; 10:13–16 EP	Stephen A. Hayner	Mark 13:28–31 TP; 13:32–37 TP
Thomas W. Currie	Mark 14:1–2, 10–11 TP; 14:3–9 TP; 14:12–16 TP	William R. Herzog II	Mark 2:23–28 EP; 3:1–6 EP; 3:7–12 EP
Shannon Daley-Harris	Mark 14:17–21 PP; 14:22–25 PP; 14:26–31 PP	Ernest Hess	Mark 15:21–32 EP; 15:33–41 EP
		Allen R. Hilton	Mark 13:14–23 HP; 13:24–27 HP
William J. Danaher Jr.	Mark 14:17–21 TP; 14:22–25 TP; 14:26–31 TP	Elizabeth L. Hinson-Hasty	Mark 15:6–15 TP; 15:16–20 TP
David A. Davis	Mark 14:66–72 PP; 15:1–5 PP	M. Jan Holton	Mark 4:35–41 PP; 5:1–20 PP
D. Mark Davis	Mark 14:32–42 TP; 14:43–52 TP; 14:53–65 TP	Paul K. Hooker	Mark 1:14–15 EP; 1:16–20 EP; 1:21–28 EP
Katie Day	Mark 14:66–72 TP; 15:1–5 TP	Leah McKell Horton	Mark 1:1–8 HP; 1:9–11 HP; 1:12–13 HP
Patricia E. de Jong	Mark 14:32–42 PP; 14:43–52 PP; 14:53–65 PP	Paul Junggap Huh	Mark 1:14–15 PP; 1:16–20 PP; 1:21–28 PP
Mark Douglas	Mark 12:35–37 TP; 12:38–40 TP; 12:41–44 TP	E. Elizabeth Johnson	Mark 1:29–34 EP; 1:35–39 EP
Musa W. Dube	Mark 9:30–32 EP; 9:33–37 EP; 9:38–41 EP	Mariam J. Kamell	Mark 4:26–29 EP; 4:30–34 EP
		Catherine L. Kelsey	Mark 15:21–32 TP; 15:33–41 TP
Matthew Flemming	Mark 12:13–17 HP; 12:18–27 HP; 12:28–34 HP	Steven J. Kraftchick	Mark 13:1–8 EP; 13:9–13 EP
Mary F. Foskett	Mark 12:13–17 EP; 12:18–27 EP; 12:28–34 EP	Timothy Andrew Leitzke	Mark 1:40–45 TP; 2:1–12 TP
		Bill J. Leonard	Mark 3:13–19a TP; 3:19b–30 TP; 3:31–35 TP
Bridgett A. Green	Mark 10:17–22 EP; 10:23–31 EP	W. Carter Lester Jr.	Mark 8:1–10 PP; 8:11–21 PP
A. Katherine Grieb	Mark 14:32–42 EP; 14:43–52 EP; 14:53–65 EP	B. Diane Lipsett	Mark 14:17–21 EP; 14:22–25 EP; 14:26–31 EP
Marsha Snulligan Haney	Mark 8:31–33 PP; 8:34–9:1 PP	Michael Lodahl	Mark 10:46–52 TP; 11:1–10 TP
Daniel J. Harrington	Mark 4:1–9 EP; 4:10–20 EP; 4:21–25 EP	Dwight M. Lundgren	Mark 12:35–37 HP; 12:38–40 HP; 12:41–44 HP
Tracy L. Hartman	Mark 5:24b–34 TP		

Mary Luti	Mark 15:42–47 PP; 16:1–8 PP; 16:9–20 PP	Pheme Perkins	Mark 8:1–10 EP; 8:11–21 EP
Fumitaka Matsuoka	Mark 11:11–26 TP; 11:27–33 TP; 12:1–12 TP	Karen Pidcock-Lester	Mark 7:1–23 PP; 7:24–30 PP; 7:31–37 PP
Shelly Matthews	Mark 10:17–22 HP; 10:23–31 HP	Nancy Claire Pittman	Mark 14:66–72 HP; 15:1–5 HP
Donald K. McKim	Mark 1:14–15 TP; 1:16–20 TP; 1:21–28 TP	Neta Lindsay Pringle	Mark 9:2–8 EP; 9:9–13 EP; 9:14–29 EP
Joyce Ann Mercer	Mark 9:42–50 TP; 10:1–12 TP; 10:13–16 TP	Marjorie Procter-Smith	Mark 4:35–41 HP; 5:1–20 HP
		Charles Raynal	Mark 14:32–42 HP; 14:43–52 HP; 14:53–65 HP
Nancy Mikoski	Mark 13:1–8 HP; 13:9–13 HP	Mitchell G. Reddish	Mark 15:6–15 EP; 15:16–20 EP
Stephen R. Montgomery	Mark 13:28–31 HP; 13:32–37 HP	Robb Redman	Mark 8:22–26 TP; 8:27–30 TP
Martha Moore-Keish	Mark 7:1–23 TP; 7:24–30 TP; 7:31–37 TP	Leanne Pearce Reed	Mark 9:2–8 HP; 9:9–13 HP; 9:14–29 HP
D. Cameron Murchison	Mark 6:30–44 TP; 6:45–52 TP; 6:53–56 TP	André Resner	Mark 8:22–26 HP; 8:27–30 HP
Carmen Nanko-Fernández	Mark 14:1–2, 10–11 PP; 14:3–9 PP; 14:12–16 PP	Gail A. Ricciuti	Mark 8:1–10 HP; 8:11–21 HP
vanThanh Nguyen	Mark 6:1–6a EP; 6:6b–13 EP; 6:14–29 EP	Cynthia L. Rigby	Mark 13:1–8 TP; 13:9–13 TP
		V. Bruce Rigdon	Mark 8:22–26 PP; 8:27–30 PP
Frederick Niedner	Mark 9:2–8 TP; 9:9–13 TP; 9:14–29 TP	Matthew S. Rindge	Mark 5:21–24a, 35–43 EP; 5:24b–34 EP
Rodger Y. Nishioka	Mark 13:28–31 PP; 13:32–37 PP	Christophe D. Ringer	Mark 12:13–17 TP; 12:18–27 TP; 12:28–34 TP
L. Roger Owens	Mark 9:2–8 PP; 9:9–13 PP; 9:14–29 PP	Nelson Rivera	Mark 15:42–47 TP; 16:1–8 TP; 16:9–20 TP
Lance Pape	Mark 5:21–24a, 35–43 HP; 5:24b–34 HP	John B. Rogers	Mark 15:6–15 PP; 15:16–20 PP
Julie Peeples	Mark 2:13–17 PP; 2:18–22 PP	Art Ross	Mark 5:21–24a, 35–43 PP; 5:24b–34 PP
Pete Peery	Mark 6:30–44 PP; 6:45–52 PP; 6:53–56 PP		

Kristin Saldine	Mark 15:6–15 HP; 15:16–20 HP	John K. Stendahl	Mark 10:17–22 PP; 10:23–31 PP
Stanley P. Saunders	Mark 10:32–34 EP; 10:35–45 EP	Richard Stern	Mark 9:42–50 HP; 10:1–12 HP; 10:13–16 HP
Bernard Brandon Scott	Mark 7:1–23 EP; 7:24–30 EP; 7:31–37 EP	Laird J. Stuart	Mark 4:1–9 HP; 4:10–20 HP; 4:21–25 HP
Bob Setzer Jr.	Mark 6:1–6a PP; 6:6b–13 PP; 6:14–29 PP	Laura S. Sugg	Mark 4:26–29 HP; 4:30–34 HP
J. Barrie Shepherd	Mark 7:1–23 HP; 7:24–30 HP; 7:31–37 HP	Hal Taussig	Mark 13:28–31 EP; 13:32–37 EP
Bruce E. Shields	Mark 6:30–44 HP; 6:45–52 HP; 6:53–56 HP	Dean K. Thompson	Mark 11:11–26 HP; 11:27–33 HP; 12:1–12 HP
Jeffrey S. Siker	Mark 8:22–26 EP; 8:27–30 EP	James W. Thompson	Mark 12:35–37 EP; 12:38–40 EP; 12:41–44 EP
Judy Yates Siker	Mark 15:42–47 EP; 16:1–8 EP; 16:9–20 EP	L. Casey Thompson	Mark 13:14–23 PP; 13:24–27 PP
G. Malcolm Sinclair	Mark 6:1–6a HP; 6:6b–13 HP; 6:14–29 HP	Leonora Tubbs Tisdale	Mark 1:40–45 HP; 2:1–12 HP
		Jeffery L. Tribble Sr.	Mark 4:26–29 PP; 4:30–34 PP
Thomas B. Slater	Mark 8:31–33 TP; 8:34–9:1 TP	Darryl Trimiew	Mark 9:30–32 TP; 9:33–37 TP; 9:38–41 TP
Laura A. Smit	Mark 4:35–41 TP; 5:1–20 TP	Thomas H. Troeger	Mark 3:13–19a HP; 3:19b–30 HP; 3:31–35 HP
Shively T. J. Smith	Mark 10:46–52 EP; 11:1–10 EP		
Sheldon W. Sorge	Mark 4:26–29 TP	Leanne Van Dyk	Mark 4:1–9 TP; 4:10–20 TP; 4:21–25 TP
Richard E. Spalding	Mark 8:31–33 EP; 8:34–9:1 EP	Allen Verhey	Mark 5:21–24a, 35–43 TP
O. Benjamin Sparks	Mark 9:30–32 PP; 9:33–37 PP; 9:38–41 PP	Richard W. Voelz	Mark 14:17–21 HP; 14:22–25 HP; 14:26–31 HP
Wolfgang H. Stahlberg	Mark 10:46–52 PP; 11:1–10 PP	Carol L. Wade	Mark 12:13–17 PP; 12:18–27 PP; 12:28–34 PP
Mark W. Stamm	Mark 9:30–32 HP; 9:33–37 HP; 9:38–41 HP	Paul W. Walaskay	Mark 6:30–44 EP; 6:45–52 EP; 6:53–56 EP
Thomas R. Steagald	Mark 8:31–33 HP; 8:34–9:1 HP		
Thomas D. Stegman, SJ	Mark 4:35–41 EP; 5:1–20 EP	Jon M. Walton	Mark 4:30–34 TP

Richard F. Ward	Mark 2:13–17 HP; 2:18–22 HP	Karyn L. Wiseman	Mark 14:1–2, 10–11 HP; 14:3–9 HP; 14:12–16 HP
Rebecca H. Weaver	Mark 13:14–23 TP; 13:24–27 TP		
Annette Weissenrieder	Mark 1:40–45 EP; 2:1–12 EP	Steven Toshio Yamaguchi	Mark 4:1–9 PP; 4:10–20 PP; 4:21–25 PP
Wain Wesberry	Mark 1:40–45 PP; 2:1–12 PP	Oliver Larry Yarbrough	Mark 15:42–47 HP; 16:1–8 HP; 16:9–20 HP
John Wilkinson	Mark 2:23–28 TP; 3:1–6 TP; 3:7–12 TP	Mark E. Yurs	Mark 1:1–8 PP; 1:9–11 PP; 1:12–13 PP
Dena L. Williams	Mark 2:23–28 PP; 3:1–6 PP; 3:7–12 PP	Randall C. Zachman	Mark 2:13–17 TP; 2:18–22 TP

www.ingramcontent.com/pod-product-compliance
Lightning Source LLC
Chambersburg PA
CBHW080747071125
35098CB00005B/13